MW01556111

Understanding
and Overcoming
the Inequality That
Limits Our Lives

GREED
and good

Sam Pizzigati

THE APEX PRESS
NEW YORK

©2004 by Sam Pizzigati

Published by The Apex Press, an imprint of the
Council on International and Public Affairs
777 United Nations Plaza, Suite 3C
New York, New York 10017
Telephone/fax: 800-316-APEX (2739)
E-mail: cipany@igc.org
Web Page: www.cipa-apex.org

Library of Congress Cataloging-in-Publication Data

Pizzigati, Sam.
Greed and good : understanding and overcoming the inequality that limits our lives /
Sam Pizzigati.
   p. cm.
Includes bibliographical references and index.
ISBN 1-891843-25-7 (alk. paper)
1. Income distribution--United States. 2. Wealth--United States. 3. Avarice--United
States. I. Title.
HC110.U6P598 2004
339.2'2'0973--dc22
              2004043728

Cover and interior graphics by David M. Barnum
Jacket and interior design by Mary Ellen McCourt
Printed in the United States of America

For Karabelle and Nick
in memory of Tony

Contents

INTRODUCTION   vii

BOOK ONE: THE CASE FOR GREED   1

WHY WE 'NEED' INEQUALITY   3

For 'Progress'
GREED AS AN INCENTIVE   5

For 'Justice'
THE GREEDY AS DESERVING   51

For Sweetness and Light!
THE GREEDY AS BENEFACTORS   93

JOBS AND PAYCHECKS   95

CHARITY AND COMPASSION   127

CULTURE AND ART   139

A CASE NOT MADE   153

BOOK TWO: THE COST OF GREED   155

THE PRICE WE PAY FOR INEQUALITY   157

Economically
THE INEFFECTIVE ENTERPRISE   159
GRUESOME GROWTH   195

Individually
EXCESS WITHOUT HAPPINESS   237
PROFESSIONS WITHOUT PRIDE   273
SPORTS WITHOUT WINNERS   295
WEALTH WITHOUT HEALTH   311

Socially
A FRAYING SOCIAL FABRIC   331

Environmentally
AN IMPERILED NATURAL WORLD   359

Politically
A DYING DEMOCRACY   379

A PRICE TOO HIGH   409

BOOK THREE: AN END TO GREED? 411

ALTERNATIVES TO INEQUALITY   413
    HISTORIC STRUGGLES   415
    CONTEMPORARY OPTIONS   457
   Enter the Ten Times Rule
    A MAXIMUM WAGE?   479
    LIFE IN A TEN TIMES RULE AMERICA   503
    A STRATEGY FOR CHANGE   527
LOOKING FORWARD   549

NOTES   553
ACKNOWLEDGEMENTS   637
INDEX   639

INTRODUCTION

NO GOOD AND DECENT SOCIETY, most Americans would agree, accepts poverty. A good society sees poverty — the absence of wealth — as a clear and present danger, a social ill that all good people ought to unite to overcome. People in a good society, we note, may differ on *how* to overcome poverty. They do not differ on the necessity. Decent societies, we believe, never rest so long as some among us have much too little.

But what if some among us have much too much? What if we have, in our midst, a significant number of people who hold more wealth, considerably more wealth, than anyone needs to live a comfortable life? Should the presence of such wealth concentrations upset us, unnerve us, outrage us? Should a good society fear concentrated wealth? Indeed, can anyone ever have too much wealth?

In American public life today, we seldom ask these questions.

This disinterest would be understandable if wealth in the United States were becoming less concentrated. But wealth in the United States is, in fact, becoming more concentrated — and at record rates. Our twentieth century ended with the single most colossal amassing of grand fortunes in American history. These fortunes, and the gap they open between wealthy Americans and everyone else, "should scare any thoughtful person," observed one alarmed commentator, Molly Ivins, at century's end. But that gap, she lamented, "isn't even part of the mainstream political debate."[1]

Our mainstream has been too busy applauding. Grand accumulations of wealth, our top pundits and political leaders inform us, signal an America that's doing just fine.

"A society that values individualism, enterprise, and a market economy," as conservative columnist George Will puts it, "is neither surprised nor scandalized when the unequal distribution of marketable skills produces large disparities in the distribution of wealth."[2]

"We are not a people who object to others being successful," Bill Clinton has agreed, "we do not resent people amassing their own wealth fairly won in a free enterprise system."[3]

This conventional wisdom has, over recent years, gone largely unchallenged. In contemporary America, even steadfastly liberal lawmakers feel compelled to emphasize their comfort with grand fortune.

"The problem in America today isn't that some people are getting rich," liberal stalwart David Bonior from Michigan declared as the 1990s boom began to gain momentum. "The problem is, most people are getting nowhere."[4]

Liberals. Moderates. Conservatives. All seem to agree that the misfortune of the poor, but not the wealth of the fortunate, merits the nation's attention.

"What public policy should be concerned about is poverty, not inequality," argues Martin Feldstein, the conservative who chaired President Ronald Reagan's Council of Economic Advisers. If a society's total wealth is rising, Feldstein assures us, any wealth that amasses at a society's summit "isn't a bad thing."[5]

Laura D'Andrea Tyson, Feldstein's counterpart in the Clinton administration, sings much the same song. She asks Americans to imagine the nation's economy as an apartment building. Some people live in penthouse luxury, others in the rat-infested basement. What should the nation do? Pillage the penthouse? Forget the penthouse, advises Tyson.

"We need to do something," she contends, "about that rat-infested basement."[6]

In the meantime, commentators caution us, let the wealthy be. Rich people, as economist Michael Weinstein has opined in the *New York Times*, are "fun to watch, fun to ridicule, perhaps even fun to envy." But they aren't, continues Weinstein, "much to worry about."[7] Poverty may pose problems, in other words, but economic inequality — the inevitable outcome whenever grand fortunes accumulate — need not detain us.

"Inequality is not inequity," sum up two widely published commentators on wealth in America, economist W. Michael Cox and journalist Richard Alm. "What Americans ought to care most about is maintaining our growth, not the red herring of gaps in income and wealth."[8]

These pages will disagree. We will argue that the gap that so deeply divides the wealthy from the rest of our society does matter, and not just for the poor. The greater that gap, we will show, the greater the greed, the greater the grasping for dreams that can never be attained, the greater the strain on the bonds that make societies good, communities human. That some people have too much, we will contend, is not just *a* problem. It is *the* problem, the root of what ails us as a nation, a social cancer that coarsens our culture, endangers our economy, distorts our democracy, even limits our lifespans.

If we want to lead longer lives, if we want more time in these lives for those we love and the work we love to do, if we want our society to have the wherewithal — and the will — to address the challenges we see all around us, we need to narrow the gap that separates the wealthy from everyone else. If all men and women are indeed created equal, these pages will hold, then any society that winks at the monstrously large fortunes that make some people decidedly more equal than others is asking for trouble. To become a good and decent society, or at least a significantly better society, we need to stop — and reverse — America's increasingly intense concentration of wealth at the top.

BY EVERY MEASURE, we have more wealthy people in the United States today than ever before. Millionaires, once an exotic species, now live "next door." In 1969, one hundred thousand American households could legitimately claim millionaire status.[9] By the 1980s, the United States was minting nearly one hundred thousand new millionaires every year.[10] By 2000, America's economy was generating millionaires at a rate over ten times faster, more than a million a year.[11]

We ought, perhaps, not read too much into these numbers. By century's end, after all, millionaire status no longer connoted colossal wealth. In 1984, most Americans felt that anyone worth just half a million dollars could be safely considered rich. By 2000, according to a *Money* magazine survey, Americans earning $50,000 or more felt real wealth didn't kick in until a fortune hit $3 million.[12]

Still, even at this loftier standard, the ranks of the wealthy have been multiplying mightily. The numbers of fortunes worth multiple millions, notes New York University economist Edward Wolff, actually rose faster in the 1990s than the numbers of mere millionaires. Between 1989 and 1998, our millionaire household population jumped by a bit more than half. Over that same span, America's population of "deca-millionaires," households worth at least $10 million, quadrupled.[13]

Some fiscally fortunate Americans have graduated to even higher levels of affluence. The richest of these rich we call billionaires.

A billionaire is a millionaire a thousand times over. America's first billionaire, John D. Rockefeller, emerged about a century ago.[14] He would remain, for years, America's only billionaire. In 1978, well over a generation after John D.'s passing, analysts could only identify one honest-to-goodness billion-dollar fortune in the entire United States.[15]

That would soon start to change. In 1982, *Forbes* magazine would count just over a dozen billionaires for its first annual list of the four hundred richest Americans.[16] By 1996, the richest four hundred on the *Forbes* list *averaged* $1 billion.[17] In 2000, *Forbes* identified 267 billionaires, twenty times the 1982 total.[18]

Fortunes were accumulating so rapidly, commentators started musing in the late 1990s, that America might soon see the world's first trillionaire. That historic figure, *Wired* magazine suggested, would almost certainly be Bill Gates, the software entrepreneur who co-founded Microsoft.[19] Gates, by century's end, had come to personify great wealth in America.[20] Over stretches of the 1990s, his fortune was expanding by some $400 million *every week.*[21] How grand a sum is $400 million? Turn-of-the-century America's greatest lottery payoff, scored on May 9, 2000, came in at $363 million.[22] Gates was, in effect, hitting the lottery jackpot — beating the lottery jackpot — fifty-two times a year.

The Bill Gates fortune would be no isolated, freak phenomenon in the late twentieth century. Over the century's last decade, the grand fortunes that took root in the United States overwhelmed the world. On the *Forbes* 1990 list of the world's ten grandest accumulations of wealth, Americans only appeared twice.[23] By 1993, Americans made up, for the first time, a majority on the *Forbes* global top ten, with seven American fortunes on the list. In 1995, Americans occupied the list's top three slots, in 1998 the top four. In 1999, Americans swept the top seven slots on the *Forbes* list. The net worth of their combined fortunes — nearly $200 billion — helped the total net worth of the world's richest two hundred people hit $1 trillion for the first time ever. These fortunes would dip some after the stock market collapse that began in 2001. But the prominence of America's wealthy would see no dip. In 2003, *Forbes* researchers counted eight Americans among the world's richest top ten.[24]

AT SOME POINT, WISE PEOPLE have observed down through the years, accumulating ever greater sums of wealth makes no practical, personal sense.

"The money doesn't matter — not after the first million," financier Joseph Hirshhorn once noted. "How could it? You can't wear more than two shirts in a day, or eat more than three meals."[25]

At some point, presumably, even the richest among us will have nothing left to buy, or not enough time to consume what they have already bought. That point has not yet come. America's most fortunate have proved far more imaginative than Joseph Hirshhorn could have ever imagined. They have adapted. They have learned how to spend in a style that befits their financial good fortune.

Monumental fortunes must, of course, be housed monumentally. Toward that end, our wealthy spare no expense. They build and buy individual homes that cost as much as neighborhoods. Realtors in Florida's Palm Beach, early in 2001, proudly listed one attractive abode at $75 million. Seven other homes across the country, available at the same time, listed at or over $40 million.[26] Some homes of our wealthy amount to neighborhoods in and of themselves. In the Hamptons, the East Coast's most sumptuous summer getaway, construction crews spent 2003 finishing up a personal "compound" for billionaire industrialist Ira Rennert.[27] Among the site's charms: twenty-nine bedrooms and thirty-nine baths. Rennert's original plans also called for a twenty-car garage and "a reconstructed pub, transported stone by stone," from England.[28]

Other multimillionaires have opted for the majesty of castle life. New Jersey banker Alan Wilzig, for one, built himself a $10 million Medieval-style castle, complete with six suits of armor.[29] For well-endowed American turret-lovers who covet the real thing, Europe beckons. Several European real estate agents even specialize in castles. Early in 2001, Alexander Kraft of Sotheby's International Realty had a half dozen for sale. His prize: a winsome thirteenth-century beauty just outside Salzburg. A steal at $20 million.[30]

Anything less than a castle, in some posh neighborhoods, now gets the wrecking-ball. Wealthy buyers routinely spend millions on luxury homes, then knock them down to build homes even more luxurious. In San Francisco, realtors have dubbed this buy-demolish two-step the "scraper" phenomenon: You "buy a house, scrape it off the lot and build a bigger one."[31]

The magnificent new homes that arise from teardown lots need, of course, to be suitably accessorized, inside and out. Wealthy Americans have relished this responsibility. They have confronted — and conquered — one accessorizing challenge after another.

The challenges can be formidable. Take landscaping, for instance. Can any sight be more pitiful than a grand new home surrounded by tiny young saplings? Ordinary Americans might be content to wait twenty years for saplings to mature. But why plant little trees when you can buy big ones? In 1999, wealthy homeowners up and down the East Coast were handing New Jersey's Halka Nurseries up to $20,000 for a single thirty-foot tree — and another $40,000 to put each tree's thirty-five-thousand-pound root ball in the ground. At peak planting season that year, Halka had enough orders to fill eight truck trailers a day, with each trailer carrying up to fifty trees.[32]

Other wealthy homeowners devote their energies to creating fitness-friendly landscapes. Backyard tennis courts? Always nice, but sometimes too noisy. The solution? The affluent with net smarts sink their courts six feet below ground level.

"People don't want to hear the bounce," explains Frank Newbold, a realtor in the Hamptons.[33]

Indoors, of course, the wealthy face equally daunting accessorizing challenges. Ever try decorating a dozen bedrooms? At century's end, New York's ABC Carpet & Home offered some help, with bedsheets at $1,300 for a set of two.[34] And what about all those closets that need filling? Wealthy Americans can find plenty of expert advice at such establishments as Bijan, the Manhattan shopping mecca considered by some "the most expensive store in the world." In 1998, the store's showroom, open by appointment only, featured racks of $1,500 silk shirts.[35] Not far from Bijan, at Harrison James, a prosperous shopper could pick up an alligator duffel for $17,500.[36]

Late in 2001, the Milanese fashion house known simply as Prada would open still another Manhattan shrine to "unique luxury items." Prada's new $40 million emporium featured two sets of doors, one for normal mortals and another for V.I.P.s. Once safely inside, a swell could slip into a celebrity-only dressing room and strut about in a white mink cape. The privacy came free. The cape cost $13,200.[37]

America's most affluent, amid their ongoing struggles to find suitable shelters and fill them, have never lost sight of other basic human needs, most notably transportation. The challenge here? Moving in style, avoiding the rabble. Those crowded airport check-in counters can be so unpleasant. To the rescue, the private jet, little time-savers that can carry big creature comforts. In the new century's first year, the $48-million Boeing Business Jet, a favorite among the power-suit set, offered a dining room that seats six, two full bathrooms, and two large-screen televisions. By October 2000, Boeing had sold a small fleet of these jets to corporations — and twenty more to individuals.[38]

Soaring through the skies can, of course, get tiresome. All clouds eventually start to look alike. That may help explain why yacht makers, in recent years, have enjoyed such a fabulous run. Over the last half of the 1990s, the number of mega-yachts — boats at least eighty feet long — nearly doubled. Shipyards strained to keep up with the amazing demand. Waiting lists for new mega-yachts could stretch three years.[39]

The yachts were stretching, too. Back in 1986, publisher Malcolm Forbes had caused quite a stir when he unveiled a personal yacht that ran half the length of a football field. By 1997, the "largest American-owned pleasure vessel afloat," owned by the founder of The Limited retail empire, stretched over twice as long.[40]

What do you put on boats measured in football fields? Everything you can. In 2001, Trinity Yachts of New Orleans outfitted its *Seahawk* with a baby grand piano, a dining room for twelve, and "an air-conditioned deck, complete with an eight-person whirlpool."[41]

Where could America's yachtsmen take their floating whirlpools? In the early twenty-first century, a fabulous assortment of resorts offered even the most world-weary wealthy destinations truly worth remembering. Hong Kong's Peninsula Hotel welcomed the well-heeled with the $5,065-per-night Peninsula Suite. Guests could enjoy a marvelous harbor view and every possible convenience. The thoughtfully appointed bathroom, for instance, came with a hands-free phone system, the ultimate antidote, one travel writer noted, to "that age-old fear of dropping the Nokia in the tub."[42]

Wealthy Americans, at the turn of the century, would not be content to merely choose between resorts. They would create, in their zest to be best, entire new categories of destination, most notably the "destination wedding" — just you, your dearest, and several hundred of your closest friends in Bali or some other equally exotic locale. A New York couple, Valesca Dost and Mathias Guerrand-Hermes, set the matrimonial standard. Their wedding opened with over 450 guests in Paris, then ended five days later in Morocco. The reception highpoint? A friendly match of polo — on camels.

"Everyone," gushed one suitably impressed journalist, "felt like a pasha."[43]

Paul Allen, the Microsoft billionaire, would fabricate his fantasies around celebrities, not camels. In 1996, Allen started inviting America's greatest superstars, people like Carlos Santana and Robin Williams, on all-expense-paid junkets to some of the world's most dazzling destinations. The first of Allen's junkets went to the Riviera, the second to Venice, the third to Alaska. The fourth, in August 2001, took Allen and his celebrity pals on a long weekend excursion from Helsinki to St. Petersburg in the $1,400-per-night suites of a luxury liner.

The invitations to this Augustfest, delivered in a gold-embossed wooden box "with a faux Fabergé Easter egg nestled in a satin pillow," reportedly went to a list of notables that included everybody from Paul McCartney to Dan Aykroyd. The cost of these junkets? Allen's Alaska cruise set the billionaire back $9 million.[44]

Junkets with superstars, stretch yachts, big weddings, even grand expensive homes, do not, in the final analysis, bestow true distinction upon a person of significant means. To achieve true upper crust status, your upstairs needs a downstairs. You need, in a word, servants. Servants of fine bearing and perfect deportment, just like those famous British butlers. Servants with class, the ultimate marker of every self-respecting class society.

Immediately after World War II, amid frightfully high taxes on people of means, servants seemed to be going extinct, on both sides of the Atlantic. The number of butlers in Britain, about eighteen thousand in England's glory days, shrank into the hundreds.[45] Butlers, at one point, appeared destined to live on only in Agatha Christie mysteries. That did not happen. The last quarter of the twentieth century would see servants make a remarkable comeback. In the United Kingdom, the number of agencies supplying domestic staff tripled in the 1990s. By century's end, the British Isles boasted twice as many domestic servants as at the start.[46] But the most dramatic servant explosion came in the United States, the new home of the wealthiest of the world's wealthy.

In the Hamptons, the home away from home for New York's glitterati, the new social norms called for four domestic staff per household: a laundress, a chef, a housekeeper, and a houseman, for changing light bulbs and other chores.[47] Many wealthy families that summered in the Hamptons also employed, back home in New York City, multiple social secretaries. Why more than one? Servants, one careful observer of the Manhattan social scene informed a reporter, are like cats.

"When you're not home all day," he explained, "you need to get another one to keep the first one company."[48]

To meet the mounting demand for servants, veritable butler boot camps started emerging in the 1990s. Denver's Starkey International Institute for Household Management charged students $7,200 for an eight-week course in the care and feeding of wealthy people. By 1999, this "Harvard of high-end household help" was graduating sixty household managers a year. Graduates could expect to earn, annually, up to $120,000.[49]

By 2000, these certified servants actually constituted only a small fraction of the new army of Americans who earned their daily bread pampering the wealthy. Manhattan, observed one jaded journalist, "has become an island of modern maharajahs trailed by their processions of body servants, couturiers, accountants, drug pushers, personal trainers, closet arrangers, chefs, plastic surgeons, architects, lawyers, interior designers, head waiters, pimps, estate planners, therapists, jewelers, flatterers and flunkies."[50]

Full employment, mogul-style.

WE LIVE TODAY, MANY AMERICANS have come to feel, amid a greed that seems to define our culture, to taint almost everything we touch.

"The expansion of our greed," the ninety-three-year-old historian, Jacques Barzun, noted early in the new millennium, "is not lovely to look at."[51]

That greed has become unavoidable. Newsstands "feature a gaggle of glossy magazines with cover articles trumpeting one or another Ultimate Mutual Fund Guide, as if the subject has the sex appeal of supermodels in bikinis on Polynesian beaches."[52] On television, Americans can tune in to a steady diet of programming that has transformed greed, as one Midwest reporter notes, into "a source of entertainment."[53] *Who Wants to Be a Millionaire*, the first new series in this genre, would quickly beget *Greed: The Series, Who Wants to Marry a Multi-Millionaire*, and then, after a brief respite, 2002's huge bat-out-of-hell hit, *Joe Millionaire*.

"Is it wrong to want to have enough money to live comfortably?" asked one distressed onlooker, *Washington Post* columnist Michelle Singletary. "Certainly not. But it is pitiful that the desire to become rich has become a national pastime."[54]

Pitiful or not, that desire to become wildly wealthy has sometimes seemed to infect everybody in America.

"There's nothing left to do but go out and get rich," Bob Dole quipped, only half-joking, after talkshow host Jay Leno asked the 1996 Republican Presidential candidate, six weeks after the election, about his future plans.[55]

At century's end, many Americans didn't just *want* to become millionaires. They felt they *had* to become millionaires, or be judged a failure by the standards of the wealth-obsessed society that considered the Dow ticker the heartbeat of America. Older Americans, those who still remembered a world where wealth was not the measure of all things, looked on helplessly, hopelessly out of sync with an America they neither understood or wanted to understand.

"The message is in the air. If you don't care about money, you don't count," observed Thomas Boswell, one of the nation's top sportswriters. "The only occasion I'm brought up short is when I talk finances with my father. He doesn't say anything, but the more authoritative I sound, the more an expression of disappointment passes over his face."[56]

These older Americans had begun their adult lives in an America that knew no awe-inspiring fortunes. The fabulously wealthy, by the 1950s, had largely faded from the American scene. In New York, the most visible markers of their wealth, the grand private mansions that lined Fifth Avenue in the early 1900s, had become grand public places, impressive headquarters buildings for important cultural and educational institutions. Americans considered this sort of turnover irreversible. Private excess, they believed, had birthed public benefits that future generations would enjoy for years and years to come. There would be no going back. The plutocrats had been routed.

By century's end, the plutocrats would be back.

"Someone has just bought the International Center of Photography, a grand old mansion on Fifth Avenue, in order to turn it back into a private house," the *New Yorker* noted in early 2000.[57] Public institutions, in the new America, were now becoming private mansions. The twenty-first century was beginning just as the nineteenth century had ended, with unimaginable wealth concentrated in a few fortunate pockets.

"The plutocracy," the *New Yorker* marveled, "has never been so plutocratic."

A half-century ago, in the 1950s, no one in America imagined that the United States would ever again witness the rise of a new plutocracy. No one, absolutely no one, envisioned a new age of grand fortunes in America, fortunes grand enough to rival the towering accumulations of wealth that defined, in the decades after the Civil War, the epoch we now know as the Gilded Age.

In those Gilded Age years, "robber barons" of steel and rail and oil squeezed gargantuan fortunes out of workers and consumers alike — and changed the face of America. In 1861, millionaires were as uncommon a sight as billionaires would be a century later. Only a handful dotted the American landscape. By 1900, over four thousand fortunes had reached seven figures.[58] Some reached much higher. In 1876, William Vanderbilt inherited $90 million from his father's $105 million estate.[59] It took his father over thirty years to build his fortune. Son William proceeded to nearly double it in just seven.[60]

Few contemporaries found William particularly brilliant. Neither have historians. One dubbed him "a plodding, penny-pinching watcher of detail to whom brains and money meant the same thing."[61] But you didn't need to be brilliant to swindle rivals with secret rebates or fix prices with cartels or dodge taxes with payoffs to politicians. In the Gilded Age, you just had to be rich and powerful. Never before, in America, had so few become so rich so fast — amid such sleaze. Of his day's business tycoons one United States senator noted: "When they speak they lie; when they are silent, they are stealing."[62]

The names of the biggest robber barons — Carnegie, Morgan, Rockefeller — remain familiar to us today. But their excesses have been largely forgotten. Railroad magnate Jay Gould boasted a palatial five-hundred-acre estate on the Hudson, complete with the world's largest orchid collection.[63] Tobacco king James Buchanan Duke's New Jersey manor fielded a lawn that took a crew of forty to tend.[64] William Vanderbilt delighted in $75,000 costume balls.[65] At one, guests found dogs wearing diamond-studded collars.[66]

Vanderbilt keeled over in 1885. His children carried on. Son George spent $6 million — and kept three hundred stonemasons busy for three years — erecting a two-hundred-and-fifty-room palace on a North Carolina mountainside. Son Cornelius spent his dollars building a $5 million mansion on Manhattan's Fifth Avenue. To make space for "three beds of blossoms and a few square yards of turf," he had the brownstone next door torn down and replaced with a $400,000 garden.[67]

Meanwhile, elsewhere in Manhattan, half the city's people spent their days and nights in always crowded, often deadly tenements. Some neighborhoods averaged close to one thousand people per acre, an obscenely high density then matched, notes one historian, only by "parts of Bombay."[68] Cornelius Vanderbilt and his friends never noticed. They stood firmly convinced that all Americans, even the poorest among them, were sharing the grandeur of Gilded Age prosperity.

"The very beggars in our metropolitan cities, and the 'tramps' sleeping in our fields or under the roof that shelters our cattle," one comfortable observer cheered in 1880, "wear a finer fabric than kings could boast a century ago."[69]

Vanderbilt's crowd may not have been discomforted by the enormous gap that distanced his era's wealthy from the rest of America. But many of their fellow Americans were. In the 1890s, notes one student of Vanderbilt's era, books decrying the "massing of private economic power" would become "not only bestsellers but national events." Influential writers like William Dean Howells would be "joined by dozens of lesser novelists in excoriating the moral consequences of gilded avarice."[70]

No novelist would make more of an impact than Edward Bellamy, the frail son of a New England Baptist minister.[71] Bellamy's 1888 novel, *Looking Backward*, became, after *Uncle Tom's Cabin*, America's best-selling secular book of the nineteenth century.[72] *Looking Backward* told the tale of a wealthy Bostonian who went to bed in 1887 and awoke a century later, in 2000, to find an America that had uprooted inequality. In this new America, every adult earned the same annual income. Americans bid for their jobs, and, if no one bid for a particularly unappetizing job, then the hours of work required for it were reduced until the job became appealing enough to attract bidders.

Bellamy's egalitarian vision proved immensely popular, as did the vision advanced, about the same time, by an even more beloved advocate of greater equality in America, author and activist Henry George. At his death in 1897, George may have been the nation's third most admired man, "eclipsed in public recognition only by Mark Twain and Thomas Edison."[73] A self-educated economist, George gave voice to the apprehensions — and shame — Americans felt about their nation's growing inequality.

"We have prohibited hereditary distinctions, we have forbidden titles of nobility; yet there is growing up an aristocracy of wealth as powerful and merciless as say any that ever held sway," George told one audience.[74] "There are in the United States," he told another, "some few people richer than it is wholesome for people to be."[75]

George's most famous work, *Progress and Poverty*, attacked the concentration of land ownership and proposed the abolition of all taxes, save those on land values. This "single tax" prescription won the popular economist enough adherents to run a competitive campaign for mayor of New York in 1886.[76] George would lose that race, a three-candidate contest, to the Democrat on the ballot, but George's supporters claimed the election had been stolen from him

— and many observers agreed. George did top the Republican in the race, an up-and-comer by the name of Theodore Roosevelt.

At George's death, eleven years after his mayoral run, over a hundred thousand people marched in his funeral procession.[77] Theodore Roosevelt, meanwhile, would go on to make some plutocracy-busting history of his own, as President of the United States.

Roosevelt, a man of means himself, never saw fit to genuflect before the great fortunes of his day. "I have to talk to millionaires but I wish I didn't. They bore me," he noted in 1903. "Outside of money-making they're dumb."[78] Such "dumb" men, Roosevelt felt, should not be allowed to dominate American democracy. In 1906, Roosevelt would push for an estate tax, a levy on the assets the rich leave behind at death. Taxing estates, he explained, would "put a constantly increasing burden on the inheritance of those swollen fortunes which it is certainly of no benefit to this country to perpetuate."[79]

For Roosevelt, for millions of other Americans of his time, the notion that "swollen fortunes" were "certainly of no benefit to this country to perpetuate" seemed indisputable. In this conviction, in this revulsion against stark economic inequality, Roosevelt and his contemporaries would echo a long and noble tradition.

TOO MUCH INEQUALITY, philosophers and prophets have argued down through the ages, tears at the ties that bind the human community.

"An imbalance between rich and poor," contended Plutarch, an ancient Greek historian, "is the oldest and most fatal ailment of republics."[80]

The Greeks, notes Thomas Palaima, a University of Texas-based authority on antiquity, believed strongly that hard work produces personal prosperity. "But they held an equally strong belief," he adds, "that the concentration of exorbitant wealth in the hands of a small class ultimately divides communities and invites disaster for one and all."[81]

In the ancient East, as in the ancient West, in the New World, as in the Old, the thoughtful have always feared the consequences of letting wealth concentrate. "Excess and deficiency," taught Confucius in China, "are equally at fault."[82] Across the Pacific, in North America, Native American communities "ritualized the fair distribution of wealth." Indians of the old Pacific Northwest, notes one contemporary writer, "honored the rich only when they threw huge parties to give everything away."[83]

The world's great religious traditions have all echoed this wariness about wealth. Sages from Buddha to Muhammad, historian Arnold Toynbee once observed, disagreed with each other on "the nature of the universe, the nature of the spiritual life, the nature of ultimate reality." But they all shared, pointed out Toynbee, the same perspective on the chase after fortune: "They all said with one voice that if we made material wealth our paramount aim, this would lead to disaster."[84]

"There is enough wealth to meet everyone's need," as Mahatma Gandhi would later explain, "but not everyone's greed."

Western religious traditions have sounded the same note. "Give me neither poverty or riches," the Old Testament tells us in Proverbs.[85] Such injunctions rebound throughout the Judeo-Christian heritage. Indeed, contends Jim Wallis, an evangelical theologian, no theme resonates more compellingly in the Bible than "the immorality of inequality."[86]

"The profit of the earth," as *Ecclesiastes* exclaims, "is for all."[87]

At various points in the history of ancient Israel, powerful men chose to challenge this clear injunction. They devoted themselves to accumulation, against the ancient traditions. At exactly these points, those epochs when wealth concentrated, the great prophets — Isaiah, Amos, Hosea, Jeremiah — emerged onto the Biblical scene and thundered for justice. And no Biblical figure, adds Rev. Jim Wallis, would have more to say about inequality than Jesus.

"Jesus speaks more about the gap between rich and poor," the theologian observes, "than he does about heaven and hell."[88]

Thoughtful, and sometimes courageous, clergy have been revisiting that gap ever since.

"Our incomes are like our shoes," as one English cleric, Charles Colton, reminded his congregation in 1822, "if too small, they gall and pinch us; but if too large, they cause us to stumble and trip."[89]

Sir Francis Bacon, the English scholar who helped develop the basics of scientific reasoning, would no doubt have enthusiastically embraced Colton's homespun imagery. Two centuries earlier, Bacon had advanced his own homespun perspective on wealth.

"Money is like muck," Bacon noted, "not good except that it be spread."[90]

Sir Francis made this observation at about the same time English subjects were starting to populate the colonies that would become the United States. These subjects would later, as the revolutionary generation of 1776, take to heart Bacon's apprehensions about unequal distributions of wealth. Not for them the aristocratic inequalities of England. They would create a new nation where fortunes would not be privileged. Everything America's original revolutionaries knew about the world, everything dear to them from their religious traditions, everything they learned from their study of antiquity, had led them to believe that wide gaps between the wealthy and everyone else endangered the good society they wanted their new nation to become.

America's revolutionary leaders, explains historian James Huston, understood "the necessity of securing and then maintaining a nearly equal distribution of wealth among the voting citizenry."[91] Benjamin Franklin "argued that no man ought to own more property than needed for his livelihood." Noah Webster of Massachusetts, he of later dictionary fame, declared in 1787 that "a general and tolerably equal distribution of landed property is the whole basis of national freedom," the "very soul of a republic."[92]

The nation our revolutionary generation created did at first maintain, by and large, that "tolerably equal distribution of landed property." Great fortunes, over the new nation's first century, did not dominate the young republic. But neither did a consistent commitment to real equality, as abolitionists, trade unionists, early feminists, and legions of other reformers continually pointed out. Still, compared to the fortresses of aristocratic inequality in Europe, the young United States did stand apart. Fourth of July orators could proudly — and credibly — proclaim the United States a nation where the people, not privilege, ruled.

That claim, with the unfolding of the Gilded Age after the Civil War, would no longer remain credible. The emergence of giant industrial empires, social critics noted, perverted the values that made America a special place.

"The greatest country, the richest country, is not that which has the most capitalists, monopolists, immense grabbings, vast fortunes, with its sad, sad foil of extreme, degrading, damning poverty," wrote Walt Whitman, the greatest poet of the time, "but the land in which there are the most homesteads, freeholds — where wealth does not show such contrasts high and low, where all men have enough — a modest living — and no man is made possessor beyond the sane and beautiful necessities."[93]

The grand fortunes of Gilded Age America would trigger almost equally grand citizen movements that aimed to cut the wealthy down to democratic size. In 1892, the "Populists" burst into the nation's consciousness, electing governors and members of Congress, challenging racism in the old Confederacy, challenging the domination of great wealth everywhere. That wealth, argued the farmers who launched the Populist crusade, imperiled all Americans.

"Plutocracy should be called the great national crime," proclaimed Milford Howard, a Populist congressman from Alabama. "The spirit of avarice is devouring the great heart of this nation. The greed for gain gets such possession of men's souls that they become demons. They rush into the maelstrom of money-getting, and soon lose all fear of God and love for their fellow-men, and before they realize it, they have become slaves to a passion which is as cruel as fate and remorseless and unrelenting as death."[94]

In the early twentieth century, a new generation of reformers, the middle-class Progressives, would pick up where the Populists left off.

"We can either have democracy in this country," as attorney Louis Brandeis, later a Supreme Court justice, thundered in near-Biblical cadences, "or we can have great wealth concentrated in the hands of a few, but we can't have both."

Men and women inspired by reformers like Brandeis would keep the pressure on outsized fortunes throughout the first half of the twentieth century. They battled for checks on "trusts," the grand accumulations of companies that created even grander accumulations of wealth. They battled for taxes on the incomes of the wealthy. They battled for taxes on estates stiff enough to prevent tycoons, at death, from giving birth to new dynasties. They helped focus America's political discourse on inequality. "As late as the 1940s," notes one business journalist, "it was possible to talk without irony of 'soaking the rich.'"[95]

And the rich did get soaked.

A half-century of unrelenting struggle against privilege would climax, during and right after the Great Depression, in new values for America. The selfless, not the selfish, would set the nation's tone. In the 1930s and 1940s, under pressure from organized and angry average citizens, lawmakers would tax the nation's wealthy at rates considerably higher than ever before. Working people, for the first time, would win basic rights to bargain for a larger share of the wealth their labors created. Historian Claudia Goldin has dubbed these years the "Great Compression." Higher taxes on the wealthy, the first national minimum wage, Social Security, and collective bargaining would all combine to dramatically narrow the gap between America's wealthy and everyone else.[96]

What emerged, in full glory, after World War II would be the world's first truly middle class nation, "the first genuine mass prosperity in the history of humankind."[97] America's post-war economy boomed — for nearly everyone. Home ownership, pension plans, and health insurance became commonplace facts of life for average Americans.[98] The nation, by every economic measure, was becoming more equal, and those not yet "equalized" seemed to be on their way. In the 1960s, just to make sure, we would even start a war against poverty.

In the quarter century after World War II, the real incomes of American families — all families, rich, poor, and every one in the middle — rose substantially. But middle class and poor families actually saw their incomes, on an annual basis, rise faster than the incomes of rich families.[99] Throughout these years, average Americans made steady progress to the good life that had become the American dream. A decent home. A dependable paycheck. Time to enjoy families and friends. Opportunities for children. These all seemed attainable in the years after World War II.[100]

In these prosperous times, average Americans did not feel particularly diminished if they weren't rich. Americans lived in a society that celebrated the middle class, and most could entertain reasonable hopes of becoming part of that vast middle. Vast inequality, by the 1950s, seemed a relic of America's economically primitive past. Earlier eras of greed, economists began pronouncing, simply reflected the immaturity of America's industrializing economy. Wide disparities of wealth and income, they assured the nation, would continue to dissolve as America's economy continued to evolve.[101]

The executives who managed corporate America after World War II would, in this relatively egalitarian atmosphere, keep a low profile. They wore gray flannel suits, not TV make-up. They hid in nondescript office buildings. They wouldn't think of building palaces, even if they could afford them.

And then, early in the 1970s, the drive toward a more equal America suddenly started sputtering. The nation's great and growing middle class, the moving force of modern American life, stopped growing. Almost overnight.

We can measure how well, or how poorly, a middle class is growing in any number of ways. We can, for instance, define a range of incomes as "middle class" and then count — and compare over time — the number of families that fall within this range. One analysis along these lines, conducted in 1998, defined as middle class those families that earn between $30,000 and $80,000. In 1973, this analysis found, families earning between $30,000 and $80,000, as measured in 1998 dollars, made up nearly two-thirds of all American families. In 1998, they made up only half.[102]

We can also define middle class as a fixed ratio. Economists who take this approach typically compute an overall income median — the point at which half a society makes more, half less — and then label as middle class everyone who makes at least half the median but no more than twice. In 1969, the number of Americans in the middle class, as defined by this standard, constituted 71.2 percent of the American people. Three decades later, in 1998, only 61.5 percent of Americans fit this middle class standard.

What happened to those Americans who no longer lived in the middle? Some fell below middle class income levels. The share of Americans making less than half the median wage, notes the Economic Policy Institute, expanded from 18 percent of the nation in 1969 to 22.3 percent in 1998. Other refugees from middle-income ranks jumped up in earnings. The number of people making at least twice the median wage rose from 10.8 percent in 1969 to 16.2 percent in 1998.[103]

Measuring the middle class, to be sure, is no exact science. All sorts of people, after all, define themselves as middle class, including people who strike others as poor and people who strike others as rich. Ultimately, argues economist Paul Krugman, a middle class nation cannot adequately be defined purely by numbers. A truly middle class nation, he suggests, is "a society in which most people live more or less the same kind of life."

"In 1970 we were that kind of society," notes Krugman. "Today we are not, and we become less like one with each passing year."[104]

By THE OPENING OF THE TWENTY-FIRST CENTURY, the United States had gone a decade without recession, the longest stretch of peacetime prosperity in the nation's history. America had never before generated so much wealth. Yet most Americans felt anything but flush.

"About 75 per cent of American families are caught in an Alice-in-Wonderland world," as economist Barry Bluestone had observed a few years earlier, "working enormous hours but not getting anywhere."[105]

America's typical middle class families, the Federal Reserve Board would report in 2003, were actually losing ground. Between 1998 and 2001, Fed data showed, typical middle class families saw the total value of their financial assets — everything from their mutual funds and bank savings to the money in their retirement accounts and the cash value of their life insurance — drop, from $17,600 to $17,100.[106]

How could that be? How could so many families, amid such massive new wealth, be struggling to hold their own? So many families were struggling, careful analysts pointed out, because most families were not sharing in America's bounty. Our nation's new wealth was enriching only a small and fortunate few.

Who made up this fortunate few? In 2001, the *New York Times* would define "the winning upper crust" as those households worth at least $250,000, a category that encompassed about one in five American households.[107] In the 1980s and 1990s, this most affluent fifth captured almost all of America's gains in household net worth — 91 percent, according to economist Edward Wolff.[108] By 2002, the Census Bureau calculated, America's top fifth was raking in over half the nation's annual personal income, its highest share ever.[109]

But these "top fifth" statistics, many analysts argue, actually cloud more than they clarify. Not everyone in America's richest fifth, they note, has been realizing the same king-sized prosperity. Indeed, these analysts add, America's most fundamental economic divide doesn't sit between the nation's most affluent 20 percent and everybody else. America's real divide has become the gap that separates the immensely wealthy, not the merely affluent, from everyone else.

On average, to be sure, those households in America's most affluent fifth have been doing quite well over recent years. In the 1980s and 1990s, after adjusting for inflation, the "average" income for this top fifth rose a sweet 70 percent, to $196,500.[110] But averages can deceive. Consider, for instance, a baseball team with one star making $15 million and twenty-four other ballplayers earning $250,000 each. The *average* salary on that club would be $840,000, but twenty-four of the twenty-five players would be making less than one-third the average.

In the 1980s and 1990s, America's most affluent 20 percent resembled a top-heavy baseball team.[111] By the turn of the century, in 2000, most households in this affluent 20 percent didn't earn anywhere near the group's $196,500 average. Three quarters of the households in the richest fifth, in fact, only earned between $58,400 and $108,400.[112]

America's most affluent 5 percent were doing considerably better than that, Congressional Budget Office research revealed in 2003. The Americans in these households saw their average pretax incomes leap, after adjusting for inflation, from $205,500 in 1979 to $434,300 in 2000, an imposing 111 percent increase. Overall, between 1979 and 2000, the incomes of America's richest 5 percent jumped over three times faster than the incomes of America's next richest 15 percent.

But these numbers still don't tell the full story. To really understand who gets what in the United States today, we need to look closer at America's top 5 percent. That closer look offers up a striking picture: Within our top 5 percent, the richest 1 percent outpace, by astonishingly wide margins, the next richest 4 percent.

Households in America's richest 1 percent saw their *average* annual income soar, after adjusting for inflation, from $454,200 in 1979 to $1,290,800 in 2000, a 184 percent increase. Households in the next richest 4 percent saw, by contrast, their average incomes rise only 64 percent, from $139,668 to $229,485.[113]

The gap between America's richest 1 percent and everybody else becomes even more striking when we shift our spotlight from annual income to accumulated wealth.

In 1998, the nation's wealthiest 1 percent sat on nest-eggs worth an average $10.2 million. Their wealth had increased 42 percent since 1983, after taking inflation into account.[114] The richest 1 percent, between 1983 and 1998, actually *gained* in wealth more than double what the next richest 4 percent *owned*.[115] In all, economist Edward Wolff concluded in 2001, America's wealthiest 1 percent accumulated more than half, 53 percent, of the nation's "total gain in marketable wealth over the 1983-1998 period."[116]

The new wealth generated by the American economy in the "prosperous" 1980s and 1990s had, in effect, come to rest in the pockets of a tiny elite. The most celebrated among this elite went by an acronym. We called them CEOs.

BACK IN THE EARLY 1970S, if asked to name even a single current corporate chief executive, most Americans would have been hard-pressed. Fewer still would have known what "CEO" stands for. A generation later, almost all Americans would know. The shorthand for "chief executive officer," by century's end, had come to symbolize — epitomize — America's growing polarization of income and wealth.

CEOs first started gaining the public's attention in the 1980s, for an understandable reason. Something strange was happening. Average wages were stagnating, but paychecks for top corporate executives were soaring. In all, over the course of the 1980s, top executive pay would more than triple, rising 212 percent.[117]

But the real eye-opening gains in CEO compensation were yet to come. Between 1990 and 2000, top executive pay soared another 571 percent.[118] The new century began with top corporate CEOs routinely averaging over $10 million a year.

Average worker pay, meanwhile, had barely outpaced inflation. If production worker pay in America had grown as fast as CEO pay, one study pointed out, production workers would have averaged $120,491 in 2000, not the $24,668 they actually took home.[119]

These two trends — soaring executive pay and stagnating paychecks for average workers — created remarkably stark disparities. In Silicon Valley, janitors made $8.40 an hour cleaning the offices of top executives making $10,000 a day.[120] Or more. Cisco CEO John Chambers pulled in $121.7 million in 1999, over $333,000 a day if he worked every weekend and Christmas day, too.[121]

General Electric CEO Jack Welch, the next year, would do even better. He carted home $144.5 million in 2000, a payout nearly three hundred times greater than the compensation his CEO predecessor at G.E. earned in 1975.[122]

Things had changed at G.E. — and in America, too. In 1975, the G.E. chief executive's $500,000 paycheck equaled the combined incomes of thirty-six American families earning the nation's median income. Jack Welch's $144.5 million equaled the year 2000 median income of nearly thirty-five hundred American families.[123]

In new millennium America, a top executive could — and did — make in one year what an average employee would have to work almost two millennia to equal. To match the year 2000 take-home of Sprint CEO William Esrey, for instance, a Sprint telephone line repair person would have had to labor for the next 1,891 years.[124]

Such disparities amazed — and shocked — business people who had devoted their careers to the nitty-gritty of making America work.

"Top management increasingly seems to view itself as a group of demigods entitled to dwell in the financial pantheon once reserved for nobility," a *Machine Design* magazine editorial writer would angrily note. "In the face of massive layoffs and hardship inflicted on the work force in general, corporate management is on an upward spiral of greed that seemingly has no bounds."[125]

No bounds indeed. In 2000, the top three executives of MedImmune Inc., a Maryland biotech company, personally pulled in over $20 million each. Their company's good fortune depended on a drug designed to treat the "symptoms of a respiratory virus in high-risk infants."[126] Making millions off of high-risk infants, wasn't this a bit unseemly? Certainly not, retorted company spokesperson Lori Weiman.

"Our company, like everyone else," the corporate flack explained, "looks at what's standard and customary."[127]

Standard and customary. What would the biotech giants of earlier ages have thought about America's new compensation standards?

"Jonas Salk never sought to patent his polio vaccine," notes journalist William Greider. "He thought his reward was knowing how greatly his work had advanced all of humanity."[128]

Silly Salk. What did he know.

IMAGINE IF A PRESIDENTIAL CANDIDATE had stood before voters, in 1976, and promised to make life worse for average Americans. Imagine this candidate, in the first debate of the fall campaign, making a pledge that went like this:

"If I'm elected, I promise that you're going to work longer hours than you've ever worked before, for the next twenty-five years. But, hey, that won't matter because you won't be able to afford to go out much anyway. You're going to have less job security. You're going to be bounced around. And your local communities are going to have less to spend on schools and parks. Why am I asking you to tolerate all this? For the good of the country? Are you kidding? I'm asking you to do more and take less because I want to create an America that works for the privileged. Yes, sir, you may have it tough over the next twenty-five years, but your fellow citizens who happen to be wealthy are going to have a grand time. How does that sound? Do we have a deal? Can I count on your vote?"

Any candidate who delivered such a speech in 1976 would surely have been hooted off the stage. Newspapers would have railed against this candidate's nightmarish vision. The candidate's party faithful would have deserted. On election day, our loudmouth candidate would have been buried by America's greatest landslide ever. Average Americans would have gone to sleep that night smiling and content, secure in the knowledge they had soundly defeated an outrageous attack on their future well-being.

No candidate in 1976, of course, ever ran for office pledging to help the already affluent grab a greater share of the nation's income and wealth. No candidate over the last quarter-century has ever run on such a platform, or anything close to it. Yet America's affluent *have* increased their share of the nation's income and wealth, and enormously so, at the same time average Americans have seen their economic fortunes stagnate. The vision that would have been seen as a nightmare in 1976 has come true.

"No country without a revolution or a military defeat and subsequent occupation," economist Lester Thurow has noted, "has ever experienced such a sharp a shift in the distribution of earnings as America in the last generation."[129]

How sharp? If households in America's poorest fifth of households had received at the end of the twentieth century the same share of the nation's after-tax income as they received in 1977, each poor household would have taken home $3,300 more in 1999 than it actually did. If average American households had received in 1999 the same share of America's income they received in 1977, families in our middle fifth of households would have earned, after taxes, $3,500 more per household than they actually did.

And at the top? If America's wealthiest 1 percent had closed the century with the same share of the nation's income that this top 1 percent received in 1977, our wealthiest would have made $226,000 *less* per household than they actually did earn in 1999.[130]

The bottom line from America's generation-long shift in who gets what: By the early twenty-first century, Federal Reserve Board research would document in 2003, America's top 1 percent had accumulated over $2 trillion more in wealth than everyone in America's bottom 90 percent combined.[131]

America had become, analysts agreed, "the most unequal rich nation on earth."[132]

Must we in the United States remain as unequal as we are now? Is our nation's wealth destined to remain forever concentrated? Perhaps. But earlier generations of Americans faced inequality that seemed just as stark, just as embedded, as ours. They made a difference. They created a more equal America, a society where wealth did not concentrate, a society where average people could significantly improve their lot in life.

These earlier generations could not, in the end, sustain the momentum for a more equal America. But we can learn from their efforts. We can avoid their mistakes and build upon their triumphs. We can make a lasting difference, these pages will contend, if we dare to be bold. We will propose, in this spirit, that our nation needs to stop the concentration of wealth where it starts, by capping the incomes of those Americans at our nation's economic summit. We will propose what might be called, in effect, a "maximum wage."

A *maximum* wage? Americans who care about economic inequality can today barely generate enough political momentum to raise the *minimum* wage. How can we possibly talk about a *maximum* wage and expect to be taken seriously? In our contemporary United States, isn't any talk about income limits simply ludicrous?

Maybe not. In 1942, a President of the United States, Franklin D. Roosevelt, actually proposed the equivalent of a maximum wage — and no one laughed.

President Roosevelt asked Congress that year to impose a 100 percent tax on all individual income over $25,000, about $300,000 in current dollars after adjusting for inflation. Roosevelt's plan to cap incomes didn't pass, but his proposal did have an impact. By 1944, Congress had voted to tax income over $200,000 at a 94 percent annual rate, not a cap, to be sure, but not too far distant from one.

Would an income cap make sense for us today? And if so, at what level? At $300,000, the equivalent of FDR's $25,000? At half a million dollars a year? At a million? The pages ahead will spend no time arguing that any one of these numbers makes more sense as a limit than any other. Whether the richest people in our society earn $300,000 a year or $1 million a year does not really matter. What matters, these pages will contend, is the *gap* between the rich and everyone else. That gap is what needs limiting — before our social fabric stretches so far it tears.

If our problem is indeed our gap, as the pages to come will argue, then any "maximum wage" worth fighting for ought to be about reducing the distance between top and bottom, and not just about placing ceilings on the top. The maximum wage approach we propose aims in this direction. We call our approach the Ten Times Rule. In a Ten Times Rule America, no American would be able to earn more than ten times the income of any other. Any income above this ten times limit would be subject to a 100 percent tax.

If this Ten Times Rule were ever to become the law of the land, our nation's richest would only be able to become richer if our poorest became richer first. America's wealthiest and most powerful, in this ten times environment, would suddenly have a personal, deep-seated, vested self-interest in improving the well-being of America's poorest and least powerful.

These musings about a maximum wage will no doubt strike many contemporary ears as sheer madness. We live at a time, after all, when great fortunes are accepted as a given, a basic fact of life. To be is to accumulate. What journalist Richard Todd calls "the original American dream" — "the fragile idea that there is an equality based on worth that transcends net worth" — seems to have no place in early twenty-first century America.[133]

In our current climate, to try to attend to inequality seriously, to even consider placing limits on accumulation, is to invite ridicule. Limits on income? In a free country? How dare anyone suggest such an attack on our freedom!

In our free country, truth be told, we set limits all the time. We tell hunters they can shoot only so many ducks. We tell motorists they can drive only so fast. We tell developers that their skyscrapers can sport only so many floors. We set limits to protect our well-being.

That well-being, these pages will argue, demands that we set limits on income as well.

But incomes, the retort will come, cannot be lumped together with ducks and speed limits. Greed may be ugly, the retorters will argue, but the craving to become rich motors our civilization, all civilization. To progress as a people, we must accept greed. To place limits on accumulation, to shackle greed in any significant way, shape, or form, would be to throttle the engine that drives all human progress.

This strain of thinking echoes powerfully throughout the United States today and, to a lesser extent, throughout the rest of the world as well. To make the case for a more equal America, we need first to carefully consider, not dismiss, this case for business as usual, this case for greed.

Book One

The Case for Greed

WHY WE 'NEED' INEQUALITY

EACH AND EVERY SPRING, at graduation ceremonies across the United States, many hundreds, even thousands, of commencement speakers deliver noble calls to arms. Do good by others, the speakers urge graduates, give back to your communities.

Few commencement speakers ever stray from these earnestly virtuous themes — and none of them ever advise the opposite course. None of them urge graduates to go forth out into the world, behave selfishly, and get rich. Yet out there in the real world where graduates venture, we celebrate those who have become fantastically rich, those never too tired to grasp for more. We buy their books. We elect them to high office. We envy their success, and, perhaps most disturbingly, we dare not imagine a society without them.

A century ago, even a half-century ago, we did not fawn so. What changed? What made avarice attractive? How did celebrating wealth and the wealthy become so socially respectable? Give credit to the apologists for greed. They have made a cogent, powerful case. They have a seductively simple story to tell and they tell it well. Their basic storyline now shapes how we Americans see the world: Without rich people striving to become richer — without everyone else striving to become rich — progress would cease and civilization, as we know it, would simply collapse.

So argue today's most distinguished defenders of great fortunes, gentlemen like P. George Benson, the dean of the business school at the University of Georgia.

"A natural product of the wealth creation process of our capitalistic system is unequal incomes and unequal net worths," Dean Benson posited in 2001. "Our competitive private sector rewards individuals differently according to their talent and productivity. Some do well, some not so well. A few become very wealthy."[1]

Their wealth, added Benson, enriches us all.

"Inequality of results is the incentive for creating the wealth that is necessary for a civilized society," he explained. "It provides the motivation for all of us to excel at whatever our business is. And in the process of excelling, we cure diseases, build world-renowned educational institutions, invent technologies that improve the quality of our lives, produce enough food to feed the hungry, and create artistic masterpieces that inspire and entertain."

We will forever prosper, concluded Dean Benson, so long as we pursue wealth and honor those who pursue most successfully.

"So the next time you hear someone bashing the wealthy," concluded the good dean, "remember the wealthy are, have been, and always will be an integral part of the incentive structure that drives our economy and our American way of life."

Behind these stirring sentences sit three basic ideas that drive the case for greed.

The first: We need people to be greedy, to want to become fabulously wealthy. Greed makes for a wonderful incentive. Without a shot at becoming wealthly, people would simply laze their lives away.

The second: Those who do achieve wealth fully deserve their good fortune. If the greedy were to be denied their just desserts for all the striving that they do, who would ever continue striving to succeed?

The third: We all benefit when some of us become far wealthier than others, when the greedy fulfill their ambitions to become rich.

We will examine, in the pages ahead, each of these claims. We will explore the reasonableness of greed as an incentive. We will consider the greedy as deserving. We will examine, finally, the greedy as benefactors to society at large.

In this endeavor, we will focus considerable attention on America's corporate CEOs, that small exclusive group that has come to personify greed and grasping. Corporate chief executives are not, to be sure, the only greedy people in America. But corporate CEOs manage the companies that dominate the world. Their decisions impact our lives, and today, more than ever before, pure simple greed seems to drive these decisions. That's how it should be, insist the apologists for our current corporate order. We shall see.

GREED AS AN INCENTIVE

NO SOCIETY CAN ADVANCE, inequality's defenders have always asserted, without incentives. If we want talented people to do great things, these defenders submit, we need to offer equally great rewards. Great rewards prompt great deeds. Societies that choose to limit rewards, say by taking steps that make accumulating wealth more difficult, reduce the incentive to achieve. These societies, the argument goes, will stagnate. The most talented within them will simply not offer all they have to give.

Any society that heaps rewards on the talented, the argument continues, will certainly end up with some people who hold far more wealth than others. But these differences in wealth can become powerful and positive incentives in their own right. They send the message that those without wealth need to shape up and work harder. The wider the disparities in wealth, the more powerful the message.[1] Imbalances of wealth and income, in short, grease America's economic gears. Eliminate these imbalances, apologists for inequality warn, and you eliminate the incentives that keep us going and growing.

These pages will certainly not challenge the notion that incentives can keep us on our toes. As individuals, we do need incentives. We use them every day. We offer our kids the opportunity to stay up an extra half-hour if they'll eat all their broccoli. That half-hour amounts to an incentive. We give our dogs treats when they obey our entreaties to sit and fetch. We scan newspapers for sales, the incentives that merchants offer us to part with our dollars. Incentives work. They change behavior. We couldn't get by without them.

But some incentives, we know from experience, work better than others. We might offer a lollipop to get a three-year-old to sit and listen. That lollipop would likely make no impact whatsoever on a refrigerator repairman. Some incentives, we also understand, might be inappropriate because they make too much of an impact. We do not, for instance, reward our canines with foot-long franks. Our pooches, if so rewarded, might learn how to sit and fetch quite nicely. But they would also become dangerously obese. So we fill our fanny packs with bite-sized biscuits. These make appropriate training incentives. Foot-long franks do not. In a different context, of course, hot dogs could serve as a perfectly appropriate incentive: To encourage ten-year-olds to attend a practice, a Little League coach might reasonably promise a hot dog cookout after the workout.

With incentives, in other words, context is everything.

In America's executive suites, over recent years, incentives have been everything. Corporate America has been engaged, in fact, in human history's most costly incentive experiment ever. This experiment has, since the early 1980s, awarded America's top corporate executives over half a trillion dollars.[2] Has this enormous transfer of treasure — perhaps the single biggest reason why wealth in the United States has concentrated so intensely — served as a reasonable incentive? Are the lavish rewards that corporate boards continue to bestow upon executives legitimate? That depends.

We need to look at the context.

MOVERS AND SHAKERS IN CORPORATE AMERICA, and those who write about them, have always spent a great deal of time thinking about incentives. Large, modern enterprises, by their very nature, raise questions about incentives that small enterprises simply do not face.

Consider, for example, America's classic small enterprise, the mom-and-pop shop. In a corner candy store, the incentives never blur. Mom and pop work for themselves. If they work hard, and if their enterprise prospers, they know they'll prosper, too. But most of us don't work for ourselves. We work in large enterprises. Our paychecks come every two weeks, even when we're sick or on vacation. If a mom-and-pop has a bad day, mom and pop might not see any income at all. If our enterprise has a bad day, our paychecks still come. We are employees, not owners.

CEOs, in this broad sense, sit in the same boat as the newest corporate mailroom hire. CEOs don't own the companies where they work. They draw paychecks, just like any other employee. This employment relationship has always troubled scholars who study how businesses operate. If executives are mere employees and if executives can pocket paychecks whether their enterprises are doing superbly or just getting by, why would any sane person in an executive slot put out the extra effort needed to create a superb enterprise? Clearly, scholars have concluded, we have a problem here. Moms and pops will naturally work hard because what they get depends on how hard and how smart they work. Executives have no such natural incentive. How then can enterprises go about getting executives to exert themselves and truly do their best?

The answer, a generation ago, seemed obvious. How can enterprises keep their executives performing at the highest levels? Keep them happy! Enterprises succeed, argued analysts who advocated a "human resources" approach, when they find and hang onto talented executives. Wise enterprises, consequently, should do whatever they can to keep their talented executives content. Above all, they should pay well.

This human resources perspective suited executives, predictably enough, just fine. They appreciated any approach that stressed the need to keep executives smiling.[3] But other business analysts challenged this keep-them-happy perspective. Forget about keeping executives happy, these skeptics advised.

Keep an eye on them instead. Executives, after all, do not own the corporations they manage. They function merely as "agents" for the shareholders who do. As agents, executives do not necessarily share the same interests as shareholders. They have their own agendas, and that reality creates an ever-present tension between executives and shareholders.[4] How can this tension, this "agency problem," be overcome? Companies must introduce incentives, analysts known as "agency theorists" advised, that tie an executive's self-interest directly to the interests of the executive's firm. Sure, they argued, executives should be paid well — but only if the enterprises they manage are doing well.

After World War II, and into the early 1970s, with American goods dominating world markets and corporate profits holding up quite nicely, the hard-boiled cynicism of the agency theorists seemed woefully shrill. Executives were delivering. So why not just pay them well and keep them happy? Why rock the boat? Few corporate boards of directors did. America's top business executives would enter the 1970s the most generously paid in the world. The critics could only mumble from the sidelines. But the mumblers, in the 1970s, would find an audience. Throughout the decade, in industry after industry, American corporations were losing market share to foreign competitors. Profits were dipping, share prices stagnating. By 1980, many investors had come to agree, "a great many American companies were in a sorry state and in need of serious restructuring."[5]

America's executives, for their part, didn't seem to be up to that "serious restructuring" task. They had adapted themselves, Wall Street suspected, "to the special habits of working inside large, stable bureaucratic structures." They refused to "take big risks or initiate major changes." They acted like stodgy bureaucrats.[6] And corporate executives were acting like stodgy bureaucrats, critics hastened to add, because they were paid like bureaucrats. Executives were cashing healthy paychecks whether their companies were soaring or sinking. Corporate America had given top executives no real incentive to perform.[7] The agency theorists, big-time investors came to believe, had been right all along. Executives would not work to maximize corporate earnings until their pay — and their future — depended on the performance of their company.

BY THE EARLY 1980s, America's biggest investors had become absolutely convinced that America's corporations were being atrociously mismanaged, so convinced that a new breed of entrepreneurs would be able to begin making billions off that certainty.

These new entrepreneurs — "bright, insolent, cocksure individuals responsible only to their financial backers" — would soon become celebrated as "corporate raiders."[8] America's top executives, these dashing raiders pronounced, were not doing nearly enough to "maximize shareholder value." Corporate America needed to be completely restructured, under new management totally committed to making money for shareholders. The raiders, naturally, proudly presented themselves as just the ace restructurers America needed. They began their ambitious corporate crusade, in the early 1980s, by buying modest interests in targeted companies, then threatening full takeovers. The targeted companies would either panic and buy out the raider's modest stake — at a price much higher than the raider originally paid — or be swallowed up by the raider. This "greenmail" would evolve into a full-fledged takeover industry, almost all of it financed by bankers and bond traders anxious for a piece of the lucrative restructuring action. Corporate raiders soon found themselves controlling, as owners, a significant chunk of America's corporate assets.

Once in control, these raiders delivered on their promises. They shook up business as usual, mostly by breaking their newly purchased companies up into pieces. Some pieces they sold. Some they kept. In the pieces they kept, they ordered all operations managed to maximize cash flow, by any means necessary, a logical step since the raiders needed cash to pay back their debts to banks and bondholders. After a few years, raiders would typically place their "restructured" pieces back on the market and sell them off, usually at top dollar, making huge personal fortunes in the process.

Mainstream corporate America, dazzled by this derring-do, would adopt the bold raider mantra — "maximize shareholder value" — in remarkably quick order. In America's boardrooms, everyone now seemed hot to trot down the restructuring road, to gobble up companies, break them apart, and swap the pieces. From 1982 through 1988, American business would see over ten thousand mergers and acquisitions, over $1 trillion worth of wheeling-and-dealing.

The corporate raiders would actually stimulate, directly, only a small portion of these restructuring transactions. Their real impact would be indirect. Corporate decision makers, in the face of the raider challenge, simply decided to do their own "restructuring." This self-restructuring, notes Wall Street veteran Roy Smith, who watched the action as an investment banker, almost always followed the same script. A corporation would begin by "selling off divisions and other assets that no longer fit into a highly focused, back-to-basics strategy." The new "lean and mean" enterprise that remained would then emphasize operations that generated quick cash. Finally, to guarantee that everything went as intended, the restructured enterprise would "provide substantial incentives to management to work their butts off to make all this happen."

What sort of incentives? Incentives for maximizing shareholder value. Executives, the new conventional wisdom held, would only maximize that value if they saw themselves, first and foremost, as shareholders themselves, as part of ownership, not just the hired help.[9] Incentives in corporate America would now link executive rewards, directly, to share price. How shares fared in market trading would determine executive compensation. And how exactly would this compensation be tied to stock performance? Through stock options.

Stock options, on paper, merely give whoever receives them the right to buy shares of stock, at some specific time in the future, at some specific price. In practice, an option can be much more than a right. An option can be a chance to make a killing, by buying stock "at a cut-rate price" and selling at a premium profit.[10]

Imagine yourself an executive. Shares of your company's stock are currently trading at $50. You are granted the option to buy, four years from today, one hundred thousand of these shares at this same $50 per share. You do some quick calculations. If your company's share price rises to $100 over the next four years, you could "exercise" your option to buy those one hundred thousand shares at $50, then immediately sell them, on the open market, at their $100 value. You would make a profit of $50 per share, or $5 million. You smile. This option business could be a hugely good deal.

A good deal, investors agreed, for shareholders, too. Executives, with option sugarplums dancing before their eyes, would surely move heaven and earth to "maximize shareholder value." Who could doubt that? Who could doubt that corporate America had solved, once and for all, "the agency problem"?

STOCK OPTIONS, BY THE 1980s, had actually already become a familiar corporate fixture. Historians, in fact, have traced option incentives back to the 1920s.[11] But options remained little more than curiosities until 1950, when Congress "liberalized" how options could be treated for tax purposes.[12] Under the new law, and a subsequent ruling by the national board that then set accounting standards, companies could count options as deductions for tax purposes, yet not have to count options as expenses against earnings.[13] This accounting sleight-of-hand made a dollar's worth of options more attractive than a dollar's worth of straight salary, since any dollars shelled out for salaries had to be counted before profits could be figured. Options carried no such baggage and came somewhat "into vogue," after 1950, as an executive incentive.[14] Still, throughout the 1950s and 1960s, options remained a distinctly second-tier incentive. Corporate boards granted options "sparingly" and in modest numbers.[15]

This second-tier status would begin to fade in the 1970s, particularly in the emerging new electronics industry. Influentials in electronics had latched onto options early on. The founders of Intel, for instance, stocked their new company with talent by offering options, not higher salaries, to the executives and engineers they wanted to recruit from other firms. In 1971, to lure one top marketing executive, Intel offered options for twenty thousand shares, about 1 percent of the company. Intel gave that executive the right to buy the shares at $5 apiece. Later that same year, Intel's stock went public at $23.50.[16]

Options could be equally rewarding in more mainstream business circles. In 1978, Lee Iacocca, America's first modern celebrity CEO, humbly accepted from his new employer, the troubled Chrysler, the option to buy four hundred thousand company shares at just over $11 a share.[17] Iacocca would later turn his options into a $42 million personal payday.[18] But most top executives, unlike Iacocca, would show little interest in options in the 1970s, and for good reason. Options only pay off when share prices are rising. But share prices had stopped rising in the early 1970s, and the subsequent bear market lasted the entire decade. In a bear market, executives argued, stock options no longer make for effective incentives. In a bear market, the argument went, executives could break their backs, do fantastic work, and still not see any significant upward tick in their company's share price. Corporate boards obligingly agreed. They would, throughout the 1970s and into the 1980s, offer executives a variety of incentives not linked to share prices.[19]

These incentives often blossomed one on top of the other. Warner Communications, for instance, bestowed seven different long-term incentive plans on its CEO, Steve Ross, from 1973 through 1989. Among the incentives: an annual bonus that handed Ross a fixed percentage of the company's after-tax profits, as much as $4.2 million a year.[20] In all, the "prince of pay," as Ross was dubbed by one compensation analyst, took home about $275 million from 1973 through 1989, a $16 million annual average.[21]

IN THE 1980S, THE PRINCE OF PAY would have plenty of amply compensated company. CEO pay overall jumped 212 percent over the decade, at the same time corporate profits were rising only 78 percent.[22] To press and investing public alike, that seemed utterly ghastly. Something needed to be done. Executives had to be held more accountable, and that accountability could be achieved, critics asserted, only if stock option incentives finally became, once and for all, the dominant centerpiece of executive compensation.

This option drumbeat would intensify as the 1990s began, and no one would pound away any harder than America's "institutional investors," the pension funds, endowments, and other entities with huge conglomerations of cash that need to be invested.[23] These institutional investors had good reason to worry about executive pay and performance. They often owned such large stakes in individual companies that they couldn't afford to simply sell off their shares in an underperforming company, as a typical unhappy investor might. Any big sell-off on their part might send the sinking price of an underperformer's stock sinking even faster. Institutional investors, in effect, had no choice but to hold their huge stakes in poorly performing companies and try to get the poor performers to shape up. Stock options, these investors came to believe, might just be the incentive needed to light a fire under an underperforming management team.[24]

Options also held all sorts of attractions for corporate directors. For starters, option awards could be easily justified, from a public relations perspective. By granting options, corporate boards could reward executives without having to take flak for shelling out lavishly high salaries and bonuses.[25] This flak had hit hard against Reebok in 1988, a year company earnings fell, after the athletic shoemaker awarded CEO Paul Fireman an $11.1 million bonus. In 1989, Fireman's bonus soared even higher, to $14.2 million, prompting still more negative publicity. In 1990, Reebok's directors finally wised up. They renegotiated Fireman's incentives and limited his bonus to $1 million per year. Fireman wouldn't mind. Reebok stuffed his pockets with a 2.5 million-share stock option grant.[26]

For Reebok, and every other top company, options neatly shifted the responsibility for executive pay excess from corporate boards — and the individuals who sat on them — to the stock market. If executives do well by options, corporate boards could reasonably argue, their good fortune merely reflects the market's impartial judgment. The more highly the market values an executive's performance, the higher the executive's eventual option payoff will be, and vice versa, as Sprint would later take pains to emphasize after critics questioned its executives' high option earnings. "The less they make the stock price rise," Sprint explained, "the less they get paid."[27] What could be fairer?

Option grants still carried useful accounting magic, too. They amounted to "free money."[28] Companies could grant options to executives right and left, not record the options as expenses that count against profits, and end up paying less in taxes, because options, once cashed in by executives, became tax-deductible expenses for the companies that granted them. By the mid 1990s, such deductions were "chopping billions off corporate tax bills." In one year alone, this tax bonanza saved Microsoft $352 million in taxes, Cisco $198 million, and PepsiCo $145 million.[29] Stock options, one analysis concluded, "let companies have their cake, eat it too, and get a second helping."[30]

A few lonely business voices did dare to speak out against this voodoo accounting.

"If options aren't a form of compensation, what are they?" investor guru Warren Buffet protested. "If compensation isn't an expense, what is it? And if expenses shouldn't go into the calculation of earnings, where in the world should they go?"[31]

Corporate boards had little interest in Buffet's quibbles. But they did pay attention, in 1993, when the Financial Accounting Standards Board, the accounting industry's national rulemaking body, tried to demystify the option magic act. The board proposed that options "be charged against earnings as a compensation expense." Outraged corporate leaders immediately "protested en masse," claiming that the board's change would send corporate profits, stock prices, and the nation's economy into a cataclysmic tailspin.[32]

The standards board chairman, Dennis Beresford, did his best to defend his agency. In one particularly "heated" discussion aboard a corporate jet, Beresford "scoffed at the doomsday arguments" against the Board's option stance. The executives Beresford was debating, the *Wall Street Journal* reported, then "invited him to exit the craft — at 20,000 feet."[33] The standards board would eventually agree, under duress, "to exempt the cost of stock options from being reported as an expense."[34] Options would keep their magic.

By the early 1990s, top executives, no less than corporate boards themselves, had fully fallen under the option spell. Corporate executives, the "underperformers" that investors wanted option grants to "shape up," were now enthusiastically willing to swallow any option medicine investors wanted swallowed. The 1970s bear market that had soured executives on options had ended. Share prices, in the 1980s, were rising again.

But something else changed in the 1980s as well. Executives suddenly realized they were missing out on the real money to be made in America's booming economy. Top executives like Steve Ross might indeed be doing quite well. But Ross took seventeen years to cart home his $275 million from Warner Communications. Michael Milken, the junk bond king, cleared twice that, $550 million, in just one year.[35]

All the real money, top corporate executives saw clearly, was going to the wheelers and dealers, clever operators like former Treasury Secretary William Simon, who bought Gibson Greeting in 1982, with other people's money, and then cleared a quarter-billion personal profit on an "initial public offering" — an IPO — of the company's stock.[36]

Everybody on Wall Street, simply everybody, seemed to be making multimillions wheeling and dealing. On the biggest "leveraged buyouts," or LBOs as the insiders called them, just the transaction fees alone were enough to generate fortunes. In one classic mid-1980s buyout deal, involving Revlon cosmetics, lawyers and investment bankers walked off with $110 million in fees.[37]

These multimillions made an enormous impact on corporate CEOs. Their investment banker advisors were making fortunes that put their own executive bonus plans to shame.

"Once executives realized what their advisers were making," notes Charles Morris, an investment banker who watched the frenzy from a front-row seat, "they insisted on a share of the pie."[38]

But to get that share, executives first needed to get equity — an ownership stake — in their companies. Stock options could give them that equity stake.

"CEOs learned two things from LBOs," as New York corporate lawyer Dick Beattie would explain to the *Wall Street Journal*. "First, the way to build significant wealth was through equity ownership, not salary and bonuses, and second, you didn't need to do an LBO to build equity: You could give yourself options."[39]

Technically, of course, executives couldn't give themselves options. Only corporate boards of directors could bestow options upon executives — but these corporate boards now had absolutely no reason not to. Their critics, on the one hand, were demanding options as a "reform" that would keep executives accountable. Their executives, on the other hand, now saw options as a risk-free ride to windfall glory. For corporate boards, in short, options had become the ultimate no-lose proposition. Reformers demanded them. Executives welcomed them. Accountants winked at them. Uncle Sam blessed them with favorable tax treatment. Options seemed to please everybody.

By the mid 1990s, in nearly every important industry, most American top executive pay would be coming from stock options, not salaries and bonuses. In 1980, stock option grants represented less than 20 percent of total CEO pay.

By 1997, CEOs at the nation's top two hundred firms were taking home 55 percent of their pay from options.[40] Three years later, in 2000, that share of top executive pay from stock options had jumped to nearly 75 percent[41] — and sometimes much more. In 1999, America Online CEO Steve Case earned $575,000 in annual salary, a bonus worth $750,000, and $115.5 million by "exercising" — cashing out — his options.[42]

For corporate America's top executives, observed the *Wall Street Journal*, stock options had become "a virtual cash machine." In 1997, top executives at the 350 firms tracked by the *Journal* cashed in $1.02 billion in option gains — and carried in their pockets unexercised options worth $7.2 billion more.[43] A year later, Compaq Computer CEO Eckhard Pfeiffer found himself sitting on unexercised options valued at $410.4 million.[44] In 2000, the nation's biggest stash of unexercised options belonged to Oracle CEO Larry Ellison. He ended the year sitting on options valued at $3.4 billion. Eight other CEOs that same year could boast stashes worth at least half a billion dollars.[45]

Some of these billions in potential personal profit, to be sure, did evaporate early in the new millennium, when the stock market nosedived. But relatively few big-time CEOs would end up significantly stiffed. Most had cashed out option windfalls regularly throughout the 1990s. On average, top executives gained $2.9 million each exercising options in 1995, $8 million in 1999.[46] And some top execs, most notably Walt Disney CEO Michael Eisner, did spectacularly better. In 1993, option incentives pushed Eisner's total compensation to over $200 million, a staggering sum *Business Week* called the most any CEO "has made in a single year — or probably in an entire career in the history of American business." Eisner's $203 million take-home added up to $78,081 an hour or "more than a half-million dollars a day, every day, for an entire year."[47]

Four years later, Eisner would again make headlines. On December 3, 1997, he registered the single "biggest payday for an executive in history" by exercising options for 7.3 million shares of Disney stock. Eisner's incentive agreement gave him the right to buy those shares for $130 million. On that December day, the shares were actually worth $695 million. By exercising his options, Eisner cleared a $565 million personal profit.[48]

Executives from earlier eras could barely recognize this new business landscape.

"I have a difficult time relating to the compensation today," Donald E. Petersen, the former chairman of Ford Motor Co. told reporters in 1999, "and I've really only been out of the full-time part nine years."[49]

Not everyone, of course, was sharing in corporate America's compensation largesse. In 1999, the same year America Online's Steve Case cleared $116 million, three of the many individuals who had helped AOL become the nation's most popular Internet gateway filed suit against Case's cyberspace money-machine. The three had been AOL chat room "volunteers." In exchange for monitoring AOL's chats, the volunteers had received free Internet access, but no compensation, and that, their lawsuit charged, violated labor law, since

AOL treated the "volunteers" as employees. AOL both gave them assignments and required them to work a minimum number of hours every week.[50]

This lawsuit against AOL would draw little media attention — or sympathy. Yes, Steve Case and his fellow executives were raking in dollars by the tens of millions. Yes, not everyone connected with AOL was sharing in the dollar deluge. But didn't those ungrateful volunteers understand that the system was working just as intended. America Online, business journalists gushed, demonstrated just how marvelous an incentive options could be. Early on in their entrepreneurial journey, Steve Case and his right-hand man, company chairman James Kimsey, had each "negotiated tens of thousands of stock options" from the private lenders who bankrolled their new venture. The options gave them the right to purchase AOL shares "for prices ranging from 50 cents to $3.50 each," a nice right to have once the shares soared past $50 dollars a share. And credit that soaring, the *Washington Business Journal* declared, to options. Stock options gave Case and Kimsey "a powerful incentive to maximize share price."[51]

With stock options, corporate America had an incentive that truly seemed to work. Year after year, corporate America would keep working it.

"In the war for executive talent," enthused compensation consultant Ira Kay of Watson Wyatt, "the bullets are stock options, and there's plenty of ammo."[52]

With all that firepower on the loose, some less enthused observers did wonder whether corporations might be shooting themselves in the foot. Might nine-digit payoffs for executives be a tad excessive? Not to worry, advised option advocates. Talented executives, they insisted, "can often add so much value to a company that their outlandish pay, in the grand scheme of things, amounts to a small tip."[53] These small tips, business analysts declared, were solving corporate America's longstanding "agency" problem. Thanks to option incentives, executives were finally thinking like shareholders, not hired help.[54] "CEO pay is aligned with company performance more closely today than ever before," crowed *Chief Executive* magazine.[55] "A bigger percentage of CEO compensation is coming from stock and stock options," cheered Scott Page, a top executive headhunter. That's "good for Americans," he added, and "good for American business."[56]

THAT AMERICAN BUSINESS WAS DOING WELL certainly seemed indisputable in the 1990s. By century's end, shareholder value had been "maximized" to a degree that no bullish prognosticator would have ever dared predict back in the early 1980s. At the start of that decade, about five thousand companies had their stock publicly traded on Wall Street.[57] The shares of these companies were worth a combined $1.3 trillion. By the end of 1999, about nine thousand companies were trading on Wall Street. Their combined share value: an amazing $16.7 trillion.[58]

But some observers, as the 1990s moved along, found their attention grabbed by other, more troubling sets of statistics. Companies were certainly doing well. But executives continued to be doing even better. In 1996, *Business*

Week pointed out, corporate profits increased a healthy 11 percent and share prices an even healthier 23 percent. But CEO pay gains for the year — up 54 percent — "far outstripped" both profits and shareholder returns.[59] In 1998, the *New York Times* commissioned a survey that compared the gains registered by shareholders with the compensation of top executives. Between 1993 and 1997, the survey found, shareholders in large firms saw their average annual return jump 19 percent. The chief executives at those same firms saw their annual pay leap 38 percent, twice the shareholder gain.[60] The *Wall Street Journal* conducted a similar analysis on 1999 executive pay and found a similar story. Median shareholder return, down 3.9 percent. CEO compensation, up 23.5 percent.[61]

What was going on here? Option incentives were supposed to align the interests — and rewards — of executives and shareholders. In an "aligned" environment, if share prices were rising, executives and shareholders would prosper together, or so the theory went. But if options had indeed "aligned" the interests of executives and shareholders, how could rewards for executives be rising so much faster than rewards for shareholders?

Simple arithmetic could supply some answers. Executives, by the mid 1990s, were routinely receiving such large grants of options that only a small tick up in share price could trigger a mammoth windfall. Suppose, for instance, you were an executive fortunate enough to have been granted the option to buy 10 million shares at $80 each. If your company's share rose just $2 annually, a modest increase of 2.5 percent, you would stand to make $20 million for every year the share price rose this meager $2.[62]

Critical observers also pointed out another reason why executive pay was rising so steeply. Executive pay reformers had originally expected that their cherished stock options would essentially *replace* more traditional executive incentives. That didn't happen. The new waves of stock option grants were simply layered on *top* of the salary, bonuses, and other forms of compensation executives were already receiving. In effect, executives simply gained a new revenue stream. This new stream, coupled with the old streams, virtually guaranteed that executive pay would far outpace shareholder return.

Some companies, to be sure, were so committed to option magic that they did abandon more traditional executive revenue streams. In 1998, for instance, Steve Jobs, the once exiled founder of Apple Computer, came back to the company as interim CEO for a token $1 annual salary. In January 2000, Apple granted Jobs 20 million options to take the company's CEO reins on a permanent basis. The options would be worth $1.39 billion if Apple's shares increased 10 percent a year over the decade ahead. Unfortunately for Apple, this bold stock option incentive produced no surge in the company's share price — and no great displays of executive aptitude on Jobs' part either. Apple shares, worth over $43 when Jobs became CEO, sank below $20 over the next fifteen months.[63]

Industry observers blamed that decline, in part, on the "Cube," an eight-inch-square computer that Apple expected would fly off store shelves after its year 2000 release. But the Cube, a product that Steve Jobs had pushed relentlessly, didn't fly anywhere. Sales met just a third of expectations. Jobs, analysts quipped, had made just two mistakes: He had targeted a bad product to the wrong market. Apple discontinued the Cube halfway through 2001.[64] Option magic, apparently, had its limits.[65]

That magic, critics argued, rested on a deeply flawed premise. Those who touted options as a magical performance-enhancing incentive assumed that steeply rising share prices reflect outstanding executive performance. But share prices can rise in the real world, and rise significantly, without an executive doing anything outstanding or even merely astute. Share prices, in a complex modern economy, reflect all sorts of factors that may have nothing whatsoever to do with executive performance.[66]

Factors like supply and demand.

Prices rise, textbooks tell us, when demand exceeds supply. In the stock market, demand started rising significantly in the 1980s. Paycheck deductions for 401(k)s, an entirely new retirement savings vehicle, were pouring hundreds of millions into the market for shares of stock, rain or shine, every two weeks. Millions of Americans, made stock-savvy by their 401(k)s, were also investing on their own, many for the first time. All this cash cascading onto Wall Street generated enormous upward pressure on share prices. By 1997, the S&P 500 stock market index had gained, in just fifteen years, an incredible 1,026 percent.[67]

In this bull market, Wall Street's greatest ever, the stock options awarded to America's top executives quickly became sure tickets to fortune. The swelling bull market, observers noted, had created a rising tide that was lifting all executive boats. In this awesome market, explained New York University's David Yermack, even executives "with mediocre or below-average performance" couldn't help but "end up making a lot of money."[68] Executives, *Business Week* charged, were winning rich rewards "for stock market performance, not business performance." Corporate America had committed "the classic error of confusing a bull market for genius."[69]

Could corporate America undo that error — and figure out a way to make sure that options rewarded only the truly worthy? Many investors felt certain the bull market-raises-all-boats dilemma could be overcome. Standard grants of stock options do not automatically connect rewards to actual performance, these optimists conceded. But stock option incentives could reward performance — if options came with "strings."

These strings could come in various sizes and shapes. Executives, some investor advocates proposed, should be expected to outperform their peers at other companies before they can collect any compensation windfall.[70] Options ought to be worthless, suggested the Council of Institutional Investors, unless a company outperforms a market or industry index. Steps like these would help ensure that "a CEO doesn't get paid just because the stock market rises."[71]

Other critics pushed even tougher option reforms. Advocates of "premium-priced options," for instance, wanted executives to have to hike a company's shares to a specified target price before they could cash in on their options.[72]

Some corporate boards of directors did take this advice to heart. In New Jersey, the RCN Corporation, a telecommunications start-up, awarded top executives options that could only be cashed in if company shares hit a target price and rose faster than the S&P 500 index.[73] But such string-laden options came with complications that gave most corporate boards pause. Normal "no-strings" stock option grants, for one, did not have to be factored into corporate earnings statements. Corporate boards could reward all the standard options they wanted without cutting their profit rates. "Out-perform" options carried no such accounting benefits. Under a 1972 accounting rule, these options are charged against earnings — and lower a company's reported profits. Such charges cost RCN, the New Jersey telecom, $50 million in one year alone.[74] This discriminatory treatment against options that carry performance targets could easily have been remedied, by having accounting standards treat all options the same, as charges against earnings. But executives continued to lobby diligently, and successfully, against that change throughout the 1990s and beyond, ensuring, noted the *New York Times*, that "the stock market's tide — be it rising or falling — will continue to have as much of an effect on most option values as a company's performance does."[75]

In the end, few corporate boards would place any strings on their executive stock option plans. One 1999 survey found that only a quarter of CEO option grants "contained any sort of link to performance."[76] For America's top executives, no strings, no sweat.

THE SEARCH FOR THE PERFECT EXECUTIVE INCENTIVE would take one other turn in the 1990s. If the goal is to get executives to behave like owners, some corporate boards started wondering, why not just insist that they become owners? Why not require executives to buy — and hold — shares of the company they managed?

The idea would catch on.[77] In the early 1990s, hardly any large corporations insisted that their executives own shares. By decade's end, according to pay consultants at Pearl Meyer, over one hundred of America's two hundred biggest companies were requiring executives "to buy and hold sizable blocks of stock." Some demanded that top executives own stock valued at fifteen times their basic paycheck.[78]

These stiff ownership requirements initially caused a bit of a stir, but they would eventually make little impact.[79] Few corporate boards that set ownership standards actually bothered to enforce them. Companies with ownership requirements, the *Wall Street Journal* reported in 1999, would "simply extend deadlines or cut the requirements for executives who don't comply."[80] In other situations, corporate boards thoughtfully structured their ownership mandates to make sure executives wouldn't lose their shirts if the company's share price

— and the value of the executive's ownership stake — started sinking. Baxter International, an Illinois medical products company, started an ownership incentive program in 1994 that required the firm's top executives to buy company stock. But the company didn't expect these executives to risk their own money to make these required stock purchases. Instead, Baxter International "guaranteed" $122 million in personal bank loans, and the executives used this risk-free cash to buy company shares.[81]

Other corporations, to help their executives meet stock ownership requirements as painlessly as possible, actually went into the executive loan business themselves. In 1993, for instance, Eastman Kodak required its new CEO, George Fisher, to own Kodak stock worth four times his annual base pay within five years. Fisher met that requirement — without having to spend hardly any of his own dollars. Kodak loaned Fisher $8.2 million to buy the required company shares, then waived interest payments on the loan, then, incredibly, forgave principal payments for a five-year period.[82]

Still other companies simply forgave loans to their executives completely. Priceline, a dot.com darling in the late 1990s, loaned $3 million to the firm's chief financial officer, Heidi Miller. Less than a year into her CFO tenure, with the company's share price down 90 percent, Miller left Priceline. The company forgave her $3 million loan.[83]

At several corporations, loan programs would lurch even more out of control. One financial services giant, Conseco, handed its top officials $575 million in loans and loan guarantees to purchase company shares. The borrowers, naturally, figured these shares would appreciate. By selling off the appreciated shares, they would then be able to pay off their loans and profit handsomely. But Conseco's share price didn't rise. The price tumbled — the "incentive" of stock ownership apparently not working too well — and executives suddenly could not afford to repay their loans.[84] Conseco's executives and shareholders were now fully, and perversely, "aligned." They were all in hot water together. Conseco would eventually show CEO Stephen Hilbert, the nation's fourth most highly paid chief executive in 1999, the door.[85] In 2002, the company went bankrupt.[86]

In that same year, President George W. Bush would sign into law legislation that prohibits sweetheart loans to top executives. But the legislation "grandfathered" in all corporate loans to executives currently in place.[87] At the bill's signing, on July 30, 2002, over a third of America's fifteen hundred largest companies still had executive loans outstanding. The loans totaled $4.5 billion.[88]

OUT-PERFORM OPTIONS. Premium-priced options. Ownership requirements. All these attempts by corporate America to shower incentive rewards *only* on worthy, high-performing executives share, with plain vanilla stock options, the same basic assumption: that the price of a company's stock does indeed represent a reasonable measure of executive performance. If a company's stock market share price is rising, Wall Streeters believe, that company must surely be on the right track. The market, after all, is always right. But this faith in market wisdom, this absolute confidence in the ability of markets to render valuable judgments about company performance, rests on several shaky propositions that can't be "fixed" with any amount of incentive plan fine-tuning.

The first, and most basic, of these propositions: Investors know what they're doing.

If investors chose stocks by throwing darts at the financial pages, no one would argue that these dart-throwing investors were making reasoned judgments. Investors, of course, don't choose stocks by flinging darts. But no one who follows the stock market, not even the most ardent believers in market wisdom, would seriously argue that individual investors always make informed judgments when they purchase stocks. In real life, stock purchases sometimes reflect sober judgments — and sometimes hot tips from brothers-in-law. Some individual investors do pore over corporate reports, but most investors remain unsure about even the most fundamental of investing basics. In 1997, the National Association of Securities Dealers asked a cross-section of Americans if they could describe the difference between a load and no-load mutual fund. Only 12 percent could.[89]

Champions of market wisdom readily acknowledge that most individual investors are in no position to evaluate corporate performance and prospects. But these clueless individual investors, the market faithful argue, make only a marginal impact on the ultimate judgments the stock market makes about individual corporations. Most decisions to buy and sell shares of stock, these cheerleaders claim, are made by experts, either professional stockbrokers or the skilled investment managers of mutual funds and pension plans. Share prices reflect the market wisdom of these experts.

How much "stock" should we put in this claim? Not much. In the contemporary stock market, even with "experts" teeming all about, a company's share price can rise and fall for reasons that have nothing to do with the overall performance of the company or the individual performances of the company's top executives. Consider, for instance, the fascinating phenomenon sometimes known as the "Dow Jones effect."

Dow Jones and several other Wall Street firms currently compile what are called stock market "indexes." Each index tracks a different representative sample of stocks. One index might track utilities, another transportation companies. The Standard & Poor's 500, one of Wall Street's most influential indexes, tracks the five hundred companies that boast the largest market value within their industries.

Indexes, historically, have given investors a sense of which way the overall market, or a section of it, is headed. Today indexes do more than that. They actually drive investment decisions, through mutual funds that mirror specific stock market indexes. The experts who manage these "index funds" don't try to outsmart the market by picking individual stocks. Instead, they buy all the stocks in a particular index. An index fund tied to the S&P 500, for example, will own the shares of every company the S&P 500 tracks.

Here's where the investing plot thickens. Indexes regularly add new companies and delete old ones, as companies come and go, grow and shrink. These decisions to add or delete can carry enormous market implications. If a new company is added to Standard & Poor's list of America's top five hundred companies, for instance, all the index funds that track the S&P 500 must go out and buy shares in that company. Such index-driven purchases can give a company's share price a powerful jolt. One example: In 1995, Standard & Poor's added Comerica Inc., a banking company, to the S&P 500 list. Over the next two days, the number of Comerica shares sold soared fifteen-fold. Comerica shares rose a swift 6 percent.[90] By the late 1990s, just the anticipation of a company's addition into the S&P 500 could be enough to send its shares zooming. In 1999, the market price of Yahoo rose 24 percent in just one day, as investors "snapped up shares of the Internet service before it was added to the Standard & Poor's 500-stock index at the close of trading." The big winners: Yahoo founders David Filo and Jerry Yang. Filo's stake in Yahoo jumped $1.6 billion in value, Yang's $1.5 billion.[91]

Another common stock market phenomenon, the "Fidelity effect," can also distort market "wisdom." Some Wall Street stock traders have become so huge that, just like bulls in china shops, they can't turn around without wrecking something, even if they have no intention of causing trouble. By the mid 1990s, the Fidelity mutual fund family had become one of these china shop bulls. Fidelity managed over one-half trillion dollars worth of stock, more than a quarter of all the stock held in America's mutual funds.

All these shares gave Fidelity a huge stake in many individual corporations, stakes so large that a simple decision by Fidelity to sell shares in a company that had been doing well — a decision that might allow Fidelity to pocket some profits — could send the company's share price into a tailspin. In early fall 1995, for instance, Fidelity's Magellan Fund held 12.2 million shares of Motorola. Over the next two months, Magellan sold 8 million of these shares. Motorola's share price promptly dropped 18 percent, at a time, the *Washington Post* reported, "when the company announced no bad news and Wall Street analysts issued no sell recommendations."[92] Executives at Motorola, in other words, had done nothing wrong, at least in Wall Street eyes. But their share price took a hit anyway. Against Fidelity's size, market "wisdom" would be no match.

Big market players like Fidelity eventually realized that, given the immense volume of their stock trading, trying to pick individual corporate winners out of the stock market pool might not always be worth the effort. Instead, Fidelity and other big players started picking sectors. Was technology going to be hot? Fine, the big players reasoned, let's buy tech. Let's buy tech companies across the board. If some of these companies don't pan out, no problem, as long as the tech sector, as a whole, does well.

That reasoning made eminent sense for big market traders like Fidelity. But the impact of that reasoning gave poorly performing executives a free ride.

With Fidelity buying up every tech company in sight, high- and low-perform-ing companies alike would see an increased demand for their shares. That would be good news for executive underachievers in technology and other "hot" sectors, bad news for executives, competent or not, in sectors that investors were writing off. And in the late 1990s, even at the height of the stock market boom, investors were writing off plenty of sectors.

"Never have so many industries been out of favor with investors during a stock market boom," *Chief Executive* magazine complained in 1999. "In one of the most bullish years ever, 10 of the 17 industries we studied suffered negative shareholder returns."[93]

These negative returns in autos and other out-of-favor industries meant that executives in these sectors were missing out on the juiciest option windfalls. Corporate boards of directors in these disfavored sectors reacted predictably. They panicked. To keep their executives from jumping ship and flocking to industries where the options were greener, corporate boards started dishing out incentives less dependent on market "wisdom." Ford Motor, for instance, handed CEO Jacques Nasser a multi-year cash bonus. Under the terms of Nasser's pay agreement, he would be able to collect that bonus even if Ford's share price sank.[94] Option magic, with a twist.

INDIVIDUAL INVESTORS WHO HAVEN'T the slightest clue about which executives are performing well and which aren't. Companies whose shares go up in price simply because they've been added to a market index. Shares that go down in price simply because a king-sized player like Fidelity has decided to pocket profits. Executives who win stock option jackpots because they're lucky enough to work for a company in a sector the market defines as "hot." Executives rewarded with extra compensation goodies because they work in a sector the market dismisses.

Something surely must be missing from our picture. Where are the experts paying attention to how well individual companies — and their executives — are performing? And if no one is paying attention, how can anyone possibly claim that share prices represent a fair measure of executive performance? We must have omitted some element of Wall Street market reality. And indeed we have. We have yet to consider that key financial world player known as the stock market research analyst, Wall Street's single most important source of wisdom about corporate and executive performance.

Stock market research analysts specialize in specific industries and compa-nies. They parse company balance sheets line by line, ever vigilant for indica-tors that reveal just how well, or poorly, a company may be doing or about to do. Every so often, they share their wisdom. Buy these shares, they tell those of us who haven't the time to identify emerging corporate winners, sell those oth-ers. Every major securities firm on Wall Street maintains a stable of well-paid analysts. These analysts can be enormously influential. A good word from the right analyst can send a company's shares into the stock market stratosphere —

and turn executive option incentive awards into eight- and nine-digit fortunes.[95] This dynamic gives executives, in turn, an incentive to give stock analysts more than a good bit of their time and attention. Top executives seem to understand almost intuitively that a calculated burst of CEO charm and charisma, carefully targeted to just the right stock analyst, can work wonders for their bankrolls.

"I do know from my own experience watching how security analysts respond to CEOs that the personality of the CEO has a significant effect on the price of the stock," noted T. J. Dermot Dunphy, one former CEO, in a 2001 interview.[96]

CEOs also understand that analysts can be as easily intimidated as charmed. Among the most notable intimidators: Enron CEO Jeff Skilling. "If you didn't act like a light bulb came on pretty quick, Skilling would dismiss you," one big trader told *Fortune* after the energy giant went belly-up. Enron "had Wall Street beaten into submission."[97]

But charisma and browbeating only partly explain why stock analysts so seldom discomfort the companies they are supposed to be rigorously rating.[98] Much more significant have been the institutional pressures — the powerful conflicts of interest — that encourage analysts to swallow any discouraging words a truly independent analysis might lead them to utter.

These institutional pressures have built up significantly over recent years. A generation ago, Wall Street brokerage houses gained much of their revenue from stock-trading commissions, and out of those commissions came the funding for analyst research. In that commission-driven environment, Wall Street firms didn't particularly care whether their analysts recommended that investors "buy" or "sell" a particular stock. The firms made money as long as investors kept buying and selling, since every transaction generated hefty commissions. But these transactions, in the 1980s and 1990s, became less and less profitable as first discount brokers and then the Internet captured significant stock-trading market share. With commissions fading, the Wall Street houses that used to count on commissions would come to depend more on investment banking for their revenues.

As investment bankers, these Wall Street firms took the shares of stock their clients — individual corporations — had to sell and sold these shares to the investing public. Naturally, the Wall Street underwriters wanted the investing public to pay premium rates for these shares. Just as naturally, the Wall Street firms expected their analysts to help the process along, by issuing judgments about the shares that were suitably enthusiastic. But the conflict of interest didn't stop there. Wall Street companies were constantly on the prowl for new stock issues to take public. Analysts who regularly made negative judgments about companies were, in effect, alienating possible future clients. The fewer clients, the less investment banking profit, the smaller the firm revenue — and, eventually, analyst paychecks.[99]

All these pressures — the fear, the greed, the infatuation with charismatic executives — would combine, by century's end, to make stock analysis about as credible as pitches from carnival barkers. No matter the stock, no matter the circumstance, stock analysts had just one word for the often unsuspecting investing public: buy. One analyst, from Salomon Smith Barney, didn't stop recommending that investors buy Enron until shares had sunk to $15.40, a price down nearly $70 from the stock's high.[100] One survey, conducted in 2000, examined 27,000 different analyst recommendations. Fewer than 1 percent recommended "sell."[101]

America, by 2001, had seen enough. Midway through the year, even before Enron collapsed, stock analysis would emerge as a national op-ed issue, in both the business and general press. Congress would feel compelled, in June, to call the securities industry onto the carpet.[102] Why all the concern? Why had stock analyst conflicts of interest become such a major sore point? Stock analyst conflicts of interests, acute observers understood, threatened much more than the reliability of "buy" and "sell" recommendations. Problematic stock analysis subverted corporate America's entire incentive structure. This structure rested on the simple notion that share prices rise when executives perform well. But if share prices could be sent soaring by factors that have nothing to with executive performance — by, for instance, bogus "buy" recommendations from stock analysts with hidden agendas — then executives could be rewarded even if they performed poorly.

Conflicts of interest in stock analysis, commentators urged, needed to be swept away, and, midway through 2002, Congress would finally do some sweeping, enacting legislation to "protect the objectivity and independence of stock analysts."[103] The unspoken assumption behind this reform legislation: Share prices, once established in a transparent, conflict-of-interest-free market, would accurately indicate how well, or how poorly, a corporation is performing. But what if share prices, even if set by an entirely "honest" market, are not the only important measure of corporate performance? What if judgments about corporate "success" need to take other indicators besides "return to shareholders" into account? And if other indicators beyond shareholder return do indeed need to be taken into account — before any company, or chief executive, can be judged successful — then wouldn't any compensation system that bases incentives on share prices end up rewarding executives who might actually be poor or mediocre performers?

Good questions. Inside corporate America, at century's end, no one was asking them.

PEOPLE USUALLY ONLY ASK QUESTIONS when they need answers. Corporate America's movers and shakers aren't asking questions about corporate success because they don't feel they need answers. They already *know* what success is. In corporate America today, success equals maximizing shareholder value. End of discussion. CEOs are expected to labor toward one goal and one goal alone: to make sure shareholders get their due.[104] No other stakeholders matter. Any executive who increases shareholder value, American corporate leaders believe, is performing nobly and ought to be suitably rewarded.

Elsewhere in the corporate world, by contrast, other stakeholders do matter. In Japan, in continental Europe, shareholders are considered just one stakeholder among many.[105] Only in the United States and the United Kingdom, note finance scholars David Collison and George Frankfurter, "are shareholders' interests regarded as preeminent."[106]

What gives shareholders in the United States the right to such all-encompassing preeminence? Corporations, one argument holds, desperately need the dollars shareholders invest in them. Without these dollars, companies would never be able to grow and prosper. In fact, few of the dollars modern corporate enterprises use to do business come from shareholders. Most of the dollars that investors shell out to buy stocks go to other investors who happen to own the shares, not to the corporation whose shares have been traded. Shareholders only rarely buy shares directly from a corporation.

So where do corporations get the money they need to operate? Not from stocks. In 1993, corporations whose stock traded publicly needed $555 billion to do business. Proceeds from equity — money corporations raised by selling their stock directly to investors — accounted for a mere 4 percent of that $555 billion, according to Federal Reserve figures. The overwhelming bulk of the operating capital corporations needed, 82 percent, came from "retained earnings," company income from selling products and services. Another 14 percent came from borrowing.[107] Revenues from the sale of shares can sometimes, to be sure, play a significant role, particularly for young companies. But overall, notes *Business Ethics* editor Marjorie Kelly, equity capital's limited contribution to business success in no way justifies a limitless shareholder claim on corporate earnings.

"Equity capital is one relatively minor source of funding, vital at a certain point," she points out. "Yet it entices holders to suck out all wealth, forever."[108]

Outside America's corporate suites, some critics have begun challenging this logic of privileging shareholders at the expense of consumers, employees, communities, and other stakeholders. An overbearing fixation on shareholders, notes columnist Ellen Goodman, isn't even ultimately in the best interests of shareholders themselves. After all, shareholders are people, too, "stakeholders in society," not just owners of stock.[109]

Corporate leaders usually dismiss such sentiments as do-gooder raving. But sometimes even corporate leaders openly acknowledge that corporations amount to more than share prices. These moments, curiously, only seem to materialize when corporate leaders are asking society at large to bail out a failing enterprise. Those who seek bailouts, and those who try to justify them, never argue the government must save a troubled corporation to "maximize shareholder value." They argue, instead, that the greater community has an important stake in a failing enterprise's survival. These arguments resonate powerfully, because communities *do* have a stake in corporate success.

If communities do have a stake in corporate success, then, of course, shareholders are not the only stakeholders that matter. And if shareholders are not the only stakeholders that matter, then executives should not be rewarded for pleasing only shareholders. Executives should be expected to please all an enterprise's stakeholders — and be rewarded only if they are successful in that endeavor.

In the 1990s, some corporate boards did actually embrace this notion that executive incentives need to consider more than shareholder return.[110] At Ford, for instance, the board of directors added a product "quality" incentive into CEO Jacques Nasser's compensation package. But skeptics suspected that Ford was only going through the motions. They soon had ample evidence. In 1999, Ford failed to meet its vehicle warranty and customer satisfaction "quality" target. No big deal. Ford would hand CEO Nasser $10.2 million anyway, a 48 percent raise over his pay in 1998, when Nasser headed up Ford's auto operations. So much for quality as job one.

By century's end, in boardrooms the nation over, America's corporate elite would worship shareholder value and shareholder value alone — and nowhere more so than at Computer Associates, a New York software company. Directors at Computer Associates would dangle more than a billion dollars in incentives before the company's top three executives. To realize that billion, the executives needed only to give the company share price a healthy boost up. What happened next warrants a few moments of our time.

COMPUTER ASSOCIATES, BY THE MID 1990S, had become a classic corporate success story. The company, just a three-person start-up in 1976, had achieved world-class status.[111] In the entire software industry, only a handful of companies stood any taller. Could Computer Associates grow even bigger? The company's board believed it could, if only the firm's three top executives — CEO Charles Wang, President Sanjay Kumar, and Executive Vice-President Russell Artzt — were extended just the right incentives. No garden-variety incentive plan, the board felt, would do. The company's new incentives would have to be grand enough to inspire lofty new levels of executive performance.

The board's new incentive plan, approved in 1995, would promise CEO Wang and his top two colleagues more than 20 million shares of company stock if the Computer Associates share price, in just one twelve-month period over the next five years, closed above $53.33 for at least sixty days.[112] To reach that milestone, the company's share price would have to jump 20 percent a year, twice Wall Street's historic rate of return.

Beating that ambitious marker would turn out to be mere child's play for Wang, Kumar, and Artzt. On May 21, 1998, the three hit the "jackpot" — and ahead of schedule. The company's shares that day closed at just over $55, their sixtieth day over $53.33 in the previous year. That close triggered an incentive windfall worth more than $1.1 billion.[113] The lion's share, over 12 million shares worth $670 million, went to the fifty-four-year-old Wang. Kumar pocketed shares worth $334.9 million, Artzt $111.6 million.[114]

Computer Associates shareholders, for their part, weren't complaining. The incentive plan seemed to have worked admirably. Shareholder value had been maximized!

That maximization would be brief.

The Computer Associates up-escalator, after the May 21 jackpot day, would suddenly reverse direction. By late July, company shares had dropped 31 percent off their May high. The reason? To offset the grants of actual stock to Wang, Kumar, and Artzt, the company had been compelled to book a $675 million charge against earnings. Before the charge, the company had claimed a $194 million profit. After the charge, the company stood $481 million in the red.[115] That did not please Wall Street — or shareholders. The incentives intended to enhance shareholder value, they suddenly realized, had instead sent that value sinking. The angriest of the shareholders, in a series of lawsuits, would charge that Wang and friends had scored their $1.1 billion windfall by "artificially inflating the company's stock price."[116] A year later, a Delaware judge, citing a technicality, ordered the three executives to give about half the windfall back.[117]

Throughout this litigation, the Computer Associates board of directors would remain thoroughly unrepentant. Their incentive plan, directors insisted, had worked as intended.

"It was a very good plan," explained the chairman of the board's compensation committee, Willem F. P. de Vogel. "I have never seen three people work harder."[118]

But what exactly did the Computer Associates top executives work hard at? Producing great products? Not quite. Among the company's primary customers, the managers of mainframe computing operations, Computer Associates was striking out badly. At technology conferences, where these managers gathered, "probably 95 percent of the hands" in the room would go up when attendees were asked if they wanted to drop Computer Associates products, the *New York Times* reported.[119] These product failings never seemed to interest CEO Wang or any other top Computer Associates executives. They were too busy scheming to keep the company's share price inflated.

The most creative of these schemes involved the fees that customers paid to use the various Computer Associates software products. Computer Associates, under Wang, would regularly claim as immediate current income the total value of long-term, multi-year software contracts. This hocus pocus worked wonderfully as long as Computer Associates could get customers to keep signing long-term contracts. But moving Computer Associates software, as the 1990s wore on, became a harder and harder sell. The big mainframes that

Computer Associates software served no longer dominated business computing. In response, Computer Associates executives could have carefully analyzed
the computing marketplace, made some judgments about the software their
customers would need down the road, and then worked to create these new
products. But why bother? Computer Associates executives had a more lucrative solution. They would buy up, by the hundreds, their smaller rivals. What
these smaller rivals had, and what Computer Associates coveted, were customers with long-term contracts. Each of these contracts could be extended, or
"rerolled," into new revenue for Computer Associates. A $2 million, five-year
contract with two years to go might become a new $4 million ten-year con-
tract. Computer Associates would then book the additional millions as fresh
cash. Computer Associates, in the 1990s, would turn this rerolling into a sleazy
corporate art form. The company, one former executive revealed, made a practice of hiring "young, cute girls to basically resell maintenance contracts."[120]

But the "cute girls" wouldn't be enough. CEO Wang and his gang figured
out early on that they would only meet their personal incentive plan targets if
Computer Associates had really big long-term contracts to reroll. And they
could only get these really big contracts, the executives understood, by buying
out their largest rivals. Wang and his colleagues would pursue exactly this
course. In 1995, in "the largest takeover in the history of the software business,"
Computer Associates would buy out Legent software for $1.8 billion, then
spend $1.2 billion the next year to grab Cheyenne Software. The scheming
would continue even after Wang and friends scored their $1.1 billion windfall
in 1998, since Wang and his fellow executives apparently knew no other way
to keep their money-machine rolling. In 1999, Computer Associates would
buy out Platinum software for $3.5 billion, then top that the next year by
snatching up Sterling software for $4 billion.[121] All these buy-ups, essentially a
high-tech pyramid scheme, would goose the Computer Associates share price
after its post-windfall tumble — and help CEO Wang to still more mammoth
personal paydays. He would gross $445.7 million in 1999.[122]

The Computer Associates share price comeback would be short-lived. After
peaking at decade's end, the company's share price again plummeted. Wang
would step down as CEO in 2000. Over his last three years as chief executive,
Business Week calculated, he had earned $698.2 million. In those same three
years, the return to Computer Associates shareholders had dropped 63 percent.[123] No other executive in America, *Business Week* pointed out, had given
shareholders, over those three years, less for their money.

THE ENORMOUS WINDFALLS at Computer Associates signaled, for many business observers, a corporate incentive system gone more than slightly haywire.
The link between pay and performance, *Business Week* concluded in 1999, "has
been all but severed in today's system."[124] Incentives that tied pay to share
prices, some thoughtful business leaders had come to realize, inevitably produced executives who spent more time manipulating the market than manag-

ing enterprises for success. But most business observers saw nothing amiss. Incentives tied to share prices remained corporate America's wonder drug.

"We really made it worth people's while to drive stock prices up, and they found ways to do it," exulted Jude Rich, a "human capital" consultant with Sibson & Co.[125]

Some observers put the blame for this sort of mindless cheerleading on corporate boards of directors, the bodies responsible for determining executive incentives in the first place. In the post-mortems after the Computer Associates billion-dollar windfall, for instance, critics faulted the company's directors for accepting a sixty-day trigger in the incentive plan for their top executives. How could sixty days, critics wondered, ever be considered enough time to demonstrate real improvement in a company's fortunes?[126]

Why do members of corporate boards accept such flawed incentive plans? They have their own incentives. The Computer Associates board, for instance, included Shirley Strum Kenny, the president of the State University of New York at Stony Brook. In 1996, Kenny's university received a $25 million donation from Computer Associates CEO Charles Wang.[127]

Such flagrant boardroom back-slapping, organized labor would note in 1998, infests the entire executive incentive-setting system. Corporate boards, the AFL-CIO charged, "are rigged to overpay CEOs."[128] Researchers would back up labor's charges. One study of almost twelve hundred companies, conducted by the Investor Responsibility Research Center, found intricate business ties between directors and the executives they were supposed to be making independent judgments about.[129] At MBNA Corp., a national credit card company, the board of directors compensation committee was chaired by the college roommate of MBNA's top executive, Alfred Lerner. The roommate's law firm supplied MBNA legal services. Between 1993 and 1997, MBNA CEO Lerner's pay increased 147 percent a year, three times faster than the company's share price.[130]

Board compensation committees, a leading National Association of Corporate Directors official would acknowledge in 2001, simply aren't very adept at setting pay standards.

"They don't spend enough time on it," noted Roger Raber, "and a lot of this is done by the seat of your pants in a clubby atmosphere."[131]

In this clubby boardroom atmosphere, chief executives set the dominant tone.

"Sixty percent of the directors of companies are the CEOs of other companies," corporate pay watchdog Graef Crystal estimated in 1999, "and they don't come to the table with a predisposition against high pay."[132]

The top executives who sit on each other's boards of directors, *Los Angeles Times* commentator John Balzar would add two years later, "solemnly tell each other they need all this money or they couldn't possibly be motivated to get out of bed and come to the office." And then, adds Balzar, "they hire factotums to step forward with straight faces and tell the rest of us that this is so."[133]

The most significant of these factotums: the executive pay consultants who do the statistical legwork for board compensation committees. Graef Crystal, before becoming an executive pay whistle-blower, spent more than twenty years as one of these consultants.[134] Crystal, like most of his consultant colleagues, would actually be hired by the corporate executives whose incentive plans he would be recommending, not by the corporate board committees charged with setting executive pay.

"Therein lay the problem," notes Crystal. "If the CEO wanted more money, and I didn't want to recommend to the board that he should get more money, well, then, there was always a rival compensation consultant who could be hired."[135]

NOT ALL CHIEF EXECUTIVES have their incentives set by corporate boards they totally dominate. Board members do occasionally take the upper hand. At other moments neither side may hold clear control. Turnover also clouds the power picture. Over time, within individual corporations, casts of characters will change. A particularly dominant CEO might retire. New board members might flex some muscle. Corporate power, as a consequence, is almost always flowing, sometimes running into the boardrooms where corporate directors meet, sometimes ebbing out into executive suites.

Could reforms in how corporations are required to operate help channel more power into boardrooms? Could these reforms produce incentive plans less stacked in executives' favor? Some observers believe so. Boards of directors would display more independent judgment, they argue, if CEOs were prevented from chairing the boards of their own companies, or if the individuals who serve on a corporation's board were not allowed to have any business dealings with the corporation. But other observers doubt that such steps would put much of a brake on escalating CEO pay. The sorts of individuals who serve on corporate boards, these doubters point out, all share the same underlying perspective. They all assume that chief executives can — and will — make bottom-line miracles happen *if* they are offered enticing enough incentives.

Where boards differ, researchers have shown, is on how they *justify* the lush incentives they offer executives to keep these miracles coming. Boards that seldom exert much independent judgment typically describe their executive incentive plans "as a means of retaining scarce leadership talent."[136] Directors on these boards tend to talk about their CEOs as "uniquely talented leaders" or "valuable human resources" that the company can't possibly afford to lose. On the other hand, where boards function somewhat more independently, often the case at companies where the CEO and the chairman of the board are not one and the same person, board members seldom spend much time blessing the brilliance of their executives. Directors on these more independent boards stress, instead, the importance of keeping executive noses to the grindstone. Incentive plans, these boards contend, should only reward executives if they deliver the goods.

Directors at companies that don't fit snugly into either of these two categories — firms where "board control over management is neither particularly high nor low," about a fifth of the companies examined by Northwestern University researchers Edward Zajac and James Westphal — go both ways. These boards of directors laud their executives as talents the company can't afford to lose *and* insist that, without performance incentives, executives would likely go off and feather their own nests at corporate expense.[137]

Do any of these differences actually make a difference? Are "independent" boards that insist that executives "perform" before they are rewarded less likely to shovel dollars into executive pockets than kowtowed boards that hand executives rewards just to keep them from leaving? In a word, no. "Independent" boards of directors that orate endlessly about the importance of only rewarding performance are posturing, the research suggests, nothing more. These "independent" boards, in practice, demonstrate no rock-solid commitment to holding executives accountable.[138] By demanding performance-based incentives, these boards are merely signaling, to the rest of the business world, that they call the shots, not the top executive. Lions roar to proclaim their dominance. Corporate boards insist that their executives "perform."

And if those executives don't perform? Their corporate boards will reward them anyway. The boards know it — and their executives know it, too. Poor performers in executive suites can almost always count on their boards to be ever so understanding. America's top executives, in effect, now find themselves sitting in "an absolutely no-lose situation." CEOs who underperform, notes long-time compensation consultant Donald Sullivan, can count on continued rewards "as a goad to improve their results." And if those rewards don't improve results, chief executives can then count on boards to say "we have to stay 'competitive,' so let's ignore performance."[139]

At Time Warner, for instance, shares sank over 15 percent from 1993 to 1996, at the same time the S&P 500 was rising nearly 60 percent. But that poor performance didn't stop Time Warner from handing CEO Gerald Levin a $4 million bonus in each of those three low-performing years. The reason? Time Warner, the company explained, had to consider the rewards offered by its "most direct competitors for executive talent."[140]

In the 1990s, this imperative to be competitive would sweep through America's corporate boardrooms. By the early twenty-first century, 96 percent of S&P 500 companies were "benchmarking" their executive pay against the compensation of rival executives.

"Company boards figure that if a CEO doesn't earn as much as his peers," *Business Week* explained, "he'll take a hike."[141]

But who should be considered a top executive's "peers"? That would become, in corporate boardrooms, a $64 million question. Should corporate boards strive to make sure their top executives are paid as well as their industry's average-paid CEOs or as well as their industry's best-paid CEOs?

Executives about to be "benchmarked," naturally, always want their rewards keyed to what their more highly paid "peers" are making. They usually get their way. In America today, everyone involved in the benchmarking process has a vested interest, an incentive, to set the benchmark high, not low.

Executive compensation consultants, the people who compile peer group pay statistics, have an incentive to keep their consulting contracts. These consultants almost always recommend that top executives be paid at a rate higher than their average-paid peers, smart thinking since consultants owe their contracts to those top executives.[142]

Members of corporate boards, meanwhile, have an incentive to keep their CEO happy. That CEO, after all, must be above-average. Why else would the board have hired him — or, ever so occasionally, her — in the first place? Boards almost always agree to benchmark their CEO at some above-average level, most typically somewhere between the fiftieth to seventy-fifth percentile of all comparable executives. If they didn't set this above-average benchmark, board members fear, their CEO might just pick up and leave, forcing the board to go through the "time-consuming job of finding a successor."[143]

"Read the directors' rationale for CEO pay, contained in the annual proxy statement, and you're likely to find that the goal is to keep pay in line with that provided by the top half of the industry," notes *Philadelphia Inquirer* business analyst Jeff Brown. "That doesn't sound extravagant, but if all companies seek to offer above-average pay, simple math says the average must constantly rise."[144]

Competitive benchmarking gives corporate America, in essence, a perpetual upward motion CEO compensation machine.

"We want to make our CEO happy," as one corporate director told *Business Week* in 2001, "and the best way to make him happy is to pay him commensurate with our competitors."[145]

CORPORATE BOARDS PLAINLY FIND penalizing poor performance — by executives — a distinctly distasteful chore. They much prefer devoting their creative energies to more positive pursuits, like coming up with incentive packages sweet enough to keep their executives from looking elsewhere.

These "retention" incentives have taken various shapes. Some boards simply give their favorite executives shares of stock outright. These "restricted" stock grants — so named because the executives who receive them cannot do anything with the shares for a specified period of time, typically four years — hold charms ordinary stock options cannot match. With stock options, executives gain merely the *right* to buy stocks at a certain fixed price. An option to buy a hundred thousand shares at $20 a share, for instance, will only be valuable if the stock's actual market price rises above $20. Grants of restricted stock eliminate all downside. An executive with restricted stock owns an actual asset, not merely the option to buy an asset. This asset will have value even if the company's share value sinks. If, for example, a hundred thousand restricted shares originally worth $20 each crash to $10, those shares are still worth $1 million, and all the executive with these shares needs to do to collect that $1 million is sell the shares at $10.

"With restricted stock," as compensation watchdog Graef Crystal puts it, "you just have to breathe 18 times a minute to make a profit."[146]

Plenty of executives in corporate America can do that, and their boards seem determined to reward them for it. By 1999, more than a third of America's corporate boards, 38 percent, were dispensing restricted stocks to executives.[147] These grants, proclaims Jan Koors, a prominent compensation consultant, give corporate America "a strong retention tool." Executives who jump ship *before* they can cash out their restricted stock, he explains, stand to lose millions.[148]

In theory perhaps. In actual corporate life, restricted stock grants have proved a pitifully poor "retention" incentive. Companies on the prowl for executive talent simply up their offers to make up for whatever retention incentive executives might have to forfeit by exiting their current companies. In 1999, for instance, Fort Worth's Sabre Holdings Corp. snatched executive hotshot William Hanningan out from SBC Communications with a pay package worth $20.9 million. That package, a Sabre official told the *Dallas Morning News*, was designed to be cushy enough to make up for any compensation Hanningan lost when he left SBC.[149]

Restricted stock grants, in other words, work wonderfully as a retention incentive — so long as a company that grants the restricted stock has an executive nobody else wants. If, on the other hand, a company has an executive other firms lust after — in short, an executive worth keeping — restricted stock and other retention incentives make no impact whatsoever, except, of course, to raise the overall level of executive pay another several notches.

Boards of directors absolutely convinced that they must retain their top executive at all costs do occasionally change their minds. Sometimes quickly. In 1996, computer hard-drive maker Seagate Technology wanted desperately to lock up the services of its top executive, the sixty-five-year-old Al Shugart. The California company pledged to hand Shugart 150,000 shares of stock if he stuck around as CEO another five years.[150] Two years later, Seagate's board had become desperate once again, this time to show Shugart the door. The company had slumped, and the board that had locked up Shugart's services for five years now wanted him out after just two. Shugart refused to go. To give him an incentive to change his mind, the Seagate board would eventually accelerate the vesting of Shugart's restricted shares, extend the amount of time he could sit on stock options previously awarded him, and agree to pay him $750,000 a year over the next three years for consulting. Shugart would eventually walk away with $10 million.[151]

CORPORATE AMERICA, BY CENTURY'S END, had perfected executive pay incentives for every occasion. Executives could earn king-size compensation if they "performed" in their jobs, if they stayed in their jobs, or if they, like Seagate's Al Shugart, exited their jobs.

Corporate America's exit incentives, otherwise known as "golden parachutes," first started unfurling in the 1980s when corporate raiders began buying up stock in their takeover targets at increasingly inflated prices.[152] Big shareholders at the targeted companies welcomed the raider interest. Top executives, understandably, didn't. Any takeover could cost these executives their suites, and this unnerving prospect gave CEOs an incentive to battle takeover bids, even those bids that would make their shareholders fortunes. Corporate boards figured they needed to give executives a counter incentive, some contract sweetener that would encourage executives to approach takeover bids more open-mindedly. Enter the golden parachute, an agreement to award a displaced executive what amounts to super severance. Executives outfitted with golden parachutes need not fear whatever a takeover could bring. The new owners might shove the old executives right out of their top-floor offices. But no one, at least no one who mattered, would be hurt. The executives shoved out, buoyed by their multimillion-dollar canopies, would float softly down to earth and land, safely and securely, on their feet.

By the 1990s, golden parachutes had become standard corporate operating procedure. Companies of all sizes and shapes, *Nation's Business* magazine noted in 1994, were routinely using golden parachutes "to attract new talent and to retain key people."[153] Nearly three out of five major companies, added *Executive Compensation Reports* two years later, were offering their top executives super severance.[154]

These golden parachutes were soon funneling hundreds of millions of dollars out of corporate coffers. Leonard Abramson, the founder and CEO of USHealthCare, floated down from his lofty corporate perch with $56 million when Aetna gobbled up his company in 1996. In 1998, Bank of America chief executive David Coulter had a most comfortable landing after his enterprise merged with Nationsbank. Coulter walked off with $4.97 million a year for life, *plus* another $48 million in assorted extra severance.[155]

David Coulter and his fellow executives had come to reside, by century's end, in a truly wondrous world. In this special place, executives with incentives to perform didn't have to perform to become extravagantly wealthy, and executives with incentives to stay didn't have to stay to become wealthier still. Corporate America, in a sense, had gone far beyond the realm of incentives. Boards of directors were no longer *incentivizing* executives. They were *insuring* them — against even the remotest possibility that their executive service would leave them with anything less than a dynasty-sized fortune.

Golden parachutes served as insurance. Grants of restricted stock served as insurance. But the most imaginative insurance of all only began popping up, with any frequency, in the mid 1990s. The insiders called this newest twist "repricing."

Repricing addressed a most aggravating aspect of power-suit life, the annoying reality that stock options do not automatically translate into compensation windfalls. Share prices must rise over time for options to pay off, and share prices, despite an executive's best manipulative efforts, sometimes do not rise. Corporate boards can sidestep this built-in flaw, as we have seen, by going the "restricted stock" route — and rewarding executives with actual shares of stock, not just options to buy. But grants of restricted stock leave unsettled the predicament of option-laden executives stuck at companies with sinking shares. These executives hold worthless paper. How could they be expected to perform nobly, or even stick around, without an option windfall to dream about?

Corporate board compensation committees, fortunately, have the wherewithal to remedy the situation. They can simply cancel existing options and reissue new ones, usually without shareholder approval, "repricing" these new options at a lower price.[156] The compensation committee at Cendant, the financial services giant, did a good bit of this repricing in 1998, after the discovery of what *Business Week* called "massive accounting irregularities" sent the company's shares tumbling, from over $30 to less than $10. That tumble shoved the 25.8 million options held by the company's CEO, Henry Silverman, "underwater." Silverman had been granted the options when Cendant shares were selling in the $17 to $31 range. With the share price at $10, his options had become worthless. But not for long. The Cendant compensation committee, undoubtedly unnerved by the realization their company might soon have a sulking CEO, repriced "a big chunk" of Silverman's options to $9.81. The stock then rebounded to $15, enough to turn Silverman's worthless options into an asset worth over $54 million. Silverman ended the year in ninth place on *Business Week*'s annual list of America's best-paid CEOs.[157]

Repricing does carry risks. Corporate boards that reprice can count on rumblings from shareholder ranks. For some reason, many shareholders cannot understand why executives should get worthless options "repriced" while ordinary shareholders, if they bought a sinking stock before it sank, are simply stuck. In response, repricing corporate boards insist they have no choice. If they didn't reprice, they would no longer be "able to compete." They would "lose employees."[158] And perish that thought, particularly if the employees who might be lost happen to occupy a CEO seat.[159]

The ongoing competition for executive talent, in other words, makes repricings unavoidable, or so goes the corporate spin.[160] Some companies, in their haste to insure executives against any unfortunate eventuality, have even spun themselves into repricing circles. Metro-Goldwyn-Mayer Inc., for instance, repriced the options held by a *former* CEO. But weren't repricings, reporters wondered, a stratagem meant to *retain* CEOs? Why reprice the options of an executive already departed? MGM scrambled for a rationale. The repricing was only fair, a spokesperson finally blustered to *Business Week*, since the company had repriced options for other executives the year before.[161]

MGM-LIKE INANITIES, by the end of the 1990s, had corporate America's image-*meisters* advising boards of directors to steer clear of repricing.

"Option repricing is a justifiable flashpoint for CEO pay critics," *Chief Executive* magazine concluded in 1999. "The simplest rule for boards and compensation committees to follow is never to reprice options. The public relations danger is simply too great and it will only feed the critics' worst suspicions."[162]

Most corporate boards have ended up taking *Chief Executive*'s advice, particularly after the Financial Accounting Standards Board changed the accounting rules. Under the new rules, adopted in the late 1990s, companies that canceled underwater options and replaced them with new repriced opportunities stood to face a "substantial charge against earnings."[163] Some corporations, of course, did try to end run the new regulations. Sprint, for instance, canceled worthless underwater options and promised to issue the employees who held them, in six months and a day, new repriced options. Six months and a day just happened to be the length of time a company had to "wait to avoid extra expense charges under the new accounting rule."[164] But companies like Sprint were careful not to apply this end run to the underwater options held by their topmost executives. The negative public relations fallout would simply have been too great — and, besides, why chance that fallout when the flaws of standard stock option plans could be addressed by so many other less controversial approaches?

These alternative approaches were soon proliferating across the corporate landscape. Some companies with sinking share prices simply issued their executives stuck with underwater options huge new quantities of options, at an attractive low price.[165] Other boards gave executives more time to exercise their options, a move designed to give underwater options a chance to float back to the surface. In 1999, for instance, Sears gave CEO Arthur Martinez and other top executives an extra year to get the company's share price up. The company's incentive goals, Sears spokesperson Peggy Palter told the *Chicago Tribune*, needed to be "more realistic."[166]

But time extensions, as welcome as they might be, couldn't insure underwater executives an option payoff, one big reason why some boards opted for more direct guarantees. The ever-imaginative directors at Philip Morris, for their part, started paying executives "dividends" on their option grants, a most thoughtful gesture since the company's shares, worth over $58 in 1998, were down by more than half two years later. The dividends — on shares the executives did not actually own and might never own, if they chose not to exercise their option — didn't bring the Philip Morris shares above water, but executives, *Business Week* pointed out, could at least "look forward to a quarterly check."[167]

Other companies tried to insure their executives against option anxiety with a neat little trick known as the option "reload." Executives blessed with reloadable options would automatically receive new options whenever they exercised old ones. Executives with reloadable options could make money, and lots of it, despite precipitous drops in their company share price. "Executives at Alcoa, American Express, Morgan Stanley Dean Witter and Sprint," the *New York Times* reported in 2001, "all were able to cushion their losses because they reloaded their options back when their shares were flying high."[168]

But even reloads don't *guarantee* windfalls at the end of the option rainbow. To *fully* insure that options pay off, a company would have to agree to pay an executive even if the company's shares do not rise. No company, of course, could possibly agree to reward an executive who *fails* to raise the company's share price, could it? Nonsense. We live in a free country. Corporations can do anything they want, even explicitly promise to reward an executive for failing. Some businesses, the *Wall Street Journal* reported early in the new century, were actually protecting executives against stock depreciation "with guaranteed cash payments if their stock price fails to reach a certain level."[169] Amazon, for instance, lured Joseph Galli from Black & Decker with a $7.9 million cash bonus and 3.9 million stock options. Amazon *guaranteed* that the options would generate a $20 million payoff. If Amazon's shares didn't jump enough to enable Galli to cash out a $20 million personal profit, the company promised to give Galli the $20 million outright.[170]

No one, of course, demanded the heads of the Amazon directors who had approved the Galli deal. Those directors were merely playing the game as corporate America had come to expect it to be played. Companies throughout the United States, *Business Week* noted early in the new century, are "frantically piling on more options and scrambling to make sure their execs come out on top — no matter what happens to their share prices."[171]

Close observers of corporate America could only shake their heads.

"It's insane to think that these 'incentives' worth millions of dollars are buying anything extra," charged former pay consultant Graef Crystal. "When it comes to pay, too many of these guys have no off-button — that's the greedy part."[172]

Who could argue?

BACK IN THE EARLY 1990S, amid the first major rumblings about overpaid CEOs, reformers advanced a host of specific proposals to end executive excess. At the time, the typical CEO at a major American corporation was earning about $2 million a year — more than three times what executives were making in the early 1980s. What could be done to bring this excessive pay under control? Executive incentive plans, *Business Week* urged, should be simplified. Limit executives to "a salary, a bonus, and a single stock-option plan that encourages ownership." To make sure that corporations don't pass options out cavalierly, change the accounting rules and make all options count as charges against earnings. Require executives to hold on to their stock for some extended period of time. Disclose to shareholders exactly what executives are making.[173] Could changes like these really rein in executive pay? *Business Week*, even back in 1992, wasn't particularly sanguine.

"Compensation is a complex and controversial issue," the magazine noted. "Few critics agree even about the precise nature of the problem, let alone its solutions."

But those critics, in the early 1990s, had caught the nation's attention. Executive pay had become an *issue*. In 1992, even candidates for the White House, both Democratic and Republican, felt compelled to express their concern.[174] That concern, in the next year, would actually translate into action. In 1993, the new President, Bill Clinton, signed into law legislation that denied corporations the right to deduct from their income taxes any executive pay over $1 million. The Securities and Exchange Commission, in the same spirit, mandated that companies must reveal more information about just how much their executives are making. Reform finally seemed to be "taking hold."[175] One group that had been railing against excessive CEO pay, the United Shareholders Association, actually "declared its mission accomplished" and closed up shop.[176]

The release of the next year's executive pay statistics seemed, at first glance, to confirm that move's wisdom. In 1994, executive pay would indeed fall, by 25 percent from the previous year.[177] But 1994's modest executive pay levels, *Business Week* would unhappily conclude the following year, represented merely the "calm before the storm." Pay levels had dropped, the magazine explained, because few executives had bothered to cash out their stock option incentives in 1994, an understandable decision since the year's "weak stock market made their options less lucrative." Any surge in the stock market, *Business Week* predicted, would inevitably trigger another wave of windfalls.

The 1993 executive pay reforms, most analysts soon agreed, had made no appreciable difference. Corporate America had not kicked the high-pay habit. In fact, the most visible of the 1993 reforms — the $1 million tax deductibility cap on executive pay — actually fed that habit. The cap, it turned out, only applied to an executive's base salary. Stock options and any other "performance" incentives were all exempted, and that gave corporate boards an even greater incentive to shovel options into executive pay plans. And even the $1 million cap on straight salary could be sidestepped. Corporate boards could simply "defer" salary above the $1 million limit until after an executive retired. At that point, the cap would not apply.[178]

The irrelevancy of the 1993 reforms would come into still sharper relief after the release of the annual executive pay figures for 1995. Average big-time CEO pay, noted consultants at Pearl Meyer, would leap to $4.37 million for the year, up 23 percent over 1994. "Performance-based" incentives, the pay category exempted by the 1993 deductibility cap, accounted for almost all that increase.[179]

Once again, critics from within corporate America raised their voices in protest.

"Compensation inflation is running riot in many corner offices of Corporate America," *Business Week* editorialized. "This has simply got to stop."[180]

But the riot didn't stop. After 1995, in fact, the riot spilled totally out of control. In 1996, executive compensation at the 365 top corporations tracked by *Business Week* rose an average 54 percent.[181] In 1997, average executive pay soared again, to $7.8 million, up 35 percent over 1996. In 1998, the pay parade would march on to even loftier heights. Average chief executive pay topped $10 million for the first time, jumping 36 percent.[182] Top executives, the *Wall Street Journal* reported, cashed out their largest stock option profits ever in 1998. And those option profits figured to swell even higher in the years ahead, since over two hundred major companies had handed their CEOs "megagrants," stashes of stock options worth at least three times an executive's annual salary and bonus.[183] Executives, thanks to such megagrants, were now counting their windfalls not by tens of millions, but by the hundreds. The Gap's chief executive, Millard Drexler, saw his personal bottom-line jump $494.6 million in 1998, a total that included base pay, bonuses, exercised stock options, and unrealized gains on accumulated stock options.[184]

The next year, 1999, brought more of the same. The top twenty CEOs in the United States, *Business Week* reported, averaged $112.9 million each, and that average did *not* include the value of unexercised stock options.[185]

Just how much incentive, angry observers from outside the business community asked, did executives need anyway?

"Is someone not going to work for you if he gets $50 million instead of $100 million?" wondered Tim Smith, the director of the New York-based Interfaith Center on Corporate Responsibility. "How rich do they have to be?"[186]

WOULD ANY PLAYER IN CORPORATE AMERICA have the moxie to step up to the plate and challenge greed in the suites? Reformers, by century's end, saw only one possible countervailing force with enough muscle to make a difference: the institutional investing community. By 2000, America's institutional investors — mutual funds, pension funds, university endowment funds — controlled half the U.S. equity market.[187]

These investors, corporate America's most savvy insiders understood, could pull the plug on incentive excess any time they so chose.[188] In the boom years, they chose not to. Part of that reluctance, noted Robert A. G. Monks, a pioneer shareholder advocate, may have been personal. University decision makers, for instance, routinely "pal" around with the corporate executives they ought to be confronting. But a big part of that reluctance also reflected pure institutional conflict of interest. Universities would rather not upset their corporate contributors.[189]

Other conflicts of interest also come into play. By law, every corporation that sells stock to the public must publicly report to — and face — shareholders once a year. Shareholders can bring resolutions on executive incentives to these annual meetings. Shareholder votes then determine whether these resolutions pass or fail. They usually fail. Why? Mutual funds and other large institutional investors typically give voting responsibility for their holdings to money managers. These money managers vote these shares, almost always, to support corporate management positions.

This pro-management bias may be unavoidable. From the money manager perspective, after all, every corporation could be, someday down the road, a client looking for a new outfit to manage its pension money or 401(k). Why vote against a management position and risk alienating a potential client?[190] And money managers who *already* manage a corporation's retirement fund are seldom going to vote against that corporation, on behalf of some other institutional shares they may manage. Why risk losing a current client?[191]

So no one risks anything.

"We are all victims," financial analyst Marcy Kelly told the *Wall Street Journal* in 1999, "of the excesses and greed the institutional investors allow to take place."[192]

By century's end, some institutional investors were trying to undo the damage. The nation's largest pension system, TIAA-CREF, adopted new policy that called on boards of directors to adopt only "rational" executive compensation policies.[193] America's other giant pension fund, the California Public Employees' Retirement System, also started flexing more muscle. In 1999, Bank of America CEO Hugh McColl took home $76 million, in a year when Bank of America axed nineteen thousand jobs. CalPERS, in protest, vowed to withhold its support from four directors seeking re-election to Bank of America's board.[194] CalPERS, the pension fund's president, Sean Harrigan, would tell Congress in 2003, "is deeply concerned over what appears to be an attitude of entitlement in the executive suite of corporate America."[195] The California pension giant, Harrigan added, would be developing — and sharing — analytical tools that "help identify on a more systematic basis where compensation abuses are occurring."

But few activists within the institutional investment community see these stirrings as a sign of significantly more accountable corporate days to come. One reason: The shareholder resolutions that institutional investors can bring before annual corporate meetings are not binding on corporate boards. Companies can legally ignore shareholder resolutions, even if they pass. In 2002, for instance, ninety-eight shareholder resolutions gained majority support at corporate annual meetings. Corporate boards, reports the Council of Institutional Investors, ignored eighty-four of them.[196]

What corporate managements cannot legally ignore are the votes cast by shareholders for board of directors candidates. Institutional investors have the power, should they ever choose to organize collectively, to depose corporate boards that shower millions upon their executive elites. But corporate governance rules work against that organizing. Opposition candidates for corporate boards, to have their supporters counted, must print up and get into the hands of shareholders their own ballots, an incredibly costly process.

Over the first half of 2003, various public interest groups lobbied hard for rule changes significant enough to democratize corporate board elections. Midway through the year, in July, the federal Securities and Exchange Commission did announce a series of reforms in that direction. But the SEC's changes, even fully implemented, would leave a solid majority of corporate board members, at least three-quarters, "elected" as they always have been elected, in shareholder voting that lacked even the basic trappings of democracy.[197] Insiders would continue to call the corporate shots.

INSTITUTIONAL INVESTORS OPERATE, ultimately, in a business environment where all the "incentives" encourage them to play lapdog, not watchdog. Still, throughout the 1990s, corporate America didn't need to count on conflicts of interest or rigged corporate governance rules to keep potential whistle-blowers quiet and ineffective. Something else, something stronger, gave corporate America a blank check for incentive outages. Something else guaranteed that ridiculously overpaid executives would have no trouble swatting away whatever brickbats came their way. That something else would be the great stock market boom that closed out America's twentieth century. "Good times" made the irrationality of executive excess actually seem rational.

Incentives, after all, are about outcomes. Those who extend incentives intend certain outcomes to take place. If those outcomes do take place, the incentives have succeeded. In the 1990s, the incentives so profusely extended to America's top executives certainly seemed to have succeeded. Shareholder value had unquestionably been increased. Great rewards *for* executives, just as intended, had inspired great deeds *by* executives.

Critics could — and did — dispute this simple-minded cause-and-effect between booming executive pay and booming share prices. To no effect. Share prices were *up*. Executive pay was *up*. The simple-minded, insisted corporate America, were those who disputed the link. And those who disputed the link could only mutter in frustration. The corporate case for excessive incentives would remain credible and powerful, they understood, so long as share prices kept climbing.

"When everybody is making money," conceded one pay critic, Nell Minow, "it's hard to get people upset because some people are making too much."[198]

But what would happen if share prices stopped climbing? If executives were indeed compensated for performance, as corporate America's flacks constantly insisted they were, then executive pay ought to stop rising if stocks started stumbling. Conversely, if stocks seriously stumbled and executive pay continued soaring, who could honestly claim that stock options and retention bonuses, that restricted shares and golden parachutes, that excessive executive incentives, in all their generous glory, "worked" — or were necessary to make America "work"?

A falling stock market, in short, would either confirm that corporate America had finally come up with an incentive system that linked pay and performance or expose that system as a fraud. Which would it be?

The curious, at century's end, would not have to wait long for an answer. In 2000, the millennial year, share prices fell. By every measure, shareholder value plunged. The S&P 500 index, the standard benchmark of corporate well-being, dropped 9 percent. The Nasdaq composite index, the prime thermometer for hot high-tech companies, fell 39 percent. The Dow Jones industrial average, the yardstick for America's most stable companies, down 5 percent. Mutual funds overall, down 15 percent.[199]

Precious few corporations dodged the dip. For shareholders, 2000 was absolutely and undeniably a year to lament. And for America's top executives? What kind of year did they enjoy? The answer would come the following spring.

IN THE 1990S, SPRINGTIME STARTED giving birth to a new media ritual. Every spring, after corporations released their required annual financial statements, major media outlets in the United States would tally up the year's executive pay statistics and rank order the nation's most generously rewarded CEOs.[200] Nationally, *Business Week*, the *Wall Street Journal,* the *New York Times*, the *Washington Post, Forbes, Fortune*, and *USA Today* all published annual executive pay studies, each one charting a slightly different set of executives, each one defining compensation slightly differently. At the regional level, the *Chicago Tribune*, the *Baltimore Sun*, the *Philadelphia Inquirer*, the *Seattle Times*, and nearly every other major metropolitan newspaper generated local executive pay scorecards, each one spotlighting the biggest local CEO compensation winners.

In the spring of 2001, all these media listmakers essentially had one question on their minds: Would CEO pay reflect the stock market's wretched 2000 — or would CEO pay continue on its merry way? The answer stunned even the most jaded Wall Street observers. Despite the wretched market, executive compensation would once again soar.

In 2000, the *New York Times* reported, chief executives averaged 22 percent raises in salary and bonus — and took home new grants of stock options worth an average $14.9 million. In total compensation, the CEOs at the two hundred corporations the *Times* surveyed averaged more than $20 million.[201] *Business Week* looked at 365 top corporations — and found the same upward momentum. The average CEO, the magazine reported, "earned a stupendous $13.1 million last year."[202] The *Wall Street Journal* reported an 8.2 percent total pay increase.[203] *USA Today*, looking at a different corporate sample, estimated that top executives in 2000 saw their personal bottom lines boosted by 62 percent, to a $36.5 million average.[204]

"Falling stock prices, disappointing earnings and other bad news," the *Washington Post* told readers, "don't seem to be hurting the compensation of many U.S. executives."[205]

Did rising CEO pay *averages* conceal slumping paychecks in those specific industries hit hardest by Wall Street's downturn? Good question. The San Jose *Mercury News*, the newspaper of record in Silicon Valley, offered an answer. Few industries had enjoyed 2000, the year of the dot.com collapse, less than high tech, the paper noted. Over the course of the year, Silicon Valley's 150 top firms saw their shares drop 20 percent.[206] But tech execs did not share that pain. They registered, in fact, their best year ever. The area's top eight hundred-plus executives walked off with $4.8 billion in 2000, averaging just under $6 million each, more than twice what they received the year before.[207]

Individually and as a group, nationally and regionally, across the board and industry by industry, top executives did exceedingly well in 2000 — and no one, a *Washington Post* analysis made clear, could reasonably consider their immense good fortune a reward for performing well. The "base pay" for executives in 2000, the straight salary they received just for showing up at the office every day, accounted for just 10 percent of total executive pay, the *Post* pointed out.[208] This base pay brought the executives the *Post* studied an average of $1.13 million for the year. The remaining 90 percent of the pay executives received, about $9 million, came from *incentives* of various sorts. In other words, America's top executives received, on average, $9 million for "performance" in a year when their performance, by every standard measure, reeked of absolute failure.

Compensation consultants who had in earlier years defended executive excess as "logical and fair" didn't bother trying to justify the stunning new numbers.

"I'm actually a little disappointed," Ira Kay of the Watson Wyatt Worldwide consulting firm told the *New York Times*.[209]

Corporate America's watchdogs, for their part, felt betrayed. Veteran shareholder activist Nell Minow had, earlier in her career, actively pushed for stock option incentives. The more options executives held, she and like-minded reformers had believed, the more attention executives would pay to shareholder interests.

"In my young and innocent days, I really did think that stock options would be a good thing," Minow noted after the release of the 2000 executive pay figures. "But what did I know?"[210]

How did incentives meant to "align" executives with shareholders end up keeping executives floating high while shareholders sank? Options, America discovered in 2000, gave executives as much cushion to coast as incentive to perform. By cashing out options awarded in previous years, executives could comfortably ride out a year or two of poor share price performance.

In the new century's first year, executives would cash out options by the mega-millions, with the most megas going to executives with enough "vision" to sense what the future might bring — or enough inside knowledge to get out while the getting was good. In Silicon Valley, Intel's top five executives exercised over 3 million options in the first half of 2000, "more than seven times the number of options they had exercised the year before," noted San Jose's *Mercury News.* These shrewd option moves gained the five executives $160 million by September, just three weeks before Intel started announcing bad news about sales.[211] By the end of the year, Intel shares would be down a third.[212]

Executives at Cisco Systems played the same option games. CEO John Chambers alone scored $156 million by unloading options early.[213] Together, the top half dozen executives at Cisco cashed out almost 7 million options before Cisco shares peaked in late March 2000. They cleared $307.8 million in option profits.[214]

Not all executives, of course, could match the exquisite sense of timing of the power suits at Intel and Cisco. With the stock market sinking, some top executives did indeed find themselves holding millions of options they could no longer exercise at a profit.[215] Many options executives had considered sure-fire windfalls at the start of 2000 had become, by year's end, no more valuable than lottery tickets. In lotteries, of course, most people lose. But corporate America was not about to let executives lose out, even if they had underperformed. In boardroom after boardroom, companies did everything they could, the *Washington Post* reported, "to give their top executives a helping hand."[216]

Out of Black & Decker's helping hand came a million new options for CEO Nolan Archibald, five times more options than he received in 1999. Black & Decker shares had dropped 25 percent. Lucent Technologies doubled the annual option grant award to CEO Richard McGinn. Lucent shares were off 81 percent. In 2000, overall, companies awarded CEOs 55 percent more stock options than the year before.[217]

Other corporate boards went back to the future in 2000 and blessed their executives with simple, old-fashioned cash bonus incentives. That took some doing, since executives over the course of the year hadn't done much worth rewarding. Still, corporate boards were able to rise to the challenge. Some awarded executives bonuses "for implementing Y2K computer bug initiatives." One company actually gave its CEO a bonus for "making sure transition managers were in place once the CEO retired." Overall, CEO bonuses jumped 21 percent in 2000 and added almost $2 million to the typical top executive paycheck.[218]

THE AMAZING CEO PAY FIGURES FOR 2000, careful business observers realized, would be no one-year anomaly. CEO pay figured to stay high well into the new century, even if the stock market kept stumbling. Top executives still sat, these observers explained, on millions of unexercised options, many originally granted while share prices were still rising. Share prices had since peaked — and fallen — but good chunks of the unexercised option stashes would generate sizable profits should stocks up tick even slightly.

"Local executives will likely keep winning the options' jackpot for years to come — regardless of how their stock performs," concluded Silicon Valley's *Mercury News.*[219]

The first executive to hit that jackpot, after 2000, would be Larry Ellison, the CEO of software giant Oracle. In January 2001, Ellison cashed out options granted him in earlier glory days and pocketed $706 million.[220]

Corporate boards took one other little-noticed step, as the new century began, that promised to keep executives in compensation clover for years to come. They redefined the "long" in "long-term" compensation. Throughout the 1990s, top executives had received both annual and "long-term" pay. Salaries and bonuses would come annually, new options and other stock incentives would be awarded once every several years. With share prices rising, as they did throughout the 1990s, these "long-term" plans left CEOs suitably satisfied. Salaries and bonuses guaranteed them a healthy annual cash flow, and, as share prices rose, their options that had not yet vested became more valuable year by year. In 2000, with share prices suddenly falling, everything changed. Executives, in effect, were stuck with "long-term" incentives that now offered no incentive. A most intolerable situation. In response, executives started demanding new long-term incentives *every year*. And corporate boards graciously agreed.[221]

Annual "long-term" incentive awards hand top executives — passionate golfers all — what amounts to performance mulligans, executive suite do-overs.[222] Your company's share price down? If you're the CEO, no need to worry. Your thoughtful board of directors will give you a new batch of options, all exercisable down the road at the current low share price. And if share prices sink even lower next year, your board will give you still another batch of option incentives, all exercisable at an even lower price. Your board, in effect, will keep lowering the performance bar until it finds a height you can jump over — and win the windfall that is your due.[223]

Corporate boards would go a long way down this mulligan road in 2000. The new "long-term" incentive plan deals cut over the course of the year were worth, on average, 49 percent more than the long-term plans set in 1999.[224]

"In other words," the *New York Times* would note in 2001, "2003 is already looking like a good year for executive pay."[225]

SHAREHOLDER VALUE WOULD CONTINUE to droop in 2001 and 2002. Executive compensation would not. In 2001, at the two hundred major companies surveyed by the *New York Times*, profits would be down 35 percent. Median CEO pay at these same companies: up 7 percent.[226] In 2002, a repeat performance. At the one hundred top corporations analyzed by *Fortune*, pay for "middle-of-the-road" CEOs jumped 14 percent, to $13.2 million, in the same year the S&P 500 sank over 22 percent.[227] But these ample CEO pay figures, insiders knew, actually understated the rewards heaped upon America's top executives. Upon America's executive class, over the previous dozen years, corporate America had created a veritable parallel incentive universe, an amazing array of perquisites, or "perks," each one explicitly intended to make life at the top as worry-free as turn-of-the-millennium life could possibly be.

These perks, corporate America believes, make sound business sense. Perks, the argument goes, free executives from life's inconveniences. Executives, freed from daily distractions, have no "incentive" to think about anything else other than corporate success. Perks pump performance! Consequently, within corporate America, no consideration for the welfare of top executives has become too small to be overlooked.

Do executives need help keeping up with life? How about a person, or two, to help? In 1998, MBNA Bank handed CEO Charles Cawley $144,415 for "personal assistants." In 1999, Cawley's personal assistants cost MBNA $159,055. The next year, MBNA's expenditure for CEO assistants dropped to just $123,022. Perhaps Cawley made up the difference from his own pocket. He did take home, in 2000, about $45 million.[228]

Every major U.S. corporation also reimburses executives for whatever financial planning services they might require. In 2000, Citigroup gave chairman Sandy Weill $74,000 — almost twice the income of a typical American family that year — to pay experts to do his personal financial planning. Those experts undoubtedly had their hands full. In 2000, Weill earned $28.2 million in pay and restricted stock, made $196 million more by cashing out options granted in previous years, and collected grants of new stock options valued at $301.7 million.

Executive perks, all together, now add tens of millions of dollars into executive pockets each and every year. These perks, most inconveniently, also add to executive tax liabilities, since many of them count as "income" at income tax time. This poses a problem. How can executives feel appropriately incentivized if they have to pay taxes on their perks? Many corporate boards don't bother finding out. They simply hand their executives the extra cash they need to offset any taxes that might be due on the perks.[229]

Despite such thoughtful gestures, taxes still present an enormous aggravation for America's top executives, the prime reason why corporate boards have perfected still another perk, the most lucrative executive perk of all: "deferred compensation."

All 401(k) plans — the deferred pay plans open to average corporate employees — are subject to strict limits. A plan participant can defer and invest, tax-free, only so much salary each year. In 2002, for instance, no employees, be they CEOs or stock boys, could defer more than $11,000 in earnings through a company 401(k) plan. Yet individual CEOs that year, unlike average employees, were able to defer taxes on many millions more than that $11,000. And how is that possible? Under current law, corporations can establish special pay deferral plans only open to top executives. No limits apply to these plans. Executives can shelter as much of their cash compensation as they please.[230] Individual tax-avoiding CEOs, the *Wall Street Journal* reported in 2002, have turned these deferral accounts into parking lots for "tens of millions of dollars."[231] Just how many dollars overall have poured into deferred executive pay accounts? The estimates, the *New York Times* notes, run from "the tens of billions" to "the hundreds of billions."[232]

In theory, all these dollars in executive deferral plans sit at risk. If a company goes belly-up, an executive could lose every deferred dollar.[233] Corporate boards have moved, predictably, to eliminate this unfortunate risk. They simply reimburse executives for the cost of insuring their deferred pay stashes. One example: The CSX transportation company handed CEO John Snow — later named U.S. secretary of the treasury by President George W. Bush — $421,000 to offset the cost of insurance Snow bought to guarantee his deferred pay should CSX be taken over by another company.[234]

Corporate deferred pay thoughtfulness doesn't end here. Corporations don't just sit on the money executives divert into their deferred pay accounts. They pay interest on it, at higher than standard market rates. General Electric, in the mid 1990s, guaranteed CEO Jack Welch a sweet 14 percent on his deferred pay dollars.[235] G.E. could be even sweeter. In 2000, Welch's last full year before retirement, General Electric gave him $65.5 million in pay and restricted stock as well as new options that could be worth as much as $274 million. Welch realized another $57 million by exercising options already in his pocket.[236] Was all that enough to show G.E.'s appreciation for services rendered? Not by a longshot. G.E. shelled out another $1.3 million to pay Welch's life insurance premiums.[237] God forbid he should drop dead and leave his heirs without a meal-ticket.

"Why does an executive need to be so well compensated and then have all these various and sundry things paid by the company?" Ann Yerger, the research director at the Council of Institutional Investors, would ask at century's end. "Most of us pay our expenses out of our own pockets — that's what our salary is for."[238]

Added Jamie Heard, the head of Proxy Monitor, an adviser for institutional investors: "There's just one word for most of this — greed."[239]

AMID THE PERKS, AMID THE OPTIONS, amid the bonuses, amid the greed, corporate America has continued to insist, right into the new century, that rich rewards remain absolutely essential to business success. How else, if not with lavish incentives, can tip-top performance be coaxed out of America's executive suites? Year after year, corporations have kept pumping up the windfalls, dumping millions upon millions on executives already sated with billions. By early in 1998, for instance, Dell Computer CEO Michael Dell already owned $2.34 billion worth of his company's shares.[240] Enough incentive? Apparently not. The Dell board awarded CEO Dell options worth $33.5 million in 1998 and another $105.4 million worth in 1999.[241] "We pay for performance here," a Dell flack proudly proclaimed, "and Michael is a phenomenal CEO."[242]

But what possible purpose, asked *Business Week* columnist Allan Sloan, could more options serve — "other than enriching Michael Dell"?

"He already owns 190 million shares, his name is on the building and his $16 billion stake offers him ample incentive to get the stock price up," Sloan observed. "Will he defect to Gateway or Compaq if he doesn't get options?"[243]

"How much more incentive do you need," adds Patrick McGurn of Institutional Shareholder Services, "when you already own billions of dollars' worth of stock?"[244]

Is it true, a business journalist asked Tyco International chief executive L. Dennis Kozlowski at a CEO forum, before his 2002 tax evasion indictment, "that at a certain level it no longer matters how much any of you make, that you would be doing just as good a job for $100 million less or $20 million less?"

"Yeah," replied Kozlowski, "all my meals are paid for."

So why was he still striving for tens of millions more? In the game of life, Kozlowski explained, the money is "a way of keeping score."[245]

At the turn of the century, Kozlowski would by no means be the only top executive "keeping score." "How much the boss makes," *Business Week* would note, "has become something of a scorecard."[246] A scorecard with a difference. Most games we play at some point end. In bridge, you make rubber, you win. In baseball, you score more runs in nine innings, you win. In basketball, you hit more points by the final buzzer, you win. But the game never ends in corporate America. No buzzer ever sounds. No CEO, consequently, can ever make enough to win. Some other CEO is always just ahead, waiting to be caught. Some other CEO is always right behind, threatening to catch up. In this game without end, no incentive reward can ever be enough. CEOs will always need more. On corporate America's playing fields, under current rules, they'll always get it.

Some observers felt these rules would change, and dramatically so, after Enron's collapse late in 2001 triggered over six months of almost daily corporate scandal headlines. The rules would actually change, somewhat, the summer after Enron, with the passage of the Sarbanes-Oxley corporate accountability bill. This legislation did ban a host of accounting and corporate governance practices that had contributed, over the years, to executive excess.[247] But the Sarbanes-Oxley reforms would place no quick or meaningful brake on executive incentives. That became readily apparent a year later, when news reports tallied the first executive pay scorecards for the 2003 corporate fiscal year.[248]

At H.J. Heinz, the ketchup king, top executive W. R. Johnson saw his bonus jump 316 percent in 2003 at the same time the company's shares were sinking nearly 29 percent. Annual incentives at Heinz, the company insisted, reflect "clear performance measures aligned with the creation of shareholder value."

At Applied Micro Circuits, a computer parts maker, share values dropped 59 percent in fiscal 2003. The company rewarded CEO David Rickey with 8 million new stock options. This option generosity, potentially worth $56.6 million, would "serve as a meaningful incentive," the company explained, "for employees to remain."

At cereal giant General Mills, share prices actually increased in fiscal 2003, by 3.3 percent. The company's directors, to show their gratitude, upped CEO

Stephen Sanger's bonus 73 percent and threw in new options worth $35.4 million. These rewards, General Mills asserted, were "reasonable in light of performance and industry practices."

Late in August 2003, two weeks after these outrages surfaced, one familiar and well-respected figure in corporate America, Richard C. Breeden, would release what he hoped would be an antidote to over two decades of executive incentive excess. Less than a year earlier, the federal judge overseeing fraud charges against WorldCom, the telecom giant that had gone bankrupt midway through 2002, had asked Breeden, a veteran corporate consultant and a former chairman of the federal Securities and Exchange Commission, to recommend reforms to fix the deeply troubled WorldCom.

Breeden took his task to heart. He saw an opportunity, as WorldCom's official "corporate monitor," to fix what ailed all of corporate America, not just one company. And what ailed WorldCom and the rest of corporate America, Breeden concluded, was an incentive system run totally amuck. WorldCom encapsulated everything wrong with corporate incentives.[249] Lavish stock option grants had made WorldCom CEO Bernard Ebbers one of America's richest men. WorldCom relished handing out "retention" grants as well. The company had incentivized Ebbers and other WorldCom executives with a retention "slush fund" that totaled nearly a quarter-billion dollars. Golden parachutes — $50 million for Ebbers alone — and sumptuous perks also abounded. All these incentives, Breeden noted in his August 2003 report to U.S. District Court judge Jed Rakoff, did not encourage excellence. These incentives, instead, had encouraged a "reckless pursuit of wealth." And that reckless pursuit, Breeden found, had "created a climate conducive to the fraud that occurred," a fraud that ultimately cost investors $200 billion in share value.

The fix? Breeden recommended, and U.S. District Court judge Rakoff subsequently ordered, nothing less than the wholesale dismantling of WorldCom's entire executive incentive structure. In the new MCI, the company that would arise from WorldCom's bankruptcy, stock options would be banned for five years — and could not be reinstituted unless shareholders approved their use in advance. Retention bonuses and "all personal use of corporate aircraft and other corporate assets" would also be prohibited, and executive severance agreements would be subject to strict limits.[250]

Breeden's report would not reject totally corporate incentive orthodoxy. The new MCI, his report would note, would need pay incentives to "ensure that compensation is linked to superior performance." Toward that end, Breeden encouraged the MCI board to consider performance targets that link executive pay directly to profitability, growth in market share, and several other specific yardsticks. But Breeden would not completely swallow corporate America's pay-for-performance mantra. Even the most outstanding performance, his report would caution, must not be used to justify levels of compensation that violate "overall reasonableness."

To ensure this "reasonableness," Breeden proposed his most unexpected recommendation of them all. The new MCI board, his report declared, must set a lid on "total compensation from all sources" for its top executive, a "maximum dollar amount for any single year." Breeden would set this maximum — the first ever for the CEO of a major American corporation — at a generous level. The MCI chief executive, he noted, should receive "not more than $15 million" a year, though the board, he added quickly, would "be free to set a lower number."[251]

WorldCom's new incentive structure, Breeden urged business leaders at the official release of his 149-page report, ought to become a model for every major American corporation.

"We hope all of corporate America," he noted, "will look at it very carefully."[252]

Other observers, that same summer of 2003, would echo Breeden's call for a cap on executive pay. *Washington Post* business columnist Steven Pearlstein, for one, called excessive pay "the original sin of corporate malfeasance," the incentive that "warps the judgment and the ethics of executives."[253] He implored shareholders at America's largest corporations to insist that annual executive pay be limited, for the next five years, "to $1 million in salary and fringe benefits, $1 million in performance-based bonuses and $1 million in restricted stock." Only this sort of $3 million cap, Pearlstein noted, "would end the arms race that companies use to justify sky-high pay."

Corporate America's movers and shakers would blissfully ignore Pearlstein's cap proposal — and Breeden's as well. They would, instead, spend 2003 arguing that the entire corporate reform movement triggered initially by Enron's collapse made higher executive pay more necessary, and justifiable, than ever.

"CEOs," noted Ralph Ward, the publisher of *Boardroom Insider* newsletter, "are saying that because of reforms, there's more risk and more time on the job, and that justifies more pay. Boards tend to go along with that."[254]

In other words, later for incentives. In post-Enron America, top executives simply *deserve* more.

Our society's most generously rewarded, to be sure, have always felt they deserve more. Do they? We take that question next.

THE GREEDY AS DESERVING

IF YOUR SALARY WERE DOUBLED, would you work twice as hard? What if your earnings were quintupled? Would you become five times more productive? Probably not. Even the most rewarding of rewards, at some point, no longer make any sense as incentives.

Corporate America reached — and passed — that point some time ago. An executive who stands to make $100 million, most reasonable observers would agree, is not going to work twice as hard as an executive who stands to take home only $50 million.[1] Nor, for that matter, is an executive with a shot at $10 million going to work ten times harder than a colleague with a chance to make only $1 million. Why then would any corporation let an executive walk off with $100 million in annual compensation? Or $50 million? Or any princely sum that has, in the real world, little practical incentive value? Corporate America has an answer. Those who are paid considerably more than the rest of us simply deserve considerably more than the rest of us.

At century's end, few top corporate executives — and few Americans of any significant means — doubted they fully deserved their good fortune. In one survey of America's most affluent 1 percent, conducted by *Worth* magazine, 98 percent of the wealthy people polled attributed financial success to "greater determination."[2] Almost as many of the wealthy surveyed, 95 percent, credited success to "greater ability or talent," and 91 percent told pollsters that the financially successful have "greater intelligence."

All this hard work, talent, and intelligence, the wealthy appear to believe, contribute much more to financial success than mere happenstance — or unsavory personal qualities. The wealthy polled by *Worth* rated intelligence over twice as important to accumulating wealth as "knowing the right people" and talent twice as important as "luck." A willingness to take risks, they suggested, makes success in life four times more likely than "being born into privilege." What about ruthlessness? Only 2 percent of the wealthy polled called "being more ruthless" a significant key to success.

In sum, the wealthy agree, people worth millions are determined, smart, able, and bold.

And rare.

Or so corporate America would add. People who combine determination, intelligence, ability, and boldness, corporate leaders believe, aren't standing at every corner. CEOs, *Corporate Board* magazine explains, "are all individuals with a scarce talent." They deserve to be compensated as the "scarce high-talent individuals" they are.[3]

So quit quibbling, America, about excessive executive salaries.

"It's easy to paint these salaries as bad for society," one corporate insider, executive-placement expert Jeff Christian, argued midway through the 1990s, "but these are truly people with rare skills."[4]

"If you have a strong chief executive, be thankful," agreed Albert J. Dunlap, then the chief executive at Scott Paper. "There are damn few good ones out there."[5]

FOR MOST OF THE 1990S, almost everyone in corporate America counted Al Dunlap as a truly "rare" talent, one of the "damn few good ones" who deserved whatever good fortune came his way. At his prime, Dunlap would be as admired as any executive in America. Business magazines plastered his picture on their covers.[6] Universities and lawmakers jostled for his wisdom.[7] Fellow corporate executives envied his gumption.[8]

Dunlap even awed corporate America's watchdogs. In 1995, *Newsweek* asked one of these watchdogs, executive pay critic Nell Minow, about a nine-digit windfall Dunlap had just scored at Scott Paper.

"He deserves," Minow replied, "all the money he gets."[9]

By the mid 1990s, Dunlap had been dazzling corporate America for the better part of two decades. He had vaulted, with ease, from one executive suite to another, his legend growing at every stop along the way. Here was a West Point-trained, take-no-prisoners trouble-shooter willing and able to take on bloated corporate bureaucracies — and make stockholders money.

"Al goes in like a chainsaw," one Dunlap admirer noted. "He goes in and cuts away all the fat and leaves a great sculpture."[10]

The more Dunlap carved, the wider Wall Street smiled. At struggling paper-cup maker Lily-Tulip, for instance, "Chainsaw Al" fired over a quarter of the company's salaried employees. Lily-Tulip shares soared by more than 1,100 percent.[11] Dunlap epitomized, for Wall Street, the ideal CEO. He would do battle for shareholders first, last, and always. What anybody else thought, he delightedly insisted, would not interest him in the least.

"The price of leadership is criticism," Dunlap loved quipping. "If you want to be liked, get a dog."[12]

In Philadelphia, the Scott Paper board of directors lapped up Dunlap's *shtick*. He seemed just what their once dominant, now struggling, company needed.[13] In 1993, the company had lost $277 million.[14] Something had to be done. Something big. In April 1994, Scott Paper's directors made the big move. They named Dunlap the first Scott Paper CEO ever hired from outside company ranks. Dunlap, as Scott Paper's new CEO, would waste no time. Just two months after arriving, he announced plans to slice the company's workforce by 35 percent, over eleven thousand jobs.[15] He also almost immediately deprioritized — and deep-sixed — expenditures that didn't directly pump up Scott Paper's quarterly earnings. The company's budget for research and development would be halved. The company's charitable contributions would be ended. The new Scott Paper even reneged on a company pledge to the Philadelphia Museum of Art.[16]

This gesture of less than brotherly love would soon be topped by another. Dunlap decided to yank Scott Paper out of Philadelphia, the company's home ever since 1879, and open a new headquarters in Florida's Boca Raton. From Dunlap's perspective, the move made perfect sense. He already owned a $1.8 million Boca Raton mansion.

For consumers, neither the move to Boca Raton nor any other Dunlap maneuver would ever make much sense. During Dunlap's tenure, prices on Scott Paper household staples jumped repeatedly, some at double-digit rates. Consumers would not be pleased. Scott Paper products, under Chainsaw Al, actually lost market share.[17]

Wall Street didn't care. Dunlap had Scott Paper's share price soaring, up 225 percent.[18] And the best, the confident CEO told investors, was yet to come. Scott Paper, he proclaimed, had "a great future ahead."[19]

In fact, Scott Paper had no future at all. Dunlap had not been improving the company. He had been "prettying" it up for sale to the highest bidder, as savvy observers had realized early on.[20] In July 1995, just fifteen months after taking charge, Dunlap clinched the deal that would, later that year, end Scott Paper's long history as an independent enterprise. Competitor Kimberly-Clark, the Kleenex company, would buy out Scott Paper and swallow the company up whole — all except Dunlap and a handful of his executive pals. They would be handed, under the terms of the merger deal, ample severance packages.[21]

How ample? Dunlap's marketing chief, Richard Nicolosi, would walk off with $17.2 million for his sixteen months of distinguished Scott Paper service. Basil Anderson, the company's chief financial officer, would leave with $14.9 million. Russell Kersh, a Dunlap confidant since the glory days at Lily-Tulip, would exit with $16.4 million.[22]

Dunlap, naturally, would do considerably better.[23]

"After 20 months of intense work — and thanks in part to my own stock purchases, options, and other incentives — I left Scott $100 million richer than when I arrived," Dunlap would later tell the world proudly.[24]

Other Scott Paper employees would not fare as well. Jerry Chambless, a $60,000-a-year plant supervisor, was forty-nine when he lost his job in Dunlap's chainsaw massacre.[25] Unable to find another job, he suffered a stroke that left him in a wheelchair.

"I hold Al Dunlap fully responsible for what's happened to my husband," the stricken supervisor's wife told reporters. "Look at all the lives he's destroyed."[26]

Dunlap would have little trouble deflecting such angry attacks, thanks, no doubt, to years of training by the nation's finest public relations talent.

"I had a corporation where every person stood the chance of losing their job, so I got rid of 35 percent of the people," a well-prepped Dunlap would tell critics. "But 65 percent of the people have a more secure future than they've ever had."[27]

What about his $100 million windfall? A little excessive perhaps?

"I created six and half billion of value," Dunlap informed a Lehrer News Hour audience. "I received less than 2 percent of the value I created."[28]

Dunlap's clever counters would all be baloney. The 65 percent of Scott Paper employees who survived his chainsaw, for instance, enjoyed no job security. Just one day after the merger, Kimberly-Clark announced plans to eliminate eight thousand more jobs.[29]

And that $6.5 billion of "new" value Dunlap claimed he created?

"What galls many former executives, employees, and union leaders," *Business Week* would report, "is their belief that Dunlap and his team took credit for improvements that had been in the works for months, if not years."[30]

Dunlap, in the end, added no real value to Scott Paper. He merely, as the Wharton business school's Peter Cappelli would explain, "redistributed income from the employees and the community to the shareholders."[31] The company's shares did soar — but not because Dunlap had made the company more effective. Wall Street bid up Scott Paper because investors figured Dunlap would do what he always did: "cut jobs, divest assets, and then ditch the company at a tidy profit."[32]

Midway through 1996, six months after Dunlap's grand "success" at Scott Paper, Wall Street would exult in the news of still another Dunlap investing opportunity. Sunbeam, a famous but lackluster appliance maker, had just named Dunlap its top executive. The announcement came on July 18. The next day, Sunbeam shares leaped nearly 50 percent. In just a day, Dunlap had made Sunbeam shareholders more than half a billion dollars.[33]

That was good news, of course, for Sunbeam shareholders — and not so bad news for Dunlap either. He had received 2.5 million in stock options to join Sunbeam and another million shares of restricted stock. Dunlap, noted one analysis, made $48 million from Sunbeam before he "fired anyone or barked a single order as the new chief executive."[34]

But no one had to wait very long for Dunlap to start firing. Just a few months after taking over, the new CEO announced plans to shut down two-thirds of Sunbeam's factories and eliminate six thousand jobs, half the company's workforce.[35] Why the rush? At Scott Paper, cutting a workforce by a third had earned Dunlap $100 million in twenty months. Was he simply too eager to see how much he could make if he cut a workforce in half?

In any case, Sunbeam would pose a challenge Dunlap had never before encountered. The company had already been chainsawed — before Dunlap arrived.[36] Dunlap would only be able to get Sunbeam moving again, observers predicted, if he faced up to the challenge of actually overseeing real product development.[37] But how was Sunbeam going to roll out great new products, skeptics wondered, with a workforce that had been cut in half?[38]

Sunbeam couldn't. The company, Dunlap had promised, would be "making money" within a year.[39] But Dunlap's first anniversary came and went with the company still stumbling. Dunlap's antics now became even more frenetic. He shelled out $2.5 billion to buy up three small companies and then announced more job cuts "to absorb the newcomers."[40] Employees grimaced, not Dunlap. Early in 1998, Sunbeam had doubled his salary — and added in new stock considerations worth $70 million.[41]

Dunlap would do little to "deserve" these new millions. In the spring, Sunbeam reported huge first-quarter 1998 losses.[42] Dunlap, Wall Street began to fret, might be "failing in his turnaround mission."[43] In early June, Sunbeam shares would be down 65 percent.[44] Dunlap, by that point, had begun flailing about furiously for loans — or a buyer willing to take the Sunbeam turkey off his hands. Nothing worked. Finally, on June 15, a dispirited Sunbeam board gave Dunlap the heave-ho. He had, board members agreed, "terrorized underlings, refused to listen to suggestions, overrated his own intelligence, and adopted arbitrary rules."[45] More charges would start emerging in the months ahead, and, in 2001, the Securities and Exchange Commission would file suit against Dunlap and four of his management buddies. Nearly a third of Sunbeam's 1997 operating earnings, the SEC charged, "came from accounting fraud."[46] In January 2002, Dunlap would agree, without admitting guilt, to lay out $15 million to settle a Sunbeam shareholder suit. Sunbeam, by that time, had gone into bankruptcy.[47]

Sunbeam effectively ended Albert Dunlap's executive career. But what a career it had been. For close to thirty years a bully had swaggered his way across the business landscape, wreaking havoc in the lives of tens of thousands of employee families, accepting the accolades of corporate and political leaders, all the while puffing up companies with smoke and mirrors and piling up an enormous personal fortune.

Albert J. Dunlap no longer graces the covers of business magazines. He has become a corporate nonperson, rarely mentioned and, if mentioned, quickly dismissed as an unfortunate aberration. But Dunlap is no aberration. His career typifies corporate America's boundless faith that inordinate business success lies just one "rare talent" CEO away. Dunlap was one such rare, "deserving" talent.

Jerry Levin is another.

In 1997, the struggling Coleman camping equipment company named Jerry Levin the firm's new CEO. Levin quickly pledged to turn the company into a winner.

"I am 100 percent confident that Coleman will be a very successful growth vehicle," he announced. "This company is not for sale."[48]

The next year, Levin sold the company — to Al Dunlap and Sunbeam. The sale, Levin noted, would "clearly" benefit Coleman shareholders by creating both "immediate value and longer-term growth potential." But most of that benefit seemed to go only to Levin. He cleared $10 million in option profits shortly after the sale announcement. Coleman shareholders, after Sunbeam tanked, would end up empty-handed.

Sunbeam's very own rare talent, Albert J. Dunlap, had failed to measure up. Now, to replace the disgraced Dunlap, the directors on Sunbeam's board would have to find a new rare talent. They found him. In June 1998, shortly after firing Dunlap, Sunbeam's struggling board proudly announced the hiring of a new CEO, a true rare talent.

Jerry Levin.

RARE TALENTS TAKE GREAT RISKS. Rare talents work tirelessly at onerous tasks. Rare talents make incredibly wise and weighty decisions. Rare talents deserve rich rewards. Corporate America is sticking to this story, the Al Dunlap disasters notwithstanding. Dunlap's sorry saga, we are told, merely signifies that corporate America can occasionally be snookered.

Did Dunlap snooker corporate America? He certainly did — but that wasn't particularly difficult to do. The corporate boards that hired Al Dunlap apparently didn't even bother to check his résumé.[49] But whether scam artists like Dunlap can snooker corporate America matters, in the end, far less than another, considerably more fundamental, question: Is corporate America snookering us? Does *anyone* who sits in an executive suite deserve to walk away with tens — or even hundreds — of millions of dollars?

Just how deserving, in other words, are the executives and entrepreneurs who have accumulated America's greatest fortunes?

These executives and entrepreneurs are eminently deserving, business folklore assures us, because great fortunes begin with great risks. Nothing ventured, nothing gained. Those who do venture merit gain. After all, upon venturing out, they may encounter great pain. Don't they deserve, given that danger, whatever gain comes their way? A potent argument. But what if that prospect of pain should disappear? Would the venturesome then deserve any great gain that comes their way? Surely not, for how can risk justify reward if the "risk" carries no downside?

Defenders of America's greatest fortunes insist, of course, that dangerously real downsides lurk around every corporate corner. Executive life, they tell us, comes with no guarantees. Top executives can be fired. Or their stock holdings can suddenly lose value. So goes the mythology. In real corporate life, hardly anyone fortunate enough to sit behind a top executive's desk ever loses — not with golden parachutes in one desk drawer, repricings, reloadings, and restricted stock over in another. Corporate America has created, as we have seen, what amounts to a risk-free womb for "truly rare talents."

"Welcome aboard the Chief Executive Gravy Train," the *Wall Street Journal* proclaimed in 1998. "It overflows with treasure when things go well — and even when they don't."[50]

In 2000, things most definitely did not go well for Office Depot. Net income for this Florida-based chain dropped an incredible 81 percent. Bad news for the company's top executive, David Fuente? Yes, in a way. He lost his job. The Office Depot board canned him halfway through the year. But Fuente left, after thirteen years as CEO, with $8.6 million in severance, on top of $1.4 million worth of regular compensation for a half year's worth of work.[51] In "losing," Fuente pocketed more income in one year than most Americans could earn in two hundred and fifty.

"There is no longer," notes Carol Bowie, one top national executive pay expert, "any risk financially to being a CEO."[52]

America's top executives have achieved, in effect, the risk-free nirvana business titans have been seeking ever since the modern corporate order first emerged in the decades after the Civil War. In boardrooms back then, as in boardrooms today, astute captains of industry have always understood that grand fortunes come most expeditiously to those who eliminate risks, not those who take them. A century ago, corporate giants rigged "trusts" to crush any rivals that might place their enterprises at true competitive risk. Today's corporate giants endeavor to squash rivals with much the same zeal. Microsoft, a federal judge would rule in 1999, illegally and repeatedly manipulated "its prodigious market power and immense profits to harm any firm that insists on pursuing initiatives that could intensify competition against one of Microsoft's core products."[53]

America's business leaders simply despise risk. They will do most anything to avoid it. They will collude. They will connive. They will conspire. And if they get caught rigging the marketplace? No great risk in that. The antitrust laws enacted generations ago — to prevent corporations from eliminating competitive risk — can almost always be sandbagged by clever lawyers. Corporate America's sharpest business operators, in other words, can eliminate marketplace risks without taking any.

The exceptions only prove the rule. In the 1980s, Michael Milken amassed hundreds of millions — $550 million in 1986 alone — by diligently conniving to drive risk out of the bond market.[54] Government investigators did eventually catch up with Milken and filed, in 1989, over one hundred felony charges against him. The junk bond king wound up pleading guilty, serving nearly two years in jail, and paying $1.1 billion in fines and penalties. An object-lesson powerful enough to scare other executive lawbreakers straight? Probably not. Milken left prison, in many eyes, a business folk hero. By century's end, his net worth still hovered close to $1 billion.[55]

Average Americans, unlike top executives, cannot so easily eliminate risk from their daily working lives. Millions of Americans, in fact, regularly face serious risks in their workplaces. We sometimes, as a society, recognize the dangers these Americans face. But we never, as a society, claim these risk-takers deserve to be rich.

America's average workaday risk-takers don't wear power suits. They are fire-fighters who rush into burning buildings and ironworkers who walk on I-beams forty floors up. They're nurses on midnight shifts and clerks in robbery-prone convenience stores. They're men and women who encounter real haz-ards, some because they welcome risk, most because they have no choice. Corporate America seldom rewards these everyday risk-takers particularly well. Corporate America seldom even feels compelled to reduce the risks that put these risk-takers at peril. Risk-free wombs remain for executives only.

Mere working folk get "clean rooms."

Workers in "clean rooms," the workplaces where computer chips are made, wear head-to-toe protective clothing. They labor in air their employers have carefully made dust-free, since a single dust particle can compromise the entire chip-making process. But chemical fumes are another matter. Fumes don't endanger the chip-making process, and clean room air filters, consequently, aren't configured to trap any chemical fumes that may be floating about.

In 1998, after various cancers started claiming "clean room" worker lives, concerned California health department officials tried to find out just how much risk chip-making workers were actually facing. But the health officials didn't get very far, mainly, critics charged, "because semiconductor manufac-turers refused to cooperate."[56] Three years later, in 2001, British health author-ities had more success. They were able to complete a comprehensive clean room risk assessment and found, among workers at a Scottish semiconductor plant, "elevated levels of breast, lung, brain, and stomach cancer."

"Clean room" workers in the United States, the British study's results made plain, were taking risks every day, for paychecks that averaged, at century's end, about $25,000 a year.[57] Top computer industry executives like IBM's Lou Gerstner — $102 million in total 1999 compensation — could make more than that in a couple hours.[58]

Who deserves, in the final reckoning, more compensation for taking risks, a Lou Gerstner or an IBM clean room employee, perhaps a worker like Armida Mesa, a nonsmoker who was diagnosed with cancer sixteen years after she start-ed working for Big Blue?[59]

To meaningfully consider such a question, notes British philosopher Alex Callinicos, a serious analysis "would have to come up with a way of comparing the moral worth of, say, the risks that rich people face when they play the stock market with that of the hazards confronting workers compelled to undertake dangerous tasks in a polluted workplace because of the absence of alternative employment in their area."[60]

Corporate America has not yet undertaken this sort of comparative analy-sis. Any such study would, undoubtedly, be too risky.

HARD WORK PAYS. Just ask any business card-carrying member of America's corporate elite, someone like New York bank CEO John K. Castle. In the 1990s, Castle built up a personal fortune worth $100 million. He deserved every dollar. Hard work, he told one journalist at decade's end, made him worthy.

"None of this happens without working 60 hours a week," Castle noted proudly. "But I work 60 hours a week because I want to, not because I've got a time clock."[61]

Castle may want to rethink his aversion to time clocks. He seems to have trouble keeping track of how many hours he actually works. That became apparent, in 1999, after a *Wall Street Journal* reporter followed the New York executive around for a day in the middle of a winter work week. That day opened, in Florida, with Castle showing off his $11 million Palm Beach estate. Later, the *Journal* watched Castle wile away the afternoon hours jumping hurdles "astride one of his show horses at his nearby 10-acre farm." The day ended on the water, with Castle nibbling cheese and crackers aboard his yacht. This busy day, the *Journal* reported, was by no means out of character for Castle. During the winter months, he spent a few days on and around his Florida estate every week.

CEO Castle, the *Journal* added, had also found time in his hectic business schedule to organize a private expedition to the North Pole, climb his way up and down mountains in Africa and the Himalayas, and send his yacht on a two-year voyage around the world. Castle, the hard-working executive that he is, naturally didn't have the time to personally skipper his yacht the entire way. Instead, about a dozen different times, he would fly overseas to meet up with the yacht at some exotic port of call, then captain the vessel for a week or so of sailing until duty called him back to New York. Castle logged almost 150,000 air miles in the process. All time well spent. Chief executives, Castle told the *Journal*, "need some time to step back and get the broader perspective."

How many wealthy people labor at schedules as grueling as John K. Castle's? A healthy number, apparently. One 1998 study of Americans who make at least $1 million a year found that more than 20 percent take two months or more of annual vacation.[62]

More specific numbers, unfortunately, are somewhat hard to come by. Executives, after all, punch no time clocks. And if they did, would they punch out *before* joining a potential investor for dinner? Would they log as work time the hours they spend on golf links mixing putts and patter with potential takeover targets? Would they count as office hours the morning commutes they spend chatting on cell phones in chauffeured limousines? Profound questions. We seem destined to never know exactly how many hours top executives keep their noses to the grindstone.

But even if we could calculate such a figure, and if that figure were sixty or eighty or one hundred hours a week, would high-ranking executives then *deserve* millions of dollars a year for their labors? That case would be hard to make. Average Americans who moonlight at second or even third jobs routinely work sixty to eighty hours a week, without receiving anything remotely close to the robust rewards executives receive. If these average Americans don't deserve king-sized rewards for their long hours, then why should "hard-working" executives deserve regal rewards for theirs?

Our society obviously places no particular premium value on sheer hard work alone. Nor should it.

"It is not enough to tell me that you worked hard to get your gold," as Henry David Thoreau once noted. "So does the devil work hard."[63]

IF THE DEVIL WERE TO GO STRAIGHT, and put his talents toward legitimate pursuits, would he deserve a fortune in return?

That, a human resources specialist might respond, depends. The specialist would likely want to subject the devil's new responsibilities to some close analysis. How much decision-making authority does the devil enjoy in his new position? How complex are the decisions the devil will be called upon to make? How many people will be impacted by those decisions? In short, how difficult, how weighty will the devil's new work be?

By any reasonable measure, the chief executives of major business corporations do difficult, weighty work. They manage enterprises that may employ thousands of people. They make decisions that involve billions of dollars. They interact with important people from all walks of life. For performing these complex responsibilities, most reasonable people would agree, top executives certainly deserve to be well rewarded.

So, perhaps, do school superintendents.

The superintendents of big-city school districts also manage enterprises that employ thousands of people. Superintendents also make decisions that involve billions of dollars. They also interact with important people from all walks of life. Superintendents, in addition, must also do their work with press, parents, and politicians intently scrutinizing their every move. And all these onlookers demand results. Schools must be safe, test scores must rise, and all children must be educated.

A tall order. In 1997, for agreeing to take on this challenge, New York City's top school executive took home $245,000. He managed a system that boasted seventy-five thousand employees, over 1 million students, and an $8.1 billion budget. In that same year, corporate chief executives who led businesses in the same budget range managed, on average, fourteen thousand employees — and took home $25 million, more than one hundred times the salary of New York City's top school official.[64]

Who had the more complex and demanding job, the New York City school chief or the corporate chief executives? Who deserved more reward?

A fair comparison? Maybe not. Big-time business executives operate on the world stage, school superintendents are strictly local players. Business executives hobnob with United States senators, superintendents with city councils. Top corporate executives make decisions that shape the fates of nations. Superintendents shape junior high curricula. Superintendents, a corporate human resources office might argue, cannot possibly deserve to earn as much as top business executives. The "scope" of the work they do is simply not broad enough.

Should "scope," then, be our yardstick for determining who deserves the greatest rewards? Should the greatest rewards go to those who work on the grandest stage? That certainly seems reasonable. But if scope makes for a sensible standard, why do today's corporate executives make more, colossally more, than a President of the United States?

In 1995, that question popped up to Raymond and Carla Baechle, a Florida couple who happened to own some shares of BellSouth stock — and also happened to share some discomfort about the lofty rewards then bestowed upon BellSouth's most prominent executives. Why should these executives, the Baechles wondered, make a lot more money than the President of the United States when the President, as they put it, had "a much more demanding job" than any BellSouth corporate officer? The Baechles, unable to think of any valid reason for that pay discrepancy, advanced a shareholder resolution that asked BellSouth to limit executive compensation to just $400,000 a year, twice the $200,000 then paid to Presidents of the United States.[65]

The company was not amused. Limiting executive salaries to $400,000, BellSouth officials informed the Baechles, "would have an adverse impact" on leadership, operations, and "shareholder value."

The Baechle proposal, not surprisingly, sank without a trace. BellSouth, meanwhile, went on to boost CEO John L. Clendenin's annual compensation for 1995 to $4.8 million — twenty-four times then President Bill Clinton's White House salary — and tossed in, as an extra treat, an option grant valued at $2.3 million. All this generous compensating took place while BellSouth was announcing the latest of over twenty-one thousand job cuts.[66]

Did John L. Clendenin deserve to earn more in one year than the President of the United States would have had to serve nine four-year terms to equal?

Defenders of chief executives naturally object to any comparisons along these lines. A reasonable society, they believe, ought not compare apples to oranges, or CEOs to distinguished figures from other fields. Presidents and corporate chief executives operate in distinctly unique contexts. They face different challenges, different institutional cultures, different dangers. Why should we expect them to receive the same rewards?

A reasonable enough position, except for one inconvenient historic reality. Years ago, Presidents and CEOs *did* receive the same rewards. In fact, for a good bit of the twentieth century, the typical big-time corporate CEO took home less than the President of the United States, not more.

In the 1930s, the newly created federal Securities and Exchange Commission coordinated the nation's first systematic survey of CEO compensation. The typical chief executive of a publicly traded firm in the United States, that research revealed, earned $60,000 in 1934.[67] In that same year, the President of the United States, Franklin D. Roosevelt, earned $75,000.[68]

A generation later, Presidents were still earning more than corporate chief executives. In 1970, the typical American CEO walked off with $154,427.[69] Richard M. Nixon that year earned $200,000.[70]

Over the next decade, the tables did turn somewhat. In 1980, Jimmy Carter made the same $200,000 Richard Nixon made in 1970. But corporate CEOs had in the meantime seen their compensation increase. The typical 1980 CEO took home $313,028, half again more than the President.[71] Still, given the free room and board at the White House, Presidents were doing just about as well as corporate chief executives.

The big picture? For at least half a century, from the 1930s through the 1970s, America's most distinguished political leader, the President of the United States, and America's most distinguished business leaders, corporate CEOs, earned comparable incomes.

Over these years, corporate CEO pay remained remarkably stable, at least after taking inflation into account. In 1934, CEOs took home $60,000, a sum equal to about $790,000 in 2001 dollars.[72] In 1970, the typical American chief executive earned $154,427. That compensation, in 2001 dollars, would have equaled $717,365.[73] A decade later, in 1980, the typical CEO took home $313,028, a sum that would have amounted, in 2001 dollars, to $733,037.[74] Again, no appreciable change from the 1930s.

The bottom line: Over the course of the 1930s, 1940s, 1950s, 1960s, and 1970s, American business, in its infinite wisdom, did not see fit to raise the real compensation of the nation's top executives. For nearly fifty years, America's most typical CEOs took home, in earnings adjusted to 2001 purchasing power, about $750,000 a year.

After 1980, this executive pay stability would shatter. Over the next twenty years, CEO real incomes would double once, double twice, double a third time, and then nearly double again. In 2001, typical CEOs were earning $10.2 million — fourteen times more than the $750,000 CEOs averaged for the half-century before 1980.[75] By century's end, top American business leaders were routinely making more in a week than the President of the United States could earn in a year.

Do America's modern CEOs deserve this incredible good fortune? Are they performing at levels that put their executive predecessors to shame? Do they face stiffer challenges? Are they working more efficiently? Are they making weightier decisions? Do they deserve more credit for enterprise success than executives deserved in days gone by?

These are not easy questions.

In other fields of endeavor, we can make credible performance comparisons across generations. We can confidently contend, for instance, that basketball players today perform more effectively than their Depression-era counterparts. Today's hoopsters stand taller, jump higher, and shoot better. With CEOs, we can make no such clear, incontrovertible judgments. Do CEOs today operate in a more demanding environment than CEOs a generation ago? Perhaps. Is that environment twice as demanding as the business landscape thirty years ago? Ten times more demanding? Who knows? No one can say for sure whether executives today face challenges substantially more daunting than executives yesterday.

Some observers try anyway. And they make, at first glance, a good case. The economy has changed, these defenders of modern executive pay argue. Yesterday's Industrial Age has become today's Information Age. Executives no longer dictate letters at leisurely paces. They juggle e-mails and cell phones and make complex judgments at split-second intervals. Plop a 1930s executive in a twenty-first century executive suite and that executive would sink faster than an original Celtic in a modern-day NBA arena. Today's executives, corporate cheerleaders insist, do fundamentally more demanding and difficult work than yesterday's. They should, as a result, reap greater rewards.

Let us test this case. If CEOs do indeed deserve their current good fortune because the Information Age has transformed the work they do, then all corporate executives who operate — and succeed — in the difficult, demanding Information Age ought to be reaping grand rewards. But, in fact, not all Information Age CEOs are reaping grand rewards. Successful CEOs today who operate outside the United States — in Germany, Japan, France, Britain, and every other developed nation in the world — all make appreciably smaller rewards than American CEOs.

These successful foreign executives operate in the same globalized economy as American executives. They face the same Information Age obstacles and opportunities. But they are not compensated at the same lofty level. Top corporate executives in the United States make more, massively more, than executives anywhere else in the world.

The world saw vividly just how much massively more when Chrysler, the classic U.S. automaker, merged into Daimler-Benz, the equally classic German company in 1998. Daimler-Benz, at the time the merger was announced, outpaced Chrysler by every standard corporate measure. Daimler-Benz raked in considerably more revenue than Chrysler. Daimler-Benz also generated considerably higher profits. But executives at Chrysler, remarkably, took home considerably bigger paychecks than their German counterparts.[76] In 1997, Daimler Chairman Juergen Schrempp earned an estimated $2.5 million. Chrysler Chairman Robert Eaton that same year made over six times more, $16 million. Chrysler's top *five* executives, together, collected $50 million in compensation in 1997. Daimler's top *ten* executives pulled in only $11 million.[77]

Elsewhere in the world, the same basic story. Foreign CEOs simply don't play in the same compensation sandbox as their American rivals. In 2000, the average pay for all the CEOs of companies listed on the New York Stock Exchange more than tripled the average pay of the top executives of all the companies listed on the Tokyo Stock Exchange. The Japanese executives averaged between $300,000 and $500,000. The U.S. average: $1.5 million.[78] In

2000, the highest-paid chief executive in British banking, the Royal Bank of Scotland's Fred Goodwin, pulled in $3 million. His American counterpart, Citigroup CEO Sandy Weill, took in $127 million, forty-two times more.[79]

These huge gaps between American executives and their competitors overseas are beginning to narrow somewhat. Many top European and Asian executives, who see themselves as every bit as worthy as their American counterparts, are demanding U.S.-style remuneration. They feel they deserve more. Maybe American CEOs deserve less.

SOME AMERICAN CEOS, business commentators in the United States agree, do definitely deserve less compensation than they are currently collecting. Executives who fumble away shareholder value, most commentators believe, ought to be getting warnings, not windfalls. By contrast, these analysts are quick to add, those executives who successfully enhance shareholder value deserve our deepest thanks. They have created wealth. They deserve wealth in return.

But how much wealth? Corporate America has not, by and large, given this question much quality time.

"If shareholders gain a billion in market value, what percentage should go to management?" wonders one pay consultant, Eric Scoones, a principal at William M. Mercer Inc. "I don't think many people have sat down and asked that question."[80]

Corporate leaders, instead, simply assume that the road to business success starts and ends at the top. CEOs, America's standard boardroom wisdom holds, deserve substantial, indeed almost total, credit for corporate achievement. CEOs frame the vision. They inspire the troops. They ride to the rescue, white knights in blue power suits. They need no help. They seek no help.

At America's finest business schools, tomorrow's top executives are taught to marvel at the individual magnificence of CEOs past and present.

"A business school case in strategy," notes the British economist John Kay, "characteristically features a named CEO struggling, frequently alone, to resolve the fundamental issues of his company's strategic direction."[81]

Those CEOs who succeed in this epic struggle, corporate America takes as a given, deserve whatever rewards they may gain. "Successful" executives, in effect, have a right to outsized fortunes. Remarkably, even critics of executive pay excess often buy into this heroic worldview. In 1996, for instance, reporters rushed to Graef Crystal, America's most-quoted executive pay critic, after reports surfaced that Andy Grove, the top executive at Intel, the world's largest computer chipmaker, had just cashed out $94.6 million worth of stock options. Reporters expected Crystal to be outraged. He wasn't.

"I told the reporters," Crystal would note later, "that Grove was one of my compensation heroes and that, if anything, he was being paid far too little for his magnificent contributions to the shareholders of Intel of which, I am happy to say — nay, ecstatic to say — I am one."[82]

A shareholder who spent $100 on Intel stock in 1987, Crystal explained, would have seen that $100 grow, in just a decade, to over $1,800, a 34 percent annual compounded return. By contrast, the S&P 500 Index, over those same ten years, returned a mere 14 percent per year.[83] Any executive who creates such immense value for shareholders, analysts like Crystal believe, can hardly ever be overpaid.

The enormously wide gaps that mega-million-dollar rewards open between executives and everybody else do at times give these analysts pause. "How can a society continue to operate," Crystal once mused, "if this gulf gets wider and wider, year in and year out?"[84] But if an executive really does perform for shareholders, he adds, companies have no choice but pay up and cheer. We need, Crystal proclaimed after Grove's $94.6 million payday, "to celebrate his triumph and pray that those turkey CEOs running the other companies in my investment portfolio call up Grove and ask him how he did it."[85]

And how did Grove do it? Not alone, as Grove himself has freely acknowledged. In 1998, at his retirement as Intel CEO, Grove had nothing but the highest possible praise for his successor Craig Barrett, the company's chief operating officer since 1993. Barrett, Grove noted, deserved all the credit for Intel's chip-making prowess.

"Craig has been the architect of Intel's operations throughout the last decade," summed up a magnanimous Grove. "Craig keeps the Intel machine running."[86]

That observation, if accurate, does raise some questions. If Craig Barrett deserves such significant credit, then his boss, CEO Andy Grove, was clearly not single-handedly responsible for Intel's success. And if Andy Grove was not single-handedly responsible for Intel's success, isn't it also possible that Craig Barrett was not single-handedly responsible for the kudos that Grove so generously showered upon him? Isn't it possible that behind Craig Barrett stood legions of hard-working, unheralded assistants? And if those unheralded assistants did indeed deserve significant credit for Intel's success, why did the rewards for that success go so disproportionately to Andy Grove?

SO WHO REALLY DOES DESERVE CREDIT for corporate success? Outside the United States, in even the most Americanized of foreign lands, business leaders and commentators give a straightforward answer. They define corporate success as a collective endeavor.

"Profits are brought in by everyone in the firm," a *Times* of London analysis noted soberly in 2001, "not just the chief executive."[87]

Businesses in most of the industrialized world tend to share, much more than in the United States, both credit and rewards. The pay gaps between top executives and average employees, outside the United States, have remained relatively modest. In Japan, near century's end, chief executives at big Japanese companies averaged about $350,000, not quite seven times the $56,000 the average Japanese white-collar "salaryman" took home.[88] A 1997 survey estimated a sixteen-to-one pay gap between Japanese CEOs and average Japanese blue-collar workers.[89]

The differentials between executives and workers run higher in Europe than Japan, but only slightly so. Most Germans, a *Wall Street Journal* report noted in 1998, fear that excessive executive pay — and wider income gaps — would "endanger social peace."[90]

"It's the European mentality," one shareholder activist told the *Journal.* "The enrichment of an individual on the backs of the workers is considered exploitation."

Even, sometimes, among executives themselves.

"Many European executives still pride themselves on their egalitarian sensibilities and lack of ostentation," a *Forbes* reporter concluded in 1999. "The farther north, the more this attitude prevails."[91]

That same attitude once prevailed, to a point, in the United States. Back in the middle of the twentieth century, pay gaps between American executives and American workers approximated pay gaps elsewhere in the industrial world. In 1965, American CEOs took home forty-four times more than average factory workers, according to *Business Week's* Annual Executive Pay Survey.[92] That gap about doubled the differential between German workers and German executives, but American workers made more, in real purchasing power, than their German counterparts.

The story started changing in the 1980s. By 1997, *Business Week* put the gap between American CEOs and average workers at 326 to 1. That divide soared to 475 to 1 in 1999 and then, in 2001, to an even more remarkable 531 to 1.[93] The German pay gap ratio, by contrast, expanded only marginally. By 2001, to add insult to injury, average German workers were making more, in real purchasing power, than their American counterparts.

By century's end, America's top executive pay packages were routinely outpacing minimum-wage paychecks by multiples of a thousand times and more. But these executives weren't just speeding past unskilled workers. They were zooming past rigorously educated professionals as well. Early in the 1980s, chief executives averaged twenty-three times the average engineering paycheck.[94] In 2000, top executives in the United States scored over one hundred and fifty times the pay of their engineers.[95]

By the late 1990s, even many of those who benefited from such gaps were starting to gag. In a 1997 *Business Week* poll, nearly half the four hundred senior executives surveyed said they felt CEO pay at America's biggest companies had gone beyond "acceptable limits."[96] Other business leaders, like Gregory Pierce, a Chicago publishing executive, expressed a deeper outrage.

"From a spiritual point of view," Pierce preached, "it cannot be true that the work of the CEOs of some companies is worth a thousand times that of some other of their employees, just as it cannot be true that because you can get people to work full time for minimum wage they are justly compensated."[97]

HOW CAN EXECUTIVES MORALLY MERIT a hundred or a thousand times more compensation than average working stiffs? How can executives, with a clear conscience, lay claim to such a disproportionate share of the nation's economic wealth? What can possibly justify such a cascade of corporate treasure into CEO pockets?

Genius can justify that cascade. The nation's most richly rewarded executives aren't just smarter than everyone else, apologists for over-the-top corporate compensation assert, they are masterminds. These men of genius don't take wealth someone else should have. They create wealth that otherwise would not exist. The rest of us may not always be able to fully fathom the moves these masterminds make. We should not be discouraged. After all, we aren't the masterminds. They are.

"Up to the point of bankruptcy or incarceration we regard the rich man and his work as complex beyond our understanding," notes author Michael Lewis, a Wall Street-trained chronicler of the ways and wiles of the wealthy. "All highly public business decisions made by rich men are, at the time of the decision, not evaluated on their own terms but widely applauded as strokes of genius."[98]

The grander the decision maker's fortune, the more enthusiastic the applause. And no one would gain more curtain calls — or rewards — in the boom years than Michael Eisner, the superstar CEO of Walt Disney, the world's mightiest entertainment empire.

Back in 1984, the year Eisner took on Disney's top executive slot, that empire looked anything but mighty. Uncle Walt, the founding genius, had packed it in. Mickey and Goofy were getting on. Shareholders were grumpy. But Eisner would restore the Magic Kingdom. Hit movies, under Eisner, would once again start tumbling out of Disney's studios. The movies would spin off Broadway shows and theme park attractions. The attractions would make Disney World "the most popular vacation destination" in the United States.[99] On Wall Street, Disney's market capitalization, the total value of the company's shares, would leap more than tenfold, in less than a decade.

Michael Eisner reaped the credit — and a lion king's share of the rewards. In 1992, Eisner cashed out over $200 million in option gains.[100] The immensity of that windfall amazed America, even the Disney insiders who had negotiated Eisner's pay package.

"None of us in our wildest dreams ever imagined we'd be looking at a $200 million payday," Raymond Watson, the chair of the Disney board of directors compensation committee, would note. "But then again, we never thought we'd be talking about a market cap of $22 billion, either."[101]

That market cap just kept climbing. Through Eisner's first thirteen years as CEO, Disney shares averaged 27 percent annual gains.[102] In early 1997, a grateful Disney board bestowed upon the magical Eisner a new, even more generous compensation agreement.[103] Eisner celebrated his good fortune, on December 3, 1997, by cashing out a pile of the stock options he had collected under his old contract. The day's transactions left him, as we saw earlier, with a $565 million personal profit, the biggest single payday, up until then, in American business history.[104]

That payday certified Eisner's genius. Every move he made now only added to his glory. Disney's Major League Baseball team, the Anaheim Angels, guaranteed the bulky Boston first baseman, Mo Vaughn, $80 million for six years. Reporters labeled the deal, on Eisner's part, "a stroke of genius."[105]

But what exactly was Eisner a genius at?

Certainly not what would, by most people, be considered "management." No one, not even the most eager-to-please Disney flack, would ever label Eisner a managerial genius. The nuts-and-bolts of running a modern, complex enterprise — identifying good people, nurturing their talents, keeping them happy and productive — didn't interest Eisner in the least. Business magazines duly noted his "arrogance" and "inability to keep key people."[106] Hollywood gossip columnists regaled readers with the juicy inside stories behind his classic feuds with former friends and colleagues, feuds that cost the Disney empire tens of millions of dollars. In 1995, for instance, Eisner brought in, as Disney president, Hollywood superagent Michael Ovitz, his "best friend for 25 years." The move surprised just about everyone in entertainment, including Ovitz.

"I was floating around looking for something to do," Ovitz later related. "To this day I don't know why he brought me in here."[107]

Eisner, apparently, didn't know either. Fourteen months after hiring Ovitz, Eisner sacked him. Ovitz walked off with a severance package estimated at $94.5 million.[108]

Some executives with "people problems" stake their claims to genius on visionary brilliance. Eisner could make no such claims. He badly bungled the Internet. His flagship cyberspace initiative, Go.com, an effort to give computer users a jumping off point, or "portal," into the Web, proved a miserable flop that cost Disney over $100 million.[109] Eisner the would-be visionary blew tens of millions more on merchandising, with a mad rush to plant Mickey in every mall. He spent a fortune blanketing — and ultimately boring — America with Disney retail stores. Disney, analysts would later scold, had "opened too many stores" and stuck too long with tired old merchandising characters.[110]

"They didn't rejuvenate characters or go out and develop new characters, and most importantly they didn't get Harry Potter," one industry insider explained to the Disney empire's hometown newspaper, the *Orlando Sentinel.*

That last failure stung. How could Eisner have fallen so out of touch with changing public tastes? The ability to connect, to recognize popular culture that could capture the public's imagination, was supposed to be Eisner's very special genius.[111] Eisner's "instincts," at the start of his career, had brought America such soap opera smashes as *All My Children* and *One Life to Live.*[112] Now, with a new century beginning, Eisner's instincts seemed to be failing him. Disney once had a lock on animated hits. Now those hits were coming from other studios. Worse yet, the biggest animated blockbuster of the new century, *Shrek*, openly lampooned Disney's most-beloved cartoon creations. Disney's network TV operation, meanwhile, was stumbling, too. Eisner had acquired ABC to give Disney's studios a network to showcase their product. A hit product, a comedy like *The Simpsons*, could spin out years and years of rerun profits. Disney needed one of those hit comedies. But Eisner couldn't deliver. "Disney hasn't developed a hit sitcom," *Fortune* pointed out in 2002, "since *Home Improvement* in 1991."

ABC, under Eisner, would register one megahit, the game show *Who Wants to Be a Millionaire*. But the network proceeded to ride that hit to viewer exhaustion, running episodes as many as four times a week.[113] By late 2001, *Who Wants to Be a Millionaire* was drawing yawns and ABC had dropped down to last in the prime-time ratings. ABC's operations in 2002, one analyst predicted, would cost Disney $400 million.[114]

What had happened to the legendary Eisner genius? Even the Mo Vaughn baseball deal soured. In 2002, after three disappointing years, a bitter Vaughn exited the Angels.

Can genius suddenly disappear? Or did Eisner, perish the thought, not have genius to lose? Maybe Eisner, business analysts started suggesting, hadn't been single-handedly responsible for Disney's grand successes of the 1980s and early 1990s. After all, he did have "a strong wind at his back during his glory days at Disney."[115] In the 1980s, that wind blew VCRs into tens of millions of American homes, creating a huge new market for home videos. Disney, with a half-century of children's classics in its vaults, was able to profitably feed this new market. Eisner played no part whatsoever in the VCR explosion. He contributed nary a creative thought to *Bambi*, *Sleeping Beauty*, or any of the other classics that would pump up Disney's revenue streams.[116]

Could Michael Eisner legitimately claim genius status at anything? Most certainly. At reaping rewards, he remains unparalleled. Eisner, noted *Forbes* midway through 2003, had annually "averaged $122 million in pay since 1997." Disney shareholders, in those same years, had averaged a minus 5 percent annual return.[117] Despite that woeful performance, *Forbes* marveled, Eisner actually received a $5 million bonus in 2002.

That must be genius.

MICHAEL EISNER DIDN'T HAVE THE "VISION" to see the Internet coming. Other executives — the pioneers of Internet commerce — did. Were they geniuses? At century's end, a good bit of America thought so. *Time* magazine even gave one of these pioneers American journalism's ultimate individual tribute. *Time* named Jeff Bezos, the executive behind Amazon, the Internet's most illustrious retailer, its 1999 "Person of the Year."[118]

"Every time a seismic shift takes place in our economy," the magazine explained, "there are people who feel the vibrations long before the rest of us do."[119]

Bezos apparently felt those vibrations.

In 1994, Bezos had been just another ambitious young financial manager in New York when he happened to stumble upon a fascinating fact. Traffic on America's new "information superhighway," the Internet, was rising by over 2,000 percent a month. Suitably impressed, the young Bezos set out for Seattle to start an Internet bookstore. In less than three years, his Amazon had become the Web's hottest shopping destination. By December 1999, Bezos had built a fortune worth $13.3 billion.[120]

"A rich reward, to be sure," acknowledged *Time*, "but how on earth can you compensate a man who can see the future?"[121]

America's investors were every bit as impressed as *Time*. By December 2000, they had valued Amazon at $36 billion. At the time, the company still hadn't turned a dime of profit.[122] No cause for concern, commentators declared. The Internet had changed the rules. Profits no longer really mattered. Losses merely signaled "the New Economics of Internet commerce."[123] Bezos played by these new rules. In fact, he wrote them.

"Amazon's plan, imitated by hundreds of other Internet companies, was to grow first and to figure out how to profit later," as one observer noted.[124]

The profits would come, Bezos insisted, by the end of 2000.[125] They didn't. In 2000, Amazon sold $2.8 billion worth of merchandise — and lost $1.4 billion in the process.[126] But then, in early 2002, a sudden about face. America's business press trumpeted the good news. Amazon, the headlines shouted, had finally made a profit! Genius redeemed? Not exactly. Amazon, a closer look revealed, had gone into the black by the barest of margins, eking out just a $5 million profit on sales of $1.2 billion.[127] And that profit only reflected the company's fourth quarter business operations. For all of 2001, Amazon once again lost big, going $567 million deeper into the red.[128]

Still, a profit was a profit.

"It's a major turning point for us," Bezos boasted.[129]

What triggered the turnaround? A special free shipping offer, analysts noted, helped some. So did shifts in foreign currency values. Amazon gained an unexpected $16 million from currency exchanges alone in the fourth quarter of 2001, more than three times the quarter's eventual — and much-ballyhooed — $5 million bottom-line profit.[130]

Other analysts credited Amazon's sudden profitability to an aggressive new company commitment to reducing expenses. Amazon was now cutting costs at every opportunity. Among the company's most significant cost-cutting moves: a massive layoff of thirteen hundred employees, 15 percent of the company's total workforce.[131]

These pink slips shut down Amazon's original customer service center in Seattle, where workers hadn't been particularly happy with Amazon even before the layoff notices. In fact, workers at the Seattle center, frustrated by low wages and mandatory overtime, had been trying to organize a union.[132] The company, explained one worker, a single parent named Nancy Becker, expected employees to put in fifty hours a week at crush times, a requirement that was more than just inconvenient for single moms like herself.

"If we are unable to meet that," Becker noted, "our benefits get docked."[133]

True geniuses, of course, aren't supposed to have to squeeze workers to make money, and Bezos, the New Economy genius, now found himself scrambling to sugarcoat his distinctly Old Economy maneuvers. To blunt the shock from Amazon's first mass layoff, Bezos would have his company announce plans to create a special trust fund — with $2.5 million worth of Amazon stock — for the laid-off workers. The trust fund shares, Amazon explained, would be cashed out in 2003 and distributed to the thirteen hundred workers who lost their jobs. The payout would "give these employees a chance to share in the long-term success of the company, even if they were no longer working for it."[134]

That "long-term success," to be sure, could not quite be guaranteed. Amazon, by the end of 2001, had registered seven consecutive years of losses, spilling, along the way, $2.86 billion worth of red ink. At some point, presumably, Amazon might run out of red ink to spill. But that prospect, reporters found, couldn't seem to darken the perpetually sunny Jeff Bezos disposition. Interviewers almost always found him chortling and chuckling, as *Newsweek* put it, "like an overcaffeinated Norwegian tickled to within an inch of his life."[135] If you were Bezos, you might feel tickled, too. On the *Forbes* 2002 list of the world's richest people, the Jeffrey Preston Bezos fortune would be worth $1.5 billion.

THE INTERNET BOOM CAME, THE INTERNET BOOM WENT. But one executive still stood tall, amid the dot.com wreckage. He had come to embody, more than any other single individual, American business brilliance. This executive, swooned his admirers, always brought good things to life — for shareholders. He was Jack Welch, the long-time CEO of the most successful "Old Economy" company in America, General Electric.

Business journalists, by the end of the twentieth century, were acclaiming Welch's wisdom at every imaginable opportunity. Indeed, noted one nationally syndicated columnist, "you can hardly open a business magazine nowadays without seeing a salute to Jack Welch. The man's a bloomin' genius."[136] Not just a genius. The "manager of the century," or so *Fortune* tagged him in 1999. And who could better lay claim to that honor? Under Welch's leadership, G.E., once a predictable appliance maker, had become the world's largest nonbank financial corporation, with annual profits that no company anywhere could match — or even dream about matching.[137]

In the face of such achievement, even crusty CEO critics genuflected.

"Jack Welch of General Electric made $75 million last year and he is a brilliant, brilliant chief executive," CEO gadfly Graef Crystal told reporters in 2000. "You could make the case that if anyone deserves to be paid $75 million, it's him."[138]

Actually, the General Electric board of directors came to believe, a mere $75 million couldn't do Welch justice. The man needed a raise. He got it. In 2000, the G.E. board hiked Welch's base salary by 20 percent, upped his bonus 27 percent, and awarded him almost $50 million worth of free shares of G.E. stock to "recognize his 20 years of outstanding service as chief executive."[139]

What brand of genius could be worth so much? America's biggest book publishers felt America would pay to find out. In 2000, they staged a spirited bidding war for Welch's memoirs. The eventual winner, Time Warner, offered Welch a $7.1 million advance, an unprecedented sum for nonfiction.[140]

Welch's book, published in 2001, went on to become a bestseller. But would-be captains of industry didn't have to read *Jack: Straight from the Gut* to learn the great man's secrets. The "big ideas" behind Welch's phenomenal success had already filtered through America's corporate suites. Welch's most admired contribution to corporate wisdom? His competitiveness dictum. If you're not competitive in a particular market, Welch advised, don't compete. And Welch practiced what he preached. Early in his tenure as G.E. chief executive, he directed his managers to "sell off any division whose product was not among the top three in its U.S. market."[141] They did. G.E. would unload or shut down operations that impacted tens of thousands of workers.

Welch played few favorites. He could be as ruthless with his white-collar help as his blue-collar factory workers. In fact, corporate human resources professionals consider Welch the "brains" behind what may be corporate America's most brutal office personnel practice, the annual firing squad known as "forced rankings."[142] At General Electric, under Welch, this approach to supervision forced managers to rank their professional employees, every year, by category. Each one had to be placed in the top 20 percent, the middle 70, or the bottom 10.[143] The top got accolades. The bottom got fired.

"Not removing that bottom 10 percent," Welch would tell G.E. shareholders, "is not only a management failure but false kindness as well."[144]

Jack Welch's General Electric would have no room for "false kindness." You were either competitively successful, as an employee or a division, or out. You had to deliver.

Except at the top. Jack Welch delivered nothing. He built nothing. He became the twentieth century's most celebrated executive by identifying challenges — and running the other way. A G.E. division struggling to make a market impact? Dump it. An employee who isn't putting up the numbers? Fire away. Jack Welch did not turn marginal General Electric business operations into market leaders. He did not endeavor to transform weak staff into standouts. He, instead, surrounded himself with the already successful — already successful divisions, already successful employees — and rode their successes to his own personal glory.

We need to be fair here. Jack Welch did sometimes try to develop something new. In the late 1990s, for instance, at the height of corporate America's Internet frenzy, Welch decided that G.E. needed to stake out a claim in cyberspace. General Electric, he told *USA Today*, has "got to have more 'dot.coms.'"[145] Welch set out to get those dot.coms. He poured cash into iVillage, Promotions.com, and a host of other cyber sites that promptly, within a matter of months, lost 90 percent of their value. G.E.'s television network, NBC, also tried to launch an Internet portal. "NBCi" proved to be an even feebler entry into the portal sweepstakes than Michael Eisner's Go.com. The NBCi shares, worth $88.50 when they first started trading, ended at $2.19. Business journalists had a field day ridiculing G.E.'s fumbling.

"The NBCi story is a hoot and a half," wrote one, Allan Sloan, in the *Washington Post*. "I can't give you Jack Welch's side of all this, because GE wouldn't return my calls."[146]

JACK WELCH, TRUTH BE TOLD, never once asked people to label him a genius. Nor did he, in his decades at the top, ever credit his personal good fortune to his own earth-shattering mental brilliance. Welch credited his success, instead, to the genius of the free market.

"Is my salary too high?" Welch asked in 1999, his $75 million year. "Somebody else will have to decide that, but this is a competitive marketplace."[147]

Translation: "I deserve every penny. The market says so."

In the world that top executives like Jack Welch inhabit, impartial, unbiased markets — not suspect, unreliable people — determine executive compensation. Markets can't be tricked. Talents in short supply and high demand will always fetch a premium price. That price will be fair, that price will be deserved, because markets don't make mistakes. Smart businesses simply play by market rules. They pay their executives what the market says their top executives deserve.[148] If they don't, they risk losing their executive talent.

Corporate boards tend to worry obsessively about losing "talent." To avoid that horror, Motorola's directors handed their company's CEO, Christopher Galvin, the lushest 1999 pay package in the entire Chicagoland business world, $58.9 million in cash and stock.[149] If Motorola had chosen to be less generous, explained Samuel Scott, the chair of the company's compensation committee, another firm might have stolen Galvin away.

"Motorola," Scott noted, "has been a good company for others to take talent from."[150]

A less obsessed corporate board might not have considered CEO Galvin much of a flight risk. Galvin's granddaddy founded Motorola. His daddy had been the company's CEO.[151]

Still, corporate directors believe, modern companies can't afford to take any chances. Quality CEOs just don't grow on trees. If you believe your company has one, you need to hold on to that executive — at any cost. Multiple millions for CEOs make perfect market sense, notes Pearl Meyer pay consultant Steven Hall, simply because "not many people have the God-given gift to run a corporation successfully."[152]

In the 1990s, in the considered opinion of corporate America, God appeared to be giving out fewer gifts. Throughout the decade, business leaders anguished about what they saw as a shrinking supply of top executive talent.[153] And that shrinking supply, they insisted, explained why CEO pay packages were soaring even where share prices were sinking. So why couldn't Americans get this supply-and-demand business straight and quit carping about excessive CEO pay? The public, as one business analyst at *Barron's* noted, needed to understand once and for all "that there's a sellers' market for executive talent and a scarce supply of people who can manage multibillion-dollar corporations."[154]

American business leaders take this scarcity as a given. How else, in a market economy, to explain rapidly rising CEO compensation? If quality CEOs were plentiful, executive compensation would not be soaring. But executive compensation *is* soaring, so qualified CEOs obviously must be few and far between — and totally deserving of whatever many millions they receive. That's simple market logic.

And simply wrong. American corporations today confront no scarcity of executive talent. The numbers of people qualified to run multibillion-dollar companies have never, in fact, been more plentiful then they are now.

These numbers have been growing steadily over recent years, in part because America's graduate schools of business, the world's most-admired prep schools for business leaders, have been graduating, for decades now, thousands of rigorously trained executives every year. America's first graduate school for executives, the Tuck School of Business at Dartmouth, currently boasts an alumni network over seven thousand strong. Alumni from the equally prestigious Harvard Business School total some sixty-six thousand.[155] Add in the alumni from other widely acclaimed institutions and the available supply of executives trained at top-notch business schools approaches several hundred thousand.[156]

Just how many of these academically trained executives have the skills and experience really needed to run a *Fortune* 500 company? Ten percent? Five? Let's assume, conservatively, that only 1 percent of the alumni from America's best business schools have enough skills and experience to run a big-time corporation. If this assumption were accurate, the seven or eight dozen Fortune 500 companies that go looking for a new CEO every year would be able to choose, at minimum, from between two and three thousand eminently qualified candidates. Do the math. Several thousand qualified candidates, less than a hundred vacancies. No supply shortage here.

Not all corporate insiders, to be sure, consider elite business schools a suitable source for top-notch executive talent. Some skeptics openly disparage the book learning that goes on in academic business training. They only trust and admire executives who have spent long years working their way up corporate ladders, learning lessons at corporate life's always demanding schools of hard knocks. These skeptics may or may not be right in their judgments about academic business schools. But they still have no valid reason to worry about a scarcity of executive talent. In today's globalized world economy, quality "graduates" from schools of hard knocks abound more plentifully than ever before.

Years ago, American corporations seldom looked beyond the borders of the United States for executive talent. That tunnel vision made sense. Executives inside the United States and executives outside worked in different business environments. Foreign executives could hardly be expected to succeed in an unfamiliar American marketplace, even if they did speak flawless English. But today, in our "global" economy, distinctions between domestic and foreign executives no longer matter nearly as much. In dozens of foreign nations, in hundreds of foreign corporations, executives are competing in the same global marketplace as their American counterparts. They're using the same technologies, studying the same data, and strategizing toward the same business goals. They are, in short, learning the same hard-knocks lessons. Together, taken as a group, executives from elsewhere in the world constitute a huge *new* pool of talent for American corporations.

Pay consultants in the United States already acknowledge the reality of this global marketplace for executive talent. In fact, they cite global competition as one important reason why executive pay in the United States is *rising*.[157] American companies now have to compete against foreign companies for executive talent, the argument goes. This competition is forcing up executive pay in the United States.

Really? What ever happened to market logic? If corporations all around the world paid their executives at comparable rates, market competition would certainly force up executive compensation worldwide. But corporations don't all pay executives at comparable rates. American executives take home far more compensation than their foreign counterparts. By classic market logic, any competition between highly paid American executives and equally qualified but more modestly paid international executives ought to end up lowering, not raising, the higher pay rates in the United States. Why, after all, would an American corporation pay $50 million for an American CEO when a skilled international CEO could easily be had for one-fifth or even one-fiftieth that price? We have here, in short, a situation that Jack Welch's deep, abiding faith in the "market" does not explain. In the executive talent marketplace, American corporations face plenty, not scarcity, yet the going rate for American executives keeps rising — even as more and more "low-wage" executives from foreign nations enter the competitive fray.[158] Has someone repealed the laws of supply and demand? How else could executive pay in the United States have ascended to such lofty levels?

Some analysts do have an alternate explanation to offer. Markets, they point out, still operate by supply and demand. But markets don't set executive pay.[159]

"CEOs who cheerlead for market forces wouldn't think of having them actually applied to their own pay packages," explains *Los Angeles Times* commentator Matthew Miller. "The reality is that CEO pay is set through a clubby, rigged system in which CEOs, their buddies on board compensation committees and a small cadre of lawyers and 'compensation consultants' are in cahoots to keep the millions coming."[160]

Markets didn't pay Jack Welch $75 million in 1999 — and over $50 million more than that in 2000. The old boys network did, and that network, unlike the fair, impartial market of Jack Welch's dreams, plays favorites all the time.

AMERICA'S CLUBBY, RIGGED SYSTEM does have its defenders. These candid insiders do not insult our intelligence with paeans to the eternal wisdom of the market. They concede the abundance of quality candidates for top executive positions. But corporate boards, these insiders contend, can't afford to gamble on an unproven talent, someone who *may* turn out to be a good chief executive. Boards simply can't risk placing a billion-dollar company in what may prove to be less than competent hands. They need, in effect, to insure themselves against failure — by hiring only top-notch, already proven talent.

Bill McClellan, a *St. Louis Post-Dispatch* writer, learned all about this play-it-safe approach in 1999, after he wrote a column blasting excessive executive pay.[161] A CEO of a major area company, a bit alarmed, gave McClellan a call and invited him to lunch. The chief executive didn't want to rant. He merely wanted to help McClellan better understand the facts of corporate life.

Stock options, the CEO admitted, are indeed soaring out of control, and corporate boards often do get too cozy with their hired help. Even so, the executive noted, a smart company can't ever "pay a good CEO too much" because the alternative, having a bad CEO, can send a good, decent company to ruin.

"If you have a boss who just doesn't get it," the CEO explained, "he's not going to appreciate people who do. He will be drawn to people like himself. He certainly won't be promoting people who disagree with him."

"Soon, then, you'll have a culture of bosses who don't get it," the CEO continued. "The company will begin to flounder. Morale will plummet. Talented people will begin to leave. The company will go into a free fall."

Such could be the unhappy fate of any company that ends up with just "one bad boss." To avoid this sort of calamity, a responsible corporate board must always move heaven and earth to hire the best boss possible and only the best. By paying top dollar, and higher, the CEO explained to McClellan, "you're ensuring quality."

In the 1990s, venture capitalists and other significant investors subscribed wholeheartedly to this "one bad boss" theory. These investors insisted on proven, top-notch, top-dollar CEO talent for the start-ups they bankrolled. Start-ups like Webvan, the high-profile Internet retailer that humbly aimed "to revolutionize the grocery industry."[162]

Price would be no object in Webvan's search for a CEO talented enough to lead the company to corporate glory. Webvan would find and hire the best, most capable chief executive available. And who might that most capable executive be? Who could possibly be more capable, Webvan's underwriters reasoned, than the CEO of a company that makes money telling other CEOs how to run their companies? That chief executive was George Shaheen, then the $4-million-a-year top executive at Andersen Consulting, "one of the largest, richest and most prestigious management-consulting firms on earth."[163]

Shaheen did not come cheap. To bring him on board, Webvan had to shell out a $13.5 million signing bonus and stock options valued at $123 million.[164]

"Essentially, Webvan was paying up front for Shaheen's cachet, his experience and his connections in the high-technology and financial worlds," an industry trade journal noted. "Webvan hired him because he was George Shaheen."[165]

Shaheen, brought on in 1999, had big plans for Webvan. By the end of 2002, he pledged, the company would be delivering groceries ordered over the Internet in twenty-six markets across the United States. Investors were thrilled. Cash poured into Webvan, $393 million in venture capital and then $402 million more from an IPO of the company's stock.[166]

With $800 million raised, with executive superstar Shaheen sitting in the CEO chair, Webvan couldn't miss. Or so Wall Street thought. But success was not to be. Webvan proceeded to lose more than $600 million in less than two years, including $453 million in 2000 alone. By the following spring, the company found itself having to raise another $60 million just to have a prayer of sticking around another year. Those extra dollars never materialized. In April 2001, Shaheen resigned. Webvan's stock, once sailing along at $34 a share, had dropped to 8 cents.[167] Glory would have to wait.

Shaheen, meanwhile, walked off with his own personal insurance policy, a retirement package he had negotiated before he started as Webvan's CEO. That package, on paper, guaranteed the fifty-seven-year-old Shaheen $375,000 a year from Webvan for the rest of his life.[168] Unfortunately for Shaheen, Webvan went belly up three months after his resignation, ending, somewhat prematurely, his guaranteed "lifetime" annuity.[169] George Shaheen, Webvan's costly insurance policy against failure, couldn't, in the end, even insure himself against failure.

IN ANY LARGE, COMPLEX ORGANIZATION, one person can always make a meaningful contribution to the enterprise's eventual success. But no single individual, not even a chief executive, can guarantee enterprise success, no matter how many dollars are stuffed into that one person's pocket. In generations past, business leaders accepted this simple insight as a matter of course. They expected hard work from the executives they put in positions of authority, not miracles. Top executives could make a positive difference. But so could any other company employee. All were hired hands. No more, no less. Chief executives deserved more, of course, than other employees, but not that much more.

A century ago, America's most powerful business leader, the financier J. Pierpont Morgan, actually quantified how much more. In the companies Morgan controlled, chief executives would earn, at most, twenty times the compensation of the companies' most lowly paid workers. A hundred thousand dollars for a CEO? A million dollars for a CEO? Morgan would have considered such sums totally undeserved. The millions were for corporate America's owners, not their hired help.

In Morgan's time, America's most powerful corporations still largely belonged to the men who initially launched them. These founding owners, the nation's business leaders believed, fully deserved whatever immense wealth their corporations brought them. This divine right of founder to fortune lives on today, in our contemporary celebration of the entrepreneurial spirit. Anyone with enough vision and spunk to create a grand enterprise, we believe, deserves an equally grand reward. We see entrepreneurs as heroes. We salute their achievement. We honor their memory.

Mere "managers" — top executives who make their fortunes by running grand enterprises, not creating them — have a much harder time winning our admiration. Indeed, the hundreds of millions earned by these top executives, CEOs like Disney's Michael Eisner, may even leave us a bit uneasy. A board of directors, after all, handed Michael Eisner the keys to the executive suite. But nobody ever handed *the* Walt Disney — Uncle Walt — anything. He built a great company by dint of individual effort. So hats off to the great entrepreneurs like Uncle Walt. They did it their way. That they be richly rewarded for their achievement is the American way.

But just how much credit for their success do our nation's greatest entrepreneurs really deserve? Just how individual is *their* achievement?

We ought to ask. The answer makes a difference. If entrepreneurial achievement is not as heroically individual as entrepreneurs claim it to be, then the massive rewards that flow to the executives who *create* corporate giants ought to give us as much pause as the massive rewards that go to executives who *manage* corporate giants.

In our era, no executive has created a grander corporate giant than Bill Gates. At a ripe young age, this remarkable entrepreneur co-founded what would go on to become the world's most highly valued enterprise. In the process, Gates became the world's wealthiest single individual, amassing more money in twenty years than the average American could accumulate in half a million lifetimes. Is this fortune an appropriate reward for an exceptional individual effort? Let's review the record.

Bill Gates came into the world, in 1955, as the son of a stable, caring, well-educated family of means. Young Bill would attend the finest schools, winding up as an undergraduate at Harvard. He would develop, as a student, an abiding passion in computers. Other students his age developed passions, too. Most had to shunt them aside. They needed to graduate, find a secure job, and pay off college loans. Young Bill Gates, scion of a secure family, had the freedom to follow his muse. He would drop out of Harvard and start a computer software business with a friend.

The business, Microsoft, would bob along, jostling for attention with hundreds of other fledgling new businesses. Then, in 1980, young Bill Gates would get a break. IBM couldn't be bothered to develop a software "operating system" for the new personal computer Big Blue was about to bring to market. Gates, ever alert, would convince IBM to let his Microsoft supply the operating system. Just one problem: Microsoft didn't have one. Gates neatly sidestepped that dilemma by buying an operating system, for less than $100,000, from another fledgling entrepreneur.[170]

Over the next few years, IBM's personal computers would introduce computing to tens of millions of Americans. Microsoft would collect a royalty on every computer IBM sold. Business analysts would later call IBM's agreement with Microsoft "one of the biggest business blunders of modern times."[171]

IBM, as part of that blunder, gave Microsoft the "exclusive right" to market the new operating system for IBM computers, MS-DOS, to other computer makers.[172] Microsoft would make the most of that right. Other computer makers, to gain the right to use MS-DOS, had to agree to pay Microsoft a licensing fee on *every* computer they sold, even those computers they sold without Microsoft's operating system installed inside.[173] The U.S. Justice Department would later, in 1994, ban all the agreements that required computer makers to pay fees for Microsoft's operating system even if they didn't use it. Too late. Microsoft's monopoly had already taken firm hold. The company had become a money machine.[174] Bill Gates had become phenomenally rich.

And deservedly so, some might say. Bill Gates made his own breaks. At every turn, he outsmarted his competition. True enough. But young Bill had some help along the way. Help, in the first place, from his loving parents whose resources opened up one wonderfully enriching opportunity after another. But help also from people not so near and dear, help from the taxpaying public of the United States.

American taxpayers bankrolled the computer technology that so captured the imagination of young Bill Gates. The first real computer produced in the United States was built for the U.S. Census Bureau. Microprocessors — and the software necessary to use them — were evolved by the scientists working on guidance systems for federally funded ICBMs and NASA rockets.[175] In all, over the first dozen years of the modern computer age, the federal government financed eighteen of the twenty-five "most significant advances in computer technology."[176] A few years later, the Internet would begin as a taxpayer-funded project designed to help scientists "share research and computing resources."[177]

Without tax dollars, the computer opportunities that Bill Gates so artfully seized would not have existed. Nor would a market have existed for the software Bill Gates sells. Tax dollars financed the schools that created the literate public necessary to sustain the new Information Age that so enriched Bill Gates and his fellow entrepreneurs.

The simple truth in all this? No achievement, not even the greatest entrepreneurial success of our times, is ever entirely individual. All achievement is shared, even if rewards may not be.

History's most creative achievers, to their credit, have always recognized the social roots of their success.

"If I have been able to see further," Sir Isaac Newton once noted, "it was only because I stood on the shoulders of giants."

"Many times a day," Albert Einstein would add centuries later, "I realize how much my outer and inner life is built upon the labors of my fellow-men, both living and dead."[178]

Great thinkers like Newton and Einstein could see the social realities behind their individual achievement. Most contemporary wealthy achievers cannot. Wealth tends to blur their vision. They have trouble noticing, as their wealth accumulates in ever higher piles, the contributions that others have made to their individual good fortune. They come, over time, to credit themselves for their awesome financial success. An understandable conclusion, at least psychologically speaking. After all, if multiple people stand behind each wealthy person's individual achievement, then whatever rewards that achievement might bring ought to be shared broadly, not concentrated in the pockets of one person. And if rewards should concentrate in one person's pockets, by what right can that one person claim to deserve them? If you yourself should have overstuffed pockets, why even raise this discomforting question? Better to assume that grand fortunes come, like gold medals to speedy sprinters, only to those who simply outrun the competition.

In every age, some people of ample means do dare ask discomforting questions. In our age, several have emerged. In 2003, one of these free-thinkers barnstormed the United States, asking these tough questions at gatherings big and small. That freethinker? None other than Bill Gates Sr., the father of the world's richest man.[179] Gates Sr., now retired from a successful Seattle law practice, currently runs the $24 billion foundation his son created. In that capacity, Gates Sr. has traveled the world and witnessed, first-hand, the social advantages that accrue to some people and not to others.

"There are a lot of Americans," Gates Sr. has concluded, "who do not recognize that their financial comfort is a consequence of conditions and programs in this country that made it possible for them to be wealthy."[180]

What proportion of their great fortunes do the wealthy owe to their social surroundings? In 2001, during Senate debate on the future of the federal estate tax, the only tax in the United States levied on accumulated wealth, Gates Sr. ventured an estimate.

"Imagine that two infants are about to be born," he suggested to a Senate subcommittee. "God summons their spirits to his office and makes them a proposition. One child will be born in a prosperous industrialized country, the United States. Another child will be born into a country of society-wide abject poverty. God proposes an auction for the privilege of being born into the United States. He asks each new child to pledge a percentage of his earthly accumulation at the end of his life to the treasury of God. The child who writes the highest percentage will be born in the United States. Does anyone think either child would pledge as little as 55 percent, the current top estate-tax rate?"[181]

The Senate would be duly unimpressed. Several months later, a Senate majority would endorse the Bush administration's proposed repeal of the estate tax. The vote disappointed, but did not surprise, Bill Gates Sr. A "myth of individual merit and success," he believes, now dominates America's public discourse about wealth and wealth-holders. But great wealth, he points out at every opportunity, "is never entirely the result of individual achievement."[182] To maintain the fiction that it is, we must by necessity "dismiss the incredible contribution our society makes to creating the fertile soil for successful private enterprise."

We make other misjudgments about wealth as well.

"We underestimate," notes Gates Sr., "the role of luck, privilege and God's grace in our good fortune."

And what a huge role that is.

JOHN D. ROCKEFELLER ONCE DESCRIBED becoming rich as a three-step process. "One, go to work early," he's reputed to have noted. "Two, stay late. Three, find oil."[183] Many millions of people in the world today routinely follow John D.'s advice. They go to work early and stay late. A few "find oil" and move on to become wealthy. Most, the overwhelming majority, do not. Why not? Do people in the non-wealthy majority not work as diligently as the wealthy few? Are they less disciplined? Less focused? Less tenacious? Less, in short, deserving? Some people may think so, but most of us have come to understand, as we grow older, that virtuous habits cross class lines. Hard-working, disciplined, focused, and tenacious people, we have learned, can be found at every income level. Noble efforts, we realize as we mature, do not guarantee great fortune. Nor do dishonorable, even contemptible, behaviors necessarily shove riches out of reach. Lazy, lying, and larcenous people, we know from experience, can and do regularly become rich.

But lazy, lying, and larcenous behavior, we also understand, does not guarantee great fortune either. Most despicable people we know, or have known, aren't particularly rich. So what does separate the rich from the rest of us? Just dumb luck, the vicissitudes of happenstance? To a large extent, yes. Dumb luck determines, to a surprisingly huge degree, who amasses massive wealth.

Ask Ralph Roberts. In the early 1960s, Ralph ran a belt-making business. But then along came Sansabelt pants — the beltless trouser fashion sensation — and Ralph felt sure this new craze "was going to wipe out the belt business."[184] So Ralph sold off his belt-making operation. Ralph now needed a new line of work. He found it, at a friendly poker game. A "two-bit" cable television start-up in Mississippi, he learned, was looking for investors. Ralph took the plunge. He sunk a chunk of his belt-business proceeds into the Tupelo cable system. Thirty years later, Ralph's cable business, renamed Comcast, would be worth billions.[185]

"I begin every day saying, 'Thank God he sold the belt business,'" Ralph's son, Comcast President Brian Roberts, would later note.[186] Sansabelt pants never did wipe out belts, demonstrating once again, as Brian Roberts readily points out, that "luck is a big part of life."

Scholars who study entrepreneurial success have come to the same conclusion, notes Roy C. Smith, the former investment banker who became a professor of entrepreneurship and finance at New York University. "Academics have been studying self-made businessmen for a few decades, looking for the keys to success and a methodology to teach to young, would-be entrepreneurs," writes Smith, but that search has not yet found "a simple, repeatable formula."[187]

"Indeed," Smith adds, "many academics have come to believe that great entrepreneurial success is usually a random event, influenced as much by luck as by skill."

That same luck, other academics point out, has been driving up executive paychecks. Two of them, economists Marianne Bertrand of Princeton and Sendhil Mullainathan of MIT, have actually computed the precise impact of luck on executive pay. The two focused their research on the oil industry. They identified the factors that impact stock prices that oil executives can't do anything to influence, everything from the world price of oil to the dollar's exchange-rate value, then calculated the share of oil executive pay that comes from events oil executives cannot control. Their conclusion, as summed up by one reporter: CEO pay "goes up from luck as much as from performance."[188]

In the 1980s and 1990s, Bertrand and Mullainathan's oil executives were lucky enough to be at the right place at the right time, as were almost all America's top executives. CEOs at the end of the twentieth century didn't need to "find oil." They just needed to ride Wall Street's bull market. The higher that market rose, the richer their rewards.

But dare we call *all* the multi-million fortunes executives have amassed over recent years lucky? Don't some of these fortunes reflect admirable intelligence and insight, not just fortuitous chance? How can anyone, for instance, dismiss as merely "lucky" the fortune accumulated by someone as dedicated and diligent as Eric Schmidt?

Not many executives entered the twenty-first century more widely respected, within American business circles, than Eric Schmidt. His vita shouted merit on every page. Schmidt, forty-five years old at the century's turn, had studied electrical engineering at Princeton and Berkeley, two of the world's most demanding educational institutions. After school, he had honed his high-tech skills at the Xerox Palo Alto Research Center in California, the legendary computer science hotbed that birthed the drop-down menu and the desktop mouse. Schmidt had then translated his technical expertise into business success, first as chief technology officer at Sun Microsystems, later as chief executive of Novell, what had been a troubled computer networking company. Novell, under Schmidt, did an abrupt about-face, and close observers gave Schmidt the credit.[189]

For his labors at Novell, Schmidt took home $7 million in 1999, on top of $4 million in 1998.[190] His financial future would soon turn even brighter. In 2001, Google, the hot new search engine company, would name Schmidt its CEO.

How could anyone possibly dismiss as "luck" Eric Schmidt's personal achievement? Whose career success could be more "earned," more deserved, than his?

None of us, in one sense, have the right to judge anyone's personal achievement. We do not know — we cannot know — all the defining moments that shape the trajectory of an individual life. We cannot know if a principal's random decision placed Eric Schmidt into the classroom of a teacher inspiring enough to turn young Eric on to technology. We cannot know if Schmidt had a chance encounter with a colleague who just happened to mention an interesting job opening at Sun Microsystems. Nor do we have any idea if Schmidt, early in his tenure at Novell, received an insightful, unsolicited e-mail that may have helped him understand just where the struggling company had been going wrong. Only a person who lives a life can truly know all the chance moments that may have shaped it. Wise people remember these moments as they look back on their lives. Eric Schmidt may be one of these wise people.

"Lots of people who are smart and work hard and play by the rules don't have a fraction of what I have," he told a reporter after making his fortune. "I realize I don't have my wealth because I'm so brilliant. Luck has a lot to do with it."[191]

And the grander the wealth, the more important luck's role will likely have been, as even the lustiest cheerleaders for concentrated wealth sometimes acknowledge.

"Want to get rich?" as *Forbes* headlined a 1997 story about the four hundred richest Americans. "Don't get born in Afghanistan."[192]

And don't forget, *Forbes* added, that "even folks who are gifted, and did it all themselves, cannot possibly end up with a net worth of $475 million (the cutoff on this year's list) without having won some huge crapshoots along the way."

SURELY THERE MUST BE MORE to becoming wealthy than luck. There surely is. There are connections. You don't need to be particularly smart, industrious, or even lucky enough to find oil to become rich. You just need to know the right people.

Business mythologists have, down through the years, always tried to minimize the role connections play in the lives of the economically successful. Good ideas, they hope we believe, will eventually be rewarded. Invent a better mouse-trap and the world will beat a path to your door. To succeed and become wealthy, American business folklore insists, you don't need to come from "proper" society. You don't, any more, even need to be the "right" color. American business only cares about one color, green. If you have a clever enough business proposition, you'll always be able to find someone willing to bankroll your idea and set you on the road to riches. You don't, in short, need to know the "right" people. If you're good enough, if you're deserving, the right people will find you.

In the 1990s, business boosters prattled endlessly about the historic opportunities open to anyone with genius and grit. Financial angels and venture capitalists — rich people with plenty of spare cash to invest — stood ready to make our entrepreneurial dreams come true. The rest of us just needed to be bold enough to do the dreaming. We had evolved, as a nation, into the ultimate economic meritocracy. Visionary sees the future. Investors capitalize the vision. Visionary hits the jackpot.

"Yeah, right, anybody can raise capital for an Internet company," one skeptical chief executive deadpanned in response, "if they know the same guys that I do."[193]

That skeptic was Eric Schmidt, our CEO wise man. Schmidt looked over the business landscape and didn't see triumphant visionaries. He saw a business world where the right connections, not the best ideas, separated flops from fortunes.

In 1993, San Francisco entrepreneur Halsey Minor seemed destined to become one of those flops. His high-tech information service, CNET Inc., wasn't making any money. Investors wouldn't give him the time of day. Bills went unpaid. Minor did everything he could to keep his vision treading water. He sacrificed. He "maxed out his credit cards." Nothing worked. All seemed lost. He was ready, then and there, "to throw in the towel." Then, to the rescue, came a connection, "a well-to-do friend" with "a last-minute cash infusion." CNET would survive. By 1997, Halsey Minor would be worth $73 million.[194]

Minor, of course, didn't succeed *only* because he had a connection. Minor did have an idea. But ideas, in the pursuit of wealth, are optional. Connections, and connections alone, can build grand fortunes. If you are well enough connected, you need not bring any ideas, knowledge, or talent to the task at hand. You need only to know how to schmooze.

In 2000, for instance, Washington lawyer Vernon E. Jordan Jr., a mover and shaker in and around the Clinton Administration, agreed to become a partner at Lazard Freres & Co., a private Wall Street banking firm. Jordan, at the time, had not one iota of banking experience. He had connections. He was someone, as one Lazard Freres executive explained, "who could get CEOs on the phone." For this talent, Lazard Freres promised Jordan $5 million a year for five years, plus a suite in one of New York's most expensive hotels and a bonus "based on performance."[195]

Connections can take the connected to far loftier heights than penthouses in Manhattan. Witness the remarkable career of America's most famous multimillionaire of distinctly modest talents, the forty-third President of the United States, George W. Bush.

The grandson of a United States senator from Connecticut, the son of a rising political star within Texas Republican ranks, young George W. began his rise to wealth, power, and fame by compiling an undistinguished prep school academic record. His grades and test scores would show no great promise — or sign of diligent individual effort. Young George would matriculate at Yale anyway, where his family connections guaranteed him a "legacy" admission.[196] At Yale, George W. would compile another undistinguished academic record. Nor did he engage himself, extracurricularly, as either a participant or critic in the turbulence of late 1960s college life. He would sail through four years at Yale, evincing little interest in anything collegiate outside elite secret societies.

After graduation, in 1968, young George sidestepped Vietnam by slipping into the Texas Air National Guard. Connections greased the way. He then worked, for a time, at an agricultural conglomerate run by one of his dad's former employees. Another connection. In 1977, George W. finally struck out on his own, more or less. He started his own oil company, Arbusto Energy Inc. Arbusto, the Spanish word for "bush," did not actually try to find any oil. Arbusto, instead, invested in wells drilled by other firms. Where would Arbusto obtain the money to make these investments? The money would come from connections — wealthy Bush family and friends.

"The list of investors," one later analysis would note, "was remarkable for a young company owned by a man of 32 with scant experience and virtually no track record."[197]

Arbusto would eventually totter toward bankruptcy and only be saved, in 1984, by a timely merger with another company. Two years later, this merged company would be bought out by still another company, the Dallas-based Harken Energy. Halfway through 1990, after a murky series of wheels and deals, George W. would cash out of Harken with nearly $850,000 in stock profits, not long before the company "reported a $22-million loss."[198]

That neat little profit would later come in handy — for George W.'s career change. A few years earlier, George had been longing for something more substantial in life than gooey black gold. Fortunately, to help him set out on a new path, he had still more connections, namely Eddie Chiles, the owner of the Texas Rangers baseball team and a long-time supporter of George W.'s daddy. All was not well for Eddie Chiles. He had been ailing and needed, for health and financial reasons, to sell his Rangers. George wanted them. Unfortunately, George did not have nearly enough cash on hand to buy them. Chiles, fortunately, would be understanding.[199] He would give young George the opportunity to raise the needed purchase price. George W. would promptly collect financial commitments "from a Yale classmate, the classmate's business partner, one of his father's campaign aides and the husband of a Bush cousin."[200] But these commitments only took him half way home, and the other half appeared out of reach after Richard Rainwater, a deep-pockets investor from Fort Worth, rejected George's invitation to ante up. George's bid for the Texas Rangers seemed dead in the sage brush.

Outside Texas, this sad news would upset a powerful man, Peter Ueberroth, the commissioner of Major League Baseball. Ueberroth liked the idea of having the son of a President of the United States own a baseball team. Ueberroth went to work. He would personally persuade George's balking investor, Richard Rainwater, to fork over the additional dollars George needed. In April 1989, thanks to that help, George W. Bush would become a baseball owner. In all, he had put up, out of his own pocket, $606,302, which he had borrowed. That gave him, mathematically speaking, a 1.8 percent stake in the team. His grateful investor teammates would grant him an additional 10 percent share — and a $200,000 salary as the managing general partner.[201] Later, after his Harken wind-fall, George would have the cash to pay back the $606,302 he had borrowed.[202]

With the Texas Rangers, George W. had finally found his element. As part-ner numero uno, he could schmooze to his heart's content. He would represent the Rangers at baseball meetings. He would give speeches to fans. He would even get to approve player trades. What incredible fun. The team, meanwhile, would start climbing in the standings. Attendance would climb, too, thanks in no small part to a beautiful new stadium, The Ballpark at Arlington, built with $135 million kindly supplied by taxpayers.[203]

George W. had become a high-profile businessman, successful, he would proudly note, "by any objective measure." Boosted by this high profile, George would soon spring into state politics. He would run for governor in 1994 as a can-do business executive. He would win. He would also become an extreme-ly rich man, after the 1998 sale of his beloved Texas Rangers. The team's value had tripled. George W. would clear a $14.9 million personal profit, not a bad return on a $606,302 original investment.[204]

To what did George W. owe all this good fortune? Mere connections? He would scoff at this insulting insinuation, in 1999, as he geared up to run for President.

"Thanks to the integrity of my dad and mom, I've inherited a great name that has sometimes opened doors and sometimes slammed them shut," he explains. "But the business world is a world of results and performance, and having a famous last name didn't strike oil or conceive and build The Ballpark at Arlington, or help the team's win-loss record. And my name hasn't made any decisions for me as governor."[205]

The gospel according to George W. Bush. He didn't connect his way to suc-cess. He delivered, on his own. Such are the ways the wealthy see the world. They must surely deserve their good fortune. Why else would they have it?

WHAT IF GEORGE W. IS RIGHT? What if these pages are somewhat exaggerat-ing the role chance plays in human affairs? After all, an admirer of George W. might argue, some people do find themselves in the right place at the right time. But that good fortune does not guarantee them a grand fortune. Nor does knowing the right people automatically make anyone fabulously wealthy. Happenstance merely creates opportunities. Those lucky enough, or well con-nected enough, to have opportunities still have to *do something*, in some way, before they can cash in. George W. Bush had to win taxpayer approval for a new ballpark. He deserves credit — and considerable reward — for doing what had to be done, doesn't he? Not just anybody could have done what he had to do.

Actually, many of us *could* have done what George W. had to do, and just as well as he did, if not better. In fact, a great many of us, if good fortune were to suddenly pluck us up and sit us at the top of some *Fortune* 500 enterprise, would do just fine — because we would have help. The same help that executives currently at the top receive.

Individuals, as they rise in corporate hierarchies, make more money. We all know that. But rising executives don't just make more money. They get more help. The higher up in an enterprise any executive sits, the more help that executive will receive. At the summit, for those who occupy a *Fortune* 500 chief executive suite, extraordinary amounts of help are available. Corporate America surrounds executive suites with legions of people compensated, some quite handsomely, to help those at the top succeed — and look good doing it. Chief operating officers are on hand to make sure, day by day, the company runs smoothly. Chief financial officers keep and cook the books. Chief information officers peer into the technological future. Executive vice-presidents develop strategic plans.

But the buck stops at the chief executive's desk, right? And life's lonely at the top, right? And no one else is paid to see the big picture, right?

Actually, plenty of people are paid to see that big picture. They're called management consultants. Executives at the top tap the talents of these consultants all the time, so much so that management consulting has become, on an annual basis, an $89 billion industry worldwide, with three-fifths of that business in the United States.[206]

"We live in paradoxical times," marvels one *New York Times* business analyst. "Executive compensation is spiraling out of control, yet the more companies pay their chief executives, the more help they seem to need with basic questions like 'What business are we in?' and 'Where do we go from here?'"[207]

Think you might need still more help than all this to succeed as a chief executive? Fine. The help is there. Not just speechwriters to make you sound smart, but speech coaches to help you enunciate more forcefully. Not just secretaries to keep your schedule, but fashion experts to help you dress your best. Not just executive search companies to help you hire qualified people, but executive assistants to drop the bad news on people you want to let go. In this incredibly supportive environment, large numbers of us would probably be able to function just fine. We would make blunders. We would make lucky guesses. We would muddle through — just like the executives who currently sit at the top. And why should that surprise us? In our most basic capacities, we *are* just like the executives who currently sit at the top.

Take it from an unlikely source, Alan Greenspan, the chairman of the Federal Reserve Board, a hero, for most of the 1990s, to almost every executive who sat in a CEO seat.

"The vast majority of things which human beings can do," Greenspan once told a San Francisco audience, "everyone can do, and the difference between those basic skills relative to what the base is, is really very small."[208]

And if the differences between us are so very small, and if many of us, given the small differences between human beings, could function reasonably well if chance or connections placed us atop a grand enterprise, then by what stretch of reason can someone currently atop a grand enterprise deserve to earn more in a week than any average American could earn in a lifetime?

Maybe George W. knows.

INTELLIGENCE DOES NOT GUARANTEE WEALTH. Nor does hard work. Nor vision. Nor good looks, hustling, miserly behavior, or simple ruthlessness. All these factors may help grow grand fortunes. None assure them. Even luck and connections don't guarantee that riches will be forthcoming. All incredibly wealthy people may at some level be lucky. But not all lucky people are incredibly wealthy.

Is there, then, any sure route to wealth? Just one. Inheritance. People born into families of great wealth tend to become, with unfailing regularity, wealthy themselves.

Inheritances leave defenders of inequality uneasy. Great wealth, these defenders tirelessly proclaim, encourages and rewards great effort. But those who inherit great wealth need not make any effort at all.

"To the extent that resources are distributed on the basis of inheritance," as historians Robert Miller, Jr. and Stephen McNamee point out, "they are not distributed on the basis of merit."[209]

Inheritances cannot be defended, in any credible way, as "earned." But they can be dismissed — as increasingly unimportant, in the modern world, to economic success. Apologists for inequality have rushed, in recent years, to make just this case. Inheritances, they argue, may once have been a big deal. No longer. Rich people today make themselves rich.

"Forget old money. Forget silver spoons," *Forbes* exclaimed in 1996, introducing the magazine's annual list of America's richest four hundred. "Great fortunes are being created almost monthly in the U.S. today by young entrepreneurs who hadn't a dime when we created this list 14 years ago."

"More than ever before, today's wealth is a product of personal achievement rather than inheritance," marveled conservative commentator Dinesh D'Souza four years later. No one can responsibly argue, added D'Souza, "that most of today's affluent got that way by choosing their parents carefully."[210]

Some recent social science research appears, at first glance, to bolster this conservative case. In the mid 1990s, for instance, studies by the Rand Corporation and the Brookings Institution concluded that rich people, for the most part, owe their fortunes to their own personal labors. But these studies focused on upper middle class professionals and managers, people earning

$100,000 to $300,000 a year, and ignored, as political scientist Michael Parenti points out, the very rich.[211]

Scholars who do include the very wealthy in their calculations find that inheritances do make a significant contribution to America's total personal wealth. How much of a contribution? The scholarly estimates vary wildly. Americans, taken as one group, owe somewhere between 20 and 80 percent of their personal wealth to inheritance.[212]

But scholars do agree on one point. The bulk of the wealth that is inherited slides into relatively few pockets. Hardly any Americans ever see an appreciable inheritance. One study, on the 1983-85 period, estimated that only 4 percent of Americans had ever received a bequest.[213] More recent research, discussed in a paper published in 2000 by the Federal Reserve Bank of Cleveland, found that 92 percent of Americans have never seen an inheritance. Just 1.6 percent, the study found, have inherited more than $100,000.[214]

Statistics can only tell us so much. Case studies — financial life histories of the very wealthy — can help us understand far more clearly just how important inheritances are to great fortunes. Researchers from the Boston-based United for a Fair Economy compiled a good number of these life histories for an analysis of the 1996 *Forbes* list of America's most affluent. Just over half of these four hundred wealthiest Americans, this research found, inherited at least $50 million. Another 20 percent were born into families wealthy enough to sit in America's most affluent tenth.[215]

"This is what most people might call," the researchers noted, "a 'head start.'"

In any pursuit of great fortune, head starts can be remarkably valuable, mainly because the easiest way in the world to amass wealth is to have some.

"To turn $100 into $110 is work," as Seagrams billionaire Edgar Bronfman once put it. "To turn $100 million into $110 million is inevitable."[216]

Money makes money. In the closing decades of the twentieth century, money made money at astonishingly rapid rates. Consider, as the *Economist* magazine has, a typical wealthy Manhattanite circa 1983, a millionaire with $500,000 in stock holdings and a $500,000 apartment. That Manhattan millionaire, if he sat in that apartment for the next fifteen years and did nothing more strenuous than glance at the stock tables in the daily paper, would have seen his net worth increase by $5 million.[217]

Suppose that millionaire had inherited that original $500,000 in stock and $500,000 apartment. How much of that subsequent $5 million should be considered "earned" — and deserved? Should the millionaire's entire $6 million fortune be credited to his inheritance? Or should the $5 million from stock and real estate appreciation be credited to the millionaire's "good sense" to hang on to his stock and apartment? Answers to questions like these can vary, one reason why scholarly estimates on the impact of inheritances on personal wealth also vary.

Some people, of course, would have no problem classifying the entire $6 million accumulated by our Manhattanite millionaire as eminently earned. Some people, as Texas populist Jim Hightower likes to explain, "were born on third base and think they hit a triple."[218]

THOSE UNTROUBLED BY INEQUALITY invariably end up ascribing unequal outcomes to individual behaviors. Those who have little wealth, the comfortable argue, have no one to blame but themselves. They have squandered away opportunities and loafed while others were laboring. Those who did that labor, those who seized their opportunities, have considerable wealth to show for their noble efforts, as by all rights they should.

This assumption that merit determines how societies distribute their bounty convincingly explains, for some people, why certain individuals enjoy more wealth than others. But this explanation, the unconvinced point out, starts wobbling whenever people's economic fortunes suddenly change on a mass scale, as they invariably do. In the 1930s, for instance, the jobless rate in the United States tripled. Did millions of Americans suddenly become lazy? Similarly, in the last twenty years of the twentieth century, the richest 1 percent of Americans more than doubled their share of the nation's wealth. Did America's wealthy suddenly become twice as smart or hard-working, twice as worthy?[219]

Perhaps the wealthy, some reasonable people conclude, did become twice as worthy. How else to explain the massive rewards that have been flowing to the top?

"The numbers are so big, you just have to wonder if anyone is worth that much money," muses David Larcker, a business professor at the Wharton School. "But in some cases, maybe they are."[220]

Or maybe people at the top of the economic ladder didn't become more deserving. Maybe they just became more powerful.

Some academics seem headed toward this conclusion. These scholars can't find any rational business reason why America's top business executives have been able to quintuple their pay over recent years. Executive pay increases have outpaced profits, outpaced rising share prices, outpaced revenues from sales. Researchers, these scholars suggest, perhaps ought to pay less attention to balance sheets and more attention to corporate power dynamics — to the many different ways, political and economic, that executives manipulate power to bolster their personal bottom lines.[221]

Graef Crystal, the pay consultant turned academic, sometimes sees rewards at the top in these same power-dynamic terms. His research has also unearthed no rational links between how executives perform and how, over recent years, they have been rewarded.

"Most of it is simple piggery," Crystal told one reporter in 1996, "they grabbed what they could."[222]

And kept it.

"How do you distinguish," the conservative columnist George Will once asked, "between money earned and money merely taken?"[223]

Will's question matters. That you deserve everything you can take, you can grab, is the law of the jungle. We deserve better.

THE GREEDY AS BENEFACTORS

THE GOOD THINGS IN LIFE, apologists for inequality would have us believe, we owe to greed. The greedy benefit us all. They bring us sweetness and light, progress and hope. Their tireless strivings to accumulate wealth leave us more prosperous, compassionate, and cultured than we otherwise would be. We are all enriched, friends of fortune insist, when some of us become far wealthier than others. Societies where wealth concentrates need not apologize. They should, instead, encourage even greater concentration.

"Too often we forget that economic inequality is not a moral imperfection to be cut out of society by doctors of economic and social healing," the business journal, *Barron's*, assured its corporate readers in 2001. "It is a practical and moral mechanism for the increase of human wealth and the advancement of the human condition."[1]

"Greed is healthy," as Wall Street financier Ivan Boesky, amasser of a $300 million fortune, once noted. "You can be greedy and still feel good about yourself."[2]

You can feel good about yourself, defenders of inequality posit, for several reasons.

First, great fortunes don't just sit in treasure chests. Great fortunes fuel investment and create jobs. The more freely wealth accumulates, the stronger our economy.

Second, contributions from the wealthy drive charitable good works. The greater the fortunes of the fortunate, the more good work charities can do.

Third, the wealthy, as generous patrons of the arts, nurture cultural achievement. The wealthier our wealthy, the finer our culture.

Great wealth, in other words, may not make a reliable incentive. The rich may not truly deserve their riches. But we need inequality anyway, assert those who fawn over fortune, because inequality

93

"works." We all benefit when some of us have more, much more, than others.

Do we? If inequality does indeed benefit us all, then we ought to be living today in the best of times. We have, after all, become far more unequal here in the United States than we used to be. Our inequality has been growing, and rapidly so, for well over a generation. If concentrations of great wealth truly benefit us all, we ought now, as Americans, to feel more financially secure than we have in quite some time. A million points of light ought to be warming our hearts. Great art ought to be dazzling our senses.

How secure, how warm, how dazzled, in our actual lives, have we become? Let us see.

JOBS AND PAYCHECKS

A CENTURY AGO, IN ROBBER BARON MANHATTAN, a wealthy banker's daughter invited a *New York Herald* reporter by for a sneak preview of her latest new wardrobe. Out for viewing came one magnificent gown after another. Magnificent dresses in silk, chiffon, satin, and lace, "hand-embroidered, beaded, ribboned, and encrusted with diamonds."[1] The crowning touch: a coat cut from white unborn baby lamb, lined with ermine.

The price tag for the new wardrobe? About $2 million, a stupendous sum in 1906.

"Money spent in this way is not lost," the banker's daughter hastened to assure the reporter, "for if the dressmakers and milliners and shoemakers had no demand for their work the wheels of progress would necessarily be hampered."[2]

This banker's daughter would feel right at home, ideologically, if not fashionably, in twenty-first century America. In our corporate boardrooms, in our legislative chambers, even, sometimes, in our union halls, we have convinced ourselves, beyond a shadow of a doubt, that wealthy people spin our nation's economic wheels. Without rich people, and plenty of them, the economy would sputter to a stop.

Don't count me as an "enemy of the wealthy," Pennsylvania's most powerful Teamster leader told the *Philadelphia Inquirer* in 1998, "poor people don't build companies that hire people."[3]

Having rich people among us, we have come to believe, helps poor people — and everybody else, too. Rich people spend more than the rest of us, our leaders inform us, and the spending they do creates jobs and prosperity. Rich people also save more than the rest of us, and the savings they make stimulate investment. That investment creates still more prosperity. Want that prosperity to continue? Just boost the capacity of rich people to spend and save — by reducing tax rates on the wealthy. Want to jeopardize whatever prosperity we have already achieved? Ask the rich to pay more in taxes.[4]

"They say, 'Tax the rich,'" one wealthy Californian, actor Mickey Rooney, complained midway through the 1990s. "Don't they understand that the rich are the only people who can afford to give them jobs?"[5]

Ludwig von Mises, an Austrian economist who taught in the United States after World War II, made much the same point a half century earlier, in somewhat more ponderous prose. Societies that accept and applaud growing gaps between the wealthy and everyone else, he contended, actually improve the lives average people live.

"Inequality of wealth and incomes is the cause of the masses' well-being, not the cause of anybody's distress," von Mises argued in 1955. "Where there is a 'lower degree of inequality,' there is necessarily a lower standard of living of the masses."[6]

Did Mickey Rooney, back in the 1950s, ever read von Mises on the masses? Not likely. Few people paid much attention to Professor von Mises when he lectured at New York University. The Austrian was considered, at the time, somewhat old-fashioned, a throwback to less enlightened days. But times change. Our most politically powerful economists today revere Ludwig von Mises. His observations about inequality now drive our economic policies.[7] Rich people, our policy makers assume as self-evident fact, "grow" the economy. The richer they become, the bigger the economic pie. The bigger the pie, the more for everyone, even if the wealthy walk off with the biggest pieces.

In the closing years of the twentieth century, America's rich did become richer, phenomenally so, and America's economic pie did grow, just as the policy makers had predicted. But what about those "masses"? Did America's growing economy usher in the new epoch of mass well-being the cheerleaders for concentrated wealth had promised? Many observers, at century's end, were firmly convinced it had. Wealth, they reported, wasn't just "trickling down" from on high. Wealth was gushing into average American households. Inequality, they rejoiced, had "worked."

"As the American Century draws to a close, times have rarely been better," *Business Week* rhapsodized in 1999. "Eight years into an expansion that just won't quit, the robust U.S. economy is the envy of the world."[8]

This expansion would become, one year later, the longest uninterrupted period of economic growth in America's history. This record-breaking blast of prosperity, commentators proclaimed, had essentially wiped out unemployment.

"This boom has been so long and so good that it has reached down to virtually every person in society," Cornell University economist Richard Burkhauser concluded. "Almost all the able-bodied people who are looking for jobs can find them."[9]

Boosters of America's economic status quo could barely contain their glee. Were rich people getting richer in this boom that would not end? Yes, "inequality is increasing," economists Ken Deavers and Max Lyons acknowledged, but what of it? Living standards, the two crowed, "are rising across the entire income distribution."[10]

Was the middle class disappearing, as the worry-worts kept charging? Absolutely, gloated *Investor's Business Daily*.

"The middle class is shrinking," the journal smugly noted, "because it's getting richer."[11]

America, other celebrants exulted, had become a nation of investors.[12] Over half of America's middle class families, 53 percent, held stocks in 1998, up from less than a third, 31 percent, at the end of the 1980s.[13] Shares of stock now accounted for 54 percent of all household financial assets.[14] The new ownership of corporate America, smiled Chrysler Chairman Robert Eaton, "is rapidly becoming most of America."[15]

These new "owners" were speaking a vocabulary that most Americans would have found unintelligible before the 1980s. Mutual funds, IRAs, 401(k)s, Keoughs — one new option after another for amassing wealth. And amassing wealth seemed to be just what average Americans were doing. Between 1984 and 1997, the dollar value of the stocks held by mutual funds multiplied thirty times over.[16] By 2001, over 37 million Americans were regularly stashing away dollars in 401(k)s.[17] And middle class families were buying more homes, too. By September 1999, almost two-thirds of America's 103 million households owned their own homes. America had never seen such high home ownership rates.[18]

Could a more robust prosperity even be imagined?

"These are the best of economic times," noted Marc Zandi, the chief economist at one respected economic consulting firm, "by any measure."[19]

Who could doubt that? Certainly not the President for most of the 1990s, William Jefferson Clinton. "America's middle class," the President told the nation in 1997, "is rising fast."[20] America, President Clinton added in his 1999 State of the Union, "is working again" — "with nearly 18 million new jobs, wages rising at more than twice the rate of inflation, the highest home ownership in history, the smallest welfare rolls in 30 years, and the lowest peacetime unemployment since 1957."[21]

Two years later, just days before leaving office, President Clinton would cast a final proud look back.

"Unemployment is at a 30-year low," the President told a student group, "we have 22.5 million new jobs, the longest economic expansion in history, the lowest minority unemployment ever recorded, the lowest female unemployment in 40 years."[22]

All this should have been cause for a raucous national celebration. But Americans, strangely enough, weren't celebrating. Amid American history's "longest economic expansion," inside the workplaces and neighborhoods where average Americans labored and lived, journalists could find few people cheering.

"This is America's Golden Age," a puzzled *New York Times* noted early in the new Bush Administration. "So if things are so great, why don't we seem pleased?"[23]

"Circumstances just keep getting better," the *Times* added, "and Americans just keep complaining."

What was going on here? Grousing, the *Times* concluded, must be hard-wired into human nature — or, at the least, the central nervous system of the American character.

"The American character may be so fundamentally entwined with striving," the *Times* hypothesized, "that we will grouse no matter how much better circumstances get."

Had Americans fallen victim to some debilitating post-success syndrome? Is that why they weren't cheering America's record prosperity? Or was there some other, some simpler explanation behind why average Americans weren't celebrating? Could it be that inequality had *not* improved average American lives? Could it be that average Americans had little, if anything, to celebrate?

LITTLE TO CELEBRATE? What about all those statistics? The rising family incomes. The millions of new jobs. The record homeownership rates. The over-flowing mutual funds. Economists had never seen such numbers. Average Americans, they believed, ought to be down on their knees, thanking their lucky stars. But average Americans, *even before* the economic downturn that began in 2001, were thanking no one. How could that be? How could average Americans and economists see the world so differently?

That difference might have been a matter of perspective. Economists read statistics. Average Americans have to live them. That can be hard.

Consider, for instance, those statistics on rising family incomes. The key numbers here, the annual figures for household income, do show increases over time.[24] In 1980, the nation's most typical households earned $17,710. This national "median household income" did indeed double, and then some, to $42,151 over the next twenty years.

An impressive leap? Not quite. These dollar figures don't take inflation into account. If we adjust for inflation, the picture changes. Household income still increases over the course of the 1980s and 1990s, but only by $7,000. How significant an increase, over twenty years, is $7,000? Not very. To move from $35,238, the inflation-adjusted 1980 household income, to the $42,151 median income of 2000, household revenues inched up, on average, a meager $346 a year — a less than 1 percent annual income increase.

Still, an increase is an increase. So can we conclude, along with corporate America's cheerleaders, that average Americans were, at century's end, making more money than they made back in 1980? We could, but we would be wrong.

Average Americans were actually making *less*, on an hourly basis, at the end of the 1990s than they made in 1980. In fact, Americans were earning less for their labor at the end of the 1990s, after nearly twenty years of "prosperity," than they earned in the early 1970s.

In 1973, American "production and nonsupervisory employees" — about 80 percent of the nation's workforce — averaged $13.91 an hour, in dollars inflation-adjusted to 1999 levels. This hourly rate, over the next twenty years, shriveled all the way down to $12.50 in 1995, before bouncing back up a bit, to $13.24, in 1999.[25]

Business commentators, at the time, enthusiastically hailed this late 1990s uptick in wages. The same prosperity that was enriching the rich, they exclaimed, was also enriching average Americans. A premature conclusion. In 1999, after factoring in inflation, most average Americans were still making over $56 less a week, almost $3,000 less a year, than what they earned in 1973.[26]

The widely lauded late 1990s uptick in wages would not, in any case, last particularly long. Wages for average Americans would be stagnating once again by century's end. In 1999, only employees making more than $65,000 a year, less than a tenth of the total workforce, actually saw their paychecks register a real increase.[27] In 2000, the median wages of America's 90 million nonsupervisory workers, "ground to a virtual halt, climbing by less than a tenth of a percent."[28] In 2001, production and non-supervisory workers in America's private sector would still be earning less, in average weekly earnings adjusted for inflation, than they earned in 1973.[29]

All these wage numbers do raise an obvious question: If hourly wages have been sinking and stagnating, how could typical American household incomes be rising, even by a paltry 1 percent a year? What can explain this apparent discrepancy? Only sheer hard work. American household incomes rose slightly between 1980 and 2000, despite lower real wages, because average Americans devoted more of their hours to working.

Once upon a time, an average American family could live a middle class life off the paycheck of a single breadwinner. By the 1990s, that once upon a time had disappeared. At century's end, according to Census Bureau data, only 28 percent of middle-income families were getting by with just one wage-earner — and most of these single-earner families had no choice in the matter. They sported only one parent.[30]

In the 1990s alone, average couples upped their hours on the job the equivalent of seven extra workweeks a year — and all these added hours, one business journal noted, didn't count into the mix "commuting or the time spent dealing with e-mail or talking on cell phones."[31] Americans, by the end of the 1990s, were spending "more time on the job than workers anywhere else in the industrialized world."[32] One 1999 report from a United Nations agency concluded that Americans were working two weeks a year more than the Japanese, once considered the world's leading workaholics, and an incredible eleven more weeks, or over four hundred more hours a year, than average Germans.[33]

No wonder average Americans weren't cheering their good fortune. They were too exhausted to exult.

THE CHEERLEADERS FOR INEQUALITY are certainly a persistent bunch. Real hourly wages may still trail their early 1970s levels. Breadwinners may be working many more hours. But none of this, the ideologues assure us, means that average Americans aren't better off. After all, they point out, *total* compensation is up.

Total compensation, the argument goes, tells us much more about the actual well-being of average Americans than hourly wages — or even household income totals. Hourly wage and household income figures don't include fringe benefits. *Total compensation* numbers do. American workers, Jerry Jasinowski, the president of the National Association of Manufacturers, noted proudly midway through the 1990s, "nowadays receive a much greater share of their compensation in the form of various benefits." If you take these benefits into account, Jasinowski contended, workers were actually better off in the 1990s than they were in the early 1970s, when hourly wages were higher.[34]

W. Michael Cox, the chief economist at the Federal Reserve Bank of Dallas, could not have agreed more. He spent a good part of the late 1990s — in his book, *Myths of Rich and Poor*, and on the interview circuit — arguing that increases in nonwage benefits helped prove that average Americans were doing quite a bit better than simple wage and income data might suggest.[35]

Were cheerleaders like Cox on to something? Have more generous nonwage benefit packages offset, for average Americans, years of falling and stagnant real wages? The numbers, at first glance, appear to make a persuasive case for the Cox best-of-times contention. Employers, by century's end, *were* spending more money on employee benefits than they did back in the early 1970s, when wages were peaking. But these increasing employer outlays for fringe benefits were not actually improving the benefits employees received.[36] Companies did not spend more on benefits because they were adding new benefits or enhancing old ones. Companies spent more on benefits primarily because the most costly fringe benefit in American workplaces — health care — was costing them more to provide. Throughout the 1980s and early 1990s, companies that offered health care benefits found themselves forced to expend more and more dollars just to maintain their existing health insurance benefit programs.

Many businesses, as the 1990s progressed, simply stopped making this maintenance effort. They began shifting the cost of providing health care insurance onto the backs of their employees. After 1992, employer outlays for health insurance actually dropped.

The numbers tell the story. Throughout the 1980s and early 1990s, with health care costs rising rapidly, employer expenditures for health care benefits steadily increased, from $1.07 an hour in 1979, in inflation-adjusted dollars, to $1.35 in 1989, then to $1.52 in 1992. That 1992 figure would mark the high-water. By 1998, employers had cut back on their health care expenses significantly, despite continuing increases in the cost of health care. In 1998, employers shelled out, on average, only $1.30 an hour to provide health care benefits for their employees.[37] With fewer employer dollars going into health care benefits, fewer employees could count on health care coverage. By 2003, the Robert Wood Johnson Foundation would later report, nearly a third of Americans under sixty-five were going regularly without health insurance for months on end.[38]

With retirement benefits, the second biggest "fringe" historically available to American workers, the erosion process started even earlier. In 1979, employers expended $1.13 an hour on retirement benefits, after adjusting for inflation. They spent, ten years later, only 95 cents an hour on retirement security and even less, just 84 cents an hour, in 1998.[39]

Employers realized this fairly massive savings by fundamentally restructuring their retirement systems. Up until the 1980s, most major companies had tied their pension benefits to years of service and average final pay.[40] In these "defined benefit" plans, employees knew exactly where they stood. A typical plan, for instance, might guarantee employees who hit age sixty a pension that equaled 2 percent of their final pay for each year they had spent on the job. A sixty-year-old with thirty years could, under such a plan, retire with an annual pension that equaled 60 percent of that employee's final pay.

To finance such "defined benefits," employers and employees typically each made contributions into a single, company-wide pension fund. The dollars in the fund would be invested. If the investments did well, the company would have more than enough to meet its ongoing pension obligations. If the investments did poorly, the company still had to mail retirees their checks. In traditional defined-benefit plans, in other words, employers carried responsibility for their workers' retirement security.

In the 1980s and 1990s, a growing number of corporations decided to sidestep this responsibility. They created new-style retirement programs. No longer would management guarantee workers a specific pension benefit. Companies, instead, would guarantee only a specific annual contribution into an individual investment account for each worker. In these new "defined contribution" plans, workers would bear full responsibility for investing the dollars in their individual accounts. Those workers who invested their account dollars wisely, the theory went, would eventually be rewarded with an overflowing pot of retirement gold. But if that pot was not overflowing, employees would have to make do with whatever dollars the pot was holding.

Some employees welcomed these new "defined-contribution" plans. But many others, particularly veteran workers, felt far better off under their employer's traditional defined-benefit plan. This plan already guaranteed them, after all, a specific, significant pension once they hit retirement age. Why put that guaranteed retirement security at risk?

To be fair to all employees, those corporations that wanted to go the defined-contribution route ought to have let older workers, if they so chose, remain with the company's original defined-benefit plan. But that would have increased, considerably, the corporate outlays necessary to meet pension obligations. Companies would have had to maintain, far into the future, both defined-benefit and defined-contribution programs. Companies eager to go with defined-contributions, as a result, faced a dilemma. They could spend more on pension benefits — by giving veteran workers the right to choose the retirement plan that best fit their needs — or they could "give long-term workers a raw deal."[41]

Many corporations chose the raw deal. In 1978, defined-benefit plans covered 30 million workers. That number had slipped to 23 million by 1998. Over those same years, the number of workers in defined-*contribution* plans zoomed from under 20 to over 50 million.[42] These numbers thrilled business commentators. They saw, in the soaring numbers of new, individual defined-contribution retirement accounts, a brave new world of mass investing. Workers were taking control of their own retirement futures! In this brave new world, mere workers could become millionaires, simply by setting aside a few dollars a month in their 401(k)s.

The 401(k) would become, in the closing decades of the twentieth century, America's most celebrated fringe benefit. This simple variation on the defined-contribution model had begun, humbly enough, as a minor provision in a 1978 tax bill.[43] Workers, Congress concluded that year, might save more if they were allowed to defer taxes on their savings. The newly created 401(k) made these deferrals easy, by allowing workers to park a chunk of their paychecks in a special personal account that would grow, tax-free, until retirement time. Congress never expected the 401(k) to replace the traditional, company-guaranteed pension. The 401(k) would merely, Congress figured, supplement traditional retirement plans. But corporate America had different ideas. The new 401(k)s, companies quickly realized, gave them a means to provide retirement benefits at less than half the cost of traditional pensions.[44] Instead of maintaining costly defined-benefit plans, companies could contribute relative pittances to employee 401(k) accounts and be done with their retirement security obligations.[45]

The 401(k) retirement rush would soon be on. By 1998, over a quarter of America's 100 million private-sector workers, 27 percent, had a 401(k) at work but no pension. Only 15 percent of America's workers had what Congress originally intended, both a traditional pension and a 401(k).[46]

Those 401(k) millionaires, in the meantime, would be few and far between. The average individual 401(k) account, the National Defined Contribution Council reported in 2000, held a $49,160 balance.[47] The Employee Benefit Research Institute added, in a report released the next year, that 44 percent of individual 401(k)s held less than $10,000 and another 14 percent not more than $20,000.[48]

Some older workers, to be sure, did accumulate somewhat larger 401(k) nesteggs. Workers in their forties, the Employee Benefit Research Institute noted, averaged about $62,000 in their 401(k)s at the start of the new century. But this $62,000 hardly guaranteed an uninterrupted string of happy, secure golden years, as an analysis conducted by T. Rowe Price, a Maryland-based financial services company, rather vividly demonstrated. Suppose, this analysis noted, that a forty-five-year-old with $62,000 in a 401(k) had the wherewithal to put an additional $5,000 into this account every year until age sixty-five. Suppose that the investments in the 401(k), over these years, returned 9 percent. At age sixty-five, based on these rosy assumptions, the worker would have a 401(k) worth about $600,000. Even if this worker then limited retirement spending to $36,000 a year, T. Rowe Price concluded, the worker would still have a three out of ten chance of running out of money after twenty years of retirement.[49]

In short, the only way average forty-five-year-olds with 401(k)s could ensure their retirement security would be by planning to die early.

Most Americans, of course, don't want to have to die early to enjoy their golden years. But they may have to reconsider. So suggests research on retirement savings that New York University economist Edward Wolff released in 2002.

Wolff examined *all* the wealth, not just the 401(k) nesteggs, that working Americans age forty-seven and over had accumulated for their retirements by the end of 1998, the latest year with full statistics available. Wolff expected these older Americans to be better prepared than their counterparts in the early 1980s. After all, a sizeable proportion of them were covered by 401(k)s or some other sort of defined-contribution plan, most of these dollars in these plans were invested in stocks, and stocks, between the early 1980s and the end of 1998, had soared, up 248 percent from 1989 to 1998 alone.[50]

But Wolff did not find what he expected. Working Americans who were forty-seven to sixty-four in 1998 actually held less retirement wealth than Americans who were forty-seven to sixty-four in 1983.[51] Between 1983 and 1998, the typical American household headed by an adult nearing retirement saw an 11 percent dip in accumulated retirement wealth, from $184,200 to $171,600.[52]

To live comfortably in retirement, financial counselors often advise, a typical family needs an income flow that equals about 80 percent of the family's pre-retirement income. Relatively few American families nearing retirement at century's end, Wolff's data show, came anywhere close to meeting this 80 percent standard. In 1998, only 38.2 percent of families nearing retirement had the wherewithal, between their accumulated wealth and their expected pension and Social Security benefits, "to replace at least three-quarters of their current income at retirement."[53]

By century's end, typical American families faced less retirement security, not more, just as they faced less health security, not more. The increasing share of "total compensation" devoted to fringe benefits had not, in the closing decades of the twentieth century, offset the pinch — and pain — of stagnant real wages. Benefits, as experienced by average Americans, did not advance in the 1980s and 1990s. They eroded.

GOOD THINGS HAPPEN WHEN JOBS BECOME PLENTIFUL. With jobs abundant, lousy jobs no longer seem such deadend traps. Workers know they can always just leave a miserable job — and likely find a better job elsewhere. Employers know that, too. So they do their best to keep their jobs attractive and their workers happy. The result? Higher wages, heftier benefits, a better deal for all working people.

So what went wrong in the 1980s and 1990s?

These two decades saw an amazing string of "boom" years. For all but twenty-two months in the 1980s and all but eight months in the 1990s, the U.S. economy expanded year after year, creating jobs by the millions.[54] The nation's official unemployment rate dipped below 5 percent in 1997 and kept falling, almost sinking under 4 percent, on an annual basis, in 1999 and 2000.[55] Jobs, at century's end, would be more plentiful than they had been in over a generation. Wages, as a consequence, should have been soaring. And new and improved fringe benefits should have been raining down upon workers. But they weren't. Wage rates, even after a run-up at the end of the 1990s, still didn't match, in real purchasing power, wages from the early 1970s.[56] And benefits were shrinking, not expanding.

How could this be happening? In the past, more jobs had always meant more smiles. Why wasn't America smiling this time around? The sharpest analysts knew the answer. America wasn't smiling because jobs had changed. Over the course of the 1980s and 1990s, corporate America essentially redefined the character of work in the United States.

A job, back in the 1960s, had meant forty hours of work a week — and a reasonable expectation that you could keep working those forty hours week after week, year after year, if you did your work well. A job had meant serious side benefits as well. A decent pension to reward your years of loyalty. Enough health insurance to protect your family.

In the 1980s and 1990s, fewer and fewer jobs matched this classic, all-American workplace standard. The nation's biggest companies, the firms that had historically provided the good jobs that Americans coveted, suddenly stopped creating the jobs that prosperity was supposed to bring. Between 1980 and 1992, America's five hundred largest corporations more than doubled their assets — from $1.18 trillion to $2.68 trillion — and, at the same time, slashed their payrolls by over a quarter. The number of jobs at the nation's top five hundred companies dropped from 15.9 million in 1980 to 11.5 million in 1993.[57]

This massive job-shedding introduced a new concept, downsizing, into America's business discourse. In downsizings, jobs disappeared, the work remained. That work could be accomplished, corporate America came to realize, without the bother — and cost — of having to keep full-time staff on the payroll. And this realization helped popularize still another new approach to getting work done, outsourcing. By 1996, 86 percent of America's large companies were farming out regular work to subcontractors, up from 58 percent of companies in 1992.[58]

Much of the work that wasn't outsourced would go to "temps" or part-time workers. In 1982, only 5 million Americans worked in a temporary or part-time capacity. That total increased more than fivefold over the next fourteen years, to nearly 28 million in 1996.[59]

Temps averaged, near the end of 1996, $8.79 an hour. Full-time workers, at the same time, averaged $11.44.[60] Corporations, naturally, seized this savings opportunity. By 1999, according to American Management Association research, 70 percent of America's businesses had replaced regular full-time employees with temporary workers.[61]

Temps, by the mid 1990s, could be found doing almost any task that needed doing, from the menial to the mindful. Companies could, for instance, pick and choose from among eighty-five thousand temporary accountants. These calculating temps earned as much as 20 percent less than full-time accountants — and received few or no benefits to boot.[62]

Part-timers, like temps, also hardly ever qualified for any benefits. Simply by splitting full-time work into part-time halves, companies could virtually eliminate, not just halve, their benefit outlays.[63]

Part-timers and temporaries would together make up, at century's end, a big part of what some economists came to call the "contingent workforce," the universe of people who held "nonstandard" employment.[64] All told, in 1999, almost a quarter of all working Americans labored in the contingent workforce, nearly always at jobs that were less financially attractive than comparable full-time work.[65]

Many more workers labored in "full-time" jobs that bore scant resemblance to the full-time jobs from days of yore. These *faux* full-time positions proliferated, most noticeably, in America's fast-growing retailing sector, and nowhere more so than at America's fastest-growing retailer, the mighty empire known as Wal-Mart.

WE TEND, AS A NATION, NOT TO PAY MUCH attention to retail workers. A marginal group, we assume. Lots of teenagers. Stay-at-home moms looking for diversions. Some bored retirees, too. Just a bunch of people trying to make an extra buck or two.

Retail workers don't deserve this casual indifference. Retail workers may actually be, in twenty-first century America, our single most significant employee group. One worker in five, outside of government service, now works in retail. Teenagers? At one recent count, only 16 percent of retail workers were teens. Almost half, 44 percent, were at least 35.[66]

"In working-class and inner-city communities across the country," notes Annette Bernhardt, a University of Wisconsin analyst, "retail is in fact the main employer."[67]

And not a very good one. A half-century ago, retail employees worked regular full-time hours, the same forty-plus hours a week that factory workers averaged.[68] By the end of the 1990s, manufacturing jobs still offered, week in and week out, more than forty hours of wages. But retail workers could only count on just over thirty.[69] Retail jobs, increasingly, paid less, too. In 1973, retail workers earned three-quarters of the national average wage. In 1999, they earned just over two-thirds the national norm.[70]

Retail jobs didn't just "happen" to deteriorate. Corporate America made this slide inevitable, points out analyst Annette Bernhardt, by consciously adopting a high-tech, low-wage model for retail work, a model "defined, almost single-handedly, by one company."[71] Wal-Mart, that one company, started out in the early 1960s as an Arkansas five-and-dime. Forty years later, Wal-Mart stores would blanket the nation and employ over 1.2 million workers, more than any other private employer in the United States.[72] These workers, at the start of the twenty-first century, were helping Wal-Mart to about $7 billion a year in profits.[73]

The key to Wal-Mart's success? In business circles, Wal-Mart flacks continually trumpet their company's super-sophisticated inventory-management technology.[74] Wal-Mart's television ads, meanwhile, credit the company's good fortune to the chain's ever grinning employees, the men and women who keep Wal-Mart store shelves stocked and register lines moving. These Wal-Mart "sales associates," the company notes proudly, have plenty of reason to grin. Seven of ten, Wal-Mart boasts, work "full-time."[75] And these full-time workers qualify for a variety of benefits, even health insurance and 401(k)s.[76]

Is Wal-Mart single-handedly saving the middle class? Not exactly. Wal-Mart employees work "full-time" only because Wal-Mart defines full-time work as twenty-eight hours a week. This curious definition does carry some advantages — but only for Wal-Mart. If business is brisk at any particular retail outlet, Wal-Mart managers can have their "full-time" associates work more hours, without having to pay time-and-a-half for overtime.[77] Federal law mandates time-and-a-half for full-time workers asked to work overtime, but that mandate only kicks in above forty hours a week.

Still, doesn't Wal-Mart deserve plaudits for offering benefits to employees who work just twenty-eight hours a week? Many Wal-Mart workers might not think so. At Wal-Mart, new hires do not immediately qualify for Wal-Mart's health insurance. Huge numbers of veteran employees who do qualify simply can't afford it. That's because Wal-Mart expects workers to pay health insurance premiums, out of their own pockets, that equal about half Wal-Mart's total cost for providing health care benefits. Nationally, companies that offer health insurance recoup from employees only a quarter of the insurance cost.[78]

Early in 2002, Wal-Mart upped its employee health insurance payroll deduction rate still higher, by 30 percent.[79] With the increase, workers would have to shell out $2,600, over twelve months, for family coverage.[80] How could Wal-Mart workers averaging less than $11,000 a year for "full-time" work possibly afford such costly health insurance? Company officials had some helpful advice. They suggested that employees withdraw money from their 401(k)s to offset the hefty health insurance premium increase.

"We want to give our associates," a Wal-Mart spokesperson explained to the *Wall Street Journal,* "as much flexibility as we can."[81]

Workers who took the company's advice — and started emptying their 401(k)s to pay for health insurance — would have been taking quite a gamble with their futures. Wal-Mart has never offered a pension plan, and the employee stock ownership plan the company touts as a substitute hardly secures many golden years. Less than 2 percent of Wal-Mart associates, by the end of the 1990s, had amassed more than $50,000 worth of stock in their individual stock ownership account.[82]

Wal-Mart workers might not enjoy much retirement security, but they could at least, in the 1990s, count on a proper burial. Midway through the decade, Wal-Mart announced a special $5,000 death benefit for the company's loyal associates. A noble gesture? Not according to the *Houston Chronicle.* The real "benefits" from the deaths of Wal-Mart workers, the paper would later reveal, were going to Wal-Mart, not to worker families. Wal-Mart had secretly taken out life insurance policies, payable to the company, on well over a quarter million employees. These "dead-peasant" policies, as they're known inside insurance circles, awarded Wal-Mart $64,000 whenever any covered worker kicked the bucket. Amazingly, these secret policies didn't cost Wal-Mart much of anything. The company "borrowed money from the insurers to pay the premiums" on the policies, then wrote off the premiums on its tax returns as a business expense. The entire package, one lawyer explained to the *Houston Chronicle,* amounted to an "elaborate tax dodge."[83]

Actually, Wal-Mart had stumbled on to more than a tax dodge. The company had found a way to make even dead workers productive.

"I never dreamed that they could profit from my husband's death," the widow of one of those workers, Jane Sims, told the *Chronicle.*[84]

Sims ended up receiving not a penny of the $64,000 Wal-Mart collected after her husband's heart-attack.

The heirs of Wal-Mart founder Sam Walton, meanwhile, have fared a good bit better than the widow Jane Sims. Of the ten richest people in the world, on the *Forbes* magazine annual list published in 2002, five were Waltons. Sam Walton's sons Jim, John, and S. Robson, daughter Alice, and widow Helen together sat on a fortune worth a combined $103 billion.[85]

Jobs in modern America do pay after all, just not for the workers in them.

IN THE QUARTER CENTURY AFTER WORLD WAR II, a full-time job at General Motors — or any other major corporation in the United States — meant a passport to a better life. Over the course of the next quarter century, corporate America essentially revoked that passport. That revocation made some Americans, like the Waltons, billionaires. That same revocation left millions of other Americans deep in poverty.

Poverty in America used to be something that happened to people who didn't have jobs. That changed in the 1980s and 1990s. By century's end, the driving force behind poverty had been transformed, from unemployment to under-paid work.[86] In the 1980s and 1990s, corporate America turned low-wage jobs into low-wage careers, with immensely profitable corporate giants like Wal-Mart leading the way. Wal-Mart, as founder Sam Walton explained, always paid workers "as little as we could get by with at the time."[87]

"I was so obsessed with turning in a profit margin of 6 percent or higher that I ignored some of the basic needs of our people," Sam Walton would later write in his autobiography, "and I feel bad about it."[88]

Not bad enough to correct it. Wal-Mart's low-wages survived Sam Walton's 1992 death. At century's end, about half of Wal-Mart's workers could qualify for food stamps.[89] In 2002, a single mom with two kids could work all year at Wal-Mart, in a $7.50 an hour "full-time" job, and still come out $2,000 *under* the official poverty line.[90]

Corporate America's cheerleaders did their best, throughout the boom years, to ignore numbers like these. Ignore all that carping about "low" wages, they argued. Trickle-down really does work. America, they announced, is conquering poverty!

The official statistics partly supported the cheerleaders' claim. Poverty, as measured by the Census Bureau, did shrink in the 1990s. In 2000, only 11.3 percent of Americans lived in poverty, the lowest rate since 1973.[91] America didn't just have *fewer* poor people, the cheerleaders argued, America had the world's most fortunate poor people. Almost every poor family in the United States — 97 percent of them, to be exact — owned a color TV, the conservative Heritage Foundation noted in 1998. Two-thirds of poor families lived in air-conditioning. Seven of ten had their own cars.[92]

"Poverty, understood as the absence of food, clothing, and shelter," one top right-wing commentator, Dinesh D'Souza, argued near the boom's end, "is no longer a significant problem in America."[93]

America's poor, in other words, aren't really poor. Sure, America has the world's richest rich. But America's "poor" are rich, too. Their homes boast microwaves, VCRs, stereos, dishwashers, an array of consumer goods unimaginable to the vast bulk of the world's people. How could any poor people so rich, conservative commentators wondered, possibly be labeled poor?[94] If even the "poor" were so blessed, what more proof could be needed that inequality, in the end, benefits everybody, not just the wealthy?

Those who take this perspective seriously tend to see "poverty" as nothing more than a set of simple absolutes. A family with a roof over its head, food on the dinner table, and a television in the living room, the absolutists believe, cannot possibly be poor. But poverty, more careful analysts point out, cannot be reduced to a roof or a meal or a TV set. Poverty has always been — and will always be — a *relative* reality. If substantial numbers of the people around us own things we cannot afford to own, we will be poor, even if our families own goods that might be considered "luxuries" by families in other societies. If substantial numbers of the people around us can do things we cannot afford to do, we will be poor, even if our incomes would seem ample to families elsewhere.

Poor people are, at root, excluded people.[95] They lack the wherewithal, as one British observer puts it, "to do the things that society takes for granted."[96] What any particular society "takes for granted" will, of course, evolve and change over time. Back in 1980, for instance, American families didn't need a home computer to feel part of the society around them. Now computers help define contemporary American life. To be unable to afford one is to be excluded from the ebb and flow of the lives most Americans live.

Just how much income, in modern America, do families need to afford the basics that constitute what our society considers a decent life? We need to know the answer. People who can't afford the basics are poor. If we want to know whether *real* poverty in the United States is decreasing, we need to know how much people need to earn to be able to afford these basics. Unfortunately, the federal government's official poverty numbers, as maintained by the Census Bureau, don't help us much here.

The Census Bureau currently sets the poverty line at three times the income a family needs to afford a minimally adequate food budget.[97] If your income falls above this line, you are not officially poor. The federal government first applied this three-times rule to poverty back in 1963. At that time, the rule made sense. Various studies conducted in the early 1960s had demonstrated that average families spent a third of their incomes on food.[98] That's no longer the case. Food, at the start of the twenty-first century, only consumes one-seventh of an average family's basic expenses.[99]

The lives average families live have changed in all sorts of other ways, too. Many more women work now outside the home. Child care and other work-related expenses loom much larger in the typical family budget.[100] And housing costs currently eat up a much larger share of family income than they did in 1963.[101] The federal government's poverty calculations reflect none of these changes — and, as a result, these official calculations do not define as poor millions of Americans who cannot afford "to do the things that society takes for granted."[102]

Just how outdated have the federal government's official poverty guidelines become? Sharon Daly, a Catholic Charities official, put a flesh-and-blood face on the inadequacy of the federal poverty numbers when she testified before Congress in 2001. Daly related the story of a single mom with two young children who had come for emergency food assistance to a local Catholic Charities agency in Allentown, Pennsylvania. The mother, at the time, was working fifty hours a week, at $8.50 per hour. Under the standard federal poverty standard, Daly noted, this young mother was not "poor," not even close to poverty. Her $18,000 annual income put her more than $3,000 over the $14,630 poverty threshold for a family of three. But how much would this mother have had to earn to really meet her family's basic needs, without having to resort to a food bank and other charitable assistance? She would have needed to earn, Daly observed, at least $14.98 an hour, almost double the young woman's actual wage rate. [103]

Daly's $14.98 wage estimate came from one of the many research efforts conducted, over recent years, to calculate just how much income American families need to meet their basic needs.[104] Researchers involved in these efforts have developed, as alternatives to the official poverty line, "basic family budgets" for households of varying size in different parts of the country. In 2000, analysts from the Economic Policy Institute in Washington, D.C. reviewed nearly two dozen of these "basic family budgets."[105] Each of the budgets EPI studied defined the "basics" a little bit differently. Some included, for instance, school supplies and checking account fees. Others didn't. The budgets also covered different geographic areas. Given these differences, the bottom lines for these basic budgets, not surprisingly, varied widely. For a single parent with two kids, the monthly income required to live a minimally decent life ranged from $1,605 a month in Kentucky to $3,484.44 in the District of Columbia, in dollars inflation adjusted to 1996 levels.[106] Overall, according to the twenty-three studies, the annual income a three-person family required to live a minimally decent life averaged a bit over $29,500.[107]

How many of America's actual single-parent, two-kid families met this $29,500 standard in 1996? Not many. In that year, the median income for single-parent, two-child households stood at $16,389. The "official" poverty level that same year? Just $12,636 for a three-person family.[108] In other words, single-parent families with two kids in 1996 could have earned considerably more than twice the official poverty threshold and still not have earned enough to meet minimal levels of decency.

What about two-child families with two working parents? In 2000, Economic Policy Institute researchers created their own "basic needs budget" and keyed that budget to actual 1998 living costs, the latest figures then available, in Baltimore. The EPI researchers defined their "basics" conservatively. A two-parent, two-child family living on EPI's Baltimore "basic budget" would have no pets and no cable TV and take no vacations. The family would never go out to the movies or eat at a restaurant, not even for fast food. The family would rent a two-bedroom apartment but buy no renter's — or, for that matter, life — insurance. The family would never use a credit card or be able to save a dime for retirement, college, or emergencies.

In 1998, this basics-budget family would have needed to earn $34,732 to get by, over twice the official poverty threshold.[109] How difficult would reaching $34,732 have been in 1998? The adults in a two-parent, two-child Baltimore household could have worked, year round, at jobs that each paid $3 *above* the minimum wage and *still* not have made enough to reach the basics-budget threshold.

In 2001, researchers from Ms. Foundation for Women calculated an update on the basic cost of living for a two-parent, two-child family. Such a family, these researchers found, needed $36,835 in 2000 to be able to afford the minimal basics.[110] The adults in this family of four could have worked, year round, at jobs that paid *$3.50 above the minimum wage,* the Ms. Foundation researchers concluded, and still have not made enough to reach a minimum needs budget threshold.

In 1998, in other words, the parents in a family of four needed jobs that paid $3 an hour *over* the minimum wage to give their kids a minimally decent life. In 2000, these parents needed jobs that paid $3.50 an hour over the minimum wage to provide, at a minimal level, for their families.

At century's turn, after a generation of widening inequality, such was the progress that poor people were making.

"PEOPLE ARE REALLY HURTING," Philadelphia Mayor Ed Rendell noted early in 1999, at the height of the 1990s boom, "and no one's paying attention."[111]

The year before, the number of local families seeking housing from city shelters had jumped 17 percent. Requests for help from local food banks had leaped 22 percent.[112] Poverty in Philadelphia, official or otherwise, did not appear to be shrinking. The benefits from America's great boom years hardly seemed to be trickling down to those who needed them most.

The ideologues of inequality begged to differ. Over the course of the boom years, they trotted out one new argument after another to counter those, like Rendell, who dared suggest that trickle-down America wasn't working as advertised.

Factor in all the handouts poor people get from the government, went one standard counter, and poor families turn out to be doing just fine.[113] Households weren't getting poorer, other ideologues contended, just smaller. "If two people earning $20,000 each divorce," one of these ideologues explained, "the result is two households of $20,000 instead of one with $40,000."[114] And that hand-wringing about all those struggling families in the poorest fifth of households? Take those numbers about the bottom fifth of households with a grain of salt, advised the conservative Heritage Foundation. The poor families in the lowest-income fifth actually have fewer people in them than the richer families in any of the upper fifths.[115] Add up the actual numbers of people in each household quintile, the argument went, and you'll find many more Americans at the prospering top than the struggling bottom.[116]

Other trumpeters of America's economic triumph blasted the nation's inflation statistics. The consumer price index, one panel of conservative economists argued, has been "overstating inflation by at least a percentage point." Real wages, these economists insisted, were actually rising, not declining.[117]

In sum, people at the bottom were doing quite well, thank you, so well, in fact, that maybe America needed to become more unequal, not less. As a matter of fact, some economists were arguing by century's end, America's rich weren't prospering at the expense of the poor. America's poor were prospering at the expense of the rich!

Indeed, contended economists like Robert Rector of the Heritage Foundation, if you add up the taxes rich people pay, add into the mix the benefits that cascade down to the poor, and then adjust incomes for family size and hours worked, all those severe inequalities between household incomes at the top and bottom simply disappear, leaving the hard-working affluent with a "remarkably low" share of the nation's after-tax income.[118]

The arguments of Robert Rector-types would fill the nation's op-ed pages throughout the boom years and beyond.[119] Economists less bedazzled by the boom, from think tanks like the Economic Policy Institute and the Center for Budget and Policy Priorities, would labor valiantly to carry less ideologically loaded numbers to the public and policy makers.[120] They would eventually get some formidable help, from landmark independent research prepared by the nonpartisan Congressional Budget Office.[121] This CBO research, published initially in 2001 and updated in 2003, gave income data from the 1980s and the 1990s by far their closest scrutiny and, in the process, put to rest any and all claims that rising inequality had somehow left average and poor Americans significantly better off.

The CBO researchers defined income broadly. They included every significant category of income, from the obvious (wages and salaries, interest and dividends) to the often overlooked (retirement benefits and employer contributions to 401(k)s). They took into account categories of income that primarily benefit the affluent (capital gains and rental income) and categories that primarily benefit the middle class (employer-paid health insurance premiums). And they took special care to include all categories of income, both cash and in-kind, that primarily benefit the poor (Medicaid health insurance coverage, food stamps, school lunches, and housing and energy assistance). In sum, the CBO totaled all the resources that "low-income households have at their disposal," even the dollars they receive from the Earned Income Tax Credit, the fastest-growing source of aid for poor people in the 1990s.[122]

The researchers also adjusted incomes for differences in household size, recognizing that if two households have $20,000 in income, a one-person household with $20,000 will be better off than a four-person household with $20,000. On top of that, to guarantee that the income going to the bottom fifth of the population was not somehow understated, the CBO placed the same number of people, not the same number of households, into each of its analytic income fifths, a departure from normal Census Bureau practice.[123]

The CBO researchers, in effect, had all their statistical ducks in order. They were counting all the income Americans, rich and poor, receive. They were adjusting for changing demographics. They were comparing equally sized quintiles. And what did they find, after all these calculations? Had America's increasingly unequal economy significantly benefited poor and middle-class Americans? Not even close.

Average incomes for the poorest fifth of Americans, after adjusting for inflation and after taxes, rose only $52, or less than one tenth of 1 percent, per year between 1979 and 2000.[124] Average incomes in the middle fifth of households also rose by less than 1 percent a year, from $36,400 in 1979 to $41,900 in 2000.

Households in the top 1 percent, meanwhile, saw their after-tax incomes more than triple, from an inflation-adjusted $286,300 in 1979 to $862,700 in 2000.

The significance of the CBO numbers, the best statistical evidence available, could not be any clearer. *Some* Americans were benefiting appreciably from America's increasingly unequal economic order. But precious few of these *some* lived in average- or low-income households.

CORPORATE AMERICA'S CHEERLEADERS, try as they might, have not been able to get the nation's income data to cooperate. They have sliced the data. They have diced the data. But the data have still not offered up the numbers the cheerleaders so desperately covet, the evidence, the proof, that all Americans do better whenever rich people get richer.

Some cheerleaders, in response, have essentially given up searching for evidence. Instead, they scapegoat. The United States, they argue, does not have growing inequality. The United States has growing immigration. Immigrants, the scapegoaters contend, are making America's economy look bad.

"I would challenge anybody to find a middle-class family in this region whose economic condition has declined," Stephen Kagann, the chief economist to New York Governor George Pataki, huffed after news reports in 2001 revealed that typical New York family incomes had dropped $2,876 over the course of the 1990s. "Nobody's real income goes down during periods of prosperity."[125]

So how could Kagann account for his state's declining median family incomes? Middle-class people had moved out of New York in the early 1990s, Kagann asserted, and immigrants, making less, had moved in.

"That by itself would bring the median down," Kagann told the *New York Times.* "But that does not mean that a middle-class person is less well-off than they were in 1990. That would simply be untrue."[126]

Kagann's protestations echoed themes that other economists had been circulating for several years.

America's "ever-higher immigration rates" are contributing mightily to the nation's "increasing income disparity," W. Michael Cox, the chief economist at the Federal Reserve Bank of Dallas, and Richard Alm, his frequent co-author, had asserted in an analysis published in 2000. Immigrants, Cox and Alm noted, constitute a significant presence in each of the nation's seven most unequal states. These unequal states — New York, Arizona, New Mexico, Louisiana, California, Rhode Island and Texas — average about 13 percent foreign-born. In the nation's seven least unequal states, immigrants average only 3.8 percent of the population.[127]

If you adjust America's wage data to account for immigration, chimed in American University economist Robert Lerman, you find that the nation's wage-earners did just peachy in the 1980s and 1990s. Without adjusting for immigration, Lerman maintained, the real wages of workers in the United States show a 1 percent drop from 1979 to 1999. After adjusting for immigration — by including the 1979 home-country incomes of immigrants who worked in the United States in 1999 — real wages show a 6 percent increase.[128]

Poor immigrants, in short, make the United States *look* poor. But both immigrants and the United States overall, the cheerleaders argue, are actually doing quite well economically.

"Let us say someone earning $2,000 per year in Guatemala in 1980 immigrates to the U.S.," *Forbes* magazine conjectured in 1999. "If this person ends up in a U.S. job that pays $10,000 per year, he would certainly be richer. However, since $10,000 is in the poverty range for the U.S., the number would show up in U.S. statistics as both an increase in the poverty rate and earnings inequality."[129]

The message to economists who worried about poverty and inequality: Wise up, the country's fine.

"If economists could concentrate more on simply doing economics better," *Forbes* concluded, "we could all relax and simply enjoy the fruits of the market economy."[130]

In the 1980s and 1990s, of course, those market economy fruits were most likely picked by low-wage immigrant workers. By the end of the 1990s, about 30 million foreign-born individuals lived in the United States, with over a million more arriving each year.[131]

These immigrants did little relaxing. They worked, nearly every available hour they could. In Maryland's Montgomery County, just outside the nation's capital, one immigrant from Latin America told an interviewer he was working "part-time." How many hours a week, the interviewer wanted to know, was the immigrant working?

"About sixty," came the reply

Sixty? How could you be "part-time," the confused interviewer asked, and be working sixty hours a week? The worker couldn't understand the confusion. He considered himself a part-time worker. After all, he was still looking for more work.[132]

A continent away, in California, millions of immigrant workers assembled computer chips, built houses, and served meals for wages so low that few could afford, on their own, a roof over their heads. In booming San Jose, immigrants lived as many as twenty-six men to a house.[133]

Were these low-wage immigrants, just by their presence, making the United States appear more unequal than the nation really was? Corporate America's cheerleaders certainly nurtured that claim. More perceptive observers disagreed. What was making America appear — and be — more unequal, they explained, was not the presence of immigrants, but their exploitation. America's low-wage immigrants, these observers noted, were creating wealth — and not getting much of it back.

This exploitation of immigrant labor gives the United States a distinct competitive advantage, as even some conservative analysts acknowledge.

"It's a form of reverse foreign aid," notes the Cato Institute's Stephen Moore. "We give less than $20 billion in direct aid to Third World nations and we get back $30 billion a year in capital assets."[134]

These "assets," explains journalist Greg Palast, are immigrants, "workers raised, fed, inoculated and educated by poorer countries, then shipped at the beginning of their productive lives" to the United States, where they add enormous value to corporate America's bottom line.[135] At little cost. Unskilled immigrant workers, particularly those without proper papers, can be worked hard and paid little. Workers inside the United States illegally, after all, can hardly stand up and object to ill-treatment. They might as well write up their own deportation orders.

Skilled immigrant labor may be, for corporate America, an even better deal. By 1997, skilled immigrants made up 21 percent of the computer scientists in the United States and 21 percent of the nation's chemical engineers.[136] These immigrant professionals arrived in the United States already thoroughly trained — on someone else's dime.

"The habit of siphoning off other countries' high-skilled workers," Palast observes, "permits America's monied classes to shirk the costly burden of educating America's own underclass."[137]

Corporate America has, in effect, created a system that works with a perverse brilliance.

"Bangalore-born programmers in Silicon Valley," Palast notes, "design numberless cash registers for fast-food restaurants so they can be operated by illiterate Texans."[138]

Not exactly the American dream.

OUR REAL AMERICAN DREAM, of course, revolves much more around homeownership than any particular job. What matters most, Americans agree, is having a home to call your own, a place to raise a family — and build equity for the future. In the booming 1990s, almost everybody in the United States, except perhaps illiterate Texans, seemed to be able to realize this homeownership dream. Homeownership rates set records throughout the decade, to the delight of America's economic pom-pom squads. Weren't these rates undeniable proof, they argued, that wealth at the top was indeed trickling down? Average Americans must be getting wealthier. How else could they afford to buy so many homes of their own?

How else? Simple. In the 1990s, America's real estate industry changed the homeownership rules.

Mortgage lenders in the United States, up until the 1990s, had always insisted that first-time homebuyers must come up with a substantial downpayment before any home loan would be advanced. Saving enough to afford a downpayment, in the years after World War II, became a rite of passage for

American families. Not every young family, to be sure, made enough to meet the real estate industry's stiff downpayment requirements, but enough could, in America's postwar decades, to keep the lending pump primed.

By the mid 1990s, the lending world had changed. After a generation of falling real wages, few young families were now making enough to prime the mortgage pump. Most families starting out could not come close to affording, no matter how hard they scrimped and saved, the substantial downpayments that lenders had traditionally insisted upon.

What did the lenders do? They stopped insisting. Can't afford 15 percent down? How about 5 percent?

In 1989, about 93 percent of mortgages required downpayments that ran *above* 10 percent of the purchase price. Ten years later, over 50 percent of mortgages went to families that put down, as their downpayment, *less* than 10 percent.[139] The typical downpayment, about 15 percent in the mid 1980s, slid to 5 percent in the late 1990s.[140] Many young couples couldn't even afford that. Lenders, ever considerate, ratcheted down the required downpayment still another notch, to 3 percent. Early in the new century, Fannie Mae, the giant mortgage investor, made the predictable final leap. To its standard loan product line, Fannie Mae added a "zero down" mortgage.[141]

These shrinking downpayment requirements meant that more young working families could "afford" to buy their own homes. But lower downpayments also meant that young working families, once they had mortgage in hand, would face crushingly high monthly payments. "A zero-down mortgage," as one consumer reporter warned prospective homebuyers, "is going to cost you more in payments every month, not just in higher principal and interest charges, but in mortgage-insurance fees as well."[142]

Younger families had no choice. They took whatever mortgages they could get. They gained, in exchange, a financial burden they could not sustain.

A prudent family, Fannie Mae had once traditionally suggested, ought not spend more than 25 to 28 percent of its gross income on housing. By the end of the 1990s, more and more families found themselves routinely outspending that standard, spending so much on housing, scholars from the University of Texas and Harvard reported, that they were "placing their financial security in jeopardy."[143] By century's end, according to the 2000 Census, nearly a third of American homeowners — 31.2 percent — were paying more than a quarter of their incomes on housing.[144]

These homeowners, to make matters worse, were gaining less economic security for their housing investment dollars. Homeownership, in years past, had always carried families up the economic ladder.[145] A family might start out with an $85,000 mortgage on a $100,000 home. A decade later, that family might still owe $50,000 on the mortgage, but the value of the home might have appreciated to $150,000. The fortunate family now held $100,000 in home "equity," and this equity, as the family continued to pay down the mortgage, would only swell higher, giving the family a long leg up on lifetime financial security. By the end of the 1990s, home ownership no longer delivered this automatic security. Homes were still appreciating in value, but average families were no longer building significant equity. Families under age 45, concluded a study by Freddie Mac, the nation's top housing finance enterprise, held 14 percent less equity in their homes in 1999 than families under 45 had held a decade earlier.[146]

"Despite a booming economy," observed Stephen Brobeck, the executive director of the Consumer Federation, the sponsor of the Freddie Mac study, "many middle-class families have built no wealth."[147]

Why wasn't home ownership helping families build wealth?

In the 1990s, more and more families simply couldn't afford to sit back and let their homes "build wealth." With incomes stagnating, families needed more cash to pay their bills. They took that cash from their homes — by "leveraging up," borrowing against their home value via home-equity loans and lines of credit. In 1981, only 4 percent of outstanding home mortgage debt came from second mortgages. By 1991 — after the introduction and proliferation of home-equity loans and lines of credit — the second mortgage share of total mortgage debt had tripled.[148]

Overall, between 1983 and 1998, mortgage debt nearly doubled, from 21 percent of the value of homeowner property to 37 percent.[149] By the turn of the century, warned the Consumer Federation's Stephen Brobeck, far too many homeowners were "standing on the edge." They might be able to make their payments, he explained, "but if anything goes wrong — job loss, illness, divorce — they could end up in bankruptcy and possibly lose their house."[150]

Many did. Between the early 1980s and the end of the 1990s, the number of homeowning Americans in bankruptcy proceedings more than quadrupled.[151]

EVERY THREE YEARS, THE FEDERAL RESERVE conducts in-depth survey research on the financial well-being of American consumers. In early 2000, Fed officials released the data from their 1998 survey research. The average American family's consumer debt, the Fed reported, had increased by almost $10,000 in just three years.[152]

In Washington, Congress and the White House took these new debt numbers in stride. Home equity down? Consumer debt up? No need, our movers and shakers believed, to fret. Average Americans, despite shrinking home equity, were still building brighter financial futures anyway — in the stock market.

Over the course of the 1980s and 1990s, the years of Wall Street's greatest bull market ever, a number of average Americans did indeed parlay stocks into brighter financial futures for their families, just as some average Americans, over those same years, parlayed some good fortune at casino blackjack tables into brighter financial futures. But most Americans, the vast majority of Americans, saw no appreciable gains from the great bull market that opened on Friday, August 13, 1982 and ran into 2000. Many American families may have owned stock by century's end, but few families owned much.[153] Among America's middle-income families, 52.1 percent owned shares of stock in 2001. This 52.1 percent's most typical families held just $15,000 worth of shares.[154]

The real rewards from stock market wheeling and dealing had gone, by century's end, to a narrow band of affluent households, as IRS data released in 2001 showed plainly. In 1997, the latest year with full stats then available, Americans who made at least $1 million — about one-tenth of 1 percent of the nation's taxpayers — made more money buying and selling stock than all other Americans combined. Overall, Americans made over 61 million stock market transactions in 1997, according to the IRS. All this buying and selling generated net gains of $136.4 billion. Over half this enormous trading profit, 54 percent, went to households that reported incomes of at least $1 million.[155]

In that same year, families that earned under $100,000 made up 89 percent of the taxpaying public. These under-$100,000 households received just 11 percent of all gains from the year's stock market trading.[156]

And whose fault was that? Why average Americans, of course, at least according to Wall Street. American families, Wall Streeters lamented right before the stock market bubble started bursting in 2000, were making a big mistake. They were not rushing fast enough into the market. Newspaper, television, and radio analysts urged those Americans not yet "in the market" to get with it. They detailed, with example after example, the dollars flowing to those brave enough to take the market plunge. A "stone-broke" family in mid 1989, as commentator Scott Burns pointed out, could have amassed a $28,000 nest egg, in just nine years, simply by investing $100 a month in common stocks.[157]

"At least half the families in America," Burns concluded, have "missed the easiest ticket to wealth in two generations."[158]

But lamentations like these did some missing of their own. They missed the one inconvenient reality — the absence of spare cash — that the great majority of American families could never forget. Most families not yet "in the market" couldn't afford to be "in the market." They couldn't afford to set aside $100 a month in stocks. They had nothing close to the initial stake necessary to make real money in stocks.

"If you had put $10,000 in the stock market in 1983, you could have more than $110,000 today," as journalist Holly Sklar noted in 1999. "Unfortunately, most Americans didn't have the $10,000 to invest then, and they don't have it today."[159]

And those struggling Americans who did their best to raise that $10,000, those who, by the late 1990s, finally did have a significant stake to invest, these struggling Americans, as things turned out, would have been better off keeping their money in a bank savings account. *Money* magazine, in 2002, looked back upon Wall Street's previous four years, and tried to calculate just how well average Americans had actually fared with their stock market investments. Not too well at all, *Money* concluded. Average mutual fund investors, for the four years, had earned just 1 percent a year on their investments.[160]

Main Street, corporate cheerleaders enthused in the 1990s, was going Wall Street. Wall Street, unfortunately, turned out to be a dead-end.

IN THE 1990S, MOST AMERICANS did not make a killing in the stock market. So what *did* most Americans get out of the boom years?

Not much.

In 2001, typical families in the poorest quarter of American families earned $19,700 in income. These families had all of $1,100 to their names, after subtracting everything they owed from everything they owned. This $1,100, their "net worth," amounted to an increase of just $500 over what typical families in America's poorest quarter were worth in 1992, after adjusting for inflation, according to Federal Reserve Board data.[161]

Typical families in the second quarter of America's wealth distribution, that quarter just below the national average, took home $34,900 in 2001. These families ended that year worth $40,800, a per family increase of $11,800 over 1992. Should we be impressed by this $11,800 increase? If these families had been able to put their 1992 net worths in a savings account paying a little over 4 percent annual interest, they would have ended up 2001 wealthier than they actually did.

Typical families in the next quarter up, the quarter just above the national average, earned $50,900 in 2001. These families averaged $156,100 in net worth that year, a $47,700 increase over 1992. But much of that increase came from the appreciation of homes and other assets these families already owned. Between 1998 and 2001, typical families in this third quarter actually lost money with their stock market investments.[162]

For average Americans, the national data make plain, the boom years brought no miraculous gains.

But maybe we have this all wrong.

Inequality, we have argued, has not delivered for average Americans. These Americans had been promised that great days would surely multiply if the nation only did more to help rich people become richer. With more dollars in rich people's pockets, the promise went, the economy would expand, prosperity would settle down upon the land, and average Americans would end up, if not rich themselves, significantly better off than they had ever been before.

Some of this promised sequence did, in fact, unfold. The economy did indeed expand, throughout the 1980s and 1990s, as the rich became richer. But that expansion left most average Americans, the national stats make abundantly clear, only marginally better off.

But why should our focus be *national*? Wealth in the boom years, after all, did not concentrate uniformly all across the nation. Great fortunes accumulated much more rapidly in some parts of the United States than others. If we

want to explore whether helping rich people become richer does indeed benefit average people, don't we need to focus our attention on those areas of the
country where rich people became the richest?

After all, if the ideologues on inequality are correct, if growing the fortunes
of rich people does indeed grow good times for everybody, then those places
where great fortunes are growing the fastest ought to be the places where average people are prospering the most exuberantly.

Fair enough. Let's look beyond the *national* numbers. Let's zero in on those
places where rich people have accumulated wealth most impressively. In these
places, according to greed economics, we should find average families thriving,
not just surviving.

And where exactly should we look to find all these happy campers? We have
an obvious choice. Throughout the 1980s and 1990s, one state consistently
grew more fortunes than any other. This one state became, in the process, more
thoroughly unequal than any other — became, by century's end, a virtual heav-
en on earth for the wealthy.

And average people? How did they fare, economically, in this inequality
heaven? How did they fare, in California?

OVER THE LAST QUARTER OF THE TWENTIETH CENTURY, American computers
and American entertainment thoroughly dominated global markets. Those
computers and that entertainment came, overwhelmingly, from California, the
nation's most populous state. Out of Southern California came television,
movies, and music. Out of Northern California came the computers and semi-
conductors that, midway through the 1990s, accounted for nearly half of
America's industrial growth.[163] By 1997, the seven thousand or so electronics
and software companies around Silicon Valley — the corridor south of San
Francisco — were valued at nearly half a trillion dollars.[164] Never before, proclaimed the Valley's biggest boosters, had so much wealth been created in such
a short time.[165]

"You've got the biggest wealth creation machine," exclaimed one Menlo
Park investment expert, "man has ever seen."[166]

And all this wealth filled Santa Clara County, Silicon Valley's hometown
jurisdiction, with more rich people in one place than America had ever seen. In
1996 alone, the county "minted" sixty-two new millionaires every day.[167] In
1999, some sixty-five thousand county households, about 11 percent of the
Santa Clara total, were worth more than $1 million, without even having to
count the value of their homes.[168] At least thirteen local households, that same
year, could claim billionaire status.[169]

Statewide, incomes for the wealthiest Californians soared in the years before
century's end. Between 1993 and 1997, after taking inflation into account, the
state's richest 1 percent saw their incomes, on average, leap over 57 percent,
from $537,168 to $844,991. The taxpayers in this lofty 1 percent, a California

Budget Project report noted in 2000, were reporting more income than the entire bottom 60 percent of state taxpayers.[170]

In no other state, outside California, would wealthy people be doing so well.

That should have been good news for California's average-income people, according to trickle-down economic doctrine. Average Californians ought to have been following rich Californians straight up the economic ladder. They weren't. In the 1990s, the incomes of average four-person families in California actually lost purchasing power, $1,069 in all, after adjusting for inflation.[171] Between 1989 and 1999, the number of Californians living in *official* poverty increased, from 24 to nearly 29 percent.[172]

Over the longer timeframe, taking into account both the 1980s and the 1990s, the same trend line appeared. The more affluent Californians, those in the top fifth of the state's families, saw their incomes rise, after inflation, 49 percent between the end of the 1970s and the end of the 1990s. The middle fifth of California families, meanwhile, saw their incomes drop 3 percent — $1,538 in purchasing power — over the same period.[173]

By century's end, fewer, not more, average Californians could afford the basics of middle-class life.

"Seven million Californians have no medical insurance — not just the greatest number but the highest percentage of medically uninsured of any state," Harold Meyerson, a veteran political observer, pointed out in 2000. In Los Angeles, he added, "an entire city council district — that's a quarter-million people — could comprise Angelenos who live, all quite illegally, in family-home garages."[174]

Further north, in booming Silicon Valley, life certainly appeared more pleasant, at least by conventional measures. Jobs abounded in Santa Clara County, and these jobs paid an amazing $18,000 more, on average, than jobs nationally.[175] Overall, about a third of Santa Clara households made between $75,000 and $150,000, more than double the national norm.[176] Silicon Valley "seemed to have it all." The area, by century's end, ranked first nationally for annual spending on home furnishings, third nationally on travel expenditures, and fifth nationally in dining out. But most Santa Clarans, even those with incomes that doubled the national average, did not share in this good life. Silicon Valley, the San Jose *Mercury News* would report in 1999, "is becoming a place where only the top tier can live comfortably."[177]

The Silicon Valley squeeze started with the most basic of middle-class basics, housing. Nationally, in 1998, the cost of a typical American home ran about three times the income of a typical American family. In Santa Clara County, the median home price — $364,740 in 1998 — more than quintupled the local median income. Fewer than 30 percent of Santa Clara households could afford to buy a typical county home.[178] And those who could didn't get much home for their money. One tiny ranchette in West San Jose, an undistinguished property with a small dirt backyard and no central air, listed for $508,000 and sold for over $650,000 after the owners received thirty-seven offers.[179]

Journalist Karen Breslau, a writer for *Newsweek* and *Wired*, considered herself thoroughly middle class, until she moved to Silicon Valley in 1998.

"In Silicon Valley, I am a have-not," she would write a year and a half later. "It seems no amount of saving, of macaroni-and-cheese eating, of settling for vinyl instead of Italian tile can put me within a comma and three zeros of owning a house here. My friends suffer from the same shelter psychosis, that pervasive distress experienced by upper-middle-class migrants who on the cusp of middle age suddenly find themselves unable to afford even the cheesiest 'starter home.'"[180]

Silicon Valley rents did their share of squeezing, too. If you worked as a pharmacy technician, a tax preparer, a dietitian, an elementary school teacher, or an insurance underwriter, the San Jose *Mercury News* pointed out in 1999, you couldn't afford the rent on an average Santa Clara County two-bedroom apartment. If you labored as a local department store sales clerk, the paper added, you "would have to work more than 112 hours per week, every week" to afford a decent apartment.[181]

By the late 1990s, runaway housing costs had helped turn Silicon Valley into the nation's most expensive place to live.[182] That cost of living — 37 percent higher than the national average — shoved most local families onto a treadmill that never seemed to stop.

"I always thought that making over $100,000 meant that you wouldn't have to worry about anything," noted one area resident, Randy Wigginton, a thirty-nine-year-old San Jose software consultant with two kids. "I thought you'd light cigars with $100 bills. I found out it allows you to go to the grocery store."[183]

How did Silicon Valley families keep up? By going into the red. By 1998, Santa Clara County ranked number one nationally in average household debt.[184] Nearly 90 percent of county families owed money, above and beyond whatever mortgage debt they may have carried. Their average debt load: $12,237.[185]

In Silicon Valley, at the turn of the century, you either left the area or did whatever you had to do to keep from falling off the treadmill. One evening in 2000, long after midnight, a *New York Times* reporter found herself among a dozen locals riding Santa Clara County's No. 22 bus. The passengers, mostly workers with full-time jobs, rode that bus all evening long, just as they rode it every evening. They would nap along the way, waking up every two hours, when the bus had to be emptied between roundtrips. For someone trying to make ends meet in Silicon Valley, the "rent" on the No. 22 couldn't be beat. Only $3 for a ticket good all day — and night.[186]

THROUGHOUT THE 1980S AND 1990S, inside California and outside California, average Americans did their worst where rich people did their best.[187] In those places where magnificent fortunes took root for a few, frustrations took their toll on the many.

Places like Fairfax County, the pricey Virginia suburb outside Washington, D.C.

In the 1990s, no county in the entire United States boomed any better than Fairfax County, home to hundreds of high-tech fortunes in telecom and cyberspace. By 2000, the county median household income had topped $90,000.[188] In Fairfax County's trendy malls, shoppers could find $2,800 wine racks and $12,000 ovens.[189] The proud parents at one local high school, to send the Class of 2000 off in style, threw a $60,000, all-night graduation party. They handed out, as door prizes, televisions and stereos.[190]

Nearly a million people lived amid this gilded Fairfax County prosperity. But only a fortunate few shared in it. Lisa and Steve Pagliocchini and their two young children were not among them. Lisa and Steve together earned $90,000, well over the national average. But Lisa and Steve didn't feel above average. In Fairfax County, they felt trapped.

"I'm at war with myself half the time," Lisa told a local reporter in 2001. "There are times when I would love to be a home mom, but we can't afford it. It would be tight, very tight."[191]

Life would be tight even *with* Lisa working. She and Steve drove a "well-worn minivan" and an "aging Chevy Blazer." They scoured "discount stores for bargain detergent and consignment shops for $1.50 jeans." They rose before dawn to get their daughter to a free preschool. Still, they found themselves considerably better off than most young Fairfax County families. Thanks to an inheritance, Steve and Lisa had manageable mortgage payments, only $1,280 a month. That left them enough extra cash to add a deck to their home and drive into the mountains for hiking vacations.[192] But Steve and Lisa, even with that inheritance, didn't live a middle class life nearly as comfortable as the life that Lisa's parents had enjoyed.

Lisa's folks had raised their family only a few blocks from where Lisa was now raising hers — in a bigger house. Lisa's dad, a federal employee, had been able to buy and pay off that house on just his salary alone. Lisa's parents didn't seem to need a second income. They "always took nice vacations" anyway, "traveling throughout North America."

Lisa could not provide those sorts of experiences for her children. She ended the boom years wondering what she and Steve had done wrong. They hadn't been "wild spenders." They had worked hard. So why was middle-class life in Fairfax County so much sweeter for her parents? How could her parents, on one public employee salary, afford a lifestyle that Lisa and her family, on two full-time salaries, couldn't come close to matching?

LISA PAGLIOCCHINI IN THE 1990s and her parents in the 1960s raised families in decades that were, on one level, amazingly alike. Both decades saw record-breaking economic expansions. The 1960s boom started in February 1961 and didn't end until over a hundred months later, in December 1969.[193] The American economy had never before expanded for so many consecutive months. This 1960s record would not be broken for a generation, not until the boom of the 1990s opened in March 1991 and marched along, triumphantly, for ten full years.

Two decades, two booms. In both decades, gross domestic product soared. In both decades, jobless levels sank. But the two decades would not be identical. In only one of them — the 1960s — would average Americans prosper.

Lisa Pagliocchini's parents, in the 1960s, lived through a middle-income golden age. The median family income in this golden age, the income earned by the typical American family, zoomed 39.7 percent over the course of the decade, *after* taking inflation into account.[194] In the 1990s boom, by contrast, American median family income inched ahead, after inflation, just 3.9 percent.[195]

In the 1960s, wages and salaries rose substantially across the occupational landscape. In the 1990s, jobs that used to help people climb up the economic ladder didn't even pay enough to outpace increases in the cost of living. Teachers, airline pilots, and clergy all lost ground in the 1990s. Over the course of the decade, overall, about one fifth of America's most common occupations "saw wages decline after adjusting for inflation."[196] Most other occupations barely held their own. Real-estate brokers, registered nurses, and construction workers saw pay hikes that amounted, after inflation, to less than 1 percent a year.[197]

In the 1960s, poor people did just as well as their middle-income neighbors. The official poverty rate, 21.9 percent in 1961, dropped more than 40 percent over the next seven years, to 12.8 percent.[198] The 1990s boom gave poor people no such hefty helping hand. The official poverty rate dropped only marginally in the 1990s, from over 13 percent at the start of the decade to a bit under 12 percent in 2000.[199]

Throughout the 1960s, in other words, average Americans raced ahead economically. In the 1990s, average Americans made no significant progress whatsoever.

How could that be? How could average people benefit so substantially from 1960s prosperity and benefit so meagerly from the prosperous 1990s? Distribution, in the end, would make the difference. In the 1960s, most all the new wealth created would be shared across the economic spectrum. In the 1990s, by contrast, the benefits from the booming economy would not be shared. The goodies from the good times would concentrate, overwhelmingly, in the pockets of people at the top.

The 1960s and the 1990s actually help tell a broader story. Each decade climaxed an era.

The first of these eras began right after World War II and lasted into the early 1970s. Throughout this quarter century, the gains from America's growing economy swelled the wallets and pocketbooks of low- and middle-income Americans.

Between 1947 and 1973, a family at what researchers call the twentieth percentile — that is, a family at the top of the poorest fifth of American families

— saw its income just about double, from $10,270 to $20,214, in dollars infla-tion-adjusted to 1996 levels.[200]

During these years, America's lowest-income families, the bottom fifth of income-earners, increased their total share of America's national income by 10 percent.[201]

Middle-income Americans, in this first quarter century after World War II, would do even better. Families at the fortieth percentile — the bottom of the middle class — saw their incomes *more* than double, from $16,572 to $33,355. So did families at the sixtieth percentile, the top of the middle class. Their incomes leaped from $22,472 to $46,538.[202]

And wealthy families? Between 1947 and 1973, affluent family incomes rose, too, but not as rapidly as did the incomes of poor and middle-class fam-ilies. By 1973, the total share of the nation's income pulled in by wealthy peo-ple had actually fallen. In that year, the most affluent 5 percent of American families took in 11 percent less of the nation's income than they did in 1947.[203]

The 1990s climaxed a substantially different era. In this second era, the years from the mid 1970s through the end of the century, the gains generated by America's growing economy did not enrich Americans up and down the eco-nomic spectrum. These gains concentrated — at the top. Over the first half of this second era, between 1977 and 1990, nearly 80 percent of all the nation's income gains, according to one estimate, "fell into the pockets of the top 1 per-cent of families."[204] America's richest 1 percent received 62 percent of all new wealth created between 1983 and 1989 and an even greater share, 68 percent, of the wealth created between 1989 and 1992. [205]

"If these trends continue," NYU economist Edward Wolff predicted mid-way through the 1990s, "the super rich will pull ahead of other Americans at an even faster pace in the 1990s than they did in the 1980s."[206]

The super rich would essentially do just that. Between 1992 and 2001, the households in America's richest 1 percent increased their share of the nation's income by 71 percent.[207] In 2001, the Census Bureau would report, the share of the nation's income going to the poorest fifth of Americans and the middle fifth of Americans dropped to the lowest levels ever recorded.[208]

So what happened to Lisa Pagliocchini's shot at the American dream? In the prosperous 1990s, why couldn't she and her husband, with two incomes, bring their family the same middle-class comforts that Lisa's parents, with just one income, had been able to bring theirs? The two families simply lived in differ-ent times. In the era Lisa's parents enjoyed, the era climaxed by the 1960s, aver-age Americans shared in their nation's prosperity. In the era that saw Lisa start her family, gains concentrated at the top. That considerable share of the nation's prosperity that went to Lisa's parents in the 1960s — and millions of middle-income people like them —went, in the 1990s, to Lisa's bosses.

In 1968, the best-paid boss in the entire United States, General Motors chief executive James Roche, made 142 times the pay of America's average worker. Thirty years later, America's best-paid boss, Disney CEO Michael

Eisner, took home twenty-five thousand times more than the average American worker.[209]

The corporate executives who employed Lisa's generation, the financiers who bankrolled these executives, the corporate raiders who played footsie with the financiers — all these movers and shakers captured, as the last quarter of the twentieth century unfolded, an ever greater share of the wealth that working Americans created. They turned the middle-class golden age of the 1960s into a 1990s gilded age that only the affluent could truly enjoy.

Average Americans, back in the 1960s, would never have imagined that this sort of turnaround could ever take place, not in the United States of America. In their America, the fruits of prosperity seemed to be more widely shared each and every year. The days when elites could hoard America's rewards, they believed, had passed and could never return, not in a society as democratic, as just, as sensible as theirs. Only depraved civilizations let great wealth concentrate at the top.

Even Mr. Spock said so. In 1969, in one of the last original *Star Trek* episodes, America's most popular pop philosopher calmly explained why life on the planet Ardana was most certainly headed down the wrong path. On Ardana, *Star Trek* viewers had learned, rulers lived amid luxury in a cloud city while miners toiled in wretchedness below.

"This troubled planet is a place of the most violent contrasts," Mr. Spock noted. "Those that receive the rewards are totally separate from those who shoulder the burdens. It is not a wise leadership."[210]

Millions of 1969 viewers no doubt gave Mr. Spock's analysis a knowing nod. Rewards, they agreed, ought to be shared. Nothing good could come from any society where they weren't. So assumed average Americans in the 1960s. They were right.

CHARITY AND COMPASSION

IN COLUMBUS, OHIO, at the start of the twenty-first century, the richest man in town lived a relentlessly paranoid life. Billionaire Leslie Wexner, a retail king, would not set foot off his massive estate — nearly fifty thousand square feet of living space — without his trusted bodyguards. And he wouldn't set foot into any local event that sought his presence until dogs had first had a chance to sniff the grounds for bombs.[1]

And what did the good people of Columbus feel about this peculiar behavior? No big deal, a lifelong local told *Worth* magazine. Down through the years, Wexner had been, "so charitable," on everything from education to medical research, that people essentially didn't care how he behaved. Wexner wasn't just the richest man in town, he was the most generous, too, "a wonderful plum for the city."[2]

Societies where great fortunes grow, the admirers of affluence have always argued, will regularly produce "plums" like Leslie Wexner, millionaires and billionaires eager to enrich their communities with an unending stream of philanthropic dollars. The greater the fortunes, the greater the philanthropy.

And who could dispute that?

Certainly not the zookeepers of San Diego. By century's end, Joan Kroc, the widow who inherited the original McDonald's fortune, had given her local zoo and assorted other good works nearly a quarter billion dollars.[3]

Certainly not literacy activists in Mississippi. Early in 2000, they had corralled the "largest private donation ever to promote literacy," a $100 million gift from former Netscape CEO James Barksdale and wife Sally.[4]

And certainly not the medical educators at UCLA. Movie magnate David Geffen awarded them $200 million in 2002, the biggest single gift ever made to an American medical school.[5]

Big fortunes, big gifts. In our contemporary United States, land of the world's most king-sized fortunes, nearly every community seems to be able to claim a plum or two.

Louisville, for instance, claims Owsley Brown Frazier, a billionaire who made his fortune off Jack Daniel's and Southern Comfort, then poured millions into local health care, museums, and education.[6]

"The guy is just awesome," smiles a former mayor of Frazier's fair city, Jerry Abramson. "Louisville is a far better community because of his involvement."[7]

Want awesome? How about Warren Buffet, the world's second-richest man. Buffet has indicated that his massive fortune in equities will, after he and his wife pass on, all be given away.[8] Bill Gates, the world's richest man, has done Buffet one better. He has let it be known that most of his immense fortune, as much as 95 percent, will be given away *before* he dies.[9] The Bill and Melinda Gates Foundation, had already become, by 2002, the "wealthiest philanthropic organization in the world," annually spending more money fighting malaria and other world health problems than the government of the United States.[10] Gates has repeatedly described himself as just "a steward of his immense wealth" and has noted, just as frequently, "what a great privilege" it will be to meet his steward's responsibility and return that wealth "to society."[11]

In the meantime, of course, Gates and other awesomely affluent people will continue to accumulate. The more they amass, the more they will be able to give away, as Steve Kirsch, an aspiring Silicon Valley billionaire, explained to an inquiring reporter in 1999.

"It would be fun to be a billionaire," Kirsch acknowledged, but the ultimate benefit of amassing a billion, he quickly added, "would be the ability to pass more money on to charity."[12]

The more money people like Steve Kirsch have, people like Steve Kirsch hope we understand, the better off the rest of us will be.

AMERICANS TODAY, BY AND LARGE, have come to see great and generous philanthropy as something that just happens — naturally — whenever wealth concentrates. The wealthy make money. The wealthy, sooner or later, give that money away. So why get alarmed about great fortunes? Within every great fortune sits a cash cow for charity.

Our republic's earliest citizens, by contrast, found great fortunes distinctly alarming. Any concentrations of wealth left unchecked, they believed, would doom their young democracy to the same aristocratic decadence they had taken up arms against the British to reject. In the early 1800s, these widely held apprehensions about grand concentrations of wealth had prosperous men of commerce — and their fledgling fortunes — on the defensive. In New England, by the 1830s, grand new textile mills had generated "an embarrassment of riches" for Boston's wealthiest families, note two scholars of the era, Peter Hall and George Marcus. These wealthy families "became increasingly preoccupied" with justifying their good fortune. They needed, somehow, to square "the fact of possession" with America's "dominant egalitarian and democratic values."[13]

Boston's wealthy "Brahmins," to a significant degree, would succeed in their squaring effort, largely by filling their city with America's first great charitable works. The glorious institutions made possible by Brahmin philanthropy — the Massachusetts General Hospital for one — demonstrated clearly that the "generous rich" were exerting their influence "only for beneficent purposes,"

Harvard's Samuel Atkins Eliot would argue in 1845.[14] Great fortunes, their most devoted admirers pronounced, were making Boston a better place to live, work, and pray.

In the decades after the Civil War, the flacks for the fortunate would once again find themselves forced to resquare the "fact of possession" with America's egalitarian values. Giant new corporations were creating the greatest fortunes America had ever seen and, at the same time, convulsing the nation. Brahmin-style philanthropy — a hospital here, a museum there — now seemed inadequate, and the greatest fortune-founders of the Gilded Age, men like Andrew Carnegie and John D. Rockefeller, came to understand that simply giving more, Brahmin-style, would just not do. These men of enormous wealth needed, as scholars Peter Hall and George Marcus note, to "explain why 'men of affairs' like themselves should have come to control such vast resources." They needed "to legitimate that control as part of the natural scheme of things." To meet that goal, their philanthropy would have to do more than merely alleviate distress. Their philanthropy would "aim to identify and eradicate the causes of poverty, dependency, and ignorance." The mighty multimillionaires of the Gilded Age would not simply justify their wealth as a means of "service to the public." They would portray themselves "as servants of Progress — midwives, as it were, of the new industrial order."[15]

Andrew Carnegie, before his 1919 death, would devote an estimated $350 million of his personal fortune, about $7 billion in today's dollars, to serving "Progress."[16] His philanthropy would reshape America. His matching grants gave thousands of communities their first public libraries. His pension system, the first ever for college professors, "transformed" scholarship in the United States. His beneficence bankrolled organs for churches and "endowed an institute for peace, that elusive heaven on earth."[17]

"The man who dies rich," Carnegie had once noted, "dies disgraced."[18]

Carnegie would not die disgraced. America was impressed.

John D. Rockefeller did some impressing, too. He stepped back from his oil empire in 1897 and spent his last forty years giving away a fortune worth, in today's dollars, about $6 billion.[19] Rockefeller's dollars helped create America's national park system. He gave birth to Colonial Williamsburg and the University of Chicago. His Rockefeller Foundation, established in 1913, set out to do nothing less than "promote the well-being of mankind."[20] If that "well-being" could not, in the end, be assured, the fault — many Americans came to believe — was certainly not John D.'s. He had tried.

Three generations later, the flacks for America's newest men of fortune would proclaim a new golden age of giving. America could once again see grand-scale philanthropy, the flacks promised, if we as a nation cheered on the creation of Carnegie-sized fortunes. To inspire and enable more giving, more splendid good works, we needed merely to let the wealthy amass more wealth.

"Many people still think that commerce and charity are at opposite poles," Steve Forbes, the heir to one of America's greatest publishing fortunes, observed in 2001. "They are actually two sides of the same coin — the coin of serving others."[21]

The annual charitable giving numbers from America's top charity score-keeper, the Center on Philanthropy at Indiana University, seemed to document this direct connection between commerce and compassion.[22] In the booming 1990s, Americans set new records for charitable giving year after year. In 1998, individual contributions to nonprofits in the United States jumped over 10 percent, to a record-busting $134.8 billion.[23] In 1999, donations by individuals climbed substantially once again, to $144 billion.[24]

"Clearly," announced Bruce Reed, a top White House executive, in 2000, "America is in a charity boom."[25]

The flacks for America's grand fortunes smiled. Their case had been made. In an America that let the wealthy be, the needy, not the greedy, were emerging as the biggest winners of them all! Or so they claimed.

THE WHITE HOUSE AND THE FLACKS FOR FORTUNES would only be wrong on two counts. At century's end, charities were not booming, and the truly needy were not winning.

America's wealthiest had indeed become wealthier over the course of the boom years. America's charities had not. Americans, the *New York Times* reported at century's end, were actually giving "to all forms of philanthropy" at a less, not a more, generous rate.[26]

That conclusion came out of data collected in 1999 by the Independent Sector, a coalition of philanthropic organizations. *Total* giving may have been rising, the Independent Sector data documented, but giving *rates* were actually dropping. In 1998, for instance, American households contributed 2.1 percent of their incomes to charity. A decade earlier, by comparison, American households had given away to charities 2.5 percent of their incomes.[27] Giving, as a percentage of income, had actually been falling for years. In 1960, sociologist Robert Putnam pointed out, Americans donated to charity "about $1 for every $2" they spent on recreation. Americans, in 1997, gave away less than fifty cents for every $2 spent on leisure.[28]

How could the economy be booming and giving rates dropping? Those benefiting the most from the boom, observers started pointing out midway through the 1990s, just did not seem to be in a giving mood.

"The real problem," conservative columnist James Glassman charged in 1996, "lies squarely with the upper brackets."[29]

Between 1980 and 1991, a *Wall Street Journal* commentary had noted the year before, the incomes of people earning more than $1 million a year had soared by about 80 percent, after adjusting for inflation. Over these same years, the average charitable contributions out of the million-plus crowd dropped 57 percent.[30] Over twenty thousand households with incomes more than $500,000, sociologist Andrew Hacker added in a 1995 analysis, did not list a single charitable deduction on their tax returns.[31]

What were all these wealthy households waiting for? The hereafter? Apparently not.

"By one count," the *Economist* reported in 1998, "eight in ten Americans earning more than $1 million a year leave nothing to charity in their wills."[32]

Some observers blamed the high-tech new rich for the absence of generosity in deep-pocket circles. A 1999 survey, conducted by the Community Foundation of Silicon Valley, "found that 45 percent of the wealthiest contributors in the region give just $2,000 or less a year to charity" — and 6 percent "give nothing at all.[33]

One long-time local big giver, the seventy-six-year-old Leonard Ely, faulted Silicon Valley's young whippersnappers for this dismal philanthropic performance.

"They're all millionaires and billionaires by the time they're 30," Ely growled in an interview. "Look," he recalled one wealthy whippersnapper telling him, "I don't have my Ferrari and my place in Tahoe, and you're telling me I should give money away?"[34]

But Silicon Valley's young fortune-makers weren't the only fakers on the corporate scene come giving time. Mature, sober, respected captains of industry could be equally closefisted. Among these less than generous captains of industry: Dick Cheney, George W. Bush's choice for the nation's second-highest office. As a corporate executive in the 1990s, Cheney donated a microscopic 1.01 percent of his $20.7 million income to charity. Reporters revealed this embarrassing little fact during the 2000 Presidential campaign, and an angry Cheney immediately charged that the press numbers shortchanged his actual giving. His charitable contribution total should be adjusted, Cheney claimed, to include the $89,500 in speaking fees he had earmarked directly to charity and the $143,820 his company shelled out in contributions to match his personal giving. Reporters did the quick math. Adding these additional donations brought Cheney's giving rate up to all of 2.14 percent.[35]

Some mature, sober, respected captains of industry, to be sure, did not follow Cheney's parsimonious lead. In Los Angeles, the admirers of the awfully affluent could point proudly to their own local $6 billion man, the home-building and life insurance magnate, Eli Broad. In 1999, Broad put $100 million into education. In 2000, he upped his total charitable giving to over $137 million.[36]

"If he were emulated by other rich people," Jill Stewart, a local political columnist, wished out loud, "my God, we'd have a truly great society."[37]

But Eli Broad, as generous as his giving appeared, hardly deserved this sort of unabashed adulation. Even headline-grabbing donors like Eli Broad, truth be told, were giving "far less to charity than they should — or could."[38]

One wealthy man spent the twentieth century's last decade working tirelessly to get that message across. He failed.

CLAUDE ROSENBERG, IN THE 1990S, was a man on a mission. America's wealthiest families, he was convinced, could easily afford to give far more to charity than they were actually giving. Why weren't wealthy people giving more? No one who knew how wealth works, Rosenberg believed, had ever told the wealthy how much they could comfortably afford to give. He would.

Rosenberg expected the rich would listen. He was, after all, no crackpot. Over four decades, Rosenberg had forged an admirable reputation in investing circles. He had built up, at J. Barth & Co., the largest regional investment research operation in America. He had authored five books on finance, including one classic, *Stock Market Primer*, that went on to sell over half a million copies. He had founded two successful investment companies. One eventually managed over $60 billion in assets.[39]

These business triumphs had, naturally enough, generated a substantial personal fortune for Rosenberg, a fortune he went on to share generously with his family foundation. By century's end, the Rosenberg family foundation had amassed $32 million in assets.[40]

With this exemplary background, Claude Rosenberg felt he could speak about fortunes and philanthropy with as much credibility as anyone. And the frustrated Rosenberg had plenty to say. Over the years, to help his favorite charities solicit contributions, Rosenberg had often approached acquaintances with substantial fortunes. He had expected suitably substantial checks. These checks didn't come.

"I was disappointed, even angry, that people I knew were giving little compared to their estimated wealth," Rosenberg would later note.[41]

Wealthy people, Rosenberg eventually concluded, were basing their giving decisions on their annual income, not on the combination of that income and their already accumulated wealth.[42] If the wealthy took this wealth into account, not just their incomes, they would realize that they could afford to contribute far more to charitable causes.[43]

In fact, Rosenberg's calculations revealed, if America's most fortunate took their already accumulated wealth into account, they could increase their annual giving enormously and still end up each year richer than when they started.

Just how enormously? In 1991, the over fifty thousand Americans who made over $1 million for the year contributed, on average, a modest $87,000 a year to charity. These wealthy Americans, Rosenberg's data showed, could have upped their contributions to charity by ten times and still ended the year with more wealth to their names than when the year opened.[44] And if all these wealthy families had, in 1991, boosted their giving tenfold, America's charities would have received an astonishing $40 billion more in charitable contributions than they actually did![45]

Rosenberg explained all this, patiently and clearly, in a 1994 book, *Wealthy and Wise: How You and America Can Get the Most Out of Your Giving*. A few years later, in 1998, he would found an advocacy and research organization, the NewTithing Group, to spread the book's message. This new group would quickly pick up a host of celebrity endorsements, with notables from mutual fund wizard Peter Lynch to former President Jimmy Carter saluting the effort.[46]

"Our main point is that generosity has been based too much on income," Rosenberg would point out at every opportunity. "With capital for many people being so much larger than income, there is enormous untapped capacity to give."[47]

Rosenberg did everything he could, as the 1990s moved along, to help affluent families better understand their "untapped capacity." His NewTithing Web site would even offer a charitable capacity calculator.[48] Wealthy families, the calculator exercises demonstrated, could live normally, in the lifestyle to which they had become accustomed, and still, at the same time, significantly increase their giving.

Rosenberg would also appeal, throughout his tireless outreach efforts, to the hopes and dreams of his target audiences.

"I am trying to convince people, especially wealthy people, that it is very much in their interest to give away much more and to create a society where they can live safer, happier, better lives," Rosenberg told one reporter. "They just need to change how they think about how much they can afford to give."[49]

And if the wealthy didn't do that rethinking, Rosenberg warned, then darker days would surely be ahead.

"America's lopsided distribution of resources could one day result in heavier taxation of the wealthy," he cautioned. "And in difficult economic times, growing inequality could lead to more frequent threats of violence and even destruction of property aimed at the affluent."[50]

By the end of the 1990s, no single individual could have possibly done more than Claude Rosenberg to convince affluent Americans to up their charitable contributions. His ideas had been featured in the *Wall Street Journal* and a host of other major publications. He had delivered speeches coast to coast. He had even pushed his cause out into cyberspace.

The wealthy, for their part, didn't push back. They simply, as a group, ignored Rosenberg's message. Almost completely.

In the 2000 tax year, according to data NewTithing released in 2002, Americans as a whole gave about $150 billion to charity. They could have actually afforded to give, without losing any net worth, more than twice that amount, $320 billion in all.

The bulk of that extra $170 billion that could have been given — but wasn't — should have been given by America's wealthiest households, those households making at least $1 million for the year. These households each gave, on average, only $122,940 to charity in 2000.[51] They could have given nearly ten times that amount, $1,031,000 to be exact, and still not lost a cent off their net worth.

In all, households that made over $1 million in 2000 could have that year afforded to give over $128 billion more to charity than they actually did.[52] In 1991, by comparison, the superwealthy could only have easily afforded to give $40 billion more than they did.

So what had Claude Rosenberg's valiant campaign accomplished? Wealthy Americans, after years of exposure to NewTithing proselytizing, were most probably wiser about their wealth. But they were not the least bit more generous.

CLAUDE ROSENBERG AND HIS FELLOW RESEARCHERS at the NewTithing Group, in the course of their work, pumped out a steady stream of data that reinforced their main thesis, that wealthy Americans could painlessly afford to significantly increase their charitable giving. But NewTithing's data also documented another, equally important reality. Wealthy people, the data showed, are less generous with their dollars than low- and middle-income Americans — and the wealthier families become, the less they give, as a share of their income and wealth.

In 2000, for instance, average households at each income level below $100,000 contributed, according to NewTithing's calculations, every dollar they could comfortably afford to give. They, in effect, "maxed out" on their charitable contributions, as measured against the NewTithing standard.

America's more affluent households did not come anywhere close to maxing out. Those households that earned between $100,000 and $200,000 in 2000, for instance, gave to charity only 70 percent of what they could have comfortably afforded to give.

But these households making between $100,000 and $200,000 were veritable Mother Theresas compared to families higher up on America's economic ladder. In 2000, households making between $200,000 and $500,000 a year gave away to charity just 36 percent of what they could comfortably have afforded — and those that reported income between $500,000 and $1 million gave a mere 21 percent.

And what about the top, those families earning over $1 million a year? Households at this loftiest level gave away only 12 percent of what they could have given without crimping their lifestyle or shrinking their net worth.[53]

In these numbers, a profound lesson: The more wealth concentrates, the fewer the dollars that make their way to good causes.

Over recent years, other researchers have documented the same dynamic. One 1996 study, commissioned by Independent Sector, found that Americans earning less than $10,000 a year in 1995 gave a higher proportion of their pretax incomes to charity than households earning more than $100,000, by a 4.3 percent to 3.4 percent margin.[54] About the same time, British researchers compared the charitable giving rates of the nation's five hundred richest donors with the giving rates of modest suburban families. The suburbanites gave at a rate "three times higher" than England's wealthiest donors.[55]

In 2003, new research would dramatically deepen our understanding of exactly who gives what. The researchers behind this new work, published by the *Chronicle of Philanthropy*, had sifted through itemized tax returns filed for 1997, the only year with tax data then available by zip code. From these returns, the researchers computed "discretionary income" totals, by subtracting household expenses for housing, food, and taxes from total incomes. The researchers then calculated, for taxpayers who had earned at least $50,000, charitable giving as a percentage of discretionary income.

The result? In state after state, county after county, taxpayers in wealthy communities gave less of their income to charities than taxpayers in poorer communities.

In the Washington, D.C. metro area, residents of Fairfax County, the nation's most affluent county, gave 6.3 percent of their discretionary income to charity. Residents of Prince George's County, the least wealthy of Washington's large jurisdictions, gave 16.7 percent of their discretionary incomes to charitable groups.[56]

In California, Marin County residents claimed more discretionary income than residents from any other major local jurisdiction. But the county, the *Chronicle of Philanthropy* found, ranked next to last in share of income devoted to charity. Marin County residents gave away only 6.5 percent of their discretionary incomes.[57] California's most generous spot? That appeared to be Solano County, where local residents donated 12.4 percent of their discretionary incomes to charity. These Solano County residents had fewer discretionary dollars than the residents of any other county in California.[58]

In Texas, residents of the state's most affluent jurisdiction, Collin County, outside Dallas, donated 6.5 percent of their discretionary incomes to charity. Only one jurisdiction in Texas donated at a stingier rate. Residents of the much poorer Johnson County donated nearly twice as much, 12.5 percent, as their wealthy Collin County brethren.[59]

Numbers like these tell us a great deal about out of whose pockets charitable contributions come. But they don't tell us where charitable contributions go — and that's information we need to know, in the final analysis, before we can make any reasonable judgment about the importance of the charitable contributions that wealthy people make.

Wealthy people, for instance, might do a better job targeting their contributions to the truly needy than average donors. If this were the case, then America's concentrated wealth would still be cause for celebration, even if less affluent Americans donate more of their incomes to charity than wealthy people do. But this is not the case. America's wealthy, as a group, aren't just less generous than average Americans. America's wealthy are also less likely, with the donations they do make, to help needy people.

"It's a mistake to believe that the wealthy are contributing mainly to causes that help the poor," as Teresa Odendahl, the director of the National Network of Grantmakers, told *American Benefactor* magazine in 1997. "The majority of their money goes to their churches, their universities and schools, and to the arts — these are nonprofit organizations that serve them."[60]

Slate, the online magazine, helped drive home the same conclusion after the magazine started compiling annual lists of America's biggest donors. The listings helped show "that when wealthy Americans give, they tend to give to universities, medical research centers, and cultural institutions — not organizations to help the poor."[61] On one annual *Slate* biggest donor list, not a single top donor "gave money to provide for social-welfare services, such as homeless shelters."[62]

Wealthy people typically devote their charitable energies to the good causes that make them feel most at home. At the end of 1998, for instance, Eckhard Pfeiffer, the CEO of Texas-based Compaq Computer, sat on the boards of four nonprofits: the Houston Symphony, the M. D. Anderson Cancer Center in Houston, Southern Methodist University, and the Greater Houston Partnership, that city's leading advocate for the business community. Pfeiffer had personally taken in pay and stock options worth $192.5 million the previous year. His company, that same year, made charitable contributions that totaled all of $4.2 million.[63]

Pfeiffer by no means stood alone. His fellow elite CEOs, in the boom years of the 1990s, exhibited the same philanthropic priorities and proclivities.

"These guys cut the wages, cut the health benefits, raid the pension funds, eliminate the jobs and pocket all the profits," thundered *New York Observer* columnist Nicholas Von Hoffman. "They share nothing, they give nothing away except to the cancer clinics they go to, the colleges they send their kids to and the business schools they get their junior henchpersons from. The museums they do favor have been turned into annexes where they throw their private parties."[64]

BY THE END OF THE 1990S, two decades of unshared prosperity had left America's wealth concentrated in the pockets of men like Eckhard Pfeiffer. These same years had left the United States less, not more, charitably inclined to those who needed charity the most.[65]

In 1998, out of all the dollars donated to nonprofits, fewer than one in ten, only 9.2 percent, went to groups dedicated to providing basic human services, according to Indiana University's Center on Philanthropy. In 1970, by comparison, Americans gave to human service charities at a rate more than 50 percent higher.[66]

Why the difference? Americans, back in 1970, lived in a society where wealth had not yet concentrated in prodigious piles. Middle-income people controlled a much greater share of the nation's assets and income in 1970 than in 1998, and America's charitable giving patterns in 1970 reflected this greater middle-income influence. By century's end, with wealth considerably more concentrated, America's most fortunate had come to set the philanthropic tone. Our nation's increasing insensitivity reflected their dominance.

Back in 1931, after the Roaring Twenties, another time of unshared prosperity, America's wealthy also set our nation's philanthropic tone. In that year, with the Great Depression well under way, the governor of Pennsylvania came before Andrew Mellon, the then U.S. secretary of the treasury and, in his own right, one of the nation's richest men. The governor had a desperate request. Would Secretary Mellon, he asked, be willing to make a $1 million *personal* loan to help Pennsylvania meet its "welfare needs"?

Secretary Mellon, the history books tell us, never did make that personal loan to Pennsylvania. But he did proudly show the good governor his latest art purchase, a grand master painting that had set Mellon back $1.7 million.[67] Secretary Mellon, in one of the greatest philanthropic gestures in American history, would later donate that painting and the rest of his magnificent art collection to the nation. The National Gallery of Art, in Washington, D.C., today testifies to his generosity.

So maybe we shouldn't get so cross with the wealthy. At giving time, they might not dig down as deep in their pockets as the rest of us. And their philanthropy might not show much in the way of compassion for the less fortunate. But wealthy people sure do appreciate the finer things in life. Without their commitment to the arts, and the fortunes they invest in art, where would our culture be?

Where indeed.

CULTURE AND ART

ART MUSEUMS. CONCERT HALLS. OPERA HOUSES. These remain today our standard symbols of high culture. These are the places, from generation to generation, where great art survives. They define us. They showcase the best of the human spirit. And they wouldn't exist, we are constantly reminded, without rich people.

Affluence and the arts have always gone — and will always go — together, or so the friends of fortune have always contended, down through the centuries. To create, artists need patrons, individuals who can both appreciate great art and support the artists who create it. Only wealthy people can adequately fit this patron bill. Only wealthy people, the classic "leisure class," have the time to cultivate a sophisticated appreciation for art. Only wealthy people have the wherewithal to keep starving artists from starving.

"The rich make life more interesting: they are a luxury a civilized society should be able to afford," as William Davis, one admiring chronicler of the ways of the wealthy, has noted.[1] "Walk around any museum and look at the treasures they have left us, and ask yourself what there would be to see if Communism had arrived four centuries earlier."[2]

An art lover so inclined might start this walk-around exercise at New York's glorious Metropolitan Museum, the perfect place to reflect upon the cultural contributions of J. P. Morgan, the greatest business kingpin — and art collector — of his time. Morgan, before his 1913 death, spent over $900 million, in today's dollars, buying artwork. He literally stocked America, most notably the Metropolitan Museum, "with the world's great art."[3]

An art lover in a reflective mood might next want to drop in on New York's Museum of Modern Art and contemplate here the far-flung legacy of banker David Rockefeller, the grandson of J. P. Morgan's contemporary, John D. Rockefeller. David, the museum's chairman emeritus, devoted years of his life "acquiring fine art, especially Impressionists and early Modern masters like Picasso" and years more "creating a corporate art program that today numbers over 20,000 works in 350 locations."[4]

What would art in America have done without David Rockefeller? And what would art in America do without the men of means who have followed in his art-collecting footsteps, the billionaires like Bill Gates who, in 1994, transformed "himself from a role model for nerds into a cultured gentleman" by laying out $30.8 million for a celebrated notebook of jottings and drawings by Leonardo da Vinci.[5] Four years later, for $36 million, Gates added Winslow Homer's *Lost on the Grand Banks* to his increasingly impressive collection. No one had ever paid more for a painting by an American.[6]

The love of fine art, some observers believe, just comes naturally to the very rich.

"Billionaires almost cannot help becoming art collectors," noted one recent survey on the art-collecting scene in *Forbes* magazine. "With so much money and, usually, so many houses to decorate, it only makes sense that they would surround themselves with much of the world's finest artworks, furniture, porcelain and other objects of beauty."[7]

Once imbued with this love of beauty, rich people just seem to have to share it. They simply cannot bear the thought of a museum going without. In 1999, for instance, high-tech multimillionaire Jonathan Ledecky found himself attending a fundraising dinner for the famed Phillips Collection. The museum, Phillips officials explained, needed a few dollars for a refurbishing project. "Ledecky leaned over to a high-tech pal," the *Washington Post* would later report. "'I'll go half if you go half,' he whispered. 'Let's announce it right now at this little dinner.' 'Done,' said his friend."

"And the museum had an additional $375,000," the *Post* related. "Just like that."[8]

In the closing years of the twentieth century, rich people seemed to be making it happen — "just like that" — for cultural institutions all across the United States, and all the arts, performing as well as visual, seemed to share in this generous benevolence. In New York, financial services mogul Sanford Weill took over as the chairman of the Carnegie Hall board in 1991. Over thirty fellow CEOs would eventually join Weill on that board, with each expected to donate $100,000 a year. Midway through the 1990s, Weill upped the ante. He announced a $75 million fundraising goal for Carnegie Hall's endowment and "almost immediately raised half of it from the board, the average director contributing nearly $600,000."[9]

Weill's high-minded, high-octane philanthropy reflects, according to art critic Hilton Kramer, "a well-established American tradition."

"Anyone familiar" with America's great cultural and educational institutions, Kramer argued in 2001, "knows that most of our major art museums, concert halls, libraries, universities, and research institutions were created by private wealth."[10]

The more private wealth in the pockets of wealthy people, cultural guardians like Kramer believe, the more secure our culture will be. Wealthy Americans, at least as far as the arts are concerned, may be the ultimate "good hands people." They preserve and protect our cultural patrimony. They can be counted on — unless the rest of us do something stupid, like tax their fortunes away — to make America not just rich, but beautiful.

FOR WELL OVER A GENERATION NOW, ever since the late 1970s, the rest of us have cooperated. We have taken no steps toward taxing great fortunes. Instead, we have reduced the taxes the wealthy are expected to pay. We have sat back and watched new J. P. Morgan-sized fortunes emerge, one after another, right in the heart of America's greatest cultural centers. We should now, as a result, be witnessing a flowering of fine art in America, a veritable renaissance. Are we? Some observers think so.

These observers marvel at the amazing new additions to America's cultural landscape. In Los Angeles, they applaud the visually stunning J. Paul Getty Museum, "a Shangri-La and Starship Enterprise rolled into one."[11] The Getty opened in 1998. That first year, 1.8 million visitors "would brave the rigors of limited parking" to ogle the masterworks assembled by Texas oilman J. Paul Getty's billions. So many people came — "by car pool, by shuttle bus, by taxi" — that museum officials found themselves forced to launch "an anti-attendance advertising campaign." That campaign worked. Attendance at the Getty dropped to a more manageable 1.4 million in 1999.[12]

The next year, in Getty's home state, the Houston Museum of Fine Art would open a new wing named after Audrey Jones Beck, the granddaughter of Jesse H. Jones, Houston's most celebrated business leader. Over the course of the new wing's first twelve months, 2.2 million visitors rushed in.[13]

Overall, across America, museum attendance jumped 45 percent in the 1990s. Curators counted 900 million visits in all, and that was more, art enthusiasts exclaimed, than the total attendance for all the decade's pro baseball, basketball, and football games combined.[14] And Americans who weren't walking through art museums seemed to be taking their seats in theaters and concert halls. The performing arts, one report noted in 2001, "appear to be booming." More arts organizations were offering live performances than ever before.[15]

Even symphony orchestras, by the end of the 1990s, were sounding happy notes. A dozen years earlier, orchestral leaders were all but convinced their art form wouldn't make it to century's end. "The symphony orchestra as we know it is dead," Ernest Fleishmann of the Los Angeles Philharmonic had declared in 1987.[16] "There is little doubt," music critic Samuel Lipman had added, "that the long-expected terminal crisis of American orchestras is upon us."[17] But by century's end, the "terminal crisis" had passed, and the American Symphony Orchestra League trumpeted the news. In the 1999-2000 symphony season, the League noted, ticket sales hit nearly half a billion dollars, up 53 percent from 1990-1991. In this same 1999-2000 season, over two-thirds of America's top orchestras ran their budgets in the black. The 109 orchestras that shared their data with the League ended the year with a combined $12 million surplus.[18]

"Nine years before," the League crowed, "the same orchestras reported a combined survey deficit of $26.7 million."[19]

Did all this add up to a renaissance? Who knew for sure? But those atten-dance numbers certainly looked good and, at least in America's concert halls, sounded even better.

FANS OF AMERICA'S GREAT FORTUNES tend to see the history of the arts in America as a history of the wealthy in the arts. Artists make art. The wealthy buy it. The wealthy share it. Curtain down. A standing ovation from a grate-ful American public.

In real life, America's most wealthy, even in their flushest moments, have never made the sorts of investments the arts in America have needed to keep going and growing.

Americans first learned that lesson in the 1920s. In the Roaring Twenties, as in the 1980s and 1990s, new grand fortunes appeared to be popping up everywhere. The performing arts groups of the time had great hopes for these grand new fortunes. America's new super rich, they figured, would rescue art from grimy fiscal pressures. Artistic brilliance would shine anew. Culture would captivate America.

But the new super rich, in the 1920s, never rode to the rescue. They gave what they wanted, not what they could. The age's wealthiest individuals, one subsequent study of the arts noted, would prove "unable or unwilling" to sub-sidize "such high-cost performing organizations as symphony orchestras and opera companies."[20] Major arts groups, consequently, spent the decade scram-bling. They aggressively solicited donations from whatever deep-pockets they could convince to serve on their boards. At the same time, they redoubled their ticket-selling efforts. But neither deep-pockets nor ticket sales would deliver the needed results. Chronic underfunding seemed destined to be the arts community's eternal burden.

At least until the 1950s. After World War II, arts activists began challeng-ing the old funding formulas. The arts community, activists argued, needed to develop funding sources outside the ticket marketplace and traditional phi-lanthropy. The arts, they believed, needed — and deserved — government support. In 1960, the activists would score their first breakthrough. In Albany that year, lawmakers would okay the creation of the New York State Council on the Arts, the first state arts agency in the nation.[21] Four years later, Congress would establish the National Endowment of the Arts. The federal government would now become, for the first time, a significant player in arts funding.[22]

In 1966, two leading scholars would blow away what remained of the polite fiction that live performing arts could "support themselves in the mar-ketplace."[23] In a landmark study, economists William Baumol and William Bowen would help policy makers understand that the arts in America could make no real headway without help from tax dollars.[24] That understanding, in fairly short order, would speed historic increases in government aid to the arts. In community after community, federal dollars would begin leveraging growing "private and state and local government support for the arts through a system of matching grants and grants-in-aid to states."[25]

But this generous flow of public tax dollars would not, in the end, survive the Reagan era. In the 1980s, amid rising federal budget deficits and angry attacks from cultural conservatives, arts funding would start losing its political appeal on Capitol Hill. By the early 1990s, states and localities, not just Congress, would be cutting back on aid to the arts.[26]

With government support fading, the arts now needed new patrons. Once again, arts advocates would look to the super rich. Once again, they would be disappointed. Total individual contributions to performing arts organizations would increase over the course of the 1990s, but these increases would come largely from arts lovers of modest means, not from rich donors. And these smaller donations required "higher development costs" to obtain.[27] The bottom line for performing arts groups: After subtracting fundraising costs, the net revenues from individual contributions weren't nearly enough to keep pace with rising general operating expenses.

Corporate contributions would not make up the difference. Corporations, overall, did boost their total arts giving in the 1990s, but the executives who made these contributions tied them more tightly than ever before "to individual corporate marketing campaigns."[28] General operating deficits within arts groups continued to grow wider.

With individual and corporate contributions inadequate, with direct government subsidies evaporating, arts groups had no choice but to hunt for money in the marketplace. That meant, essentially, selling more tickets — at higher prices. And that meant, in turn, making artistic decisions based purely on economics. Who could fill the most seats at the highest prices? Arts groups knew the answer. Only big names could fill high-priced seats. So arts groups jumped on the big-name bandwagon. They increasingly produced "lavish programs featuring celebrity artists to attract large audiences."[29] Stagings of familiar, tried-and-true classics could also fill seats. So arts organizations increasingly recycled old "warhorses," in what would become known as the *Nutcracker* strategy. These old favorites delivered good bang for the buck. They could be produced cheaply — no need to bother with new sets — and arts groups, by producing warhorses instead of nurturing new work, could avoid paying royalties to creators.

Celebrity blockbusters and endless warhorse reruns would not, everyone involved understood, elevate America's general artistic levels. But blockbusters and warhorses weren't expected to have any elevating effect. They were only expected to give arts organizations a badly needed fiscal shot in the arm. Unfortunately, they didn't do that either. The marketplace, in the 1990s, would not deliver. The blockbusters and the warhorses would not raise enough revenue to offset shrinking support from government sources. By century's end, arts groups were receiving no more revenue from marketplace initiatives, as a share of total revenue, than they had back in the late 1970s.

"In the aggregate," researchers from RAND, America's original think tank, would note in a major 2001 study, "performing groups are about as dependent upon the market as they have been in the past, despite intensive efforts at marketing and audience development, and despite sharp rises in the cost of tickets."[30]

The RAND research, conducted for the Pew Charitable Trusts, analyzed America's entire theater, opera, dance, and music scene — and sounded some rather discouraging notes.[31] The researchers acknowledged that overall attendance at arts productions had increased somewhat between 1982 and 1997. But this increase, the researchers concluded, reflected population growth and related factors, "not an increase in the percentage of the population that engages in the arts."[32] And the population that did engage in the arts, the researchers found, was aging. In 1982, people under forty made up 27 percent of the audience for classical music. By the end of the 1990s, concert-goers under forty constituted just 14 percent of the classical music audience.[33]

On stage, among performers, researchers uncovered other troubling trends. The emphasis on blockbusters had tilted the rewards for performing to a few select superstars. The rest of America's performing professionals faced rising economic insecurity.

"On average," the study noted, "performing artists earn less, work fewer weeks, face higher unemployment and are much more likely to take jobs outside their profession than other professionals with comparable education."[34]

These trends, the RAND analysts argued, were driving a "fundamental shift" in America's "performing arts system." That shift, they explained, couldn't really be seen in America's biggest cities — or smallest towns. In the nation's largest urban centers, the nation's premiere arts organizations were continuing "to grow by focusing on star-studded productions that pull in the crowds." In small communities, meanwhile, the arts emphasis still remained on "low-budget live productions that rely largely on volunteer labor."[35] The changes were taking place everywhere else, in the mid-size metropolitan areas that had once employed the vast majority of professional performers. Arts groups in these mid-sized areas, the RAND researchers documented, "are facing the greatest difficulty in attracting enough of the public to cover their costs."[36] These mid-sized arts groups "lack the resources to put on blockbusters."[37] Many "are likely to disappear."[38] Those that hang on are likely to survive by eliminating almost everything but "traditional programming and fairly mainstream artistic endeavors."[39]

Do those who care about culture need to worry about these mid-sized arts organizations? After all, if elite arts groups in America's biggest cities are continuing to prosper and if volunteer arts groups are continuing to put on productions in small communities, what's the big deal? The big deal, the RAND researchers stressed, is the role that mid-sized arts groups in America have historically played. These mid-sized arts groups offer talented young performers the stages they need to get serious about their art and develop their skills.[40] But that's only the half of it. If mid-sized arts groups can only survive by relying on the stale warhorses of America's performing arts repertoire, innovation will likely become a luxury our culture simply cannot afford.[41]

In the 1980s and 1990s, the RAND research demonstrated plainly, America had experienced no renaissance in the performing arts — and no renaissance loomed.

"The world of the performing arts is sick and needs attention," Michael Kaiser, the president of the Kennedy Center for the Performing Arts, would agree late in 2002. "The arts world is moving close to becoming a virtual cartel of a few large mainstream organizations that survive and thrive. This would be catastrophic. A healthy arts ecology demands that we have large and small organizations, mainstream and edgy, and of all ethnic backgrounds."[42]

The RAND analysts, for their part, saw ahead an America "likely to make it more difficult for talented actors, composers, musicians, and dancers to mature artistically."[43] And this bleak future beckoned even in those places where wealth in the United States had concentrated the most, places where potential patrons of the arts could be found around every corner, places like Silicon Valley.

On June 4, 2002, in the capital city of Silicon Valley, the San Jose Symphony Orchestra announced plans to file for bankruptcy. The orchestra, a fixture in San Jose for over 120 years, faced debts that amounted to "more than a third of its annual $7.8 million budget." Many of the eighty-nine musicians in the orchestra, violinist Kristen Linfante told reporters, will be "going back to school to begin new careers."[44]

In San Jose, as in most of the rest of America, the renaissance would have to wait.

THE PEOPLE WHO RUN VISUAL ARTS ORGANIZATIONS, unlike those who run performing arts groups, don't have to worry about filling seats. They don't have to pay musicians, dancers, or actors either. But they do face chronic budget pressures every bit as tight. By the end of the 1990s, these pressures had created in the visual arts a mirror image of the performing arts.

In the visual arts, as in the performing arts, government funding support started ebbing in the 1980s and 1990s. In the visual arts, as in the performing arts, America's ever-wealthier wealthy sat, for the most part, on their checkbooks and offered no substantial relief. In the visual arts, as in the performing arts, arts groups then rushed off to the marketplace for any and all dollars they could capture.

These visual arts groups had several money-raising marketplace options. They could sell reproductions of the art that hung on their walls, for instance, and they could sell food and drink in their museums. Most lucratively of all, they could sell tickets, and that's just what they set out to do.

The art museum experience in the United States had traditionally been, in much of America, a free experience. People walked into museums the same way they walked into public libraries. They couldn't "take out" art, as they could take out books, but they could linger before an artwork, no charge, for as long as they wanted. In the last quarter of the twentieth century, this library-like era ended, almost everywhere in the United States.

In many cases, admission fees would follow directly on the heels of cutbacks in government support. In Los Angeles, after the 1978 passage of Proposition 13, America's first major statewide tax cut initiative, the Los Angeles County Museum of Art imposed its first general entrance fee. Adults would have to pay $1.50 to enter inside.[45] The fee would make an immediate impact. Within a month, attendance at the Los Angeles museum dropped 44 percent. Within a year, average daily attendance would fall from 1,400 visitors a day to 370.[46]

Still, despite these attendance losses, there would be no going back, in Los Angeles or anywhere else. Museums would either succeed in the marketplace — by selling more and more tickets, at higher and higher prices — or have to pack up their paintings. And how would museums endeavor to sell more tickets? They would follow the performing arts script. They would produce "blockbuster" shows based on "warhorse" art that had already demonstrated clear drawing power.

The script, on one level, "worked." Blockbusters — "exhibitions on Impressionism, Egyptian art, Picasso and most of all van Gogh" — did generate ticket sales.[47] In 1996, only fourteen art shows in the United States attracted more than two hundred thousand customers. That total rose to eighteen in 1997 and twenty-one in 1998. In 1999, thirty-one blockbusters drew at least two hundred thousand people.[48]

These sorts of blockbusters undeniably multiplied revenues. But they did not, in any meaningful sense, expand the audience for art. The Los Angeles County Museum of Art offered a typical example. In 1977, before entrance fees, the museum counted about half a million visitors. Not a bad figure for a metro area with 7.5 million people. By 2001, that metro area population had grown to 10 million. How many visitors stopped by the Los Angeles County Museum of Art in 2001? About half a million, the same number the museum had welcomed back in 1977.[49]

Blockbusters had not, in Los Angeles, worked any magic. Nor did they work any magic anywhere else. How could they? Museums across the country, over the course of the 1990s, had raised their entrance fees to heights that all but eliminated the casual visitor. In Los Angeles, the county museum's original $1.50 admission fee in 1978 had been hiked, by 2002, to $7.[50] But that would be a bargain compared to the $12 charged, in 2000, at the Guggenheim in New York and the Museum of Fine Arts in Boston.[51]

These fees didn't just eliminate huge swatches of the population from regular museum going. They radically changed — for the worse — the museum-going experience.

In free public museums, notes *Los Angeles Times* art critic Christopher Knight, people can experience art casually, as part of everyday life. They come, over time, to see this art as belonging to them, part of their "cultural patrimony." Stiff entrance fees have ended this sense of common ownership. We pay to see art, just as we pay for a movie, a ballgame, or any other "commercial entertainment."[52]

By century's end, America's museum directors could care less about nurturing an appreciation for humanity's common "cultural patrimony." Museum directors had become entertainers, ever on the lookout for "popular attractions geared toward drawing crowds rather than nourishing the soul."[53] These "popular attractions" would include an exhibit on the history of the sneaker — nourishment for the sole? — that appeared at San Francisco's Museum of Modern Art in the summer of 2000.[54] And these popular attractions would also include, perhaps most profitably of all, air conditioning. Pumping up the AC, the *Wall Street Journal* would report in 2001, "is helping fill galleries" across the United States.[55] To lure sweating passers by, art museums were turning thermostats down, to as low as 69 on the hottest days, and running "cool rules" ad campaigns.

"Our air conditioning," the marketing director at Kansas City's Kemper Museum of Contemporary Art, boasted to the *Journal,* "is a huge selling point for us."

BLOCKBUSTERS, WARHORSES, AND AIR CONDITIONING all helped up arts attendance in the boom years. But they brought no artistic renaissance, no greater role for the arts in American life, and no guarantee that the arts would survive to thrive in the years ahead.

Real security for the arts, analysts note, can only come from a widening of the audience for artistic excellence. And that audience, they believe, can be widened — not by blockbusters, but by education, not by air conditioning, but by a systematic effort to support teaching about and appreciation for the arts in America's schools.[56]

Educators, not surprisingly, have been making this same recommendation for years.

"Because of the role of the arts in civilization, and because of their unique ability to communicate the ideas and emotions of the human spirit," notes the national society that represents music educators, "every American student, preK through grade 12, should receive a balanced, comprehensive, sequential, and rigorous program of instruction in music and the other arts."[57]

A "balanced, comprehensive, sequential, and rigorous program of instruction" in the arts, music educators know, is just what America's public schools are *not* providing. The National Assessment for Educational Progress, the testing arm of the U.S. Department of Education, would document — and come to symbolize — this neglect in the mid 1990s.

The National Assessment for Educational Progress, or NAEP, had for years regularly tested students across the United States in reading, math, and other subjects. But not the arts. In 1996, NAEP officials finally set out to remedy that situation. They prepared broad samples of fourth, eighth, and twelfth grade students for an arts assessment. But the assessment had to be postponed when the Department of Education couldn't find the dollars to pay for it. The testing eventually did take place, the next year, but in truncated fashion. Federal Education Department officials could only find enough budget dollars to assess arts knowledge among eighth graders.[58]

The results from this limited assessment would prove valuable nonetheless. They confirmed what arts educators had long suspected: America's schools were offering students precious little contact with the arts. Only 25 percent of eighth graders, the assessment showed, were "actually singing or playing an instrument at least once a week."[59] The same percentage attended schools where visual arts classes were only offered once or twice a week. Another 17 percent attended schools where visual arts classes were *never* offered.[60]

"This NAEP assessment verifies that most American children are infrequently or never given serious instruction or performance opportunities in music, the arts, or theater," Secretary of Education Richard Riley told reporters. "That's wrong."[61]

The NAEP arts assessment, and Secretary Riley's anguished response to it, would get no rise out of America's champions of culture, those men and women of private wealth and exquisite taste who see themselves as noble protectors of humanity's fine arts heritage. These wealthy patrons of the arts, in the wake of the NAEP report, made no massive move to rescue America's young people from artistic illiteracy. These patrons of the arts simply did not have time to focus on schools and art education. They had more important work to do. They were too busy underwriting artistic monuments — to themselves.

These monuments — luxurious new concert halls and art museums, or new wings for old buildings — proliferated wildly in America's turn-of-the-century years. In 2002, *USA Today* counted "at least" sixty major arts building projects over $10 million "either underway, in planning stages or just completed." These sixty projects, by conservative estimate, together cost $5.1 billion.[62]

Not all Americans of means, to be sure, cheered this building boom. Some worried that edifices and air conditioning, in the absence of arts education, might not be enough to give the arts a fighting chance for the future. One such worried American of means, cable TV multimillionaire John Sykes, would actually move to change that future.

Sykes, midway through the 1990s, had volunteered to serve as a "principal for a day" at a public school in Brooklyn. The school's students had welcomed him with a musical show, and their energetic effort left Sykes, the president of cable television's popular VH1 music network, all smiles. But those smiles faded when a music teacher told Sykes the school couldn't afford to keep its music program going. A shocked Sykes promptly decided to "adopt the school" and outfit the kids with new instruments. His philanthropy at this single school would soon turn into a citywide program and then, in 1998, into a national philanthropic effort, the VH1 Save The Music Foundation.[63]

The Foundation's goal: to help restore instrumental music programs in America's schools and increase children's access to music education. Toward this end, Save The Music would enlist a long list of partners and sponsors, outfits of substance ranging from the National School Boards Association to Subaru.[64] By May 2002, Save The Music had donated $21 million worth of musical instruments to nine hundred public schools. In just five years, the program had touched the musical lives of four hundred thousand children.[65] By 2008, Save The Music officials noted, an estimated 1 million public schoolchildren would regain access to music education *if* Save The Music were able to raise enough donations to successfully complete its ten-year plan.[66]

But even this success, Save The Music officials understood, would be limited. At the start of the new century, only one quarter of America's schools offered music as a basic part of the curriculum.[67] If Save The Music were able to reach 1 million kids, that would still leave about 35 million more children yet to be reached.

"We've helped so many children and schools these past five years," acknowledged Bob Morrison, the Save The Music executive director, early in 2002, "but the need to restore music education programs unfortunately continues in the face of significant education budget cuts across the country."[68]

Save The Music, gallant though the effort, was not making much more than a minor dent.

IN THE 1990S, VH1 PRESIDENT JOHN SYKES HAD ONE IDEA — his Save The Music program — on how the affluent ought to go about nurturing public appreciation for the arts. Steve Wynn, the stylish, art-collecting chairman of Mirage Resorts, had another.

In 1998, amid massive fanfare, Wynn opened a "Gallery of Fine Art" inside his luxurious new Las Vegas resort hotel, the Bellagio. Over the next two years, an average of two thousand customers a day would pay $12 a head to take a peek at Wynn's $400 million worth of "paintings and sculpture by the likes of Renoir, van Gogh and Picasso."[69]

Elsewhere in Las Vegas, on and around "the Strip," Wynn's fine arts derring-do would quickly inspire a mini-boom in masterworks.

"Strip moguls recognize," noted one reporter, "that art is entertainment, just like golf or nightclub acts or gambling."[70]

In 2001, to cap off this artistic flurry, a new casino and resort known as The Venetian, an even grander palace than Wynn's Bellagio, opened an opulent art gallery all its own, after teaming up with New York's Guggenheim Museum and Russia's venerable Hermitage.[71]

"It's a great combination — high kitsch and high art at the same time," noted The Venetian's proud president, Rob Goldstein.[72]

Other observers, like Dave Hickey, a University of Nevada at Las Vegas art critic, weren't so sure. Hickey had the quaint notion that museums ought to offer a "refuge" from commerce, not opportunities for new profit centers.

"All of this is based on the presumption that art is a spectator sport, like a tractor pull," noted Hickey, after surveying the burgeoning Las Vegas fine arts scene. "You're not in the museum business anymore. You're a carnival."[73]

Some American cities, in the boom years, did try to stick to the museum business — and offer all people, not just those who could afford the price of admission, a refuge where fine art could be experienced, not just consumed. Of these cities, none would make a more admirable effort than St. Louis.

A democratic people, leaders within the St. Louis arts community believed, ought not count on the whims of the wealthy to protect and preserve the best their culture has to offer. That perspective had deep local roots. A century earlier, after the 1904 St. Louis world's fair, local citizens — "working-class European immigrants who smarted from the memories of the elitism of their homelands' cultural institutions" — had converted the fair's only permanent structure, the Palace of Fine Arts, into the St. Louis Art Museum. They carved into stone their new museum's mission — *Dedicated to Art and Free to All* — and hoped the generations ahead would never forget that motto.

Those generations never did. The St. Louis Art Museum, down through the decades, has remained free.[74] City and county local residents pay, as part of their property taxes, a "museum tax." At one point, local political leaders did propose an admission fee to pay for capital improvements. City and county residents rejected the fee. They voted, instead, to double their museum tax, "to keep the free admission policy."[75]

The St. Louis museum tax — at century's end, $220 on a home assessed at $100,000 — came to supply nearly 80 percent of the city art museum's general operating revenue.[76] That solid base of support, in turn, gave museum officials the creative freedom to think beyond warhorses and blockbusters.

"The great challenge for museums," as Brent Benjamin, the St. Louis Art Museum's director, noted in 2000, "is to build an audience for exhibitions that are not Impressionism or antiquities."[77]

The St. Louis Art Museum seemed, at century's end, to be doing a fairly good job at that. The museum, throughout the 1990s, consistently topped attendance lists for touring exhibitions, perhaps the art world's best comparative attendance measure.[78] The museum was surviving, even thriving — without depending on the wealthy.

The fine arts in St. Louis have always, to be sure, welcomed contributions from the city's most affluent, but the arts in St. Louis, more so perhaps than the arts in any other city, have never *had* to have those contributions to stay alive and thrive. The direct result? The arts in St. Louis have never been left in the lurch when the priorities of the privileged didn't quite match up with the needs of arts organizations. The arts in St. Louis have never had to rush wildly into the marketplace to make up for the dollars the wealthy have not seen fit to throw their way.

Elsewhere in America, arts community leaders have, for the most part, never stopped counting on the wealthy. They have been systematically disappointed. Amid that disappointment, they have turned to the marketplace — and only compounded their problems. Arts leaders have ended up shrinking the public for fine art and giving this shrunken public an arts experience that is decidedly less than fine.

The "accumulation of wealth," President Calvin Coolidge, a dependable friend of wealthy people, once declared, inevitably brings forth a "widening of culture." [79]

Not necessarily.

Not if that accumulated wealth sits concentrated, at the top.

A CASE NOT MADE

WE HAVE, IN THE PAGES just concluded, examined the classic claims made on behalf of concentrated wealth.

Societies that welcome great fortunes, the case for concentrated wealth asserts, give their most deserving individuals the incentives they need to refine their talents and work harder, longer, and smarter than they otherwise would. And societies that richly reward their deserving are, in turn, themselves rewarded — with prosperity, charity, and beauty.

Civilized societies, in sum, need great wealth. The wealthy deserve their wealth. The rest of us all benefit from it.

A simple story. A comforting story.

As comforting as any fairytale.

Fairytales, unfortunately, do not reveal reality. They obscure it. Those of us who go about living as if life were a fairytale will always inevitably be disappointed. Life cannot deliver what fairytales promise.

Over the past quarter-century, the fairytale spun by the fortunate has not delivered. Aiding and abetting wealth concentration has not energized genius, rewarded the worthy, or left those of us unworthy of great fortune any better off. We have not benefited from increasing inequality. We have not come to live in a more secure, compassionate, or lovely land.

But we cannot and should not attempt to judge concentrated wealth — or any social phenomenon, for that matter — on the basis of "deliverables" alone. To appropriately analyze any human endeavor, as America's schools of business have taught us, we need to look at costs, not just benefits.

In modern life, we perform "cost-benefit" analyses all the time, in everything from our businesses to our debates over public policy. "Costs" and "benefits," we understand, must each be evaluated before we reach any final judgments on any endeavor's ultimate value.

An endeavor that delivers all its promised *benefits*, after all, could quite rightfully be declared a dismal failure if the *costs* incurred to make that delivery have proven outrageously monumental. By the same token, an endeavor that doesn't, at first, deliver on its promises might still be worth continuing — if that endeavor exacts no appreciable cost. Change sometimes does take considerable time. With more time, a suspect endeavor might eventually deliver.

America's growing inequality has not yet, we have seen, delivered. How should we react? Should we sit back and give inequality more time to produce the benefits so far denied us? Or should we take steps — now — to roll back inequality and start anew.

Hold that question, a freshly minted MBA might suggest. We have yet to examine the "cost" side of America's social ledger. Great fortunes may not, at least so far, have benefited us. But what have they actually *cost* us?

Good point. We need to answer our MBA's question.

Book Two

The Cost of Greed

THE PRICE WE PAY FOR INEQUALITY

IF THOSE WHO FAWN OVER FORTUNES were right, if letting wealth accumulate were indeed the prime prescription for a healthy, vigorous society, we ought today to be enjoying a new American golden age. Never before, after all, have grand fortunes accumulated as prodigiously as they have over recent decades, at least not in modern times. Our economy, given this awesome accumulation, ought to be vibrant, full of opportunity at every turn. Our enterprises should be generating wealth at extraordinary rates. We ourselves ought to be feeling stoked and energetic, confident that our hard work will be duly rewarded. Compassion ought to be flowing for the unfortunate, the arts ought to be blooming. We should be feeling absolutely terrific about ourselves and our country.

But we aren't. So what went wrong? What really happens when societies stand back and let great wealth accumulate in the pockets of a few? What has inequality cost us?

The pages ahead will search for answers to these questions, in places both self-evident and somewhat surprising. We'll explore the worksites where we labor and the neighborhoods where we live. We'll look at our families and our friendships. We'll examine what makes us happy and what makes us sick. We'll probe why our professions no longer leave us proud, why our pastimes no longer bring us pleasure. And we'll end our exploration by peering into two important worlds that now stand dangerously at risk, the natural world we have inherited and the democratic political world we have struggled to create.

Inequality impacts all these worlds, all these places. Now we see how.

The Ineffective Enterprise

Most Americans today work, either directly or indirectly, for enterprises, for large organizations that employ specialized workforces and multiple layers of management.

Enterprises have been driving the American economy for well over a century, and Americans have been debating, for almost as long, just what needs to be done to make enterprises effective. The debates have revolved, for the most part, around a single simple question: How do you turn dozens, hundreds, or thousands of people who don't know each other — and may not even know much about the work they have been hired to perform — into an operation that efficiently produces goods or provides services?

At the end of the nineteenth century, one American felt sure he knew the answer. To make enterprises effective, industrial engineer Frederick Winslow Taylor asserted, managements needed to manage — down to the most minute details of the work to be done. Taylor called his approach to enterprise effectiveness "scientific management."

In a scientifically managed enterprise, Taylor taught, management does the thinking. All of it. Managers, he advised, should always "fully" plan out every single task every single worker "is to accomplish, as well as the means to be used in doing the work."[1]

Taylorism — the notion that workers need to be carefully scripted, motion by motion — would go on to flourish in the new twentieth century. Businesses hustled to organize themselves, as best they could, along "scientific management" lines. Total management control over the work process, executives believed, would make for enterprises that functioned efficiently, with no effort ever wasted, no minutes ever lost.

Today, a century later, the nostrums of "scientific management" seem a quaint, even barbaric, relic of a distant past. No contemporary business leader would dare suggest, at least not in polite company, that employees only do good work when management tells them exactly what to do and how to do it. Instead, modern executives orate, at every opportunity, about *empowering* workers, about the importance of creating workplaces that encourage employees to exercise their creativity.

Almost every high-level corporate manager now knows, by heart, this empowerment mantra: In generations past, they have learned at innumerable management seminars, command-and-control might have made some business sense. In the old days of mass production, with workers standing at assembly lines, performing the same mindless tasks over and over, corporations didn't really need to know what workers thought. They just needed workers to do what they were told. But that mass-production world, the story continues, no longer exists. The Industrial Age has given way to an Age of Information.

In the old days, enterprises could prosper churning out the same product by the millions. Customers were expected to buy what manufacturers produced — and they usually did. "You can have any color you want," as automaker Henry Ford once quipped, "so long as it's black." In the new Information Age, by contrast, enterprises only do well when they *customize* products to what customers want. And who knows what customers want? The workers at the front lines, the employees who interact directly with consumers. These workers, through their contacts with customers, gain incredibly significant information. An effective enterprise values this information — and the employees who have it.

The effective enterprise, adds the empowerment mantra, also values workers on the production line, because modern production operations must be constantly changing to keep up with evolving consumer preferences. Who better to help figure out how to change, how to produce products ever faster, smarter, and more efficiently, than the workers actually involved in the producing?

For Information Age business success, in short, workers simply must be engaged and involved. In our modern world, command-and-control no longer makes any sense.[2]

Think of modern enterprise life, suggests British economist John Kay, as a basketball game. If a basketball game were entirely predictable, coaches could succeed merely by defining what they want each player to do at each exact moment. But no coach ever tries to script an entire game. No script, coaches understand, could ever anticipate "the almost infinite variety of situations that might arise."[3] Smart coaches prepare players — and expect players — to make their own decisions.

Expectations like these, notes Edward Lawler, the director of the Center for Effective Organizations at the University of Southern California, go against the "old logic" grain of corporate America. In the old logic enterprise, management makes all the decisions. Management, the old logic assumes, creates most value. What Lawler calls the "new logic" enterprise subscribes to a quite different set of assumptions. Corporate success, the new logic enterprise understands, requires that all employees, not just managers, "must add significant value."[4]

And just how can corporations maximize this added value? In the late twentieth century, experts rushed forward with guidance. Their strategies would go by a host of different labels. Participative management. Quality circles. Total quality management. Experts would talk endlessly about "reengineering" corporations to effect "high-performance organizations." Employee involvement, the experts stressed over and over, gives corporations smart enough to try it the "ultimate competitive advantage."[5]

This empowering ethos swept through corporate America in the 1980s and 1990s. Managers and their staffs sat together, in meeting after meeting, drafting, discussing, and debating "mission" and "values" statements. And journals, magazines, and newspapers noticed. They celebrated, year after year, the triumphs of enterprises that were said to have successfully empowered their employees.

One typical triumph came at Ironite, an Arizona fertilizer company. An Ironite customer had asked for the company's fertilizer in boxes instead of bags, a reasonable enough request. But Ironite didn't have a boxing machine, and buying one would have cost the company far more than the firm could have comfortably afforded. No problem. Ironite's employees simply built a box-maker themselves, at a tenth of the cost of buying one.

That sort of employee creativity, Ironite's chief executive pointed out proudly, does not just happen out of the blue.

"You get this only if you involve and respect employees," explained Ironite CEO Heinz Brungs. "You can't order them to build a machine."[6]

Every company, "effective enterprise" gurus insisted throughout the 1980s and 1990s, could become an Ironite. But few companies, researchers agreed by century's end, had actually reached anything close to Ironite status. Study after study reached the same dispiriting conclusion. Enterprises, by and large, were not empowering workers.[7]

Just 10 percent of *Fortune* 1000 corporations, Edward Lawler would report in 1996, were managing "according to the new logic."[8] And only a small fraction of the companies that claimed to be empowering workers, a *Journal of Business* study would reveal two years later, were actually engaging in any serious empowerment work.[9] Another study, published in 2000 by *Administrative Science Quarterly*, found executives across the United States quick to proclaim their allegiance to the new logic, but slow to practice it. On empowerment, concluded Barry Staw and Lisa Epstein, the study's authors, top executives are essentially going through the motions.[10]

But why? Why aren't top executives giving empowerment strategies a real go?[11] Empowering employees, the experts all agree, can enhance enterprise efficiency. Why aren't executives making any real effort to see whether the experts are right? What CEOs, after all, wouldn't want their enterprises to be more efficient?

Strange. Something is stopping American business from creating the employee-empowering, customer-focused "new logic" enterprises that the Information Age so clearly demands. What is it?

ALMOST ANYONE WHO HAS EVER WORKED in a large company would probably agree, in a heartbeat, that the obstacles to enterprise effectiveness can almost always be summed up in just one eleven-letter word. Bureaucracy. Average employees experience frustrating doses of "bureaucracy" each and every day, in everything from turf wars between managers to the endless delays while ideas go up and down the decision-making ladder.

Bureaucracies, sociologists tell us, grow naturally — and inevitably — in enterprises organized along hierarchical lines. In the classic corporate hierarchy, workers sit at the base of a steep pyramid. Above them rest layers upon layers of management. The more layers, the steeper the pyramid, the greater the distance between actual workers and ultimate corporate decision-making authority. To succeed in the Information Age, analysts contended in the 1980s and 1990s, enterprises needed, above all else, to "flatten" these towering pyramids.[12] Many top executives readily agreed, some intensely.

"Rigid hierarchies," exclaimed one such executive, J. Burgess Winter, the CEO of an empowerment-minded Tucson copper company, "are the corporate cholesterol of organizations."[13]

Reformers like Winter urged executives to do battle against hierarchy. Deflate that management bloat, they beseeched, and free your employees to become the creative contributors to enterprise success they most certainly can be. For a time, in the early 1990s, corporate America claimed to be following the reformers' advice. America's corporations, observers pronounced, were shearing off management fat layer by layer. But these claims, once subjected to review, would not hold up. American companies weren't becoming leaner, as economist David Gordon documented, just meaner. Corporate America remained, he concluded, as "middle-management-heavy as ever."[14]

Other research reinforced Gordon's findings.[15] The total number of middle managers, one investigation found, actually increased between 1989 and 1995.[16] Corporate America's demand for managers, the *Wall Street Journal* reported in 1996, "is booming."[17]

The "new logic" war against hierarchy had clearly fizzled. Years of seminars and books and speeches had made virtually no impact. Organizational pyramids had not been flattened. Employees remained shut out from decision-making. And none of this, careful analysts pointed out, should have surprised anyone. Reformers tend to see corporate hierarchies as anachronistic, easily disposable hangovers from bygone days of command-and-control. But hierarchies are no feeble anachronisms. In contemporary business, they still serve a real purpose. They help ensure that excessive executive pay remains excessive. They amount, in essence, to income-maintenance programs for top executives.

Peter Drucker, the father of modern management theory, had detected and described this income-maintenance dynamic years before, back in the early 1980s. In any hierarchy, Drucker noted, every level of bureaucracy must be compensated at a higher rate than the level below. The more levels, the higher the pay at the top.[18] Hierarchies would remain appealing to executives, he argued, as long as they prop up and push up executive pay. His solution? To make hierarchies less appealing to executives, Drucker suggested, limit executive pay. No executives, Drucker wrote in 1982, should be allowed to make more than twenty times the compensation of their workers.[19]

Few other prominent scholars in the boom years would dare to suggest, following Drucker, a specific ratio between executive and worker compensation. But many did make clear their concern that wide pay gaps fouled the "atmosphere of trust and confidence between workers and management" so essential to successful employee empowering. "Large differences in status," concluded a Brookings Institution analysis, "can inhibit participation."[20] "Extreme wage differentials between workers and management," agreed four other researchers in a major study published in 2000, "discourage trust and prevent employees from seeing themselves as stakeholders."[21]

Those who care deeply about building effective enterprises have drawn one clear conclusion from these realities. To be serious about reducing bureaucratic bloat, about ending command-and-control, about creating effective organizations for a modern economy, enterprises simply must narrow wide reward differentials. Enterprises that crave the best their employees have to offer, but ignore gaping differentials in compensation between top and bottom, do so at their peril.

IN THE EARLY DAYS OF THE COMPUTER REVOLUTION, in the heady air of America's unofficial capital of high tech, Silicon Valley, some companies did do more than just crave the best their employees had to offer. These companies openly declared war on corporate business as usual. The founders of these firms, executives like Bob Noyce, forty when he helped launch Intel in 1968, had experienced command-and-control hierarchies earlier in their careers. They were determined not to let command-and-control habits define their new enterprises. They would empower employees. They would flatten hierarchies.

An early hire of Intel, a company history notes, once stopped co-founder Noyce in an office hallway.

"I'm not really clear on the reporting structure of this outfit," the new hire asked. "Can you just draw me a quick organization chart?"[22]

Noyce gladly obliged. He walked to a nearby blackboard, drew an X and then a circle of Xs around that first X. The X in the middle, he explained, was the employee. The Xs that circled the employee were Intel's executives. The employee, Noyce told the new hire, could interact with any one of them he chose.

In Intel's earliest years, circles, not pyramids, would define the workplace. Intel would nurture a culture that encouraged "anyone who had a good idea to speak up, anyone with a question to ask it."[23] In a "fast-moving industry where speed of response to change was all-important, and where information had to flow as swiftly as possible if the company was to make the right decisions," no other approach seemed appropriate, or even rational.

New companies throughout Silicon Valley shared Noyce's perspective. One of them, Hewlett-Packard, actually predated Intel. That company's co-founders, Bill Hewlett and Dave Packard, preached what would become known as the "HP Way." Their company, they pledged in 1966, would "maintain an organizational environment that fosters individual motivation, initiative and creativity, and a wide latitude of freedom in working toward established objectives and goals."[24]

Silicon Valley's start-ups of the 1970s would share this same contempt for corporate command-and-control. Curiosity and creativity, not profits and empire building, seemed to drive them. Steve Wozniak, the designer of the first Apple computer in 1976, wasn't out "to get rich or launch a *Fortune* 500 company," as one journalist fascinated by Silicon Valley's early history has noted. Wozniak "just wanted to have fun and impress the guys down at the local computer club."[25] Wozniak and his soulmates felt they were forging new ways of doing business, not just new products. Their companies would operate on a free and open basis. Worklife in the companies they founded would be exciting and fun.

And lucrative, too. Extremely so. People liked the products that shipped out of Silicon Valley. Computing's founding executives may not have set out to make themselves wealthy, but they soon amassed millions anyway. Would these millions spoil the creative, open-minded enterprises that dotted Silicon Valley? The founders didn't think so. They had a strategy for keeping their employees engaged and creative. They would share the wealth their companies were creating. They would give their employees stock options.[26] These options, they felt sure, would motivate everyone in their enterprises to strive for enterprise success. Inspired by options, executives and employees would bust down bureaucratic barriers. They would work, innovate, and prosper — together.

Options would go on to propagate wildly throughout Silicon Valley's corporate culture. Everybody in Silicon Valley, from receptionists to engineers, soon seemed to be cashing in on the option cascade. At one digital giant, Cisco, employees in 1998 held "an average of $200,000 in unvested options." Not everyone in computing, to be sure, would be sitting on such comfortable option stashes. Options were clearly enriching some far more than others. One late 1990s survey of twenty Silicon Valley companies, conducted by the National Center for Employee Stock Ownership, found that 49 percent of all options granted had gone to management. Senior executives at these companies had accumulated option grants that averaged $2 million. Administrative workers, in the same companies, held options that averaged just $18,000.[27]

These sorts of gaps, as startling as they might be, would raise few eyebrows in Silicon Valley. Options, high-tech's cheerleaders opined, made gaps irrelevant. Everyone was benefiting. Any inequality in the distribution of rewards simply didn't matter.

But that inequality, in the end, would matter — to the ideal of the open, empowering, creative workplace that Silicon Valley's original pioneers held so dear. By distributing options to all or most all employees, these pioneers had believed, young high-tech companies could cancel out any resentment that windfalls for executives might otherwise engender. But they were wrong. Options would not cancel out inequality. Inequality would cancel out the open, creative, empowering workplace.

Silicon Valley's *disempowering* dynamic would unfold initially at Intel, the first of the high-tech giants where huge pay gaps emerged between executives and everyone else. By 1971, Intel co-founders Bob Noyce and Gordon Moore had amassed shares of company stock worth nearly a combined $20 million. But they weren't selling, not a share.

"Both men," notes Tim Jackson, a *Financial Times* correspondent who authored a 1997 history of Intel, "clearly believed that Intel still had far to go."[28]

To get there, Noyce and Moore entrusted Intel's daily operations to the company's most hard-driving, least empowering-minded executive, Andy Grove. From 1971 on, Grove ran Intel — and arrogantly ran roughshod over the creative freedom that had typified Intel's earliest days. The command-and-control ethos that Intel had so famously rejected would now become Intel's standard operating procedure.[29]

One Grove contribution to Intel's workplace culture, the "Late List," came to symbolize the company's increasing regimentation. Security officers, operating under Grove's direct orders, were required to collect, and circulate to top Intel executives, the names of all employees who arrived at work after eight in the morning. This Late List infuriated Intel's engineers. They deeply resented any implication they were shirking. In the mornings, after long nights spent working, the engineers would scribble angry notes on the Late List sign-in sheets — "I was here until midnight last night, damnit!" — and subversively identify themselves as Mickey Mouse or even Andy Grove himself.[30]

Year after year, deep into the 1980s, Intel employees would chafe under Grove's heavy-handed management. Thousands of them, notes Tim Jackson, regularly put up "with more regimentation, more inconvenience, more indignity than people in other companies."[31] But they stayed on. They had to stay. They were trapped, locked in place by their options. Stock options have to vest before they can be cashed out, and vesting takes time. In the interim, employees disgruntled by Grove's petty tyrannies had no choice but to swallow their pride. Grove and his fellow executives could essentially manage however they saw fit, secure in the knowledge that their subordinates couldn't afford to walk away from unvested options. The options meant to encourage professionals to perform at the highest levels had created instead, at Intel, legions of bitter, resentful, humiliated employees who gave the company not their all, but their least.

Intel would evolve eventually into just another command-and-control workplace, a "second-rate manufacturer by world-class standards" that would sooner tie up rivals in court battles over patents than risk engaging them in fair and open competition. Intel's notorious litigation offensives would pay off handsomely for the company. By the end of the 1980s, notes company historian Tim Jackson, "Intel was making so much money that it didn't *need* to be an efficient producer."[32]

By the end of the 1990s, the empowering spirit that had once animated high-tech's pioneers had almost totally disappeared, and not just from Intel. Wealth now ruled.

"Silicon Valley used to care more about innovation than getting rich," shouted out the January 2000 cover of *Red Herring,* a Bay Area-based business magazine. "No longer."[33]

The last Silicon Valley bulwark against corporate business as usual, Hewlett-Packard, threw in the towel near century's end. Hewlett-Packard had done more to keep Silicon Valley's original egalitarian vision alive than any other big-time high-tech player. The company, in the hard times of the late 1970s, had avoided layoffs by cutting pay 10 percent across the entire board, executives included.[34] The company's CEO, into the 1980s, worked out of "a cubicle in the midst of a vast room instead of a corner office."[35] HP top executives did make good money, but nowhere near the magisterial sums pulled in by executives elsewhere. This "egalitarian" HP, by the mid 1990s, had started to fade. Some signs of the fade, most notably a private office for the HP CEO, would be obvious to all.[36] Other signs would be considerably less visible. In the 1970s, HP workers who boxed the company's calculators made decent money and benefits. In the 1990s, temps from Manpower were doing HP assembly work, with no benefits and making the same $1,000 a month HP workers had made back in the 1970s, despite decades of inflation.[37]

The final insult to the "HP Way" would come at decade's end. Midway through 1999, Hewlett-Packard would award its new chief executive, Carly Fiorina, the biggest no-strings stock grant in U.S. corporate history. The $66 million worth of shares handed to Fiorina, added to her base salary and assorted bonuses, brought the total value of her new, four-year pay package up to $90 million.[38] A small price to pay, the HP board figured, for a CEO who could rev up Hewlett-Packard's declining fortunes.

Fiorina would rev up nothing. Within two years, HP's stock shares had dropped more than 50 percent.[39] But Fiorina had a plan. To jump start the company, she would ask HP's ninety-three thousand worldwide employees to accept voluntary cutbacks. Employees would be able to pick their poison, either a 10 percent pay cut, a 5 percent pay cut and the loss of four vacation days, or the loss of eight vacation days. Workers could also choose none of the above. Remarkably, 86 percent of HP's workforce picked one of the three cutback options. One company spokesperson "chalked up the high participation rate" to the legacy of the HP Way.[40] The voluntary cutbacks would save HP $130 million.

Less than a month after HP employees made this noble collective sacrifice, the company rewarded them for it. Management, in a surprise announcement that would kill any vestigial remains of the HP Way, revealed plans to lay off six thousand workers. Inside HP's workplaces, observers found an immediate "bitterness" backlash. Employees, noted Rice University's Steven Currall, would have taken CEO Fiorina's fourth option — no voluntary cuts — if they thought they were "in jeopardy of getting laid off anyway."[41]

The voluntary pay cuts and the six thousand layoffs would produce no turnaround in HP's fortunes. Fiorina, in still another desperate gambit, proceeded to broker a merger with rival Compaq Computer, then spent millions of corporate dollars to sell the controversial merger to shareholders. She eventually won a shareholder green light for her merger and, as CEO of the newly merged company, moved quickly to make her new enterprise profitable — by eliminating 15,000 of the merged company's 150,000 jobs.[42]

Fiorina and her Compaq counterpart, Michael Capellas, had made sure during merger negotiations, of course, that their new company would have plenty of room for them, Fiorina as chief executive, Capellas as president. They would work under two-year contracts worth a combined $117.4 million in salary, bonuses, and stock options.[43]

Years before, back in Silicon Valley's earliest days, Carly Fiorina's predecessors thought they could make their fortunes and still, at the same time, maintain enterprises that fostered "individual motivation, initiative, and creativity." They could not. Silicon Valley had promised to empower employees. Silicon Valley, instead, betrayed them.

AMERICA'S BUSINESS LEADERS, IN PRACTICE, have never really accepted the notion that empowering employees makes enterprises effective. Empowering workers, after all, requires that power be shared, and the powerful, in business as elsewhere, seldom enjoy sharing their power.

The powerful enjoy sharing rewards even less. Corporate leaders have never accepted, either in theory or practice, the notion that enterprise effectiveness demands some sort of meaningful reward sharing. Rewards, business leaders have always believed, don't need to be shared. They only need to be targeted — to those employees who do good work. If high-achievers are rewarded, the traditional corporate calculus holds, more workers will strive to become high-achievers. Want to grow a high-performance organization? Simply offer individual workers rewards for high performance.

Researchers, down through the years, have repeatedly challenged this corporate devotion to "pay-for-performance." Rewards, they have shown, simply cannot guarantee that employees will perform at higher levels. People are simply too different, and motivations too complex, for any reward to make an automatic impact.[44] Indeed, as *Business Week* pointed out in 1999, researchers have not as yet unearthed a single case where singling out high-achieving individuals for extra pay has made an enterprise more effective.[45]

Why doesn't simply paying people for "good" performance work very well? The difficulties start with defining just exactly how performance will be measured. Employees usually, and understandably, balk at any performance measures they see as subjective. Managers, employees know from experience, can let everything from favoritism to outright racism cloud their judgments about performance. As a result, most employees would usually rather see "objective measures, such as sales volume or units produced," used to evaluate them.[46] But "objective" measures carry their own baggage. Employees, once they know they will be rewarded based on how well they meet a specific objective, tend to work toward meeting that objective — and only that objective.

"Pay customer-service reps to answer the phone on the first ring," quips *Fortune* management analyst Geoffrey Colvin, "and they'll answer it — and then put it down."[47]

At best, adds Colvin, performance rewards like these "will get people to do more of what they're doing. Not better, just more."

But just *more* no longer cuts it, not in the Information Age. The modern enterprise needs workers thinking — and caring about — their work. Such thinking and caring cannot be "bought" by dangling rewards for individual performance. In fact, many analysts believe, individual workplace rewards push enterprises in exactly the wrong direction. They discourage the collaboration and cooperation *between* employees so essential to Information Age enterprise success. Where companies target rewards to individual employees, explains economist Matt Bloom, individual employees quite logically "concentrate only on their own performance — to the exclusion of organizational goals."[48] Individual awards, in the end, undermine the cooperative spirit. They are, as analyst Edward Lawler notes, "counterproductive to individuals working together."[49]

So counterproductive, experts on motivation have concluded, that they deserve no place in the modern enterprise. Abraham Maslow, the influential twentieth century psychologist, held that individual rewards inevitably generate dysfunctional behavior.[50] W. Edwards Deming, the twentieth century's top workplace quality guru, agreed.[51] Effective enterprises, thinkers inspired by Deming continue to contend today, unite employees around a common goal. Individual rewards for performance divide them.[52]

But must rewards for performance always have this effect? Couldn't rewards be structured to encourage, not frustrate, cooperation and collaboration? A small but hardy band of labor and business analysts have made just this case. Rewards for performance, these analysts believe, can lead to greater enterprise effectiveness — so long as these rewards are shared on an enterprise-wide basis. This "gain-sharing" perspective, the brainchild of a union leader named Joseph Scanlon, first took significant root in the 1940s. Businesses, Scanlon argued, only thrive when labor and management join together and cooperate "to solve production problems and improve productivity."[53] And workers *will* cooperate, Scanlon argued, if the gains realized from cooperation are shared among all workers, not parceled out to a few.

Scanlon's influence would peak in the early 1950s, with "Scanlon plans" scattered widely throughout American industry.[54] The plans followed a similar outline. Performance goals would be identified.[55] Employee committees would generate, receive, and approve ideas for reaching these goals. Any profits generated by these ideas would then be split, typically fifty-fifty, between the company and the workers as a group.[56]

Joseph Scanlon would pass away in 1956, but his ideas would linger. In the 1990s, corporate reformers would still see in group bonus plans a healthy, team-building antidote to command-and-control.[57] Some CEOs even totally reconfigured their enterprises around the group-bonus spirit. In 1992, for instance, CEO Rob Rodin completely eliminated individual pay-for-performance rewards at his California company, Marshall Industries. All eighteen hundred employees would receive instead a share of Marshall's overall profit, and that share, as a percentage of salary, would be the same for everyone. Six years later, chief executive Rodin proudly reported that the productivity of his industrial electronics company had tripled.[58]

But successes like Rodin's would not change many minds in America's executive suites. In the 1990s, in corporate America as a whole, individual performance rewards would remain more than twice as common as group gain-sharing.[59] And of the 15 percent of companies that did claim to be engaged in some form of gain-sharing, few had actually been at it very long. Indeed, researchers seem to agree, few gain-sharing plans have ever lasted very long. Most gain-sharing efforts, the research suggests, typically go through the same depressing cycle. They launch with smiles all around. Workers enthusiastically pinpoint the obvious inefficiencies they see everyday in their workplaces, these inefficiencies are fixed, earnings jump, and everyone shares in some robust rewards. But workers can only fix obvious inefficiencies once. After this once, new productivity gains become steadily harder to realize. The "low-hanging fruit" has already been picked. The rewards from gain-sharing start to shrivel.[60]

That shriveling, in the 1990s, would put a particularly tight squeeze on workers involved in gain-sharing plans, mainly because many of the companies that did give gain-sharing a try over the course of the decade used gain-sharing bonuses to replace, not supplement, other forms of compensation. At Dupont Chemical's fibers division, for instance, workers agreed to trade all raises in exchange for three years of gain-sharing. At other companies, gain-sharing substituted for regularly scheduled cost-of-living inflation adjustments.[61]

In all these situations, essentially only workers stood at risk. If gain-sharing failed to generate appreciable cost reductions, workers could easily end up receiving less total compensation than they had earned before the gain-sharing went into effect. Top executives, meanwhile, faced no such risk. Their personal compensation, as we have seen in earlier pages, would continue to grow no matter how well their companies performed.

Gain-sharing plans that left only workers at risk, of course, totally subverted the trust between bosses and workers that Joe Scanlon had considered so basic to gain-sharing success. Plans that "shared" gains but not risks did not nurture more participative, empowering enterprises. They reinforced hierarchical distinctions.

Still, not every gain-sharing effort in the boom years would fizzle. Some enterprises did register meaningful, ongoing benefits from gain-sharing in the 1980s and 1990s. These enterprises all shared one distinction: They were small.[62] Most of them resembled Kay Manufacturing, an Illinois auto parts manufacturer with just 125 employees. Kay Manufacturing launched gain-sharing in 1993. By 1996, the company had halved factory rejects and reduced its accident rate from fifty a year to one.[63]

What makes small companies more hospitable to gain-sharing than large companies? Smaller companies, analysts note, carry fewer levels of management than larger companies and smaller pay gaps between executives at the top and workers at the base. These smaller gaps make cooperation easier to come by.[64] And individual workers at smaller firms can see clearly that their efforts really do make an impact on the enterprise bottom line. In larger companies, notes Edward Lawler, "profits are so far beyond the direct influence of most employees that profit-based bonuses are simply not likely to be an effective motivator."[65]

The evidence from America's workplaces, many analysts have concluded, all points in one direction. To keep hierarchies flat, to enhance cooperation and performance, keep enterprises small. In enterprises, as corporate reformer and later Supreme Court justice Louis Brandeis observed a century ago, human scale is small scale. Businesses, Brandeis noted, "may keep growing bigger but human beings come in the same size."[66] And that same size is overpowered, not empowered, when businesses bulge.

But businesses in the 1980s and 1990s kept bulging anyway. No one could credibly argue that this bulging, this swallowing up of former competitors into bigger and bigger single enterprises, was giving workers a more "direct stake in corporate performance." So why did businesses keep bulging ever larger? Businesses kept bulging simply because rewards kept concentrating — at the top.

RESEARCHERS FIRST DOCUMENTED the link between bigness and big pay in the 1950s. The corporate executives who made the most money, analysts discovered, didn't always have the most profitable companies. They had the biggest. Executive compensation, concluded one 1959 study, appears "to be far more closely related to the scale of operation of the firm than to its profitability."[67]

In the years to come, researchers would repeatedly reconfirm this size-compensation connection. Corporate performance, pay analyst Graef Crystal found at century's end, usually explains "only 2 to 4 percent" of the difference between what top executives make. "The rest," he reported, "largely depends on the size of the company."[68]

The larger a company, the more that company's top executives take home. Corporate moguls have understood this direct relationship ever since the dawn of corporate time — and done their best to act upon it. A century ago, they would get carried away. They would go on a bigness binge, between 1898 and 1902, that forged industrial behemoths many times greater in size than any the world had ever seen. These giant "trusts" generated astounding fortunes for the corporate titans at their summits — and bullied millions of average Americans, workers and consumers alike.

Average Americans did not take kindly to this fearsome corporate concentration. They struggled mightily to bust the trusts, and out of those struggles would emerge a body of "antitrust law" that essentially placed limits on just how big and powerful individual corporations could become. These limits would remain in place for over half a century, but, in the 1970s. they would start to unravel. By decade's end, several key industries — the airlines, trucking, natural gas, and banking — would all be significantly "freed" from government rules and regulations.

Wheelers and dealers would move quickly to profit off this "deregulation." Piece by piece, they began assembling little companies into big empires. Reagan administration officials, in the early 1980s, would help move this process along, by essentially refusing to enforce the nation's remaining antitrust statutes. The United States would soon see, in the wake of this law enforcement failure, a merger wave "that would have been inconceivable under prior administrations."[69]

Bigger corporate enterprises would bring bigger corporate executive paychecks. By the 1990s, America's corporate elite had achieved levels of compensation that dwarfed the pay of executives at any other time or in any other place. This lavish compensation, in turn, would only *increase* the pressure on enterprises to bulge even bigger, since executives awarded incredibly immense pay packages now found themselves prodded to justify their exalted status. Wall Street investors wanted results. And right away.[70]

How could executives deliver the fast and dramatic results investors expected? Certainly not by paying attention to the lofty ideals of the effective-enterprise crowd. A truly effective enterprise, a collaborative enterprise, could not be fashioned quickly and dramatically. So why should a richly rewarded top executive even try to fashion one? Why wrestle with the aggravations and uncertainties of trying to make an enterprise work more effectively and efficiently? Wall Street, after all, wasn't demanding that executives make their enterprises bigger *and* better. Just bigger would do.[71]

Bigger it would be. In the 1990s, top executives would go out and consummate mergers with a passion — and in a quantity — unseen since the heyday of the original trusts. U.S. corporate executives became, as Yale's Jeffrey Sonnenfeld would later quip, "serial acquirers" of other businesses.[72] They cut, from 1994 through 1998, merger and acquisition deals that involved, in all, more than thirty-six thousand companies.[73] They didn't stop there. In 1999, corporate America cut another $1.75 trillion worth of merger deals, nearly ten times the total merger action of 1990.[74]

"The industrial world," concluded the *Washington Post* just before the new millennium, "has approached the turn of the century in a frenzy of merger madness."[75]

Corporate leaders, naturally, did not consider their merging "madness." By assembling ever larger enterprises, executives argued, they were consolidating "overlapping networks," helping companies realize economies of scale, and, above all, creating "synergy." [76] Formerly separate companies, CEOs crowed, were now "synergistically" cross-promoting — and growing — each other's products.

These claims, inside America's newly merged companies, soon became little more than sick jokes. In actual workplaces, mergers were spreading havoc, not synergy. And how could they not? Many of the mergers had been assembled in haste, sometimes in just a matter of days. [77] Once assembled, the newly merged mega-corporations required top executives to "manage" far more than any executive could comfortably handle. [78] These executives were in no position to manage anything. They had spent so many years doing their best "to swallow their peers and grow through buying rather than building," business journalist Ken Kurson explained, that none of them "knew how to manage." [79]

America's corporate giants would enter the twenty-first century as bloated, top-heavy caricatures of the effective, quality-conscious enterprises that the Information Age demanded. Intel, again, would lead the way.

IN 1998, LONG-TIME INTEL CEO ANDY GROVE handed his famous company's reins to his veteran deputy, Craig Barrett. Barrett, eager to make his own mark on Intel, would promptly go on a merger-and-acquisition tear. He would spend, over the next two years, some $7 billion to buy out more than twenty other companies. [80]

This fearsomely rapid expansion would take, inside Intel, a heavy toll. The company would soon start stumbling with one core product after another. In May 2000, Intel recalled a million faulty computer motherboards. Three months later, the company recalled a new chip. In October, executives postponed the launch of one long-awaited new processor and canceled plans for another. That same month, Intel outraged computer makers by shoving back, on the eve of the Christmas shopping season, the release of still another new processor. [81]

Industry observers blamed Intel's manic merging for the company's problems. Intel executives were spending much too much of their time, one Intel-watcher told *eWeek*, "reviewing takeover targets, negotiating deals, reviewing contractual agreements." [82]

"I think it's an interesting coincidence that Intel's having these problems at the same time they're venturing into all these other areas," agreed an analyst from *Microprocessor Report*. "I don't think you can underestimate the importance of staying focused." [83]

CEO Barrett's frantic wheeling-and-dealing had left Intel a bigger enterprise, not a better one. His mergers had not delivered. Computer industry mergers, one distinguished high-tech guru would add in 2001, *never* deliver.

"I know of no computer merger anywhere," observed David Caminer, the brain behind the world's first business computer, "where there has been added value from the merger of competing forces of engineers, marketers and programmers."[84]

Outside the computer world, other business insiders offered similar judgments about the negative impact of mergers on enterprise effectiveness. The maverick chief executive behind Southwest Airlines, for instance, credited his company's success to its refusal to play merger games. Southwest, CEO Herb Kelleher pointed out in 2002, had explicitly rejected taking the merger-and-acquisition road to king-sized status.

"We've never been focused on gigantism," Kelleher explained. "We've focused on being the best."[85]

Mergers, some analysts noted, may actually destroy more shareholder value than they create. In 2001, researchers from Stern Stewart & Co., a global consulting firm based in New York, ranked how well over five thousand major companies worldwide were doing at creating shareholder value.[86] The most striking finding: European enterprises were creating significantly more value than American enterprises. Why the difference?

"One possible reason is Europeans' smaller appetite for big mergers," suggested the British *Economist* magazine. "One lesson from the rankings is that costly acquisitions are a good way to destroy value."[87]

Another lesson would be that outsized compensation rewards for top executives are a good way to stimulate costly acquisitions. Executive pay in Europe, throughout the 1980s and 1990s, had lagged substantially behind executive pay in the United States. European executives, consequently, faced far less pressure to justify their exalted status — by making grand merger maneuvers — because their status was nowhere near as exalted.[88]

And a variety of stakeholders in Europe were eager to keep things that way. European unions, shareholders, and politicians all frowned on American-style CEO pay — and the merger games U.S. executives played to keep that pay soaring. These stakeholders acted as a constant constraint on executive behavior in Europe. Euro CEOs could fantasize about the lovely personal windfalls a megamerger might bring. Relatively few had enough power to pull them off.

CEOs in the United States faced no such constraints. American executives, from their command-and-control corporate perches, were free to play whatever corporate shell games caught their fancy. And why not play these merger games? These were games American executives could not possibly lose.

Some U.S. executives would "win" simply by gobbling up other companies as rapidly as possible. The fastest gobbler may have been L. Dennis Kozlowski, the CEO of Tyco International. Over one three-year span, "Deal-a-Day Dennis" engineered the acquisitions of *seven hundred* companies.[89] For his efforts, Kozlowski took home $140 million in 1999 and $205 million more in 2000.[90] His house-of-cards would start collapsing just over a year later. In 2002, Tyco would lose over $80 billion in value in just six months.[91]

Other American executives won their merger windfalls not by gobbling, but by being gobbled. They wheeled and dealed themselves out of jobs and into fortunes. Sometimes quite sizable fortunes. Richard Adams saw his Virginia-based company, UUNet Technologies, bought out by MFS Communications in 1996. MFS, a year later, was bought out by WorldCom. Adams ended 1997 with a personal fortune estimated at $500 million.[92] He went on to devote his spare time to a new company, Cello Technologies, which filed for bankruptcy in 2000. Despite this unfortunate setback, *Forbes* that same year valued the Adams fortune at $1 billion.[93]

Still other executives tried to get gobbled, failed, yet still walked away a good bit richer. In 2001, the chairman and CEO of Honeywell, Michael Bonsignore, was ousted after a deal to merge Honeywell into General Electric fell through. Bonsignore left with $9 million in severance on top of a $2 million annual pension slated to start in 2004. He did have to pay a price for all this Honeywell honey. The company demanded that Bonsignore stipulate that he would not work for a competitor — "or badmouth Honeywell" — after his exit.[94] With his severance and retirement, some wondered, why would Bonsignore ever want to?

And why would any American CEO of sound mind and body not want to follow in Bonsignore's footsteps and try to plot the biggest mergers they could possibly imagine? And if those mergers backfired and cost their companies a fortune — Quaker Oats CEO William Smithburg lost his company $1 billion in the mid 1990s after buying up and then having to sell off the sinking Snapple soft drink company — who cared?[95] The merger-and-acquisition action, after all, wasn't about building better enterprises. The action was all about, and only about, building fortunes. The grandest merger deal of the 1980s, the RJR Nabisco buyout, "gathered steam," journalist Michael Lewis would later write, "for no better reason than that a rich man — Henry Kravis, in this case — wanted to call attention to his capacity to get richer."[96]

And the richer, of course, could never get rich enough.

"If we're going to be big, we might as well be big," billionaire Ted Turner, a gobbler-turned-gobbled, exclaimed late in 1999. "I want one of everything."[97]

AT SOME POINT, FOR EVERY WHEELER-DEALER CEO, the dust eventually settles. At some point, these executives run out of companies to snap up and swallow. Their grand enterprises, at some point, need to operate profitably enough to keep their creditors and investors happy.

But how? The "economies of scale" the executives had so cavalierly promised quickly turn out to be mirages. And those "synergies"? Just phony illusions. The executives find themselves trapped. They sit at the summit of bureaucratic monstrosities, huge unworkable, inefficient, top-down, direction-less enterprises that bear absolutely no resemblance to the participatory, empowering, high-performance enterprises they give speeches lauding. From this summit, the executives cannot move their enterprises forward — toward "new logic" status — because that would mean unplugging the personal wealth-creation machines their corporations had become. From this summit, America's executives can only move their enterprises in one direction. Backwards.

The retreat — from the basic precepts of "Information Age" enterprise success — would begin before the twentieth century ended. America's top executives would not focus their enterprises on serving consumers. They would, instead, seek to bamboozle consumers at every turn. They would not empower workers. They would, instead, squeeze workers at every opportunity. Their new enterprises would be effective — but only at exploiting.

American consumers would be subject to this exploitation, by century's end, almost every time they dropped a dollar, or a credit card, on a counter. These dollars and credit cards came from banks and other financial institutions, and that's where the exploitation of America's consumers began.

In the late twentieth century, no sector of the economy experienced more frantic wheeling-and-dealing than what has come to be known as the "financial services" industry. Industry observers, by 1996, counted seventy different banking mergers valued at more than $1 billion. By the end of 1998, they counted three hundred. Each merger, along the way, seemed to feed a merge-at-any-cost fever. In 1996, NationsBank paid 2.6 times "book value" to buy Boatmen's Bancshares in St. Louis. In 1997, NationsBank paid four times book value for Florida's Barnett Banks. Later that year, First Union paid a record $17 billion — 5.3 times book value — to buy CoreStates, a lackluster bank that hadn't upped earnings in over a year. "By that time," *Fortune* magazine would later note, "the bidding had become so frenzied" that lackluster numbers "just didn't matter."[98]

Banking executives raised the billions they needed to keep the bidding going by promising Wall Street that "the new deals would generate spectacular earnings growth."[99] They could only deliver those "spectacular earnings" in one way: by spectacularly fleecing consumers.

Automated teller machines did a good bit of the fleecing, through an assortment of new surcharges and higher fees. By 1997, banks were routinely charging extra fees to customers who used another bank's ATM. In 1996, before these new surcharges, consumers typically paid $1.01 per transaction. By 2001, the average cost had jumped to $2.86.[100] In some big cities, transaction costs hit $4.50, for withdrawals as low as $20.[101]

America's banking giants were squeezing even more dollars out of customer pockets, the *Wall Street Journal* would report in 2002, by "racheting up late fees." In 2001, credit card issuers pulled in $7.3 billion in late fees, a five-fold leap from the $1.7 billion in late fees they collected in 1996.[102] By 2003, banks were charging late fees that averaged $30.04. Late fees, five years earlier, had averaged only half that.[103]

Banking mergers, Americans had been assured, would bring "economies of scale" that would help consumers save. In real life, mergers simply made gouging consumers easier.

And not just in banking. Media executives played the same merger-and-acquisition games as bankers, and consumers could feel the media M&A impact every time they opened up their monthly bills for cable and Internet or turned on their TVs and radios. The most blatant gouging would come from the most blatantly bone-headed media merger, the turn-of-the-century marriage of America Online and Time Warner.

The supergiant that would become known as AOL Time Warner had actually started to take shape back years before, when Time took over Warner in the most celebrated media merger of the 1980s. Warner CEO Steve Ross made $200 million off the deal. Time Warner then swallowed Ted Turner's media empire, a deal that gave Turner a new title, vice chairman, and $111 million for five years of vice chairing.[104] Time Warner next moved to tie the knot, in 2000, with the biggest on-ramp to the Internet, America Online. That deal brought under one roof media properties that ranged from HBO, CNN, and Looney Tunes to CompuServe and Netscape — and also triggered $1.8 billion worth of option cash-out clauses in the contracts of the top five executives who did the dealing.[105]

Those executives didn't have much time to savor their windfalls. They needed, quickly, to figure out how to post enough earnings to justify their mega-merging. Their solution? Squeeze consumers. Midway through 2001, they hiked America Online's basic monthly subscription rate, already the highest in the industry, from $21.95 to $23.90, a move that figured to boost company revenues by $150 million. About $100 million of that new revenue, company officials told Wall Street, would be "pure profit."[106]

America Online's rivals blasted the price boost, in public — and cheered lustily in private. AOL's price hike meant they could jump their own Internet rates as much as 20 percent and, as one industry analyst noted, "still be in the same relative pricing position vis-à-vis AOL as they were before!" Added the analyst: "It's almost like free money!"[107]

Free money from the pockets of America's consumers. But consumers, by century's end, were used to having their pockets picked by media giants. In 1996, these giants had convinced Congress to sweep away most of the remaining government regulations that covered the communications industry. This deregulation, members of Congress cheerfully predicted, would stimulate competition and save consumers millions. The legislation, instead, gave a green light to greater industry concentration — and consumer gouging. In the five years after the passage of the Telecommunications Act of 1996, basic rates for cable TV jumped 36 percent, well over twice the inflation rate.[108]

That same Telecommunications Act had an even greater impact on radio. Before the act's passage, no company could legally own more than forty radio stations nationally. The act erased this national limit. Five years — and $100 billion worth of radio station mergers later — just two companies totally dominated the nation's airwaves. One of the two, Clear Channel Communications, had amassed nearly twelve hundred local radio stations.[109] These five years of gobbling added $72.5 million to the personal fortune of Clear Channel's chief executive, L. Lowry Mays.[110]

Clear Channel felt the same pressure to deliver big-time earnings as banks and AOL Time Warner. And Clear Channel responded in exactly the same fashion — by thumbing its nose at consumers. Radio's new giant gave listeners just what they didn't want to hear: automated, homogenized programming stuffed with incredible numbers of commercials. By the end of the 1990s, some Clear Channel stations were running uninterrupted blocks of commercials that lasted *eight minutes* long.[111]

The same dynamics played out in network television, where prime-time programming, as the 1990s wore on, gave viewers less and less program and more and more commercials. The more ads that media giants like Disney, owner of ABC, could squeeze into each prime-time hour, the higher the earnings they could waltz before Wall Street.

In 1999, Disney CEO Michael Eisner needed to do a good bit of that waltzing. Disney earnings had dropped 27 percent. Wall Street was grumbling. Eisner responded. To make way for more commercials — and more commercial revenue — he had the producers of ABC's prime-time programming ordered to "trim their shows by at least 30 seconds per episode." At the time, ABC already sported more "non-program time" than any other major network, almost sixteen and a half minutes of commercials per hour, over ten minutes more of commercials than prime-time programs sported in the 1970s.[112]

In industry after industry, the same storyline kept repeating. Companies merge. Company executives hit the jackpot. The huge new merged company scrambles to make enough money to pay off creditors and keep investors happy. Consumers take it on the chin.

Or sometimes, if the consumers were flying, their butts.

By the late 1990s, America's deregulated airlines had been merging and purging for twenty years. Those mergers fattened executive wallets — and ended up squeezing passengers into seats much too small for the standard American tush. Continental, to maximize passenger revenue, bolted its airplane seat rows all of thirty-one inches apart, with the width of the seats just over half that.[113] But airlines like Continental weren't completely heartless. They actually did their best to help passengers fit into those silly little seats. They stopped feeding them. At century's end, passengers could spend twelve hours getting on and off planes and not get anything to eat more substantial than a bag of pretzels.[114] Plane travel had clearly become, for many Americans, the ultimate expression of corporate indifference to the consuming public.

For other Americans, the ultimate indifference tag belonged, hands down, to America's telephone giants. And no phone giant seemed to deserve that tag more than US West, the Denver-based Baby Bell the *Arizona Republic* labeled "the company everyone loves to hate."[115] Plenty of people had good reason to hate US West, among them Maggie Wilson, an elderly rural Arizonan. Wilson had ordered a $99 phone installation in June 1997. She promptly received a bill for $13,000 but no phone. She complained and was curtly informed she would personally have to sign up twenty-five customers for US West before the company would do her installation. Two and a half years after Wilson first asked for phone service, she still had none. Stories like Maggie Wilson's would be so common that three states would eventually levy substantial fines against US West. Two others debated yanking the company's license to do business.[116]

US West CEO Solomon Trujillo, amid the blistering criticism, solemnly promised service improvements. But the promised improvements never seemed to come. Trujillo, lawsuits against US West would later charge, never intended them to come. He was purposefully shortchanging customers to jack up US West's bottom line and make the company a more appealing merger partner.[117] In 2000, US West did merge, into Qwest Communications. Trujillo, from the merger deal, would clear $30 million.[118]

Making phone calls, watching TV, flying home for the holidays — America's middle class basics would all seem less attractive and more aggravating as the twentieth century ended. No simple pleasure seemed able to escape the relentless corporate pressure to maximize earnings at consumer expense. Not even duckpin bowling.

Duckpins have survived, over the years, as an acquired taste peculiar to the mid-Atlantic and parts of New England. Bowlers in duckpins put their hands around their bowling balls, not their fingers in. The balls weigh less than four pounds, and even little kids can roll them. Baltimore gave birth to duckpins in the early 1900s, and the game spread, "like canasta," into blue-collar communities up and down the East Coast.[119] The number of duckpin alleys would peak, at about twelve hundred, in the early 1960s.[120] Duckpins and the more standard "tenpin" game would both start fading after that. Locally owned lanes would plod along, sustained by devoted if not growing cohorts of practitioners.

Then suddenly, midway through the 1990s, everything changed. Bowling caught the fancy of the power suits at Goldman Sachs, a Wall Street investment bank. Here was a business, Goldman Sachs figured, ripe for consolidation. In 1996, Goldman Sachs spent $1.1 billion buying control over bowling's biggest business, the Richmond-based AMF, and then proceeded to grow that business considerably bigger. AMF, moving fast, bought up some two hundred bowling alleys across the country.[121] But even bigger bowling markets beckoned, most notably in China. AMF rushed onto the Chinese bowling scene, investing millions in lane construction. Bowling seemed to be going big-time!

The big-time didn't last. The Chinese bowling bubble would pop in 1998, amid the Asian financial crisis, and the popping sent AMF's overall profits "into the gutter." Company executives now needed to shore up investor confidence back in the United States. They demanded big earnings numbers from their American lanes. The duckpin alleys couldn't comply. They were profitable, but not profitable enough. AMF, in short order, "all but abandoned duckpins." By early 1999, only eighty duckpin lanes remained open.[122]

"Eventually," noted a discouraged John Shanahan, the president of the Baltimore Duckpin Bowlers Association, "there won't be any ducks."[123]

Effective enterprises, preached the organizational development prophets of the latter twentieth century, care about people like John Shanahan. They care about all their customers. Effective enterprises, the prophets agreed, talk to customers, study customers, do everything they can to discern what they can do to make their customers' lives easier and more pleasurable. This knowledge in hand, effective enterprises then endeavor to deliver on what consumers want — by providing products and services at a quality and cost that customers will find impossible to pass up.

An effective enterprise, in other words, concentrates on customers, first, last, and always.

In the closing years of the twentieth century, America's enterprises could not keep that concentration. The executives of these enterprises had something more important on their minds, their own personal fortunes. They sold out their customers. No one should have ever expected otherwise. Where we allow executive wealth to concentrate, without limit, executives will forever concentrate on maximizing that wealth. First, last, and always.

HOW CAN ENTERPRISES, IN THE INFORMATION AGE, really know what consumers want and address those wants efficiently? Effective enterprise theorists almost all advance variations on the same answer: To end up with loyal customers who value their products and services, enterprises first need to value their employees.

Employee commitment and creativity, effective enterprises understand, determine how well customer needs can be met.[124] Effective enterprises, consequently, do everything they can to keep employees committed and creative. They invest in employee training. They ask employee advice. They treat employees as their most important competitive advantage.

In the 1980s and 1990s, corporate executives spent significant sums to send their managers to a never-ending series of training sessions where earnest organizational consultants patiently explained these ABCs of effective enterprise success. And then these same corporate executives turned around, without a moment's pause, and took steps that rendered totally null and void all the lessons the consultants taught. The consultants urged that managers respect employees. The executives ordered, instead, that managers systematically discard them — as part of a calculated corporate strategy that had never before been employed on a massive scale. Observers eventually came up with a word to describe this new discarding phenomenon. They called it *downsizing*.

American workers had, of course, been discarded before. But downsizing, as begun in the 1990s, represented something quite different, a new departure for American business. Companies had traditionally discarded workers — "laid them off" — when sales went sour. Executives generally tried to avoid layoffs.

Every layoff, after all, signaled a management failure. A company that found itself forced to lay off workers had clearly misread market demand.[125] Companies that did lay off workers hoped, and expected, to be able to hire them back. Managements considered layoffs *temporary* measures.

By the early 1990s, in America's biggest corporations, these classic attitudes about layoffs had started to wither away. Employers were no longer laying off workers, on a temporary basis, because they faced shrinking demand for their products. Perfectly healthy, profitable companies were now consciously dismissing workers — permanently discarding them — solely to boost their short-term bottom lines.

In 1991, a recession-scarred year, American companies laid off an estimated 550,000 workers. By 1992, the recession had ended. The economy was growing again. Goods were flying off shelves. But layoffs continued: 500,000 in 1992, over 600,000 in 1993, over 500,000 in 1994.[126] These layoffs had virtually nothing to do with sluggish consumer demand. They had everything to do with the games executives play. Corporate executives were downsizing to make their mergers and acquisitions pay off — for themselves.

In August 1995, for instance, executives at Chemical Bank announced plans to merge with the Chase Manhattan Bank. Both banks had been profitable before the merger announcement. The new merged bank, the executives promised, would be even more profitable. Downsizing would see to that. The workforce of the merged bank would be sliced by twelve thousand employees, a move that would reduce the new bank's annual expenses by $1.5 billion. The personal bank accounts of Chemical Bank's former top officers and directors, in the meantime, would be increased, by just under $10 million.[127]

Not all the companies that downsized in the 1990s, to be sure, were merging. Nonmerging companies downsized, too — to keep pace with their merging competitors. By downsizing, they could create their own labor "efficiencies."

"Downsizing is not an event any more," as one business observer, Mitchell Marks of New York's Delta Consulting Group, put it. "It's become a way of business life."[128]

In 1998, near the height of the decade's boom, American firms sacked over two-thirds of a million workers, over one hundred thousand more workers than they cut loose in the recession year of 1991.[129] Simply by announcing a downsizing, executives found, they could build "earnings momentum." A single job eliminated, went the Wall Street rule of thumb, adds $60,000 to future annual earnings. A company with 500 million shares selling at ten times earnings could, investors figured, hike its stock price $1.20 a share just by downsizing a thousand workers.[130]

What executive sitting on top a pile of stock options could resist the lure of numbers like these? Certainly not Bernard Ebbers, the Mississippi entrepreneur who built an unknown telecommunications company, WorldCom, into the nation's second largest long distance phone company. Ebbers danced his way to the top with a corporate two-step. Step one: Cut a merger deal with another company. Step two: Slash costs at the new merged company by downsizing workers. Ebbers started two-stepping in 1983. Over the next sixteen years, he engineered sixty-five acquisitions.[131] After nearly every one, he dropped a downsizing ax on the newly merged workforce.[132]

Unfortunately for Ebbers, his two-step eventually danced straight into an unforgiving wall. In 2000, the U.S. Justice Department and European antitrust officials nixed his biggest merger of all, a $129 billion hook-up with Sprint.[133] With no more grand merger partners in sight, Ebbers suddenly found himself forced, one industry reporter noted, "to generate growth in a fashion he has never had to master: simply running the company."[134]

Ebbers didn't have a clue. He tried spinning off some of the companies he had so energetically acquired. He tried more downsizing, by trumpeting, in 2001, plans to eliminate up to 15 percent of his seventy-seven thousand employees. Layoffs, he reportedly explained to insiders, were his "most straight-forward option."[135] His management team, meanwhile, explored options that fell in the less straightforward column. Their accounting subterfuges would go on to make front-page headlines in 2002 — and drive WorldCom into bankruptcy. On June 27, 2002, the newly bankrupt WorldCom began laying off another seventeen thousand workers.[136]

Chronic downsizers like WorldCom could be found all across America's corporate landscape. Their downsizings were supposed to leave their companies lean and efficient. They did no such thing. Instead, thoughtful insiders agreed, the downsizings unleashed dynamics that left America's workplaces less effective, not more.

One such insider, Alan Downs, "personally fired hundreds of employees and planned for the batch firings of thousands more" during his corporate career.

"Slowly," Downs would later note, "I began to see what *really* happens after a layoff. Morale hits rock bottom. Lines of communications within the company shatter. Productivity ebbs, while high-priced consultants try to patch the business back together." Downsizing leaves behind, summed up Downs, "a sluggish, bumbling organization that must relearn even the most basic functions."[137]

The workers left behind, meanwhile, are seldom in the mood to do any relearning. What downsizing companies might gain through lower labor costs, researchers have found, they lose "through diminution in the loyalty and enthusiasm of remaining employees." Workplace survivors tend to "exhibit less entrepreneurship, stay out sick more often, and show little enthusiasm about meeting the company's production goals."[138]

Other employees react to the insecurity that downsizing evokes by rushing in the opposite direction. These employees start working every hour they possibly can, desperately hoping to earn enough to cushion themselves from the inevitable downsize ax.[139] One worker who felt this excruciating pressure, Brent Churchill, a thirty-year-old lineman with Central Maine Power, would be accidentally electrocuted to death in 2000 after "clambering up and down poles" for nearly twenty-four hours straight.

"In his last two and a half days of life, Brent Churchill slept a total of five hours," one news report noted. "The rest of the time he was working."[140]

Churchill, before his death, had seen thirty-seven of his fellow linemen downsized.

Brent Churchill may or may not haunt his former employers at Central Maine Power. Many other employers, in the 1990s, *would* be haunted. Lawsuits did the haunting. Downsized older workers, minorities, and women all brought unprecedented numbers of discrimination suits against their former employers in the decade before the century ended. The settlement and attorney costs of this massive legal action, two scholars noted in 1998, were making a significant impact on corporate bottom lines. Corporate America's "job massacres," they concluded, were helping to "undercut the very cost and productivity advantages they are supposed to create."[141]

The American Management Association would reinforce that conclusion with data that actually came from downsized companies themselves. Only about a third of companies that had downsized, the AMA reported, dared to claim any increases in productivity. An amazing 86 percent of these same companies admitted a fall-off in worker morale.[142]

Downsizings, in short, left enterprises *defective*. No CEOs, by the end of the 1990s, could credibly justify downsizings as a matter of efficiency or business necessity. Downsizings served only one purpose. They helped top executives keep their sweet deals sweet.

At the crest of the 1990s downsizing, the man who had invented modern management theory, Peter Drucker, was nearing ninety years old. Drucker was no ivory-tower academic. He knew, from personal experience, just how cruel life could be. In Germany, as a young man, he had watched the Nazis rise to power. But even Drucker, as world-wise as he was, would be taken aback by downsizing. The "financial benefit top management people get for laying off people," he told an interviewer in 1996, is "morally and socially unforgivable."

"There is no excuse for it," Drucker admonished. "No justification."[143]

The downsizers would not even blink. Downsizing would continue, as rewardingly as ever, into the twenty-first century. Top executives at the fifty U.S. companies that did the most downsizing in 2001 averaged 44 percent pay increases the next year, researchers from United for a Fair Economy and the Institute for Policy Studies would report in 2003.

Compensation for these energetic downsizers, the researchers noted, increased more than seven times faster than compensation for CEOs overall.[144]

SMART EXECUTIVES HAVE ALWAYS UNDERSTOOD that managerial success ultimately depends on having workers willing to contribute their best.

"Executives succeed," as business commentator Dale Dauten puts it, "when employees decide to bestow the gift of excellence upon them."[145]

But employees do not — and will not — bestow this gift when they feel others are capitalizing unfairly on their labors.[146] Employees, be they white-collar, blue-collar, or pink-collar, do not expect to make as much as their bosses. But they do expect to share fairly in the wealth they create. Employers who do not share wealth fairly violate the most basic of unspoken workplace understandings.

"The rational worker's response to the shredding of that understanding," as AFL-CIO President John Sweeney has noted, "is what we in the unions call work to rule — do the minimum and use your brain to help yourself, not your firm."[147]

The vast majority of us would, most definitely, rather *not* work to rule. We typically start out every job wanting to do our best, not our least. We want to feel part of a team, a good team. We humans are, after all, social creatures. We live and work in social situations. In good situations, we feed off each other's strengths. We help others and others help us. We learn. We grow. The group success becomes our success.

Most of us, at one point or another in our lives, have been part of a team that really worked — a team on a ballfield perhaps, or a team of volunteers building a playground, or a team of friends planning a surprise party. We know how satisfying, even thrilling, a good team experience can be. We want, not surprisingly, to experience this satisfaction, this thrill, at our workplaces. Few of us ever do.

Mike Daisey, for one short, shining moment, thought he had become one of the lucky ones. Mike had found a job — at Amazon.com, the Internet retailer — that did give him thrills. A twenty-something with a degree in aesthetics and several years of comedy troupe experience, Mike didn't figure to be someone who could get much satisfaction out of working for a big company. But Mike enjoyed his work at Amazon talking to customers and writing business plans. He felt part of something big, something important. He devoted himself to his job. He worked seventy hours a week, handled as many as twelve hundred e-mail messages in a single day.

"I had fallen in love with an idea, a dream of a company," he remembers. "I really thought I would change the world."[148]

Then the dream ended. Mike came across a spreadsheet listing the salaries and stock options people were making in the corner of Amazon where he worked. Mike found himself at the bottom of that list, a long way from the top. Amazon, he saw, was not sharing wealth with any real fairness. Mike suddenly felt betrayed. He no longer took any satisfaction from his job. The joy had evaporated. He left Amazon not long afterwards.[149]

Why did the inequities of that spreadsheet bother Mike Daisey so? What made the inequality he discovered so demotivating for him — and what makes inequality, in the business world at large, so poisonous to the values that make for healthy enterprises? Why are people less likely to give their best when rewards are unequally distributed?

Scholars and psychologists can help us here. We do our best work, they tell us, when we enjoy what we are doing, when our motivation comes from within. Most of us know this from our own experiences. Some of us cultivate magnificent flower beds. Some of us cook indescribably delicious dinners. Some of us restore rusted old clunkers into marvelous motoring machines. We invariably seem to do marvelous work like this for the pleasure we take from it, not for any monetary reward. Indeed, monetary rewards can sometimes get in the way, make what we enjoy doing seem *less* pleasurable.

One classic experiment, conducted in 1971, demonstrated rather dramatically just how quickly rewards can sap the joy out of activities that bring us pleasure.[150] The experiment placed inside a puzzle-filled room a group of people who had all previously indicated that they enjoy solving puzzles. In the first segment of the experiment, the investigator asked the puzzle people to do their puzzle thing. They all did. Then the investigator ended the first segment and announced a break before the second segment would begin.

"I shall be gone only a few minutes," the investigator announced. "You may do whatever you like while I'm gone."

The investigator, as promised, left the room. The puzzle people were now alone with their puzzles. Some merrily continued puzzle solving. But others pushed their puzzles aside. This contrast between players and abstainers would turn out to be anything but random. The investigator had, before the experiment began, divided the participants into two groups. One half would be paid, the other not. Neither half knew the other was getting different treatment. The subsequent behaviors during the break neatly tracked this division between paid and unpaid. Those who were getting paid for participating in the experiment spent much less of their break time playing with the puzzles than those who weren't getting paid. All the participants, remember, had initially described themselves as people who enjoy doing puzzles. So why didn't the people in the paid category continue, during the break, doing an activity they enjoyed? Pay, psychologists tell us, had essentially turned what had been *play* — and pleasurable — into *work*, something that we do for a reward, not for the simple pleasure of just doing it.

Pay almost always has this impact. Pay signals, at a most basic level, *compulsion*, that we are performing an activity not because we want to perform it, but because we must perform it, to earn enough to live.[151]

Workers who worry the most about making enough to live, who fear what will happen if their kids get sick, who scramble every month to meet the mortgage or pay the rent, never forget for an instant that they *must* work to live. They never stop feeling compelled to work. And the more that these workers, that any of us, feel pressured to work, the less pleasure we will take from the work we do. The less pleasure we take from our work, in turn, the less likely we are to do our work with any creativity or imagination.

No enterprise, of course, can turn work into play. But enterprises can, by helping employees feel more secure in their lives, take employee minds off the pressures that compel them to work. Enterprises that pay well and offer benefits that bring peace of mind can free employees to concentrate on the job at hand — and maybe even take some pleasure from it. But good pay and good benefits do not guarantee a workplace where employees take pleasure from their work. Inequality can poison any workplace. Where workers see rewards distributed unequally, and grossly so, pleasure will seldom proliferate.[152] Why should that be the case? Unequal rewards remind us that we are working under compulsion. Why, after all, would any sane person labor to make someone else rich? We enrich someone else with our labor — we let ourselves be exploited — only because we have no choice. We must do that labor because we must get that paycheck. So we labor on. We take a paycheck from our work, but no pleasure.

The starker the inequity in any workplace, the less pleasurable the work becomes. The less pleasurable the work, the less workers will likely contribute to enterprise success. The less workers contribute, the less effective the enterprise will be. In the workplace, in other words, justice matters. The "sense of injustice," as the British political scientist Harold Laski noted in 1930, "acts as an inhibition fatal to the doing of one's best."[153]

Not all employees, of course, *must* continue laboring in situations where they see and feel inequity. Many employees can afford to leave. They have nest-eggs large enough to tide them over — or good prospects for quickly finding another job. These employees, if they find themselves in situations where executives monopolize rewards, have the freedom to simply walk away. And they do. In workplaces where justice disappears, so does loyalty.

"What you see are people leaving who know a lot about the firm and the industry," the Stanford Business School's Charles O'Reilly would observe in 1998. "If they feel they are inequitably treated, then they are gone."[154]

And they are missed. Enterprises pay a heavy price for high turnover, and auditors can actually calculate the cost. They start with the unused vacation time that must be converted into dollars, add in the severance that must be shelled out, the recruitment ads that must be placed, the staff time that must be spent interviewing applicants, the training that must be conducted when the new hire finally comes on board. How much does all this total? Some human resources experts "place the cost of a single turnover at between 100 and 300 percent of the employee's annual wages or salary." Other estimates run higher. Modern enterprises, one analyst concludes, almost always experience serious damage "every time an experienced, competent, talented worker leaves the firm voluntarily."[155]

That damage can be particularly devastating when the exiting employee happens to have been an important part of a company's management team. In the 1990s, as pay gaps between CEOs and their subordinates within management widened, these sorts of exits became more and more frequent. Pay disparities within management ranks, the Harvard Business School's Jay Lorsch argued in 1999, were fostering "unspoken jealousy" at the top management level and creating a situation that "undoubtedly prompts the most talented executives to seek high paying positions elsewhere."[156]

Two Notre Dame researchers, the next year, would detail that exodus. The two scholars had analyzed turnover rates, over a five-year period, among executives at nearly five hundred companies. They found that senior executives at firms with wide management pay gaps were twice as likely to exit as senior executives at companies where pay was more equally distributed.[157] A company that spends "big dollars attracting and retaining a top CEO," Notre Dame's Matt Bloom noted, winds up "reducing the cohesion, knowledge and experience of the managerial team it relies on to make key decisions."

"Unless a board can provide compelling evidence for why one person is overwhelmingly more important than all the other employees," concluded Bloom, "shareholders and employees probably have good reasons to be very concerned about large pay gaps."[158]

These sorts of warnings from business school professors have made little impact on corporate America's top decision makers. The typical adult American today, runs the conventional corporate boardroom wisdom, will work for six or more companies by the time retirement comes. So why worry obsessively about loyalty? Why bother bending over backwards to keep employees contented and staying put? If employees aren't happy, they can leave. They'll leave anyway. That's life in the Information Age.

Corporate America, once again, has enterprise reality absolutely backwards. In the Information Age, organizational loyalty actually matters more, not less, than ever.

Generations ago, in the heyday of command-and-control, enterprises could survive high turnover. New employees just came in and did what they were told. But today, in the Information Age, enterprises need employees able and willing to do far more than what they are told to do. Modern enterprises need employees who can collaborate with colleagues and co-workers in problem-solving, high-performance teams. But teams only perform well when the people on them trust in each other. Trust building takes time. Employees in high-turnover workplaces never get to take that time. Nor do they want to take that time. Who in their right mind would pour their heart and soul into a company that doesn't expect them to be — doesn't want them to be — around for the long haul?

Enterprises that devalue loyalty, that welcome high turnover, will always be defective. Inequality will always make that devaluing inevitable.

OVER THE COURSE OF THE BOOM YEARS, loyalty would not get much respect in America's corporate boardrooms. Inspiration would be a different matter. Corporate boards lionized the ability to inspire. Truly great chief executives, they believed, captured imaginations. They united employees behind clear, vibrant, energizing visions of enterprise success.

This conventional boardroom wisdom appealed mightily to America's corporate elite. Top executives enjoyed thinking of themselves as visionary leaders. But the visions they would typically express, as top executives, would seldom stir any employee souls. In the boom years, America's top executives would display precious little visionary leadership. What they displayed, instead, would be tunnel vision.

By century's end, top executives had come to focus almost exclusively on what brings them individual wealth, not what makes their enterprises effective. And what brought them wealth were rising share prices. These share prices had become, for America's executive class, the only significant enterprise reality that demanded their attention. Offer leadership to their employees? Who could make the time?

"Top managers," astutely noted one mutual fund official, T. Rowe Price's Richard Howard, in 1999, "are almost more managers of their stock than they are managers of their own companies."[159]

"And why not," *Business Week* would ask three years later, "when every upward tick of the stock means massive gains for option-rich executives?" The personal net worths of corporate executives, *Business Week* would add, are "so closely tied" to the company share price that maintaining that price had become "the highest corporate value."[160]

Those responsible for America's corporate enterprises, in this environment, no longer saw organizations that needed to be led. They saw fortunes to be made. By any means necessary. By century's end, everybody who was anybody inside corporate America knew exactly what was going on. For anyone not in the know, *Fortune* magazine in 1999, more than two years *before* the Enron scandal surfaced, offered a guided tour.

"Someplace right now, in the layers of a *Fortune* 500 company, an employee — probably high up and probably helped by people who work for him — is perpetrating an accounting fraud," noted *Fortune*. "Down the road that crime will come to light and cost the company's shareholders hundreds of millions of dollars."[161]

In 2002, after Enron's spectacular collapse, these frauds would fill America's front pages. They came in a bewildering assortment. Some involved fudging revenues, in schemes that ranged from the simply sneaky — keeping "the books open at the end of quarters" to record enough sales to meet earnings targets — to the crudely criminal.[162]

Gregory Earls, the chief executive of U.S. Technologies, fell on the crude side. He would be indicted in 2003 for diverting, in two separate scams, nearly $15 million raised from investors to his ex-wife and other similarly noble causes. Few executives would be more brazen than Earls. A former director of the FBI, William Webster, chaired his company's audit committee![163]

Xerox fell between crude and sneaky. The copier giant, between 1997 and 2000, "prematurely" counted some $2 billion in revenue from its leasing operations, a sleight-of-hand that concealed company problems — and gave CEO Paul Allaire the time he needed, in 1998 and 1999, to sell off a stack of his own Xerox shares and pocket $16 million from the proceeds.[164]

Other companies, like Priceline, the Internet travel ticket company, claimed as revenue money they had no right claiming. Travel agencies had traditionally booked, as their own revenue, only the commissions they received from selling airline tickets. Priceline claimed, in its revenue totals, the entire ticket sales price.[165] America Online played the same sort of games, in its brokering of online advertising space.[166] Starting in 2000, these slick maneuvers padded America Online revenues by over a quarter of a billion dollars.

"Without the unconventional deals," noted a later *Washington Post* investigation, "AOL would have fallen short of analysts' estimates of the company's growth in ad revenue."[167]

With the unconventional deals, AOL chief executive Steve Case was able to take home $73.4 million in 2000.[168]

Still other companies, like Lucent, the technology spin-off from AT&T, "channel stuffed" their way to greater earnings. These companies reported, as sold, products that "had merely been placed in a warehouse or on a retailer's shelf."[169] A few companies, in an interesting twist on the channel-stuffing notion, essentially bribed "wholesalers to buy more of their products than retailers are selling" by stuffing wholesaler pockets with special "incentives." Bristol-Myers Squibb, the health care products kingpin, found this approach particularly promising.[170]

In telecom, the world of voice and data transmission, executives "swapped" their way to fortunes. "Swapping," the exchange of cable capacity between telecom companies, began as a legitimate business transaction. Swaps let telecoms with more customers than cable capacity transmit the messages their customers wanted to send. But none of the telecom giants, by 2000, were worrying about having too many customers. In their rush for riches, executives at all the big telecoms had vastly overbuilt their cable networks.[171] The resulting glut of cable capacity had shoved the telecoms into a bind. They needed to show Wall Street enough revenue growth to prove their businesses were viable. But revenues could only rise if customer traffic filled their networks, and the telecoms faced a distinct customer shortage. How could they possibly increase revenues without customers? Not to worry. They would become each other's customers! One telecom would wire money to fellow telecoms. The fellow telecoms would wire the same amounts back. Each telecom in on the phony transactions would record the wired dollars as revenue.[172] In 2001 alone, the telecoms swapped their way to revenues worth an estimated $2.5 billion.[173]

The swaps wouldn't be enough, in the end, to keep the telecom bubble from bursting. But they did enrich executives, their intended purpose all along. Before the bubble burst, Global Crossing chairman Gary Winnick walked off with $750.8 million, $735 million of that from selling off company shares propped up in price by swaps and other schemes.[174]

Top executives, in the boom years and beyond, would manufacture revenues from whatever source they could find. Pension funds became one favorite revenue candy jar, as soon as executives realized how they could get the jar open. Pension funds, over time, accumulate huge caches of cash. These are invested, with the returns from the investments used to pay retirees their pensions. Corporations cannot legally count, as corporate income, any pension fund investment earnings needed to pay retirees their promised benefits. But corporations can count as corporate revenue any pension fund investment income that might "exceed" those promised benefits.[175] This loophole, in the 1990s, gave corporate executives a sweet incentive to cut benefits. They couldn't resist.

In 1995, IBM shifted the bulk of its workforce into a new retirement plan that reduced pension benefits — and gave IBM the ability to claim hundreds of millions in pension fund revenue as company income. Five years later, this new plan was contributing $1.2 billion to IBM's bottom line, over 10 percent of the company's pretax income total.[176] Similar pension-driven revenue windfalls multiplied all over corporate America.[177]

By puffing up revenues, tunnel-visioned executives could enhance almost any bottom line. And where revenues couldn't be easily enhanced, expenses could always be hidden. The champ here would be WorldCom, the phone giant. In 2001, WorldCom concealed nearly $4 billion by recording ordinary operating expenses as capital expenditures, a blatantly dishonest maneuver that let the company "report higher profit and more favorable cash flow than honest accounting would have allowed."[178]

In the boom years, executives from all across corporate America played games like these, making sure, wherever necessary, that everyone around them played along. This executive rush to riches would corrupt entire corporate cultures, not just accounting departments, and nowhere more so than in the software industry, the home to most of the world's biggest fortunes.

By the 1990s, software giants like database king Oracle had become notorious for aggressively shoveling out into the marketplace software nowhere near ready for prime-time. Oracle salespeople would routinely tout new software features that didn't work well — or didn't even exist. Businesses that bought Oracle software would regularly find themselves spending "far more to fix the product than the original cost of buying it."[179] Some victims filed lawsuits, but, overall, few bothered. What good would complaining do? The entire software industry operated Oracle-style.

Behind these aggressive, customer-unfriendly tactics, industry observers noted, stood "Wall Street's relentless demands to meet earnings targets."[180] Oracle CEO Larry Ellison made sure his salespeople felt those pressures — and shared his tunnel vision.

"The management theory was simple," one former Oracle sales rep, Marc Benioff, would later note. "Go out and don't come back before you have a signed contract."[181]

Sales managers who didn't meet their quotas, by any means, fair or foul, could expect furious phone calls from Ellison, at any time, on any day. Ellison, one ex-Oracle employee told reporters, "treated people like chattel."[182] These chattel would help Ellison to over $700 million in personal stock option profits in 2001.

In their single-minded zeal, America's top corporate executives didn't just cheat customers and browbeat employees. They shortchanged the government, too, out of billions in taxes due. In 1991, corporations reported to the government, as taxable income, 91 cents for every $1 of profit they reported to stockholders. By 2000, for every dollar of profit reported to shareholders, corporations were reporting less than 70 cents to the IRS. In 1997 alone, the *New York Times* reported, this profit underreporting saved corporations $60 billion.[183]

Stock options accounted for some of this underreporting. Companies could legally deduct from their taxable income the huge options awards cashed out by their executives. These same awards didn't have to be subtracted from profits reported to Wall Street, a shady double-standard that helped keep share prices artificially high. But this "legal" loophole wouldn't be enough for America's corporate leaders. They cheated the IRS out of billions more through fraudulent tax shelters. The top tax avoiders, in the 1990s, would include some of corporate America's most respected names. UPS, for instance, "engaged in a long-running sham to evade more than $1 billion in taxes."[184]

Up until the 1990s, one high-ranking IRS official noted to the *New York Times* at the turn of the century, executives had feared getting caught cheating on their corporate taxes. They worried that cheating charges would blemish their company image. By the 1990s, image concerns no longer mattered. Top executives now saw their corporate tax offices as profit centers pure and simple. They entrusted these offices with just one obligation, to "aggressively reduce the tax burden."[185]

No company would pursue that goal more "aggressively" than the Houston-based Enron, as federal investigators would show in a three-volume report released in 2003.[186] Enron's various tax avoidance scams, the federal research revealed, enormously padded the profits the company reported to investors — and enabled Enron to pose, on Wall Street, as a going and growing concern. That posing, in turn, enabled Enron's top two hundred executives, in 2000 alone, to personally clear a combined $1.4 billion in earnings, most of that from stock options. And these option windfalls, in turn, enabled Enron to save still more in taxes. Overall, from 1996 through 1999, Enron would claim $2.1 billion in profits in its financial reports and pay no federal taxes on a dime of these profits. In 2000, Enron would claim another $979 million in profits and pay only $64 million in taxes.

Enron, to pull off this incredible heist, needed plenty of advice. America's top banking, law, and accounting firms were more than willing to provide it.

"Wall Street banks, acting on the advice of leading lawyers and accounting firms, helped Enron devise shelters that let the company operate tax-free for years," reporter David Cay Johnson would later note, "while exaggerating its reported profits by billions."[187]

Between 1995 and 2001, in all, Enron shelled out over $88 million in fees for tax-avoidance advice and hand-holding.[188]

Within corporate America, everyone seemed to be doing their part — to keep executive fortunes growing. Bankers. Accountants. Lawyers. Salespeople. Even a former FBI director. Everyone would be either looking the other way or greasing the skids.

Slowly and steadily, under the unrelenting pressure to keep share prices rising, an ethic of double-dealing and dishonesty was oozing out from America's executive suites and poisoning America's business culture. The executives who ruled from those suites were supposed to serve, according to their job descriptions, as the ultimate good "stewards" of their enterprises. To employees, they came across, instead, as looters. Employees saw, at every turn, behavior from their "betters" that violated every cliché about integrity, hard work, and honesty that ever appeared in a corporate "values" statement. Many employees responded in kind. They stole, too. Greed, after all, is "infectious," as Federal Reserve chairman Alan Greenspan reminded the nation in America's first post-Enron summer.[189] Workplace frauds, the Association of Certified Fraud Examiners estimated in 2002, were costing the American economy $600 billion a year, "or about $4,500 per employee."[190]

Not every disgruntled employee stole. Some just stewed — and then exploded. Management worried a good bit about these potential blow-ups, so much so that one former CIA staffer felt he could make a lucrative living selling corporations software that they could use to "detect anger and mood changes in employee e-mail."[191]

"Language becomes more simplified when we are angry or stressed," the ex-CIA hand, a psychologist named Eric Shaw, explained in 2001. "Angry people use words that denote judgment, good or bad, and they refer to individuals more frequently and are more emotional, more evaluative and more personal."

But Shaw was smart enough to put his software's eggs in more than one basket. Besides looking for complex, emotionally charged word patterns, his software would also search out simple single words, like *kill, fire,* and *bomb.*

American executives, in the new century, might not have much vision. At least they would have advance notice.

WE HUMAN BEINGS, UNLESS SOME CATASTROPHE sends us back to the Stone Age, will spend the rest of our existence as a species working in enterprises. How well we do as humankind will depend, in no small part, on how effectively these enterprises are able to function. If our enterprises learn how to truly tap the talents of everyone involved in them, if our enterprises efficiently and responsibly develop and deliver quality products and services that speak to deeply felt individual needs, then all our lives, as consumers and producers, will no doubt dramatically improve.

What sort of enterprises will help us reach these noble goals? No serious students of organizational effectiveness disagree on the basics. We need enterprises, they tell us, that hunger to know what their eventual customers or clients have to say. We need enterprises that unite employees behind a common vision, that empower employees with the tools, training, and decision-making authority they need to make creative contributions, that help employees cooperate and collaborate with each other. We need enterprises guided by leaders who respect their workers and are respected by them.

Inequality within the enterprise, the evidence from late twentieth-century America suggests, subverts all these elements of enterprise success. The more rewards are allowed to concentrate at enterprise summits, the less likely that consumers will be valued, workers will be empowered, and executives themselves will be respected.

Some do challenge this evidence. The rewards pumped to the top, these skeptics argue, couldn't possibly make as much of a difference as critics of executive pay charge. The rewards showered upon executives, their argument goes, are simply too tiny, relatively speaking. Executive pay, one *Barron's* business writer smugly explained in 1998, "is always an insignificant sum compared with workers' total compensation or to any other cost of doing business."[192] For a mega-billion company, mega-million executive windfalls amount to mere peanuts, not dangers.

But the danger comes not from the "peanuts," but from what executives will do to grab as many peanuts as they can. To keep their pockets stuffed, executives will nurture the hierarchies that frustrate enterprise empowerment. They will devote themselves to making their companies bigger, not better. They will dishonor customers and discard employees. They will create enterprises where workers take little satisfaction from the work they do — and, when nobody's looking, any valuable they can walk away with.

Corporations that lavish multiple millions on their executive superstars, even if those millions be mere "peanuts" in the grand corporate scheme of things, create great fortunes for their executives. They do not create great enterprises.

Ask Jim Collins, a former scholar at the Stanford Graduate School of Business who launched his own management laboratory in 1995. In the 1990s, Collins led a research team that spent five years trying to determine "what it takes" to turn an average company into a "great" one. Collins and his colleagues "systematically scoured a list of 1,435 established companies to find every extraordinary case that made a leap from no-better-than-average results to great results." No fly-by-night stock market bubble baby could qualify as a "great" enterprise on the Collins list. A company, to be defined as great, "had to generate cumulative stock returns" that, over fifteen years, had "exceeded the general stock market by at least three times" — and had to have made this remarkable showing "independent of its industry."[193]

The Collins research team eventually identified eleven firms that had successfully made the leap to "great." The researchers then went about discovering "what it took to make the change." They paired each "great" company with another company with similar attributes that could have made the leap to great "but didn't."[194] They combed through years of data, interviewed senior managers and board members, and examined compensation and employment patterns.[195] And what did they find?

"I want you to forget everything you've ever learned about what it takes to create great results," Collins would report in 2001. "I want you to realize that nearly all operating prescriptions for creating large-scale corporate change are nothing but myths."[196]

His research results, Collins explained, totally demolished "The Myth of Acquisitions," the idea that corporations could buy their way to greatness. None of the companies on the Collins list had made the leap to greatness by gobbling up other companies. His research results also refuted, just as convincingly, "The Myth of Stock Options," the idea that options, high salaries, and bonuses are valuable incentives that can "grease the wheels of change."[197] None of the companies that had made their way onto the great list, Collins pointed out, boasted a high-paid, celebrity CEO.

A celebrity CEO, Collins would explain, turns a company into "one genius with 1,000 helpers." The presence of a celebrity in the chief executive suite "creates a sense that the whole thing is really about the CEO."[198] And that sense, the Collins research concluded, will always make for enterprise mediocrity.

Corporate leaders, after the Collins research appeared, would make no rush to abandon the myths his research so deftly punctured. Nor would they make any serious effort to refute what the Collins study had to say. They had no choice, their apologists explained, but to continue along with corporate business as usual. After all, if CEO rewards aren't pegged at lavish levels, how else would corporations be able to motivate aspiring junior executives to work the brutishly long hours necessary to make their way to the top? CEOs, as Stanford economist Edward Lazar acknowledges, might not really contribute anything to their enterprises that justifies their outlandish pay. Still, Lazar argues, the outlandish pay they take in does serve an important purpose.

"The CEO gets to enjoy the money," he notes. "But it's making everybody else work harder."[199]

True enough, but at what cost to the "everybody else"? The dash for the jackpot at the end of the corporate rainbow, journalists noted at century's end, was brutalizing white-collar America. Up-and-comers who saw themselves as top executive material saw in that jackpot all the justification they needed to work and never stop working. The outrageous numbers of hours they labored would create, in corporate cubicles all across the United States, new norms and expectations. These expectations encouraged, even applauded, workaholism.[200] The inevitable results, as tallied by the *Economist* magazine: "burnt-out" employees, "low morale," "dulled creativity."[201] And more *defective* enterprises.

Effective enterprises simply cannot be bought or bribed or bullied into being. We expect money for our work. But we do not do our best work for money.

So what's the best way to pay people? *Fortune* asked that question late in the 1990s, then offered an answer from Alfie Kohn, a writer once labeled "America's most biting critic of money as motivator." Kohn's essential guidance: "Pay well, pay fairly, and then do everything you can to get money off people's minds."[202]

Inequality, within the enterprise, keeps money *on* people's minds. Deeply unequal enterprises have never been effective. They never will be.

GRUESOME GROWTH

NO ENTERPRISE IS AN ISLAND.

Every enterprise sits within a larger social reality, what we call society. From society, enterprises draw sustenance, everything they need to survive. Take this sustenance away, enterprises founder, then die, just like fish out of water.

What do enterprises need from society? They need, of course, people able to perform enterprise work. The more able employees a society has to offer, the better off enterprises will be. To make the most of these employees, this "human capital," enterprises also need financial capital. They need money for equipment and supplies, for offices and payroll, for production and marketing. Without adequate capital, human and financial, no enterprise can hope to succeed.

Not all enterprises with adequate capital, of course, always succeed. Many fall short. Some fail because they do not organize themselves for effective operation. But even wonderfully effective enterprises can — and do — fail. An enterprise can assemble a wonderfully talented workforce. An enterprise can outfit that workforce with the finest tools and resources. An enterprise can sweep away the hierarchical underbrush that keeps employees from doing their best. An enterprise can get everything right and still flop miserably for one reason and one reason alone. If not enough customers who want an enterprise's products can afford to buy them, the enterprise will fail. Always.

In desperately poor societies, nations where people have precious little wealth to spend, enterprises will always struggle to gain a foothold. The same struggling will take place in societies where the wealth available to spend suddenly starts shrinking, during, for instance, a recession or depression. A society where wealth contracts severely may see even its grandest enterprises fumble and fail.

Modern societies, naturally, do their best to prevent their stocks of wealth from contracting. But no modern society aims merely to maintain existing wealth. Modern societies, even those that have already amassed considerable wealth, all aim to generate new wealth. And this drive for greater wealth makes sense. No society, after all, has yet achieved perfection. We all live in societies that can be improved, and wealth helps the improvement process along. Opportunities for progress, as economist Robert Frank points out, "are greater in a rich society than in a poor one."

"A richer society," Frank explains, "has more resources for medical research, more resources for rapid transit, more time for family and friends, more time for study and exercise — and more resources for better insulated houses and cleaner, more fuel-efficient automobiles."[1]

If we want our lives to be improving, we need our economies to be generating new wealth. Almost all economists, whatever their political inclinations, start from this assumption. But economists, after starting from this assumption, soon part company — over questions about how wealth, new and old, ought to be distributed. No society can generate significant stocks of new wealth, many economists argue, without allowing existing wealth to concentrate. Other economists vigorously disagree.

How exactly *should* wealth be distributed? Does existing wealth need to be concentrated — or shared — to create new wealth? Or does distribution matter at all? These are important questions. They've been vexing economists — and societies — for centuries.

THE CLASSICAL ECONOMISTS, THE THINKERS who laid the foundations of modern economic thought, cared deeply about distribution. Two hundred years ago, these early economists saw the distribution of income between social classes "as a central determinant" of how rapidly new wealth would accumulate.[2]

David Ricardo, the English businessman who would author, in 1817, one of the most important early texts of economics, placed considerable emphasis on the distribution of wealth between landlords and capitalists. Landlords, argued Ricardo, wasted their wealth on personal luxuries. Capitalists, by contrast, invested whatever wealth came their way in productive enterprises, where more new wealth could be created. Economies, Ricardo concluded, grow more efficiently when dollars accumulate, as profits, in capitalist pockets. The more rent money fills landlord pockets, the less vital an economy will be.[3]

Karl Marx, writing a generation later, would share Ricardo's assumption that distribution matters. But Marx, writing early in the Industrial Age, saw the relationship between capitalist and worker, not the link between landlord and capitalist, as modernity's driving force. That relationship — "the distribution of income flows going to labor and capital" — determined, for Marx, how rapidly wealth accumulates.[4]

Marx and like-minded critics of the world's new industrial order would raise unsettling questions about these income flows, questions about justice and injustice that more status quo-oriented economists, later in the nineteenth century, would do their best to slide off the table. These new "neoclassical" economists broke with the classical tradition. They dismissed distribution as essentially irrelevant.[5] A thousand dollars in one pocket, they believed, would always buy the same amount of goods and services as a thousand dollars in ten pockets. So why bother with distribution? Their new orthodoxy — that distribution need not trouble serious students of how economies grow — soon dominated the emerging academic discipline of economics. Discussions about income and wealth distribution, notes historian James Huston, largely "disappeared from economics texts."[6]

Outside the ivory tower, meanwhile, concerns about distribution would not disappear. In the late nineteenth century, with giant fortunes rising across the industrial world, with enormous power concentrating in the hands of small numbers of exceedingly affluent people, many less than exceedingly affluent people were beginning to consider questions about distribution among the most relevant a society could ever ask.

The exceedingly affluent could hardly ignore this growing public unease. They needed to be able to rebut their critics. They needed an unapologetic justification for the widely unequal distributions of income and wealth that had so many people around them apprehensive and upset. This justification would emerge in the late 1800s. Economies, admirers of grand fortunes began to argue, need capital to grow and prosper. But capital can never accumulate without some people becoming wealthier than others. The resulting inequality, friends of the fortunate contended, ought to be welcomed, not feared. If wealth was concentrating, then capital was accumulating.[7] If capital was accumulating, better tomorrows were sure to follow.

This aggressive, in-your-face defense of inequality thrilled the colossally wealthy. But reasonable and responsible business and political leaders recoiled from it. Intense inequalities, these more sober leaders understood, gave radical critics of the existing social order powerful ammunition. Society's elites could not afford to be seen cheering on inequality. The Russian Revolution, and the later onset of the Cold War, would only reinforce this conviction. The capitalist West, clear-headed business and political leaders realized, could never win Cold War hearts and minds by defiantly defending inequality. The inequalities of Western capitalist society didn't need to be defended. They needed to be placed in context.

The context would come, midway through the twentieth century, from Simon Kuznets, a widely respected, Ukrainian-born Ivy League economist. Kuznets, as part of a body of work that would earn him a Nobel Prize, essentially delinked modern market economies and inequality. Kuznets described inequality as an inevitable, but purely transitional, consequence of industrialization. Agricultural nations moving into the industrial age, he counseled, would always see levels of inequality rise, mainly because people working in the emerging modern sector of the economy would always outearn people still working in the traditional agricultural sector.[8] But this inequality eventually fades away, Kuznets argued, as industrializing nations mature. More and more people, as economies develop, become part of the modern wage economy. Incomes, across society, start equalizing. The more market economies evolve, the more equal they become.[9]

The eminent Kuznets made his case in a landmark 1955 presidential address to the American Economic Association. His thesis proved enormously appealing to America's Cold Warriors. Market economies now had no need to feel defensive. Inequities might still scar the United States, but America would ultimately outgrow them.

"Equity will follow growth," Kuznets seemed to be saying to the Cold Warriors, "so there is little reason to worry about it."[10]

American economic realities, meanwhile, seemed to be proving Kuznets right. In the 1950s, America was becoming more prosperous *and* more equal. The nation could stand tall, a proud beacon to the world. Just follow us, America's leaders could say proudly to the Cold War world, we know the way to tomorrow.

That way, two decades later, would seem less certain. By the mid 1970s, America's march to shared prosperity had stalled. Poverty, noted one esteemed economist, Arthur Okun, a former chairman of the Council of Economic Advisers under Lyndon Johnson, "remains the plight of a substantial group of Americans." Large disparities in income distribution, Okun wrote in 1975, "continue to mar the social scene."[11]

Inequality, apparently, wasn't just some nasty, transitional phase that market economies, once mature, put behind them. Indeed, the liberal Okun argued, inequalities come naturally to market economies. These inequalities, he added quickly, need not — and should not — be meekly accepted. Smart societies can — and should — take steps to lessen inequality. But any steps that reduce inequality, Okun argued, also reduce economic efficiency. The more a society pushes for an equitable distribution of income and wealth, the less robustly that economy will create wealth, "largely because income redistribution reduces the incentives for work and investment."[12]

Personally, Okun noted, he might prefer otherwise, but, in real life, "the conflict between equality and efficiency is inescapable."[13] A wise society, he contended, accepts the inevitability of this conflict and goes about making do by making tradeoffs, sometimes accepting less growth to help make society more equal, sometimes accepting less equality to keep the economy growing. Decent societies, Okun believed, search for balance between equality and growth. Out of these balancing acts, he hoped, would come more decency. By making smart tradeoffs, Okun contended in his 1975 book, *Equality and Efficiency*, an affluent nation like the United States could even eradicate poverty.[14]

Equality and Efficiency did not, as Okun had hoped, help eradicate poverty. The book instead helped eradicate the campaign against poverty. Conservatives turned Okun's carefully argued case for thoughtful tradeoffs into an admission, by liberals, that any attempts to make America more equal — by, for instance, expanding aid to poor people — would inevitably backfire on everyone, the poor included, by slowing economic growth. Armed with Okun, conservatives confidently blamed the "stagflation" of the 1970s on excessive social spending and "invoked" Okun, in the years ahead, to rationalize America's "growing concentration of wealth."[15]

"By the mid-1980s," economists Randy Albeda and Chris Tilly would later point out, "most economists agreed that the key problem facing the U.S. economy was stagnant growth, not rising inequality."[16]

America needed to get growing again, mainstream economists in the 1980s asserted, and that meant accepting inequality. An America that prudently embraced inequality — that gave the wealthy ample incentives to become wealthier — would, over time, bring joy to all Americans. Everyone would become richer, mainstream economists agreed, if only we let some people become richer than others.

Conservative politicians loved this simple formulation. Liberals would be intimidated by it. Any step toward a kinder, gentler society now seemed suspect. So liberal leaders, for the most part, stopped stepping. They would join with conservatives, in the late 1970s and early 1980s, to make America safe for great fortunes. Conservatives and liberals, together, would vote to reduce taxes on the rich and regulations on corporations. They then sat back and waited for the payoff, the "bigger economic pie" America's mainstream economists promised, a pie big enough to ensure average Americans much larger servings than they had ever before enjoyed.

The payoff did not come, not in the 1980s, not in the early 1990s. By the mid 1990s, a new generation of economists was doubting that inequality would ever pay off. Inequality and growth do not, these skeptical scholars began demonstrating, march hand in hand. Nations that smile on concentrations of wealth and income, they amassed evidence to show, do not automatically become more productive.

One major study, published in 1994, compared growth and income distributions in fifty-six different nations. Those nations that displayed the widest income gaps, the study found, actually grew their gross domestic economic pies the most slowly.[17] Other studies piled up similar findings. By 1997, Princeton economist Roland Benabou could count at least thirteen different "cross-country empirical analyses," all performed in the 1990s, that demonstrated "a negative effect of inequality on growth."[18]

Statistics gathered from within the United States backed up these international findings. Economist Larry Ledebur compared growth rates in eighty-five U.S. urban areas. The wider the income gap between cities and their suburbs, he found, the slower the growth in income and jobs.[19]

By century's end, the evidence appeared overwhelming. Clearly, noted a 1998 paper for the Federal Reserve Bank system's annual summer retreat, "the older view, that greater inequality is associated with faster growth, is not supported by the data."[20]

America's corporate leaders would pay these new findings next to no attention. They would continue to toast the same concentrations of wealth economists were now roasting. The hundreds of millions of dollars pouring into America's executive suites, business commentators exclaimed, were working miracles. They amounted to a "secret weapon contributing to the unprecedented recent growth of the U.S. economy."[21]

"Rather than demonstrating rampant greed," *Chief Executive* magazine would exult in 1999, "today's CEO pay packages have helped the U.S. achieve glory as the unchallenged leader of the world's economy."[22]

CHIEF EXECUTIVE, WE NOW KNOW from our post-Enron perspective, had everything backwards. The "glory" the American economy achieved in the 1990s — the gloriously high corporate earnings, the gloriously soaring share prices — did indeed demonstrate "rampant greed," a greed that drove executives, accountants, bankers, and lawyers to lying and larceny and whatever else it took to keep their personal gravy trains rolling.

We also know, from the 1980s and 1990s economic record, that growth and inequality run on separate tracks. During these two decades, inequality rose over periods of years when the economy grew and also rose during periods when the economy contracted.

"The lesson is simple," note economists Randy Albeda and Chris Tilly. "The relationship of growth to distribution is neither a tradeoff nor an automatic cause-and-effect."[23]

Economies can grow in societies that are becoming more equal. Economies can shrink in societies where wealth is concentrating. Equality does not automatically frustrate growth. Inequality does not automatically spur it.

Given these realities, does the distribution of wealth and income, within a society, really matter? Does the level of inequality within a nation make a substantial impact on how well, or poorly, a nation creates wealth? Levels of inequality most certainly do make an impact, argue Albeda and Tilly and likeminded economists, but that impact depends, within each society, on the overall institutional and political environment, on who gets to define the ground rules.[24] Different rules produce different rates of economic "growth."

Why should that be? If we pause to consider just what economists mean when they say an economy is "growing," the reasons become fairly clear. Economies that are "growing" are simply producing more goods and services than they previously produced. Economies that are producing fewer goods and services are shrinking, not growing.

How can economies produce more goods and services? In several ways. An economy can grow if more people within a society start working. With more people working, more goods and services will be produced. An economy can also grow if people already working start working longer hours. Finally, and most importantly, an economy can grow if the people in it become more productive, if they can produce more goods and services in the same amount of time.

How can people become more productive? They can receive training that improves their skills. They can reorganize how they work and become more efficient. They can get their hands on better tools and equipment. They can explore exciting new technologies. They can be pushed to work harder or, conversely, inspired to work more creatively.

In the abstract, any of these steps can increase the volume of products and services a society produces. In actual practice, societies mix and match these approaches to economic growth, and no two societies ever come up with the same mixes. These varying approaches to growth, in turn, have varying impacts on equality. Some game plans for growth will tend to increase economic inequality. Others will leave societies more equal.

In the early days of the Industrial Age, in the United States and in Europe, the powers that be followed what might be called a brute-force game plan. They would grow their economies — that is, produce more goods and services — by working as many people as long and as hard as they could possibly work them. Early industrializing societies threw everyone they could into the workforce, even children. We look back today on these societies and shake our heads in disbelief. Twelve-year-olds working dawn to dark. How could civilized nations countenance such brutality? In fact, at the time, the powerful didn't just countenance such brutality, they lustily defended it.[25] They resisted, with all their might, any attempts at outlawing child labor. If children were not permitted to work, elites argued, who would bring home the bacon for families headed by widows?

No widows, the opponents of child labor shot back, should be forced to sacrifice their children to the industrial mammon. Society had a moral obligation to guarantee a basic level of decency to every family.

Back and forth went debates just like this, in every nation that stepped into the Industrial Age. New rules had to be set for this new age, rules that would determine just how goods and services would be produced — and each rule would have consequences for the distribution of wealth and income. If, for instance, a society resolved to stretch a well-knit safety net, to make sure all widows and children were guaranteed sustenance, resources would have to be found to hold that net in place. New revenues would have to be raised. New taxes would have to be levied. The wealthy might even have to part with a substantial share of their incomes. Any societies that resolved to take these steps, to protect the weak and tax the wealthy, would, over time, move toward greater equality.

On the other hand, in societies that strung only half-hearted safety nets, fewer families at the economic margins would ever see help. More people would feel pressured to seek work, at whatever wage they could get. Desperate new workers would flood the job market, depressing wage rates and, in the process, enriching the owners of industrial empires. These societies, over time, would become more unequal.

Battles over safety nets, over taxes, over every economic rule imaginable, would be fought — and refought — throughout the nineteenth and twentieth centuries in all the societies we now call the developed nations. By the 1990s, these years of conflict had produced two fundamentally different sets of rules in the market economies of the developed world, two decidedly different perspectives on how best to produce more.

In most of Western Europe, the rules would privilege equality. In the United States, the rules would welcome and encourage the concentration of wealth and income.

On nearly every significant rule-making question, Western Europe seemed to answer one way, the United States another.

Would the safety net be taut or torn? The Europeans stretched safety nets taut and strong enough to cushion most all of life's stumbles and slumps. Unemployed European workers, for instance, could collect jobless benefits that equaled up to 90 percent of their last paychecks.[26] These benefits could run, in nations like Belgium and Denmark, as long as the workers remained jobless.[27] In the United States, by contrast, two-thirds of the workers who lost their jobs in the 1980s and 1990s collected no unemployment benefits whatsoever.[28] Those fortunate enough to find help received no more than 50 percent of the previous pay — and that benefit would be cut off after six months.[29]

What about jobs themselves? How secure would they be? In the United States, government placed almost no restrictions on a company's ability to dismiss workers "at will," without any meaningful advance notice or severance.[30]

In Europe, workers could not be cavalierly fired. Under French and German law, employers had to be able to demonstrate, in a court of law if necessary, the economic necessity or "social acceptability" of any layoff. In most of Europe, no worker could be laid off without advance notice, with the length of the notice usually tied to a worker's job tenure. An experienced white-collar worker in Belgium, for instance, would be entitled to a year's advance notice before any layoff could take place. Many European nations also *mandated* severance pay, more than a half-year's worth in some cases.[31]

And how much would jobs pay? In market economies, of course, governments don't determine wage levels, not directly at least. But governments can have a huge indirect influence on wages, based on the rules they establish for labor relations. In nations where workers can organize themselves into unions, free from employer and government interference, workers will always make more in wages than workers in comparable nations where rights to organize are not respected.

In the United States, by the 1980s, laws no longer adequately protected basic worker rights to create and join unions. Employers, throughout the closing decades of the twentieth century, routinely fired rank-and-filers active in union organizing campaigns. If these illegal firings weren't enough to intimidate workers, employers would threaten to shut down their operations if workers opted for union representation, another illegal maneuver. And if workers were somehow able to win union representation, despite these illegalities, they still had to get their employer to sit down and bargain in good faith. Many employers in newly organized workplaces, some 40 percent of them, didn't.[32] Workers could file complaints against all these "unfair labor practices," of course, but complaints typically took years to work their way through the legal process.[33]

By 1985, not surprisingly, only 17 percent of America's civilian wage and salary employees belonged to unions. In Germany, that same year, 40 percent of employees belonged to unions.[34] But even these figures understated the incredibly wide difference between union influence in the United States and union influence in Europe. In the United States, unions typically bargain contracts that apply only to the employees of a specific employer. In Europe, unions typically bargain collective wage agreements that apply to entire industries. At century's end, just 14 percent of workers in the United States were covered by union-negotiated wage agreements. The coverage rate in France, Germany, and Belgium: 90 percent.[35]

The ongoing assault on worker rights in the United States, Ohio Congressman Dennis Kucinich would tell a labor gathering in 2001, amounted to "a means of redistributing the wealth upwards."[36] And in the United States, as opposed to Europe, most wealth that worked its way upwards stayed there. The tax rules saw to that. In 1997, wealthy taxpayers in the United States paid, on paper, 39.6 percent of their income over $263,750 in national income taxes. The top marginal tax rate in Germany that year ran 53 percent. The top rate in France: 57 percent.[37]

All these many different rules — on safety nets, on wages, on taxes — would create by century's end one distribution of income and wealth in Western Europe, quite a different distribution in the United States. By the early 1990s, American men in the top 10 percent of income-earners took home 5.6 times more per hour than men in the bottom 10 percent. In France, that gap stood at 3.2 times, in Germany 2.7 times.[38] By the mid 1990s, 27 percent of American households fell within a generally accepted definition of middle-class status. That is, just over a quarter of households in the United States had incomes no more than 25 percent less or 25 percent more than the income of the typical American household.[39] In Germany, by contrast, 44 percent of households could claim this middle-class status. In Sweden, 53 percent of households made within 75 and 125 percent of the nation's median household income. In other words, the middle class share of Swedish society almost doubled the middle class share in the United States.[40]

European nations, clearly and without a statistical doubt, sliced their economic pies into pieces that were considerably more similar in size than the pieces of America's economic pie. But the cheerleaders for corporate America, we need to remember, never promised Americans a pie with equal pieces. They promised a bigger pie. If America cheered on the rich in their efforts to become even richer, the promise went, those rich folks would bake up a pie big enough to give everybody a king-sized piece. The pieces in that pie wouldn't be anywhere near equal in size, but why care about that? Even the smallest piece in

America's pie would be bigger than the pieces people elsewhere would be getting. That was the promise. That promise would not be met. The unequal American economy did, as promised, grow in the 1980s and 1990s. But so did the more equal economies of Western Europe.[41] And those more equal economies delivered, for average people, bigger pieces of pie than the pieces served up to average Americans.

In 1995, the wages and benefits of manufacturing workers in the United States, once the world's highest, ranked thirteenth in the world. German workers pulled in the equivalent of $31.88 in wages and benefits in 1995, American workers only $17.20. Workers from throughout Western Europe — from Switzerland, Belgium, Austria, Finland, Norway, Denmark, the Netherlands, Sweden, Luxembourg, and France — all outpaced American manufacturing workers.[42]

The next five years would see the U.S. economy boom to record levels. But that boom did not send American workers back to the top of the international scale. In 2000, according to U.S. Bureau of Labor Statistics data, hourly compensation costs for manufacturing workers in the United States still averaged 17 percent less than costs in the former West Germany.[43] And that was after adjusting the figures to dollar equivalencies, a statistical move that exaggerated compensation in the United States, because the value of the dollar had risen considerably against other currencies.

The United States, to be sure, remained the richest nation in the world. No nation produced more goods and services than the United States. And therein lay the irony. In the richest nation in the world, as economists Gary Burtless and Timothy Smeeding would note, the "incomes of low- and even middle-income Americans are below those of residents in industrialized countries that are poorer than the United States."[44]

Indeed, if the value of what America's economy produced in the 1990s had been distributed more equally, say as equally as in Germany, the average American worker would have been nearly 20 percent better off than the average German worker.[45]

European workers, amazingly, weren't just earning higher incomes than comparable workers in the United States. They were working fewer hours to make those higher incomes. Americans, the International Labor Organization reported in 1999, were putting in, on average, eight more weeks worth of time on the job every year than their counterparts in France and Germany.[46]

Americans, by century's end, were eating from the developed world's most unequal economic pie. But who had time to measure?

WESTERN EUROPEAN NATIONS, WE SHOULD PAUSE TO NOTE HERE, had not become paradises on earth by the start of the twenty-first century. Europeans did not live equal or problem-free lives in the 1980s and 1990s. They just led lives that were *more* equal and *more* problem-free than lives led in the United States. But inequalities in Europe remained profound, as the continent's critics were quick to point out. The distribution of wealth, columnist Robert Samuelson correctly noted midway through the 1990s, is "wildly unequal in all advanced societies."[47]

Commentators like Samuelson argued that whatever equality Europe had achieved had come at the expense of jobs for European workers. Europe's high taxes, tough restrictions on business, and strong labor unions, they contended, had "discouraged job creation" in the name of enhancing "economic equality and job security."[48] Americans might have a less equal society, the argument went, but at least they had jobs.

Americans defensive about inequality in the United States found this notion — that Europe had traded off jobs for greater equality — irresistibly attractive. They held to it with an almost religious intensity, in total disregard of the actual official unemployment numbers. One top analyst from Wall Street's Goldman Sachs, interviewed for a *New York Times* article published early in 2002, asserted, for instance, that "there's not one country in Europe that doesn't have a higher unemployment rate" than the United States.[49] In fact, the actual figures told an entirely different story. Official unemployment in the United States, at that moment, was running at 5.7 percent. At the same time, the United Kingdom (5.1 percent), Sweden (4.7 percent), Portugal (4.4 percent), Denmark (4.4 percent), Austria (4 percent), Ireland (3.9 percent), Norway (3.6 percent), and the Netherlands (2.2 percent) were all running lower official rates of unemployment.[50]

European nations, by doing more than the United States to keep incomes equal, had not created perfect places to live and work. But Europe had managed to create, in the late twentieth century, societies that worked substantially better for average Europeans than the United States worked for average Americans. Working people in Europe made more than working people in the United States and labored fewer hours. Most average Europeans could move through their lives, from cradle to grave, seldom if ever feeling financially desperate. Even in rough times, their incomes would be protected, their health care covered. They could be doing better economically, of course, but they were doing, overall, just fine, thank you, particularly compared to their American counterparts.

Their bosses could not make the same claim. By every measure, corporate movers and shakers in Europe lagged behind their counterparts in the United States. American business leaders made more than European business leaders, had considerably more influence over the political process, and just generally enjoyed more leeway to do what they wanted when they wanted to do it.

Europe's elites knew what they were missing. At Davos, the Swiss resort where global corporate and government leaders started gathering annually in 1982, as well as at other forums and venues, elite Europeans imbibed the American way — and chafed at their second-class status. They resolved, throughout the 1980s and 1990s, to roll back the rules that made doing business on their continent so much more difficult than doing business across the

Atlantic. And they made progress in that effort. Rallied on by free marketeers like Britain's Margaret Thatcher and Germany's Helmut Kohl, the member nations of the European Common Market would approve "radical changes" in their economic governance. They would push down European throats as big a dose of Americanism — anything-goes markets stripped of government regulation — as they could get the people of Europe to swallow.[51] They would bring into being a European Central Bank that would follow tight-fisted interest rate policies, even if that meant, as it did, pushing up jobless rates.[52] And they would slash tax rates on the highest European incomes.[53]

European executives, with these new incentives in place, would soon start playing American-style "restructuring" games with their companies and their employees. They would plot and consummate mergers, $800 billion worth in 1999 alone.[54] They would downsize.[55] They would catch up, as best they could, with their U.S. counterparts. Some, like Jean-Marie Messier, would mimic the every move of their American CEO heroes.

Messier, in the late 1990s, wheeled and dealed an obscure French water utility into a global media giant, Vivendi Universal. Along the way, he "parroted American business jargon with the exuberance of a convert," taking on massive corporate-America-style debts as he merged his way to "synergy" and greatness.[56] Messier enjoyed the perks of greatness, too, with a $17.5 million corporate pad on New York's Park Avenue.[57]

Messier's good buddy, Thomas Middelhoff, the top executive at Bertelsmann, a German media company, went even further down the American corporate road. Middelhoff described himself as "an American with a German passport" and made English his company's official language.[58] He would follow the U.S. corporate model step by step, buying up companies to inflate Bertelsmann's revenues, always maneuvering for his ultimate endgame, a massive public offering of his company's stock. His wheeling and dealing would turn Bertelsmann into the world's third-largest media company.[59]

In Switzerland, another ardent admirer of American executivedom, Percy Barnevik, styled himself Europe's answer to Jack Welch, the fabled General Electric CEO. Barnevik chaired the Zurich-based ABB Ltd., one of the world's biggest engineering companies, and preached an American-style gospel of maximizing shareholder value.[60] He also did his best to maximize his own personal value, awarding himself a $120 million pension.

For Europeans, all this American-style executive grasping would be too much to bear.[61] Average Europeans fought back. In France, where polls showed that nine of ten adults considered downsizing by profitable companies "unacceptable," consumers would boycott Danone, a food company that slashed payroll to boost earnings. The boycott so infuriated the powerful chairman of one key French bank, Jean Peyrelevade, that he promptly announced he would double his consumption of Danone's yogurt products.[62]

But Europe's top executives would have to do a lot more than up their yogurt intake to get their continent aboard an American-style corporate express. In the end, they would not prove equal to the task. By 2003, Europe's top American-style executives had almost all flamed out. In Switzerland, CEO Barnevik resigned after ABB's share prices dropped 60 percent.[63] Shareholders took back more than half his $120 million pension, and Swiss government officials began a criminal investigation against him. Barnevik would claim he was guilty only of giving himself an "American payment system in a European environment."[64] In France, Jean-Marie Messier lost his CEO perch, midway through 2002, after a year that saw the heavily indebted Vivendi lose $41 billion.[65] Messier, an American-style CEO to the bitter end, walked off with $17.8 million in severance.[66]

But the most fascinating flameout would belong to Thomas Middelhoff, the top executive at Bertelsmann. Middelhoff was ousted shortly after Messier, but Bertelsmann, unlike Vivendi, had not yet started to implode before the ax came. The ax fell on Middelhoff, a *Wall Street Journal* analysis would later explain, because the good burghers on the Bertelsmann board feared that their American-style CEO was, by placing profits first, last, and always, destroying their venerable company's "corporate philosophy of using business as a means of paying for good deeds."[67]

That philosophy meant a great deal to the Bertelsmann board. Back in the mid nineteenth century, company founder Carl Bertelsmann had envisioned his new publishing business as an instrument "to better society, not increase profits." The company would become, before 1900, one of the first German firms to provide employees pensions and disability protection. Bertelsmann workers would later become the first in Germany to enjoy paid vacations. Under Reinhard Mohn, the great-grandson of founder Carl Bertelsmann, this tradition would continue. Deep into the twentieth century, just about half the company's annual earnings went into employee profit-sharing plans.[68]

Mohn, eighty-one in 2002, felt that tradition threatened by CEO Middelhoff's American ways. He would engineer, halfway through the year, Middelhoff's ouster by the Bertelsmann board.[69] A worker representative on the board, Erich Ruppik, would later explain where Middelhoff had gone so wrong.

"When he stepped on the gas," Ruppik noted, "he forgot about taking the employees along."[70]

In Europe, as Jean-Marie Messier, Percy Barnevik, and Thomas Middelhoff would learn to their chagrin, an equality-minded culture had simply become too embedded to be swept away by corporate executive superstars. Going forward, Europeans believed, was something that executives and employees ought to do together, not apart.

THE CORPORATE SCANDALS THAT BROKE into the headlines early in the twenty-first century would make a powerful impression on European public opinion. Europeans, already intensely suspicious of American-style approaches to economic growth, saw the Enrons and the WorldComs — and their European clones — as the inevitable outcomes of a capitalism "that rewarded greed and short-term gain and turned high-flying chief executives into celebrities."[71]

In the United States, the scandals elicited a far different reaction. Few political or corporate leaders felt any obligation, in Enron's wake, to question America's basic approach to wealth creation. They blamed bad apples instead. They also worried. Americans, they feared, might overact and, in their zeal to prevent future Enrons, change the basic rules that America's elites had spent a generation perfecting, rules that locked into place what some economists had come to label "the Wall Street model."[72]

This Wall Street model started taking shape in the 1970s, America's years of economic "stagflation," a time when interest rates, prices, and jobless rates were all, for the first time ever, rising at the exact same time. Most economists, ever since the work of John Maynard Keynes in the 1930s, had become convinced that governments could keep economies on a more or less even keel by increasing government spending whenever the private economy turned sluggish. But stagflation did not seem responsive to what had become the standard solutions.[73] Government couldn't solve stagflation, critics from Wall Street charged, because government had become the problem. Government needed to get out of the way, to free the free market from years of red tape and regulations.

At one level, this Wall Street critique merely recycled themes that elite interests had been expounding ever since the earliest days of the Industrial Era. On another level, this critique offered something new, a more sophisticated case for embracing inequality.

This new case for inequality — the "Wall Street model" — argued that America's future prosperity would depend on the nation's ability to become more productive. We would only grow the economy, the model's champions contended, if we first increased productivity. And how could we increase productivity? Nations become more productive, the Wall Street model postulated, when they invest in technologies that help workers produce more goods and services.[74] Consequently, the Wall Street model posited, smart societies do everything possible to encourage increased investment.[75]

But investments can't increase unless a society boasts a growing pool of savings that investments can be drawn from. Americans, the Wall Street model argued, weren't saving enough. Indeed, the model charged, the government was making the problem worse — by spending too much and taxing incomes at too high a rate. High taxes, Wall Street insisted, keep affluent families from saving as much as they otherwise would. High spending levels, they added, generate budget deficits, and the government, once in deficit, has to borrow to keep operating. The more the government borrows, the more demand for the dollars that banks have available for lending. The greater this demand, the higher the interest rates on loans. The higher these interest rates, the less borrowing by businesses — and the less investing business will be likely to do.[76]

How to break this grisly cycle? Just stop taxing and spending. Be nice to businesses. Encourage them to invest.

In the closing decades of the twentieth century, America's political leaders would swallow and follow the Wall Street model. They would lower taxes and federal spending. They would "free" business from regulations that limited profit potential. They would take steps that kept wages depressed. Rising wages, Wall Street preached, would only encourage inflation. In the name of fighting that same inflation, political leaders would even applaud Federal Reserve Bank moves that kept the economy from "overheating," even if those moves jacked up jobless totals.

All these policies, to the naked average citizen eye, could sometimes appear contradictory. To encourage savings, for instance, lawmakers would enact tax cuts that put more dollars into wealthy people's pockets. But lawmakers, at the same time, would refuse to boost the minimum wage — and place more dollars in poor people's pockets. What sense did that make? And if higher wages needed to be resisted because they might inflame inflation, why give corporations tax breaks for raising executive pay?

The more average Americans tried to find the rhyme to Wall Street's reason, the more curious the Wall Street model began appearing. How could so many clever and celebrated people be following such an internally incoherent set of policies?

In reality, the Wall Street model did have an internal logic to it, a consistency that never flagged. Within the Wall Street model, any course of action that might end up concentrating more wealth into the pockets of rich people would be good. Any course of action that might narrow the gap between rich people and everybody else would not.

Welfare "reform" that would shove poor moms into the job market, good. A job market flooded by former welfare recipients would depress wages, increase corporate earnings, keep share prices — and, naturally, executive stock option windfalls — rising.

Trade agreements that would smooth the way for U.S. corporate investment in foreign lands, good. American companies, after the passage of the North American Free Trade Agreement, wouldn't even have to move their plants to take advantage of lower wages outside the United States. They could depress wages just by threatening to move.

Lower spending on domestic social programs, good. In the name of balancing the budget, safety net programs for working families would be sliced to inadequate shreds, increasing the pressure on bread-winners to work more hours, at rock-bottom wages.

Deregulation, good. In deregulated industries, a handful of corporations would soon come to totally dominate the market. A sure prescription for higher corporate earnings, higher share prices — and more top executive windfalls.

Tax cuts for the wealthy, the best of all. In the short run, such cuts would mean immediate increases in the annual disposable income of wealthy households. In the longer run, cuts in the taxes levied on wealthy people would shrink government revenues and make deep cuts in safety net programs inevitable. That, of course, would mean more desperation out among working families — and a workforce even more agreeable to whatever wages employers might choose to pay.

By century's end, America's political elites had delivered almost everything Wall Street wanted. And these Wall Street-friendly policies had their intended effect: They helped wealthy Americans amass incredibly large fortunes. Immense new pools of capital were now available for investing in a more productive America. These pools of capital should have, according to Wall Street theorists, fueled a productivity revolution. But the significantly more productive America promised by the Wall Street model never appeared. In 2000, the Economic Report of the President would note that productivity in the United States had increased 2.05 percent a year in the 1990s, an increase over the 1980s rate, but a rate well under the 3.07 percent annual productivity gain of the 1960s.[77]

In the 1960s, Wall Street's critics noted pointedly, the United States had followed economic policies that violated almost every basic precept of the Wall Street model. In that 1960s decade, wages rose and great fortunes didn't, an economic cardinal sin according to 1990s Wall Street economic orthodoxy. To add insult to injury, careful analysts were able to trace much of the productivity growth that did take place in the 1990s to decisions made back in the 1960s and 1970s, *before* boosters of the Wall Street model started calling all the nation's economic shots.[78]

Overall, productivity gains in the last quarter of the twentieth century, years of growing inequality, amounted to less than half of the productivity gains of the century's third quarter, years of growing *equality*.[79] The United States, by following the Wall Street model, by encouraging, wherever possible, the concentration of wealth, had actually ended up placing a brake on productivity growth. Something had gone terribly wrong. But what? The Wall Street model's champions didn't stop to ask. We should.

MANY OF US HOLD, IN OUR MIND'S EYE, a delightful image of how science leaps ahead. There, beside a gorgeously sunlit meadow, sits young Isaac Newton under an apple tree. With a bonk, a red delicious bounces off Newton's noggin. What's this, he wonders. Gravity, he exclaims! One thing leads to another, and three centuries later people are standing on the moon.

We tend to overlook, in our popular culture and political discourse, everything that comes between the bonk and the moon ride. In the real world, scientific progress requires relentless research, not sunlit meadows. And relentless research, in our modern world, has always required government support. Historically, over the past hundred years, government dollars have bankrolled most of the scientific research that has fueled America's productivity progress. In fact, according to one 1997 study, nearly three-quarters of the "main science papers cited in American industrial patent applications" are based on research financed by government or nonprofit agencies.[80]

Private corporations, over the years, have generally made a much more limited contribution to basic research and development, or "R&D." Such research takes both time and money, and few corporations feel inclined to spend either on ideas that may or may not work out profitably.

"Really good research has always been the stepchild of the corporation," notes David Isenberg, himself a veteran of one of the handful of corporations, AT&T, with a well-regarded R&D history.[81]

Good basic research, scientists like Isenberg contend, can only thrive in institutions with enough patience to stick with research over the long haul. Government agencies and universities can fit that bill. So can private companies without any real competition in their industries. AT&T, for instance, built the world-acclaimed Bell Labs — where Isenberg worked — during its years as the government-regulated telephone monopoly. IBM and Xerox, two other companies with long R&D histories, spent decades without serious competition in their respective industries. They "provided stable, comfortable homes for many of the nation's brightest minds."[82]

These corporate homes, by century's end, no longer offered scientists much comfort. In a corporate America almost completely preoccupied with generating king-sized quarterly earnings gains, research that might deliver productivity gains down the road in some distant future held somewhere close to zero appeal.

"We've reached a point where R&D inside a corporation is fundamentally impossible," Peter Cochrane, the former chief technologist at BT Labs, a telecom think tank, noted bluntly in 2001. "The financial people want you to pick the winners. You can't."[83]

America's corporate executives, at the turn of the century, desperately needed winners now, not later. What good was research that might translate into breakthroughs twenty years down the road? In twenty years, someone else would be CEO, someone else would be reaping a stock option windfall if that research actually paid off. In this environment, top corporate officials had no patience whatsoever with researchers who yearned to follow their hunches, to whatever deadends or brilliant inventions those hunches might lead. Corporate America, instead, pointed researchers to the quarterly bottom line and ordered them to produce. These marching orders, within corporate research centers, would produce considerably more frustration than insight. Top researchers, by the early twenty-first century, were mourning an era that appeared forever lost.

"In the old days, there was a spirit about it — a spirit of free innovation," Robert Lucky, a distinguished scientist at Bell Labs, would tell reporters in 2001. "Research was an end in itself. Today, that's not true at all. Profitability is the end."[84]

Research that couldn't deliver profits, on a timely regular schedule, held no allure for corporate executives, who, on a timely regular schedule, expected to be cashing out one ample option payoff after another. These ample payoffs both outraged and enticed corporate scientists. On the one hand, these researchers couldn't stomach what windfall-driven decision making meant for their freedom to pursue their intellectual curiosity. On the other hand, many researchers were intrigued by the prospect of hitting some option jackpot themselves. Over one eighteen-month period near century's end, 15 percent of the Bell Labs research team jumped ship "after glamorous startups promising quick-hit riches lured them away."[85]

"Research for the sake of research gave way to innovation with a payoff," summed up the high tech trade journal, the *Net Economy*. "Greed won out."[86]

The lure of big payoffs actually devastated intellectual research communities both inside *and* outside corporate America. Greed, after all, could not be quarantined to the private sector. In the late 1990s, at the height of the boom years, academic research centers the nation over watched researchers bail out to grab their piece of the windfall action. Academics "who had the skills," noted Sreenath Sreenivasan, a Columbia University tech guru, "wanted to be out there making money."[87]

And if you wanted to be making money, education was certainly not where you wanted to be. In the boom years, education would not boom. Federal expenditures on education and training, over the century's last quarter, actually dropped, as a share of gross domestic product, by 50 percent.[88] That decline, a stunning marker of education's true "priority" status in the 1980s and 1990s, would frustrate educators enormously.

But many economists would be frustrated, too, especially those who had been studying just what makes one society more productive than another. These "New Growth" economists directly challenged the core assumption of the Wall Street model, the notion that capital investments drive productivity growth, end of story. Investments, the New Growth economists readily agreed, surely do play a significant role in enhancing productivity, but so do several other equally important factors, most notably the presence of a skilled, well-educated workforce. New technologies, the New Growth economists explained, cannot by themselves make a workplace more productive.[89] New tools and techniques need to be massaged in the workplace, adopted to real life situations, refined and tweaked in ways that make them more useful. That massaging only takes place if employees bring a quality set of skills to the workplace.[90] Investments in new technologies, in effect, only pay off if employees have been well educated and trained.

At one level — the rhetorical level — America's top corporate leaders understood this connection between productivity progress and education. The 1980s and 1990s saw an enormous outcry, from corporate suites, for better schools. In 1983, the release of *A Nation At Risk*, a landmark report engineered by the U.S. Department of Education, triggered a barrage of special commissions that aimed to improve the quality of American education, many of them chaired by corporate leaders. These executives would intone, at every opportunity, the absolute centrality of education to America's economic future. For the United States to prosper, they agreed, every child had to be educated.

But education, in the end, costs, and corporate America would not be willing to pay the price. The Wall Street model did not envision a bigger federal commitment to education. Federal spending needed to be slashed, not increased. If spending were increased, after all, how could taxes be cut, how could wealth be accumulated? In the 1980s and 1990s, the nation's leaders would talk the talk about education. They would not walk the walk.

By century's end, fewer young Americans, not more, would be getting a full and complete education. The federal Pell Grant program, an effort designed to help low-income families send their kids to college, covered 98 percent of public college tuition in 1986. In 1999, the program covered only 57 percent.[91] Many low-income families could not afford to pick up the difference, even with loans. The predictable result: In 2002, research by economists Michael McPherson and Morton Owen Schapiro documented "that the percentage of high-achieving students who do not enroll in college is five times higher among those who are poor than those who are rich."[92]

Numbers like these, argue economists not enthralled by the Wall Street model, help explain why unequal nations don't grow economically as well as nations where wealth is more equitably distributed.[93] In nations where wealth concentrates at the top, more people lower down on the economic ladder simply "lack access to the education and training that would enable them to contribute to economic growth."[94]

WISE GOVERNMENTS, THE NEW GROWTH THEORISTS TELL US, invest in education. But wise governments also understand that productivity gains won't blossom without a wide range of investments in other public goods as well. Some of these investments — government support for cutting-edge scientific research, for instance — create the knowledge we need to become more productive. Other expenditures, like dollars for plugging potholes, make more prosaic contributions. These create and maintain the "infrastructure" that helps us work more efficiently. Without an adequate infrastructure, modern economies crumble.

"Consider what would happen to economic growth," economists Barry Bluestone and Bennett Harrison asked at the turn of the century, "if the interstate highway system were suddenly to disappear, or narrow down to one lane in each direction."[95]

In the decades right after World War II, the United States systematically invested in infrastructure, in everything from sewage to cyclotrons, and the nation would become substantially more productive. In the closing decades of the twentieth century, the nation would shortchange these investments. In the 1970s, federal spending on infrastructure averaged over 2.5 percent of the nation's gross domestic product. By the late 1990s, that share had dropped to just 1.5 percent, an investment shortfall that equaled hundreds of billions of dollars — and amounted to a huge drag on technological progress.[96]

A perhaps even more significant drag, some analysts suggested, was coming from *within* enterprises. A healthy economy, these analysts noted, certainly needs a solid, supportive infrastructure. But the infrastructure that supports our workplaces may not, in the end, limit our technological progress as much as the relationships within our workplaces. A solid educational infrastructure, for instance, can keep enterprises supplied with employees who have the knowledge and skills that enterprises need. But enterprises need to be able to tap this knowledge effectively, or else these skills will go to waste.

New technologies, analysts explain, can't just be forced *upon* a workplace. They need to be fine-tuned *in* the workplace, with the active involvement — and cooperation — of workers and managers alike. In modern corporate America, unfortunately, workers and managers have not been in a cooperating mood. Decades of growing economic inequality have, as we have seen, nurtured defective, not effective, enterprises. In these defective enterprises, enterprises where loyalty had been downsized and looted away, workers have little reason to help with fine-tuning new technologies.[97]

But corporate America's productivity problem actually goes far beyond sullen workers. In a corporate America more interested in squeezing workers than involving them, employers have as little incentive to think seriously about improving productivity as employees. The more depressed employers are able to keep wages, the less their incentive to invest significantly in higher productivity. Why invest in new technologies when old technologies, thanks to cheap labor, remain quite profitable?

Employers who share rewards with workers, by contrast, must think seriously about improving productivity. To compete successfully in the marketplace, Barry Bluestone and Bennett Harrison have pointed out, companies that pay higher wages "have to find ways to use their workers more effectively."[98] Rising wages, adds *Business Week's* Aaron Bernstein, can actually "spur productivity growth."[99]

If Bernstein's observation accurately reflects reality, productivity gains should be meager in those economic sectors where wages are low — and that is, in real life, exactly the case. In the United States, the two economic sectors with the worst wages, the service and retail sectors, have registered the smallest gains in productivity.[100] Could this low productivity in service and retail simply reflect the hard-to-automate, one-on-one nature of service and retail work? Possibly. But if that were the case, then service and retail work the world over, and not just in the United States, would lag in productivity. The service and retail sectors, however, do not lag behind in productivity everywhere across the world. In some societies, service and retail show significant productivity gains. These societies share one common trait: They pay decent wages for service and retail work.

In Germany, service sector productivity, in the 1970s and 1980s, grew seven times faster than service sector productivity in the United States. Over this same period, service sector wages rose in Germany more than twice as fast as they rose in the United States.[101]

LOW WAGES CAN POWERFULLY UNDERMINE whatever incentive an employer may have to make investments in productivity. Low wages also have a broader and, perhaps ultimately, even more damaging impact: They reduce the demand for goods and services an economy produces.

Demand matters, and much more so than the Wall Street model suggests. The model, as we have seen, treats interest rates as the essential element that determines economic growth. If businesses can borrow money at reasonable interest rates, they will. They'll use this borrowed money to make investments. These investments will grow productivity and, eventually, the economy. All will be well — if interest rates are only kept low. But businesses, in actual practice, will only make investments that will help them produce more products if they see a demand for these additional products. If that demand appears unlikely to materialize, businesses simply don't invest, no matter how low interest rates may be. In the Great Depression, interest rates crashed to under 1 percent. But businesses did not rush to borrow, even at these low rates. They saw no demand.[102]

During the 1930s, the years of the Great Depression, British economist John Maynard Keynes helped policy makers understand this demand dynamic. If average people had more income, Keynes argued, they could afford to buy more goods and services, in the process boosting demand and restoring the overall economy to better health. In this demand equation, Keynes and his followers added, the distribution of a society's income mattered mightily. Dollars in average people's pockets would always do more to rev up demand than dollars in rich people's pockets because poorer people tend to spend a larger *share* of their income on goods and services than richer people. The more shared a nation's income, the less concentrated a nation's wealth, the greater the demand for goods and services.[103] Inequality, simply put, saps demand. Equality boosts it.

In an economy where demand is rising, businesses see sales to be registered, if they can only produce more goods. So they invest in their workers. Productivity advances. More goods are produced. And these goods sell, because people can afford to buy them. Businesses prosper. They hire more workers. Workers prosper. The more workers prosper, the more goods and services they buy — and businesses prosper even more, all thanks to a distribution of wealth and income that encourages a healthy flow of dollars into average people's pockets. No rocket science here. Just plain common sense.

"Indeed," as economists Barry Bluestone and Bennett Harrison have quipped, "most business leaders would like to see higher wages — at every company save their own."[104]

This tension stalks every modern market economy. In the abstract, every business wants customers with lots of cash in their wallets. The more cash available to be spent, the more sales likely to be recorded. But businesses don't see all people as customers. Businesses see some people — the people they hire — as workers. The more dollars individual businesses put in the pockets of these people, their workers, the fewer dollars these businesses may see in profits.

Individual businesses, as a consequence, have an ever-present incentive *not* to raise wages. But if every business were to succumb to the low-wage temptation, all businesses would be worse off, since one employer's workers are another employer's customers.

So what do businesses do? Do they act in their overall best interest or in their individual self-interest? Left to their own devices, history has shown, individual businesses almost always follow their individual self-interest. They seek to minimize their wage obligations. They create, in so doing, an enormous downward pressure on demand that, sooner or later, sends the overall economy into a tailspin.

History also shows, fortunately, something else. Societies do not leave individual businesses to their own devices. Countervailing social forces, most notably trade unions, emerge. These unions organize to take wages out of competition. Where they succeed, individual businesses cannot gain a competitive advantage by shortchanging their workers. They must compete on some other basis, by producing, for instance, better quality goods and services or by producing goods and services more efficiently. Societies that set stiff wage standards, in other words, give all businesses an ongoing incentive to pay close attention to what consumers want — and operate as productively as possible.

In the United States, right after World War II, stiff wage standards would be set. Unions would set them. By the mid 1950s, over one out of every three private sector workers in America belonged to a union. The nation's labor movement had never been stronger. Unions, with this strength, would help stretch a tight safety net all across the American economy. The minimum wage climbed steadily in the 1950s and 1960s, reaching, in 1968, its highest inflation-adjusted point ever. Minimum wage workers that year made $1.60 an hour, enough to push a family of three 18 percent *over* the official poverty line.[105] This rising floor under wages, coupled with stiff tax rates on the nation's highest incomes, created by the end of the 1960s the most equal income distribution in modern American history, a distribution that kept demand high and steady. Between 1947 and 1973, points out long-time Labor Department analyst Paul Ryscavage, every family seemed to be "sharing in the income-producing capacity of the economy."[106]

"The nation's economic pie was getting bigger," adds Ryscavage, "and everyone was helping themselves to a larger and larger piece of the pie."[107]

But then, in the 1970s, the tide turned. American businesses, for the first time in years, began facing real competition in global markets, from the newly vibrant European and Japanese economies. Cheap fuel, meanwhile, had disappeared, after the OPEC nations flexed their oil-producing muscles. The decent wages that America's major corporations had been paying suddenly appeared to be unnecessary extravagances. By the mid 1970s, corporate leaders were talking openly about creating a "union-free environment." Together with like-minded politicos, they pressed for a new American economic order.

The Wall Street model gave the campaigners for this new order all the ideological cover they would ever need. Rising wages, the model argued, ought to be seen as a catalyst for inflation, not as an essential source of demand. The new Reagan Administration would take this advice to heart. The minimum wage would rise, nineteen days before Ronald Reagan's 1981 inauguration, to $3.35. That would be the last minimum wage hike for nearly a decade. By 1991, the real value of the minimum wage had fallen 16 percent below 1981 levels.[108] By 2001, minimum wage workers earned, after adjusting for inflation, 35 percent less than minimum wage workers earned in 1968.[109] In the new century, minimum wage workers who worked full-time, year round, ended up with incomes that left them 22 percent *under* the poverty line for a family of three.[110]

The sinking real value of the minimum wage would place downward pressure on all wages.[111] Still more downward pressure would come from two decades of outright assault against organized labor. President Reagan would set the tone, in 1981, by hiring "replacement workers" to permanently displace over eleven thousand striking air traffic controllers.[112] That move signaled a landmark about-face in America labor relations. For over forty years, ever since the 1935 passage of the Wagner Act, the basic legislation that protects workers' right to organize, employers had rarely tried to break strikes by permanently replacing strikers.[113] President Reagan's open defiance of this established labor relations practice gave corporate threats to fire strikers a powerful credibility — and that credibility would blunt the effectiveness of the strike as an antidote to corporate power. In 1995, only thirty-two strikes involving at least a thousand workers took place in the United States. Twenty years earlier, eight times that many strikes involved a thousand workers.[114]

Year by year, in the 1980s and 1990s, the wage standards established in the 1950s and 1960s collapsed a little bit more, and with this collapse came a widening gap in America's income distribution. More income concentrated at the top. Fewer dollars trickled down to the bottom. Between 1980 and 1999, the value of the minimum wage fell 18 percent. CEO pay rose, those same years, by 882 percent.[115] By century's end, in a United States where unions represented less than 10 percent of America's private sector workers, decent wage standards could simply not be maintained.

Some policy makers did worry deeply about this collapse of wage standards. They feared a potentially catastrophic drop in consumer demand. Workers, U.S. Labor Secretary Robert Reich reminded the nation halfway through the 1990s, "are also consumers, and at some point American workers won't have enough money in their pockets to buy all the goods and services they are producing."[116]

Even some business leaders worried about America's enormous income imbalances.

"This is going to blow up in our faces," Lucent Technologies chairman Henry Schacht warned in 1998, "There is no way a society can have this much of its accumulated wealth distributed to these few people."[117]

But the blow-up did not come. Demand did not drop precipitously, or even at all. The economy kept growing right into the new century. Why no collapse? Why no horrible stumble? What happened?

Debt happened. Working families kept demand up for America's products and services by racing deeper and deeper into debt. By 1998, America's average household carried "a debtload that approaches its annual income."[118] The entire American economy balanced perilously on an ever-growing stack of credit cards and home equity loans.

This massive debt should have started alarm bells ringing on Wall Street. By century's end, after all, champions of the Wall Street model had been banging the drums for savings, not spending, for over twenty years. America would prosper, they had asserted over and over, when savings started accumulating, savings that could be translated into productivity-boosting investments. But America's massive indebtedness in the 1980s and the 1990s rang no bells, mainly because the debtors, to Wall Street eyes, didn't matter. The debtors were working families, and Wall Street had never expected working families to do any savings heavy lifting. Wall Street had always expected savings to come from affluent families. The growing indebtedness of working families simply became, for Wall Street, another excuse to target more tax breaks to the affluent. How else would the United States be able to increase the pool of savings available for investment?

So the tax breaks — for the wealthy — continued to flow. America continued to become more unequal. This growing inequality, in turn, stimulated still more indebtedness. Households, as economist Ted Schmidt points out, don't make consumption decisions just on how much money they have. They base their consumption decisions, to a large degree, on how much affluent households are spending.[119] The greater the level of inequality in a society, the more powerful the pressure on lower-income families to spend what they don't have. In the boom years, this pressure helped push indebtedness in average American households to record levels — and helped ensure that the sum total of savings in the United States would not rise. Debt at the bottom, in effect, canceled out surplus at the top. The glory years of the Wall Street model would end without any aggregate gain in American savings.

Wage cuts, giveaways to wealthy taxpayers, and smaller safety nets, Wall Street had promised, would deliver unto America massive new accumulations of capital for productive investment. Wage cuts, tax giveaways, and smaller safety nets would deliver, in the real economy, no such thing.

In fact, the Wall Street model would deliver unto America the exact opposite of productive investment. The Wall Street model would deliver speculation.

DOWN THROUGH HISTORY, WEALTH HAS at times concentrated at enormously rapid rates. Down through history, societies have also at times gone off on spectacular speculative binges. These times almost always turn out to be one and the same.

Inequality seems to inevitably breed speculation. Let great wealth accumulate at a society's summit and great speculative bubbles will soon blot out the economic horizon. In the 1630s, the huge fortunes that had found their way into the purses of Holland's finest families fed a tulip bubble so outrageous — a handful of flowers could cost $40,000 — that the bursting of that bubble sent the Dutch into deep depression.[120] Eighty years later, the fantastically flush French and English deep-pocket set chased after New World land with a manic intensity that sent deeds soaring to tulip-like levels. In the 1840s, another speculative frenzy exploded, this time around railroads, as the great fortunes of the early Industrial Revolution stoked the fires of the Great British Railway Mania. In the United States, after the Civil War, the first American men of fortune in the modern Industrial Age would catch the same railroad mania. Their speculative fever would rage on and off for thirty years. America's railroad bubble would finally burst, for good, in 1893 — and help trigger a depression that lasted a good part of a decade.[121]

The 1920s would see another epoch of rapidly concentrating wealth in the United States, an epoch that would end with America's most fabled bursting bubble of them all, the 1929 stock market crash. In that bubble's wake would come the longest and deepest depression in American history.

What explains this link between speculation and concentrating wealth? Why does an overabundance of dollars in a limited number of pockets almost always produce wild flights of economic fancy?

To understand speculative fevers, we actually need to look first at households where pockets *aren't* overflowing. In societies where wealth is concentrating at the top, households further down the economic ladder will have less wealth to spend on goods and services. Those with wealth, in turn, will have little reason to plow that wealth into productive investment, simply because little demand will exist for the goods and services that productive investment might produce. But large wealth-holders have to do something with all their dollars. They can, after all, only personally consume so much. So what happens with these dollars that wealthy people cannot consume and cannot invest productively? The wealthy plow these dollars into speculation. The speculative schemes they "invest" in may pay off, and if they do, how wonderful for the wealthy. The schemes, of course, may also flop. But if they do flop, no big deal. The money lost doesn't really matter — not to wealth-holders who have money to burn.

Most of us never experience this sensation of having "money to burn." We work hard for our paychecks. We depend on every dollar. We can't afford to risk any significant chunk of our savings. The wealthy can. They can afford to chase speculative investments that offer big returns — and so they do. Chases can be thrilling.

People of modest means do sometimes find themselves in a similar situation — the same situation that wealthy people experience every day — and these people of modest means typically behave, in these rare situations, the same way rich people behave. Consider the $2 racetrack bettor who cashes out a totally unexpected $100 daily double winner. What normally happens next? Our lucky winner, who seldom ever bets more than $2 in any one race, suddenly turns around and starts laying down $10 and $20 bets. And why not? Our bettor did no work to earn that $100 of daily double winnings. Our bettor has no sweat equity invested in that $100. Those dollars amount to "play money," so our bettor plays. All lucky bettors act the same way. They routinely risk their surprise winnings in ways they would never risk a paycheck.

Wealthy people are life's lucky bettors. They may indeed work hard, but no one makes megamillions punching a time clock or billing hours. Grand fortunes only emerge when someone somehow is able to leverage someone else's labor. A factory owner pockets a dollar on every item workers fabricate. A department store magnate pockets a dollar on every purchase sales clerks register. An heir inherits a great many dollars all at once. These are dollars that can be risked freely, even wildly. They are less than real. They are, in every unequal society, the kindling wood for speculative fires.

The more unequal a society, the more kindling wood, the more fires. In the 1980s and 1990s, kindling wood abounded — and so did speculation.

The wealthy of these years speculated on commodities. In 1994, for instance, trading in crude-oil futures and options on the New York Mercantile Exchange quadrupled the total amount of crude oil the entire world that year actually produced.[122]

They speculated on currencies. The World Bank, by the latter years of the century, was estimating that 95 percent of the thousand-plus billions of dollars in daily global currency flows amounted to pure speculative trading.[123]

They speculated on real estate. In Manhattan, wealth's world capital, clothing mogul Tommy Hilfiger picked up a Fifth Avenue apartment for $10 million in 1999. The next year, he put that same apartment up for sale at $20 million.[124]

But, most of all, the wealthy speculated on stocks. The closing years of the twentieth century will forever be remembered for the wildest, zaniest, most bizarre speculative binge in American financial history.

The binge began, innocently enough, in 1982. On Friday morning, August 13, the Dow Jones Industrial Average, the marquee measure of Wall Street's daily ups and downs, stood at 776.92, after a modest drop the day before. The Dow would never sit that low again. Friday's trading brought gains, so did the next week's. More gains came in the months ahead. By year's end, the Dow would top 1,000. The "greatest bull market ever" had begun.[125] Nothing would stop this raging bull. The market would drop suddenly in 1987. But that drop would prove only a pause. By August 1989 the market had regained all the ground lost in 1987. Half a dozen years later, in 1995, the steady climb would take an even steeper turn up — into territory not seen since the 1920s.

That turn would come when Netscape Communications, the company behind the first commercial software for browsing the World Wide Web, stunned Wall Street with the first dot.com initial public offering. On August 9,

1995, Netscape offered 5 million shares to investors at $28 each. By day's end, those shares would be selling for more than twice that. Netscape, a company that had never made a profit, would suddenly be worth $2.2 billion.[126] No major company, in stock exchange history, had ever debuted so stunningly.

The wild bull ride would now be on, with steady helpings of fresh IPOs keeping the bull suitably energized. The Nasdaq composite index, the best measure of the high-tech sector, jumped 23 percent in 1996.[127] The next year saw still more gains. Veteran Wall Streeters were starting to get alarmed. Such increases, they feared, could not be sustained.

"Today," Peter Bernstein, a mutual funds director, told the press midway through 1997, "the market has begun to penetrate into zones of irrationality."[128]

Bernstein hadn't seen anything yet. In 1997, Nasdaq would finish up 22 percent for the year, then follow that with an even more incredible 40 percent advance in 1998. The next year couldn't possibly top that. It did. The Nasdaq rose 86 percent in 1999.[129]

High-tech telecommunications and software companies led the way. Qualcomm ended 1999 up 1,882 percent, Sprint PCS up 357 percent, Oracle up 263 percent.[130] Even more amazing were the run-ups of companies that were fledgling, at best, by every normal economic measure. Yahoo, the Web search engine, boasted all of 803 employees in February 1999, a smaller workforce than a run-of-the-mill manufacturing plant. Wall Street valued Yahoo at $34 billion. E-Bay, the online auction house, employed only 130 people. Wall Street investors valued E-Bay at $11 billion, a total that made each employee worth $86 million.[131]

Share prices couldn't possibly climb any higher. Of course, they did. Priceline, a dot.com that hawked cut-rate air travel tickets, would be "worth more at its peak than every U.S. airline put together."[132]

Over the second half of the 1990s, *Business Week* would later note, all stocks together "racked up five consecutive calendar years" of annual returns that topped 20 percent, "three years more than ever before."[133] By March 2000, the ratio of stock prices to corporate earnings had "reached more than twice its historic average." The bubble, measured by that historic average, had inflated the value of stocks "on the order of $10 trillion, more than $30,000 for every person in the country."[134]

Some Wall Street watchers, amazingly, were convinced that nothing but even brighter stock market days lay ahead. In August 2000, one of the most celebrated of these optimists, James Glassman, the co-author of *Dow 36,000*, would debate one of Wall Street's few wet blankets, Barton Biggs, a Morgan Stanley strategist, before an audience of well-heeled listeners at a resort in Idaho's Sun Valley. Biggs preached caution and gloom — and lost the debate, in an audience vote, by an 85 to 3 margin. Afterwards, one of the eighty-five came up to Biggs's wife Judith.

"I'm worried about your husband," the listener noted caringly. "I think he's lost touch with things. He's out of date."[135]

Investors had little patience for skeptics like Biggs, little patience for anyone who stood — or fell — in the way of hitting still another big stock market score. In the middle of the market mania, on March 25, 1997, one market veteran, a forty-eight-year-old trading assistant named Paddy Grieve, fell suddenly to the New York Stock Exchange trading floor, right next to the spot where he had been working the past twenty-five years. Grieve's co-workers gave him CPR. The rest of his fellow traders nearby paused for a moment, then went on shouting out their trades. Doctors at a downtown hospital would later pronounce Grieve dead from a heart attack.[136] Who could blame the traders for ignoring Grieve? They couldn't help him. But they could certainly help themselves. There was work to be done, there were fortunes to be made.

Fortunes for Wall Street players of every sort.

"Everybody here is overpaid, knows they are overpaid, and is determined to continue to be overpaid," as one Wall Street player, Julian Robertson, told the *Washington Post.*

Robertson, the top gun at Tiger Management, a high-risk investment house, expected to personally score, the *Post* reported in 1998, "well above $500 million this year."[137]

Few of Robertson's colleagues and competitors would be *that* overpaid. But they did quite nicely nonetheless. In 1999, one securities company alone, Merrill Lynch, handed five top executives at least $14 million each.[138]

The market would peak one year later, in March 2000. By April 2001, stocks had lost $4 trillion of their peak, an amount that topped the combined gross domestic products of Britain, France, and Italy.[139] By June 2002, the market was off $6 trillion, a third of its total value.[140] Smiley-faced commentators did their best to minimize this loss. Nobody actually lost $6 trillion, they argued. The lost value had only existed "on paper." True enough, but the modern world revolves around paper. Wall Street's collapse meant that millions of workers would have to delay their retirements — or start them with a fraction of the nest-eggs they thought they had accumulated. Thousands of other Americans lost their jobs, as companies rushed to cut costs and get their share prices inching up again.

Other Americans lost their dream — of becoming rich.

Throughout the boom, fast-talking operators had peddled that dream all across America. One of these operators, Wade Cook, America's top promoter of "investment self-help instruction," conducted thirty-two hundred investing seminars in 1997 alone. Investors, to attend one of these seminars, paid $5,695 per person. Students could also, of course, invest in handy investment vehicles Cook was happy to make available to his budding investing talents. In all, observed *New York Observer* columnist Christopher Byron, Cook "talked nearly 400,000 would-be investors out of $100 million in 1997."

"What we're seeing here, folks," an amazed and amused Byron noted, "is the birth of America's first vertically integrated moron-milking machine."[141]

Scam artists have been milking "morons," of course, ever since time began. Here in the United States, scam artists even occupy an honored place in our folklore. We all enjoy Hollywood movies about dashing fast-talkers who can, just by flashing a smile, separate the unwary from their wallets. But fast-talkers like Wade Cook aren't, in the final analysis, what made the great 1990s stock market boom the greatest scam of all time. The Cooks were just small fry. The real schemers weren't two-bit grifters. The real schemers were the deep-pockets behind America's most revered financial institutions.

BY THE FINAL QUARTER OF THE TWENTIETH CENTURY, the United States had evolved the most sophisticated system for generating investment capital the world had ever seen, or so proclaimed America's business elites. America was creating wealth, they marveled, because America appreciated the wealthy — and had created a financial superstructure that enabled the wealthy to translate their fortunes into investments that enrich the lives of all Americans. Thanks to this marvelously efficient superstructure, they continued, any American with a business idea worth exploring could get a shot at success. America had created, in a sense, an entrepreneurial heaven on Earth.

Throughout the boom years, appropriately enough, any would-be entrepreneurs entering this heaven would usually be met first by a class of wealthy individuals known collectively as "angels." These angels sported no halos, only thick money belts. By the mid 1990s, federal officials had accredited some 250,000 of them. These angels had the green light to invest in "unregistered securities," to buy, in other words, a piece of the action in fledgling new companies. And invest they did. By 1996, wealthy angels were plowing about $20 billion a year into start-ups.[142]

Additional dollars for fledgling companies would come from "venture capitalists," professional investors who rounded up chunks of investment cash from various deep-pocket sources and, like individual angels, bought stakes in new businesses. Venture capitalists would emerge, in the 1990s, as the princes of America's financial landscape. The most celebrated of them, John Doerr of Silicon Valley's Kleiner Perkins Caufield & Beyers, began venturing in 1980. By 1990, his venture capital firm was claiming credit for birthing new companies that had created over $30 billion in stock value.[143]

Angels and venture capitalists prepped up-and-coming entrepreneurs for the big time. But to break into that big time — to actually issue stock to the investing public — entrepreneurs needed to tap into still another key financial player, the Wall Street investment bank. These "banks" did no normal banking. They took new companies "public," by selling shares in them to outside investors. From these sales, the theory went, new companies would gain the wherewithal to revolutionize the marketplace with bright new ideas. The economy, infused with these ideas, would throb with new energy. Businesses would grow more productive. Everyone would benefit.

But everyone would benefit, business leaders lectured lawmakers, only if government also did its part — by helping wealth accumulate. By following the Wall Street model, lawmakers were informed, they could keep America's financial system suitably greased and running smoothly. Tax cuts would ensure that angels and venture capitalists had enough spare cash to invest. Low wages would help keep corporate earnings rising. Rising earnings, in turn, would keep corporate stocks attractive to investors and expand the market for the new companies Wall Street investment houses brought "public."

Lawmakers, suitably impressed by this Wall Street logic, did their best to cooperate. They did their greasing, then sat back and watched capital surge through America's private investment channels. In 1990, venture capitalists invested $3.7 billion in fledgling companies. In 1999, venture investments totaled $45 billion, a twelve-fold increase.[144] In 2000, some seven hundred venture capital firms were sitting on $105 billion.[145]

"Venture cash is transforming half-formed ideas into world-beating products and services," *Business Week* exulted.[146] Venture capital, exclaimed *Worth*, is playing "a vital role in the U.S. economy, funding start-up companies and nurturing them with money, experience, and connections."[147] And investment banks, cheerleaders added, were taking those companies the final mile, getting them to market where they could raise the cash they needed "to finance growth or crucial research and development."[148] Over the course of the boom years, investment banks would bring the shares of more than five thousand companies to market, in stock offerings that raised over $300 billion.[149]

"We're the only country in the world," joked Clinton Treasury Secretary Lawrence Summers, "where you can raise your first $100 million before you buy your first suit."[150]

The picture the cheerleaders painted could hardly have been more appealing. Bright, talented, energetic entrepreneurs overflowing with revolutionary, paradigm-smashing great ideas. Angels and venture capitalists, wise in the ways of business, sharing their dollars and wisdom with tireless but inexperienced entrepreneurs. Investment bankers taking young entrepreneurs by the hand onto Wall Street, showcasing their fresh and exciting new ideas to investors all across the nation and even the world.

A pretty picture indeed, but one that in no way reflected reality. The American capital-generating process that evolved in the 1980s and 1990s had next to nothing to do with nurturing up-and-coming entrepreneurs or bringing world-beating products to market. America's capital-generating process did not generate a more productive economy. The process generated, instead, big paydays for the financial movers and shakers involved. Nothing else mattered.

Venture capitalists, flush with the cash the Wall Street model kept pumping into their pockets, behaved like any $2 bettor after a big daily double win. They laid bets — big bets — on as many fledgling companies as they could find. They then pushed these new companies to "go public" and start selling shares of stock as soon as possible. Why delay? Why waste time trying to figure out if the new company had a product or a service people really wanted to buy? Windfalls awaited, just an IPO away.[151]

Mentoring? Who had time for mentoring wet-behind-the-ears entrepreneurs? Venture capitalists, the Harvard Business School's D. Quinn Mills would later point out, were more into "bullying" their eager young entrepreneurs than mentoring them.[152] They demanded that entrepreneurs make ridiculously premature investments in mass marketing. Million-dollar Super Bowl commercials always made sense to the venture capitalists. How else was a company that hadn't yet proved any ability to survive in the marketplace going to be able to create a buzz loud enough to attract investors' attention?

Investment bankers played equally unhelpful games. Out the windows went the standards — the "due diligence" — meant to assure that only legitimate companies were brought before the investing public. Investment bankers were supposed to set a fair initial share price for any new issue they brought to market. In the boom years, notes D. Quinn Mills, they "grossly underpriced" their IPOs instead, then used that bargain-basement price in an "elaborate system of favor-trading" that "diverted money away from the entrepreneurs" into the pockets of the bankers' "high-roller clients." These high-rollers, typically the top executives of major corporations, would be allotted IPO shares at below-market rates. They would promptly unload these shares, scoring huge personal profits, when the IPO actually went public and started soaring. And investment bankers, naturally, did their best to make sure the IPO shares would soar. They promoted the new stocks "with hype dressed up as research" and aggressively marketed the shares to mutual funds that "were all too happy to goose their own near-term results by providing buy-side support."[153] These games could be incredibly lucrative, for almost everyone involved. One investment bank client, WorldCom chief executive Bernie Ebbers, made a crisp $10.6 million between 1996 and 2000 just by flipping IPO shares allocated to him by Citigroup. Officials at Citigroup would later deny they had done anything in the least bit improper. Rewarding wealthy clients with IPO shares, they told reporters, was simply standard Wall Street operating procedure.[154]

Venture capitalists did quite nicely as well, as the rise and fall of eToys, a typical overhyped dot.com retailer, would illustrate. In 1997, a venture capital firm named Idealab shelled out a half-cent a share to buy a $100,000 stake in the fledgling eToys. The dot.com would go public almost two years later, opening at $20 a share and closing its first day at $76. Later in 1999, Idealab would unload over 3.8 million of its eToys shares, at prices as high as $69. Total profit for the venture capitalists from Idealab: $193 million.[155] eToys would later go bankrupt.

America's financial movers and shakers did not, of course, only bankroll fresh-faced entrepreneurs and fledgling start-ups. Wealthy individuals and investment bankers stood equally ready to supply the capital that established companies needed to expand their operations. These investments in established concerns, the claim went, enhanced productivity and created jobs. But wealthy

individuals and investment bankers had no more interest in nurturing productivity than they had in nurturing start-ups. In their investing, they targeted precious little capital into long-term investments that could result in significant,
long-term productivity gains. They rushed instead to make the investments
that promised the quickest and fastest payoffs. In the process, they would generate some of the most colossal — and wasteful — marketplace gluts the world
had ever seen.

ONCE UPON A TIME, the residents of the United States had to make do with just
one major long-distance telephone company, AT&T. The 1980s added MCI
and Sprint to the mix. By the mid 1990s, that mix had multiplied many-fold.
Phone lines, corporate America had discovered, weren't just for talking anymore. In the emerging Information Age, they could carry data, too, huge globs
of bits and bytes. And the amount of data flowing through Wired America,
anyone in an executive suite with a mouse and half a brain could clearly see,
was only going to expand exponentially. Yesterday's wires brought voices into
America's homes. Tomorrow's wires would bring, via broadband connections,
the grandest fortune-making opportunity since Microsoft!

Into America's neighborhoods, to seize this opportunity, would rush over a
dozen telecommunications companies, each with grandiose visions for national fiber optic cable networks. Miles and miles of fiber would go down, in, and
under America's byways and highways, in a furious race to string together the
fastest, widest national networks money could buy.

Money would prove to be no object. By the 1990s, after all, America's
wealthy had plenty to burn. They poured these plentiful dollars into "telecom,"
the shorthand for America's hottest investment ticket. No one with cash
seemed to want to sit on the sidelines. Microsoft co-founder Paul Allen invested $1.65 billion in a broadband company called RCN. Cable TV magnate
John Malone poured $1.5 billion into a pair of telecoms known as ICG and
Teligent.[156] Telecoms would borrow billions more from wealthy investors via
the bond market. The industry's outstanding debt, $75 billion in 1995, would
shoot up to $309 billion in 2000.[157]

The more cash Wall Street raised, the more cable telecoms kept laying. They
would lay, in all, about 80.2 million miles of optical fiber from 1996 through
2001, enough to loop the globe over three thousand times.[158] Traffic to fill all
these lines, the telecoms believed, at least initially, would surely materialize. But
the traffic would never come, not in amounts near heavy enough to fill all the
new cables dug into America. By early 2002, only 2 to 5 percent of all the fiber
laid down by the telecom building boom would actually be carrying any voice
or data.[159] The entire telecom boom, a J. P. Morgan analyst would tell the *New
York Times*, had been "a phenomenal miscalculation."[160]

Telecom executives would do everything they could to stave off the
inevitable popping of their bubble. They would try slashing prices to boost traffic and revenue. But the price cuts only led to price wars that, the *Washington*

Post later reported, "eventually left many companies with barely enough revenue to pay operating expenses, let alone interest on their huge mounds of debt."[161] With revenues shrinking, the wire-happy telecoms would become even more desperate. They would, as we have seen, cook their books. But that move backfired, too, in a string of headline-grabbing scandals that would eventually deflate the telecom balloon by an incredible $2 trillion.[162]

Telecom's wire woes would soon spill over into the wireless world. Cellular companies, facing competition from desperate, rate-cutting land-line telecoms, would find themselves forced to slash rates, too. Their revenues soon plummeted, as did revenues at Cisco Systems and other big telecom equipment suppliers. Cisco had invested hundreds of millions in ambitious telecom national networks and, on top of that, had loaned telecoms hundreds of millions more to buy Cisco equipment. The tanking telecoms would eventually leave companies like Cisco holding the bag.[163] In the first quarter of 2001, Cisco revenues fell 30 percent. The company laid off eighty-five hundred workers. Nortel, the top supplier of fiber optic networking gear, would see even more striking revenue reverses — and lay off twenty thousand workers.[164]

Overall, analysts reported in March 2002, close to six hundred thousand workers saw their jobs disappear when the telecom bubble burst.[165] American business had never seen an industry collapse so dramatically. On the list of the twenty-five biggest bankruptcies in U.S. history, telecoms, by August 2002, held ten slots.[166]

Amid the carnage, a host of telecom notables would walk away bruised but content. Qwest chairman Joseph Nacchio and co-chairman Philip Anschutz pocketed nearly $2.3 billion dumping big chunks of their Qwest shares before their company, one of the industry's giants, started collapsing. Top executives scored phenomenal paydays even at second-tier telecoms. James Crowe, the CEO at Level 3 Communications, walked into the sunset with $115 million.[167] Jack Grubman, the Wall Street research analyst who kept urging investors to buy up telecom shares even as the industry was collapsing, averaged $20 million a year during telecom's biggest bubble days. He left his Wall Street employer, Salomon, in 2002. As a parting present, Salomon forgave a $19 million personal loan Grubman had received from the company. Citigroup, Salomon's owner, also handed Grubman a reported $12 million worth of Citi stock.[168]

Reporters started detailing these sorts of giveaways midway through 2002 in a series of thoughtful analyses that tried to trace just how the telecom debacle had unfolded. But one aspect of the story puzzled perceptive journalists like Gretchen Morgenson of the *New York Times*. They could understand why analysts like Jack Grubman would keep pushing telecom shares as a "buy" long after he knew the telecom game plan no longer made any business sense. They could understand why the investment banks like Salomon, Grubman's employer, did their part to keep up pretenses. Grubman helped Salomon collect nearly $1 billion in investment banking fees. And reporters could even understand why deep pockets like Paul Allen and John Malone so unquestioningly poured billions into hare-brained telecom business plans. In any mad rush for fortune, reporters reasoned, sound judgments will always be suspended. But what about the telecom executives, the CEOs who kept announcing plans to lay more wires even after they knew, beyond any possible doubt, that the industry had already laid far more capacity in the ground than consumer demand could possibly fill. Why did these CEOs behave so irresponsibly?

In August 2002, this final puzzling piece fell into place. Gretchen Morgenson discovered that top executives of established telecom giants like Qwest, under the table and out of sight, had been cutting purely personal "sweetheart deals" with start-ups that supplied telecom equipment. The start-ups, Morgenson revealed, would sometimes give big-time telecom executives stock options "in exchange for an established executive's participation on an upstart company's advisory board."[169] Other times, start-ups would let executives in on IPO shares at bargain-basement prices. The telecom executives, however they received their start-up stakes, now had a personal incentive to help their favorite start-up's shares shoot up in price — and they had, at the same time, the power to provide the start-ups exactly the contracts they needed to build share price momentum. Nearly every contract to lay unneeded and unjustifiable cable capacity sent some start-up's share price soaring — and enriched the telecom CEO who had the contract let.

The industry analysts who helped Morgenson piece together this incredible story of telecom conniving and corruption could, in retrospect, only shake their heads.

"Looking back," noted one, Susan Kalla, "it looks more and more like a pyramid scheme."[170]

THE STOCK MARKET ISN'T, OF COURSE, supposed to be a con game. The stock market is supposed to be America's investment crown jewel, the source of the capital American businesses need to become ever more productive. In the 1980s and 1990s, this widely accepted notion — that the stock market actually serves a vitally important productive function — turned out to be the biggest con of them all.

In modern American business life, as opposed to modern American business folklore, corporations seldom look to the stock market for the capital they need to enhance their operations. Companies raise most of the capital they need internally, out of their own revenues. To raise any additional investment dollars, firms typically go first to commercial banks, or sell bonds. But companies do also float occasional new issues of their stock. And these new issues, in the twentieth century's closing years, did serve a definite business function. They served, in case after case, to bail executives out of the messes they had made with their mergers.

Big-time merger-and-acquisition sprees, in the closing years of the twentieth century, almost always left America's big-time executives saddled with staggering loads of corporate debt. Early on in the boom years, executives realized they could neatly offset, or at least reduce, those staggering debts by playing games with Wall Street. The process couldn't be simpler. An executive multimillions in debt would have his company issue new shares of stock that, once gobbled up by investors, would return multimillions to company coffers. The executive would then use these multimillions to pay down the company debt, in effect trading creditors for shareholders. The multimillions these shareholders paid for their shares, analyst Christopher Byron noted in 1997, essentially provided indebted companies with "a free loan that never has to be paid back."[171]

Those who celebrate Wall Street as a marketplace miracle that keeps companies well stocked with capital never seem to pay much attention to this sort of wheeling and dealing. They simply assume that dollars investors spend to buy shares of stock end up helping companies produce more goods and services. But the overwhelming bulk of stock market trades do not even involve transactions between a company and investors who want to buy shares of the company's stock. The overwhelming bulk of trades are simply transactions between one temporary owner of shares and another. Ninety percent of all stock market trades, notes St. Johns University economist Gary Mongiovi, "involve nothing more than the speculative reshuffling of the ownership of corporations."[172]

In effect, notes Columbia University's Louis Lowenstein, stock trading has become a game of "musical shares." The same shares are traded again and again. In the process, Lowenstein points out, "nothing is created."[173] Nothing useful. Nothing but fortunes.

The more trading, naturally, the more opportunities for making fortunes. The more bets you make, the more likely one bet will pay off big. In the boom years, bets on stocks bounced back and forth between investors at dizzying rates. In the early 1960s, shares on the New York Stock Exchange turned over at a 14 percent annual rate. By the late 1980s, stocks were turning over, going from one owner to another, at a 95 percent annual rate.[174] At century's end, shares of the very hottest stocks, like Amazon.com, would be turning over at a 100 percent rate *every two weeks*.[175]

None of this feverish speculation added an ounce of productive value to America's economy. In fact, this feverish speculation subtracted from America's productive might. Every trade, every churn of shares from one share owner to another, swallowed up time and resources that could have been put to far more productive use. The billions upon billions wasted away on this speculative trading amounted, as Adrian Slywotzky, a partner at Mercer Management Consulting noted in 2002, to "a massive redeployment of capital and people from fundamentally productive activities to fundamentally unproductive activities."[176]

How much capital, how many people hours, have been wasted away over the last quarter century? Economists may one day give us an answer.[177] We need here note only that Wall Street promised us economic growth, not economic waste. Let wealth concentrate, we were assured, and America's incredibly sophisticated financial markets would render unto us investments that would keep the United States the most productive of nations. Our representatives in Congress and our leaders in the White House believed in the Wall Street model. They took steps — everything from cutting taxes on the wealthy to freezing the minimum wage — that encouraged great wealth to concentrate. And great wealth did concentrate, at levels not seen in the United States since just before the Great Depression.

In return, great wealth gave us speculative waste, not productive investment, more economic waste than any generation of Americans had ever seen.

We should have expected no less. Con games never serve any productive purpose. Con games never create wealth. They concentrate it.

WEALTH THAT CONCENTRATES MUST BE PROTECTED, and protection costs. A great deal.

In early twenty-first century Manhattan, the ultimate in protection for wealthy households, a "safe room," ran $400,000 and up. A typical bulletproof, steel-reinforced safe room sported its own phone line and power generator, a computer that could lock and unlock almost any door in the house, and an "oxygen scrubber" to keep air inside the safe room from getting stale. A wealthy household could, if so inclined, accessorize a safe-roomed house with floor board stress detectors, burglar alarms for dresser drawers, and motion detectors that could tell the difference between pets and people.[178]

Security experts who install safety accessories like these now make up one of the nation's fastest-growing professions. Over one and a half million Americans currently work in private security. Over a half-million other Americans work in public law enforcement.[179] None of these security personnel, private or public, work at jobs that produce any of the goods and services we normally associate with a growing economy. Instead, they work to make sure that other people end up in a place — prison — where they can't make much of a productive contribution to the economy either. And that mission they have completed exceptionally well. America's inmate population jumped from just under two hundred thousand in 1970 to just under 2.2 million in 2002.[180] Law enforcement, overall, cost the nation $6 billion in 1968. The 2003 estimate: $210 billion.[181] The nation's *total* annual protection bill, the outlay for both public *and* private security, has surpassed a quarter trillion dollars.[182]

This oversized sum, analysts note, represents an enormous missed opportunity. The dollars we spend on security — if spent on something other than security — could make an important contribution to helping the economy become more productive. Just imagine "the boost in productivity that might occur," ask economists Randy Albeda and Chris Tilly, "if the money spent both privately and publicly to hire additional security and police were spent to hire child care workers."[183]

So what conclusion should we draw? Are we as a nation just wasting all the hundreds of billions we spend on "additional security and police?" Or do outlays for security, unlike outlays for speculation, serve a useful and absolutely essential social purpose?

That depends — on the level of outlay. Expenditures on security certainly do carry a socially redeeming value that speculative outlays can never match. No decent society can possibly stand by and let people be mugged and robbed. To be productive, people need to be safe. Resources spent keeping people safe do make an economic contribution, and a necessary one at that. But the resources we devote to security also exact a price. Societies that are fixated on protecting wealth are not creating wealth. The more societies have to spend on security to keep people safe, the less their capacity to help people become more productive. Societies that *don't* have to devote massive resources to security clearly have an economic leg up on societies that do.

We live today, the adage goes, in a dangerous world. Yet some nations in this dangerous world have been able to keep their populations safe *without* having to spend massively on security. Indeed, many societies that don't spend massively on security appear distinctly safer than other societies that do. The United States, for instance, spends far more on prisons than all other industrial nations. Six hundred of every hundred thousand U.S. residents lived behind bars in 1995. France only incarcerated ninety-five people per hundred thousand population, Sweden only sixty-five, and Japan only thirty-seven.[184] Did going to the immense expense of keeping all these law-breakers behind bars leave Americans safer? In the mid 1990s, a girl or a woman in the United States was four times more likely to be murdered than a girl or woman in Sweden, five times more likely to be murdered than a girl or a woman in France, and seven times more likely to be murdered than a girl or woman in Japan.[185]

How can some nations spend so little on security and still be safe? Some nations, analysts answer, are more equal than others. Crime rises in unequal societies. Where "the rich have more to protect and the poor have less to lose," note economists Randy Albeda and Chris Tilly, "crime goes up."[186] And crime keeps going up, other analysts add, as the gap between rich and poor widens. That gap, not poverty itself, is what drives crime rates. Indeed, poor societies can be safe societies, if people in them see that life's hardships are shared more or less equally. But where "rewards are inequitably distributed," as psychologists Martin Daly, Margo Wilson, and Shawn Vasdev have observed, "escalated tactics of social competition, including violent tactics, become attractive."[187]

Over the years, several other scholars, including the Nobel Prize-winning economist Amartya Sen, have traced the relationship between murder, the most violent of crimes, and income inequality. High poverty rates, these studies have shown, don't necessarily produce high homicide rates. High rates of inequality do. How equally or unequally resources are distributed, concluded one review of this research published in 2001, more powerfully impacts "levels of lethal violence in modern nation states" than "the average level of material welfare."[188]

For a case in point, look south. Look to Brazil.

By global standards, Brazil can actually claim to be an affluent nation. On a per capita income basis, Brazil rates higher than 77 percent of the rest of the world, and many nations, in proportional terms, have more people living in poverty than Brazil.[189] But no nations display a more striking gap between rich and poor. In Brazil, the richest 10 percent of families make nearly 50 times what the poorest 10 percent make.[190]

Amid this stark inequality, Brazilians spend $2 billion a year on private security arrangements.[191] In Sao Paulo state, a third of local residents "pay security guards to watch over their homes."[192] Sao Paulo's people have reasons to be nervous. The homicide rate in Sao Paulo city tripled in the 1990s. Kidnappings in Sao Paulo have become so common that some plastic surgeons now "specialize in treating wealthy victims who return from their ordeals with sliced ears, severed fingers and other missing body parts that were sent to family members as threats for ransom payment."[193]

Meanwhile, over in Brazil's second largest city, Rio de Janeiro, carjackings were taking place so often, by the late 1990s, that police officials assured affluent drivers that they wouldn't "be fined for running red lights at night." Thousands of those drivers took no chances. They armored their cars, typically at $35,000 per automobile. Motorists interested in "anti-explosive gas tanks," sirens, and other extras had to pay double.[194]

"Soon the haves will circulate throughout the city in personal tanks," Sao Paulo novelist Ignacio de Loyola Brandao predicted right before the century turned.[195]

That prediction would turn out to be somewhat off base. Brazil's wealthy took to the air, in the early years of the twenty-first century, not tanks. By mid 2002, Sao Paolo could claim the world's busiest helicopter traffic, with twenty-four times more helipads than New York. Sao Paulo businessmen rode helicopters every day, a *Washington Post* correspondent reported that year, "from their fortified offices to their fortified homes." In their walled neighborhoods private armies patrolled "behind electrified fences."[196]

"We have become prisoners in our own homes," Ellen Saraiva, the wife of one top Brazilian executive, admitted to a reporter. "One of my daughters is studying abroad right now, and as much as I miss her, it makes me feel at peace to know she is not here living through this nightmare."[197]

Thoughtful Brazilian economists had nightmares, too. In some countries, they knew, people woke up every morning thinking about what they could be doing at work to be more productive. Brazilians woke up thinking about what they could be doing to survive.

IN JAPAN, AT CENTURY'S END, few people woke up worrying about survival. And nobody was making fortunes armoring cars, mainly because the Japanese entered the twenty-first century with one of the world's lowest crime rates.[198] Families in Japan did not live behind electrified fences, shielded by private security armies. They lived, instead, about as equally as any people in the developed industrial world. In Brazil, the richest tenth of families made almost fifty times more than the poorest. In Japan, people at the top tenth of the income ladder made just over four times more than people at the bottom.[199]

Just 2 percent of Japanese households, in 1997, lived on less than $16,000 a year — and the exact same percentage, only 2 percent, made more than $160,000. Most Japanese families, over half, lived right in the middle, on between $35,000 and $75,000 a year.[200]

None of this equality evolved by accident. The modern Japanese did not inherit a remarkably equal society. They created it, after 1945, in a nation that had been pounded into rubble. World War II, points out journalist Kevin Sullivan, had destroyed nearly "all personal wealth" on the Japanese islands, "leaving Japan's aristocrats and peasant farmers alike struggling for the same food scraps in the bombed-out ruins."

"From that starting point," Sullivan notes, "Japan set out to rebuild itself as a land where everyone was equal."[201]

The American army of occupation would help drive the equalizing process, by breaking up Japan's massive rural estates and sharing the land with average farmers.[202] Japan's new lawmakers would do their part as well. They taxed the wealthy at stiff rates and stretched a well-knit safety net for the poor.[203] Even Japanese business leaders, prodded by labor and public opinion, made important contributions to a more equal Japan. Their companies offered workers lifetime job security. And Japanese banks, notes American economist Dean Baker, "were expected to extend loans to major employers, even those losing large amounts of money, to keep unemployment low."[204] All these steps, taken together, created a society with no "exclusive Beverly Hills or desperate Bronx slums."[205]

This equality would help nurture an incredibly productive society. In the 1970s and 1980s, Japanese enterprises won world-wide reputations for quality and efficiency. Japanese products captured growing shares of one global product market after another, in everything from stereos to motorcycles. Year by year, exports rushed out of Japan at ever faster rates. Japan's trade surpluses mounted, as did the value of the Japanese yen. Interest rates, meanwhile, dropped to the developed world's lowest levels. The nation's bankers could hardly believe their good fortune.

"Japanese banks overflowed with money," writes economist William Stewart, "much more than they could accommodate by relending in Japan itself."[206]

Bankers, in other words, had "money to burn," and, in the late 1980s, this money did what money to burn always does: ignite a wild speculative fire. In Japan, that fire raged from 1986 into 1991 and ended with a substantial collapse in real estate and stock market prices. Banks were suddenly left holding portfolios thick with burnt-out investments.

Japan's economy spent the rest of the 1990s trying to recover. Shares on the Japanese stock exchange never did. They lagged the entire decade — at the same time share values in the United States were soaring. What was Japan's problem? Smug American corporate leaders felt they knew exactly what was wrong. Japan had become too equal. The Japanese, American business observers asserted, needed to wake up to modern global realities. They could-n't possibly "continue to subsidize the poor through a 50 percent income tax on wealthy citizens" and expect to grow their economy. Japan needed to real-ize, once and for all, that a 70 percent tax on inherited wealth represents "out-dated and excessive government interference" on the incentive to invest.[207]

"Nothing in America or Europe matches the rot in the state of Japan," echoed an editorial in the British *Economist*. Japan "needs to make the difficult choices that will bring efficiency and long-term growth." And that meant pri-vatizing public services and deregulating businesses.[208] Many high-ranking Japanese office-holders would agree with this diagnosis. Japan, they concluded, could no longer afford equality.

"It's difficult for a government official to advocate income inequality," acknowledged Kenji Umetani, a director in Japan's economic planning agency. "But when we are designing the future structure of the Japanese economy, we have to make some adjustments to the existing structure that will necessitate an acceptance among Japanese people of greater income dispersion."[209]

Early in the twenty-first century, Japan's new prime minister, Junichiro Koizumi, would set about to make these adjustments. He would encourage Japanese corporations to downsize, just like American corporations. He would applaud policy moves that promoted "wage restraint" and kept job growth depressed.[210] Business leaders exulted.

"In seven or eight years," predicted Shoji Hiraide, the general manager of one of Tokyo's grandest department stores, "Japanese society will look much more like Western society, with gaps between rich and poor that can be clearly seen."[211]

That prospect left the people of Japan singularly uneasy. Some Japanese business executives might be upset "about the tiny gap" between their pay and the pay of their employees," noted Hiromitsu Ishi, a Japanese university presi-dent, "but most Japanese people like the notion of a not-so-uneven income dis-tribution."[212]

The Japanese people had reason to appreciate their nation's unusually equi-table income distribution. Equality had been good to average families in Japan, even during the "crisis" years of the 1990s. Joblessness in Japan, the *National Catholic Reporter*'s John Cort would note in 1998, had increased over the decade, but, at 4.3 percent, still stood lower than joblessness in the "booming" United States. And Japanese workers earned more than their American coun-terparts, 17.7 percent more for factory work.[213]

"Japan's problems," agreed Ezra Vogel, the director of Harvard University's Asia Center, "have been grossly exaggerated." Most Japanese "are happy with their quality of life, which includes a low crime rate, low unemployment and excellent schools."[214]

But what about Japan's stagnant stock market? What about the economic "crisis" that Prime Minister Koizumi insisted could only be fixed by adopting America's Wall Street model? That "crisis," observers like John Cort charged, impacted "mainly the rich and those who aspire to be rich."[215] Average Japanese faced no crisis. In the 1990s, they held their own.

Japanese elites did not. On the global stage, they lost ground. In the 1990s, top Japanese executives watched their American counterparts take home paychecks that tripled — and then tripled again — executive paychecks in Japan. Prime Minister Koizumi promised relief for these frustrated Japanese corporate leaders. He would force a break with hide-bound Japanese traditions. He would totally overhaul Japan's "crisis"-ridden economy.[216] Or so he pledged. But Koizumi would fall short. By 2003, his efforts to engineer a seachange in Japan's economy had failed. Japan would not swallow the Wall Street model. The Japanese people would taste Wall Street's medicine and spit it out.

In growing inequality, average Japanese people sensed a threat to their economic well-being. But they sensed other dangers as well. And they were right to worry. Unequal societies pay a price that can't always be measured in mere dollars and cents and yen. To these costs we now turn.

EXCESS WITHOUT HAPPINESS

NO ONE, AT LEAST NO ONE WHO claims to be leading a rational life, pursues wealth simply to become more wealthy. As individuals, and as societies, we treat wealth as a means to an end. We strive to become more productive, to create more wealth, only because we believe that wealth, at some level, can improve our lot in life, can make us, in a word, happier. Are we fooling ourselves? Can wealth actually bring happiness? And if wealth can bring happiness, does that mean that still more wealth will bring still more happiness, that those individuals who accumulate the most wealth will be the happiest of all?

Various thinkers, both grand and grinning, have pondered these questions down through the centuries. They seem to agree, more or less, on the basics: No amount of wealth can ever guarantee happiness. In all things, including wealth, moderation.

"Many very rich men are unhappy," as the ancient Greek historian Herodotus intoned, "and many in moderate circumstances are fortunate."[1]

"It's pretty hard to tell what does bring happiness," quipped Frank McKinney Hubbard, the early twentieth century Indiana humorist, over two millennia later, "poverty and wealth have both failed."[2]

Few of us today would quibble with either Herodotus or Hubbard. We generally look askance at people who turn their lives into a single-minded race after riches. In one 1996 Gallup poll, 80 percent of us said flatly we would not sacrifice significant family time to become rich.[3] Four years later, in another national survey, that same share of us, 80 percent, "expressed fears" that wealth might turn us "into greedy people."[4]

Do these attitudes mean that Americans don't want to become wealthy? Not exactly. In fact, not at all. In 2000, in the same poll that found people fearful about wealth, two-thirds of us said we "would like to give wealth a shot."[5] An earlier national survey, conducted in 1994 for *Worth* magazine, uncovered remarkably similar attitudes. Half of all Americans, *Worth* found, agreed wholeheartedly that "money can't buy happiness." Yet at the same time, almost 70 percent of Americans also felt "that doubling their earnings would make them a lot or somewhat happier."[6]

These sorts of conflicted attitudes fascinate social scientists. Some of them have spent years digging at the roots of these attitudes. They've explored, through surveys and interviews, observations and experiments, the possible ties between wealth and what psychologists call "subjective well-being," what the rest of us call happiness. The results from their research, interestingly, both confirm and reject a link between wealth and what makes and keeps us happy. Increases in income, the research makes clear, definitely do make people significantly happier — when these increases lift people out of deprivation. But once people have escaped deprivation, researchers have concluded, additional increases in income don't appear to make people any happier. The world's richest nations do not necessarily boast the world's happiest people.

"One of the central findings in the large scientific literature on subjective well-being," notes Cornell University economist Robert Frank, "is that once income levels surpass a minimal absolute threshold, average satisfaction levels within a given country tend to be highly stable over time, even in the face of significant economic growth."[7]

So does money not really matter to happiness, except when people need more of it to hurdle out of poverty? Things aren't that simple. People in rich nations may not be happier, on average, than people in nations that aren't as rich, but, within individual societies, money *does* matter. Affluent people, in every society, are happier, as a group, than their not-as-affluent neighbors. Not everyone making $200,000, of course, is happier than everyone making $20,000. Six-figure incomes do not, by themselves, turn sour cynics into smiling romantics. But six-figure incomes do make a difference. Someone with a sour disposition and a $200,000 annual income will almost always be happier than someone with that same sour temperament who takes home just $20,000.

We seem to have a bit of a contradiction here. On the one hand, according to the best statistical evidence, people in richer nations are, on average, no happier than people in nations that cannot claim quite as much wealth. On the other hand, *within* nations, richer people are, on average, happier than everybody else. How can this be? How can income differences *within* nations make a difference in how happy people feel when income differences *between* nations don't? Is there a logical explanation for this distinction? Indeed there is. Our friend context. In the lives we lead, money doesn't make us happy. Context does.

Imagine yourself a traveler. What do you need to be happy? A comfortable seat? Sounds reasonable. How can you be a happy traveler, after all, if you're crowded for hours in a tight, severely cramped space? Actually, you *can* be a happy traveler in a tight, cramped space. In fact, you can be a happy traveler in a tight, cramped space even if you're soaked and shivering. You wouldn't mind one bit that cramp and damp if you had been shipwrecked and just spent an hour treading water. You would be happy beyond belief to find any space at all, no matter how tight, in a lifeboat. You would shiver and smile.

Now imagine yourself flying high above those chilly waters, sitting comfortably in a airline aisle seat. You have plenty of room to stretch out. No one is sitting next to you, or in front of you or behind. Sitting in your infinite comfort, you strike up a conversation with the passenger across the aisle. He seems even happier than you are. You ask him why. You learn that he had found a fantastic deal on his ticket. He paid one-third of what you paid. Suddenly, despite your comfort, you don't feel happy at all. Context.

Are we happy? This simple question almost always begs another: Compared to what? We define our happiness by our position. And we define our position by comparing ourselves to others — or to ourselves, at an earlier stage in our lives.

Researchers have repeatedly documented the importance of this comparative dynamic. In one famous study, psychologists asked different groups of people to assess how happy they feel about themselves. One group was surveyed with a disabled person present in the room, the other group without a disabled person present. The people surveyed in the presence of a disabled person always turned out to feel happier about their own lives than the people quizzed in a room without a disabled person present.[8] Context.

This same comparative dynamic drives how we feel about our economic fortunes. If we grew up under a leaky roof, with rats underfoot, any clean apartment, even a tiny clean apartment, will make us happy. But if we grew up in a tiny clean apartment, worked hard all our lives, and still found ourselves unable to afford one of the roomier homes we see all around us, we are not likely to feel particularly content in our tiny clean apartment.

"The happiness that people derive from consumption," as researcher Alan Durning notes, "is based on whether they consume more than their neighbors and more than they did in the past."[9]

And that's why differences in wealth *within* nations make a difference in how happy people feel, why, as economist Robert Frank notes, the "upper classes in any society are more satisfied with their lives than the lower classes are, but they are no more satisfied than the upper classes of much poorer countries."[10] We compare ourselves to the people around us, the people whose lives we see and hear about every day. We don't normally compare ourselves to people from foreign lands, or to people from bygone days, because we don't experience their lives as part of our own daily lives.

All this suggests a possible economic formula for happiness: If most people in a society can sit back, think about their personal situation and conclude that they're doing significantly better than they used to be doing, and if most people can look around their society and conclude that they're doing just fine compared to most everybody else, then you have the makings of a generally happy society.

At the end of the twentieth century, the wealthiest nation in the world, the United States, did not fit this profile. Average Americans, as the new century dawned, were not sitting back and contentedly contemplating how nicely their personal fortunes had improved. They were, instead, struggling to maintain their economic status quo. Nor were average Americans feeling good about themselves compared to other people around them. Everywhere they looked, at century's end, average Americans could see signs that some Americans — afflu-ent Americans — were doing incredibly better than they were.

America, in short, did not have the makings of a happy society.

Did the absence of these makings actually lead to an unhappier America? Over the final decades of the twentieth century, social scientists carefully tabu-lated the answers Americans gave, year by year, to the old chestnuts of happi-ness research, questions like "Taken all together, how would you say things are these days — would you say that you are happy, pretty happy, or not too happy?" and "How do you feel about your life as a whole?" These queries, acknowledges Yale political scientist Robert Lane, make for "imperfect meas-ures," but they do help us determine whether a society's level of subjective well-being is undergoing any significant change.[11]

In the 1980s and 1990s, the level of subjective well-being in the United States did undergo a significant change. That level dropped.

Should this drop concern us? Or should we consider rising unhappiness an inevitable consequence of modern life? The hectic pace of Information Age life, some might argue, may simply dispose people to be less happy. An interesting conjecture, but if modernity were making people less happy, social scientists would be finding significant declines in subjective well-being in both Western Europe and the United States. They are not. Researchers have found, Yale's Robert Lane notes, that "the decline in happiness is largely an American phe-nomenon."[12]

"Something has gone wrong," Lane concludes. The United States is simply "not as happy as it is rich."[13]

HULA HOOPS GENERATED PLENTY OF SMILES in the 1950s. And so did Milton Berle. But clever toys and antic comics weren't why most Americans were feel-ing good about their lives in the decades right after World War II. In these post-war years, unlike the end of the twentieth century, Americans were feeling good because the United States fit the happiness profile. Average Americans were doing better, significantly better, than they had ever done before. And average Americans also seemed to be doing just as well as everybody else. Most people seemed to be living remarkably similar lives. A couple kids, a home in the sub-urbs, a car by the curb.

Every evening, throughout the 1950s and 1960s, these kids, these homes, these cars would flash across America's TV screens. The television families that Americans followed, from the Andersons on *Father Knows Best* to the Cleavers on *Leave It to Beaver*, lived lives that most Americans either led — or could see themselves leading. In America's postwar decades, the "good life" meant a mod-est, comfortable life, and most Americans could afford all the basic comforts.

That would all change, drastically, in the 1980s and 1990s. With more wealth concentrating at the top of America's economic ladder, luxuries, not basic comforts, would come to define the good life. Fancy watches. Expensive cars. Vacation homes. Most Americans could see this new good life all around them, but they could only ogle. This good life they could not afford.

But why should that, cheerleaders for the new America wondered throughout the boom years, make any difference to the happiness people feel?

"If you drive a Mercedes and I have to walk, that's a radical difference in lifestyle," argued Dinesh D'Souza. "But is it a big deal if you drive a Mercedes and I drive a Hyundai?"[14]

That difference, in fact, is a "big deal." A monstrously big deal. Luxury impacts everyone, even those who don't want to be impacted.

In the 1990s, reporter Peter Delevett counted himself one of those who didn't give one whit about luxury. In Silicon Valley, at the height of the dot.com wealth-amassing frenzy, he drove a plain car. He had always driven a plain car. But that plain car, and his modest lifestyle, would come to seem painfully inadequate in the boom years.

"As time went on, I began to feel, well, self-conscious pulling up to cover millionaire-packed dinner parties in my practical little Toyota Tercel," remembers Delevett. "We bought a red convertible. Silicon Valley, circa 1999, made you covet."[15]

Middle class Americans, at century's end, didn't need to sit at fancy dinner parties to feel compelled to covet. The explosion of wealth at the top of America's economic ladder had scattered this covetousness — what economist Robert Frank calls "luxury fever" — almost everywhere in American life.[16] In the twentieth century's final years, "super-spending by the super-rich" essentially raised the price of admission to the good life.[17]

Affluent Americans, those households that made up the topmost 20 percent of the income distribution, could meet this price, at least occasionally. The vast majority of American families could not. In a starkly unequal United States, Americans of modest means found themselves comparing the quality of their lives to the lives led by people of considerably more ample means, and, against that standard, their lives simply didn't measure up.

But haven't Americans always measured their lives against the lives led by more affluent people? Haven't Americans always tried to "keep up with the Joneses"? Most certainly. So what was so different, so happiness deflating, about the 1980s and 1990s? The difference would be the extent of inequality that emerged over the course of these years, the significantly larger gap that opened between affluent Americans and everybody else.

In every society, in every age, people compare themselves to others around them. These others make up what researchers call a "reference group." If people feel they're doing well compared to their reference group, they're likely to feel good about their lives, happy in their circumstances. In the years right after World War II, average Americans typically found their reference group in their neighborhoods — and the idealized version of those neighborhoods they watched on TV. With this reference group, average Americans could keep up.

They might not make as much as the Andersons on *Father Knows Best*, but they didn't fall that far short. The affluent lived within hailing distance.

By century's end, after two decades of increasing inequality, America's affluent no longer lived within economic hailing distance of average families. The distance between the average and the affluent had substantially widened.[18] Television still brought us into the comfortable lives of affluent people. But the comforts of these affluent households had become luxuries most American families would never be able to easily afford.

"TV mainly shows people in the top 20 percent of the income distribution," Harvard economist Juliet Schor would note late in the 1990s. "A family that is supposed to be an ordinary middle-class family on TV has a six-figure lifestyle. That has had a profound impact on our sense of what normal spending is."[19]

How profound? In the mid 1990s, research conducted by Schor among employees at a major American corporation found that "each additional hour of television watched in a week" ups a viewer's annual consumer spending by an additional $208.[20] Watching affluent people in affluent settings, Schor concluded, inflates "the viewer's perceptions of what others have, and by extension what is worth acquiring — what one must have in order to avoid being 'out of it.'"[21]

These televised images of affluence would be reinforced by real life — as experienced in America's workplaces. In the late twentieth century, the workplace would come to replace the neighborhood as America's middle class reference standard, mainly because many millions of American women had begun working outside the home. In 1980, less than half America's moms worked for paychecks. By 2000, two out of three moms were stepping outside their neighborhoods for work.[22]

Neighborhoods, Juliet Schor notes, generally bring together households of comparable incomes. If you compare yourself to your neighbors down the street, as Americans typically did back in the 1950s and 1960s, you're comparing yourself to people with incomes not likely to be much different from your own. Workplaces, by contrast, bring together people of significantly different income levels, particularly when workplaces are offices. In the 1980s and 1990s, Americans of modest means spent their days in these mixed-income workplaces. They encountered, week after week, "the spending habits of people across a wider economic spectrum" than they had ever encountered before.[23] They sat in meetings with people who wore "expensive suits or 'real' Swiss watches." They could see, up close, just how much the affluent own and just how well the affluent live. And they couldn't match that affluent lifestyle, not even come close, especially in places where riches were rapidly concentrating. Places like South Florida.

"It's very difficult not to look down at your shoes and sigh," noted one South Florida sociologist, Lynn Appleton, in a 2001 interview. "You see car after car after car that costs more than your yearly income." The Joneses, added

Appleton, who taught at a university in Boca Raton, never "used to be so hard to keep up with."[24]

Wealth in the United States had become, in effect, not just more concentrated, but more visible. The inevitable result: a general ratcheting up of the sense of what it takes to live a decent life. One research project, in the boom years, asked people to estimate how much money they needed to fulfull their dreams. Between 1986 and 1994, that estimate doubled. Desires, as Juliet Schor pointed out, had clearly outrun incomes.[25]

"In order to be middle class as our culture is coming to understand the term," concluded author Barbara Ehrenreich in 1997, "one almost has to be rich."[26]

IN THE QUEST TO BECOME "ALMOST RICH," Americans, as we have seen earlier, are now devoting more of their waking hours to work than people anywhere else in the developed world. We typically accept this national workaholism as simply a natural, inevitable "fact of life." But these long hours are no natural phenomenon. They represent an enormous change in the rhythms of everyday American life. A half-century ago, Americans spent far fewer hours at work, so many fewer that some observers, back in the 1950s, actually worried about a national "leisure crisis." Work-free weekends. Nine-to-five jobs. Pensioned retirements. Would average Americans, commentators asked, become bored with all the time they had on the hands?[27]

By the 1990s, no one was worrying any more about excess leisure. In 1997, married couples with one or two kids were spending over six hundred more hours on the job — the equivalent of over fifteen forty-hour weeks — than they spent on the job in 1979.[28]

The American dream wasn't supposed to work this way. Progress in the United States was supposed to bring more leisure, more time for family, more time for fun. And progress *had* brought more leisure, before the final decades of the twentieth century. Americans in the 1960s spent considerably fewer hours on the job than Americans in the 1910s. But leisure time stopped expanding in the late 1960s and then started shrinking, a turnaround that went largely unnoticed, by press and public, until Juliet Schor's eye-opening 1991 book, *The Overworked American*. By the 1990s, as Schor detailed, almost a third of men with kids under fourteen were working fifty or more hours a week. Employed mothers in one big city, Boston, were *averaging* over eighty hours of work a week on housework, child care, and employment. Between 1973 and the late 1980s, poll data indicated, the typical American's "free time" had dropped 40 percent.[29]

American families, Schor argued, had become trapped in "an insidious cycle of 'work-and-spend.'"[30] To afford America's ever-inflating middle class lifestyle, Americans were spending ever more hours at work.[31]

"Clearly, middle-income families in America have acquired more possessions than their parents and grandparents had," *New York Times* reporter Louis

Uchitelle would note in 1999. "But the middle-class comforts of an earlier day were accessible to families with just one earner; today, middle-income families find that they must combine at least two incomes, and often three, in pursuit of a life style that seems always out of reach."[32]

How out of reach? In one 1998 Marist College survey, 63 percent of Americans told pollsters they had difficulty paying monthly bills. A poll conducted later that same year by Peter Hart Research found that 67 percent of Americans felt their earnings weren't enough to keep up with the cost of living.[33]

Americans kept up anyway, as we have seen, by going into debt. On average, by midway through the 1990s, credit card holders were paying $1,000 a year in interest and fees.[34] In 1996, for the first time ever, over a million Americans filed for personal bankruptcy.[35]

"These are the people I'm seeing in bankruptcy court," one bankruptcy judge noted that year. "The guy loses his job and finds another one. It's a dead-end job, but at least it pays the mortgage. He gets depressed with his life and finds himself lured by the ads touting 'pay no interest for a year,' and so he buys a big screen TV and a satellite dish. He loses his job again and can't pay for the luxuries he's charged. Interest charges cause the balance to skyrocket. He finds another job and the cycle repeats. Eventually he finds himself with one option — to file for personal bankruptcy. I can't fault him."[36]

Most American families, of course, would not go bankrupt in the boom years. But they wouldn't become happier either. The game of life, more and more Americans had come to feel, was rigged against them. No matter how many hours they worked, no matter how much debt they risked, they could not "make it" to the bar that defined the good life. That bar kept rising. The affluent saw to that. These affluent, in an increasingly unequal America, could always afford to ratchet their consumption up to another level. And they did, to keep their distance from the mere middle class. By century's end, reporters were chronicling a product-by-product consumption spiral that seemed destined to never end.

"One year, a wealthy person's kitchen must have a $3,800 Sub-Zero refrigerator hidden discreetly behind wood paneling," journalist Richard Connif noted. "The next year, Sub-Zeros become 'middle-class,' and the better kitchens tend to have $30,000 Traulsens."[37]

Granite countertops, added reporter Margaret Webb Pressler, had for years defined the truly classy kitchen. But then tract-house developers "began offering granite as an upgrade, enabling the merely comfortable to buy in." The rich "moved on," to countertops fabricated from poured concrete.[38]

"And when those become too widely dispersed among the middle class," Pressler predicted, "the rich will rip apart their kitchens and start over again, continuing the lavish cycle."

The comfortably affluent could afford to laugh about this rising consumption pressure.

"I've learned that Abraham Maslow got it wrong," one analyst joked. "The eminent psychologist thought that once we satisfied our basic need for food, clothing and shelter, we would seek a higher happiness through art, human fellowship and the life of the mind. Spiritual transcendence would be the ultimate payoff of prosperity. But it hasn't worked out that way. Instead, everyone would rather go shopping."[39]

But not everyone could afford to chortle. For the millions of Americans "just struggling to get by," Juliet Schor noted, the game wasn't just rigged. The game was brutalizing. People, Schor explained, "are suffering tremendously because this is a system that says to be somebody, you have to wear these shoes and drive this car and live in this house."[40] In an unequal America, those who could not afford to accumulate ever more and better things would not find much happiness.

Neither, sadly, would those who could afford things aplenty.

WHY DO WE PUT SO MUCH FAITH in the power of "stuff" to make us happy? We believe that the things we buy can make us happy for a perfectly understandable reason. Things sometimes *can* make us happy, and almost all of us have experienced, at some point in our lives, the happiness that things can bring.

But not all things are equal. Only *some* things can bring us happiness, things that serve a real function and fill a real void in our lives.

Consider, economist Robert Frank suggests, the situation of a struggling, low-income grad student with a washing machine on its last legs. Laundry is one aggravation after another. The student, unfortunately, can't afford a new washer or even a servicing visit. He searches instead for replacement parts, wasting the better part of two weekends in the process. In the end, the student's do-it-himself repairs break down.

Would this student have been happier if he had been able to afford a new washer? Of course. A new washer would have filled a real need.[41]

Things that serve real needs can significantly enhance our subjective well-being. A working washing machine makes us happier not so much because other people have washers but because, outfitted with a working washer, our lives will be easier. By the same token, in a neighborhood ill-served by public transportation, a car can bring happiness. We need reliable transportation.

People in poverty typically can't afford enough of the things they need to function successfully in the society that surrounds them. That's why increases in income, for people in deprivation, can significantly enhance well-being. Added income enables people in poverty to purchase the things that serve basic unmet needs.

On the other hand, for people who live comfortably above the poverty level, most purchases do not involve the meeting of previously unmet needs. The purchases most of us make, most of the time, either replace or supplement something we already own. We trade in an adequately functioning old car for a brand new one. Our ability to move ourselves from place to place is not enhanced. We add another topcoat to our closet. We have not enhanced our ability to stay warm in the winter.

The brand-new car, the extra topcoat, to be sure, do bring pleasure. But this pleasure soon fades, as quickly as the aroma from a new car's upholstery. New cars and topcoats have introduced no new functional value to our lives. They fill no lasting need. They give us no lasting pleasure. We quickly adapt to their newness. And the more affluent we are, the more often we can afford to buy a new car or a new coat, the smaller the pleasure we take from each new purchase. Newness, by itself, no longer gives us much of a thrill when we experience newness all the time.

Eventually, to get any thrill at all, the affluent must go beyond the new. To keep themselves satisfied, they need not just another new car, but a BMW, not just a new coat, but an ermine. They cycle endlessly through ever more costly exotics, pushing ever harder for a satisfaction that always seem to elude them. They are trapped, the psychologists tell us, on a treadmill, a "hedonic treadmill" where "the pleasures of a new acquisition are quickly forgotten."[42] Like addicts, they crave new fixes. And each new fix only accelerates the treadmill — for everyone. Formica, granite, poured concrete. The wealthier the wealthy, the faster the treadmill.

The faster the treadmill, the less the satisfaction.

In 1975, at the depths of America's worst economic downturn since the Great Depression, nearly three quarters of the American people, 74 percent, were still able to agree that "our family income is high enough to satisfy all our important desires." By 1999, after nearly two decades of the most robust economic expansion in American history, the share of Americans who felt they could satisfy their most basic desires had actually dropped, to 61 percent.[43]

OUR PURCHASES, WE HAVE NOTED, can sometimes make us happy. But the accumulation of more purchases, once we have met our basic functional needs, doesn't make us happier. What does? Many Americans, after all, still walk around smiling, despite America's ever faster treadmill. What's their secret? Are these smiling people drugged? Have they discovered some secret path to happiness?

Some of these smilers, of course, may be drugged. But the addict's high never lasts. Nor do any of the other highs, financial or sexual, promised by the happiness hucksters who cram spam into our e-mail in-boxes. In the end, suggests political scientist Robert Lane, only one aspect of life always delivers satisfaction over the long haul. And that aspect is companionship, the solidarity and fellowship of family and friends.[44] From webs of companionship, or community, adds sociologist Amitai Etzioni, we take "profound contentment."[45]

Authentic companionship and community cannot be bought. They must be nurtured, by an ongoing stream of interpersonal interactions. A shared meal. A neighborhood struggle to get a new stop sign. An evening spent volunteering. A good laugh watching a ballgame with friends. Over time, enough such interactions "bind people together and strengthen the places they live." They create what Harvard's Robert Putnam calls "social capital."[46] They foster happiness.

In 2001, Putnam released a massive national study that documented just how powerful a difference community and companionship can make. To complete this study, researchers had surveyed over twenty-six thousand people in forty communities and interviewed three thousand other Americans selected from a random national sample. People who live amid high concentrations of social capital, the researchers found, live happier lives than residents of financially wealthier communities that sport less in the way of social capital. Putnam's conclusion: Social capital, "much more so than financial status," makes for "a very strong predictor of individual happiness."[47]

Yale political scientist Robert Lane, in his research, had reached much the same conclusion the year before. Commodities, Lane noted, "are poor substitutes for friends."[48]

That sounds right, most Americans would no doubt agree. But who has time, they might add, for friends — or family or community? And therein lies the ultimate irony of our times. To be able to afford the good life, and the happiness we feel sure the good life must bring, we devote ever larger chunks of our lives to making as much money as we can. In the process, we end up with less time for the things that really do make us happy.

Less time for friends. On a typical day in 1965, Robert Putnam notes, about two-thirds of Americans, 65 percent, spent at least some time informally socializing. Thirty years later, in 1995, only 39 percent of Americans devoted any time to socializing on a typical day.[49]

Less time for family. At century's end, nearly 7 million children five to fourteen regularly cared for themselves, all alone, while their parents were working.[50]

Less time for community. In the 1960s, about half the American people "invested some time each week in clubs and local associations." In the 1990s, less than one quarter of Americans devoted time to community groups.[51]

Not every American, of course, was racing through life as the millennium ended, shortchanging friends, family, and community, "feeling hurried and rushed every day, getting annoyed at long lines, going to bed wired, waking up tired."[52] But enough were to produce a remarkable social shift. In 1973, a Harris poll asked a random sampling of Americans how much time they needed to earn a living, attend school, and care for home and family. Half the Americans surveyed said they needed more than 40.6 hours a week to meet these responsibilities, half said they needed less. A generation later, in 1999, that halfway point, the median, had climbed to 50.2 hours, nearly a 25 percent increase.[53]

No wonder leisure suits bombed.

ARE AMERICANS OVERWORKED AND OVERSTRESSED? If they are, various commentators routinely declare, they have no one to blame but themselves. These distinctly unsympathetic observers, notes economist Robert Frank, "insist that if middle-income families can't afford to keep up with the consumption standard set by others, they should simply spend less and stop complaining."[54]

W. Michael Cox, the chief economist at the Dallas Federal Reserve Bank, has been among the busiest of these critical commentators. His book, *Myths of Rich and Poor: Why We're Better Off Than We Think*, co-authored with Richard Alm in 2000, helped spell out the spend-less-and-stop-complaining mantra.

"It's not the high cost of living that gets us," Cox argues, "it's the cost of living high."[55]

Want more quality time with your kids? More hours for relaxation? A less stressed existence? Just do it. No one forced you onto the treadmill. No one's keeping you from stepping off. The choice, Cox-like commentators assert, is up to every individual. It's a free country. So suck it up, be an adult, and live with the consequences of your decisions.

Some people, to be sure, have been able to step off America's hedonic treadmill. But their example has touched off no mass exodus. How could it? America's entire economy — entire culture, for that matter — is geared toward defining happiness as the sum total of goods and services consumed. Every day, in malls, on television, and almost everywhere else as well, average Americans are constantly updated on the acquisitions that define the life that any self-respecting American ought to strive to reach. Average Americans have no say in this standard setting. But they strive to meet these standards anyway. In the marketplace that is America, they have no real choice. Average households may be absolutely free, in theory, to ignore society's consumption standards, but, in real life, they ignore these standards only at their peril.

"When upper-middle-class professionals buy 6,000-pound Range Rovers," explains Robert Frank, "others with lower incomes must buy heavier vehicles as well, or else face greater risks of dying."[56]

Parents who fail to spend what society says they should, adds Frank, expose their loved ones to dangers "few families could comfortably tolerate." Unwilling to buy a "nice" house because you don't want to have to assume a back-breaking mortgage load? What real option do you have? "Living in a house priced well below average," Frank notes, "can mean living in a dangerous neighborhood, or having to send one's children to a substandard school."[57]

In an increasingly unequal America, agrees economist Juliet Schor, average Americans work and spend at rising rates not to "live high," but to protect themselves.

"Americans did not suddenly become greedy," she notes. "Upscaling is mainly defensive."[58]

Americans spend defensively, Schor points out, for both practical and psychological reasons. In some occupations, consumption standards simply must be met, no matter how high these standards might shoot. Salespeople, professionals, and the self-employed, to make anything close to a decent living, "have to dress, drive, even eat the part." Nothing projects "failure," says Schor, more than a salesperson in a twelve-year-old car.[59]

Salespeople, in turn, bring the same attitudes about consumption into interactions with their customers. Researchers have documented, notes Schor, "what most people already know: the way you dress affects how salespeople treat you."[60] What you own, researchers have also shown, can make a powerful impact in even the most fleeting of daily encounters. Studies have demonstrated, for instance, that motorists who delay at a green light "are less likely to be honked" from behind if they're driving a luxury automobile."[61]

Some of us can tolerate occasional intemperate honking. Few of us can tolerate the full psychological cost of jumping off the hedonic treadmill. Honking only costs us a moment's peace of mind. Once off the treadmill, we risk losing something far more important, our status in the groups that matter most to us. And our most valued group identity, in any society split into economic classes, usually involves where we stand, or seek to stand, in the class structure. Consumption defines that standing.

"We display our class membership and solidify our class positioning," notes Juliet Schor, "in large part through money, through what we have."[62]

In a relatively equal nation, a society where relatively minor differences in income and wealth separate the classes, people will typically not obsess over meeting consumption standards. If nearly everyone can afford much the same things, things overall will tend to lose their significance. People are more likely to judge you by who you are, not what you own, in a society where incomes and wealth are distributed somewhat equally.

The reverse, obviously, also holds true. "As inequality worsens," as Schor puts it, "the status game tends to intensify."[63] The wider the gaps in income and wealth, the greater the differences in the things that different classes are able to afford. Things, in markedly unequal societies, take on greater symbolic significance. They signal who has succeeded and who has not. You are judged, in these societies, by what you own, by what you consume, not who you are. In these unequal societies, if you are willing to risk getting labeled a loser, you can decline to play by the consumption rules. You can step off the treadmill. But you don't. After all, what right do you have to expose your child to the loser label? What right do you have to force your friends to choose between you and the stigma of hanging out with a failure? You keep treading. We all keep treading.

We tread with no illusions. We know we will never be able to achieve all the trappings of success, not when the incomes of the most "successful" are increasing at much faster rates than our own. But we can, if we keep treading, afford at least a taste of that success.

"At Starbucks," as journalist Peter Grier put it at the turn of the century, "coffee costs twice as much as at a no-name carry-out, yet it's only $1.45."[64]

That container of coffee at Starbucks, says the University of Florida's James Twitchell, amounts to "luxury on the cheap."[65] We can't have it all, but we can have some.

NOT ALL OF US, OF COURSE, GET THRILLS FROM TRIPLE LATTES. Nor do we all need fancy cars to feel good about ourselves. Many of us buy only at sales. We study *Consumer Reports*. We are proud of our consumption prudence. The high-pressure consequences of living amid gross inequality may mess with other people's heads, we tell ourselves, not ours.

Or so we think. We think wrong. In an unequal society, no consumer escapes inequality. Where wealth concentrates, average people only have one choice. They can live like hermits or spend more than they want — on products they don't really need.

An exaggeration? Consider this exercise. Imagine yourself an automaker in a nation with 100 million households. The vast majority of these households, some 80 percent, earn middle class incomes between $30,000 and $50,000. The rest of your nation's households split evenly between affluence and poverty. Ten percent earn over $50,000, 10 percent below $30,000.

Your nation's middle class households have adequate, not affluent, incomes. They're extremely sticker-price conscious. As an automaker, you can't expect to make much more than $1,000 per car profit selling to this middle class market. Still, you *can* make a lot of money marketing to your middle class. If every middle class household bought a new car once every five years and you cornered just one quarter of the middle class market, you could sell 4 million new cars a year — and make a $4 billion profit.

What about your society's affluent households, that 10 percent of families making more than middle class incomes? These families are not as price sensitive. You can sell them more car. You can earn, in fact, a $2,000 profit on every "luxury" car you sell an affluent household, twice as much as you can earn selling to a middle class household. If you could capture a quarter of this affluent market, you could clear $800 million a year.

So which market would get your prime attention, as an automaker, the middle class market or the affluent market? Both would surely be profitable, but, in a middle class-dominated society, you would likely choose to focus on the middle class market, because that's where the biggest returns would be. You would work hard to build the best modest-priced cars you could. Your prize — a meaningful share of the immense middle-class new car market — would be well worth your effort.

Now imagine yourself an automaker in a considerably *less* equal nation of 100 million households. In this more unequal nation, the middle class makes up only half the total 100 million households. About 20 percent of households make over $50,000, with 30 percent making less than $30,000.

In this nation, middle class families are struggling. They'll still buy new cars, but they're more sticker-price conscious than ever. You can't expect to move cars off the showroom floor in this market unless you keep prices way down. On each new car sale to these middle class households, you figure to average just $500 in profit. If you capture a quarter of this middle class market, you stand to register a $1.25 billion profit.

Meanwhile, in this more unequal society, affluent households aren't just more plentiful, they're also wealthier. For just the right automotive experience, these wealthier households are willing to pay a premium. A savvy automaker can now earn a $3,000 profit on every new car sale to an affluent household. Ka-ching! These sales add up fast. An automaker who captured a quarter of this luxury market could walk off with $3 billion. So where are you, as an automaker in an unequal society, going to place your automaking energy? You would, of course, choose to focus on the luxury market.

A far-fetched scenario? Not hardly. In fact, in the closing years of the twentieth century, automakers in the United States faced essentially these exact inequality dynamics.

Until the 1980s, these automakers had historically, ever since Henry Ford, always focused their factories on "building cars for everyday American families."[66] But this middle class-oriented approach, by the late twentieth century, no longer made any business sense. In an increasingly unequal America, as *Washington Post* automotive expert Warren Brown would note in 1997, the wealthy had become "practically the only customers the automakers can count on."[67]

By century's end, the mass middle class market for new cars had essentially evaporated. The bottom two-thirds of American income-earners, people making under $50,000, were buying just one-third of the nation's new cars, and most of the new car buyers in this bottom two-thirds weren't really people of modest middle class means at all. They were, observed W. Van Bussmann, a DaimlerChrysler economist, either young people with prosperous parents or retirees with a lifetime of assets to draw from.[68]

In this new market environment, with fewer families able to afford new cars, automakers felt they had little choice. If they wanted to continue making big money, they would have to start making much more money on each car sold. And that they proceeded to do — by "supersizing" their products. In the 1990s, automakers made cars bigger. The bigger the vehicle, the more option-laden, the bigger the per-vehicle profit.[69] The new strategy worked wonders. Ford, G.M., and Chrysler, amid record levels of inequality, all registered record earnings over the decade's last six years.[70]

Middle class motorists who still yearned for that new car aroma, in the meantime, found themselves paying through the nose for that most essential of American middle class entitlements, the basic family sedan.[71] Back in the mid 1960s, the most popular sedans, the Chevy Impala and Ford Galaxie, had cost consumers about $2,600, or around $13,000 in 1996 dollars. Most middle class households could, without much squeezing, afford that cost. By contrast, the comparable 1996 vehicle, the Ford Taurus, ran about $20,000, a price that shoved the Taurus "out of the reach of many middle-class consumers."[72]

Consumers who went looking for more affordable vehicles, by the end of the 1990s, found their choices limited. The inexpensive Ford Escort, for instance, "faded away without much notice" in 1999, as Keith Bradsher, the *New York Times* Detroit bureau chief, would later note. Ford replaced the Escort "with the taller, fancier Focus."[73]

America's auto industry had, in effect, totally reverted to the bad old days *before* Henry Ford, a time when average Americans could only daydream about becoming new car owners. In 1914, Henry Ford had attacked that reality. He had upped the wages of his autoworkers to $5 a day. On this Spartan, barely middle class wage, his workers could afford a spanking new Model T by saving up the equivalent of five months pay.

In 2000, to buy an average-priced new car, America's middle class families would have to set aside the equivalent of more than six months pay.[74]

Detroit didn't care. The middle class had become irrelevant. America's affluent didn't just buy more expensive cars, they bought more cars per person. By century's end, Keith Brasher would note, the hawking of "third and fourth automobiles to high-income families" had become one of the auto industry's "fastest-growth" market segments.[75]

BY THE END OF THE 1990s, nearly every major consumer industry in the United States, not just automakers, had come to grips — or ruin — with the phenomenon retailers had come to label the "two-tier market." America's growing concentration of wealth had essentially divided consumers into two camps, a luxury market at the top, a bare-bones market for everyone else. America's single, giant, dominant middle class market had vanished.

"The middle class, which once seemed to include almost everyone, is no longer growing in terms of numbers or purchasing power," noted *Business Week* in 1997. "Instead, it's the top and bottom ends that are swelling."[76]

As a retailer, you either recognized that reality or went under. America's classic middle class emporiums, department stores like Gimbel's, could not survive in a two-tier world.

"You could run the perfect store," explained economist Lester Thurow, "and if your customers go broke, you go broke with them."[77]

Those stores that didn't want to go broke targeted the swelling top and bottom. Discounters claimed the bottom. Everybody else dashed for the top, in the greatest retail gold rush ever. Retailers had seen bottoms swell before, but no one, anywhere, had ever seen the swelling at the top that American retailers witnessed in the 1980s and 1990s.

Outfits like the New York-based Spectrem Group, a research and consulting firm, began specializing in helping retailers understand the massive new affluent market. About 18.4 million households, Spectrem reported in 2000, could claim either an annual income over $100,000 or at least $500,000 in net worth, over and above the value of their primary residence. But the real explosion in affluence, researchers made plain, was breaking out at the tippy top.

Millionaire households, analysts at the Tampa-based Payment Systems Inc. related, were growing almost twenty times "faster than the general population."[78] The ranks of "pentamillionaire" households — families worth at least $5 million — were jumping even more rapidly. They totaled six hundred thousand by 2000.[79]

The wealthy, for the first time ever, now constituted a mass market in and of themselves, an enormous "rich niche," to use *Fortune*'s phrase.[80] By 1997, the Merrill Lynch financial services empire alone could count 125,000 customers with $1 million in their accounts. The bankers at Citicorp could claim, that same year, 75,000 customers with accounts worth at least $3 million.[81] By 2005, predicted the Affluent Market Institute, America's millionaires would control "60 percent of the nation's purchasing dollars."[82]

Amid this affluence, spending on luxury goods and services spiraled upward at rates marketers had never before imagined possible. Some thirty-seven hundred Porsches rolled out of U.S. showrooms in 1993. In 1999, dealers unloaded almost twenty-one thousand of these luxury sports cars, an increase of 476 percent.[83]

Retailers rushed to partake in the luxury feeding frenzy. In the fashion world, the *Boston Globe* reported, Giorgio Armani began "a new clothing line targeted at upper-strata status seekers." The gowns in this new line started at $12,000.[84] In hardware and appliances, Home Depot unveiled a chain of Expo Design Centers, well-appointed warehouses designed, the *Washington Post* noted, "to display and sell home furnishings you didn't know you wanted." Among these furnishings: chandeliers at $5,595 each, refrigerators at $3,996, and hand-painted tiles at $145 apiece. By 2005, Home Deport hoped to have two hundred Expo Design Centers up and running across the United States.[85]

Best of all, this luxury market appeared recession-resistant. In March 2002, two years after Nasdaq started tanking, waiting lists for $13,000 Hermes Birkin handbags still stretched for more than a year.[86]

No business, in the entire United States, would exult in this new, mass luxury market more joyously than banking. Bankers, of course, could count. By 1993, they knew that individual Americans with at least $1 million to invest owned assets worth about $4 trillion, "the near equivalent of all pension and mutual funds combined."[87] America's bankers rushed in to serve this gigantic new market. By the end of 1999, affluent households were handing financial services companies $270 billion a year to manage their money.[88]

"There's nothing but upside in this business," gushed Geoffrey von Kuhn, the chief of Citibank's American private-banking operations.[89]

For their new well-heeled clients, bankers were happy to provide almost any service imaginable. "Wealth management" would come to cover everything from checking accounts to advice on buying art and pearl necklaces.[90] And banks would be amply compensated for their thoughtful assistance. Profit margins in wealth management, a PricewaterhouseCoopers survey revealed in 2001, would run 35 percent.[91]

"It's simply easier," *Fortune* concluded, "to make money dealing with rich people."[92]

So why, if you were a retailer, would you bother dealing with anybody else? Why indeed? Bankers, for their part, spent as little time dealing with the hoi polloi as they possibly could. At the same time bankers were helping swells find just the right pearls, people in poor neighborhoods, the *Washington Post* reported, were finding it "harder than ever to find a bank branch or even an ATM within walking distance."[93]

By 2001, wealth had become so concentrated that even mere millionaires could find themselves treated as second-class consumers. To qualify for high-class handholding from Goldman Sachs, for instance, an affluent household needed $25 million. Households with only $1 million, sources inside Goldman Sachs told *Investment News*, would "soon be able to come on board," but these less affluent households would not be able to expect much in the way of personal attention. Mere millionaire households would "be asked to do most of their business online."[94]

IN AN UNEQUAL SOCIETY, living amid a marketplace of goods and services gone upscale, average consumers always lose. In a luxury market, goods and services cost more than they need to cost, often much more. Among the reasons: simple supply and demand.

"No matter how rich Seattle gets," as columnist Michael Kinsley would explain at the turn of the century, "the number of people who can enjoy a house on Lake Washington will stay about the same. What increases, of course, is the price."[95]

And the wealthy don't particularly care about that price, because they don't have to care. If you have to ask how much a bauble costs, as the old saw goes, you can't afford it. New York banker John K. Castle was asked, in 1999, how much he paid for his yacht and its plush interior decoration. He couldn't say. "One of the things about my lifestyle is that I don't want to know what anything costs," Castle explained to a *Wall Street Journal* reporter. At the top of the economic ladder, he added, price "doesn't really make any difference. That's part of the freedom."[96]

In a marketplace dominated by concentrated wealth, more than prices change. Products themselves change. Manufacturers and merchants, in markets dominated by the wealthy, come to lavish their attention, their creativity, their quality on the luxury market. Everything else goes to seed. Some analysts call this phenomenon "model feature creep." Year by year, economist Robert Frank explains, "products embody more and more costly new features." Over time, one year's high-end models become the next year's base models.[97] "And as this happens," Frank adds, "simpler versions of products that once served perfectly well often fall by the wayside."[98]

We see this marketplace dynamic all the time. We set out to buy a simple, sturdy barbecue grill to replace a now rusted grill we bought a dozen years ago.

That simple, sturdy model no longer exists. We find ourselves paying for racks and ash collectors we don't want and probably will never use. We grumble, but we buy that feature-laden grill anyway. But the extra features, the extra costs, eventually add up to too high a price. At some point, we start cutting back on the middle class basics.

"More families can no longer afford things that were once seen as the birthright of the middle class — the occasional new car, the new clothes, the annual vacation," *Business Week* would report in 1997. "Many have cut back in areas their counterparts wouldn't have considered skimping on in decades past."[99]

Inequality, the sage British social commentator, R. H. Tawney, observed back in 1920, "diverts energy from the creation of wealth to the multiplication of luxuries."[100] And that diversion invariably undermines, in every unequal era, the social capacity to satisfy basic consumer needs.

Especially that most basic consumer need of all, a home.

HOMES ARE THE SINGLE BIGGEST PURCHASE the typical American family ever makes. The entire American dream revolves around having a home to call your own.

By the late twentieth century, vast numbers of American families could only afford that home by going far deeper into debt than average Americans had ever before gone. In some areas of the country, even a willingness to take on massive debt wouldn't be enough. In turn-of-the-century San Francisco, only 12 percent of local families could swing a mortgage for one of the city's median-priced homes.[101] Bay area housing costs were running so high, in 2000, that one nonprofit group was relocating low-income families as far away as Reno, Nevada, the closest place with affordable housing. Complained the group's director: "The whole housing system is breaking down."[102]

In 2002, researchers from the National Low Income Housing Coalition would document the extraordinary extent of that breakdown. Across the country, on average, anyone working full-time had to earn at least $14.66 an hour, about triple the federal minimum wage, "to be able to afford to rent a modest two-bedroom home."[103]

In earlier years, an affordable, comfortable home had been an American middle class given — and an achievable goal for many lower-income households. Younger families would typically rent for a while, set aside money for a downpayment, then buy a home and start building up equity. By the 1990s, this pattern no longer played out. Housing simply cost too much. Renters could not save up for downpayments. Homeowners could not build up equity.

What had happened to America's middle class housing market? Middle class housing had been done in by the luxury dynamic, the same inequality-driven dynamic that had distorted everything else from cars to barbecue grills. In a market environment where price is no object for some people, prices will eventually be higher for all people.

In places like metro San Francisco, middle class families should have been living quite comfortably at the end of the 1990s. They earned, after all, about 33 percent over the national average. But they weren't living quite comfortably. They were struggling — with home costs nearly four times the national average. Why did homes cost so much in the San Francisco area? The "intensely competitive bidding from freshly minted millionaires," concluded the *San Francisco Chronicle,* after a lengthy investigation.[104] These freshly minted millionaires, *USA Today* added, frequently think "nothing of plunking down $500,000 for a San Francisco tear-down with a view."[105]

The new homes that replaced the tear-downs — and filled virgin spaces — would be grand homes. In the 1980s and 1990s, developers built homes the same way automakers built cars. They built them big, to maximize the profits they could expect to receive from their affluent customers. In 1984, just 7 percent of new homes topped three thousand square feet, the size usually thought large enough to require household help to maintain. Fifteen years later, 17 percent of America's new homes sprawled over three thousand feet.[106] Even garages were getting bigger. By century's end, 16 percent of all new homes came with garages that held three or more cars.[107]

Homes with super-sized garages concentrated, of course, wherever wealth concentrated. And in those areas where wealth concentrated, average families could seldom find anything affordable, not anywhere close. Where wealth congregated the most conspicuously of all, in America's trendy beach and mountain resorts, the unavailability of affordable housing created entire towns off limits to working families. In the Hamptons, the East Coast's ritziest summer resort, small cottages that went for $5,000 in the 1940s were fetching up to $900,000 by the mid 1990s."[108] People who worked in the Hamptons — plumbers, teachers, sanitation workers — couldn't even afford to rent locally.[109] Many simply gave up and left. At one point in 2000, half the thirty-six jobs in East Hampton's town road crew were going unfilled. Workers couldn't afford to take the $25,000 jobs, a town official explained, because local housing cost too much.[110]

The deep pockets who descended upon the Hamptons every summer — and made the area unaffordable for working families — would return every fall to Manhattan, another locale largely off limits to working families. In 2000, Manhattan apartments south of Harlem averaged more than $850,000.[111] In the Manhattan apartment market, one amazed realtor would note, "if you have a terrace and you have a view of Fifth, there is no number that you could put on your apartment that is impossible to obtain."[112]

What would be impossible to obtain, in end-of-millennium New York, would be an affordable place for an average-income family. A quarter of New York City's households ended the 1990s paying more than half their income on rent.[113] In the 1990s, even reasonably affluent families could no longer afford Manhattan addresses. Many would cross the river to Brooklyn — and set Brooklyn's housing market on fire. In 1997, thirty-five of Brooklyn's thirty-six zip codes registered double-digit hikes in home prices.[114]

In Brooklyn, and elsewhere in America, many middle class families would refuse to go deep into debt to buy a luxury-priced home. Instead, they would leave the neighborhoods where they had grown up. They would leave the communities where they worked. They would find housing they could afford in distant suburbs and small towns. These families would escape the mortgage squeeze. They would pay a different price for inequality.

To some inconveniences, we never adapt. Loud sudden noises always make us irritable, no matter how many times we hear them. Traffic congestion makes a similarly unpleasant impact. People who travel long distances, in traffic, to arrive at work don't "get used" to long commutes. They die from them. Literally. Commuters in heavy traffic, researchers have found, are more likely to quarrel with co-workers and loved ones, more likely to have high blood pressure, and more likely, economist Robert Frank notes, "to experience premature deaths."[115] Traffic saps smiles out of life.

Unfortunately, Americans now spend more time in traffic than we ever did before. Between 1982 and 1999, a Texas A & M research team has estimated, the number of hours Americans spent "stalled in traffic" tripled.[116] Morning and evening rush hours, combined, averaged six hours a day in 2000, twice as long as they lasted in 1980.[117]

Why have America's roads become so congested? More people? Population growth only explains an inconsequential portion of the nation's increased traffic flow. In the 1980s and 1990s, traffic congestion actually rose eleven times faster than population.[118] So what's clogging America's highways? Commuters are clogging our highways. Americans are driving many more miles on them — to get to work.

Robert Frank calls the phenomenon the "Aspen effect," after the Colorado mountain resort. The phenomenon's stage one: Wealthy families bid up real estate in a desirable community. Stage two: With rising home prices, people who provide basic services in that community, everybody from cops to cooks, can no longer afford to live locally. Stage three: Service workers buy and rent housing far from where they work — and start commuting considerable distances. The end result? In Colorado, by the late 1990s, all roads in and out of "Greater Aspen" were almost always "clogged morning and night with commuters, many of whom come from several hours away."[119]

"The lower you are on the wage scale," explained Rick Stevens, the mayor of one Greater Aspen community, the town of Basalt, "the farther away you have to live."[120]

By century's end, Greater Aspen-like situations could be found all over America. Workers in California's Santa Clara County, the heart of Silicon Valley, found themselves commuting from Livermore and Tracy, communities about a hundred miles away.[121] In 1999, one worker at a Hewlett-Packard plant in San Jose, Santa Clara's biggest city, would leave his home in distant Stockton at 3 a.m. to "beat the traffic." The worker, according to a *San Francisco*

Chronicle profile, would arrive at the plant at 4:30 a.m., nap for an hour, then work a full shift. He would clock out at 2:30 p.m. and typically arrive home in time for dinner — but only if traffic were light.[122]

A continent away, on Long Island, another harried commuter, David Kavanagh spent his days fixing cooling systems for the Grand Union supermarket chain. He usually worked at a different store in the New York metro area every day. Management would let him know which one the night before. Kavanagh would leave home at 4:30 in the morning and not be home until 10 at night. He would eventually sue Grand Union over the company's refusal to compensate him for his travel time. He lost the case. An appeals court ruled that employers are under no legal obligation to pay for "normal" commutes.[123]

Workers with commutes as horrible as David Kavanagh's still make up a distinct minority of America's commuters, but their ranks are growing. The number of Americans who spend at least forty-five minutes driving to work every day jumped 37 percent between 1990 and 2000, according to Census figures. The number of Americans who spent at least ninety minutes driving to work, those same years, soared by 95 percent, to over 3.4 million unfortunate souls.[124]

Some of these souls, to be sure, may not consider themselves unfortunate. Some people chose to commute long distances. To spend weekends close to nature, they happily endure brutal commutes during the week. But millions of other Americans endure these brutal commutes with teeth gritted. And some Americans can't endure them at all. Road rage, in the late twentieth century, would become a mass social reality. Between 1990 and 1995, road rage incidents increased by over 50 percent.[125] By 1999, lawmakers in seventeen states were debating anti-road rage legislation.[126]

At century's end, no one could be totally shielded from road rage and traffic congestion, not even the affluent. And the affluent didn't appreciate that. In Southern California, midway through the 1990s, highway officials felt their pain — and came up with a solution to their distress. That solution, "congestion pricing," debuted on a privately operated highway in Orange County. For a fee, up to $4 a ride, motorists could zoom along in special "High Occupancy Toll" lanes. These "Lexus lanes" quickly caught the attention of transportation planners elsewhere. They also outraged many middle-income motorists. Pay-for-speed lanes, complained one, are really about "giving the rich people an advantage." With Lexus lanes, added Maryland commuter Rob McCulley, "you don't have to sit in traffic if you have enough money to pay your way out of it."[127]

True enough, of course. But Lexus lanes, as a solution to America's traffic snarls, did offer a certain social symmetry. Inequality had, after all, helped create traffic jam America. Why not let more inequality fix it — at least for the affluent?

SITTING IN TRAFFIC, WATCHING CARS ZOOM PAST IN A LEXUS LANE, we daydream about how sweet life must be for people who can always afford convenience. We imagine never having to settle for second-rate, never having to deny ourselves a simple pleasure, never having to make do because we don't make enough. The wealthy, we imagine, live that sweet life. We envy them for it, and we race to grab, in our own daily lives, as much of that sweetness as we can.

Some do counsel us against making that race.

"We need to have the idea that you can have growth in your life," Millard Fuller, the founder of Habitat for Humanity, tells us, "without having growth in the size of your home or bank account."[128]

We appreciate the concern. But we are torn. We are of two minds about wealth. On the one hand, we gape at how easily rich people can make their dreams come true — and their disappointments go away. We see, for instance, a Steve Hilbert, the CEO of the Indiana-based financial services company, Conseco. As a boy growing up, Hilbert wanted nothing more out of life than to play basketball for Indiana University. He would never make the team. But he did make so much money at Conseco that he was able to build, at home, his own exact replica of the Indiana University basketball court. Weekends in the 1990s would find Hilbert dribbling away on his $5.5 million replica, playfully experiencing the hoop glory he never knew.

"On Saturdays," Hilbert would tell *Forbes*, "I hit the winning shot to beat everyone from UCLA to Michigan."[129]

On the other hand, we know that rich people sometimes shoot and miss. Every week, thumbing through the tabloids at supermarket checkout counters, we read about the wrecked and wretchedly unhappy lives rich people can lead. We read about Herbert Haft, the patriarch of the Trak Auto and Shoppers Food Warehouse empire, living alone in a huge mansion, divorced from his wife, totally estranged from his daughter, oldest son, and five grandchildren.[130] We scan the stories about Alice Walton, the Wal-Mart heiress who had become, before she hit fifty, the world's richest woman. Poor Alice suffered through three auto accidents before the 1990s ended. In the last of the three, she nearly lost a leg after smashing her SUV. The police charged her with drunken driving.[131]

"You know who I am, don't you?" she slurred to the arresting officer. "You know my last name?"[132]

Anne Scheiber didn't inherit billions nor snare, in her lifetime, any headlines. But riches dominated Scheiber's unhappy life every bit as much as Alice Walton's. Scheiber had begun pursuing her fortune back in the Depression, after her brother, a stockbroker, had invested and promptly lost all her savings.

"She was bitter with my father for the rest of her life," that brother's son would later relate. "In fact, she got more bitter the older and richer she got."[133]

After the loss, Scheiber started all over. She scrimped and saved in every way imaginable. She lived alone, skipped meals, walked to work, and wore worn-out clothes. By 1944, Scheiber had accumulated a $5,000 nest egg. Over the next half-century, she grew that $5,000 into a portfolio worth over $22 million. Nurturing this portfolio would be all that ever mattered to Scheiber. She would never marry or get close to anyone.

"A big day for her," Scheiber's stockbroker would later recall, "was walking down to the Merrill Lynch vault near Wall Street to visit her stock certificates. She did that a lot."

Scheiber died in 1995, at the age of 101. Over the last five years of her life, she didn't receive a single phone call.

In the closing years of the twentieth century, a rather sizable cottage industry emerged to help people of means avoid the unhappy fates of the Herbert Hafts, the Alice Waltons, and the Anne Scheibers. A host of organizations, by century's end, specialized in helping the affluent bear the "emotional burden of opulence."[134]

More than Money, a nonprofit launched by assorted younger heirs and dot.com millionaires, offered counseling and workshops. The Sudden Money Institute fielded a range of specially trained advisers. The Money, Meaning and Choices Institute zeroed in on "the psychological challenges and opportunities that accompany having or inheriting money."[135] In Chicago, an annual "Ministry of Money" retreat for those worth over $5 million, hosted by Father John Haughey, S.J., a Loyola University professor, encouraged the well-endowed to talk candidly about the burdens wealth imposes.[136]

This notion that wealthy people can bear terrible "burdens" strikes many people of modest means as outrageously silly. Chris Mogil, a New Englander, would see this outrage after, as a young man, he inherited a fortune from his grandfather.

"I was haunted by the question why I should have this privilege," says Mogil, who later started his own nonprofit to help wealthy people "take charge of their money and their lives." But Mogil found that he couldn't expect much sympathy from his nonwealthy friends. Their typical reaction: "Well, if the money bothers you, give it to me."[137]

But wealth does impose burdens, as Mogil and almost all thoughtful wealthy people so clearly understand. These burdens can weigh heavily on nearly every aspect of daily life, from the search for meaningful relationships to the ambition to achieve. Living with great wealth can be like living amid funhouse mirrors. Wealth distorts. You can never be sure about what you see. Is this person nodding approvingly at what I say because I have expressed a keen insight or because I might contribute to her cause? Is the smile on his face a sign of undying affection or a lust for my fortune?

"After I've gone out with a man a few times, he starts to tell me how much he loves me," heiress Doris Duke, worth $1.2 billion at her death in 1993, noted back in her thirties. "But how can I know if he really means it?"[138]

Someone who holds great wealth, suggests philosopher Philip Slater, can never know.

"If you gain fame, power, or wealth, you won't have any trouble finding lovers," Slater notes, "but they will be people who love fame, power, or wealth."[139]

The wealthy respond to this reality in various ways. Some become angry, upset "that money rather than affection or love seems to attract people to them."[140] Others become wary of any intimate relationship. And still others respond by seeking a safe refuge. They find intimacy in their fortunes.

"Money," as the industrialist Armand Hammer once boasted, "is my first, last, and only love."[141]

Sports impresario Jack Kent Cooke, the real estate and media tycoon who owned four different pro sports teams, might have chuckled at that line. Over his eighty-four years, Cooke amassed a near-billion-dollar fortune — and four wives. He died in 1997. In his will, Cooke mentioned every wife by name and left not a penny to one of them.[142]

J. Paul Getty, mid-century America's oil king, outdid Cooke. He divorced five times.

"A lasting relationship with a woman is only possible," Getty concluded, "if you are a business failure."[143]

Brutish patriarchs like Jack Kent Cooke and J. Paul Getty, some might argue, reflect their times more than their wealth. Both grew up in unenlightened, pre-feminist times, amid paleolithic attitudes toward women. In more modern times, the assumption goes, more sensitive and successful family relationships can unfold in wealthy households. But great wealth, author Ann Crittenden notes, can distort healthy, loving relationships just as easily in enlightened as unenlightened times. In the 1980s and 1990s, Crittenden notes, wealth concentrated overwhelmingly in male pockets. Men "struck it rich" much more frequently than equally competent women because few women were either willing or able to devote most all their waking hours to the money chase. And that dynamic created — and still creates — an enormous earnings gap between affluent men and their wives.

"Whether or not she works outside the home, the wife of a high-income man risks becoming a privileged employee rather than an equal partner," Crittenden observes. "As an exceedingly rich man once told me: 'My first wife was like my housekeeper.'"[144]

Men with fortunes don't need wives who do housekeeping. They can afford housekeeping staffs. So why keep a housekeeping wife around? They often don't. Not when a trophy wife can look ever so much better beside the mantel.

ALL RELATIONSHIPS, NOT JUST ROMANTIC COUPLINGS, tend to be twisted by wealth. Rich people "possess and enjoy early," as novelist F. Scott Fitzgerald once famously wrote, "and it does something to them, makes them soft where we are hard, and cynical where we are trustful, in a way that, unless you were born rich, it is difficult to understand."[145]

Even someone born rich might be unable to understand a J. Paul Getty. In 1973, mafiosa kidnapped his sixteen-year-old grandson, John Paul III, then in Italy. The kidnappers demanded a ransom the boy's father, Getty's son, could not pay. Getty did eventually come through with the money, but only after his son agreed to pay him back, at 4 percent interest.[146]

How can such behavior possibly be explained? The wealthy, speculates columnist Nicholas von Hoffman, "grow up convinced everybody around them is after their money."

"They're right, of course," he adds, "which only warps their personality the more."[147]

Out of this suspiciousness that comes so naturally to rich people almost always grows, equally as naturally, an isolation from all those who aren't rich, because all those who aren't rich are always suspect. The greater the wealth, the greater the isolation. The greater the isolation, the more perverse the efforts to rejoin the human family, as historian M. H. Dunlop notes in her recent study of Gilded Age New York at the start of the twentieth century. In New York's original Gilded Age, with wealth concentrated as never before, strange new rituals evolved to reconnect the wealthy to the greater society they kept at arm's length. Men of means, relates Dunlop, "went on midnight slumming tours and sneaked peaks at the dirty feet of the unimaginably poor."[148]

These slumming tours would be fastidiously organized. Guidebooks even carried listings of them. But wealthy New Yorkers sometimes took their cheap thrills in less formally organized outings. Some would drop by "the toy departments of New York City's great department stores" to watch poor children gaze longingly through the windows at "toys they would never have a chance to touch."[149] Such behavior by the wealthy, historian Dunlop concludes, reflected a basic boredom with life. The rich had "retreated to the close company of their own," then "wearied of seeing only persons like themselves who owned the same things they owned." Out of ennui, New York's Gilded Age gentlemen "moved in new and risky directions." They "sought the thrill of watching other beings suffer in ways that were closed to them."[150]

Contemporary commentators have observed a similar mental exhaustion among the gentlemen and ladies of America's new Gilded Age. Wealthy people, they find, are subject to "consumption fatigue." Philosopher Philip Slater traces this fatigue to the control that wealth enables wealthy people to exercise over their lives.

"When you can control what comes to you in life," Slater points out, "life itself loses most of its excitement."[151]

Stanley Marcus spent his entire adult life working feverishly to put that excitement back in to wealthy lives. The original brains behind Neiman Marcus, the Dallas-based retailer to the rich, Marcus "sought to rekindle interest in possessions among those who wanted for nothing," as one obituary noted after his death in 2002, at the age of ninety-six. Toward that end, the famous Neiman Marcus holiday catalog each year endeavored to offer ever more outrageous extravagances, from his-and-her miniature submarines to his-and-her matching camels. Marcus even marketed silver-plated barbecues complete with live bulls. His fame grew world-wide.[152]

"He never let up in his mission," the British *Economist* magazine eulogized, "to save the very rich from the wasting disease of boredom."[153]

Marcus never succeeded, not in any lasting fashion. His "stuff" could not guarantee happiness, not to the daughters of quick-rich Texas oilmen his early retail empire set out to serve, not to digital economy dot.com wonderboys two generations later.

These dot.com'ers, notes psychologist Stephen Golbart, had no idea what they were getting into when they pulled in their first windfalls. Many would go out on spending extravaganzas, buying up two or three houses, cars, and assorted other "stuff" before binging out. But the spending would never "do it" for them. They would, Golbart found, "become depressed, empty and uncertain about what to do with the rest of their lives."[154]

Sudden new wealth, adds Irwin Rosen, a psychoanalyst at the Menninger Clinic in Kansas, always at first seems the ultimate answer to all prayers. "How many people," he asks, "say, 'Boy, if I had a million bucks, all my problems would be solved?' But when they acquire wealth, they learn that all their problems aren't solved."

Indeed, those who come upon significant wealth find they face new problems. They face "the envy of others." Perhaps even worse, observes Rosen, they face their own guilt, the sense "they don't deserve the money at all."[155] This guilt can become particularly intense among those born into exceedingly good fortune, people like the clients of Myra Salzer, a financial adviser in Colorado who runs a four-day seminar on inherited wealth. Her clients, says Salzer, feel "undeserving." And that doesn't surprise her. "They've almost been denied an opportunity to see what they can do for themselves," she explains.[156]

Those wealthy individuals who speak candidly in programs like Salzer's seminar have, at some point, made a decision to try to confront the guilt their fortunes make them feel. Other wealthy people do not confront guilt. They deny it. If I am far more wealthy than most all other people, they tell themselves, I must be deserving. If I weren't deserving, I wouldn't be so favored by fortune. In 1997, researchers at Roper Starch polled a national cross-sample of America's most affluent 1 percent. Everyone surveyed made at least $250,000 in income or held $2.5 million in assets. These wealthy Americans were asked to agree or disagree with a simple statement: "I deserve all my financial success." Nearly 90 percent agreed, 54 percent "strongly" and 32 percent "mostly."[157]

A harmless self-delusion? Unfortunately, no, because those of ample means who believe they fully deserve their good fortune usually also come to believe, come to insist, that those not blessed with abundance must deserve their ill-fortune. These self-satisfied wealthy come to see poverty "as a sin of the lazy" and great wealth "a reward for hard work."[158] If the poor were deserving, they would not be poor. The unfortunate get the little they deserve.

This contempt for the poor becomes increasingly vicious as societies become increasingly unequal. The more bountiful the wealth of the fortunate and the more vile the deprivation of the unfortunate, the greater the pressure on those at the top to see their society's starkly unequal distribution of wealth as based on a just system that rewards superior work — and punishes sloth. How could the fortunate come to feel otherwise? If they acknowledged that hard-working people could still be poor, then their society would not be just and their good fortune in it might not be deserved. How much easier to assume that society works justly — and blame the poor for being poor.

In America's original Gilded Age, historian M. H. Dunlop reminds us, one orator by the name of Russell Conwell made a considerable name for himself by delivering, over five thousand times, a lecture entitled "Acres of Diamonds." Conwell told his audiences a century ago that "it is your duty to get rich."

"While we should sympathize with God's poor — that is, those who cannot help themselves — let us remember," orated Conwell, "that there is not a poor person in the United States who was not made poor by his own shortcomings, or by the shortcomings of someone else."[159]

About one hundred years later, in America's second Gilded Age, this same contempt would return, only delivered by syndicated columnists, not itinerant lecturers. In 1995, a liberal pollster, Stan Greenberg, had called on Democrats to push policies that appeal to downscale voters. How outrageous, shot back columnist Robert Novak. Greenberg, Novak asserted, was asking America to coddle "the country's losers."[160]

These losers didn't deserve help, in the eyes of America's smug — and they didn't get it in the boom years of the 1980s and 1990s. The rich did not share their good fortune with the less fortunate. Instead, notes author Michael Lewis, "the rich man's empathy for the nonrich" dwindled. Lewis, a Wall Street refugee, found this absence of empathy repugnant but understandable. After all, he explained, "you can't give money to anyone you don't respect, and you can't respect anyone who doesn't make money."[161]

In fact, if you're rich enough, you can't really respect anyone who isn't rich. You become contemptuous, not just of the poor, but all the rest of America's freeloaders.

"Let's face it," as one affluent entrepreneur told *Worth* magazine. "In this country the destructive behavior is done by the bottom 5 percent. The productive behavior comes from the top 5 percent. Everybody in the middle just eats the food."[162]

Worth's Richard Todd would report these comments in a 1997 analysis of wealth in America. Wealthy people, Todd related, hardly ever utter such sentiments in mixed company. But the entrepreneur's explicit comments, he added, were not isolated ravings. They represented, Todd noted, "something that one often senses at the top ranks of our country but seldom hears: a true abhorrence of the people in the middle."[163]

AVERAGE PEOPLE, WE HAVE ARGUED IN THESE PAGES, are of two minds about the wealthy. The reverse, interestingly, also holds true. The wealthy, for their part, are of two minds about average people. Many may abhor people in the middle, but, deep down, many would also feel more at ease if their children lived a middle class life. Wealthy people, at least wealthy people with any sense, worry all the time about the dangerous impact wealth may have on the happiness of their kids.

In 2000, one fascinating survey of wealthy people, conducted for U.S. Trust, a wealth-management services company, revealed just how deeply many wealthy parents worry. Those polled had either a $300,000 annual income or a net worth of more than $3 million. Of those surveyed, 61 percent acknowledged worrying that their children would grow up overemphasizing material possessions. Many also feared their children would "have their initiative and independence undermined by material advantages."[164]

These apprehensions, note caregivers who work with children, are well-placed. Spoiled children, psychologists explain, are children who come to expect their environment to always respond as they want.[165] These sorts of environments, of course, can be created by overly doting parents in homes of any income. But these environments evolve most readily in households where anything desired can be afforded. Those born rich, notes London psychiatrist Trevor Turner, grow up all too often "never having known what it is to want something and not have it."[166]

Children so "blessed" can grow up without a clue about the real world that everyone else calls home. The *New York Times*, in 2000, would publish a riveting and revolting profile of one of these "born rich," a twenty-nine-year-old Upper East Sider who had enrolled in a Chase Manhattan Bank management training program after she figured it would be "chic to have a career." The young woman's well-to-do father had found the training slot for her, and she started on the job in March. But things didn't quite go right. Supervisors didn't like the young woman's Park Avenue princess outfits. They asked her to conform to the bank's dark-suits-and-stockings dress code. She did, despite firmly believing that stockings were "especially middle class." Soon enough, summer neared. The young woman informed her immediate boss she needed three months off for her family's annual vacation in the south of France. The supervisor approved one week's leave.

"That was so ridiculous," the frustrated trainee would later tell a reporter. "That's not even enough time to shop."

New York's affluent circles, notes *New York Times* reporter Monique Yazigi, abound with similarly clueless young people, children of privilege who "lack the drive and the discipline of their hungrier peers."[167] Robert Elliott, an executive vice president at a trust company that serves old-line wealth, has seen this same story, over and over.

"It's hard for someone who has several million dollars, which produces income of over $100,000 or so, to be interested in a job that pays $40,000," says Elliott. "Ultimately they become less committed to their career than their peers, which obviously produces less success in their career and ultimately less satisfaction with their lives."[168]

Over the years, some immensely wealthy parents have gone to great lengths to shield their children from this dissatisfaction. They have simply refused to pass their progeny their wealth.

"I would as soon leave to my son a curse," Andrew Carnegie once thundered, "as the almighty dollar."[169]

In our own time, Warren Buffet, the billionaire investor, has followed Carnegie's lead. To set up his three children with "a lifetime supply of food stamps just because they came out of the right womb," he has informed the world, would be "harmful" and "antisocial." New York entrepreneur Eugene Lang took a similar stance. He announced that his three children would receive just "a nominal sum" from his $50 million fortune.

"I want to give my kids," Lang told *Fortune*, "the tremendous satisfaction of making it on their own."[170]

So does James Rogers, the chairman of Sunbelt Communications, a chain of television stations that helped him build a personal net worth of $500 million.

"Leaving children wealth," Rogers once noted, "is like leaving them a case of psychological cancer."[171]

Kids from wealthy families, parents like James Rogers believe, can be saved from this horrible fate by denying them fortunes they have not earned. Insist that sons and daughters make their own fortunes, they assume, and these sons and daughters will turn out fine. But in real life, more astute observers point out, denying wealthy children their due in no way guarantees these children happiness or fulfillment. Wealthy parents can refuse to pass on wealth. But they can never avoid passing on the high expectations their great wealth creates.

These expectations, San Jose family therapist Dale Lillak points out, can be as burdensome as any inherited bankroll. Kids from wealthy families who have been brought up to "make it on their own," explains Lillak, quite naturally want to emulate the success of their wealthy parents. But their chances of matching that success "are slim," no matter how well-adjusted and hard-working they may be. Their parents, after all, didn't become fabulously wealthy just because they were hard-working. They became fabulously wealthy because, at some point in their lives, fortune smiled their way. All riches, Lillak continues, represent "luck on some level," and all the healthy child rearing in the world can't teach luck.[172] And that means that children encouraged to make their own way in the world will never measure up to the standard of "success" their parents have achieved — unless lightning somehow strikes twice. Wealthy parents who expect their children to "make it" fully on their own, as a consequence, are doing their children no great favor. They have set their children up for failure, not fulfillment.

Wealth, in the end, traps wealthy parents. If they lavish wealth on their children, they risk steering their kids into empty, unsatisfying lives. If they expect their children to forge their own way in life, they risk dooming their kids to disappointment.

The saddest irony in all this? Giving, in human affairs, can be a wonderful source of joy, perhaps the greatest source of joy of all, and the wealthy, by dint of their fortunes, certainly have more to give than anyone else. But the dollars the wealthy can so easily afford to give too often bring no great joy, no joy at all. For the wealthy, giving becomes just another burden, partially because they fear the impact of that giving on their loved ones — and partially because they are expected to give, even hounded to give, by nearly everyone they encounter. Billionaire Larry Tisch, a fixture on the *Forbes* 400 list of the richest Americans, once complained he received "thirty requests for money a day."[173]

That constant drumbeat of entreaties makes giving an obligation, not a source of satisfaction. If you resist that obligation, you will be resented. If you accept that obligation, then *you* start feeling the resentment. You gave because you felt forced into it.

Over the course of a wealthy person's lifetime, the resentments, the frustrations, the burdens add up. For George Bernard Shaw, the most acclaimed playwright of his time, the mix did not paint a pretty picture.

"You can easily find people who are ten times as rich at sixty as they were at twenty," Shaw would note in his seventies, "but not one of them will tell you that they are ten times as happy."[174]

SOME AWESOMELY AFFLUENT AMERICANS consciously set out to overcome the burdens and strains that must always come with wealth. These affluent steel themselves against wealth's temptations. They set out to lead normal lives. To a remarkable extent, some of them succeed. The world's second richest man, Warren Buffet, drove his own car and lived in an eminently nondescript house throughout the 1990s, even as his billions mounted. Mitchell Fromstein, the CEO of Manpower Inc., ended the 1990s living in the same four-bedroom suburban Milwaukee home he and his wife had purchased back in the mid 1970s, before Fromstein started pulling in several million a year. He was driving a twelve-year-old Mercedes when the *Wall Street Journal* profiled him in 1999.

"I'm not trying to keep up with anybody," the seventy-one-year-old executive explained. "We don't need a lot of things to be happy."[175]

Any wealthy person in America can follow the path blazed by Buffet and Fromstein. But hardly any do. Why not? If wealth makes for such a burden, as these pages have contended, then why do so few wealthy people ever attempt to put that burden down? America's sociologists of wealth suggest an answer. Great wealth, they contend, may indeed distort and poison normal human relationships. But great wealth also empowers, on a variety of intoxicating fronts. Wealth gives the wealthy, sociologist Paul Schervish contends, the capacity to "overcome the usual constraints of time."[176] Wealth can add extra hours to the days of the wealthy, extra years to their lives.

"By hiring accountants, housekeepers, gardeners, and personal secretaries to perform various mundane tasks," Schervish explains, "the wealthy expand the portion of the day they can devote to doing what they want or what they deem important."

Wealth also empowers spatially. Riches enable the wealthy, notes Schervish, "to physically move about the world as they wish while, at the same time, insulating themselves from the movements or intrusions of others." And, finally, wealth empowers psychologically, by encouraging the wealthy to believe that their "self-determined goals are more important" than any other goals, that they have the right to pursue whatever goals they choose.

In our modern America, we all seek to become empowered. Our society, from right to left, considers empowerment a basic core value, an unalloyed good. We all should become "agents," as scholars might put it, empowered to shape our own personal destinies.[177] But the empowerment the wealthy find in their fortunes, sociologist Paul Schervish submits, goes far beyond mere agency. Wealth grants the wealthy "that extraordinary attribute of hyperagency."[178]

"As agents," Schervish explains, "most people search out the most suitable place for themselves in a world constructed by others." As "hyperagents," the wealthy construct their own world. Most of us spend our lives accommodating ourselves to the world. The wealthy, if wealthy enough, can accommodate the world to themselves.

Hyperagency means never having to tolerate any inconvenience. Why, for instance, miss the comfort of sitting in your own special chair when you go out for a fine meal? One July night in 1995, billionaire Marvin Davis had his favorite brass and green-leather armchair brought into the trendy Hamptons hotspot, Nick & Toni's. Three men carried the chair in from a van. After dinner, the three returned to carry the armchair back out.

"Mr. Davis," the *New York Observer* reported, "lumbered out of the restaurant under his own power."[179]

Hyperagency in refuges like the Hamptons also means never having to take anything, even Mother Nature, as a given. The Hamptons too cold in the winter for palm trees to survive? A mere trifle, easily overcome. In the 1990s, one deep-pockets couple had palms installed at their Southampton estate, then had the trees flown to Florida for the winter.[180]

Wherever the wealthy congregate, they bend the world to their priorities, their schedules, their pleasures. In palm tree-friendly Florida, billionaire H. Wayne Huizenga apparently couldn't bear the thought of having to apply for country club membership. He founded his own private country club, with only himself and his wife as members. The club featured an eighteen-hole golf course, three helicopter pads, and sixty-eight boat slips for invited dignitaries.[181] In California, the rich and the regal can't bear the thought of having eyebrows go unplucked, not for a moment. Anastasia Soare, the proprietor of one exclusive Beverly Hills salon, marched into the new millennium ready to pluck, any time, any place. She did local house calls that ran at least $400 for a five-minute pluck-cut-and-wax. For $3,000, she would even fly cross-country.[182]

In 1996, actor Charlie Sheen didn't want anybody to fly to him. He wanted a fly ball. For a Friday night baseball game that year, he bought a $5,000 block of seats behind the left-field fence at Anaheim Stadium. He and three friends then sat in the middle of that block all by themselves, for the entire game.

"Anybody can catch a foul ball. I want to catch a fair ball," Sheen explained. "I didn't want to crawl over the paying public."[183]

Hyperagency does sometimes have its limits. On that Friday evening in Anaheim, for instance, a homerun ball never came Charlie Sheen's way. Not everything can be bought, not all the time. In some rare situations, the world the wealthy encounter simply refuses to be shaped. Author Fran Lebowitz once found herself in a museum with a quite wealthy man. After twenty minutes, the man had to leave. He felt it, Lebowitz noted, "too irritating to see things that he couldn't buy."[184]

But the wealthy, over time, find that most of what they want in life can be bought. And with that understanding comes an arrogance peculiar to those who never need to compromise to get their own way, an arrogance that places their happiness and comfort first, whatever the impact on others might be.

Public officials in San Jose would encounter that arrogance, first-hand, in the late 1990s. These officials, to help ensure homeowners a "good night's sleep," had adopted regulations that restricted late-night jet landings at the local airport.[185] But billionaire CEO Larry Ellison saw no reason why the regulations should apply to him. He refused to abide by the local rules and kept landing his $38.7 million Gulfstream GV at all hours of the night. After the first violation, city officials sent Ellison a polite letter reminding him of the anti-noise ordinance his jet had violated. Eighteen months later, after the violations continued, officials issued a stiffer warning, then, late in 1999, threatened to sue.[186]

"San Jose has no right to tell me when I can land my airplane," Ellison retorted. "It's like saying people who weigh more than 200 pounds can't go into a store after 6 p.m."[187]

Ellison took the city to court. In June 2001, he won. A federal judge gave him the right to land his forty-ton private jet at the San Jose airport after the 11:30 p.m. curfew that all other big jets were still expected to honor.[188]

Hyperagency, of course, doesn't turn every phenomenally rich person into an arrogant, immature, totally self-centered boor. But hyperagency does seductively steer all who enjoy it down that same direction. To step back, to refuse to engage in and enjoy the hyperagent life that great wealth enables, is no easy task. We would all rather shape our world than be shaped by it.

Occasionally, of course, a wealthy person will not be seduced. In 1999, for instance, a Michigan-based construction mogul, Bob Thompson, sold his asphalt and paving business and shared $130 million of the proceeds from the sale with his 550 employees.[189]

"What was I going to do with all that money anyway?" asked the sixty-seven-year-old Thompson. "There is need and then there is greed. We all need certain basic comforts, and beyond that it becomes ridiculous."[190]

Why can't all rich people be like that, we wonder. If we were rich, we tell ourselves, *we* would certainly be like that. Nonsense. If we were rich, we would feel the same burdens rich people feel — and be seduced by the same pleasures. The wisest among us, people like the essayist Logan Pearsall Smith, have always understood this reality.

"To suppose, as we all suppose, that we could be rich and not behave as the rich behave," as Smith wrote in 1931, "is like supposing that we could drink all day and keep absolutely sober."[191]

"I have known some drunks who were happy at times," philosopher Philip Slater added half a century later, "but I've known no one who devoted a long life to alcohol and didn't suffer from it, and I believe the same to be true for wealth."[192]

THE CANADIAN SOCIAL SCIENTIST ALEX MICHALOS, a president of the International Society for Quality of Life Studies, once calculated from data on subjective well-being that nothing has a greater overall impact on an individual's satisfaction with life than an individual's sense of financial security. And this sense of financial security, he concluded, largely emerges from how individuals appraise three basic gaps in their lives: "the gap between what one has and wants, between what one has and thinks others like oneself have, and between what one has and the best one has had in the past."[193]

Over the closing decades of the twentieth century in the United States, decades of growing inequality, average Americans saw each of these three gaps widen. Our wants escalated as America's most affluent set new and higher standards for the good life. Our sense of what most of the people around us own inflated as we spent fewer hours with friends and neighbors and more hours in the workplace. Our past looked brighter than our present as we contemplated our stagnant paychecks and worried about our escalating health insurance premiums. Don't worry, the song said, be happy. We worried.

And we worried even if we were fortunate enough to sit on the other side of the great divide in income and wealth. Affluence, we found, brought new burdens.

"New wealth is rewriting relationships with friends, family and co-workers, and heightening everyone's sensitivity about where they fit in," journalist Michelle Quinn reported at the end of the 1990s, after interviewing what seemed to be half of Silicon Valley. "It's raised expectations and fueled frustrations. No matter what their economic status, people are on edge."[194]

On edge and not happy. Playwright Neil Simon could have predicted as much.

"Money brings some happiness," Simon had quipped years before. "But after a certain point it just brings more money."[195]

And trouble.

Still, as George Bernard Shaw once noted, some wealthy people do seem to be able to live lives largely trouble-free.

"Perhaps you know some well-off families who do not seem to suffer from their riches," Shaw observed in 1928. "They do not overeat themselves; they find occupations to keep themselves in health; they do not worry about their position; they put their money into safe investments and are content with a low rate of interest; and they bring up their children to live simply and do useful work."

In other words, concluded Shaw, the happy rich "do not live like rich people at all." They "might therefore," he concluded, "just as well have ordinary incomes."[196]

And if they did, we all would be happier.

PROFESSIONS WITHOUT PRIDE

THE THINGS WE BUY BRING US, at best, only limited satisfaction. The work we do, by contrast, can add enormous and lasting satisfaction to our lives.

Unfortunately, only some among us spend our lives working at jobs that bring us significant pleasure. These fortunate souls stand out. We recognize them immediately. These are people who have studied and practiced and mastered a body of knowledge and skill. They perform their work at high levels. They take great pride in it. In fact, they take such great pride in the work they do that they cannot bear to watch this work performed poorly by others around them. Within their trade, they correct the beginner who may not know better. They rebuke the sloppy who do.

The people who approach their work in this spirit, the people who practice and perfect and protect their trade, whatever that trade may be, we call professionals. Over time, in any modern society, professionals tend to unite with like-minded colleagues. They create professions. These organized professions, the British social thinker R. H. Tawney once noted, typically take on two noble missions. Within them, professionals strive to maintain the quality of the services they provide and prevent the frustration of that quality by "the undue influence of the motive of pecuniary gain."[1]

Professions, Tawney argued in 1920, differ markedly from ordinary business operations. Ordinary businesses seek to maximize financial return. Professions do not. True professionals, Tawney contended, measure their success by the service they perform, "not the gains which they amass." Professionals do certainly owe their incomes to their professional positions, but "they do not consider that any conduct which increases their income is on that account good."[2] Professions, agrees a more contemporary observer, journalist Stephen Metcalf, "encourage in the good professional a certain gentility regarding money, an old-fashioned prudishness."

"Professionals aren't supposed to haggle: they set standard fees, then bill you," adds Metcalf. "They're allowed to be very well-off, but not very rich."[3]

Historically, in return for this genteel moderation, professionals have expected from society the power to control the conduct of their profession. They value this control enormously, not because they thirst for power, but because they relish the autonomy, the ability to make informed and independent judgments, that makes professional practice so pleasurable. This autonomy thrives best within self-governing professions. Where societies deny autonomy to professions, individual professionals must practice their professions as outsiders see fit — and that practice brings no great joy.

Societies, for their part, will grant professions the autonomy they seek, but only if they trust the professions that seek it. To gain this trust, and keep it, wise professions police themselves. They deliberately prohibit, as R. H. Tawney observed, conduct that, though "profitable to the individual," would bring the profession "into disrepute."[4] If a profession succeeds in this self-policing effort, if a profession is able, in other words, to consistently prevent disreputable behavior within its own ranks, everyone benefits. The public is shielded from professionals who choose to abuse their expertise.[5] Honest professionals get to freely practice the work that brings them pleasure.

These sorts of mutually beneficial arrangements can endure only so long as professionals keep their professional balance. Should they lose that balance, should they let private self-interest trump professional responsibility, all bets are off. If a public senses that professionals are prospering extravagantly at public expense, that public will no longer trust professionals to set their own rules. Exit autonomy — and the professional pleasures autonomy brings.

In the closing decades of the twentieth century, America's most influential professionals would put these pleasures at risk. They would look away as individuals within their professions abused the public trust. They would look away because great wealth beckoned. They would find that great wealth. They would lose everything else.

BEHIND EVERY SIGNIFICANT CORPORATE DECISION made in the United States today stands a lawyer. Lawyers advise and lawyers bless. Their nods give go-aheads. Their thumbs down can give even the most determined chief executive pause.

Attorneys who practice corporate law have constituted, ever since the rise of the modern corporation, the elite of the legal profession. Their rewards have always been ample. Still, until recent times, attorneys in corporate law did not earn terribly more than lawyers practicing in less lucrative fields. In 1954, the year that future Harvard president Derek Bok graduated from law school, he could have taken a job with a top Wall Street law firm for $4,200 a year. He also could have gone to work in the Justice Department "for almost as large a salary as private law firms were offering."[6] Attorneys a half-century ago could live comfortably working in or out of corporate law. Top lawyers at the biggest corporate law firms collected impressive, but not staggering, rewards.

The same could be said for the top corporate executives that top corporate attorneys advised. A half-century ago, they collected impressive, but not staggering, rewards. That would change, as we have seen. Executive pay would explode upwards over the last quarter of the twentieth century. Corporate lawyers watched the explosion. Actually, they did more than just watch. They lit the fuse. With every regulation and tax they helped corporations sidestep, with every merger they packaged, with every workplace they kept "union-free," these attorneys helped inflate corporate earnings — and executive incomes.

These rising executive incomes, in turn, raised pay expectations within America's top corporate law firms. Senior partners at these firms saw no reason why pay for executives should far outpace their own compensation. These attorneys considered themselves every bit as sharp and savvy as the executives they advised. Why shouldn't fortune smile just as sweetly on them as on corporate executives?

Executives, these lawyers understood, did hold one specific compensation advantage. Simply by manipulating shares of stock, executives could fashion for themselves enormous fortunes. Law firms, as private partnerships, could engage in no such lucrative stock maneuvers. Top partners in these firms, to keep pace with the pay of their corporate executive counterparts, would have to develop a different set of wealth-amassing techniques. And so they did. Over the last quarter of the twentieth century, America's elite attorneys would redefine and restructure how private law firms operate.

Law practices in the United States, even the most prestigious, had traditionally been modest in size. But modestly sized operations, in law as in business, can support at the top only modest compensation. Law firms would now shed their historic size limitations. In 1978, only fifteen law firms in the entire nation could claim as many as two hundred attorneys. A decade later, over seven times as many firms sported two hundred or more lawyers.[7] By 1997, just one law firm alone, the New York-based Skadden, Arps, Slate, Meagher & Flom, employed twelve hundred lawyers in twenty-one cities.[8]

These new supersized law firms did not "practice" law. They manufactured it, factory style. Legions of young attorneys staffed the new legal assembly lines. These "associates" labored sixty, seventy, even over eighty hours a week. They would be paid handsomely for these hours — associates at Skadden, Arps, Slate, Meagher & Flom, for instance, started at $101,000 in 1998 — but their employers, the partners in America's top law firms, could afford to be generous. Associate labor was making them rich.[9]

Between 1970 and 1990, after adjusting for inflation, per-partner profits at the nation's elite law firms leaped by 75 percent and more.[10] The profits would keep flowing in the 1990s. Midway through the decade, the 360 partners at New York's Cravath, Swaine & Moore were averaging more than $1 million each.[11] In 2001, Cravath's per-partner profits totaled twice that, $2.14 million. That same year, at Wachtell, Lipton, Rosen & Katz, partners averaged $3.17 million.[12]

By century's end, any "gentility regarding money" had been thoroughly purged from America's top law firms. A new money culture had taken root. Top attorneys no longer served their clients. They scrambled to squeeze them. In this scramble, notes Derek Bok, who would serve as the dean of the Harvard Law School before becoming the university's president, nothing would matter more than the billable hour.

"The more associates a firm could maintain for every partner, and the more hours they worked," explains Bok, "the larger the pool of profits would become."[13]

And that pool seemed limitless. If corporate clients balked at excessively high hourly rates, their law firms could simply smile, moderate the rate, and bill more hours. Two-minute phone calls could be rounded up to billable quarter-hours. Extra witnesses could be interviewed. Extra lawyers could be brought into meetings.[14] In this environment, inefficiency paid. The more time spent on a task, the more hours to be billed.[15]

Billable hours, as lucrative as they could be, would actually constitute only one prime revenue stream for America's top firms. In the 1980s and 1990s, they would start exploiting another, equally lucrative source of fortune, the contingent fee.

Lawyers had started practicing contingency fee law, years before, as a strategy to help people of limited means. Through a contingency arrangement, a litigant with a good case but no money could secure an attorney's services. That attorney would typically receive, instead of standard hourly fees, a third of whatever settlement the case produced. These contingency arrangements could make sense for both litigant and lawyer. They could also invite abuse. Lawyers who came to specialize in contingency fee law had to "win" to be paid. Some attorneys, under this pressure, would start to do anything to win. They might "harass defendants with endless requests for documents and interrogatories to extract a settlement" or "even manufacture evidence to inflate the amount of damages."[16]

Such tactics could be profitable. Contingent fee settlements and judgments could total tens of millions of dollars, a fact that did not go unnoticed in the plush offices of America's most prestigious law firms. Why should these contingent fee fortunes, top partners wondered, be left to ambulance chasers? In the 1980s, these top partners moved to cut their firms into the contingent fee action.[17] Litigants who could afford to pay standard legal fees would now have their cases handled on a contingent fee basis.

America's top firms would have, in contingent fee law, a promising new revenue stream. The general public would be no better served. Observers would be struck by "how few individuals with deserving claims receive anything at all." One major investigation of malpractice cases found that "only one in eight or ten meritorious claims ever reaches a lawyer, and only half of these result in any payment of money to the victim."[18]

In this client-be-squeezed, public-be-damned legal environment, America's biggest and best law firms found themselves, not surprisingly, stumbling to keep their moral bearings. The professionals America trusted to uphold the law would, at the height of the boom years, work diligently to subvert it — and then even flaunt their subversion.

In 2001, for instance, the Houston-based firm of Vinson & Elkins openly boasted, on its Web site, about the firm's pivotal role in creating off-balance-sheet partnerships for the nation's most innovative company — and its biggest client. That client was Enron. In 2001 alone, the Enron account earned Vinson & Elkins $36 million. By year's end, the off-balance-sheet partnerships that Vinson & Elkins had helped create, partnerships "structured to enrich a few Enron insiders at the expense of company shareholders," had sunk the energy giant into bankruptcy.[19] Unhappy Enron shareholders would later charge that Vinson & Elkins, with its work at Enron, had engaged in outright racketeering.

In earlier generations, few young people had gone into the law expecting to practice racketeering — or amass multimillions. The law offered other, more professional satisfactions, the opportunity to practice an honorable trade, to build lifelong, collegial relationships. These pleasures would all erode in the 1980s and 1990s. Inside the profession's huge new law firms, young associates working eighty-hour weeks made "good" money, but had little time to enjoy it. That time, they told themselves, would come when they "made" partner. The pleasures of the profession would then be theirs. But partnership, once made, would turn out to bring no great pleasure either.

The profession had changed. In years past, partners could and did take great pride from their practice. The hours they spent mentoring young colleagues and sharing insights with fellow partners they respected and esteemed kept their careers professionally satisfying. Partners seldom squabbled about money. Seniority rules determined the shares each partner took from the firm profit pool.

In the late twentieth century, with hundreds of millions of dollars filling law firm profit pools, ambitious partners would come to see these traditional rules as silly and unfair. They demanded that firms shift to "performance" distributions. Let the most rewards go to the partners who brought in the most business. Partners who didn't spend their time bringing in new business, who wasted potential billable hours mentoring colleagues, now came across as fools. And if you were a partner who asked colleagues for their insights about a case, you would be seen as an even bigger fool. Any insights those partners might give you, after all, would entitle them to a share of what should have been your profits.

Professional pleasures could not endure in an atmosphere this strained. Fewer partners mentored, fewer partners collaborated. Partners, instead, hoarded clients. And if those clients, as a result, didn't receive the best possible representation, then so be it. The practice of law was now about profits, not clients, about selfishness, not service.[20]

Meanwhile, outside the exquisitely paneled confines of America's largest law firms, in small practices and legal clinics, individual lawyers would also be working long hours, but not to get rich.[21] They would be working their long hours to pay back their enormous student loans. By century's end, over half of America's law school graduates would be starting their careers more than $75,000 in debt, with one in every five over $105,000.[22] Some young lawyers, those who signed on with high-profile private firms, could handle these debt loads. Half of all new private-practice lawyers, after all, would be taking home starting salaries over $90,000 a year by the late 1990s. And law schools knew that. By century's end, notes economist Dean Baker, the high salaries available in elite private practice had become "the driving force behind rising tuition."[23] Law schools would charge what the market would bear. In the 1990s, tuitions would soar 140 percent.[24]

Salaries for government and public-interest lawyers, over those same years, would rise 37 percent. By decade's end, the typical attorney for a public interest group would only be earning $35,000. Median incomes for government lawyers would go somewhat higher, but not enough to offset six-figure student debt loads. With salaries outside elite private-practice law so limited, the national association of public interest lawyers would charge in 2003, two-thirds of law school graduates could not afford to even consider a job in the government or public interest sector.[25]

Those young lawyers who did go into public interest work would do the best they could in understaffed and underbudgeted legal offices. They would, on a regular basis, have to say no to people who needed legal help. And they would be resented for it. Lawyers, increasing numbers of Americans were convinced, were just out for themselves.

"Has our profession," asked a 1986 American Bar Association report, "abandoned principle for profit, professionalism for commercialism?"[26]

By century's end, the answer would be in little doubt.

OUR SOCIETY'S SUSPICIONS ABOUT LAWYERS DO, of course, have roots that go deep into history. Let us first, as Shakespeare suggested, kill all the lawyers. Accountants carry none of this classic baggage. The founding fathers of accountancy, men like the legendary Arthur Andersen, left their successors a trade with an awesome aura of professional probity.

"Think straight and talk straight," Andersen would advise his colleagues in the early years of the accounting profession. He took his own advice to heart. In 1915, for instance, Andersen demanded that a steamship company formally acknowledge the sinking of a freighter that had sunk *after* the company's fiscal year had ended.[27] The investing public, Andersen insisted, had a right to the full story. Accountants had a responsibility to determine — and present — the unvarnished truth in every business situation.

The American people would come, after the stock market crash in 1929, to understand the importance of this honorable accountancy mission. In the 1930s, the federal government "gave the accounting industry the valuable franchise to audit companies that sell shares to the public."[28] Accountants, notes journalist David Hilzenrath, were expected "to do their best to make sure investors can trust corporate financial statements." That meant more than crunching numbers. That meant checking inventory and contacting customers. And that meant, most importantly, making judgments.

Any audit of a modern corporation demands thousands of judgment calls. Is an asset fairly valued? Is a liability understated? Is a revenue collectible? The

best accountants have always taken great pride in making these judgments —
and getting them right.

Those who do judging, of course, must be impartial and independent.
Auditors, accounting's founding fathers agreed, could not objectively audit a
company's books and, at the same time, participate actively in that same company's business operations. Honorable auditors must avoid any trace of conflict
of interest.

Down through the years, in practice, this ethic of independence would
prove difficult to sustain. In the late twentieth century, with corporate executive compensation escalating at record rates, sustaining this ethic would
become impossible.

In the 1980s and 1990s, partners at America's top accounting firms would
see the same executive pay extravagances that partners at America's top law
firms saw. They would feel the same envy. And to keep their own personal
rewards rising, at a corporate executive-like pace, partners at top accounting
firms would take the same steps that partners at top law firms took. They
would supersize their partnerships.

Accounting firms actually supersized considerably faster than their law firm
counterparts. By the 1980s, just eight accounting firms were conducting virtually all the audits of companies listed on the New York Stock Exchange. In
1989, two megamergers brought this "Big Eight" down to the "Big Six," and
eight years later still another merger left the accounting profession dominated
by the "Big Five."[29]

But in accounting, unlike law, supersizing alone could not ensure the
princely earnings that Big Five partners had come to see as their natural right.
Corporations, after all, were merging, too, and each merger created fewer big
companies to be audited. Accounting firms, in a consolidating corporate
America, would need new revenue streams, and these new revenues, top
accounting firm partners concluded, could only come from the hot new field
of management consulting. That quaint old professional ethic — that auditing
firms ought to keep at arm's length from the companies they audit — would
simply have to go.

In the accounting profession that would emerge in the 1980s, auditing
would fill a new and considerably less elevated role. Audits would no longer be
about helping the investing public unearth business truth. Audits would now
be "loss leaders," a strategic maneuver accounting firms could employ "to get
their foot in a client's door and win consulting contracts."[30] Revenues from
these contracts would come eventually to overshadow totally revenues from
auditing. In 2001, PricewaterhouseCoopers would bill the Tyco International
conglomerate $13 million for auditing services and nearly triple that total, $38
million, for consulting work on taxes, acquisitions, and technology. Raytheon,
the military hardware company, paid PricewaterhouseCoopers $3 million for
auditing that same year — and $48 million for consulting.[31]

All this consulting, notes corporate researcher Philip Mattera, "flew in the face of the accounting profession's independence rules." The guardians of the profession didn't seem to mind. Accounting professional groups actually lobbied hard *against* any moves that might reimpose traditional accounting values.[32] The profession's movers and shakers, now routinely averaging over $1 million each, had found a most lucrative niche in corporate America.[33] They were not about to let it go.

Accounting had finally become, at least at the top, a profession that paid. But making your way to that top still took time. Young accountants usually had to spend ten years at a Big Five firm before earning partner status — and the half-million dollars or so in annual compensation that typically came with it.[34] Not bad, but ambitious young partners found they could do considerably better by crossing over and crunching numbers *inside* the corporate world, as corporate financial officers. Corporate CFOs, by the 1990s, were routinely taking home $1.5 million in annual compensation.[35] Some were doing considerably better. Mark Swartz, for instance, left his professional home at one Big Five accounting firm, Deloitte & Touche, and became the chief financial officer at Tyco International. In 2001, Swartz earned nearly $35 million.[36]

Back in the accountant cubbyholes at Deloitte & Touche, Ernst & Young, and the rest of the Big Five, ambitious auditors watched this desk-swapping closely. They would come to see, naturally enough, each audit they conducted as a lucrative career-changing opportunity. Smart auditors, by making just the right impression on the company they were auditing, could end up hired to a cushy company executive slot. And smart auditors didn't need to be told how to make that right impression. To get along, they played along — with the sorts of corporate financial sleights-of-hand that old Arthur Andersen would have delighted in exposing.

The entire auditing process, from the corporate perspective, now worked beautifully. Accounting firms, the supposed corporate "watchdog," no longer had any interest in subjecting the companies they audited to searching, tough-minded audits. The senior partners at these firms saw every auditing relationship as a first step toward a lucrative consulting contract. Why spoil the chances for that contract by giving an audited company a hard time? The lowly accountants who did the actual auditing work, meanwhile, had little reason to blow the whistle on their solicitous superiors. Why make a scene and risk spoiling a corporate job opportunity? Why can't we all just be friends?

In this clubby environment, accountants no longer stood at arm's length from their clients. Indeed, auditors frequently found themselves interacting with corporate officials who used to be their supervisors or colleagues. Such incestuous relationships, one academic observer, the University of Richmond's Paul Clikeman, pointed out, practically invited shenanigans. Accountants doing audits, he explained, could hardly be expected to maintain "proper professional skepticism when questioning their friend and former colleague."[37] These former colleagues, in turn, knew all the tricks of the auditing trade.

"The former auditor's knowledge of the audit firm's testing techniques," Clikeman observed in 1998, "may allow the client to manipulate the financial statements in ways that are least likely to be detected."[38]

By the time Clikeman made that observation, corporations had plenty of reason to want their financial statements manipulated. Real corporate profits had soared between 1992 and 1997, and those soaring profits had kept share prices — and executive stock option jackpots — soaring, too. But real profit growth, by 1998, had stalled. In fact, as economist Paul Krugman notes, the after-tax profits of the S&P 500 grew barely at all over the last three years of the century. For corporate executives, now fully accustomed to option windfalls, this would not do. If real profits weren't rising, they would just have to find some fake profits. And they did. Between 1997 and 2000, the corporations that make up the S&P 500 were able to report out, thanks to creative accounting, a whopping 46 percent jump in corporate earnings. Accounting smoke and mirrors, explains Krugman, had created "the illusion of profit growth."[39] And that illusion drove executive earnings to all-time record levels.

This most helpful illusion came courtesy of the accounting profession.

At Xerox, for instance, executives created a $1.5 billion phony profit, between 1997 and 2000, by faking $3 billion in nonexistent revenues.[40] The gyrations Xerox went through to fake these revenues clearly violated standard accounting rules, and one brave auditor at KPMG, the accounting firm handling the Xerox audit, had the temerity to point this violation out. Xerox executives were displeased. They asked KPMG for a new auditor. KPMG supplied one. KPMG would receive $62 million in fees from Xerox over the century's last three years, over half from consulting.[41]

Not everyone would turn a blind eye to this rampant faking and fraud. Arthur Levitt Jr., the Securities and Exchange Commission chairman, charged at the start of the new century that auditors and corporate executives had joined "in a game of winks and nods." In corporate financial reports, Levitt asserted, "integrity may be losing out to illusion."[42] Nobody paid Levitt much mind. Congressional leaders shrugged. Who cared?

And then came the collapse of Enron. Within a year, the most noble accounting firm of them all, Arthur Andersen, the firm that embodied the heart and soul of the accounting profession, had ceased to exist as an auditing entity.[43] Enron and Arthur Andersen had been joined at the hip. Former Andersen employees filled Enron's executive offices, in slots ranging from treasurer to chief accounting officer. Andersen accountants and Enron executives, a report released by Enron's board of directors would later note, worked side-by-side to inflate revenues and conceal liabilities. Personnel who would not cooperate were shunted aside. For professional services rendered, over the course of this collaboration, Andersen would take in from Enron $1 million a week.[44]

In the wake of Enron's spectacular collapse and Andersen's equally spectacular professional misconduct, accounting industry flacks endeavored to dismiss Andersen as some foul rotten apple in an otherwise healthy barrel. The face-saving would not wash. Within months after Enron's crash, every giant accounting firm in the nation had come under suspicion and serious investigation. KPMG for work with Xerox. Deloitte & Touche for Adelphia. PricewaterhouseCoopers for MicroStrategy. Ernst & Young for PeopleSoft.[45] Accounting as a profession stood disgraced.

And humiliated. In Portland, Oregon, a minor league baseball team staged an "Arthur Andersen Appreciation Night." Fans were handed $10 receipts for $5 tickets.[46] In Congress, reformers rushed to snatch away from the accounting profession all regulatory autonomy. The resulting Public Company Accounting Reform and Investor Protection Act, enacted midway through 2002, created a powerful new board to oversee the auditors of public companies. The new board, Senator Paul Sarbanes proudly noted, would have "the authority to set standards" and "investigate and discipline accountants." It would be answerable to the Securities and Exchange Commission, not the accounting profession. The Public Company Accounting Reform and Investor Protection Act, Sarbanes summed up, "will mark the end of weak self-regulation on the part of public company auditors."[47]

Out across the nation, average Americans applauded the new legislation. Accountants, after all, could not be trusted. Accountants, meanwhile, wondered what had happened to their profession. The older the accountant, the deeper the shock.

"I'm heartbroken," one retired Arthur Andersen accountant, Albert Pollans, told a reporter. "We were the best of the best, and we took a great deal of pride in our work."[48]

BY THE EARLY YEARS OF THE TWENTY-FIRST CENTURY, many physicians felt the same distress, as professionals, as accountant Albert Pollans. These doctors labored in large institutions where basic decisions about patient care, decisions they had invested years of their lives to learn how to make, were now made by "bean-counters," financial analysts who had never ever taken a pulse or written out a prescription. Doctors in these institutions felt pressured and second-guessed, at every turn. They could be berated if they lingered with individual patients, scolded if they didn't empty out hospital beds rapidly enough. In short, they felt they could no longer practice as they saw professionally fit.

This humiliation would be, for doctors, an exceptionally bitter pill to swallow. No professionals in the entire United States, perhaps the entire world, had worked harder, or more successfully, to control the practice of their profession. American doctors, by the mid twentieth century, had achieved near total autonomy. Doctors themselves essentially determined how physicians were trained, how they were judged, even how they were paid. And lay Americans accepted these arrangements. They trusted doctors and valued their expertise. Politicians, for their part, feared doctors' collective clout. On medical matters, they largely let doctors, as a profession, determine public policy.

That, for American society overall, would prove to be a mistake. Doctors practice a profession that directly and regularly impacts everyone. In any modern society, as a consequence, everyone holds a vital, personal stake in basic decisions about medical care. No society should default this responsibility to doctors, or any one group.

Outside the United States, industrial nations have generally listened to doctors on matters of public policy, but not defaulted to them. Over time, these nations have all created health care systems that guarantee their citizens access to affordable medical care, usually through some form of national health care coverage. In the United States, by contrast, no national health coverage system would ever take hold. The United States, instead, would offer only Medicare and Medicaid, one program for the elderly, one for the poor. These two programs, both created in the 1960s, would not guarantee all Americans affordable health care. But they did guarantee doctors a wider paying clientele.

America's doctors, before Medicare and Medicaid, had practiced in an environment where some patients could afford to pay for services rendered and others, most notably the elderly and the poor, could not. In this America, a great deal of medical work either went uncompensated or compensated at less than the going rate. Medicare and Medicaid would modify these medical fee realities. Doctors would now be guaranteed, via tax dollars, "payments from millions of patients who previously were unable to afford the cost of their care."[49] These guarantees gushed new revenues into medicine — and gave doctors a powerful incentive to see as many patients, and perform as many procedures, as possible. The more "care" doctors could provide, the more they could earn.

In earlier ages, similar economic temptations had led to shockingly unprofessional medical messes. In the 1700s, for instance, authorities at the English Royal Hospital at St. Bartholomew famously decided to pay surgeons by the limb. The more limbs they amputated, the higher their total fees. This new pay-for-performance approach to compensation would not long endure. After a significant leap in the number of London limbless, hospital authorities changed course and required their suddenly saw-happy surgeons to obtain advance approval before moving ahead with any amputation.[50]

By the 1970s, American surgeons were no longer doing much amputating. But they did seem eager, especially after Medicare and Medicaid, to cut into patients at the slightest provocation. By the mid 1970s, researchers had begun keeping statistics on unnecessary operations. By the mid 1980s, an extensive academic literature was demonstrating "that perhaps 10 to 30 percent of diagnostic tests, procedures, and hospital admissions are unnecessary."[51] These procedures, necessary and unnecessary alike, were paying off handsomely. Top medical specialists could command, by the 1990s, $500,000 a year and more — and that for just performing three operations a week.[52]

Such stunning rewards would, not surprisingly, help swell the number of medical specialists in the United States. Why become a general practitioner when specialty practice could be so much more lucrative? Doctors in the United States, by the late 1980s, accounted for about the same percentage of the overall population as doctors in Canada. But specialists in the United States would make up a far greater percentage of the physician population. In Canada, 52 percent of doctors would engage in primary care general practice. In the United States, only 33 percent.[53]

American doctors who couldn't become famed specialists could still find fortune — by investing in clinical laboratories and other ancillary medical services, then referring their patients to these facilities. "Self-referrals," by the 1990s, had become a national scandal. A quarter of the nation's independent clinical labs, federal investigators found, "were owned at least in part by physicians who made referrals of items or services to them."[54] Florida doctors with an ownership interest in radiation therapy units, one federal investigation found, were referring patients to radiation at a rate 50 percent higher than the national radiation referral average — and their patients were paying, for therapy, over 40 percent more than average radiation patients elsewhere.[55]

"Not infrequently, when we find cases of abnormally high and questionable utilization," a top official in the Health and Human Services Department's Inspector General Office would later tell Congress, "there is a financial reward at work."[56]

Not all physicians, of course, were chasing recklessly after financial rewards, but enough were to keep incomes of physicians increasing far faster than the incomes of their patients. In 1973, private practice physicians earned four times the U.S. median income. Two decades later, in 1994, physicians averaged over eight times the national median.[57]

An angry public would lash back. Society had granted doctors autonomy. Doctors, the public felt, had abused it. Society, in moves big and small, would now start taking that autonomy away, telling doctors what they could and could not do. In 1989 and 1993, Congress would go after "self-referrals," enacting legislation that prohibited Medicare payments for lab services when the physician who ordered the services had a "financial relationship" with the lab.[58] The entities footing the bill for most of American health care, the federal government and large employers, also began implementing programs that subjected doctors to "case-by-case assessments" of the care they were providing.[59] These "utilization management" programs infuriated physicians. Case-by-case reviews, they charged, were squeezing professional judgment out of the practice of medicine.

"Conscious of being watched," noted Dr. George Dunea, a physician at Chicago's Cook County Hospital, "many doctors are beginning to practice an undesirable brand of defensive medicine, ordering tests with an eye on the reviewers, admitting or discharging patients merely because the criteria say so, calling in consultants to cover all bases."

All this, Dr. Dunea added, went totally against the grain of what the professional practice of medicine ought to be about.

"How can medicine be practiced by the book," he lamented, "when each new day calls for intuitive decisions, short cuts, compromises, strategies designed for this patient only and nobody else?"[60]

Physicians would soon face even greater pressures on their professionalism — from for-profit corporate medical empires. Medicine had become so intensely lucrative, by the 1980s, that entrepreneurs suddenly saw no reason to leave health to the nonprofits that had traditionally operated America's hospitals. These entrepreneurs quickly started buying up and privatizing community hospitals. Then, to shake profits out of hospitals that had always functioned on a nonprofit basis, the new investor-owned chains began standardizing medical care. What they couldn't standardize, they eliminated.

This standardizing and squeezing would work wonders for the bottom lines of the new health care corporate empires. Their imperial CEOs would be suitably rewarded. In 1994, the top executive at U.S. Healthcare, Leonard Abramson, would sit on a personal stash of company stock worth over $784 million.[61] Fortunes this imposing could often only be maintained via outright fraud. Columbia/HCA chief executive Richard Scott would resign in 1997 amid a massive federal probe into kickbacks and overbilling. By that time, he had accumulated $338 million worth of Columbia/HCA shares.[62]

Major employers did not smile upon all this health care profiteering. Their health care costs were spiraling totally out of control. They demanded relief. Health maintenance organizations — HMOs — promised to deliver it. HMOs rejected the traditional fee-for-service model of medical care in the United States. They charged large employers fixed lump sums for each employee. In return, they guaranteed employees all the care they needed. This approach to financing health care, HMO enthusiasts proclaimed, would give medical professionals an incentive to keep people well. The healthier people became, the fewer health services they would require, the lower overall medical spending.

The theory sounded fine. But, in an unequal America, the theory would not work. In America's traditional fee-for-service system, *unnecessary* services proliferated. Under HMOs, *necessary* services would simply not be performed. Big money for HMO kingpins, in a "managed care" environment, could only be made if expenditures for health care services were kept down as low as possible. And they would be kept down — by pressuring doctors to practice by the book and avoid any and all "intuitive decisions."

HMO executives, not practicing doctors, would reap the subsequent rewards. Dr. Malik Hasan, the neurologist who ran Health Systems International Inc., would end up Colorado's highest-paid executive in 1995. He took home $20.5 million that year.[63] He made, in effect, more in two days than average doctors could earn in an entire year.

Physicians who actually spent their days with patients noticed, and resented, these sorts of disparities. In 2002, *Medical Economics* magazine asked doctors in general practice if they were sorry they had gone into primary care. An astounding 73 percent said yes.[64]

Patients, one young doctor, Cynthia Howard, told *Medical Economics*, had little patience with her in the new medical marketplace. They would even balk, Dr. Howard explained, if she tried to collect a $10 Medicare copayment.

"You already make a million dollars a year," the patients would tell her, "so why do you need my money?"

Howard, a practitioner in Texas, didn't make a million dollars, or anything close.

"Where else but in medicine in 2002 can you find a job that has no vacation pay or sick time; no retirement benefits or health care coverage; and no certain paycheck?" Howard asked. "No wonder med school admissions are down."

For doctors who just wanted to be doctors, to enjoy the respect of their communities and make a decent living, the profession no longer worked. The concentration of the dollars Americans spend on health care had left a wound that medicine could not heal.

IN A THRIVING, VIBRANT CULTURE, talented young people follow their hearts. They seek out professions that catch their imaginations. Some choose to teach. Some become chemists. Some nurse. Some preach. Some raise cut flowers. Wise cultures encourage young people to choose professions that tickle their fancies. Economies only develop to their fullest, these cultures understand, when people are working at trades they enjoy.

In societies that tend toward equality, young people will naturally tend to gravitate to the professions that bring them the most satisfaction. If no one line of work offers *substantially* more compensation than any other, most talented young people will pick as their life's work the profession they find most personally appealing.

Professions themselves, in more equal societies, must always strive to remain appealing or risk watching talented young people go elsewhere. Equality, in effect, gives professions an extra incentive to manage their affairs professionally. Professions that let down their professional guard and fail to discipline misbehavior within their ranks will lose public respect — and the interest of young people who might otherwise have chosen to enter into them. And professions that neglect their responsibility to maintain a pleasant working environment for practitioners will also turn off young people. Only rare birds will willingly devote a career to a tense and distasteful daily grind. More equal societies, in short, keep professions on their toes, anxious to please both public and practitioners.

In less equal societies, the incentives all run in the opposite direction. In societies that tolerate significant gaps in compensation within and between professions, talented young people have a rational reason *not* to follow their hearts. If some lines of work can offer their practitioners five times more, or perhaps even fifty times more, than others, then monetary rewards will eventually dominate young people's career decisions.

Roy Smith made his life's work decision in 1966, right after graduating from the Harvard Business School. Smith chose to go into investment banking. Only one other graduate from his business school class made the same choice, a not particularly surprising statistic. Investment banking, at that time, offered rewards not appreciably higher than any other business field. Smith's starting salary at Goldman Sachs would be a mere $9,500, with no guaranteed bonus.[65]

Three decades later, graduates from top business schools could start an investment banking career at as much as $235,000 a year.[66] And almost all of them seemed to want to do so. Investment banking, once a yawner, had suddenly become a magnet. One investment house, in 1990, received thirty-six thousand applications.[67]

Only a handful of these applicants would, of course, ever manage to get a foot in the door. But investment banking and other professions that offered jackpot earnings would continue to lure America's "most talented young people to pass up careers in engineering, manufacturing, civil service, teaching and other occupations."[68] Societies, economists Robert Frank and Philip Cook argue, suffer mightily when young people are so tempted.

"The economic pie would be larger," the two explain, "if more bright students abandoned their quest to become multimillionaire personal-injury lawyers for the more modest paychecks of electrical engineers."[69]

Individual young people, not just societies, suffer when outsized rewards bias career choices. Those who choose work they don't relish for a paycheck they do can often end up stewing in affluence. And those who choose work that speaks to their hearts, not their wallets, can end up feeling devalued — by a society that rewards other professions at levels far higher than theirs.

No profession in the United States, by century's end, would count in its ranks more of these devalued professionals than education.

Education in America has never paid particularly well. Educators have always earned less than comparably educated professionals in other fields. For years, that didn't much matter to the nation at large. The schools could still attract significant numbers of talented young people, despite poor pay, simply because significant numbers of talented young people — women and people of color — were effectively barred from entering most other careers. American education enjoyed, in effect, a captive talent pool.

The great social struggles of the 1960s and 1970s would topple many of the barriers that kept minorities and women captive. In the new, more socially equal America, schools would now have to compete for talent with other professions. In this competition, they would prove unable to keep up. The gap between educator salaries and compensation in other fields would actually widen. Between 1990 and 2000, the average salary of a veteran New York City teacher would rise seven times slower than the compensation of a partner at a top New York law firm — and four times slower than the average salary of a computer science grad from a top university.[70] In the 1990s, years of low inflation, teaching salaries in New York would not even keep up with the cost of living.[71]

"If you don't have a competitive compensation program, talented people will not give you a second look," the *School Administrator* journal noted in 2001. "In the war for talented employees, organizations outside education seem to be winning all the battles."[72]

In the 1990s, elected leaders and education policy makers desperately searched for "work-arounds" that could somehow offset the impact of widening pay gaps. Early in the decade these policy makers would cheer when one recent Princeton grad suggested a bold new program to place talented young people into teaching. Her new "Teach for America" effort would invite grads from top universities to take two years off their march up the career ladder to teach in an impoverished public school. Those self-sacrificing, idealistic young grads who accepted the offer would then receive six weeks of summertime training to get them ready to enter the classroom and make a difference for kids.

Teach for America, the claim went, would bring into America's most hard-pressed schools the energy and enthusiasm of some of America's most talented young people. In return, the claim continued, these talented young people would receive a priceless, life-enriching experience. They could do good, in Teach for America, and then go on to do well — in some more financially fitting profession.

The claims would not pan out.[73] Many of Teach for America's young people would not stick out their two-year stints. Those who did left their assignments with mixed feelings.

"Did I change my school? No." noted one, who went on to attend Yale Law School. "Did I change the lives of some of my kids? I hope so. Is that enough? I don't know."[74]

Many career teachers, on the other hand, had no mixed feelings whatsoever about Teach for America. They considered the program an insult, plain and simple, to their profession. Few young people of talent, Teach for America assumed, could ever be expected to devote a career to a profession as unappealing as teaching. So schools ought to be grateful, ran the program's unspoken subtext, that at least some talented young ones were willing to give teaching two years of their valuable time, especially since these bright young folks have actually spent six whole weeks learning how to teach.

Most career educators at disadvantaged schools resented that subtext, but they swallowed hard and welcomed unprepared teachers into their schools anyway. What choice did they have? In an unequal America, efforts like Teach for America would be the best that public schools could realistically expect.

GROWING INEQUALITY, IN THE LATE TWENTIETH CENTURY, worked to devalue almost everyone who labored in the public sector, not just educators. Even the most highly rewarded of public sector professionals would end the century feeling distinctly second-class.

A number of these professionals worked at the federal Securities and Exchange Commission. These lawyers and accountants labored nobly to protect investors from stock market scams. They could have chosen careers on Wall Street. They chose public service instead. The Securities and Exchange Commission certainly did have its attractions. SEC service, as one proud staffer noted, offered "opportunities not easily found elsewhere: the chance to work on novel and important issues, the opportunity to collaborate with an unusually nice group of colleagues (especially rare for lawyers!) and, not least, the chance to feel good about what you do for a living."[75]

But these pleasures would be largely canceled out, in the boom years, by the vast pay gap that separated SEC staffers and their counterparts on Wall Street.

"Every day," SEC staffer Martin Kimel would later explain, "my colleagues and I speak with securities lawyers in the private sector who are earning two to three times our salaries (not counting bonuses and stock options)."

These exchanges, not surprisingly, left staffers like Kimel feeling like saps. Many would leave the SEC. And those who gritted their teeth and hung on anyway, because they valued the work they were doing too much to leave, came to be seen as losers. If they actually had anything on the ball, the industry scuttlebutt went, they would be working on Wall Street. Summed up Kimel: "It is as if those of us who stay too long — and I am talking years, not decades — risk being labeled as spoiled milk."[76]

The same pressures would bear down on the nation's judiciary in the 1990s. Over the course of the decade, fifty-four federal judges discarded their judicial robes for greener pastures in the private sector. In the 1960s, years of far smaller pay gaps between public and private service, only three federal judges left the bench to work elsewhere.[77]

"Something is horribly wrong," exclaimed one frustrated federal judge in Florida, Edward Davis, "when my law clerks can leave me, after serving two years, and go to New York and make more money than I made as a judge."[78]

A great deal more. In 1990, the sixty-odd partners at the law firm of Cravath, Swaine & Moore, on average, each earned "more than the nine justices of the U.S. Supreme Court combined."[79]

These sorts of discrepancies, Supreme Court Chief Justice William Rehnquist would argue early in the new century, endanger the very quality of justice in America. Judges needed to be totally independent, not beholden to litigants who might be their future employers. The "large and growing disparity" between public and private sector pay in the legal profession, Rehnquist would entreat, simply "must be decreased if we hope to continue to provide our nation a capable and effective federal judicial system."[80] The nation cannot afford to have a judiciary "limited to the wealthy or the inexperienced."[81]

Rehnquist delivered this lament in 2002 before a blue-ribbon National Commission on the Public Service chaired by Paul Volcker, the former Federal Reserve Board chairman. The panel's hearings actually attracted not just one, but two, Supreme Court justices. The judiciary, Associate Chief Justice Stephen Breyer asked the commission to remember, was by no means "the only sector of the government with problems."

"Salaries do matter," Breyer testified. "If you keep cutting and cutting and cutting, you will find the institutional strength sapped. You will find morale diminished. You will find it harder to attract and keep people."[82]

Breyer's answer: Professional salaries in the public sector needed to be raised. A most reasonable position. But salaries in the public sector, in a nation where compensation at the top of the private sector had leaped to stratospheric heights, could never be raised high enough to compete effectively. The taxpaying public would not stand for it. In a deeply unequal nation, Breyer failed to see, public sector professions would always have to beg for respect — and talent.

Or would they? In a 2001 column, a *Wall Street Journal* commentator, Holman W. Jenkins Jr., argued that great concentrations of wealth actually promote quality public service. The more wealthy families about in the land, Jenkins contended, the bigger the pool of financially secure sons and daughters who can afford to labor in worthwhile but low-paying public service positions. His policy prescription? Keep those fortunes growing and inheritances flowing!

"With sizable inheritances to supplement their earnings," Jenkins noted, "more people from privileged backgrounds might become policemen, teachers, botanists or park rangers without making a big sacrifice."[83]

Trickle-down with a professional face.

MANY MILLIONS OF PROFESSIONALS IN THE UNITED STATES, from scientists to social workers, practice their professions neither in the public sector, for the government, nor in the private sector, for profit-making enterprises. These millions of professionals work in America's nonprofit sector.

Organizations in this nonprofit "independent sector" in some ways mirror their for-profit counterparts. In the nonprofit world, for instance, boards of directors set compensation levels for top executives, just as in the for-profit world. These compensation decisions, over recent years, have become increasingly contentious, again just as in the for-profit world. The reason? With pay rising so rapidly in the executive suites of corporate America, many board members in the independent sector have begun to feel that nonprofits simply must discard their traditionally modest executive pay standards — or risk becoming unable to attract top-flight executive talent. If nonprofits do not significantly increase their upper-most compensation, these board members have argued, they would "become employers of last resort" and find themselves stuck with leadership unable to "juggle multiple tasks and motivate both professionals and volunteers."[84]

These arguments for higher executive pay resonate well on the boards of most big-time nonprofits. Many members of these boards, after all, are themselves corporate executives in the private sector. And these arguments also resonate, naturally, with the executives of big-time nonprofits. These executives are constantly rubbing shoulders with their corporate counterparts, at board meetings, at fundraising galas, on blue-ribbon commissions. They consider their jobs every bit as demanding as executive jobs in the for-profit sector. They feel they deserve comparable rewards.

These rewards would start coming in the late twentieth century. By the mid 1990s, America's most generous private universities were paying their top executives one-half million dollars a year.[85] Foundations, another category of big-time nonprofits, would keep pace.[86] One top foundation executive, the Lilly Endowment's Thomas Lofton, took home $450,000 in 1997 salary, plus another $163,648 in benefits.

"We have to compete," explained one Silicon Valley foundation official, Colburn Wilbur, "to get qualified people."[87]

This competition would soon drive top nonprofit salary packages over the million-dollar mark. The president of the Sloan Kettering Cancer Center would draw $1,077,500 to open the twenty-first century.[88]

The Internal Revenue Service, the nation's arbiter of which organizations qualify for tax-free, nonprofit status and which do not, did not find such paychecks unreasonable. Under IRS regulations, any compensation amount "as would ordinarily be paid for like services by like enterprises under like circumstances" could not be defined as "excessive." With executive compensation at "like enterprises" in the private sector soaring, nonprofits would have no problem justifying their bountiful executive rewards.[89]

But nonprofits would have problems footing the bill for this generosity. Nonprofits, unlike their for-profit counterparts, have no stock jackpots to award. Any generosity they opt to extend to executives has to come out of actual — and limited — budget dollars. Major nonprofits might have enough of these dollars to be able to significantly hike executive pay. Few have the dollars, or the inclination, to raise average employee pay at the same significant rate. The result: widening pay gaps between the executives at top nonprofits and their professional staffs.

These gaps can sometimes tear nonprofit institutions into warring camps. In 1995, at Long Island's Adelphi University, an angry faculty voted 131 to 14 to demand the firing of the college's president, Peter Diamandopoulos. Adelphi's board of trustees had made Diamandopoulos the country's second highest-paid college president — the first, Boston University's John Silber, sat on Adelphi's board — and supplemented his ample $523,636 salary by outfitting him with a $1.2 million apartment in New York City and a $401,000 condo closer to campus in Long Island's Garden City.[90]

Similar pay scandals would erupt throughout the nonprofit world in the 1990s, in organizations ranging from the United Way to the Baptist Church.[91] Each took a heavy organizational toll — and not just on the individual nonprofit in the headlines.

"The whole nonprofit sector suffers for the 'highly publicized' transgressions of a few," the lead association of the nonprofit world, the Independent Sector, would note in a report published in 2000. "The public holds the nonprofit sector to a 'higher standard.'"[92]

Astronomically high salaries for nonprofit executives, Harvard analyst Peter Frumkin would add, erode that "higher standard" in any number of ways. They weaken "a community's confidence in the motives of nonprofit workers." They shake "the confidence of clients." They undermine "the ability of donors to assume a link between the size of their gift and the amount of charitable services delivered."[93]

Without community, client, and donor confidence, nonprofits cannot thrive. Lower levels of confidence translate, inexorably, into lower revenues, into program cutbacks and salary freezes for the professional staffers who do the actual day-by-day work of every major nonprofit. These professionals didn't go into nonprofit work to become rich. But they also didn't expect to work under nonprofit executives who *are* getting rich — or with clients and donors upset by these executive riches. These professionals went into nonprofit work to do good and feel good about the work they are doing. In an America more and more unequal, this work would bring fewer and fewer of these good feelings.

WE TEND TO THINK ABOUT *THE* PROFESSIONS, in our everyday discourse, as medicine and law, as accounting and architecture, as teaching, the ministry, or nursing. We typically, on hearing *profession*, visualize fields of identifiable work with special schools and degrees, specific standards and certificates. But we also use *profession*, informally, to describe almost any body of skilled work. Law enforcement can be a profession, dressmaking a profession, child care a profession. And we recognize, as well, that people in every line of endeavor yearn to be considered — and treated — as professionals in the work they do, for good reason. To be treated as a professional, in our life's work, is to be respected, is to be given the autonomy to make basic decisions that affect our work. To be a professional is to make judgments, not just take orders. To be a professional is to take pride in what we do, to share our expertise, to insist on quality.

Wise societies welcome and nurture professional attitudes. Wise societies want the people who labor within them, all people, to approach their work as professionals. Indeed, the wisest of societies recognize that professionalism knows no collar color, that blue-collar work, or pink-collar work, can be every bit as professional as white-collar effort. In human labor, as the English social critic R. H. Tawney told us more than four score years ago, there is no distinctive difference "between building schools and teaching in them when built, between providing food and providing health."

"The work of making boots or building a house is in itself no more degrading than that of curing the sick or teaching the ignorant," Tawney explained. "It is as necessary and therefore as honorable. It should be at least equally bound by rules which have as their object to maintain the standards of professional service."[94]

A wiser America would, following Tawney, treat all workers as potential professionals.

Some, no doubt, will object to any characterization of all working people as potential professionals. How can workers on an auto assembly line, these skeptics might ask, ever be considered "professionals"? These workers, after all, just turn same bolt day after day, year after year. They have no body of knowledge to master, no skill to perfect. They just turn bolts. They will never merit, in some people's minds, true professional status.

But these workers, if treated as just bolt-turners, will never perform truly good work either. Indeed, as the effective enterprise literature teaches us, any enterprise that keeps people endlessly engaged in mind-numbing repetitive work will never operate effectively. Effective enterprises don't treat autoworkers as bolt-turners. They treat them as automakers. They encourage them to collaborate with their fellow automakers to come up with new ways to make cars. In an empowered environment, workers do not turn bolts, they craft cars. They can take pride in their work. They can be professionals.

But few workers will ever behave professionally in a plant, in a company, in a nation, where inequality is rising. Few workers will behave professionally in situations where they are expected to be clever so someone else can become disproportionately richer.

Inequality, at every turn, subverts the professional spirit. Every worker, in every workplace, should be a professional. In a more equal world, and only in a more equal world, every worker could be.

SPORTS WITHOUT WINNERS

IN A GOOD SOCIETY, people derive great pleasure both from the work they do and the games they play. In troubled societies, where work brings little pleasure, we flee to our games. Indeed, the less pleasure we take from our work, the more we seem to sink our psyches in the games we play — and watch.

In modern America, many millions of our lives now revolve, almost exclusively, around the games we call sports. We awake to the radio and listen for the latest scores. We troop down to the den, or out to a gym, and pedal away on a stationary bike to game highlights flashing on the twenty-four-hour sports network of our choice. At breakfast, we pore over the sports pages. In the car, on the way to work, we tune in our favorite sports-talk show. On the job, we talk sports at the water cooler — and rue the upset that cost us a big win in the weekly office football pool. On weekends, we could, if we wanted, watch ballgames from noon to midnight. In modern America, "SportsWorld" never ends.[1]

Our sports-obsessed lives have become easy to mock. But we cannot deny the pleasure that sports can bring. We delight in the drama of never knowing how a game will end. We marvel at athletic artistry honed over years of practice. And we learn. We learn, through watching and participating in sports, lessons worth treasuring, lessons about loyalty and trust, about diligence and courage, about the bonds that link people, about the barriers that keep people apart. Sports can even nurture democratic values. In sports bars, everyone is entitled to an opinion. In short pants, at the starting line of a 10K run, everybody's equal.

The ancient Greeks knew the pleasures that sports can bring. So did our grandparents. But sports played a considerably different role in their social orders. Sports rumbled along at the margins of their societies, an economically inconsequential enterprise. Sports offered escape and little more. Now sports offer fortunes. Sports have become a driving economic force, a high-stakes business, an essential corporate sector.

How essential? The games we play and watch have become a $213 billion annual operation.[2] How corporate? Of the 116 major league franchises in baseball, football, basketball, and hockey, publicly traded corporations control 84, either wholly or partly.[3] Pro sports teams no longer muddle along as economic small-fry. The single most lucrative franchise in American sports, the New York Yankees, pulled in $800 million in revenues from 1996 through 2000.[4]

Sports fans, at century's end, didn't need to be told that sports had become big business. Sports pages seemed, at times, to carry more about the money athletes were making than the games they were playing. The numbers, year after year, would escalate ever higher. Baseball's highest salary in 1988: $2.4 million for catcher Gary Carter. In 1993, $6.2 million for outfielder-first base-man Bobby Bonilla. In 1998, $10 million for outfielder Albert Belle. In 2003, $22 million for shortstop Alex Rodriguez.[5]

Owners of franchises, for their part, could receive even more impressive rewards. Sports could pay, from an ownership perspective, in any number of ways. Owners could reward themselves, or their family, with multiple-digit salaries and consulting agreements. Yankees owner George Steinbrenner once paid himself $25 million for negotiating a cable television deal.[6] In 2001, one pro football owner paid himself $7.5 million.[7] Such sums counted as "business expenses." They could be deducted from a franchise's tax bill.

Owners enjoyed an assortment of other fortune-enhancing tax breaks as well. They could "depreciate" much of what they paid their players.[8] They could also play back-scratching games between their teams and their other properties. Owners with both a team and a television outlet in their portfolios could, for instance, have the rights to telecast their team's games sold dirt-cheap to the TV outlet. The TV property would then have cheap programming, the sports team a convenient year-end operating "loss" for tax purposes.[9]

But the real windfalls in American sports would not come from operating teams. The real windfalls would come from selling them. Pro sports leagues operate as cartels. As such, they limit supply, in this case, the number of teams. These limits make pro franchises scarce, and incredibly valuable, commodities. In the boom years, franchise values jumped even more rapidly than stock values. In 1997, according to *Forbes*, the nation's football, basketball, baseball and hockey franchises were worth an average $146 million. The next year, *Forbes* tabbed their average value at $196 million.[10] By 1999, for just one fabled fran-chise, the Washington Redskins, bidders were offering $800 million.[11]

The buyers and sellers of sports franchises, and the athletes who play for them, seemed to inhabit, by century's end, their own special world. Owners had always been well-to-do. Now players appeared to be living at levels of lux-ury equally distant from the everyday lives of everyday fans. In 1956, baseball's flashiest star, Jackie Robinson, earned $42,500, a salary nine times the income of the average household. Just over four decades later, baseball's flashiest star, Ken Griffey Jr., would make over $8.5 million. Griffey's 1997 earnings would top average household incomes by about two hundred times.[12]

Fans, by Griffey's era, had begun seeing players and owners as members of the same exclusive club, multimillionaires all. And the frequent squabbles between players and owners would leave fans, even the nation's number one fan, totally mystified.

"It's just a few hundred folks trying to figure out how to divide nearly $2 billion," President Bill Clinton would complain during the 1995 baseball lockout. "They ought to be able to figure that out."[13]

But they couldn't, and that didn't make any sense, not to fans. With all that money flowing about, why couldn't players and owners get along? And why weren't owners and players, with all that money they were getting, giving fans their money's worth and more? Why weren't they treating fans to a new golden age of sports?

For fans, at the start of the twenty-first century, the sports experience had come to feel anything but golden. Average fans, in fact, seemed to be taking less pleasure from the games they followed, not more. Most fans couldn't articulate exactly *why* sports so often left them disappointed, not in so many words, but they had their suspicions. Money, too much money, many suspected, had made a real mess out of sports. They suspected right. America's workplaces couldn't escape the poisons that spread whenever too much money collects in too few pockets. Neither could America's pastimes.

IN SPORTS, DOWN THROUGH THE GENERATIONS, wealthy people and average working people have always coexisted rather uneasily. Wealthy people owned the teams, working people rooted for them. This relationship could sometimes sour. A tightwad owner might dump a popular player. Tempers would flare. Hearts would be broken. Storm clouds would circle.

The storms would usually pass. Owners and fans would forgive and forget. But not always. A particularly upset owner might, in a huff, yank his team out of one city and plop it into another. But owners, however unhappy they may have become with one city, always realized they needed average working people. If they couldn't win the hearts of average fans in one town, they would just have to find another town where they could. Rich people might *own* the nation's sports franchises, the movers and shakers in sports understood, but their teams, to be successful, had to *belong* to average people. A sports franchise simply could not flourish, assumed the conventional wisdom in mid twentieth century America, without the support of fans from average working families.

America would change over the last half of the twentieth century. So would the assumptions of America's sports franchise ownership. In the new America that emerged in the 1980s, the economy would no longer revolve around average, middle class households. In the new America, income and wealth would tilt toward the top, and owners would tilt that way, too. Owners would no longer covet the average fan. The average fan spent only average money. The real money, in a much more unequal America, now rested in affluent pockets. Franchise owners, in the 1980s and 1990s, would move heaven and earth to get these pockets picked.

A great deal of earth. Bulldozers and backhoes would redefine American sports in the late twentieth century. Across the United States, wherever professional sports were played, deluxe new ballparks and arenas, veritable sports palaces, would rise up to host the nation's favorite games. This unprecedented "stadia mania" added fifty-one new facilities to America's urban landscape in the 1990s alone, at a cost of nearly $11 billion. By 2005, experts estimated at the turn of the century, twenty-five additional new ballparks and arenas, costing another $7 billion, were likely to open.[14]

These new sports palaces replaced, in most cases, stadiums built in the 1960s and 1970s, facilities that still had years of useful life ahead. But these older facilities had been built for a different America. They lacked what owners now craved and demanded: luxury accommodations for America's affluent.

Ballparks, of course, had always offered special seating for fans with deeper pockets. Patrons who wanted to sit up close to the action would pay a few dollars extra per ticket for a "box seat." Anybody could buy one. Almost anybody, by saving up a little, could afford one. These box seats would remain the ultimate in ballpark luxury until 1965, the year the Houston Astros introduced a new twist on the premium seat notion.[15] The Astrodome, the world's first domed ballpark, that year began offering "luxury suite" seating. These first "luxury suites" sat far from the field, high up along the Astrodome's upper rim. They amounted, essentially, to an afterthought, a maneuver to make money off an otherwise undesirable section of the stadium.

Three decades later, luxury suites would no longer be an afterthought. They would become the main motive for billions of dollars of new stadium construction. Any ballpark or arena that couldn't be reconfigured to prominently position luxury suites would now be considered obsolete. The new facilities that replaced these "obsolete" stadiums would be designed, from top to bottom, to maximize luxury seating opportunities.

In the nation's capital, the new MCI Center would open in 1997 with over one hundred luxury suites, available from $100,000 to $175,000 a year, and three thousand "club seats," each costing $7,500 on an annual basis.[16] Two years later, the new American Airlines Arena in Miami would raise the luxury seating bar. Miami's twenty special suites would feature dining rooms, lounge areas, plasma-screen TVs, computers, DVD players, and outside terraces with views of the city's downtown and harbor.[17]

In Washington, Miami, and the rest of America's pro basketball world, deep pockets more interested in watching than dining could also cheer from special courtside seating. In 1997, these front-row seats at New York's Madison Square Garden went for $1,000.[18] These same courtside seats, for the 2002-2003 season, ran $1,500 each.[19]

Pro football teams, in their vast stadiums, couldn't offer intimate "courtside" seats. They would make do with luxury suites and club seating sections. By the 2003 season, all but three teams in the National Football League would boast facilities that enabled them to offer some sort of "premium-level tickets."[20] Football fans, of course, didn't *have* to pay "premium" prices for their seats. All the new stadiums had plenty of standard seating options available. But these new standard seats would often come with a catch. In many of the new facilities, fans actually had to pay for the right to buy a seat. Owners called these rights "personal seat licenses." In Charlotte's new football stadium, the "right to buy a season ticket" cost $2,500.[21]

Not all standard seats in the new America would require seat licenses. But all standard seats would require, almost without exception, thick wallets. In the 1990s, analysts at the Team Marketing Report started tracking a "Fan Cost Index" that calculated, for a family of four, the cost of a day or a night out at a game. Included in the calculation: four average-price tickets, four small sodas, two small beers, four hot dogs, two game programs, two souvenir caps, and parking. In the 2002 season, the analysts found, families of four paid, on average, $145.21 to watch a Major League Baseball game in person. Attending a National Basketball Association game, in the winter of 2002, would set an average family back $277.19. The following fall, on the gridiron, a family of four paid, on average, $290.41 per game to see NFL football.[22] This "average," researchers noted, did not take into account the cost of "premium-level" tickets.[23] Overall, the prices on *regular* tickets for NFL games rose 77 percent between 1992 and 2002.[24]

In baseball, virtually the same ticket story played out. Prices for all seats catapulted over the closing decades of the twentieth century. In 1967, a field-level box seat to a Baltimore Orioles game cost a mere $3.25. A seat in the bleachers could be had for 75 cents.[25] For the 2003 Orioles season, a bleacher seat cost $13. Baltimore's bleacher seats, between 1967 and 2003, jumped in price four times faster than the inflation rate. Baltimore's field level box seats cost $35 each in 2003, more than twice as much as they would have cost if seat prices had just matched inflation.

In an economically top-heavy America, pro sports teams could always find enough fans to pay the new prices. And those willing to pay the highest going rates could look forward to royal treatment. At Washington's MCI Center, the high rollers in luxury seating enjoyed their own separate parking, their own separate entrance, their own separate restaurants, and even their own separate concourse, all "barred to the arena's 15,680 ordinary ticket holders."[26]

These "ordinary ticket holders" would not include many ordinary people. In the new America, sports arenas would essentially be off-limits to average people, even the workers who built them. The Washington Wizards charged an average $51 per ticket when the MCI Center opened. "At those prices," Percell Spinner, a carpenter who worked on the arena, told a reporter, "only the rich people can afford that."[27]

Even players would have problems paying for seat space. In Oakland, strong safety Lorenzo Lynch walked into the ticket office for his team's new football stadium and asked about buying eight seat licenses for his father and family. Lynch walked out empty handed. "Even with his $375,000 annual income," the San Jose *Mercury News* would later report, "he decided he couldn't swing the tickets."[28]

Going to ballgames, in mid twentieth century America, had been a basic rite of middle class passage. By the 1990s, few average families would be making that passage.

In America's new sports environment, rabid but unwealthy fans could occasionally still get a chance to go to a ballgame. Someone at work might know someone down in accounting with two extra tickets in the corporate box. Two buddies might score a good ticket deal on eBay. And if you waited until the second inning, a scalper might give you a break. But none of that helped parents who wanted to share with their kids the same memorable ballpark experiences their parents had shared with them. For working families, opportunities to enjoy an outing at the ballpark essentially no longer existed.

"So far," *Washington Post* sportswriter Thomas Boswell would note in 1996, "nobody has the first hint of a solution of how to get the average fan, and his family, back into the ballpark in the next century."[29]

SO WHAT'S THE BIG TRAGEDY? Fans can't afford to see a game in person? All they have to do, if they care that much about sports, is turn on the television. Every game worth seeing, by the 1990s, could be found somewhere on TV. And television coverage, all fans would have to agree, had gone ballistic! More cameras on the action, more stats on the screen. Add in remotes and picture-in-picture and fans could spend a Sunday on the couch and never miss a single important play. Throw your feet up, grab a beer. Sheer rapture!

Television executives would pay dearly to bring these rapturous moments to American fandom. In 1997, the Fox television network agreed to pay the NFL $17.6 billion to broadcast pro football games through 2004. The deal more than doubled each NFL team's TV income.[30]

For owners and star athletes, these TV dollars translated into enormous income gains. For fans, the high-priced TV rights meant more commercials. Many more commercials. Television executives, to make an adequate return on their investments, stuffed all the games they televised with as many ad minutes as they could possibly squeeze in. Football and basketball timeouts, from time immemorial, had lasted only a minute. Baseball players took about the same sixty seconds to change sides between innings. Now TV stretched these one-minute breaks to two minutes and more.

Even worse, TV producers, not coaches, started dictating the flow of game action. In football and basketball, TV now called most timeouts. "Commercial timeout" became as familiar a phrase to fans as "first down!" Games sputtered. The multiple commercial timeouts threw game rhythms out of kilter. Teams in football, before commercials totally took over, would line up quickly after a momentum-shifting interception, eager to run a play while they still held the psychological edge. TV now dulled that edge.

Longer commercial breaks also meant longer games. NFL games once fit nicely into three-hour time slots. By the late 1990s, the league was setting aside three hours and a quarter for each game telecast. To make sure games didn't spill over this expanded time frame, the NFL and the TV networks would have to take other steps as well. They would shorten halftimes — and also keep game clocks running in situations that had previously stopped the clock. The running game clocks made for fewer plays, on average, in NFL games. Better fewer plays, the networks figured, than fewer commercials.

Did fans have any right to expect anything better? The televised games were still free, weren't they? And what right did fans have to complain about a free product? Actually, by the 1990s, "free" games would be disappearing from America's TV screens. By 1997, for the first time ever, teams were streaming more games over paid cable than "free," over-the-air TV. This cable trend, observers agreed, only figured to increase. They pointed to the growing numbers of franchise ownership groups scrambling to create their own premium cable networks. Yankees principal owner George Steinbrenner started the stampede, in a 1999 deal that merged his club with the basketball New Jersey Nets and the hockey New Jersey Devils. The move created a year-round package of cable programming — and cleared Steinbrenner an estimated $200 million.[31] Other owners quickly figured out that they didn't really need to start their own cable network to boost their telecast earnings. They could extort higher rights fees out of the TV outlets currently carrying their games just by threatening to start up a new network.

All these ownership maneuvers — the new stadiums, the premium-priced seating, the television wheeling and dealing — would help baseball owners double their revenues between 1996 and 2001.[32] But the record revenues came at a price. The game was turning off fans. In Baltimore, Denver, Milwaukee, and Cleveland, all cities with sparkling new stadiums, attendance in 2002 hit new-ballpark record lows.[33] Baseball's "fall classic" the same year ended with the worst TV ratings of any seven-game World Series ever. Between 1991 and 2002, baseball's World Series ratings fell an amazing 50 percent.[34]

Other sports faced similar ratings woes.

"Broadcast television ratings for the four major professional sports — baseball, basketball, football and hockey — have been generally decreasing for more than a decade," a *New York Times* survey would note in 2001.[35]

Industry analysts groped for explanations. Pro sports, some suggested, had become too black for white audiences. Video games were distracting kids. Too many sports on too many channels were confusing viewers. Other analysts saw a more profound transformation at work. Owners, they argued, had turned sports into just another commodity. Owners and their minions no longer saw *fans*. They saw *consumers*.

"Teams aren't in cities anymore," explained the *Baltimore Sun*'s Michael Hill, "they're in markets."[36]

Consumers, the most astute sports observers began pointing out, simply do not see sports through the same emotional lens as *fans*.

"Instead of hoping that your team wins, you begin to demand it," notes NBC sportscaster Bob Costas. "It's like you bought a car and if it doesn't work, you want to know why. When a team doesn't win, instead of disappointment or heartbreak, you now have anger and resentment."[37]

In 1999, one careful observer, sports columnist Thomas Boswell, inventoried a month's worth of that anger. He noted a variety of incidents that had recently taken place in stadiums across America. Fans heaving ice chunks in Denver. Ten fans arrested and twenty ejected in Minneapolis. A mini-riot in Boston.

"Once, we went to games to let off steam. Now, we get steamed," Boswell lamented. "Whatever level of raw rage you think is circulating in our sports arenas, I promise you, it's higher."[38]

Why did the rage run so deep? Why did fans resent athletes so and not movie stars, one reporter asked a spectator at an NBA playoff game?

"Because," the fan shot back, "we don't have to pay $113 to get into a movie."[39]

WHAT IF MOVIE-GOERS DID HAVE TO PAY $113 to get into a movie? And what if, on top of paying that $113, they also had to pay, with their own tax dollars, the cost of building the theater they saw the movie in? How resentful might movie-goers get then?

Average American families, both those that follow sports and those that do not, have actually subsidized the transformation of professional sports into a luxury commodity. The tax dollars of working families, directly and indirectly, have bankrolled America's "stadia mania" — and shifted hundreds of millions of dollars into the pockets of some of America's richest people.

In 1997, for instance, billionaire Paul Allen asked Washington State to underwrite three-quarters of the cost of the new $425 million stadium he wanted built for his Seattle Seahawks football team. If the money weren't forthcoming, Allen noted, the Seahawks just might have to move elsewhere. The money came.[40]

Overall, between the mid 1980s and the end of the 1990s, governments at the state and local level expended some $7 billion on "new homes" for forty-one professional teams.[41] In the early 2000s, in Houston and also in Philadelphia, the tabs for new sports palace projects topped $1 billion, with much of that coming from public purses.[42]

Tax dollars from public purses did give government agencies of various stripes ownership rights over most of America's new sports stadiums. But the profits from these palaces flowed, almost exclusively, to team owners. In Maryland, state officials coaxed Art Modell, the owner of the Cleveland Browns, to move his team to Baltimore by building, to Modell's specifications, a new stadium that would eventually cost over $200 million. Under the terms of the deal, Modell gained the right to all profits from game concessions, parking, tickets, and advertising, plus half the gate receipts from any nonfootball event held in the new stadium. Modell paid no rent to use the stadium, only operating expenses, and also walked off with permission "to keep up to $75 million" from the sale of the new facility's "personal seat licenses."[43]

Meanwhile, over in Cleveland, public officials cut a desperate deal of their own. They agreed to replace Modell's operation by subsidizing a new stadium for a "new" Cleveland Browns franchise. The reborn Browns, in this stadium's opening year, would score a $36.5 million profit — for the team's private owners, not Cleveland.[44]

In some cities, angry taxpayers somehow found the backbone to stop schemes that would finance new ballparks at their expense. Franchise owners, in several instances, then went ahead and built their own stadiums, or at least that's what the public thought was happening. In fact, public tax dollars were pouring into these "privately" funded projects, through "government funded highways, off-ramps, rail connections, and parking lots."[45]

By 2001, with most of the construction dust settled, observers could finally get a clear look at what had transpired. No professional team, urban analyst Neal Peirce would note, "has failed to snare, ultimately, a subsidized stadium it wants."[46] And all these subsidies, other observers added, had diverted public tax dollars from more pressing public needs.

"How did government get in the business of entertaining its citizens," asked one Maryland lawmaker, "as opposed to educating them, providing roads and building bridges?"[47]

Most public officials did their best to ignore such questions. In Cleveland, exactly one day before the City Council voted to bankroll a ballpark for the "new" Browns, officials of the city's underfunded school system announced plans to eliminate interscholastic sports and lay off 160 teachers.[48]

The owner of the "old" Browns, Art Modell, most likely found nothing amiss in the priorities of his former city's top officials. How could anyone, after all, possibly doubt the value of a big-time sports franchise?

"The pride and the presence of a professional football team," as Modell had once proclaimed, "is far more important than 30 libraries."[49]

Libraries would have to do without, in more ways than librarians might immediately realize. Those luxury suites that meant so much to patrons of fine football like Art Modell would be rented, by and large, by large corporations. These corporations would write off, as tax deductions, half of whatever they paid for their suites. By the 1990s, according to one estimate, luxury suite deductions were cutting corporate tax bills by about $80 million a year.[50] That "savings" meant $80 million less for libraries — and playgrounds and schools and every other ill-funded public service.

A small price to pay, as Art Modell might say, for "pride and presence."

AND WHAT ABOUT THE PLAYERS? How have they actually fared in a more unequal America?

Avid sports fans hardly ever agree on anything about players. They argue, and relish arguing, about which players "have game" and which players don't, about which young players will grow up to become stars, about which star players rate Hall of Fame honors. Fan arguments about players never end. Except on one topic. Money. Modern big-time sports stars, all fans seem to agree, have life incredibly sweet. Even ordinary athletes, fans now assume as a given, can and do become multimillionaires.

Who could argue the point? Did not all Major League Baseball player salaries average, in 2001, over $2 million? They most certainly did.

But numbers, as sports fans know better than most, can sometimes mislead. In an unequal America, players have not been the incredibly big winners they seem. Athletes who play professionally are, in fact, more likely to end their careers in pain than in mansions. And the superstars of sports, as many millions as they may have accumulated, have yet to crack the topmost sanctums of American income and wealth.

Consider Sammy Sosa, the Chicago Cubs slugger. In 1999, the year after Sosa's homerun duel with Mark McGwire made baseball history, Sosa earned $9 million.[51] That same year, fifteen Chicagoland CEOs pulled in pay packages that totaled at least $10 million.[52]

On the annual *Forbes* listings of the four hundred richest Americans, not one professional athlete has ever appeared. Not even Michael Jordan, the planet's most famous athlete throughout the 1990s. To match the fortune of media mogul Rupert Murdoch, one analyst calculated at decade's end, Jordan would have to match his own peak annual athletic and endorsement earnings for 140 consecutive years.[53]

Jordan's actual professional playing career spanned about two decades. Few big league professional athletes now have careers that span much more than two or three years.

In pro football, for instance, rookies quickly learn that "NFL" stands for "Not For Long."[54] NFL player careers, notes one study, typically last 3.3 years. Running backs can look forward, on average, to 2.57 years in the league. Only 6 percent of players who make an NFL roster can count on lasting ten years.[55] Major League Baseball careers, as of 2002, averaged four years, NBA basketball careers four and a half.[56]

Pro athletes did not always come and go so quickly. In the 1950s and 1960s, players, once established, returned year after year. Fans who followed football in those years could name, thirty years later, their favorite team's entire defensive line. Today, only the most compulsive fans can name more than a lineman or two on their favorite team. Players simply cycle in and out too hurriedly to make an impression.

Many players these days exit as casualties of pro football's "salary cap." The cap keeps each team's total payroll at a certain prescribed limit. With the cap in place, teams cannot retain on their rosters both a handful of marquee star players *and* a significant core of veterans. The veterans cost too much. They can be replaced by inexperienced rookies at prices far less expensive. And so they are. Every preseason, around Labor Day, NFL teams now routinely ax from their rosters a steady stream of skilled, seasoned veterans.

These axed veterans often hold "long-term" contracts worth multiple millions, contracts that made headlines when the veterans originally signed them. But insiders knew, at the time, that the headlines distorted the dollars the players would actually be receiving.

"Teams call news conferences to announce long-term, multi-million-dollar deals," sportswriter Leonard Shapiro explained in 2002. "A player does get a large signing bonus — his guaranteed money — but most don't get to the final few years of the contract when they're due to be paid the big money."[57]

Football's revolving door keeps most players virtually anonymous to average fans. Only stars get to hang around long enough for fans to feel they know them. Stars, of course, have always grabbed the lion's share of fan attention. But by the 1990s, in the new world of American sports, they would get almost all of it. Everybody's eyes would now fix upon stars — and their fortunes. And the bigger the fortunes, the more unrelenting the pressure on stars to prove their "worth" whenever they took the field or rink or court.

Tennis star Andre Agassi and his equally famous tennis star partner, Steffi Graf, once found themselves giving a lesson to a fan who had bid, at a charity auction, $125,000 for an hour's worth of the two stars' time. The pair delivered an hour's lesson, but then, feeling "sheepish," kept going. They spent all day with the bidder.

"You try to be worth $125,000," Agassi explained later, "and you realize you can't be."[58]

Most all stars felt this same pressure and strained constantly, on the field, to demonstrate their multi-million dollar "worth." Their performance, all too often, would slip as they strained. One study of baseball free agency, published in 2001, compared star player performance before and after stars signed big new contracts. In every offensive category, the researchers found, player numbers tailed off. Newly minted baseball millionaires banged out fewer homers, drove in fewer runners, and hit for significantly lower averages.[59]

At century's end, each big new contract megadeal would up the compensation strain, and not just for the stars who signed the big new contracts. Other stars, particularly those who had inked long-term contracts two or three years earlier, would feel underpaid — and underappreciated — as they watched players of no greater ability or accomplishment sign contracts that put their own salary to shame. In 2001, superstars throughout baseball grumbled about how "disrespected" they felt after Alex Rodriguez cut a ten-year deal for $252 million. Frank Thomas, a stellar player who had been among baseball's high-salary elite, suddenly found himself making only a third of the salary earned by the game's top-paid player. He demanded that his contract be renegotiated and refused, in the meantime, to check in at spring training. Thomas insisted he wasn't "asking to be the richest man in baseball." All he wanted, he explained, was to be "at least in the top 20."[60]

Thomas would eventually rejoin his team, but he never really recovered from the slight. His career would nosedive.

Some superstars, like Chicago's Sammy Sosa, would be able to get the new deals they wanted. But their struggles for the big money would isolate them from fellow players and fans alike. "Any day now, Sosa is expected to sign a contract extension that will make him wealthier than he ever could have imagined," *Chicago Tribune* sportswriter Rick Morrissey observed just before the 2001 season. "But he looks so very alone, him and his money."[61] Sosa's stormy, distracting contract battles the summer before had alienated "half of the Cubs' fan base." Was that battle, Morrissey wondered, worth it? Would Sosa even "notice the thick layer of permafrost between himself and some of his teammates, upset at how the Sosa contract watch helped send the Cubs into a free fall last year."[62]

The richer the contracts sports stars signed, the greater their isolation. Superstars, by century's end, would live and travel and party in their own universes. They could sometimes be spotted, sportswriter Steve Rushin would note, in one of "the nightclubs that so many stars inhabit, with the inevitable glassed-off VIP room, inside of which is a smaller roped-off VVIP section, and so on, until the biggest star in attendance can be found standing alone in a kind of VVVVIP phone booth, dolefully sipping a mai tai."[63]

The biggest stars trusted themselves and hardly anyone else. And that made sense. The people they met, after all, didn't want them. They wanted a piece of their fortune. Up-and-coming stars would learn this lesson quickly.

"The way I handle it is really simple," Eddy Curry, a young Chicago Bulls basketball pheenom, explained. "I don't make any new friends."[64]

The superstars would have their wealth and little else. Out in the playgrounds and the sandlots, youngsters with little saw only the wealth. And that wealth seemed to be within their reach. Just a quicker cross-over dribble away. But that wealth was a mirage, as anyone who studied the odds would quickly see. Only 1 percent of high school athletes could expect to play big-time college ball. Only 1 percent of college ballplayers could expect to become pros. Only 1 percent of pros could expect to reach stardom.[65]

Athletes would, at times, become rich in the late twentieth century. But America's new Gilded Age would bring gold — and fulfillment — for precious few of them.

SPORTS, SOME COMMENTATORS LIKE TO SAY, MIRROR LIFE. In the boom years, the sports scene most definitely did mirror American life — in the depth of its inequality.

During the boom years, in America at large, gaps in income and wealth between affluent Americans and everyone else reached modern records. In sports, these same gaps also widened, between owners and players, between players and fans, and, in some sports, between teams themselves. Indeed, within baseball, the financial gaps between teams extended so wide that the game's high priests sometimes seemed unable to pronounce on anything else.

"Fans in a number of markets have been forced to watch their teams become chronically uncompetitive," baseball commissioner Bud Selig told Congress after the 2000 season. "During my 32 years in baseball, I have never witnessed the type of despair that competitive imbalance is causing so many of our clubs."[66]

In baseball, as in America, "markets" ruled supreme. And that, for baseball, created a real problem. Teams in the nation's biggest urban markets were cutting for themselves far more lucrative local TV and radio deals than teams in smaller cities could ever hope to cut. At the start of the 1990s, richer baseball franchises were collecting four times more revenue than the poorest. By decade's end, revenues for richer teams were outpacing revenues for poorer teams by twenty-to-one.

Amid inequalities this striking, baseball's traditional approaches to ensuring "competitive balance" no longer worked. The amateur player draft, for instance, had originally been designed to give losing clubs first dibs on the most promising stars of tomorrow. The teams with the worst records would choose first, the powerhouses last. But poorer teams, in the boom years, found they couldn't afford the bonuses the top blue-chip players were demanding — so they simply stopped drafting them.[67] Poorer teams that did stumble onto young talent soon lost it. Emerging stars on poor clubs would almost invariably jump to rich clubs as soon as they had played enough years to qualify as "free agents."[68]

Baseball teams with the highest revenues, most notably the New York Yankees, would dominate the 1990s. Poorer teams would struggle. In 1999, only one of the ten lowest-payroll teams in baseball ended the season with more wins than losses. Of the ten highest-payroll teams, eight had winning records.[69] In April that year, fans in Kansas City, one of the bottom clubs, actually organized to demonstrate their displeasure. During a game against the Yankees, some two thousand Royals fans marched out of the ballpark, carrying banners and chanting, to protest baseball's "staggering salary gap."[70]

But most fans in the poorer "markets" didn't stage protests. They just lost interest. In 1998, attendance dropped for half the teams in baseball. Most teams, conservative columnist and rabid baseball fan George Will noted the next year, "have no realistic hope of contending, ever." Eventually, Will warned, the fans of these teams would catch on and "baseball's spell will be broken."[71]

Pro football, interestingly, did not share baseball's competitive imbalance woes. Teams in the vast majority of NFL cities *did* have a "realistic hope of contending." Throughout the boom years, one year's losers in the NFL would become the next year's winners. The reason? Football's owners rejected the pure "market" approach. They shared, *equally among themselves*, all the revenues from their immense network TV contracts.

"Without that socialistic, communistic approach to business that we have," the ever clever Art Modell, owner of the Baltimore Ravens, proclaimed in 2001 at the Super Bowl, the biggest annual spectacle in sports, "we wouldn't have this colossal event."[72]

The football hierarchy's commitment to "socialist equality" would only go so far. Among themselves, club owners would share and share alike. But within their individual teams owners would remain firmly wedded to the corporate assumptions that had, in America at large, done so much to concentrate wealth and widen inequality. The owners assumed that teams, like corporations, absolutely must have top talent to succeed. The owners would pay a premium for that top talent, even if that meant compensating some players at rates far, far higher than others. These basic assumptions, in football and every other major sport, would keep player salaries soaring — at the top end of the income scale.

"Average" salaries, amid this soaring, would rise substantially, too, pulled up by the megasalaries at the top. But *median* salary figures, the numbers that show what typical players are actually making, would increase at far less rapid rates. Teams, in other words, were becoming far more unequal internally, and nowhere more so than in baseball.

Early in the 1980s, before the income explosions at the top, *average* and *median* salaries in baseball would vary only modestly. In 1983, the "average" baseball salary stood at $289,000. The median ballplayer that year made $207,500. By 2000, over a million dollars would separate baseball's "average" and "median" salaries. Ballplayers, thanks to giant megadeals at the top, "averaged" $1,789,556 in 2000. But the typical ballplayer took home $550,000.[73] The gap would continue growing in the new century. In 2002, Alex Rodriguez would take home $22 million, but a third of baseball's Major Leaguers would earn $300,000 or less. How wide had the baseball gap become? In 1988, ballplayers at the exact middle of baseball's income distribution had earned $10 for every $100 earned by baseball's top-paid players. In 2002, baseball's "middle class" made $4 for every $100 top players made.[74]

What impact did this gap have? Not the impact owners hoped. Throwing megamillions at stars did not create winning ballclubs. In fact, the more dollars owners threw at top players, at the expense of their teammates, the poorer their teams performed. Matt Bloom, a management expert at the University of Notre Dame, would document this reality at the end of the 1990s. He had set out, a few years before, to use baseball to test whether "unequal rewards induce greater individual effort and performance." Bloom would subject nine years' worth of baseball salary and performance data to close analysis. His research would draw one clear conclusion.

"The bigger the pay difference between a team's stars and scrubs," as the *Wall Street Journal* summed up Bloom's findings, "the worse its record."[75]

The 1998 season would prove typical. In that season, three of the five major league teams with the most unequal payrolls finished last in their divisions, three of the five most equal teams finished first.[76] On the field, equality seemed to work.

But baseball would pay Bloom's research no heed whatsoever. Owners would continue to lust after superstar saviors. The Texas Rangers would ink Alex Rodriguez to ten years and $252 million — and promptly finish last the next three years. The team that lost Rodriquez, the Seattle Mariners, would promptly tie the Major League record for wins in a season.[77]

NEAR THE END OF THE 1990s, ESPN, America's top all-sports television network, began running weekly documentaries about the twentieth century's greatest sports heroes. The series caught on. Sports fans young and old found these profiles fascinating, perhaps because every episode reminded viewers just how much sports in America had changed. Once upon a time, the profiles helped viewers remember, money didn't dictate *everything* in sports. But now money did.

"Money makes those who pay it resentful and impatient and makes those who receive it feel guilty or inadequate," laments sportswriter Thomas Boswell. "Money makes fans cranky, the media sarcastic. Money warps judgment and sours dispositions, in the locker room and the stands."[78]

What could end the dollar's dominion over sports? Boswell would speculate, at times, about the difference a better order of owners could make. Owners, he understood, could do great harm to the games they controlled. The worst of them, men like video rental mogul Wayne Huizenga, could ruin sports for an entire city.

Huizenga had come into baseball, as the owner of the Florida Marlins, eager to show off how a "real" businessman makes money. Huizenga moved quickly. He convinced, in the mid 1990s, "all the weak-spined owners to get tough with the union, bring salary costs down and, then, make serious money."[79] The owners' subsequent showdown with the players union, a showdown Huizenga helped incite, ended up canceling a World Series but changing, from the owners' perspective, relatively nothing in baseball labor relations.

Huizenga then changed course. He would now seek to make his "serious money" by trying to "monopolize the market" for good players. Huizenga flung open his checkbook and signed up an assortment of accomplished veteran players. He would shell out, before his checkbook spree ended, $89 million on multi-year contracts. Huizenga's solid new players, none of them huge superstars, would make an immediate impact. The Marlins would actually go all the way in 1997, winning the World Series.

Attendance at Marlins games would rise too, from 1.7 to 2.3 million. But that leap would not be large enough to offset the cost of Huizenga's free agent splurge.[80] That would frustrate Huizenga no end. He soon started whining that his team's "2.3 million patrons weren't buying enough luxury boxes."[81] He demanded a fix: a new stadium.

South Florida would not go along. Something about building another stadium for a billionaire apparently didn't appeal to the locals. An angry Huizenga would now retaliate. He unloaded, one by one, the players who had thrilled Miami with their World Series heroics. In 1997, the World Series year, the annual Miami payroll had run $53 million. By the next summer, the payroll would be down to $24 million, with about $10 million more in cuts planned for 1999.[82]

On the playing field, the new bargain-basement Marlins would tank. Their veterans gone, the team sank to last place. Miami, a city that should have been a baseball hotbed, would become a baseball graveyard. Fan attendance dropped, in 1998, to baseball's second-worst total.[83] Few individuals, sportswriter Thomas Boswell would note, had ever "done the game more harm" than Wayne Huizenga.

"Maybe, someday," Boswell mused, "baseball will attract a core of owners with a sense of balance in their expectations."[84]

To prosper and bring pleasure at the same time, in other words, sports would seem to need a better class of super rich. Maybe. But another alternative does exist. Imagine how good sports could be if we had a society with no super rich at all.

WEALTH WITHOUT HEALTH

ALL OF US OF SOUND MIND, even the most sports-crazed among us, *really* care deeply about only one reality in our lives, our own individual health and the health of our loved ones. We want everyone close to us to live a long and healthy life.

But if we are truly of sound mind, we also care deeply about the health of everyone we encounter, not just everyone dear to us. We care about our neighbors, our co-workers, even the people we pass on the streets. None of us, after all, want to live among sick, unhealthy people. Self-interest and altruism reinforce each other here: The healthier those around us, the healthier we individually and those we love are likely to be.

All people around us, unfortunately, are not healthy. We typically cite several reasons. Some people, we note, are born unhealthy. Some people engage in unhealthy behaviors. And some people, we acknowledge, have much less money than others.

This last reality, public health researchers have helped us understand, is "powerfully related" to longevity and illness.[1] People with lower incomes are more likely to suffer heart attacks and strokes, more likely to develop diabetes and cancer, more likely to become disabled.[2] Older Americans in excellent health have, on average, two and half times more income and five times more wealth than older Americans in poor health.[3]

Why are people without much wealth less healthy than people of means?

Low-income people, some analysts contend, simply don't have access to decent health care. Poor people with health problems in the United States are "only half as likely to see a doctor" as more affluent people.[4] But access alone doesn't seem to explain why people with more money tend to be healthier than people with less money. Health varies by income bracket, researchers have shown, "even in countries with universal access to care, where health care resources seem to be distributed justly."[5]

If lack of access to care doesn't adequately explain why lower-income people suffer poorer health, what does? Other analysts have an answer: poverty itself. Deprivation breeds chronic ill-health. Poor kids breathe more polluted air and get more asthma. Poor adults, after lives spent working in jobs that expose them to environmental hazards, end up with elevated blood-lead levels.[6]

311

Better access to health care, these analysts point out, cannot by itself undo the daily insults to good health that a life without money inevitably engenders. Only by ending deprivation — only by ensuring all people decent housing, clean air and water, nutritious food, adequate clothing — can societies make significant strides against ill-health. Help poor people out of squalor and health outcomes will improve appreciably.

So have argued insightful champions of public health ever since the middle of the nineteenth century. And history has affirmed their wisdom. Medical science "breakthroughs" have typically won the popular culture credit for triumphs over disease, but rising standards of living have actually mattered much more than medical fixes. A vaccine, for instance, did end the scourge of smallpox in nineteenth century England. But nineteenth century English doctors had no vaccines for diphtheria, pneumonia, and a host of other infectious killers. Yet death rates for all these diseases, over the course of the nineteenth century, fell as dramatically as death rates from smallpox.[7] Medicines didn't stop these other infectious diseases. Better incomes did. People who could afford to live in decent homes and eat decent diets developed stronger immune systems. Their more adequately nourished bodies could, for the first time, fight off disease.

Rising incomes, by the mid twentieth century, had essentially eradicated mass malnutrition throughout the developed world. Diseases that had once routinely killed children, like measles, now meant little more, in developed nations, than a few days off from school. In the world's poorly nourished nations, meanwhile, diseases like measles remained killers. To public health advocates, a half century ago, the prescription for better health seemed obvious. Incomes needed to rise. Greater wealth would lead to greater health. If nations kept living standards rising, health outcomes everywhere, in nations rich and poor, would continue to improve.

This certainty would not last. Epidemiologists — researchers who study how and why diseases spread within populations — soon began to have second thoughts. Yes, rising living standards did seem to work wonders against the classic infectious diseases. But infectious diseases, in economically developed nations at least, no longer posed the prime medical challenge. In these nations, degenerative, not infectious diseases, now ravished populations. By the late twentieth century, heart disease, cancer, diabetes, and other degenerative conditions accounted for three-quarters of all deaths in the United States.[8] Against these ailments higher per capita incomes seemed to make no difference.

The statistics told a striking story. Economically developed nations with higher per capita incomes — per capita incomes, remember, are simple averages computed by dividing total income by total number of people — did not necessarily register lower death rates than economically developed nations with lower per capita incomes.[9] The Dutch, for instance, lived longer than Americans despite living in an economy that generated about 30 percent less per capita wealth.[10]

The conclusion from these numbers? Rising income levels, researchers would agree, do make a significant contribution to better health — but only in societies where most people live amid horrible material deprivation.[11] In societies that have conquered this deprivation, societies where most people can count on decent living conditions, more income and wealth do not automatically translate into longer, healthier lives.[12]

Had income and wealth, in developed economies, become irrelevant to health? In one sense, yes: More money did not guarantee better health. But money, investigators in the late twentieth century began to argue, did certainly still matter a great deal, only in a different way. In developed societies, what matters most to health is not aggregate wealth, but wealth distribution. The more concentrated a developed society's wealth, the less healthy the society. Populations of people who live "in countries and regions with smaller gaps between rich and poor," as one researcher would note, "are, in general, healthier than the populations of countries and regions in which the gap is larger."[13]

Christopher Jencks, a widely known and respected Harvard sociologist, would come late to this research into the links between health and the distribution of income and wealth. "If you had asked me a year ago," he told an interviewer in 1998, "if there was evidence that income inequality had some social consequence, I would have said, 'Gee, I don't know.'" But Jencks found his attitudes changing after he began studying the epidemiological research. The data, he noted, "seem to say that if you are of average income, living among people of average income, you are less likely to have a heart attack than if you live more stressfully in a community where there is you in the middle, and a bunch of rich people and a bunch of poor people."[14]

Inequality, in effect, could kill.

"That seems hard to believe," observed Jencks, "but it is the direction in which the evidence seems to point."

THE EVIDENCE, BY THE MID 1990S, had been accumulating for some years. Even the world's top medical authorities had begun taking notice. In 1996, the prestigious *British Medical Journal* would inform readers that "studies have related income inequality to infant mortality, life expectancy, height, and morbidity, with a consistent finding that the less equitable the income distribution in a country, the less favourable the health outcome." The studies, the journal added, "seem to show that inequality per se is bad for national health, whatever the absolute material standards of living within a country."[15]

The more unequal a country, the less healthy its people.[16] And by "people," researchers emphasized, they meant all people, not just the poor. Low-income people suffer poorer health in unequal societies, investigators explained, but so does everyone else. People with modest incomes in an equal society could actually look forward to longer, healthier lives than people with higher incomes who lived in an unequal society.[17]

Researchers, by century's end, had demonstrated this "inequality effect" on health in one comparative study after another. The first wave of these studies compared countries. People lived longer, investigators found, in nations with narrower income gaps. In the late 1980s, the nation with the developed world's lowest level of income inequality, Japan, boasted the world's highest life expectancy. And that relationship between inequality and life expectancy didn't appear to be a coincidence. The nation with the developed world's second-lowest level of income inequality, Sweden, held the world's second highest life expectancy.[18]

British epidemiologist Richard Wilkinson, in a powerful 1996 book, *Unhealthy Societies: The Afflictions of Inequality*, would collect this mounting international evidence for "a strong relationship" between income distribution and mortality.[19]

"In the developed world," he would conclude, "it is not the richest countries which have the best health, but the most egalitarian."

This conclusion, noted Wilkinson, rested on a wide and deep pool of research data.[20] Some "eight different groups of researchers," working on "ten separate sets of data," had clearly demonstrated linkages between national mortality rates and income inequality.[21]

Investigators would find the same relationships between inequality and death rates when they compared states within the United States. In 1996, two separate high-powered research teams published landmark studies. One team, led by George Kaplan, later the top epidemiologist at the University of Michigan School of Public Health, gathered state-by-state mortality data, adjusted that data by age, and stirred into the mix other health-related data on everything from low birth weight to homicides. The researchers found "a significant correlation" between death rates and the share of income received by each state's bottom 50 percent of households — and substantial correlations between inequality and "a large number of other health outcomes" as well.[22]

These results, the Kaplan team concluded, did not "prove that income inequality causes poor health." But their findings, the researchers quickly added, ought to be a "cause for alarm given the increasing inequality of income and wealth in the United States."

A second study, published simultaneously, pounded home the same point. Researchers Bruce Kennedy, Ichiro Kawachi, and Deborah Prothrow-Stith calculated a state-by-state inequality index and then examined the relationships between income distribution and specific causes of death. This Harvard-based team found "strong associations" between inequality and "all of the indicators of treatable causes of mortality." In states with greater inequality, all people, from a health standpoint, appeared worse off.[23]

Researchers from both research teams, in explaining their work, took care to distinguish the impact of poverty from the impact of inequality. The conventional wisdom, as George Kaplan pointed out, assumed that the states with the highest death rates would be the states with the most poor people. But that assumption did not hold. The research, Kaplan observed, "suggests that the

increased death rates" in more unequal states "are not due simply to their having more poor people." In more unequal states, he noted, "income inequality
seems to be increasing mortality rates among nonpoor people as well."[24]

That point would be reinforced repeatedly, by new studies, over the next
several years. In 1998, an expanded Kennedy team sought to determine
whether inequality alone could account for differences in health outcomes
between states, or whether those differences could be better explained by other
factors ranging from smoking habits and obesity to level of schooling and
health insurance coverage. Or, the researchers asked, were still other factors —
age, sex, and race, for instance — the key determinants? The investigators took
all these factors into account. Their finding: Inequality in and of itself, separate
from all other factors, does indeed significantly matter. People in states with the
highest income inequalities turn out to be 30 percent "more likely to report
their health as fair or poor than individuals living in states with the smallest
inequalities in income."[25]

Inequality, in short, could help explain why people in some states lived
healthier lives than others. Could inequality also help explain health differences
in jurisdictions smaller than states? The answer would come, in 1998, after
researchers compared health outcomes in America's metropolitan areas. The
analysts, based at the University of Michigan, collected data from all but one
of the 283 official metro areas in the United States.[26] Their aim: to test whether
"the size of the gap between the rich and the poor in a society is importantly
related to health." Their finding: The more unequal a metropolitan area, the
higher the area's death rate is likely to be.

"Given the mortality burden associated with income inequality," the health
researchers would conclude, "business, private, and public sector initiatives to
reduce economic inequalities should be a high priority."

Other epidemiological investigators, meanwhile, drilled down even deeper
than metro areas. In New York, Peter Arno and two colleagues at the Albert
Einstein College of Medicine, Chee Jen Chang and Jing Fang, plowed through
four years of infant-mortality data from every zip code in the nation's largest
city.[27] These zip codes included some of the richest neighborhoods in the entire
United States and some of the poorest. In which zip codes did the fewest babies
die? The answer proved an eye-opener. The fewest babies did not die in the
city's highest-income zip code. The fewest babies died in a zip code that sported one of the city's most narrow income gaps between top and bottom, Staten
Island's overwhelmingly middle-class South Beach.[28]

Nations. States. Cities. Zip codes. The evidence, notes James Lardner, a former *US News & World Report* journalist who has written widely on health and
inequality, tells a consistent story. Societies divided by deep economic inequality "are more unhealthy — not just in some highfalutin moral sense but in the
plain old medical sense, and not just for the poor (as anyone would suspect)
but for the bulk of the population."[29]

"To put it more baldly, if you live in a place where differences in income and wealth are unusually large," adds Lardner, "your chances of escaping chronic illness and reaching a ripe old age are significantly worse than if you live in a place where differences are not as large."[30]

OF ALL THE COMPARISONS RESEARCHERS have made between equal and unequal, healthy and unhealthy, the most compelling of all may well be the contrast between the world's richest nation, the United States, and the nation that has been, over most recent decades, the world's most equal, Japan.

By all rights, the United States ought to be the healthiest place in the world. The United States spends more money to keep people healthy — over $1 trillion annually — than any other nation on the face of the globe. Americans make up less than 5 percent of the world's population, yet our medical bills add up to 42 percent of what the world spends on health care.[31] And we Americans don't just spend money on health care. We mount mammoth mobilizations against unhealthy habits. We have waged war against smoking and fatty foods and drunk driving. We invented aerobics and mass marathons.

"We should be pretty healthy," notes Dr. Stephen Bezruchka, a veteran observer of the international health scene from the University of Washington School of Public Health.[32]

We should be, but we're not.

In 1970, the year Bezruchka started medical school, the United States ranked fifteenth in the world on the most significant health measures. By 1990, the United States had dropped to twentieth place. Over a decade later, in 2001, Americans occupied the twenty-fifth rung in the world's health ratings. We trailed nearly every other rich nation in the world and even, notes Bezruchka, "a few poor ones."[33]

First place, meanwhile, belonged to Japan, the world's most equal developed country.

Japan's lofty health status, of course, could conceivably have nothing to do with its distribution of income and wealth. The Japanese could simply, for instance, be the fortunate beneficiaries of a healthy gene pool. A possibility? Certainly. But back a few decades, in 1960, Japanese people had the same genes they have now, and their health status only ranked the world's twenty-third best.[34]

How about diet? Could Japanese people owe their longevity to the healthy food they eat? Nutritionists certainly do give Japanese cuisine high marks for healthfulness. But this cuisine didn't change much between 1965 and 1986, yet life expectancy in Japan, over these two decades, soared seven and a half years for men and eight for women.[35]

Maybe the Japanese are healthier because they've done a wonderful job eliminating unhealthy behaviors. Actually, the Japanese have some way to go on the unhealthy behavior front. Japanese men smoke at twice the rates of American men. Yet deaths attributable to smoking in Japan run at only half the

American rate.[36] Smokers in Japan simply live longer than smokers in the United States.

Everybody in Japan lives longer. Life expectancy in Japan, now almost eighty years, stretches three and a half years longer than life expectancy in the United States.[37] These three and a half years, in epidemiological terms, amount to an enormous gap. How enormous? If Americans stopped dying from heart attacks tomorrow, life expectancy in the United States would only jump up to levels the Japanese have already achieved.[38]

People in Japan, of course, are still dying from heart attacks and cancer and lung disease and all the other ailments that are killing Americans, but they are dying at substantially lower rates. What explains this gap? Has Japanese medicine become that much more effective than ours? No serious observer makes that claim. Japanese doctors have discovered no super cures. Only one Japanese medical scientist has ever won a Nobel Prize. Sickly people across the world do not flock to Tokyo for treatment. Medical science, in short, has not marched faster in Japan than anywhere else.

Japan, as a society, has marched fast and far only in one area important to health. The Japanese, since the 1940s, have done more than any other people to create a society where, relatively speaking, only narrow gaps of income and wealth separate the affluent from the average.

Japan had been, before World War II, just an ordinary unequal country. But the war left Japan's traditional hierarchies battered and discredited. A "flood of egalitarian ideas" soon swept over the country — and swept out of economic power the old elites. By 1949, 95 percent of the directors of Japanese companies were people who had worked their way up through the ranks.[39] The Japanese companies that these new directors helped shape valued workers and their ideas — and their need for stable, secure employment — more than companies anywhere else in the world. Corporate Japan, in compensation patterns, in job security, in employee involvement, would in no way resemble corporate America. By the 1980s, the two nations, Japan and the United States, had evolved two different economies, two different societies, and two different health outcomes.

But can the economic organization of a society actually make a difference in how long people live? Apparently so. Researchers have reviewed the medical records of Japanese people who have emigrated to other countries. If something peculiarly "Japanese" explains why Japanese people are living longer than people elsewhere, emigrants from Japan would be outliving their neighbors in their new homes. But Japanese emigrants, the research shows, are no healthier in their new countries than their new neighbors.[40]

Must we conclude, from all this evidence, that inequality somehow "causes" disease? How foolish this question sounds to American ears. We who have been raised on the germ theory of disease can readily understand how deadly to our health a virus can be. But inequality is no virus, no saturated fat, no carcinogen. How can inequality "cause" disease? The honest answer: We don't yet know for sure, just as, generations ago, we didn't know exactly why foul water makes people sick. Still, researchers and analysts do have some ideas on how inequality is doing us in. We turn now to these ideas.

HAPPY WITH YOUR CHIN? Feel that you're projecting enough grim determination? Or does that chin of yours make you seem indecisive? Not a problem. Legions of cosmetic surgeons, in every major American metropolitan area, now stand ready to recast your countenance. Or straighten your droopy eyelids. Or trim your thunder thighs. All, of course, for a price. A price only the affluent can afford.

In the United States today, the "needs" of these affluent have come to drive — and distort — the distribution of our health care services. Physicians who could be providing prenatal care for frightened young mothers are instead performing tummy tucks.

We should not be surprised. Where wealth concentrates, health care providers will invariably concentrate on the wealthy. Inequality, notes Mark Cullen, a professor of public health at Yale, even warps our medical research priorities. In a United States ever more unequal, research dollars are increasingly flowing into "developing treatments only the rich can afford."[41]

This disproportionate attention to the affluent makes, from a medical perspective, no sense. Affluent people face fewer daily insults to their health than less prosperous people. They are less likely to work around hazardous chemicals, less likely to encounter people with untreated illnesses, less likely to lose heat in their homes. Any distribution of health care resources that privileges wealthy people will, consequently, inevitably undermine a society's overall level of healthfulness. And this privileging is exactly what plays out in unequal places. In the United States, medical "specialties" that cater to high-income people have proliferated the fastest in the nation's most unequal states. By contrast, notes a research team led by Leiyu Shi of Johns Hopkins University, states with narrower gaps between rich and poor provide their citizens with many more primary care options.[42]

Unequal societies, in other words, get health care backwards. They devote valuable health care resources to people who need these resources the least. Such misplaced priorities, many researchers believe, help explain why people in unequal societies live, on average, shorter, unhealthier lives than their counterparts in more equal societies.

Overwork may also help explain how inequality "causes" ill-health. Average Americans spend far more hours at work today than Americans who lived in earlier, more equal decades. Families of workers on the job more than fifty hours a week, research shows, have more "severe" interpersonal conflicts.[43] Family conflicts can lead to health-deflating depression or alcoholism. Overwork, to make matters worse, invites overeating. Obesity comes naturally when time-squeezed people are continually grabbing bites on the run. Nearly 100 million Americans now carry enough extra pounds to increase their mortality risk.[44]

But frazzled Americans are grabbing bites on the run all across the United States, not in any one particular state. So why then in some states, the more economically equal states, do residents lead longer, healthier lives? Something basic about life in more equal places must be offsetting the strains, the daily pounding, of modern life. Researchers have a label for this something. They call it *social cohesion.*

Social cohesion — the sum total of human relationships that help people feel respected, valued, and safe in their everyday lives — cannot be bought over the counter or prescribed by any doctor. Social cohesion can only be nurtured, over time, by and between people who care about each other, who support each other, who trust each other. Social cohesion, many epidemiologists contend, makes societies healthier places. If we can go about our daily routines knowing we can count on others, these researchers posit, we feel better about life. Feeling better, we do better — in our physical health.

People who live outside supportive, cohesive networks lead lives that are, in effect, socially "malnourished." They suffer, suggests Yale's Robert Lane, from a "famine," not of food, but "of warm interpersonal relationships," a "malnutrition" that leaves them weak and vulnerable to disease.[45]

Some of the most dramatic early evidence for "social malnutrition" came from a nine-year project that traced individual health histories in California's Alameda County. The most socially isolated of the seven thousand county residents studied turned out to be "two to three times more likely to die of all causes" than their more socially connected neighbors, even after taking cigarette smoking, drinking, and other health-impacting factors into account.[46]

Other early evidence, even more dramatic, came from a small town nestled in the foothills of Pennsylvania's Pocono Mountains. Immigrants from southern Italy had started settling this community, a town named Roseto, in the 1880s. Roseto's residents led lives that appeared, at least outwardly, not much different from the lives led by immigrants in nearby towns. Rosetans smoked. They ate fatty sausages. They seldom exercised.[47] In other Pennsylvania small towns, as in the rest of America, this sort of lifestyle invariably generated waves of heart attacks. But doctors in the 1950s discovered something strange about little Roseto. Rosetans weren't dropping dead, at standard rates, from heart attacks, nor from anything else. Roseto's heart attack rate ran 40 percent under what medical experts figured the rate should be, and the town's overall death rates were also "substantially lower" than rates in neighboring towns.[48]

Why weren't people in Roseto dying off as regularly as everybody else? Researchers eventually came to credit the town's good health to its deeply rooted social cohesion.[49] The original Rosetans had all come from the same Italian village. Their community had remained, over the years, especially close. People didn't just know each other, they protected each other from whatever bad breaks life could throw their way.[50] Rosetans displayed deeply seated egalitarian sensibilities. Some of them did come to earn more than others, but few people ever did anything to flash their financial success.

"Practically everyone," one reviewer of the literature on Roseto would later write, "dressed in the same simple clothes and lived in similar square, clapboard houses with front porches, screen doors, and small gardens."[51]

Roseto's more prosperous locals, medical researchers Stewart Wolf and J. G. Bruhn found, paid close attention to the "delicate balance between ostentation and reserve, ambition and restraint, modesty and dignity." Should they lose their balance, and show themselves too preoccupied with making money, the local priest would point out the error of their ways. The town's entire culture, investigators concluded, "provided a set of checks and balances to ensure that neither success nor failure got out of hand."[52]

Roseto's cohesive, egalitarian culture, by the 1970s, would start to unravel. The more affluent third-generation Rosetans "started building newer, bigger houses on the outskirts of town." They "hired interior decorators, walled off their gardens, and no longer invited their relatives to move in."[53] The "social taboos against conspicuous consumption began to weaken," as Rosetans moved steadily deeper into the American mainstream.[54]

"Roseto became a lonelier place," analyst Helen Epstein sums up. "There were fewer picnics, the brass bands performed less frequently, membership in social clubs and other organizations dropped off."[55]

Rosetans in these lonelier years actually began adopting, along with the rest of America, some healthier habits. They started watching their diets. They started smoking less. They also started dying, despite these healthier habits, at ordinary American rates. Within a decade, heart attacks were striking down Rosetans as often as people in neighboring towns.[56] Roseto, a truly unique place, had become, rather swiftly, just another place, a town no more healthy, no more cohesive, no more equal, than any other.

CLOSE, WARM, CARING RELATIONSHIPS, the evidence suggests, are seldom sustained in communities where differences in income and wealth keep people far apart. Inequality stretches the bonds of friendship and caring that keep people close. At some point, even the closest bonds snap. Individuals no longer "cohere." They become less trusting, as they have in the United States. At the height of America's post-World War II equality, in 1968, 55 percent of Americans said they trusted others. Three decades of increasing inequality later, in 1998, only 35 percent called themselves trusting.[57]

The larger a society's income gap, many investigators now agree, the less trust, the less cohesion, the less healthy the lives that people lead. But again the same question, why? Why should people in less cohesive, less trusting environments end up less healthy?

The answer may rest in how, at the most fundamental level, we experience inequality.

Within all societies, however equal or unequal they may be, we experience inequality through hierarchy. We are all born into humanity's oldest hierarchy, the family. We move on through school, another hierarchy, and then into the workplace, still another. We may play on a sports team or serve in the army or join a theater company. More hierarchies. Some hierarchies we experience may be benign, others cruel. All share one commonality: All hierarchies involve positions of higher and lower status. These differing levels of status may seriously impact our health. Even seemingly minor inequalities in hierarchical status, researchers have found, can make a substantial difference on how long and how healthily people live. Just how substantial only became clear after British epidemiologists began publishing results from a massive study of about seventeen thousand men employed in Britain's civil service.

University of London epidemiologists began what became known as the "Whitehall study" to learn why heart attacks hit some people and not others. The civil servants at Whitehall, the British seat of government, offered a nearly ideal research sample. In the late 1960s, when the study started, these civil servants constituted a remarkably undiverse group — one white, middle-class, Anglo-Saxon man after another, all between the ages of forty and sixty-four. The massive uniformity of the Whitehall sample, investigators believed, would help them zero in on the exact factors that generated heart failures.[58]

The researchers would work diligently — for years. They examined all the "obvious risk factors for heart disease," everything from diet and exercise to smoking. They checked blood pressures. They measured cholesterol levels. They even compared health outcomes between civil servants at various rungs of the civil service ladder. The lead researcher in this latter effort, Michael Marmot, soon uncovered a consistent phenomenon. White-collar employees at the bottom of the civil service hierarchy were many times more likely to die from heart attacks than employees at the top. And lower-grade employees also appeared to be much more prone to other ailments, including cancer and stomach disease.

Marmot found more as well. Health outcomes improved, rung by rung, as civil servants moved up the employment grade ladder. Clerks had three times as many fatal heart attacks as the supervisors immediately above them in the civil service hierarchy. These supervisors, in turn, had twice as many fatal heart attacks as the administrators above them. The most modest of distinctions, Marmot and fellow investigators discovered, could produce striking differences in death rates. Senior assistant statisticians suffered fatal heart attacks at almost twice the rate of chief statisticians.

The conventional risk factors for heart disease — poor diet, lack of exercise, smoking, high blood pressure — could only account, the investigators determined, for less than half of the health differences, overall, between Whitehall employment grades. Hierarchical status, in and of itself, clearly seemed to be making a health impact.

"If a clerk and a manager both smoked twenty cigarettes a day," as Helen Epstein, a reviewer of the Whitehall literature, would note, "the clerk was more likely to die of lung cancer."[59]

Other studies, from Massachusetts to Finland, would later find similar patterns.[60] Social standing everywhere, not just Whitehall, appeared to shape health outcomes. The lower an individual's slot in a workplace hierarchy, the worse the individual's health. Subordinate status, somehow, some way, was "causing" ill-health.

And just how was subordinate status making this impact? Some clues would emerge from research conducted far from Whitehall's white collars, out in the wilds of Africa, among the baboons of the Serengeti plains.

Baboons, like people, interact within hierarchies. Males at the bottom of these hierarchies, researchers have found, exhibit far higher levels of hormones called glucocorticoids than male baboons at or near the top. Glucocorticoids typically release out through the body whenever primates encounter stressful situations. These hormones serve a necessary function. At threatening moments, they divert a body's resources away from tissue repair and other "non-urgent tasks" and help the body mobilize for action.[61] A threatened baboon, flush with glucocorticoids, either fights or takes flight. Without these hormones flowing, an individual baboon would never last long out in the wild.

But glucocorticoids, if they're *always* flowing, create a different set of problems. In a baboon awash with glucocorticoids, the body never ends up devoting enough resources to needed maintenance work. Blood pressure rises. The immune system eventually starts to break down. These breakdowns, interestingly, never seem to afflict baboons that sit high in baboon hierarchies. The explanation? High-ranking baboons can go for appreciable periods of time without feeling particularly threatened. Baboons lower in the hierarchical order, by contrast, live much more stressful existences. They find themselves, as British epidemiologist Richard Wilkinson observes, "constantly faced down by more dominant" baboons. This chronic stress eventually blunts the body's feedback mechanisms that regulate glucocorticoids.[62] Hormone levels run out of whack. Health deteriorates.[63]

Chronic stress, the Whitehall researchers found, can make the same sort of negative biochemical impact on human bodies. With civil servants, as with baboons, body chemistry varies with status. Levels of low-density lipoproteins, chemicals that make blood vessels more likely to clog, ran higher in both low-status civil servants and low-status baboons. High-density lipoproteins, substances that help bodies clear cholesterol, displayed exactly the reverse pattern. These health-enhancing chemicals ran at higher levels among civil servants and baboons at the top end of their hierarchies.[64]

Primates, people and baboons alike, may share the same chemistry. But the exact stresses we primates face obviously differ enormously. Low-ranking baboons face physical violence. They worry about getting bitten. In human workplaces, we rarely encounter threats of violence. Our stresses come instead from the emotional ebb and flow of nine-to-five life, from getting passed over for promotions or having our ideas belittled, from worrying about job security, from struggling to meet impossible deadlines.

But doesn't everyone within a workplace hierarchy feel stress, even CEOs at the summit? Top executives, after all, have quarterly earnings expectations to meet. What could be more stressful? And if everyone in a modern workplace is stressed and if chronic stress really does make people sick, why should high-ranking executives be any healthier than low-ranking clerks? Just one reason: High-status executives, researchers believe, do not experience the *same* stress as low-status clerks. The pressure they feel from having too many appointments on their calendar or having to make an important decision, explains analyst Helen Epstein, "is very different from the kind of stress a clerk feels when he thinks that he is stuck in a routine, under someone else's often arbitrary authority."[65]

Some people within a hierarchy, in other words, control their own fates, or feel they do. Others experience little or even no control at all over the work they do. The lower the hierarchical rung, the less control, the more damaging the stress. In the Whitehall research, Michael Marmot found feelings of low control "associated with lower civil service rank, greater risk of heart attack, and higher blood levels of a substance called fibrinogen, which is associated both with stress and with heart attacks."[66] Other studies in Sweden, the United States, Germany, and elsewhere in Britain have demonstrated comparable links between health and the control people feel they have over their work.[67]

Outside the workplace, meanwhile, individuals also experience control and lack of control issues, only here, off the job, hierarchies are defined not by employment rank but by the distribution of income and wealth. Those with appreciable income and wealth simply have a much greater wherewithal to control how their lives unfold than those without.[68] The less wealth, the less control, the more stress.

These stresses build over time, one upon another, stirring up, in the process, a toxic biochemical brew. People at the lower end of hierarchies, on and off the job, can come to "feel depressed, cheated, bitter, desperate, vulnerable, frightened, angry, worried about debts or job and housing insecurity."[69]

"Prolonged stress from any of these sources," notes Richard Wilkinson, "is often all it takes to damage health."[70]

How potent are these chronic stresses? They can, contends Wilkinson, "dominate people's whole experience of life."[71] They can even, over time, *physically* alter our insides, as Stanford neurochemist R. M. Sapolsky has so deftly illustrated.

Throughout the nineteenth century, Sapolsky relates, cadavers for medical anatomy classes in London came from local poorhouses. The adrenal glands anatomists found in these cadavers became the adrenal gland textbook standard. But every so often doctors would get a chance to dissect a cadaver from a wealthier life. The adrenal glands found in these more affluent cadavers seldom met the textbook standard. They were too small. Doctors subsequently "invented a new disease" to account for these smaller adrenal glands, and this new disease "flourished" until physicians came to realize, early in the twentieth century, that smaller adrenal glands were actually "the norm" — and the larger adrenals of the poor "the result of prolonged socioeconomic stress."[72]

Doctors made the same mistake with the thymus gland, with more tragic results. In poor people's cadavers, the thymus appeared small. Doctors classified the larger thymus glands of more affluent people "as a disorder." They "treated" this disorder with radiation. The doctors eventually realized their error. Too late. The radiation treatments they had administered "later caused thyroid cancer."[73]

Inequality had killed still again.

IN THE UNITED STATES, OUTSIDE ACADEMIC CIRCLES, the vast upsurge of epidemiological interest in inequality has made relatively little impact on our ongoing national discourse over health care policy. In Britain, by contrast, the notion that inequality, not just poverty, can significantly undermine health, has actually become a matter of somewhat heated public debate. In 1998, for instance, a well-publicized report by the British government's former chief medical officer, Sir Donald Acheson, talked about the struggle for better health outcomes as "fundamentally a matter of social justice."[74] Nonsense, critics charged. Sir Donald, fumed one commentator in London's *Sunday Times*, actually "blames ill-health on economic inequality."[75] Such an "absurd" conclusion, the critique continued, could only come from an "equality fanatic." And why was this conclusion so absurd? Acheson had totally failed, the *Times* would disdainfully charge, to take into account the "choices" about health that people in modern societies make.

"The most likely reason for the widening health gap is that better-off people have changed their behaviour, for example by stopping smoking or choosing to breast-feed, whereas worse-off people have not," the *Times* critique concluded. "Behaviour associated with poor health is concentrated among poor people, but this has nothing to do with the earning power of the better-off."[76]

The poor, in short, have no one to blame for their ill-health but themselves.

This blame-the-victim message can and does resonate powerfully within modern societies, largely because the core "fact" at its root turns out to be absolutely true. Many habits we now know as unhealthy — smoking, overeating, engaging in substance abuse — *are* practiced more by people who rank low in wealth and income. All these unhealthy behaviors, from smoking to obesity, carry what epidemiologists call a "social gradient." Their frequency increases as social and economic status decreases.

So do low-income, "low-status" people simply "choose" to be unhealthy? Many researchers think not. The same stresses that enlarge adrenal glands, they suggest, can help us understand why people low in hierarchical status seem to hang on to unhealthy habits with more tenacity than their "betters." Lower-status people practice unhealthy behaviors not because they want to be unhealthy, but because they need relief — from social stress.[77] People typically respond to stress, investigators note, by increasing their intake of our society's readily available relaxants, disinhibitors, and stimulants. They smoke. They do drugs. They "increase their consumption of various comforting foods," digestibles that "usually have high sugar and fat content."[78] The more chronic the stress, the more likely a reliance on one or another of these comforting props.

And the more chronic the stress, the harder to end that reliance. Researchers, for instance, have found a clear "social gradient" in smoking cessation programs. People of lower social and economic status who attend such programs are less likely to give up smoking than people of higher status. But "the desire to give up smoking," interestingly, carries no social gradient.[79] Clerks turn out to be just as eager as CEOs to stop smoking. What then explains the economic differentials in cessation success rates? Stopping an unhealthy habit may simply be easier for people of means. They can always afford, after all, to engage in other forms of relief. People whose prospects seem hopeless, on the other hand, often cannot. Smoking may well be their "only relaxation and luxury."[80] Do they "choose" to smoke? Literally speaking, yes. Is their "choice" a purely individual decision, totally unrelated to their subordinate place in the social and economic hierarchy? Clearly not. The stresses that hierarchical life generates, in other words, don't just wreak biochemical havoc. They encourage behaviors that can contribute, *over the long run*, to poor health outcomes, to reduced life expectancies.

These same chronic stresses, researchers note, help drive the behaviors — homicide, for instance — that reduce life expectancies *in the short run*.

Homicide statistics reflect as strong a social gradient as the numbers on smoking. People on society's lower rungs commit more murders than people higher up. Why do people commit homicides? Research has identified "loss of face" as the largest single "source of violence."[81] People lose face when they feel humiliated by others. Everyone, of course, feels humiliated at some point or another. But our social status conditions how we respond to the humiliation. People of means, of "larger reserves of status and prestige," will likely "feel less fundamentally threatened by any particular loss of face" than someone whose life seems to be tumbling out of control.[82]

No homicide records ever list inequality as the cause of death. Maybe they should.

AND NOW THE GOOD NEWS. Hierarchies may figure to be with us for many millennia to come, but the biochemical stresses hierarchies generate can be mitigated, even neutralized, by the caring, compassionate, public-spirited social cohesion that thrives whenever inequalities of income and wealth are significantly narrowed.

"It seems likely," notes epidemiologist Richard Wilkinson, summing up the evidence, "that social support may be important in changing the way people respond to stressful events and circumstances."[83]

Epidemiologists found that social support in Roseto, the town where local customs helped nurture a deeply embraced egalitarian ethos. And they have found that same social support, even more strikingly, in war-time Great

Britain. Life expectancy in England and Wales actually increased more during the 1940s, the years that included World War II, than in any other decade of the twentieth century.[84]

The 1940s added six and a half years to the life expectancy of British men, seven full years to the lives of British women. British life expectancy, overall, jumped over three times faster in the 1940s than in the 1980s.[85] These numbers, analyst Helen Epstein suggests, should astound us. British life expectancies in the 1940s rose despite "hundreds of thousands" of battlefield deaths and bombings that killed thirty thousand civilians.[86]

But more than bombs, notes Richard Wilkinson, dropped in Britain over the course of World War II. The war years also saw a "dramatic" drop in inequality. Higher taxes on high incomes and lower unemployment levels kept income gaps narrowing. People at the top and bottom of British society moved closer to the middle. Overall, the number of people making less than 50 percent of Britain's median income may have dropped by as much as half.[87] And that, in turn, nurtured an egalitarian spirit that lifted people's hearts.

"Inequality did not disappear, but something changed," Helen Epstein points out. "There was an ethos of cooperation and common striving. For a time, most of the nation was of one mind."[88]

By war's end, most British felt inspired to take the next step, to do whatever they could to build a society that "took better care of its members."[89] Voters, after the war, sent war-time Prime Minister Winston Churchill packing. The new Labor Party government that succeeded him promptly created a national health system that guaranteed every British man, woman, and child free basic care. Britain had become, despite the horrors and deprivation of a war-ravaged decade, a more cohesive, caring place. A healthier place.

THE WORK OF EPIDEMIOLOGISTS LIKE Michael Marmot and Richard Wilkinson, many scholars believe, "provides a direct biological rationale" for how inequalities impact health.[90] But not all scholars consider their emphasis on hierarchies and biochemistry, on "psychosocial pathways," an appropriate explanation for the stark differences in health outcomes that widening inequality inevitably seems to generate.

These skeptical scholars focus their attention on the *material* realities of life in unequal societies. Growing economic inequality within any society, they contend, will always mean that more people will lack access to "education, health care, and other services, with long-term consequences for health."[91] And more people will lack this access because unequal communities tend to invest less in the medical, educational, and other public services vital to health than do more equal communities.

"Increases in income inequality go hand in hand with underinvestment, which will reap poor health outcomes in the future," as George Davey Smith has argued in the *British Medical Journal.* "In the United States, poor investment in education and low expenditure on medical care is seen in the states with the most unequal income distribution."[92]

John Lynch, George Kaplan, and several University of Michigan colleagues deepened the case against the centrality of psychosocial factors in research they published in 2001.[93] Using newly available international data, Lynch and colleagues found that some psychosocial measures, like levels of distrust, do not always match up with the health outcomes. France, Italy, and Spain, for instance, show high levels of social distrust, but low incidences of coronary heart disease and relatively long life expectancies. Psychosocial factors like trust between people and the control people feel over their own lives, Lynch and colleagues conclude, "do not seem to be key factors in understanding health differences" between many wealthy countries.

That may be the case, the researchers advise, because many wealthy nations have made "investments in public health relevant goods and services" that tend to equalize the basic medical care all people receive. In societies where most people receive similar health care services, the argument goes, the psychosocial stresses generated by economic inequalities will be offset — and become less important to health outcomes.

To illustrate this point, some investigators contrast health outcomes in the United States and Canada. In the United States, public officials have chosen not to make the investments that equalize access to health care. Americans at different income levels receive widely varying levels of care. Health outcomes in the United States, not surprisingly, *do* match up with income inequality data. The more unequal an American state or metropolitan area, the higher the mortality rate.

In Canada, provinces also vary by level of income inequality, just as states do in the United States. But these provincial differences in inequality do not translate into significantly different death rates, as do state-level inequality differences in the American context.[94] What explains the difference? In Canada, health care and other material resources are "publicly funded and universally available." In the United States, health resources are distributed through the market, based largely on ability to pay. In Canada, as a result, income inequality appears to matter less for health.[95]

Case closed? Do we have proof here that psychosocial factors are not that central to differences in health outcomes? Maybe not. Analyst Stephen Gorin asks us to consider the differences between *how* health care is provided in the United States and Canada. In the United States, the poor only gain access to health care "through public assistance or charity, in short, through programs that differentiate them from the rest of the population." These programs have a stigma attached, and that stigma, notes Gorin, "is undoubtedly a source of stress, and possibly poor health, for the individuals relying on them."[96] In Canada, with everyone covered by government health insurance, no stigma applies to health care. In short, Gorin suggests, even investments in health care can have psychosocial dimensions.

We live in a world, apparently, where psychosocial and material factors continually interact to keep some people healthier than others. Epidemiologists will no doubt continue to debate which of these factors carry greater causal weight. The psychosocial camp, for its part, readily acknowledges the significance of material underinvestment, but contends that the most telling impact of inequality on health goes deeper.

"If, in the spirit of neo-materialism, you give every child access to a computer and every family a car, deal with air pollution, and provide a physically safe environment, is the problem solved?" as Michael Marmot and Richard Wilkinson ask. "We believe not."[97]

Not if people remain trapped in subordinate status, they argue, not if widening inequality is making that status an ever heavier weight to bear. That status will generate terribly debilitating stress — and undermine health — even if living standards are rising. How else to explain, wonder Marmot and Wilkinson, the "dramatic mismatches in living standards and health between societies"?[98]

Contrast, for instance, the situation of black men in the United States and men in Costa Rica, historically the most equal of Latin American nations. By absolute level of material well-being, black American men far outdistance their Costa Rican counterparts. In 1996, black males in the United States, with a median income that stood at $26,522, had over four times the purchasing power of Costa Rican men, whose median income barely topped $6,400. Yet Costa Rican men, on average, could look forward to nine more years of life expectancy than black men in the United States.[99]

The explanation for this difference, note Marmot and Wilkinson, "must have more to do with the psychosocial effects of relative deprivation" — the stresses of subordinate-status daily life in a racially and economically unequal society — "than with the direct effects of material conditions themselves."[100]

"To emphasize psychological pathways," Wilkinson takes pains to make clear, "does not mean that the basic cause of the problem is psychological or can be dealt with by psychological interventions."[101] The base problem, to his perspective, remains economic inequality. Greater inequality "increases the burden of low social status." Greater inequality dissolves social cohesion. Better health outcomes can never be attained, or maintained, in societies that grow more unequal.

On this last point, at least, most all researchers who have delved deeply into the links between economic inequality and health seem to agree. No good, in health terms, can come when a society becomes more unequal.

IF GROWING INEQUALITY WITHIN A SOCIETY leaves people less healthy, can people only get more healthy if their society becomes less unequal?

Some health professionals, based on the epidemiological evidence, argue that the struggle for healthier societies must, first and foremost, be a struggle for more equal societies. All people will have a meaningful chance to "get well," these health professionals believe, only in societies that are striving to get more equal.

"If we share the resources of our country more fairly," as Scottish medical educator George Watt has put it, "we shall have a more cohesive society and reduce inequalities in health. It will not happen the other way around."[102]

Other health care professionals disagree. They do not dispute the epidemiological evidence that links inequality and health. But they see the struggle against overall economic inequality as a long-term matter. What about, they ask, the here and now? Improvements in the health of the American people, these experts argue, will never begin to be made if these improvements must wait until America first becomes more equal.

"Those of us dedicated to a more just society find the American public's toleration of gross — and growing — inequalities in income and political power puzzling and frustrating," notes National Institutes of Health bioethicist Ezekiel Emanuel. "Yet this is the reality in which changes will have to be fashioned."[103]

"Income redistribution is important," agrees Barbara Starfield from the Johns Hopkins University School of Public Health, "but it is unlikely to happen any time soon."[104] In the meantime, conscientious health advocates ought to be promoting "more practical and feasible" strategies, by working, for instance, to increase access to primary health care.

Health advocates, adds Yale's Ted Marmor, should be addressing "the doable but difficult task of making medical care more fairly distributed before taking on the more utopian task" of narrowing economic inequality.[105]

These voices all seem eminently reasonable. But their logic is not without flaws. Access to medical services certainly does deeply impact our individual health. But the stresses and strains, disappointments and deprivations of everyday life in a deeply unequal society, taken cumulatively, seem to impact our overall health far more significantly.

"By the time a sixty-year-old heart attack victim arrives at the emergency room, bodily insults have accumulated over a lifetime," as researchers Norman Daniels, Bruce Kennedy, and Ichiro Kawachi have noted. "For such a person, medical care is, figuratively speaking, 'the ambulance waiting at the bottom of the cliff.'"[106]

The basic social and economic inequalities that drive people over that cliff, these three analysts contend, simply must be seriously addressed, as impractical and utopian as that task may feel in an increasingly unequal society.

Daniels and his colleagues also make another point, a more "practical" observation about access to health services. Champions of better and wider health care services, they note, have exerted enormous energy over recent years to extend access to affordable, quality care. Yet more, not fewer, Americans now go without health care services. This shameful situation, contends the Daniels team, could have been predicted. In times of growing inequality, advocates for social decency seldom make significant progress in any realm, health included.[107] To be truly "practical," to actually improve people's health, Daniels and his colleagues argue, advocates must not "*choose* between expanding coverage of health care and devoting our energies to changing the social distribution of other resources."[108] They must do both.

"Popular support for universal health care coverage," the Daniels team concludes, "*arises* (when it does) out of a shared egalitarian ethos that is itself a product of maintaining a relatively short distance between the top and bottom of the social hierarchy."

Where no egalitarian ethos exists, neither will a consensus that society ought to work to keep all people well. Where the "haves" and "have nots" stand wide apart, those with health security simply do not care, enough, about those without. In these sorry places, no secure health safety net will ever be strung. In these sorry places, the social fabric, in essence, has frayed. We move now to how — and why.

A Fraying Social Fabric

Weavers can almost always distinguish, without much difficulty, quality from second-rate fabric. Quality fabrics will typically be tightly knit. You can tug and twist them. They will not tear. In our everyday speech, we talk about quality *social* fabrics in much the same way. People within a healthy social fabric, we say, lead *tightly knit* lives. They care about each other. They join together in community improvement efforts. They give of their time to help others not as fortunate as themselves. They enjoy each other, too. Within a healthy social fabric, people relish spending time with friends. They welcome neighbors over for dinner. They mingle in parks. They dawdle over bake sales.

Within a tightly knit social fabric, people seem to routinely "experience joy in the completion of ordinary life tasks."[1] They don't just do their work or run their errands. They forge relationships. Colleagues at work turn into teammates on an after-hours softball team. Chance encounters picking up kids at a day care center start up long-lasting friendships. Afternoons spent raking leaves end up with neighbors sharing ideas. These sorts of relationships between people, over time, build "social capital," a special sort of grease that keeps the wheels of society rolling smoothly.[2] Societies that accumulate social capital, researchers tell us, aren't just more pleasant places to live. They seem to function more efficiently as well.[3] People in these societies don't waste time constantly worrying about whether they can trust other people — because they know these other people, or know people who know them, or know their paths will cross again.

These thick webs of relationships do not, of course, *guarantee* that people will behave fairly and effectively with each other. But they do increase the odds. They make civility the social norm. They foster "the sense of well-being and security that come from belonging to a cohesive society."[4]

Most of us, if we had the choice, would choose to make our home in a society of this sort. We sense, almost instinctively, that tightly knit communities make for good places to live. Many of our parents and grandparents can vouch for that. They lived in such communities.

We don't.

Harvard sociologist Robert Putnam has, over recent years, chronicled the "ebbing of community" in America, the fraying of our social fabric, more thoroughly than any other observer of our contemporary scene. He has tracked, through mountains of data, the eroding of our social capital. He has documented the fading frequency of "neighborhood parties and get-togethers with friends," the increasingly rare "unreflective kindness of strangers," and, most tellingly, our long-abandoned "shared pursuit of the public good."[5]

Putnam's work on the collapse of community in America first caught public attention midway through the 1990s. He labeled the phenomenon, in a brilliantly evocative phrase, America's "bowling alone" syndrome. Bowling in the United States, Putnam pointed out, used to be a social activity. People did most of their bowling in leagues, as part of teams that competed every week. League bowlers socialized between strikes and spares. They laughed, they bonded. They even sometimes shared points of view about civic issues.

By the 1990s, Americans were still bowling, but not much any more in leagues. Between the 1960s and the mid 1990s, league bowling dropped off over 70 percent for men, over 60 percent for women.[6] Bowling no longer meant bonding.

Researchers have found the same pattern in nearly every aspect of American life, from card playing to eating dinner. By virtually every meaningful measure, not just bowling, Americans have come to enjoy each other less. Between the mid 1980s and the end of the 1990s, according to one set of national polls, the readiness of average Americans "to make new friends" declined "nearly one-third."[7] A subsequent study, conducted in 2000 by Harvard University and the Center on Philanthropy at Indiana University, found that a third of all Americans simply no longer engage in "informal socializing, such as inviting friends to their homes or visiting relatives."[8]

Americans don't even seem to be enjoying the people closest to them, their spouses and their children, as much as they once did. Working couples, in one mid 1990s survey, reported only having twelve minutes per day "to talk to each other."[9] The kids of working parents found themselves alone so much, in the late twentieth century, that a new social category — "latch-key children" — had to be invented to account for them.[10]

Average Americans, the various data streams show, also seem to care less about their communities than they once did. Between the mid 1970s and the mid 1990s, "the number of Americans who attended even one public meeting on town or public affairs in the previous year" fell 40 percent.[11] Over these same years, local organizations saw their active memberships drop by more than half.[12]

These declines in civic involvement, in social interactions of any sort, happen to correspond, almost exactly, to another trend line in American life, our nation's rising levels of economic inequality. Indeed, the American social fabric seems to have begun fraying, begun tearing, at exactly the same time inequality in America began accelerating.

Must social fabrics always tear when societies become more unequal? Must inequality always isolate us from each other when gaps in income and wealth widen? Must widening gaps always leave our communities less caring and more cold-hearted?

These questions deserve America's attention. They have not yet received it.

PEOPLE WHO ARE QUITE WEALTHY, the sort of people who proliferate whenever income and wealth start concentrating, have always had a difficult time understanding their fellow human beings who happen to be less fortunate than they. The least fortunate the wealthy understand hardly at all.

"Poverty is an anomaly to rich people," as the nineteenth century English economist Walter Bagehot once noted. "It is very difficult to make out why people who want dinner do not ring the bell."[13]

Today's wealthy face similar comprehension deficits. In abstract theory, they share the same world as the less fortunate. In daily reality, they live within an entirely separate space. They move through a world of "Four Seasons suites" and "$500 dinner tabs," a world so comfortable that any other existence becomes almost impossible to even imagine.[14] In 1997, business journalist Richard Todd noted at the time, the typical American household had to make do on $31,000 worth of income for the entire year. How could the wealthy, Todd wondered, possibly comprehend what living on $31,000 must really be like? For wealthy Americans in 1997, Todd pointed out, $31,000 amounted to "a price tag, not a salary," the cost of "a low-end Land Rover, a year at Brown, a wedding, a dozen or so Prada dresses."[15]

In the boom years, America's most affluent routinely went about their lives with "very little sense that they live in the same country as anyone who is poor."[16] If reminded, they lashed out. The unfortunate, they insisted, needed to get their slothful little acts together. The nation, America's most fortunate agreed, needed to show some tough love. No more pampering. Poor people needed to be shoved off the dole, into jobs if they could find them, into oblivion if they could not. Decades earlier, in the 1960s, America had made war on poverty. America, in the 1980s and 1990s, would make war on the poor.

Those who led the 1960s war against poverty would never have understood this new offensive against the poor. They lived, after all, in a different America, a more equal America. They saw poverty as a horrible stain on a proud nation's social fabric. We will, President Lyndon Johnson pledged in 1964, wash that stain away. The United States would become a place where people truly care about each other, a "Great Society." Congress would buy into that noble vision. Lawmakers created medical care programs for the poor and the elderly. They widened Social Security coverage. They invented Food Stamps and created new subsidies for low-income housing.[17] And they didn't just create new programs for America's least fortunate. They funded them. Between the mid 1960s and mid 1970s, total outlays on medical, housing, food, and cash support for the poor "rose nearly 400 percent," after adjusting for inflation.[18]

"By the late 1960s," notes journalist James Lardner, "responsible officials looked toward a day when the last pockets of poverty, as they were quaintly known, would be eliminated."[19]

Sargent Shriver, the nation's top-ranking anti-poverty official, even had a year in mind when this noble goal would finally be realized.[20] That year, 1976, would eventually come and go without the ultimate triumph Shriver had expected. His War on Poverty did reduce indigence, and substantially so, but poverty would persist.

What would not persist, beyond 1976, would be any effort to wipe the poverty stain, once and for all, off America's social fabric. The year 1976 would mark, in budget terms, the War on Poverty's last all-out charge. Total anti-poverty cash assistance that year, in inflation-adjusted terms, would hit an all-time high. By the mid 1980s, that assistance would be down 14 percent.[21] By 1991, the purchasing power of a typical poor family's welfare benefits had crashed 42 percent from 1970 levels.[22] By 1994, in not one state in the entire nation did "welfare benefits plus food stamps bring recipient families up to the poverty line."[23] By 1996, America's political leaders would be ready to "end welfare as we know it." The welfare reform they would enact that year, the Personal Responsibility and Work Opportunity Reconciliation Act, eliminated the welfare system created by the original Social Security Act. In its place came a new program for "Temporary Assistance to Needy Families." The emphasis would fall on the "Temporary." Under the new law, poor families would be allowed to receive benefits for no more than five years. Within two years, any head of a family accepting benefits would need to be working.[24]

The new law accomplished exactly what lawmakers had intended. Welfare reform drove people off welfare rolls, at incredibly rapid rates. Within five years after the reform legislation's 1996 passage, the number of families on welfare had dropped almost 60 percent, from 5 million to 2.1 million.[25] What happened to these millions of families no longer on welfare? The government didn't know, or particularly care. The welfare reform legislation included no provisions for tracking what happened to former recipients.

Private groups did their best to fill in the informational void. The Children's Defense Fund had interviews conducted with over five thousand former recipients. Nearly 60 percent of former recipients who had found jobs, the research revealed, were earning weekly wages that kept their families *below* the poverty line. Over half the former recipients who had left welfare for work, the research added, had found themselves "unable to pay the rent, buy food, afford medical care, or had their telephone or electric service cut off."[26] Other survey work would reinforce the Children's Defense Fund findings.[27] Some former welfare recipients might be "better off today," Children's Defense Fund founder Marian Wright Edelman would tell Congress in 2001, "but millions are not thriving and are struggling simply to survive."[28]

Welfare reformers sloughed off Edelman's critique. In states where governors and lawmakers really understood how to make the new system work, they insisted, public policy miracles were taking place. Among the miracle makers: Wisconsin's Tommy Thompson, the governor who would later ride his reputation as a welfare reformer to the top slot at the federal Department of Health and Human Services. Journalists would rarely challenge Thompson's miracle-working claims. Those who did dare glance behind the curtain found more messes than marvels. In Wisconsin, noted the *Milwaukee Journal Sentinel's* Eugene Kane, some thirty thousand poor families just "disappeared" under Thompson's widely lauded welfare reform.[29]

Thompson's reform, Kane pointed out, had been billed as an endeavor "to build a bridge to meaningful work for the poor."[30] But any program truly devoted to "meaningful work," Kane observed, would bend over backwards to help recipients get the education and training necessary to qualify for decent-paying jobs. In Wisconsin, as well as elsewhere throughout the nation, welfare reform did no such thing. Poor mothers, under welfare reform, could not attend postsecondary classes and still qualify for basic benefits.[31]

Welfare reform didn't just prevent poor moms from going to college. In some places, welfare reform actually drove poor kids out of high school. In New York City, in 1998, local welfare officials told Keith Keough, a senior on the Grover Cleveland High basketball team, that he'd have to leave school and report to workfare once he turned eighteen — or else forfeit the benefits he had been receiving ever since his mother died the previous summer. An outraged math teacher immediately rallied to the boy's aid.

"I am a high school teacher in Queens," the educator wrote reporters, "and today an 18-year-old boy cried because he was told to leave school and go to work."[32]

Amid the resulting furor, city officials did an about-face. They dismissed the entire affair as "an isolated incident." Not quite. Earlier that same year, reporters discovered, a local judge had ruled that city officials had systematically "set up unconscionable obstacles" for poor young people who wanted to finish high school. Instead of giving students time to do homework, the judge found, officials were "requiring them to travel late at night on subways, to empty trash baskets in deserted municipal buildings."[33]

Mean-spirited acts of cruelty against the poor, in the welfare reform age, would multiply far beyond New York. In Colorado, a mother lost her family's Medicaid coverage after state officials discovered she owned a car. The mother, it turned out, had bought a used car to shuttle her six-year old asthmatic daughter back and forth to day care. The mom, before the car, had been taking her child to day care via light rail and a bus, leaving home at 6:30 a.m. to make all the right connections. But the mom feared that the early morning cold was making her daughter's asthma worse. A used car seemed a rational solution. But not to local officials. In Colorado, any mom with an asset worth more than $1,500 could no longer qualify for Medicaid.[34] A sick daughter made no difference.

Colorado's Medicaid officials were taking their cues from a state and a nation that had defined insensitivity to the unfortunate as perfectly appropriate behavior. Those who would suffer the most, from this insensitivity, would be those who had the nerve not to have been born in the United States. Congress would, in the 1990s, deny Food Stamps and Medicaid benefits to America's *legal* immigrants.[35]

Overall, Food Stamp rolls dropped by nearly 8 million people after the 1996 welfare overhaul, mainly, critics charged, because new procedures had turned the applications procedure into an intimidating obstacle course. In Ohio, Food Stamps went to 80 percent of the state's eligible poor in 1994, only 59 percent in 2000.[36]

"Every day, too many of our children have too little to eat," Marian Wright Edelman would report to Congress in 2001.[37] We in America live in the "world's wealthiest" nation, she would add, yet "millions of our children are still being left behind."

NO SOCIETY THAT PURPORTS TO BE CIVILIZED can ever justify leaving poor children behind. Children are our innocents. They cannot possibly be held "accountable," as poor adults so often are, for their poverty. Decent societies simply do not tolerate child poverty.

Unequal societies do.

At century's end, the most unequal nations in the developed world carried the highest child poverty rates. In the United States, over one in four children — 26.3 percent — lived in households that UNICEF, the United Nations children's agency, defined as poor, that is, households making less than half a nation's median income. The United States, the world's most unequal developed nation, did not, at the time, boast the developed world's highest child poverty rate. That dishonor belonged to Russia, possibly the only nation in the world, over the course of the 1990s, where wealth concentrated at a faster rate than in the United States. Russia's child poverty rate stood at 26.6 percent.[38]

Meanwhile, at the other end of the child poverty scale, researchers found the world's most equal nations. In France, just 9.8 percent of children lived in poverty by century's end. In the Netherlands, 8.4 percent. In Sweden, 3.7 percent.[39]

What explains these inexcusable differences in child poverty rates between less unequal and more unequal nations? Elite isolation, analysts note, certainly plays a pivotal role. In countries where wealth is concentrating the fastest, the wealthy and the powerful simply lose touch with the rest of society — and no small bit of their humanity in the process. A disconnected elite, observes University of Texas economist James Galbraith, will be much more likely to rush into public policies that end up punishing the poor.

"The 'end of welfare as we knew it,'" he points out, "became possible only as rising inequality insured that those who ended welfare did not know it, that they were detached from the life experiences of those on the receiving end."[40]

But elite isolation, analysts like Galbraith are quick to add, does not fully explain why poverty overall, and child poverty specifically, stains the social fabric of unequal nations much more markedly than the fabric of more equal nations. Something else, some other powerful social dynamic, must be at work, particularly in the United States and Britain, the two wealthy nations with the highest child poverty rates. In these two ostensible democracies, wealthy elites cannot unilaterally determine public policy toward the poor. These elites do not have enough votes, or even enough money, to impose their insensitive vision of what government should and should not do on the rest of us. Yet that insensitive vision has prevailed anyway.

To mend our social fabric, to create a society where cruelty can never be enshrined as policy, we need to understand why.

EVERY SUNDAY BEFORE ELECTION DAY, somewhere in the United States, a minister is earnestly reminding congregants that we are indeed our brother's keepers. The congregants all nod approvingly. An appreciable number of them, the following Tuesday, will then proudly vote — for candidates who pledge their eternal enmity against the "government handouts" meant to help our brothers, and sisters, who may be poor.

Why do such pledges work so well politically in the United States? Why do people of average means in America vote "against" the poor much more frequently than people of average means vote against the poor in the Netherlands, France, Sweden, or any one of a dozen other modern societies? Does some basic flaw in the American character doom us to a politics of insensitivity — and make attacks on poor people inevitable?

Economist James Galbraith most certainly does not believe so. Forget character flaws, he advises. Concentrate, instead, on America's economic flaws. Concentrate, above all, on what America's increasingly unequal distribution of income and wealth has meant for people in the middle.

Middle-income working people who vote against poor people are not by nature, Galbraith contends, "nasty, mean-spirited, ignorant, brutish."[41] They are instead responding somewhat rationally to an ugly and unequal world. In this unequal world, ever since the 1970s, a fortunate few have been gaining a greater share of America's treasure. This greater share at the top has meant a smaller share of income and wealth — greater poverty — at the bottom. Greater poverty, in turn, increases the cost of ongoing government programs to help the poor.

Who bears this cost? The wealthy easily could. In an increasingly unequal society, after all, they have more income and wealth, much more. But in an increasingly unequal society the wealthy also have more political power, and they use that power to "insulate" themselves from tax collectors. They convince lawmakers to reduce or even eliminate the taxes that most directly impact their affluent selves. The tax burden, ever so steadily, shifts onto middle-income people. These families in the middle, James Galbraith argues, soon become "ripe for rebellion against the burdens of supporting the poor."[42]

In America, the rebellions would start flaring in the late 1970s. They would flame throughout the rest of the century.

These rebellions, notes Galbraith, rarely emerged spontaneously. They would typically be stoked by sophisticated, lavishly financed ideological offensives that followed "a fairly standard form." In the early stages, the people who benefit from anti-poverty programs would be "stereotyped and demonized." They would be "presumed to be 'trapped' in a 'spider's web of dependency.'" Aid programs for poor people, the claim went, only encourage this dependency. Over time, this drumbeat would intensify. In reports and books bankrolled by wealthy donors, and in op ed columns and speeches based on these reports and books, "reformers" would declare that anti-poverty initiatives have been abject failures. They would pound home these declarations "so loudly and persistently" that those who disagreed would eventually "simply recede from public view."[43]

Individual anti-poverty programs, their defenders effectively silenced, would then stand defenseless. In budget battles, they would lose the dollars they needed to operate effectively. Without dollars, these anti-poverty initiatives would lose constituent support. In due time, some of these initiatives would be totally wiped off the public policy slate.

"Public housing suffered this fate in the early 1980s," observes Galbraith. "Welfare went away in 1996."[44]

Outside the United States, in Europe, conservative ideologues watched as this daring offensive against the modern welfare state unfolded. They thrilled to the battle cries that rallied conservatives in America to victory. No more handouts! No more big government! No more high taxes on the incomes of the successful! Emboldened, the European conservatives would launch their own offensives against the welfare state. But these offensives would all largely fail. In Europe, unlike the United States, conservative ideologues would not be able to turn middle-income people against programs that ensured decency for poor people.

The European conservatives, in their zeal to match the conservative triumph in America, had made a colossal miscalculation. They believed that average people, suitably enlightened by conservative insights, would see the poor as conservatives see them, as undeserving freeloaders. But contempt for the poor, the European conservatives failed to realize, only flourishes and festers where inequality has upset the basic security of middle class life. Their European nations, in the 1980s and 1990s, were simply not unequal — and insecure — enough.

Danish conservatives would learn that lesson the hard way.

Danish right-wingers had been stewing about Denmark's "overly generous" welfare state for quite some time. Everywhere they looked, they saw "handouts." Bums were making out like bandits. They didn't have to pay a cent for medical, child, or home nursing care. Or college either. They could even get paid family leave if they stayed home from work.[45] To make matters worse, the affluent had to pick up the bulk of the bill. Wealthy Danes paid taxes at rates that infuriated their conservative admirers. A most shameful situation.

In 1982, for a variety of somewhat unique political reasons, Danish conservatives would at long last gain an opportunity to set Denmark "right." Elections that year would give a coalition of conservative parties clear majority status. The conservatives would hold this status for over a decade, ample enough time to challenge — and start undoing — the welfare state created by their Social Democratic Party rivals.[46]

That undoing would never take place. In 1993, the Danish conservatives would leave office, their agenda unfulfilled. "Big government" had not been routed. Their nemesis, the Danish welfare state, still thrived. The conservative-led governments between 1982 and 1993, observers noted, had proven almost completely "unable to change Danish society" in any "profound way."[47] Poorer people in Denmark did not lose services and benefits, despite over a decade of conservative rule in Denmark.

What explains the conservative failure to smash the Danish welfare state? What made Danish social programs so resistant to right-wing "reforms"? What kept poorer Danes protected?

Many observers credit the survival of the Danish welfare state to the egalitarian spirit that animates it. The Danes, in creating their welfare system, had not set about the business of "eradicating poverty." They aimed instead to "improve the social welfare of the entire population."[48] The social welfare programs they created guaranteed *every* Dane important benefits and services, not just the poor. Every Dane could take advantage of free medical care and education through college. Every Dane could count on home nursing support, if needed, and an adequate pension.[49] Every Dane, even the most affluent, could receive child allowance payments four times every year.[50]

Within the Danish welfare state, all citizens had both a *right* to benefits and services and an *obligation* to support these benefits and services, to the best of their ability. And that meant that wealthy Danes, those most able to help support the Danish welfare state, paid more of their incomes in taxes than anyone else. These high tax rates on the wealthy, in turn, helped keep affluent incomes relatively modest – and gave affluent Danes reason to use and appreciate the same public services and social benefits every other Dane enjoyed.

Average Danes paid taxes, too. But these taxes fueled no massive taxpayer rebellion. Middle class people in Denmark depended too much on public services to do anything foolish that would jeopardize the funding of these services. In this sort of environment, compassion for poor people came naturally, not because average Danes were "naturally" compassionate, but because compassion, in a more equal society, tends to serve every average person's rational self-interest.

No analyst, in Denmark or anywhere else, has done more to clarify the essential rationality of this self-interest than John Rawls, the Harvard scholar many consider to have been the most important political philosopher of the twentieth century.

Suppose, Rawls once famously asked, that a group of people could create the society they were going to be born into, but not their place within that society. What sort of society would these people choose to create, a society where wealth was distributed unequally, and deeply so, or a society that distributed wealth much more evenly?

Most thoughtful people faced with this choice, Rawls argued, would tilt toward equality. In a more equal society, after all, even if you were unlucky enough to find yourself born into the ranks of your new society's least fortunate, you would still be able to look forward to a decent and tolerable life, since the least fortunate in a more equal society would never be that much *less* fortunate than anybody else. In a deeply unequal society, on the other hand, you could win big, that is, be born into a fabulously rich family, but you could also lose big. You could find yourself wretchedly poor. By opting to enter a more equal society, you could avoid, close to absolutely, this latter wretched outcome — and ensure yourself at least a modicum of personal social security.

In real life, of course, we cannot choose either the society or family we are born into. We all enter the world amid grand uncertainty about our prospects. For some of us, those of us born into wealth, this uncertainty ends fast. Great wealth ensures us security. We can confidently face the future with life's basics guaranteed. We will never go hungry or homeless. We will never suffer indignity should we suddenly become incapacitated by illness or accident. We will never have to deny our children what they need to succeed. Our great wealth will shield us from dangers and open doors to opportunity.

Unequal societies, societies where wealth has concentrated significantly, will always boast plenty of people affluent enough to live these sorts of self-assured, confident lives. In more equal societies, by contrast, few of us will have enough personal wealth to secure our futures against whatever unexpected obstacles life may throw our way. Without these personal fortunes, we will naturally worry about what could happen to us and our loved ones should we be forced to face a long bout of unemployment. Or a crippling ailment. Or a steep bill for college tuition.

But these worries need not incapacitate us. We can still live securely, even without sizeable individual personal fortunes to fall back upon, if we know we can count on help from others should times get difficult. We will support, consequently, programs that insure us this help. We will rally enthusiastically to proposals that guarantee us income when we lose our jobs, medical care when we lose our health, and old-age pensions when we lose the bounce in our step. In an equal society, the vast majority of us will spiritedly support all these initiatives because, simply put, someday we may need them.

In more unequal societies, no consensus on the importance of mutual support ever develops. Significant numbers of people in unequal societies — those people fortunate enough to be wealthy — need never worry about their basic security. These affluent have enough personal resources to weather any illness or accident. They can afford any tuition bill. Their savings will generate income long after old age has withered their individual earning power. These wealthy require no public safety net. They feel themselves totally self-sufficient — and wonder why everyone else can't be self-sufficient, too.

In an unequal society, in short, the most fortunate usually feel no vested self-interest in maintaining strong and stable social safety nets. The more unequal the society, the more people without this vested self-interest, the less the support for safety net programs. In other words, as James Galbraith sums up, rampant inequality "weakens the willingness to share" and, even worse, concentrates the resources that could be shared in the "hands least inclined to be willing."[51]

"In this way, and for this reason," Galbraith continues, "inequality threatens the ability of society as a whole to provide for the weak, the ill and the old."

AMERICANS OF MEANS, AND THEIR MANY ADMIRERS, usually object mightily to any suggestion that America has become, over recent years, a less compassionate place. Widening gaps between the affluent and everyone else, they assert, have not left America more cold-hearted. The weak, the ill, and old still tug at our heartstrings. As evidence, apologists for inequality point to programs like the Earned Income Tax Credit, a relatively new federal initiative designed to help the working poor.

The "working poor" make up about a quarter of employed Americans.[52] These low-wage workers take home paychecks that leave them, over a year's time, below or only slightly above the poverty line. In the United States today, these workers can count on the Earned Income Tax Credit to help them make ends meet. The program works on what might be called a "rebate-plus" principle. Workers who qualify for the Earned Income Tax Credit can get back, at tax return time, some or even all the income tax deducted from their previous year's paychecks. They can even, depending on their income and number of dependents, get additional cash back. In 2000, if the Earned Income Tax Credit had not existed, a couple with two kids making $20,000 a year would have owed a bit more than $200 in federal income tax. With the Earned Income Tax Credit in place, that same family could apply for and receive a $2,100 cash refund.[53]

The Earned Income Tax Credit, originally created in 1975, only came into its own after the 1986 Tax Reform Act substantially hiked the tax benefits that low-income workers could receive from it.[54] A few years later, in the 1990s, Congress expanded the program still again. By 1997, a low-wage worker with several dependents could collect as much as $3,656 via the credit. For parents working full-time in minimum-wage jobs, the Earned Income Tax Credit could "increase net earnings nearly 40 percent."[55] By century's end, the credit was funneling low-wage Americans $26 billion a year in cash refunds.[56]

The Earned Income Tax Credit, cheered *Fortune* magazine, "is first-rate social policy."[57] Few public figures disagreed. In the Earned Income Tax Credit, American business and political leaders had an anti-poverty program they could wholeheartedly embrace. And they did. The expansions of the credit enacted in the 1990s sailed through Congress with wide bipartisan majorities. This overwhelming support struck champions of America's unequal economic order as proof certain that grand fortunes and graciousness can advance hand in hand. The Earned Income Tax Credit demonstrated, at least according to inequality's champions, that affluent America had not turned its back on poor people.

But the various expansions of the Earned Income Tax Credit, in fact, signaled no great new wave of compassion toward the poor. By century's end, even with the billions spent on Earned Income Tax Credit refunds, the United States was still spending on poor people, as a share of gross domestic product, only half what other developed nations were spending.[58] And the Earned Income Tax Credit refunds, at the recipient level, offered considerably less than met the eye. The same low-wage workers who were receiving income tax rebates under the credit were also paying considerably more in Social Security and other payroll taxes.[59] These increased payroll taxes, in the 1980s and 1990s, ate significantly into the rebates poor families gained through their income tax credit.

To make matters worse, many low-wage workers eligible for Earned Income Tax Credit rebates never received them, largely because the government never worked particularly hard to simplify the tax credit application process.[60] One official pamphlet explaining just who was eligible for the credit ran fifty-four pages.

The bottom line: Despite the Earned Income Tax Credit, the *net* incomes of poor working people have hardly increased at all over the last two decades. In fact, according to Congressional Budget Office data released in 2003, the after-tax incomes of America's poorest 20 percent rose less than one-half of 1 percent, on average per year, between 1979 and 2000. CBO researchers included all federal support programs in their calculations, including Earned Income Tax Credit refunds. They found, after adjusting for inflation, that total incomes for the poorest 20 percent of Americans moved from $12,600 in 1978 to $13,700 in 2000, an average increase of $1 per week over the twenty-one years.[61]

The Earned Income Tax Credit has plainly worked no wonders for low-wage workers. Indeed, critics have charged, the credit is really only working wonders for employers fond of exploiting low-wage labor. The Earned Income Tax Credit actually gives these employers an incentive to continue paying low wages. For every $6 an hour these low-wage employers pay workers with families, the Earned Income Tax Credit adds about $2 to the worker's bottom line. If these employers were to pay appreciably higher hourly wages, the government would add nothing. Low-wage employers, in effect, are receiving what amounts to billions of dollars a year in outright corporate welfare subsidies.

Meanwhile, America's "other" welfare program, welfare for the poor, is no longer subsidizing poor moms. Under the 1996 welfare reform act, poor mothers with children are now required to enter the workforce and essentially take any job available, no matter how low the wage. This requirement, by flooding the job market with poor moms, is also working wonders for low-wage employers. With a growing labor pool of poor mothers available, low-wage employers are under no pressure to raise their wage rates.[62] The rush of poor moms into the job market serves, quite efficiently, to keep wages depressed.

The federal government, of course, could undo this downward pressure by raising the minimum wage. But minimum wage hikes enjoy no support in corporate circles, perhaps because business leaders and their friends in Congress have exhausted their compassion quota with the Earned Income Tax Credit. Throughout the boom years, business and political leaders sat back and did nothing as inflation steadily and significantly eroded the minimum wage. In 1968, minimum wage workers earned, in inflation-adjusted dollars, $8 an hour. In 2001, even after a minimum wage hike in 1996, they earned only $5.15.[63]

The modest 1996 increase in the minimum wage did help spark a brief surge in wage rates at the end of the 1990s. But that increase wasn't high enough to boost low-wage workers back up to where they had been in the late 1960s. Indeed, the 1996 legislation that increased the minimum wage actually *widened* the gap between low-wage Americans and America's most affluent. That's because Congress, without much fanfare, included in the minimum wage increase bill a provision that helped wealthy Americans "sidestep taxes on big stock market gains."[64] With this provision in effect, America's most fortunate could donate stocks to their own personal foundations, deduct from their incomes the stocks' current value, not what they originally paid for them, and, through this maneuver, totally avoid capital gains taxes on their stock market earnings.

Their personal foundations could then sell the donated stock, pocket several million dollars profit from the sale, and, if they so chose, use those millions to subsidize still another scholarly tome dedicated to exposing the uselessness of minimum wage laws and the silliness of those who support them.

IF YOU WANT TO SEE REAL COMPASSION IN AMERICA, the most ardent defenders of America's current unequal economic order argue, don't look at government "welfare" programs. Look instead straight into the hearts of Americans. There you'll see a "thousand points of light," countless examples of goodness and mercy that have nothing to do with government handouts. Let other nations depend on government to help the downtrodden. In America, the claim goes, the fortunate help the unfortunate directly.

Take, for instance, the battle against hunger. No one can deny that vast numbers of Americans have engaged themselves, over the past quarter-century, in anti-hunger campaigns. Since the early 1980s, notes Janet Poppendieck, a sociologist at Hunter College in New York, "literally millions of Americans" have volunteered their time in "soup kitchens and food pantries" and the "canned goods drives, food banks, and 'food rescue' projects that supply them."[65]

Poppendieck herself has been actively involved in anti-hunger activism since the late 1960s. Over the years, she has interviewed hundreds of volunteers at food banks across the United States. She knows the anti-hunger world, personally and professionally, as well as anyone. And she is troubled by what she knows. America's heavy emphasis on volunteer efforts to fight hunger, she fears, may be dulling, not feeding, our national commitment to compassion.

This anti-hunger volunteerism, Poppendieck notes, has become part of everyday American life. Boy Scouts go door-to-door collecting spare cans of food. Supermarkets place collection barrels for foodstuffs near their entrances. Restaurants sponsor anti-hunger fundraisers. Surrounded by all this activity, many of us quite logically assume that hunger must surely be "under control." Those who actually coordinate anti-hunger volunteer programs know that not to be true. The most important organizations in America working against hunger — Second Harvest, Food Chain, Catholic Charities, the Salvation Army — have all stressed that they play only a supplemental role in the struggle against hunger. The real heavy-lifting in that struggle, these groups have testified repeatedly, must come from government food assistance programs.

But many lawmakers no longer deem these programs essential. If government food programs were so needed, these lawmakers ask, why do so many poor people convert their Food Stamps into cash or resell items they pick up free at food pantries? If people were really hungry, the lawmakers argue, these poor families wouldn't be turning food aid into dollars they can spend on something other than food.

Are these lawmakers exaggerating the "fraud" that goes on in food programs? They may be, but many poor people, the fact remains, *do* turn food aid into cash. Does this mean that hunger really isn't a problem anymore? Wrong question, answers Janet Poppendieck. We ought instead, she argues, to be asking what makes modern life in the United States so miserably difficult for poor people. The key culprit, she contends, is not hunger.

"Many poor people are indeed hungry, but hunger, like homelessness and a host of other problems, is a symptom, not a cause, of poverty," Poppendieck notes. "And poverty, in turn, in an affluent society like our own, is fundamentally a product of inequality."

Only by confronting that inequality, adds Poppendieck, can we overcome social misery. The key issue, she argues, "is not whether people have enough to survive, but how far they are from the median and the mainstream."

That observation, at first take, doesn't ring true. Surely, at least with food, the issue must be whether people have enough to survive. What, after all, could be more misery-inducing than having to go hungry? Poppendieck understands how odd her contention — that inequality, not hunger, matters most — might seem. She helpfully offers an analogy to clarify her point. In many tropical nations, she notes, "children routinely go barefoot." But no mother in these nations feels "driven to convert food resources into cash to buy a pair of shoes, or to demean herself by seeking a charity handout to provide them."

But a poor mother in the United States, "where children are bombarded with hours of television advertising daily," faces a quite different set of pressures. Her child must have shoes, and not just any shoes, but the *right* shoes, "the particular name brand that her child has been convinced is essential for social acceptance" at the local junior high. To get her child the right shoes, to protect her child from ridicule, an American poor mother may well feel driven to convert Food Stamps into cash, even if that means going hungry.

The quality of life that poor people lead depends, in the end, not on how much food is on their plate, but on the gap that separates them from the social mainstream. If that gap is widening, poor people will see more misery, more hunger, even as cans of green beans are piling up in food banks.

Far too many anti-hunger activists, Janet Poppendieck charges, have ignored America's growing gaps in income and wealth. These activists, "diverted by the demands of ever larger emergency food systems," have essentially left conservative lawmakers free "to dismantle the fragile income protections that remain," free to "concentrate ever greater resources at the top." The result: Those "who want more inequality are getting it, and well-meaning people are responding to the resulting deprivation by handing out more and more pantry bags, and dishing up more and more soup." Ladling soup may make us feel noble, Poppendieck notes, but we ought not confuse our comforted consciences with real progress for people shunted to our society's bottom rungs.

"It is time," she concludes, "to find ways to shift the discourse from undernutrition to unfairness, from hunger to inequality."

THE OBLIGATIONS OF A GOOD SOCIETY go far beyond insuring decency for the hungry, the ill, the old, and the weak. All truly good societies, all societies that knit strong social fabrics, take great pains to offer and maintain public amenities for everyone. These societies cherish what some call the "commons," those shared aspects of public life that impact all people, not just the unfortunate.

In societies that cherish the commons, people breathe clean air, drink safe water, and gaze out over landscapes free from blight. The schools of these societies are joyously inspiring, their parks well manicured, their streets walkable without worry. In these societies, commuters don't sit and fume in endless traffic jams, and kids and seniors always seem to have plenty of pleasant places to go.

Public amenities, most Americans would agree, help make life worth living.[66] Yet today, all across the United States, these amenities are going neglected. In city after city, county after county, frustrated citizens can point sadly to signs of a deteriorating commons — to worn-out parks, to traffic-clogged roads, to libraries operating on scaled-back hours. These deteriorating public services, in the booming 1990s, would exasperate millions of American families. America had never been wealthier. So why couldn't our communities keep parks clean and libraries open? Why were local elected leaders neglecting the public goods and services that make our lives easier and more enjoyable? Were these officials vile — or simply incompetent?

Or could there be another explanation? Could we be expecting our local officials to do the impossible, to maintain the commons, for all Americans, at a time when growing inequality had left Americans with not much in common?

A commons, any commons, brings people together. We cannot benefit from public parks and public libraries, or public schools and public transportation, without rubbing elbows with other people. In more equal societies, no one gives this elbow rubbing much of a second thought. In less equal societies, the situation changes. In less equal societies, some people — the wealthiest among us — are not at all eager to come together, face to face, with other people. This hesitance, in societies divided by wide gaps in wealth, almost always arises, not because the wealthy are born snobbish, but because wealth inevitably generates pressures that induce the wealthy to withdraw from general company.

"Economic disparity," as journalist Michele Quinn has noted, "has always made socializing awkward."[67]

This awkwardness, Quinn has shown in her reporting on life in Silicon Valley, can spoil even the most casual of encounters. Just going about "picking a restaurant to meet friends," she explains, can end up sparking considerable social static if some acquaintances in a group can easily afford a hot new dinner spot and others can't. Wealthy people, once singed by such static, tend to take steps to avoid it in the future. They start, sometimes consciously, sometimes not, "making friends with those whose economic profile is similar to theirs."[68]

Author Michael Lewis, another acute observer of life amid wealth, sees in this self-segregation an eternal truth: "People tend to spend time, and everything else, in the company of others who possess roughly similar sums of money."[69]

Wealthy people see this separation as self-protection. They come to feel, often with good reason, that the nonwealthy envy and resent them.

"We've had five sets of friends who have turned on us since we made our money," one newly minted multimillionaire told the *Houston Chronicle* in 2000. "Some of them demanded a cut, saying they helped us, so we should help them."[70]

Wealthy people, this multimillionaire concluded from his experience, are better off hanging out with other wealthy people.

"You don't have to worry that they want something from you," he explained, "because, well, they're rich, too."[71]

The wealthy, not surprisingly, come to have little patience with the rest of us. Sooner or later, they withdraw. They cluster with their own kind, in affluent surroundings, luxury condominiums like New York City's Ritz-Carlton Downtown. In these surroundings, the wealthy no longer need the commons. They no longer depend on publicly provided goods and services. They can afford to provide their own.

At the Ritz-Carlton Downtown, for instance, the payment of a $4,500 monthly condo fee would entitle residents, early in the twenty-first century, to almost any service they could imagine. They could have condo staff arrange child care or do laundry or fill a refrigerator. They could even have staff talk to their plants while they were away on vacation. Not far from the Ritz-Carlton Downtown, at the Trump International Hotel & Towers, suitably wealthy families could buy into an equally lavish and self-contained world. Janet and Christopher Hassett, multimillionaires from California, made their home there in the late 1990s. They found everything they needed, all under one roof. Never any crowds, never any waiting. They could have lobster risotto delivered just by "pressing an extension" on their phone. If they ever wanted to cook for themselves, staff would be happy to bring by anything from porcelain chop sticks to a non-stick wok.[72]

"Here it's private and exclusive," Janet Hassett beamed in an interview. "It's la-la land."

Would she ever leave, a reporter wondered? Only in a pine box, she laughed.[73]

IN THE SELF-CONTAINED WORLDS OF WEALTHY PEOPLE like Janet and Christopher Hassett, public goods and services hardly ever make an appearance. The exceedingly wealthy don't need public parks for recreation or public transportation to get to work. They don't browse at public libraries or send their children to public schools. They never sit in public hospital waiting rooms. They don't even call on public law enforcement officers for protection. Their homes are monitored, day and night, by private security.

Exceedingly wealthy people, in short, don't use public services. They have no personal stake in supporting them. They come, over time, to resent any government that insists they help pay for them.

"The poor have sometimes objected to being governed badly," as the English writer and critic G. K. Chesterton noted years ago. "The rich have always objected to being governed at all."[74]

These objections never much matter, to the regular providing of quality public services, so long as a society's rich people are neither particularly plentiful nor wildly wealthy. In societies where grand fortunes are few and far between, the overwhelming majority of people will always depend on the commons. This overwhelming majority will actively partake of public services — and frown on those who seek to wiggle out of their obligation to help support them. In these more equal communities, isolated wealthy families may grumble about paying for public services they don't use, but their grumbling will be dismissed. Public life will move on.

But everything changes when wealth starts concentrating, when fortunes start proliferating. In these societies, more and more people start inching away from the normal, everyday social life of their communities. More and more people start living in their own private and separate wealthy worlds. At some point, if wealth concentrates enough, the society begins to tip. Private services come to seem necessary not just for the awesomely affluent but for the modestly affluent as well. These affluent, in every community becoming more unequal, also come to feel they're better off going life alone, on their own nickel — better off joining a private country club, better off sending their kids to private school, better off living in a privately guarded gated development.

Over time, the greater the numbers of affluent who forsake the commons, the greater the danger to the public services that most people still depend on. The affluent, in more equal communities, may grumble about paying taxes for public services they do not use. But grumbling is usually all they can do. In communities where wealth is concentrating, by contrast, the affluent have the clout to go beyond grumbling. They can press politically for tax cutbacks, and succeed, because fewer people, in an unequal community, have a stake in the public services that taxes support.

With every such "success," with every tax cut, with every subsequent budget cutback, with every resulting deterioration in public services, the constituencies for maintaining quality public services shrink. Those who can afford to make the shift to private services do so. With fewer people using public services, still more budget cutbacks become inevitable. Services deteriorate even further. People of distinctly modest means now find themselves depending on private services, even if they really can't afford them. Deteriorating public services leave them no choice.

This dynamic unfolds so predictably, whenever wealth concentrates, that one economist, the University of Chicago's Sam Peltzman, has even formulated a "law" to account for it. Growing income *equality*, holds Peltzman's Law, "stimulates growth of government."[75] Growing *inequality* has the exact opposite effect. In societies becoming more unequal, taxpayers are less likely to support spending that enhances a society's stock of public goods and services.

"If wealth and income are unequally distributed, the 'winners,' so to speak, will want to maintain their advantage," explain historians Carolyn Webber and Aaron Wildavsky. But "if substantial equality already exists, then citizens will want still more of it."[76]

Over the last half century, government spending in the United States has followed Peltzman's Law as assuredly as if that law had been enacted by Congress. Spending for public goods and services increased in the 1950s and 1960s, years of growing equality, and fell significantly in the 1980s and 1990s, years of growing gaps in income and wealth. In California, America's egalitarian middle class heaven after World War II, $1 of every $100 state residents earned in the 1950s went for the commons, for building schools, roads, water systems, and other public goods and services. By 1997, California had become the nation's most unequal state. In that year, of every $100 Californians earned, only seven cents went for public services.[77] The result: a massive deterioration of the California commons, from schools to roads. In the late 1990s, three-quarters of the teachers hired by the Los Angeles school district, the state's largest, "lacked teaching credentials." Freeways in the area remained "among the most clogged in the country."[78]

Americans, by century's end, could see the same sort of disinvestment in public goods and services throughout the United States. Drinking water systems that served more than 50 million Americans violated basic health standards. In nine major metro areas, the air people regularly breathed was polluted enough to spread serious respiratory disease.[79]

Our commons had been fouled — and nobody seemed to be cleaning the contaminants up, not in the air, not in the water, not even in our food. The federal government's Food and Drug Administration inspected food-processing plants twenty-one thousand times in 1981. By 1997, despite widespread fears about E-coli, listeria, and other dangers, the FDA only had enough funding to conduct five thousand annual inspections.[80]

This collapse of the commons, this fraying of the social fabric, would seldom inconvenience America's most fortunate. One way or another, affluent Americans could always arrange to get those public amenities they felt they absolutely must have.

In New York City, for instance, visitors in the boom years would marvel at how beautiful the city seemed. "The city looks good, quite good indeed," economist William Tabb would observe early in the twenty-first century. "For the more affluent, the city is a fine place."[81] Tabb would give the credit to a clever financing maneuver that had become exceedingly popular in New York corporate circles. This maneuver gave quasi-public entities, called "Business Improvement Districts," the power to levy taxes on businesses within a particular neighborhood and spend the proceeds on various public amenities, from litter removal to refurbishing park benches, within the confines of each district. These Business Improvement Districts appeared to work admirably. The New Yorkers who lived and worked within them raved about the quality public services they delivered.

Had New York City stumbled onto a formula for successful urban revitalization? No such luck. Corporate tax dollars, as economist William Tabb would explain, had once gone to support the entire city. Through Business Improvement Districts, corporate tax dollars could now be targeted to the specific enclaves that corporate interests, for one reason or another, wanted "spruced up." Corporate New York, in effect, was now off the hook for maintaining a city-wide commons. With Business Improvement Districts, noted Tabb, the same companies that had for years been demanding lower taxes — lower taxes that left city schools without playgrounds and libraries — had "found a privatized way of paying for the services they want."[82] What they didn't want, they didn't have to support.

New York's affluent, by century's end, would see no litter on the streets they walked. Everyone else would see a cleaner, better New York only when they stepped into the neighborhoods that attracted affluent New Yorkers.

IN OSLO, UNLIKE NEW YORK CITY, Norwegians of means do not get to pick and choose the neighborhoods, or the public goods and services, their tax dollars will support. And they don't seem to mind. All Norwegians consider themselves part of one commons.

"Here, if you have money or no money, it doesn't make a difference," Ansgar Gabbrielson, a leader in Norway's Conservative Party, told a *New York Times* reporter in 1996. "We all go to the same doctors; we all get the same services."[83]

The services of the Norwegian commons make for quite a pleasant existence. Parents in Norway can receive up to forty-two weeks of paid maternity leave. Lifelong homemakers receive retirement pay. Norway even pays children an annual stipend. In the mid 1990s, each Norwegian child under seventeen, whatever that child's family income might have been, was entitled to $1,620. Norwegian families also enjoy full medical security. All medical bills, above a few hundred dollars per person, are reimbursed. In their bountiful commons, adult Norwegians can also find wonderful opportunities to advance their careers. Norway's Lifelong Learning Program gives all working men and women the option to take paid annual leave, once every decade, to improve their job skills.[84]

Norwegians credit the generosity of their society to a "national commitment to egalitarianism."[85] They work diligently to maintain this commitment. To keep income differences narrow, they tax higher incomes at higher rates. Few Norwegians grumble. Most all are proud of the caring society they have created.

Outside observers are not as universally impressed. Generosity comes easy, critics sneer, when a nation sits aside offshore oil fields that are gushing black gold at volumes and rates only topped by Saudi Arabia.

But oil bonanzas, more sympathetic observers note, don't guarantee a bountiful commons. Within the United States, oil-rich Texas rates lowly on nearly every measure of a quality commons. Nearly a quarter of children in Texas, 24.1 percent, lack health care coverage, according to federal data released in 2003, a higher percentage than in any other state.[86] Way south of Texas, in oil-rich Venezuela, petroleum wells generate about $9 billion a year in revenues, yet over half that nation's 23 million people still live in dire poverty, without any decent public amenities.[87]

In Texas and Venezuela, no bountiful commons has ever taken root, despite oil riches. Both locales have, historically, allowed those riches to concentrate. They have welcomed and embraced colossal concentrations of wealth that would, in Norway, bring only shame. They have made a beleaguered commons inevitable.

In Norway, in other words, equality, not oil, keeps the nation caring.

"Even if we didn't have oil," as Norwegian Health Minister Gudmund Hernes noted defiantly midway through the 1990s, "we would not rethink the notion of the welfare state."[88]

That may be true, skeptics snicker, but that's only because social solidarity comes as second nature in a nation as ethnically homogeneous as Norway. It's easy for Norwegians to behave as if they were their brother's keepers, these skeptics charge. Norwegians share a common culture. They look alike. They speak the same language. They don't have to deal with cultural and racial differences. They can treat everybody fairly because racist attitudes and assumptions never tear at their social fabric.

In the United States, by contrast, racist attitudes and assumptions have been ripping us apart for hundreds of years. These attitudes and assumptions prevent the sort of social solidarity that matures so easily in nations like Norway. Homogeneous nations, the skeptics sum up, deserve no special plaudits for their benevolence. If their populations were more diverse, they would be no more generous and caring than any other nation.

Racism, of course, does rip social fabrics — and probably more viciously than any other social divider. But racism does not survive and thrive in isolation. Racism, many analysts note, cannot be separated from inequalities in income and wealth distribution. Indeed, maldistributions of income and wealth may well be what keeps racist stereotypes and hostilities alive in our modern age, an age that repeatedly declares, in every official international pronouncement, zero tolerance for racist behavior.

We Americans have by and large separated racial and economic inequality. We see lingering racism and concentrating wealth as two totally distinct phenomenon. Rich people, we know from our experience, can be bigots and rich people can be noble humanitarians. That some Americans have accumulated substantially more wealth than others, we consequently assume, makes no difference to whether America is winning or losing the struggle against discrimination, intolerance, and hate.

We have paid, and continue to pay, an enormous price for this most faulty assumption.

YEARS AGO, IN SEGREGATED AMERICA, African Americans occupied essentially only the bottom rungs of our national economic ladder. Racism, both virulent and subtle, kept better jobs off limits to black people — and kept wages depressed in the jobs where blacks dominated. Civil rights activists in these segregated years could and did argue, with unassailable logic, that black poverty reflected ongoing discrimination. End that discrimination, people of good will agreed, and black people would finally be able to realize the American dream.

The struggle against segregation and racial discrimination would take generations — and many lives. That struggle would finally triumph, in the 1960s, with a series of landmark civil rights acts. People of color, under these new laws, could no longer be denied jobs or housing, an adequate education or the right to vote.

These stirring victories, most of white America believed, would clear away the obstacles that had blocked black people from full participation in American life. With discrimination at long last illegal, racial gaps in social and economic well-being would surely start vanishing, or so white America assumed. But gaps between blacks and whites would not vanish in the decades after Jim Crow died. By almost every measure of social and economic well-being, black Americans would continue to lag behind white Americans, often by significant margins. Black Americans didn't make as much money. They suffered through higher jobless rates. They spent more time in poverty. They lived shorter lives. And they didn't do as well in school.

The school achievement statistics would be the most distressing of all, for schools were about the future. If black young people weren't succeeding in school, they didn't figure to succeed later in life — and racial gaps would never narrow. For America's political leaders, white and black alike, and for millions of parents, poor black student performance in education would emerge in the late twentieth century as the single most visible symbol of America's failure to come to grips with racial inequalities.

And just who or what was to blame for inequalities in school performance? Answers varied. Many community activists blamed low black test scores on poverty and the poor schools that most black kids attended. But some experts argued that other factors had to be at work. How else to make sense out of the most troubling academic achievement gap of all, the gap between middle-income kids of color and middle-income white kids? Black students were scoring lower than white kids, researchers reported, even when they shared the same socio-economic status.[89]

"How do we explain the underproductivity of middle-class kids, of able and gifted minority youngsters who come out of situations where you would expect high achievement?" asked Edmund Gordon, a distinguished psychologist at Yale. "This is not something a lot of people feel comfortable talking about."[90]

That discomfort, of course, reflected the racial dynamite in the middle class achievement gap numbers. These numbers cheered only the heirs to America's vilest racist traditions. If blacks from middle-income families were scoring less on their SATs than whites from middle-income families — and even less than whites from low-income families — that "proved," to racist minds, that blacks must be intellectually inferior, exactly the claim that white supremacists had been making for generations.[91]

Halfway through the 1990s, two academics, Richard Herrnstein and Charles Murray, would give this age-old racist claim a more scholarly gloss. Their 1994 best-seller, *The Bell Curve*, argued that "intelligence is largely inherited and intractable" and linked poverty and poor school test scores to the "lower" average IQ of blacks.[92] *The Bell Curve* would find plenty of receptive readers. National public opinion polls, conducted about the same time, suggested that one in five whites still believed that "blacks are genetically less intelligent than whites."[93]

Educators and community leaders, deeply alarmed by *The Bell Curve* mindset, would launch an all-out search for the real reasons behind the achievement gap between black and white students from comfortable families. The College Board, the nation's premiere testing organization, would create a special blue-ribbon panel, the National Task Force on Minority High Achievement, to investigate.[94] Meanwhile, out across the United States, parents, pundits, and politicians would be in no mood to wait for declarations from blue-ribbon panels. Some would blame white teachers for the achievement gaps between black and white middle class students. These teachers, critics contended, were making racist assumptions about black kids.[95] Other critics blamed black parents.[96] They didn't "care enough" about learning. Still other critics blamed black students themselves. These students, the charge went, equated success in school with "acting white" and ridiculed those black students who did dare to concentrate on their studies.[97]

In 1998, after a three-month investigation, the *San Francisco Examiner* would enter the fray. A major *Examiner* analysis would trace the achievement gap between middle class black and white students to a "complex" set of factors, everything from low teacher expectations to differences in parenting styles.[98] Nothing new here. But this *Examiner* analysis would go a bit further. The paper would offer, almost as an afterthought, another observation on the achievement gap between middle class black and white students. Black middle class families may have the same income as white middle class families, *Examiner* reporter Annie Nakao noted, but they have "less accumulated wealth."

"This, along with segregation patterns, can affect where a family buys a home," Nakao added, "and result in children having to attend school in less desirable districts, where peers are less likely to aspire to higher education."[99]

The *Examiner* reporter had hit upon a vitally important but almost universally ignored reality: Families with the same income do not necessarily live in the same economic world. Families really only belong to the same socio-economic class when they earn about the same incomes *and* own about the same wealth.

In the late 1990s, one researcher, Yale's Dalton Conley, would document just why this insight matters. Taking income *and* wealth into account, Conley reanalyzed the data that purported to show a clear achievement gap between "middle class" black and "middle class" white students. He would discover that no achievement gap actually existed. Black and white students from comfortable families of the same income *and* same wealth, he found, actually scored about the same on standardized tests.[100]

By ignoring wealth, Conley noted, previous educational researchers had ignored a key determinant of educational success. A family that earns $50,000 a year and owns a home, he explained, will almost always be able offer its children more in the way of educational advantages than a family earning the same income that rents. The family that owns will likely live in a better neighborhood. That better neighborhood will likely have a better school, because local property taxes still largely determine how much individual schools have to spend. That better school will likely have lower teacher-to-pupil ratios, better textbooks and supplies — and more qualified teachers. Students in that better school will likely do better. Almost always.

A family's level of wealth also determines other educational supports as well. Families with wealth can afford extracurricular resources and activities that

families without wealth cannot. And families with wealth, adds education journalist Alain Jehlen, can offer their children an even more important leg up, a
sense of confidence.

"Parents who own their home or other forms of wealth are imbued with a
sense that 'their kind' of people can make it in America," he notes. "Children
soak up this feeling at the dinner table and in a thousand other little interactions that have more impact than any amount of preaching."[101]

Wealth, in short, matters to education. And because wealth matters, how
wealth is distributed ought to matter, too, especially to Americans who want to
narrow and erase, once and for all, the gaps that divide white Americans from
Americans of color. These gaps rest, above all else, on differences in wealth.

IN 1995, TWO RESEARCHERS, Melvin Oliver and Thomas Shapiro, would publish
a major study that set out to compare the wealth of black and white households.[102] On one level, their findings would prove rather unremarkable. Black
households overall, the two sociologists would show, owned less wealth than
white households.[103] Everyone, of course, already knew that, and everyone also
thought they knew why. The breadwinners in black households, the conventional wisdom went, did not have the education that breadwinners in white households had attained. Consequently, white breadwinners could find better jobs and
earn higher salaries. Black breadwinners, once they had earned the same degrees,
would be able to compete for the same good jobs. Eventually, they would make
the same incomes and have the same wealth. The gap would disappear.

But Oliver and Shapiro's work would directly challenge this conventional
wisdom. Blacks in the United States didn't just hold less wealth overall than
whites. Blacks who had achieved the same educational degrees as whites held
less wealth. Indeed, blacks who had the same degrees, the same jobs, and the
same salaries as whites owned on average "dramatically lower levels of
wealth."[104]

Subsequent research would find no significant changes in these distribution-
al patterns. The wealth gap between white and black families, Dalton Conley
would sum up in 2001, "is far greater than racial differences in education,
employment or income." And this wealth gap, Conley would add, had actually
been growing "in the decades since the civil rights triumphs of the 1960s."[105]

How could that be? How could wealth gaps between white and black
households be growing if blacks now had access to the better-paying jobs previously denied them? The wealth gap between black and white households
could be growing, analysts noted, because most of the wealth Americans accumulate doesn't come from our job earnings. We spend the bulk of our earnings
on day-to-day expenses. Most of our household wealth, from 70 to 80 percent,
comes from "family gifts in one form or another passed down from generation
to generation."[106]

"These gifts," notes Dalton Conley, "range from a downpayment on a first
home to a free college education to a bequest upon the death of a parent."[107]

Gifts like these help young families gain an economic foothold. With help on a downpayment, families just starting out can buy a first home and spend years building equity instead of paying rent. With a free college education, they can be saving money instead of paying back student loans. With an unexpected bequest, they can invest in a bond or a mutual fund and watch their wealth grow.

In the latter decades of the twentieth century, the years after the civil rights revolution, family wealth did grow. Homes and other real estate, stocks and bonds leaped ahead at record rates. Those families that entered the 1970s with household wealth would see that wealth multiply nicely over the next thirty years. But few black families would share in this multiplication. Most black families did not enter the 1970s holding any significant household wealth. They had nothing to multiply. Their parents and grandparents had not left them much wealth, in any form, because their parents and grandparents had little wealth to share. And they had little to share because they lived in a society, the United States, that had systematically prevented them, and their parents, and *their* parents, from accumulating wealth in the first place.

That prevention process had begun, generations back, in slavery. Black slaves were denied any share of the immense wealth they created. But the expropriation of the wealth that black people created did not end when slavery ended. The slaves freed by Lincoln's generals had been promised "forty acres and a mule." They never got them. They ended up instead as tenant farmers squeezed by sharecropping arrangements rigged to keep them in perpetual debt.[108] And if they could somehow save up some cash, despite these arrangements, they still couldn't count on being able to buy their own land. Whites who sold land to blacks, in some parts of the South, would be "physically attacked" after the Civil War.[109] In 1870, less than 5 percent of America's black families would own their own land.[110] Blacks that year made up a third of the South's total population. They would own 1.3 percent of the South's total wealth.[111]

By the early 1900s, a half-century after slavery, not much had changed. In the Deep South's Black Belt, fewer than one-fifth of black farmers owned the fields they worked with their families.[112] And the land and wealth they did accumulate could be snatched away at any time, as one successful South Carolina black farmer, Anthony Crawford, learned in 1916. One day, at a local store, the prosperous Crawford — his farm extended over four hundred acres — fell into an argument with the storekeeper. Word spread that Crawford had cursed a white man. A mob came for him. He fought back. The local sheriff whisked him away to jail, where a second mob grabbed him, tied a rope around his neck, hung him up, and "riddled his swaying body with several hundred bullets." Soon afterwards, the remaining Crawfords "packed up their belongings and left."[113]

Millions of black families picked up stakes like the Crawfords. But they would find limited opportunity elsewhere. In Northern cities, the government agencies set up to help Americans become homeowners would routinely keep black families out of housing and credit markets. The Home Owners' Loan Corporation, in the 1930s, would institutionalize "redlining," a practice that denied home loans to residents of black neighborhoods. The Federal Housing Authority and the Veterans Administration would later shut blacks out of homeownership by funneling most of their loan dollars to suburbs where African American households were unwelcome. Between 1930 and 1960, less than one of every hundred mortgages issued in the United States would go to black families.[114]

America's most important wealth-enhancing program of the twentieth century, Social Security, would also shortchange African Americans. To get Social Security through Congress in 1935, New Dealers needed the support of white Southern Democrats. The price of that support: no Social Security coverage for farm laborers and domestics, the two job categories that employed the most black workers. This initial exclusion, not remedied for years, meant that millions of black working people would exhaust during old age whatever savings they had been able to accumulate during their working years. They would die with little wealth to hand down to their family's next generation.[115]

That next generation, by the 1990s, would find itself on the economic outside looking in. By the end of that decade, just one man, Microsoft's Bill Gates, would hold more wealth in stocks and bonds than all the African Americans in the United States together.[116]

In the late 1990s, Gates would pledge to spend $1 billion over the next twenty years on minority scholarships. That "one white man can possess more securities wealth than all 33 million African Americans combined," observed *Washington Post* columnist Courtland Milloy, "suggests something so wrong that it's going to take much more than a billion dollars' worth of schooling opportunities to fix it."[117]

NO SOCIAL SCIENTIST HAS EVER BEEN ABLE TO CALCULATE just how far, before tearing, a social fabric can be stretched. But people within an unequal society, note economists Gary Burtless and Timothy Smeeding, can often sense danger "when the gulf separating rich, middle class, and poor grows too large."[118] In the closing decades of the twentieth century, many Americans did sense danger. They felt like targets. They believed that a disturbing number of their fellow Americans could no longer be trusted to live by the rules that define civil behavior. Some ascribed this refusal to play by the rules directly to growing inequality.[119] What else could society expect, they asked, when some did unimaginably well while others could imagine only more misery?

"There is," as *New York Observer* columnist Michael Thomas would put it, "one very simple rule in life: Boast about your wealth, lifestyle and possessions, and it will occur to others either to get the same for themselves, or to deprive you of yours. The more remote a possibility the former becomes, the tastier the latter will seem."[120]

Affluent Americans, in the 1980s and 1990s, felt themselves much too tasty. They demanded protection. Political leaders rushed to provide it. They locked up every suspicious character in sight. By century's end, the United States would have 5 percent of the world's population and 25 percent of the world's prison inmates.[121] In California, America's most unequal state, public officials built one new university in the twentieth century's last two decades — and twenty-one new prisons.[122]

These building priorities would satisfy few Californians.

"The people in the inner city feel like they're being left out," Miguel Contreras, a top labor official in Los Angeles, would observe early in the new century. "And the people who live in the gated communities want higher gates."[123]

Rick Hilton, an heir to the Hilton hotel fortune, couldn't find gates high enough in Los Angeles. He wound up moving his family, in 1996, to New York City and an apartment that came with two cameras inside and six more outside in the hallway.[124]

"I feel completely safe in the middle of the night," Hilton's wife Kathy would note.[125]

Other affluent Americans couldn't feel completely safe without turning their homes into private fortresses. Architects caught on quickly. By 1998, the Neo-Fortress Movement — "towers and turrets, walled yards, locked gates, and tall, narrow windows" — had become a trendy and stylish look.[126]

In the end, affluent Americans would learn that no home fortress, no gates, no hallway cameras, could protect them from random violence. On September 11, 2001, all Americans would suddenly come to realize that we live in a horribly unsafe world — and cannot escape it.

That horribly unsafe world, like the United States, has become considerably more unequal over recent years. The latest studies of global income distribution, Robert Wade of the London School of Economics would note in 2001, all confirm "a rapid rise in inequality" among the earth's 6.2 billion people.[127] This inequality, he observed, is polarizing the world, creating entire regions where the social fabric has shredded, leaving behind scores of nation states "whose capacity to govern is stagnant or eroding." In these nations, "a rising proportion of people find their access to basic necessities restricted at the same time as they see people on television driving Mercedes cars."

"The result," Wade would add perceptively, just months before the horror of September 11, "is a lot of unemployed and angry young people, to whom new information technologies have given the means to threaten the stability of the societies they live in and even to threaten social stability in countries of the wealthy zone."

IN THE AFTERMATH OF THE ASSAULT on New York's World Trade Center, Americans would briefly step back into the commons that had been all but abandoned over the course of the previous quarter century. We all saw, in the heroic willingness of firefighters and other public employees to put their lives on the line for others, a world where people took seriously their obligations to one another. We liked what we saw. We saw community. We saw caring. We cheered.

But then life went on, as before, amid a social fabric that continued to fray, a commons that continued to collapse.

In New York, a year and a half after September 11, city officials would begin gearing up to shut down local firehouses, the homebases of 9/11 heroism, to help cover a mammoth budget deficit.[128] To avert the shutdowns, labor groups in the city rallied behind a proposal to impose a "transfer tax" on Wall Street stock transactions. Such a tax had actually been on the books until the early 1980s. Advocates for the tax noted that if this levy were reimposed, at just half the rate that had been in effect back in 1981, the city treasury would gain $3.8 billion, more than enough to eliminate the city's budget deficit without shutting firehouses and shredding other city services. But Wall Street balked. A transfer tax, the biggest brokerage houses charged, would be "disastrous." The mayor agreed. Stock trading would not be taxed. Firehouses, instead, would start closing.[129]

A continent away, wealthy Californians would be equally oblivious to the dangers of living in an unequal world. Their landgrabs along the California coast, throughout the boom years, had turned a series of coastal communities into resorts that middle class families could no longer afford to live in. Local city councils, if not the wealthy, worried mightily about the potential impact.

"So many firefighters, paramedics and other public safety employees on the coast are moving so far away because of housing prices," one journalist reported, "that there is new concern they might not be able to get back to town in an emergency such as an earthquake, when they would be needed most."[130]

We all, in the final analysis, need each other, whether we be rich or poor or anywhere in the middle. We never know when the earth might crack — or our homes go up in flames. We all really do need others to care about us, and that means, logically speaking, we ought to care about them. Deeply unequal distributions of income and wealth keep us from caring. Deeply unequal distributions keep us apart.

"Where wealth is centralized," as Confucius once noted, "the people are dispersed. Where wealth is distributed, the people are brought together."[131]

And social fabrics seldom tear.

AN IMPERILED NATURAL WORLD

IN A CARING COMMUNITY, people think about the future. What kind of society, they wonder and worry, will we leave our children and their children? Greed, by contrast, knows no tomorrow. Accumulate. Consume. Toss. Disregard the consequences.

But consequences, we know now, decades after Rachel Carson first rang the alarm against "the contamination of air, Earth, rivers, and sea," cannot be disregarded.[1] We are spinning through space on a distinctly fragile planet. This planet, our home, can only take so much abuse. Most of us, in our day-to-day lives, ignore this reality. Some of us fear it.

"Our house is burning down and we're blind to it," French President Jacques Chirac told world leaders gathered in Johannesburg for the 2002 Earth Summit. "Nature, mutilated and over-exploited, can no longer regenerate, and we refuse to admit it."[2]

This sense of despair, the more optimistic among us believe, may not be entirely warranted. On every continent, the optimists note, people at the grass-roots level are working to avert environmental catastrophe — and making an impact. Their sheer numbers have compelled the world's political leaders to conduct Earth summits. Their consumer dollars are changing how companies go about their business. No major corporation today dares to be seen as hostile, or even indifferent, to our planet's well-being. Almost every top business currently spends a small fortune performing — and promoting — environmental good deeds.

These good deeds, to be sure, will not save our Earth, as eco-entrepreneurs like Paul Hawken are quick to point out.

"If every company on the planet were to adopt the best environmental practices of the 'leading' companies," Hawken notes, "the world would still be moving toward sure degradation and collapse."[3]

But business, Hawken and other eco-entrepreneurs argued in the 1990s, can be reconfigured to go beyond mere good deeds. Markets, they acknowledged, have traditionally ignored the environmental impact of what business takes, makes, and wastes.[4] But markets can be fixed, they argued, to factor into account the environmental costs of business activity. "Green taxes" can be levied on business operations that do damage to the natural world. To avoid these green taxes, businesses would need only pollute less and waste less. And they would, because such ecologically appropriate behavior, in a world of green taxes, would make eminent bottom-line sense.[5]

Hawken and like-minded thinkers had good reason, in the 1990s, to believe that their ideas might help inspire an environmental turnaround of unprecedented proportions. All the pieces for a breakthrough appeared to be in place, especially in the United States. Over two decades of environmental activism had changed how Americans think about their natural world. On top of that, times were "prosperous," the economy was "booming." What better time for an upsurge in selfless environmental behavior? A prosperous people could afford to be magnanimous to Mother Earth.

But no magnificent environmental turnaround would ever take place in the United States, or the world for that matter, in the 1990s. Freshwater aquifers continued emptying, rainforests vanishing, species dwindling.[6] In 1992, only 10 percent of the Earth's coastal reefs were "severely damaged." By late 2000, that percentage had soared to 27 percent. Fewer healthy reefs, in turn, meant less protection from the storms "associated with climate change."[7] Our global environment, as a cranky French President Chirac would conclude at the 2002 Earth Summit, still stands "in danger."[8]

How could the Earth have come to this sorry pass? Why had progress against environmental degradation been so halting, despite decades of growing environmental awareness? Chirac had no answer. Some environmental activists did. Progress against environmental degradation has been so halting, they suggested, because gaps in wealth and income have become so wide.

OUT IN THE WILD, IN THE NATURAL WORLD, most creatures within a species lead remarkably similar daily existences. Some squirrels may stash away an extra acorn or two, but few squirrels live significantly better than any others. The same could once be said of us. The vast majority of the world's people, for most of human history, led lives that were roughly comparable. Relatively few families consumed terribly more than any others, wherever we lived, whatever the continent. That situation, of course, did begin to change as human civilizations began to emerge and evolve. Even so, until just a few centuries ago, the daily differences in living standards around the world remained, for the most part, modest. In the 1750s, notes demographer Paul Bairoch, most people in those nations we now consider "poor" lived just as well as most people in those nations we now call "rich."[9]

The Industrial Age would begin to alter this reality. By 1820, a few decades after industrialization began reshaping the global economy, the world's richest countries would claim, on a per person average, three times more wealth than the world's poorest countries.[10] By 1900, the world's richest nations would be averaging nine times more per person income than the world's poorest.[11] By 1960, the richest fifth of the world's people would claim thirty times more income than the poorest fifth. Over the next three decades, that margin would more than double, to sixty-one times.[12]

This colossal gap would widen even more rapidly in the twentieth century's final years. In 1991, the world's wealthiest 101 families would make more money than the entire populations of India, Bangladesh, Nigeria, and Indonesia combined.[13] In 1999, U.N. researchers would report that the world's two hundred richest individuals had amassed a combined $1 trillion.[14] If this fortune returned a mere 5 percent a year, the world's two hundred richest people would have averaged $684,932 in *daily* income — at the same time the world's poorest 1.3 billion people were subsisting on less than $1 a day.

The world's two hundred wealthiest lived in both rich and poor nations. Mexico, for instance, would boast the world's fourth highest billionaire contingent, with twenty-four in all, midway through the 1990s. Half the rest of Mexico, 45 million people, lived in poverty.[15]

"The Latin American brand of inequality is not for the timid," analysts from the Carnegie Endowment for International Peace and the World Bank would note in 1999. "The richest 10 percent of families are richer than their counterparts in the United States, while the poorest 10 percent are 10 times as poor."[16]

Do gaps so gaping matter to the global environment?

Mainstream economists, even those who think of themselves as environmentally aware, have generally sidestepped this question. Most environmentally minded economists do care about equity, but the equity they care about involves generations, not classes. To be fair to generations yet to come, they rightfully insist, we must consider the eventual environmental cost of what we do today, even if the bill for that cost won't come due until after we've gone.

These conventional environmental economists do not inquire whether the producer of a particular environmental cost "is rich and its victims are poor, or vice versa."[17] Instead, they spend their time adding up overall "costs" and "benefits." If the total "cost" of an environmentally degrading economic activity tops the "benefit," they sound warning bells. If the benefit tops the cost, they conclude that all's well with the natural world.

But all may not be well. Activities that degrade the environment, economist James Boyce reminds us, "do not merely benefit those alive today at the expense of future generations. They also typically benefit some living people at the expense of others."[18]

Standard cost-benefit analyses, by discounting income and wealth distinctions, essentially ignore the pressures that drive environmental degradation in the first place. Central American cattle ranchers, to offer one example, level rain forests because they stand to benefit personally from the destruction. These cattle ranchers, if wealthy and powerful enough, will continue to level rain forests, whatever the "costs" of that leveling to society. Even worse, on an unequal globe, the desperation of those without wealth and power, and not just the greed of those with it, will also come to despoil the natural world.

We see this desperation — and despoilation — wherever wealth concentrates. In Guatemala and El Salvador, environmental author Tom Athanasiou observes, the wealthiest 2 percent of the population owns over 60 percent of available arable land.[19] Should we be surprised, he asks, when landless peasants in outrageously unequal nations like these "migrate into rain forests or onto fragile uplands" to find land to farm?[20]

In our increasingly unequal world, such migrations are degrading our globe.

"Dispossessed peasants," notes author and activist Alan Durning, "slash-and-burn their way into the rain forests of Latin America, hungry nomads turn their herds out onto fragile African rangeland, reducing it to desert, and small farmers in India and the Philippines cultivate steep slopes, exposing them to the erosive powers of rain."[21]

In an unequal world, the Earth fears the poor.

OUR EARTH, OF COURSE, also has ample reason to fear the rich. In the Philippines, for instance, President Ferdinand Marcos and his business associates virtually wiped out what may have been the world's most glorious tropical hardwood forest.[22] The Marcos gang sawed down, stacked up, and shipped out enough hardwood to keep First Lady Imelda Marcos in world-class luxury for decades.

We remember Imelda for her fantastic footwear, her 1,200 pairs of shoes that became, in the 1980s, the world's most visible symbol of contemptuous consumption. We have largely forgotten the excess that defined the rest of the Ferdinand Marcos fortune, his dozens of country houses throughout the Philippines, the second presidential palace he had constructed in his home province, his waterfront Long Island estate half the world away.[23] How many kilowatts were wasted cooling and cleaning, lighting and guarding the enormous personal empire of Ferdinand Marcos? We don't know. But we don't need exact numbers to understand that our Earth winces whenever wealthy people begin to consume — and waste. Excess always exacts an environmental price.

Still, no one wealthy family by itself can ever waste enough, no matter how excessive its consumption, to seriously threaten our environmental well-being. We could multiply the Marcos excess by four hundred or so — the number of billionaires in the world at the start of the twenty-first century — and still not come up with enough wasteful consumption to give the Earth more than a moment's pause. The enormously wealthy may be wasteful, but they are not plentiful. In 2001, of the world's 6.2 billion people, only 7 million owned more than $1 million in financial assets.[24] If every one of those 7 million lived in a mansion that wasted several thousand square feet of space, if every one bopped about town in a luxury auto that burned ten miles to a gallon, if every one filled closets with clothes that were only worn once, the globe would likely muddle through quite nicely. In a world of 6.2 billion people, the personal habits of 7 million people, as environmentally degrading as these habits might be, will never make much of a dent.

This may be why so much environmental advocacy literature focuses on rich nations and not rich people. Those of us who live in rich nations are, relatively speaking, plentiful. We make up a large enough group to make a significant impact on the Earth. Our 20 percent of the world's population, U.N. researchers have reported, accounts for 86 percent of the world's consumption. The world's poorest 20 percent accounts for 1.3 percent. Those of us in the richest 20 percent use seventeen times more energy than the bottom 20 percent and seventy-seven times more paper. We eat eleven times more meat, seven times more fish. We own 145 times more cars. [25]

Within the rich nations, we Americans stand out. We produce nearly a quarter of the world's greenhouse gases and ten times more hazardous waste than the world's next largest producer. We generate over 330 pounds of municipal waste per person, 36 percent more than the world's rich-nation average.[26] We have become, many expert observers believe, an enormous drain on the world's life-blood.

"The environmental impact of 2.6 million newborn Americans each year," notes Thordjorn Bernsen, a former Norwegian environment minister, "far exceeds that of the 34 million new Indians and Chinese."[27]

Bernsen may be exaggerating, but not by much, suggests the work of two scholars at the University of British Columbia, Mathis Wackernagel and William Rees. Midway through the 1990s, the two calculated how many acres were needed, per person, to support America's "consumption of food, housing, transportation, consumer goods, and services." They tallied all the "garden, crop, pasture, and forest space" necessary to produce everything that Americans buy. They factored in fossil energy and land use. Individual Americans, they concluded, leave an "ecological footprint" that totals about twelve and a half acres per person. Individuals in India require, by contrast, just two acres each.[28]

These sorts of dramatic contrasts tend to frame the ecological challenge facing our globe as a simple conflict between a rich north and a poor south. The nations of the north, in this framework, become one undifferentiated mass of affluence, the nations of the south one monstrous sinkhole of poverty. In the north, households spend $17 billion a year on pet food. Meanwhile, in South Asia, half of all kids under five go malnourished. In Africa, south of the Sahara, a third of the continent's people die before they hit forty.[29]

These contrasts shock. But they do not tell the whole story. Indeed, the gaps between north and south may not be the biggest obstacle to environmental sanity. That biggest obstacle may well be the gaps *within* "rich" nations, between the rich and everyone else. These gaps accelerate the consumption that takes place within rich nations. Where these gaps grow, as wealth concentrates, so does our consuming. And so does our waste. The wider these gaps, the deeper we stamp our footprints into the Earth.

But that's not the worst of it. In an unequal world, everyone else in the world wants to follow in our rich nation footsteps. Or, at the least, ride in our SUVs.

BACK IN THE MID 1970S, Americans suffered through a gasoline crisis. The memories, for many of us, remain vivid. Long lines of idling cars snaking their way into gas stations. Drivers sitting — and fuming — in their cars, sometimes for hours. If, back then, you had walked down one of those gas station lines, clipboard in hand, and asked the frustrated drivers what sort of automotive future they envisioned, the answers would have no doubt come quickly. Tomorrow's vehicles, most motorists would have confidently predicted, will definitely be much more fuel-efficient than the dumb gas-guzzlers we have now.

Those motorists could not have been more wrong. America's vehicles have not become considerably more fuel-efficient. In 2000, a generation after the gas crisis, America's cars would only average 23.6 miles per gallon. And that average would actually overstate how many miles America's drivers were getting to the gallon, since millions of Americans were doing their everyday driving in vehicles officially classified as "light trucks," not cars. The biggest of these, SUVs like the king-size Ford Expedition and Dodge Durango, averaged 12 miles per gallon, and less, in city driving.[30]

Vehicle fuel efficiency in America, in other words, had gone backward, not forward — and at quite an environmental price.

"If you switched today from the average American car to a big SUV, and drive it for just one year," environmental author Bill McKibben noted in 2001, "the difference in carbon monoxide that you produced would be the equivalent of opening your refrigerator door and then forgetting to close it for six years."[31]

What had happened to America's more fuel-efficient future? Technology certainly didn't fail us. By 2000, America's automakers certainly knew *how* to make fuel-efficient cars. But they didn't. In an unequal America, they felt they couldn't. In an unequal America, fuel efficiency didn't pay.

Automakers had once been able, back in the middle of the twentieth century, to make decent dollars by selling modestly priced cars. Automakers may not have made a ton of money on every car sold, but they sold a ton of cars — to the middle class households that dominated America's mid-century marketplace. But that mass middle class market, as we have seen, had disappeared by the 1990s. Wealth in America had concentrated. Far fewer average families now made enough to be able to buy their autos new. Automakers, in response, devoted their attention to the affluent — and reconfigured their product lines. Out went the modest-margin, high-volume marketing strategy that had worked so well in a more equal America. In a more unequal America, automakers couldn't count on ever higher volume. They would have to start making more money on each vehicle sold. And that meant building bigger vehicles. Automakers could make, on each SUV sold, as much as ten times the profit from the sale of a standard sedan.[32]

These bigger vehicles carried, naturally enough, bigger appetites. They burned fuel at astonishing rates. But this higher fuel consumption gave no pause to the affluent 20 percent of American households now buying the bulk of new vehicles. In the 1980s and 1990s, their incomes were rising 44 percent faster than prices at the pump.[33]

The affluent could afford not to worry about fuel economy. The atmosphere couldn't. America's growing fleet of king-sized vehicles, environmentalists warned, was fouling the air and warming the globe. Environmental groups, throughout the 1990s, pressed Congress to take action. They asked lawmakers to eliminate the gas-guzzler tax exemption for "light trucks," a move that would "provide tremendous financial incentives for automakers to improve the fuel efficiency of their light trucks and SUVs." They backed tax breaks for carmakers that seriously set about hiking fuel efficiency. They promoted tax credits for consumers who purchase fuel-efficient vehicles.[34]

All these reforms made environmental sense. But they promised, at best, only to slow, not reverse, environmental degradation. To truly shrink America's ecological footprint, many analysts noted, we Americans would need to do more than shun SUVs. We would need to fundamentally rethink our society's bedrock economic assumptions – about growth, about accumulation, about personal satisfaction.

Pleasure, we modern Americans assume, increases as we accumulate. Our economy, we believe, will keep improving our lives so long as we take care to keep the economy "growing." And this economic "growth" has always meant "more," as in more goods. More goods will bring more pleasure. More makes better. Make more. Consume more.

Herman Daly imbibed this faith in growth as a bright young economist in the 1950s. He had come out of Texas eager to do good for people of limited means. Economic growth, as conventionally defined, seemed just the ticket. In an economy that grows, Daly's professors taught him, more becomes available for the poor. In a growing economy, the poor grow richer. Daly would not start second-guessing this growth-equals-progress equation until, in the late 1960s, he spent two years living among intensely poor people in Brazil. Amid this poverty, and amid Brazil's natural splendor, Daly suddenly started grasping the immensity of the gap between north and south, the fragility of the Earth, and the inadequacy of standard "more-is-good" economics. He would later emerge, after subsequent stints at Yale and the World Bank, as one of the world's most astute champions of a truly sustainable Earth. And he would argue, in a widely acclaimed body of scholarship, that the fight for a sustainable Earth must become, at the same time, a fight against inequality.[35]

HERMAN DALY BEGINS HIS CASE FOR AN EQUITABLE EARTH with the basics. Every economy, he notes, faces certain common problems. The first revolves around the allocation of productive resources. How should these resources be allocated? What should be produced? Bicycles or jellybeans? In market economies, prices guide these decisions. Prices help product makers and service providers understand what people want.[36] Manufacturers take signals from these prices. If the price on an item spikes, they'll produce more of it, to meet the obvious demand.

Distribution poses the second problem all economies — and societies — face. How should the benefits from production be apportioned? Goods, most people would agree, ought to be distributed fairly. A few people shouldn't get everything. But markets can't help us here. They cannot price fairness. Responsible societies, as a result, don't leave fairness to the market.[37] They establish rules, on everything from minimum wages to child labor, to guide how markets operate. The more democratic the society, the more fairness these rules are likely to generate.

Economists, Daly points out, have wrestled for ages with questions about both production and distribution. But they have given the third challenge all economies face — scale — virtually no attention at all. Scale raises questions about size, about how large an economy can grow within any given ecosystem, about how much economic activity an ecosystem can sustain. Conventional policy makers consider these questions irrelevant. They take the abundance of the Earth for granted. We humans, as U.S. Treasury Secretary Henry Morgenthau once asserted, live "on an Earth infinitely blessed with natural riches." On such an Earth, "prosperity has no fixed limits."[38] Today, notes Herman Daly, we know better — or at least should. Years of ecological research have made plain that no nations can assume they will always remain "infinitely blessed with natural riches."

We encounter "natural riches," Daly reminds us, in one of two forms. Some — oil, copper, coal, and the like — exist as fixed quantities. We use them up, they're gone. Other natural riches flow continuously, as renewable resources. The sun shines, rain falls, green plants manufacture carbohydrates. These resources do not exist as fixed quantities. But if these resources are depleted faster than nature can renew them, they can be used up and extinguished just as surely as copper and coal. We can cut down trees, for instance, faster than nature can grow them.[39]

Those resources we use up don't actually disappear, of course. They remain with us, as wastes. Our Earth, fortunately, has natural systems to handle these wastes, systems that go largely unseen. Termites break down wood. Earthworms recycle termite wastes into soil. The soil nourishes new trees. The world is renewed.[40] But natural waste-removal systems can be overwhelmed. Our economic activity can, at some point, produce more waste than the Earth can absorb. Where does that point sit? Just how much waste can the Earth absorb? We Americans appear intent on testing the limits. Directly and indirectly, we currently generate twenty-three tons of waste — each — per year.[41]

Scientists used to believe, observes author David Korten, that our first catastrophic environmental crisis would come when we as a world depleted our stocks of oil or some other nonrenewable resource. But we now seem more likely, he notes, to hit other limits first, among them our Earth's capacity "to absorb our wastes."[42]

These wastes, in contemporary America, no longer spew predominantly from factory smokestacks. We're "slowly fixing," notes commentator Bill McKibben, these traditional sources of pollution. Our new waves of wastes, unfortunately, are coming from sources that cannot be so readily "fixed." Our new wastes are coming from the unfolding of our normal daily lives, "from things going as they're supposed to go — but at such a high volume that they overwhelm the planet."[43]

Take for example the five-plus pounds of carbon that shoot out of car exhausts, as carbon dioxide, whenever an engine burns a gallon of gasoline. No filter of any sort, Bill McKibben points out, "can reduce that flow — it's an inevitable by-product of fossil-fuel combustion." This carbon dioxide, in turn, is trapping enormous amounts of heat on the Earth's surface. The greenhouse effect. We are "turning the Earth we were born on into a new planet."[44]

We as a species weren't built for a new planet. We were built for the one we have. And that planet, Herman Daly stresses, cannot sustain our insults forever. We can only shove so much economic activity through our Earth's ecosystems before they break down. If we keep increasing our "throughput" — the sum total of energy and materials we drive through the human economy — we make that breakdown, at some point, inevitable. At that point, the "natural systems that support all life," everything from the recycling of wastes to the atmosphere's capacity to filter out excessive ultraviolet radiation, would no longer be able to support all life.[45] We would be toast.

When would the toaster bing? No one can give an exact date. But we do know that we cannot produce more forever. Simple math tells the story. Between 1970 and 1990, notes the University of Oregon's John Bellamy Foster, world industrial production grew at a rate of 3 percent a year. If that rate were to continue, world production would double in twenty-five years, multiply sixteen-fold within one hundred years, and soar 250 times in two centuries.[46]

"Anyone who believes exponential growth can go on forever in a finite world," as the distinguished British-born scholar, Kenneth Boulding, once put it, "is either a madman or an economist."[47]

And that raises, for Herman Daly, what may be the most fundamental question of all.

"If the economy cannot grow forever," Daly has asked, "then by how much can it grow? Can it grow by enough to give everyone in the world today a standard of per capita resource use equal to that of the average American?"[48]

In 1987, an international commission chaired by the prime minister of Norway, Gro Harlem Brundtland, offered up a calculation that helps us answer this most basic of questions. The Brundtland Commission concluded that the world economy would need to grow by a factor of five to ten to give everyone in the world a shot at living an average American life. But the world's current level of human economic activity, Daly notes, is already showing "clear signs of unsustainability." To multiply this level of economic activity by five to ten — to double what we make and what we consume, then double and double again this production and consumption —"would move us from unsustainability to imminent collapse."[49]

WE CANNOT, CONCLUDES HERMAN DALY, "grow" forever. Current human economic activity is already preempting one-fourth of what scientists call "the global net primary product of photosynthesis."[50] This economic activity cannot possibly be multiplied five- to ten-fold without forcing a fundamental environmental breakdown. The economics of "more" simply cannot deliver an American standard of living to everyone on Earth. For everyone's sake, Daly and other ecological economists contend, we need to reject "growth" as our be-all and end-all.

But if we were to say no to "more," wouldn't we be consigning the world's poor to perpetual second-class status? And if we tried to narrow global lifestyle differentials, in a world that wasn't producing great amounts of more, wouldn't average people in rich nations have to be content with less? To improve the lives of the poor, in a no-growth world, wouldn't we, in effect, have to degrade the lives of everybody else? Are we faced, in the final analysis, with a choice we don't want to make? Must we either brutalize people to protect the Earth or brutalize the Earth to protect people?

In fact, argues Herman Daly, we do not face this choice. We do not face a choice between more and less. We face the choice, as a world, between more and better, between economic *growth* and economic *development*.

These two notions, growth and development, often get confused, a confusion that may stem from how we think about growth in our everyday lives. We speak, for instance, about children growing. Children who grow, we all understand, are becoming larger in size. But we also talk about adults growing. We might say, for instance, that a newly elected office-holder has "grown" in office. We don't mean, of course, that this elected official has become larger in size. We mean simply that this official has matured — developed — as a person. Herman Daly draws this same contrast between economies. An economy that "grows" gets larger. An economy that "develops" gets better.

Conventional economists do not distinguish between more and better, between growth and development. They simply assume that more always makes for better. They don't evaluate the outputs of economic activity, to separate the potentially harmful from the possibly helpful. They just count them. The more things we make, the higher they say our standard of living rises. Our current single most important conventional measure of economic vitality, gross domestic product, simply tallies the sum total of economic activity that takes place within a geographic area over a given period of time. Economies "grow," in standard economist-speak, when gross domestic product increases.

But "growing" economies are not always producing better lives for the people who live within them. The economic "outputs" that increase our gross domestic product do not necessarily increase our individual well-being. Our gross domestic product, to give one example, includes the value of all the products our chemical factories manufacture for sale. That's fine. Better living through chemistry. Chemical factories, on the other hand, also generate toxic wastes. That's not so fine. Toxic wastes do not improve our lives. They fill dumps that need to be cleaned up. They give us cancer. No matter. In the calculation of gross domestic product, a dollar spent on cleaning up a toxic waste dump — or burying a cancer victim — counts as economic growth.[51]

Or consider food. The food industry, notes analyst Jonathan Rowe, spends $21 billion a year "to entice people to eat food they don't need."[52] The commercials, coupons, and supermarket aisle displays that this $21 billion buys all raise our gross domestic product. And so does the $32 billion of goods and services the weight loss industry offers to help people dump the excess pounds they gain consuming food they don't need to consume. And so do the liposuctions that people have performed when weight-loss products don't work exactly as advertised. Every spin of this "grueling cycle of indulgence and repentance, binge and purge," economically speaking, "grows" our economy.[53]

Our "growth" economy has, in effect, spun out of control. In countless instances, we don't need the "more" we're getting. Indeed, adds psychotherapist Marc Burch, our homes are becoming "warehouses" for possessions we never use — or even remember.[54]

"We accumulate for the sake of accumulation to the point where we no longer really know what we own," he notes. "We trip over this junk, insure it, maintain larger-than-needed houses to shelter it, pay for security services to keep it from being stolen, fret over its safety, curse its oppressive effects on our emotions and activities, search through it to find what we really need to get on with our lives, trip over it in the dark, and then, at last, relegate it to a landfill."[55]

Up to a point, of course, adding more to what we possess can most certainly improve how good we feel. If we have no place to sleep, any bed will help us survive another night. If our bed has lumps, a new mattress will bring us comfort. But at some point down the consumption road, Marc Burch observes, "spending more and more for additional luxuries" eventually starts detracting from whatever fulfillment we might feel.[56] To make the money to buy the "more" we do not need, we work ourselves too hard and too long. We don't feel fulfilled. We feel stressed.

What we really need, to feel fulfilled, are the "goods" that standard growth economics doesn't count. We need to be surrounded by people we care about and who care about us.[57] We need more time for the personal pursuits that bring us pleasure. We need safe streets, clean parks, easy commutes. We don't need our already "rich" economy to grow and give us "more." We need our economy to develop and give us better.

In an economy that focused on better, not more, goods providers would make their mark and their money "by adding ingenuity, tasteful design, and efficiency improvements to products," not by pushing people to buy more and bigger products. The emphasis, notes Marc Burch, would be on making products "more durable, repairable, and aesthetically pleasing." Large numbers of

people would be employed "in maintaining, repairing, rebuilding, and recycling."⁵⁸ A no-growth economy, adds environmentalist Alan Durning, would
place a premium on "permanence" and make the all-important distinction
"between physical commodities and the services people use those commodities
to get." Few people, for instance, buy cars because driving gives them immense
pleasure. Most people buy cars to gain easy access to the places they want to go.
In an economy devoted more to better than to more, thoughtfully designed
housing and public transportation systems could give people easy access to
where they want to go as conveniently as cars.⁵⁹

Societies absorbed in development, not growth, would aim to *reduce* the
amount of energy and materials we drive through the human economy, our
"throughput." They would seek, as economist E.F. Schumacher once noted, to
"meet real human needs ever more efficiently with less and less investment of
labor, time, and resources."⁶⁰

But how would we know, how would we measure, if we were making
progress toward this noble goal of truly meeting human needs? Conventional
economic yardsticks wouldn't be able to help us. These measures only see value
in more. They make no allowance for better. Other measuring options, fortunately, do exist. Over recent years, scholars have fashioned several alternative
yardsticks that treat life as something more than the sum total of all goods and
services exchanged in the marketplace. One measure developed at Fordham
University, the Index of Social Health, combines sixteen different quality-of-life
indicators, everything from high school completion and teenage birth rates to
average weekly wages. Another ambitious quality-of-life measure, the Genuine
Progress Index, calculates both the positive and negative impacts of economic
growth. This index subtracts from the standard gross domestic product various
costs of growth, be they social, like family breakdown and the loss of leisure
time, or environmental, like loss of wetlands or the cost of air pollution.⁶¹

The Fordham researchers have crunched annual numbers for their Index
back to 1959. The researchers behind the Genuine Progress Index have run
numbers back to 1950. Their calculations, interestingly, reveal the same basic
trends. They both show the *quality* of American life increasing up until the mid
1970s and then dropping off. What happened in the mid 1970s? We have
already noted, in earlier pages, one significant phenomenon that took place in
these years: In the mid 1970s, the march toward a more equal America sputtered and stalled. We have had rising inequality ever since.

Rising inequality, we have argued, inexorably undermines the quality of our
lives. If that be the case, might rising inequality also undermine efforts to shift
our economic focus from quantity to quality, from more to better? Many ecol-
ogists believe that inequality has exactly this effect. Inequality, they contend,
makes "growth," as conventionally defined, appealing. Inequality makes the
economics of "more" seem our only hope.

IN ANY UNEQUAL SOCIETY, THE DOMINANT, to maintain their dominance, always find themselves striving to keep the minds of the dominated off the underlying unfairness of their situation. In our modern age, a fixation on "growth" helps enormously in this effort.

Growth neatly diverts attention from troublesome questions about equity. Do some people have more, much more, than others? Not to worry. If an economy is "growing," the dominant proclaim, then everyone will eventually have more. In a growth economy, the argument goes, all will get theirs, in due time, so long as the economy keeps growing. The need to keep that economy growing, in turn, becomes a rationale that justifies economic policies that help wealthy people become wealthier: The richer the rich become, the more they will invest, the more the economy will grow. To prosper, the gospel of growth assures us, we must merely keep faith — in the all-consuming importance of more.

But if we conclude that the Earth can no longer survive on an endless "growth" diet, then everything changes. Questions about the concentration of wealth, once easily shunted aside, now thrust themselves onto center stage. If we must, for the sake of our future on Earth, place limits on growth, than how the benefits from limited growth are distributed immediately becomes a matter of no small public interest. In a society that limited how much more can be produced, we would look askance at any individuals who gathered in extravagantly more than anyone else. In a world of limited growth, what Herman Daly calls a "steady state" world, a world developing but not growing, sharing would inevitably become second-nature. A sustainable world would be a more equitable world.[62]

An inequitable world, by contrast, cannot be sustainable. In an unequal world, the wealthy chase their own private solutions to whatever problems, a degraded environment included, life may bring. Local waters too polluted? They jet off to pristine beaches elsewhere. Those without wealth, meanwhile, come to see the accumulation of wealth as their only route to personal security. "In response," environmentalist Rich Hayes has noted, "governments push economic growth even more forcefully." The politics of more.

"Can environmental values survive such a future?" Hayes asks. "I can't see how."[63]

Environmental values, our recent history suggests, thrive only in times of greater equality. America's entire basic body of environmental protection legislation — the Clean Air Act, the Endangered Species Act, the National Environmental Policy Act — moved through Congress into law in the late 1960s and early 1970s, a time of unprecedented economic equality in the United States.[64] Our years of increasing inequality, since the mid 1970s, have brought not one single grand new breakthrough for environmental protection. Environmentalists in the United States have essentially spent the last thirty years playing defense. Despite that defense, our Earth continues to erode.

We ought to be able to do better, but we won't, not within an economy, not within a society, growing more unequal with every passing year.

WHICH RAISES A FRIGHTENING THOUGHT. Are we too late? Haven't the values of "more" already triumphed, not only in the United States but all over the globe? In our media-saturated world, hasn't just about everyone been exposed to the glories of modern consumer culture? Given that exposure, how can we expect the world's poor to be content with anything less than the same consumer comforts the comfortable currently enjoy in the United States? How can we expect poor peoples to reject the growth economics that promise to deliver these comforts? How can we expect poor nations to explore more equitable, more sustainable economic alternatives, to choose development over growth?

Poor nations, clearly, will only explore these alternatives if they have evidence to believe that equity and sustainability can improve life quality today, in the here and now, better than the economics of inequality and growth. Such evidence, wondrously, does exist, in a tropical hothouse of innovation that few people outside South Asia even know exists. In this place, a coastal state within India known as Kerala, over 33 million people have created a remarkably equitable society where equity and sustainability actually offer a realistic and practical alternative to the economics of more.

Kerala, by every conventional measure, rates as a desperately poor place, "even by Indian standards."[65] Keralans average, per person, $200 less in gross domestic product than the average Indian. The comforts conventional economic growth delivers — cars, air conditioners, washing machines — grace only a tiny percentage of Keralan households.

But the people of Kerala, in social interactions, don't come across as desperately poor. They come across as proud. Keralans, men and women alike, look visitors straight in the eye. They don't beg. They don't show, notes Akash Kapur, a thoughtful observer of the Indian scene, any of the "self-abasement that so often comes with poverty."[66] Keralans have reason to be proud. On the only measure that "ultimately matters" — "the nature of the lives people can or cannot lead," a formulation introduced by Nobel Prize-winning economist Amartya Sen — Keralans have created a society that outperforms much of the rest of the world.[67] People in Kerala lead lives that are long and healthy, in vital, safe, tolerant communities.

The numbers testify to Kerala's achievement. Morocco, a nation about equal to Kerala in population, generates about three times more wealth per person than Kerala. But people in Kerala, on average, live ten years longer than Moroccans. Colombia, another similarly sized nation, generates four times Kerala's wealth. But babies die in Kerala at less than half the rate they die in Colombia.[68]

Kerala and California also carry about the same population. California, of course, overwhelms Kerala economically. California generates seventy-three times more growth per person than Kerala's. But Kerala, not California, enjoys more social peace. In the 1990s, about two hundred thousand inmates packed California's jails and prisons. The number of full-time prisoners in Kerala: five thousand.[69]

Within India, Kerala boasts the lowest rates of malaria and cholera and the highest rates of access to doctors, nurses, health clinics, and hospitals.[70] Within the world, Kerala boasts a literacy rate that tops the average of all other low-income nations — by an amazing 40 percent.[71] And the literate in Kerala, unlike most of the rest of the low-income world, include girls as well as boys. In 1994, 93 percent of high school-age girls in Kerala were enrolled in high school, more than three times the rate in the rest of India and the world's poor nations.[72]

The people of Kerala owe their good fortune, their outstanding *quality* of life, partly to the accidents of geography. On the west, Kerala stretches along the Indian Ocean. This long coastline has always left Kerala open to new ideas from abroad, everything from Christianity to communism. Meanwhile, on the east, mountain ranges have kept Kerala somewhat separate from the rest of the South Asian subcontinent. These mountains, together with the sea, helped create a land where divergent peoples – Hindus, Christians, Muslims, and Jews – have lived side by side, in tolerance, for generations.[73]

In this heady atmosphere, intolerance — and exploitation — would not go unchallenged. In the nineteenth century, Kerala saw massive protests against the indignities of India's caste system, an outrageously rigid hierarchy that subjected people in the "lower orders" to life-long humiliation.[74] In the 1930s, inspired by the teachings of Mahatma Gandhi, small but significant numbers of Kerala's wealthy Brahmins, all born at the opposite end of the caste hierarchy, began "renouncing their privileges and giving up their lands."[75] About the same time, all across Kerala, grassroot networks of landless tenants were organizing for thorough-going land reform. They would later elect, in 1957, India's first communist-led state government, and this new government would quickly enact sweeping land reform legislation. But the legislation would not go into effect. India's central government promptly dismissed the ministers who would have been responsible for its implementation. Kerala's peasant associations would not be intimidated. They kept up the pressure, and comprehensive land reform would finally come about, fourteen years later, in 1971.[76] The reform would give about 1.5 million former tenant families title to their first property.

Over the next two decades, under steady pressure from peasant groups and trade unions, elected governments in Kerala, communist and noncommunist alike, would enact still more wealth-redistributing reforms.[77] Kerala's minimum wage became India's highest. Stiff tax rates on the wealthy, meanwhile, helped underwrite the free and low-cost distribution of basic services. Keralans, by the 1990s, were paying no charge for a minimal level of electrical power.[78] In state-supported stores, Keralans could buy everything from rice to batteries at subsidized prices.[79]

All these reforms, notes environmental author Bill McKibben, helped create "a state with some of the most equal wealth distribution on Earth."[80] That suited average families in Kerala quite nicely. But outsiders, particularly outsiders with power and wealth, considered Kerala hostile territory. Industrialists avoided Kerala. They were not about to situate manufacturing plants in a state where wage rates ran three times the Indian average.[81] Kerala, as a result, would not — could not — "grow" in standard economic terms. Without capital to fund ambitious "growth" projects, no giant manufacturing plants would soar above Kerala's tropical forests. Joblessness, on the other hand, would rise, to levels that topped the average unemployment rates elsewhere in India. But Kerala did not crumble, as conventional growth economics would have predicted. Kerala, instead, developed. Kerala's communists may "have failed to spur economic growth," as a 1998 *Atlantic Monthly* analysis would observe, but "they have been singularly successful at implementing development through redistribution."[82]

Kerala would grow better, not bigger, through a variety of imaginative initiatives. One key effort, the People's Resource Mapping Program, mobilized villagers to inventory their local natural resources and then forge plans to develop these resources sustainably. Village volunteers, once trained, collected data on land use, local assets, and water resources. Scientists added other data into the mix to create "environmental appraisal maps" that villagers and scientists together could then use to fashion local action plans.[83]

These plans, note anthropologist Richard Franke and sociologist Barbara Chasin, would make real differences in people's lives. In Kalliasseri, a village in northern Kerala, the mapping helped villagers realize they were always importing, late in the dry season, expensive vegetables from elsewhere in India — at the same time their own rice fields "lay fallow for lack of water." The village decided to try an experiment. Land owners would grant unemployed young people "free use of their fallow rice fields during the dry season," to raise vegetables. The youths would then use the maps developed by the mapping project to identify the fields "that would make the best use of local water resources." The end result? The jobless youths earned income, productive land no longer went wastefully fallow, and local villagers saved money buying vegetables.[84]

The same spirit of sharing and sustainability has animated development efforts all across Kerala.[85] In the midst of one literacy campaign, for instance, teachers in a predominantly Muslim region realized that many people weren't becoming literate because they needed glasses to be able to see what they were supposed to be reading. Over a two-month stretch in 1989, local people in the region proceeded to donate over fifty thousand pairs of eyeglasses. Forty trained volunteers, note Richard Franke and Barbara Chasin, then "matched those who needed glasses with the appropriate set of lenses."[86]

Sustainable solutions also emerged to meet Kerala's energy challenges. Historically, rural Indians have used wood for fuel, a course that has leveled wide expanses of local forests and exposed families to dangerous levels of "suspended particulates" from inefficient wood-burning stoves. Cooking for three hours at one of these stoves, researchers have found, fouls lungs as grimly as smoking twenty packs of cigarettes a day. In the 1980s, activists would fan out across Kerala to educate about wood stove dangers. Scientists and engineers, meanwhile, collaborated "on improved stove design" and "seminars to bring together household cooks and scientists." All told, the project would help Keralan households install some two hundred thousand high-efficiency stoves.[87]

Kerala state officials, to conserve energy, have also encouraged architectural styles that make the most of local resources. The schools, offices, and homes designed by Laurie Baker, the British-born architect Kerala officials hired to design state housing for the poor, offer one example. Conventional builders reinforce concrete floors with steel rods. Laurie Baker's buildings use grids of split local bamboo instead, "at less than 5 percent of the cost." Baker's mostly brick-and-mud structures save even more energy by avoiding air conditioning, no small feat in an oppressively hot place like Kerala. His secret? "Gaps between bricks let air and daylight through a wall, while diffusing the glare of direct sunlight," notes Adam Hochschild, an American admirer. Baker's buildings also often feature pools of water surrounded by tiny courtyards. The evaporation from the pools keeps temperatures down, as does the shade of the coconut palms Baker strives to keep overhead. The net effect: buildings that sit beautifully in harmony with their surroundings, all reflecting a clear understanding, sums up Adam Hochschild, "that the Earth will not forever permit us to be so profligate with its riches."[88]

THE PEOPLE OF BRAZIL COULD once credibly claim they, too, lived at least somewhat in harmony with their surroundings. In the 1950s, Brazil's flagship city, Sao Paolo, offered a model of sensible urbanity. A neatly tuned network of trolleys and buses kept the city's 3.7 million people coming and going in clean, fume-free air. On Sao Paolo's streets, only 164,000 private cars, less than one for every twenty-three people, pumped out pollution.[89]

But over the next half century, years that saw Kerala choose equity, Brazil chose to take a different course. Kerala would redistribute land to poor peasants and endeavor to keep rural life a viable option. In Brazil, where 43 percent of the land belonged to less than 1 percent of the nation's landowners, authorities would make no serious effort to distribute rural land wealth.[90] Poor peasants in Brazil would react sensibly. They fled the economic dead-end the countryside had become. They filled Brazil's urban centers. Sao Paolo would jump, in the four decades after 1960, from 3.7 to 17 million people.[91]

In Brazil's new overcrowded urban environments, the affluent would create their own separate living spaces — and lose all interest in maintaining the amenities that make life livable for all. Public transportation, for instance, now made no sense. The affluent had no desire to rub elbows, in trolley cars, with people so clearly "below" them. The trolley tracks would be torn up. Once charming cobblestone streets would be widened into multilane thoroughfares. By the end of the 1990s, average people could no longer move easily about their once beautiful Sao Paolo. Some 5.1 million cars choked the city.[92]

And sewage would choke the rivers. Nearly half the families in Brazil, the nation's top statistical agency reported in 2001, do not have access to proper sewage-collecting. Over the course of the 1990s, a decade that saw Brazil's economic "growth" nearly double over the 1980s, the number of families without sewage treatment barely dropped at all.[93]

In a reasonable world, the contrast between Kerala and Brazil, a contrast so strikingly evident by the 1990s, might have sparked some serious soul-searching. Brazil's choices — wealth concentration over wealth redistribution, "growth" over sustainability — had paid no dividends for either average people or that tropical piece of the Earth they called home. Kerala's commitment to equity and better, not more, had created a nation that worked for average people and their environment. Maybe the world needed more Keralas.

The world, at least the world elites that set the rules, would have other ideas. Global policy makers would promote, throughout the closing decades of the twentieth century, economic policies that undermined Kerala-like choices at every turn. The "Kerala model" stressed self-sufficiency, making the most of local resources. The world's movers and shakers insisted instead upon "free trade." They labeled as "protectionist" — and intolerable — any actions taken to shield and sustain fragile local economic activity from competition with the world's corporate giants. The Kerala model placed "infant survival, nutrition, education, and public services ahead of consumerism and private gain."[94] The world's globalizing elites would ridicule public expenditures as inefficient and inflationary. The Kerala model promoted policies that narrowed gaps in income and wealth. The globalizers accepted inequality as natural and necessary. Without inequality, they argued, economies could never "grow."[95]

Kerala's political leaders never bought into this globalization mantra. But that didn't matter. Globalization would impact Kerala anyway. India's central government found itself in the same situation as governments throughout the "less developed" world. To gain economic assistance, these governments had no choice but to accept the policy prescriptions pushed by international economic agencies like the World Bank and the International Monetary Fund. That meant moving to privatize public services — and cutting the budgets of those services that remained public. That meant cutting taxes on the wealthy to create a better "business climate." That meant ending tariffs that kept the prices of imported goods high enough to give local industries and farmers the space they needed to survive.

Kerala would feel the impact of these "structural adjustment" policies throughout the 1990s. Budget cuts at the national level would force Kerala state officials to cut back on lunches for poor schoolchildren.[96] The state subsidies that kept rice and other basic goods inexpensive also had to be reduced. But Kerala's political leaders would fear the abolition of protective tariffs perhaps most of all. Without protection, their state's labor-intensive, sustainably managed small farms and cottage industries would be competing directly with highly mechanized, energy-devouring, resource-depleting corporate operations.[97] Kerala could not win that competition. Indeed, suggests Herman Daly, societies that treat people and environment with all due respect will always be losers in a no-holds-barred "free trade" marketplace.

In societies that respect people and the Earth, Daly explains, enterprises must take environmental and social costs into account. Such societies enforce anti-pollution laws. They set minimum wage standards. They levy taxes that fund health and other basic benefits. Enterprises in these societies have responsibilities, to people and place, that must be met. These enterprises can compete with no problems against enterprises that bear similar responsibilities. But they cannot compete against enterprises that are "free" to ignore their impact on the Earth and its people. Enterprises that can dump their wastes into rivers — and exploit their workers as easily as they exploit the Earth's resources — will always be able to sell their products for less than enterprises held responsible for their conduct. Enterprises that degrade people and earth, in an entirely "free" marketplace, enjoy a "natural" advantage.[98]

That advantage, of course, can be countered — by imposing tariffs "on goods imported from countries that refuse to internalize environmental and social insurance costs."[99] But tariffs, global elites insist as a matter of faith, infringe upon "free trade." Indeed they do, and that's why they're needed, not to protect inefficient domestic industries — the claim the globalizers always make — but to protect societies wise enough to recognize that no business can honestly calculate profit and loss without having to take all costs into account.[100]

In a world dominated by "free trade" orthodoxy, and the lure of western consumer culture, Kerala would stumble into the twenty-first century working desperately to maintain its commitment to both equity and the environment. Whether Kerala could maintain that commitment remained unclear. Many educated Keralans, by 2000, had begun emigrating to the more affluent Persian Gulf. They wanted more than their society could deliver.[101]

Kerala, critics contend, can only deliver that "more" by abandoning the Kerala model. These critics have not yet triumphed. Within Kerala, limits on the economics of more remain in place. For how much longer no one can say. In a world that worships growth and welcomes inequality, Kerala's vision of our human future will never be secure.

IS A SUSTAINABLE WORLD TRULY ATTAINABLE? Can we ever go beyond the mindset that more is always better? The experience of Kerala suggests that perhaps we can — but not on a globe where the lifestyles of the rich and famous continually tease and taunt us.

"A billion people living in dire poverty alongside a billion in widening splendor on a planet growing ever smaller and more integrated," economists

Raymond Baker and Jennifer Nordin have noted, "is not a sustainable scenario."[102]

A seriously sustainable scenario, ecological economists point out, would require us to recognize what we so far have not, that the Earth cannot be exploited endlessly, that we can only consume, only discard, so much. The Earth imposes limits on what we can do. To move toward sustainability, we need to understand these limits, accept these limits, live within these limits. But we will never succeed at that endeavor so long as we place no limits on our economic behavior, no limits on the accumulation of more.

Every year, on Earth Day, earnest speakers ask us all to think about ourselves as the stewards of our planet. As stewards, they remind us, we have the responsibility to preserve and protect. This responsibility defines the environmental ethic. The lust for "more" — gluttony — poisons it. We will never become the stewards of our Earth we need to be until we reject this gluttony. But we will never be able to reject gluttony until we first reject inequality. Gluttony grows where wealth concentrates.

Where wealth concentrates, societies accumulate. They get bigger. To save our Earth, we must have better.

A Dying Democracy

THE POLITICAL COMMENTATORS that grace America's op-ed pages don't usually agree on much. But they do agree, overwhelmingly, that democracy in America isn't working very well. Our elected representatives, the complaint goes, hardly ever show real leadership or move with dispatch. They take few risks. They have become mere slaves to public opinion polls.

Hardly any commentators argue the reverse. In fact, in the United States today, not a single prominent pundit contends that politicians regularly defy what the polls tell us. Yet today, the truth is, our elected leaders *do* often disregard even the clearest public opinion poll numbers. Not all the time, to be sure, but on a predictable basis. In modern America, our representatives regularly ignore polling results whenever these results dismay the rich and powerful. And our representatives move decisively whenever these same rich and powerful want to see movement.

Too cynical a judgment?

In the tumultuous days after the horrible tragedies of 9/11, America's entire airline industry seemed to be tottering at the verge of collapse. Over one hundred thousand airline and travel industry workers had lost their jobs, almost overnight.[1] Americans the nation over clamored for Congress to act.

In Washington, lawmakers noted solemnly that this clamor had been heard. "We need to secure," House Speaker J. Dennis Hastert pronounced shortly after 9/11, "some strong help for the American workers."[2]

Help from Congress would indeed shortly be forthcoming, but not for American workers. Airline employee unions had assembled a package of proposals designed to provide cash support, job training, and health benefits for the out of work.[3] Lawmakers ignored these proposals. Instead, just ten days after 9/11, they enacted a $15 billion bailout that left airline executives, as a *Los Angeles Times* observer would note, "free to slash more jobs and run."[4] The bailout would include no help for workers who had lost health care, no money for job training, and no extension of unemployment insurance. Airlines, under the bailout, would even be free to duck their severance obligations to laid-off workers.

Airline executives, for their part, had to agree not to raise their salaries over the next two years to qualify for the bailout's billions.[5] But that stipulation meant nothing, in practical terms, since the bailout placed no limits at all on executive stock option windfalls or any other non-salary category of executive pay.[6]

Airline executives would not be the only corporate leaders who shook their tin cups after 9/11. Shortly after the attacks, insurance industry executives met with President Bush "to press for the creation of a multi-billion dollar government safety net to limit their exposure to future terrorist incidents."[7] The President proved happy to oblige. He would later sign into law, as part of the Homeland Security Act, legislative language that committed taxpayers to foot the bill for billions in insurance company liabilities.[8]

These bailouts for the airline and insurance industries would not stir, in mainstream political and media circles, much in the way of debate. Why bother debating? The bailouts represented nothing new, just American democracy at work. Corporate leaders ask, corporate leaders get.

The telecoms want government regulators out of the way? Fine. The Telecommunications Act of 1996 gives them total freedom to wheel and deal — and set whatever cable TV rates they deem appropriate.[9]

Bankers worried about public outrage over soaring ATM fees? Congress can help. Shortly before century's end, lawmakers put the kabosh on a proposal that would have forced banks to slash ATM surcharges.[10]

Data-entry operations upset about a new federal ergonomics standard designed to protect office workers from "carpal tunnel syndrome" and other Information Age ailments? In 2001, early in the new Bush administration, Congress will smite the new rule down.[11]

Corporate leaders, of course, do not always win what they want in our modern America. They couldn't possibly. Some corporate sectors, after all, are competing against each other for congressional favors. They all can't win. But where corporate interests share common interests, their deepest desires seldom go unfulfilled. And corporations, in the closing decades of the twentieth century, would desire nothing more deeply than lower taxes. They would get them.

By statute, corporations are supposed to pay 35 cents in federal tax on every $1 of profits. In practice, by 2003, they were paying under 15 cents in taxes on every profit dollar, thanks to a friendly Congress that has delivered unto corporate America hundreds of billions of dollars in new and expanded tax-based corporate subsidies.[12]

These sorts of business tax breaks have come to be widely known — and derided — as "corporate welfare." Corporations, by the mid 1990s, were raking in over $100 billion a year worth of corporate welfare, $53 billion in tax breaks and another $51 billion from direct subsidies to industries.[13] The enormity of these subsidies disturbed even some usually pro-business conservatives in Congress.

"I don't think," noted Ohio Republican John Kasich, "we should coddle the rich."[14]

But his colleagues did. In 1995, Kasich tried to cut corporate welfare by $15 billion. The House would vote to axe just $1.5 billion, not much more than 1 percent of the total.

"House Republicans took a hard look at corporate welfare," the *Washington Post* noted, "and decided they liked what they saw."[15]

If American politics were truly "poll-driven," as the conventional wisdom holds, members of Congress would have never dared oppose Kasich's proposal for modest cuts in corporate welfare. After all, as polls showed well *before* Enron hit the headlines, most Americans do not trust corporations. In one 1996 poll conducted for *Business Week*, only 4 percent of Americans felt large corporations really cared "about what's good for America." And two-thirds of those surveyed, 67 percent, told pollsters the "government should use higher taxes to penalize companies that eliminate jobs, close plants, or pay their executives extremely high compensation."[16]

If American politics were simply poll-driven, legislation to implement penalties against misbehaving corporations would have sailed through Congress. But no such legislation would even reach the House or Senate floor. And that would not be because Congress was too busy working on other initiatives that Americans cared about more. Lawmakers have spent the last quarter-century ignoring almost everything average Americans care about.

Pensions? After Enron's collapse, and the evaporation of millions of dollars from employee 401(k)s, Americans expected government to make some effort to make their retirements more secure. But the post-Enron Congress "shunned even modest protections like rules to require companies to make promised severance payments or to let workers elect representatives to the board of their 401(k) plans."[17]

Education? Parents with kids in schools with leaky roofs want help making school buildings safe, clean, and up-to-date. By the late 1990s, the typical school in the United States had seen forty-two years of service.[18] Giving every child an appropriate learning environment, the American Society of Civil Engineers estimated in 2001, would cost the United States $127 billion.[19] Congress has made no move to appropriate any of that.

Health care? Americans, polls show clearly, worry constantly about affording quality care. But lawmakers have made no moves to give Americans what all other industrial democracies already have, a system that guarantees everyone access to affordable care.

America's political leaders, early in the 1990s, always had a ready excuse whenever an impertinent voter would ask why Congress couldn't act to insure all Americans against illness or repair leaky school roofs. The nation, the answer went, simply couldn't afford the cost, not with the federal budget running in the red. By the late 1990s, that excuse would no longer be credible. At century's end, the federal government was running huge budget surpluses, not deficits, and so were state governments. Surely the time had now come for investing in America. But the time had not come. America's working families would still not see any action on the concerns they told pollsters they cared most about. Not from Republicans. Not from Democrats. By 2000, despite bountiful budget surpluses, government investments in education, research, and infrastructure had dropped, as a share of gross domestic product, 63 percent from their 1980 level.[20]

Not all lawmakers, of course, would sit silent through all this.[21] But those who dissented would find themselves overwhelmed by corporate cash.

"We have come to the point," political reform advocates Ellen Miller and Micah Sifry would note, "where we have what amounts to a 'coin-operated Congress.'"[22]

And plenty of coins were flowing in. In 2001, the health care industry alone spent $235 million making its case to Washington politicos. Corporate America's nine biggest sectors, that same year, together invested $1.27 billion to nudge American democracy their way, forty-seven times the outlays made by all America's trade unions combined.[23]

Deluges like this, repeated year after year, would not guarantee the wealthy and powerful victories in every battle they engaged. But they would always bounce back, and quickly, from any setback. In 1993, for instance, the new Clinton administration squeaked through Congress a modest increase in the top income tax rate on high-income households, an increase that infuriated America's deepest pockets.[24] Lawmakers shared their outrage. To show how much, they would go after the IRS, first by holding a series of high-profile hearings that portrayed IRS agents as bullying stormtroopers, then by pushing through "reforms" and budget cuts that crippled the government's ability to audit high-income tax returns.[25] The end result? In 1999, for the first time ever, poor taxpayers were more likely to be audited than wealthy taxpayers.[26] Over the course of the 1990s, Syracuse University researchers would later note, IRS audit rates on America's wealthiest taxpayers actually dropped 90 percent.[27]

For the lawmaking friends of America's rich and powerful, a defanged IRS would not be enough. In 2001, after the ascendancy of George W. Bush, they would rush to pass the largest tax cut for the wealthy in American history.[28]

This first George W. Bush tax cut would have little to offer the vast majority of American taxpayers, the men and women who make up the bottom 80 percent of American income-earners. As a group, these middle- and low-income Americans pay nearly twice as much in Social Security and Medicare payroll taxes as they pay in income taxes.[29] But the 2001 tax cut would cut not one dime from payroll taxes. Instead, the act would set in motion the repeal of the estate tax, a levy that only impacts America's richest 2 percent.

"This is an administration and Congress that galloped to the rescue of the rich," the *Washington Post* would note just after President Bush signed his initial tax cut into law.[30]

Two years later, with the federal budget back deeply in the red, the administration and Congress would gallop again, to the same rescue. The Bush administration's 2003 tax cut would save households making over $1 million a year, on average, $93,530 each off their annual federal income taxes. Households making under $10,000 a year would see, from this same 2003 tax cut, an average annual tax savings of $1.[31]

In 1994, nearly a decade before this second mammoth George W. Bush giveaway to the wealthy, the *National Catholic Reporter* had openly wondered whether democracy in America has passed some point of no return.

"Has greed killed democracy in America?" asked a *Reporter* editorial. "It now appears no bill can make it through the U.S. Congress that does not first and foremost serve the nation's super rich, those 100,000 families or so who annually amass more than $1 million, who run Congress and for whom Congress works."[32]

For this wealthy slice of America, democracy in the United States continues to work well. Our elected leaders do not take their cues from the polls. They take their cues from the wealthy. Some sticklers for political precision have a word for any nation that willingly accepts the rule of the rich. We in the United States, they insist, cannot claim to have a *democracy*. We have become a *plutocracy*. We the people no longer rule.

WEALTH, OUR NATION'S MOST SAVVY POLITICAL THINKERS have from time to time noted, has always played a central role in American political life.

"There are two things that are important in politics," as Mark Hanna, the top GOP strategist of the first Gilded Age, quipped over a century ago. "The first is money, and I can't remember what the other one is."[33]

In Hanna's time, money talked. But money did not totally monopolize the discussion. Throughout the 1890s, Hanna's heyday, candidates without much money — the original Populists — raised issues that challenged corporate power and even won elections. How incredibly distant those days seem today. In twenty-first century America, no candidate without a bankroll can mount a competitive race for a meaningful elected office. In 1976, candidates typically had to spend $84,000 to win a seat in the U.S. House of Representatives. In 2000, they spent an average $840,000.[34]

In contemporary American politics, those candidates who spend more win more. A candidate's odds of winning, researchers have shown, increase in direct proportion to the money the candidate has available to spend. House candidates who campaigned on less than $100,000 in 1992, for instance, did not win a single race. Those who spent between $250,000 and $500,000 won one race in four. Those who spent over $500,000 won half the time.[35] And those candidates who spend lofty sums against opponents less amply funded win almost all the time. In the 1996 elections, House candidates who spent more than their opponents won 90 percent of their bids for office.[36]

Numbers like these, in the 1990s, would make fundraising the most important talent on the political landscape. In 2000, the Democrats formally recognized that reality. They named as chairman of their party an individual whose sole qualification for the honor amounted to his fundraising prowess. The new chair, Terry McAuliffe, had first hit the fundraising big time in 1995. In just over seven months, he raised $27 million for the Clinton-Gore re-election. Two years later, a grateful Al Gore would fly "through the snow to make it to McAuliffe's 40th-birthday bash."[37]

Back in Mark Hanna's day, money could buy votes. A century later, the sort of money that people like Terry McAuliffe could raise was making voting nearly irrelevant. Most elections today are decided not at the ballot box, but by the fundraising that takes place before voters are paying any attention to who the candidates will be. Political observers call this early fundraising the "money primary." The ability to raise large sums of cash quickly and early, analysts Robert Borosage and Ruy Teixeira note, now "separates the serious candidates from the dreamers before voters even learn their names."[38]

Serious candidates give the money primary every ounce of their political energy. Their goal: to amass enough money to scare off challengers. Money has become, explains political scientist Jamin Raskin, a means "to discourage and overwhelm political competition and debate."[39]

In the money primary, no candidate, no matter how well-known, can afford failure. In 1999, Republican Presidential candidate Elizabeth Dole, the most politically viable woman ever to run for the nation's top office, ended her campaign before a single voter in the "real" primaries had cast a ballot. Dole had raised just $1.7 million in 1999's third quarter. George W. Bush had raised $20 million over the same period. Dole had $861,000 available to spend when she quit the race. Bush, at the time, had $37.7 million.[40]

"The bottom line," Elizabeth Dole would note wistfully in her withdrawal announcement, "is money."[41]

Five Republican candidates, in all, would drop out of the 2000 Presidential race before the Iowa caucuses, the traditional opening event of the race to the White House.[42]

"We're turning the nominating process of both parties into lifestyles of the rich and famous," complained Ed Gillespie, a strategist for one of those candidates, Ohio's John Kasich. "Some very good candidates never even got to the point where voters got to say one way or another how they felt about them."[43]

In money primaries, the only people who get to have a say, to "vote," are those who open their wallets to candidates, and those who open up actually make up an incredibly narrow slice of the American public. In fact, notes the Center for Public Integrity, 96 percent of Americans make no political contributions whatsoever.[44] And of those who do make contributions, only a tiny number give enough to merit a candidate's attention at the money primary stage. How tiny? In the two years leading up to the 2002 elections, only a little over one quarter of 1 percent of adult Americans contributed over $200 to a political campaign. Only one tenth of 1 percent contributed at least $1,000.[45]

Those few Americans who do contribute generously to political campaigns, predictably enough, in no way represent a cross section of the American people. In the 1996 elections, notes a Joyce Foundation study, 81 percent of

Americans who contributed at least $200 to a political candidate made at least $100,000 a year.[46] In the general population that year, just 6 percent of Americans earned over $100,000.[47]

For candidates who play the money game well enough to win, the fundraising for the next election starts as soon as they take office. To raise enough money to scare off serious challengers, experts estimate, a House incumbent needs to raise at least $2,000 per day, Sundays included, in the year and a half after getting sworn in.

"We're in an escalating arms race here," Steve Elmendorf, chief of staff to then House Minority Leader Richard Gephardt, explained in 2001. "It would be nice to have a little break so people could do their job before they have to spend all their time calling people, asking them for money."[48]

The people called most often — rich people — have become quite accustomed to chatting regularly with America's most important elected leaders. In 1996, according to a study conducted for *Worth* magazine, 11 percent of America's richest 1 percent met personally with President Clinton. Nine percent of these affluent Americans met personally with his Republican challenger, Robert Dole.[49]

In America today, to be rich is to be chummy — with whatever elected leader you choose. In June 2001, President Bush and Vice President Cheney and several hundred tables full of their favorite deep-pocket friends packed the Washington Convention Center for a fundraising dinner that collected a record $20 million. The banquet tables went for $25,000 each. Each $25,000 check "bought the right to request a particular senator or congressman as a dinner companion."[50]

Senators, congressmen, governors, presidents, most all elected officials of national significance, now spend their days — and dinners — surrounded by men and women of wealth. Should we be surprised that these elected officials occasionally lose a bit of perspective? Take poor Fred Heineman, the former police chief of Raleigh, North Carolina. Heineman, after his 1994 election to Congress, could not believe that some people actually considered him to be a person of means. How outrageous. All Heineman had to live on was his $133,600 congressional salary and $50,000 in police pensions.

"That does not make me rich," Heineman protested. "That does not make me middle class. In my opinion that makes me lower middle class."

And who was middle class?

"When I see someone who is making anywhere from $300,00 to $750,000 a year, that's middle class," Heineman explained. "When I see anyone above that, that's upper-middle class."[51]

In Heineman's world, a swirling universe of dinners and lunches with extraordinarily well-heeled movers and shakers, that sort of income classification made eminent sense. Average voters, of course, approach life from a slightly different perspective. In the 1996 elections, they sent the candid Heineman home.

How many other "lower middle class" members of Congress feel, like Fred Heineman, put upon financially? We will never know. Most pols smart enough to get elected to Congress are smart enough to keep their financial aspirations to themselves. But not all. Senator Bob Packwood from Oregon, for instance, couldn't help but confide to his private diary his fervent desire for a thicker wallet. Perhaps someday, Senator Packwood wrote to himself, "I can become a lobbyist at five or six or four hundred thousand."[52]

Packwood would have to delay his fondest financial desire.[53] A sex scandal in 1995 would turn his career upside down and inside out — and, in the process, force the public release of his private papers.

The release of Packwood's diary no doubt left more than a few of his colleagues quietly squirming. Packwood, after all, didn't figure to be the only senator daydreaming about the great wealth that might one day come his, or her, way. In a plutocracy, with great wealth all about, most all lawmakers sooner or later come to share the same dreams.

IF THE WEALTHY SAW THE WORLD the same way everyone else sees it, then no one who cares about government of the people, by the people, and for the people would worry one whit about excessive chumminess between pols and plutocrats. But the wealthy do not see the world the same as people of more limited means. In 1996, in a fascinating opinion survey exercise, pollster Celinda Lake would document the difference.

Lake, a widely respected polling analyst, compared the political perspectives of two different random samples, one taken from the American voting public at large, the other compiled from the ranks of Americans who had given candidates at least $5,000 over the previous two and a half years. Half the large donors Lake surveyed were Republicans, half Democrats.[54] What did she find? The large donors Lake queried, by almost a two-to-one margin, agreed that "government spends too much, taxes too much and interferes too much in things better left to individuals and businesses." Only a third of the average voters surveyed shared that perspective. Most average voters, instead, told Lake they believed that "government is too concerned with what big corporations and wealthy special interests want, and does not do enough to help working families."[55]

Lake repeated her survey research four years later and found similarly stark contrasts on one issue after another. One case in point: funding Social Security.

Under current law, all Americans pay Social Security taxes at the same rate, up to a set cap that rises slightly each year. In 2001, all Americans paid a 7.65 percent Social Security payroll tax — the "FICA" deduction — on wages and salary up to $76,200. Those with income over $76,200 paid no Social Security tax on any of this income. In 2001, as a result, someone making $76,200 and someone making $762,000 paid the same exact $5,829.30 in Social Security tax. But the $5,829.30 amounted to 7.65 percent of the $76,200 person's annual salary and less than 1 percent of the $762,000 person's salary.

Before the 2000 election, Celinda Lake asked both of her sample groups, the ordinary voters and the $5,000 contributors, if they favored raising the salary cap on Social Security taxes. Solid majorities of the ordinary voters — a group including Democrats, Independents, and Republicans — agreed the cap should be lifted. Only 24 percent of these ordinary voters opposed raising the cap.

Among the $5,000 contributors, the numbers reversed. The majority of those with an opinion in this deep-pocket sample opposed lifting the cap.[56]

America's lawmakers have studiously followed the lead of these $5,000 contributors. They have avoided any talk of raising the Social Security salary cap. The cap-lifting notion, despite its popularity with rank-and-file voters, remains a non-issue.

In American politics today, on all issues, not just Social Security, our wealthy have come to enjoy almost magical powers. They can make ideas that average people find attractive disappear. In deeply unequal societies, wealthy people always wield these powers. Their regular, ongoing access to elected officials guarantees their world views a respectful hearing. Their distaste for populist approaches makes lawmakers think twice before even entertaining unconventional economic ideas. In time, if wealth concentrates enough, unequal societies become polities where only the world views of the wealthy receive any serious consideration at all. Representative government comes to represent only the rich.

In the United States, the world's most unequal rich nation, rich people would not be satisfied in the 1990s with elected officials who merely represented their interests. They would do their best to do away with the middleman — and represent their interests themselves. They would make remarkable progress.

ON NOVEMBER 8, 1994, Republicans had a very good day. For the first time in four decades, their candidates would gain simultaneous majority control of both the House and the Senate. Two months later, over eighty "freshmen" lawmakers, most of them Republicans, formally began their congressional careers. About a quarter of these newcomers shared a special bond. They were each worth at least $1 million.[57]

By the 2000 elections, six years later, Democrats had regrouped. The new century's first elections ended with Congress almost evenly split between Democrats and Republicans. The elections also ended with more millionaires in Congress. Of the candidates newly elected to Congress in 2000, one third held personal fortunes worth at least $1 million.[58]

Two years later, on Election Day 2002, neither Republicans or Democrats registered any substantial numerical gains. But millionaires did. They would make up, the Associated Press reported, "close to half the incoming members of Congress."[59]

Inside Congress, and outside Congress, American politics seems to be turning into a rich people's hobby. Rich people seem to be running for everything.

In Virginia, cell phone entrepreneur Mark Warner spent $10.5 million of his personal fortune in a losing 1996 Senate bid.[60] Five years later, Warner, a Democrat, emptied another $4.7 million from his wallet. That was enough, with some additional help from his friends, to make him governor.[61] That same year, in 2001, billionaire Michael Bloomberg, a Republican, spent $73.9 million from his own deep pockets to become mayor of New York. Bloomberg spent more on mailings, $16.6 million, than his opponent spent on his entire campaign. He spent more on his election night victory party, $45,000, than the average American family makes in a year.[62]

Not every deep-pocket candidate, over recent years, has ended up celebrating. In fact, healthy percentages of wealthy candidates have lost their election bids. In the 2000 elections, for instance, five of the nineteen candidates who spent more than $1 million of their own money to get elected fell short.[63] Some commentators see in these defeats reassuring proof that, at least in America, democracy still trumps dollars. Other observers of the American political scene beg to differ. Rich people's candidacies, they argue, are having an enormous impact on American politics, win or lose. They point, as just one example, to the 1994 California Senate race.

Into this Senate contest, Michael Huffington, the heir to an oil fortune, invested $28 million of his own considerable fortune, just two years after he spent $5 million to win election to the House of Representatives.[64] This time around Huffington's millions would not be enough, mainly because he came up against a candidate with some significant millions of her own. His opponent, Diane Feinstein, pushed $2.5 million of her family fortune into the race and spent about $14 million overall, enough to emerge triumphant.[65]

But Huffington, even in defeat, had an impact. His relentless barrage of TV ads defined the campaign's political thrust. Day after day, Huffington's ads blasted Feinstein for having voted for "the biggest tax increase in history."[66] Feinstein, in truth, had only voted for the modest tax hike on wealthy incomes that was part of the Clinton administration's 1993 deficit-reduction package. This tax increase had actually raised taxes on only 1 percent of California taxpayers. In her campaign, Feinstein would do her best to explain all this to voters. But she would never feel, despite her eventual victory, that she had truly overcome the tax-hiker stigma Huffington plastered on her.

"It hurt me the way they presented it," she would acknowledge.[67]

Feinstein, a Democrat, would not be hurt that way again. In 2001, the Democratic Party leadership in the Senate opposed the Bush administration proposal to cut total taxes on the wealthy far more than Clinton's 1993 measure had raised them. Feinstein voted for it.

The many millions that the Michael Huffingtons heave into their own campaigns don't just distort how the public perceives taxes and other issues. These millions also raise the overall campaign spending bar. They force other candidates to raise ever more money to stay competitive. Candidates who can't raise these ever higher sums will not be taken seriously, no matter how qualified they may be.

Caleb Rossiter would learn this lesson in 1998, in his race against Amory Houghton, the richest man in Congress. Houghton, a billionaire heir to the Corning Glass fortune, had already won re-election to his upstate New York district five times, outspending his Democratic rivals $2 million to $14,000 in the process.[68] Rossiter, a native of Houghton's district and a respected, experienced advocate for progressive causes, had no trouble winning the Democratic nomination to challenge Houghton's sixth bid for re-election. No one else wanted the honor. But Rossiter felt Houghton might be vulnerable this time around. The billionaire, despite his "moderate" image, had voted to weaken clean-water standards and cut Medicare. If voters could be alerted to positions like these, Rossiter figured, Houghton might have a fight on his hands.

Sounding that alert, Rossiter understood, would take cash, at least "half a million dollars." Rossiter would go at the task of raising that cash with everything he had.

"I spent so much time on the phone trying to get that money that my ears hurt and my soul ached," he later would note.[69]

Rossiter would eventually raise a respectable $250,000, not nearly enough to match what Houghton had available to spend on TV. To try to offset his TV time deficit, Rossiter would devote nearly every waking hour to meeting voters directly. He walked precincts, stood at factory gates, marched in parades. But Rossiter would need more than shoe-leather. To have any shot at topping Houghton, he needed more dollars. The only possible significant source: national liberal advocacy groups.

Rossiter would go ahead and make his case to these national organizations. They would not find that case compelling. Hardly any national groups would give Rossiter any financial support. Giving Rossiter money, they figured, would be lunacy. Rossiter was running against a billionaire. What chance did he have? In the end, Rossiter would have no chance at all. On Election Day, he would be demolished, by 68 to 25 percent.

The liberal political realists in Washington, with Rossiter's defeat, had their judgments more than amply confirmed. They had been right not to waste any of their scarce resources on Rossiter's doomed campaign. They had been, in the rational accounting of modern American politics, absolutely right to dismiss his candidacy. But the absolute rationality of their decision, on another level, merely demonstrated just how irrational American politics had become. Caleb Rossiter sported a distinguished career in unselfish public service. He exuded intelligence and dedication, compassion and commitment. All he lacked was a fortune. To insiders, that made Rossiter a joke, a hapless Don Quixote.

In 1999, a year after Caleb Rossiter's dismal race, journalists found Washington's political insiders hard at work getting ready for the 2000 elections, all doing their best, once again, to win — with wealth. "Both parties," reported analyst Robert Dreyfuss, "are busily recruiting superwealthy candidates who can either self-finance their runs or call on personal networks of rich donors."[70] In Nevada, he added, the likely GOP candidate for Senate would be former Congressman John Ensign, the son of the Circus Circus casino empire. In New Jersey, the Democratic Party's Senate nod seemed to be going to Jon Corzine, a Wall Street executive worth $300 million.

"The two candidates," Dreyfuss reported, "have scared off credible opponents."[71]

On Election Day 2000, both Ensign and Corzine would win.

Not everybody in the two winning parties, the Nevada Republicans and the New Jersey Democrats, felt like celebrating. Some party stalwarts, like Richard Sooy, a New Jersey podiatrist, felt a bad taste in their mouths. Sooy, the previous spring, had been a candidate himself, for a local office. A Corzine ally had offered him up to $50,000 for his campaign — in return for giving Corzine an endorsement in the Senate primary. Corzine would go on to spend more than $60 million, from his own fortune, to win election.[72]

"I'm not a historian," Richard Sooy the podiatrist would later note, "but I don't believe Thomas Jefferson meant for it to be like this."[73]

EARLY IN 2001, about the same time John Ensign and Jon Corzine were taking their oaths to serve in the Senate, a smiling George W. Bush was holding his first cabinet meeting. The new President, a multimillionaire, looked around the table and beheld a truly remarkable sight: a cabinet as close to all-millionaire as a cabinet could be.

Of the eighteen men and women on the new Bush administration cabinet, seventeen held personal fortunes worth at least seven digits. Seven of these each held, in net worth, at least $10 million. The lone non-millionaire, Secretary of Agriculture Ann Veneman, could lay claim to only $680,000.[74]

In the George W. Bush White House, even staffers would have bulging bankrolls. The President's top political adviser, Karl Rove, came into the West Wing with stock holdings alone worth $1.5 million.[75] Impressive. Almost as impressive as some of the incomes made and fortunes held by White House staffers in the Clinton administration. Robert Rubin, Clinton's top economics adviser and later his treasury secretary, earned $26.5 million from his Wall Street firm the year before he joined the White House staff. Franklin Raines, a Clinton pick to head the Office of Management and Budget, earned $12.8 million his last year before joining the Clinton team. Erskine Bowles, who would later become a Clinton chief of staff, came into his White House responsibilities with a personal net worth somewhere between $30 and $60 million.[76]

In modern America, administrations might come and go. Extremely rich people, apparently, would never be far from the action.

And not just in the White House — or Congress. By century's end, America's most affluent had hit the trifecta. They made laws as members of

Congress, they implemented laws from the crowning heights of the executive branch, and they sat in solemn judgment on the laws as justices of our nation's highest court. In 2000, six of America's nine Supreme Court justices held net worths comfortably over $1 million. The financial disclosure form of a seventh, Chief Justice William Rehnquist, left his millionaire status a bit unclear. Rehnquist's filing would note only that he held assets worth somewhere between $525,000 and $1.3 million.[77]

All this wealth troubled some observers. Public officials of great wealth, these observers noted, stood to benefit enormously from the decisions they would be called upon to make in public office. During the 2001 debate over the estate tax, for instance, opponents of estate tax repeal noticed that Bush administration officials pumping for repeal had somewhat of a personal stake in the matter. Repeal of the nation's only tax on the fortunes rich people leave behind at death, critics noted, would save the heirs of Vice President Cheney up to $40 million, the heirs of Treasury Secretary Paul O'Neill up to $50.7 million, and the heirs of Defense Secretary Donald Rumsfeld up to $120 million.[78]

President George W. Bush could, presumably, approach the estate tax question with a more open mind. His heirs only stood to save as much as $9.9 million if the estate tax were repealed.[79]

This sort of cynical conjecture and innuendo, America's most fortunate and their friends believe, totally misses the point. Rich people, they assert, actually improve our democracy when they give of their precious time to serve in public office. Rich people, their champions explain, "cannot be bought." They are, after all, rich already.

This argument often impresses listeners, particularly in locales where headlines about endless kickback and influence-peddling scandals have soured voters on ordinary office-holders of limited means. But simple corruption, in fact, poses *no* fundamental threat to our democracy. Kickbacks can be prosecuted. Bribe-takers can be unveiled. Democratic governments can and do eventually catch up with pols on the take.

Democracy cannot so easily survive the far more significant threat that great wealth poses. Real democracy thrives only where free and open debate engages people's imaginations, only where old ideas are regularly challenged, only where new ideas are always welcome. The presence of great wealth in politics, the domination of great wealth over our political life, endangers this debate.

"Money doesn't just talk in politics," as political analyst William Greider explains, "it also silences."[80]

Our major political parties today, to compete effectively, must either enlist wealthy people as their candidates or enlist the wealth of wealthy people on behalf of candidates the wealthy find credible. In this political environment, ideas that might discomfort great wealth are "effectively vetoed even before the public can hear about them."[81] Those who pay the freight for politics come to define the issues that politics addresses.[82]

These freight-payers, should their definitions be challenged, turn apoplectic.

"This isn't an issue that should even be on the political agenda today," Nike billionaire Phil Knight fumed after critics attacked the sweatshops that manufactured his company's sport shoes. "It's a sound bite of globalization."[83]

Knight would have his way. In the 1990s, the ongoing scandal of sweatshop labor would receive nothing more than sound-bite attention from America's political class.

But Knight and his friends would score a much greater political triumph in the closing years of the twentieth century. They would keep off America's political radar screen an even greater scandal than the reemergence of sweatshops. They would keep off America's radar screen the scandal of rising inequality, the greatest and most rapid redistribution of wealth — from bottom to top — that the United States had ever seen.

"Inequality is at levels not witnessed since before the Great Depression," as analysts Robert Borosage and Ruy Teixeira would point out midway through the 1990s. "Yet neither political party has a coherent argument or agenda to deal with this fundamental dynamic."[84]

The nation's two major parties, throughout the 1980s and 1990s, would treat the widening gap between America's rich and everyone else as a non-issue. Several thoughtful observers figured that top American political leaders would have to ditch, at some point, this see-no-evil attitude. Gaps in income and wealth, these observers believed, were simply growing too wide to be disregarded.

"Sooner or later this country's politics will get back to the core issue: economic inequality," William Greider noted in 1995. "I hope this happens in my lifetime. Actually, I think the subject is bearing down on the politicians faster than they imagine."[85]

"Eventually," agreed commentator Mark Shields in 1997, "public attention must turn to the widening gap in income between those at the very top and everyone else."[86]

But mainstream American politics would never turn to the widening gap, never consider how that gap was impacting America, never contemplate steps that might slow, or, heaven forbid, even reverse America's growing economic divide. America's political leaders would simply never raise any questions about inequality, at least never raise them loud enough for Americans to hear.

Why this reluctance? Big Money, critics charged, had "metastasized" throughout the American body politic.[87] In this sick body, noted physicist Barry Casper, a former policy adviser to Senator Paul Wellstone, democracy was dying.

"We now have a political system in which a public policy proposal can have enormous popular support and the potential to garner an electoral majority," Casper explained, "but it may not even get a fair hearing, much less a vote, in the Congress or anything approaching adequate coverage in the media."[88]

Can America's body politic be revived? Many activists feel they have the medicine that can do the trick. They call their medicine campaign finance reform.

IN A DEMOCRACY, THE PEOPLE RULE. They rule, most basically, by deciding who gets elected to office. In the United States, by century's end, Big Money seemed to be deciding elections, not the people. How could the people regain control? Get tough on Big Money, came the answer from reformers. Shove Big Money out of America's election process.

In the 1990s, public interest activists would work indefatigably to get this message across to the American people. They would finally score, in 2002, a landmark victory when a reluctant George W. Bush signed into law campaign finance reform legislation co-sponsored by his arch Republican rival, Arizona Senator John McCain, and Wisconsin Democrat Russell Feingold. Only once before in American history, back in 1974, had Congress ever attempted such a comprehensive election campaign reform.

The original reformers, lawmakers sickened by the Watergate scandals, figured they had covered all the bases with their 1974 legislation. They had limited contributions. Individuals, under the new reform law, could give no more than $2,000 within a single election cycle, political action committees no more than $10,000. They had also limited expenditures. Their legislation capped how much candidates and their supporters could spend on their campaigns. Big Money, the reformers felt confident, had been checked.

But not checkmated. The new 1974 law would quickly start to unravel.

The Supreme Court took the first hard yank. In 1976, the High Court would rule that the caps on campaign spending in the 1974 reform violated the First Amendment right to free speech. Candidates, the court ruled in this *Buckley* decision, could not be prevented from spending their own money on their own behalf. Nor could supporters of a candidate be prevented from spending whatever they wanted to spend. Any spending limits, the Court determined, would have to be optional to pass constitutional muster.[89]

Candidates and political parties, in the wake of *Buckley*, could now *spend* however much they wanted. But wealthy donors still couldn't *give* whatever they wanted directly to candidates. The contribution limits set by the 1974 reform legislation still remained legally in place. Legally, perhaps, but not practically. By law, political parties could not accept unlimited contributions for campaigns on behalf of specific candidates. But they could accept unlimited "party-building" contributions to strengthen their infrastructure. These contributions, known as "soft money" because they skirted the "hard" $2,000 contribution limit, would soon start soaring. In 1980, at the onset of the "soft money" era, Republicans raised $15 million in soft cash, the Democrats $4 million. Two decades later, in 2000, Republicans and Democrats together raised nearly half a billion dollars, $487 million to be exact, from soft money contributions.[90] More than 90 percent of these dollars, Georgia Rep. John Lewis would note, "came from corporations and wealthy individuals whose interests are often at odds with those of average Americans."[91]

Big Money would find other loopholes to exploit as well. After the 1974 election reforms, wealthy individuals could legally fork only $2,000, per election cycle, to a specific candidate. But corporations could "invite" their executives to "max" out to the $2,000 limit and then "bundle" the resulting checks off to the candidates of their choice.

Corporate special interests and wealthy individuals could also, under the law, finance as many election-oriented TV ads as they wanted, so long as these ads were produced independently of any specific candidate's campaign. This "independent expenditure" loophole, coupled with "soft money" and bundled contributions, would create a new political environment that corporate America quickly came to dominate. In the 1998 election cycle, business interests would outspend labor interests by eleven to one. In just the first year and a half of the 2000 election cycle, business would outspend labor by sixteen to one — and overwhelm environmental groups by even wider margins.[92]

The reform legislation of 1974 had, in essence, failed miserably. Big Money dominated American politics as powerfully as ever. McCain-Feingold, the reform enacted in 2002 to fix the reform enacted in 1974, set out to limit that domination. Soft money contributions to national parties, under McCain-Feingold, would be illegal. Interest groups would not be allowed to flood the airways with TV spots in the weeks right before elections. Disclosure requirements would be tougher. A new era.

"The political landscape," announced a proud Senator Carl Levin from Michigan, "will be filled with more people and less influence, more contributors and smaller contributions, more democracy and less elitism."[93]

"This will be a landmark piece of legislation that I think will be written about in the history books for years to come," added Senate Majority Leader Thomas A. Daschle.[94]

But other observers worried that Congress was just repeating history, not making it. McCain-Feingold, they argued, would not pass what some fair election advocates called the "Fannie Lou Hamer standard." Fannie Lou Hamer had been a civil rights hero, the leader of the struggle that challenged Mississippi's all-white delegation at the 1964 Democratic National Convention. Any campaign finance reform, skeptics about McCain-Feingold argued, would have to make the political system fairer for people like Fannie Lou Hamer — "a poor woman, a person of color, a stranger in the halls of power" — to be considered an important step toward.[95]

McCain-Feingold, these activists believed, did not make America fairer for today's Fannie Lou Hamers, mainly because backers of the legislation, to win passage, had agreed to double the amount of "hard" money wealthy donors can give directly to candidates. In the 2000 federal elections, critics of McCain-Feingold pointed out, soft money contributions had accounted for about a third of all the money spent. The rest came from hard money. If wealthy contributors doubled their hard money contributions in 2004, to max out at the new limit, they would be able to flood the political process with more money than flooded the process in 2000, even with the ban on soft money.

"In short," noted one public interest group, "there will be more money spent after McCain-Feingold than ever before, only now politicians will claim this is OK since it's all hard money."[96]

The ban on soft money, other activists noted, wasn't likely to work particularly well either.[97] The "soft" dollars that had been going to the national parties, they predicted, would simply start going instead to state parties, to more independent expenditures, or to non-party entities known, by their tax code loophole, as "527 committees."[98]

Senators McCain and Feingold, to their credit, had never claimed that their legislation would "solve" the Big Money challenge. Party strategists, McCain had acknowledged, would be hard at work "trying to figure out loopholes" as soon as the bill became law.[99] McCain-Feingold, agreed Russell Feingold after the bill's passage, would have just a "modest impact." Only the "public financing" of election campaigns, he noted, could ever prevent candidates from having to rely on wealthy Americans.[100]

Growing numbers of activist reformers agreed with Feingold's perception. Proposals for publicly financing election campaigns would mushroom in the late 1990s. Two states, Maine and Arizona, would actually enact and implement "Clean Money" public financing systems in time for their 2000 state elections.

In the Maine system, candidates who opt for public financing must agree to limit their spending and not accept private contributions. To qualify for public support, candidates must initially collect a specified number of $5 contributions from voters. If a "Clean Money" candidate's opponent chooses not to seek public financing, to avoid having to abide by spending limits, the Clean Money candidate can receive extra public financing.[101] Arizona's public financing works in a similar fashion.

Both laws are so far proving popular, with more candidates running "clean" in each successive election. And cleanly elected lawmakers in both states say they feel they can legislate without having to kow-tow to special interest lobbyists.

"It is too soon to say that money no longer talks in either state capitol," one observer noted in 2001, "but it clearly doesn't swagger as much."[102]

Is "Clean Money" the antidote to Big Money that American democracy needs? Can public financing of elections offset the advantages that concentrated wealth carries onto the political playing field? Like Senators McCain and Feingold, interestingly, the nation's top Clean Money advocates have never described their reform as a solution that will "solve" America's Big Money problem once and for all. Clean Money systems, these advocates understand, have yet to secure anything close to a solid foothold. Even in Maine, they point out, the public financing dollars available for statewide candidates aren't enough to run a competitive race against opponents who opt not to run "clean."[103]

But Clean Money public financing, even if more adequately funded, would still not level the political playing field. Indeed, note thoughtful reformers, the political playing field will never be level so long as some players — by dint of their bankrolls — remain far bigger and stronger than every other player on the field. In a deeply unequal America, we can change the rules that determine how political campaigns are run. But we cannot prevent the very rich from using their grand fortunes to distort how candidates — and the public — think about political issues.

IN 2002, ACCORDING TO THE ANNUAL GALLUP POLL on education, 3 percent of America's public school parents felt their local public schools were failing.[104] That figure may have surprised casual observers of American politics. Over the previous two decades, after all, the debate over what we ought to do about "failing public schools" had almost completely dominated America's political discourse on education.

In that discourse, most grassroots American educators shared a common perspective. To fix failing schools, they believed, you start with qualified teachers. You give these teachers small classes so they can give students individual attention. You give them supportive principals, time to plan lessons and collaborate with colleagues, and an opportunity to impact the decisions that affect learning. And you recognize parents for what they are, a child's first teachers, and treat them with respect. Do all this, grassroots educators believed, and "failing" schools will significantly improve.

These prescriptions, of course, raise countless questions. Just how small do classes have to be? How can schools effectively attract and retain quality teachers? What can schools do to help time-squeezed parents become involved in their children's education? To improve education, questions like these need to be thoughtfully discussed and debated. Throughout the 1990s and into the new century, unfortunately, America's mainstream political debate would give these sorts of questions little attention. Instead, in state after state, lawmakers and voters would find themselves preoccupied with an entirely different proposition, the notion that public schools can best be improved by giving parents taxpayer dollars, or "vouchers," to send their children to private schools.

Where did this voucher notion come from? Not from teachers or principals. Not from educational researchers. Not even from dissatisfied parents. None of these groups shoved vouchers into the political limelight. The shove would come instead from the upper reaches of America's economic firmament, from some of America's deepest pockets.

These zealously wealthy individuals came to the debate over education with an ax to grind. Public education, by its very existence, violated their sense of free-market decency. Public schools, as Wall Street financier Theodore Forstmann put it, were merely "monopolies" that "produce bad products at high prices."[105]

Over the course of the boom years, wealthy ideologues like Forstmann would pay any price necessary to thrust an alternate vision of education onto America's political agenda. Public tax dollars, they argued, should not subsidize "monopolies." Parents should be able to "choose" where they send their children to school. They should be able to spend public tax dollars to pay private school tuition.

No single individual would do more to advance this notion of taxpayer-subsidized vouchers for private school tuition than billionaire John Walton, heir to the Wal-Mart fortune. Walton would pump $250,000 into the 1993 ballot initiative that would have, if passed, created a voucher system in California.[106] That measure didn't pass. California voters drubbed it, by 70 to 30 percent.[107] Walton would not be deterred. He pumped still more of his fortune into a 1998 Colorado initiative that would have let parents take a tax deduction for private school tuition.[108] Voters drubbed that idea, too, 76 to 33 percent.[109]

But billionaires seldom have to take "no" for an answer. Two years later, Walton shipped still more dollars to Michigan, where Dick DeVos, son of Amway co-founder Richard DeVos, was trying to get voters to buy his version of Walton's California voucher plan.[110] Voters still weren't buying. They rejected vouchers by 69 to 31 percent.[111]

Walton and Wall Street's Ted Forstmann, even before the Michigan vote, had realized that they needed to do more than wage referendum campaigns to gain public support for vouchers. In 1998, Walton and Forstmann would each invest $50 million from their own personal fortunes to underwrite private school tuition for kids from low-income families.[112] The goal: to gin up a demand, among poor people, for publicly financed vouchers for private schools.

This new effort would not make the impact Walton and Forstmann hoped. Veteran advocates for inner city parents refused to be bought. In 1998, the NAACP would go on record against all voucher-type initiatives.[113] In 2000, NAACP activists in California helped defeat still another statewide voucher initiative, this one bankrolled by Silicon Valley venture capitalist Timothy Draper, who had spent $2 million to put vouchers on the statewide ballot.[114] Voters would crush Draper's initiative, 71 to 29 percent.[115]

No matter. Deep-pocket voucher proponents would keep up the pressure, out of their own wallets and out of the budgets of the foundations they controlled. The $2 million seed money for the first national group promoting vouchers would come from the Walton Family Foundation, the "philanthropic" arm of the Wal-Mart fortune. Out of other foundations would come subsidies for think tanks and special university centers that churned out an endless stream of voucher-boosting reports and press releases.

By 2002, Walton and his wealthy friends had little to show, by some measures, for their decade of effort. Voters had repeatedly rejected vouchers, by wide margins, in every voucher referendum. In only two states, Florida and Colorado, and two cities, Milwaukee and Cleveland, had lawmakers voted to establish voucher programs — and only on a limited basis. But by other measures, perhaps more significant measures, the wealthy champions of private school vouchers had achieved considerable success. Their legal teams had scored, in June 2002, a major victory when the U.S. Supreme Court ruled that taxpayer-funded vouchers for religious school tuition do not violate the

Constitution. Their unrelenting referendum campaigns, though all losers, had drained millions of dollars and thousands of volunteer hours from groups supporting public education. And their ad campaigns — the biggest a $20 million blitz announced by Ted Forstmann in 2000 — had begun to soften up the opposition to vouchers in public opinion polls.[116] The wealthy zealots opposed to public education, in a sense, had succeeded. They had redefined America's political debate on education, altered America's political climate.

The climate change that men like John Walton engineered on education would not be unique. Over the closing decades of the twentieth century, America's wealthy would significantly transform America's political climate on issue after issue.

Social Security, for instance, used to be known as the "third rail" of American politics. No politician would dare suggest meddling with the basic inner workings of America's most popular social program. But Wall Street, by the 1990s, had come to see a reason to meddle. If Social Security could be "privatized," if dollars withheld for Social Security could be diverted into stocks, bonds, and mutual funds, Wall Street would have the ultimate cash cow. If just 2 percent of the dollars withheld for Social Security were instead invested in Wall Street securities, the resulting fees and commissions for Wall Street banks and brokerage houses would total $10 billion a year.[117]

Wall Street-subsidized think tanks would spend the closing years of the twentieth century convening conferences and churning out reports that sang the glories of privatizing Social Security.[118] The steady drumbeat of their underlying message — you can't count on Social Security — would eventually convince large majorities of American young people they would never live to see a Social Security check. In fact, Social Security faced no debilitating crisis. The system, independent experts agreed, "could operate without any changes at all — no cuts in benefits, no additional revenue — until 2041."[119] And the system would face virtually no shortfall at all, even then, other analysts pointed out, if the bottom two-thirds of Americans "had the same share of national income in 1998 that they had in 1978."[120] Rising inequality, these analysts noted, meant fewer dollars for the Social Security trust fund, since high income above the Social Security salary cap weren't subject to any Social Security payroll tax.

These facts would not matter much in the public debate over Social Security, not when the movers and shakers behind the push to privatize Social Security had tens of millions of dollars available for spreading Social Security doom and gloom. Their privatizing push would seem, by century's end, unstoppable. Even Clinton administration operatives started hinting about compromises that would start funneling Social Security tax dollars into Wall Street's outrageously eager clutches. These compromises, in the end, would not be struck. The sudden burst of the stock market bubble, starting in 2000, would shunt privatization off the immediate political agenda.

But the privatizers, observers figured, would be back in force. And they would likely dominate the political debate over Social Security once again, even if rigorous campaign financing reforms became the law of the land.[121] In an America top heavy with concentrated wealth, even with Clean Money-type reforms in place, think tanks subsidized by wealthy ideologues would still be pumping out white papers.[122] Top corporations would still be offering plum positions for ambitious political leaders with careers in temporary holding patterns. And, perhaps most significantly of all, America's media empires would still be making celebrities out of flacks for the wealthy's pet causes.

"FREEDOM OF THE PRESS," the irreverent journalist A. J. Liebling once quipped, "is guaranteed only to those who own one."

A half century ago, few Americans affluent enough to own a press actually owned only one. America's newspapers and magazines, and television and radio stations as well, would belong for the most part to ownerships of multiple media properties. Still, throughout the 1950s and 1960s, independent media voices could and did arise. Journalism, for most of the twentieth century, would always sport at least some owners who considered their media properties a sacred public trust. These owners would take seriously their responsibility to keep Americans informed and alert. Not all, or even most, owners would feel that sense of responsibility. But that didn't matter. Widespread competition between media ownership groups tended to keep individual media outlets honest — or at least give readers and viewers someplace else to go if they weren't.

By century's end, that had all changed. In the early 1980s, media critic Ben Bagdikian had counted about fifty different owners of major media outlets. Twenty years later, merger mania had left only six different ownerships in control of America's most important sources of information.[123] The media had become just another business, and a lucrative one at that. Newspapers, by century's end, regularly averaged profit rates that doubled the *Fortune* 500 average.[124] Top media executives could stand tall in any executive gathering. In 2000, for instance, Gannett CEO John J. Curley took home $9.4 million in compensation and held, on top of that, $112.3 million in unexercised stock options.[125]

Within America's media empires, as in the rest of corporate America, steady doses of downsizing would help keep Wall Street happy and stock prices up. These downsizings would exact a steep price journalistically. In understaffed newsrooms, harried reporters now had little time to do their own digging.[126] The "news," not surprisingly, would lose bite. Across the country, again not surprisingly, ratings for traditional "news" would sink. But these low ratings would engender no soul-searching among media executives. They simply devoted their news programs and pages to non-newsy filler and fluff. Out would go coverage of ongoing political debate. In would come the latest on murder and mayhem. If it bleeds, "news" executives exulted, it leads.

Democracy, America's founders had believed, cannot prosper without free and open public debate. Only a free press could keep a free people free. America's media barons, by century's end, hardly bothered to even pay lip service to this noble ideal. They would feel accountable only to their quarterly bottom line. Not a good situation. But things, some American media critics noted, could be worse journalistically. We could be in Italy.

Italy, by century's end, boasted the Information Age's ultimate plutocrat, a billionaire who had become as familiar as family to every Italian. This media magnate, Silvio Berlusconi, had built a colossal media empire by conniving with politicians to win special favors — and then gone into politics, at least partly to keep prosecutors from nailing him for the favors. Berlusconi carried a host of overwhelming advantages into Italy's political arena. He owned Italy's three biggest private TV networks, its biggest publishing conglomerate, its biggest newsmagazine, two nationally circulated daily newspapers, not to mention Italy's biggest investment firm and most popular sports team.[127] His total fortune would reach, at one point, $12.8 billion, enough to place him fourteenth on the 2000 *Forbes* wealthiest people in the world list.[128]

Berlusconi's national TV networks would give him, in any election campaign, a virtually unbeatable advantage.

"This is the only country in the world," one of Berlusconi's political foes would note in 1999, "where the political parties must pay their political adversary in order to run an election campaign."[129]

In 1994, Berlusconi would be elected Italy's prime minister. He would prove a flop his first time around Italy's political track. But he would be back. In May 2001, Italian voters went to the polls and once again elected Silvio Berlusconi, their nation's richest citizen, to their most powerful office.[130]

CAN A DEMOCRATIC SOCIETY, WITHOUT VIOLATING the basic freedoms a democracy is supposed to hold dear, limit the influence of someone as wealthy and powerful as a Silvio Berlusconi? Several political commentators would find themselves, by the 1990s, grappling with this perplexing question. The *Washington Post*'s David Broder, the dean of America's political commentators, would end his grapple by concluding that "it is damnably difficult to devise a system that will effectively reduce the role of money in politics and still not trample on constitutional rights to express political views."[131]

Damnably difficult indeed. A democratic nation can, quite legitimately, prohibit one person from owning multiple media networks. But a free nation cannot deny a rich person the right to endow a school of journalism — and shape the minds of a generation of journalists. A democracy can choose to limit campaign contributions and still remain a democracy. But a free society cannot prevent multimillionaires from winning friends and influencing people by making generous donations to their favorite charitable causes.[132] A nation committed to free and open debate can regulate TV political advertising, to prevent one side from monopolizing the limited resource of pre-election air-time. But a free society cannot stop rich people from bankrolling think tanks that drown the public debate in misinformation.

In an unequal society, a society dominated by concentrated wealth, democracy will always be "damnably difficult." And we will make no progress toward overcoming these difficulties, the British political scientist Harold Laski argued years ago, until we recognize that the primary problem in a deeply unequal democracy isn't the influence we allow the wealthy to bring to bear on our politics. The primary problem is concentrated wealth itself, the huge gap between the wealthy and everyone else.

"A State divided into a small number of rich and a large number of poor," as Laski noted in 1930, "will always develop a government manipulated by the rich to protect the amenities represented by their property."[133]

To practice democracy, to realize democracy, we need to narrow inequality. That does not mean abandoning efforts to change the political rules. Serious rule-changing efforts, like the continuing Clean Money campaign, *can* throw the armies of great wealth off balance — and, in the process, create political space for working to narrow the inequality that stains our nation. But Americans today are so turned off to politics that campaigns for election reform, in and of themselves, are unlikely to rally the public support necessary to change the political rules significantly. After all, if you believe politics doesn't matter, then why bother to change the political rules?

Generations ago, at several different points in American history, Americans did have a reason for caring about politics. They saw political life as an opportunity to cut the overbearing wealthy down to democratic size and improve the lives of America's vast, non-wealthy majority. If those times ever came again, so would the public support needed to enact real reform in the political rules of the game. Americans would then see a reason for fighting for political reforms that put people before corporate special interests.

In other words, argues analyst Robert Dreyfuss, if we want to see real political reform, we need to refocus America's political debate on the class wars that only the rich are winning. This notion that we need to take on America's wealthy corporate elite, Dreyfuss acknowledges, does not particularly interest mainstream political leaders, "or even some foundations that support campaign finance reform." These foundations would "rather see reform that tinkers with the system, preserving the power of the affluent while smoothing out some of the system's rough edges."[134]

Democracy, these tinkerers assume, can survive amid rampant inequality. But no historical evidence, notes economist Lester Thurow, supports that assumption. Some deeply unequal societies, he points out, have indeed survived for centuries. But none of these societies, not "ancient Egypt, imperial Rome, classical China, the Incas, the Aztecs," ever "believed in equality in any sense — not theoretically, not politically, not socially, not economically."[135]

"Democracies have a problem with rising economic inequality precisely because they believe in political equality," Thurow explains. "No one has ever tried survival-of-the-fittest capitalism for any extended period in a modern democracy, so we don't know how far rising inequality and falling wages can go before something snaps."

And what may snap may well be our democracy.

NO NATION, OBSERVERS LIKE LESTER THUROW SUGGEST, can over the long haul remain both deeply unequal and deeply democratic. Severe inequality and meaningful democracy cannot coexist. But why? The answers may lie in Latin America. Democratic aspirations and deeply unequal economic realities have commingled longer in Latin America than anywhere else in the world.

Great wealth, political thinkers in Latin America have noted, always privileges politically those who hold it. Democracy presupposes legal equality — we're all equal under the law — but wealth makes the wealthy substantially more equal. Carlos Vilas, a political theorist from Argentina, asks us to consider Carlos Slim, Mexico's wealthiest single individual. Slim's holdings have included the controlling interest in Mexico's biggest telephone company, largest bank, and most profitable financial services corporation.

"Are Slim's political power and efficacy restricted to just the ballot he casts every two or three years?" Vilas asks. "Hardly."[136]

But inequality, Vilas argues, creates a danger to democracy that goes far deeper than power imbalances. Democracies, he points out, require citizens. And inequality, most poisonously of all, undermines citizenship.

To be a citizen, in any democratic sense, an individual must have autonomy. You must be free to speak your own mind. Most all nations that call themselves democracies have written the right to speak freely into their basic constitutions. But this right, on paper, does not guarantee an individual the autonomy necessary to speak freely. People who fear losing their jobs should they speak what they see to be truth do not feel autonomous — or free. They feel dependent, on others.

To feel autonomous, and free, individuals must enjoy at least a basic level of economic security. Economic security, in turn, requires certain limits on the behavior of a society's most powerful economic players. If employers are able to threaten to pull up stakes and move elsewhere unless their current communities deliver the subsidies the employers seek, individuals in these communities will not feel autonomous and not behave freely. The decisions they make will be made under duress, not in the democratic spirit of free and open debate. The more inequality, the more duress. The more that wealth concentrates, the more dependent those without it become on those who have it. In the most severely unequal societies, these dependencies force people without wealth onto their knees, turn them into submissive clients looking for powerful patrons.

"Patron-client relations of domination and subordination," notes Carlos Vilas, "tend to substitute for relations among equals."

In environments like this, the most dominated, the most deprived, come to believe that only the most powerful of patrons can guarantee their security. Vilas notes one example among many from Latin American history: In Peru's 1995 presidential election, the vast majority of Peru's poorest people voted for Alberto Fujimori, a power-hungry strongman bitterly opposed by the Andean nation's democratic political parties and trade unions.

In societies deeply split by income and wealth, people also become less and less able to visualize life on the opposite side of the economic divide. People at the bottom increasingly identify only with kith and kin, their own narrow religious or ethnic group, not with any broader community. People at the top, meanwhile, increasingly pledge allegiance to the corporate entities that provide them wealth, not the society they share with their less fortunate neighbors. Amid these social dynamics, all sense of "shared belonging" to a single common society tends to fade. Democracy, to thrive, needs this sense of shared belonging, the conviction that you and your adversary, however much you disagree, share some elemental basic interests. In severely unequal societies, few feel these common interests. Democracy withers.

Historically, Carlos Vilas observes, Latin America's two most consistently democratic nations — Uruguay and Costa Rica — have also been Latin America's two most equal nations. Contemporary public opinion surveys, he adds, show "the greatest preference for democracy" in these two countries "and the greatest tolerance for authoritarian rule in Brazil, Guatemala, Paraguay and Ecuador, where wealth is concentrated in the hands of a small percentage of the population."[137]

In the United States, our level of inequality has not yet reached Guatemalan levels. But our inequality is already encouraging the same anti-democratic habits of mind scholars like Carlos Vilas have identified and explored in Latin America. In the United States, as in deeply unequal nations elsewhere, the wealthy become accustomed to getting their own way. These wealthy can buy, outside of politics, everything they want. Why, they wonder, can't they buy what they want in politics?

Sometimes, if wealthy enough, they can.

In 1997, Microsoft co-founder Paul Allen, already the owner of the Portland Trailblazers pro basketball franchise, expressed an interest in purchasing Seattle's pro football team, the Seahawks. But billionaire Allen wanted some help from taxpayers — and insisted on a new stadium and a host of other revenue-producing enhancements. To help state lawmakers see the wisdom of providing this help, Allen would spend $1 million on lobbyists. The lobbyists would do their job well. They convinced lawmakers to hand Allen $300 million in state subsidies and another $300 million to cover interest and finance charges for a new stadium. Taxpayers, under the deal the lawmakers signed off on, would pick up almost all of the tab.[138]

But the deal, under Washington State law, would have to be approved by taxpayers before any dollars could change hands, and this requirement left Allen and his lobbyists more than a little apprehensive. They feared that voters would reject the deal they had brokered if the deal's opponents had until the next Election Day in November to mobilize. The solution? Allen's lobbyists wrote into the stadium subsidy package a provision calling for an early special election five months before the normal Election Day. That unusual timing, they figured, would keep turnout low and deny opponents the time they needed to organize. The lobbyists would turn out to be right. Allen would win his new stadium.

"Microsoft millions," one computer industry trade journal would later note, had turned "a state into a banana republic where election laws can be altered to suit one person's interests."[139]

Not all wealthy people, of course, behave so selfishly self-centered in the political arena. Phenomenally wealthy people do sometimes take actions and positions that actually place the public interest first. Cable TV impresario Ted Turner would perform, for instance, a series of highly publicized good deeds over the course of the boom years. In 1997, after what he called "a spur of the moment decision," he decided to donate $1 billion to the United Nations over the next ten years.[140]

"The federal government, the state government, the municipal government — they're all broke," Turner had noted the year before. "All the money is in the hands of these few rich people and none of them give any money away. It's dangerous for them and for the country."[141]

Other supremely rich people felt similarly. Billionaire currency trader George Soros spent the 1990s underwriting democracy-building projects. Jon Corzine, the Wall Street multimillionaire New Jersey voters elected to the Senate in 2000, would speak out strongly as senator against the repeal of the estate tax, America's only tax levy on concentrated wealth. In this effort to save the estate tax, he would join with Bill Gates Sr., the father of the wealthiest man in the world. Gates Sr. would emerge, in 2001, as America's most visible public advocate for taxing accumulated fortunes.

Could wealthy people actually be good for democracy? To anyone watching wealthy people like Turner and Corzine and Gates Sr. in action, that almost seemed to be the case. Here were truly "autonomous" people making decisions, taking stands, as public-spirited as anyone could ask. What could be wrong with that?

In a democracy, a great deal.

Democracy is about we the people making decisions, not about hoping that people of great wealth and power do the right thing. Bill Gates Sr. and the other wealthy people who joined his call to save the estate tax do most certainly deserve the thanks of all people who care about fairness. Without their intervention, in the winter of 2001, a permanent repeal of the estate tax would have sailed through Congress. But the powerful impact that fairness-minded wealthy people made on the estate tax debate dramatizes exactly what's wrong with our democracy, not what's right. Lawmakers paid no attention to the case against estate tax repeal until several rich people started making it. America's media considered estate tax repeal a boring done deal until the daddy of the world's richest man raised his voice in protest.

In America, wealthy people make things happen, or stop things from happening, as the case may be. That's plutocracy, not democracy. Plutocracy can sometimes deliver up a result average people value. But so can monarchy. We the people of the United States made a choice, a long time ago, to practice democracy. We have practiced democracy for over two hundred years. Maybe someday we'll get it right. But that day will never come, the evidence suggests, until we have a less, a significantly less, unequal nation.

BUT YET, SOME MIGHT OBJECT, what about America's foundations? Our nation currently hosts hundreds of forward-thinking foundations, each one originally endowed by a rich person's grand fortune. These foundations are funding innovative approaches to public policy problems. They are nurturing cutting-edge ideas and initiatives that our lawmakers seem much too timid to explore. We wouldn't have these foundations if we didn't have wealth that had concentrated at some point in the past. If we took steps as a society to prevent the concentration of wealth in the future, wouldn't we be throwing out the baby with the bath water? Wouldn't we be undermining our common good if we discouraged the concentrations of wealth that bankroll foundation endowments?

We could note, in response, that foundations are as likely to subvert as promote the public good. Foundations founded by wealthy right-wing ideologues do regularly — and massively — bankroll initiatives that serve only to advance special, not common, interests. But the problem with treating foundations as a reason for tolerating, or even welcoming concentrations of wealth, goes far beyond the machinations of right-wing zealots. Foundations, the public-spirited and the mean-spirited alike, have a much more debilitating impact on our democracy. They bias our democratic political discourse — against a careful consideration of how we are impacted, and hurt, by concentrated wealth.

America's foundations, explains foundation analyst Mark Dowie, depend for their funding on an unequal distribution of America's wealth. They generally do not, as a consequence, "directly address the injustices created by disproportionate wealth."[142] They sidestep, not confront, inequality, and that sidestep, notes Dowie, reflects the "central contradiction of foundation philanthropy."

Mainstream foundations, adds economist Robert Kuttner, can articulate wonderfully about "social-change goals" that "are impeccably liberal — empower the poor, clean up the environment, improve the welfare of children — but the political dimension leaves many senior foundation executives uneasy."[143] They assume, notes Kuttner, that "social problems have technical solutions," that research, if rigorous enough, will somehow result in social change. Almost universally, they simply would rather not dip their toes in political waters and risk causing waves that might unduly upset America's powers that be. And that reluctance is "reinforced by the composition of mainstream foundation boards, which tend to be patrician and corporate."

Some foundations, to be sure, do break beyond these limits. Kuttner himself helps edit a magazine, *The American Prospect*, that owes its capacity to challenge concentrated wealth in no small part to foundation support. But activists for a democratic society, Kuttner suggests, will never make adequate progress expecting "large private fortunes," however noble their originators may have been, "to underwrite progressive politics."[144]

If we are to have systemic reform in our democracy, we have no choice but to cut to the chase and confront power and wealth. A democratic society does not wait for crumbs to fall from rich people's tables. A democratic society identifies the public interest, through free and open debate, then moves to meet it. And that will mean, more often than not, having to advocate steps likely to discomfort those with wealth and power.

As "nice as it is that Bill Gates gives money to libraries," notes Randy Cohen, the resident ethicist at the *New York Times*, "a decent country would tax Microsoft at a rate that lets cities buy their own books."[145]

IN ANY COMPLEX MODERN NATION, identifying the public interest can be incredibly difficult work. Inequality makes this hard work all the harder.

"The wider the disparities in Americans' economic circumstances," as Harvard political analyst John Donahue has pointed out, "the more their policy priorities are likely to diverge, and the harder it becomes to stake out common ground."[146]

The public agenda that does get set, in an increasingly unequal America, most often reflects the interests of those at the top end of those disparities. Average Americans know that — and resent it. In 1996, 60 percent of Americans agreed that public officials don't care much about what they think.[147] In 1960, a considerably more equal time, only a quarter of Americans held to this alienated perspective.

Citizens, Carlos Vilas has argued in the Latin American context, only participate politically when they feel their participation matters. In the United States, by century's end, most citizens felt their participation no longer mattered — and no longer participated. In 1996, the voting turnout among *eligible* voters came in at just 49 percent, the lowest level since 63 percent of eligible voters voted in 1960.[148] In the 1998 midterm elections, nearly two-thirds of Americans, 64 percent, did not vote.[149] In the 2000 Presidential primaries, nearly 80 percent of Americans did not vote.[150] In the 2000 Presidential general election, turnout did bump up slightly over the previous Presidential general election, by 2.2 percent. But Curtis Gans, America's most-quoted expert on voter turnout statistics, would not be impressed by the slight increase.

"When you have one of the three closest elections of the last 125 years, when you have the stimulus of polls telling you how close it is and you still have nearly half the nation not showing up," Gans noted, "you haven't fundamentally changed the motivation of the American people."[151]

Two years later, in the 2002 congressional midterm elections, despite massive get-out-the-vote efforts by both parties, 61 percent of voters would not go to the polls.[152]

Americans, observers note, aren't just stiffing the ballot box. They aren't even following politics any more. In 1960, 60 percent of the nation's households watched John F. Kennedy debate Richard Nixon. In 2000, under 30 percent of the nation watched Al Gore and George W. Bush go at it.[153]

Levels of citizen participation in American political life, analysts lament, figure to sink even more in the years to come. More than half the kids in America, Curtis Gans noted in 2000, are currently growing up in households "where neither parent votes."[154]

Some observers see in these staggering statistics no reason to get alarmed. If people aren't voting, these observers contend, they must be satisfied with the way things are. An interesting theory. But if nonvoters are "the satisfied," then affluent people ought to be *not voting* at levels higher than anyone else. Affluent people have, after all, the most reasons to feel satisfaction. In fact, researchers agree, affluent people in the United States are voting at rates much *higher* than everyone else, not much lower. In 1996, for instance, 76 percent of voters in families making at least $75,000 a year voted. Voters from families earning under $10,000 cast ballots at just a 38 percent rate.[155]

The wider the gaps between top and bottom, researchers have also found, the less voting overall. In the 1996 elections, the ten states with the smallest income gaps averaged a 57 percent voter turnout. The ten with the widest income gaps averaged 48 percent.[156]

"Income gaps," notes political analyst Holly Sklar, "translate into voting gaps."[157]

These voting gaps, adds economist Paul Krugman, quickly generate "disproportionate political weight" for well-off people. America's major political parties do not compete for the votes of average Americans. They compete for the votes of those who vote. They compete, notes Krugman, "to serve the interests of families near the 90th percentile or higher, families that mostly earn $100,000 or more per year."[158]

That competition, naturally, has consequences for society at large.

"A family at the 95th percentile pays a lot more in taxes than a family at the 50th, but it does not receive a correspondingly higher benefit from public services, such as education," Krugman explains. "This translates, because of the clout of the elite, into a constant pressure for lower taxes and reduced public services."[159]

Average Americans see, in these reductions, a government that doesn't work for them. More reason not to pay attention to government. Amid that inattention, the plutocrats tighten their grip. Plutocracy by design and default.

WE CANNOT AND SHOULD NOT, OF COURSE, *totally* reduce the problems of our democracy, our "inequalities of power," to "inequalities of wealth."[160] Unequal distributions of power, we have learned over the years, can certainly exist in societies not skewed dramatically by great differences in income and wealth. We saw that reality in the Soviet Union.

To function democratically, as Nobel Prize-winner Amartya Sen has noted, a modern state must have "established and protected forums of public criti-

cism" and "regular elections admitting rival parties." Without these democratic structures, small elite groups in a society may be able to do great "social
harm," even without holding a personal level of wealth that can simply overwhelm their opposition.[161]

Greater equality, in short, may not always and absolutely ensure greater
democracy.

But greater inequality, always and absolutely, ensures less democracy.

A PRICE TOO HIGH

EARLY IN THE TWENTY-FIRST CENTURY, a distinguished CEO, Pepsi-Cola's Roger Enrico, made somewhat of an unexpected remark to author Jeffrey Garten.

"We have to care about the distribution of wealth," Enrico noted, "because the fact of the matter is if there's a shrinking middle class, that's not a good thing."[1]

Not a good thing. Four words that summed up decades of research into inequality by scholars from nearly every academic discipline, from economics to epidemiology. Societies that let wealth concentrate at the top, these scholars have shown, pay an incredibly high price. Societies that stand by idly as middle classes break apart and sink have no future, at least no future their people will ever rush to see.

Roger Enrico may not have read this research. He really didn't need to read it. He understood, at some gut level, that societies work best when most people live their lives at a level of abundance not outrageously higher or lower than their neighbors.

Our basic human common sense, as evolved over many millennia, has imprinted us with this understanding. Our best human societies recognize the common bonds we all share. Our worst frown on sharing — and honor, with power, those who share the least. In these distinctly unequal societies, concentrated wealth overpowers common sense and leaves us lusting for what the wealthy have and we do not. In our lust, we pay no attention to cost. We pay any price. We eventually bankrupt our societies and our souls.

Those who champion inequality, despite its cost, sometimes do acknowledge that inequality may not always be a "good thing." But inequality, they insist, is the only thing. The march of civilization demands it. We have no choice but to accept it.

They are wrong. Alternatives do exist. We have been less unequal in the past. We can be less unequal again.

Book Three
An End to Greed?

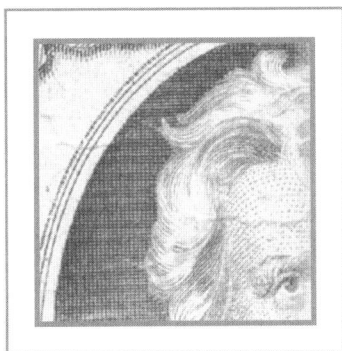

Alternatives to Inequality

Of all the Americans alive today, only those retirees old enough to be receiving Social Security can remember a time when most Americans, even a President of the United States, considered concentrated wealth a clear and present danger.

The rest of us have lived our lives in an America that accepts the proliferation of grand fortunes as an inevitable fact of life, as natural as boredom on the job, as traffic at rush hour. We simply cannot envision an America without enormously rich people.

Earlier generations of Americans certainly could. In fact, over our nation's first century and beyond, no American political figure of any consequence ever openly and unabashedly welcomed the presence of great fortunes in our midst. We Americans, back in those days, considered concentrated wealth a menace to everything that made us special as a people. We would struggle, generation after generation, to limit the presence and the power of grand accumulations. That struggle, to a degree unimaginable today, would define our political life.

To move forward, to create an America where inequality no longer limits our lives, we today need to understand that historic struggle — and why that struggle failed. Only with that understanding can we compare and contrast more modern approaches to closing the enormous gaps that divide us. Only with that understanding can we set ourselves back on course to where we need to be.

HISTORIC STRUGGLES

ON APRIL 27, 1942, only months after Pearl Harbor, President Franklin D. Roosevelt presented to Congress a proposal to limit the income of any one American. At a time of "grave national danger," the President advised, "no American citizen ought to have a net income, after he has paid his taxes, of more than $25,000 a year."[1] The nation's "discrepancies between low personal incomes and very high personal incomes," FDR urged, "should be lessened."[2]

Not all Americans would agree. The *New York Herald Tribune* quickly labeled FDR's $25,000 limit — about $300,000 in current dollars — "a blatant piece of demagoguery."[3] Many wealthy Americans, adds historian Kenneth Davis, felt "angry outrage." But few newspapers across the country would, in the end, echo the *Herald Tribune*'s fury, and wealthy Americans, by and large, would keep their outrage "prudently muted."[4] Hardly any average Americans, the wealthy realized, shared their anger. The President, most Americans believed, was merely stating what needed to be said. At a time of national crisis, the rich needed to pay more in taxes, a great deal more.[5] No one in their right mind, most Americans agreed, could possibly object to that notion.

Sixty years later, another American President, George W. Bush, *would* object to that notion. Amid a new national crisis, a war against terror, this President would insist that America's wealthiest citizens should pay not more in taxes, but less, a great deal less.

In January 2003, President Bush would propose a $674 billion tax cut — and target 32 percent of that cut to America's richest 1 percent. Taxpayers in this top 1 percent, under the Bush proposal, would enjoy $66 billion more in savings than the entire bottom 80 percent of the American taxpaying public.[6]

Two Presidents, two eras, two strikingly different responses to national crisis. Franklin D. Roosevelt moved to soak the rich, George W. Bush to shower still more riches upon them. What explains the difference?

As individuals, interestingly, both FDR and George W. shared a great deal in common. Both were born into wealth. Both had names made familiar to the American people by previous Presidents. Both had made their way, without distinction, through elite private schools. Both had been governors. Both had experienced life, to a remarkable extent, in the same luxury lane. The two shared just about everything — except eras.

415

George W. Bush would take his oath of office in an America that celebrated men of fortune as the engines of our prosperity.

Franklin D. Roosevelt, by contrast, would enter the White House after an intense half-century of citizen struggle against the people his distant cousin, Theodore Roosevelt, had repeatedly blasted as the "malefactors of great wealth."

All those years of struggle against concentrated wealth had dramatically shaped Franklin Roosevelt's America, probably much more than he ever understood. Today, early in the twenty-first century, struggles against concentrated wealth no longer shape how we see the world. But they could. They should. To move forward, we need to look back.

AMERICA'S FOUNDING GENERATION, the generation of 1776, waged and won a war for independence. But the revolutionaries who led this war effort did not just seek to separate from England. They sought to establish an entirely new social order, a nation of citizens, not subjects, a republic, not an aristocracy. In their new nation, the people would rule.

This attempt at republic would not be the world's first. History had seen, in ancient and more recent times, a series of efforts to establish republican rule. Athens. Rome. Venice. Florence. All had failed. Why? America's founders carefully studied the historical record to find out. Republics, they concluded, require an equitable distribution of wealth.[7] Where wealth concentrates, political power can never be democratically shared.

"The balance of power in a society," John Adams would explain in 1776, "accompanies the balance of property in land. The only possible way, then, of preserving the balance of power on the side of equal liberty and public virtue, is to make the acquisition of land easy to every member of society; to make the division of the land into small quantities, so that the multitude may be possessed of landed estates."[8]

To America's revolutionary founders, equity seemed nature's way. Most of their fellow colonials lived on small, semisubsistence family farms. In this overwhelmingly agrarian setting, grand fortunes hardly ever accumulated. Some farmers did work harder than others, but the Earth could yield, no matter how much work was performed upon it, only so much wealth. That reality, notes historian James Huston, kept gaps in colonial income and wealth relatively limited. And those gaps would stay limited, the generation of 1776 believed, so long as all who labored were guaranteed the "fruits of their labor."[9] If those who toiled received their due, significant inequalities of wealth would never emerge in the new American republic. The new republic would prosper, in liberty, for all.

This catchphrase, "fruits of their labor," would pepper revolutionary era speeches and broadsides.[10] Republican liberty would surely fail, the revolutionaries agreed, if their new nation ever let elites expropriate what average Americans labored so hard to earn.

To prevent failure, the new nation would have to be vigilant. Fortunes would have to be divided at every opportunity. In Europe, the laws of primogeniture and entail enabled wealthy aristocrats to pass on their fortunes, undivided, to their firstborn male heirs. By ending these laws, America's founders believed, the young United States could prevent grand concentrations of wealth from accumulating — and threatening republican rule.[11] State by state, in the decades after the Revolution, advocates of republican virtue would press tirelessly to abolish entail and primogeniture. These dangerous principles, as Senator James Barbour from Virginia would argue in 1820, "concentrate the property of the country, and with it the power and influence of a few."[12]

But efforts to end aristocratic inheritance laws, America's early leaders believed, could not by themselves keep property and power dispersed. Good republicans, the revolutionaries agreed, must attack aristocratic wealth at its source — by keeping the economy free from government interference. America's revolutionaries subscribed, in effect, to the doctrine of *laissez-faire*. Egalitarians today, of course, consider *laissez-faire* an inherently conservative doctrine, a convenient fiction that those of wealth and power propagate to hoard what they have. But America's revolutionaries saw the matter in a quite different light. They believed that politics, not economics, concentrates wealth and power. Wide disparities in wealth could only result when an elite manipulates politics to extract from hard-working citizens the fruits of their labor.

If the economy were just let alone, America's original revolutionaries believed, equality would grow naturally. Nobody could become fabulously wealthy in an economy where labor, and labor alone, determined a man's worth.[13]

THIS BASIC WORLD VIEW — what James Huston calls the republican theory of wealth distribution — would hold clear sway in America's early years. A democratic republic, Americans agreed, must ever strive to avoid, in Thomas Jefferson's phrase, the "numberless instances of wretchedness" that inevitably arise whenever some hold far more property than others. Jefferson did acknowledge, notes historian Sean Wilentz, that a completely equal division of property would be "impracticable." But he believed deeply that "enormous inequality" had left humankind with "much misery." A republic, Jefferson would write, "cannot invent too many devices for subdividing property."[14]

Some early leaders of the American republic, to be sure, did not share Jefferson's apprehensions. Alexander Hamilton, the nation's first treasury secretary, considered significant income and wealth disparities inescapable — and even preferable. The more liberty men enjoyed, Hamilton felt, the more unequal in economic circumstance they would likely become.[15] Hamilton's sympathies lay with America's moneyed classes, with urban investors, not semi-subsistence farmers. Hamilton's policies, as treasury secretary, would be about "rousing America out of its semicommercial slumbers."[16]

Toward that end, Hamilton would urge the very first Congress, in 1789, to assume responsibility for redeeming, at face value, a broad array of national and state-level debts going back to the Revolutionary War. To get America moving, he believed, investors needed to be rewarded. Hamilton also asked Congress to charter a national bank, an institution that would be backed by the full faith and credit of the federal government but run by private investors. Hamilton would get what he wanted — and so would America's financiers. The more enterprising among them had been buying up Revolutionary War and state debt at rock-bottom prices. The new federal government's decision to redeem these debts, at their original value, guaranteed these enterprising speculators enormous windfall earnings on their investments. The new national bank, meanwhile, gave the nation's commercial interests control over a key lever of economic life. They would now have the power to privately determine the new nation's investment priorities, a power, critics feared, that could nurture a new moneyed aristocracy.[17]

The young American nation, once Hamilton's ambitious agenda had been adopted, would need revenue to foot the bill. That revenue would come largely from America's yeoman farmers. In 1790, on Hamilton's recommendation, Congress would levy an excise tax on the manufacture of distilled liquor. The tax amounted, in a young rural nation, to a tax on backwoods farmers, since these farmers did much of the nation's distilling. Farmers distilled because they had little economic choice. In America's interior, where they farmed, poor road systems made shipping wagons full of grain to market prohibitively expensive. Farmers, instead, would distill their excess grain into more easily transportable whiskey products. By taxing the stills the farmers used to manufacture these products, Hamilton's federal government was essentially shifting wealth out of farmer hands into the pockets of the financial speculators who held America's debt.

But Hamilton, in a nation still devoted to the spirit of 1776, had gone too far. His "use of government banking and debt to reward a wealthy elite," notes political analyst Kevin Phillips, had "trespassed on the Revolutionary credo."[18] Bitter disputes over Hamilton's economic policies would soon split America's political class into warring parties — and, in the 1800 elections, sweep Hamilton's party, the Federalists, out of power forever.

The sorry events of the 1790s, the victorious Jeffersonians believed, had confirmed the wisdom of 1776. If the people were not vigilant, if the people let elites manipulate politics, an aristocracy of wealth would re-emerge in their young republic and eventually destroy it. No republic, the Jeffersonians argued, can tolerate inequality and survive. The new United States, as James Madison had noted, needed to become more equal, through laws that, "without violating the rights of property, reduce extreme wealth towards a state of mediocrity, and raise extreme indigence toward a state of comfort."[19]

Aristocracy equals inequality, republicanism equals equality. In early nineteenth century America, no public figure would challenge these basic equations. Every actor on America's political stage, radicals and conservatives alike, took this egalitarian attitude toward property as a given. Aristocracy, pronounced the utopian-minded William Leggett in the 1830s, served to "concentrate all wealth and privilege in the hands of a few."[20] "In monarchies and aristocracies," pronounced a far more conservative New Jersey Whig, Congressman Joseph Fitz Randolph a few years later, "there are classes of the very wealthy and of the very poor; in a Republic both extremes are avoided."[21]

This conviction — that concentrated wealth endangers republican virtue — so dominated American political life before the Civil War that every side to every great political controversy would invariably justify its position by claiming that the opposition viewpoint, if followed, would leave America dangerously unequal. In 1832, for instance, President Andrew Jackson would place his opposition to rechartering a national bank squarely in the Jeffersonian tradition.

"It is to be regretted," Jackson opined, "that the rich and powerful too often bend the acts of government to their selfish purposes."[22]

National bank supporters in the 1830s, unlike Alexander Hamilton in the 1790s, would take pains to present their case through the same Jeffersonian prism. Bankers, financiers, and bondholders, they stressed, toiled at their trades just like everyone else. They deserved the "fruits of their labor," too.[23]

In early America, even defenders of slavery — the ultimate denial of the right to the fruits of your own labor — painted themselves as principled opponents of concentrated wealth. Slavery, the Virginian George Fitzhugh argued in 1857, made for a more equal society than social relations in the "free" North. Capitalists in the Northern states, he posited, expropriated value created by their workers and, in return, paid only subsistence wages. Under slavery, Fitzhugh asserted, masters willingly ensured slaves decent living standards. Slaveholding practices that kept slaves well-fed and healthy, Fitzhugh claimed, helped masters protect their capital investment.[24]

Slavery's critics, for their part, had little trouble demolishing these slaveholder claims. Slavery, they pointed out, had outrageously skewed the South's distribution of income and wealth. Nearly half the South's personal income flowed to a mere one thousand families.[25] Slavery, Senator William Seward from New York noted, had poisoned the Roman republic. The same fate, he warned, awaited a United States that tolerated slaveholding. In slavery, "the rich and great" grow "always richer and greater and the poor and low always poorer and more debased."[26]

A free republic, almost all Americans took as a matter of faith, wherever they stood on slavery, could not safely accept great gaps between rich and poor. Most Americans also believed that the young United States had so far prevented these gaps from developing. Throughout the nation's first century, historian James Huston notes, Americans continually celebrated "the egalitarian nature of the American distribution of wealth."[27] The United States, crowed the economist Theodore Sedgwick, had achieved an equal division of property "such as has never been known among mankind."[28] Equality, authors proudly proclaimed, made America different — and better. "Unlike the European States,"

Baltimore's John Pendleton Kennedy would note in 1845, "we have no piles of hoarded wealth destined to be transmitted in mass to our posterity."[29]

Visiting Europeans would echo the same sentiments. They continually marveled at the level of equality they found in the new American nation. American society, noted Michel Guillaume Jean de Crèvecoeur, "is not composed, as in Europe, of great lords who possess everything, and of a herd of people who have nothing." In the United States, the "rich and poor are not so far removed from each other as they are in Europe."[30]

Americans would see for themselves, when they visited Europe, the same stark distinctions. In 1859, for instance, an in-person glimpse at English inequality would leave one visiting American of substantial means, John Sherman, shocked and overwhelmed.

"The idea that all this stock and property belonged to a few, that the great mass of people merely labored for others, and that the whole government was conducted and a system of laws passed simply to continue and intensify this state of things, and that the favored class had the possession of all the powers of government," Sherman noted, "made me feel a rebel from the beginning."[31]

In mid-nineteenth century America, even an affluent American could feel like a rebel with a cause. That cause was equality.

CELEBRATIONS OF AMERICAN EQUALITY would be commonplace in America's earliest years — and preposterously premature. The young nation had not achieved an equal social order, or anything close. Millions of American families held no more personal property than Europe's most wretched households. But these families — slave families and Native American families — didn't count. Those who did the counting, historian James Huston notes, simply "did not factor into their calculations people whom they considered to be exceptions or insignificant."[32]

But even among white men, Americans who clearly did "count," wealth did not sit equally distributed, as working class orators would start pointing out in the late 1820s. Advocates for urban workers, in their books and journals, would actually publish the first figures on wealth distribution to ever appear in the United States.[33] Workers, these advocates argued, were not getting their due, the fruits of their labors.[34] America, urged one fledgling trade union in 1828, needed to do much more active battle against the "evils which result from an unequal and very excessive accumulation of wealth and power in the hands of a few."[35]

In pre-Civil War America, wealth and power were indeed accumulating, especially in urban areas. In New York City, the richest 4 percent would claim 63 percent of local wealth in 1828, 81 percent in 1845.[36] Still, despite this growing inequality, urban workers demanding their just due would not make, overall, much of an impact. Fourth of July orators would continue to celebrate, as indisputable fact, American equality. And their claim — that America had become a land of opportunity where all could enjoy the fruits of their labor —

would still ring true. Most Americans, after all, still lived on farms, not in cities. With so much cheap land readily available, a farmer struggling in the East could always reasonably expect to achieve commercial success in the West.[37]

Off the farm, in urban centers, new industrial enterprises were beginning to employ substantial numbers of Americans in wage labor. But in the United States, unlike England, these new industrial enterprises would typically remain small-scale operations.[38] In these smaller enterprises, gaps in income and wealth did grow, but not nearly as wide or as fast as they did in England. America, on the whole, would remain a land of small shops and farms, the original basis of the Jeffersonian equality ethic. If you worked hard, your labor would bear fruit. If you worked hard enough, you could even become wealthy, but not too wealthy, since one person's labor could only produce so much fruit.[39]

Only politics, good Jeffersonians reminded each other, could upset this natural economic equilibrium. So government needed to be kept small. A larger, more active government, along the lines of what America's commercial and financial interests periodically demanded, would only mean more patronage, more taxes, more opportunities for enlarging "the fortunes of the favored few at the expense of the laboring multitude."[40] Small governments amassed no great debts, levied no great taxes — and gave great fortunes no easy entry into American life.[41] In other words, to maintain the equality that republican life required, the government needed to do next to nothing.[42]

But republican equality had, of course, already been poisoned, by the most poisonous aristocratic seed imaginable. Slavery had left huge swatches of America "controlled by a small opulent elite that discouraged the wide diffusion of property among nonslaves."[43]

The United States would eventually stumble into war and, in the heat of that war, make the political choice to end slavery. But merely ending slavery, thoughtful Americans understood, would not end the inequality slavery had wrought. To guarantee freed slaves the fruits of *their* labor, America would have to do what the young nation had never done before. America would have to make a conscious political choice to redistribute wealth, in this case land, from those who had too much to those who had none at all. The slaves had been promised forty acres. America would either keep that promise or doom the South to deep and corrupting inequality for generations to come.

The promise would not be kept. America blinked, after the Civil War, and looked away. The former slaves would get no forty acres. The fruits of their labor would continue to be expropriated. Inequality in the South, nurtured over slavery's decades, would survive slavery's smashing.[44]

AMERICA WOULD NOT TAKE FROM THE WEALTHY to undo the legacy of slavery. But America would take from America's most privileged, albeit modestly, to win the war that ended slavery as an institution. During the Civil War, taxes on affluent incomes and inheritances would make their first appearance on America's national political stage.

In 1861, Congress would enact the first of several Civil War income tax levies. This initial measure placed a modest 3 percent tax on incomes over $800, then a considerable sum. Most Americans approved. If some among them were going to be asked to give up their lives for the union, the general feeling went, the least people of means could do was pay a little tax.[45] The 1861 revenue legislation also included America's first inheritance tax. Millionaires, the *New York Herald* approvingly noted, "will henceforth contribute a fair proportion of their wealth to the support of the national government."[46]

Actual income tax collections would not begin until 1862, after new legislation set a 3 percent tax on all income between $600 and $10,000 and a 5 percent tax on income over $10,000.[47] America's first commissioner of internal revenue, working "day and night in a small room in the Treasury building with three clerks borrowed from other departments," was soon pulling in revenue by the bucket. One clerk collected $37 million in just six months.[48] But the war was costing $2 million a day, and Congress quickly found itself upping the income tax ante. An act in 1864 raised the top tax rate to 10 percent.[49] That top 10 percent rate, the next year, would be applied to all income over $5,000.[50]

These new taxes did have some critics. Income taxes, charged Rep. Justin Morrill from Vermont in 1864, "were seizing the property of men for the crime of having too much."[51] But the grumblers, by and large, held their tongues — until the war ended. At that point, inside Congress and out, they would mince no words. Academic Goldwin Smith, in 1866, denounced the income tax's "socialistic tendency." The income tax, added Vermont's Morrill, "can only be defended on the same ground the highwayman defends his acts."[52]

Defenders of the income tax did their best to counterattack. A Pennsylvanian, Rep. Washington Townsend, charged that the "clamor in favor of the abolition of the income tax" had been cynically orchestrated by "men of colossal fortunes."[53] But postwar income tax advocates were fighting a losing battle. Congress would soon start reducing income tax rates.[54] By 1872, the year the Civil War era income tax expired, less than a fifth of 1 percent of the nation's population were paying any taxes at all on their incomes.[55]

In 1873, THE YEAR AFTER AMERICA'S FIRST INCOME TAX DIED, Mark Twain published his first novel. His book, *The Gilded Age*, described an America where "the air is full of money, nothing but money, money floating through the air."[56] In this new America, grand fortune now held dominion. The United States, Twain's bestseller helped Americans understand, had been transformed.

Grand fortunes had, of course, existed before the Civil War. A decade before the war, at least two hundred millionaires called the United States home.[57] But these millionaires dominated neither politics nor the economy. In a proud republic, they seemed curiosities, not threats to the good and welfare of everyday life. The Civil War would change that, leaving in its wake a "cyclone-like realignment of wealth and power."[58]

No modern nation had ever waged, before 1861, a conflict as costly as America's Civil War. To pay the bill, a modest income tax would not suffice. By war's end, the North would borrow over $2.5 billion. Millions of these borrowed dollars, in turn, cascaded back into the American economy, as payments for war contracts. Bullets had to be manufactured, uniforms stitched, cannon balls shipped. An enterprising young gentleman could make a fortune. Enterprising young gentlemen did make fortunes. The men who would become the giants of American commerce — J. P. Morgan, John D. Rockefeller, Andrew Carnegie, Marshall Field — all started out, political analyst Kevin Phillips reminds us, as "young northerners who avoided military service, usually by buying substitutes, and used the war to take major steps up future fortune's ladder."[59] Between 1861 and 1865, federal officials let about $1 billion worth of contracts to private companies. Contractors, one historian suggests, pocketed nearly one-half that billion in pure profit. By war's end, the number of millionaires in New York City had tripled.[60]

Wealth would continue to concentrate after Appomattox, with ample help from the nation's lawmakers. The 1869 Public Credit Act guaranteed speculators gold for the government bonds they had bought, with far less valuable paper money, during the war. Financiers could end up making a 150 percent return on bonds that originally yielded only 6 percent interest.[61] For investors more interested in railroads, lawmakers would prove equally generous. By 1871, federal and state officials had dispensed to America's private railroads about $100 million in financial subsidies and 200 million acres in land grants.[62]

All these subsidies, in due course, would help fuel an enormous expansion of America's industrial might. The capital invested in American manufacturing would leap from $1 billion in 1860 to $10 billion in 1900.[63] An agrarian nation, in the span of a few short decades, would become the world's greatest industrial power. Giant corporations, led by America's railroads, now dominated the economic scene. These corporations, wherever possible, pooled their resources. They rigged cartels, fashioned "trusts," invented holding companies.[64] They created, in industry after industry, monopolies that simply overpowered any small businesses and farms that stood in their way. And they amassed the greatest fortunes the world had ever seen.

By 1896, America's largest individual family fortunes had tripled in value from 1873.[65] Americans of more limited means could not help but notice. The wealthy flaunted their good fortune at every opportunity, and the nation's newspapers chronicled the flaunting. At one party frequented by a host of swells, guests delighted to find cigarettes wrapped in $100 bills.[66] Wealthy matrons would routinely buy two seats at the opera, "one for them, and one for their day's purchases."[67] William K. Vanderbilt, for his "summer cottage" in Newport, spent a sum that would equal over $365 million in our modern dollars.[68]

In the great new mansions now emerging, Americans saw the moneyed aristocracy they had always feared. Commentators now filled books and journals with anguished descriptions of a democracy endangered. America, a new generation of reformers argued, needed to regain its egalitarian equilibrium. Economic inequality, orators like Henry George reminded their fellow citizens, violated nature's most eternal laws.

"No person, I think, ever saw a herd of buffalo, of which a few were fat and the great majority lean," George noted in one Iowa address. "No person ever saw a flock of birds, of which two or three were swimming in grease, and the others all skin and bone."[69]

America's men of wealth, and their admirers, would not let these attacks go unanswered. For the first time in the republic's history, gentlemen of substance openly celebrated the presence of concentrated wealth in America. Inequality, argued apologists for grand fortune, evolved naturally in human affairs, just as naturally as men from apes. In successful species and societies, the "Social Darwinists" posited, the strong survive — and prosper. Millionaires, famed Yale political scientist William Graham Sumner maintained, "are a product of natural selection."[70]

"The aggregation of large fortunes is not at all a thing to be regretted," Sumner assured Americans. "On the contrary, it is a necessary condition of social advance."[71] Americans needed to shunt aside, Sumner urged, the "old ecclesiastical prejudice in favor of the poor and against the rich."[72] Government "had no business interfering on behalf of the downtrodden."[73] No reason existed "to limit the property which any man may acquire."[74]

Many of Sumner's contemporaries, to the contrary, would see reason to limit the property "any man can acquire." Among them would be one of America's wealthiest men.

IN 1868, A YOUNG RISING BUSINESS TYCOON, Andrew Carnegie, wrote himself a memo. Carnegie had reason to feel elated. He had already organized his first successful company. But young Carnegie felt no cause for celebration. He felt soiled by his new wealth. No idol, he wrote, could be "more debasing than the worship of money."[75] Beyond $50,000, Carnegie urged himself, "never earn."[76]

Andrew Carnegie would not follow his own advice. By 1900 he would be taking home over $23 million a year.[77] Still, Carnegie would never feel comfortable with fortune. This son of Scottish social reformers would wrestle with wealth intellectually his entire life. In 1889, he would share his intellectual grappling in a widely read essay, *The Gospel of Wealth.*

In the past, Carnegie noted, small enterprises had ensured America a relatively equitable distribution of wealth. No one individual could amass a colossal fortune in a small-enterprise economy. But that smallness, Carnegie contended, was actually holding America back. Small enterprises could not achieve efficiencies of scale. Their goods cost too much. Large-scale enterprises, by contrast, could operate efficiently, and, through their efficiency, make goods available to consumers at reasonable cost.

Large-scale enterprises, Carnegie acknowledged, also exacted a price. Wealth could never be distributed equitably in a large-enterprise economy, since large-scale enterprise demanded "the concentration of business, industrial and commercial, in the hands of a few."[78] These fortunate few, Carnegie maintained, were, in effect, benefiting from economic necessity. To remain honorable, these fortunate must see themselves as merely the stewards, not the owners, of the great wealth that industrial concentration had enabled them to amass. As stewards, they have a responsibility to dispense their wealth for the benefit of society. If successful as stewards, by death they will have given their fortunes entirely away. "The man who dies rich," Carnegie proclaimed, "thus dies disgraced."

Carnegie himself actually would give away his fortune in the decades after *The Gospel of Wealth* appeared. But Carnegie would have little faith in the innate generosity of his fellow tycoons. They, he believed, needed to be nudged. Carnegie cheered America's "growing disposition to tax more and more heavily large estates left at death." No one should be allowed to inherit a fortune, he argued. A stiff tax on bequests, he believed, would give the wealthy an incentive to give away what they had while they still had it.[79]

Carnegie's musings had a powerful impact on American attitudes toward the great new fortunes, but not the impact Carnegie might have hoped. His hostility toward inherited fortunes left Americans more convinced than ever that enormous concentrations of wealth had no place in a free republic. Average Americans understood, with Carnegie, that the nation had evolved a new economy. But they refused to accept, notes historian James Huston, the "concentration of economic power in a few hands." Concentrated economic power meant monopoly, and monopoly denied workers the fruits of their labor.[80]

A *laissez-faire* approach to the economy, the heirs to America's Jeffersonian tradition now realized, no longer made sense. Unless government stepped in, unless government regulated the railroads, took on the trusts, taxed the wealthy, the monopolists would tighten their death grip ever more firmly upon the still fragile republic.[81] To ensure the equity so essential to a healthy republic, more and more Americans believed, the nation needed a new politics. The struggle against entail and primogeniture had done noble work against the aristocracy of old, observed journalist Henry Demarest Lloyd late in the nineteenth century. But new noble work demanded to be done.

"We have nearly finished democratizing kings," exclaimed Lloyd, "and now we are about to democratize the millionaire."[82]

AMERICA'S IMMENSELY WEALTHY, REFORMERS agreed by the 1890s, needed to be whittled down to democratic size. Their whittling instrument of choice: a federal income tax. A "graduated" levy that taxed high incomes at high rates, reformers believed, would be the key to redistributing America's wealth — and restoring America's democracy.

Congress had killed America's first income levy, the Civil War era income tax, in 1872. Almost immediately, reformers had started pressing to bring the tax back. Between 1873 and 1879, lawmakers introduced fourteen bills to reenact a national tax on incomes.[83] In 1883, crusading newspaper publisher Joseph Pulitzer made the demand for an income tax part of his *New York World's* ten-plank platform for social reform.[84] In 1886, the Knights of Labor, then American labor's largest national organization, announced its support for a graduated income tax.[85] By the 1890s, the income tax had become part and parcel of every significant American reform agenda.

The advocates for these agendas — radical farmers from the South and West, labor activists, members of the Nationalist Clubs inspired by Edward Bellamy's best-selling novel *Looking Backward*, followers of Henry George — would join in 1891 to start taking serious steps toward creating a third party devoted to the income tax and other social reforms. In May, at a convention in Cincinnati, these activists would adopt a common platform that demanded, in phraseology that had become familiar to reformers the nation over, "a just and equitable system of graduated tax on income."[86]

The following February, an even broader assemblage of reformers would gather in St. Louis to launch the new "People's Party."

"The fruits of the toil of millions," the preamble to the party's St. Louis platform would read, "are boldly stolen to build up colossal fortunes, unprecedented in the history of the world, while their possessors despise the republic and endanger liberty."[87]

Over the next several years, "Populist" candidates from the new People's Party would run for offices high and low — and be elected, even in some gubernatorial races. The movement's leaders, men like the fiery Georgia lawyer Tom Watson, made the progressive income tax an ongoing centerpiece of their organizing. An income tax, Watson explained in 1893, "would discourage the accumulation of enormous fortunes and would afford a legal method of checking the growth of concentrated wealth."[88] The income tax, Watson believed, helped define the difference between the People's Party and America's old, corrupt parties of privilege. A Congress packed with Democrats and Republicans, he told his fellow People's Party activists, would never let a graduated income tax see the light of day.

"As long as the Old Parties are dominated by the influences which now control them," Watson charged, "the Income Tax will remain a dead issue — a monument to the servile party spirit which makes laws in the interest of plutocracy."[89]

But that "servile party spirit" was cracking. Young lawmakers in Congress like Nebraska's William Jennings Bryan were taking up the income tax call. In 1890s America, you didn't need to be a rabble-rousing radical like Tom Watson to worry what great fortunes were doing to your country. A tax on high incomes seemed, to many Americans, entirely appropriate — and long overdue.

"The most effective weapon against Plutocratic policy," as Charles H. Jones, the editor of the *St. Louis Republic*, would note in 1893, "is the graded income tax."[90]

That same graded income tax, some men of substance believed, could also be an "effective weapon" against rabble-rousing radicals. In the shadows cast by America's great fortunes, men of means saw fearsome anarchists lurking, "foreign" ideologies taking root. This would not do. America had lived through a Civil War. Now a class war loomed. A tax on wealthy incomes, many in Congress felt, could help avert that war, by denying rabble-rousers an exploitable issue. Passage of an income tax, declared Rep. Uriel Hall, a Missouri Democrat, would help "kill anarchy and keep down socialists."[91]

By 1894, income tax advocates on Capitol Hill had hit critical mass. They included determined critics of America's new corporate order, resolute defenders of republican virtue, and politicians sick of plutocrats one day, scared by anarchists the next. These lawmakers, Democrats and Populists, coalesced behind legislation that would tax the incomes of only the most affluent Americans. Their modest proposal, a 2 percent tax on incomes above $4,000, would immediately elicit cries of outrage from fortune's friends.

"In a republic like ours, where all men are equal," exclaimed Senator John Sherman, "this attempt to array the rich against the poor or the poor against the rich is socialism, communism, devilism."[92] Other opponents charged that taxing income would lower wages, dampen incentive, and generate corruption.[93] The income tax, they roared, would take from the "thrifty and enterprising" and give to the "shiftless and sluggard."[94]

Income tax advocates shrugged off the opposition's heated rhetoric. They had the votes. Their income tax proposal would pass as an amendment to the 1894 tariff bill, legislation that President Grover Cleveland, an income tax opponent, couldn't afford to veto. The Democratic hen, the *New York Tribune* roared, had "hatched a Populist chicken."[95] On August 28, 1894, the nation, for the first time since the Civil War era, had an income tax.

But not for long. On May 20, 1895, only nine months after the income tax became law, a five-to-four Supreme Court majority would rule the tax unconstitutional.

This ruling against the income tax, argued one anguished dissenter from the court's decision, Justice John Harlan, invited "the dominion of aggregated wealth."[96] Outside the high court's chambers, outraged Americans agreed. Indignant critics likened the income tax ruling to the infamous Dred Scott decision of 1857, the case that denied Congress the right to outlaw slavery anywhere within the United States.[97]

"Today's decision," noted an angry *St. Louis Post-Dispatch*, "shows that the corporations and plutocrats are as securely entrenched in the Supreme Court as in the lower courts which they take such pains to control."[98]

More fuel for the firestorm against the Supreme Court's income tax ruling would come from a widely circulated 1895 book, *The Present Distribution of Wealth in the United States*. Out of America's 63 million population, author Charles B. Spahr noted, only two hundred thousand families made over $5,000 a year. These affluent Americans, he noted, actually faced a tax burden four times *lower* than the tax burden on average Americans.[99]

The United States, millions of Americans firmly believed, needed a graduated income tax now more than ever. They would soon have a chance to express that opinion at the ballot box. Reform forces, in 1896, gained control over that year's Democratic National Convention. They chose as their candidate William Jennings Bryan, the leading congressional champion of the 1894 income tax. The Populists then cross-endorsed Bryan's candidacy. The reformers seemed united at last. The 1896 Presidential election, they exulted, would give Americans a clear choice, the people or the plutocrats.

The plutocrats would be ready.

BY 1896, AMERICA'S GREAT MEN OF WEALTH had become accustomed to treating elections as a recurring business expense. Eight years earlier, many of them had opened up their wallets to Republican Presidential candidate Benjamin Harrison. They feared, notes historian Michael Kazin, that the Democrats "might cut the steep tariffs that protected their firms from foreign competition."[100] In 1892, many men of wealth would switch horses and give the Democrats their financial support. The Democratic Presidential candidate that year, Grover Cleveland, seemed perfectly willing to be helpful.

Cleveland would go on to win the 1892 election, but the real triumph belonged to America's men of substance. In the Presidential race, they couldn't lose.

"I am very sorry for President Harrison," as industrialist Henry Clay Frick noted to his partner, Andrew Carnegie, "but I cannot see that our interests are going to be affected one way or the other by the change in administration."[101]

The 1896 Presidential race would be a different story. This time, all men of wealth agreed, a change of administration *would* matter. William Jennings Bryan posed a menace. He had to be stopped. Not because of silver, the centerpiece of Bryan's campaign. Bryan's call for the free and unlimited coinage of silver did indeed strike America's men of money as foolishly insane public policy. But this campaign, every politically aware American agreed, would be about much more than silver or gold.

"It is the people against the dollar, men against money, the public good against the privilege of accumulating wealth that others create," explained Frank Parsons, a leading contemporary academic.[102]

The privileged few essentially concurred with that assessment. Republican candidate William McKinley's campaign manager, Mark Hanna, would have no trouble dunning corporate leaders for whatever sums he needed.[103] The McKinley forces would eventually spend, notes historian Louis Koenig, close to $16 million, about $320 million in contemporary terms, or over $130 million more than George W. Bush spent to win the 2000 election.[104] Bush the younger outspent Al Gore by a three-to-two margin. McKinley would outspend William Jennings Bryan by twenty to one.[105]

With the McKinley campaign war chest overflowing, Republicans were able to circulate over 250 million flyers and pamphlets, send thousands of campaign speakers all across the nation, and, notes historian Michael Kazin, stage parades "in nearly every big city."[106] The industrialists bankrolling McKinley's campaign would keep up the pressure in other ways as well. Your job security, they warned their employees, would depend on the election results. The owner of one New England company even covered the front of his factory with giant placards: "This factory," the signs read, "will be closed on the morning after the November election if Bryan is elected."[107]

On Election Day, amid widespread charges of ballot box fraud, McKinley would capture a narrow victory, collecting just over half, 50.88 percent of the recorded vote. Bryan actually won more states, but McKinley swept all of America's industrial centers.[108] Reformers felt devastated. "The people" cried the widely revered Henry George, have "lost again."[109]

The people would lose still again the next year, in 1897, after the new President and Congress took office. America's huge "industrial combines," the trusts, now presented their bill for services rendered. They wanted tariffs on foreign goods raised, and raised high enough to help them consolidate their monopoly hold over America's domestic markets.[110] Congress would promptly enact and McKinley sign into law a new tax law that sent the tariffs on foreign imports to all-time record highs.

Wealth now sat firmly in the saddle. Even the outbreak of war, in 1898, would do little to discomfort America's affluent. This latest conflict, the Spanish-American War, would see no renewed push for an income tax. Congress, instead, would adopt a weak tax on inheritances, mainly because conservatives, as historian Sidney Ratner would later note, "felt that a concession on the inheritance tax was far less of a danger to the wealthy classes than one on the income tax."[111] The 1898 inheritance tax adopted by Congress applied only to those bequests over $1 million left to distant relatives or private bodies.[112] But even this modest attempt to limit wealth wouldn't outlast the war. In 1902, Congress repealed the war-time inheritance levy.

Corporate America, by the twentieth century, had essentially swept away all competitors, economic and political. Individual corporate entities were now free to conduct their business as they, and only they, saw fit. And these enterprises saw fit, between 1897 and 1904, to "concentrate" as never before. They unleashed a stunning merger wave that would turn 4,200 of America's largest companies into 257 corporate Goliaths.[113]

In the early 1900s, a new popular opposition would emerge to challenge these incredibly huge new concentrations of wealth and power. The great farmers' movements that had undergirded the People's Party may have been broken, and the dreams inspired by utopians like Edward Bellamy may have been dashed, but different players were now entering the fray. From the ranks of America's burgeoning immigrant communities would come skilled and savvy socialist agitators. From the mines and factory floors of America's industrial giants would come a more vibrant, aggressive labor movement. And from the ranks of America's middle class professionals would come a new, more determined reform spirit. The stage would once again be set for an epic battle between people and plutocrats. The people, this time, would have a champion in the White House.

THEODORE ROOSEVELT MADE A MOST UNLIKELY PEOPLE'S CHAMPION. But then again, he made a most unlikely President. Republican party bosses had never intended to make Roosevelt America's chief executive. They had plopped "TR" onto McKinley's 1900 re-election ticket to bury him politically. As governor of New York, TR had stepped on too many toes. He had refused to play patronage ball. He had pushed a tax on corporations. The local powerbrokers wanted him out of New York. The Vice Presidency seemed a safe enough place to stick him — until President McKinley was assassinated less than a year after he was re-elected. The hero of San Juan Hill now sat in the White House.

As President, Roosevelt would begin to grow on the American people. He brought suit, under the Sherman Antitrust Act, against a huge new railroad holding company that was trying to lock up effective control over transportation in the Northwest.[114] No President had ever before sought to break up a corporate giant. Roosevelt would go on to challenge dozens more. Rich and powerful people did not impress him. He would not be their lackey. But Roosevelt would not be impractical either. He needed to be renominated in 1904 to be able to continue on in the White House. He could, he knew, only go so far with his people's agenda. He could thunder on about trusts, but he would sidestep debates over tariffs and taxes.[115]

Meanwhile, out across the country, reform-minded journalists were rousing the reading public with alarming exposés of corporate power gone dangerously amuck. Angry voters, in response, would seed the Congress elected in 1904 with a new generation of progressives. Voters would also cast an unprecedented 400,000 votes for the Presidential candidate of the still fledgling Socialist Party, the veteran labor leader Eugene Victor Debs. The nation's political climate was clearly changing.

And Roosevelt, ever the savvy pol, was changing with the times. He began fulminating, first softly, then more loudly, against "malefactors of great wealth." He would call, in 1906, for a "progressive tax on all fortunes beyond a certain amount."[116] The nation needed, TR pronounced, "to put a constantly increasing burden on the inheritance of those swollen fortunes which it is certainly of no benefit to this country to perpetuate."[117]

Later that same year, Roosevelt would begin cautiously promoting a new stab at enacting an income tax. "The man of great wealth," said Roosevelt, "owes a peculiar obligation to the state because he derives special advantages from the mere existence of government." Roosevelt would keep this drumbeat going for the rest of his second term. The nation needed new taxes on income and wealth, he noted in 1907, because "most great civilized countries have an income tax and an inheritance tax."[118]

None of Roosevelt's tax-the-rich sentiments would, in the end, be written into law while TR remained in the White House. The friends of fortune still controlled both the House and Senate. Roosevelt, ever the practical pol, would not take them on. "The income tax," notes Steven Weisman's recent history of the period, "was clearly a cause for which he was prepared to take a stand, but not to stake his presidency."[119] Still, observes analyst Kevin Phillips, Roosevelt's rhetoric would help warm "the Progressive climate."[120]

By 1909, with Roosevelt's successor, William Howard Taft, in the White House, that climate would feel warm enough for progressives in Congress, both Republicans and Democrats, to make a move. The progressives would attach an income tax to the new tariff bill then working its way toward passage. Their maneuver would complicate life for conservatives. These conservatives wanted desperately to keep the nation's tariff laws rich people-friendly. But they could hardly expect to prevail with their latest tariff wish-list if they continued to oppose all moves to start taxing wealthy incomes. To prevail on tariffs, conservatives would have to take a more nuanced approach toward taxing incomes. And they did. Senate Finance Committee Chairman Nelson Aldrich, working with President Taft, agreed to endorse a proposed resolution calling for a constitutional amendment that would expressly allow Congress to levy an income tax.

This amendment, to be enacted into the Constitution, would have to be approved by three-quarters of the states. That, a confident Aldrich believed, would never happen.[121] By shunting the income tax question to the states, Aldrich and his allies figured, they could kill any prospect of an income tax for years to come and, as an added benefit, campaign credibly in 1910 as champions of the common man.[122] No conservative could challenge the wisdom of this political logic. The resolution to add an income tax amendment to the Constitution would pass the Senate 77-0 and the House 318-14.

But the old guard had misread the public mood. Americans had tired of the games rich people play. In the 1910 elections, in one state after another, voters opted to replace the old-line order.[123] State legislatures, now filled with more reform-minded lawmakers, soon started *ratifying* the income tax amendment that Congress had cynically enacted. In New York, John D. Rockefeller was aghast. The unthinkable — an income tax on the rich — could now actually become reality. Rockefeller rushed to mobilize opposition to the income tax ratification drive. "When a man has accumulated a sum of money within the law, that is to say, in the legally correct way," pronounced Rockefeller, "the people no longer have any right to share in the earnings resulting from the accumulation."[124]

The people disagreed. By 1913, enough states had ignored Rockefeller to make the right to levy an income tax the sixteenth amendment.[125] Woodrow Wilson, meanwhile, had been elected President in a 1912 election that saw three tax-the-rich candidates — Wilson himself, the "Bull Moose" Teddy Roosevelt, and the Socialist Eugene Debs — grab 74 percent of the vote.[126] The stage was now set, in Congress, for the passage of income tax legislation that would take advantage of the Constitution's newest amendment.

The congressional old guard, now a distinct minority, did make a last stand. Senator Henry Cabot Lodge from Massachusetts bitterly denounced one income tax proposal on the table — a plan that would have taxed incomes over $1 million at a 20 percent rate — as "confiscation of property under the guise of taxation" and "the pillage of a class."[127]

In the end, the old guard could not stop the enactment of the nation's first tax on incomes since the Civil War era. But Lodge and his friends could still hold their heads high in high-income circles. The income tax that would finally be enacted in 1913, thanks to their unrelenting protestations, would not place too heavy a burden on America's well-to-do. The 1913 legislation would subject income over $500,000 to just a 7 percent tax.[128]

AVERAGE AMERICANS, IN 1913, WOULD HAVE MUCH PREFERRED a considerably higher tax rate on wealthy incomes. Most Americans, by that year, had become acutely aware of the inequality all around them. Great strikes in the urban centers of the East had dramatized the massive gap between capital and labor — and blue-ribbon committees and commissions had documented that gap. In 1912, for instance, the House Banking Committee, chaired by Arsene Pujo from Louisiana, revealed that just two financial groupings, the Morgan and Rockefeller empires, controlled a tenth of the nation's wealth.[129] America, the Pujo Committee charged, faced "a vast and growing concentration of control of money and credit in the hands of comparatively few men."[130]

Between 1895 and 1910, a study by Dr. Willford Isbell King would note a few years later, the wealthiest 1.6 percent of Americans had essentially doubled their share of America's national income.[131] Most laborers in America, a government Industrial Relations Commission would add in 1915, earned less than $10 a week. America's top forty-four families, by contrast, were averaging well over two thousand times that.[132] The commission's research director, Basil Manly, felt that only a tax that limited inheritances from any estate to $1 million could make a dent on inequality so monstrous. The need for some sort of tax on great wealth, average Americans agreed, had become inescapable.

And urgent. The 1914 outbreak of war in Europe had sent the demand for U.S. products soaring. War profits were stuffing the pockets of America's corporate elites. Over a twenty-two month period, the shares of one industrial giant, Bethlehem Steel, jumped from just over $46 a share to $700.[133] The wealthy needed to be taxed, now more than ever, most Americans believed.

And America, more than ever, needed revenue, to prepare for a war that seemed day by day more likely. In 1916, the logic of these twin pressures would push Congress to levy, for the first time ever, a significant set of taxes on America's fortunes and those who held them. The 1916 tax act would more than double the tax on incomes over $1 million, to 15 percent, and would also include an estate tax of up to 10 percent on any bequest over $5 million.[134]

The legislation brought predictable jeers — the *New York Times*, for instance, declared the new estate tax a "frank project of confiscation" — but the momentum behind taxing the rich had never been stronger.[135] And that momentum would build still more after the United States entered the war in 1917. From Harvard, O.M.W. Sprague proposed that those enriched by war-time profits should have 95 percent of those profits taxed away. Taxing away excess earnings, Sprague argued, would keep rich people from wasting dollars on the luxuries that businesses, in war-time, had no business producing.[136]

In Congress, some lawmakers would introduce even stiffer tax-the-rich proposals. Rep. Edward Keating from Colorado proposed a 96 percent "surtax" on incomes over $150,000, on top of a 4 percent normal tax. The effect, he explained to his fellow lawmakers, would "be to tax all incomes above $150,000 100 percent."[137]

Out across the country, accomplished and distinguished Americans would enthusiastically endorse Keating's call for a 100 percent top tax rate. An "American Committee on War Finance" spent 1917 mobilizing public support for a "conscription of wealth" that would cap individual incomes at $100,000.[138] The committee's heavyweights would range from millionaire Amos Pinchot, who testified on the group's behalf before Congress, to newspaper magnate E. W. Scripps, who wired President Wilson his support for taxing away all incomes above $50,000.[139]

Pinchot's War Finance Committee took out ads in major newspapers to advocate the income cap notion and claimed endorsements from organizations representing millions of Americans. These organizations, Pinchot noted in his Senate testimony, "have expressed the belief that the war can not be either justly or efficiently carried on unless people who do not fight but have plenty of money are made to realize their responsibility."[140]

The income limits advanced by Pinchot's committee and Congressman Keating would not get enacted into law, but they did help create a climate of opinion that encouraged Congress to escalate, significantly, the top tax rates on America's richest taxpayers. The War Revenue Act of 1917, signed into law in October, would up the top tax rate on incomes over $2 million to 67 percent.[141] That same year, Congress would also raise the top estate tax rate up to 25 percent.[142] A year later, the 1918 Revenue Act would raise the maximum tax rate on top incomes still higher, to 77 percent.[143]

This 77 percent rate would apply to incomes over $1 million, and just sixty-seven taxpayers filed returns that placed them in that top bracket.[144] But these sixty-seven and their less but still staggeringly wealthy friends would make an enormous contribution to war finances. Between 1917 and 1919, less than 1 percent of the tax returns Americans filed reported incomes over $20,000. Yet this elite group would supply 70 percent of the nation's total income tax revenue.[145]

To most Americans, that share seemed about right. Young men were sacrificing their lives. The wealthy could afford to sacrifice some fortune.

THE END OF WORLD WAR I, in November 1918, would also end America's first great offensive against plutocracy. By 1920, in fact, apprehensions about "plutocracy" had almost totally vanished from mainstream political discourse. A new vocabulary now dominated American politics. Americans no longer worried about the wealthy. They feared "Bolsheviks." That fear, stoked into hysteria, would smother the egalitarian reform spirit — and usher in the most rich people-friendly years America had ever seen.

The hysteria that did the egalitarian spirit in had actually begun during the war. The struggle against the Kaiser's armies, President Wilson had proclaimed, would "make the world safe for democracy." The war, instead, would imperil democracy within the United States. Throughout the war years, lawmakers and judges would systematically trample basic civil liberties. Dissent would be treated as disloyalty. Agitators would be silenced, even lynched. By war's end, federal and state officials, egged on by national "loyalty" groups, had blanketed America's political landscape with a thick, stagnant smog of suspicion. In this foul atmosphere, social reformers could not see, or even breathe.

Trade union activists would try to persevere anyway. They had little choice. Workers were hurting. Millions had lost their jobs when the war ended. Those with jobs faced an inflation that had slashed purchasing power by over half since 1913.[146] Workers, in response, hit the bricks. The year 1919 saw one of the greatest strike waves in American history. Over 4 million workers walked off their jobs.[147]

Many never walked back. America's industrialists, notes historian Robert Murray, were "spoiling for a fight."[148] They had been on the defensive for years, scorned by muckraking journalists, reformers, and even Presidents of the United States. Now they would go on the attack. Striking trade unionists, they charged, were fomenting Russian-style Bolshevik revolution. America's wartime superpatriots, organized in groups like the new American Legion, would quickly pick up the theme, and the "Red Scare," as 1919 advanced, would start to feed heatedly upon itself. Teachers lost their jobs for not evincing appropriate levels of patriotic fervor.[149] The Methodist Church Federation for Social Services and other reform-minded religious agencies were denounced as "leaning toward Bolshevism."[150] In the South and Midwest, the Klan re-emerged as a major presence.[151] Race riots destroyed entire African American communities. In this atmosphere, wrote a visiting English journalist, no one could venture "the most innocent departure from conventional thought" without risking the "horrid" radical label.[152]

The "Red Scare" hysteria would eventually, by mid 1920, subside. But the forces of reaction, historian Robert Murray points out, could be pleased with the "normalcy" the hysteria had left in its wake. Labor had been "badly mauled," capital had been bolstered, and "complete antipathy toward reform" had been "enthroned" throughout the land.[153]

Amid this "antipathy toward reform," few mainstream lawmakers would dare defend the plutocrat-soaking taxes enacted during World War I. In Washington, a new Congress and a new President, elected in 1920, now began undoing the war-time taxes. They would be prodded on by the new treasury secretary, Andrew W. Mellon, a gentleman who just happened to be at least the third-richest man in the nation.[154] Mellon would serve as treasury secretary throughout the 1920s and guide one tax cut after another into law. The first, in 1921, reduced the maximum income surtax down to 40 percent.[155] That move saved Mellon's own family an estimated $1 million in taxes.[156] By the end of 1926, the top total rate on high incomes had dropped from 77 to 25 percent.[157] And many millionaires would pay taxes at rates well below that 25 percent.[158] Under Mellon's watch, special interest "loopholes" would for the first time start shredding the tax code. The oil and gas industries would be among the earliest beneficiaries.[159]

"Never had there been a better time to get rich," economist John Kenneth Galbraith would write thirty years later, "and people knew it."[160]

BY THE MID 1920S, NOTES HISTORIAN BEN SELIGMAN, "peace and prosperity everlasting" seemed to have "descended on America."[161] New whiz-bang technologies were changing how Americans lived their daily lives. They listened to radios and records. They ate frozen food. They took Sunday drives in Model T's. Life, for millions of Americans, seemed amazingly good. And the credit for the good times, America's political leaders claimed, belonged to business — and a government smart enough to leave business alone.

No other country in the world, President Calvin Coolidge told his fellow citizens, "ever approached ours in the equal and general distribution of prosperity." And the reason? Unlike other countries, Coolidge argued, the United States had stopped worrying about inequality. The nation had taken a much wiser course. We had stopped "penalizing" business leaders, Coolidge noted. We understood "that if production be encouraged and increased, then distribution fairly well takes care of itself."[162]

Production did increase in the 1920s, as all sorts of technological advances diffused through the economy. Between 1919 and 1929, the horsepower behind wage earners in manufacturing shot up 50 percent.[163] The output per hour of wage labor in manufacturing jumped, consequently, 72 percent.[164] But the fruits of that incredibly productive labor would not be shared. Workers would spend the "Roaring Twenties" struggling, not flapping, as 1929 Brookings Institution research would make clear. Over a fifth of American families, researchers revealed, were having to make do on less than $1,000 a year,

42 percent on less than $1,500.[165] And what could families afford on such incomes? Not much. One 1925 study had set $1,000 as the minimum subsistence level for a family of five. At that level, a family could meet daily physical needs but have "nothing left over for emergencies or pleasures." To meet "the American standard," that is, to partake in the good life of motorcars and radios, required at least $2,000.[166] For most Americans, the 1920s good life, even at minimal levels, remained a good bit beyond their grasp.

The twenties did roar, in other words, but mostly only at the top. Once again, as after the Civil War, the dismantling of a war-time tax structure had set the stage for a vast new concentration of wealth in the hands of America's most fortunate. In 1919, just sixty-five Americans registered at least $1 million in income. In 1929, over five hundred Americans would be making $1 million a year.[167] That same year, the nation's richest 2 percent would hold 60 percent of America's $362 billion in personal wealth.[168] The richest one-half of 1 percent would hold about a third of that $362 billion.[169] At the time, four of every five Americans could claim no savings at all.[170]

In the 1920s, as in the 1980s and 1990s, the vast sums amassing at the lofty upper reaches of American society would fuel an explosion of luxury spending. One well-heeled Philadelphia banking family, the Stotesburys, equipped its bathrooms with gold fixtures. "You don't have to polish them you know," a family spokesperson pointed out.[171]

Americans of modest means would do their best to keep up with this upsurge in luxury spending, mainly by going into debt or diverting money for necessities into the radios, automobiles, and other consumer goods that now defined the decent standard of life that every American ought to be living.[172] The economy, meanwhile, tottered precariously. The decade's tax cuts, by concentrating more of the nation's wealth in wealthy people's pockets, had helped spark a speculative boom in the stock market. Average Americans, meanwhile, were no longer earning enough to absorb the products rolling off the nation's assembly lines. This unequal, unstable state of affairs could not be sustained. In October 1929, Wall Street's bubble popped. The economy deflated. The United States, after a decade of the starkest inequality in American history, now slid into depression, the longest, deepest economic downturn Americans had ever experienced.

NEAR THE HEIGHT OF THE 1920S BOOM, one of America's most illustrious financiers, John J. Raskob, had penned an article for the *Ladies' Home Journal*. "Everybody Ought To Be Rich," the article's headline proclaimed.[173] By 1932, few Americans were daydreaming about becoming rich. The Great Depression had taken hold. The rich, more and more Americans believed, ought to be held responsible, not in awe.

The men who sought to be elected President that year, in 1932, openly acknowledged the new mood. Franklin Roosevelt, accepting the Democratic nomination, announced that Americans "look to us for guidance and for a more equitable opportunity to share in the distribution of the national wealth."[174] President Herbert Hoover, seeking re-election, told a rally at New York's Madison Square Garden that he longed for an America "where wealth is not concentrated in the hands of a few, but diffused among the lives of all."[175]

The 1932 Revenue Act represented a step in that more equitable direction. The measure upped the top tax rate on millionaire incomes to 63 percent.[176] That rate seemed high enough to most elected leaders. But one wanted to go further, much further. In the early Depression years, this particular politician, Huey P. Long, the governor of Louisiana, would stand up and speak out — and, in the process, electrify millions of Americans. Huey Long, a contemporary noted, "dared put his fingers into the real ulcer of social evil in American life," the nation's inequitable distribution of wealth.[177] He denounced that evil in a political language Depression America could readily understand.

"Unless you redistribute the wealth of a country into the hands of the people every fifty years, your country's got to go to ruination," Long warned. "Too many men running things that think they're smarter than the Lord."[178]

Long would enter the United States Senate in 1932 and immediately begin urging action to limit concentrated wealth. The tax laws, he proposed, ought to "be so revamped that no one man should be allowed to have an income of more than one million dollars a year" and "no one person should inherit in a lifetime more than five million dollars."[179]

Long's initial Senate proposals would collect only a handful of votes. One of that handful would come from Arkansas Senator Hattie Caraway, a political novice appointed, in 1931, to fill the term of her late husband. Hattie Caraway would have to run on her own in the 1932 elections, and no one gave her much of a chance. No woman, after all, had ever been elected to the United States Senate, and Caraway faced six other candidates. Huey Long endorsed her anyway, and, in the closing weeks of Hattie Caraway's campaign, he brought his tax-the-rich and share-the-wealth message into Arkansas.

"Think of it, my friends!" Long told one cheering Caraway rally. "In 1930 there were 540 men in Wall Street who made $100,000,000 more than all the wheat farmers and all the cotton farmers and all the cane farmers of this country put together." No wonder, the homespun Long thundered, "your belly's flat up against your backbone!"[180]

On Election Day, Hattie Caraway would pull off a political miracle. Her upset triumph put political Washington on notice. Huey P. Long had become a national phenomenon. After Caraway's victory, he would reintroduce his Senate share-the-wealth resolution. This time around, his proposal to cap wealth and income would receive twenty votes.[181]

The "Long Plan" for American economic renewal would go through several variations. But the plan's basic thrust remained constant. America, Long proclaimed, needed a ceiling on the income and wealth of the very rich to create a floor of decency for everyone else. One iteration of Long's plan proposed a 1 percent tax on all individual wealth between $1 million and $2 million, with the rate rising to 100 percent on all fortunes over $100 million. This same version featured a $1 million cap on annual income.[182]

Long, early after the 1932 elections, felt sure that America's newly elected President, Franklin Roosevelt, shared his tax-the-rich commitment. But the early New Deal made no significant moves toward wealth redistribution, and Long would quickly sour on FDR. In 1934, he would launch his own national opposition, the "Share-Our-Wealth" movement.

"In order to cure all of our woes," Long told the nation in a February 1934 radio address, "it is necessary to scale down the big fortunes, that we may scatter the wealth to be shared by all the people."[183]

Share-Our-Wealth took off as no grassroots movement in America ever had. By mid 1935, Share-Our-Wealth clubs claimed 7 million members. Even allowing for "considerable exaggeration," noted one critical journalist, this total "represented the largest active political organization ever put together in this country."[184] Secret polling by FDR's political strategists would confirm Long's growing influence. A Long candidacy in 1936, the polling found, might pull millions of votes away from Roosevelt.[185]

Long would make no secret of his Presidential ambitions. In mid 1935, he busied himself writing a novel later published as *My First Days in the White House*. Those first days, he pledged, would be momentous. After his inauguration, Long wrote, Congress would declare it "against the public policy of the United States for any one person to possess wealth in excess of one hundred times the average family fortune."[186]

Meanwhile, on Capitol Hill, Long's attacks on concentrated capital found growing company. Inequality, many lawmakers now believed, had ushered in the Depression. Only serious efforts to diminish that inequality would end it. The foundation of the nation "has collapsed," charged New York Congressman Fiorello LaGuardia, "and there will be nothing left unless we provide an economic readjustment, a better distribution, and that we can do by breaking up those fortunes."[187] Taxes on the fortunate, progressives urged, needed to rise substantially to subsidize relief programs for America's impoverished majority. Senator Robert La Follette Jr. of Wisconsin promised "to fight for increased inheritance and income taxes — the likes of which we have never heard of — so that those with huge incomes will have to cough up to help pay" for relief.[188]

By 1935, the heyday of Huey Long's Share-Our-Wealth movement, tax-the-rich sentiment seemed everywhere. "It did not require much deep thinking for the average person to deduct that there must be something drastically wrong when people are starving in the midst of plenty," noted Minnesota Governor Floyd B. Olson.[189] "If these fortunes are not broken up by law," a distraught Senator George Norris of Nebraska confided in a private letter, "the time will come when they will be broken up by the mob."[190]

By late spring 1935, FDR had come to share that sense of alarm. The previous January, the President had seen no need to introduce any new tax-the-rich legislation. By May, he had become convinced that he needed to take steps to steal Huey Long's thunder. Taxes on the wealthy, Roosevelt concluded, would have to be increased.

That spring, historian Arthur Schlesinger, Jr. relates, Roosevelt sat down with an emissary from William Randolph Hearst, the aging newspaper publishing magnate, to explain what he was about to propose to Congress. To combat Huey Longism, "to save our system, the capitalistic system," FDR told Hearst's agent, "I want to equalize the distribution of wealth."[191]

"The thinking men, the young men, who are disciples of this new world idea of fairer distribution of wealth," FDR added, "they are demanding that something be done to equalize this distribution."[192]

In June 1935, Roosevelt would move to realize that "fairer distribution." He would launch what historians have dubbed the "Second Hundred Days," the months that defined and enacted into law what we now think of as the New Deal.[193] For workers, FDR backed legislation to guarantee the right to join and build effective unions. For the elderly and those unable to work, the President called for a new system of "Social Security." And in the name of America's most basic democratic ideals, Roosevelt demanded the passage of stiff new taxes on the nation's greatest fortunes and incomes.

"The transmission from generation to generation of great fortunes by will, inheritance or gift is not consistent with the ideals and sentiments of the American people," the President explained. "Great accumulations of wealth cannot be justified on the basis of personal or family security. Such inherited economic power is as inconsistent with the ideals of this generation as inherited political power was inconsistent with the ideals of the generation which established our country."[194]

Wealthy Americans gagged. A furious William Randolph Hearst ordered his editors to start calling the New Deal the "Raw Deal." Roosevelt's tax proposals, Hearst papers began charging, would only "soak the successful." But lawmakers would pay Hearst and his fellow deep pockets little mind. These lawmakers, like Roosevelt, were far more concerned about Huey Long and the millions mobilizing behind him. Congress, in 1935, would end up hiking the highest estate tax rate to 70 percent, on bequested fortunes over $50 million.[195] On incomes, lawmakers upped the top marginal tax rate to 79 percent.

This new tax legislation, while a step forward, left most progressives in Congress distinctly underwhelmed. The new top tax rates, they noted, only applied to handfuls of wealthy taxpayers.[196] "As finally passed," many progressives believed, "the Wealth Tax Act of 1935 did little either to redistribute wealth or to raise revenue."[197]

The nation's strongest champion of a more equal America, in the meantime, would be unable to mobilize the public behind tougher tax measures. On September 8, 1935, Huey Long would be assassinated in Baton Rouge, one day after he boasted that only by enacting his Share-Our-Wealth program could they "keep me from being President — unless I die."[198] After Long's assassination, no politically potent attempt to up taxes on the wealthy would surface for the rest of the 1930s. It would take a new war, as the decade ended, to force the nation to confront the appalling inequality of wealth and income that Depression-era politics had failed to adequately address.

FRANKLIN ROOSEVELT, BEFORE WORLD WAR II, had never been particularly chummy with America's corporate leaders. FDR had never been able "to sympathize with the ambitions and drive of much of the American business fraternity," Secretary of Labor Frances Perkins would later note, mainly because he "couldn't see why a man making enough money should want to go scheming and plotting, sacrificing and living under nervous tension, just to make more money."[199]

In 1940, with Europe at war, the already cool relations between Roosevelt and America's business fraternity would become even cooler. The United States, FDR believed, needed to prepare for conflict. And that meant more than making armaments. That meant making sure that average Americans felt good about their country. To emerge victorious, Roosevelt felt fervently, America would have to do battle against both Nazism abroad and inequality at home.

"Not a single war millionaire," the President flatly pledged in 1940, "will be created in this country as a result of the war disaster."[200]

Corporate interests would have other ideas. They mobilized, in late spring 1940, to stop Roosevelt's proposal for a stiff excess profits tax on corporate earnings. That summer, business leaders would actually refuse to enter into defense contracts until Congress gave them a more business-friendly tax bill.[201] They would get their way. But the attack on Pearl Harbor, over a year later, would give Roosevelt the upper hand.

In April 1942, about twenty weeks into the war, the President would send Congress the most radical tax initiative in American history. Roosevelt proposed a "supertax" on affluent incomes. Under this proposal for a "100 percent" tax, single persons with before-tax incomes of $40,000 would be left with $25,000 after standard tax rates had been applied. Any income above $40,000 would be subject to FDR's new 100 percent tax. For married couples, the 100 percent supertax would kick in on all income over $110,000.[202]

On April 28, 1942, the day after FDR sent his tax plan, just one part of a broader economic plan, to Congress, the *New York Times* would make the President's $25,000 income limit the day's lead story. The idea for the limit, the *Times* reported, had come from the United Automobile Workers union.[203] Actually, the idea may have come from any number of sources. Roosevelt himself had probably not forgotten the campaign for an income cap during World War I. In the 1930s, various economists had resurrected the case for caps.[204] Roosevelt's own economic advisers, in the winter of 1942, had huddled for weeks and come back with an economic plan that included a $50,000 income limit.[205] Capping income had become an idea with broad appeal.

That appeal, to be sure, had its limits. On Wall Street, share prices would dip sharply after the President revealed his income-capping proposal.[206] But even some business leaders would rally to the President's proposal. "I think this will help to prevent the inflationary spiral," the president of the American Cotton Manufacturers Association, W. N. Banks, told the Associated Press.[207]

Business leaders less enthused by the President's call for an income cap generally clipped their comments. They didn't dare come out swinging against a proposal that enjoyed considerable public support.

"My first reaction to a $25,000 limit is that it would cause dislocations that would be most unfortunate," Albert Hawkes, the president of the U.S. Chamber of Commerce, told reporters. "But I would prefer to analyze the situation carefully before I could make a well considered and definite statement."[208]

The opposition to FDR's cap would go about its business behind the scenes. The key congressional panel with jurisdiction over the President's plan, the House Ways and Means Committee, would quietly refuse to give the supertax any serious consideration.

Roosevelt would not be deterred. Shortly after Labor Day, FDR repeated his call for a $25,000 maximum income, "the only practical way of preventing the incomes and profits of individuals and corporations from getting too high."[209] Congress would once again ignore the President's 100 percent super-tax, but the Revenue Act of 1942 that Congress did pass would raise the rates on America's highest incomes to all-time record levels. The top surtax, which had been raised to 77 percent in 1941, jumped to 82 percent. High incomes were also subject to a 6 percent normal tax and a new 5 percent "Victory Tax." The combination meant, on all income over $200,000, a 93 percent tax rate.[210]

The new Victory Tax provision would also apply the income tax, for the first time ever, to average Americans.[211] All workers earning over $12 a week would now have income tax withheld from their paychecks.[212] Only 7.1 percent of Americans had been paying federal income taxes at the war's start. By war's end, nearly two-thirds of Americans, 64.1 percent, would be paying taxes on their incomes.[213]

But the new taxes on both wealthy and average Americans would come nowhere close to meeting the war's insatiable appetite for revenue. In fiscal 1943, the government still had to borrow $60 billion.[214] Congress would respond, in 1944, by upping the tax rate on the wealthy still again. The new rate schedule would place a 94 percent top rate on all income over $200,000, a rate that significantly exceeded the very highest rates in effect during World War I (77 percent on incomes over $1 million) and the Depression (81 percent on incomes over $5 million).[215] The years 1944 and 1945, concludes historian John Witte, would be "the most progressive tax years in U.S. history."[216]

These same years would bring millions of American families a sense of real prosperity. Between 1939 and 1945, wages in manufacturing soared nearly three times faster than the cost of living.[217] "At war's end, Americans were rolling in cash," notes political analyst Kevin Phillips. "Many families had their first discretionary income."[218]

The war had equalized incomes. Americans liked the result.

WHAT DO AMERICA'S CONSERVATIVES WANT? All we want, conservative religious activist Pat Robertson once noted, is "a return to the kind of government America had during the Eisenhower Administration in the 1950s."[219]

In reality, any sudden return to the Eisenhower era would leave Robertson, and every other contemporary conservative who has ever demanded lower taxes on wealthy incomes, absolutely appalled. Wealthy Americans spent the 1950s paying taxes at top rates that exceeded 90 percent. And Dwight D. Eisenhower, over the eight years of his Presidency, made not one political move to cut those rates. Ike knew better. He knew history. The history of the years right after World War II.

In 1946, with the war over, Republicans in Congress figured the time had come to roll back Roosevelt's war-time taxes. They didn't anticipate much problem, particularly after they won control over Congress in the November elections. GOP leaders interpreted that victory as a mandate to cut taxes. In rapid-fire order, they enacted one across-the-board tax cut after another. President Harry Truman, more interested in retiring the remaining war debt than tax relief for millionaires, would veto them all. In 1948, Republicans would enact still another tax cut. Truman would turn thumbs down once again, but this time Republicans had the votes to override his veto. The new Revenue Act they enacted over Truman's veto dropped the nation's top marginal tax rate, 94 percent at its war-time high, down to 82 percent.[220]

Truman would make the Republicans pay for their victory. In the 1948 Presidential election, he would make their tax cut a centerpiece of his campaign. The GOP, Truman would charge, "helps the rich and sticks a knife in the back of the poor."[221] In November, Truman would score a stunning victory, and not just for himself. Republicans would lose both the House and Senate, notes Kevin Phillips, "in a landslide repudiation influenced by Democratic charges of GOP favoritism to the rich." That whopping defeat, adds Phillips, would convince "the GOP to leave the nominal top rate alone through all eight years of the Eisenhower administration."[222]

Dwight Eisenhower would take office in 1953. By that time, Congress had already hiked the top marginal rate on high incomes back up over 90 percent. The rate would stick at 91 percent, on income over $200,000, throughout the 1950s. Stiff taxes on high incomes had become, for mainstream Democrats and Republicans alike, accepted public policy.[223]

Those who challenged this tax-the-wealthy consensus would come across as cranks. Their claim, that "confiscatory taxes" on high incomes undermined initiative and investment, rang hollow. America in the 1950s seemed to be working just fine. Throughout this tax-the-rich decade, Americans could see, almost everywhere they looked, nothing but good times.[224] Higher profits, higher wages. A more secure safety net.

America, in so many ways, appeared to be thriving as never before. America was becoming more equal, and equality was making America a better place, just as America's revolutionary founders had figured.

"American labor," the nation's most visible union leader, George Meany, would pronounce in 1955, "has never had it so good."[225]

And for once the good seemed to be extending, at least somewhat, to African Americans. Before World War II, black males took home 41 percent of white male wages and salaries. By 1960, black paychecks averaged 67 percent of white.[226] America, an emerging civil rights movement proclaimed, must do better. America, a growing number of Americans believed, could do better. Growing economic equality was working wonders on America's psyche.

AVERAGE AMERICANS, BY THE 1950s, had been struggling to reconcile Jeffersonian ideals with the realities of modern industrial life ever since the initial rise of corporate power after the Civil War. They would realize, early on in this struggle, that only concerted government action could prevent a new aristocracy of wealth from overwhelming American life. They would, in the 1890s, mobilize for that government action. They would be crushed, in 1896, by the sheer weight of wealth's reaction.

In the early twentieth century, a new offensive for a more equal America would arise and achieve, by the end of World War I, America's first significant limits on concentrated wealth. These limits would not stick. A burst of hysteria, after the war, would restore men of wealth to unquestioned economic and political power. The Depression would shake that power, and a new war would then subject great fortunes, and those who held them, to the stiffest limits on wealth America had ever seen. In the 1950s, with these limits still in place, a new, more equal America would finally flower. The American dream, for millions of average Americans, had finally come true.

But America's wealthy, in the middle class golden age that emerged in the 1950s, would never resign themselves to limits on their own personal fortunes. A frontal assault on high tax rates, the wealthy understood, would be politically impractical. So they worked the backdoor instead. They nibbled away at the egalitarian tax structure that the 1940s had bequeathed America. Throughout the Eisenhower years, notes Kevin Phillips, "the perfection and enactment of tax loopholes, credits, and exemptions became one of Washington's principal cottage industries."[227]

These new tax-avoiding subterfuges should have set alarm bells ringing. Tax avoidance maneuvers, if left free to multiply, could clearly undermine America's egalitarian tax structure. But few voices in American public life would jump up and make that point. America's traditional watchdogs, the nation's academics, journalists, and elected officials, would remain largely silent about the tax avoidance games America's most affluent were playing. These watchdogs had been scared silent, by a new hysteria, by "McCarthyism." This second Red Scare had begun in the late 1940s and would not taper off appreciably until the mid 1950s. By that time, the nation's most determined social critics — radical professors, progressive religious leaders, left labor activists — had either lost their voices or their audiences.

More moderate advocates of a more equal America, meanwhile, had ample reason not to make waves. This new Red Scare, unlike the first after World War I, did not turn into an all-out assault against the right of trade unions to exist. Nor did men of wealth and their minions, under cover of the scare, go directly after egalitarian tax rates. Both unions and progressive tax rates, the two most basic building blocks of mid-century American equality, had become too deeply entrenched to openly challenge in a frontal assault.

The international political dynamics of the Cold War only reinforced this reluctance. In the ongoing ideological competition with the Soviet bloc, America's most thoughtful political leaders understood, unions and progressive tax rates helped the United States win hearts and minds. Who could believe Soviet claims about the evils of capitalism when American workers, flush with the good wages made possible by good union contracts, were buying homes in the suburbs? Who could give much credence to Soviet rhetoric about "ruling classes" when high taxes on high incomes were relegating Rockefeller-sized fortunes to history's dust-bin?

Capitalism may have once meant child labor and plutocratic fortunes, commentators now enthused, but the United States had gone beyond all that. Robber Barons had become ancient history. America's class struggles had ended. America, liberal academics and policy makers agreed, now needed simply to concentrate on "growing" the economy. "Growth" would bring into America's prosperous, all-encompassing middle class anyone unfortunate enough to have been historically left out.

For mainstream politicians, particularly mainstream liberals, this emphasis on "growing" the economy had enormous appeal. Growth offered these liberals, notes historian Robert Collins, an easy way out of their Cold War box. By chanting the "growth" mantra, they could talk about progress without having to talk about inequality — and risk getting labeled a parlor pink or worse. By granting "growth" star billing, they could ride out the Cold War unpleasantness, "avoiding hard questions and evading tough decisions about the distribution of wealth and power in America."[228]

America's first new President of the 1960s, John F. Kennedy, would embrace "growth" with the same passion he brought to his secret private life. His administration would dare what the Eisenhower administration dared not. The Kennedy administration would seek to slash high tax rates on high incomes. These high taxes, Kennedy proclaimed, inhibited growth. An economy "hampered by restrictive tax rates," he told the prestigious Economic Club of New York in 1962, "will never produce enough revenue to balance our budget, just as it will never produce enough jobs or enough profits."[229]

Kennedy, in January 1963, would send Congress a proposal to cut America's income taxes across the board. The top rate on high incomes, 91 percent on income over $200,000, would drop to 65 percent under the Kennedy plan.[230] In February, Kennedy's secretary of commerce, Luther Hodges, would detail the administration's case. He heaped upon the House Ways and Means Committee heavy helpings of statistics to buttress his argument that the administration's proposed tax cuts for average taxpayers would increase consumer demand and employment. He would, interestingly, present no comparable statistics to buttress the administration's case for high-income tax cuts. Congress would just have to take the claimed benefits from these cuts on faith.[231]

Most lawmakers, in Kennedy's Cold War America, shared that faith. Levying heavy taxes on rich people, they had convinced themselves, no longer made sense. Only commies still wanted to "soak the rich."

Congress would eventually approve most of what Kennedy wanted. The nation's top tax rate on income would drop from 91 to 70 percent.[232] President Kennedy's successor, Lyndon B. Johnson, would sign the new rates into law early in 1964.

Over the next four years, Johnson would evince no further interest in cutting tax rates. LBJ, unlike Kennedy, had cut his political eyeteeth in New Deal Washington. He had grander dreams in mind than tax cuts. He saw a "Great Society," a "war on poverty." But these echoes of the New Deal, veteran Capitol Hill observers soon realized, were now reverberating in a fundamentally different political context. The nation's political elites, reformers included, no longer thought or talked like New Dealers.

"A generation ago," America's premiere political columnist, Walter Lippman, noted in 1964, "it would have been taken for granted that a war on poverty meant taxing money away from the haves." But America's current elected leaders had rejected that idea. They believed, Lippman observed, that social and economic progress no longer required high taxes on wealthy people, that the "size of the pie can be increased by invention, organization, capital investment, and fiscal policy."[233]

The 1960s would remain, nonetheless, a time of growing equality in the United States. The momentum from the 1940s and the 1950s would continue throughout the decade. Wealthy Americans still faced substantial high tax rates, even after the Kennedy tax cut. Collectively bargained union contracts still defined wage rates in much of the private sector. But the stage had been set for a grand reversal. By the 1970s, champions of equality no longer graced America's political scene. Apprehensions about plutocracy had vanished, as they had in the 1920s. America's top political leaders wanted growth. America's men of wealth assured these politicos they could deliver that growth — if the politicians did their best to help the process along. They would.

AMERICA'S LONG MARCH TOWARD GREATER ECONOMIC EQUALITY, the defining phenomenon of the nation's mid-century years, ended sometime between the late 1960s and the early 1970s. No elected leaders, in these transition years, ever asked Americans if they wanted their country to become more unequal. Elected leaders simply began pursuing policies that made greater inequality inevitable. Tax policies. Budget policies. Labor policies. Banking policies. Antitrust policies. Trade policies. Decision by decision, a new American economy started to evolve in the 1970s, an economy that privileged rich people and the grand enterprises that generated their fortunes. All in the name of growth. If the nation provided the privileged enough incentives to innovate and invest, the architects of the new inequality assured the nation, the economy would grow. All would be well.

But the economy didn't grow. The vibrant, job-generating, wage-enhancing economy of the 1950s and 1960s would fade away in the 1970s. Inflation, recession, and stagflation would define America at the start of the twentieth century's last quarter — and the "cures" advanced for these ailments just seemed to make everything worse, at least for average Americans. Inflation too high? Interest rates would have to be raised.[234] Wouldn't higher interest rates generate higher joblessness? That couldn't be helped. Investors couldn't be expected to invest if they were worried about inflation. Investors still not investing, even after interest rates had been raised? More tax breaks for investors would have to legislated. Wouldn't these tax breaks translate into fewer dollars for public services? Couldn't be helped. The nation couldn't afford to let investors get discouraged.

The discouraged, by the mid 1970s, would be average Americans. Some political leaders would notice. One of them, an obscure Southern governor named Jimmy Carter, promised a fresh start. In his 1976 campaign for the Presidency, Carter would blast away at America's loophole-ridden tax system. A "disgrace to the human race," he called it. A Carter administration, he vowed, would make taxes more progressive. The powerful would no longer sip their way through tax-deductible two-martini lunches.[235] In less than a year's time, Carter would move from obscurity into the White House.

But President Carter, once in office, could not deliver on his promises. Congress would continue to pander to the privileged. A new tax act, enacted in 1978, actually left the "disgrace to the human race" more disgraceful. This legislation would hand business and the affluent a host of new "incentives," including a hefty reduction in taxes on capital gains.[236] For average Americans, Congress had virtually nothing to offer.

Average Americans needed — and deserved — much more than that. Inflation had shoved millions of working families into higher tax brackets. These families were now paying taxes at higher rates at the same time they were earning, in real purchasing power, the same as before, or even less. That didn't seem fair.

This time, Republicans, not Democrats, would speak more convincingly to the frustrations average Americans felt. They would promise to fix the tax system, once and for all, by cutting everybody's taxes. What could be fairer?

In 1977, New York Congressman Jack Kemp and Delaware Senator William Roth would drop the first bombshell. They proposed an enormous, unprecedented 30 percent, across-the-board cut in personal income tax rates. Under their proposal, the top tax rate on America's highest incomes would fall, over three years, down to 50 percent.[237] Veteran political observers gasped. Tax rates on rich people hadn't been that low since the start of the Great Depression. Kemp and Roth, most observers agreed, couldn't possibly expect Democrats, even the most fervid fans of "growth" incentives, to go along.

Four years later, Democrats would go along. In 1981, America's newly elected President, Ronald Reagan, would win substantial Democratic support for a tax cut that took as its inspiration the 1977 Kemp-Roth initiative.

America's classical political discourse on wealth and inequality had, in effect, been turned upside down. Back in the early nineteenth century, notes historian Sean Wilentz, Americans had feared that their government might "unjustly transfer wealth from the middling classes to the wealthy."[238] The Ronald Reagan right, in the late twentieth century, convinced Americans that they needed to fear the exact opposite. The government, the right charged, was unjustly shifting wealth from the middle to the poor. America's good-for-nothings, with government help, were stealing the fruits average Americans had labored so hard to earn. That government help had to be ended and could be ended — by cutting taxes. If taxes were slashed, working Americans would be free from government programs that rewarded the shiftless, free to reap the rewards working Americans so richly deserved, free even to become rich.

With Ronald Reagan in the White House, a new vision now dominated American politics, a vision that unapologetically welcomed grand fortune.

"More than anything else," the newly elected Ronald Reagan announced, "I want to see the United States remain a country where someone can get rich."[239]

That would mean, above all else, ending high tax rates on high incomes, the heart and soul of America's progressive income tax. Reagan had despised progressive taxation ever since his years as a Hollywood star.[240] The progressive income tax, Reagan would charge earnestly and erroneously in the early 1960s, had descended on America "directly from Karl Marx who designed it as the prime essential of a socialist state."[241]

As President, Reagan would waste no time trying to undo what Karl had wrought. But average Americans, the administration understood, would never accept a tax cut that only benefited rich people. To slash tax rates on high incomes, consequently, the administration would have cut rates on all incomes, even if these cuts sent the government into record debt. That didn't matter. Only rates at the top mattered. The tax cutting on average incomes in the Reagan plan, administration budget director David Stockman would later confide, "was always a Trojan horse to bring down the top rate."[242]

Under the Reagan tax plan, the Economic Recovery Tax Act of 1981, the top rate on individual high incomes would sink from 70 to 50 percent.[243] Corporations, meanwhile, would receive a grab-bag of additional tax reduction goodies, ranging from higher tax credits for investments to new depreciation schedules that enabled companies to write off, much more quickly than ever before, their biggest purchases. The legislation even included a provision for "safe-harbor leasing," a neat trick that let corporations with tax deductions they couldn't use transfer these deductions to other corporations that could.[244]

"The hogs were really feeding," budget director Stockman would afterwards acknowledge. "The greed level, the level of opportunism just got out of control."[245]

For working Americans, the savings from the 1981 cut would soon be offset by hikes in the FICA payroll tax. The Social Security Amendments of 1983 would leave Americans paying more for Social Security protection — and receiving less.[246]

All these tax changes, taken together, would help engineer, within a decade, the single largest redistribution of wealth in American history. In 1983, the year the Reagan cuts took full effect, the 500,000 families that made up America's richest 0.5 percent held a combined $2.5 trillion in wealth. By 1989, these same families held over twice as much. The families in this elite echelon "could have paid off the entire national debt" and still have owned, noted Rep. David Obey, 10 percent more in 1989 "than they did in 1983."[247]

These wealthy families, of course, did not pay off the national debt. That debt would continue to mount and limit, for the rest of the century, the permissible in American politics. In a debt-ridden United States, few lawmakers would even consider bold new initiatives that might help average American families improve their life chances.

By the mid 1980s, no serious lawmaker could deny that the 1981 tax cut had created enormous fiscal chaos. But the Democrats, who still controlled the House of Representatives, were in no mood to raise taxes, on the wealthy or anybody else. Their 1984 Presidential candidate, Walter Mondale, had hinted he might, if elected, have to raise taxes — and had been crushed for his candor. Mondale's defeat would shove any proposals to tax the rich, or anybody else, totally off the table. Leading Democrats would now talk only about tax "simplification." In 1986, they would join with Republicans to advance a "simplification" agenda. Their joint venture, the Tax Reform Act of 1986, would reduce the number of basic tax brackets down to two. The top tax rate on high incomes, 70 percent as recently as 1980, would now fall to 28 percent.[248]

The 1986 act, to be sure, did boast some redeeming features. The act, for instance, ended the favorable tax treatment of capital gains income. Proceeds from the sale of property and stock would now be taxed at the same rates as ordinary income. Lawmakers celebrated this change as a grand step toward common sense tax reform. Reformers who read the fine print did no cheering. "Behind the facade of eliminating 'tax preferences for the rich and powerful,'" Kevin Phillips later pointed out, the 1986 act shoved into the tax code some 650 new provisions that benefited special interests.[249] Most incredibly of all, the legislation imposed the highest tax rate not on the wealthy, but on the upper middle class. Income between $70,000 and $170,000 would be taxed at a special "bubble" rate of 33 percent. Income above $170,000 would face only a 28 percent levy.

Two years later, in 1988, George Bush the elder would inherit the Republican nomination and campaign as the upholder of the Reagan tax cut orthodoxy. "Read my lips," Bush would tell America. "No new taxes." But Bush, as President, would soon have to abandon his macho pledge. By 1990, after a decade of tax cuts for the privileged, red ink had thoroughly soaked the federal government's budget books. Bush had no choice but to bless a bipartisan congressional compromise. Taxes on the affluent would be raised, ever so slightly, to reduce the budget deficit. The 28 percent top tax rate on earned income would nudge up to 31 percent, the first tax rate hike on top incomes in a generation.[250] The Reagan revolution, the new tax hike seemed to signify, had finally run its course.

That revolution, millions of average Americans had believed, had been waged on their behalf, to save them money. The revolution, by that measure, failed miserably. In 1980, American families at the exact middle of the nation's income distribution paid 23.7 percent of their incomes in income, Social Security, and other federal taxes. In 1990, middle-income families paid these taxes at a 24.6 percent rate.[251] The Reagan revolution had left the American middle class paying more, not less in federal taxes. Average Americans had been taken for a ride. The Reagan revolution had been a fraud.

GEORGE H. W. BUSH WOULD PAY POLITICALLY for the fraud of the Reagan years. In the 1992 election, maverick billionaire H. Ross Perot would spend a significant chunk of his significant fortune deriding the fiscal irresponsibility of the Reagan era. The Democratic nominee, Bill Clinton, would campaign on a pledge to reverse course and "put people first." This one-two punch knocked the Republicans flat. Bush would receive just 37 percent of the popular vote, a remarkably abysmal showing for a sitting President.

Clinton's emphasis on "putting people first" had been promoted, within his campaign, by some of the same progressives who had worked diligently throughout the 1980s to raise public consciousness about growing inequality. These progressives wanted to see a massive new program of "public investment" in America's dilapidated infrastructure — and higher taxes on the wealthy to help foot the bill for that investment.

Clinton, as President, would follow through, partially, on some of the policy initiatives these progressives proposed, but not in the spirit of "putting people first." The new President would instead put investors first, investors nervous about the mammoth federal budget deficits run up during the Reagan-Bush years. The annual federal budget deficit had nearly quadrupled between 1981 and 1992, from $79 billion to $290 billion.[252] To restore investor confidence, Wall Street insisted, these deficits would have to be reduced.

New public investment initiatives, outside of a few token efforts, would now be out of the question. In the plan President Clinton presented Congress in 1993, overall federal spending would be cut. Taxes on the affluent, at the same time, would be increased, from 31 to 39.6 percent on income over $250,000. The Clinton administration would package this increase as a budget-balancing move, nothing more, nothing less. The wealthy, under the Clinton plan, would see their income taxes rise, but they would still be paying less in taxes, much less, than they did before Ronald Reagan took office.

Republicans in Congress would erupt in outrage anyway. They mounted an all-out assault on Clinton's Omnibus Budget Reconciliation Act. If the Clinton economic plan were enacted, they charged, the economy would collapse. They almost prevailed. The Clinton plan passed the Senate by one vote.

The tax increases in the Clinton legislation, retroactive to the start of 1993, would only apply to households making more than $100,000, about 4 percent of the nation's total.[253] Even so, the new legislation would quickly begin to hike federal revenues substantially, mainly because, in late twentieth century America, the nation's most affluent households had become so affluent that any increase in the tax rate applied to their incomes could produce a fiscally staggering result. By 1998, the nation's enormous annual budget deficit had become a surplus. Analysts credited this surplus to the revenues generated from higher tax rates on America's highest incomes.[254]

These new revenues would not go into new programs to "put people first." Average Americans, in Clinton's first term, would continue to see their economic fortunes stagnate. In October 1994, new federal data would reveal that median household income had fallen for four straight years.[255]

Numbers like these left some top Clinton administration officials distinctly alarmed. They pleaded for a new commitment to fighting inequality.

"Unless we turn this situation around," Labor Secretary Robert Reich pronounced, "we're going to have a two-tiered society; we can't be a prosperous or stable society with a huge gap between the very rich and everyone else."[256]

But Reich was beating a drum few influentials in the Clinton White House wanted to hear. The administration would take no step to raise, as a national concern, America's widening maldistribution of wealth and income. And that unwillingness, historian James MacGregor Burns and political scientist Georgia Sorenson would charge at century's end, may have been the most avoidable tragedy of the Clinton years.

"Clinton failed to exhibit the moral outrage," noted Burns and Sorenson, "that could have put inequality at the top of the nation's agenda."[257]

And Clinton's disinterest in equality, adds historian Sean Wilentz, would set the 1990s tone for the entire rest of the Democratic Party mainstream.

"From time to time, liberal officials and office-seekers would rail against the monopolistic corporate special interests — Big Oil, the pharmaceutical companies — but with less consistency and conviction than their Progressive and New Deal predecessors," Wilentz observes. "Outside the liberal and left-wing margins, virtually no one seemed willing to make the case that even mild redistribution was essential to the health of our political system."[258]

In the meantime, the political right would regain the offensive. In the 1994 elections, Republicans led by House Minority Leader Newt Gingrich painted the 1993 Clinton tax hike on the wealthy as "the greatest tax increase of all time" and regained control of both the House and Senate for the first time in four decades. The Reagan boys were now back, ready for tax-scrapping bear. The entire federal progressive income tax, agreed the new House majority leader, Dick Armey of Texas, and the new chair of the House Ways and Means Committee, Bill Archer, another Texan, ought to be stomped into the dust.[259]

But first things first. The exuberant Republicans, bursting with ideas on how to end the oppression of America's rich people, needed to come to a consensus on where to start. Some wanted to slash the tax rate on capital gains income, a key proposal advanced by the GOP's 1994 campaign credo, the Contract with America.[260] Others, like Armey, wanted to push for a "flat tax," a single tax rate on all income, a neat little trick that would cut the tax bill of a $500,000-a-year household in half.[261] Lurking in the wings were still other tax-cutters who had their hearts set on going after the hated estate tax, America's only levy on grand fortunes. In 1995, to sort through all these options, Republicans would establish a special tax commission, chaired by Jack Kemp of Kemp-Roth fame.[262] A year later, in 1996, Kemp's National Commission on Economic Growth and Tax Reform would recommend the entire GOP tax-cutting smorgasbord, everything from a flat tax on regular income to the abolition of all taxes on dividends, capital gains, and estates.[263] The Republicans wanted it all. Piece by piece, they would start to get it.

In 1997, Congress would pass and President Clinton would sign a "Taxpayer Relief Act" that extended some Americans quite a bit more "relief" than others. Under the legislation, America's wealthiest 1 percent would receive $1,189 in tax savings for every $1 in tax savings that went to America's bottom 80 percent. The bulk of those savings for the wealthy would come from a Tax Relief Act provision that cut the tax rate on capital gains income from 28 to 20 percent. The households in America's richest 1 percent, at century's end, collected about two-thirds of the nation's capital gains income.[264]

With capital gains taxation now suitably "reformed," Republicans in Congress would now take aim at bigger prey, the estate tax. Few average Americans knew anything about the estate tax, for an understandable reason. The estate tax simply didn't impact middle class people. At century's end, only 2 percent of Americans were leaving behind, at death, estates large enough to incur any estate tax liability.[265]

For friends of fortune, that was 2 percent too many. Early in the 1990s, as Bill Gates Sr. and Chuck Collins would later show in their analysis of estate taxation, *Wealth and Commonwealth*, some of America's wealthiest families joined with conservative ideologues to orchestrate a crusade against what they would call, after appropriate focus group testing, "the death tax."[266] They would portray this "death tax" as an onerous levy that kept struggling farmers and small businesspeople from bequeathing their life's work to their deserving children. In reality, the federal estate tax statute gave farms and small businesses special treatment. Families that inherited farms and small businesses large enough to be subject to the estate tax — a distinct minority of all farms and small businesses — could pay off the tax owed in installment payments, over fourteen years, at below-market interest rates.[267]

The crusaders against the estate tax conveniently ignored these inconvenient details. In fact, when challenged, they could not produce a single case where the estate tax had forced heirs to unload a family farm or small business they wanted to keep.[268] They marched on with their repeal campaign anyway. By summer 2000, they had enough votes to drive repeal legislation through both the Senate and House. President Clinton would veto the repeal bill, and his veto would be narrowly upheld, but the repealers would not be terribly disappointed. They still had, they were convinced, history on their side. One year later, they would have a more tangible asset. A President.

AMERICANS, GEORGE W. BUSH DECLARED on the 2000 Presidential campaign trail, deserve a break. A tax break. "After eight years of Clinton-Gore," he declared early on in his campaign, "we have the highest tax burden since World War II."[269] A Bush administration, he pledged, would lighten that burden. Voters who wanted to see by just how much, Bush aides noted, could click their way to the Internet where the official Bush campaign Web site featured a "Bush Tax Calculator" that families could use to compute the tax savings they would realize if George W. were elected. This calculator, unfortunately, had a flaw: No family making over $100,000 could use it. The calculator couldn't compute tax savings for any high-income household.[270] If you earned $250,000 or $250 million, you would get no help from the official "Bush Tax Calculator."

Of course, if you were making $250,000 or $250 million, you didn't need a calculator to understand just how nicely the election of George W. Bush would enhance your personal bottom line. Bush's pledge to drop the top tax rate on income from 39.6 to 33 percent, coupled with his promise to repeal the estate tax, amounted to a gift that would keep on giving — to wealthy households — forever.[271]

Delivering this gift would become the new Bush administration's first priority. Less than a month after his inauguration, the new President would call for a $1.6 trillion tax cut. His tax cut plan, he announced, would save "the average family" some $1,600. Indeed it would — if the total tax cut were divided by the total number of America's taxpaying families. But the White House had no intention of dividing the benefits from his tax cut equally among all America's taxpayers. Under the Bush plan, analysts quickly noted, a taxpayer earning $31,100 would pocket a tax cut of $501, about 1.6 percent of income. A taxpayer making $915,000 would clear a $50,166 savings, 5.5 percent of income.[272]

The President and his millionaire advisers, charged critics like the Rev. Andrew Greeley, were proposing "to make the rich richer, to continue the steady growth of income inequality in our country — an inequality that is profoundly immoral."[273] Similar denunciations, some from unexpected sources, would multiply over the course of George W. Bush's first winter and spring as

President.[274] But President Bush would continue, despite the growing opposition, to stay "on message." In speech after speech, he would orate over the desperate need to cut income taxes to help hard-working Americans like the $22,000-a-year waitress trying to raise two kids. But $22,000-a-year single parents with two kids, the President never bothered to note, didn't owe any federal income taxes.[275] Struggling low-income waitresses paid federal payroll taxes, for Social Security and Medicare, not federal income taxes. The Bush tax plan offered low-income Americans not one cent of payroll tax relief.

Congress would pass the Bush plan anyway, late in spring 2001.[276] The legislation, as finally enacted, would prove to be the most bizarre, complex, and confusing tax legislation ever enacted. The estate tax would be repealed, but only for 2010, after which the 2001 estate tax rates would come back into effect, unless, of course, the estate tax was totally repealed in the meantime.[277] The already existing child tax credit would rise, then go back to its original level.[278] The alternate minimum tax, a tax code provision originally enacted to make sure everyone paid at least some taxes, would sink between 2001 and 2004, a move that would help upper middle class families. But this relief would end in 2005.[279] Meanwhile, the showcase of the Bush plan, a $600 tax rebate, evaporated into the fine print. Only families making at least $12,000 would get the full rebate. Half the bottom 60 percent of America's income earners would receive no rebate at all.

"The people who are excited about this rebate aren't going to get it," Robert McIntyre, the director of Citizens for Tax Justice, would note after the Bush plan's passage. "And the people who aren't excited about it are going to get it."[280]

McIntyre's group would complete, months later, a fuller analysis of the Bush 2001 tax cut. From 2001 to 2010, the group's study revealed, America's richest 1 percent would pocket "almost half a trillion dollars" from the tax cuts enacted in the Bush administration's first year. The Bush tax cut, over the course of the decade, would save the average family in the richest 1 percent $342,000, or $657.69 a week.[281]

By contrast, a family in the middle fifth of American income-earners would realize $5,402 in savings over that same period, an average of $10.38 a week. A family in the bottom 20 percent would see just $1.43 per week in tax relief.[282]

The controversies over the 2001 Bush tax cut would soon fade from the public mind, shoved off the political stage by the horrific September 11 assault on the Wall Trade Center and the Pentagon. But President Bush would reignite the controversy, less than two months after 9/11, by announcing his intention to ask Congress to speed up the income tax rate reductions scheduled by the 2001 tax cut legislation for later in the decade. The news astounded observers. The President had declared a war on terrorism, a war whose cost would surely be enormous. How could he possibly be asking for more tax cuts that would primarily benefit America's most comfortable?

In 2002, some Democrats would pick up on this theme. In the Senate, Edward Kennedy offered a plan to delay, not speed up, the tax cuts already in the works for the wealthy. In the House, a group of representatives urged that the top tax rate be restored to 39.6 percent, its year 2000 level.[283] "It's a choice between bailing out billionaires at Enron or providing unemployment benefits for laid-off workers," noted Bernie Sanders, the Independent congressman from Vermont. "If Democrats want to do anything this session, they have to have the guts to take on the tax cut."[284]

The Democrats, as a party, didn't want to do anything. In the 2002 congressional session, the top Democratic leaders in the House and Senate would not push to undo the tax relief for the wealthy enacted in 2001. The Democratic National Committee chair, Terry McAuliffe, declared taxing the wealthy "off the table."[285]

That fall, in the 2002 midterm election campaign, Democrats would make no sustained effort to challenge the President's upper crust priorities. They would suffer, on Election Day, embarrassing losses. President Bush, naturally, would quickly claim a mandate for pressing ahead with still another round of tax cuts. This new round of cuts, introduced early in 2003, would be configured to hand America's richest 1 percent, taxpayers making at least $374,000 a year, another $30,127 in tax savings in 2003 alone.[286] Overall, analysts noted, the new Bush plan would, if enacted, completely or substantially eliminate federal taxes on every revenue source that makes rich people rich, from inherited estates to interest, capital gains, and dividend income. The package, observed one *Washington Post* reporter, advanced "tax changes Ronald Reagan could only dream of."[287] President Bush and his friends were "going for broke," charged Rep. George Miller from California. "Their goal," he added, "is to force feed as much of the economic productivity of this country to the richest people of this country as fast as they possibly can before the nation catches up with them."[288]

Miller would oppose that force-feeding, but the majority of his colleagues would go along. The House and Senate would adopt a "compromise" that actually left the Bush tax plan *more* wealthy-people friendly. Under the tax cut, as finally enacted, households making over $1 million a year would average $93,500 in 2003 tax savings. At the other end of America's income ladder, over a third of America's households, 50 million in all, would see no savings at all from the Bush plan. Tax savings for households in the exact middle of America's income distribution, meanwhile, would average $217 in savings.[289]

Middle-income families with children would do somewhat better than that average, since the Bush plan did increase, by $400, the income tax child credit. But that $400 would be little consolation for families with kids in college. State budget cuts had already forced major tuition hikes at almost all America's public colleges and universities. In New York, for instance, a week before lawmakers in Congress gave the Bush tax cut their blessing, state lawmakers had adopted a budget that boosted annual tuition and fees by $950.[290]

More college tuition hikes, in New York and elsewhere, seemed inevitable. The new federal tax cut legislation did include $10 billion in emergency aid to hard-pressed state governments for each of the next two years. But that $10 billion didn't figure to help many states avoid new tuition hikes. State governments were facing an estimated $100 billion budget shortfall just for 2003 alone.[291] GOP leaders in Congress, some observers contended, weren't interested in helping fiscally squeezed states. The $10 billion in state aid, these observers pointed out, had only been added to the tax cut legislation at the last minute, as a desperate maneuver to win enough Senate votes to get the legislation passed.

"The new tax cut is about cutting taxes on the rich," University of Texas economist James Galbraith would note. "The tax bill throws peanuts at the fiscal crisis of the states."

And what could average folks expect after states get those peanuts? Galbraith saw not a pretty picture: "Sales taxes will keep going up. Poor people pay those. Property taxes will rise relentlessly, as they are doing down in Texas. Middle-class folk pay the property tax. Funds for schools, health care, transportation and the environment will be cut." The ultimate "train wreck," Galbraith predicted, would come after the 2004 election.[292]

"What I really want to know is this," an exasperated Congressman George Miller had asked a few months earlier, in February 2003. "What is it that the Bush Administration has against working middle class people? What the hell is it?"[293]

AMERICA'S EARLY LEADERS, NOTES HISTORIAN JAMES HUSTON, always "prided themselves on the difference between their republican, egalitarian society and the class-ridden aristocratic societies of Europe."[294]

"To find rampant crime, utter hopelessness, a permanent poverty class, and magnificent fortunes residing next to indescribable hovels," Huston points out, "Americans went to Europe."

Today, generations later, the roles have reversed. Europeans, Huston observes, now "come to the United States to witness the social distance between rich and poor, to observe homelessness and unendurable poverty, to see a political system of republicanism that elicits either apathy or outright hostility from the majority of its citizens, to research rampant crime and the world's largest population of prison inmates, to record the antics and frivolities of the inordinately wealthy." This may be, concludes Huston, the ultimate irony. The United States, not Europe, now "exhibits the traits that the revolutionists found loathsome in the eighteenth century." The United States, not Europe, has become "the aristocratic disgrace of western European civilization."

In America's political mainstream, a mainstream defined by politicians bought by the wealthy, by a media owned by the wealthy, by public policy think tanks bankrolled by the wealthy, hardly anyone acknowledges this disgrace — or worries much about it. But outside America's legislative halls and executive offices, off the front pages, many Americans *are* worrying. These Americans are discussing and debating alternatives to greed. They deserve our attention.

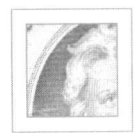

CONTEMPORARY OPTIONS

ADVOCATES FOR A MORE EQUITABLE AMERICA, a century ago, saw their campaign for social justice as essentially a two-front struggle. A good and honorable republic would emerge, these advocates believed, if more wealth accumulated at the bottom of America's social order, less at the top. Wise nations, James Madison had argued years earlier, seek to "reduce extreme wealth towards a state of mediocrity, and raise extreme indigence toward a state of comfort." Social justice activists one hundred years ago shared Madison's perspective. The fewer tycoons, the fewer paupers, the better the republic would most certainly be. For progressives, the task appeared straightforward. They needed to "level up" the lowly, "level down" the high and mighty.

Today, a century later, crusaders for social justice have largely given up on "leveling down." Contemporary social justice activists devote their energies, almost exclusively, to strategies that might help America "level up." And who can fault them? In today's political environment, thinking about "leveling down" can seem a colossally futile waste of time. The "extreme wealth" that so worried generations past now worries virtually no one of import in American public life. America once had Presidents who railed against "malefactors of wealth" and "economic royalists." In modern America, grand fortunes go unchallenged. No American under sixty has ever heard a prominent elected leader, in an important public forum, express a case, any case, against concentrated wealth.

Most people serious about social justice, as a consequence, don't think much about leveling down. They concentrate instead on "level up" activism, on advancing initiatives that can help poor people amass income and wealth. This single-minded attention to "leveling up," as a strategy for reducing inequality, can certainly be justified. "Leveling up" approaches, after all, *can* help close the gaps that separate the wealthy from everyone else. If poor people are improving their economic status faster than rich people are improving theirs, gaps between top and bottom will most assuredly narrow. Leveling up, as an approach to fighting inequality, also carries another attraction. No one prominent in American public life "supports" poverty. Everyone, all American political leaders agree, deserves an opportunity to get ahead.

Advocates for low-income families have worked diligently to translate this broad consensus for "equal opportunity" into political support for programs that give poor people a meaningful helping hand. But they have had, at best, limited success. Poor people, many influential American politicos believe, don't particularly need a helping hand. They need a kick in the butt. America, these influentials insist, remains *the* land of opportunity. In America, if you work hard enough, you will succeed. We have no "fixed" economic classes. Ours is a socially mobile society. You work, you climb. A lowly start does not condemn you to a lowly finish. That's what makes America great.

In truth, we are not today as mobile people as we think ourselves to be. Children from families in the nation's highest-income 10 percent, economists Samuel Bowles and Herbert Gintis documented midway through the 1990s, are twenty-seven times more likely, as adults, to end up in that top 10 percent than children from the bottom 10 percent. Out of every thousand children born into America's lowest-income tenth, their research revealed, only four will make it into the highest.[1]

"Individuals of all races and ethnicity are constantly moving from one class to another," a *Washington Post* survey of mobility research concluded in 1997. "But upward mobility is not automatic and is far less common, regardless of race, than is often assumed."[2]

Subsequent studies have only reinforced that conclusion. Annette Bernhardt, a researcher in Wisconsin, reviewed data that tracked 5,200 wage-earners over sixteen years. Increasing numbers of workers, she observed in 2002, "are permanently stuck in low-wage and dead-end careers, with little chance of entering the middle class."[3] Overall, the *New York Times* would add early in 2003, "experts report that mobility up and down the income ladder has diminished significantly recently in the United States."[4]

America's diminishing mobility has begun to alarm conservatives and liberals alike. Society, more academic analysts are proclaiming, needs to do something.

"Never has the accident of birth mattered more," Nobel Laureate economist James Heckman noted early in the new millennium. "I am a University of Chicago libertarian, but this is a case of market failure: children don't get to 'buy' their parents, and so there has to be some kind of intervention to make up for these environmental differences."[5]

"Many factors that lead to high or low incomes are beyond individuals' control," agreed a much more liberal Northwestern University political scientist, Benjamin Page. "We can and should help the unlucky."[6]

America's unlucky are still waiting for that help. Despite an overwhelming consensus in America that everyone deserves equal opportunity, despite growing evidence that obstacles are blocking that opportunity, despite growing support for "interventions" to increase opportunity, America has seen precious little "leveling up." People at America's economic bottom do not today enjoy any greater economic security than they did five, ten, or twenty years ago — or feel any less poor. The "practical" political approach to social justice — ignore concentrated wealth at the top of society, devote all possible political energy toward helping society's unfortunate — has not delivered. Leveling up, in the absence of any effort to "level down," seems to have failed.

In an unequal society, these pages will contend, any struggle for a more equal society that emphasizes "leveling up" over "leveling down" will always fail. The question is not whether we must level up or level down to fight inequality. We must do both. The real question is, how can we do both best?

AMERICANS HAVE BEQUEATHED TO WORLD CIVILIZATION two magnificent gifts fundamental to social progress. We have demonstrated that a nation can survive as a republic — and we invented free, universal public education.

These two gifts, we Americans once understood, work best in concert: Only an educated people can effectively govern themselves. But we have, over recent decades, tended to disregard this civic role of public education. We have emphasized instead education as an economic imperative. No one can succeed in the Information Age, we proclaim at every opportunity, without an adequate education. In high-tech times, we all agree, a poor education almost always guarantees economic failure, a life at the margins. Poor schools, seen in this light, constitute America's single biggest obstacle to equal opportunity. The obvious remedy: To make opportunity real for everyone in America, the schools poor kids attend simply must become better.

In the mid 1980s, this need to improve schools for poor kids became America's preferred response to growing inequality. Through better schools, experts and elected leaders agreed, America's unfortunate could be "leveled up" into middle class comfort.[7] A "better-trained workforce" would cure what ails low-income America. "One finds this mantra," economist Robert Kuttner would note midway through the 1990s, "in speeches of CEOs, declarations of business groups, White House pronouncements on the social role of corporations, and pleas by advocates of disadvantaged youth."[8]

Throughout the 1980s and 1990s, blue-ribbon commissions would swamp America with ambitious plans for improving the nation's most beleaguered public schools. But few of these plans, by century's end, had translated into significant achievement gains for disadvantaged students. Why so little progress? Schools by themselves, advocates for poor families did their best to explain, cannot undo the deficits that hold back children who live in or near poverty. Kids without a place at home to do homework will always have trouble keeping up. Kids in families always on the move from rental to rental, from school to school, will always keep falling further behind. To succeed in school, poor kids need a healthy learning environment, a stability, that a life in poverty cannot provide.

Kids who somehow beat the odds and make their way successfully through school, advocates added, face still another huge barrier to completing their education. Their families can't afford to send them to college.

Clearly, some analysts began arguing, poor kids need more than just good schools to get ahead. They need to live in families with "assets," families with enough household wealth to provide everything from a stable home environment to a reasonable shot at a college education. "Asset building" would soon become an important new addition to the "leveling up" dialogue. By the mid 1990s, specific "asset building" proposals would be proliferating in academic and political circles all across the United States.[9]

One version, the Individual Development Account, or IDA, advanced by Washington University's Michael Sherraden, took the already familiar Individual Retirement Account, or IRA, as a model, and proposed giving asset-poor families a tax incentive to save for their children's futures.[10] The Clinton administration would contemplate creating "Universal Savings Accounts" that would give families earning less than $40,000 an annual $600 tax credit and a federal matching grant of up to $700 a year.[11] Nebraska Senator Bob Kerrey suggested that every newborn be awarded a $1,000 savings account and then $500 a year more until the child's fifth birthday. At age twenty-one, after sixteen years of compounding interest, the grown child would have $20,000 — and a head start on life.[12] Republicans, meanwhile, advanced a "Savings for Working Families Act," a bill that aimed to reward families that save with matching federal dollars.[13]

The most sweeping of the asset-building prescriptions would come from two Yale Law School professors. Bruce Ackerman and Anne Alstott. Their 1999 book, *The Stakeholder Society*, proposed that the federal government extend to all Americans, on their twenty-first birthday, a no-strings-attached $80,000 grant, a sum about equal to the cost of a quality four-year college education.[14]

No top politicians would rush to embrace this notion of a universal $80,000 grant. But a host of top politicos, in 2000, would maneuver to position themselves as asset-building advocates. In their 2000 election bids, both George W. Bush and Al Gore pledged to advance, if elected, bold new asset-building approaches.[15]

Bush and Gore, in their campaigns, would make even louder pledges around education. Both promised, in nearly every stump speech, to make America's schools their highest priority. This matching campaign rhetoric reflected, in effect, an elite consensus on "leveling up," a consensus that had been twenty years in the making. Government, America's movers and shakers agreed, must bust down the barriers that block poor people from economic success. Schools must be improved. Nest-eggs must be nurtured.

But this elite consensus, in the early years of the twenty-first century, would not move anywhere beyond rhetoric. Low-performing schools would not be significantly improved. Millions of poor kids would continue to walk every morning into overcrowded, ill-equipped classrooms and find inexperienced, unqualified teachers. And nest-eggs would not be nurtured. More families would continue to drop out of America's middle class than in. These outcomes could have been predicted. Schools for poor kids can indeed be improved, nest-eggs can be nurtured. But not on the cheap. "Leveling up" efforts, whenever *seriously* pursued, cost. A great deal. America's movers and shakers, in the opening years of the new century, would simply not be willing to foot the bill.

How big a bill would real "leveling up" demand? Michael Sherraden's original 1991 asset-building proposal would have cost $28 billion to implement in its first year alone. In 1998, Democrats and Republicans joined to enact a pilot program somewhat along the lines Sherraden suggested. The congressional appropriation for this initial asset-building effort: a grand total of $300 million *for five years.*[16]

In education, federal officials would need just look in their own backyard to see how much a real "leveling up" effort would cost, since the federal government itself is currently running the nation's most successful school system for kids from low-income backgrounds. This school system, the Department of Defense schools for kids from military families, boasts better test scores from low-income students than any other school system in the country. How do the DoD schools produce these outstanding results? Money, educators point out, certainly helps. In the 1990s, Department of Defense schools spent 23 percent more per pupil than the national per pupil average.[17]

In the 2000-2001 school year, local, state, and federal authorities spent nearly $400 billion overall on public elementary and secondary education. Bumping that figure up 23 percent, to match the per pupil investment in Defense Department schools, would require about another $100 billion a year.[18] And that $100 billion would still not guarantee equal educational opportunity. College would remain beyond the grasp of millions of students from low-income families. That added $100 billion would also do nothing to give poor children an equal opportunity in their early years, before school. How much more does the nation need to spend on quality preschool services? More, suggests Johns Hopkins University educator Robert Slavin, than America is even willing to consider.

Slavin came to that conclusion after examining results from an ambitious North Carolina experiment in quality preschool education that had begun in the 1970s. This experiment gave a randomly selected group of poor kids, from infancy to age eight, a comprehensive set of social supports. Later tested as teenagers, these poor kids "scored substantially higher on measures of IQ, reading, and mathematics" than kids who hadn't enjoyed the same support.[19] Good news? Not really. The project, Slavin observed, was "too expensive under current conditions to replicate widely."[20] How expensive? The program cost, on average, $13,000 per child, in 2002 dollars, about twice the per child cost of the federal government's existing Head Start program.[21] And Head Start, as funded in 2002, was only reaching three-fifths of the three- to five-year-old poor children eligible for it.[22]

In an America where a "leveling up" program as popular as Head Start could not gain full funding, Slavin understood, preschool programs robust enough to make a significant difference for all poor kids would remain sheer fantasy. And other interventions needed to guarantee equal opportunity — the programs to turn around low-performing schools, the assistance needed to make college affordable — would remain fantasies, too. They all cost too much. Lawmakers in turn-of-the-century America would only fund, at best, token efforts. To do otherwise, to raise the hundreds of billions necessary to provide real equal opportunity, lawmakers would have to take a step they have been unwilling to take. They would have to insist that America's wealthy ante up. A nation as wealthy as America can afford a leveling up agenda, but not without reaching into America's deepest pockets. To "level up," America first needs to level down.[23]

So note the authors of the *The Stakeholder Society*, the most ambitious text of the asset-building movement. The United States, Bruce Ackerman and Anne Alstott point out, could bankroll an $80,000 nest-egg for every twenty-one-year-old simply by enacting a 2 percent tax on the wealth of America's more comfortable households.

"The wealth of America is distributed so unequally," they observe, "that stakeholding can be financed by a tax that hits only the top 41 percent, with the top 20 percent contributing 93 percent of the total."[24]

America's elites, in the early years of the twenty-first century, would evince no interest in this sort of tax. They would evince no interest in any "leveling up" activity that required, to succeed, any sort of "leveling down." In an unequal America, the stakeholder society, any serious effort to level up people at America's economic bottom, would have to wait.

ANY SOCIETY THAT AIMS TO HELP POOR PEOPLE climb up life's economic ladder, up past the obstacles that have blocked their way in the past, must be willing to devote significant time and treasure to the effort. But time and treasure, even if adequately expended, can go for naught. Few will ever climb *up* life's ladder, even with help, if they live and labor in an economy that's constantly shoving *down* the people above them.

Our current economy does just that. In fact, our nation's movers and shakers have been shoving people down America's economic ladder ever since the 1970s. These movers and shakers have changed the rules that determine how our economy plays out. The old rules gave working people a shot at getting and keeping good jobs. The new rules reward those who snatch good jobs away.

Our corporate elites, not surprisingly, would rather we not pay much attention to the rule changes. They enjoy the new playing field. Under the new rules, they no longer have to bother with pesky government regulations that require them to protect workers and consumers. They can merge and purge their industries without suffering antitrust prosecution. They can deny workers the right to organize without getting prosecuted for violating labor laws. They can collect subsidies, financed by public tax dollars, for downsizing and sending jobs overseas. They can count, most of all, on government — as the economy's "referee" — to make sure every close call goes their way. Should taxes on the affluent be raised or public services cut and privatized? Should Medicare be extended or insurance companies guaranteed new markets? Should trade agreements respect environmental standards or give companies that exploit the environment the competitive edge? Under the new rules, the ultimate decisions always seem to tilt the same way.

Corporate America started demanding, and winning, these new rules for the economy over a quarter century ago, in the nation's "stagflation" years. If America's economic playing rules were changed, business leaders then assured lawmakers, the resulting prosperity would swoop working Americans up into a new era of good times. That didn't happen. The new rules shoved millions of Americans down, not up, and left dazed families wondering anxiously how they would ever get themselves back to where they had been.

To Americans who complained about this economic duress, corporate America had a two-part retort. Your problem, those in distress were informed, sits with your education. You aren't educated enough. Your problem is your bank account. You don't save enough. You haven't built up a big enough nest-egg. This clever spinning of the two "leveling up" strategies that came into vogue in the 1980s and 1990s — education and asset building — essentially transferred the responsibility for disappointing living standards off the economy and onto people living disappointing lives.

People like Christopher Audet. In 1999, a *Christian Science Monitor* article presented the story of Audet, a Florida man, as a cautionary tale about what inevitably happens whenever people don't take their life's choices seriously enough. Under the headline, "The Growing Cost of Skipping College," the piece noted that Audet had "tried college, but he couldn't stick with it." The result? Audet had become a toll-taker in Ft. Lauderdale making $5.75 an hour. Audet's fate, the article suggested, awaits any worker who gives school the straight-arm. Real wages for America's unskilled workers, the article noted, had actually dropped over the previous ten years.[25]

Articles like this *Christian Science Monitor* piece, the media watchdog group FAIR would later note, never seem to mention an equally telling fact. Real wages for unskilled males most certainly did fall over the course of the 1990s, but so did the entry-level wages of men with college degrees. If Christopher Audet had finished college, he would have stepped into a job market that paid college grads 8 percent less, in real dollars, at the end of the 1990s than they made at the decade's start.[26] In the boom years, if you worked for a living, you were making no leaps up the ladder — even if you had worked hard to get yourself an education.

Indeed, if education could drive people up the economic ladder all by itself, the last quarter of the twentieth century should have seen an unprecedented upward explosion in average American household incomes. In the three decades after 1973, the share of American workers with college degrees doubled.[27] But average Americans saw no income explosion. Between 1973 and 2001, the real hourly wages of Americans with college degrees rose all of 11 cents per year.[28]

People like Christopher Audet aren't rotting the American economy. Our economy is rotting from stagnating wages. And nothing will change so long as work does not pay. Assets will not accumulate in average households. Kids will not even do appreciably better in school. Raising incomes in America's poorest households, note sociologist Mike Miller and activist Chuck Collins, "would do more for raising educational performance than would the current nostrum of raising standards." Higher wages, they point out, "make it easier for families to keep their children in school for longer periods."[29] In the years right after World War II, the higher wages bargained by strong unions elevated millions of mass production workers into the middle class, "despite their blue-collar occupations," and, note Miller and Collins, "propelled many of their offspring into higher education."[30] Between 1945 and 1970, years of rising wages, college enrollment in the United States more than quadrupled, from 1.5 to 8 million students.[31]

Over the course of those years, from 1945 to 1970, our nation's basic economic rules kept us on what progressive economists have labeled the "high road." Lawmakers, prodded by strong unions, anxious to score Cold War debating points in the struggle with the Soviet Union, insisted on rules for the economy that really did "put people first." Employers were expected to bargain with their employees. Affluent people were expected to pay their fair share of taxes, and these tax dollars would help fund investments in schools, in housing, in roads and bridges, in research that developed new technologies and created new industries and jobs. Under these postwar rules, the minimum wage would regularly rise. Under these rules, working people would prosper. They would rush up America's economic ladder.

The United States, progressive economists advise, needs to get back on this "high road" — and start once again following policies that privilege average people. If we could set ourselves back on the "high road," economists Barry Bluestone and Bennett Harrison have estimated, we might as a nation be able to "regain the more equal income distribution that existed in the 1960s" within a dozen years.[32]

America's top economic decision makers have ignored this "high road" counsel. They have kept America, with only an occasional detour, rolling down the "low road," the road that privileges the powerful and leaves the rest of us to fend for ourselves. They justify this low-road course, year after year, with the same numbing, lifeless prose.

"We must pursue monetary conditions in which stable prices contribute to maximizing sustainable long-run growth," Federal Reserve Chairman Alan Greenspan tells us. "Such disciplined policies will offer the best underpinnings for identifying opportunities to channel growing knowledge, innovation, and capital investment into the creation of wealth that, in turn, will lift living standards as broadly as possible."[33]

America's average living standards, after over a generation of such "disciplined policies," remain unlifted. So why do we, as a nation, stick to the low road? We stick because the low road can be comfortable — for those who ride down it in limos. The low road has carried America's wealthy wherever they have wanted to go. Not surprisingly, they have resisted, with gripping determination, any national change of direction.

Back before the 1970s, by contrast, the wealthy and powerful did not resist the high road. Corporate leaders played along, under "high road" rules, and they actually did quite well. The gap between the wealthy and everybody else did narrow substantially in the quarter century after World War II, but not because wealthy people stopped making more money. The incomes of the affluent actually rose during the "high road" years, just not as rapidly as the incomes of average people.[34]

So why do today's corporate leaders fiercely oppose the same "high road" policies that yesterday's corporate leaders accepted so readily?

No great mystery here. Yesterday's corporate leaders could afford to be accepting. In the postwar years, decades of rebuilding in war-torn Europe and Asia, American businesses enjoyed little competition. Executives could amble along, pay decent wages, abide by regulations meant to protect the public interest, meet their tax responsibilities, and still, at the end of the day, tally handsome profits. But that world of easy earnings started crumbling in the 1970s. Corporate America could no longer effortlessly dominate markets, either in the United States or across the world. Corporate leaders now faced real competitors — and a choice. They could sit down with government and labor and jointly rethink and retool to meet the challenges of a new world economy. Or corporate leaders could keep their own good times going by ending good times for everybody else. They would choose the latter course. They would press for and win new "rules" for the economy. They would gain everything from a "union-free" environment to deregulation, everything from "free trade" agreements to lower tax rates.

Under these new rules, wealth — and power — would concentrate ever more grandly at the top of America's economic ladder. And that power would keep the new rules firmly in place, despite clear and mounting evidence that these new rules had created an America that was failing most Americans.

We as a nation cannot hope to steer America back onto our abandoned "high road," cannot begin creating an America that works for most Americans, unless we confront and reduce this power of concentrated wealth, the power that keeps America on the "low road." To put into place the policies necessary to create an economy that works for everyone, we need, in short, to "level down."

Down through history, in the United States and elsewhere as well, average people have at times been able to "level down" severe inequalities. But those times, history shows us, have almost always come amid intense social crises, amid wars and depressions that have left societies — and their upper crusts — deeply shaken. Must we today wait for war and depression before we can make any serious inroads against concentrated wealth? Or can we level down, seriously and significantly, without having to first undergo cataclysmic social dislocation?

That just may be, in the century ahead, the most important question we all face.

WISE PEOPLE HAVE BEEN THINKING ABOUT how best to "level down" concentrated wealth ever since the dawn of recorded history. How do we know? The Bible tells us so. The giants of our biblical narratives, the great prophets from Moses to Jesus, obsessed about the need to keep wealth from concentrating — and poisoning the good and just societies they hoped to hasten into reality.

Moses and the Israelites, after escaping Egypt and bondage, faced the challenge of sustaining themselves as a new nation. How would they choose to structure their new society? Would they recreate the hierarchies they had fled? Moses, notes theologian Ched Myers, urged his people to think anew.[35] Gather for your needs, Moses advised, and no more. Strive not to endlessly accumulate. Pharaoh had accumulated. The Israelites, Moses insisted, must not go down that road. Future prophets would echo Moses. They understood, as Ched Myers explains, that oppressive regimes draw "labor, resources, and wealth into greater and greater concentrations of idolatrous power." They urged Israel "to keep wealth circulating through strategies of redistribution, not concentrating through strategies of accumulation."[36]

And how could a just society keep wealth from accumulating? The Bible offers a course of action Myers has termed "sabbath economics." All who do honor to God, the Bible advises, should regularly rest from their labors, from their accumulating. "Six days you shall gather," Exodus tells us, "but on the seventh, which is a Sabbath, there will be none."[37] Those who observe the Sabbath must rest from accumulating not just every seventh day, but every seventh year. In this Sabbath year, Exodus advises, "You shall let the land rest and lie fallow, so that the poor of your people may eat."[38] All debtors, insists Deuteronomy, must be released from their burdens in this same Sabbath year.

Ancient prophets, Ched Myers explains, saw debt release as "a hedge against the inevitable tendency of human societies to concentrate power and wealth in the hands of a few." In ancient societies, wealth would often first start concentrating in significant accumulations when deeply indebted families had to sell off their lands to service their debts. The creditors, landowners themselves, would add the lands of indebted families to their own personal holdings, creating ever larger fortunes. For shame, prophets like Isaiah would thunder in response, as they berated wealthy creditors who had added "house to house and field to field, until there is room for no one but you."[39]

The Bible's Sabbath logic, notes theologian Ched Myers, would reach its "fullest expression" in the "Jubilee," the grand remission that marked the year after every seventh Sabbath year, or the fiftieth year of the biblical cycle. In the Jubilee year, the Book of Leviticus proclaims, all shall be released from their debts, all lands shall be returned to their original owners, and all slaves shall be freed. A leveling down, a leveling up.[40]

This Jubilee vision, Myers suggests, can help us understand the clashes between Jesus and the authorities of his day.[41] Jesus claimed "the authority to cancel debts and restore the Sabbath." This "revisioning of Sabbath economics," notes Myers, "lay at the heart of his teaching — and stood at the center of his conflict with the Judean public order."[42] "Many who are first will be last," preached Jesus, in wisdom inspired by the Jubilee tradition, "and the last first."[43]

Those uncomfortable with this tradition, down through the years, have argued that biblical urgings for Sabbath years and Jubilees were never taken seriously, even in biblical times. But the Bible, Ched Myers notes, presents ample evidence to the contrary. The Bible's prophets — Isaiah, Amos, Hosea, Jeremiah — repeatedly rail against violations of the Sabbath spirit.

"If we are going to dismiss the Jubilee because Israel practiced it only inconsistently," adds Myers, "we should also ignore the Sermon on the Mount because Christians have rarely embodied Jesus' instruction to love our enemies."[44]

In ancient Israel, a simple agrarian society, the Sabbath economics of rest, relief, and remission could and did provide a standard for realizing a just and good society, a "leveling" frame of reference. In our more complex times, Sabbath economics can still offer us inspiration. But we need to look elsewhere for an operational leveling plan. The agrarian Jubilee does not fit our modern age. Those who would do honor to the Jubilee spirit, notes Ched Myers, "have hard work to do."[45] We have an obligation to develop a leveling approach that does fit our times.

What might that leveling approach be?

WE HAVE NO THUNDERING PROPHETS TODAY. We do have thoughtful theologians. Many of these theologians believe that our age can lay claim to a leveling instrument worthy of our biblical heritage. They see in "progressive taxation" — tax systems that pinch the wealthy at higher rates than everyone else — a modern match for the Jubilee spirit.

"In a just society, those with more have an obligation toward those who have less," notes Patricia Ann Lamoureux, a Baltimore-based professor of moral theology. "This outlook supports a proportional and progressive tax structure."[46]

Progressivity, America's Catholic bishops agreed in their landmark 1986 pastoral letter on economic justice, brings to tax policy "an important means of reducing the severe inequalities of income and wealth."[47]

Our age's most important progressive tax levy, the federal income tax, boasts roots that run deep in both secular and religious thought. Karl Marx certainly did, as Ronald Reagan used to complain, support the progressive income tax. But he was merely following in the footsteps of the most celebrated hero of Ronald Reagan's conservative movement, the eighteenth century thinker Adam Smith.

"It is not very unreasonable," wrote Smith in his most famous work, *The Wealth of Nations*, "that the rich should contribute to the public expense not only in proportion to their revenue, but something more than in that proportion."[48]

Social justice crusaders have been echoing that idea ever since.

"The progressive income tax," as commentator Molly Ivins summed up in 2001, "is the single fairest form of taxation ever invented."[49]

This cheering, to be sure, has dimmed somewhat in recent decades. The federal income tax, many observers charge, no longer makes much of a progressive impact. Loopholes have become so large, tax rates on high incomes have fallen so low, that income taxes no longer tend to even out America's income inequalities. These inequalities, Joseph Pechman lamented in his 1989 American Economic Association presidential address, have become "even more pronounced after tax than before tax."[50] The wealthy, liberal commentator Mickey Kaus has argued, have never paid income taxes at the high progressive rates the tax laws say they should. They simply exploit loopholes to slash their tax bills.[51]

Conservatives have welcomed these liberal critiques. High tax rates on high incomes, they cheerfully chime in, will always backfire. "History shows that the ability to extract higher revenues from the rich is extremely limited," Bruce Bartlett, a former Treasury Department official, contended in 1993. "Higher rates simply cause the rich to shift their income from taxable forms to nontaxable forms or to forms that are taxed at a lower rate."[52] If the wealthy can accumulate fortunes with or without high tax rates in effect, conservatives ask, why bother taxing progressively?

Attacks on tax progressivity gained wide currency in the late twentieth century. But these attacks misread history. The federal progressive income tax, until neutered by the Reagan administration, *did* impact the concentration of wealth in the United States, and enormously so. That became undeniably obvious in 1998, after researchers Michael Klepper and Robert Gunther calculated an inflation-adjusted list of the forty richest Americans of all time.[53] The four fortunes Klepper and Gunther found at the top of their list wound up belonging to John D. Rockefeller (1839-1937), Andrew Carnegie (1835-1919), Cornelius Vanderbilt (1794-1877), and John Jacob Astor (1763-1848). All four of these tycoons made their fortunes *before* the heyday of high progressive tax rates on high incomes, a heyday that began in the 1930s and gamely hung on into the 1970s.

The list's fifth richest American of all time, Microsoft's Bill Gates, made his fortune *after* the demise of the stiffest progressive rates on high incomes, as did the eleventh richest on the list, Wal-Mart's Sam Walton, the thirteenth richest, investor Warren Buffet, and the twenty-second richest, Microsoft's Paul Allen.

Of the forty richest men in American history, not one made the bulk of his fortune during America's half century of high progressive tax rates. In effect, over the course of this half century, the American economy almost entirely stopped generating colossal concentrations of wealth and power. Awesome fortunes emerged in the United States *before* the 1930s and the onset of high progressive taxes. Awesome fortunes emerged *after* the Reagan administration eliminated high progressive rates in 1981. But no colossally grand fortunes emerged *during* the years the U.S. tax code subjected high incomes to progressive high rates.

Must we attribute the absence of colossal fortunes in the mid twentieth century to the progressive income tax? Alternate explanations could certainly be feasible. Maybe entrepreneurs in mid-twentieth century America simply gave up trying to make money, because Uncle Sam was snatching so much of it away. Maybe high tax rates drained the incentive to succeed out of the business world. Maybe entrepreneurs, lacking "incentive," just became lazy and stopped behaving entrepreneurially, stopped working hard to excite American consumers with new products and new technologies. That would explain, some might argue, why the computer industry didn't start generating excitement — and billionaires — until the Reagan years ripped progressivity out of the U.S. tax code.

Actually, these alternate explanations explain nothing. Entrepreneurs did not "give up" during the high tax years. They innovated on a grand scale throughout the high tax era. Indeed, they brought to market, right in the heart of that era, the single most exciting product in consumer history, the product that became the single "greatest form of mass entertainment" ever.[54] That product? Television. In 1948, only 1 percent of American households owned a TV. Within seven years, televisions graced the homes of 75 percent of the American people.[55] Those TV sets didn't just drop into those homes. They had to be designed, manufactured, packaged, distributed, marketed. An entire new broadcasting industry had to be invented. Programming had to be produced. Imaginations had to be captured. All of this demanded an enormous outlay of entrepreneurial effort. And that effort was made, despite progressive tax rates that taxed away income over $200,000 at a 91 percent rate. The progressive income tax in the early 1950s didn't prevent innovation and entrepreneurship. The progressive income tax simply prevented that innovation and entrepreneurship from generating dynasties of gargantuan wealth and power.

We must acknowledge, at this point, that some great fortunes did emerge in the heyday years of progressive tax rates. None of these fortunes would grow large enough to rank among America's forty richest of all time. But some did reach grand proportions. Do these fortunes prove that high progressive tax rates cannot prevent great wealth from concentrating? Not in the least. These fortunes amount to the exception that proves the rule. Some Americans did indeed become fabulously wealthy during the high tax years. But they only became fabulously wealthy because America's lawmakers essentially exempted them from high taxes. The great fortunes that emerged over the course of the high tax years almost all arose in one industry. The oil industry. Oil men, over the mid-century years, led a charmed political existence. They had what no one else had, a special tax code preference that amounted to a "get out of jail free" card. That preference, the "oil depletion allowance," would give oil men the single most lucrative tax loophole ever.

The oil depletion allowance, first introduced in the 1920s, would be institu-tionalized and expanded in the 1930s.[56] Over the next half century, oil tycoons essentially escaped the tax rates that applied to every other industry.[57] By the 1980s, the end of the progressive tax era, America's wealthiest individuals had either inherited their wealth, from fortunes originally amassed before high pro-gressive tax rates went into effect, or made their fortunes in and around the oil business. *Forbes* magazine began its annual "400 richest Americans" calculations in 1982. Of the thirteen billionaires on that first 1982 list, five owed their for-tunes to one daddy, oil man H. L. Hunt.[58] The very richest Americans, besides little Hunts, also included oil offspring from Sid Bass and John Paul Getty.[59]

In the years after that initial *Forbes* annual list, oil would lose its special sta-tus. The 1981 tax cut that slashed the top tax rate from 70 to 50 percent, fol-lowed by the 1986 cut that dropped the top rate to 28 percent, cleared the decks for super fortunes across the entire economy. America's early computer entrepreneurs would take full advantage of that opportunity. In the 1950s, with progressive tax rates in effect, the introduction of television into American homes had created no megafortunes. In the 1980s and 1990s, with progressive tax rates no longer in effect, the introduction of computers into American homes would create one new megafortune after another.

Elsewhere in the industrial world, progressive tax rates did not disappear in the 1980s. In Europe and Japan, tax rates on top incomes would remain rela-tively high. Megafortunes in these nations would remain rare. America's four hundred richest, *Forbes* would note in 1997, "are clearly lucky to be Americans." The richest of the rich in the United States, the magazine explained, pay taxes at "nowhere near" the rates applied to the wealthy in other developed nations.[60] "You don't have to be a rocket scientist," *Washington Post* political analyst David Broder would agree, "to know that the U.S. tax system has helped the top brackets amass their wealth."[61]

Progressive income tax rates, Broder understood, clearly do make a differ-ence. They can prevent huge concentrations of wealth from amassing. But do progressive tax rates make enough of a difference? Can progressive rates be sus-tained, over time, at high enough levels to keep a democratic society free from immense pockets of wealth and power? For egalitarians, unfortunately, history cannot offer a comforting answer.

"A PROGRESSIVE TAX CODE," notes *Los Angeles Times* columnist John Balzar, "dampens greed."[62] But high tax rates on high incomes also have another inevitable impact. They make rich people see red.

Wealthy people, as a group, have never accepted the basic principle behind tax progressivity, the notion that all citizens should be taxed according to their ability to pay. Wealthy individuals, by and large, have always seen progressive tax rates as intolerable sanctions on success, vile nuisances to be hated, avoid-ed, and, God willing, ultimately eliminated. Not all rich people, of course, have shared this embittered attitude. In every progressive tax era, a few brave affluent souls have spoken out *for* progressive taxation — and risked "class traitor" stares from their wealthy peers.

"Why shouldn't the American people take half my money from me?" as Edward Filene, the department store merchandising giant, once quipped. "I took all of it from them."[63]

Edward Filene and his ideological heirs have never set the tone for America's upper crust. In the United States, and elsewhere as well, efforts to initiate seriously progressive income tax systems have always met relentless resistance from wealthy people and the politicians in their pockets. In these standoffs, the wealthy usually prevail. But not always. Not during times of national crisis. Wars and economic catastrophes tend to upset politics as usual. They make the previously unthinkable — high taxes on high incomes — suddenly achievable. Still, crises never last forever. The wealthy eventually regain their political footing. They then, typically, take dead aim against any progressive tax rates the previous crisis may have left behind. They struggle, with all their might, to ax these rates. After World War I, they succeeded. In the 1920s, in the United States and most other industrial nations, the wealthy seized back the ground they had lost during the war.

With the wealthy back in the saddle, the world would stumble backwards, back toward inequality, to depression, to another world war. After World War II, notes University of Colorado political scientist Sven Steinmo, most observers expected more of the same. They felt sure that governments would "roll back taxes to somewhere near prewar levels." That didn't happen. Western governments proved able to hold "on to the high levels of taxation that the war had made politically possible."[64] That achievement would subsequently reshape the entire postwar world. In the years right after World War II, revenues from high progressive taxes would bankroll the initiatives, in everything from education to housing, that created the modern middle class — and the most equal societies the developed world had ever seen.

This progressive tax momentum, unfortunately, could not be sustained. In the United States, as we have seen, elites during the Eisenhower years didn't have the political strength to confront tax progressivity directly. They would work behind the scenes instead, trying to carve loopholes in the tax code. The Kennedy years would see the beginnings of actual rollbacks in tax rates. Still, despite the new loopholes, despite the Kennedy rate reductions, America's tax code would retain considerable progressivity until the Reagan years essentially ended tax progressivity in the United States.

The rest of the world would soon start following suit, slowly at first, then more rapidly in the late 1990s. Most governments in Europe and Asia felt they had no choice, not in a tightly globalized world economy. In this economy, dominated by a low-tax United States, political leaders feared that capital would abandon their countries if they dared try to maintain tax rates at high progressive levels. They found themselves, consequently, "forced to redesign their tax systems — largely irrespective of the preferences or desires of the majority of citizens."[65]

By 2000, every major European nation had reduced taxes on the wealthy.[66] Tax rates on wealthy incomes in these nations still remained higher than tax rates on wealthy incomes in the United States. But the gap, by century's end, had shrunk. Progressive income tax systems, throughout the world, were now no longer making the equalizing impact they once had. They no longer functioned as much of a brake on concentrated wealth.

In the 1990s, especially in the United States, egalitarians would begin searching for alternatives. Their exploration would come to focus on another longstanding, but sparingly practiced, leveling down option, the "wealth tax."

AMERICANS HAVE BEEN PAYING TAXES on "wealth," or property, ever since colonial days. But we have, down through the years, defined "property" rather narrowly. Our contemporary "property tax," in fact, only taxes one category of property, real estate. This narrow definition tends to generate a fundamental unfairness. Average families must pay taxes on the value of their homes, the chief source of their household wealth, but more affluent families pay no tax on the value of their stocks and bonds, the chief source of their wealth. Our current "property tax," in effect, privileges the property of wealthy people — and, in the process, serves to concentrate still more wealth in wealthy people's pockets. This property tax special privilege could be swiftly ended, many egalitarians have argued, simply by imposing a "wealth tax," an annual levy on all property, not just real estate.

If a wealth tax were enacted in the United States, each household would simply tally up assets and liabilities to compute a "net worth." Households with little net worth would pay no "wealth tax." Households with a modest net worth would pay a tiny percentage of that net worth in tax. Households with hefty net worth would pay considerably more.

Wealth taxes already exist elsewhere in the world, mostly in Western Europe. These levies subject appreciable accumulations of wealth to a small annual tax rate, typically around 1 or 1.5 percent. Switzerland taxes its largest wealth accumulations at an even lower rate, just one third of 1 percent.[67] In the United States, notes New York University economist Edward Wolff, even rates as low as these could generate quite substantial annual revenues. In 1995, Wolff proposed a wealth tax that would exempt every family's first $100,000 in assets, then tax wealth above that level at rates that ranged from a miniscule 0.05 percent to a still tiny 0.3 percent on the highest accumulations. An annual wealth tax so configured, Wolff calculated, would have then raised $50 billion.[68]

In the 1990s, Wolff's new research on America's increasing maldistribution of wealth would help build support for his wealth tax notion, some from important quarters. Midway through the decade, AFL-CIO secretary-treasurer Tom Donahue would call for a tax on all fortunes worth over $10 million.[69] "A progressive tax on wealth," former U.S. labor secretary Robert Reich would argue in 1998, "should not be beyond imagination."[70]

Support for a wealth tax even came from unexpected quarters. In 1999, multimillionaire developer Donald Trump suggested a wealth tax that would subject every fortune worth at least $10 million to a one-time 14.25 percent tax. If that tax were imposed, Trump asserted, the resulting revenue would be enough to retire America's entire national debt.[71]

No modern nations have ever seriously contemplated taxing wealth at a level anywhere near that 14.25 percent. The wealth tax, in practice, has remained a modest levy, a levy so modest that no contemporary wealth tax actually does much to level down inequality. A $100 million fortune averaging a 10 percent annual return on investments will, if subjected to a 1 percent annual wealth tax, continue to amass in size at quite a steady clip.

Why have wealth taxes, where they exist, remained so modest? Why do wealth taxes exist in so few nations? One reason may be the administrative headaches that inevitably accompany any effort to tax property. To be taxed, property must first be assigned a dollar value. Some forms of property — stocks and bonds, for instance — carry a regularly updated dollar value. These create few assessment problems. But other forms of wealth, from fine art to expensive jewelry, can take considerable effort to assess fairly. That reality poses a dilemma for lawmakers. If they choose to tax only those forms of wealth that can be easily assessed, then rich people will have an incentive to shift their fortunes into forms of wealth not easily assessed. If lawmakers choose to apply a wealth tax to all forms of wealth, including the difficult to assess, then a new assessment bureaucracy would have to be created, to keep rich people honest.

None of these administrative headaches make wealth taxes unworkable. But these headaches must be addressed, and that can take time. In moments of national crisis, the only moments when nations have historically contemplated placing new tax burdens on wealthy people, time cannot be wasted. Governments at crisis moments need revenues immediately. They can, almost always, collect these revenues more quickly and efficiently from taxes on income than taxes on wealth.

Still another reason, a perhaps more consequential reason, helps explain why wealth taxes have not advanced much beyond the curiosity stage. Any effort to establish and maintain a progressive *wealth* tax faces the same challenge as any effort to establish and maintain a progressive *income* tax: Rich people will always fight more forcefully to stop the taxation of excess wealth — or income — than average people will fight to make sure that excess wealth, or income, is taxed. Rich people, whenever taxes on excessive wealth or income are proposed, have a direct stake in the decision to be made. That's *their* money at issue. A tax on excessive wealth takes money directly *out* of wealthy pockets.

For the nonrich majority, by contrast, the benefits from progressive taxation, on either wealth or income, will always seem less tangible. A tax on excessive wealth never places dollars directly *into* the pockets of the nonrich majority. The most obvious benefits from taxing excessive income — more revenue dollars for programs that improve the quality of the lives that nonrich people live — can certainly be concrete. But these benefits are never immediate, and average people, as a result, seldom feel an urgent need to press for them, *except* during wars and other moments of national crisis.

These crisis moments totally transform the political environment. Everyone in society suddenly feels a sense of engagement, of urgency. Revenues, people understand, must be raised to win the war or solve whatever the crisis may be. And these revenues, average people also see clearly, will only be raised at adequate levels if all people contribute what they can, especially those who can afford to contribute the most. Wealthy people, in this atmosphere, can seldom prevail politically. Progressive tax proposals they could have swatted away with ease in more "normal" times — and perhaps did — now become law. The wealthy grit their teeth and pay their taxes. Their time will come. After the crisis.

The crisis over, the wealthy make their move. They launch aggressive struggles to render progressive tax systems ineffectual. Eventually, history shows, they prevail, unless and until some new crisis restores urgency and passion to the case for progressive taxation.

We now have, in the United States, nearly a century of experience with the progressive income tax. In all that time, non-rich majorities have never been able to sustain tax progressivity, absent war or depression, for more than a few decades. Could some other approach to progressive taxation prove more lasting, over the long term, than the progressive income tax? Could some other approach give non-rich majorities as much incentive to fight *for* "leveling down" as rich people have to fight against it? Perhaps. Wealth taxes weren't the only unusual "leveling down" idea championed in the 1990s.

FEW SCHOLARS HAVE DONE MORE TO HELP us understand how inequality limits our lives than Cornell University economist Robert Frank. Wealth that concentrates at excessive levels, Frank has shown, invariably fuels a wasteful conspicuous consumption that leaves average people gasping for breath on a never-ending "hedonic treadmill." In his 1999 book, *Luxury Fever*, Frank suggests a tax strategy that could slow that treadmill — and channel concentrated wealth into spending for the public good.

Frank's strategic suggestion, the "progressive consumption tax," essentially calls rich people's bluff. High taxes on high incomes, the wealthy have always claimed, sap a nation's economic vitality. If rich people are taxed heavily, the argument goes, they can't save and invest as much as they otherwise would. That's bad news, the argument continues, for entrepreneurs looking for investment capital. If these entrepreneurs can't find capital, they can't expand existing operations or create new ones. Everyone loses.

Advocates for tax progressivity have always considered this argument basically bogus. If wealthy people were taxed at lower levels, they note, the resulting dollars that would stay in wealthy pockets would not all be responsibly "invested." Many of these dollars would be wasted, on speculation or luxury spending. But let's assume, for argument's sake, that wealthy people really would save and invest, at significantly higher levels, if tax collectors would only give them a break. These eager-to-invest wealthy people, Robert Frank suggests, ought to welcome enthusiastically the prospect of a progressive consumption tax. Such a tax, he posits, would reward savers and investors — and penalize only those self-absorbed rich who squander their treasure on luxury baubles.

A progressive consumption tax, Frank notes, could work simply. If a progressive consumption tax replaced the traditional progressive income tax, Americans would still report to the IRS how much they earn every year, but they would also report how much they save every year — in everything from bank accounts to mutual funds. The difference between income and savings would represent a family's consumption. Each family would be able to claim a standard deduction, for basic living expenses, off that consumption total. The remaining consumption would be taxed, at low rates for low amounts, at high rates for high amounts.[72]

Under a progressive consumption tax system, wealthy people who save and invest their excess cash would pay far less in taxes than wealthy people who spend lavishly. This penalty on luxury, Frank believes, would encourage wealthy people to spend less and save more.[73] Less luxury spending by the wealthy would, in turn, reorient the economy. Carpenters, Frank predicts, would "spend less of their time building mansions for the superrich" and more time building homes for regular people. Fewer dollars would be "spent on liposuction and tummy tucks," more on "people who actually have illnesses."[74]

The rates for a progressive consumption tax, Frank adds, could be calibrated at levels that raise the same revenue from people at different income levels that the federal income tax does now. But if consumption tax rates were set more progressively than the current federal income tax, a course Frank favors, a progressive consumption tax could raise more revenue than the income tax does now. Tax rates on consumption, notes Frank, ought to go as high as income tax rates went before the Reagan revolution, to 70 percent.[75] Rates this high, he believes, could raise enough revenue to fund a renaissance in America's long-neglected "inconspicuous consumption," our nation's outlays for transportation, health, and other public goods that ease life's daily aggravations.

Consumption taxes amount to an indirect tax on luxuries, and taxes on luxuries, Frank acknowledges, generally have an abysmal track record. Taxes on jewelry, yachts, fancy sedans, and other luxuries typically raise much less revenue than expected, mainly because affluent people merely shift their spending from goods taxed as "luxuries" to goods not yet subject to a luxury tax.[76] And traditional luxury taxes, Frank adds, seldom stay in effect particularly long. Taxpayers quite naturally disagree, sometimes emotionally so, on whose luxuries ought to be gored.

"Is a $300 ticket to an evening performance by the Metropolitan Opera a frivolous luxury?" the Cornell economist explains. "Perhaps for some people, but what about the Des Moines school teacher who has saved 20 years for the thrill of a lifetime? No two of us are alike, and what is one person's luxury is another's necessity."[77]

A progressive consumption tax, Frank argues, avoids the problems inherent in taxing individual luxuries. A consumption tax would apply to spending on *all* goods and services. A consumption tax can operate, as a result, without any lawmaker having "to define and tax specific luxury goods on a case-by-case basis."[78] In other words, in theory at least, a consumption tax can do what a luxury tax cannot, actually discourage spending on luxuries and raise revenue at the same time. But to have this impact, to raise revenue and slow the consumption "arms race," consumption tax rates must be configured progressively. Rich people who consume lavishly, Frank emphasizes, must be taxed at far higher rates than average people who consume at much more modest levels.

"If a progressive consumption tax is to curb the waste that springs from excessive spending on conspicuous consumption," he notes, "its rates at the highest levels must be sufficiently steep to provide meaningful incentives for the people atop the consumption pyramid. For unless their spending changes, the spending of those just below them is unlikely to change either, and so on all the way down."[79]

Would lawmakers in the United States actually consider enacting a progressive consumption tax? They actually already have. During World War II, Treasury Secretary Henry Morgenthau advanced a proposal for a graduated "spendings tax." The proposal anticipated, in all major particulars, the progressive consumption tax Robert Frank would propose over a half-century later. All families would pay a tax on the amount of money they spent during the year, after deducting the cost of necessities. Rich families would pay this "spendings tax" at far higher rates than anyone else.[80]

Congress, in the end, would give Morgenthau's proposal only cursory attention, but modern lawmakers, Frank believes, might be more open to the notion. Indeed, he notes, "the progressive consumption tax is hardly a fringe idea." The evidence: In 1995, Senators Pete Domenici, a New Mexico Republican, and Sam Nunn, a Georgia Democrat, introduced legislation — the Unlimited Savings Allowance Tax Act — that would have exempted all personal savings from tax.[81] This bill's introduction, to Frank, signals that progressive consumption taxes have finally become politically viable.[82] But the "USA tax" proposal advanced by Domenici and Nunn amounted to only a pale reflection of Frank's progressive approach to consumption taxation, as Frank himself notes. "For the USA tax to stimulate significant alterations in our consumption patterns," he notes, "its rate structure would have to be much more steeply progressive."[83]

Indeed, in 1995, many progressive tax reformers would see absolutely no redeeming social value in the Domenici-Nunn proposal. If enacted, charged Robert McIntyre of Citizens for Tax Justice, the "USA tax" would have merely amassed existing tax loopholes for the rich and powerful "into one giant, all-encompassing loophole."[84]

The consumption tax notions advanced by Senators Nunn and Domenici in their USA tax proposal would find a more hospitable welcome among conservatives opposed to high taxes on the wealthy in any way, shape, or form. In its 1996 final report, the Republican National Commission on Economic Growth and Tax Reform, chaired by Jack Kemp, concluded that America needed a new tax system that "either let savers deduct their savings or exclude the returns on the savings from their taxable income."[85] Seven years later, in his proposed budget for the 2004 fiscal year, George W. Bush would advance a series of initiatives to accomplish that same goal. Conservatives had, in effect, squeezed out of the USA tax proposal just what they needed — a bipartisan justification for making all investment income tax-free — and discarded the rest.

Must all "progressive consumption tax" proposals face the same fate? Probably. Affluent taxpayers are not likely to embrace the sort of steeply progressive rates on their consumption that Robert Frank advocates, concludes Aaron Bernstein, a veteran *Business Week* observer of economic inequality. Advocates of truly progressive consumption taxes like Robert Frank, Bernstein notes, expect America's most affluent "to consume less so that all of us can live better lives."[86] America's most affluent, Bernstein argues, would be more likely to take the same attitude toward steeply progressive consumption tax rates that they have taken toward steeply progressive income tax rates. They would oppose these rates with every ounce of their being.

"People of privilege," as John Kenneth Galbraith once quipped, "will always risk their complete destruction rather than surrender any material part of their advantage."[87]

And that brings us back to the essence of our leveling down dilemma. Leveling down proposals will always face stiff and fervent opposition from the wealthy. This opposition from the wealthy will always prevail, eventually if not at first, unless average working people demonstrate an even greater fervor on behalf of leveling down than wealthy people demonstrate against it. Average people would indeed have reasons to support a steeply progressive consumption tax — more revenues for public goods and services, a possible slowdown in the consumption "arms race" — but these reasons don't seem more likely to energize Americans into action than proposals for a steeply progressive income or a steeply progressive wealth tax.

To move forward to a less unequal America, we need a new approach to leveling down, a new approach on two levels. We need, first, an approach that offers America's nonrich majority a tangible, direct, personal stake in leveling down. With a personal stake in the outcome of leveling down debates, working Americans might finally be able to mobilize the political determination necessary to cut concentrated wealth down to democratic size.

But to maintain wealth accumulations at democratic proportions, we would need an approach to leveling down that does more than just inspire the nonrich majority to noble struggle. We would need an approach that gives our wealthy a reason to care more about "leveling up" the bottom of society than ending "leveling down" limits on the top, a reason to believe that even they, as wealthy people, would be better off in a society with a more modest gap between top and bottom. We would need, in effect, an approach to fighting inequality that directly links leveling up and leveling down.

Creating this link would, of course, demand an ambitious new set of rules for our economy. Or maybe just one rule. The Ten Times Rule.

A MAXIMUM WAGE?

ON SEPTEMBER 11, 2002, exactly one year after history's most deadly assault on American civilians, a distinguished gentleman stepped to a simple podium at the front of Trinity Church, a grand old edifice that sits along New York's fabled Wall Street. The gentleman, William J. McDonough, would be the featured speaker in a ceremony to commemorate the tragedy that had shaken New York and the world.

McDonough had not been a 9/11 rescue worker, nor a near victim, and his remarks would not speak directly to the horror and heroism of that awful day. McDonough, the president of the Federal Reserve Bank of New York, would note instead the challenges ahead, the need to rally the wounded, to comfort the grieving, to rebuild the city, all endeavors that require us, at a basic moral level, to love each other as we would have others love us.

"Loving our neighbor as ourselves," the New York Fed president would then contend, "requires that the remaining imperfections in our democracy be corrected." [1]

McDonough asked his Trinity Church listeners to devote their attention to one imperfection "in particular": the gap between America's most privileged and everyone else. Two decades ago, he observed, top American corporate executives earned forty-two times more than average production workers. Today's top executives, he pointed out, earn over four hundred times the income of average workers.

"I am old enough to have known both the CEOs of 20 years ago and those of today," McDonough told the memorial assemblage. "I can assure you that we CEOs of today are not 10 times better than those of 20 years ago."

The vast increases in executive compensation over recent years, McDonough continued, have been "terribly bad social policy and perhaps even bad morals." Amid gaps as wide as these, he noted, how can the privileged purport to be loving thy neighbor as thyself?

"Is not my fellow worker," McDonough wondered, "my neighbor?"

Those of us who lead "lives of great comfort and success," the New York Fed president would go on, need to acknowledge that "our good fortune" has "very little to do with our own virtue." We have been lucky, he added. We have had fine genes, good health, loving parents, great teachers —"any and all of these got us where we are." Yes, McDonough noted, a market economy does require that some people "be rewarded more than others." But, he appealed, "should there not be both economic and moral limitations on the gap created by the market-driven reward system?"

America's economy, McDonough concluded, does need limits. Business leaders, he advised, "should simply reach the conclusion that executive pay is excessive and adjust it to more reasonable and justifiable levels."

In Trinity Church, on that day of commemoration, William J. McDonough did not speak on behalf of his fellow movers and shakers in American business. These movers and shakers do not share, not in public at least, McDonough's conviction that market-driven rewards can be economically and morally unjustifiable. But McDonough did give voice, on that solemn day in Trinity Church, to many millions of other Americans, fellow citizens who share his revulsion at our nation's "recent explosion of claimed privilege," and who believe, with him, that we must regain our "moral balance." These millions of Americans are ready — and willing — to limit "the gap created by the market-driven reward system." But they don't know how. Maybe these pages can help.

AMERICA'S BUSINESS LEADERS, William J. McDonough believes, have a moral responsibility to end compensation excess. If society appeals to this moral responsibility, he also believes, business leaders will see the light and take steps to limit the gaps that divide us. Society, in other words, need not legislate specific limits on excessive incomes. We can trust those who sit in executive suites to do, eventually, the right thing. The market, McDonough has faith, will in the end produce just outcomes.

Most Americans, over the last century, have not shared this faith. The marketplace, we concluded long ago, cannot separate right from wrong, cannot guarantee fairness and justice. Markets, experience had taught us, mix the weak and the strong. Without limits in place, the strong define what "fairness" should be — on wages and everything else — and then impose their decision.

We Americans did not want to live in that world. We insisted instead on new rules for the economy. We demanded legal protections for workers, for consumers, for the environment. In 1938, in one early rule-making triumph, we established a national minimum wage, a mandatory floor under wages.

A floor under wages made sense in the 1930s. That floor makes equal sense today. Markets simply cannot be trusted to determine how much constitutes too little. But what about too much? Can any marketplace where some have far more power than others be trusted to determine at what point rewards become excessive? If the strong, in the absence of limits, have the power to deny minimal wage decency to the weak, don't they also have the power to exceed decency for themselves, to accumulate income and wealth at inappropriate levels? Over recent decades, with income and wealth concentrating at unprecedented rates, this thought has troubled more than a few observers.

"Something seems wrong to me," as Lynn Shellenberger, a Minnesota community activist, noted deep in the boom years, "when we have a minimum wage and not a maximum wage for executives who make so much money."[2]

"Why have a floor," asked *St. Louis Post-Dispatch* columnist Bill McClellan about the same time, "and not a ceiling?"[3]

The notion of a maximum wage, a national income cap, actually first surfaced in the original Gilded Age. Back in 1880, amid the starkest inequality America had up until then ever seen, moral philosopher Felix Adler called for "an income tax graduated up to 100 percent on all income above that needed to supply all the comforts and refinements of life."[4] Adler, the founder of the Ethical Culture movement, would be a leading crusader for social justice in New York and the nation for the next fifty years. A young Franklin D. Roosevelt may have heard him speak, or read his work. In any case, as we have seen, FDR would propose his own maximum, a 100 percent tax on all income over $25,000.

Roosevelt, the greatest politician of his time, would prove unable to assemble much of a political coalition behind his income cap proposal. His allies likely saw FDR's "supertax" as a politically impractical declaration of war against the rich, a war that Roosevelt could not win. If income were capped at FDR's $25,000, after all, the wealthy would have felt themselves locked in place, fiscally frozen, left with no prospect of improving their material well-being. In that situation, the wealthy would have had but one choice: to battle against Roosevelt's cap by any means fair or foul. No cap would have been able to withstand their subsequent pressure.

But suppose FDR had proposed a cap, a maximum allowable income, *not* fixed at a particular dollar amount. Suppose FDR had asked Congress to set this cap, this maximum, not as a set amount, but as a multiple of the nation's minimum wage. If that approach had been proposed and adopted, if we had an income ceiling tied to an income floor, a maximum tied to a minimum, then the wealthy, to increase their earnings, would not have had to subvert or sidestep the 100 percent tax. They would have needed only to convince Congress to raise the minimum wage. By working to help others, they would have helped themselves. America's income tax system, if all this had taken place, would have become reciprocal, not just progressive. Wealthy people, by playing within this tax system's rules, would have been able to see their own individual income status improve.

Systems where all people can see themselves benefiting, at some level, are systems that can stand the test of time. An approach to leveling down that combined both progressivity and reciprocity just might have a fighting chance.

IF WE WERE, AS A SOCIETY, TO ACCEPT THIS NOTION that a maximum linked to a minimum might indeed help us, in James Madison's words, to "reduce extreme wealth towards a state of mediocrity, and raise extreme indigence toward a state of comfort," we would immediately face an obvious question. How wide a gap between top and bottom makes sense? How much income is enough? How much is too much?

Many economic analysts deem these questions inherently silly. As a society, they note, we cannot agree on what works of art ought to be labeled obscene. How could we possibly agree on the level of income we ought to label as obscenely excessive?

"Obscene," pay expert Graef Crystal has quipped, "is $1,000 more than I am making."[5]

But some denizens of the business world have been willing to take a stab at defining too much. In 1998, *Fortune* magazine asked a sampling of people in and around American business to pinpoint where they believe excess begins. The answers, predictably, varied.[6]

"Above $5 million I have serious questions," the Harvard Business School's Howard Stevenson responded. "That's the equivalent of earnings on between $50 million and $100 million in capital. That's $13,000 a day."

"One million dollars per year," Katie Herbert Douglass, a former CEO, opined, "is more than any person can spend."

To Stevenson and Douglass, anything more than $13,000 a day or $1 million a year simply *felt* too much. Do judgments as subjective as these have any value? Indeed they do, suggests ethicist Michael Josephson, a successful entrepreneur who left the business world to lead a national character-building campaign. The "ethical concept of too much," Josephson argues, derives from two sources. The first involves proportion. Income that *feels* unfair, that *seems* disproportionate, can legitimately be considered excessive. The second source involves economic markets. We can label as "too much," Josephson notes, any income "no longer driven by the marketplace but by artificial escalation."[7]

And what constitutes "artificial escalation"? Scholars have been wrestling with that question for years. They have poured over data, from all over the world, to discover whether any natural laws determine the distribution of income and wealth. This research carries enormous implications. If certain distributions do prove to be "natural," then concentrations of income and wealth beyond these natural distributions would be "artificial" — and in the interest of healthy societies to level down.

In 1988, a British economist, Sir Henry Phelps Brown, offered up a magisterial summary of much of this scholarly research.[8] Four years later, two Americans, economist Sidney Carroll and physicist Herbert Inhaber, jointly delved even deeper into the data.[9] The work of these scholars, taken together, may not prove *the* final word on income distribution. But their work does suggest a useful standard for determining where excess begins.

Henry Phelps Brown and the Carroll-Inhaber team, to help us understand how societies distribute income, both invoke the "parade" imagery of the Dutch economist Jan Pen. In a "Pen parade," every income earner in a society marches past us, in income order, lowest to highest, each person shrunk or stretched in height in proportion to the person's income. In these imaginary Pen parades, average income-earners march past us at what we would consider average height. The poor, proportionately sized, parade across as dwarfs, the rich, also proportionately sized, as monstrously tall giants.

Statisticians can reduce this dramatic Pen parade imagery to paper by charting what they call "cumulative frequency functions."[10] But we can create the same effect, more simply, by imagining all our society's income-earners lined up as marchers on a wide sheet of graph paper, the poorest and shortest to the left, the richest and tallest to the right. If we were to mark a dot above each marcher's head, then connect our dots, we would have a chart that tells the same story as a set of cumulative frequency figures.

Our chart, by connecting the dots from the short and poor on the left to the tall and rich on the right, would, of course, display a line that slopes upward. But here's the fascinating part. This line will always slope upwards at the same angle, no matter what existing society we choose to chart. Societies, in effect, all parade alike.

Up to a point, that is. In all societies, our parade chart line would slope gently upwards — until nearing the parade's richer end. At that point, the line would no longer maintain anything close to "a steady and gentle gradation."[11] The slope, at the rich end, would suddenly steepen. What had been a line gently sloping up would suddenly "kink" up dramatically.[12] This kink can vary, in the angle of incline, from society to society. But in all societies this sudden kink upwards amounts to a striking departure from the gentle slope that tracks the incomes of everyone except the very rich.

Below the kink, no income gaps of any consequence separate people at different income levels. People at the twentieth percentile level of income — that is, people who make more than 19 percent of a society's income-earners but less than the rest — always earn just slightly more than people at the nineteenth level, people at the fiftieth percentile level just slightly more than people at the forty-ninth. Everyone below the kink, notes Henry Phelps Brown, "rubs elbows with others who are a little better or worse off than he or she is."[13] Income gaps, Brown notes, do start to widen a bit at the eighty-fifth percentile, as incomes start reflecting not just wages and salaries from work, but return from property — dividends, interest, rents, profits from a business. But the gaps do not become terribly significant, do not widen precipitously, until much higher up the income distribution, at the ninety-seventh percentile. In the United States, Herbert Inhaber and Sidney Carroll have found, people at the ninety-seventh percentile level don't just make slightly more than people at the ninety-sixth percentile, they make enormously more.[14] Above the ninety-seventh percentile, these scholars show clearly, "the concentration of income rises at an exceedingly fast pace."[15]

Modern societies have, in effect, "two patterns of income distribution."[16] The first covers just about everybody, the second only the rich. If the first pattern covered everyone, if incomes above the ninety-seventh percentile only increased at the same gradual pace as incomes below, the rich would collect far less income than they actually do, particularly in the world's most unequal rich nation, the United States. The difference between what wealthy Americans would receive in income, if the first pattern of income distribution applied to everyone, and what they actually do receive constitutes what Inhaber and Carroll define as "too much," what we might call an "artificial escalation."[17]

A wise society, these two scholars suggest, would not tolerate this "too much." Nor would a wise society tolerate "too little" at the other end of the income scale. A wise, decent society would accept only that range of income inequality that seems to unfold, naturally in all societies, between too little and too much. And how wide is this "natural" range of inequality? Inhaber and Carroll offer some clues. In their 1992 book, *How Rich Is Too Rich?*, these two researchers focus their calculations on the 1987 tax year in the United States. The 1987 "too much" kink, they found, began at about the $112,000 income level. In that same year, the official poverty rate, for a family of four, stood at $11,611. The gap that year between the official federal figure for "too little" income and the Inhaber-Carroll estimate for "too much"? About ten to one.

That same ten-to-one ratio jumps out from the Pen parade analyses of Henry Phelps Brown. Indeed, before inequality in the United States started exploding in the 1980s, this same ten times ratio defined income distribution patterns in nearly every major American workplace, as Yale law professor Boris Bittker pointed out in 1977. Noted Bittker: "In virtually all institutions of our society — the universities with which we are especially familiar, the federal civil service, and business organizations save at the very top — the salary scale from bottom to top is confined to a ratio of 1 to 10 or thereabouts."[18]

In the ancient world, interestingly, philosophers defined a much narrower ratio as natural and appropriate. Plato pronounced the ideal ratio between the wealth of the richest and the wealth of the poorest to be four to one. Aristotle deemed the ideal ratio five to one.[19] But let's assume, for the moment, that a ten times ratio fits our modern world more appropriately. Could we ever apply a "Ten Times Rule," efficiently and simply, to incomes in a complex modern economy? Most certainly — if we keyed our Ten Times Rule to an already existing and widely accepted given of modern American economic life, the minimum wage. Ten times this minimum, if we took this approach, would become our maximum. All income above this maximum would then be subjected to federal income tax at a 100 percent rate. No American would have, after paying federal income tax, more than ten times the annual income of a minimum wage worker.

What about people earning incomes *below* the maximum but *above* the minimum?

A Ten Times Rule society could easily key *all* tax rates to the minimum wage, not just the tax rate applied to the wealthiest incomes. A maximum tied to a minimum, we have noted, would give rich people a vested interest in improving the well-being of poor people. Creating tax tables that linked all tax rates to the minimum wage would give everyone else in society that same vested interest.

In such a Ten Times Rule America, if you earned exactly ten times the minimum, you would pay 10 percent of your income in taxes. If you earned five times the minimum, you would pay a 5 percent tax. And if you made exactly the minimum wage, you would pay 1 percent of your income in taxes. The ultimate in tax simplicity. And also the ultimate in reciprocity. If you earned five times the minimum wage, you would do better personally — your tax rate would go *down* — if the minimum wage went *up*.

Do the math. Suppose the federal minimum wage stood at $6 an hour. Over a year's time, a minimum wage worker working full-time would earn $12,480. Let's round that off to $12,500, to keep our calculations simple. A couple working at minimum wage jobs would make twice $12,500, or $25,000 a year. Our "maximum" income would then be $250,000 for a couple filing jointly. A couple making half that, or five times the minimum wage, would be earning $125,000 a year. This couple would pay 5 percent of that $125,000 in federal income tax if the Ten Times Rule were the law of the land.

Now suppose a year passes. Congress raises the minimum wage, to just over $7 an hour. A minimum wage couple would then be earning $30,000 a year, and the 5 percent tax rate would, at this point, only apply to annual incomes five times the *new* minimum wage. That five times point would start at $150,000.

What would this mean for our couple that made $125,000 the previous year? That couple could see its income *increase* and its tax rate *decrease* all at the same time. If, for instance, the couple registered a 10 percent pay increase in the new year, bringing its income to $137,500, the tax rate applicable to that income would be just 4 percent, since the couple would no longer be making five times the minimum. Thanks to a higher minimum, this family would be paying taxes at a lower rate, despite a higher income.

In a Ten Times Rule America, all families would have reason to cheer higher minimum wages. For the poorest, a higher minimum would mean more income. For middle class people, a lower tax rate. For the rich, a higher permissible income. The better poor people would do, the better middle class people would do. The better the poor would do, the better the rich would do. Trickle down in reverse.

CAN WE ACTUALLY BE SERIOUS ABOUT setting a limit on annual income? Wouldn't an income limit be against the Constitution or something? Don't we live in a "free" country? Wouldn't a limit on our individual incomes amount to an attack on our individual freedoms?

Actually, in our modern world, no "free" people live without limits, not even in the United States. On our interstate highways, for instance, we enforce limits right and left. We limit who can use an interstate. No bicycles allowed. We limit how fast people can drive. We even limit the size of the signs that merchants can set aside the road. These limits all curb the "freedom" of individuals to engage in perfectly legitimate activities — to ride bikes, to accelerate cars, to advertise wares. But we accept these limits. Unlimited individual "freedom," we understand, can undermine our overall well-being.

Over recent decades, in our economy, we have operated on a contrary assumption. We have assumed, in economic matters, that all will turn out perfectly well if all of us just follow our own individual self-interest. Within our economy, consequently, we have relaxed limits on what individuals can do. We have reduced taxes on high incomes to encourage rich people to accumulate as much as they possibly can. A society where people are vigorously pursuing their own individual self-interests, our leaders preach, will ultimately evolve into a good and noble place. Greed, we assume, creates good.

But in real life, as opposed to market theory, greed — the single-minded pursuit of individual self-interest — creates more social chaos than social good. Behavior that may seem smart for an individual can prove incredibly dumb for society, or any social grouping, as economist Robert Frank has vividly noted.

"The individual who stands up at a concert achieves a better view, until everyone else stands," he points out, "then no one can see very well, and everyone pays the price of tired legs. Those who can't hear at a cocktail party raise their voices; soon all ears are ringing and everyone is hoarse."[20]

The unbridled pursuit of individual self-interest, thoughtful societies acknowledge, will always perversely impact community well-being. To protect this well-being, wise societies set limits. In our everyday lives, we take these limits, on everything from highways to hunting, for granted. We do not feel "less free" with these everyday limits in place. Would we somehow feel "less free" if *incomes* were limited?

Certain Americans, interestingly, already face income limits of sorts. In the United States, poor people confront income limits all the time. Medicaid recipients, for instance, are only allowed to earn so much. If they earn "too much," they lose their health insurance coverage and end up worse off. We also impose limits on certain incomes that sit further up the income distribution. Under IRS rules, for instance, nonprofits that compensate their executives at "excessive" levels can face stiff penalties.[21] The IRS even watches out for "excessive compensation" in the private sector. The owners of a small company, for instance, cannot pay themselves exorbitant salaries as a scheme to avoid paying out dividends to their fellow shareholders.[22]

Of late, some public officials have even dared set income limits at the summit of corporate America. Midway through 2002, in a highly unusual move, the Securities and Exchange Commission asked the federal judge overseeing the WorldCom bankruptcy to limit executive pay at the company. U.S. District Judge Jed Rakoff went along with that request. He directed an independent monitor to prevent WorldCom executives from raking in "unjust enrichment"— and barred WorldCom from paying any executive more than $100,000 until the monitor was able to set up operations.[23]

All these "limits," to be sure, have remained largely invisible in American society at large. But one facet of American life does boast limits on income that have become familiar to tens of millions of Americans. Those tens of millions are America's sports fans. The professional football and basketball players these fans avidly follow all labor in a marketplace that has set rigid limits on incomes.[24]

These limits on pro athlete incomes enjoy the full support of football and basketball team owners. These incredibly rich men battled long and hard to impose salary caps on their players. They did not consider that battle an offensive against "freedom." They were merely trying, they explained, to save their sports from the chaos of compensation that had spun out of control. Sports would be more enjoyable for everyone, the owners argued, if owners and players operated in a marketplace where incomes were capped. Sports fans today accept this case for caps. For the sake of the game, most fans see absolutely nothing wrong with limiting player pay. Income limits in sports have become the American way.

Some nationally syndicated commentators would like to see this new American way extended into other areas of American life. Economist Robert Samuelson, for instance, feels America would be better off if we placed a cap on attorneys' fees. Lawyers, the conservative Samuelson argues, have come to care more about making fortunes than justice. "Every trial lawyer now dreams of a pot of gold," he asserts. To mine that goal, attorneys search high and low "to discover some 'deep pocket' from which immense damages — and legal fees — can be extracted."[25] The lawsuits these attorneys are filing, Samuelson charges, are squeezing billions of dollars out of law-abiding corporations, disrupting, in the process, the normal ebb and flow of commerce.

"The best way to stop the spread of self-enriching suits," he concludes, "is to remove the pot of gold or, at least, reduce it to a small pile."

Samuelson's solution?

"Let's put a cap on lawyers' pay," he impishly suggests. "If you're an attorney, you can make $1 million a year from lawyering or, perhaps, $2 million. Above that, the tax rate is 100 percent."

A $1 million or $2 million ceiling, says Samuelson, "would be high enough to attract bright, hard-working and even greedy people into the law." At the same time, that ceiling would be low enough to "curb predatory lawyering, which uses the law to amass personal fortunes of hundreds of millions of dollars."

How can Samuelson, a champion of free markets, justify *not* leaving attorney compensation to whatever the market will bear? The compensation lawyers receive, he explains, must "rightly yield to a larger public interest."

"The court system is not a proper arena for capitalist ambition," he notes. "Its integrity should not be mortgaged to the quest for personal riches."

Besides, adds Samuelson, only a relatively few people would be affected by a $1 million cap on attorney pay. If a $1 million cap were in place, lawyers "could still sue wayward companies and could still ask for huge awards for deserving victims." Only one thing would change: "Lawyers simply couldn't collect as much for themselves. They could become rich but not stupendously wealthy. There would be ample incentive for justice — and less for plunder."

Samuelson's case for limiting attorney pay makes some powerful points. And almost all these points could be applied, just as compellingly, to the business sectors that Samuelson so desperately wants to protect from greedy lawyers.

Is the health system, after all, a "proper arena for capitalist ambition"? The judicial system is supposed to do justice. The health system, America's biggest industry, is supposed to keep people well. Isn't there a "larger public interest" in keeping people well? Should the executives of America's HMOs and for-profit hospital chains and pharmaceutical companies be allowed to amass huge fortunes, as they do, by taking advantage of sick and vulnerable Americans? In health as in law, wouldn't there be more "incentive" to provide quality care — and less incentive "for plunder" — if the kingpins of America's health care corporations could only make so much and no more?

And don't Samuelson's arguments for income limits apply equally well to the communications industry? After all, don't we have a "larger public interest" in making sure Americans receive the news and information they need to govern themselves effectively in a democracy? And what about the transportation industry? Don't we have a "larger public interest" in making sure people can move safely from place to place?

Don't we, in fact, have a "larger public interest" in all industries? Doesn't every industry, at some level, exist to meet the needs of real individuals? Don't we, as a society, have an interest in making sure that these real needs, and not possibilities for plunder, remain uppermost in the minds of all industry executives? And if we do have this "public interest" in discouraging plunder everywhere in our economy, how can we justify subjecting only some people to income limits, be they athletes or attorneys?

SALARY LIMITS ON PROFESSIONAL ATHLETES, and professional athletes alone, may not be particularly fair, but they have become a fixture on the sports scene, as routine as layups. Modern-day sports fans see salary caps as good for the games they love. Could sports fans — and everybody else in America — someday come to see income limits on all high incomes as equally routine and necessary?

That could happen, but only if a broad American public first came to see grand concentrations of income and wealth as not a good to be encouraged but a danger to be avoided. The amassing of unlimited fortune, notes physicist Alan Cottey, would have to become "socially unacceptable, in much the same way that having an unlimited number of spouses is socially unacceptable."[26]

Naturally, if the idea of a "Ten Times Rule" ever began to capture public attention, many of our society's most wealthy would do whatever they could to make sure the rest of us considered limits on income — and not unlimited wealth — "socially unacceptable." The wealthy and their hired help would immediately and incessantly raise exactly three basic objections to the prospect of a "Ten Times America."

How can we be so sure? The eminently comfortable, whenever they face a challenge to their comfort, *always* raise three basic objections. So notes economist Albert Hirschman, a veteran analyst of the word games powerful people play. Apologists for an unjust status quo, Hirschman points out, invariably trot out three dire alarms the moment any serious proposal for social change surfaces.[27]

Bold attempts to transform society, influentials will first argue, are futile. These bold moves never really "alter the natural order of things." Second, influentials continue, those who persist in these futile exercises will come to see their handiwork "actually backfire and have the opposite of their intended effect." Third, influentials assert, campaigns to change society radically endanger the progress we have already achieved. Hirschman labels these "three staple claims of reactionary rhetoric" the *futility, perversity,* and *jeopardy* theses. Down through the ages, friends of fortune have regularly invoked variations on these themes to denounce any proposals that smack of "leveling down." Attempts at redistribution, they have argued repeatedly, amount to futile gestures that will, if pursued, only leave the poor poorer and civilization in shambles.

Apologists for greed particularly enjoy invoking the first of Hirschman's three theses, the futility thesis. Efforts to redistribute wealth, to help the poor by taking from the rich, make no sense, influentials for injustice relish arguing, because the wealthy simply don't own large enough fortunes. Billionaire oilman J. Paul Getty, the story goes, once received a letter that asked him to make the world a better place by sharing his wealth with every man, woman, and child on Earth. Old J. Paul sent back a check for 30 cents.

"Here's your share," read his cover letter.[28]

In 1997, one of America's most admired business leaders, Charles S. Sanford, Jr., made the same point, a bit less smugly, in an address to future business leaders. Sanford, the retired CEO of Bankers Trust, acknowledged the depth of America's unmet needs, then shifted to an offensive against leveling down.

"Could these immense social needs be satisfied by redistribution of existing or even foreseeable wealth?" he asked. "The answer is no. To totally redistribute all that we have now would simply result in poverty for all."[29]

That's not quite true. In fact, that's not true at all. By the mid 1990s, wealth in the United States had become so concentrated that a serious bit of redistribution could have actually made quite a sizable dent on poverty. Indeed, by the mid 1990s, a bit of redistribution could have eliminated poverty, as political scientist Andrew Hacker revealed in a book published the same year Charles Sanford dismissed redistribution as an exercise in futility. Hacker performed a series of calculations on income figures from 1994, then the most current year with data available.[30] In 1994, 1.1 million households in the United States made over $200,000, more money than the President of the United States. These 1.1 million households averaged, *after* taxes, $340,000 each.

Suppose, Hacker asked, people in 1994 had paid their normal taxes. Then suppose that the incomes remaining had been capped at $200,000, with all the dollars above that amount handed to the IRS and applied to redistribution. How much of a difference could those special redistribution dollars have made? Quite a difference. If incomes in 1994 had been capped in this fashion, the IRS would have collected, above and beyond normal tax collections, enough money to *double* the average income of America's poorest 19.8 million households, the households that then constituted the bottom fifth of America's income distribution. With this doubling, these households would have escaped poverty. Their average incomes would have jumped from $7,760 per household to $15,530.

In 1994, before taxes, households making over $200,000 averaged sixty-one times more income than households in the bottom 20 percent averaged. If Hacker's redistribution exercise had actually been conducted, that gap from top to bottom would have shrunk dramatically, down to thirteen to one.

Andrew Hacker did not have a Ten Times Rule in mind when he conducted his income-capping thought experiment. But what if we updated his exercise, on incomes from a more recent year, and keyed our calculations to the notion that no American, after paying taxes, should earn more than ten times any other? How significant an impact would Ten Times tax rates make on America?

We'll use as our reference year 2003.[31] Over the course of this year, a full-time worker making the federal minimum wage — $5.15 an hour — earned $10,712. A couple, with each spouse earning the minimum wage, would have earned twice that, or $21,424. If the Ten Times Rule had been in effect in 2003, our "maximum wage" for the year would have been ten times this annual minimum, or $214,240, for a couple filing jointly.

In 2003, America's richest 1 percent took home a great deal more than $214,240. These top income-earners averaged $1,082,000 for the year. If the Ten Times Rule had been the law of the land in 2003, households in this richest 1 percent would have paid a 10 percent tax on their first $214,240 of income and a 100 percent tax on all income above that $214,240.[32] The total federal tax due: $889,184, an amount that would have equaled 82 percent of the total income of the average top 1 percent household.

America's next richest 4 percent of households, in 2003, averaged $217,000 for the year, just a hair more than the $214,240 that would have been the 2003 maximum income. In a Ten Times Rule America, the average household in the next richest 4 percent would have paid $24,184 in federal income tax, a sum that would have equaled 10 percent of $214,240 and 100 percent of the tiny excess over that. These households would have paid 11 percent of their total incomes in federal income tax.

In 2003, the next most affluent 15 percent of America's households averaged $103,000, not quite five times the minimum wage for couples. These taxpayers would have, consequently, paid only 4 percent of their incomes, or

$4,120, in federal income tax under the Ten Times Rule. Down a rung, in the second most affluent 20 percent of Americans, households averaged $59,800 in 2003, a bit more than twice the annual minimum wage for couples. These households would have paid 2 percent of their incomes in federal income tax, or $1,196, in a Ten Times Rule America.

Our next 20 percent of Americans — the statistical "middle class" — averaged $36,600 per household in 2003, less than twice the annual income for a minimum wage couple. Middle-bracket taxpayers, under the Ten Times Rule, would have paid federal income taxes at just a 1 percent rate in 2003. They would have owed $366 in income tax.

The 20 percent of Americans below this middle fifth averaged $22,000 in 2003. They also would have been subject to just a 1 percent federal income tax in 2003. Their total Ten Times Rule tax bill would have come to $220.

Finally, households in America's poorest 20 percent averaged only $9,900 in income in 2003. Average households in this group made less, over the year, than the annual income of a full-time minimum wage worker. Under the Ten Times Rule, they would have owed no federal income tax at all.

Let's step back a moment. Let's compare these Ten Times Rule tax bills with the actual taxes due, in 2003, from Americans in these same income categories. An interesting pattern emerges. If the Ten Times Rule had been in effect in 2003, all households in the United States would have paid fewer dollars in federal income taxes than they actually did — all except the households in the richest 1 percent.

The tax savings for most households, under the Ten Times Rule, would have been substantial. Households at the exact middle of America's income distribution would have paid, in a Ten Times Rule America, 1 percent of their income in federal income taxes. They actually paid taxes in 2003, *after* the year's Bush administration tax cut, at a rate over three times as high, 3.6 percent.[33]

In a Ten Times Rule America, even affluent households just below America's economic summit would have seen a tax break in 2003. Households in America's ninety-sixth through ninety-ninth richest percentiles would have paid 11 percent of their average $217,000 incomes in Ten Times Rule income tax. These households actually paid federal income taxes in 2003 at a 16.9 percent rate.

In other words, if the Ten Times Rule had been in effect in 2003, average families would have seen their federal income taxes cut by almost three-quarters and families making around $200,000 would have seen their taxes cut by over a third.

Must be a catch, right? Wouldn't the federal government simply have gone broke if the Ten Times Rule had been effect in 2003? You couldn't cut taxes for 99 percent of Americans, increase them for just 1 percent, and expect the government to do everything it did before, could you? Actually, you could. If the Ten Times Rule had been applied to American incomes in 2003, the *increase* in revenues the government would have collected from the richest 1 percent of

Americans would have offset, and then some, the *decrease* in revenues from the bottom 99 percent of America's taxpayers.

In 2003, if all income over the $214,240 Ten Times annual maximum had been subject to a 100 percent tax, the richest 1 percent of Americans would have paid $1,200 billion in federal income taxes.[34] The rest of American taxpayers, under the Ten Times Rule, would have paid a bit over a fifth of that, bringing total Ten Times Rule federal income tax revenues to $1,463 billion.

For 2003, under our existing individual income tax rates, the federal government will actually end up collecting about $1,006 billion in revenues, *over $450 billion less* than the government would have collected had the Ten Times Rule been in effect.[35]

In budget terms, how significant could this added $450 billion have been? Consider this: In 2003, the entire federal budget, outside of spending for the military, Social Security, and Medicare, only amounted to $388.7 billion.[36] Adding $450 billion to the federal budget in 2003 would have more than doubled the federal government's capacity to provide services to the American people.

And what could the federal government have done with all this new budget capacity? Those additional hundreds of billions could have guaranteed all working parents safe, quality, low-cost child care. Those billions, shared with local governments, could have rehabilitated old housing stock and expanded the availability of affordable places to live. Those billions could have funded afterschool programs that keep teenagers out of trouble. Or lowered the cost of bus fares. Or placed reading aides in every first grade classroom. Or halved tuitions at America's public universities. Or bankrolled health insurance for every American family. In fact, with nearly a half trillion new dollars, our nation would have had the resources to do, in some variation, all of the above. In 2003, if the Ten Times Rule had been in effect, we could have begun renewing the American dream.

IN A TEN TIMES RULE AMERICA, on paper at least, we could raise enough new revenue to make an incredible difference in the lives of every working family. But what about the real world, not the paper version? In real life, would the Ten Times Rule actually raise the revenue our calculations suggest? That would depend — on America's rich people.

The Ten Times Rule would only be able to renew America if the IRS successfully collected hundreds of billions of new tax dollars out of the incomes of America's richest 1 percent. And the IRS, in turn, would only be able to collect those hundreds of billions if America's rich continued earning annual incomes far above the Ten Times maximum. But why, if the Ten Times Rule ever became law, would rich Americans bother earning money above the Ten Times maximum? Why would they work to earn income that would be completely taxed away? What sense would that make?

Friends of fortune would immediately, and gleefully, raise questions like these if the Ten Times Rule were ever to become a matter of serious public debate. If the wealthy behaved rationally and stopped working once they hit the maximum income threshold, the skeptics would note, the IRS would have no "excess" income to tax. Tax collections overall would not rise. They would sink. New government programs would be out of the question. With a Ten Times Rule in effect, friends of fortune would insist, the government wouldn't even be able to afford old programs!

In other words, the classic perversity thesis: A cap on our highest incomes wouldn't raise government revenues. A cap would lower them. Slicing the economic pie to give rich people smaller pieces would merely guarantee smaller pieces for everyone!

In the 1990s, apologists for inequality invoked this perversity thesis whenever they felt a need to swat away talk about capping incomes. In 1998, for instance, *Barron's*, a business journal, cast a skeptical eye at Andrew Hacker's what-if experiment with a $200,000 income cap. A 100 percent tax on all income over $200,000, *Barron's* commentator Gene Epstein pronounced, would never raise much revenue. A cap on income over $200,000 would instead "impose crippling disincentives on risk-taking and work effort" — and "soon diminish the size of the pie the redistributionists so enjoy slicing."[37]

"Why struggle to become the CEO," Epstein added, "when you won't be compensated for taking on his headaches?"[38]

Income caps, agreed conservative columnist George Will a year later, will always perversely impact the public purse. Consider the likely outcome, Will asked in a 1999 column, if incomes above $1 million were subject to a 100 percent tax.

"No one would earn the one-millionth dollar, thereby triggering the confiscation," Will predicted, "so the revenue yield from the 100 percent rate on millionaires would be zero."[39]

Zero? George Will's "zero" prediction would certainly be right on the mark if rich people, like average people, actually *worked* for their income. No rational person is ever going to labor for dollars that will all be funneled to a tax collector. But America's highest incomes don't come from labor, from work, from sweat, from personal effort. America's highest incomes come, overwhelmingly, from the ownership of property.

Wealthy Americans, unlike average Americans, owe most of their incomes to their fortunes. Wealthy people don't have to punch time clocks or fill out timesheets to earn a living. They can live quite luxuriously without ever having to move a muscle, "except, perhaps," as Robert Reich quips, "to speed-dial their brokers."[40]

Indeed, in America today, the higher your income, the less you rely on actual "work" to make ends meet. In 2000, for instance, Americans making between $200,000 and $500,000 received 58 percent of their incomes from wages and salaries. Americans who made $1 million or more that same year received just a third of their incomes, 33 percent, from wages and salaries. Most of their income came from other sources — everything from dividends and interest to capital gains and business profits. Taxpayers who reported at least $10 million in 2000 received even less of their incomes from paychecks, just 25 percent.[41] And the very richest Americans? In 2000, wages and salaries accounted for only 16.7 percent of the income of America's 400 richest taxpayers.[42]

What do these figures mean for our Ten Times Rule? A great deal. Income from labor can be turned off, like water out of a spigot. Income from wealth never stops flowing. In a Ten Times Rule America, wealthy people angry about paying taxes at a 100 percent rate could certainly choose to stop working. But they could not stop their wealth from working. That wealth would continue to generate income. And that income, above the Ten Times maximum, would be taxed 100 percent.

OVER RECENT YEARS, MORE SOPHISTICATED PURVEYORS of the perversity thesis have given the classic arguments against high taxes on high incomes a new twist. These more sophisticated apologists for inequality do not prattle on about wealthy people losing their incentive to work.[43] High taxes on high incomes, this new perversity school argues, will always fail to raise revenue for a different reason. Wealthy people taxed at high levels, the argument goes, merely maneuver to take their income in less taxable forms, as nontaxed perks, for instance. These maneuvers reduce the total amount of income a government can tax. The government, as a result, collects fewer overall tax dollars.

As proof, these new perversity theorists point to the 1993 federal legislation that raised the top individual income tax rate from 31 to 39.6 percent. Despite a growing economy, they note, taxpayers in America's top income brackets reported less taxable income in 1993, after the increase, than they had reported in 1992.[44] The conclusion: The rich, in the face of higher tax rates, will rearrange their personal finances to deny tax collectors the increased revenues they expect to receive from higher tax rates on high incomes.

But the data from 1992 and 1993, University of Chicago economist Austan Goolsbee later demonstrated, prove nothing of the sort. Upper bracket taxable income, Goolsbee's work would show, did drop off dramatically in 1993, but largely because corporate executives, at the end of 1992, had rushed to cash out stock option windfalls before the newly elected Clinton administration could take office and raise tax rates.[45] Taxable income did not disappear. Instead, this income merely showed up in a different year.

Hiking tax rates on the wealthy, Goolsbee would go on to note, "can lead to dramatic shifting of taxable income in the years immediately surrounding a tax change," and that shifting may allow many wealthy people "to avoid taxation for a short period of time." But, over a longer span, taxable income totals don't change much. The taxable incomes of the rich, Goolsbee concluded after analyzing upper-bracket incomes throughout the twentieth century, do not increase when tax rates become less progressive and do not diminish when tax rates become more progressive.

Would that same finding hold true if America's wealthy faced, at tax time, a tax as drastic as a 100 percent levy on all income above a Ten Times maximum? Or would the wealthy feel impelled, in the face of a tax this drastic, to take drastic action of their own, action that might indeed significantly diminish America's sum total of taxable income? Might rich people simply flee a Ten Times Rule America — and take their fortunes with them?

Wealthy people have, to be sure, threatened to flee America in the past. Over a century ago, in the 1894 debate over whether America needed an income tax, high society doyen Ward McAllister made that threat explicit. If members of Congress levied a 2 percent income tax, he declared, they would drive "rich men to go abroad and live."[46]

The wealthy today still play McAllister's exit card. In fact, suggests British philosopher Alex Callinicos, the exit threats of the rich have come to dominate our global political and economic life. We live, he notes, "in the shadow of the blackmail of capital."[47]

"A small group of corporate rich," Callinicos explains, "move their money from country to country in the search of the highest return. They are able, with a large degree of success, to demand that public policy is tailored to suit their needs."

If their demands are not met, if they are subjected to taxes they deem too high or any other inconvenience, these wealthy power brokers threaten to invest their dollars elsewhere. Don't let that happen, they urge governments. If we and our dollars exit, they predict, your poor will lose jobs and opportunity. This "prediction," notes Callinicos, amounts morally to extortion. Corporate leaders who predict the pain they have the power to inflict, he points out, occupy the same moral plane as the "kidnapper who predicts that the child he has taken will suffer unless his parents come up with the ransom money."

In a Ten Times Rule America, or an America about to enact a Ten Times Rule, would the wealthy resort to this sort of extortion? Would they threaten to leave? And would they actually make good on that threat? Would they exit the United States en masse, fortunes in hand, if America's lawmakers ever enacted any measure that resembled the Ten Times Rule? Almost certainly not. In a Ten Times Rule America, a mass exodus of the wealthy would be about as unlikely as a mad rush by CEOs to take jobs in mailrooms.

WE LIVE IN A WORLD WHERE FEW RICH PEOPLE keep their fortunes under mattresses. In the United States, as elsewhere around the globe, wealthy people have their fortunes invested in marketable assets, everything from stocks and bonds to real estate. America's wealthy hold staggeringly enormous quantities of these assets, several trillions of dollars worth.

The passage of a Ten Times Rule — a tax on *income*, not wealth — would actually leave all these assets completely untouched. A Dallas real estate magnate who owned ten square blocks worth of downtown Dallas on the day a Ten Times Rule first became law would still own those same ten square blocks one year later — unless, of course, that Dallas real estate magnate had decided, in the meantime, to get out of the Dallas real estate business. Would our office building king, in a Ten Times Rule America, make that decision? To avoid paying Ten Times tax, would he pull up stakes and relocate himself and his fortune somewhere else?

Exiting Dallas whole hog might strike our real estate tycoon, at first blush, as an eminently sensible option. If he stayed put in Dallas, all those millions in rents he had been making, all his income above ten times the minimum wage, would be taxed away. And that income would be taxed away even if he moved his personal home address to another country. Governments tax income where income is earned. Our magnate, if he wanted to hold on to his Dallas office buildings, would have to pay a Ten Times tax on the income from them, even if he went off to live in a country without a Ten Times Rule.

So our Dallas deep pocket wistfully concludes he has no choice. He starts making plans to pull out of town entirely. He will sell his office buildings, pocket the profits, and reinvest his fortune in some convivial, less taxing nation. That won't be so bad, he tells himself. He can always watch his beloved Cowboys on satellite TV.

Hold on a minute. Our magnate suddenly realizes that leaving might not be such a good idea after all. If he sells his buildings, his profits from that sale, his capital gains, would count as income and be subject to the Ten Times tax. Those millions in profits he planned to invest abroad would almost all be taxed away. He might as well stay put in Dallas.

But hold on just another minute. If our real estate magnate had done some thinking in advance, couldn't he have avoided the Ten Times tax on his capital gains — by unloading his assets as soon as he realized that a Ten Times Rule was about to be enacted? If he went that route, if he sold his buildings before the Ten Times Rule actually went into effect, he would have paid taxes on his capital gains at pre-Ten Times Rule tax rates. Our magnate then could have left the United States with suitcases stuffed with cash, invested his bundle overseas, and lived happily ever after.

Nice try. But that dog won't hunt either. In an America about to implement a Ten Times Rule, all wealthy people, not just our clever Dallas office king, would be thinking about selling off their assets to avoid Ten Times taxes. But if all these wealthy went ahead and tried to cash out, or even if just a good many of them went ahead, the marketplace would be awash with the assets of the wealthy — office buildings, shares of stock, mansions, fancy cars, whatever. A marketplace awash with these assets would be a buyer's market, and in that buyer's market the assets of the wealthy would plummet in value. America would see a veritable fire sale on grand fortunes. Wealthy refugees from a Ten Times Rule America, after selling off their assets at fire-sale prices, would have to start their new lives on foreign soil with only a fraction of their former net worth.

And these wealthy refugees would face, in their new homes, one inevitable final insult. They would have escaped the Ten Times Rule. But they would not have escaped high taxes on high incomes. The nations where Americans fleeing the Ten Times Rule would most likely want to relocate — nations where they could invest their pared-down fortunes safely and securely — would be the nations least likely to give wealthy Americans a significant tax break. The safest and most stable havens for investment, outside the United States, have been and will be, for years to come, the developed nations of Western Europe and Japan. All these nations have, over the last quarter century, levied higher taxes on the wealthy than the United States. These higher taxes did, to be sure, drop some in the late 1990s, but only because, in a globalized economy, European and Japanese lawmakers could not maintain high taxes on high incomes at the same time the world's greatest economic power, the United States, was taxing the wealthy at rock-bottom rates.

If the United States were to change course and adopt a Ten Times Rule, Western Europe and Japan would no longer feel pressured to lower taxes on their own wealthy. Their tax rates on high incomes would likely rise, at least back to their previous levels. Wealthy refugees from a Ten Times Rule America would face, in Europe and Japan, tax rates considerably stiffer than the rates they once enjoyed back in the United States.

Some nations, of course, *would* lay out a low-tax welcome mat for refugees from a Ten Times Rule America. But these would be the nations where wealthy Americans would be least likely to want to settle and invest. These would be economically and politically unstable nations, with little to make themselves attractive outside puny tax rates on wealthy people's incomes. More stable nations would see no need to lower tax rates to attract wealthy Americans, not in a world where the United States had enacted a Ten Times Rule.

All this would no doubt eventually become clear to our Dallas real estate magnate, clever man that he is. In a Ten Times Rule America, Dallas would remain his home. No other choice would make sense. If he moved overseas, but left his assets back in Dallas, the income from those assets would still be taxed at Ten Times rates. If he sold his assets, he would pay Ten Times rates on his capital gains — and then have to pay lots of taxes on his new real estate empire in downtown Düsseldorf. And if he tried to outsmart the Ten Times Rule, by selling off his assets before Ten Times taxes went into effect, he would take a bath on the sale. But if our magnate stayed put in the Big D, he'd be making as much money as anybody else in town. And he'd still have his Cowboys.

This Ten Times Rule America, our clever magnate might just conclude, may not be such a bad place after all.

ALL AMERICA'S WEALTHY PEOPLE might not prove as reasonable as our Dallas real estate magnate should the Ten Times Rule ever become the law of the land. Some might even try to dupe the IRS. In fact, many might try to dupe the IRS, especially at first.

How many would succeed? Those wealthy tax avoiders who tried garden-variety tax fraud — padding executive expense accounts, for instance — would likely soon see the error of their ways. In a Ten Times Rule America, the IRS would be able to concentrate enforcement resources almost entirely on wealthy people. In a Ten Times America, these would be the only people with tax liabilities large enough to risk cheating to avoid.

Most families, in a Ten Times America, would be paying only 1 or 2 percent of their incomes in federal income taxes. Even more affluent families, those earning $200,000 a year, would be paying taxes at rates far below what they currently pay. Few of these families would see Ten Times tax rates as unfair abominations that deserve to be flouted. Most Americans, in this environment, would honestly pay their taxes. IRS tax fraud investigators would be free to devote their attention almost totally to taxpayers at the top.

Still, even with this focus, IRS investigators would not have an easy time of it. In our wired world economy, with currency constantly flowing in and out of countries as bits and bytes, IRS agents would face a bewildering array of subtle subterfuges. These maneuvers would pose a significant danger to a Ten Times Rule America, a danger historically known as "capital flight," the shady transfer of financial assets out of a country to avoid taxes, instability, or any other unpleasantness that might spook people with appreciable asset holdings.

"Capital flight" typically afflicts deeply troubled and deeply unequal economies. Russia, for instance, saw enormous capital flight in the 1990s, as suddenly wealthy entrepreneurs schemed to conceal their new fortunes. Various nations have, at times, tried to crack down on capital flight. Some have placed controls on short-term transfers of financial assets. Others have limited foreign currency purchases. But such measures, no matter how carefully drawn, seldom completely eliminate capital flight.[48]

A Ten Times Rule America, given these realities, would be foolish to expect too much from capital flight controls. Some wealthy income *would* escape the IRS. Some wealthy people *would* be able to cheat the Ten Times Rule. If that *some* became *many*, of course, the Ten Times Rule would collapse.

Would that some become too many?

If wealthy people want to avoid taxes *intensely* enough, history warns us, they will ultimately find a way. They will commit fraud. They will carve loopholes into the tax laws they detest. They will pound on politicians until they undo the laws that impose high rates on high incomes. No democracy on earth, over the long haul, has ever been able to buck this sort of pressure. No democracy has ever been able to maintain, generation after generation, tax rates progressive enough to keep income equitably distributed, tax rates effective enough to prevent dangerous concentrations of wealth and power.

So why should we expect things to be any different in a Ten Times Rule America? For one reason and one reason alone: The Ten Times Rule would add a new incentive into the political mix, an incentive that would give high-income people a reason to work *within* a progressive tax system, not just *against* it. In a Ten Times Rule America, society's most affluent wouldn't have to carve loopholes, pound on politicians, or sneak their wealth overseas to enhance their own personal financial well-being. In a Ten Times Rule America, society's most fortunate would always be able to enhance their own well-being simply by enhancing the well-being of society's least fortunate.

The numbers tell the story. Under the Ten Times Rule, every $1 of increase in the hourly minimum wage would immediately translate into an extra $41,600 a year into the pockets of America's most affluent.[49] In a Ten Times Rule America, wealthy people would have a powerful incentive to do good, not just well.

And how much good would they do? How high would the minimum wage climb in a Ten Times Rule America? We cannot say for sure. We do know that millions of affluent families would have ample reason to keep the minimum wage rising. At $7 an hour, a minimum wage would generate a $291,200 maximum for a couple filing jointly. An $8 minimum would generate a $332,800 maximum. Families currently making $332,800 pay about a quarter of that in federal income tax. In a Ten Times America, if the minimum wage were $8, they would pay just a tenth of their income in federal tax. In a Ten Times America, might not these families work, until they drop, for an $8 minimum?

AN $8 HOURLY MINIMUM WAGE. In an America debating the pluses and minuses of adopting a Ten Times Rule, that prospect would certainly cheer advocates for poor families — and immediately be denounced by friends of fortune. An $8 minimum, these friends of fortune would argue, would irresponsibly place America's entire economy in jeopardy. Yes, they would acknowledge, a "maximum" income tied to the minimum wage might increase the pressure for a significantly higher minimum. But that significantly higher minimum would jeopardize the job security of low-income people. Employers would never be able to afford an $8 minimum. America's lowliest workers would find themselves jobless. The economy, in a Ten Times America, would lurch into recession.

This, of course, is the "jeopardy" thesis, the third and final classic argument against bold attempts at social change. The higher minimum wages that would accompany a Ten Times Rule, apologists of privilege would argue, would inevitably place our nation's very economic foundation at intolerable risk.

Nonsense. Our nation has actually survived, quite nicely, with an hourly minimum wage worth *more* than $8. In 1968, in fact, the federal hourly minimum stood at $1.60 an hour. That $1.60 would have equaled in 2003, after adjusting for inflation, over $8.25 an hour.[50] What economic "damage" did this minimum worth over $8.25 wreak? None. The American economy sparkled throughout the 1960s, 1968 included. The decade saw jobs proliferate, poverty shrink, and average wages soar. All with a minimum wage that ran, in real value, about 50 percent higher than the $5.15 minimum wage on the books in 2003.

Our current lowly minimum wage would, in a Ten Times America, almost certainly rocket up quickly. How could it not? In a Ten Times America, the traditional advocates for higher minimum wages would suddenly be joined by legions of affluent people who never before had any reason to give the minimum wage a second thought. And if the minimum wage did jump to $8.25, society's maximum income would leap to $343,200. At that maximum, *fewer* than 1 percent of America's households would be paying more in federal income taxes under the Ten Times Rule than they actually paid in 2003.[51]

Indeed, with a minimum wage at $8.25, families in a Ten Times Rule America could earn $100,000 *over* the $343,200 max and still wind up at the end of the year with a tax bill no higher than their actual bill in 2003. The result: In a Ten Times America, only the top half of America's richest 1 percent would pay appreciably higher taxes. The income tax burden would fall, almost exclusively, on those who make fortunes from their fortunes.

These fortunes, under America's current tax laws, are constantly compounding, year after year, creating colossal concentrations of wealth and power that endanger almost everything we hold dear. In a Ten Times America, new colossal concentrations of wealth would no longer rise up. And already existing concentrations of wealth, in an America that adopted the Ten Times Rule, would grow no larger. All income from these concentrations, above the Ten Times maximum, would be taxed away.

Over time, all concentrations of wealth that existed at the adoption of the Ten Times Rule would begin cracking and splitting. At the death of their owners, these concentrations would be divided up among family members, becoming smaller with each successive division. Eventually, several generations down the line, *no* colossal private fortunes would cast a shadow across America's economic and political landscape.

But what about the years until then? In these intervening years, immensely wealthy people would still control great fortunes. Wouldn't these wealthy individuals still be free, in a Ten Times America, to invest their fortunes wastefully and irresponsibly? And wouldn't any wasteful, irresponsible decisions they might make negatively impact the sort of society the Ten Times Rule would have been adopted to help create?

In a Ten Times Rule America, some wealthy people would most definitely still control dynastic fortunes, for many decades. A Ten Times Rule would not be able to dictate the investment choices these wealthy individuals choose to make. But a Ten Times Rule could influence these choices — and give America's wealthy an incentive to build America up, not waste America away. The key to this building-up process would be a rather prosaic category of income that most Americans never encounter, the income from state and municipal bonds.

In the United States today, states and cities, sewer and school districts, and various other taxing authorities regularly issue bonds to raise funds for costly special projects. Bonds amount to loans. Someone who buys a $5,000 ten-year municipal bond is lending the city that sells that bond $5,000. In return, the city pays the lender interest. The lower the interest rate that needs to be paid to attract the lender, the better, of course, for the city.

State and local governments have, historically, counted on federal help to keep their interest costs low. That help comes through the tax code. The federal government levies no federal income tax on the interest income that state and local governments pay to people who buy their bonds. This "tax-free" feature makes state and local bonds most attractive to investors in upper-income brackets. For investors in these top brackets, tax-free municipal bonds can be better buys than taxable bonds that offer higher interest rates.

In 2002, for instance, affluent Americans in the top tax bracket paid a 38.6 percent tax on income over $307,051. For these Americans, a tax-free bond yielding just 4 percent interest would have been a better buy than a taxable bond yielding 6.5 percent interest.

Every so often, usually at times of intense budget crunch, some senator or White House official will make noises about ending the tax-free status of state and local bonds. State and local officials immediately raise holy hell. Without tax-free status for the bonds, they exclaim, state and localities would have to offer higher interest rates to attract investors. Countless important projects would quickly become far too expensive to afford.

These arguments always carry the day. The tax-free status of state and municipal bonds has become, in modern American politics, as sacred a cow as a cow can be.

How would a Ten Times Rule America — how should a Ten Times Rule America — treat income from state and local bonds? Should a Ten Times Rule continue to grant special treatment to state and local bond income?

That would be a tough call. Part of the appeal of the Ten Times Rule would be its simplicity. You make five times the minimum wage, you pay 5 percent of your income in federal income tax. You make ten times the minimum, you pay 10 percent. You make more than ten times, you pay a 100 percent tax on the excess.

That's it. No loopholes. No special deductions that privilege one group of taxpayers over another. Granting state and local bond income tax-free status would, of course, upset this basic simplicity. If municipal bond income were declared tax-free, affluent individuals would be able to sidestep the standard Ten Times income limit. But a Ten Times Rule America would have good reason, despite all this, to keep state and local bond income tax-free anyway. Keeping municipal bond income exempt from federal taxes would enable a Ten Times Rule America to steer the fortunes of the super rich into investments that directly benefit working Americans.

Imagine, for a moment, the dynamic that would be created if state and local bond income amounted to the only "loophole" to the Ten Times Rule. America's wealthy would rush to buy as many bonds as they could possibly afford. The income from these bonds, after all, wouldn't be taxed away, even if that income fell above the Ten Times maximum. The demand for tax-exempt state and local bonds would quickly soar to record levels.

This rising demand would place state and local governments squarely in the driver's seat. They would be able to offer miniscule interest rates and still find wealthy people eager to buy their bonds. Their bonds would be the only show in town, the only way wealthy people could make and keep money, above the maximum wage, inside the United States.

How low could interest rates go in this sort of investing environment? In 2002, with the top tax rate on high incomes at 38.6 percent, municipal bonds were yielding as low as 2 and 3 percent. In a Ten Times Rule America, with a 100 percent top tax rate, states and localities would likely find eager investors for bonds that yielded only a small fraction of 1 percent. These states and localities would, at that point, have hundreds of billions of dollars of rich people's money at their beck and call — at virtually no cost.

Those billions could be invested, in a thousand different ways, to restore and renew America's long-neglected infrastructure. New schools could be built. New water purification plants. New bridges. New transit lines. Each of these new projects would mean new jobs, more income for working people, more tax revenues to support public services. We would see, in effect, a Ten Times Rule chain reaction that would leave America stronger, healthier, cleaner, safer.

And what about our rich people? Would their tax-exempt income from state and local bonds undermine the Ten Times maximum limit? Not much. At a 0.25 percent rate of return, tax-free municipal bonds would generate little excessive income in a Ten Times Rule America. A wealthy individual over the maximum would have to buy $10 million dollars worth of municipal bonds to earn $25,000 worth of annual tax-free income. Fine. This $25,000 would be a small price to pay to access, for the public good, $10 million.

The municipal bond "loophole," in a Ten Times Rule America, would benefit average Americans in other ways as well. Low yields on state and local bonds would dampen interest rate levels throughout the economy. Mortgage rates would fall. Housing would become more affordable. More chain reaction. More reason to cheer a Ten Times Rule.

OVER A CENTURY AGO, A TRADE UNION editor, an immigrant named Karl Dovai, made what may be the first recorded case for a Ten Times Rule in America. Dovai had emigrated to the United States from Germany in 1848. In 1883, with the original Gilded Age in full bloom, he testified before the U.S. Senate Committee on Education and Labor. Sewing women, Karl Dovai told the Senate hearing, are currently earning 9 to 11 cents a day, tycoons like Jay Gould $10,000 an hour.[52]

"Suppose the difference between the highest and lowest wages will be as one to ten — that will perhaps be the most that will occur — would not that be better than it is now?" Dovai asked the assembled senators.

Life would have been better then, with a ten times income differential. Life would be better now. We turn now to better understand how.

Life in a Ten Times Rule America

MOST OF US CAN GO YEARS, even lifetimes, without ever coming face to face with grand fortunes. We know, of course, that great concentrations of wealth exist. But we pay them no mind. We have more important things to think about. Our families. Our work. Our homes. Our health. These matter to us, enormously. We worry about them all the time.

About everything else, about matters unrelated to how we go about our daily lives, we have little time to worry. And what could be more unrelated to our daily struggles than the unreal world of those who can earn more in a day than we can earn in a year, more in a month than we can earn in a lifetime. We might sometimes daydream about how nice life could be if we lived in that luxurious world. But we seldom, in our thinking about wealth and the wealthy, go any deeper. Why bother? That world doesn't concern us.

These pages have endeavored to argue otherwise, to make the case that huge concentrations of wealth weigh down heavily on nearly every aspect of our daily existence, in the process squeezing joy from our jobs, hope from our dreams, sometimes even love from our lives. A Ten Times Rule, a limit on the accumulation of grand fortune, would lift this heavy burden. Not immediately. Not completely. But enough to improve, fundamentally, the quality of our lives.

We Americans have spent these lives, for some time now, in a land of trickle down. Let wealth accumulate at the top, we have been assured, and significant benefits will trickle down to the rest of us. We're still waiting.

A Ten Times Rule would end that wait. In a Ten Times America, an America that ended the unlimited accumulation of wealth, benefits wouldn't just trickle down. They would pour. An America where the wealthy could no longer amass ever larger fortunes would be a thoroughly different America. Average Americans would feel that difference every day.

So would, of course, America's wealthy. We need to start our survey of life in Ten Times Rule America with them. Trickle down, after all, always starts at the top.

YOU'RE A CEO. YOU'VE BEEN SUCCESSFUL all your life. You went to the best schools, rushed up the job ladder, became a hot commodity, and eventually won the keys to a chief executive's suite. You make millions of dollars a year. Your life couldn't be sweeter. And then America adopts the Ten Times Rule. What happens next?

Would you choose to stay on as your company's chief executive? If you do, you will almost certainly have to swallow a pay cut. An enormous pay cut. Your company's board of directors, with a Ten Times Rule in effect, is no longer going to shower you with millions. That would make no sense, since the IRS would simply tax away any millions you receive over the ten times maximum.[1]

Would you look for a CEO position elsewhere, in some nation without a Ten Times Rule? You could, but corporations everywhere else in the world all pay their top executives considerably less than what CEOs have been receiving in the United States. These foreign corporations have had no trouble finding qualified executive candidates locally. Why would these corporations now consider hiring an American, especially an American accustomed to making much more money than they have ever had to pay?

Would you simply retire, fly off into the sunset? You could, of course, easily afford to go that route. You could, if you so choose, spend the rest of your days napping on a beach, dangling your toes in the surf.

So what, in the end, would you do? And what would your fellow CEOs be likely to do if they suddenly woke up in a Ten Times America? Some no doubt would simply take their money and run — and be content to sun on the sand. But most top executives, particularly those with real talents, could never be content doing nothing. They might exit their executive suites, but not to fly off to some tropical isle. These "high-achievers," if they ever left their executive suites, would likely only exit to take on some other endeavor they had always wanted to try their hand at. These executives just might see the Ten Times Rule as a liberating opportunity, a chance to follow their dreams.

Just like Anthony Grassi followed his.

In 1990, at the age of 46, Anthony Grassi did what countless high-achievers only fantasize about. He walked away. Grassi, a top First Boston investment banker, had become, after several years of beneficent bonuses, "comfortably rich" and suddenly realized that he and his family simply didn't need any more money. At that point, Grassi started planning his exit from corporate America. Piece by piece, he parceled out his wealth: so much for his children's college education, so much for a new home in the country, the rest for a savings plan that would return him $250,000 a year tax-free for the rest of his life. Grassi figured he could afford to give away half that $250,000 to charity and still have more than enough to live on quite pleasantly.

Grassi's time, after his exit, became his own. He chose to devote it to volunteering. He would go on to serve as the board chairman of two important environmental groups.

"Working for something bigger than just you and your pocketbook gives rewards that are just bigger," Grassi would later tell the *Wall Street Journal*. "I regret I wasn't able to do this when my children were younger."[2]

In our current world, talented, hard-charging executives are constantly day-dreaming about walking down the same path that people like Anthony Grassi have so boldly blazed. Many of these executives talk incessantly, among themselves, about hitting the "number," about amassing a fortune large enough to let them leave their high-pressure careers behind and live the sort of human life they have always, deep down, wanted to live.[3]

But the hard-chargers, in today's corporate world, hardly ever walk away. If they did, no matter how wealthy they might remain, they would be *less* wealthy than their colleagues who kept racing ahead, kept racking up additional millions. They would be second-rate. That prospect, deep down in their competitive souls, they cannot abide.

In a Ten Times Rule America, this sort of status tension would melt away. High-powered executives who walked away would be able to spend their time doing whatever work they wanted to do and still, if they configured their wealth carefully, have incomes every bit as high as anyone else. They could make the leap and remain "winners."

Not every top executive in an America that adopted the Ten Times Rule would want to make a leap into another life. Some would be quite content to stay put, to continue on as before, even at a reduced level of compensation. These non-leapers would be executives who actually enjoy their executive work, who feel they have unfinished business to complete. But these executives, in a Ten Times Rule America, would face a daunting challenge. In a deeply unequal America, they knew how to function. To grab the help they needed, they merely waved money. To the talent they wanted on their team, by their side, they held out the prospect of becoming phenomenally wealthy. Work here, work hard, they told the talent, and someday great fortune will be yours.

In a Ten Times Rule America, that promise would fall flat. In a Ten Times America, no one would be gaining great fortune. Given that reality, chief executives would have to offer top talent something more than money. They would have to offer the talented a quality work environment, a comfortable yet challenging place to labor.

In our current business workplaces, top executives need only pay lip service to the quality of corporate life. They know full well that talented people, if promised a shot at vast fortune, will put up with most anything — with eighty-hour workweeks, abusive bosses, arbitrary decision making, even outright thievery. In a Ten Times Rule America, by contrast, talented people would no longer be chasing after windfalls. They would be searching for satisfying places to work. Corporate leaders would either have to make their workplaces more satisfying or find themselves surrounded by second-rate people.

Workplaces become more satisfying, researchers tell us, when companies give employees more autonomy, when they offer staff more opportunity to shape decisions, when they ensure everyone enough time off to restore creative juices, when they distribute rewards fairly. In a Ten Times Rule America, top executives would finally have to start paying attention to all these elements that make workplaces more satisfying. They would have no choice, not if they wanted to attract and retain talented people.

To move down this road, to seriously involve staff in decision making, to share rewards fairly, to ensure people a "life" off the job, most enterprises in America would have to totally revamp how their corporate offices operate. They would have to reject expectations that top staff work twelve-hour days, reject the myths of CEO omnipotence that justify top-heavy reward systems, reject the traditional mindsets that encourage corporate intellectual conformity. In a Ten Times Rule America, those firms that took on these changes, that became serious about creating new corporate cultures, would be the firms that thrive. In these firms, even executives might enjoy coming to work.

OVER TIME, IN A TEN TIMES AMERICA, the environments where the wealthy work would begin to change. So would the environments where the wealthy, and the rest of us, live.

We live today, all of us, within a housing market split dramatically in two. At the one end, America's most affluent routinely enjoy not just one home, but two or three. At the other, average families sweat to meet their mortgages. The adoption of a Ten Times Rule would turn this split housing market upside-down. In an instant, America's largest, most lavish, most desired homes would become burdens, not trophies.

Consider the dilemma, in a Ten Times Rule America, that would face an extravagantly affluent couple with a condo in Manhattan, a stately summer home in Southampton, and a cute winter getaway in the Bahamas. All these residences carry costs. Condo fees, property taxes, insurance, utilities, gardeners, plumbers, not to mention a mortgage or two. How much might these costs total? A half-million a year? A million? No big deal. What's a million or so out of an annual income of $5 or $10 million?

That same million, in a Ten Times Rule America, would suddenly loom large. With a Ten Times income ceiling in place, our extravagantly affluent couple might suddenly find the upkeep of three wonderful homes a bit too much to bear. Our wealthy couple might even decide, with a heavy heart, to place one of its multiple abodes on the market. But our couple wouldn't be alone. In a Ten Times America, thousands of other wealthy households would face the same squeeze. They would likely make the same choice. They would rush to unload the residences they could no longer comfortably afford to maintain.

Here's where things would start to get interesting. With all these excess luxury homes on the market, prices on top-end residences would inevitably start to fall. These falling prices on luxury homes would quickly ricochet throughout the rest of the housing market. With a home that had been worth $1 million now selling for $750,000, a less luxurious home that would have sold for $750,000, before the Ten Times Rule, might now sell for $500,000. A home that would have sold for $500,000 might now fetch only $400,000. Down, across the board, would go prices on America's most expensive homes.

This downpricing would immediately impact how homebuilders see the world. In our current unequal America, developers quite logically concentrate on concentrated wealth. They erect edifices for America's affluent. They ignore America's middle. In a Ten Times Rule America, that course would no longer make sense. Why build *new* luxury homes in a housing market flooded by existing luxury homes for sale at attractively reduced prices? Nimble developers, in this housing market, would look elsewhere for homebuyers. And they would find them in the middle class. Middle class households, in a Ten Times Rule America, would once again appear attractive. In a more equal America, these households would have a greater share of the nation's income and wealth. Year by year, in a Ten Times America, developers would seek to serve this growing middle class market. Year by year, the stock of affordable housing would swell. More families would be able to find — and afford — decent homes of their own.

Not all wealthy families, to be sure, would rush to sell their surplus housing in a Ten Times Rule America. Those families with immense fortunes would still be able to afford to maintain multiple luxury homes *if* they were willing to spend their fortunes down. Fine. The more homes they try to maintain, the quicker their fortunes would shrink.

Affluent families earning just under the Ten Times maximum would find themselves in a somewhat different position. Suppose a couple with an excess luxury home had an annual income of $250,000. This family, if the Ten Times maximum stood at $300,000, could still report another $50,000 in income before any 100 percent tax would kick in. Let's assume this family could clear a $250,000 capital gain by selling off one of its homes. Would the family sell? And what would happen to that $250,000 profit if the family did sell? Would $200,000 of that profit be taxed away immediately, as excess over the $300,000 annual maximum?

In a Ten Times Rule America, this would become an important question because many households might find themselves in a similar situation — that is, many households earning less than the Ten Times maximum might have a one-year spurt of income that places them above the maximum for only one year. It won't seem fair to these families to have most of this one-year spurt subject to a 100 percent tax, not when that same spurt if received over several years in smaller chunks would have avoided the 100 percent rate.

What would a Ten Times Rule America do in these one-year-spurt situations? A Ten Times America would restore into the tax code the same special treatment for sudden and dramatic increases in annual income that existed years ago, in an era when the United States taxed incomes more progressively than our nation does now. That special treatment went by the name of "income averaging."[4] In "income averaging" days gone by, households with income spurts could average their incomes over a multi-year period. A Ten Times Rule America would follow the same tax logic.

How would this income averaging work? Let's return to our household earning $250,000 a year. If this household sold one of its homes and cleared $250,000, its annual income would jump, for one year, to $500,000, well above the $300,000 maximum. Suppose this household had earned $250,000 in each of the four years before the sale. This family, under income averaging, would be able to average out the five years, four years of $250,000 income and one of $500,000. The average, in this case, would come to $300,000 a year. The household would then owe a Ten Times Rule total tax for the five years of just $150,000, a sum that would equal 10 percent of the $300,000 annual average for the five years.[5] Households in this situation would have ample reason to sell off any excess housing they might own.

Still other wealthy households might choose, instead, to hang on to their excess properties and rent them out, not necessarily for profit, because whatever income they might make beyond the Ten Times maximum would be taxed away, but just to meet their maintenance expenses. The wealthy households that went this route would retain title to their property. Later, in retirement, if their income dipped below the Ten Times limit, they could sell the excess property and use the income from the sale to augment their retirement income.

Wealthy families would have another option as well. They could choose to donate their excess properties to some local charity — and claim the donation as a tax deduction.

Current tax rules allow taxpayers to claim charitable deductions that equal no more than half their annual incomes. A Ten Times Rule America would be wise to continue this practice, for the same reason a Ten Times America would be wise to allow income from state and municipal bonds to remain tax-free. Letting taxpayers deduct charitable contributions, as they do now, would help leverage *private* fortune for *public* benefit.

Take, for example, a couple with a fortune worth $10 million that reports $500,000 a year in income. With a $300,000 maximum in effect, this couple would pay $230,000 in federal income tax on its $500,000 income, a sum that would equal 10 percent of the couple's first $300,000 in income and the $200,000 the couple took in over the $300,000 ceiling. But if this couple chose to carve $150,000 off its $10 million fortune and donate this $150,000 to charity, its tax bill would shrink. Only $150,000 of the couple's first $300,000 in income would now be taxable. On this $150,000, a sum five times the minimum, the couple would pay only a 5 percent tax, or $7,500. The new total tax bill for our wealthy couple: $207,500. The bottom line: By making a $150,000 charitable contribution, our wealthy couple would save $22,500 in Ten Times taxes.

How might this dynamic work with the donation of an excess home? Let's assume that our wealthy couple has a spare home worth $750,000. Under current tax law, taxpayers can divide, for tax purposes, a large charitable contribution made in one year into pieces and then claim, over a several year period, each individual piece as an annual deduction. If this practice continued under the Ten Times Rule, our wealthy couple would be able to donate a $750,000 home to charity, then claim a $150,000 charitable deduction for each of five years. The couple, over the five years, would realize $112,500 in tax savings.

Tax savings this robust would help inspire a significant transformation in the housing market of a Ten Times America. Year after year, to be able to claim charitable tax deductions, wealthy households would be donating excess high-end homes to nonprofit organizations. Grand old homes of the wealthy would be reborn as college dormitories and halfway houses. Or nonprofits might simply sell or rent the homes donated to them as a means to raise operating revenues. In any case, the end result — an increase in America's stock of affordable housing — would be the same. The more excess luxury homes sold, the lower the sale prices on homes overall. The more excess luxury homes rented, the lower rentals overall.

Housing heaven? Not entirely. Some middle-income households, those counting on big profits from selling homes they've owned for years, might grumble at first as overall home prices, in a Ten Times Rule America, began deflating. Homes that these households had expected to sell for $400,000 might, in a Ten Times America, only return $250,000. But the grumbling wouldn't last. Middle class households that sell their homes, after all, have to find new places to live, and these new places, in a Ten Times Rule America, would cost them less. What these middle class households might lose on the sale of an old house they would gain on the purchase of a new one.

Professional housing speculators, to be sure, might not enjoy the housing market in a Ten Times America. The vast majority of everyone else would have abundant reason to cheer.

IN A TEN TIMES RULE AMERICA, average consumers would find more products, at lower prices, in all big-ticket consumption categories, not just housing.

The reason? In a Ten Times America, marketers would no longer have any incentive to target the top end of America's income and wealth distribution — and ignore everybody else. That top end would no longer have enough income and wealth to make targeting worthwhile. Marketers, instead, would reorient themselves to America's middle class. They would start flooding America's marketplace with products and services specifically geared for average-income families, just as they did in the 1950s and 1960s, the twentieth century's golden age of American income equality.

But the shrinking importance of the luxury market, in a Ten Times Rule America, would almost certainly prompt an even more fundamental sea change in consumption. The end of luxury's dominance over American retailing would lower, significantly, the level of spending that signifies the "good life."

In America today, as in all societies where wealth concentrates, the affluent define the good life. They set the consumption standard. Those who want to be seen as successful do their best to meet this standard. We all, of course, want to be seen as successful. So we do whatever it takes to reach whatever consumption bar the affluent set. We work extra hours. We max out our credit cards. But that bar never seems to get any closer — and never will, not in societies where deep divides separate the most affluent from everyone else. The affluent, in unequal societies becoming more unequal, just keep raising the bar.

In a Ten Times America, by contrast, the gaps that separate the affluent from America's middle class would be narrowing, not expanding. The bar would be more reachable. More people, many more people, would be able to afford the consumer goods that signify the good life. These goods, in this more equal environment, would soon start to lose their "must-have" significance. In societies where most people can afford the same consumer goods, these consumer goods eventually — and always — become less important to have.

Old habits, of course, die hard. In a Ten Times Rule America, some people would continue to obsess over what they buy and own. But fewer people, in a Ten Times America, would crave consumer goods they can barely afford. In a Ten Times America, the middle class, not the wealthy, would come to set the consumption standard — and most families would be able to meet that standard, without working themselves to exhaustion, even most families at the lower end of America's income ladder.

These bottom-rung families, in a Ten Times America, would have more income at their disposal. Under the Ten Times Rule, the minimum wage would regularly be rising, and each hike in the minimum wage would trigger wage increases in jobs paying just above the minimum. All lower-wage work, in short order, would begin to pay more. At the same time, the most basic costs of the good life would be sinking, as the luxury market became less dominant. These twin trends — higher wage income, a lower entry fee into the good life — would give millions of low-income families financial breathing space, their first ever. These families would find themselves able to afford lifestyles that bring them self-respect without having to work second jobs or endless and exhausting overtime.

And if fewer people felt compelled to work beyond the standard work week, more jobs would become available. If ten people working forty-eight hours a week, for instance, were to feel comfortable working just forty hours a week, full-time jobs for two other workers would suddenly become open. In a Ten Times Rule America, given dynamics like these, jobless rates would start dropping. More people would be working. Fewer would require support from the social safety net.

Those workers in a Ten Times America who felt comfortable reducing the time they devote to work would have more time — after work — for activities they find personally rewarding. This added time might prove the greatest blessing of all. The Ten Times Rule could not guarantee everyone a fulfilling job.

But a Ten Times America would leave people with more time to find fulfillment outside work, to engage in pastimes that satisfy our primal urges to learn, to create, to master new skills.

Today, in our unequal America, far too few of us have this opportunity to devote significant time to the pastimes we truly enjoy. We spend our days, instead, on our hedonic treadmills, racing to meet a standard for the "good life" that inequality keeps driving ever further beyond our reach. In a Ten Times Rule America, this treadmill would slow. We would no longer spend our time, waste our time, getting nowhere fast.

IN A TEN TIMES RULE AMERICA, our workplaces would be more humane, our home lives less hedonically hectic. But what of the third great sphere of our daily existences, that space outside work and home, the realm we usually call "community"? How would our communities fare in a Ten Times America?

Community life in America is currently languishing almost everywhere. In our rush to "catch up" to society's affluent pacesetters, in our frenzy to keep from falling further behind, we have little patience, or energy, for activities that seem to make no contribution to our personal financial bottom-lines. We neglect those aspects of our lives that don't translate into dollars. We neglect, most of all, our communities.

In a Ten Times America, a more equal America, we would feel *less* pressure to make every moment financially rewarding. We would have *more* time to devote to community — to joshing with neighbors or bowling with friends, to joining organizations and serving on committees, to writing letters to the editor or even running for office ourselves.

But would we actually devote this additional time, in a Ten Times America, to our communities? Or would we just look inward and devote all our new time to ourselves?

Some commentators actually see looking inward as a logical — and perhaps inevitable —response to the unavoidable tensions of modern life. Information Age stresses and strains, the argument goes, drive us inexorably into "cocooning." In a tense, high-speed world, we retreat from community. We turn our homes into safe, secure, self-contained family redoubts. Would the adoption of a Ten Times Rule override this cocooning impulse? Maybe not. In a Ten Times Rule America, after all, home theaters, pizza delivery vans, broadband Internet, and all the other devices we can use to cut ourselves off from having to rub shoulders with other people would still surround us. So why should we expect our community lives to flower under the Ten Times Rule? Why should we expect people in a Ten Times America to invest time in their communities, not just themselves, to pursue public, not just private, solutions to life's problems?

We should expect this investment in community, this interest in public solutions, for one compelling reason. In a Ten Times Rule America, a more equal America, public solutions will make more sense.

Private solutions can indeed always "solve" life's problems, but only at a significant cost. Your family need a place to go for fun? Your children need good schools? You want to read all the latest bestsellers? Or feel safe when you lock your door at night? Or commute without aggravation? If you have enough wealth, you can get what you want by yourself, without joining in community with others. You can jet off to an exclusive resort. You can send your kids to an elite private school. You can buy every new book that tickles your fancy. You can hire a security service to guard your home — or a limo service to take you to work. If you have enough wealth, you have no need to engage in your community, no need to press for better public parks or better public schools or better public libraries or better public law enforcement or better public transportation.

Inequality encourages people to seek private solutions. The more wealth concentrates, the more affordable — for society's affluent — private solutions become. And the more eagerly a society's elites invest in private solutions, the less diligently that society will pursue public solutions. These public solutions, over time, come to atrophy. Public parks get dangerous. Public schools get crowded. Public libraries are open less often. More families, in response, abandon community-minded approaches to problem solving. They come to feel they have little choice.

In a Ten Times Rule America, the pressures would reverse. The wealthiest households in a Ten Times America would still, of course, be able to afford tuition at elite private schools. But private tuition on top of country club dues on top of private security service fees on top of chauffeur salaries would quickly add up and overwhelm any income capped at a ten times maximum. In a Ten Times America, wealthy families would have to be willing to spend down their accumulated wealth, year after year, to be able to solve their problems privately. Some would do that. Others, especially those with less robust fortunes, would not. And the fewer people who sought private solutions, the more expensive those solutions would become.

Most affluent people, under the Ten Times Rule, would no longer be able to comfortably afford, all at once, the private schools, the country clubs, and the assorted other private amenities that currently fill their lives. These affluent families would have to start *caring* about public amenities. The quality of these amenities would suddenly start to matter to them. The local public school can't afford an art teacher? A guidance counselor? Uniforms for the girls' softball team? These "frills" become outrages when they impact your own child. The affluent, in a Ten Times America, would not tolerate these outrages. Their caring, their unwillingness to settle for second-best, could not but help to improve the quality of public amenities, be they schools or parks or libraries, for all Americans.

PUBLIC SERVICES PROVIDE ONE ESSENTIAL SUPPORT for vital, vibrant communities, independent nonprofit organizations another. Nonprofits — the clubs for boys and girls and runners and gardeners, the centers for seniors, the councils for the arts, the societies for historic preservation — abound in healthy communities. In a Ten Times America, these nonprofits would flourish. Volunteers would be plentiful. Average-income people, off the hedonic treadmill at last, would have more time for engaging in the volunteer pursuits that interest them. Affluent people, with no more incentive to keep piling up millions, would increasingly choose to devote their careers to the nonprofits they most admire.

If the Ten Times Rule were to become the law of the land, nonprofits would also be able to count on generous flows of charitable contributions, from families both above *and* below the ten times ceiling. In a Ten Times America, with lower taxes on their incomes, average families would have more income to donate. Wealthy families, for their part, would have a strong incentive to donate regularly at high levels. By donating away hefty slices of their accumulated wealth, as we have seen, families with income *above* the ten times maximum would be able to hang on to more of their income *below* that maximum.

Bequests at death, in a Ten Times Rule America, would add considerably to the nonprofit revenue stream. Wealthy Americans do already, of course, leave sizable sums to charities, mainly to limit their estate tax liabilities.[6] The more money that wealthy people earmark for charities in their wills, the less their estates will pay in tax. But wealthy people also have another important deduction they can claim under current estate tax law, a deduction that steers bequests *away* from charities. Wealthy individuals can currently have deducted from their estates however much they choose to leave their surviving spouse. In 1997, America's biggest taxable estates, those worth $20 million or more, left $7.47 billion to charity but even more, $7.57 billion, to surviving spouses.[7]

Under current law, the more a departing wealthy individual leaves a spouse, the better off that individual's estate will be. Surviving spouses can take a generous bequest, invest it, and end up with an even more generous fortune to bestow upon their sons and daughters. In a Ten Times Rule America, this fortune compounding would cease. A surviving spouse would not be able to grow an inherited fortune, since any income from an inherited fortune above the ten times ceiling would be taxed away.

The fortune itself, meanwhile, would shrink, not grow, as the expenses of maintaining it — annual security fees to safeguard the family fine art collection, insurance for the family fleet of luxury cars — eat away at the size of the fortune. In a Ten Times America, in short, a huge bequest to a surviving spouse might often prove more burden than benefit.

So why would a mogul, in a Ten Times America, ever leave a huge fortune to a surviving spouse? Why leave a spouse a couple hundred million when a far smaller bequest would be enough to guarantee any spouse a life-long annual income at the ten times maximum? Wealthy people living under the Ten Times Rule would almost certainly leave their spouses considerably less fortune than they leave them now. And who would get that money that would have gone to spouses? Most likely the charitable sector. Charitable organizations, in a Ten Times America, would be among the biggest winners.

But what about the offspring of the wealthy? Wouldn't the wealthy be far more likely to leave fortune to offspring than charities? Not at all. What would be the point? In a Ten Times Rule America, wealthy offspring with incomes already above the maximum would have little to gain from inheriting additional assets. Wealthy people sitting down to do their wills would surely recognize this reality. They would be less likely, as a result, to leave their assets to their already wealthy offspring and more likely to leave these assets to charity — or to people who aren't already wealthy, people earning under the ten times maximum, people who would be able to retain any income these assets might generate. Who would these lucky people be? They might be long-lost cousins. They might be trusted chauffeurs. They might even be beloved, never-forgotten third grade teachers. They could be anybody — anybody not already wealthy. Only the most perverse wealthy, in a Ten Times Rule America, would leave significant fortune to the already fortunate.

Over time, this steady asset transfer from the highly privileged to the less privileged would inexorably narrow the gap between our most fortunate and everyone else. The Ten Times Rule, a tax on *income*, would help end the concentration of America's *wealth*.

IF A TEN TIMES RULE WERE EVER TO BECOME a matter of national political debate, friends of fortune would readily acknowledge, right at the outset, the capacity of an income maximum to *break up* wealth. But societies, these skeptics would argue, only advance when they *create* wealth. To serve as a vehicle for progress, a Ten Times Rule would have to build up wealth, not just break it down.

A point well-taken. Societies do need to create wealth to advance. Would a Ten Times Rule help create wealth? More specifically, would enterprises, our modern world's engines of wealth creation, become more productive and efficient under a Ten Times Rule? No question, for a nation considering whether to adopt a ten times ceiling, would be more important. For wealth to build in a Ten Times America, a Ten Times Rule would have to help enterprises become more effective and efficient.

What makes enterprises effective and efficient? The same sorts of qualities, researchers tell us, that make workplaces satisfying places to work. High-performing enterprises empower workers with decision-making authority. They help staff collaborate. They reward workers fairly. In effective enterprises, executives respect workers and, in turn, are respected by them.

American business leaders pay homage to these noble ideals at every opportunity. They spend tens of millions of dollars every year on conferences and courses designed to instill these ideals into managers and workers alike. But these investments, we have seen, have failed to pay off. America's most important enterprises have not become more effective over recent years. They have, if anything, become more deeply defective, as America's executives, in their rush for riches, have merged and purged their way to fortunes, blathered about synergy while shoving companies into bankruptcy, and mouthed commitments to quality while committing criminal conspiracies. The antics of our executives have left workers demoralized, not empowered, consumers suspicious, not satisfied. Our executives have not created wealth. They have expropriated it. The resulting inequality, within the workplace, has subverted and perverted enterprise success.

A Ten Times Rule would set off a quite different set of organizational dynamics. A Ten Times Rule would, almost immediately, end the incentives for executive behaviors that sap enterprise vitality. With an income ceiling in place, top-ranking executives would be less likely to rush into silly mergers, less likely to downsize away employee loyalty, less likely to shortchange consumers, less likely to hopscotch from one company to another, less likely to spend more time managing their company's share price than their company's operations. These behaviors have all proliferated, in our current deeply unequal America, because these behaviors all promise jackpot payoffs. In a Ten Times America, jackpots would no longer juice executive behavior. A Ten Times Rule economic landscape would be a jackpot-free economic landscape.

In a Ten Times Rule America, top executives would make, at most, ten times more than their lowliest employees. With only a ten times spread between top and bottom, enterprises would no longer be able to sustain corporate America's current abundance of hierarchical levels. Enterprise hierarchies would flatten. And with that flattening would come behaviors that nurture enterprise effectiveness. "Flatter" hierarchies would encourage the free and candid exchange of information that steep hierarchies stifle.[8] The more modest the compensation of "higher-ups," the less pressure on workers to defer to higher-up opinion. The less deference, the more dialogue, the more sharing of ideas, the more seizing of opportunities that employees closest to customers — or production — so often see first. The end result? Better enterprises. More productive enterprises.

Compensation compression, the smaller gap between top and bottom, would not just compress hierarchies. Compensation compression would shrink overall enterprise size. Oversized, sprawling corporate empires, with imperial CEOs lording over complex webs of divisions and branches, would almost inevitably start to subdivide once a Ten Times Rule reset the economic rules. Corporate emperors, in a Ten Times America, would lose their coin of the realm, their ability to dish out rewards large enough to keep the executives of subsidiaries content in subordinate roles. In a Ten Times America, these subordinates would likely chafe at taking orders from CEOs now earning not much more, if any more, than what they would be earning. Imperial CEOs, for their part, would have nothing to gain from struggling to hold their corporate empires together. They would earn just as much — the ten times income maximum — overseeing two subsidiaries as twenty.

Over time, under a Ten Times Rule, these new institutional realities would "splinter" America's corporate empires. More modestly sized business operations would come to dot the nation's economic landscape.[9] In these smaller companies, strategies that involve and empower workers in decision making have a much better shot at taking root. These smaller enterprises would be more likely to be effective enterprises.

The benefits from this corporate empire shrinkage, in a Ten Times Rule America, would spill even beyond this increased enterprise efficiency. Smaller enterprises would be less politically powerful enterprises. Smaller enterprises would not have the clout to extort tax subsidies — "pay us what we want or we'll take our ten thousand jobs elsewhere" — from overmatched state and municipal governments. Smaller enterprises would not have the political punch to ram through state legislatures statutes that exempt their operations from environmental safeguards. Smaller enterprises would not have the wherewithal to fix and rig marketplace prices. Smaller enterprises, most important of all, would be closer to the communities where they do business. Their executives would be more aware of the impact their decisions might have — and more accountable for those decisions.

What could America do, a young Ralph Nader once asked, "to direct corporate resources toward respecting the values and pleas that are beyond the balance sheet morality?"[10] America could enact the Ten Times Rule. No other single step would do more to make corporations more responsible organizations. Or more productive. The Ten Times Rule would unleash a corporate chain-reaction that would significantly level America's economic playing field. On that new field, we could create the wealth America needs.

A TEN TIMES CHAIN-REACTION might actually produce workaday changes far more fundamental than enterprises that are flatter and smaller. A Ten Times Rule might even help us address some of America's most intractable problems, among them the subordinate roles that people of color and women continue to play, despite years of law making and court decisions that have ruled discrimination against the law.

People of color and women in America already labor under an income ceiling of sorts, a "glass ceiling." The upper reaches of America's economy remain, a generation after the historic rights struggles of the 1960s and 1970s, overwhelmingly male and white. In 2002, of the top five hundred chief executives in America, only six weren't men. Women in corporate management started the new century earning 65 percent of what their male counterparts earned. During the biggest of the boom years, between 1995 and 2000, the earnings gap between men and women in corporate management actually widened.[11]

The statistics for people of color fit a similar pattern. Minority men and women, a federal Glass Ceiling Commission reported midway through the 1990s, make up just 3 percent of American corporate senior management. They earn 21 percent less than white senior managers doing the same work.[12]

The adoption of a Ten Times Rule would shatter this glass ceiling — from above.

At century's end, women overall constituted just over 9 percent of income-earners making between $500,000 and $1 million and just under 7 percent of income-earners making over $1 million.[13] In a Ten Times Rule America, corporations would no longer be compensating anyone over $500,000. High-ranking executives, over 90 percent of them male and white, would suddenly find themselves tumbling from the tops of flattening corporate hierarchies. They would smash, on the way down, into corporate America's glass ceilings. With hierarchies compressing, with income gaps between people of different genders and colors suddenly narrowing, women and people of color would likely feel less demoralized, and more willing to give their all for enterprise success. Enormous gaps in rewards, in a Ten Times America, would no longer "rub in" — or cement — their socially subordinate status. At the same time, throughout America, opportunities for executive leadership would be increasing. The proliferation of enterprises in a Ten Times America, as large enterprises subdivided into smaller operations, would give women and people of color many more chances to play leadership roles.

The Ten Times Rule, to be sure, would not magically wave away deeply ingrained biases. But the Ten Times Rule would erode the economic privilege that arbitrarily empowers some Americans over others. Toward justice, we could take few more significant steps.

NO ENTERPRISE, NOT EVEN an incredibly efficient and effective enterprise, can ever succeed solely on its own initiative. An enterprise can boast an enlightened management, a committed workforce, a wonderful product and still experience sheer, sad, and even sudden failure. Effective enterprises, to become and stay effective, need to do business in effective economies.

In effective economies, enterprises can count on obtaining the capital they need to start up and expand, the technology they need to operate efficiently, the qualified employees they need to get their work done, and the safe and secure business environment they need to produce and distribute their goods and services. Most of all, in an economy working effectively, enterprises can count on having a market, customers able to afford the goods and services they produce. Enterprises trapped in an economy that cannot supply these needed supports will not create wealth. Enterprises so trapped will likely not even survive. Healthy enterprises, in short, require a healthy economy.

Would a Ten Times Rule help create this economic health?

In any national debate about the viability of a Ten Times Rule, skeptics would delightedly seize upon this question. A Ten Times Rule, they would charge, would collapse the economy of any nation foolish enough to adopt it. That collapse, they would argue, would begin with the disappearance of the capital enterprises need for investment, since wealthy people save and invest a greater share of their income than average people. If the incomes of the wealthy were leveled down, where would investments for innovation come from?

The somewhat surprising answer: In a Ten Times Rule America, enterprises would find investment capital from essentially the same places they find capital today.

In our current economy, only a small share of investment capital actually comes directly out of the pockets of wealthy people. Investment capital comes, in large part, from the collective savings of average people, savings that have been institutionalized through pension funds and other retirement vehicles. Huge amounts of investment capital also come from the endowments of universities and other nonprofit institutions.

What about all those venture capitalists? Don't they play an essential investment role? They certainly do, but the venture capital companies these venture capitalists run get most of the dollars they funnel to entrepreneurs from retirement funds and large nonprofit endowments, not from private wealthy individuals. "Private equity," as business journalist Michael Peltz notes, "is largely an institutional market."[14] In the boom years, America's most celebrated venture capital company, Silicon Valley's Kleiner Perkins Caufield & Byers, annually handed entrepreneurs $100 billion a year. Those dollars came, in overwhelmingly numbers, from "university endowments and other institutions."[15]

In a Ten Times America, pension funds and other institutional sources of investment capital would have more, not less, to invest.

Consider, as an example, the pension funds that cover America's public employees. In a Ten Times America, public employment would enjoy a remarkable renaissance. A 100 percent tax on incomes over the ten times maximum would generate hundreds of billions of new federal revenue dollars. These dollars would likely fund a massive upgrade of education and other public services. More teachers would be staffing America's schools, more highway workers would be filling potholes, more rangers would be protecting parks. More public sector workers would be receiving paychecks, and more paychecks would translate into more pension fund contributions from public sector workers.

Private sector pension funds would keep pace. In a Ten Times Rule America, the redistribution of income *within* private enterprises — lower pay packages at the top, higher pay packages at the bottom — would leave average employees significantly more able to up their retirement contributions. And top executives, under the ten times income ceiling, would no longer have any powerful incentive to play games with employee pension fund dollars. Top executives currently can and do steer dollars out of pension funds to jack up corporate quarterly earnings — and their own personal option windfalls. The windfalls would disappear in a Ten Times America, and so would the incentive to deny pension funds the dollars they ought to be holding. Retirement funds, in a Ten Times America, would be exceptionally robust sources of needed investment capital.

But what about our other key institutional sources of investment capital, particularly foundation and university endowments? Don't these endowments get most of their dollars from wealthy people? If the Ten Times Rule leveled down the incomes of the wealthy, wouldn't these endowments suffer financially? Not really. In fact, probably not at all.

Under the Ten Times Rule, foundations and universities would continue to collect significant contributions from America's deepest pockets. Wealthy Americans earning income above a ten times ceiling, earlier pages have noted, would be able to reduce taxes on their income *under* the ceiling by making large charitable contributions. Foundation and university endowments would no doubt benefit from these contributions. Foundation and university endowments would likely benefit even more, under the Ten Times Rule, every time a wealthy person passes on. In a Ten Times America, we have seen, wealthy people would be writing out wills that leave more dollars to charities and fewer to already rich spouses and offspring, since, with an income ceiling in place, the already rich would be in no position to benefit from grand bequests. Alma maters, by contrast, would.

Some dollars that today go to promising young entrepreneurs do, of course, come straight from the pockets of wealthy people. These dollars would most certainly be less bountiful in a Ten Times Rule America. Would worthy entrepreneurial efforts, as a consequence, have to go without the capital they need to get going? Not hardly. Legitimate investments in worthy entrepreneurial efforts don't increase as dollars concentrate in the pockets of wealthy people. Speculation increases. In a Ten Times America, with wealth less concentrated, more dollars would be carefully invested and fewer dollars would be wasted — on silly schemes that promise quick fortunes.

In the boom years of the 1990s, as wealth concentrated at record rates, we saw these schemes "flower." One of these schemes even tried to drive America's neighborhood florists out of business.

In 1998, a small gang of wealthy Americans actually set out to redefine — and take over — the retail flower industry, one of America's most vibrant small business strongholds. The gang's leaders included the former top executives of the Blockbuster video chain. These execs had already made a fortune shoving local video stores out of business. They could make an even greater fortune, they figured, in the $15 billion retail flower industry. Their plan: buy up the top one thousand local florists in the nation's one hundred biggest local flower markets, create America's first-ever national flower store chain, then "go public" on Wall Street and make a stock trading killing.[16]

The Blockbuster boys had more than enough cash in their own pockets — some $10 million — to get the ball rolling. With that as leverage, they were on their way. In no time at all, they were wining and dining local florists all across the country. Locals who sold out to the new national flower chain, the Blockbuster gang leaders hinted, could look forward to magnificent stock option bonanzas. Hundreds of local florists took the bait. By April 1999, the gang had snatched up enough local outlets to start selling shares of stock on

Wall Street. These shares soon shot up 33 percent. This new flower empire, Wall Street figured, would streamline the flower business the same way Blockbuster had streamlined video rental. Economies of scale. One size fits all.

But that one size, in practice, pinched. The local florist shops bought up by the new chain now had to toe a strict national corporate line. That meant no more generous donations of flowers to local charities. No more letting regular customers pay on sixty-day schedules. No more free deliveries to hospitals. No more buying from anyone but chain-approved wholesalers, even if that meant peddling flowers of inferior quality. No more conducting business the way neighborhood florists had been conducting business for generations.

By spring 2000, the new flower chain's local outlets were losing customers right and left. The chain, in response, turned the screws even tighter. Layoffs. Cost-cutting. The customers kept disappearing. Finally, in April 2001, America's first floral empire filed for bankruptcy. Six months later, the empire folded.

In a Ten Times Rule America, none of this speculative waste would ever have taken place. With an income cap in effect, the Blockbuster boys would not have had the personal capital necessary to launch a credible takeover bid of America's flower stores. Nor would have the Blockbuster boys been able, in a Ten Times America, to seduce local florists to sell out simply by dangling stock options in their faces. Get-really-rich-quick schemes can only seduce in societies where people can indeed get really rich quick. In a Ten Times America, people would still be able to become rich, but not quick, and not really rich. In a United States that adopted the Ten Times Rule, speculators would find capital — and dupes — in short supply.

ENTERPRISES LOOKING FOR THE BASICS, not dupes, would find them in a Ten Times America. An educated workforce? The federal government, with revenues swelled by a 100 percent tax on income above the ten times ceiling, would be able to fund a total overhaul of American public education. Schools could be modernized, class sizes reduced, preschools expanded, college tuitions minimized, quality teachers recruited and retained. Access to new technology? Those same increased federal revenues could fund more in-depth R&D programs in America's labs and universities. A dependable infrastructure for bringing goods and services to market? A Ten Times America that kept the income from state and municipal bonds tax-free would have at its disposal, at virtually no cost, billions upon billions of dollars for public works projects to rebuild and renew long-neglected bridges, ports, railroads, and roads. Those projects would create jobs, those jobs would generate paychecks, and those paychecks would bestow upon enterprises the most important business basic of all: a steady supply of customers.

Customers would be plentiful in a Ten Times Rule America, partly because jobs would be more plentiful, but more because average people overall would simply have more income at their disposal. The Ten Times Rule, by taxing away the excess income of the rich and lowering taxes on everyone else, would steer a far greater share of America's income dollars into the pockets of average Americans. This redistribution, in turn, would have a powerful and positive impact on America's economy.

We can illustrate that impact with a picture, any picture — or painting — worthy enough to hang on a museum wall. A Rembrandt perhaps. A Cézanne maybe. Rich people like to purchase Rembrandts and Cézannes. They pay millions for them. The rest of us don't buy Rembrandts. Our big-ticket items are more likely to be refrigerators. With one million dollars, the cost of a modest Rembrandt, a thousand of the rest of us could replace our old refrigerators with new energy-efficient models.

Any society that opted for a Ten Times Rule would be opting for refrigerators — and a job-friendly economy. What, after all, creates more work, one thousand consumers buying energy-efficient refrigerators or one consumer buying a Rembrandt? A Ten Times Rule, by limiting the flow of dollars into the pockets of the already rich, by increasing the flow of dollars into the pockets of everyone else, would consistently and significantly enhance what economists call "mass purchasing power." Wealth, like manure, only does good when you spread it around. A Ten Times Rule would spread wealth — and give our slumbering economy a much-needed wake-up call.

Apologists for inequality, needless to say, have never appreciated analogies that equate great concentrations of wealth to great piles of manure. Societies that spread wealth, they insist, are doomed to perpetual slumber. Limit the ability of rich people to spend, their argument goes, and no one will do much spending. Innovative consumer goods, one conservative commentator, Tony Snow, tells us, always start off as expensive luxuries only the rich can afford. The rest of us wait "until the prices come down." Without free-spending rich people, Snow argues, few innovative products would ever make it to market and excite consumers. These rich, in effect, "shoulder the development costs of most new products and technologies."[17] Rich people, Snow concludes, carry "most of our economic weight."[18]

But that weight, in a Ten Times Rule America, could be shared. Public enterprises and agencies could easily provide markets for promising new products. Municipal transit authorities, for instance, could purchase fleets of vehicles that feature efficient new engine designs. School systems could put in bulk orders for desk furniture that incorporates new approaches to ergonomic design. NASA officials could commission the development of flame-retardant materials. Innovative products, in a Ten Times America, would have little trouble finding their way to market.

Innovative products, of course, require more than markets before they can become social realities. Innovative products require innovators. All new products need to be invented, developed, then championed. That process can demand a great deal of effort. Who would ever undertake this effort, opponents of a Ten Times Rule might likely shout, without the prospect of grand reward at the end of the day? Would we today, they ask, have computers on our desktops and software in our computers if our society a generation ago had shut the door to the accumulation of billion-dollar fortunes? Let Bill Gates have his billions, the argument goes, he has given us Windows. Inequality nurtures progress. The triumphs of our glorious Information Age, exult the friends of fortune, "prove" it.

The advances of the computer revolution actually do have a lesson for us, but not the lesson apologists for inequality suppose. We can have innovation, the computer revolution in fact teaches, without embracing greed, without smiling upon a deeply unequal distribution of riches.

Just ask Linus Torvalds, exhibit A in the case for equality and economic innovation.

Linus Torvalds cannot lay claim to having a household name. But this Finnish computer programmer has made contributions to innovation every bit as striking as any ever advanced by a Silicon Valley billionaire. Back in 1991, Torvalds, then a student in Helsinki, bought his first computer. His new PC carried a Microsoft operating system, as most computers still do, and Torvalds soon found himself frustrated by the Microsoft system's limitations. He could have simply gritted his teeth, like fellow frustrated users, and made do. But Torvalds chose not to take that course. He decided to write his own operating system. He tagged his new system, with a whimsical touch, Linux.

Torvalds did not then take the typical next move. He did not rush to cash in on his work. Instead, he posted Linux on the Internet and invited people to use it for free. That wasn't all. Torvalds also encouraged users to make improvements on his Linux program — and the young Finn set up a licensing system that required all improvements to be shared, for free, with all other users. This sharing strategy worked marvelously. Sharing, Torvalds found, begets sharing. Linux quickly evolved into a robust operating system that many computer experts rated as more stable and efficient than the Microsoft systems that dominate the PC market. By century's end, over 7 million people worldwide were using Linux, and that number was growing at double-digit annual rates.[19]

Torvalds himself opened the new century contentedly writing software in California. He had no billions to his name. That didn't matter. He had never sought billions.

"My main goal," as Torvalds once explained, "has always been to be in the position that I'm not ashamed of what I've done or am doing, and that I'm doing the best I can."[20]

Torvalds and Linux stand in the middle of what has become known, within the computer industry, as the "open source" movement. All over the world, experts and enthusiasts are writing computer code, sharing their work openly and freely, and watching others, operating in the same spirit, improve their initial work and advance it to higher levels of sophistication and quality. Some observers dismiss "open source" as a do-gooder protest against corporate computing's powers that be. But "open source" amounts to much more than that. The "open source" spirit amounts to a return to computing's roots, a return to the collaborative spirit that has generated the Information Age's greatest leaps forward, in everything from graphic interfaces to the Internet.

William McGill, who would later become the president of Columbia University, experienced this collaborative spirit early on, as a colleague of computing's first grand innovators, scientists like the widely admired J.C.R. Licklider of the Massachusetts Institute of Technology. "Few of these innovators are known to the public because they created the Internet in a collegial atmosphere, lacking in ego and greed," notes McGill.[21] Licklider and other innovators of the time, McGill observes, gave no thought to how rich their discoveries could make them. They were "driven by science" and "uninterested in credit." This, says McGill, "is the way it ought to be."

"I am saddened to think," he adds, "we have become so hardened by self-interest that we forget how science is supposed to work."

Innovation and invention, scientists like William McGill understand, can and do take place without the lure of great fortune. The chance to do interesting work, to feel part of something significant, offers talented people more than enough incentive to achieve and create at the highest levels. Creative people, notes psychologist Mihaly Csikszentmihalyi, don't love money. Creative people "love what they do."[22]

"It is not the hope of achieving fame or making money that drives them," this nationally respected analyst adds, "rather, it is the opportunity to do the work that they enjoy doing."[23]

Inequality *discourages* people from doing the work they most enjoy doing. In deeply unequal economies, in societies where rewards for some lines of work dwarf the rewards available from other lines of work, talented young people gravitate to the work that pays the most, not the work they find most personally appealing. They end up, for instance, in corporate law firms, spending eighty-hour weeks researching arcane points of obscure law. This work offers little intrinsic satisfaction. The work does offer, on the other hand, a chance to make partner — and annual incomes in the seven-figure range. Money trumps satisfaction. Talent goes to waste.

In a Ten Times Rule America, with a ceiling on income in place, no one field could ever astronomically outcompensate another. The nation's top figures in public interest law would earn in the same ballpark as the nation's top figures in corporate law. College presidents would make as much as bank presidents, top engineers as much as top stock analysts. Truly talented people, under the Ten Times Rule, would be more likely to go into fields they really enjoy — and be more likely to do great work in those fields.

Fewer people, meanwhile, would squander their energies lusting after jobs that promised colossal rewards for the tiny numbers of people able to make it to the top. In a Ten Times America, some lines of work might still carry higher monetary rewards than others. But no line of work would carry cash rewards dazzling enough to make talented young people stomach work they have no interest doing.

The talented simply do not need to be bribed, with colossal monetary rewards, to share their talents, a reality that apologists for inequality continually refuse to acknowledge. These apologists confuse wealth and reward. Wealth may be a reward. But rewards, to motivate, need not bring wealth. Applause can be a reward. Recognition can be a reward.

"Among the 50 states," as business commentator Daniel Akst points out, "not a single governorship has gone begging for want of bonuses and stock options."[24]

How much we earn, researchers agree, does certainly matter to us, but not as much as how much we earn compared to others around us. Most of us, economist Robert Frank notes, would rather take home $100,000 in a society where everyone else was making $90,000 than $110,000 in a society where everyone else was taking home $200,000.[25]

But what about those among us who don't just want to make *as much* as everybody else? What about the competitive among us who want to make *more* than everybody else? Would these competitive people be able to find satisfaction under the Ten Times Rule? Would a ten times economy be able to give these feverish competitors the incentive they need to perform at their best? Why not? Fierce competitors really don't care what they make. They just don't want to be beaten. They don't want anyone making more than what they earn. Fierce competitors, in a ten times economy, would still be able to climb their way to a "top." And at that top no one would be making more than they do. But that top would be a "top" with a difference. At this top — at the ten times limit — our nation's most competitively successful would not be earning colossally more than anybody else.

And that, in turn, would make an enormous difference for the rest of us. In a Ten Times Rule America, all people would be able to take pride in their work, in their contribution to society, because no one's work would be devalued by someone else's enormous compensation. In a Ten Times America, all work would have honor. All young people would have an incentive to do honorable work, the work they enjoy doing. Out of that work would come innovation. Out of that innovation would come wealth.

EARLY IN THE TWENTY-FIRST CENTURY, America's single largest organization, the AARP, asked a rather large national cross-section of adults — of all ages — what makes life worth living.[26] The vast majority of those surveyed placed earning a great deal of money near the bottom of their list. Happiness, those quizzed seemed to agree, comes instead from a combination of five much more significant factors: nurturing solid family ties, building friendships, helping people in need, getting a solid education, and having a satisfying job.

In a Ten Times Rule America, average Americans would be more likely to realize each of these five outcomes. But even this success, unfortunately, would not *guarantee* our happiness in a Ten Times America. Life does remain, to no small degree, about the money. To feel content, most of us need to see ongoing improvement in our economic circumstances. We can be content with an income of $50,000, as economist Robert Frank has noted, if we made $45,000 the year before. We will likely not be content with that same $50,000 if we earned $55,000 the year before.[27] Psychologically, we do better when we make modest, steady progress in our personal finances. Too much too soon, too little too late, leaves us sour. To keep us happy, a Ten Times Rule America would have to keep our incomes rising steadily.

And that's exactly what a Ten Times Rule would do. The reciprocity built into the Ten Times Rule, the direct link between incomes at the top and incomes at the bottom, would ensure a never-ending lobbying effort by people at the top to raise wages for people at the bottom. Rising wages at the bottom would, in turn, ripple throughout the economy and boost wages *between* top and bottom. In our current America, real wages have stagnated for three decades. In a Ten Times America, real wages would march steadily — and satisfyingly — ahead.

In a Ten Times Rule America, as a consequence, we would have in place a solid foundation for deep and lasting happiness. People would be moving up the economic ladder, modestly and steadily, within a society that values our time and our work. A Ten Times Rule would help us improve the quality of our lives.

But what about the *quantity* of our lives?

Quantity, as environmentalists have helped us understand, matters. The Earth's ecosystem can sustain only so much activity. At some point, the quantity of that activity endangers our natural ecosystems. We deplete natural resources faster than they can be replenished. We generate more waste than our Earth can absorb. Those of us around today may never live long enough to have to face a point of no return. We may be able to "grow" our economies, and then grow them a good bit more, without ever having to feel personally the environmental degradation we have wrought. But our children, or their children, will have no such luck. We ignore quantity at their peril, if not ours.

We do have an alternative. We can stop "growing" our economy in conventional economic terms, move toward what Herman Daly has called the "steady-state economy." We can shift our concentration from growth to development, from more to better. But this shift, as Daly emphasizes, will never be able to succeed without an equally momentous shift in how we think about rich and poor, about the distribution of income and wealth.

Any society wise enough to recognize that our ecosystem cannot support unlimited material production, Herman Daly notes, must also recognize that allowing 99 percent of a "limited total product to go to only one person" cannot possibly make sense — or be just. Limits on material production, in other words, at some point necessitate limits on distribution. Without limits on who gets what, limits on how much we burden the Earth become impossible to sustain. And what limits on distribution would help ensure sustainability? As a "formula for fairness," a ten times differential between minimum and maximum income strikes Daly as sensible and practical.[28]

"No one is arguing for an invidious, forced equality," he notes. "A factor of ten in inequality would be justified by real differences in effort and diligence, and would provide sufficient incentive to call forth these qualities."[29]

A ten times maximum, adds Daly, would help us create a better world, a sustainable world, a world where tomorrow's basic needs would "always take precedence over the extravagant luxury of the present."[30] How good a place might this world be? A world that rejects extravagance as a motive force, author Alan Durning suggests, would be much more than simply a world without environmental degradation. A world that lived by sufficiency, not excess, would offer "a return to what is, culturally speaking, the human home: to the ancient order of family, community, good work, and good life; to a reverence for skill, creativity, and creation, to a daily cadence slow enough to let us watch the sunset and stroll by the water's edge; to communities worth spending a lifetime in; and to places pregnant with the memories of generations."[31]

A world without excess. A ten times world.

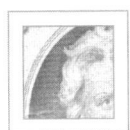

A Strategy for Change

Will anyone reading these pages ever live in a Ten Times America? Today, in these early years of the twenty-first century, that hardly seems likely. Those of us eager to see greater equity in the United States currently don't have enough clout to maintain an adequate *minimum* wage. How could we possibly hope to ever realize an income *maximum*?

So must we content ourselves with more pedestrian objectives? In a deeply unequal America, must we accept greed's golden rule — that those who have the gold rule — and simply do our best to prevent the golden from wreaking too much collateral damage? Must we resign ourselves to racing on treadmills? Must we have only plutocrats, or their pals, on our ballots? Must we bowl alone? Or dare we dream of different lives, of satisfying careers, of vibrant communities, of ballgames without three-minute breaks for commercials? Dare we believe that our society can change, and fundamentally so, for the better? Dare we imagine as bold, as thrilling, a change as a Ten Times Rule?

We can so dare. And we should. American attitudes toward compensation and fairness have changed dramatically before. They could change again.

Consider this: We still have among us people old enough to remember a time when overwhelming majorities of Americans felt comfortable in an economy that paid blacks less than whites for the same exact work, women less than men. Today, overwhelming majorities of Americans consider "equal pay for equal work" a basic core value. Within the span of a lifetime, we redefined fairness.

Our human species has already flirted with the notion that fairness may demand limits on income, via top tax rates calibrated at 100 percent. We here in the United States once had in place a 94 percent top tax rate on wealthy incomes. The British, in 1941, enacted a 97.5 percent top rate.[1] The Danes, after World War II, dabbled with an ever higher figure.[2] Civilized, perfectly rational people have discussed and debated income maximums in our past. Why shouldn't we assume that such maximums might once again be discussed in our future? In our modern world, substantial numbers of people already feel comfortable with income ceilings. One 1995 poll found over half the French people, 52 percent, supporting a salary cap, just 33 percent opposed.[3]

Decades ago, pollsters found similar sentiments right here in the United States. In December 1942, 47 percent of Americans favored a cap on the income any individual ought to be allowed to keep, after taxes. Only 38 percent opposed the idea.[4] Pollsters found this broad support for an income maximum about eight months after President Franklin Roosevelt first championed the idea. Over the years since, no American political notable has ever revisited the income cap notion, either in peacetime or war, and the concept, predictably enough, has almost totally faded from public view. In one 1992 Roper poll, only 9 percent of Americans expressed support for "limiting the amount of money any individual is allowed to earn in a year."[5] Yet many Americans, polling data also show, feel distinctly uneasy about concentrated wealth. One in three Americans, a 1990 *Fortune* poll found, believe America would be better off without any millionaires.[6] In 1996, nearly two-thirds of Americans agreed that "differences in income in America are too large."[7] Seven years later, in 2003, about the same number, 63 percent, told Gallup that "money and wealth in this country should be more evenly distributed."[8]

And how should money and wealth be more evenly distributed? Americans remain deeply unsure. The same 2003 Gallup poll that found broad support for a more even income distribution found no great outcry for higher taxes on high incomes. Only 38 percent of Americans, Gallup reported, consider taxes on wealthy people "too low."[9] Earlier polling had found similarly conflicted attitudes. In 2000, in an October pre-election survey, 46 percent of Americans agreed that "it's unfair that many people are becoming millionaires when a lot of people work very hard every day and will never be rich." But a slightly larger share of the American public, 51 percent, disagreed with that observation.[10] Yet that same year, in a September survey, 77 percent of Americans told pollsters they wanted to hear from Presidential candidates George W. Bush and Al Gore on just how they planned "to reduce the gap between rich people and poor people in this country."[11]

Americans, the polls make plain, remain profoundly unsettled about wealth and income inequality. Our conflicted attitudes toward concentrated wealth — and what to do about it — sit side by side in a murky mix of apprehension and ambivalence. And this confusion, of course, serves only to perpetuate our increasingly unequal status quo. Those who sit at the summit of America's economic hierarchy, surrounded by the greatest accumulation of wealth the modern world has ever seen, have nothing to fear from a public ambivalent about wealth and wealth holders. In this muddled political climate, no proposal for a Ten Times Rule, no proposal for any significant redistribution of wealth and income, will ever get traction. And that won't change until Americans, in large numbers, begin to consider concentrated wealth a clear and present danger, until Americans stand ready to condemn not just greed and grasping, but the public policies that encourage the greedy to grasp.

Years ago, Americans feared concentrated wealth. We today do not. We have swallowed a political perspective on wealth that would have appalled the likes of Theodore and Franklin Roosevelt — and the many millions of Americans who gave them their support. This perspective, this faith that helping the wealthy become wealthier will somehow benefit us all, has proved a fraud. But this perspective, despite its failure, remains our conventional wisdom. And that should not surprise us. Conventional wisdoms seldom collapse on their own. They collapse only when challenged, only when advocates for change thrust forward initiatives that expose the bankruptcy of the conventionally wise.

So where should advocates for a more equal America begin this challenging? What initiatives can we promote to help crystalize vague misgivings about inequality into a clear conviction that concentrated wealth endangers what we hold dear? What can we do today, and the day after, to make the struggle against concentrated wealth a campaign and a cause that challenges and engages ever larger numbers of Americans? What can we do to shove inequality onto America's political centerstage?

What can we do? What should we do? To make concentrated wealth *the* issue of our time, we need to focus on the engine that continues to concentrate America's wealth. We need to focus on the modern American corporation. The battle for a more equal America ought to begin with an assault on corporate business as usual.

This business as usual is failing us, failing to provide jobs that deliver adequate income, failing to bring us career and retirement security, failing to keep our communities vital. And at the root of this failure sits greed. More specifically, at the root of this failure sits a complex of attitudes and accepted practices, often enshrined in law, that have, for over a generation now, encouraged and enabled corporate leaders to amass incredible personal fortunes. We will not "fix" our corporate enterprises until we end this concentration of wealth within our corporate enterprises.

Any struggle against concentrated corporate wealth, to emerge triumphant, would have to involve the many millions of Americans who have a direct, intimate stake, as employees, in enterprise success. And if this struggle did involve these many millions of Americans, inequality would become, in the twenty-first century, what we need it to be. Inequality would become the central battleground of American political life.

On that battleground, a campaign for a Ten Times Rule could be waged. On that battleground, a Ten Times Rule could be won.

THE STRUGGLE AGAINST ECONOMIC INJUSTICE begins, in every modern nation, with organized labor. In nations with strong, deeply rooted trade union movements, inequality does not widen. Inequality ebbs. In the United States, for over a generation now, we have had no strong, deeply rooted labor movement presence. We have paid the price. Our wealth has concentrated, at record levels.

Wealth in the United States will no doubt continue to concentrate until labor regains a vital presence in the everyday life of our nation. But the reverse may also be true: American labor might not be able to regain a vital presence until concentrated wealth no longer holds a lock-grip over our economy — and democracy. And if that be the case, then labor faces a single overriding strategic imperative. Labor must step front and center and lead the charge, enterprise by enterprise, against concentrated wealth.

Unions, to assume this leadership role, would need to think differently about how they relate to the enterprises where union members labor. Historically, most unions in the United States have focused narrowly on wages, hours, and working conditions. American unions, unlike unions elsewhere, have typically left every other facet of enterprise life, including executive compensation, to management discretion. In recent years, labor activists and leaders have begun contesting this traditional mindset. Unions, these new thinkers have urged, need to focus more attention on the overall health and viability of the enterprises where union members work. Unions need to care, the new thinkers have argued, about how enterprises make decisions and govern themselves, about how they keep their books, even about how they pay their executives.

This new thinking has spawned a wide and innovative array of new labor initiatives. Unions are now working to leverage the union member dollars in America's pension funds. They are pressing fund managers to invest in enterprises that engage in practices that build productive relationships between labor and management.[12] They are also working, at the same time, to encourage *more* corporate enterprises to adopt these positive practices. They are urging pension funds to support corporate reform shareholder resolutions, to challenge excessive executive pay, to oppose "large workplace pay disparities that damage employee productivity and morale."[13]

"We have to find ways to get companies to act in a more responsible way," explains Ron Blackwell, the director of the AFL-CIO's Department of Corporate Affairs. "Policies that benefit only a small minority of shareholders are not sustainable — economically or socially. We want business to prosper, and to maximize long-term shareholder value, but in ways that benefit all shareholders."[14]

Many of America's biggest unions have helped advance this new labor thrust. The Communications Workers of America, in one campaign effort, called on Sprint to limit annual increases in executive pay to the average annual increases in worker pay, a move needed, the union noted, to "assure shareholders and employees that Sprint's hard-earned profits will be used for research, development, equipment modernization."[15] A Teamsters campaign called for a $1 million limit on the base salaries of General Electric's top five executives. "We still think a million dollars means something," noted the union's director of corporate affairs, Bart Naylor.[16]

Millions of other Americans, unions have discovered, feel the same way. By 2000, over 11 million Americans a year were clicking into PayWatch, the Web site the AFL-CIO launched in 1997 to help expose and battle back against executive pay outrages.[17] Americans angry about CEO pay can use Paywatch to e-mail corporate boards, message members of Congress, or lobby the Securities and Exchange Commission. Employees at America's biggest fifteen hundred corporations can even use the site to compute how many years they would have to work to match what their top executives make in just one.

"Depending on the CEO," quips AFL-CIO Secretary-Treasury Richard Trumka, "it's usually a few thousand years."[18]

Labor's corporate reform efforts, in the wake of the Enron scandal, would ratchet up still another notch. Unions rushed to the aid of workers left stranded by the bankruptcies at Enron and other corporate giants, even where those workers had never been union members. Then, late in 2002, labor helped lead a campaign to require America's mutual funds to disclose how they vote their investors' shares, on executive pay and other issues, at corporate annual meetings. The campaign triumphed. Mutual funds, federal regulators ruled early in 2003, can no longer vote their investors' shares corporate management's way — and then keep those votes secret.[19]

The same corporate scandals that helped labor win this mutual fund victory also shifted America's pension fund giants closer to labor's corporate reform perspective.[20] In the mid 1990s, the retirement funds that make up the Council of Institutional Investors had refused, as a group, to back any reforms that would require corporations to book stock options as expenses. The reforms would fail. That failure, in turn, would help executives puff up their corporate bottom lines over the rest of the decade — and score hundreds of billions in stock option windfalls. In 2002, after Enron, the Council of Institutional Investors would do an abrupt about-face and vow to support option expensing.[21]

About-faces like this struck some observers, like *Los Angeles Times* senior economics editor James Flanigan, as the dawning of a brand new day, as the beginning of a "transfer of authority from executive suites to representatives of the shareholder-employees." Workers, Flanigan noted, hold more than 60 percent of the stock in publicly traded companies, either indirectly through their pension plans or directly through their own individual retirement investments. If working people flexed their "ownership" muscles, Flanigan observed, they would no longer need to go through life "ceding control to corporate executives to manage companies as they see fit."[22]

The vote tallies on shareholder resolutions debated in 2002, after Enron's collapse, did seem to show some muscle flexing. One set of researchers tracked nearly five hundred resolutions considered over the course of the year. Just over a hundred, the researchers found, actually won majorities, the best shareholder resolution winning percentage ever.[23] And these winning votes actually forced some specific changes in corporate behavior. Managements at Bristol-Myers, Squibb and Johnson & Johnson, after shareholder voting, all agreed to end or reduce the consulting fees they pay to auditors, a move reformers had been demanding ever since Enron first hit the headlines.[24]

But other more skeptical observers saw no particular reason to celebrate the post-Enron shareholder voting. None of the resolutions enacted in Enron's wake, they noted, placed any explicit limits on executive compensation. And even if a pay-limit resolution were to gain a shareholder majority, they added, that resolution would be unlikely to change executive pay behavior, since shareholder resolutions on compensation do not carry the force of law. Managements are not legally bound to put these resolutions into effect.

Real change in corporate pay practices, many reformers argue, will only come when dissident shareholders start waging — and winning — election campaigns to unseat management-friendly incumbents on corporate boards of directors. But reformers also see no wave of these battles about to break out, mainly because board challenges can be incredibly expensive to mount. In 2001, for instance, Texas billionaire Sam Wyly waged a crusade to defeat management-backed board candidates at Computer Associates, the company where, just three years earlier, a trio of executives had cashed out an insane $1.1 billion stock option windfall. Wyly spent a whopping $10 million on his challenge against the Computer Associate management board slate. He lost anyway.[25]

Shareholder activists, in effect, have the deck stacked against them. Managements hold most all the cards.[26] Veteran shareholder activists, to be sure, know how the cards will likely play out. But they play on anyway. Even in defeat, they note, shareholder activism can make an important contribution to the struggle against concentrated wealth. Debates over CEO pay resolutions, points out shareholder strategist Scott Klinger, can always help "get a discussion going on whether the value of a company has been created by a single person or all employees."[27] But shareholder resolutions in and of themselves, most activists would agree, are unlikely to ever significantly impact actual executive pay.

Labor's corporate reformers, to make a real dent on concentrated corporate wealth, would need to extend their struggle beyond the corporate annual meeting. They would need to take the campaign against corporate greed to the one battlefield where labor can win and has won epochal victories, the one battlefield where Americans expect to see labor do most of its fighting. At this battlefield — the bargaining table — labor, not just management, holds some facecards.

TRADE UNIONS TODAY, AT CONTRACT BARGAINING time, are actually already raising executive pay excess as an issue. Savvy union negotiators will frequently use the immorally high pay gaps that divide executives and workers to dramatize the moral case for higher wages. Publicity about these gaps often helps rally public support for grossly underpaid workers.[28] But America's trade unions have so far not moved, in any significant way, to make pay gaps themselves an actual bargaining matter. These gaps remain beyond the "scope of bargaining." Executive pay has always been considered — and continues to be considered — none of labor's business, a topic unfit for collective bargaining.

Could that change? Could gaps between worker and executive pay become a bargaining matter? Why not? Labor's "business," after all, most certainly does include the setting of worker pay levels. Labor negotiators, to set these worker pay levels, routinely bargain contracts that peg worker pay to benchmarks that unions have no hand in setting. Unions regularly, for instance, bargain cost-of-living clauses. These clauses automatically boost wages by a certain rate or amount whenever the official inflation rate spikes. Unions do not determine the inflation rate. Nor do they determine executive pay. But unions could insist, in a Ten Times Rule spirit, that rewards that go to workers at the bottom of the enterprise ladder ought to be linked to the rewards that go to executives at the top, in the same way that cost-of-living adjustments link wage increases directly to the inflation rate. No workers within an enterprise, labor could argue, should ever be paid less than a specific multiple of what the enterprise pays its loftiest executive.

Any collectively bargained contract that linked compensation at the bottom of an enterprise to compensation at the top would create the same sort of healthy dynamic that the adoption of a Ten Times Rule would create for society at large. Executives within enterprises that adopted a "pay equity ratio" between top and bottom would have an ongoing incentive to raise the compensation of their lowest-paid workers.[29] In any corporation with a twenty-five times pay equity ratio in effect, no executive would be able to take home $1 million unless all workers took home at least $40,000.

Corporate flacks would, of course, do their best to paint pay equity ratios as the first step toward the end of civilization as we know it. They would no doubt blast ratio-minded union negotiators as irresponsible radicals. But those union negotiators would be able to blast right back. Was J. P. Morgan, the grandest capitalist of the late nineteenth century, an irresponsible radical? Morgan, in the many corporations he created, insisted on a twenty-to-one pay ratio between workers and top executives. And how about Peter Drucker, the eminent founder of modern management science? Drucker, over the last third of the twentieth century, consistently championed the notion that pay ratios between workers and executives ought to be kept within a fifteen- or twenty-times range. Was Morgan wrong? Is Drucker's counsel misguided?

Interesting questions. They could inspire, at America's bargaining table, some of the liveliest negotiating sessions our nation has ever seen.

MIDWAY THROUGH 2002, pollsters working for National Public Radio asked a random national sampling of Americans how they felt about CEOs "taking big bonuses and lavish perks, as their companies were failing and stockholders lost money." Over two-thirds of those surveyed, 71 percent, listed themselves as "very angry."[30]

Corporate executive pay excesses have been leaving Americans "very angry" ever since the early 1980s. America's political leaders, in the meantime, have done nothing meaningful that speaks to this anger. America's unions could do plenty. A labor movement struggle to establish "pay equity ratios" within America's biggest corporations could thoroughly shake up business as usual in America's executive suites — and perhaps capture the public's imagination more vividly than any labor mobilization since the great sitdown strikes of the 1930s.

But any bargaining-based drive for pay equity ratios would face one enormously discouraging reality. Unions today, in the private sector, only bargain for a relative handful of American workers. The overwhelming majority of America's corporations do not engage in collective bargaining with their employees. Less than 10 percent of American private sector workers currently carry union cards. Unions simply do not have enough of a workplace presence to advance an effective pay equity ratio struggle at the bargaining table alone. To advance any serious struggle against corporate concentrated wealth, to have any hope of establishing pay equity ratios throughout corporate America, American labor — and labor's allies — would have to identify points of leverage beyond the bargaining table. These points of leverage, fortunately, do exist. In the public sector.

We tend to think of private and public as two distinctly separate spheres of economic existence: the public sector, bankrolled by taxpayer dollars, over here, the private sector, bankrolled by marketplace transactions, over there. In reality, no clear, clean divide separates our private sector from our public. The two sectors, day by day, waltz through America's economic life as a couple.

Our local, state, and national governments interface with private businesses at a host of different levels. At the most basic of these levels, public bodies procure goods and services from private businesses. The federal government alone, in 2002, expended over $265 billion for private sector goods and services.[31] Government officials also hand businesses a vast array of subsidies and development grants. McDonald's has received millions to advertise hamburgers in Paris, automakers many more millions to design cars.[32] States and municipalities have, since 1953, spent over $20 billion to give professional baseball teams places to play.[33] Some corporate giants even receive tax dollars for not doing anything at all. In 1999, for instance, the state of Maryland handed Marriott, America's "hospitality" giant, a package of tax breaks and financial incentives worth an estimated $44 million. In return, Marriott simply promised not to move its international headquarters out of Maryland, across the Potomac, into Virginia.[34]

Governments bestow upon private businesses more than procurement orders and tax breaks. They give them licenses and leases that let them turn nature, at little or no cost, into generous profit-making opportunities. Television broadcasters, for instance, pay nothing for that slice of the electromagnetic spectrum the government has set aside for standard television broadcasting. Mining companies pay next to nothing, year after year, to lease mineral-rich government land.[35] If nature gets upset, government takes care of that, too. Developers can get subsidized flood insurance. Nuclear power plant operators get a great deal more. Actuaries estimate that a major nuclear power plant disaster could cause damages worth $500 billion. The federal Price Anderson Act, on the books since 1957, limits the nuclear power industry's liability to less than 2 percent of that total.[36]

How many tax dollars, overall, go to private businesses? No one knows for sure. But that doesn't matter. We don't need to know an exact figure, or even an estimate good to the nearest trillion. The reality, even without exact numbers, remains plain. No significant business in the United States today sits purely in the "private sector." Every major American business interacts regularly with the public sector, in some way, shape, or form. And that reality has created a direct link between CEOs and taxpayers. Public sector tax dollars have helped pump up every major fortune "earned" in the private sector.

"Behind every great fortune is a crime, wrote Balzac," as business columnist Michael Thomas has noted. "Had he been writing in millennial America, he might have said, behind every great fortune lies a fat deal with Uncle Sam."[37]

That doesn't have to be. Taxpayers don't have to be subsidizing CEOs. The public sector could just say no — to the "fat deals" that grow great private fortunes at taxpayer expense. Governments in the United States could nix these fat deals merely by taking one simple step. They could place pay equity ratio "strings" on every major transaction with private sector enterprises.

Does a furniture company want a contract to fill a new school with desks? Fine. To have a bid considered, that company would first have to show proof that none of its employees are paid less than fifty times — or twenty-five times or ten times — its top executive.

Does a defense contractor want a loan guarantee for a foreign customer? The government would happily consider that request, if the contractor merely adopts a company-wide pay policy that narrows internal pay gaps to some modest fixed multiple.

Does a telecom want a chunk of electromagnetic spectrum for a cell phone license? No problem, so long as the telecom pays no executive at levels that significantly outpace the earnings of their lowest-paid workers.

Pay equity ratio "strings" along these lines, applied consistently and firmly, would almost immediately start wringing excess out of the American economy. Every major enterprise would feel the impact. Every major enterprise would have to make internal compensation adjustments — or lose ground to competitors who did.

Could such "strings" ever be more than an egalitarian pipedream? They certainly could. Our local, state, and national governments already place strings of various sorts on contracts with private enterprises. Our public bodies, for instance, do not award contracts or subsidies to businesses that discriminate by race or gender in their employment practices. Such discriminatory behavior, up until the fairly recent past, did not bother our society. That behavior does bother us now. If you discriminate, you do not get to do business with Uncle Sam.[38]

In 1994, efforts to impose "strings" on government contracts and subsidies took a dramatic new turn. In that year, church and labor groups in Baltimore led a campaign that resulted in the nation's first-ever "living wage" law. Under the new statute, any contractors who wanted do business with Baltimore would have to pay their workers, by 1999, at least $7.70 an hour, a wage high enough to place a family of four over the poverty line.[39] Scores of other cities and counties would soon follow suit. By late 2003, over a hundred localities had adopted living wage ordinances. The most significant of these, in New York City, mandates that service contractors with city work must pay their employees at least $10 an hour, plus health benefits, by July 2006.[40]

All the living wage ordinances so far enacted share a common assumption: Poverty does not serve the public interest. Public bodies, living wage advocates argue, have a responsibility to make sure that tax dollars do not subsidize poverty wages.

Public bodies have another responsibility as well, a responsibility seldom recognized. Poverty does not serve the public interest. Neither does inequality. Public bodies have a responsibility to battle inequality, a responsibility to help prevent wealth from concentrating. By adding pay equity ratio "strings" to every contract, to every subsidy, to every tax break, by denying tax dollars to private businesses that pay some individuals outrageously more than others, public bodies could finally begin to meet this responsibility. And serve the public interest.

NO COLLEGE OR UNIVERSITY IN THE UNITED STATES is today legally required to spend as much on sports teams for women as on sports teams for men. Universities can field, if they choose, dozens of teams for men and none for women. But if they do, their campus will receive not one dime of federal aid in any form. Congress made this determination over three decades ago, in Title IX of the Education Amendments of 1972.

"No person in the United States," Title IX proclaimed, "shall, on the basis of sex, be excluded from participation in, be denied the benefits of, or be subject to discrimination under any education program or activities receiving Federal financial assistance."[41]

Title IX would go into effect in 1975 and, over the next quarter-century, become perhaps the federal government's most successful equalizing legislation. Before Title IX, over a quarter of men, but less than a fifth of women, completed college. That gap is now gone. Before Title IX, only thirty-two thousand young women participated in college athletics. After Title IX's implementation, that total more than quintupled.[42]

Colleges and universities, the record shows, took Title IX to heart. They really had no choice. Most couldn't survive a semester without federal support. To keep public tax dollars in the pipeline, America's colleges and universities took steps to treat all students more equally — and all Americans benefited.

America's private enterprises, at compensation time, currently face no negative consequences for choosing inequality. These enterprises can, if they so choose, pay their workers pittances and their executives millions — and still merrily collect our tax dollars. Why should we let them? Private enterprises that can "afford" to compensate executives at considerably loftier levels than their workers should be able to afford going about their business without help from taxpayers.

A labor movement that worked to drive home points like this, progressive strategists like the University of Wisconsin's Joel Rogers believe, could begin reframing America's political discourse. "Maximum wage" initiatives that deny tax dollars to firms with overpaid CEOs could be an important element, Rogers suggests, within the multi-issue reform offensives labor ought to be waging.[43]

These multi-issue offensives have begun to take shape. In 1997, for instance, Connecticut labor, religious, and public interest groups joined to make the case for an omnibus statewide corporate accountability act.[44] Their coalition, Citizens for Economic Opportunity, urged state lawmakers to deny all government subsidies and contracts to any corporations that sidestep workplace safety regulations, violate environmental laws, refuse benefits to part-time workers, or pay their top executives more than twenty-five times what their average workers earn.

"Government should not be in the business of rewarding destructive behavior," the coalition's leader, Phil Wheeler, a top United Auto Workers official, told Connecticut lawmakers. "Don't take the taxpayers' money, then give your CEO a million dollar raise while your employees get nothing."[45]

Lawmakers would not prove sympathetic. They rejected the reform coalition's entire corporate accountability package, despite evidence that the central idea behind the package enjoyed broad public support. One poll had found that 86 percent of Connecticut voters supported legislation that would have the state "only give loans, grants, and contracts to companies that behave responsibly."[46]

Other polling had discovered, about the same time, the same sort of attitudes at the national level. In 1996, pollsters Peter Hart and Ethel Klein found that Americans, by a three-to-one majority, "favor government action to promote more responsible corporate behavior and penalize bad corporate citizenship"[47] Among the research's other findings: 82 percent of Americans support the setting of standards for responsible corporate behavior and giving companies that meet these standards a lower tax rate.

On Capitol Hill, that same year, a handful of lawmakers worked to translate these sentiments into actual legislation. Senator Jeff Bingaman from New Mexico proposed that a new category of corporations be created. Corporations that qualified for his proposal's new "A Corp" status would be eligible to receive special tax advantages. These advantages would go only to corporations that invested at least 3 percent of their payroll in an employee pension plan, spent at least 2 percent on worker training, paid at least one-half the cost of employee health care coverage, and compensated no executive at a level more than fifty times the wage of the company's lowest-paid worker.[48]

This notion of establishing standards for responsible corporate behavior struck some Clinton administration officials as a promising idea. Labor Secretary Robert Reich, for one, called for a "new era of corporate citizenship" and proposed cutting income taxes for corporations that upgraded worker skills, provided decent health and pension benefits, and shared their profits.[49] But Reich's boss, President Clinton, would not be comfortable with this approach. The Clinton White House, in the end, would limit its advocacy for "responsible" corporate behavior to moral suasion. The administration would go no further than hosting a conference designed, the *Washington Post* reported, "to celebrate companies with enlightened policies in the hope that others will be inspired to follow."[50]

More skeptical old Washington hands, like veteran Minnesota Congressman Martin Sabo, figured corporations needed much more pushing than celebrating. Sabo had introduced, in 1991, legislation that aimed to close the loophole in the federal tax code that actually rewards corporations for over-paying their executives. Corporations, under the current code, can deduct from their income "reasonable salaries and benefits" as a cost of doing business. But the code doesn't define "reasonable."[51] In practice, corporations can essentially deduct whatever they pay their top executives. The more compensation they lavish on executives, the fewer dollars they pay in corporate income taxes.

This state of affairs has always offended Sabo, a native North Dakotan who grew up in what he calls the "Prairie Populist" tradition.[52] His solution? A pay equity ratio for corporate income taxes. Sabo's proposed Income Equity Act denies corporations tax deductions on any executive compensation that exceeds twenty-five times the pay of a company's lowest-paid workers. Why twenty-five times? That multiple, Sabo explains, approximates the ratio between the minimum wage and the salary of the President of the United States that existed when he first introduced his Income Equity Act legislation.[53]

How much would Sabo's Income Equity Act, if enacted, save taxpayers? Researchers have worked out estimates. In 1997, if Sabo's twenty-five times deductibility limit had been applied merely to the top two executives at the 365 companies covered in the annual *Business Week* executive pay survey, the federal treasury would have collected an additional $514 million in corporate income taxes.[54]

In 2001, Sabo toughened his Income Equity Act proposal, updating the legislation to include all forms of executive compensation, from stock options to country club memberships.[55] This update figured to up the overall revenue Sabo's Income Equity Act would raise, if enacted, into the billions. But Sabo has always emphasized that enacting his Income Equity Act would do far more than raise needed revenue. The bill, he notes, would "send a message that those who work on the factory floor are as important to a company's success as those who work in the executive suite." America's "growing economic divide," he adds, "threatens our democratic principles."[56]

Sabo's Income Equity Act does not yet threaten this economic divide. His bill, Sabo understands, will not be enacted anytime soon. But the logic behind Sabo's proposal remains compelling — and attractive to broad numbers of Americans.[57]

"My bill would not limit executive pay, nor would it dictate what a company must pay its employees," as Sabo explains. "My legislation simply asserts that our government should not, through the tax code, subsidize excessive pay. If companies want to receive larger tax deductions, they should pay their lowest-paid employees better."[58]

Lawmakers like Rep. Martin Sabo and activists like the UAW's Phil Wheeler in Connecticut have, as yet, scored no pay equity ratio victories. They have, nonetheless, made an important contribution to the struggle against concentrated wealth. Their ideas point the way to the sorts of struggles that can begin to infuse American politics with the Ten Times Rule spirit. Their proposals have not yet become politically viable. But bold ideas that threaten entrenched elites always take time to build momentum. Their time will come, particularly if we pick some battles that can be won — over elites a little bit less entrenched.

AMERICAN ECONOMIC LIFE ACTUALLY FALLS into three sectors, not just two. We have the private sector, the public sector, and what has come to be known as the "independent sector," the world of nonprofits and charities. This "independent sector," like the private sector, would collapse without public sector support.

Public sector support for nonprofits sometimes flows directly into independent sector organizations, as payment for services rendered. Taxpayer dollars, for instance, compensate nonprofit health organizations for the care they provide to poor and elderly people. The public sector also supports nonprofits indirectly, via tax breaks. Nonprofits typically do not pay taxes on their property or their purchases. Municipal and state governments, as a result, collect less tax revenue than they otherwise would. Governments also collect less revenue because individuals can deduct contributions to tax-exempt nonprofits at income tax time. Over six hundred thousand nonprofit organizations in the United States currently hold tax-exempt status.[59] Contributions to these organizations, once itemized, slice federal revenues by tens of billions every year.[60]

All this taxpayer support for nonprofits, direct and indirect, primarily benefits large charitable enterprises. These large charities dominate the nonprofit world. Charitable enterprises with at least $10 million in assets make up just 6 percent of the nonprofits that file annual reports with the IRS, but hold nearly 90 percent of nonprofit assets.[61] America's largest charities have, in effect, become enormous nonprofit empires. At their summits sit executives who often receive equally enormous salaries.

These enormous executive salaries create a delicate problem. All nonprofits, even the grandest, ultimately depend on public goodwill. Nonprofits need the public to feel good about their work, good enough to contribute dollars, good enough to volunteer time. Without contributions, without volunteers, without public good will, even the wealthiest charitable enterprise will eventually start to sputter.

Excessive salaries for nonprofit executives do not engender good will. These salaries deeply offend public sensibilities. Americans don't expect those who do "charity work" to live in poverty. But they don't expect nonprofit executives to live in luxury either. In the early 1990s, the public saw this luxury — at the United Way of America — and howled in protest. Americans felt betrayed. How could United Way, the nation's most familiar charitable namebrand, bestow upon its president a $463,000 annual pay package? How could United Way let this president, William Aramony, traipse around town in a chauffeured limousine — and criss-cross America in first-class airplane seats?[62] The scandal around Aramony would not be an isolated story. By the mid 1990s, headlines about executive excess at America's biggest charities had become a major embarrassment throughout the nonprofit world.

In 1996, lawmakers stepped into the mix. They rewrote the charitable tax rules. Up until then, the IRS could only punish charities that overly enriched their top officials by revoking their tax-exempt status. But this "death penalty" sanction always seemed overkill. The IRS seldom applied it.[63] Large nonprofits, consequently, saw little risk to escalating their executive pay. The new 1996 legislation would give the IRS a more practical sanction, the power to levy fines against charities that cut unduly generous paychecks for their top officials. Nonprofit executives, under the new law, could be forced to return excessive compensation, and the fines on these "excess benefit transactions," if not paid promptly, could soar to 200 percent of the money due.[64]

This new legislation, lawmakers hoped, would end the headlines about charitable excess. By that measure, the legislation would fail. The scandals would keep coming, bigger and more lurid than ever. In New York, reporters documented extraordinary excess in the executives suites at HIP, the state's biggest nonprofit health maintenance organization. HIP's chairman collected over $1 million in salary and bonus in 1998. On top of that, the chairman's perks included one lush apartment in New York City, another in Florida, and a Jaguar sedan. Why did the chairman need a Jaguar? "He has a real problem fitting into other cars," a spokesman for HIP explained. "Jaguars are one of the few cars that have enough play in the seat for his long legs." All told, thirty HIP executives took home over $150,000 in 1998, three over $500,000. The nonprofit, at the time, drew nearly half its revenue from tax-funded programs intended to serve poor and elderly New Yorkers.[65]

A few years later, political storms would erupt in Maryland after reports surfaced that the CEO of the state's largest health insurer, the nonprofit CareFirst BlueCross BlueShield, had collected $2.7 million in salary and bonuses in 2001 and negotiated a severance agreement that guaranteed him $15.4 million more.[66] Meanwhile, at the national level, researchers were revealing that nonprofit executive pay levels were jumping at twice the inflation rate.[67] The landmark 1996 nonprofit pay reform legislation, the *Chronicle of Philanthropy* would conclude late in 2002, "has accomplished little in the six years that it has been on the books."[68]

Some observers had fully expected that sorry result. The new law never offered a simple, clear definition of what constituted excess.[69] One member of Congress had tried, early on, to fill that definitional void. In 1998, Rep. Robert Menendez from New Jersey introduced legislation "to cap the salaries of nonprofit executives at no more than the salaries of U.S. Cabinet secretaries." His cap, if enacted, would have limited top nonprofit pay to $151,800. But Congress would not be interested in enacting a nonprofit pay cap. The Menendez proposal drew not a single co-sponsor.[70]

Could some other approach to defining excess in the nonprofit world attract more support than the Menendez proposal? Perhaps. Excess within the nonprofit world could be defined not as a fixed amount, but as a ratio between top and bottom, as any income for a nonprofit executive that exceeds by ten or twenty times the income of any other employee within that executive's nonprofit. For big-time nonprofits, opposing a proposed pay standard along these top-to-bottom ratio lines might prove a bit dicey. How can a charity in good faith argue, after all, that it must be allowed to pay an executive $500,000 if it can't "afford" to pay its receptionists more than $15,000?

Big-time nonprofits would argue against a pay equity ratio anyway. Charitable enterprises, they would patiently try to explain, need to be able to pay well enough to attract talented people, to reward outstanding performance, and to keep outstanding leaders from jumping ship. Sound familiar? In a debate over contentions like these, egalitarians would have the upper hand, even in the current political environment. Americans expect charities to do good, not to insure that executives do well. Lawmakers who ignored this deeply felt conviction — and voted against a pay equity ratio for nonprofits — would likely have to do some explaining of their own.

This political dynamic just might make the nonprofit sector the best place to initiate a legislative drive for pay equity ratios in American life. In this sector, victories could be won. Lawmakers could be pressed, as a first step, to require large tax-exempts to disclose the salaries of both their lowest- and highest-paid employees. These disclosure reports would help illustrate the depth of pay inequity in nonprofit America. The next step: legislation to impose an actual pay equity ratio mandate, perhaps twenty-five times to start. Any executive compensation above the ratio would be deemed an "excess benefit" that must be returned, with an accompanying fine.

A legislative victory or two over nonprofit executive excess would give the drive for pay equity ratios throughout American life a significant boost — and give defenders of private sector excess serious cause to be nervous. An American public upset about nonprofits enriching their top executives at taxpayer expense, these defenders would quickly realize, might soon become a public upset about *for*-profits enriching their top executives at taxpayer expense.

Taxpayers don't like to feel used. Ronald Reagan knew that. He invented "welfare queens" to play on this frustration. Advocates for a more equal

America don't need to invent "corporate kings." They already exist. They're all around us. And they're vulnerable.

IN 2003, SIX MONTHS AFTER THE IRAQ WAR BEGAN, the Bush administration asked Congress for an additional $87 billion in war-related funding. Any approval of this $87 billion request, corporate watchdog groups immediately understood, would set the stage for perhaps the biggest contracting bonanza in American history. Top American corporations figured to reap hundreds of millions, even billions, from the new war contracts. The watchdogs worried. The potential for profiteering would be enormous.[71]

Did the watchdogs have legitimate reason to worry? Could top executives get rich off the new war contracts? On paper, no. The federal statute books actually include a provision that limits the taxpayer dollars that can go, as compensation, to executives at corporations that do business with the federal government. Under this provision, the top federal procurement official each year calculates a "benchmark compensation" cap that applies to each contractor's "five most highly compensated employees in management positions."[72] In 2003, this cap stood at $405,273. No executive at a federal contractor could, over the course of the year, take in more than $405,273 from America's taxpayers.

But this federal cap only limits how much contractors can claim, directly from tax dollars, for their executive compensation. The federal cap in no way limits the total compensation that executives at corporations with federal contracts can receive. And that total can run high into the millions, particularly after contractors receive lucrative federal contracts that send their share prices soaring. In 2002, for instance, the official federal "benchmark compensation" for top executives stood at $387,783.[73] The pay totals for top executives at America's biggest military contractors that year all dwarfed this official "benchmark." Halliburton CEO David Lesar collected $7.3 million in 2002 total compensation, Northrop Grumman CEO Ronald Sugar $9.2 million, and Lockheed Martin CEO Vance Coffman $25.4 million.[74]

Coffman's $25.4 million amounted to 175 times the $144,932 pay of an American Army general with twenty years of experience — and nearly two thousand times the $12,776 base pay of an Army soldier.[75] These monstrous gaps struck Phyllis Bennis, an analyst with the Institute for Policy Studies, as somewhat unseemly. She offered up, before the congressional debate began on the Bush administration's $87 billion funding request, a straightforward antidote to profiteering off Iraq.

"No contracts should be granted to any contracting corporation," Bennis proposed, "that pays its CEO more than 100 times the base pay of a U.S. soldier."[76]

Congress would not pick up on this modest proposal. But public pressure, in the future, could make nearly every major debate in Congress — or any other legislative body — an opportunity to introduce into American political discourse the notion of pay equity ratios.

Congress won't increase the minimum wage? Advocates for wage justice could insist that congressional salaries be tied to a multiple of what minimum wage workers earn. In 1950, columnist Holly Sklar points out, members of Congress earned eight times the minimum wage. By century's end, they earned thirteen times the minimum.

"Let's cap congressional salaries until they are once again eight times the minimum wage," suggests Sklar. "That would give Congress an incentive to care as much about constituents at the bottom of the income pyramid as at the top."[77]

A governor wants state lawmakers to legalize casino gambling? We need jobs, the governor intones. We need good jobs, community and religious groups might retort, as they insist on a pay equity ratio amendment to the governor's bill. No state gambling license, their amendment to the governor's gambling bill might read, shall go to any "gaming" entities that compensate executives more than ten times employees.

A cable TV giant is asking a county council to agree to higher rates for basic service? No new contract, lawmakers could stipulate, with any cable TV company that pays executives over twenty-five times what its average workers receive.

These battles for pay equity ratios would no doubt, in the early going, fail much more often than triumph. But each skirmish would be an opportunity to discuss the terribly high price we pay, in our enterprises, in our communities, in our personal lives, when we tolerate great and growing divides between our wealthy and everybody else. Each skirmish would help pay ratios seem more plausible. Each skirmish would reinforce the resolve of trade unionists struggling for pay equity ratios at the bargaining table.

Over time, victories would start to be won. Some, at the start, might be mostly symbolic. A state legislature, for instance, might limit gubernatorial pay to ten times the annual wage of the state's lowest-paid worker. In some states, that might not be a big deal. Some governors already make not much more than ten times their lowest-paid workers. Still, symbolic victories count. They build momentum. They raise consciousness. They inspire.

At some point, isolated victories would begin to cascade into a stronger, more focused movement to limit inequality. That movement could then begin to challenge our most powerful contemporary engine of inequality, the modern corporation, head on. That movement could even struggle to deny corporations that manufacture inequality the right to do business.

Deny a corporation the right to do business? That notion strikes our modern ears as utterly bizarre, as foolish as trying to deny grass the right to grow. But corporations are not and have never been "natural" entities. Within the United States, individuals have no "right" to incorporate, to create a legally recognized entity with privileges and liabilities all its own, without state government approval. Our states have always determined who can incorporate and under what circumstances.

Two hundred years ago, states took this responsibility most seriously. Americans early on in our republic's history feared corporate power. They had fought a revolution, after all, not just to free themselves from the King of England, but to free themselves from the British "crown" corporations that dominated colonial life.[78] In the new United States, citizens would do their best to keep corporations subordinate. In state after state, they pressed for statutes and adopted constitutions that treated corporations as potential dangers to democracy. Corporations in the young republic would, as a result, be "chartered" on a case-by-case basis. These charters would typically limit a new corporation to a specific mission. That mission complete, the charter would be dissolved. Charters, at times, would even specify exactly how a new corporation would be allowed to do business. Some charters, for instance, prevented incorporated turnpike companies from collecting tolls from people traveling to vote or go to church.[79]

Throughout the nineteenth century, would-be tycoons fought fiercely to "free" corporations from this sort of state oversight. Over the century's first half, the citizens of the young republic essentially held their own. As late as 1857, Pennsylvanians would adopt a constitutional amendment that instructed lawmakers to "alter, revoke or annul any charter of a corporation" that "may be injurious to citizens of the community."[80] The tide would ultimately start turning against this rigorous corporate oversight right after the Civil War, as Gilded Age wealth increasingly lubricated America's political process. State by state, corporations "rewrote the laws governing their creation."[81] New laws essentially gave the ability to incorporate to any group that paid a filing fee. Incorporated entities could continue "in perpetuity." Their officers could not be held personally liable.

Citizen reformers, in some states, would battle back, but corporate power would eventually carry the day. By the 1920s, the corporation in America had evolved "from a subordinate legal entity created to serve the public good into a fantastic shield for property and wealth."[82] "The principal instrument of the concentration of economic power and wealth," a congressional committee would conclude in 1941, "has been the corporate charter with unlimited power."[83]

In the 1990s, a new citizen's movement would begin challenging this unlimited power. Incorporation, activists pointed out, ought to be seen as a *privilege* the sovereign people choose to bestow upon a group of individuals. In return, we the people ought to expect that individuals granted this privilege will advance our common economic well-being. Those who don't ought to have their corporate charters revoked, or be placed into receivership, until their corporate misbehaviors cease.

All states currently have on the books statutory provisions for revoking corporate charters. A corporation doing business in Maryland, for example, can have its charter yanked for failing to file required paperwork or ignoring its tax bills. Maryland can also pull the plug on any state business with a corporate officer directly or indirectly linked to "organized crime." More generally, the state attorney general in Maryland can "institute proceedings against a corporation to determine whether the corporation has abused, misused, or failed to use its powers and franchises in a manner which, in the public interest, would make proper the forfeiture of its charter."

But what's in the "public interest" and what's not?

No state has adequately answered this question. A movement for a more equal America could. Indeed, some activists are already working to spell out, in specific terms, just what our public interest entails. One national network of reformers, the Program on Corporations, Law, and Democracy, has drafted a "Model State Corporation Code" to help "make possible effective democratic control of corporations in a self-governing society."[84] This model code explicitly denies to incorporated entities key powers they currently enjoy, including the power to engage in political lobbying. The code also recognizes, with another key provision, that wide compensation gaps within a corporate enterprise do not serve the public interest. The model code's draft language denies corporations the power to provide executives "compensation in whatever form" that runs "as much or more than 20 times" the average pay of their production workers.[85]

Model corporate codes with clauses this bold have not yet emerged into America's mainstream political discourse. But that discourse, on matters corporate, is starting to broaden. In 1998, one mainstream pol, New York's Eliot Spitzer, actually ran on a platform that threatened misbehaving corporations with the ultimate sanction.

"When a corporation is convicted of repeated felonies that harm or endanger the lives of human beings or destroy our environment," Spitzer proclaimed in his campaign for state attorney general, "the corporation should be put to death, its corporate existence ended, and its assets taken and sold at public auction."[86]

Spitzer would win that election and then, as attorney general, lead a vigorous charge against corporate fraud on Wall Street. His success seems to have emboldened other elected officials. In February 2002, one such official, California Senate majority whip Richard Alarcon, introduced a "Code for Corporate Responsibility" to prohibit the directors of any corporation from performing their duties "at the expense of the environment, human rights, the public health and safety, the communities in which the corporation operates, or the dignity of the corporation's employees."[87]

Alarcon's bill gives average Californians the right to sue offending corporations — and their directors — if damaged by any violation of these prohibitions. If his bill ever became law, corporate directors who handed lavish option windfalls to executives while these executives were handing pink slips to employees could be held personally liable, under the code, for subjecting employees to indignity.

"It's hard to overstate how profoundly this could change corporate behavior," notes *Business Ethics* editor Marjorie Kelly. "Instead of rubber-stamping whatever actions fatten the bottom line — keeping a dirty power plant open, or laying off 10,000 — directors would be asking about impact on employees and the public good. They'd be trying to avoid social harm, because their own pocketbooks would be at risk."[88]

State Senator Alarcon has no illusions that bills like his will pass any time soon.

"Most significant changes in American law take some time," he notes. "But the discussion is as important as the end product."[89]

In the early decades of the twenty-first century, such "discussion" — about writing pay equity ratios into corporation codes, into procurement legislation, into collectively bargained labor contracts — could begin to erode our contemporary conventional wisdom about the top-heavy distribution of income and wealth in the United States. With discussion about pay equity ratios swirling all around us, this terribly unequal distribution would no longer seem inevitable, an unpleasantness we have no choice but to swallow. Instead of accepting inequality as a given, Americans would be debating the best path to a more equal America. Amid this debate, this long-overdue discussion, the notion of a Ten Times Rule could emerge — and be seriously considered.

A CAREFUL OBSERVER AT THE END OF THE TWENTIETH CENTURY, if diligent enough, could come upon discussion about Ten Times Rule-like proposals, about income limits between top and bottom, but only at the margins of American political life. Out in those margins, small but committed groupings of activists for economic and environmental justice were keeping alive a vision of a significantly more equal America.

Late in the 1990s, one of those groupings, the Labor Party, an organization inspired by Tony Mazzocchi, a well-respected and long-time leader with the Oil, Chemical, and Atomic Workers Union, called for "a 100 percent tax on that portion of executive salaries exceeding 20 times the average worker's pay in that corporation."[90] A few years earlier, the Greens/Green Party USA had adopted a program that advocated "a maximum wage of 10 times the minimum wage; the intent being that the income of the richest not exceed that of the poorest by more than a factor of 10."[91]

From time to time, over the course of those same years, even some groups closer to the political mainstream would dare entertain a "maximum wage" vision. In 1995, for instance, a budget justice coalition that included New York's largest public employee unions, the state social workers organization, and the New York State Council of Churches released a "Counterbudget" report that recommended a more progressive state income tax. But the coalition report also noted that addressing New York's "wealth problem" might well require a "more radical" solution.

"Why not a maximum wage that is directly linked to the minimum wage?" the coalition asked. "Drastic actions need to be taken, and taken now, to reverse the economic, political and socially destructive trend of great wealth concentrated in the hands of a few."[92]

Still, despite these occasional nods from groups close to the mainstream, advocacy for an income limit in America remained, throughout the boom years and into the early years of the twenty-first century, sublimely inconsequential, as inconsequential as advocacy for a federal income tax in the 1870s and 1880s. Back in those original Gilded Age years, a time of fearsome wealth concentration, only minor third parties wasted any time or treasure campaigning for a federal tax on incomes. An income tax, through most of the Gilded Age, seemed a political nonstarter. Not until 1894 would an income tax bill slip through Congress, and that tax only subjected wealthy incomes to a modest 2 percent tax.

For the Supreme Court, as we have seen, that would be 2 percent too much. The high court would rule income taxes unconstitutional. Activists who had spent their entire adult lives campaigning for an income tax had, at that point, nothing to show for their labors — and no hope, after concentrated wealth's smashing victory in the 1896 Presidential election, that prospects for taxing the wealthy would get any better any time soon.

Yet things did get better. By 1913, an income tax amendment had won enough state support to become part of the Constitution. By 1918, America's wealthy were paying taxes at rates as high as 77 percent. By 1944, top rates on wealthy incomes had hit an amazing 94 percent.

Somewhere in the United States that year of 1944, some eighty-odd-year-old farmer just rocking on his porch, reading his paper, may have caught a headline about that amazing 94 percent tax rate. Maybe that old farmer smiled. He would have been about twenty years old in 1880, the year he first read about the idea of a "graduated income tax," in the platform of the Greenback Labor Party. The farmer, as a young man, had liked that idea. But decades passed, with no progress on that graduated income tax. And then everything changed. Who would have ever imagined, the old farmer might have asked himself that day in 1944, that we would ever see wealthy people paying taxes at a 94 percent rate? Not me, that old farmer might have laughed, not me.

Twenty-somethings today may not live to see a Ten Times Rule America. But strange things have happened before. They could happen again.

LOOKING FORWARD

IN *LOOKING BACKWARD*, THE ENORMOUSLY POPULAR 1888 novel that dared to imagine a more equal America, author Edward Bellamy had his hero, a comfortable Bostonian by the name of Julian West, go to sleep one evening in 1887 Boston and awake in 2000 — to a new millennium and a new world. The ugly gaps in income and wealth that had divided Julian West's nineteenth century Boston had vanished. America had become a caring place, a land without inequality and injustice, a good society.

On January 1, 2000, the first day of the genuine new millennium, Edward Bellamy's great-grandson looked back at *Looking Backward.* What might his great-grandfather think, Michael Bellamy wondered in an op-ed column, about how his United States of America had actually evolved?

"Were his hero to wake up today, Bellamy might be inclined to put him back to sleep for another millennium," the great-grandson concluded. "In fact, if Julian West came to today, he might think that he had simply had a normal night's rest."

A Julian West who stepped out into the real new millennium America, Michael Bellamy pointed out, would find "mean streets" that bore "an uncanny resemblance" to his era's own. Julian West, in our time as in his, would see homelessness everywhere, wealth concentrated to a fearsome degree, and "an economic incentive system that tends increasingly to reward sitting on one's assets far more generously than actually doing a day's work."[1] Julian West would see in modern America little of the progress his creator, Edward Bellamy, had so hopefully imagined. He would see an America that has failed to come to grips with inequality.

Should we be startled by our failure? Perhaps not. Human societies, after all, have been failing to come to grips with inequality for thousands of years, as archaeologists have a habit of reminding us every so often. Recent scholarship on the ancient Roman city of Pompeii, for instance, has revealed a society seething "with massive economic inequality."[2] An elite Pompeii family, notes Antonio Varone, an Italian expert on antiquity, could spend more on a single banquet than a senior public official could earn in a year. In deeply unequal Pompeii, resentments smoldered everywhere. Pompeii's plutocrats, no fools, spent lavishly to keep the lid on their inferno. Their subsidies kept a host of diversions, from wine and prostitutes to gladiatorial extravaganzas, readily accessible. Their clever and cynical reign seemed secure, even eternal. But another inferno, from nearby Vesuvius, would eventually do in Pompeii's plutocrats. They could not keep a lid on nature. Vesuvius would eventually bury their greed.

In other cities, at other times, wise men and women have struggled to place more human limits on wealth's dominion. We can read human history, in significant part, as an ongoing struggle to place limits on power, to defend ourselves from the mightiest and the wealthiest among us. Power corrupts, our prophets have always understood, not just the individuals who possess power, but any society that lets power concentrate in the hands of an intensely wealthy few.

In a sense, intense concentrations of wealth have the same impact on our human societies as intense concentrations of matter have on our physical universe. Within the cosmos, astronomers tell us, concentrations of matter, if they become intense enough, create black holes. These black holes suck the energy out of their surroundings. They devour all. They destroy all. In our human societies, great concentrations of wealth leave the same devastation. They suck the life out of their surroundings. They devour. They destroy. The more concentrated a society's wealth, the more awesome the destruction.

None of this particularly worries our contemporary cheerleaders for inequality. We need not impose any limits on accumulation, they argue. We need only trust in "free markets." Capitalism as we know it, conservative author Dinesh D'Souza assures us, "civilizes greed, just as marriage civilizes lust."[3]

An economic order that accepts grand concentrations of wealth, these pages have argued, civilizes nothing. An economic order that celebrates these grand concentrations, as ours does, only goads greed on — and brutalizes whatever the greedy do not value.

Our contemporary America hosts many legions of good people working to undo the ravages of this brutalization. In hospitals, in courts of law, in homeless shelters, in schools, in halfway houses, in prisons and parks, we see these good people, dedicated professionals and volunteers, activists and experts, devoting their lives to fighting entrenched problems that no civilized society should have to do battle against. Health problems. Crime problems. Housing problems. Pollution problems. In contemporary America, these problems all stand separate, alone, one unrelated to the next. We fight them individually — and ineffectively. We make, year after year, painfully minor progress. Yet we seldom stop to ask why. Instead, we paper over our failures, with steady streams of reports and white papers that continue to document our continuing problems. We drown ourselves in a data deluge. But we ignore the data that matter most, the data on the gaps in income and wealth that divide us. These data tell our society's most significant story. These data determine the trajectory of our society, of any society.

Income and wealth gaps can narrow, income and wealth gaps can widen. The difference determines whether we see our lives improve or we just merely get by.

In a deeply unequal America, those of us who want to see the quality of all our lives improve, not just some but a great deal, cannot afford to have our eyes diverted from the inequality around us. Whatever our specific concern about modern American life, whatever our expertise, we all share a common interest in narrowing the gaps that divide us, in limiting concentrated wealth. Achieving a more equal America will not, to be sure, magically solve all our problems. But achieving a more equal America, limiting our concentrations of wealth, would make all our problems more solvable, and appreciably so. On a more level playing field, on a playing surface where the wealthiest can no longer dominate, good people and good causes would score more triumphs. Progress toward the American dream, on that more level field, could and would resume.

Leveling needs to become our shared mission. We need to unite to oppose any initiative that would widen gaps in income and wealth, that would concentrate still greater fortune in the pockets of the already fortunate. We need to openly discuss and debate and rally behind initiatives that would narrow our gaps. Our efforts, in our lifetimes, might not create a Ten Times Rule America. But our efforts, if pressed ahead with passion, with diligence, with savvy, even with humor, would most certainly leave America a different place, a better place.

The alternative?

If we allow the wealthy to keep their wealth a nonissue, their power will only continue to bloat. America will continue to stumble backwards. We cannot let that happen. We have stumbled too long already.

"We're back to serfs and royalty," one alarmed business school professor told *Business Week* in 2001 after the release of the latest CEO pay data.

"But even the Middle Ages," rejoined journalist Geneva Overholser, "didn't last forever."[4]

How long will our new Middle Ages endure? That remains our choice. Our choice alone.

NOTES

INTRODUCTION

[1] Molly Ivins, Inequity Gap: A Product of the Economic Boom, *Liberal Opinion Week*, May 17, 1999.

[2] "Certainly," Will added in an April 23, 1995 *Washington Post* column, "there is today no prima facie case against the moral acceptability of increasingly large disparities of wealth." Will seems to have much more stomach for inequality in the abstract than in the flesh. Four years earlier, in another *Washington Post* op-ed, he had blistered overpaid executives: "Perhaps Reebok's CEO was worth $14.8 million in 1990, but why, precisely? He would have done his job less well for a piddling, oh, $7 million?" This contrast noted by Robert A. Senser, The Growing Inequalities in Wealth and Income in the United States, *Commonweal*, December 1, 1995.

[3] Jeff Pooley, The Party's Over, *Perspective*, May 1996. "If I were against creating millionaires," Clinton quipped near the end of his second term, "I would have been an abject failure in my years as president." John Dillin, Newly Rich Escalate Estate-tax Fight, *Christian Science Monitor*, September 7, 2000.

[4] David E. Bonior, My Constituents Are Not 'Losers,' *Washington Post*, August 25, 1995.

[5] Nina Bernstein, Widest Income Gap Is Found in New York, *New York Times*, January 19, 2000.

[6] Cait Murphy, Are the Rich Cleaning Up? *Fortune*, September 4, 2000.

[7] Michael M. Weinstein, Why They Deserve It, *New York Times*, November 19, 1995.

[8] W. Michael Cox and Richard Alm, Why Decry the Wealth Gap? *New York Times*, January 24, 2000.

[9] The exact 1969 millionaire household total: 121,000. Harrison Rainie, The State Of Greed, *US News & World Report*, June 17, 1996.

[10] Jonathan R. Macey, Wealth Creation as a "Sin," The Independent Institute. Accessed from www.independent.org/tii/content/pubs/policyrep/p_macey.html.

[11] The U.S. economy, according to studies conducted for the Lincoln Financial Group, was generating "a new millionaire household approximately every 31 seconds" at century's end. John Dillin, Newly Rich Escalate Estate-tax Fight, *Christian Science Monitor*, September 7, 2000.

[12] John Dillin, Newly Rich Escalate Estate-tax Fight, *Christian Science Monitor*, September 7, 2000.

[13] Edward N. Wolff, Where Has All the Money Gone? Winners and Losers in the 1980s and 1990s, *Milken Institute Review*, Third Quarter, 2001.

[14] John D. Rockefeller amassed a fortune worth $1.4 billion. Kathy Balog, A wealth of facts on America's richest, *USA Today*, April 14, 1997. Balog's numbers are from Michael Klepper and Richard Gunther, *The Wealthy 100: A Ranking of the Richest Americans, Past and Present*. New York: Carol Pub. Group, 1996.

[15] Kevin Phillips, *The Politics of Rich and Poor*. New York: Random House, 1990, 239.

[16] *Forbes* had actually rated rich people's fortunes years before as well, but the practice never became an ongoing annual event. Michelle Conlin, When Billionaires Become a Dime a Dozen, *Forbes*, October 13, 1997.

[17] Eric Quinones, Rich Are Getting Richer, Associated Press, September 29, 1996.

[18] Maria Puente, Everyone Wants a Shot at Being a Millionaire, *USA Today*, August 16, 2000.

[19] Gates, *Wired* noted, would achieve trillionaire status in March 2005, at age forty-nine, if the value of his Microsoft shares kept increasing at the same annual rate, 58.2 percent, they had maintained since 1983. Evan Marcus, The World's First Trillionaire, *Wired*, September 1999.

[20] On the Internet, inventive analysts struggled nobly to find the right imagery that could express just how wealthy the master of Microsoft had become. At one Web site, surfers could find a Bill Gates Wealth Clock with a running total on the size of the Gates fortune. Another site, the Bill

Gates Wealth Index, asked readers to presume that Bill Gates, to secure his fortune, had "worked 14 hours a day on every business day of the year" since Microsoft had been founded. That presumption would put his hourly pay "at a staggering million dollars per hour, around $300 per second." If Gates should happen to see a $1,000 bill lying on the ground, this analysis pointed out, bending over to pick it up would be "not worth his time." Bill Gates Wealth Index. Accessed from www.temple-tons.com/brad/billg.html.

[21] Conlin, When Billionaires Become a Dime a Dozen, *Forbes*, October 13, 1997.

[22] Top-Dollar Drawings, *Washington Post*, May 14, 2000.

[23] The Walton and du Pont families were the only Americans on the *Forbes* global top ten in 1990. The global top 200 were worth $463 billion. A Decade of Wealth, *Forbes*, July 5, 1999.

[24] The World's Richest People, Forbes.com, February 27, 2003.

[25] Hirshhorn, who made a fortune on the stock market, died in 1981. Quoted in Philip Slater, *Wealth Addiction*. New York: E. P. Dutton, 1980, 95.

[26] Felicia Paik, The Most Expensive Homes In America, Forbes.com, March 30, 2001.

[27] Carissa Katz, The Real Rennert, Five Years Later, *East Hampton Star*, June 5, 2003, and Kim Goad, The Hot Zone, *New York Magazine*, May 20, 2000.

[28] Deborah Schoeneman, Deborah Netburn, and Tom McGeveran, Hamptons Headache: A Man Needs His Castle, *New York Observer*, February 26, 2001.

[29] Questions for Alan Wilzig, *New York Times*, August 17, 1997.

[30] Angelo Ragaza, Your Own Private Camelot, Forbes.com, March 2, 2001.

[31] Louis Uchitelle, More Wealth. More Stately Mansions, *New York Times*, June 6, 1999.

[32] Adrian Higgins, Instant Gratification, *Washington Post*, October 8, 1999.

[33] Monique P. Yazigi, Heard in Hamptons: 'The Earth Moved,' *New York Times*, May 23, 1999.

[34] Richard Todd, High on Spending, *Worth*, October 1998.

[35] Adam Platt, The Big Sizzle, *Conde Nast Traveler*, May 1998.

[36] Frank DeCaro, The Greenspan Who Nearly Stole Christmas, *New York Observer*, December 16, 1996.

[37] Maureen Dowd, Style Beside Sorrow, *New York Times*, December 23, 2001.

[38] A Wing and a Player, *Fortune*. October 16, 2000.

[39] Craig Wilson, Size Does Matter, *USA Today*, July 7, 2000.

[40] The length: 315 feet. Julie Flaherty, A Growing Market for Mansions of the Sea, *New York Times*, November 14, 1999.

[41] Wilson, Size Does Matter, *USA Today*, July 7, 2000.

[42] Lea Goldman, Travel Super Bowls, *Forbes*, September 4, 2000.

[43] The journalist: Kristina Stewart, the editor of *Quest* magazine. Monique P. Yazigi, With This Trip, I Thee Wed, *New York Times*, July 11, 1999.

[44] Landon Thomas Jr, Calling All Czars, *New York Observer*, July 30, 2001.

[45] Blaine Harden, Molding Loyal Pamperers for the Newly Rich, *New York Times*, October 24, 1999.

[46] Christopher Walker, Britain Has Not Been This Divided Since the Thirties, *Independent*, February 11, 2001.

[47] Monique P. Yazigi, When You Got It, Flaunt It, *New York Times*, January 26, 2000.

[48] Ibid.

[49] Starkey students were "taught to trim their nose hairs, wax their eyebrows, use a yardstick to space plates at the dinner table and always call their employers by their surnames and use the proper courtesy titles." Harden, Molding Loyal Pamperers for the Newly Rich, *New York Times*, October 24, 1999.

[50] Nicholas Von Hoffman, Rich Fear the Non-Rich May Demand a Fair Share, *New York Observer*, May 29, 2000.

[51] Linton Weeks, Culture Critic Jacques Barzun, Time Traveler, *Newark Star-Ledger*, June 25, 2000. Barzun, more than most Americans, can place today's greed in perspective. Born in France, he came to the United States in 1920 and started teaching history at Columbia University in 1927.

[52] Peter Applebome, Where Money's a Mantra, Greed's a New Creed, *New York Times*, February 28, 1999.

[53] Jan Uebelherr, Observers Say America Is Suffering 'Affluenza' Epidemic, *Star-Tribune* (Minneapolis), April 9, 2000.

[54] Michelle Singletary, The Pot of Gold At the End Of the I-Do's, *Washington Post*, February 20, 2000.

[55] As They See It, *San Jose Mercury News*, December 22, 1996.

[56] Thomas Boswell, When Money Talks, Everyone Listens, *Washington Post*, October 21, 1994.

[57] Adam Gopnick, A Hazard of No Fortune, *New Yorker*, February 21, 2000.

[58] Ben B. Seligman, *The Potentates: Business and Businessmen in American History*. New York, The Dial Press, 1971, 167.

59 Gustavus Myers, *History of the Great American Fortunes*. New York: The Modern Library, 1936 (originally published 1907), 333.

60 Ibid., 344.

61 Seligman, *The Potentates: Business and Businessmen in American History*, 138.

62 Ibid., 142.

63 Ibid., 143.

64 Ibid., 167.

65 Ibid., 139.

66 Ibid., 211.

67 Myers, *History of the Great American Fortunes*, 349.

68 Edward Chase Kirkland, *Industry Comes of Age Business, Labor and Public Policy, 1860-1897*. Chicago: Quadrangle Books, 1967, 260.

69 Ibid., 403.

70 Steve Fraser, The Gilded Age Unravels, *Los Angeles Times*, April 1, 2001.

71 Milton Cantor, "The Backward Look of Bellamy's Socialism," in *Looking Backward, 1988-1888: Essays on Edward Bellamy*, Daphne Patai, editor. Amherst: University of Massachusetts Press, 1988, p. 21.

72 Michael Bellamy, Looking Backward, 2000-1887: What Happened to Utopian Evolution? *Globe and Mail* (Toronto), January 1, 2000.

73 *The Prosperity Paradox: The Economic Wisdom of Henry George — Rediscovered*, compiled by Dr. Mark Hassed. Canterbury, Australia: Chatsworth Village, 2000, p. 159.

74 Ibid., 85. The audience was a YMHA in San Francisco.

75 Ibid., 2.

76 Daniel Aaron, *Men of Good Hope: A Story of American Progressives*. New York: Oxford University Press, 1951, 88.

77 *The Prosperity Paradox: The Economic Wisdom of Henry George — Rediscovered*, 160-61.

78 *The Macmillan Book of Business and Economic Quotations*, edited by Michael Jackson. New York: Macmillan Publishing Company, 1984, 218.

79 Paul L. Menchik and Nancy A. Jianakoplos, "Economics of Inheritance," in *Inheritance and Wealth in America*, edited by Robert K. Miller, Jr. and Stephen J. McNamee. New York and London: Plenum Press, 1998, 71.

80 Accessed from www.quotationreference.com.

81 Thomas G. Palaima, Wealth and the Commonwealth, *Austin American-Statesman*, February 1, 2000.

82 Confucius, XI.15. Quoted in Alan Durning, *How Much Is Enough? The Consumer Society and the Future of the Earth*. New York: W. W. Norton & Company, 1992, 144.

83 Paul Glover, Fair Pay Forum, *HOUR Town*, February-March 1997.

84 Quoted in Durning, *How Much Is Enough? The Consumer Society and the Future of the Earth*, 143.

85 *Proverbs* 30:8.

86 Familiar Source, Forgotten Wisdom, *Too Much*, Spring 1999.

87 *Ecclesiastes* 5:9.

88 Familiar Source, Forgotten Wisdom, *Too Much*.

89 John A. Byrne, Executive Pay, *Business Week*, March 30, 1992.

90 George Soros, The Capitalist Threat, *Atlantic Monthly*, February 1997.

91 James L. Huston, *Securing the Fruits of Labor: The American Concept of Wealth Distribution 1765-1900*. Baton Rouge: Louisiana State University Press, 1998, p. xii.

92 Ibid., 3.

93 I Sing the Body Politic, *Washington Post*, October 29, 2000, from *Intimate with Walt*, edited by Gary Schmidgall. Iowa City: University of Iowa Press, 2001.

94 Milford W. Howard, *The American Plutocracy*, quoted in *The Populist Mind*, Norman Pollak, editor. Indianapolis and New York: The Bobbs-Merrill Company, Inc., 1967, 231-232.

95 Richard Todd, Who Me, Rich? *Worth*, September 1997.

96 Paul Krugman, The Spiral of Inequality, *Mother Jones*, November/December 1996.

97 Harold Meyerson, If I Had a Hammer: Whatever Happened to America's Working Class? *Los Angeles Times*, September 2, 2001.

98 Benjamin Schwarz, Reflections on Inequality: "The Promise of American Life," *World Policy Journal*, Winter 1995.

99 Barry Bluestone and Bennett Harrison, *Growing Prosperity*. Boston: Houghton Mifflin Company, 2000, 183. Between 1947 and 1973, the poorest fifth of American households saw their real incomes, their earnings after taking inflation into account, jump a vigorous 3 percent a year. The most affluent Americans increased their income, too, but by just 2.4 percent a year. In the middle, says the U.S. Department of Labor, average Americans saw their incomes jump at an annual 2.7 percent.

100 "By 1970, 99 percent of American homes had refrigerators, electric irons, and radios; more than 90 percent had automatic clothes washers, vacuum cleaners, and toasters," note economists Barry Bluestone and Bennett Harrison, "a far cry from

the equipment in the typical home before the war." Bluestone and Harrison, *Growing Prosperity*, 182.

[101] "In 1955, Simon Kuznets set the stage for post-World War II discussions of income distribution in his American Economic Association presidential address, 'Economic Growth and Income Inequality.' He argued that as countries develop, populations move from a low-income agricultural sector to a higher-income industrial sector. Incomes are relatively equal in the early stage, when almost everybody is concentrated in agriculture, and in the late stage, when virtually all work in industry. Inequality peaks in between, when the workforce is equally divided between the two sectors." Randy Albeda and Chris Tilly, Unnecessary Evil: Why Inequality Is Bad for Business, *Dollars and Sense*, March-April 1995.

[102] The exact numbers: 63 percent and 50 percent. Louis Uchitelle, Even the Rich Can Suffer from Income Inequality, *New York Times*, November 15, 1998.

[103] Lawrence Mishel, Jared Bernstein, and John Schmitt, *The State of Working America, 2000-2001*. Ithaca, New York: Cornell University Press, 2001, 83.

[104] Paul Krugman, The Spiral of Inequality, *Mother Jones*, November/December 1996.

[105] Adele Horin, All Work, Low Pay, *Sidney Morning Herald*, December 27, 1997.

[106] These numbers reflect the median financial assets of the middle fifth of American households and take inflation into account. Ana M. Aizcorbe, Arthur B. Kennickell, and Kevin B. Moore, Recent Changes in U.S. Family Finances: Evidence from the 1998 and 2001 Survey of Consumer Finances, *Federal Reserve Bulletin*, January 2003. Accessed from www.federalreserve.gov/pubs/bulletin/2003/0103lead.pdf.

[107] Anybody "with solid home equity of say, $100,000, modest savings and investments of at least $50,000 and a retirement account of more than $100,000 belongs to the winning upper crust." Tom Redburn, Honoring, and Paying, All Those Who Serve, *New York Times*, October 28, 2001.

[108] Wolff, Where Has All the Money Gone? Winners and Losers in the 1980s and 1990s.

[109] The Census Bureau started tracking the gap between the most affluent fifth and the rest of the nation's income-earners in 1967. In 2001, the top fifth claimed 50.1 percent of the nation's total income. Carmen DeNavas-Walt and Robert Cleveland, U.S. Census Bureau, Current Population Reports, P260-218, Money Income in the United States, 2001, U.S. Government Printing Office, Washington, D.C., 2002, 19.

[110] This is a calculation based on Congressional Budget Office figures for the period from 1979 through 2000. *Effective Federal Tax Rates, 1997-2000*, The Congress of the United States, Congressional Budget Office, August 2003, 30-31.

[111] Credit for the "top-heavy" image of wealth and income in the United States belongs to Edward Wolff. See Edward N. Wolff, *Top Heavy: A Study of the Increasing Inequality of Wealth in America*. New York: Twentieth Century Fund Press, 1995.

[112] The $108,400 figure represents the minimum for entering the top 5 percent of income-earners. *Effective Federal Tax Rates, 1997-2000*, 30-31.

[113] Calculated from data presented in *Effective Federal Tax Rates, 1997-2000*, 30-31. For more analysis of the CBO data, see Robert Greenstein and Isaac Shapiro, The New, Definitive CBO Data on Income and Tax Trends, Center on Budget and Policy Priorities, September 23, 2003. Available at www.cbpp.org/9-23-03tax.pdf.

[114] These are households that were worth at least $3,352,100 in 1998. Wolff, Where Has All the Money Gone? Winners and Losers in the 1980s and 1990s.

[115] Ibid. By the end of 1998, the wealth of the average household in the top 1 percent had jumped by over $3 million. In that same year, the average household in the next wealthiest 4 percent was only worth $1.4 million.

[116] Tom Redburn, Honoring, and Paying, All Those Who Serve, *New York Times*, October 28, 2001.

[117] Teri-Ann Winston James and Thomas Li-Ping Tang, Downsizing and the Impact on Survivors: A Matter of Justice, *Employment Relations Today*, Summer 1996. Original source: John A. Byrne, The Flap Over Executive Pay, *Business Week*, May 6, 1991.

[118] Sarah Anderson and John Cavanagh, Institute for Policy Studies, Chris Hartman and Betsy Leondar-Wright, United for a Fair Economy, Executive Excess 2001: Eighth Annual CEO Compensation Survey, September 2001.

[119] Ibid. Worker pay grew 37 percent over the decade, inflation 32 percent.

[120] Robert D. Hof, Too Much of a Good Thing? *Business Week*, August 25, 1997.

[121] Noted one Silicon Valley journalist: "If Chambers took his pay in $1 bills, his cash would weigh 93 tons." Mike Cassidy, Let's Put All This Money in Perspective, *San Jose Mercury News*, June 18, 2000.

[122] The exact multiple: 289. Chris Townsend, America: Who Owns the Dream?, *UE News*, February 21, 1997. For the Welch pay figure, David Leonhardt, Executive Pay: A Special Report

for the Boss, Happy Days Are Still Here, *New York Times*, April 1, 2001.

[123] The 1975 U.S. median income: $13,719. The 2000 figure: $42,148. Carmen DeNavas-Walt, Robert W. Cleveland, and Marc I. Roemer, Money Income in the United States: 2000, U.S. Census Bureau, September 2001, 1.

[124] "Esrey took home $69.3 million in total compensation and stock options in 2000," AFL-CIO researchers pointed out, "and $64.1 million in stock option exercises from prior grants." Accessed from AFL-CIO PayWatch Web site at www.afl-cio.org/corporateamerica/paywatch/ and New E-Campaign Turns Fed-Up Shareholders Into Cyber Activists on Out-of-Control CEO Pay, PR Newswire, New York, April 5, 2001.

[125] Ronald Kohl, Executive Salaries Are Becoming a National Scandal, *Machine Design*, August 8, 1994.

[126] The three: "Chairman Wayne T. Hockmeyer, with $27.1 million total, $25.7 million of it in options; chief executive David M. Mott, with $26.3 million total, nearly $25 million of it in options; and President Melvin D. Booth, with $23.8 million, $22.8 million of it in options." Kathleen Day, How Washington's Corporate Elite Stacks Up, *Washington Post*, July 16, 2001.

[127] Ibid.

[128] William Greider, If Politics Got Real, *Nation*, November 13, 2000.

[129] "At no other time have median wages of American men fallen for more than two decades," adds Thurow. "Never before have a majority of American workers suffered real wage reductions while the per capita domestic product was advancing." Lester C. Thurow, Companies Merge; Families Break Up, *New York Times*, September 3, 1995.

[130] These data come from a 1999 Center for Budget and Policy Priorities analysis. The middle fifth of the population received 16.4 percent of total after-tax income in 1977, a projected 14.7 percent in 1999. America's changing income distribution cost the middle fifth of households $78 billion in after-tax income. The poorest fifth lost $75 billion. The nation's redistribution of income — up — handed the wealthiest 1 percent $271 billion more than it would have received, after taxes, had the nation's income distribution not changed. Isaac Shapiro and Robert Greenstein, The Widening Income Gulf, Center for Budget and Policy Priorities, September 4, 1999.

[131] Arthur B. Kennickell, A Rolling Tide: Changes in the Distribution of Wealth in the U.S., 1989-2001, Federal Reserve Board, March 3, 2003. Accessed from www.federalreserve.gov/pubs/oss/oss2/scfindex.html. In 2001, America's top 1 percent held 32.7 percent of the nation's net worth, the bottom 90 percent only 30.2 percent (Table 5). The top 1 percent's share equaled $13,849.2 billion, the bottom 90 percent's $12,775.9 billion. But this top 1 total, drawn from the Federal Reserve's triennial Survey of Consumer Finances, does not tally the wealth of America's richest households, the families of the *Forbes* 400. In 2001, Kennickell's piece points out, the *Forbes* 400 alone owned nearly a trillion dollars worth of wealth (Table 1).

[132] The phrase comes from economists Gary Burtless and Timothy Smeeding. Smeeding has been the overall director of the Luxembourg Income Study, a project that has been comparing incomes in developed countries since 1983. Gary Burtless and Timothy Smeeding, America's Tide: Lifting the Yachts, Swamping the Rowboats, *Washington Post*, June 25, 1995. A project update, published in March 2000, concluded: "Measures of social distance and overall inequality indicate that the United States has the most unequal distribution of adjusted household income among all 21 countries covered in this study, while Sweden has the most equal." Timothy M. Smeeding, Luxembourg Income Study Working Paper No. 252, Changing Income Inequality In OECD Countries: Updated Results from the Luxembourg Income Study. March 2000. Accessed from http://lisweb.ceps.lu/publications/liswps/252.pdf22.

[133] When this original idea "disappears entirely," notes Todd, "we will all suffer equal loss — the [wealthiest] 1 percent no less than the rest of us." Richard Todd, Who Me, Rich? *Worth*, September 1997.

WHY WE NEED INEQUALITY

[1] Benson holds the Simon S. Selig Jr. Chair for Economic Growth at the university's Terry College of Business. P. George Benson, In Defense of Wealth, *Georgia Trend*, April 2001.

GREED AS AN INCENTIVE

[1] Rationalizers of inequality, notes economist Gary Becker, "argue that wage and income disparities must sometimes widen to send correct signals to people to save more, work harder, change jobs, or get a better education." Poor people, by this reasoning, will actually enjoy better lives "in a society where income disparities are permitted to widen than one where law and social convention keep income differentials small." Gary Burtless, Growing American Inequality, *Brookings Review*, December 22, 1998.

[2] Roy C. Smith, a former Wall Street investment banker, has calculated that about 1 percent of the $10.6 trillion gain in total stock market value from 1980 through 1998 was paid to CEOs of publicly traded companies. He adds another $200 to $300 billion, the value accumulated by other senior managers. "Altogether a third to half a trillion dollars," Smith concludes, "has passed into the hands of . . . managers of publicly traded companies." Roy C. Smith, *The Wealth Creators: The Rise of Today's Rich and Super-Rich.* New York: St. Martin's Press, 2001, 240. Adding into that total the incentive income handed executives since 1998 — and factoring in the incomes that have gone to top executives in privately held companies — would easily nudge Smith's total over the half-trillion mark.

[3] Edward J. Zajac and James D. Westphal, Accounting for the Explanations of CEO Compensation: Substance and Symbolism, *Administrative Science Quarterly*, June 1995.

[4] Basu Sharma and Aaliya Fayyaz, The Effect of Hegemonic Power on Executive Compensation, *International Journal of Commerce & Management*, Volume 10, Issue 3-4.

[5] Smith, *The Wealth Creators*, 21-22.

[6] Ibid.

[7] Without that link, was it any wonder "that so many CEOs act like bureaucrats rather than the value-maximizing entrepreneurs companies need to enhance their standing in world markets?" Brian J. Hall and Jeffrey B. Liebman, Are CEOs Really Paid Like Bureaucrats? *Quarterly Journal of Economics*, August 1998.

[8] This discussion on corporate raiders and their impact on mainstream corporate America draws from Wall Street investment banker Roy C. Smith's eyewitness perspective. See Smith, *The Wealth Creators*, 23-24 and 91-94.

[9] The modern corporation, as the Alcoa board of directors pronounced in 1988, had to "increase key employees' personal financial identification with interests of the company's stockholders." Zajac and Westphal, Accounting for the Explanations of CEO Compensation.

[10] Jay Mathews, Their Riches Were Your Command, *Washington Post*, March 24, 1996.

[11] George Milkovich and Jennifer Stevens, 100 Years of Change, *ACA Journal* (American Compensation Association), First Quarter 2000.

[12] John Helyar and Joann S. Lublin, America 1998: High on Stock Options, *Wall Street Journal*, August 8, 1998.

[13] Graef S. Crystal, *In Search of Excess: The Overcompensation of American Executives.* New York: W W Norton & Company, 1991, 231.

[14] John A. Byrne, Executive Pay: Compensation at the Top Is Out of Control, *Business Week*, March 30, 1992.

[15] "In the old days, you got options and you sat on them for years," one veteran compensation consultant, McKinsey & Co.'s Arch Patton, points out. "You didn't get them every year or every two years." An executive whose share price doubled, over those many years, would seldom receive a payoff any higher than a single year's salary. Helyar and Lublin, America 1998: High on Stock Options.

[16] Tim Jackson, *Inside Intel: Andy Grove and the Rise of the World's Most Powerful Chip Company.* New York: Dutton, 1997, 84.

[17] Helyar and Lublin, America 1998: High on Stock Options.

[18] Crystal, *In Search of Excess*, 127.

[19] Ibid., 73.

[20] Warner also received an exotic incentive known as the "Bonus Unit." For each Bonus Unit awarded — and Ross was initially awarded 150,000 — Ross gained the right to collect, in cash, any increase in the company's share price over $27. To make these Bonus Units even sweeter, Warner invited Ross to collect "dividend equivalents" on them. Over one five-year period, these dividend equivalents — payments equal to the stock dividends he would have received had he actually owned the Bonus Unit shares — returned Ross $634,000. All these incentives came on top of stock option awards. Ibid., 56-69.

[21] Ibid., 84.

[22] Craig Cox and Sally Power, Executive Pay: How Much Is Too Much? *Business Ethics*, September-October 1991.

[23] These investors "cajoled, pressured and shamed corporate boards to tie executives' fortunes more closely to those of stockholders" in the early 1990s. David S. Hilzenrath, Options Getting a Second Look, *Washington Post*, April 1, 2001.

[24] Kathleen Day, Soldiers for the Shareholder, *Washington Post*, August 27, 2000.

[25] Hall and Liebman, Are CEOs Really Paid Like Bureaucrats?

[26] Graef S. Crystal, *In Search of Excess*, 162.

[27] Phyllis Plitch, AFL-CIO Steps Up Executive Pay Activism in Cyberspace, Dow Jones News Service, April 4, 2001.

[28] Helyar and Lublin, America 1998: High on Stock Options.

[29] Senators Carl Levin (D-Michigan) and John McCain (R-Arizona) introduced legislation that would have restricted stock option tax dodges, the Ending Double Standards for Stock Options Act, S. 576. *Economic Notes*, June 1997.

30 Adam Bryant, Some Second Thoughts on Options, *New York Times*, September 21, 1997.

31 Buffet made this point throughout the 1990s. Tony Jackson, The Long View, *Financial Times*, August 15, 1999.

32 Helyar and Lublin, America 1998: High on Stock Options.

33 Ibid.

34 Joseph DiStefano and Harold Brubaker, As the Market Mushrooms, Business Leaders Take Stock, *Philadelphia Inquirer*, August 2, 1998.

35 Smith, *The Wealth Creators*, 127-130.

36 Ibid., 111-112.

37 Ibid., 96-97.

38 Charles R. Morris, *Money, Greed, and Risk*. New York: Random House, 1999, 124.

39 Helyar and Lublin, America 1998: High on Stock Options.

40 Denis Lyons, CEO Compensation: The Whole Truth, *Chief Executive*, July 1999.

41 David Leonhardt, Executive Pay: A Special Report. New Turn on an Old Favorite, *New York Times*, April 1, 2001.

42 Shannon Henry, The Download, *Washington Post*, September 16, 1999.

43 Helyar and Lublin, America 1998: High on Stock Options.

44 Joann S. Lublin, Lowering the Bar, *Wall Street Journal*, April 8, 1999.

45 Fortunes in the Future, *Business Week*, April 16, 2001.

46 Hilzenrath, Options Getting a Second Look.

47 John A. Byrne, That Eye-Popping Executive Pay: Is Anybody Worth This Much? *Business Week*, April 25, 1994.

48 James Bates, Eisner Gets a Payday of $565 Million, *Washington Post*, December 4, 1997.

49 Janet Reingold, Special Report: Executive Pay, *Business Week*, April 19, 1999.

50 Lisa Girion, Ex-AOL Chat Room Hosts Sue for Pay, *Los Angeles Times*, October 25, 2001.

51 William A. Rodger, Call It the Millionaire Machine, *Washington Business Journal*, January 27, 1995.

52 Gary Strauss, The Billionaires Club, *USA Today*, April 5, 2000.

53 Adam Bryant, Raising the Stakes, *New York Times*, January 17, 1999.

54 Hall and Liebman, Are CEOs Really Paid Like Bureaucrats?

55 Carl R Weinberg, CEO Compensation: How Much Is Enough? *Chief Executive*, September 2000.

56 Mathews, Their Riches Were Your Command.

57 Smith, *The Wealth Creators*, 45-46.

58 Ibid., 137.

59 Total average CEO pay in 1996 jumped to $5,781,300. Jennifer Reingold, Tying Pay to Performance Is a Great Idea, *Business Week*, April 21, 1997.

60 Go Figure: Pay for Performance a No-lose Deal for Today's CEOs, *Financial Post*, November 12, 1998.

61 Equity Is King in CEO Pay, *Business Wire*, April 7, 2000 and Joann S. Lublin, Executive Pay: Dot-Com Bonanza Spills Over, *Wall Street Journal Europe*, April 13, 2000.

62 Reingold, Special Report: Executive Pay.

63 Apple Options Could Net Jobs $1.4 Billion, or Not, Reuters English News Service, March 12, 2001.

64 Ian Fried, Apple Discontinues Cube, CNET News.com, July 3, 2001.

65 Jobs, despite the Apple stock slide, would do quite well anyway. In March 2003, he was able to exchange millions of his worthless Apple options for actual shares of stock that would become his in three years. Those shares, even if Apple's share price didn't budge up an inch over the next three years, would be worth $67 million when Jobs gained title to them. Gordon T. Anderson, The Next Outrage in CEO Pay? CNN/Money, April 24, 2003.

66 Eileen P Kelly, The Continuing Debate Over Executive Compensation, *National Forum*, Fall 2000. Notes Kelly: "While managerial ability clearly is vital to a company's success, critics nonetheless contend that a variety of internal and external factors influences the firm and its stock price. Internal factors, such as employees, or external factors, such as low inflation and collapsing commodity prices, might have more to do with the increase in a company's stock than do astute managerial decisions."

67 Michael Lewis, All Money, All the Time, *New York Times*, June 7, 1998.

68 David Hilzenrath, Options Getting a Second Look, *Washington Post*, April 1, 2001.

69 Editorials: Call It Executive Overcompensation, *Business Week*, April 21, 1997.

70 Reingold, Tying Pay to Performance Is a Great Idea.

71 AFL-CIO Assails Firms for CEOs' Salary Deals, *Arizona Republic*, April 10, 1998.

72 Reingold, Tying Pay to Performance Is a Great Idea.

73 Leonhardt, Executive Pay: A Special Report. New Turn on an Old Favorite. Some executives proudly accepted tide-deflating measures. Starting

in 1994, for instance, Eli Broad, the chairman and CEO of the financial services giant, SunAmerica, only received options when his company outperformed the S&P index. "I don't think I ought to benefit just from the market going up," Broad explained. Helyar and Lublin, America 1998: High on Stock Options.

[74] Leonhardt, Executive Pay: A Special Report. New Turn on an Old Favorite. "When a company awards regular stock options, it does not have to report any cost on its earnings statements," Leonhardt explains. "An accounting rule issued in 1972 says that the cost of an option is the difference between the exercise price and the stock price on the day of the grant — which is always zero for normal options. However, because the exercise price of RCN's options is not set until a later date, the Financial Accounting Standards Board requires the company to take a charge to reported earnings."

[75] Ibid.

[76] Lyons, CEO Compensation: The Whole Truth.

[77] Daniel Gross, Owing More Than Loyalty to a Company You Run, *New York Times*, January 14, 2001.

[78] Pallavi Gogoi, False Impressions, *Wall Street Journal*, April 8, 1999.

[79] One 2002 analysis of over two hundred academic studies, conducted by Dan Dalton, the dean of the Indiana University School of Business and three other authors, found "no relationship whatsoever" between the amount of equity owned by executives and company performance. David Leonhardt, Options Do Not Raise Performance, Study Finds, *New York Times*, August 11, 2002.

[80] Gogoi, False Impressions.

[81] Ibid. The company also agreed to reimburse the executives for "half of any losses on stock held for at least three years" while, at the same time, letting them keep any gains.

[82] Ibid.

[83] Gross, Owing More Than Loyalty to a Company You Run.

[84] Ibid.

[85] Ibid. Hilbert was number four in the year's *Forbes* magazine executive pay ranking.

[86] Janice Revell, CEO Pensions: Six Sweet Deals, *Fortune*, April 14, 2003.

[87] Joseph E. Bachelder, Sarbanes-Oxley's Impact on Executive Compensation, Loans, *New York Law Journal*, August 30, 2002.

[88] Most of these loans were for buying company shares. Paul Hodgson, My Big Fat Corporate Loan, The Corporate Library. Posted December 2002.

Accessed from www.thecorporatelibrary.com/spotlight/compensation/loans.html.

[89] Ask Money Watch, *Philadelphia Inquirer*, March 30, 1997.

[90] Allan Sloan, Index Investing Makes the S&P 500 Something Less Than a Benchmark, *Washington Post*, December 5, 1995.

[91] Digest, *Washington Post*, December 8, 1999.

[92] Brett D. Fromson, Sizing Up Fidelity, *Washington Post*, January 28, 1996.

[93] Weinberg, CEO Compensation: How Much Is Enough?

[94] Ibid.

[95] A buy recommendation from a "reputable analyst," Kent Womack, a professor at the Amos Tuck School of Business at Dartmouth College, has documented, can move "a stock up an average of 3 percent over a three-day period, while sell recommendations take stocks down 9 percent." Keith Regan, Are Tech Stock Analysts Too Powerful? *E-Commerce Times*, April 10, 2001.

[96] Dunphy led the Sealed Air Corp. Jeffrey Sonnenfeld. The CEO as Captain of Industry: A Dying Breed? *Directors & Boards*, Spring 2001.

[97] Bethany McLean, Why Enron Went Bust, *Fortune*, December 24, 2001.

[98] One final dynamic, adds Ezra Zuckerman, a Stanford sociologist, tends to skew the judgments stock analysts make: worry about losing access to "inside" sources. "Analysts," Zuckerman explains, "often fear that a 'sell' warning will result in severed ties to top management sources upon whom they rely for forecast information." Boat Rocking a No-no for Stock Analysts, Say Profs, *Silicon Valley/San Jose Business Journal*, June 1, 2001.

[99] "Analysts know this," business journalist Darren Gersh noted in 2001. "They know that their year-end bonus — a very large percentage of total compensation on the street — depends on firm profitability, and that depends to a large degree on investment banking. For analysts, this is an unavoidable conflict of interest." Darren Gersh, Stock Analysts: A Bonus Question, July 13, 2001. Accessed from www.nbr.com/whoswho.htm.

[100] Gretchen Morgenson, A Bubble That Enron Insiders and Outsiders Didn't Want to Pop, *New York Times*, January 14, 2002.

[101] Over 70 percent of the recommendations were either "buy" or "strong buy." Regan, Are Tech Stock Analysts Too Powerful?

[102] To appease critics, the Securities Industry Association released new "guidelines" for stock analysis just before Congress opened hearings. The guidelines prohibited analysts from profiting directly on investment banking deals. Wall Street

Defends Stock Analysts Before Congress, Reuters, June 14 2001. Critics blasted the voluntary guidelines as beside the point. "The problem is that analysts can still be compensated indirectly through year-end bonuses, and everyone on Wall Street knows their bonus — if not the money in the bonus pool itself — is likely to depend on the money brought in by investment banking deals." Gersh, Stock Analysts: A Bonus Question.

103 Final Rules on Sarbanes-Oxley Mark End of Chapter, But Not Last Word on Securities Reform, According to CCH, January 24, 2003. News release. Accessed from www.fei.org/download/2003_SEC_Rules12403.pdf.

104 In the 1950s, this was most definitely not the case. At mid century, those who argued for shareholder supremacy played a distinct second fiddle to those who argued that corporations had community obligations. Noted Adolf Berle, Jr., a top economic analyst, in 1954: "Twenty years ago, the writer had a controversy with the late Professor E. Merrick Dodd, of Harvard Law School, the writer holding that corporate powers were powers in trust for shareholders while Professor Dodd argued that these powers were held in trust for the entire community. The argument has been settled (at east for the time being) squarely in favor of Professor Dodd's contention." Adolf A. Berle, Jr., *The 20th Century Capitalist Revolution*. New York: Harcourt, Brace & World, Inc., 1954, 169.

105 The Japanese, in fact, have historically feared that the interests of shareholders and top executives would become too closely aligned, at the expense of other stakeholders. Japanese executives have not been allowed to own shares in their companies. Executives were expected to run efficient enterprises, not spend their time conniving to maximize shareholder value. Patricia McBroom, A Key to the Inequality Enigma, *Berkeleyan*, April 17, 1996.

106 David J. Collison and George M. Frankfurter, Are We Really Maximizing Shareholder Wealth? Or: What Investors Must Know When We Do, *Journal of Investing*, Fall 2000.

107 Over one recent seven-year period, corporations actually spent more money *buying back* their shares of stock from the public than they received by selling stock to the public. The period covered the years 1987 to 1994. Marjorie Kelly, Editorial: Why All the Fuss About Stockholders? *Business Ethics*, January/February 1997.

108 Ibid.

109 Ellen Goodman, Cap Cash Flow to CEOs, *Arizona Republic*, April 16, 1999.

110 Justin Hyde, Ford CEO Received $10M in 1999, Associated Press, April 11, 2001.

111 Alex Berenson, A Software Company Runs Out of Tricks, *New York Times*, April 29, 2001.

112 John A. Byrne, How Executive Greed Cost Shareholders $675 Million, *Business Week*, August 10, 1998.

113 David Cay Johnston, A 1995 Executive Pay Plan Led to Big Bonus This Week, *New York Times*, May 23, 1998.

114 These tidy sums came above and beyond the three executives' regular annual compensation. Karen Jacobs, Enough Is Enough: Computer Associates Offers a Cautionary Example of High Pay, *Wall Street Journal*, April 8, 1999.

115 Byrne, How Executive Greed Cost Shareholders $675 Million.

116 Jacobs, Enough Is Enough: Computer Associates Offers a Cautionary Example of High Pay,.

117 Between the 1995 adoption of the Computer Associates incentive plan and the 1998 windfall trigger day, Computer Associates stock had repeatedly "split," each shareholder, on three different occasions, receiving three shares for each two shares held. The original 1995 incentive plan hadn't said anything about splits, but Computer Associates, in calculating the 1998 payoff, credited Wang, Kumar, and Artzt for the splits anyway. The Delaware judge balked at that move and ruled that the executives would have to return 9.5 million shares of stock, worth $550 million, to the company. Richard J. Dalton Jr. and Pradnya Joshi, Overcompensated: Judge Says CA Execs Must Return $550M in Stock, *Newsday*, November 10, 1999. CEO Wang later "agreed to return" more than 20 percent of his 1998 pay to settle the shareholder lawsuits over his 1998 special stock grant. Louis Lavelle, Special Report: Executive Pay, *Business Week*, April 16, 2001.

118 Jacobs, Enough Is Enough: Computer Associates Offers a Cautionary Example of High Pay.

119 Berenson, A Software Company Runs Out of Tricks.

120 Ibid.

121 Ibid.

122 Strauss, The Billionaires Club.

123 Lavelle, Special Report: Executive Pay.

124 Reingold, Special Report: Executive Pay.

125 Ibid.

126 Such poorly thought-out incentive plans, charged Carol Bowie of Executive Compensation Advisory Services, are "clearly not in the best long-term interests of shareholders." Jacobs, Enough Is Enough: Computer Associates Offers a Cautionary Example of High Pay.

[127] Alex Berenson, A First Shot Is Fired at Computer Associates, *New York Times*, August 28, 2001.

[128] "CEOs get multimillion-dollar sweetheart deals," noted the AFL-CIO's Richard Trumka. "Working families worry about downsizings and layoffs." AFL-CIO Assails Firms for CEOs' Salary Deals, *Arizona Republic*, April 10, 1998.

[129] The study found 522 directors serving on executive compensation committees despite their business links to management. Adam Bryant, The CEO Cash Machine: How a Pliable System Inflates Pay Levels, *New York Times*, November 8, 1998.

[130] Ibid.

[131] Gary Strauss, CEO Paychecks: Fair or Foul? *USA Today*, April 6, 2001.

[132] Frank Swoboda, AFL-CIO Calls Boards Too Cozy With CEO on Pay, *Washington Post*, April 7, 1999.

[133] John Balzar, Executives Get Rich, Workers Get Peanuts, *Los Angeles Times*, July 29, 2001.

[134] Crystal, *In Search of Excess*, 9.

[135] Ibid., 12. A 1998 *New York Times* investigation, conducted after Crystal ended his active consulting career, documented that corporate boards were still counting on compensation consultants who had been selected by company chief executives. Bryant, The CEO Cash Machine: How a Pliable System Inflates Pay Levels.

[136] Zajac and Westphal, Accounting for the Explanations of CEO Compensation: Substance and Symbolism.

[137] Ibid. The research examined long-term incentive plans adopted between 1976 and 1990.

[138] Ibid.

[139] Bryant, The CEO Cash Machine: How a Pliable System Inflates Pay Levels.

[140] In 1997, after three lackluster years, Time Warner's stock finally started rising. A grateful Time Warner upped CEO Levin's bonus to $6.5 million. Levin had "performed." Bryant, The CEO Cash Machine: How a Pliable System Inflates Pay Levels.

[141] Louis Lavelle, The Artificial Sweetener in CEO Pay, *Business Week*, March 26, 2001.

[142] Strauss, The Billionaires Club.

[143] Jay W. Lorsch, CEO Pay: Facts and Fallacies, *Corporate Board*, May-June 1999.

[144] Jeff Brown, Tricky Answers to a Trick Question, *Philadelphia Inquirer*, May 20, 2001.

[145] Quote from Herschel Bloom of the Russell Corp. In 1999, Russell CEO John Ward took home a 36 percent pay hike, despite a 15 percent dip in the company's share value. The share value of Russell's peer companies, that same year, rose 8.6 percent. Lavelle, The Artificial Sweetener in CEO Pay.

[146] Bernard Condon, Share Scare, *Forbes*, May 14, 2001.

[147] In 1996, according to Executive Compensation Advisory Services, 29 percent of corporate boards distributed restricted stock grants. Jennifer Reingold, Special Report: Executive Pay.

[148] Jim Bohman, Utility Execs See Pay Soar During 2000, *Dayton Daily News*, March 21, 2001.

[149] Jennifer Files, Market Forces Push CEO Pay Higher, *Dallas Morning News*, May 7, 2000.

[150] The Glare of Golden Handcuffs at Seagate, *San Jose Mercury News*, March 7, 1996.

[151] Lublin, Lowering the Bar.

[152] Mike Hughlett, Executive to Get $30 Million for Leaving Minnesota's Green Tree Financial, *St. Paul Pioneer Press*, November 3, 1998.

[153] Roberta Maynard, How to Attract Top Talent in Hard Times, *Nation's Business*, April 1994.

[154] In 1996, 59 percent of 1,100 public companies surveyed dealt out golden parachutes. The 1988 share: just 41 percent. Laura Koss-Feder, Surreys With Less Fringe: A Decline in Executive Perks, *New York Times*, January 25, 1998.

[155] Coulter's windfall was calculated by *The Crystal Report*. Hughlett, Executive to Get $30 Million for Leaving Minnesota's Green Tree Financial.

[156] Stephenie Overman, Stock Options: Reprice or Hold Fast? *HR Magazine*, April 1999.

[157] Reingold, Special Report: Executive Pay.

[158] Overman, Stock Options: Reprice or Hold Fast?

[159] Lublin, Lowering the Bar. In 1998, Applied Magnetics, a parts maker for computer disk-drives, repriced some 300,000 worthless options that had been granted to CEO Craig Crisman. But this initial repricing didn't help. The stock kept sinking, making even the repriced options worthless. Directors at Applied Magnetics then slashed the exercise price on those 300,000 shares once again — and repriced another 400,000 shares they hadn't bothered to reprice the first time around.

[160] In fact, a study by three academics at Indiana University has found, the *New York Times* reports, "no evidence that the repricing of options was associated with improvement in the financial performance of the company." Gretchen Morgenson, Dispelling the Myth That Options Help Shareholders, *New York Times*, July 29, 2001.

[161] The fortunate MGM former CEO, Frank Mancuso, had his options repriced from $24 to $14.90 per share. He also received, upon exiting MGM, a $2 million annual consulting contract. Jennifer Reingold, Executive Pay: It Continues to

[160] Explode — and Options Alone Are Creating Paper Billionaires, *Business Week*, April 17, 2000.

[162] Lyons, CEO Compensation: The Whole Truth.

[163] The new rules were retroactive to December 15, 1998. Reingold, Executive Pay: It Continues to Explode — and Options Alone Are Creating Paper Billionaires.

[164] Kathleen Day, Defying Gravity: CEO's Compensation Remains at Record Highs Despite Plunging Stock Prices, *Washington Post*, April 1, 2001.

[165] "What's happening is that they have been giving their employees dramatically more options in the past year at lower prices," one pension fund official with a Canadian union pointed out in 2001. "They're leaving the old ones as is, but they might be giving them three to four times as many options at the new lower price." Brian Gibson of the Ontario Teachers Pension Plan Board, quoted in John Partridge, Corel, Investors Set to Clash Over Options, *Globe and Mail*, March 30, 2001.

[166] Stephen Franklin and Kathy Bergen, Increase in Stock Options, Grants Triggers Explosion in CEO Pay, *Chicago Tribune*, April 23, 2000.

[167] Reingold, Executive Pay: It Continues to Explode — and Options Alone Are Creating Paper Billionaires.

[168] David Leonhardt, Executive Pay: A Special Report. Little to Risk, Much to Gain, *New York Times*, April 1, 2001.

[169] Rachel Emma Silverman, Heads I Win, Tails I Win, *Wall Street Journal*, April 6, 2000.

[170] Reingold, Executive Pay: It Continues to Explode — and Options Alone Are Creating Paper Billionaires.

[171] Ibid.

[172] Harrison Rainie, The State of Greed, *US News & World Report*, June 17, 1996.

[173] John A. Byrne, Executive Pay: Compensation at the Top Is Out of Control.

[174] Ibid.

[175] Byrne, That Eye-Popping Executive Pay: Is Anybody Worth This Much?

[176] Ibid.

[177] John A. Byrne, CEO Pay: Ready for Takeoff, *Business Week*, April 24, 1995.

[178] David Cay Johnston, Executives' Pay Soars More Than Company Profits, *New York Times*, September 2, 1997.

[179] CEO bonuses were up 39 percent in 1995, stock option earnings up 45 percent. Base salaries, by contrast, jumped just 4 percent. John A. Byrne, CEO Pay: Gross Compensation? New Pay Figures Make Top Brass Look Positively Piggy, *Business Week*, March 18, 1996.

[180] Editorials: Call It Executive Overcompensation, *Business Week*.

[181] Reingold, Special Report: Executive Pay, *Business Week*, April 20, 1998.

[182] Reingold, Special Report: Executive Pay, April 19, 1999.

[183] Lublin, Lowering the Bar.

[184] Drexler's bonanza narrowly edged out Yahoo CEO Timothy Koogle's $476.4 million and outpaced, by somewhat wider margins, IBM CEO Louis Gerstner's $336.1 million, America Online CEO Steve Case's $325.8 million, and Time Warner CEO Gerald Levin's $232.8 million. The data for the *USA Today* numbers came from Graef Crystal. Gary Straus and Del Jones, Wealth of Titans, *USA Today*, April 7, 1999.

[185] Reingold, Executive Pay: It Continues to Explode — and Options Alone Are Creating Paper Billionaires.

[186] Straus and Jones, Wealth of Titans.

[187] Day, Soldiers for the Shareholder.

[188] "I think the best chance for bringing compensation under control would be, say, a dozen really powerful institutions — organizations like Fidelity and Vanguard — stating that they're going to vote against any management that oversteps on compensation," one veteran CEO told *Fortune* magazine in 2001. "But we haven't seen that happen, and I don't think we will." Carol J. Loomis, 'This Stuff Is Wrong,' *Fortune*, June 25, 2001.

[189] In 1985, Monks founded Institutional Shareholder Services, an innovative effort to help institutional investors understand the issues that come up for votes at corporate annual shareholder meetings. Day, Soldiers for the Shareholder.

[190] Ibid.

[191] John A. Byrne, That Eye-Popping Executive Pay: Is Anybody Worth This Much?

[192] Jacobs, Enough Is Enough: Computer Associates Offers a Cautionary Example of High Pay.

[193] Dunstan Prial, TIAA-CREF Aims At Executive Pay, Associated Press, March 21, 2000.

[194] Stephen Franklin, Chicago-Based Construction Firm Faces Proxy Fight over Executives' Wages, *Chicago Tribune*, April 23, 2000.

[195] The Testimony of Mr. Sean Harrigan President, California Public Employees' Retirement System, Hearing on CEO Compensation, Senate Committee on Commerce, Science and Transportation, May 20, 2003.

[196] Richard Trumka, secretary-treasurer, AFL-CIO, Letter to Jonathan Katz, Securities and Exchange Commission, May 15, 2003. Accessed at www.sec.gov/rules/other/s71003/aflcio051503.htm.

[197] Stephen Labaton, S.E.C. to Ease Voting for Outside Directors, *New York Times*, July 16, 2003.

[198] Day, Soldiers for the Shareholder.

[199] James K. Glassman, Stocks Won't Fall Forever, *Washington Post*, January 6, 2002. Some more numbers: Investors lost 12 percent of their portfolios, "based on the Wilshire 5000 total-market index, and profits for the Standard & Poor's 500 companies rose at less than half their pace in the 1990's." David Leonhardt, Executive Pay: A Special Report for the Boss, Happy Days Are Still Here, *New York Times*, April 1, 2001.

[200] Companies that trade on the stock market "have to disclose pay information for their CEOs and four other highest-paid executives each year in reports filed with the U.S. Securities and Exchange Commission and mailed to shareholders." Drew DeSilver, It Was a Fat 2000 for Top Northwest CEOs, *Seattle Times*, June 10, 2001.

[201] The median pay for the top executives the *Times* analyzed: $6.2 million. The year's top earners in the *Times* ranking: Steven Jobs, Apple Computer, $775.0 million; Sanford Weill, Citigroup, $315.1 million; Lawrence Ellison, Oracle, $216.4 million; L. Dennis Kozlowski, Tyco International, $205.2 million; John Welch Jr., General Electric, $144.5 million. Leonhardt, Executive Pay: A Special Report for the Boss.

[202] Lavelle, Special Report: Executive Pay.

[203] The Boss's Pay, *Wall Street Journal*, April 12, 2001.

[204] Strauss, CEO Paychecks: Fair or foul?

[205] CEOs of the top U.S. companies in 2000, the *Post* noted, jumped 16 percent to "a record average of $10.89 million." Day, Defying Gravity: CEO's Compensation Remains at Record Highs Despite Plunging Stock Prices.

[206] Elise Ackerman, Cashing in at Right Time, *San Jose Mercury News*, June 17, 2001.

[207] Ibid.

[208] Day, Defying Gravity; CEO's Compensation Remains at Record Highs Despite Plunging Stock Prices.

[209] Leonhardt, Executive Pay: A Special Report for the Boss, Happy Days Are Still Here.

[210] Hilzenrath, Options Getting a Second Look.

[211] Ackerman, Cashing in at Right Time.

[212] Ibid.

[213] Strauss, CEO Paychecks: Fair or Foul?

[214] In 1999, Cisco's top six executives cleared $220.5 million in option gains. Ackerman, Cashing in at Right Time.

[215] In 1999, executives happily cashed out 23 percent of their outstanding options. In 2000, they cashed out just 10 percent. Leonhardt, Executive Pay: A Special Report for the Boss, Happy Days Are Still Here.

[216] Day, Defying Gravity: CEO's Compensation Remains at Record Highs Despite Plunging Stock Prices.

[217] Strauss, CEO Paychecks: Fair or Foul? And what about all those options granted in years past that had gone "underwater"? Executives convinced boards to lower the exercise price on many of these underwater options. Or asked for — and received — new grants of actual shares, not options to buy shares. Actual shares, of course, have value even if their price keeps sinking. Leonhardt, Executive Pay: A Special Report for the Boss, Happy Days Are Still Here. PNC Financial gave $3.9 million worth of actual shares to CEO James Rohr in 2000, after going the entire decade of the 1990s without awarding a single free share. CVS, the drug store chain, handed chief executive Thomas Ryan $5.5 million worth. Both companies said the grants were needed to retain executives in a "competitive" business environment. Condon, Share Scare.

[218] Strauss, CEO Paychecks: Fair or Foul?

[219] Ackerman, Cashing in at Right Time.

[220] Mark Schwanhausser, Option Gains Held Up Well for Top-10 Bosses, *San Jose Mercury News*, June 8, 2002.

[221] Leonhardt, Executive Pay: A Special Report for the Boss, Happy Days Are Still Here.

[222] A mulligan gives a golfer the opportunity to "do over" a bad shot.

[223] And if options don't do the trick, one veteran CEO told *Fortune* in 2001, executives will just get corporate boards to replace options with some other "incentives" that will. "Anyone who is greedy, anyone who is on the make, anyone who is aggressive about what they're being paid," the executive explained, "will get rid of formulas they don't like." Loomis, 'This Stuff Is Wrong.'

[224] Leonhardt, Executive Pay: A Special Report for the Boss, Happy Days Are Still Here.

[225] Ibid.

[226] Ibid. In 2001, "average" compensation for chief executives did fall 8 percent, to $15.5 million, but only, the *New York Times* would caution, "because the year had seen a tailing off in the number of "truly enormous paychecks."

[227] Jerry Useem, CEO Pay: Have They No Shame? *Fortune*, April 14, 2003.

[228] Gary Strauss, Many Execs Pocket Perks Aplenty, *USA Today*, May 1, 2001.

[229] In 1997, for instance, Tyson Foods gave senior chairman Don Tyson $414,817 for travel and

entertainment and another $288,859 to cover any additional taxes Don might have to fork over. Adam Bryant, New Look of Perks: From Plane Trips to Tax Preparation, *New York Times*, April 5, 1998.

230 By 1997, the late CEO of Coca-Cola, Roberto Goizueta, had accumulated more than $1 billion in his deferral accounts. Johnston, Executives' Pay Soars More Than Company Profits.

231 Ellen Schultz and Theo Francis, Well-Hidden Perk Means Big Money for Top Executives, *Wall Street Journal*, February 11, 2002.

232 Johnston, Executives' Pay Soars More Than Company Profits.

233 Executive pay deferral plans, unlike pension and 401(k) plans, are not privileged. In a bankruptcy, creditors cannot seize pension and 401(k) assets. Executive deferral plans enjoy no such protection. Christopher Drew and David Cay Johnston, Special Tax Breaks Enrich Savings of Many in the Ranks of Management, *New York Times*, October 13, 1996.

234 Ibid.

235 Ibid.

236 Strauss, Many Execs Pocket Perks Aplenty.

237 Leonhardt, Executive Pay: A Special Report for the Boss, Happy Days Are Still Here.

238 So Much Money, So Little Time, *Wall Street Journal*, April 8, 1999.

239 Strauss, Many Execs Pocket Perks Aplenty.

240 Several executives, in early 1998, owned more shares than Michael Dell. Bill Gates held $35 billion in Microsoft shares to lead the CEO pack. Sumner Redstone, with $4.1 billion of Viacom shares, and Philip Knight, with $3.68 billion of Nike shares, led Dell. David Cay Johnston, Here's How the Chiefs Stock Up, *New York Times*, February 15, 1998.

241 Allan Sloan, Clean-Up Time, *Business Week*, March 15, 1999, and Hilzenrath, Options Getting a Second Look.

242 Hilzenrath, Options Getting a Second Look.

243 Sloan, Clean-Up Time.

244 Ibid.

245 A Leader's Eye View of Leadership A Roundtable Discussion, *New York Times*, October 10, 1999.

246 Byrne, CEO Pay: Ready for Takeoff.

247 "The Sarbanes-Oxley Act," notes one summary, "requires chief executives to certify the accuracy of financial reports, increases the responsibilities of corporate board members, restricts the type of work accountants can do, and established a new accounting industry oversight board." Carrie

Johnson, Lavish Executive Pay Still a Target, *Washington Post*, July 31, 2003.

248 Gary Strauss, CEOs Still Sitting on Piles of Pay, *USA Today*, August 12, 2003.

249 This discussion about WorldCom draws from Richard C. Breeden, Restoring Trust: Report to the Hon. Jed S. Rakoff, the United States District Court for the Southern District of New York on Corporate Governance for the Future of MCI, Inc. August 2003. Accessed from www.thecorporatelibrary.com/spotlight/scandals/Restoring_Trust_Final-WorldCom.pdf.

250 Breeden did allow retention bonuses in certain situations, namely when acquisitions or facility closings are involved.

251 The maximum, Breeden's report noted, could only be exceeded by an explicit shareholder vote.

252 Barnaby J. Feder, WorldCom Report Recommends Sweeping Changes for Its Board, *New York Times*, August 26, 2003.

253 Steven Pearlstein, Capping Pay of CEOs Is the Way to Go, *Washington Post*, September 19, 2003.

254 Strauss, CEO Still Sitting on Piles of Pay.

THE GREEDY AS DESERVING

1 Pay, "doesn't really motivate" CEOs, corporate pay expert Graef Crystal has noted. "They are already working as hard as they can; they are already working as smart as they can." Reed Abelson, Who Profits if the Boss Is Overfed? *New York Times*, June 20, 1999.

2 The *Worth* poll, conducted by Roper Starch Worldwide, surveyed five hundred people worth at least $250,000 in income or $2.5 million in assets. Richard Todd, Who Me, Rich? *Worth*, September 1997.

3 Jay W. Lorsch, CEO Pay: Facts and Fallacies, *Corporate Board*, May-June 1999.

4 Christian was the president of Christian & Timbers, an executive headhunting company. Ricardo Sandoval, Over the Top or Right on the Money? *San Jose Mercury News*, June 23, 1996.

5 Dunlap made this comment to the Wharton/SpencerStuart Director's Institute. 'If You're Going to Be a Director,' *Directors & Boards*, Winter 1995.

6 "For years," noted former SEC commissioner, Philip R. Lochner Jr., "he was the greatest thing in the media's eyes that American enterprise had ever seen." Jeffrey Sonnenfeld, The CEO as Captain of Industry: A Dying Breed? *Directors & Boards*, Spring 2001.

7 The Wharton School, one of America's most pres-

tigious business schools, invited Dunlap to launch a new lecture series. Tasha Huebner, Al Dunlap: Mean Business, *Wharton Journal*, 1996. Republicans in the House of Representatives made him one of the few outsiders invited to address their retreat for freshmen lawmakers. Dunlap advised the freshmen, in January 1996, to privatize as much of government as they could. "Maybe Yellowstone should be run by Disney," he noted. Downsizing the American Dream A Staff Report of the House Democratic Policy Committee, March 11, 1996.

[8] "He has been a wake-up call to a lot of CEOs, and he has been good for American business," noted one typical admirer, Wayne R. Sanders, chairman of Kimberly-Clark. John A. Byrne, The Shredder: Did CEO Dunlap Save Scott Paper — or Just Pretty It Up? *Business Week*, January 15, 1996.

[9] Leslie Kaufman, Cashing Out Rambo, *Newsweek*, July 31, 1995.

[10] 'Chainsaw' Self-portrait, *USA Today*, August 30, 1996.

[11] In 1986, a triumphant Dunlap left Lily-Tulip with $6.5 million in personal stock-option gains. John A. Byrne, Who Is the Real 'Chainsaw Al'? *Business Week*, December 2, 1996.

[12] Andi Simmons Bolton, Sunbeam Chairman Says Mississippi Plants Poised for Growth, *Mississippi Business Journal*, February 17, 1997.

[13] The firm's founders, Irvin and Clarence Scott, had invented the bathroom tissue roll in 1879. Their company would later go on to invent the paper towel and become, by 1990, the world's largest single supplier of household paper products. Byrne, The Shredder: Did CEO Dunlap Save Scott Paper — or Just Pretty It Up?

[14] 'Chainsaw' Self-portrait, *USA Today*, August 30, 1996.

[15] Molly Baker, CEOs and Layoffs: Should Salary Be Linked? *Orange County Register*, May 30, 1995.

[16] Byrne, The Shredder: Did CEO Dunlap Save Scott Paper — or Just Pretty It Up?

[17] Ibid.

[18] Ibid. The company's total market value had soared by $6.3 billion.

[19] 'If You're Going to Be a Director ....,' *Directors & Boards*, Winter 1995.

[20] "The handwriting has been on the wall a long time," as one such observer, Greater Philadelphia First executive director John Claypool, pointed out. "Dunlap has been very clear on how important making money was to him, and the way to do that in the short term is to make the company as attractive as possible and sell it." Beth Reinhard, Paper Products Firms to Merge, *Palm Beach Post*,

July 18, 1996.

[21] Byrne, The Shredder: Did CEO Dunlap Save Scott Paper — or Just Pretty It Up?

[22] Ibid.

[23] Dunlap's reward for joining Kimberly-Clark and Scott in merger bliss will include $20 million for agreeing not to give a competing company the benefit of his wisdom, $12 million to buy out his five-year contract at Scott, 5,000 shares of stock a year for advising the new company, and about $50 million or so worth of stock options. Beth Reinhard, Scott CEO Reaps Millions from Turnaround, Merger, *Palm Beach Post*, July 19, 1995.

[24] 'Chainsaw' Self-portrait, *USA Today*, August 30, 1996. For Dunlap, who claimed he worked 100 hours a week during his 20-month Scott Paper stint, the $100 million reward amounted to $12,500 for every single hour he worked.

[25] Byrne, The Shredder: Did CEO Dunlap Save Scott Paper — or Just Pretty It Up?

[26] Ibid.

[27] Bridging the Gap, PBS Lehrer News Hour, March 20, 1996.

[28] Ibid.

[29] The total combined workforce was sixty thousand. Byrne, The Shredder: Did CEO Dunlap Save Scott Paper — or Just Pretty It Up?

[30] Ibid. The move Dunlap dubbed "the linchpin of my strategy" — the $1.6 billion sale of a Scott papermaker subsidiary — had first been scoped out a year before Dunlap arrived on the scene. The high-tech tissue mill in Kentucky that Dunlap "opened with great fanfare" in 1995 had been initiated in 1990. Several product initiatives Dunlap credited to his management team were actually "the result of years of effort by ousted staffers." Added *Business Week*: "Even many of the employee layoffs had already been approved by Scott before Dunlap came on board."

[31] Ibid.

[32] John A. Byrne and Gail DeGeorge, Commentary: Dear Al Dunlap: Put Away the Chainsaw, *Business Week*, August 5, 1996.

[33] Ibid.

[34] Ibid.

[35] The downsizing, reported the *Wall Street Journal*, appeared "to represent one of the single biggest percentage cutbacks ever announced by a major U.S. corporation." Robert Frank and Joann S. Lublin, Dunlap's Ax Falls — 6,000 Times — at Sunbeam, *Wall Street Journal*, November 13, 1996.

[36] Nobody could reasonably claim Sunbeam was bloated. Only sixty staffers worked at the firm's

Fort Lauderdale corporate headquarters. Byrne and DeGeorge, Commentary: Dear Al Dunlap: Put Away the Chainsaw.

37 Ibid. "At Sunbeam," *Business Week* advised the new Sunbeam CEO, "you won't be able to just put a blender or gas grill in new packaging — the kind of thing you often did at Scott — and hope that it sells." Neither would Dunlap, the magazine added, "be able to pass on double-digit price increases to consumers" as he did at Scott.

38 Gail DeGeorge, Al Dunlap Revs His Chain Saw, *Business Week*, November 25, 1996. "You don't cut that dramatically without creating chaos inside the company," warned management consultant Alan Downs. Robert Frank and Joann S. Lublin, Dunlap's Ax Falls — 6,000 Times — at Sunbeam, *Wall Street Journal*, November 13, 1996.

39 Barbara Sullivan, Hatchet Man or Savior? *Chicago Tribune*, January 17, 1997.

40 Sunbeam Axes 'Chainsaw Al' Dunlap, CNNfn, June 15, 1998.

41 Digest, *Washington Post*, March 10, 1998.

42 The losses total $44.5 million. Sunbeam Axes 'Chainsaw Al' Dunlap, CNNfn.

43 Ibid.

44 From their March level. Ibid.

45 Martha Hamilton, Who's Chainsawed Now? *Washington Post*, June 16, 1998.

46 Dunlap's management team, an SEC official explained, had engaged in what "appears to have been a coldly calculated plan to inflate the price of the stock, ultimately for the personal enrichment" of the executives involved. David S. Hilzenrath, Sunbeam Accused of Fraud, *Washington Post*, May 16, 2001.

47 Ben White, Dunlap, Sunbeam Shareholders Settle, *Washington Post*, January 15, 2002. Sunbeam filed for Chapter 11 protection in 2001 "after struggling under a massive $2 billion debt amassed under Dunlap."

48 This Coleman discussion draws from David Evans, CEOs Seldom Lose in Mergers, *Cleveland Plain Dealer*, September 6, 1998.

49 Dunlap, a check into his background would have found, had a history of shady dealings. At Nitec, a New York papermaker, Dunlap was credited with hiking company profits. He left the company in 1976 with an exit agreement that promised $1.2 million, a princely sum in mid-1970s America. But auditors, after Dunlap left, found expenses that hadn't been recorded and recorded sales that had never actually been made. The company, they concluded, had actually lost some $5.5 million. Nitec's

top bookkeeper later testified that the fraud had been perpetrated on direct orders from Dunlap. Floyd Norris, An Executive's Missing Years: Papering Over Past Problems, *New York Times*, July 16, 2001.

50 Joann S. Lublin, Pay for No Performance, *Wall Street Journal*, April 9, 1998.

51 Office Depot Paid Ex-CEO $8.6 Million in Severance Package, *Wall Street Journal*, March 29, 2001.

52 Bowie, when she made this comment, was the research director of the Virginia-based Executive Compensation Advisory Services company. Lublin, Pay for No Performance.

53 In 2001, a U.S. court of appeals threw out Judge Jackson's remedy for Microsoft's abuses — break up Microsoft — but upheld his finding that Microsoft had violated the nation's antitrust statutes. Court ruling accessed from http://news.com.com/html/ne/Special/Microsoft/msft_ruling.html.

54 Roy C. Smith, *The Wealth Creators: The Rise of Today's Rich and Super-Rich*. New York: St. Martin's Press, 2001, 123-130. Investors who buy a government or corporate bond are guaranteed their original investment back, by a specified future date, plus interest. Bonds from long-established companies are usually considered rock-solid safe. But not every company that tries to raise cash by selling bonds fits the blue-chip label. These riskier corporations just might default sometime down the road, and investors, to protect themselves from that danger, have historically demanded that bonds from shaky companies pay higher interest than bonds from more stable enterprises. But shaky companies, Milken's personal research revealed, seldom defaulted, and, if they did, investors could recover some of what they lost in bankruptcy proceedings. Investors could make money, Milken concluded, buying low-grade bonds and holding them, particularly because "junk bonds" could be bought at prices that reflected the financial market's soft demand for this shaky paper. If Milken could convince enough investors to rethink their distaste for low-grade bonds, a real market in junk-bond trading could emerge. And if a real market emerged, then more companies might try floating bonds to raise money. And if that ever happened, then any company quick enough to connect these companies with investors — and corner the junk bond market in the process — could make major fortunes on fees and commissions. The company where Milken worked, Drexel Burnham, did that cornering in the 1980s. In 1986, America's junk bond king pulled in $550 million.

[55] Smith, *The Wealth Creators: The Rise of Today's Rich and Super-Rich*, 123-130.

[56] Susan Stranahan, The Clean Room's Dirty Secret, *Mother Jones*, March-April 2002. The Silicon Valley Toxics Coalition (www.svtc.org) has been working to focus public attention on these high-tech hazards.

[57] Ibid. Based on a $12 median hourly wage.

[58] The Top-Paid Chief Executives, *Business Week*, April 17, 2000.

[59] Stranahan, The Clean Room's Dirty Secret.

[60] Alex Callinicos, Equality. Cambridge: Polity Press. Malden, Mass.: Blackwell Publishers, 2000, 78.

[61] Castle made his fortune as the chief executive at Castle Harlan Inc. Joann S. Lublin, Living Well, *Wall Street Journal*, April 8, 1999.

[62] The study was conducted by the Management Resource Group. Another Reason to Hate the Rich, *Washington Post*, September 20, 1998.

[63] Thoreau was dismissing arguments that the extreme exertions of gold prospectors gave them a right to their riches. Patricia Nelson Limerick, Of Forty-Niners, Oilmen and the Dot.Com Boom, *New York Times*, May 7, 2000.

[64] This $25 million was the compensation for CEOs who led $7 billion enterprises. William G. Cunningham and J. Brent Sperry, Where's the Beef in Administrator Pay? *School Administrator*, February 2001.

[65] Shareowners and Institutional Holders Fight Corporate Director Benefits, *Communications Daily*, April 17, 1995.

[66] John A. Byrne, CEO Pay: Gross Compensation? *Business Week*, March 18, 1996.

[67] The 1934 data come from the Survey of American Listed Corporations, a Works Progress Administration project "supervised by the SEC to report compensation and balance-sheet data for publicly traded firms." The survey recorded the "direct compensation of the highest-paid employee" in each firm. Austan Goolsbee. Evidence on the High-Income Laffer Curve from Six Decades of Tax Reform, *Brookings Papers on Economic Activity*, Fall 1999.

[68] Guide to the Presidency: Presidential and Vice Presidential Salaries Exclusive of Perquisites. *Congressional Quarterly*. Accessed from www.lib.umich.edu/libhome/Documents.center/fedprssal.html.

[69] The best-paid executives in 1970, those at the ninetieth percentile, averaged $250,000, the equivalent of $1,161,334 in 2001 dollars. The data are from the Forbes CEO Compensation Survey published in 1971. Austan Goolsbee. Evidence on the

High-Income Laffer Curve from Six Decades of Tax Reform, *Brookings Papers on Economic Activity*, Fall 1999.

[70] Guide to the Presidency: Presidential and Vice Presidential Salaries Exclusive of Perquisites. *Congressional Quarterly*. Accessed from www.lib.umich.edu/libhome/Documents.center/fedprssal.html.

[71] Brian J. Hall and Jeffrey B. Liebman, Are CEOs Really Paid Like Bureaucrats? *Quarterly Journal of Economics*, August 1998. The authors calculate the median direct compensation for CEOs in 1980 at $622,777 in 1994 dollars.

[72] Goolsbee, Evidence on the High-Income Laffer Curve from Six Decades of Tax Reform. The inflation adjustment for 2001 reflects an author's calculation. In 1934, corporate top executive salary and bonus packages ranged, according to contemporary survey work, from $32,000 at the tenth percentile to $126,000 at the ninetieth percentile.

[73] Ibid. The inflation adjustment for 2001 reflects an author's calculation. The $154,427 figure, to be more precise, actually represents the arithmetic average CEO pay for 1970. Top executive compensation in 1970 stood at $77,000 at the tenth percentile, $100,000 at the twenty-fifth percentile, $140,000 at the fiftieth percentile, and $190,000 at the seventy-fifth percentile.

[74] Hall and Liebman, Are CEOs Really Paid Like Bureaucrats? Author's calculation for the 2001 inflation adjustment.

[75] Gary Strauss, Why Are These CEOs Smiling? Must Be Payday, *USA Today*, March 25, 2002.

[76] Adam Bryant, Raising the Stakes: American Pay Rattles Foreign Partners, *New York Times*, January 17, 1999.

[77] Greg Steinmetz and Gregory L. White, Chrysler's Executive Pay Draws Fire from Overseas, *Wall Street Journal*, May 26, 1998.

[78] Ken Belson, Learning How to Talk About Salary in Japan, *New York Times*, April 7, 2002.

[79] Lisa Biank Fasig, CEO Pay Doesn't Break Banks, *Providence Journal*, March 14, 2001. Surveys in the late 1990s found that CEOs of moderately sized American corporations made three times more than their Spanish counterparts and more than twice the pay of French chief executives. Peter Goldstein, Compensation Packages for Executives Aren't All Alike, *Wall Street Journal Europe*, December 22, 1998.

[80] John A. Byrne, That Eye-Popping Executive Pay Is Anybody Worth This Much? *Business Week*, April 25, 1994.

[81] John Kay, *Why Firms Succeed*. New York: Oxford University Press, 1995. 243.

82 Graef Crystal, Andy's Dandy: Intel CEO Is Worth Every Penny of $94 Million, *San Francisco Business Times*, April 28, 1997.

83 Ibid.

84 Jay Mathews, Their Riches Were Your Command, *Washington Post*, March 24, 1996.

85 Crystal, Andy's Dandy: Intel CEO Is Worth Every Penny of $94 Million.

86 Andy Santoni, Intel Puts Grove on Center Stage as Chairman, *Infoworld*, March 30, 1998.

87 Philip Whiteley, Introducing the 10 Million Dollar CEO, *The Times* (London), March 22, 2001.

88 The Japanese executives averaged about $350,000. Stephanie Strom, Japan's Big Income Gap, *Pittsburgh Post-Gazette*, January 10, 2000.

89 Cindy Richards, Little Guy Fights Back, *Chicago Sun-Times*, May 16, 1997. The ratio in the United States? Two hundred to one.

90 Greg Steinmetz and Gregory L. White, Chrysler's Executive Pay Draws Fire from Overseas, *Wall Street Journal*, May 26, 1998.

91 Deborah Orr, Damn Yankees, *Forbes*, May 17, 1999.

92 Denis Lyons, CEO Compensation: The Whole Truth, *Chief Executive*, July 1999.

93 Sarah Anderson and John Cavanagh, Institute for Policy Studies, Chris Hartman and Betsy Leondar-Wright, United for a Fair Economy, Executive Excess 2001: Eighth Annual CEO Compensation Survey, September 2001. Original sources: Jennifer Reingold with Fred Jespersen, Executive Pay: It Continues to Explode — and Options Alone Are Creating Paper Billionaires, *Business Week*, April 17, 2000, and Jennifer Gill, "We're Back to Serfs and Royalty," *Business Week*, April 9, 2001.

94 Margaret M. Blair, CEO Pay: Why Such a Contentious Issue? *Brookings Review*, Winter 1994.

95 Engineers averaged $82,780 in 2000. Terry Costlow, Engineers' Pay Jumps, *EE Times*, October 10, 2001. Executives averaged $13.1 million. Louis Lavelle, Executive Pay, *Business Week*, April 16, 2001.

96 Marcy Gordon, Slim Staff Can Mean Fat Check Study, Associated Press, *The Record*, May 2, 1997.

97 Pierce helped found Business Leaders for Excellence, Ethics, and Justice. Gregory F.A. Pierce, *Spirituality @ Work*. Chicago: Loyola Press, 2001, 71-72.

98 Michael Lewis, The Rich: How They're Different . . . Than They Used to Be, *New York Times*, November 19, 1995.

99 Marc Gunther, Has Eisner Lost the Disney Magic? *Fortune*, January 2002.

100 James Bates, Eisner Gets a Payday of $565 Million, *Washington Post*, December 4, 1997.

101 Byrne, That Eye-Popping Executive Pay Is Anybody Worth This Much?

102 Gunther, Has Eisner Lost the Disney Magic?

103 Paul Farhi, Disney Chief May Reap $771 Million from Stock Options, *Washington Post*, February 22, 1997.

104 James Bates, Eisner Gets a Payday of $565 Million, *Washington Post*, December 4, 1997.

105 Bill Shaikin, A Capital Idea: Paying 'Mo' Money Merely Shows That Angels Are Intent on Fielding a Winner, *Los Angeles Times*, April 6, 1999.

106 Gunther, Has Eisner Lost the Disney Magic?

107 Bernard Weinraub, The Vehicle Is Everything, *New York Times Book Review*, June 8, 1997, review of Robert Slater, *Ovitz: The Inside Story of Hollywood's Most Controversial Power Broker*. New York, McGraw-Hill, 1997.

108 Jennifer Reingold, Where Parting Is Such a Sweet Deal, *Business Week*, March 31, 1997. The size of the severance package later became a matter of some dispute, with estimates ranging from $128 million to only $25 million. Nikki Finke, Did Ovitz Tell a Whopper About $90 Million Deal? *New York Observer*, December 23, 1996.

109 Harry Berkowitz, Media Titans Take Off Gloves, *Washington Post*, May 4, 2001.

110 Richard Verrier, Disney's Problems Run Deep Orlando, *Orlando Sentinel*, April 9, 2001.

111 Eisner wasn't, in his own mind, just a chief *executive* officer. "I consider myself the chief creative officer," as Eisner told one business magazine. Gunther, Has Eisner Lost the Disney Magic?

112 Ibid.

113 Richard Verrier, Disney's Problems Run Deep Orlando, *Orlando Sentinel*.

114 Gunther, Has Eisner Lost the Disney Magic?

115 Ibid.

116 Ibid. Nor could Eisner claim any credit for the recession-less economy that followed his hiring as Disney's CEO. That economy, notes *Fortune*, "fueled growth" at Disney's theme parks.

117 Stewart Pinkerton, Seven Ways to Solve the Executive Pay Mess, Forbes.com, July 23, 2003.

118 Only three people younger than the thirty-five-year-old Bezos — Charles Lindbergh, Queen Elizabeth II, and Martin Luther King Jr. — had ever won the *Time* honor. Jeffrey Preston Bezos: 1999 Person of the Year, *Time*, December 27, 1999.

[119] Jeffrey Preston Bezos: 1999 Person of the Year, *Time*.

[120] How Much Did They Lose? *Time*, October 23, 2000.

[121] Jeffrey Preston Bezos: 1999 Person of the Year, *Time*.

[122] Amazon was $720 million in the red when Time honored Bezos in December 1999. How Much Did They Lose? *Time*, October 23, 2000.

[123] Jeffrey Preston Bezos: 1999 Person of the Year, *Time*.

[124] Saul Hansell, A Front-Row Seat as Amazon Gets Serious, *New York Times*, May 20, 2001.

[125] Bezos claimed that profits would appear in his core book, music, and video business. Jeffrey Preston Bezos: 1999 Person of the Year, *Time*.

[126] Hansell, A Front-Row Seat as Amazon Gets Serious.

[127] Why Amazon made money, *Chain Store Age Executive with Shopping Center Age*, March 2002.

[128] Larry Dignan, Amazon Posts Its First Net Profit, CNET News.com, January 22, 2002.

[129] How Amazon Cleared That Hurdle, *Business Week*, February 4, 2002.

[130] Ibid.

[131] Stock Fund for Those Laid Off, *eweek*, February 5, 2001.

[132] Miguel Helft, Amazon.com Workers Begin Union Drive, *The Standard*, November 16, 2000.

[133] Ibid.

[134] Stock Fund for Those Laid Off, *eweek*.

[135] Quoted in Miguel Helft, The Laugh Heard 'Round the World, *Industry Standard*, June 11, 2001. Writes Helft: "Amazon.com may have had its troubles over the past year, but earnestly goofy CEO Jeff Bezos has maintained his sense of humor — and the trademark laugh that goes with it."

[136] Richard Cohen, No Way to Do News Business, *Washington Post*, November 11, 1999.

[137] Jo Ann Wypijewski, GE Brings Bad Things to Life, *Nation*, February 12, 2001.

[138] Michael Kinsman, Survey Shows Highest Paid CEO Made $655 Million, *San Diego Union-Tribune*, April 1, 2000.

[139] All this came at a time when G.E. shareholder return fell 6 percent. Compensation consultant Graef Crystal called Welch's pay package this time an "obscenity." Andrew Cave, GE Rewards Chief with 'Bonkers' Pay Award, *Daily Telegraph*, March 17, 2001.

[140] GE Chief's Book Advance Jolts Publishers, *Washington Post*, July 15, 2000.

[141] Robert H. Frank, *Luxury Fever: Money and Happiness in an Era of Excess*. Princeton: Princeton University Press, 1999, 39.

[142] Forced Rankings: Tough Love or Overkill? *HR Focus*, February 2002.

[143] Philip Kennicott, When Golden CEO Jack Welch Stepped Down, It Was Into the Mud, *Washington Post*, October 14, 2002.

[144] Matthew Boyle, Performance Reviews: Perilous Curves Ahead, *Fortune* (Asia), May 28, 2001. An estimated fifth of America's biggest companies are now following Welch's "forced ranking" lead. Forced Rankings: Tough Love or Overkill? *HR Focus*, February 2002.

[145] Allan Sloan, Demise of NBCi Shows the Dangers of Trying to Create Internet Wampum, *Washington Post*, April 17, 2001.

[146] Ibid.

[147] Group Calls for Limiting Pay Ratio Between BankBoston Execs and Work Force, Associated Press, April 23, 1999.

[148] "Boards of directors perceive there's a fairly limited number of individuals capable of running these large, complex organizations," explains Diane Lerner, a *Fortune* magazine compensation expert. "And they're willing to pay to get them." Brian Dumaine, A Knockout Year for CEO Pay, *Fortune*, July 25, 1994.

[149] Stephen Franklin and Kathy Bergen, Increase in Stock Options, Grants Triggers Explosion in CEO Pay, *Chicago Tribune*, April 23, 2000.

[150] Ibid.

[151] Paul V. Galvin founded what became known as Motorola in 1928. His son, Robert W. Galvin, was later the company's top exec. See the company history at www.motorola.com.

[152] Karen Rothmyer, Protests Rise Along With Pay of Executives, *Newsday*, April 16, 1995.

[153] The talent shortage, noted one Houston-based pay consultant, Danielle Jiacomin, at the end of the decade, had companies in a panic. "They're paying more than they used to," she told the *Dallas Morning News*. Jennifer Files, Market Forces Push CEO Pay Higher, *Dallas Morning News*, May 7, 2000.

[154] Thomas G. Donlan, Out of the Park: Soaring Executive Pay Is a Sign of Economic Health, *Barron's*, May 4, 1998.

[155] Ronald Alsop, Top Business Schools, *Wall Street Journal*, April 30, 2001.

[156] Is business school academic training any good? American business seems to think so. Corporations routinely foot the business school tuition bills for their executives-in-training — *and* give their future

leaders paid time off to take business school courses. Tuitions, for the record, can now top $100,000 at the nation's most highly regarded business school programs. Ronald Alsop, Top Business Schools, *Wall Street Journal*, April 30, 2001. About a third of the nation's 500 biggest companies are currently run by chief executives with graduate school business degrees. Becky Yerak, As Dot-coms Fall, MBAs Coming Back, *USA Today*, September 25, 2000. This story cites a survey by *Chief Executive* magazine and the Spencer Stuart executive search firm.

157 "It's not fair to compare them [top executives] with hourly workers," says Ira Kay, a pay consultant at Watson Wyatt Worldwide. "Their market is the global market for executives." R.C. Longworth, CEOs Bringing Home Bigger Bucks Than Ever, *Chicago Tribune*, August 28, 2001.

158 Pay critic Graef Crystal adds other factors into the supply-and-demand mix. "Labor economists will tell you that there shouldn't be a major change in pay without a change in supply or demand. Has there been an increase in demand for major-company CEOs? No — they keep merging. A decrease in supply? Hell, no. Harvard Business School turns out more than ever, and we have all these women we keep turning down." Thomas A. Stewart, The Leading Edge: Can Even Heroes Get Paid Too Much? *Fortune*, June 8, 1998.

159 "Market forces determine how well the firm does within the marketplace, but not necessarily how well the individuals within the firm do," writes historian James Huston, who adds that "compensation is a managerial, not a market, determination." James L. Huston, *Securing the Fruits of Labor: The American Concept of Wealth Distribution 1765-1900*. Baton Rouge: Louisiana State University Press, 1998, 388.

160 Matthew Miller, A Market All Their Own Caters to CEOs, *Los Angeles Times*, April 19, 2001.

161 McClellan, in his column, proposed a maximum wage for executives set at $171,000. Bill McClellan, OK, Here's One Argument Against a Maximum Wage, *St. Louis Post-Dispatch*, September 6, 1999.

162 Michael Liedtke, Webvan's CEO Resigns, Associated Press, April 14, 2001.

163 Christopher Byron, The Man for Yahoo!: Webvan's Shaheen, He Wuz a Contender, *New York Observer*, March 19, 2001, and Michael Liedtke, Webvan's CEO Resigns, Associated Press, April 14, 2001.

164 Shaheen also received a $500,000 salary and a bonus offer up to $250,000. Michael Liedtke, Webvan's CEO Resigns, Associated Press, April 14, 2001. Option value from Byron, The Man for Yahoo!: Webvan's Shaheen, He Wuz a Contender.

165 Keith Regan, Shaheen and Webvan Take Each Other for a Costly Ride, *E-Commerce Times*, May 18, 2001.

166 Michael Liedtke, Webvan's CEO Resigns, Associated Press, April 14, 2001.

167 Ibid.

168 Webvan, a most generous employer, "also allowed Shaheen to repay a $6.7 million loan with only $150,000 worth of Webvan stock." Michael Mahoney, Former Webvan CEO to Get $375,000 Annually - For Life, *E-Commerce Times*, May 17, 2001.

169 Tim Carvell, Adam Horowitz, and Thomas Mucha, The 101 Dumbest Moments in Business, *Business 2.0*, April 2002.

170 Ann Marsh, Meet the Class of 1996, *Forbes*, October 14, 1996.

171 Robert J. Samuelson, Gates Isn't God (or Even Henry Ford), *Washington Post*, August 27, 1997.

172 Lisa DiCarlo, The Transformers: The $100,000 Monopoly, *Forbes.com*, May 10, 2002.

173 Stephen Manes and Paul Andrews, *Gates*. Cited by Robert J. Samuelson, Gates Isn't God (or Even Henry Ford), *Washington Post*, August 27, 1997.

174 In the 2001 fiscal year, Microsoft boasts $25 billion in annual sales and $11.7 billion in profits — and ends the year with "a cash horde approaching a mind-boggling $40 billion." DiCarlo, The Transformers: The $100,000 Monopoly.

175 Barry Bluestone and Bennett Harrison, *Growing Prosperity*. Boston: Houghton Mifflin Company, 2000, 18.

176 Gar Alperovitz, Distributing Our Technological Inheritance, *Technology Review*, October 1994.

177 Douglas Rushkoff, The People's Net, *Yahoo Internet Life*, July 2001.

178 Alperovitz, Distributing Our Technological Inheritance.

179 Gates Sr. criss-crossed the United States with Chuck Collins, his co-author on *Wealth and Our Commonwealth: Why America Should Tax Accumulated Fortunes*. Boston: Beacon Press, 2002. They discussed the issues around wealth their book raises.

180 Amy Barrett, Affairs of Estate: Questions for William H. Gates Sr., *New York Times Magazine*, March 18, 2001.

181 Gates testified before the Senate Subcommittee on Taxation and IRS Oversight in late March. A version of his remarks later appeared as an op-ed. William H. Gates Sr., A Tax Break's Unfortunate Legacy, *Washington Post*, May 25, 2001.

[182] Gates, A Tax Break's Unfortunate Legacy.

[183] This aphorism has also been credited to billionaire oilman J. Paul Getty.

[184] Brian L. Roberts, Broadband, Cable, and Comcast, address to the Washington Economic Club, January 24, 2001.

[185] Frank Ahrens, Roberts A Low-Key Leader for Cable Giant, *Washington Post*, December 21, 2001.

[186] Roberts, Broadband, Cable, and Comcast.

[187] Smith, *The Wealth Creators: The Rise of Today's Rich and Super-Rich*, 37.

[188] David R. Francis, The CEO Makes What? Return of a Fair-pay Debate, *Christian Science Monitor*, March 27, 2000.

[189] Novell, cheered the *Economist* magazine in 1999, had become "Re-born.com." Betsy Schiffman, Eric Schmidt Is Gaga Over Google, Forbes.com, August 6, 2001.

[190] Accessed from Forbes.com executive pay lists.

[191] The remark originally appeared in *Forbes*. Quoted by Holly Sklar, If Only the Forbes 400 Billionaires Would Listen, *Houston Chronicle*, October 4, 1999.

[192] Dan Seligman, Want to Get Rich? Don't Get Born in Afghanistan, *Forbes*, October 13, 1997.

[193] Dinesh D'Souza, The Moral Limits of Wealth, *Forbes*, October 9, 2000.

[194] Amy Cortese, How IPOs Turn Pip-Squeaks Into Players, *Business Week*, August 25, 1997.

[195] Jeanne Dugan, Pique at a Wall Street Powerhouse, *Washington Post*, January 22, 2000.

[196] Michael Kinsley, How Affirmative Action Helped George W., *Time*, January 21, 2003.

[197] Kevin Sack, Bush Owes Success to Hard Work, Connections, *New York Times News Service*, May 9, 1999.

[198] Robert Scheer, A Fox Is About to Reassure Us Hens, *Los Angeles Times*, July 9, 2002.

[199] So says Richard Greene, the former mayor of Arlington. Kevin Sack, Bush Owes Success to Hard Work, Connections, *New York Times News Service*, May 9, 1999.

[200] Corporate Connections, opensecrets.org, Center for Responsive Politics. Accessed from www.opensecrets.org/bush/cabinet.asp.

[201] Sack, Bush Owes Success to Hard Work, Connections.

[202] Paul Krugman, Steps to Wealth, *New York Times*, July 16, 2002.

[203] Sack, Bush Owes Success to Hard Work, Connections.

[204] Ibid.

[205] Ibid.

[206] The figures, for 1998, come from the Kennedy Information Research Group. Daniel Akst, Telling Them What They'll Pay to Hear, *New York Times*, July 4, 1999.

[207] Ibid.

[208] Call Him a Cockeyed Optimist, *FOMC Alert* (Southern Finance Project), March 25, 1997.

[209] Robert K. Miller, Jr. and Stephen J. McNamee, The Inheritance of Wealth in America, in *Inheritance and Wealth in America*, edited by Robert K. Miller, Jr. and Stephen J. McNamee, New York and London: Plenum Press, 1998, 1-2.

[210] Dinesh D'Souza, The Moral Limits of Wealth, *Forbes*, October 9, 2000.

[211] Michael Parenti, The Super Rich Are Out of Sight, *Dollars & Sense*, May 15, 1998.

[212] Paul L. Menchik and Nancy A. Jianakoplos, Economics of Inheritance, in *Inheritance and Wealth in America*, edited by Miller and McNamee, 51.

[213] Ibid., 51-52.

[214] Albert B. Crenshaw, The Baby Boomers' Heir-Cut, *Washington Post*, December 10, 2000. Some observers are predicting that Baby Boomers will inherit as much as $136 trillion over the coming years. But Jagadeesh Gokhale of the Federal Reserve Bank of Cleveland and Laurence J. Kotlikoff of Boston University, in The Baby Boomers' Mega-Inheritance: Myth or Reality?, a paper published by the Cleveland Federal Reserve Bank, see little change in inheritance patterns. Baby Boomers as a group, they conclude, will inherit only marginally larger sums than their parents, for a variety of reasons. Baby Boomer parents are living longer, they point out, drawing down their wealth in the process. And much of that wealth is tied up in pensions and annuities that cannot be bequeathed.

[215] *Born on Third Base: The Sources of Wealth of the 1996 Forbes 400*, United for a Fair Economy, February 1997.

[216] Quote Gallery, www.inequality.org.

[217] Leaders: The Challenge for America's Rich, *The Economist*, May 30, 1998.

[218] "George Bush was born on third base and decided that he'd hit a triple," Hightower famously declared in a speech at the 1988 Democratic convention. Jeff Cohen and Norman Solomon, Radio Populist to Be Muzzled? *Media Beat*, September 22, 1995.

[219] "The extraordinary and sudden growth in

incomes and stock-market wealth of those at the top of the economic heap is strong evidence against the (often implicit) meritocratic perspectives of many social scientists." S. M. Miller and Anthony Savoie, Challenging Inequality/Challenging Sociology, *Contemporary Sociology*, January 1999.

220 Larcker made his comment, in April 2000, after the release of the latest executive pay figures. Gary Strauss, The Billionaires Club: New Economy Rockets CEO Pay into the Stratosphere, *USA Today*, April 5, 2000.

221 Basu Sharma and Aaliya Fayyaz, The Effect of Hegemonic Power on Executive Compensation, *International Journal of Commerce & Management*. Volume: 10 Indiana 2000.

222 Harrison Rainie, The State of Greed, *U.S. News & World Report*, June 17, 1996.

223 Quoted in Robert A. Senser, Loaded at the Top: Where Productivity Gains Land, *Commonweal*, December 1, 1995.

THE GREEDY AS BENEFACTORS

1 Thomas G. Donlan, Looking Backward: A Legacy of Foolish Inspiration, 2000-1887, *Barron's*, January 8, 2001.

2 Boesky was later found guilty of engaging in illegal "inside trading." David Oliver Relin, When Greed Was Good, *Scholastic Update*, March 8, 1991.

JOBS AND PAYCHECKS

1 M. H. Dunlop, *Gilded City: Scandal and Sensation in Turn-of-the-Century New York*. New York: William Morrow, 2000, xi.

2 Ibid. The fine gown enthusiast was Giula Morosini, the daughter of the banker who had been Jay Gould's right-hand man.

3 Henry Holcomb, Teamster Leader Morris Is Down, but He's Not Out, *Philadelphia Inquirer*, December 13, 1998.

4 "The rich carry most of our economic weight," syndicated columnist Tony Snow explained early in 2001, "and any attempts to redistribute income from wealthy to poor threaten to stall the economic engine that has brought increasing prosperity to all." Tony Snow, Cry About Fairness Is Taxing, *Baltimore Sun*, February 15, 2001.

5 Rooney was speaking at a campaign fundraiser for his buddy, Rep. Sonny Bono. Annie Groer and Ann Gerhart, Hey, Gang, Let's Put on a Show of Solidarity, *Washington Post*, January 15, 1996.

6 Ludwig von Mises, Inequality of Wealth and Incomes, May 1955. Accessed from Foundation for Economic Education, Ideas on Liberty, at www.fee.org.

7 Robert H. Frank, *Luxury Fever: Money and Happiness in an Era of Excess*. Princeton: Princeton University Press, 1999, 225-226.

8 Jennifer Reingold, Special Report: Executive Pay, *Business Week*, April 19, 1999.

9 Anna Bray Duff, The '90s Boom: Broad and Deep, *Investor's Business Daily*, January 19, 1999.

10 Their paper — "Does an Increase in Inequality Matter if Living Standards Are Rising?" — was quoted in Denis Lyons, CEO Compensation: The Whole Truth, *Chief Executive*, July 1999.

11 Duff, The '90s Boom: Broad and Deep.

12 In 1983, according to the Investment Company Institute, about 42 million Americans owned shares of stock. By century's end, almost twice as many Americans, 80 million, could call themselves shareholders. Rochelle Sharpe, After the Wild Ride, *Business Week*, April 16, 2001.

13 Toni Horst, Membership in the Middle Class, The Dismal Scientist (economy.com), January 23, 2001. Accessed from www.dismal.com/todays_econ/te_012301_2.asp. By 1995, American families — for the first time ever — held a bigger share of their household wealth in stocks than their homes. The margin: $5.5 to $4.2 trillion. Sougata Mukherjee and Paola Banchero, Does U.S. Have an Epidemic of Millionaires? *Kansas City Business Journal*, January 24, 1997. At the end of the 1980s, stocks accounted for 28 percent of family household assets. Rich Miller, Laura Cohn, Howard Gleckman, Paula Dwyer, and Ann Therese Palmer, How Prosperity Is Reshaping the American Economy, *Business Week*, February 14, 2000.

14 Miller, Cohn, Gleckman, Dwyer, and Palmer, How Prosperity Is Reshaping the American Economy.

15 That remark came in a speech to the Detroit Economic Club. Who Owns American Business? United Auto Workers news release, June 17, 1996. Accessed from uaw.org/uawreleases/jobs_pay_economy/amerbus4_96.html.

16 Michael Lewis, All Money, All the Time, *New York Times*, June 7, 1998.

17 Survey Finds 'Near Zero' Investment Growth for 401(k) Plans in 2000, *CoBiz Newsletter*, August 2001.

18 The old record, 65.8 percent, had been set in 1980. Louis Uchitelle, In Home Ownership Data, a Hidden Generation Gap, *New York Times*, September 26, 1999.

19 Zandi was with the Dismal Scientist. John Miller, Economy Sets Records for Longevity and

Inequality, *Dollars & Sense*, May/June 2000.

[20] Barbara Vobejda and Clay Chandler, Household Incomes Rise Again, *Washington Post*, September 30, 1997.

[21] President William Jefferson Clinton, State of the Union Address, the White House Office of the Press Secretary, January 19, 1999.

[22] Remarks by the President to the Northeastern University Community, the White House Office of the Press Secretary, January 15, 2001.

[23] Gregg Easterbrook, The Way We Live Now: A Hazard of Good Fortunes, *New York Times*, March 11, 2001.

[24] These statistics are generated by annual Census Bureau surveys. Historical Income Tables – Households. Table H-6. Regions — Households (All Races) by Median and Mean Income: 1975 to 2000. U.S. Census Bureau. Revised April 16, 2002. Accessed from www.census.gov/hhes/income/histinc/h06.html.

[25] The average hourly wage started dipping in the 1970s, as inequality in the United States began to widen. By 1980, most jobs averaged, in inflation-adjusted dollars, just $13.48 an hour. Lawrence Mishel, Jared Bernstein, and John Schmitt, *The State of Working America 2000-2001*. Ithaca: Cornell University Press, 2001, 120, table 2.4, Hourly and weekly earnings of production and nonsupervisory workers, 1947-99 (1999 dollars).

[26] Ibid.

[27] Louis Uchitelle, How Slow Can Your Paycheck Grow? *New York Times*, February 20, 2000.

[28] Aaron Bernstein, Back on the Edge, *Business Week*, April 23, 2001. That late 1990s wage uptick likely owed more to the modest 1996 increase in the minimum wage than any other factor. The minimum wage hike, Princeton economist Alan Krueger notes, helped boost wages at the bottom of the economy in 1997 and 1998, but the impact of that boost wore off by the end of the decade. Uchitelle, How Slow Can Your Paycheck Grow?

[29] The 2001 average weekly wage: $490.09. The 1973 average: $513.82, in 2001 dollars. Lawrence Mishel, Jared Bernstein, and Heather Boushey, *The State of Working America 2002/03*. Ithaca: Cornell University Press, 2003, table 2.4, 123.

[30] Louis Uchitelle, The American Middle, Just Getting By, *New York Times*, August 1, 1999.

[31] The estimate comes from former Labor Secretary Robert Reich. Glenn R. Pascall, Reich: New Economy Is Making Us Old Fast, *Puget Sound Business Journal*, March 23, 2001.

[32] The report came from the International Labor Organization. Kirstin Downey Grimsley, A Red,

White and Blue Time Clock, *Washington Post*, September 7, 1999.

[33] Ibid.

[34] Jerry Jasinowski, In Defense of Big (Not Bad) Business, *Washington Post*, March 17, 1996.

[35] Robert Dodge, Expert Believes Economic Growth a Myth for Most of Us, *Dallas Morning News*, December 14, 1998.

[36] In 1973, employer expenditures for fringe benefits made up 14.1 percent of total labor costs. By 1992, benefits made up 18.8 percent of the compensation employers were devoting to their workers. Employee Fringe Benefits, Economic Policy. Source: *The State of Working America 1998-99*. Accessed from www.epinet.org/webfeatures/snapshots/archive/060999/snapshots060999.html.

[37] These figures reflect dollars inflation-adjusted to 1999. Mishel, Bernstein, and Schmitt, *The State of Working America 2000-2001*, 139.

[38] Some 30.1 percent, the Foundation study found, went "uninsured at some point during 2001-2002. Almost two-thirds (65 percent) of these uninsured people were without health coverage for at least six months, and nearly one-quarter (24 percent) were uninsured throughout the two-year period." Nearly One Out of Three Non-Elderly Americans Were Uninsured for All or Part of 2001-2002, Families USA, news release, March 5, 2003.

[39] Mishel, Bernstein, and Schmitt, *The State of Working America 2000-2001*, 139.

[40] Albert B. Crenshaw, 'Cash Balance' vs. Traditional, *Washington Post*, September 26, 1999.

[41] Ibid. Companies typically reacted by "giving workers little information on how their new benefits would compare to their old ones." These raw deals gave corporations "an ideal way to cut benefits for some workers in a way that is not obvious to them."

[42] A matter of definition, *Economist*, February 16, 2002.

[43] Louis Uchitelle, Do You Plan to Retire? Think Again, *New York Times*, March 31, 2002.

[44] Pat Regneer and Joan Caplin, Can We Fix the 401(k)? *Money*, April 2003.

[45] 401(k) plans, the *New York Times* reported, were "less expensive to support than the old company-guaranteed pensions, even allowing for company contributions to the 401(k) plans." Uchitelle, Do You Plan to Retire? Think Again.

[46] Ibid.

[47] Survey Finds 'Near Zero' Investment Growth for 401(k) Plans in 2000, *CoBiz Newsletter*, August 2001.

48 Albert B. Crenshaw, Pension Changes Pose Challenges, *Washington Post*, May 5, 2002.

49 Ibid. T. Rowe Price assumed that the $36,000 annual expenditures would be adjusted to keep up with inflation.

50 Edward N. Wolff, *Retirement Insecurity*, Economic Policy Institute, 2002, 7.

51 Ibid. "Among households headed by a person approaching retirement, only households with wealth holdings above $1 million saw consistent increases in their wealth, after inflation," Wolff noted. "All other wealth classes, even those with between $500,000 and $1 million in net worth, saw their retirement wealth fall from 1983 to 1998."

52 Ibid., 7-8.

53 Ibid., 52. In 1989, by contrast, 43.9 percent of households would have been able to meet this goal.

54 U.S. Business Cycle Expansions and Contractions, National Bureau of Economic Research. Accessed from www.nber.org/cycles.html#announcements.

55 Employment status of the civilian noninstitutional population 16 years and over, 1969 to date, Bureau of Labor Standards. Accessed from ftp://ftp.bls.gov/pub/suppl/empsit.cpseea1.txt.

56 In 2000, real hourly wages would finally match their 1973 level, but average real weekly wages would remain below 1973's comparable figure. Mishel, Bernstein, and Boushey, *The State of Working America 2002/03*, table 2.4, 123.

57 David Dembo and Ward Morehouse, *The Underbelly of the U.S. Economy*, New York: The Apex Press, 1995, 6-7.

58 According to consultants at A.T. Kearney Inc. Aaron Bernstein, This Job Market Still Has Plenty of Slack, *Business Week*, June 24, 1996.

59 Cheryl Fields, The Temp Route: Tryouts That Work Both Ways, *Washington Post*, May 26, 1997.

60 Aaron Bernstein, Bigger Paychecks, Yes. Better Pay, No, *Business Week*, November 18, 1996.

61 David Moberg, Temp Slave Revolt, *In These Times*, July 10, 2000.

62 "And most [temporary accountants] don't work year-round." Aaron Bernstein, The Wage Squeeze, *Business Week*, July 17, 1995.

63 Many Americans, to be sure, wanted to work only part-time, even if that meant forgoing benefits. But plenty of Americans — 7 million in 1997, for instance, about a third of the part-time universe — found themselves working part-time only because they couldn't find regular full-time jobs. "According to Chris Tilly's fine book, 'Half a Job,' involuntary part-timers typically have family incomes fully $17,000 below those who are working part-time out

of choice." Robert Kuttner, UPS: Off the Low Road, *Washington Post*, August 8, 1997.

64 This contingent workforce included everybody from workers hired into internal temp worker pools to independent contractors hired to do work that regular staff would otherwise be doing. Mishel, Bernstein, and Schmitt, *The State of Working America 2000-2001*, 244.

65 Ibid., 245.

66 Annette Bernhardt, The Wal-Mart Trap, *Dollars and Sense*, September/October 2000.

67 Ibid.

68 In 1947, for instance, both factory workers and retail workers averaged full, forty-plus hour workweeks. The State of Workers' Incomes, 1997, Press Associates, Inc.

69 Myths and Reality, Wal-Mart Watch. Accessed at www.walmartwatch.com/info/myths.cfm?subsection_id=103.

70 The exact percentages: 74 percent in 1973 to 68 percent in 1999. Bernhardt, The Wal-Mart Trap.

71 Ibid.

72 Constance L. Hays, Enriched by Working Class, Wal-Mart Eyes BMW Crowd, *New York Times*, February 24, 2002.

73 Jim Hightower, How Wal-Mart Is Remaking Our World, *Hightower Lowdown*, April 26, 2002.

74 Bernhardt, The Wal-Mart Trap.

75 Hightower, How Wal-Mart Is Remaking Our World.

76 Bill Dedman, Employees Reject Bid to Unionize a Wal-Mart 'Family,' *New York Times*, August 10, 1997.

77 Bernhardt, The Wal-Mart Trap.

78 Myths and Reality, Wal-Mart Watch.

79 Kathy Chen, A Special News Report About Life on the Job — and Trends Taking Shape There, *Wall Street Journal*, February 5, 2002.

80 "Wal-Mart employees average about $7.50 per hour, but the majority of Wal-Mart workers make less than that." Myths and Reality, Wal-Mart Watch.

81 Chen, A Special News Report About Life on the Job — and Trends Taking Shape There.

82 Bernhardt, The Wal-Mart Trap.

83 L. M. Sixel, Profiting from Death? *Houston Chronicle*, April 15, 2002.

84 Ibid.

85 Forbes World's Richest People, 2002. Forbes.com.

[86] Steve Fraser, The Gilded Age Unravels, *Los Angeles Times*, April 1, 2001.

[87] Dedman, Employees Reject Bid to Unionize a Wal-Mart 'Family.'

[88] Ibid. The autobiography, *Sam Walton: Made in America* (Bantam), was published four years after Sam Walton's death in 1992.

[89] Wal-Mart workers averaged about $6.10 an hour in 1999. Help End the Race to the Bottom, National Labor Committee, Fall 1999.

[90] Myths and Reality, Wal-Mart Watch.

[91] D'Vera Cohn, Poverty Down, Income Steady in U.S. Survey, *Washington Post*, September 26, 2001.

[92] The numbers are from the Heritage Foundation's Robert Rector. Poor, but Not Deprived, *The Economist*, October 3, 1998.

[93] The quote appears in his book, *The Virtue of Prosperity: Finding Values in an Age of Techno-Affluence.* Quoted in Eric Alterman,Which Way W.? *Nation*, February 12, 2001.

[94] Nearly 75 percent of "poor" households, one conservative journal noted, had VCRs, 64 percent had microwaves, half stereos, and just over a quarter automatic dishwashers. Fidelis Iyebote, Which Choice? *World & I*, January 2000. Viewed from the perspective that defines poverty as "lacking adequate food for the family, clothing, a reasonably warm and dry apartment to live in, or lacking a car to get to work when one is needed," the Heritage Foundation's Robert Rector told the magazine, "there are few poor persons remaining in the United States." Fidelis Iyebote, How Poverty-stricken in the U.S.? *World & I*, January 2000.

[95] Europeans, in their discourse about disadvantage, these days talk much more about "social exclusion" than "poverty." Sociologists Hilary Silver of Brown University and Mike Miller of Boston College have written an excellent introduction to this European thought. Hilary Silver and S. M. Miller, Social Exclusion: The European Approach to Social Disadvantage, *Poverty & Race*, September/October 2002.

[96] Adds Sir Donald Acheson, Briatin's former chief medical officer, "poverty is not just a matter of money; it is a question of how far you have to walk, with a pushchair, in the rain, to a shop that sells food that you can afford to spend it on." The Giant of Poverty Still Stalks Britian, but It Can Be Slain, *Independent*, October 24, 1998.

[97] Randy Albelda, Who Is Poor? *Dollars & Sense*, November-December 1994.

[98] Toni Horst, How Poor Is Poor? *Dismal Scientist*, December 9, 1999. Accessed from www.economy.com.

[99] Census Bureau Poverty Thresholds Too Low; New Minimum Needs Budget Shows It Takes $8 an Hour to Make Ends Meet, Ms. Foundation for Women news release, September 25, 2001.

[100] Child care expenses would take a significant bite out of paychecks as the 1990s moved on. By the end of the decade, the Children's Defense Fund reported in 2000, the annual cost of child care for an urban four-year-old averaged "more than the average annual cost of public college tuition in *all but one state.*" Karen Schulman, The High Cost of Child Care Puts Quality Care Out of Reach for Many Families, Children's Defense Fund, 2000, 3.

[101] Horst, How Poor Is Poor?

[102] The quote sums up how many British analysts define what ought to be the poverty standard. The Giant of Poverty Still Stalks Britian, but It Can Be Slain, *Independent* (London), October 24, 1998.

[103] Sharon Daly, Catholic Charities, Making Ends Meet: Challenges Facing Working Families in America: Statement for the Record before the House Budget Committee, United States House of Representatives, August 1, 2001.

[104] Ibid. Daly's specific estimate came from the "self-sufficiency standards" developed by the Ford Foundation.

[105] Jared Bernstein, Chauna Brocht, and Maggie Spade-Aguilar, *How Much Is Enough?* Washington, D.C.: Economic Policy Institue, 2000, 1.

[106] Ibid., 47-50.

[107] Ibid., 64-67.

[108] Ibid.

[109] Ibid., 60-61.

[110] The official poverty threshold for a family of four that same year: just $17,463. Census Bureau Poverty Thresholds Too Low, Ms. Foundation for Women news release.

[111] E.J. Dionne Jr., A Mayoral Confession, *Washington Post*, February 26, 1999.

[112] Ibid.

[113] "Meanwhile, economists Robert Rector and Rea Hederman of the conservative Heritage Foundation argued in a study last September that the census data commonly used in income studies are flawed. Specifically, they maintained the census income data don't include the value of some welfare benefits such as food stamps, or the equalizing effects of taxation." Constance Mitchell Ford and Patrick Barta, Income Gap Broadens Amid Boom, *Wall Street Journal*, January 18, 2000.

[114] Robert J. Samuelson, The Typical Household Isn't, *Washington Post*, October 8, 1997.

115 Cait Murphy, Are the Rich Cleaning Up? *Fortune*, September 4, 2000.

116 Edwin S. Rubenstein, research director of the Hudson Institute, argued this case. "For one thing the Census Bureau quintiles represented not fifths of the population but fifths of the total count of households. This is an important distinction. It turns out that well-off households have more people in them than poor households. A top-quintile household might consist of two schoolteachers in Chicago and their three children. A bottom-quintile household might be a single woman living on Social Security. Count income per person, rather than income per household, and the income distribution flattens a good bit." Edwin S. Rubenstein, Inequality, *Forbes*, November 1, 1999.

117 Christopher Farrell, Why the Productivity Tide Will Lift All Boats, *Business Week*, October 9, 1995.

118 Rubenstein, Inequality.

119 Robert Rector's "findings," for instance, were "repeated verbatim in several newspapers" and touted by the *New York Observer* as proof capitalism had conquered poverty. Katha Pollitt, Poverty: Fudging the Numbers, *Nation*, November 2, 1998.

120 One example: the Economic Policy Institute's effort to dispel the claim that faulty inflation adjustments were making family income growth seem much lower than it really was. "One reason for skepticism about the claim of mismeasured inflation is that a revised economic history based on the view that inflation has been less than the official measures yields several implausible scenarios. If one accepts the current estimate of the poverty threshold ($15,570 for a family of four in 1995), then one would have to conclude that the equivalent threshold in 1960 was near what was actually the median household's income in that year, implying that nearly half of all households were living in poverty in 1960." *The State of Working America 1996-97*. Washington, D.C.: Economic Policy Institute, 1996. Accessed from http://epn.org/epi/epswa-in.html.

121 *Effective Federal Tax Rates, 1979-1997*, The Congress of the United States, Congressional Budget Office, September 2001, and *Effective Federal Tax Rates, 1997 to 2000*, The Congress of the United States, Congressional Budget Office, August 2003. Accessed from www.cbo.gov.

122 Isaac Shapiro, Robert Greenstein, and Wendell Primus, Pathbreaking CBO Study Shows Dramatic Increases in Income Disparities in 1980s and 1990s: An Analysis of the CBO Data, Center for Budget and Policy Priorities, May 31, 2001.

123 Census statisticians have traditionally counted households to define income fifths, with each fifth in the Census rankings having the same number of households. But this definition does tend to generate a bottom fifth that has fewer people than the upper fifths, since households near the economic bottom tend to be smaller than households closer to the top. The CBO, accordingly, adjusted for that difference, ending up with a bottom fifth that had the same number of individuals as the top or any other fifth. Shapiro, Greenstein, and Primus, Pathbreaking CBO Study Shows Dramatic Increases in Income Disparities in 1980s and 1990s: An Analysis of the CBO Data.

124 All figures here in 2000 dollars. *Effective Federal Tax Rates, 1997-2000*, 30-31.

125 The data came from a study conducted in 2000 by sociologist Andrew Beveridge, who used Census Bureau numbers to compare the incomes of real families — households made up of people directly related — at the start and the end of the 1990s. In the 1990s, Beveridge found, the typical family lost $2,876 in New York State, $3,288 in California, and $3,821 in Connecticut. Janny Scott, In 90's Economy, Middle Class Stayed Put, Analysis Suggests, *New York Times*, August 31, 2001.

126 Ibid.

127 W. Michael Cox and Richard Alm, Why Decry the Wealth Gap? *New York Times*, January 24, 2000.

128 Robert H. Nelson, Inequality — a "Massive Increase"? *Forbes*, November 29, 1999.

129 Ibid.

130 Ibid.

131 Greg Palast, Insane About Asylum, *Observer* (London), September 6, 2001.

132 Working 'Part-Time' for 60 Hours a Week, *Progressive Maryland Action*, Fall 2001.

133 Evelyn Nieves, Many in Silicon Valley Cannot Afford Housing, Even at $50,000 a Year, *New York Times*, February 20, 2000.

134 Greg Palast, Insane About Asylum.

135 Ibid.

136 Miller, Cohn, Gleckman, Dwyer, and Palmer, How Prosperity Is Reshaping the American Economy.

137 Palast, Insane About Asylum.

138 Ibid.

139 The numbers come from Graham Fisher & Co., an investment research firm. Robert J. Samuelson, Economic Casualties, *Washington Post*, September 19, 2001.

140 Uchitelle, In Home Ownership Data, a Hidden Generation Gap.

[141] Zero-Down Option Opens New Doors Kenneth Harney, *Washington Post*, February 17, 2001.

[142] Ibid.

[143] Teresa A. Sullivan, Elizabeth Warren, and Jay Lawrence Westbrook, *The Fragile Middle Class: Americans in Debt*. New Haven: Yale University Press, 2000, 218.

[144] Profile of Selected Housing Characteristics: 2000. Geographic area: United States. Table DP-4. Bureau of the Census. Ten years earlier, 28.8 percent of homeowners were paying more than a quarter of their incomes on housing. Profile of Selected Housing Characteristics for the United States: 1990. Table DP-4. Bureau of the Census.

[145] Sullivan, Warren, and Westbrook, *The Fragile Middle Class: Americans in Debt*, 200.

[146] The average American held $91,000 in home equity in 1989, after correcting for inflation, only $89,500 in 1999. Albert B. Crenshaw, Mortgaging Their Future; Study Finds Many Families Are Spending Home Equity, *Washington Post*, November 26, 2000.

[147] Ibid.

[148] Teresa A. Sullivan, Elizabeth Warren, and Jay Lawrence Westbrook, *The Fragile Middle Class: Americans in Debt*, 223.

[149] Edward N. Wolff, Where Has All the Money Gone? Winners and Losers in the 1980s and 1990s, *Milken Institute Review*, Third Quarter, 2001.

[150] Crenshaw, Mortgaging Their Future.

[151] Sullivan, Warren, and Westbrook, *The Fragile Middle Class: Americans in Debt*, 236.

[152] Nina Bernstein, Widest Income Gap Is Found in New York, *New York Times*, January 19, 2000.

[153] In 2001, "51.9 percent of families held stock in some form." Ana M. Aizcorbe, Arthur B. Kennickell, and Kevin B. Moore, Recent Changes in U.S. Family Finances: Evidence from the 1998 and 2001 Survey of Consumer Finances, *Federal Reserve Bulletin*, January 2003, 15.

[154] Middle-income here refers to families in the middle fifth of the income distribution. Aizcorbe, Kennickell, and Moore, Recent Changes in U.S. Family Finances: Evidence from the 1998 and 2001 Survey of Consumer Finances.

[155] Janette Wilson, Sales of Capital Assets Reported on Individual Income Tax Returns, 1997, *Statistics of Income Bulletin*, Summer 2001. Author analysis of data.

[156] Ibid. Author analysis of data.

[157] Scott Burns, Market, Net Worth Unequal, *San Antonio Express-News*, January 30, 2000.

[158] Burns, Market, Net Worth Unequal.

[159] Holly Sklar, Net Gains, Mass Losses, *Atlanta Constitution*, April 9, 1999.

[160] Jason Zweig, What Fund Investors Really Need to Know, *Money*, June 2002.

[161] The $1,100 represents the median net worth of families in the lowest quarter of America's wealth distribution. Aizcorbe, Kennickell, and Moore, Recent Changes in U.S. Family Finances: Evidence from the 1998 and 2001 Survey of Consumer Finances, 5 and 7.

[162] Ibid., 18-19. The combined value of direct stock holdings, mutual funds investments, and dollars amassed in 401{k) and related retirement accounts amounted, on a median basis, to $54,400 in 1998 for families in the third quartile of America's wealth distribution. Three years later, this combined value had dropped to $53,300.

[163] The exact share: 45 percent. How It Really Works, *Business Week*, August 25, 1997

[164] Ibid. The closest estimate at the time: $450 billion.

[165] Ibid. Noted L. John Doerr, the Valley's most celebrated financier of business start-ups, godfather: "This is the largest single creation of wealth and economic activity to be seen in a compressed period of time."

[166] The exuberant investment counselor was Morgan White. Michelle Quinn and Jennifer Lafleur, A Hard Look at Silicon Valley's Boom, *San Jose Mercury-News*, August 15, 1999.

[167] How It Really Works, *Business Week*.

[168] Quinn and Lafleur, A Hard Look at Silicon Valley's Boom.

[169] Ibid.

[170] Gap Between California's Rich and Poor Wide and Growing, California Budget Project, January 18, 2000. Accessed from www.cbp.org/press/pr000118.html, based on Center on Budget and Policy Priorities and Economic Policy Institute data.

[171] The figures also come from the California Budget Project. Maria Machuca, Purchasing Power of Average California Family Declined Over 1990s, *Bakersfield Californian*, September 3, 2000.

[172] Ibid.

[173] Gap Between California's Rich and Poor Wide and Growing, California Budget Project, January 18, 2000.

[174] Harold Meyerson, A Paler Shade of Gray, *American Prospect*, February 28, 2000.

[175] Quinn and Lafleur, A Hard Look at Silicon Valley's Boom.

176 Ibid. The national rate was 15 percent.

177 Ibid.

178 Ibid.

179 William Booth, A Hard Place to Call Home, *Washington Post*, January 29, 2000.

180 Karen Breslau, Unreal Estate, *New York Times Magazine*, January 30, 2000.

181 The average rent: $1,503. Quinn and Lafleur, A Hard Look at Silicon Valley's Boom.

182 "On a scale where 100 is the national average, San Jose comes in at 137.2. By comparison, the New York metropolitan area hits only 120.4." Charlie McCollum, How Costs Compare with Other Cities', *San Jose Mercury-News*, August 15, 1999.

183 Quinn and Lafleur, A Hard Look at Silicon Valley's Boom.

184 Ibid.

185 The data are from Claritas Inc., a top national market research firm. Did you know? *San Jose Mercury-News*, August 16, 1999.

186 Nieves, Many in Silicon Valley Cannot Afford Housing, Even at $50,000 a Year.

187 Andrew Beveridge, a sociologist at Queens College, tracked this trend in a 2001 report for the *New York Times*. After adjusting Census numbers from the start and end of the 1990s for inflation, Beveridge found median family income down from $2,900 to $4,400 in states where wealthy people did particularly well in the boom years. Concluded the *Times*: "The poor got a little poorer, the rich got a lot richer and the large group in the middle emerged slightly worse off than when the decade began." Janny Scott, In 90's Economy, Middle Class Stayed Put, Analysis Suggests, *New York Times*, August 31, 2001.

188 Fairfax, according to researchers from Claritas Inc., was the first of more than 3,000 jurisdictions in the United States to reach this $90,000 distinction. Dan Eggen, Tasting the High Life, *Washington Post*, March 11, 2001.

189 Ibid.

190 Dan Eggen, Pampered and Privileged, *Washington Post*, March 13, 2001.

191 Dan Eggen, Feeling Pinched on $90,000, *Washington Post*, March 12, 2001.

192 Ibid.

193 Business cycle booms are tracked by the National Bureau of Economic Research. Robert J. Samuelson, The Biggest Boom Ever, *Washington Post*, January 26, 2000.

194 Louis Uchitelle, 107 Months, and Counting, Expansion Redefines Economy's Limits, *New York Times*, January 30, 2000.

195 Ibid.

196 Of 129 common occupations, twenty-four paid wages and salaries that didn't keep up with inflation. Patrick Barta, The Longest Boom, *Wall Street Journal*, February 1, 2000.

197 Ibid. The data come from Dismal Sciences, an economic consulting firm in Pennsylvania.

198 Miller, Economy Sets Records for Longevity and Inequality.

199 D'Vera Cohn, Poverty Down, Income Steady in U.S. Survey, *Washington Post*, September 26, 2001.

200 The data come from the U.S. Bureau of the Census Annual Demographic Survey, CPS. Paul Ryscavage, *Income Inequality in America*. Armonk, New York: M. E. Sharpe, 1999, 51.

201 Ibid., 52.

202 Ibid., 51. The data come from the U.S. Bureau of the Census Annual Demographic Survey, CPS.

203 Ibid., 51-52. The top 5 percent took 17.5 percent of the nation's income in 1947, 15.5 percent in 1973. Between 1947 and 1973, families at the 95th percentile saw their incomes jump, after inflation, by 91 percent. A nice boost, to be sure, but middle-class families did even better. Between 1947 and 1997, families at the bottom of the middle class, the 40th percentile, saw their incomes increase by 101 percent. Families at the 60th percentile, saw their incomes leap by 107 percent.

204 The exact figure: 79 percent. Don L. Boroughs, with Monika Guttman, Maria Mallory, Scott McMurray, and David Fischer, Winter of Discontent? *US News & World Report*, January 22, 1996.

205 Edward N. Wolff, How the Pie Is Sliced: America's Growing Concentration of Wealth, *American Prospect*, Summer 1995.

206 Ibid.

207 The top 1 percent took 8.5 percent of the nation's income in 1992, 14.5 percent in 2000. Arthur B. Kennickell, A Rolling Tide: Changes in the Distribution of Wealth in the U.S., 1989-2001, Federal Reserve Board, March 3, 2003. Accessed from www.federalreserve.gov/pubs/oss/oss2/scfindex.html, 18, 21.

208 Census Data Show Increases in Extent and Severity of Poverty and Decline in Household Income, Center on Budget and Policy Priorities, news release, September 24, 2002. The Census Bureau began keeping track of income shares by fifth in 1967. The 2001 figures also set a record low for the second fifth and tied the record low for the fourth fifth.

209 Roche made $795,000, Eisner $576.6 million. Derrick Jackson, Falling into the Gap, *Boston Globe*, September 3, 1999.

210 Mr. Spock made these comments in "The Cloud Minders" Star Trek episode. Illusions of the Cloud Minders, *Human Economy*, Winter 1996.

CHARITY AND COMPASSION

1 Heather Byer, #33 Columbus, OH, Leslie H. Wexner, *Worth*, March 2002.

2 Ibid.

3 Kathleen McGowan, #17 San Diego, CA, Joan Kroc, *Worth*, March 2002.

4 Kenneth Cooper, High-Tech Gifts to Education Set Record, *Washington Post*, January 21, 2000.

5 Stuart Silverstein and Charles Ornstein, Record Donation to UCLA, *Los Angeles Times*, May 7, 2002.

6 Jamie Waugh, #50 Louisville, KY, Owsley Brown Frazier, *Worth*, March 2002.

7 Ibid.

8 Robert Lenzner, The Mouth of the South Puts His Foot in It, *Forbes*, October 14, 1996.

9 Joann S. Lublin, Living Well, *Wall Street Journal*, April 8, 1999.

10 Douglas Gantenbein, #13 Seattle, WA, Bill Gates, *Worth*, March 2002.

11 Les Blumenthal, Gates May Be Easy Target, but Not for Nader, *Tacoma News Tribune*, August 16, 1998.

12 Michelle Quinn, Being Well-off Comes with a Different Set of Pressures, *San Jose Mercury-News*, August 16, 1999. The second part of this quote is the reporter's paraphrase.

13 Peter Dobkin Hall and George E. Marcus, "Why Should Men Leave Great Fortunes to Their Children?" Class, Dynasty and Inheritance in America. Accessed from http://ksghome.-harvard.edu/-.phall.hauser.ksg/inheritance.html.

14 Ibid.

15 Ibid.

16 Lawrence Ingrassia, In the Money, *Wall Street Journal*, January 11, 1999.

17 David Johnston, What Bill Gates Needs to Learn About Philanthropy, *Business and Society Review*, Winter 1995.

18 Ingrassia, In the Money.

19 The Challenge for America's Rich, *Economist*, May 30, 1998.

20 Steve Forbes, Why the List, *Forbes*, October 8, 2001.

21 Ibid.

22 The American Association of Fundraising Counsel funds the Indiana University research and publishes it in the annual *Giving USA* report.

23 Lynda Gorov, Spreading the Wealth, *Boston Globe*, November 28, 1999.

24 Kent Allen, Charitable Giving Soared in '99 to Record $190 Billion, *Washington Post*, May 25, 2000.

25 Ibid. The increases slowed after 1999, but still continued, all the way up to $160.7 billion in 2001. Charitable Giving Reaches $212 Billion, news release, American Association of Fundraising Counsel, June 20, 2002, Accessed from www.aafrc.org/press3.html.

26 Peter Kilborn, Charity for Poor Lags Behind Need, *New York Times*, December 12, 1999.

27 Ibid. Other measures showed the same trend. Average family contributions to human service organizations, Independent Sector reported, were dropping, too, from $271 per family in 1994, after adjusting for inflation, to $250 in 1998.

28 Robert D. Putnam, *Bowling Alone: The Collapse and Revival of American Community*. New York: Simon & Schuster, 2000, 123.

29 James Glassman, Tightfisted at the Top, *Washington Post*, December 17, 1996.

30 Joseph Grundfest, Reasons for Giving All You've Got to Give, *Wall Street Journal*, January 6, 1995.

31 A calculation based on IRS data for 1993. The uncharitable wealthy households represented 10 percent of the total in the over-$500,000 category. Andrew Hacker, Who They Are, *New York Times*, November 19, 1995.

32 Leaders: The Challenge for America's Rich, *Economist*.

33 Lynda Gorov, Spreading the Wealth, *Boston Globe*, November 28, 1999.

34 Monique Yazigi, When You Got It, Flaunt It, *New York Times*, January 26, 2000.

35 Adam Clymer, Cheney More Generous by His Own Numbers, *New York Times*, September 6, 2000.

36 Hillary Johnson, #2 Los Angeles, CA, Eli Broad, *Worth*, March 2002.

37 Ibid.

38 This characterization about America's wealthy, as a group, comes from former SEC commissioner Joseph Grundfest, a Stanford professor, in his review of Claude Rosenberg's *Wealthy and Wise* (Little Brown, 1994). Joseph A. Grundfest,

Reasons for Giving All You've Got to Give, *Wall Street Journal*, January 6, 1995.

[39] The other became the nation's fourth largest "manager of real estate for tax-exempt clients." Our Founder, The Newtithing Group. Accessed from www.newtithing.org/frames/f_about04.html.

[40] David Cay Johnston, Can Americans Give More, and Not Hurt? *New York Times*, April 4, 1999.

[41] Ibid.

[42] Katherine Burton, Rich Give Away 8% of Income, Andria Cheng, *Chicago Sun-Times*, November 29, 1998.

[43] Johnston, Can Americans Give More, and Not Hurt?

[44] Grundfest, Reasons for Giving All You've Got to Give.

[45] Ibid.

[46] Johnston, Can Americans Give More, and Not Hurt?

[47] Ibid.

[48] Ibid.

[49] Ibid.

[50] Claude Rosenberg Jr, Sharing the Wealth, *American Benefactor*, Spring 1998.

[51] NewTithing Group's Affordable Donations Y2000 (National) by Average Tax Filer. Accessed from www.newtithing.org/content/2001national .htm.

[52] Ibid. Families on the next rung of America's economic ladder, those that made between $500,000 and $1 million in 2000, could have afforded to give about five times more than they actually gave, about $17.3 billion. The next highest rung, the taxpayers with between $200,000 and $500,000 in annual income, could have afforded to give $17.7 billion more, about three times more than they actually did. Together, these top three rungs — about 3 percent of the taxpaying public — could have given 96 percent of the charitable contributions that Americans could have comfortably made in the year 2000 but didn't.

[53] Ibid.

[54] Beth Ashley, Charitable Gifts Up, but from Fewer Donors, *USA Today*, October 9, 1996.

[55] Charles Nevin, Dishing Out the Dosh, *Guardian* (UK), December 11, 1996.

[56] Jacqueline Salmon and Hamil R. Harris, Pr. George's Leader in Giving: Residents Near Top in Rate of Charitable Donations, *Washington Post*, April 29, 2003.

[57] Jane Futcher, County Flunks Charity Test, *Marin Independent Journal*, May 9, 2003.

[58] Todd Wallack, Where They Live, How They Give: Study Finds Percentage Donated to Charity Lowest in Santa Clara County, *San Francisco Chronicle*, May 8, 2003.

[59] Bud Kennedy, Johnson County Folks Not Rich, Just Generous, *Fort Worth Star-Telegram*, April 29, 2003.

[60] Ethan Watters, The Gospel of Giving, *American Benefactor*, Spring 1997.

[61] Doyle McManus, Giving Spirit Finally Gets an Honor Roll, *San Jose Mercury News*, December 26, 1996.

[62] James K. Glassman, Tightfisted at the Top, *Washington Post*, December 17, 1996.

[63] How the Other Half Gives to Charities, *New York Times*, December 20, 1998.

[64] Nicholas Von Hoffman, Our Mighty Plutocrats Are Charity Cheapskates, *New York Observer*, December 18, 1995.

[65] "As incomes of the better-off Americans rise in this age of prosperity, with the stock market and corporate profits booming," the *New York Times* added in 1999, "charities report that both individuals and companies are donating less to organizations that support the homeless, the young and the hungry than they did in leaner times." Kilborn, Charity for Poor Lags Behind Need.

[66] Ibid. Giving USA reported "that contributions for human services, including most forms of traditional charity and some that are not, represented 9.2 percent of all giving last year, a decline from 13.9 percent in 1970."

[67] Ben B. Seligman, *The Potentates: Business and Businessmen in American History*. New York: The Dial Press, 1971, 302.

CULTURE AND ART

[1] William Davis, *The Rich: A Study of the Species*. New York: Franklin Watts, 1983, xv.

[2] Ibid., 252.

[3] Jean Strouse, *Morgan: American Financier*. New York: Perennial, 2000, 7.

[4] Charles Dubow, Billionaire Art Collectors, *Forbes*, March 6, 2002.

[5] David Johnston, What Bill Gates Needs to Learn About Philanthropy. *Business and Society Review*, Winter 1995.

[6] More millions of the Gates fortune have gone to the Seattle Art Museum. Charles Dubow, Billionaire Art Collectors, *Forbes*, March 6, 2002.

[7] Ibid.

[8] Roxanne Roberts, The New Philanthropists; Charity Networks Eagerly Woo the Region's High-Tech Millionaires, *Washington Post*, April 30, 2000.

[9] Roy C. Smith, *The Wealth Creators: The Rise of Today's Rich and Super-Rich*. New York: St. Martin's Press, 2001, 302.

[10] Hilton Kramer, Charity Doesn't Depend on the Tax Code, *Wall Street Journal*, February 21, 2001.

[11] Todd S. Purdum, Up on a Hill: The Getty Learns to Weather the Crowds, *New York Times*, May 2, 2001.

[12] Ibid.

[13] Maria Puente, Museums Exhibiting Blockbuster Expansions, *USA Today*, June 19, 2002.

[14] Daniel Costello, Waiting in Line for B-List Art, *Wall Street Journal*, July 28, 2000.

[15] Kevin McCarthy, Arthur Brooks, Julia Lowell, Laura Zakaras, *The Performing Arts in a New Era*, RAND, 2001, xvii.

[16] S. Frederick Starr, Symphony Orchestras: How Did We Get Here? Where Are We Going? *Harmony*, October 1997.

[17] Samuel Lipman Who's Killing Our Symphony Orchestras? *New Criterion*, September 1993.

[18] Quick Orchestra Facts from the 1999 — 2000 Season, American Symphony Orchestra League. Accessed from www.symphony.org/research/facts/index.shtml.

[19] Ibid.

[20] McCarthy, Brooks, Lowell, Zakaras, *The Performing Arts in a New Era*, 77-78.

[21] New York State Council on the Arts. Accessed from www.nysca.org/aboutnysca.html.

[22] James Heilbrun and Charles M. Gray, *The Economics of Art and Culture: An American Perspective*. Cambridge: Cambridge University Press, 1993. Excerpted by Monika Mokre, president of the Austrian Association for Cultural Economics and Policy Studies. Accessed from www.iwe.oeaw.ac.at/Mokre/cultec.htm.

[23] McCarthy, Brooks, Lowell, Zakaras, *The Performing Arts in a New Era*, 77-78.

[24] William Baumol and William Bowen, *Performing Arts: The Economic Dilemma*. Cambridge: MIT Press, 1968.

[25] McCarthy, Brooks, Lowell, Zakaras, *The Performing Arts in a New Era*, 77-78.

[26] Ibid., 85.

[27] Pew Charitable Trusts Announce New Study Showing Major Shifts in the Future of the Performing Arts, RAND, News Release July 23, 2001.

[28] Ibid.

[29] McCarthy, Brooks, Lowell, Zakaras, *The Performing Arts in a New Era*, 92.

[30] Ibid., xxi. Average ticket prices for orchestras increased by 70 percent between 1985 and 1995.

[31] The report, *The Performing Arts in a New Era* by Kevin McCarthy, Arthur Brooks, Julia Lowell, and Laura Zakaras, aimed "to examine trends affecting audiences, artists, organizations, and finances and to identify the policy implications of those trends." Pew Charitable Trusts Announce New Study Showing Major Shifts in the Future of the Performing Arts, RAND.

[32] McCarthy, Brooks, Lowell, Zakaras, *The Performing Arts in a New Era*, xix.

[33] Kristin Tillotson, Orchestras Seek New Faces to Supplement Aging Concertgoers, *Star Tribune* (Minneapolis), June 9, 2002.

[34] Pew Charitable Trusts Announce New Study Showing Major Shifts in the Future of the Performing Arts, RAND.

[35] Ibid.

[36] McCarthy, Brooks, Lowell, Zakaras, *The Performing Arts in a New Era*, xviii.

[37] Ibid., 105.

[38] Ibid., xviii.

[39] Ibid., 105.

[40] "If the number of midsize organizations contracts," the RAND study notes, "young artists may have fewer opportunities to gain experience in their fields." Pew Charitable Trusts Announce New Study Showing Major Shifts in the Future of the Performing Arts, RAND.

[41] Ibid.

[42] Michael M. Kaiser, How to Save the Performing Arts, *Washington Post*, December 29, 2002.

[43] McCarthy, Brooks, Lowell, Zakaras, *The Performing Arts in a New Era*, xxiv.

[44] The quoted matter is the reporter's paraphrase. John M. Glionna, San Jose Orchestra Muted by Rising Debts, *Los Angeles Times*, June 5, 2002.

[45] Christopher Knight, Why Pay to See Our Own Art? *Los Angeles Times*, June 9, 2002.

[46] Ibid.

[47] Judith H. Dobrzynski, Blockbuster Shows Lure Record Crowds into U.S. Museums, *New York Times*, February 3, 2000.

[48] Ibid.

[49] Knight, Why Pay to See Our Own Art?

[50] Ibid.

51 Cliff Rothman, The Sweetest Words of All: No Charge, *New York Times*, April 19, 2000.

52 Knight, Why Pay to See Our Own Art?

53 Daniel Costello, Waiting in Line for B-List Art, *Wall Street Journal*, July 28, 2000.

54 Ibid.

55 Brooks Barnes, America's Coolest Museums — Forget Art, Visitors Rush in for the Air Conditioning, *Wall Street Journal*, August 3, 2001.

56 In 2001, the comprehensive RAND report on the state of the performing arts in America had underlined this message. The report made increasing support for public education one if its top recommendations. Pew Charitable Trusts Announce New Study Showing Major Shifts in the Future of the Performing Arts, RAND.

57 Where We Stand. MENC: The National Association for Music Education. Adopted by the National Executive Board, March 1997.

58 Kathleen Kennedy Manzo, NAEP Paints Poor Picture of Arts Savvy, *Education Week*, November 18, 1998.

59 Ibid.

60 Hilary R. Persky, Brent A. Sandene, and Janice M. Askew, The NAEP 1997 Arts Report Card: Eighth Grade Findings from the National Assessment of Educational Progress, November 1998, 145.

61 Manzo, NAEP Paints Poor Picture of Arts Savvy.

62 Maria Puente, Museums Exhibiting Blockbuster Expansions, *USA Today*, June 19, 2002.

63 Kaija Wilkinson, Cable Station Gives Urban Schools the Gift of Music, *New Orleans City Business*, April 2, 2001.

64 VH1 Save The Music Kicks Off Its Fifth Year of Restoring Music Education to Public Schools with an Expansion into New Markets, PR Newswire, February 28, 2002.

65 VH1 Save The Music. The CBS News Early Show. Accessed from www.cbsnews.com/stories/2002/05/21/earlyshow/leisure/music/main509677.shtm.

66 VH1 Save The Music Kicks Off Its Fifth Year of Restoring Music Education to Public Schools with an Expansion into New Markets, PR Newswire.

67 "VH1 Save The Music Today." Interview between Bill Clinton and Matt Lauer of The NBC Today Show in New York City, June 16, 2000.

68 VH1 Save The Music Kicks Off Its Fifth Year of Restoring Music Education to Public Schools with an Expansion into New Markets, PR Newswire.

69 Nicolai Ouroussoff, Guggenheim Weighs Odds in Vegas Expansion, *Washington Post*, July 15, 2000.

70 Maria Puente, Move Over, Slot Machines: Make Way for Art, *USA Today*, October 5, 2001.

71 Ibid.

72 Ibid.

73 Nicolai Ouroussoff, Guggenheim Weighs Odds in Vegas Expansion, *Washington Post*, July 15, 2000.

74 Cliff Rothman, The Sweetest Words of All: No Charge, *New York Times*, April 19, 2000.

75 Ibid.

76 Of this total, $61 went directly to the St. Louis Museum of Art. The rest went to other museums and even the local zoo. 2001 Tax Rate for Real and Personal Property in the City of St. Louis, MO. City of St. Louis. Accessed from http://stlouis.missouri.org/government/proptax/2001taxrate.html.

77 Dobrzynski, Blockbuster Shows Lure Record Crowds into U.S. Museums.

78 Rothman, The Sweetest Words of All: No Charge. The good people of St. Louis had, beyond their art museum, other strange ideas about art and civic responsibility. In 1919, they had built, with their own dollars, the St. Louis Municipal Opera, the first municipally owned outdoor theatre in America. They established, as official policy, a tradition that a sizable portion of the theater's 9,000 seats would be available, for every performance, at no cost. The "Muny" continues that tradition today. On show nights, one hour before the curtain goes up, 1,620 free seats are always available. America's Most Livable Communities, http://www.livableamerica.com.

79 Quoted by George F. Will, A Few Tips for Dole, *Washington Post*, June 9, 1996.

THE INEFFECTIVE ENTERPRISE

1 Quoted in Harry Braverman, *Labor and Monopoly Capital*. New York: Monthly Review Press, 1974, 118.

2 "Companies created to thrive in mass production, stability, and growth can't be fixed to succeed in a world where customers, competition, and change demand flexibility and quick response." Michael Hammer and James Champy, *Reengineering the Corporation: A Manifesto for Business Revolution*. New York: HarperCollins, 1993, 24.

3 John Kay, *Why Firms Succeed*. New York: Oxford University Press, 1995, 68.

[4] Edward E. Lawler, III, *From the Ground Up: Six Principles for Building the New Logic Corporation*. San Francisco: Jossey Bass, 1996, 22.

[5] This phrase from the work of Edward Lawler is quoted in Barry M. Staw and Lisa D. Epstein, What Bandwagons Bring: Effects of Popular Management Techniques on Corporate Performance, Reputation, and CEO Pay, *Administrative Science Quarterly*, September 2000.

[6] Dale Dauten, Give Workers Room to Rise to Occasion, *Chicago Tribune*, June 25, 2000.

[7] "Providing frontline employees with the skills, motivation, and freedom to improve how they do their jobs can greatly increase both productivity and worker satisfaction," a Brookings Institution report concluded in 1995. Yet "substantive employee involvement remains the exception in the U.S. work force." David I. Levine, *Reinventing the Workplace: How Business and Employees Can Both Win*. Washington, D.C., The Brookings Institution, 1995, 1.

[8] Lawler, *From the Ground Up: Six Principles for Building the New Logic Corporation*, 6.

[9] George Easton of Emory University and Sherry Jarrell of Georgia State, the study authors, started with over five hundred companies reputed to be involved in "total quality management." After reviewing information on the companies, Easton and Jarrell ended up with only 108 companies they believed to be making bona fide efforts to implement total quality management. In general, the two scholars noted, "whether or not a firm has seriously pursued TQM cannot be determined by relying on the firm's public pronouncements." G. S. Easton and S. L. Jarrell, The Effects of Total Quality Management on Corporate Performance: An Empirical Investigation, *Journal of Business*, April 1998.

[10] This going through the motions, the two researchers noted, actually made some sense — for top executives. Just by talking in public about empowering employees, Staw and Epstein discovered, top executives could heighten "external admiration" of their leadership and boost their eventual compensation. Staw and Epstein, What Bandwagons Bring: Effects of Popular Management Techniques on Corporate Performance, Reputation, and CEO Pay.

[11] William Lee, a leading management consultant, estimates that "fewer than 10 percent of American employers (probably *far* fewer) work for firms that practice true, systemic employee participation." William G. Lee, *Mavericks in the Workplace*, New York: Oxford University Press, 1998, 60.

[12] "The best way to assure that decisions are made at lower levels is to have very few levels of management," one analyst noted, "so that managers can-

not make all the decisions." Edward F. Lawler III, *High-Involvement Management*. San Francisco: Jossey-Bass Publishers, 1991, 194.

[13] J. Burgess Winter, the chief executive of Tucson's Magma Copper company, was one executive in the 1990s who took empowering rhetoric seriously. He was so committed to building a real partnership with his workers that, in 1991, he signed a fifteen-year contract with their union. Most contracts run for three or four years. Magma Copper's partnership paid quick dividends. By 1995, only one metal sector company in the entire United States boasted a higher profit rate than Magma. David M. Gordon, *Fat and Mean: The Corporate Squeeze of Working Americans and the Myth of Managerial "Downsizing."* New York: The Free Press, 1996, 89-90.

[14] Quoted in Alan Downs, The Wages of Downsizing, *Mother Jones*, July-August 1996. See also Gordon, *Fat and Mean: The Corporate Squeeze of Working Americans and the Myth of Managerial "Downsizing,"* 5.

[15] Downs, The Wages of Downsizing. The American Management Association looked at just over five hundred companies that had shed employees in 1994 and 1995. The number of managers at these companies had barely dipped at all, down just 1.1 percent. At these same companies, non-managerial employees had lost their jobs at a rate seven times faster.

[16] A conclusion reached by Anthony Carnevale and Stephen Rose, described in Too Many Managers, *Economic Notes*, February 1998.

[17] Managerial joblessness was "approaching historic lows." Alex Markels, Firms' Demand for Managers Is Growing Despite Layoffs and Restructurings, *Wall Street Journal*, September 26, 1996.

[18] Peter F. Drucker, *The Changing World of the Executive*. New York: Times Books, 1982, 22.

[19] Drucker would stick to this position over the ensuing years, even as executive pay soared. In mid 1990s, with CEOs taking home compensation that outpaced worker pay by *hundreds* of times, Drucker was still contending, notes biographer Jack Beatty, "that the ratio of pay between worker and executive can be no higher than twenty to one without injury to company morale." Jack Beatty, *The World According to Peter Drucker*. New York: The Free Press, 1998, 83.

[20] Levine, *Reinventing the Workplace: How Business and Employees Can Both Win*, 53.

[21] Eileen Applebaum, Thomas Bailey, Peter Berg, and Arne L. Kalleberg, *Manufacturing Advantage: Why High-performance Work Systems Pay Off*. Ithaca, New York: Cornell University Press, 2000, 44.

22 Tim Jackson, *Inside Intel: Andy Grove and the Rise of the World's Most Powerful Chip Company.* New York: Dutton, 1997, 36-38.

23 Ibid.

24 David Packard, *The HP Way: How Bill Hewlett and I Built Our Company.* New York: HarperBusiness, 1995, 80-81.

25 Ross Laver, Takethemoneyandrun.com, *Maclean's,* January 17, 2000.

26 High-tech companies, in the 1980s, would become the first American enterprises to circulate options broadly. They didn't, however, invent the use of options for employees. The Pfizer pharmaceutical company introduced one of the "first broad-based stock-option programs" in 1952. George T. Milkovich and Jennifer Stevens, 100 Years of Change, *ACA Journal* (American Compensation Association), First Quarter 2000.

27 Evelyn Richards, Playing the Options Game, *San Jose Mercury-News,* August 15, 1999.

28 Jackson, *Inside Intel,* 84.

29 Ibid., 110-111. At meetings, Grove "seemed to take a positive delight in shouting at people."

30 Ibid., 114-115.

31 Ibid,, 318.

32 Ibid., 300-301.

33 Laver, Takethemoneyandrun.com.

34 Rachel Konrad, Layoffs May Spoil HP Workers' Allegiance, CNET News.com, July 26, 2001.

35 John T. Ward, $90 Million Package Won Hewlett-Packard a New CEO, *Newark Star-Ledger,* September 23, 1999.

36 Ibid.

37 Raj Jayadev, Silicon Valley's Underbelly, *San Francisco Chronicle,* January 20, 2002.

38 John T. Ward, $90 Million Package Won Hewlett-Packard a New CEO, 47.

39 Jon Van, Recent Moves Mar CEO's Record, *Chicago Tribune,* September 5, 2001.

40 Konrad, Layoffs May Spoil HP Workers' Allegiance.

41 Ibid.

42 Bob Batchelor, Downsize This: The Hewlett-Packard Merger with Compaq Won't Produce Any Winners, *American Prospect Online,* March 25, 2002.

43 Ibid.

44 "Employees," notes one scholar in the field, "are inherently neither motivated nor unmotivated to perform effectively; their motivation depends on the situation, how they perceive it, and what rewards they need and value." Edward E. Lawler, III, The New Pay: A Strategic Approach, *Compensation and Benefits Review,* July-August 1995.

45 "Despite the anecdotal connection," *Business Week's* Jennifer Reingold pointed out, "no academic has proven that higher pay creates higher performance." Jennifer Reingold, Special Report: Executive Pay, *Business Week,* April 19, 1999.

46 Lawler, The New Pay: A Strategic Approach.

47 Geoffrey Colvin, What Money Makes You Do, *Fortune,* August 17, 1998.

48 Employees chasing individual rewards may even "engage in deleterious activities like sabotaging the work of other employees in an effort to garner more of the organization's compensation resources." Matt Bloom, The Performance Effects of Pay Dispersion on Individuals and Organizations, *Academy of Management Journal,* February 1999.

49 Diane Stafford, Losses Reflect Pay Disparity, *Kansas City Star,* November 13, 1999.

50 Lawler, *From the Ground Up: Six Principles for Building the New Logic Corporation,* 207.

51 "The late W. Edwards Deming, a guru of quality control, was a particularly vigorous opponent of trying to pay for performance, as Andrea Gabor points out in *The Capitalist Philosophers* (Times Books). Deming believed that if you hired the right people for the right jobs and put them into the right environment, everyone would perform pretty well." Daniel Akst, On the Contrary Money Can Motivate. So Can Love of the Job, *New York Times,* April 1, 2001.

52 And the most divisive rewards of all? The reward system in place across America as the twentieth century ended. "The most extreme version of a divisive pay system occurs when only senior management is heavily rewarded for stock performance and short-term profitability." Lawler, *From the Ground Up: Six Principles for Building the New Logic Corporation,* 213.

53 Milkovich and Stevens, 100 Years of Change.

54 Ibid. By the early 1950s, Ford Motor was actually distributing Scanlon plan implementation kits to other companies.

55 Luis H. Gomez-Mejia, Theresa M. Welbourne, and Robert M. Wiseman, The Role of Risk Sharing and Risk Taking Under Gainsharing, *Academy of Management Review,* July 2000.

56 Steven T. Taylor, Gainsharing the Wealth: More Companies Turn to an Old-Fashioned Incentive, *Enterprise Reengineering,* August 1996.

57 Gain-sharing, noted economist Stephen Roach, offers "a particularly promising way" to give workers "a direct stake in corporate performance." Stephen S. Roach, The Hollow Ring of the Productivity Revival, *Harvard Business Review*, November 1996.

58 Colvin, What Money Makes You Do.

59 Milkovich and Stevens, 100 Years of Change.

60 Gomez-Mejia, Welbourne, and Wiseman, The Role of Risk Sharing and Risk Taking Under Gainsharing.

61 Ibid.

62 Scanlon Plans, notes Edward Lawler, have "tended to be limited to small, often privately owned, companies." Edward E. Lawler, III, *Pay and Organization Development*. Reading, Mass.: Addison-Wesley Publishing Company, 1981, 148.

63 Taylor, Gainsharing the Wealth: More Companies Turn to an Old-Fashioned Incentive.

64 "The lack of widespread employee involvement is almost inevitable in large organizations," notes Edward Lawler. "The hierarchies in them rob individuals of the information, knowledge, power, and rewards they need in order to feel that they are an important part of a business." Edward E. Lawler III, *The Ultimate Advantage: Creating the High-Involvement Organization*. San Francisco: Jossey-Bass Publishers, 1992, 61.

65 Lawler, *Pay and Organization Development*, 152.

66 The Businessman as Villain, *Economist*, February 16, 2002.

67 William J. Baumol, *Business Behavior, Value and Growth*. New York: Macmillan. Quoted in Basu Sharma and Aaliya Fayyaz, The Effect of Hegemonic Power on Executive Compensation, *International Journal of Commerce & Management*, Volume: 10, Indiana 2000.

68 Kathleen Day, Soldiers for the Shareholder, *Washington Post*, August 27, 2000.

69 Richard B. Du Boff and Edward S. Herman, Mergers, Concentration, and the Erosion of Democracy, *Monthly Review*, May 2001.

70 Kay, *Why Firms Succeed*, 243.

71 The "prevailing logic," noted one observer, had become: "Size is not the result of success. Size is a precondition of success." Keith Hammons, Size Is Not a Strategy, *Fast Company*, September 2002.

72 Jeffrey Sonnenfeld, Expanding Without Managing, *New York Times*, June 12, 2002.

73 Roy C. Smith, *The Wealth Creators: The Rise of Today's Rich and Super-Rich*. New York: St. Martin's Press, 2001, 26.

74 Sandra Sugawara, Merger Wave Accelerated in '99, *Washington Post*, December 31, 1999.

75 Ibid.

76 Steve Lohr, Behemoths in a Jack-Be-Nimble Economy, *New York Times*, September 12, 1999.

77 "Companies used to spend a couple of months on due diligence before considering a bid, but now buyers set their sights on a company and close the deal within days, especially if it involves smaller companies or unregulated industries." Sugawara, Merger Wave Accelerated in '99.

78 Executives, pointed out Yale's Jeffrey Sonnenfeld, "could not possibly remain knowledgeable about the changing technological and market requirements for such disparate businesses." Sonnenfeld, Expanding Without Managing.

79 Ken Kurson, Who's to Blame, *Money*, September 2002.

80 Ken Popovich, Barrett Inside: Intel Diversifies, *eWeek*, November 6, 2000.

81 Ibid.

82 Ibid.

83 Ibid.

84 It All Started with Pies, *Economist*, November 17, 2001.

85 Allan Sloan, Growth by Acquisition Often Doesn't Add Up, *Washington Post*, May 7, 2002.

86 The Stern Stewart researchers calculated how much value, in share-price increases and dividends, each of over five thousand major companies had returned to stockholders between June 1996 and June 2001, compared to the returns stockholders could have earned if they had invested their dollars in investments less risky than stocks. Marked by the Market, *Economist*, December 1, 2001.

87 Ibid.

88 In nations like Germany and Japan, the noted British economist John Kay observed midway through the 1990s, maneuvers like hostile takeovers were virtually impossible, merger and acquisitions were rare. Kay, *Why Firms Succeed*, 151.

89 Sonnenfeld, Expanding Without Managing.

90 Gary Strauss, The Billionaires Club: New Economy Rockets CEO Pay into the Stratosphere, *USA Today*, April 5, 2000 and David Leonhardt, Executive Pay: A Special Report for the Boss, Happy Days Are Still Here, *New York Times*, April 1, 2001.

91 Sonnenfeld, Expanding Without Managing.

92 Bob Starzynski, Super-rich in D.C. on Rise, *Washington Business Journal*, January 24, 1997.

93 400 Richest Americans 2000. Forbes.com.

[94] Bonsignore to Get at Least $9 Million in Severance Pay, Bloomberg News, *Star-Tribune* (Minneapolis), August 14, 2001.

[95] David Evans, CEOs Seldom Lose in Mergers Executives Collect Since They Get No Blame if Deal Goes Sour, Bloomberg News, *Plain Dealer* (Cleveland), September 6, 1998.

[96] Michael Lewis, The Rich: How They're Different . . . Than They Used to Be, *New York Times*, November 19, 1995.

[97] The Business Observer, *New York Observer*, December 27, 1999.

[98] Amy Kover. *Big Banks Debunked*, Fortune, February 21, 2000.

[99] Ibid.

[100] Ralph Nader, Double Dipping ATM Fees at Banks Continue to Rise, sfbg.com, April 9, 2001. Accessed from www.sfbg.com/nader/145.html.

[101] Michelle Singletary, As Popularity of ATM Cards Grows, So Do Fees for the Quick-Cash Habit, *Washington Post*, November 8, 2001.

[102] Charles Passy, Cranky Consumer: Dodging the Late Fees on That Credit-Card Bill, *Wall Street Journal*, June 4, 2002.

[103] Jennifer Bayot, With Interest Rates Stable, Credit Card Fees Rise, *New York Times*, April 20, 2003.

[104] Sarah A. B. Teslik, Council of Institutional Investors Newsletter on Executive Compensation, December 1995. Accessed from www.ciicentral.com/cxcc.htm.

[105] Paul Tharp, Execs Earn Optional $1.8b — Deal Leads to Record Payday, *New York Post*, January 11, 2000, 4.

[106] The revelation about AOL's hinting around on Wall Street came from analysts at Deutsche Banc Alex. Brown. Greg Lindsay, AOL Rate Hike Will Feed Voracious Bottom-Line Goals, Inside.com, May 22. Accessed from www.inside.com/jcs/Story?article_id=31398&pod_id=7.

[107] David Coursey, Dear AOL Users: Toss the Training Wheels and Save Money! AnchorDesk. Accessed from www.zdnet.com/anchordesk/stories/story/0,10738,2764462,00.html.

[108] Inflation increased just 14.5 percent over the same period. Christopher Stern, Stay Tuned for Still-Higher Cable Bills, *Washington Post*, January 10, 2002.

[109] In some areas, Clear Channel and its fellow giant, Infinity Broadcasting, took in 90 percent of local radio advertising dollars. Eric Boehlert, One Big Happy Channel? *Salon*, July 10, 2001.

[110] Forbes Best Paid CEOs. 2002. Forbes.com.

[111] Lisa de Moraes, Fox, New Owner of Channel 20, Decides Not to Go Long, *Washington Post*, November 15, 2001.

[112] Jim Rutenberg, Eisner Squeezes ABC, Adds More Commercials to Prime-Time Lineup, *New York Observer*, September 13, 1999.

[113] Nicholas von Hoffman, Whatever Happened to the Friendly Skies? *New York Observer*, September 13, 2000.

[114] Airlines spent $6.11 per passenger on food in 1992, nearly 30 percent less by 2002. Carol Sottili, Can Airline Food Get Worse? Hold onto Your Tray Table, *Washington Post*, June 30, 2002.

[115] Michael Grunwald, Ties to Phone Company Leave McCain on a Fine Line; As Arizonans Fume About 'US Worst,' Firm Fares Well, *Washington Post*, January 18, 2000.

[116] Ibid.

[117] Ibid.

[118] Chuck Green, Curbing Executive Excess, *Denver Post*, March 4, 2001.

[119] Francis X. Clines, Old Baltimore Loses Blue-Collar Playground, *New York Times*, November 19, 2000.

[120] David Segal, A Game in the Gutter; Beloved by Many, Duckpin Bowling May Be Going the Way of the Dodo, *Washington Post*, April 3, 1999.

[121] Ibid.

[122] Ibid.

[123] Ibid.

[124] Southwest Airlines CEO Herb Kelleher was once asked which comes first, employees, customers, or shareholders? "Well, I said the employees come first," he would later explain, "because if they're happy and satisfied and ennobled by what they're doing, they treat your customers better, and then the customers come back, and that's good for your shareholders." Steve Salerno, Laughing All the Way, *Worth*, September 1999.

[125] "Unemployment is not inevitable," preached quality gurus like W. Edwards Deming, "it is created by management." Sami M. Abbasi and Kenneth W. Hollman, The Myth and Realities of Downsizing, *Records Management Quarterly*, April 1998.

[126] Downsizing data, throughout the 1990s, came primarily from the private consulting firm of Challenger, Gray & Christmas. Ignoring the Costs of Downsizing, *Economic Notes*, December 1997.

[127] Downsizing the American Dream: A Staff Report

of the House Democratic Policy Committee.

[128] Steven Pearlstein, Large U.S. Companies Continue Downsizing, *Washington Post*, September 27, 1994.

[129] Overworked and Overpaid: The American Manager, *Economist*, January 30, 1999.

[130] Downsizing the American Dream: A Staff Report of the House Democratic Policy Committee.

[131] Kurt Eichenwald, For WorldCom, Acquisitions Were Behind Its Rise and Fall, *New York Times*, August 8, 2002.

[132] Noguchi and Goodman, WorldCom to Slash Workforce.

[133] Kenneth N. Gilpin, Under Pressure, Ebbers Quits as Chief of WorldCom, *New York Times*, April 30, 2002.

[134] Noguchi and Goodman, WorldCom to Slash Workforce.

[135] Ibid.

[136] Simon Romero, WorldCom Facing Charges of Fraud; Bush Vows Inquiry, *New York Times*, June 26, 2002.

[137] Downs, The Wages of Downsizing.

[138] Abbasi and Hollman, The Myth and Realities of Downsizing.

[139] The workers most worried about downsizing, research by Sam Bacharach of Cornell University's School of Industrial and Labor Relations has found, are the workers "most likely to load up on overtime." Mary Williams Walsh, As Hot Economy Pushes Up Overtime, Fatigue Becomes a Labor Issue, *New York Times*, September 17, 2000.

[140] Ibid.

[141] Abbasi and Hollman, The Myth and Realities of Downsizing.

[142] The AMA study came midway through the 1990s. Sarah Anderson and John Cavanagh, Institute for Policy Studies, Chris Hartman and Betsy Leondar-Wright, United for a Fair Economy, Executive Excess 2001: Eighth Annual CEO Compensation Survey, September 2001.

[143] Beatty, *The World According to Peter Drucker*, 83.

[144] Sarah Anderson, John Cavanagh, Chris Hartman, and Scott Klinger, Executive Excess 2003, Institute for Policy Studies and United for a Fair Economy, August 2003. Accessed from www.ufenet.org/press/2003/EE2003_pr.html.

[145] Dauten, Give Workers Room to Rise to Occasion.

[146] "It becomes difficult to espouse partnership, empowerment, and a service orientation," notes Peter Block, one of America's most widely read effective enterprise theorists, "while those at the top enhance their wealth at the expense of those at lower levels." Peter Block, Stewardship: *Choosing Service Over Self-Interest*. San Francisco: Berrett-Koehler Publishers, 1993, 65.

[147] John Sweeney, Challenging Chain Saw Management: A Common Path for Working Americans and Their Money Managers. Speech before Council of Institutional Investors, April 2, 1996.

[148] Carrie Johnson, One Man's Brief Career at Amazon Becomes a Comedy Franchise, *Washington Post*, April 22, 2001.

[149] Mike Daisey later wrote a book, *21 Dog Years: Doing Time @ Amazon.com* (Simon & Schuster) on his life at Amazon and started a companion Web site at www.mikedaisey.com.

[150] This classic experiment is described in H.M.J.J. Snelders and Stephen E.G. Lea, Different Kinds of Work, Different Kinds of Pay: An Examination of the Overjustification Effect, *Journal of Socio-Economics*, Winter 1996.

[151] Ibid. "Pay makes an activity into work. The activity becomes something that is done for its economic consequences, not because it is liked."

[152] Ibid.

[153] Harold J. Laski, *A Grammar of Politics*. London: George Allen & Unwin Ltd., 1930, 212.

[154] Joann S. Lublin, A Better Way, *Wall Street Journal*, April 9, 1998.

[155] Robert W. Moody, Going, Going, Gone, *Internal Auditor*, June 2000.

[156] Jay W. Lorsch. CEO Pay: Facts and Fallacies, *Corporate Board*, May-June 1999.

[157] The study was by professors Matt Bloom and John Michel. Rick Jurgens, Look Out Below, *Wall Street Journal*, April 6, 2000.

[158] Ibid.

[159] Albert B. Crenshaw, In the Red or in the Black? *Washington Post*, October 24, 1999.

[160] John A. Byrne, How to Fix Corporate Governance, *Business Week*, May 6, 2002.

[161] Lies, Damned Lies, and Managed Earnings: The Crackdown Is Here, *Fortune*, August 2, 1999.

[162] Ibid.

[163] Web Venture Chief Is Indicted in Fraud Case, Bloomberg News, March 25, 2003.

[164] Floyd Norris and Claudia H. Deutsch, Xerox to Restate Results and Pay Big Fine, *New York Times*, April 2, 2002 and David Leonhardt, Tell the Good News. Then Cash In, *New York Times*, April 7, 2002.

[165] Gretchen Morgenson, A Bubble That Enron Insiders and Outsiders Didn't Want to Pop, *New*

York Times, January 14, 2002.

166 "The gross sales didn't change AOL's net income, because AOL counted the payments it forwarded to eBay-minus its broker's fee-as an expense elsewhere in its books." Alec Klein, Unconventional Transactions Boosted Sales Amid Big Merger, *Washington Post*, July 18, 2002.

167 Ibid.

168 The pay total actually covers eighteen months, due to a change in fiscal year. Louis Lavelle, Executive Pay, *Business Week*, April 16, 2001.

169 When the Numbers Don't Add Up, *Economist*, February 9, 2002.

170 Alex Berenson, Tweaking Numbers to Meet Goals Comes Back to Haunt Executives, *New York Times*, June 29, 2002.

171 "Instead of a stampede of customers to fill up these fiber optic highways," as a *New York Times* analysis put it, "the industry found itself with too many vacant lanes — way too many." Simon Romero and Seth Schiesel, The Fiber Optic Fantasy Slips Away, *New York Times*, February 17, 2002.

172 The vice president was Roy L. Olofson. Julie Creswell with Nomi Prins, The Emperor of Greed, *Fortune*, June 24, 2002.

173 Gretchen Morgenson, Telecom, Tangled in Its Own Web, *New York Times*, March 24, 2002.

174 Julie Creswell with Nomi Prins, The Emperor of Greed.

175 Ellen E. Schultz, Big Send-Off: As Firms Pare Pensions for Most, They Boost Those for Executives, *Wall Street Journal*, June 20, 2001.

176 Ibid.

177 Many companies also made pension surpluses pay off by making overly generous assumptions about how much the surpluses would earn in investment income. In 2002, some companies were assuming 11 percent returns, a wildly unrealistic rate given the stock market collapse. What difference could a pollyannic projection make? A single percentage point added on to an expected pension return, noted Warren Buffet, a critic of the practice, could "increase the annual earnings a company reports by more than $100 million." Warren E. Buffett, Who Really Cooks the Books? *New York Times*, July 24, 2002.

178 Dan Gillmor, Corporate Sleaze Carves into Our Trust, *San Jose Mercury News*, June 26, 2002. See also Romero, WorldCom Facing Charges of Fraud.

179 Dawn Kawamoto and Wylie Wong, Oracle's Hard Sell Illustrates Industrywide Problems, CNET News.com June 29, 2001.

180 Ibid.

181 Mark Leibovich, The Outside, His Business and His Billions, *Washington Post*, October 30, 2000.

182 Kawamoto and Wong, Oracle's Hard Sell Illustrates Industrywide Problems.

183 David Cay Johnston, Corporate Taxes Fall, but Citizens Are Paying More, *New York Times*, February 20, 2000.

184 Ibid.

185 Ibid. The IRS official was Larry Langdon, himself a former corporate tax office director.

186 Peter Behr, Enron Skirted Taxes Via Executive Pay Plan, *Washington Post*, February 14, 2003.

187 David Cay Johnston, Wall St. Firms Are Faulted in Report on Enron's Taxes, *New York Times*, February 14, 2003.

188 Behr, Enron Skirted Taxes Via Executive Pay Plan.

189 Richard W. Stevenson and Richard A. Oppel Jr., Fed Chief Blames Corporate Greed as House Revises Fraud Bill, *New York Times*, July 17, 2002.

190 2002 Report to the Nation, Association of Certified Fraud Examiners. Accessed from www.cfenet.com/pdfs/2002RttN.pdf.

191 Road Rage, Air Rage and Now, Desk Rage, editorial, *New York Observer*, July 23, 2001.

192 Thomas Donlan, Out of the Park: Soaring Executive Pay Is a Sign of Economic Health, *Barron's*, May 4, 1998.

193 Jim Collins, Good to Great, *Fast Company*, October 2001.

194 Ibid. The eleven "great" companies: Abbott Laboratories, Circuit City, Fannie Mae, Gillette Co., Kimberly-Clark Corp., the Kroger Co., Nucor Corp., Philip Morris Cos. Inc., Pitney Bowes Inc., Walgreens, and Wells Fargo. From sidebar to Jim Collins, Good to Great, *Fast Company*, October 2001.

195 The results were written up in Jim Collins, *Good to Great: Why Some Companies Make the Leap … And Others Don't* (HarperBusiness, 2001). Sidebar to Jim Collins, Good to Great, *Fast Company*, October 2001.

196 Collins, Good to Great.

197 Ibid.

198 Great Answers to Good Questions, *Fast Company*, October 2001.

199 The Psychology of Big Salaries, *Washington Post*, September 24, 1995. "If you hold CEO pay down too low," argues, in a similar line, Steve Croos, head of the executive compensation practice at human resources consulting firm William M. Mercer in Houston, "it makes it hard to adjust pay

below the CEO to levels you need to be competitive." Jennifer Files, Market Forces Push CEO Pay Higher, *Dallas Morning News*, May 7, 2000.

200 "White-collar overtime costs the employer practically nothing," the British *Economist* magazine pointed out. "It is therefore — like other underpriced goods — likely to be consumed wastefully." Undue Diligence, *Economist*, August 24, 1996.

201 Ibid.

202 Colvin, What Money Makes You Do.

GRUESOME GROWTH

1 Robert H. Frank, *Luxury Fever: Money and Happiness in an Era of Excess*. Princeton: Princeton University Press, 1999, 102.

2 Christopher J. Niggle, Equality, Democracy, Institutions, and Growth, *Journal of Economic Issues*, June 1998.

3 Ibid.

4 Ibid.

5 James L. Huston, *Securing the Fruits of Labor: The American Concept of Wealth Distribution 1765-1900*. Baton Rouge: Louisiana State University Press, 1998, 360.

6 Ibid., 360.

7 "In Victorian economic thought," notes economist James Galbraith, "inequality was itself the spur of growth. Growth required capital accumulation, and it was the accumulations made possible by concentrating incomes that justified an unequal class structure." James K. Galbraith, A Perfect Crime: Inequality in the Age of Globalization, *Daedalus*, Winter 2002.

8 Gary Burtless, Has Widening Inequality Promoted or Retarded U.S. Growth? The Brookings Institution, Washington, D.C., February 5, 2001.

9 Economic growth in market economies, for Kuznets, "need not lead to the misery and upheaval that Karl Marx had earlier foreseen." This appraisal of Kuznets' thought comes from contemporary economist James K. Galbraith. Galbraith, A Perfect Crime: Inequality in the Age of Globalization.

10 Randy Albeda and Chris Tilly, Unnecessary Evil: Why Inequality Is Bad for Business, *Dollars & Sense*, March-April 1995.

11 Arthur M. Okun, *Equality and Efficiency: The Big Tradeoff*. Washington, D.C.: The Brookings Institution, 69.

12 A description of Okun's position by Randy Albeda and Chris Tilly in Unnecessary Evil: Why Inequality Is Bad for Business, *Dollars & Sense*, March-April 1995.

13 Arthur M. Okun, *Equality and Efficiency: The Big Tradeoff*. Washington, D.C.: The Brookings Institution, 120.

14 Ibid., 117.

15 Albeda and Tilly, Unnecessary Evil: Why Inequality Is Bad for Business.

16 Ibid.

17 Ibid. "Inequality in the distribution of income, wealth, or land," the authors of the 1994 study, Torsten Persson and Guido Tabellini, would later add, "is negatively correlated in cross-country data with subsequent growth." Torsten Persson and Guido Tabellini, *Political Economics: Explaining Economic Policy*. Cambridge: MIT Press, 2000, 372.

18 Nancy Birdsall and Juan Luis Londono, Asset Inequality Matters: An Assessment of the World Bank's Approach to Poverty Reduction, *American Economic Review*, May 1997.

19 Albeda and Tilly, Unnecessary Evil: Why Inequality Is Bad for Business.

20 Joseph E. Stiglitz and Jason Furman, Economic Consequences of Income Inequality, FRBKC Jackson Hole Symposium, August 29, 1998, published in *FOMC Alert*, Financial Markets Center, September 29, 1998.

21 Carl R. Weinberg, CEO Compensation: Greed or Glory? *Chief Executive*, September 1999.

22 Ibid.

23 Albeda and Tilly, Unnecessary Evil: Why Inequality Is Bad for Business.

24 Ibid.

25 Asa Chandler, founder of Coca-Cola, once argued that "the most beautiful sight that we see is the child at labor; as early as he may get labor, the most beautiful, the most useful does his life get to be." George Winslow, *Capital Crimes*. New York: Monthly Review Press, 1999, 117.

26 Ronald Schettkat, How Bad Are Welfare-state Institutions for Economic Development? *Challenge*, January/February 2001.

27 French workers could count on from 57 to 75 percent of their pay for almost three years, German workers on from 60 to 67 percent. Peter Kuhn, Chapter 1: Summary and Synthesis, from *Losing Work, Moving On: Worker Displacement in International Perspective*, P. Kuhn, editor. Kalamazoo, Mich.: W. E. Upjohn Institute for Employment Research. Accessed from www.econ.ucsb.edu/~pjkuhn/DW_Int/DWIndex.

html.

[28] "Recipiency rates" — the number of people collecting unemployment benefits divided by the total number of unemployed — averaged 33 percent in the 1980s. "The rate reached a low point of 28.5 percent in 1984, and since then it has stayed above 30 percent, reaching a recent high of 35.1 percent in 1996." Stephen A. Wandner and Andrew Stettner, Why Are Many Jobless Workers Not Applying for Benefits? *Monthly Labor Review*, June 2000.

[29] Schettkat, How Bad Are Welfare-state Institutions for Economic Development?

[30] Ibid.

[31] In mass layoff situations, Belgium required over a half year's severance. Peter Kuhn, *Losing Work, Moving On: Worker Displacement in International Perspective*.

[32] William Greider, If Politics Got Real..., *Nation*, July 17, 2000.

[33] Fired workers could get, at best, backpay. Unions could not file claims for broader damages. Ibid.

[34] Clara Chang and Constance Sorrentino, Union Membership Statistics in 12 Countries, *Monthly Labor Review*, December 1991.

[35] Kuhn, *Losing Work, Moving On: Worker Displacement in International Perspective*.

[36] Dennis J. Kucinich, The Soul of the Worker and the American Restoration, Iowa AFL-CIO State Convention, August 14, 2001. Accessed from www.house.gov/kucinich.

[37] Leon Friedman, A Share-the-Wealth Tax, *Nation*, January 6, 1997.

[38] The numbers are from analyses prepared by Lynn Karoly of Rand. Aaron Bernstein, Why the Gap Isn't So Giant in Europe and Japan sidebar, *Business Week*, August 15, 1994.

[39] These data are from the Luxembourg Income Study, an ongoing international effort that enables scholars to accurately compare incomes across national boundaries. Steven Pressman, Luxembourg Income Study Working Paper No. 280: The Decline of the Middle Class: An International Perspective, Maxwell School of Citizenship and Public Affairs, Syracuse University, Syracuse, New York, October 2001. Accessed from www.lisproject.org/publications/liswps/280.pdf.

[40] Ibid.

[41] Figures from Eurostat and the Organization for Economic Co-operation and Development show that the U.S. economy did better than economies in Western Europe and Japan after 1992, notes Canadian writer Peter Cook. "But that discounts an earlier U.S. slowdown while counting several years of near-stagnation in Germany and Japan," Cook stresses. "Go back 10 years instead and both German and U.S. growth are the same, at an average annual 2.5 per cent, while Japan is not far behind at 2 per cent." Peter Cook, U.S. in 1990s: Land of the Unequal, Home of the Poor, *Globe and Mail* (Toronto), March 12, 2001.

[42] U.S. Wages Slip to 13th Place, Press Associates, Inc., December 9, 1996.

[43] International Comparisons of Hourly Compensation Costs for Production Workers in Manufacturing, 2000, Bureau of Labor Statistics, September 25, 2001. Accessed from www.bls.gov/news.release/ichcc.nr0.htm.

[44] Gary Burtless and Timothy Smeeding, America's Tide: Lifting the Yachts, Swamping the Rowboats, *Washington Post*, June 25, 1995.

[45] The Richest Country in the World, *Trade Union Advisor*, May 20, 1997.

[46] Work, Work and More Work, *Washington Post*, September 11, 1999.

[47] Robert Samuelson, This Isn't Sweden, Thank You, *Washington Post*, April 26, 1995.

[48] Ibid.

[49] Dean Baker, Stock Market Projections, *Economics Reporting Review*, January 7, 2002.

[50] Ibid. The data here is from the cross-national Organization for Economic Cooperation and Development. Much of the vaunted U.S. progress fighting unemployment, careful analysts point out, has come from gaming the numbers. Over the last three decades of the twentieth century, David Dembo and Ward Morehouse from the Council on International and Public Affairs note, the United States made "six major changes in the definitions of employed and unemployed." All these decisions, they report, "tended to reduce the percentage or absolute number of unemployed." David Dembo and Ward Morehouse, *The Underbelly of the U.S. Economy: Joblessness and the Pauperization of Work in America*. New York: Apex Press, 2001, 13.

[51] Roy C. Smith, *The Wealth Creators: The Rise of Today's Rich and Super-Rich*. New York: St. Martin's Press, 2001, 331.

[52] The European Central Bank, formally begun in 1998, kept interest rates in Europe considerably higher than rates in the United States throughout the years around the turn of the century. The high rates of European central bankers, notes U.S. economist Dean Baker, did more to discourage hiring in Europe than any restrictions on business enacted by European lawmakers. Dean Baker, The European and U.S. Models, *Economic Reporting Review*, June 10, 2002.

53 In 1997, German income that fell in the top tax bracket was subject to a 53 percent tax. By 2003, the top German rate had been dropped to 42 percent. Taxing the Rich, *Washington Post*, April 24, 1998 and Hogtied, *Economist*, January 19, 2002.

54 Smith, *The Wealth Creators: The Rise of Today's Rich and Super-Rich*, 333.

55 One 1995 study found that, in the previous two years, 66 percent of German companies and 61 percent of French had done some downsizing. In the United States, the figure was 72 percent. Frank Swoboda, The Case for Corporate Downsizing Goes Global, *Washington Post*, April 9, 1995.

56 The Fall of Jean-Marie Messier, *New York Times*, July 5, 2002.

57 Ibid.

58 Mark Landler, The Fraternity of Corporate Exiles: Europe Executives Undone, *New York Times*, July 30, 2002.

59 Matthew Karnitschnig and Neal E. Boudette, History Lesson: Battle for the Soul of Bertelsmann Led to CEO Ouster, *Wall Street Journal*, July 30, 2002.

60 Mark Landler, Politics Hastens the Corporate Goodbye in Europe, *New York Times*, July 18, 2002.

61 Ibid. "Obscenely overpaid CEOs with global ambitions and bad strategies are hurting national pride across Europe," noted Jeffrey Sonnenfeld, an associate dean at the Yale School of Management. "There is grass-roots pressure for the governments to respond."

62 The bank: Credit Lyonnais. Jo Johnson and Victor Mallet, Downsizers on the Defensive at New Wave of Protests, *Financial Times*, April 27, 2001.

63 Landler, Politics Hastens the Corporate Goodbye in Europe.

64 Evelyn Iritani, U.S. Business Model a Tough Sell Overseas, *Los Angeles Times*, July 7, 2002.

65 Ibid.

66 The Fall of Jean-Marie Messier, *New York Times*.

67 Karnitschnig and Boudette, History Lesson: Battle for the Soul of Bertelsmann Led to CEO Ouster.

68 Ibid.

69 Ibid.

70 Mark Landler, The Fraternity of Corporate Exiles: Europe Executives Undone, *New York Times*, July 30, 2002.

71 Evelyn Iritani, U.S. Business Model a Tough Sell Overseas, *Los Angeles Times*, July 7, 2002.

72 Economist Barry Bluestone and his late col-

league, Bennett Harrison, offer a probing, in-depth analysis of the Wall Street model in their 2000 book, *Growing Prosperity* (Boston: Houghton Mifflin Company, 2000). This discussion owes a great deal to their insights.

73 Romesh Diwan, Relational Wealth and the Quality of Life, *Journal of Socio-Economics*, July 2000.

74 Economic growth in any modern society, the model contended, "mainly depends on the level of investment and the rate of technical progress." Kang H. Park, Income Inequality and Economic Progress: An Empirical Test of the Institutionalist Approach, *American Journal of Economics and Sociology*, January 1996.

75 "If we want to grow faster, in this view, then we as a nation have to find a way to encourage more investment, pure and simple," economists Barry Bluestone and Bennett Harrison, have noted. "If we devote more of today's resources to accumulating capital, we can have faster growth and greater prosperity tomorrow." Bluestone and Harrison, *Growing Prosperity*, 110.

76 Ibid., 111-112.

77 John Miller, Economy Sets Records for Longevity and Inequality, *Dollars & Sense*, May/June, 2000. Later revised figures would put the growth in productivity at 1.5 percent for the first half of the 1990s, 2.5 percent for the second. "America's productivity growth is higher now than it was before 1995," the *Economist* magazine would conclude, "but the gains have been exaggerated." A Spanner in the Productivity Miracle, *Economist*, August 11, 2001.

78 Bluestone and Harrison, *Growing Prosperity*, 17.

79 Frank, *Luxury Fever: Money and Happiness in an Era of Excess*, 97.

80 The research, conducted by a private research group, covered the 1987/88 to 1993/94 period. Bluestone and Harrison, *Growing Prosperity*, 217-218.

81 Meg McGinity and Dawn Bushaus, The Selling Out of Innovation, *The Net Economy*, October 29, 2001.

82 Ibid.

83 Ibid.

84 Ibid.

85 Ibid.

86 Ibid.

87 Ibid.

88 Bluestone and Harrison, *Growing Prosperity*, 223.

89 Ibid., 207-209.

90 "In nearly every industry," as *Business Week*

would note midway through the 1990s, "the spread of new technologies is creating a need for employees who know how to do more." Aaron Bernstein, Inequality: How the Gap Between Rich and Poor Hurts the Economy, *Business Week*, August 15, 1994.

91 Jacques Steinberg, More Family Income Committed to College, *New York Times*, May 2, 2002.

92 Ibid.

93 *Business Week*'s Aaron Bernstein summed up some of this research in 1994: "Brown University economist Oded Galor concludes that productivity suffers when poor families can't borrow enough to educate their kids. In another study, University of Wisconsin economist Steven N. Durlauf concludes that widening inequality hurts education in poor communities deprived of school tax dollars and the role models of professional parents. Beyond that, theorizes Columbia University economist Roberto Perotti, as the rich race ahead, they balk at the high taxes needed to educate poor children better." Bernstein, Inequality: How the Gap Between Rich and Poor Hurts the Economy.

94 Keith Bradsher, More on the Wealth of Nations, *New York Times*, August 20, 1995.

95 Bluestone and Harrison, *Growing Prosperity*, 219.

96 Included here are investments in education and research as well as physical infrastructure. Ibid., 240.

97 "You can't increase productivity," as Fred Reichheld, director emeritus of one of the world's largest strategic consulting companies, puts it, "when employees are jumping ship while they are still being trained." Harvard Business School Press, Interview with author, Fred Reichheld, *The Loyalty Effect*, Harvard Business School Press 1996. Accessed from www.loyaltyrules.com/loyaltyrules/Author_Overview.html.

98 Bluestone and Harrison, *Growing Prosperity*, 176.

99 Aaron Bernstein, Sharing Prosperity Cover Story, *Business Week*, September 1, 1997.

100 Bluestone and Harrison, *Growing Prosperity*, 247.

101 These numbers are based on the work of Lester Thurow and Louise Waldstein. Bluestone and Harrison, Ibid., 232-233.

102 Ibid., 143-144.

103 Bernstein, Inequality: How the Gap Between Rich and Poor Hurts the Economy.

104 Bluestone and Harrison, *Growing Prosperity*, 247.

105 Ibid., 249.

106 Ryscavage spent over thirty years with the Bureau of Labor Statistics and the Census Bureau. Paul Ryscavage, *Income Inequality in America*. Armonk, New York: M. E. Sharpe, 1999, 50.

107 Ibid.

108 Downsizing the American Dream: A Staff Report of the House Democratic Policy Committee, March 11, 1996.

109 Census Bureau Poverty Thresholds Too Low, Ms. Foundation for Women news release, September 25, 2001.

110 Raising the Minimum Wage: Talking Points and Background, AFL-CIO, Washington, D.C., 2001, 7.

111 "The erosion of the buying power of the minimum wage," a *Chicago Tribune* analysis noted in 1999, "has taken the bottom out of the labor market and put pressure on wages well above the federal minimum." John Schmitt, Economic 'Boom' of the 1990s Is a Bust for the Middle Class, *Chicago Tribune*, September 6, 1999.

112 Robert Collins, *More: The Politics of Economic Growth in Postwar America*. New York: Oxford University Press, 2000, 198.

113 Downsizing the American Dream: A Staff Report of the House Democratic Policy Committee. A 1995 strike by the pressmen's union at the *Washington Post* actually foreshadowed the air traffic controllers strike. The *Washington Post*, generally considered a "liberal" newspaper, took the then unheard of step of permanently replacing the striking pressmen. That precedent helped mute mainstream liberal protests against Reagan's maneuvers during the air traffic controllers strike.

114 Ibid.

115 Raising the Minimum Wage: Talking Points and Background, AFL-CIO, 7.

116 Steven Pearlstein, U.S. Finds Productivity, but Not Pay, Is Rising, *Washington Post*, July 25, 1995.

117 Hedrick Smith, How the Middle Class Can Share the Wealth, *New York Times*, April 19, 1998.

118 Richard Todd, High on Spending, *Worth*, October 1998.

119 Ted Schmidt, Why Have Savings Fallen? Rising Inequality Deserves the Blame, *Dollars & Sense*, January-February 1997.

120 Christopher Byron, Internet Hysteria Brings More Fools to Unstable Market, *New York Observer*, November 9, 1998.

121 Kevin Phillips, *Wealth and Democracy: A Political History of the American Rich*. New York:

Broadway Books, 2002, 281-282.

[122] Vanessa Baird, Money, Markets and Madness, *New Internationalist*, October 1998.

[123] David Boyle, Confessions of a Global Gambler, *New Internationalist*, October 1998. On what the British call "Black Wednesday," September 16, 1992, the greatest currency speculator of them all, George Soros, "broke the Bank of England" and scored a $1 billion personal profit. Alex Callinicos, *Equality*. Cambridge, UK: Polity Press; Malden, Mass.: Blackwell Publishers, 2000, 76.

[124] Deborah Schoeneman and Deborah Netburn, The Fifth Avenue Flip, *New York Observer*, May 15, 2000.

[125] John Cassidy, Striking It Rich, *New Yorker*, January 14, 2002.

[126] Ibid.

[127] Robert J. Samuelson, The Nasdaq Casino: Place Your Bets, *Washington Post*, January 12, 2000.

[128] Sensing a Mania in the Market, *Washington Post*, July 20, 1997.

[129] Samuelson, The Nasdaq Casino: Place Your Bets.

[130] The Rise and Fall of Technology Stocks, *Infoworld*, March 26, 2001.

[131] James J. Cramer, The $86 Million Man Shops and Trades All Night, *New York Observer*, February 8, 1999.

[132] David Streitfeld, Old-Line Retail Sense Humbles Dot-Coms, *Washington Post*, January 1, 2001.

[133] David Henry, Wall Street Risks, *Business Week*, August 20, 2001.

[134] Dean Baker, From New Economy to War Economy, *Dollars & Sense*, November/December 2001.

[135] Sridhar Pappu, Still Mr. Biggs, *New York Observer*, February 11, 2002.

[136] Cory Johnson, TheStreet.com: A Death on the Floor, *New York Observer*, April 21, 1997.

[137] Sharon Walsh and Blaine Harden, Wall Street's Season to Be Jolly, *Washington Post*, January 31, 1998.

[138] Patrick McGeehan, Wall St. Firms Reward Chiefs for Strong '99, *New York Times*, February 12, 2000.

[139] George F. Will, Bucking a Recession, *Washington Post*, April 22, 2001.

[140] Robert J. Samuelson, The Search for Scapegoats, *Washington Post*, June 19, 2002.

[141] Christopher Byron, Law Hot on His Tail, Guru Wade Cook Squeezes Morons Dry, *New York Observer*, June 22, 1998.

[142] The numbers come from the Center for Venture Research at the University of New Hampshire. Smith, *The Wealth Creators: The Rise of Today's Rich and Super-Rich*, 76.

[143] Doerr, gushed Sun Microsystems CEO Scott McNealy "burns brighter than mere mortals." John Doerr, The Coach, Digerati, The Edge, September 23, 2003. Accessed from http://www.edge.org/digerati/doerr.

[144] Rich Miller, Laura Cohn, Howard Gleckman, Paula Dwyer, and Ann Therese Palmer, How Prosperity Is Reshaping the American Economy, *Business Week*, February 14, 2000.

[145] Linda Tischler, Why VC Will Get Ugluer, *Fast Company*, November 2002.

[146] Miller, Cohn, Gleckman, Dwyer, and Palmer, How Prosperity Is Reshaping the American Economy.

[147] Michael Peltz, Investing Outside the Box, *Worth*, April 2002.

[148] David Ranii, IPO Millionaires, *News & Observer* (Raleigh), November 15, 1998.

[149] Miller, Cohn, Gleckman, Dwyer, and Palmer, How Prosperity Is Reshaping the American Economy.

[150] Ibid.

[151] "You could invest in a company, take it public and cash out before you proved your business model," one former venture capitalist, Michael Barach, told the *Wall Street Journal* after the bubble burst. Greg Ip, Susan Pulliam, Scott Thurm, and Ruth Simon, The Color Green: The Internet Bubble Broke Records, Rules and Bank Accounts, *Wall Street Journal*, July 14, 2000.

[152] Stephen Metcalf, Another Day, Another Scandal — Bitter Fruit of a Free Market, *New York Observer*, July 15, 2002.

[153] Ibid.

[154] A Golden Back Scratch, *Washington Post*, September 1, 2002.

[155] By July 2002, Idealab still held 14.5 million shares in eToys. The eToys share price had by then sunk to less than $6. Still, even with shares selling at under $6, the remaining Idealabs stake in eToys was worth about one thousand times more than the venture capitalists at Idealabs originally paid for it. Ip, Pulliam, Thurm, and Simon, The Color Green: The Internet Bubble Broke Records, Rules and Bank Accounts.

[156] Allan Sloan, Dumb Investing 101: Big Hitters Made as Many Blunders as Small-Timers, *Washington Post*, September 4, 2001.

157 Robert J. Samuelson, Greenspan vs. The Glut, *Washington Post*, April 25, 2001.

158 Steve Powers, 'Robber Barons of the Information Age,' *San Jose Mercury News*, July 20, 2003.

159 Kevin Maney, How Will USA Get More Fiber in Its Telecom Diet? *USA Today*, March 21, 2002.

160 Gretchen Morgenson, Telecom, Tangled in Its Own Web, *New York Times*, March 24, 2002.

161 Steven Pearlstein, Fiber-Optic Overdose Racks Up Casualties, *Washington Post*, May 2, 2002.

162 Gretchen Morgenson, After Criticism, a Top Analyst Quits Salomon, *New York Times*, August 16, 2002.

163 Morgenson, Telecom, Tangled in Its Own Web.

164 Robert J. Samuelson, Greenspan vs. The Glut, *Washington Post*, April 25, 2001.

165 Steve Powers, 'Robber Barons of the Information Age.'

166 Morgenson, After Criticism, a Top Analyst Quits Salomon.

167 These gains came in the period 1999 to 2001. Morgenson, Telecom, Tangled in Its Own Web.

168 Morgenson, After Criticism, a Top Analyst Quits Salomon.

169 Gretchen Morgenson, Deals Within Telecom Deals, *New York Times*, August 25, 2002.

170 Ibid.

171 Christopher Byron, Can Bahrenburg Dig Petersen Out from Under Mound of Debt? *New York Observer*, November 24, 1997.

172 Gary Mongiovi, Whose Economy Is It?, *Nation*, September 8, 1997.

173 Louis Lowenstein, Capital Gains Tax Cuts: A Better Way, *Washington Post*, April 30, 1995.

174 Ibid.

175 Robert J. Samuelson, The Nasdaq Casino: Place Your Bets.

176 David Leonhardt, The Long Boom's Ugly Side, *New York Times*, May 12, 2002.

177 One 1987 estimate that the total cost of just stock commissions and other trading costs "was about $25 billion, or more than one-sixth of all corporate earnings." Lowenstein, Capital Gains Tax Cuts: A Better Way.

178 Deborah Netburn, Panic Rooms of New York, *New York Observer*, April 1, 2002.

179 Frank, *Luxury Fever: Money and Happiness in an Era of Excess*, 241.

180 The number of inmates stood at 196,441 in 1970. Winslow, *Capital Crime*, 100. Federal, state, and local jails, prisons, and juvenile detention centers held 2,166,260 people in custody at the end of 2002. Fox Butterfield, Study Finds 2.6% Increase in U.S. Prison Population, *New York Times*, July 28, 2003.

181 Ibid., 3.

182 "Total U.S. spending on private security products and services topped $57 billion in 1996, an all-time high and a 46 percent increase since 1991." Frank, *Luxury Fever: Money and Happiness in an Era of Excess*, 241.

183 Albeda and Tilly, Unnecessary Evil: Why Inequality Is Bad for Business.

184 Americans Behind Bars: U. S. and International Use of Incarceration 1995, Sentencing Project. Accessed from www.sentencingproject.org/pubs/tsppubs/9030data.html.

185 The female murder rates: United States, 3.21, France, 0.72. Germany 0.66, Sweden, 0.80, Japan, 0.45, for data collected between 1994 and 1999. American Females at Highest Risk for Murder, Harvard School of Public Health, news release, April 17, 2002. Accessed from www.hsph.harvard.edu/press/releases/press4172002.html.

186 Albeda and Tilly, Unnecessary Evil: Why Inequality Is Bad for Business.

187 Martin Daly, Margo Wilson, and Shawn Vasdev, Income Inequality and Homicide Rates in Canada and the United States, *Canadian Journal of Criminology*, April 2001.

188 Ibid.

189 Celia Lessa Kerstenetzky, The Violence of Inequality, Instituto del Tercer Mundo, Social Watch: 2001. Accessed from www.socwatch.org.uy.

190 In 1998, the Inter-American Development Bank calculated that the top 10 percent of Brazilian families take 47 percent of the country's income. The poorest 10 percent, less than 1 percent. Greg Palast, Lights Out Across Rio? World Bank Is to Blame, *Observer* (London), December 6, 1998.

191 Anthony Faiola, Brazil's Elites Fly Above Their Fears, *Washington Post*, June 1, 2002.

192 Simon Romero, Cashing in on Security Worries, *New York Times*, July 24, 1999.

193 Faiola, Brazil's Elites Fly Above Their Fears.

194 Romero, Cashing in on Security Worries.

195 Ibid.

196 Faiola, Brazil's Elites Fly Above Their Fears.

197 Ibid.

198 Kevin Sullivan, Japanese Question Economic Equality, *Washington Post*, May 4, 1997.

199 The Japanese figure represents the ratio between

someone at the 90th percentile of the income distribution and someone at the 10th percentile. In 1992, people at the 90th percentile made 4.17 times the income of people at the 10th percentile. See Figure 1. Decile Ratios and Gini Coefficient for Adjusted Disposable Income, from Timothy M. Smeeding with assistance from Andrzej Grodner, Luxembourg Income Study Working Paper No. 252 Changing Income Inequality in OECD Countries: Updated Results from the Luxembourg Income Study (LIS), March 2000. Accessed from www.lisproject.org/publications/liswps/252.pdf.

[200] Sullivan, Japanese Question Economic Equality.

[201] Ibid.

[202] Steven C. Clemons, Sharing, Alaska-Style, *New York Times*, April 9, 2003.

[203] Sullivan, Japanese Question Economic Equality.

[204] Dean Baker, *Economics Reporting Review*, September 6, 2001.

[205] Sullivan, Japanese Question Economic Equality.

[206] William H. Stewart, Looking Back at a Period of Intense Speculation, Commonwealth of the Northern Mariana Islands, Economic Service Counsel, 1998. Accessed from www.cnmiguide.com/info/essays/economics/5.html.

[207] Sullivan, Japanese Question Economic Equality.

[208] A Dashing Disappointment, *Economist*, July 13, 2002.

[209] Stephanie Strom, Japan's Big Income Gap, *Pittsburgh Post-Gazette*, January 10, 2000.

[210] Noted James Brooke, in a *New York Times* article that appeared August 31, 2001, Accelerating Decline in Japan Evokes Rust Belt Comparisons: "Instead of encouraging firms to keep workers on their payroll through a downturn and finding areas where they could do productive work — as had been the practice in Japan — firms are being encouraged to carry through U.S.-style mass layoffs. Quoted by Dean Baker, *Economics Reporting Review*, September 6, 2001.

[211] Strom, Japan's Big Income Gap.

[212] Ibid.

[213] John C. Cort, Japanese Workers Fare Well Despite 'Crisis,' *National Catholic Reporter*, August 28, 1998.

[214] Ibid.

[215] Ibid.

[216] Japan's economy, notes Dean Baker, had actually been performing rather brilliantly in conventional terms. The country's per capita GDP "rose at a 4.8 percent annual rate over the forty-year period from 1960 to 2000. This is one of the most rapid sustained growth rates by any nation in the history of the world. It suggests that Japan's system was enormously successful." Dean Baker, Japan, *Economics Reporting Review*, October 21, 2002.

EXCESS WITHOUT HAPPINESS

[1] Thomas Benfield Harbottle, *Anthology of Classical Quotations*. San Antonio: Scylax Press, 1984. Second revised edition, 1902, 485.

[2] Hubbard died in 1930. *A Dictionary of Economic Quotations, Second Edition*, Compiled by Simon James. Totowa, New Jersey: Rowman & Allanheld, 1984, 92.

[3] Robert J. Samuelson, A Tycoon for Our Times? *Washington Post*, November 11, 1998. This column draws on research compiled by public-opinion analysts Everett Carll Ladd and Karlyn Bowman.

[4] This national survey was conducted by AARP magazine. Vivian Marino, Diary: Millionaire? No, Thanks, *New York Times*, May 21, 2000.

[5] The quoted description of the survey result is from Hugh Delehanty, editor of AARP's *Modern Maturity*. The exact figure: 65 percent. Marino, Diary: Millionaire? No, Thanks.

[6] Robert Sullivan, Americans and Their Money: An Intimate Portrait, *Worth*, June 1994.

[7] Robert H. Frank, *Luxury Fever: Money and Happiness in an Era of Excess*. Princeton: Princeton University Press, 1999, 72.

[8] Ibid., 132.

[9] Alan Durning, *How Much Is Enough? The Consumer Society and the Future of the Earth*. New York: W. W. Norton & Company, 1992, 39.

[10] Durning, *How Much Is Enough? The Consumer Society and the Future of the Earth*, 39.

[11] Robert E. Lane, *The Loss of Happiness in Market Democracies*. New Haven: Yale University Press, 2000, 19.

[12] Ibid., 21.

[13] Ibid., 10.

[14] Dinesh D' Souza, The Moral Limits of Wealth, *Forbes*, October 9, 2000.

[15] Peter Delevett, Four Years and Change in the Valley, *San Jose Mercury News*, March 26, 2002.

[16] Frank, *Luxury Fever: Money and Happiness in an Era of Excess*, 3.

[17] Margaret Webb Pressler, The High End Gets Higher, *Washington Post*, July 11, 1999. Also see Jacob M. Schlesinger, The Outlook, *Wall Street Journal*, September 13, 1999.

18 Juliet Schor, The New Politics of Consumption, *Boston Review*, Summer 1999.

19 The Overspent American, *Multinational Monitor*, September 1998.

20 Juliet B. Schor, *The Overspent American: Upscaling, Downshifting, and the New Consumer.* New York: Basic Books, 1998, 82.

21 Schor, The New Politics of Consumption.

22 These figures are from a Children's Defense Fund report. Sue Pleming, One in Six U.S. Children Lives in Poverty, Reuters, April 19, 2001.

23 Schor, *The Overspent American: Upscaling, Downshifting, and the New Consumer*, 9.

24 Nicole Sterghos Brochu, 'Affluenza' Strikes S. Florida Families, *South Florida Sun-Sentinel*, April 1, 2001.

25 Schor, The New Politics of Consumption.

26 Sam Roberts, Another Kind of Middle-Class Squeeze, *New York Times*, May 18, 1997.

27 Juliet B. Schor, *The Overworked American: The Unexpected Decline of Leisure.* New York: Basic Books, 1991, 4.

28 These working families spent 3,236 hours on the job in 1979, 3,860 in 1997. Louis Uchitelle, The American Middle, Just Getting By, *New York Times*, August 1, 1999.

29 Schor, *The Overworked American: The Unexpected Decline of Leisure*, 21-22.

30 Ibid., 9.

31 Some academics in the 1990s rejected Schor's time-bind thesis. Sociologist John Robinson, for one, relied on "time diaries" kept by adult respondents to claim that average free time had actually increased 4.8 hours a week between 1965 and 1985. But other scholars question the time-diary methodology. See Gary Burtless, Squeezed for Time? American Inequality and the Shortage of Leisure, *Brookings Review*, Fall 1999. Another critic of the time-diary approach, Dale Dauten, "questions the wisdom of trying to generalize from the behavior of people with enough time to fill out time diaries in the first place." See Frank, *Luxury Fever: Money and Happiness in an Era of Excess*, 49. Still other defenders of Schor's work, note that she and other researchers following up on our work "are looking at annual hours of work, and most of the increase in hours is due to increases in weeks worked, not hours per week," the focus of the time-diary studies. See Barry Bluestone and Bennett Harrison, *Growing Prosperity*. Boston: Houghton Mifflin Company, 2000, 283, footnote 78.

32 Uchitelle, The American Middle, Just Getting By.

33 Probing the Public's Contradictions, *Economic Notes*, March 1998.

34 Bob Thompson, Consumed: Melissa Smith, Yvette King and Carrie Szejk Are Trying to Cast Off the American Culture of Spending and Excess, *Washington Post*, December 20, 1998.

35 Robin Leonard, The Million-Debtor March, *Nolo News*, Spring 1997.

36 Leonard, The Million-Debtor March.

37 Richard Connif, The Natural History of the Rich, *Worth*, December/January 2000.

38 Pressler, The High End Gets Higher.

39 Margaret Wente, If We're So Rich, Why Aren't We Happy? *Globe and Mail* (Toronto), March 31, 2001.

40 The Overspent American, *Multinational Monitor*.

41 Robert Frank told this story during *Happiness: Theory and Pursuit*, a course taught at Cornell's Adult University, July 9-15, 2000, with psychologist Thomas Gilovich.

42 Marsha Ritchins and Scott Dawkins, A Consumer Values Orientation for Materialism and Its Measurement, *Journal of Consumer Research*, 1992, quoted in Lane, *The Loss of Happiness in Market Democracies*, 147. The hedonic treadmill metaphor came originally from psychologists Philip Brickman and Donald Campbell (76).

43 Robert D. Putnam, *Bowling Alone: The Collapse and Revival of American Community*. New York: Simon & Schuster, 2000, 192.

44 Lane, *The Loss of Happiness in Market Democracies*, 77.

45 Amitai Etzioni, Toward a Good Society, *Christian Science Monitor*, March 19, 2001.

46 Rex W. Huppke, Study: Civic Involvement Linked to Happiness, Associated Press, March 1, 2001.

47 Ibid.

48 Lane, *The Loss of Happiness in Market Democracies*, 191.

49 Those Americans who did socialize in 1995 spent less time socializing than their 1965 counterparts. The average daily time devoted to informal interactions, Putnam reports, dropped from over eighty minutes in 1965 to fifty-seven in 1995. Putnam, *Bowling Alone: The Collapse and Revival of American Community*, 107.

50 Sue Pleming, One in Six U.S. Children Lives in Poverty, Reuters, April 19, 2001.

51 Putnam, *Bowling Alone: The Collapse and Revival of American Community*, 62.

52 Don Oldenburg, Why Are You So Cranky All Day, All Week? *Washington Post*, January 25, 2000.

53 The same surveys asked Americans to estimate how much time they had left over every week, after work and their other responsibilities, for relaxation, sports, hobbies, entertainment, and socializing. Between 1993 and 1999, not surprisingly, that free time fell almost 25 percent. Gary Burtless, Squeezed for Time? American Inequality and the Shortage of Leisure, *Brookings Review*, Fall 1999.

54 Robert H. Frank, Yes, the Rich Get Richer, but There's More to the Story, *Columbia Journalism Review*, November/December 2000.

55 Quoted in Walter Updegrave, How Are You Doing? *Money*, July 1999.

56 Robert H. Frank, Market Failures, *Boston Review*, Summer 1999.

57 Frank, Yes, the Rich Get Richer, but There's More to the Story.

58 Schor, The New Politics of Consumption.

59 Schor, *The Overspent American: Upscaling, Downshifting, and the New Consumer*, 100.

60 Ibid., 38.

61 Ibid.

62 The Overspent American, *Multinational Monitor*.

63 Ibid.

64 Peter Grier, It's hip to be greedy, *Financial Post*, February 12, 2000.

65 Ibid.

66 Keith Bradsher, In This Gilded Age, Gilded Model T's, *New York Times*, November 12, 2000.

67 Warren Brown, Still Down on Detroit, *Washington Post*, June 22, 1997.

68 Keith Bradsher, In This Gilded Age, Gilded Model T's.

69 Ibid. Big cars cost not much more to design or manufacture or ship to dealers than smaller, less expensive cars.

70 Ibid.

71 By 1995, average new car prices had leaped over 70 percent in just a decade. Over that same ten years, average incomes climbed only 40 percent. Aaron Bernstein, The Wage Squeeze, *Business Week*, July 17, 1995.

72 David Leonhardt, Two-Tier Marketing: Companies Are Tailoring Their Products and Pitches to Two Different Americas. *Business Week*, March 17, 1997.

73 Keith Bradsher, In This Gilded Age, Gilded Model T's.

74 Ibid. The comparison came from Robert Casey, a curator at the Henry Ford Museum in Dearborn, Michigan.

75 Ibid.

76 Leonhardt, Two-Tier Marketing: Companies Are Tailoring Their Products and Pitches to Two Different Americas.

77 Ibid.

78 Sougata Mukherjee and Paola Banchero, Does U.S. Have an Epidemic of Millionaires? *Kansas City Business Journal*, January 24, 1997.

79 Pentamillionaire households grew by more than 45 percent a year for most of the 1990s. Kathleen Day, The Private-Banking Boom, *Washington Post*, November 26, 2000.

80 David Rynecki, Who Wants to Manage a Millionaire? *Fortune*, October 16, 2000.

81 The Business Observer, *New York Observer*, July 14, 1997.

82 Holly Sklar, Net Gains, Mass Losses, *Atlanta Constitution*, April 9, 1999.

83 Peter Grier, It's Hip to Be Greedy, *Financial Post*, February 12, 2000.

84 Mary Leonard, Too Rich? *Boston Globe*, July 27, 1997.

85 Pressler, The High End Gets Higher.

86 Every Cloud Has a Satin Lining, *Economist*, March 23, 2002.

87 Everett Mattlin, Rich Pickings, *Institutional Investor*, June 1993.

88 Day, The Private-Banking Boom.

89 Ibid.

90 Ibid. A wealth management team at one bank spent ten days helping a client figure out the best place to buy his wife a pearl necklace for their twenty-fifth anniversary.

91 John T. Mulqueenn, Wise Move, *Inter@ctive Week*, December 4, 2000.

92 David Rynecki, Who Wants to Manage a Millionaire? *Fortune*, October 16, 2000.

93 Day, The Private-Banking Boom.

94 Jeff Nash, The New, Very Rich Definition of Rich, *Money*, February 2001.

95 Michael Kinsley, The New New Money, *Washington Post*, April 4, 2000.

96 Joann S. Lublin, Living Well, *Wall Street Journal*, April 8, 1999.

97 Frank, *Luxury Fever: Money and Happiness in an Era of Excess*, 25.

98 Ibid., 11.

99 Leonhardt, Two-Tier Marketing: Companies Are Tailoring Their Products and Pitches to Two Different Americas.

100 R. H. Tawney, *The Acquisitive Society.* New York: Harcourt, Brace & World, Inc., 1948 (originally published 1920), 37.

101 The median price: $407,000. William Booth, A Hard Place to Call Home, *Washington Post*, January 29, 2000.

102 Frank Ahrens, A City Open to All Comers; San Francisco's Tech Boom Begets an Affordable-Housing Bust, *Washington Post*, November 27, 2000.

103 Housing Costs Out of Reach for Many: 2002 National Housing Wage is $14.66, National Low Income Housing Coalition, news release, September 18, 2002. Accessed from www.nlihc.org/oor2002/pressrelease.htm

104 The words are a paraphrase of the *Chronicle* report by Jacob Schlesinger, The Outlook, *Wall Street Journal*, September 13, 1999.

105 Gary Strauss, The Billionaires Club: New Economy Rockets CEO Pay into the Stratosphere, *USA Today*, April 5, 2000.

106 Blaine Harden, Molding Loyal Pamperers for the Newly Rich, *New York Times*, October 24, 1999.

107 Keith Bradsher, Nice House. Great Neighborhood. But, Honey, It Has Only a 3-Car Garage, *New York Times*, November 12, 2000.

108 Sharon McDonnell, Supplement: New York Homes & Living. Hamptons Living, *New York Observer*, July 1, 1996.

109 Locals were "competing for year-round rentals with Manhattanites willing to pay anywhere from $25,000 on up — just for July and August." Tracie Rozhon, High Costs in Hamptons Force Workers Out, *New York Times*, May 7, 2000.

110 Ibid.

111 Cait Murphy, Are the Rich Cleaning Up? *Fortune*, September 4, 2000.

112 Kate Kelly, $27 Million Won't Do! In 1999, Sellers Realize No Price Is Too High, *New York Observer*, November 22, 1999.

113 Joan Oleck, There Go the Neighborhoods, *Business Week*, August 14, 2000.

114 Joe Mathews, Wall Street Dominates Big Apple, *Baltimore Sun*, August 2, 1998.

115 Robert Frank, Traffic and Tax Cuts, *New York Times*, May 11, 2001.

116 Ibid.

117 M. W. Guzy, The Consuming American Dream, TomPaine.commentary. Accessed from www.tompaine.com/opinion/2001/06/27/2.html.

118 Ibid. Between 1982 and the end of the century, notes *St. Louis Post Dispatch* columnist M. W. Guzy, the population of the United States has grown about 20 percent, the time in traffic 236 percent.

119 Frank, Traffic and Tax Cuts.

120 Angela Cortez, Pie in the Sky: Housing Costs Out of Reach Statewide, *Denver Post*, July 19, 1998.

121 Booth, A Hard Place to Call Home.

122 Raj Jayadev, Silicon Valley's Underbelly, *San Francisco Chronicle*, January 20, 2002.

123 Mary Williams Walsh, As Hot Economy Pushes Up Overtime, Fatigue Becomes a Labor Issue, *New York Times*, September 17, 2000.

124 See P050: Travel Time to Work, Workers 16 Years and Over. Data Set: Census 1990, available at http://factfinder.census.gov/servlet/DTTable?ds_name=D&geo_id=D&mt_name=DEC_1990_STF3_P050&_lang=en and QT-P23: Journey to Work. 2000 Data Set: Census 2000, available at http://factfinder.census.gov/servlet/QTTable?_ts=5 1356626240.

125 Romesh Diwan, Relational Wealth and the Quality of Life, *Journal of Socio-Economics*, July 2000.

126 Daniel B. Rathbone and Jorg C. Huckabee, Controlling Road Rage: A Literature Review and Pilot Study Prepared for the AAA Foundation for Traffic Safety, June 9, 1999. Accessed from www.aaafoundation.org/resources/index.cfm?button=roadrage.

127 Alan Sipress, Paying for Space in the Fast Lane, *Washington Post*, May 18, 1999.

128 Phil McComba, Renaissance: One Big Happy Family, *Washington Post*, December 31, 1994.

129 Ben Pappas, Cathedrals to Sunglasses and Other Fantasies of the Very Rich, *Forbes*, October 13, 1997.

130 In a bitter business dispute, Herbert Haft publicly accused his son of stealing $7 million from him. Kara Swisher, An Empire Builder Rebuilds His Life, *Washington Post*, October 14, 1994.

131 Jim Hopkins, Rich Kids Pay Price for Silver Spoon, *USA Today*, May 10, 2002.

132 Ibid.

133 Frank Lalli, How She Turned $5,000 into $22 Million, *Money*, January 1996.

134 August Gribbin, Newly Wealthy Find Money

Has a Price: Support Groups Help Rich Cope, *Washington Times*, December 23, 1998.

[135] Richard B. Wagner, Your Friends and Neighbors, Worth.com, October 20, 2000.

[136] Harrison Rainie, The State of Greed, *US News & World Report*, June 17, 1996.

[137] August Gribbin, Newly Wealthy Find Money Has a Price.

[138] Jim Hopkins, Rich Kids Pay Price for Silver Spoon.

[139] Philip Slater, *Wealth Addiction*. New York: E. P. Dutton, 1980, 29.

[140] Gribbin, Newly Wealthy Find Money Has a Price.

[141] Connif, The Natural History of the Rich.

[142] Adrian Havil, With a Living Trust, You Don't Need a Mop, *New York Times*, July 20, 1997.

[143] Connif, The Natural History of the Rich.

[144] Rock Slide in the Income Gap, *New York Times*, May 2, 1999.

[145] Quoted in William Davis, *The Rich: A Study of the Species*. New York: Franklin Watts, 1983, frontispiece.

[146] Lucinda Bredin, Surviving the Getty Curse, *Mail on Sunday* (Toronto), November 29, 1998.

[147] Nicholas Von Hoffman, Richie Rich at the Switch, *Washington Post*, February 11, 1996.

[148] M. H. Dunlop, *Gilded City: Scandal and Sensation in Turn-of-the-Century New York*. New York: William Morrow, 2000, xvi.

[149] Ibid., xvi and 145.

[150] Ibid., xvi.

[151] Slater, *Wealth Addiction*, 28.

[152] Stanley Marcus, *Economist*, February 2, 2002.

[153] Ibid.

[154] Lee Hill Kavanaugh, Riches Do Not Reap Happiness, New Millionaires Learn, *Houston Chronicle*, June 4, 2000.

[155] Ibid.

[156] Abby Ellin, Money, Money, Money, Guilt, Guilt, Guilt, *New York Times*, March 19, 2000.

[157] Richard Todd, Who Me, Rich? *Worth*, September 1997.

[158] Catherine Ford, Money...money...money...Some of Us Are So Deserving, *Calgary Herald*, July 9, 1999.

[159] Dunlop, *Gilded City: Scandal and Sensation in Turn-of-the-Century New York*, 15.

[160] Robert Novak, The Democrats' Class Struggle, *Washington Post*, August 21, 1995.

[161] Michael Lewis, The Rich: How They're Different . . . Than They Used to Be, *New York Times*, November 19, 1995.

[162] Todd, Who Me, Rich?

[163] Ibid.

[164] Michelle Singletary, The Good Life Carries Risk of Affluenza, *Washington Post*, December 24, 2000.

[165] Rosanne Rosen, Curing Your Kids' 'Affluenza,' *Columbus Dispatch*, April 8, 2001.

[166] Trevor Turner, Croesus and the Crackpots, *New Internationalist*, September 1994.

[167] Monique P. Yazigi, Even If You're Rich, It's Uncool Today Not to Have a 'Real' Job. So You Get One. *New York Times*, February 20, 2000.

[168] Ibid.

[169] Andrew Carnegie. edited by Edward C. Kirkland, *The Gospel of Wealth and Other Timely Essays*. Cambridge: The Belknap Press of Harvard University Press, 1962, xvi.

[170] Peter Dobkin Hall and George E. Marcus, Why Should Men Leave Great *Fortune*s to Their Children? Class, Dynasty and Inheritance in America. Accessed from ksghome.harvard.edu/~.phall.hauser.ksg/inheritance.html.

[171] Diana Hendriques, Determined to Share the Wealth, *New York Times*, November 29, 1998.

[172] Randy Barrett, Connie Gugliemo, The Trouble with Money, *Inter@ctive Week*, April 24, 2000.

[173] Deirdre Dolan, New York Raw, *New York Observer*, August 26, 1996.

[174] George Bernard Shaw, *The Intelligent Woman's Guide to Socialism and Capitalism*, New York: Brentano's Publishers, 1928, 41.

[175] Lublin, Living Well.

[176] Paul G. Schervish, Introduction: *The Wealthy and the World of Wealth Gospels of Wealth: How the Rich Portray Their Lives*. Praeger Paperback. 1994. Accessed from www.greenwood.com/intro.htm.

[177] The concept of agency here is not the same concept of agency that appeared earlier in our discussion of the principal-agent debate that has coursed through debates over appropriate incentives.

[178] Schervish, Introduction: *The Wealthy and the World of Wealth Gospels of Wealth: How the Rich Portray Their Lives*.

[179] Frank DiGiacomo, The Transom, *New York Observer*, July 17, 1995.

[180] Monique P. Yazigi, When You Got It, Flaunt It, *New York Times*, January 26, 2000.

[181] Lublin, Living Well.

[182] Yazigi, When You Got It, Flaunt It.

[183] Way Out in Left Field, Sheen Waits for the Angels, *Washington Post*, April 21, 1996.

[184] James Atlas, What They Look Like to the Rest of Us, *New York Times*, November 19, 1995.

[185] Sara Robinson, Sleepless in San Jose, *New York Times*, October 31, 1999.

[186] Barry Witt, San Jose, Calif., Officials Confront Airport-Curfew Violators, *San Jose Mercury News*, December 21, 1999.

[187] Robinson, Sleepless in San Jose.

[188] Michael Kazin, The Corporation as a Way of Life, *American Prospect*, August 13, 2001.

[189] The entire sale proceeds amounted to $422 million. Michelle Singletary, Saluting a Generous Spirit, *Washington Post*, August 1, 1999.

[190] Ibid.

[191] Logan Pearsall Smith, *Afterthoughts*. New York: Harcourt, Brace and Company, 1931, 54.

[192] Slater, *Wealth Addiction*, 28.

[193] Quoted in Lane, *The Loss of Happiness in Market Democracies*, 167.

[194] Michelle Quinn, Green with Envy, Despite the Good Times, *San Jose Mercury-News*, August 16, 1999.

[195] Quoted in Slater, *Wealth Addiction*, 49.

[196] Shaw, *The Intelligent Woman's Guide to Socialism and Capitalism*, 46.

PROFESSIONS WITHOUT PRIDE

[1] R. H. Tawney, *The Acquisitive Society*. New York: Harcourt, Brace & World, Inc., 1948 (originally published 1920), 93.

[2] Ibid., 94.

[3] Stephen Metcalf, Another Day, Another Scandal — Bitter Fruit of a Free Market, *New York Observer*, July 15, 2002.

[4] Tawney, *The Acquisitive Society*, 92-93.

[5] Metcalf, Another Day, Another Scandal — Bitter Fruit of a Free Market.

[6] Derek Bok, *The Cost of Talent: How Executives and Professionals Are Paid and How It Affects America*. Free Press: New York, 1993, v.

[7] Ibid., 47.

[8] David Segal, At Skadden, It's All Systems Grow, *Washington Post*, July 31, 1998.

[9] Ibid.

[10] Bok, *The Cost of Talent: How Executives and Professionals Are Paid and How It Affects America*, 224.

[11] Susan Orenstein, Why Cravath's Polyester Superstar Left Cushy Perch for Yankee Stripes, *New York Observer*, May 26, 1997.

[12] 2001 Was a Very Good Year for the Top 20 New York Firms, *New York Lawyer*, July 1, 2002.

[13] Bok, *The Cost of Talent: How Executives and Professionals Are Paid and How It Affects America*, 49.

[14] Ibid., 149.

[15] Ibid., 265.

[16] Ibid., 141-142.

[17] Ibid., 139. Major firms, Derek Bok would note in 1993, have "begun to accept cases on a contingent basis, something almost unheard of only a few years ago."

[18] Ibid., 142-143.

[19] Lawyers Proud of Enron Work, Daily Enron, August 20, 2002. Accessed from www.thedailyenron.com/documents/20020820094250-29013.asp.

[20] Bok, *The Cost of Talent: How Executives and Professionals Are Paid and How It Affects America*, 152.

[21] Ibid., 148. The largest law firms "managed to boost their real incomes by anywhere from 20 to 100 percent in the 1970s and 1980s even as the earnings of most other lawyers hardly increased at all."

[22] James V. Grimaldi, Big Debts Keep Law Grads Out of Low-Paying Public Service Jobs, *Washington Post*, November 18, 2002.

[23] Dean Baker, Lawyers Salaries and Law School Tuition, *Economics Reporting Review*, November 25, 2002.

[24] This figure was for public university law schools. James V. Grimaldi, Big Debts Keep Law Grads Out of Low-Paying Public Service Jobs, *Washington Post*, November 18, 2002.

[25] Garance Franke-Ruta, The Indentured Generation, *American Prospect*, May 1, 2003.

[26] Bok, *The Cost of Talent: How Executives and Professionals Are Paid and How It Affects America*, 264.

[27] David S. Hilzenrath, Financial Watchdog Became an Enabler, *Washington Post*, June 16, 2002.

[28] David S. Hilzenrath, After Enron, New Doubts About Auditors, *Washington Post*, December 5, 2001.

[29] Philip Mattera, Lack of Accountability: The Enron/Arthur Andersen Scandal and the Future of the Accounting Business, Corporate Research Project's Corporate Research E-Letter, No. 21, February 2002.

[30] Hilzenrath, After Enron, New Doubts About Auditors.

[31] At century's end, one MIT study revealed, top accounting firms were collecting close to three-quarters of their revenues from consulting. Beth Healy, Under Scrutiny, *Boston Globe*, March 10, 2002.

[32] Mattera, Lack of Accountability.

[33] Kirstin Downey Grimsley, Auditors Pushed Into 'Revolving Door,' *Washington Post*, February 19, 2002.

[34] Ibid.

[35] Ibid. This estimate is from Charles Peck, an analyst who tracks executive compensation for the New York-based research group, the Conference Board.

[36] Ibid. Swartz was asked to resign in August 2002, in the middle of the scandals that surrounded Tyco International. The company agreed to pay him a $44.8 million severance package. Gretchen Morgenson, Tyco Rewarded an Executive During a Grand Jury Inquiry, *New York Times*, September 26, 2002.

[37] Grimsley, Auditors Pushed Into 'Revolving Door.'

[38] Ibid.

[39] Paul Krugman, Enemies of Reform, *New York Times*, May 21, 2002.

[40] An 'Accounting Opportunity,' *Washington Post*, June 18, 2002.

[41] Ibid.

[42] David S. Hilzenrath, Two SEC Views of Industry, *Washington Post*, December 5, 2001.

[43] On June 15, 2002, Arthur Andersen announced it would no longer conduct audits of firms listed on stock markets as of August 31. David S. Hilzenrath, Financial Watchdog Became an Enabler, *Washington Post*, June 16, 2002.

[44] Ibid.

[45] David S. Hilzenrath, Big Four Firms Face Post-Enron Scrutiny, *Washington Post*, June 7, 2002.

[46] Arthur Andersen Appreciation Night, *Corporate Reform Weekly*, July 29, 2002.

[47] Remarks of Senator Paul S. Sarbanes (D-Md.), Chairman, Senate Banking, Housing and Urban Affairs Committee on the Passage of the Public Company Accounting Reform and Investor Protection Act of 2002, July 15, 2002.

[48] Hilzenrath, Financial Watchdog Became an Enabler.

[49] Bok, *The Cost of Talent: How Executives and Professionals Are Paid and How It Affects America*, 51.

[50] Bill Glauber, London Hospital That Has Survived Nine Centuries Will Not See Another, *Baltimore Sun*, April 23, 1995,

[51] Howard L. Bailit and Cary Sennett, Utilization Management as a Cost-Containment Strategy, *Health Care Financing Review*, 1991 Supplement, Vol. 13, Issue 2.

[52] Bok, *The Cost of Talent: How Executives and Professionals Are Paid and How It Affects America*, 121-122.

[53] Ibid., 123-124.

[54] Statement of D. McCarty Thornton, Chief Counsel to the Inspector General, Office of the Inspector General, U.S. Department of Health and Human Services Testimony Before the Subcommittee on Health of the House Committee on Ways and Means Hearing on Medicare "Self-Referral" Law, May 13, 1999.

[55] Bok, *The Cost of Talent: How Executives and Professionals Are Paid and How It Affects America*, 122-123.

[56] Statement of D. McCarty Thornton, May 13, 1999.

[57] To be exact, doctors in private practice earned $218,000 in 1994, 8.3 times the median. Andrew Hacker, Who They Are, *New York Times*, November 19, 1995.

[58] Under the legislation, doctors also could not "joint venture" a clinical lab "with a group of physicians whose only relationship to the laboratory is to refer laboratory work and share investment profits." Statement of D. McCarty Thornton, May 13, 1999.

[59] Bailit and Sennett, Utilization Management as a Cost-Containment Strategy.

[60] George Dunea, Letter . . . from Chicago: Distrust, *British Medical Journal*, April 30, 1988.

[61] Abramson would take in $11.4 million that same year in income from stock dividends alone. The Needy and the Greedy, *1199 News*, October 1995.

[62] David S. Hilzenrath, 2 Top Executives Resign at Giant Health Care Firm, *Washington Post*, July 26, 1997.

[63] In 1994, according to Medical Economics, the median physician income totaled $150,000. Street Smarts: $20.5 Million Sounds Big, but It's Just $9,855 an Hour, *Denver Post*, June 2, 1996.

[64] Dorothy L. Pennachio, Are You Sorry You Went into Primary Care? *Medical Economics*, September 23, 2002.

[65] Roy C. Smith, *The Wealth Creators: The Rise of Today's Rich and Super-Rich*. New York: St. Martin's Press, 2001, 191.

[66] Careers in Finance, a part of the Careers in

Business Web site. Accessed from www.careers-in-finance.com/ibsal.htm. This informational service was run by a former Bankers Trust official.

67 "This stat came from a James Fallows report in the *New York Review of Books*, that this spring 36,000 graduating students applied for jobs at just one mergers and acquisitions house." Charles Peters, Besieged and Beleaguered on $200,000 a Year; the Rich Feel Too Poor to Pay More Taxes, *Washington Monthly*, June 1990.

68 Robert H. Frank and Philip J. Cook, The Superstar Economy, *Washington Post*, November 12, 1995.

69 Ibid.

70 Tenured New York teachers saw their pay rise 20 percent in the 1990s, to a $49,030 average. Partners at Wachtell Lipton Rosen & Katz registered a 144 percent gain from the start of the decade to the end, and Stanford computer science grads saw their starting salaries rise 81 percent. Carol J. Loomis, 'This Stuff Is Wrong,' *Fortune*, June 25, 2001.

71 Ibid. The inflation rate rose 32 percent, teacher salaries 20 percent.

72 Each battle lost, each talented person not recruited, each talented person not retained, pushed America's schools into more perilous positions. "The cost of replacing disheartened education leaders is roughly one-half of the person's annual salary," *School Administrator* explained. "When the replacement is not as strong as the person leaving the position, the costs tend to be compounded by the additional time and training needed to bring the new employee up to par." And the resulting total costs make for "an appalling drain on already-scarce resources." William G. Cunningham and J. Brent Sperry, Where's the Beef in Administrator Pay? *School Administrator*, February 2001.

73 Veteran education reformers would not be surprised. Noted Ted Sizer, a former dean at Harvard and the author of several education reform classics: "You can't run complicated schools with amateurs." Sarah Carr, Re-Thinking Teach for America: National Organization Needs Better Training, *Youth City News*, 2002. Accessed from www.jrn.columbia.edu/studentwork/children/2002/carr4.asp.

74 Ibid.

75 Martin Kimel, Regulating the Ferrari Set — on a Ford Salary, *Washington Post*, January 4, 2000.

76 Ibid.

77 Stephen Barr, Lagging Judicial Pay Gives Some People Second Thoughts About Careers on the Bench, *Washington Post*, March 11, 2001.

78 Ibid.

79 Bok, *The Cost of Talent: How Executives and Professionals Are Paid and How It Affects America*, 65.

80 William H. Rehnquist, Remarks, Public Hearings of the National Commission on the Public Service: A Time of Crisis and Opportunity, Brookings Institution, July 15, 2002. Accessed from www.brook.edu/dybdocroot/comm/transcripts/20020715.htm.

81 Ibid.

82 Associate Chief Justice Stephen G. Breyer, Remarks, Public Hearings of the National Commission on the Public Service: A Time of Crisis and Opportunity, Brookings Institution, July 15, 2002. Accessed from www.brook.edu/dybdocroot/comm/transcripts/20020715.htm.

83 Holman W. Jenkins Jr., Let's Have More Heirs and Heiresses, *Wall Street Journal*, February 21, 2001.

84 Peter Frumkin, Are Nonprofit CEOs Overpaid? *Public Interest*, Winter 2001.

85 Boston University's John Silber led the way with $564,020. He actually made $775,963 in 1993, after a $300,000 bonus. Phillip Pina, Six Colleges Pay Presidents $400,000-plus, *USA Today*, September 27, 1995,

86 Judith Havemann, Top Foundations Gave Chiefs a Bountiful Raise, *Washington Post*, July 5, 1998.

87 Ibid.

88 Frumkin, Are Nonprofit CEOs Overpaid?

89 Ibid.

90 Doreen Carvajal, Faculty Vote at Adelphi Asks Ouster of President, *New York Times*, October 6, 1995. New York State would later, in 1997, dismiss eighteen of the nineteen trustees on Adelphi's board in a move some would call "the most severe government crackdown on a private board of trustees in the history of higher education." Diamandopoulos had received over $800,000 in 1996 salary and benefits. Meanwhile, during his presidential stint at Adelphi, the university's student enrollment had dropped by half. John Sedgwick, Dire Learning, *American Benefactor*, Summer 1997,

91 Frumkin, Are Nonprofit CEOs Overpaid?

92 Public Trust and Accountability 2000, Independent Sector. Accessed from www.independentsector.org/programs/leadership/Public_Trust_and_Accountability_2000.pdf.

93 Frumkin, Are Nonprofit CEOs Overpaid?

94 Tawney, *The Acquisitive Society*, 96.

SPORTS WITHOUT WINNERS

[1] The label comes from *New York Times* sports columnist Robert Lipsyte's 1975 book, *SportsWorld: An American Dreamland*. New York: Quadrangle/The New York Times Book Co.

[2] The figure represents a *Sports Business Journal* calculation for 1997. Daniel Rascher, What Is the Size of the Sports Industry? *SportsEconomics Perspectives*, August 2001.

[3] As of 1998. Roy C. Smith, *The Wealth Creators: The Rise of Today's Rich and Super-Rich*. New York: St. Martin's Press, 2001, 273.

[4] Steve Fainaru, Yankees Are Building an Empire State, *Washington Post*, February 18, 2001.

[5] Big Money for Big Stars, *USA Today*, April 9, 2003.

[6] D. Stanley Eitzen, Public Teams, Private Profits, *Dollars & Sense*, March-April 2000.

[7] Peter Keating, Artful Dodging, *ESPN, the magazine*. January 7, 2002.

[8] "This form of tax subsidy is unique to professional sports; no other business in the United States depreciates the value of human beings as part of the cost of its operation. In a curious twist of logic, showing the bias toward capital over human rights, players whose skills diminish with age do not receive a personal tax write-off; only their owners do." Eitzen, Public Teams, Private Profits.

[9] Keating, Artful Dodging.

[10] Eitzen, Public Teams, Private Profits.

[11] Smith, *The Wealth Creators: The Rise of Today's Rich and Super-Rich*, 277.

[12] Marc Fisher, 50 Years Later, Jackie Robinson Is All Business, *Washington Post*, April 6, 1997.

[13] Mark Maske, President Extends Deadline for Mediator to Suggest Terms, *Washington Post*, February 7, 1995

[14] Eitzen, Public Teams, Private Profits.

[15] Joanna Cagan, Suite Dreams, *New York Times Magazine*, November 7, 1999.

[16] Thomas Heath, Upstairs, Downstairs, *Washington Post*, November 30, 1997.

[17] Cagan, Suite Dreams.

[18] David Leonhardt, Two-Tier Marketing: Companies Are Tailoring Their Products and Pitches to Two Different Americas, *Business Week*, March 17, 1997.

[19] The Los Angeles Lakers, in 2002-2003, charged $1,750 to sit courtside. Steve Wyche, Wizards Raise Ticket Prices, *Washington Post*, September 28, 2002.

[20] New Stadiums, Removal of Premium Seats Drive Teams Up and Down in 2002 NFL Fan Cost Index, News Release, Team Marketing Report, September 3, 2002. Accessed from www.teammarketing.com/article_details.cfm?article_id=65.

[21] Eitzen, Public Teams, Private Profits.

[22] TMR's Fan Cost Index. Accessed from www.teammarketing.com/fci.cfm.

[23] New Stadiums, Removal of Premium Seats Drive Teams Up and Down in 2002 NFL Fan Cost Index, News Release, Team Marketing Report. Full chart at www.teammarketing.com/fci.cfm.

[24] Ibid.

[25] Thomas Boswell, Fans Pressed to Pay for Big-Ticket Items, *Washington Post*, December 20, 1996.

[26] Ken Ringle, Bells and Whistles, *Washington Post*, November 30, 1997.

[27] Stephen Fehr, Pricey New Sports Venues Help Make Washington No. 1 for High-Cost Tickets, *Washington Post*, October 31, 1997.

[28] Renee Coury, How Raiders Deal Went Sour, *San Jose Mercury News*, December 22, 1996.

[29] Boswell, Fans Pressed to Pay for Big-Ticket Items.

[30] Eitzen, Public Teams, Private Profits.

[31] Fainaru, Yankees Are Building an Empire State.

[32] David Leonhardt, How to Re-energize Baseball and Win New Fans, *New York Times*, August 12, 2001.

[33] Dave Sheinin, Selig-Angelos: A Team to Watch, *Washington Post*, April 14, 2002.

[34] Leonard Shapiro, Series' Ratings Hit All-Time Low, *Washington Post*, October 29, 2002.

[35] Jere Longman, Pro Leagues' Ratings Drop; Nobody Is Quite Sure Why, *New York Times*, July 29, 2001. "Down," a follow-up *Times* analysis in 2003 would add. "That is where the ratings of most major sports events went in the past year." Richard Sandomir, The Decline and Fall of Sports Ratings, *New York Times*, September 10, 2003.

[36] Michael Hill, The Golden Age of the Oriole Way, *Baltimore Sun*, July 7, 2002.

[37] Ibid.

[38] Thomas Boswell, Sometimes, Winning Can Be a Losing Cause, *Washington Post*, November 28, 1999.

[39] Jere Longman, Pro Leagues' Ratings Drop; Nobody Is Quite Sure Why.

[40] Eitzen, Public Teams, Private Profits.

[41] Spencer Hsu, Specter Calls for Privately Funded Sports Stadiums, *New York Times*, June 16, 1999.

[42] Neal R. Peirce, Antidote to Sports Rip-Offs:

Community Organizing, *Washington Post* Writers Group, July 29, 2001.

43 Kate Davis and Chauna Brocht, Subsidizing the Low Road: Economic Development in Baltimore, Good Jobs First, September 2002. Accessed from www.goodjobsfirst.org/pdf/balt.pdf.

44 Peirce, Antidote to Sports Rip-Offs: Community Organizing.

45 Quoted from Joanna Cagan and Neil deMause, *Field of Schemes: How the Great Stadium Swindle Turns Public Money into Private Profit*. Monroe, Maine: Common Courage Press, revised ed., 1999/1998), 59, in John Rouse and Larry Lutin, Corporate Welfare, Taxpayer Subsidies, and Home Field Advantages, *Public Administration Review*, September 2001.

46 Peirce, Antidote to Sports Rip-Offs: Community Organizing.

47 Hsu, Specter Calls for Privately Funded Sports Stadiums.

48 Joanna Cagan and Neil DeMause, A Tale of Two Cities, *Nation*, August 10, 1998.

49 Quoted from Cagan and deMause, *Field of Schemes: How the Great Stadium Swindle Turns Public Money into Private Profit*. 59, in Rouse and Lutin, Corporate Welfare, Taxpayer Subsidies, and Home Field Advantages.

50 Eitzen, Public Teams, Private Profits.

51 Sammy Sosa, Baseball-Reference.Com. Accessed from www.baseball-reference.com/s/sosasa01.shtml.

52 Stephen Franklin and Kathy Bergen, Increase in Stock Options, Grants Triggers Explosion in CEO Pay, *Chicago Tribune*, April 23, 2000.

53 Smith, *The Wealth Creators: The Rise of Today's Rich and Super-Rich*, 281.

54 Stephen J. Dubner, Life Is a Contact Sport, *New York Times Magazine*, August 18, 2002.

55 The survey was conducted by the NFL Players Association in data for most of the 1990s. Mike Freeman, Draft Is Start, but End Is Usually Near, *Washington Post*, March 24, 2002.

56 State of the Union, *Washington Post*, December 15, 2002.

57 Leonard Shapiro, In Today's Free Agent Market, High-Priced Items Stay on Shelf, *Washington Post*, March 7, 2002.

58 Sally Jenkins, No Need for Greed: Philanthropic Athletes Have Dollars and Sense, *Washington Post*, March 4, 2001.

59 Richard Morin, A-Rod, Please Note, *Washington Post*, April 22, 2001.

60 Dave Sheinen, The Aftershocks of A-Rod's Deal, *Washington Post*, February 25, 2001.

61 Rick Morrissey, In the Wake of the News: Sosa's Happiness Doesn't Extend to Rest of Clubhouse, *Chicago Tribune*, March 15, 2001.

62 Ibid.

63 Steve Rushin, What Price Happiness? In Their Pursuit of More Pay and Perks, Athletes Might Pause to Ponder When Enough Is Enough, *Sports Illustrated*, November 27, 2000.

64 Jon Gallo, The NBA — It's Not Child's Play, *Washington Post*, January 31, 2002.

65 Smith, *The Wealth Creators: The Rise of Today's Rich and Super-Rich*, 255.

66 Amy Shipley, Major League Baseball Enters Foul Territory, *Washington Post*, November 11, 2001.

67 George F. Will, Field of Dollars, *Washington Post*, February 28, 1999. In the 1996 draft, two top picks each received signing bonuses that topped the entire payroll of the 1997 Pittsburgh Pirates. Tyler Kepner, For Prospects, Lucrative Bonus Is a Signing of the Times, *Washington Post*, August 14, 1997.

68 Shipley, Major League Baseball Enters Foul Territory.

69 Some Have It, Some Don't, *Washington Post*, December 17, 2000.

70 The Yankee payroll, at the time, totaled $85 million, the Royals payroll, $23 million. George Vecsey, Tax Is Funny Money for Wealthy Owners, *New York Times*, May 9, 1999.

71 Will, Field of Dollars.

72 Michael Wilbon, Parity Turns NFL's Bad into Good, *Washington Post*, January 30, 2001.

73 Hal Bodley, Average Salary Increases as Total Player Payroll Nears $2B, *USA Today*, November 9, 2000.

74 Tom Weir and MaryJo Sylwester, Baseball Salaries Top-heavy *USA Today*, October 17, 2002.

75 Gordon Fairclough, Listen Up, Managers: Fat Paychecks Don't Always Guarantee Success, *Wall Street Journal*, March 24, 1999.

76 Diane Stafford, Losses Reflect Pay Disparity, *Kansas City Star*, November 13, 1999.

77 Rodriquez was actually the third superstar lost by the Mariners in just three years. "With those superstars gone, they are better than before because they are a well-rounded team, not a star vehicle," observed ESPN sportswriter Jim Caple. "They've shown that in today's economy, it's better to invest in the entire team than in one or two superstars." Jim Caple, Stars Aligned Right in Seattle, ESPN.com, June 6, 2001.

[78] Thomas Boswell, Money Creates Expectations, Then Money Destroys Them, *Washington Post*, December 22, 2000.

[79] Thomas Boswell, Marlins' Owner Cuts Bait, *Washington Post*, November 21, 1997.

[80] Ibid.

[81] George Vecsey, Record Free Fall Would Be Monument to Huizenga's Greed, *New York Times*, March 29, 1998.

[82] Piazza Keeping His Bags Packed, *Washington Post*, May 17, 1998.

[83] Shipley, Major League Baseball Enters Foul Territory.

[84] Boswell, Marlins' Owner Cuts Bait.

WEALTH WITHOUT HEALTH

[1] Robert L. Ferrer, Comment: Tax Policies Affect Health as Well as Wallet, *San Antonio Express-News*, April 4, 2001. Dr. Ferrer teaches at the University of Texas at San Antonio.

[2] Ibid.

[3] The data are from James P. Smith and Raynard Kington, Demographic and Economic Correlates of Health in Old Age, *Demography*, February 1997. Quoted in James P. Smith, Socioeconomic Status and Health, *American Economic Review*, May 1998.

[4] Alejandro Reuss, Cause of Death: Inequality, *Dollars & Sense*, May/June 2001.

[5] Sarah Marchand, Daniel Wikler, and Bruce Landesman, Class, Health, and Justice, *Milbank Quarterly*, September 1998.

[6] Low-income men "are nearly six times as likely as high-income men to have elevated blood-lead levels." Reuss, Cause of Death: Inequality.

[7] Jeanne Winner, The Social Relations of Health and Disease, *Dollars & Sense*, May/June 2001.

[8] Stephen H. Gorin, Inequality and Health: Implications for Social Work, *Health and Social Work*, November 2000.

[9] Harriet Orcutt Duleep, Mortality and Income Inequality Among Economically Developed Countries, *Social Security Bulletin*, Summer 1995.

[10] "The United States, despite having one of the highest living standards in the world (the real gross domestic product [GDP] per capita was $24,680 in 1993), has a lower life expectancy (76.1 years in 1993) than less affluent but more egalitarian countries like the Netherlands (GDP, $17,340; life expectancy, 77.5 years); Israel (GDP, $15,130; life expectancy, 76.6 years); or Spain (GDP, $13,660; life expectancy, 77.7 years)." Ichiro Kawachi, Bruce

P. Kennedy, and Kimberly Loochner, Long Live Community: Social Capital as Public Health, *American Prospect*, November-December 1997.

[11] Norman Daniels, Bruce Kennedy, and Ichiro Kawachi, Justice Is Good for Our Health, *Boston Review*, February/March 2000. Accessed from www-polisci.mit.edu/BostonReview/ndf.html#Health.

[12] "The absence of a correlation between age-adjusted death rates and the average income levels of economically developed countries has led researchers to conclude that income does not affect the mortality levels of economically developed countries." Duleep, Mortality and Income Inequality Among Economically Developed Countries.

[13] Stephen Bezruchka, Societal Hierarchy and the Health Olympics, *Canadian Medical Association Journal*, December 17, 2001.

[14] Louis Uchitelle, Even the Rich Can Suffer from Income Inequality, *New York Times*, November 15, 1998.

[15] George Davey Smith, Income Inequality and Mortality: Why Are They Related? *British Medical Journal*, April 16, 1996.

[16] "Numerous studies" show "that inequality is strongly associated with population mortality and life-expectancy across nations." Daniels, Kennedy, and Kawachi, Justice Is Good for Our Health.

[17] Marchand, Wikler, and Landesman, Class, Health, and Justice.

[18] Helen Epstein, Life & Death on the Social Ladder, *New York Review of Books*, July 16, 1998.

[19] Richard G. Wilkinson, *Unhealthy Societies: The Afflictions of Inequality*. London: Routledge, 1996, 3.

[20] James Lardner, Inequality Meets Epidemiology, Inequality.org. Accessed from www.inequality.org/wilkfr.html.

[21] Wilkinson, *Unhealthy Societies: The Afflictions of Inequality*, 212.

[22] George A. Kaplan, Elsie R. Pamuk, John W. Lynch, Richard D. Cohen, and Jennifer L. Balfour, Inequality in Income and Mortality in the United States: Analysis of Mortality and Potential Pathways, *British Medical Journal*, April 20, 1996.

[23] "Our findings provide some support for the notion that the size of the gap between the wealthy and less well off — as distinct from the absolute standard of living enjoyed by the poor — matters in its own right," the Kennedy team added. In the light of these findings, the team concluded, "society must pay attention to the growing gap between the rich and the poor." Bruce P. Kennedy, Ichiro

Kawachi, and Deborah Prothrow-Stith, Income Distribution and Mortality: Cross Sectional Ecological Study of the Robin Hood Index in the United States. *British Medical Journal*, April 20 1996.

[24] Robert Pear The *New York Times* News Service, Study Links Income Gap, Health, Commercial Appeal (Memphis), April 21, 1996.

[25] Bruce P. Kennedy, Ichiro Kawachi, Roberta Glass, and Deborah Prothrow-Stith, Income Distribution, Socioeconomic Status, and Self Rated Health in the United States: Multilevel analysis, *British Medical Journal*, October 3, 1998.

[26] Data were not available for one U.S. metro area, Anchorage, Alaska. John W. Lynch, George A. Kaplan, Elsie R. Pamuk, Richard D. Cohen, Katherine E. Heck, Jennifer L. Balfour, and Irene H. Yen, Income Inequality and Mortality in Metropolitan Areas of the United States, *American Journal of Public Health*, July 1998.

[27] The researchers reviewed data from 1988, 1989, 1992, and 1993. They eliminated zip codes with one hundred or less births or five thousand or less residents, leaving them with zip codes that accounted for 97 percent of the city's live births during the time period they studied. Caleb Daniloff, What a Difference a Digit Makes, Inequality.org. Accessed from www.inequality.org/arnofr.html.

[28] Ibid. The zip code that included New York's posh Upper East Side had an average income that dwarfed South Beach — and an infant death rate three times as high.

[29] James Lardner, Deadly Disparities Americans' Widening Gap in Incomes May Be Narrowing Our Lifespans, *Washington Post*, August 16, 1998.

[30] Ibid.

[31] Bezruchka, Societal Hierarchy and the Health Olympics.

[32] Stephen Bezruchka, Is Our Society Making You Sick? *Newsweek*, February 26, 2001.

[33] Ibid.

[34] Ibid.

[35] Wilkinson, *Unhealthy Societies: The Afflictions of Inequality*, 18.

[36] Bezruchka, Is Our Society Making You Sick?

[37] Ibid.

[38] Lardner, Deadly Disparities Americans' Widening Gap in Incomes May Be Narrowing Our Lifespans.

[39] Wilkinson, *Unhealthy Societies: The Afflictions of Inequality*, 131.

[40] That the structure of society is key to well-being becomes evident when we look at Japanese who emigrate: their health declines to the level of the inhabitants of the new country." Bezruchka, Is Our Society Making You Sick?

[41] This is a reporter's paraphrase of remarks made by Cullen at a Capitol Hill seminar. Coralie Carlson, Sabo Renews Call for Legislation to Cut Income Inequality, *Star-Tribune* (Minneapolis), September 15, 1999.

[42] Bezruchka, Societal Hierarchy and the Health Olympics.

[43] The research was conducted by investigators at Cornell's School of Industrial and Labor Relations. Arthur Waskow, Free Time for a Free People, *Nation*, January 1, 2001.

[44] Health experts measure obesity by "Body Mass Index." An index value over twenty-five increases mortality risk. About 100 million Americans, the National Institutes of Health reports, rate over twenty-five on the Body Mass Index. Romesh Diwan, Relational Wealth and the Quality of Life, *Journal of Socio-Economics*, July 2000.

[45] Robert E. Lane, *The Loss of Happiness in Market Democracies*. New Haven: Yale University Press, 2000, 9.

[46] This research was originally reported by epidemiologists Lisa Berkman and S. Leonard Syme in 1979. Kawachi, Kennedy, and Loochner, Long Live Community: Social Capital as Public Health.

[47] Ibid.

[48] Ibid.

[49] Ibid.

[50] Epstein, Life & Death on the Social Ladder.

[51] Ibid.

[52] Quoted in Kawachi, Kennedy, and Loochner, Long Live Community: Social Capital as Public Health.

[53] Epstein, Life & Death on the Social Ladder.

[54] Kawachi, Kennedy, and Loochner, Long Live Community: Social Capital as Public Health.

[55] Epstein, Life & Death on the Social Ladder.

[56] Kawachi, Kennedy, and Loochner, Long Live Community: Social Capital as Public Health.

[57] Michael Marmot, and Richard G. Wilkinson, Psychosocial and Material Pathways in the Relation Between Income and Health: A Response to Lynch et al., *British Medical Journal*, May 19, 2001.

[58] The most vivid account of this research appears in Helen Epstein, Life & Death on the Social Ladder, *New York Review of Books*, July 16, 1998. This summary largely tracks Epstein's account.

59 Ibid.

60 Ibid.

61 Wilkinson, *Unhealthy Societies: The Afflictions of Inequality*, 193.

62 Ibid., 193-194.

63 Studies on other primates have revealed similar stress and health connections. "Downwardly mobile animals," in one study of macaque monkeys, "showed a fivefold increase in atherosclerosis over two years." Marmot, and Wilkinson, Psychosocial and Material Pathways in the Relation Between Income and Health: A Response to Lynch et al.

64 Wilkinson, *Unhealthy Societies: The Afflictions of Inequality*, 195.

65 Epstein, Life & Death on the Social Ladder.

66 Ibid.

67 Wilkinson, *Unhealthy Societies: The Afflictions of Inequality*, 182.

68 Ibid., 196.

69 Ibid., 215.

70 Ibid., 184.

71 Ibid., 215.

72 Ibid., 176.

73 Ibid.

74 Sarah Ramsay, Remedy Presented for Health Inequalities in England, *Lancet*, November 28, 1998.

75 Melanie Phillips, An Unhealthy Interest in the Wealth Gap, *Sunday Times* (London), November 29, 1998.

76 Ibid.

77 Smoking and many other common risk-taking behaviors, as Richard Wilkinson contends, "are likely to be influenced by general levels of social stress in the population." Wilkinson, *Unhealthy Societies: The Afflictions of Inequality*, 185.

78 Ibid., 186.

79 Ibid., 185.

80 Ibid.

81 Ibid., 168.

82 Ibid.

83 Ibid., 196.

84 Ibid., 114.

85 Ibid.

86 Epstein, Life & Death on the Social Ladder.

87 Wilkinson, *Unhealthy Societies: The Afflictions of Inequality*, 115.

88 Epstein, Life & Death on the Social Ladder.

89 Wilkinson, *Unhealthy Societies: The Afflictions of Inequality*, 116.

90 Smith, Socioeconomic Status and Health.

91 Lardner, Inequality Meets Epidemiology.

92 Smith, Income Inequality and Mortality: Why Are They Related?

93 John Lynch, George Davey Smith, Marianne Hillemeier, Mary Shaw, Trivellore Raghunathan, and George Kaplan, Income Inequality, the Psychosocial Environment, and Health: Comparisons of Wealthy Nations, *Lancet*, July 21, 2001.

94 Gorin, Inequality and Health: Implications for Social Work.

95 Ibid.

96 Ibid.

97 Marmot and Wilkinson, Psychosocial and Material Pathways in the Relation Between Income and Health: A Response to Lynch et al.

98 Ibid.

99 Ibid.

100 Ibid.

101 Wilkinson, *Unhealthy Societies: The Afflictions of Inequality*, 184.

102 Nicholas Timmins, Unequal Societies Are Less Healthy, *Independent* (London), April 22, 1996.

103 Ezekiel Emanuel, Political Problems: A Response to Justice Is Good for Our Health, by Norman Daniels, Bruce Kennedy, and Ichiro Kawachi, *Boston Review*, February/March 2000.

104 Barbara Starfield, First Contact: A Response to Justice Is Good for Our Health, by Norman Daniels, Bruce Kennedy, and Ichiro Kawachi, *Boston Review*, February/March 2000.

105 Ted Marmor, Policy Options: A Response to Justice Is Good for Our Health, by Norman Daniels, Bruce Kennedy, and Ichiro Kawachi. *Boston Review*, February/March 2000.

106 Daniels, Kennedy, and Kawachi, Justice Is Good for Our Health.

107 This point would be driven home, in 2002, by the Pan American Health Organization. A comparative study of the nations of the Americas by PAHO found that income distributions shape how societies approach health policies. Nations with more equitable income distributions spend twice as many tax dollars on health as less equal nations. Improvements in Health in the Region of the Americas but Inequities Persist, Says PAHO, Pan American Health Organization news release, September 23, 2002. Health in the Americas 2002

Edition, Scientific and Technical Publication No. 587, Pan American Health Organization Pan American Sanitary Bureau, Regional Office of the World Health Organization. An executive summary is available at www.paho.org/english/DBI/MDS/HIA_exec_summary.pdf.

[108] Norman Daniels, Bruce Kennedy, and Ichiro Kawachi. Daniels, Kennedy, and Kawachi Respond, *Boston Review*, February/March 2000.

A FRAYING SOCIAL FABRIC

[1] James Ronald Stanfield and Jacqueline B. Stanfield, Where Has Love Gone? Reciprocity, Redistribution, and the Nurturance Gap, *Journal of Socio-Economics*, March-April 1997.

[2] Robert D. Putnam, *Bowling Alone: The Collapse and Revival of American Community*. New York: Simon & Schuster, 2000, 288.

[3] Ibid. "Where people are trusting and trustworthy, and where they are subject to repeated interactions with fellow citizens," notes Putnam, "everyday business and social transactions are less costly."

[4] The Giant of Poverty Still Stalks Britain, but It Can Be Slain, *Independent* (London), October 24, 1998.

[5] Putnam, *Bowling Alone: The Collapse and Revival of American Community*, 402-403.

[6] Ibid., 112-113.

[7] Ibid., 100.

[8] For the study, researchers conducted three thousand random telephone interviews and quizzed over twenty-six thousand people in forty selected communities across the nation. Rex W. Huppke, Study: Civic Involvement Linked to Happiness, Associated Press Newswires, March 1, 2001.

[9] Stanfield and Stanfield, Where Has Love Gone? Reciprocity, Redistribution, and the Nurturance Gap.

[10] Ibid.

[11] Putnam, *Bowling Alone: The Collapse and Revival of American Community*, 42.

[12] Ibid., 46.

[13] Labor Quotes. Accessed from www.igc.apc.org/laborquotes/index.html.

[14] Richard Todd, Who Me, Rich? *Worth*, September 1997.

[15] Ibid.

[16] James Fallows, The Invisible Poor, *New York Times*, March 19, 2000.

[17] John Miller, Economy Sets Records for Longevity and Inequality, *Dollars & Sense*, May/June, 2000.

[18] Gary Burtless, Public Spending on the Poor: Historical Trends and Economic Limits, 56, in *Confronting Poverty: Prescriptions for Change*, Sheldon Danziger, Gary Sandefur, and Daniel Weinberg, eds. New York: Harvard University Press, 1994.

[19] James Lardner, Many Causes, One Obstacle, updated version of a paper presented at a national conference on "Income Inequality, Socioeconomic Status, and Health: Exploring the Relationships." Accessed from Inequality.org.

[20] Ibid.

[21] Definition includes AFDC, SSI/Aid to aged and disabled, EITC and all other cash aid. Burtless, Public Spending on the Poor: Historical Trends and Economic Limits, 58.

[22] Paul Taylor, When Safety Nets Leave the Needy in Free Fall, *Washington Post*, September 9, 1991.

[23] The Welfare Scam, *Nation*, December 12, 1994.

[24] Gary Burtless, Growing American Inequality in Income, *Brookings Review*, December 22, 1998.

[25] Sandra Bunch, A Future With Hope, *Bread for the World*, March 2002.

[26] Marian Wright Edelman, President, Children's Defense Fund, Making Ends Meet: Challenges Facing Working Families in America: Statement for the Record before the House Budget Committee, United States House of Representatives, August 1, 2001.

[27] In 1999, for instance, the Economic Policy Institute found that 47 percent of former recipients who had found full-time work had suffered at least one "critical hardship," a phrase used to cover having to go without food, shelter, or necessary medical care. Heather Boushey, Former Welfare Families Need More Help, EPI Briefing Paper, March 2002. Another study, released by Bread for the World in 2002, reported that less than half of all former recipients had been able to find work. Those with jobs earned, on average, $6.75 an hour, not enough to take a family with kids out of poverty. Bunch, A Future With Hope.

[28] Edelman, Making Ends Meet: Challenges Facing Working Families in America.

[29] Eugene Kane, The False Promises of Welfare Reform, *Milwaukee Journal Sentinel*, April 18, 2001.

[30] Eugene Kane, W-2 Program Itself Needs a Better Work Ethic, *Milwaukee Journal Sentinel*, April 21, 2001.

[31] "Under the 1996 law," notes Kim Phillips-Fein, "college education cannot be substituted for any part of the primary work requirement." The number of City University of New York students drawing welfare support dropped from twenty-eight thousand before welfare reform to five thousand by

spring 2002. "Today," adds Phillips-Fein, "although nearly 60 percent of welfare recipients in the city lack a high school diploma or a GED, only 2 percent are enrolled in ESL or GED programs, and fewer than 4 percent are engaged in full-time education or training." Kim Phillips-Fein, The Education of Jessica Rivera, *Nation*, November 25, 2002.

32 Dennis Duggan, Back in the Game, *Newsday*, December 12, 1998.

33 Even more amazing, this judicial finding did not end the city's "callous" policies. Another judge, acting on an appeal, had denied benefits to a nineteen-year-old still in high school only shortly before the Keough case hit the headlines. Liz Willen, Workfare Confusion Remains, *Newsday*, December 12, 1998.

34 Edelman, Making Ends Meet: Challenges Facing Working Families in America.

35 "Immigrants pay taxes to support services to others," Catholic Charities told Congress in 2001, "they too should have access to assistance when they fall ill." Immigrant status, Catholic Charities added, never lessens "a growing child's need for adequate nutrition." Sharon Daly, Catholic Charities, Making Ends Meet: Challenges Facing Working Families in America: Statement for the Record before the House Budget Committee, United States House of Representatives, August 1, 2001.

36 Elizabeth Becker, Millions Eligible for Food Stamps Aren't Applying, *New York Times*, February 26, 2001.

37 Edelman, Making Ends Meet: Challenges Facing Working Families in America.

38 Dita Smith, What on Earth? Poverty Amid Plenty, *Washington Post*, January 15, 2000.

39 Ibid.

40 James K. Galbraith, Inequality and Civil Society, University of Texas Inequality Project, 1999. Accessed from http://utip.gov.utexas.edu/web/JGarchive/1999/civilsoc.htm.

41 Ibid.

42 Ibid.

43 Ibid.

44 Ibid.

45 Denmark Votes, for Now, Against Adopting the Euro, *Washington Post*, September 29, 2000.

46 Kim Viborg Andersen, Carsten Greve, and Jacob Torfing, Reorganizing the Danish Welfare State: 1982-93; A Decade of Conservative Rule, *Scandinavian Studies*, Spring 1996.

47 Ibid.

48 Ibid.

49 Denmark Votes, for Now, Against Adopting the Euro, *Washington Post*, September 29, 2000.

50 Kim Viborg Andersen, Carsten Greve, and Jacob Torfing, Reorganizing the Danish Welfare State: 1982-93; a Decade of Conservative Rule, *Scandinavian Studies*, Spring 1996.

51 Galbraith, Inequality and Civil Society.

52 John McDermott, And the Poor Get Poorer, *Nation*, November 14, 1994.

53 Albert B. Crenshaw, IRS Is Writing More Checks to Working Poor, *Washington Post*, April 16, 2001.

54 Burtless, Growing American Inequality in Income.

55 Ibid.

56 The figures here are for fiscal 1999. Crenshaw, IRS Is Writing More Checks to Working Poor.

57 Cait Murphy, Are the Rich Cleaning Up? *Fortune*, September 4, 2000.

58 The Business Week report was based on work by economists Timothy Smeeding, Lee Rainwater, and Gary Burtless that showed that other nations were spending at least 7 to 10 percent of their gross domestic product "on social transfers to nonaged people." The U.S. outlays totaled only about 4 percent. Gene Koretz, ...And the Home of the Poor: Disturbing Stats on U.S. Poverty, *Business Week*, March 12, 2001.

59 *Effective Federal Tax Rates*, 1979-1997, The Congress of the United States, Congressional Budget Office, September 2001, 5.

60 Poor people, noted one director of a tax clinic for low-wage families, American University law professor Janet Spragens, were "just overwhelmed by the complexity." Crenshaw, IRS Is Writing More Checks to Working Poor.

61 The best analysis of the CBO data can be found at Robert Greenstein and Isaac Shapiro, The New, Definitive CBO Data on Income and Tax Trends, Center on Budget and Policy Priorities, September 23, 2003. Accessed from www.cbpp.org/9-23-03tax.pdf.

62 "In effect," notes Gary Burtless of the Brookings Institution, "public subsidies to the working poor and cuts in welfare benefits to the nonworking poor have helped keep employers' costs low and thus helped fuel employers' creation of poorly paid jobs." Burtless, Growing American Inequality in Income.

63 In 2001 dollars. The Economic Policy Institute maintains a good source for minimum wage data. See www.epinet.org/content.cfm/issueguides_minwage_minwage.

64 Charlie. We Hardly Knew Ye, *Nation*, February

17, 1997.

65 Unless otherwise noted, this discussion on inequality and hunger draws from Janet Poppendieck, Want Amid Plenty: From Hunger to Inequality, *Monthly Review*, July-August 1998.

66 Economist Robert Frank, notes *Business Week*, "cites surveys to show that people consistently say they're happier when they have more" of "such public expenditures as cleaner air and water and roads that are less crowded." Aaron Bernstein, A $50,000 Car and You're Still Not Happy, *Business Week*, February 15, 1999.

67 Michelle Quinn, Green With Envy, Despite the Good Times, *San Jose Mercury-News*, August 16, 1999.

68 Ibid.

69 Michael Lewis, All Money, All the Time, *New York Times*, June 7, 1998.

70 Lee Hill Kavanaugh, Riches Do Not Reap Happiness, New Millionaires Learn, *Houston Chronicle*, June 4, 2000.

71 Ibid.

72 Deborah Schoeneman, Putting on the Gated Ritz, *New York Observer*, April 10, 2000.

73 Ibid.

74 Quoted in David Morris, The Dark Side of Privatization, Institute for Local Self-Reliance, January 30, 1996. Accessed from http://www.ilsr.org/columns/1996/30Jan96.html.

75 Quoted from Sam Peltzman, The Growth of Government, *Journal of Law and Economics*, October 1980, in Carolyn Webber and Aaron Wildavsky, *A History of Taxation and Expenditure in the Western World*, New York: Simon and Schuster, 1986, 587.

76 Ibid.

77 The figures come from the California Budget Project. Harold Meyerson, A Paler Shade of Gray, *American Prospect*, February 28, 2000.

78 Ibid.

79 Invest in America, open letter to President Clinton, Speaker of the House Hastert, Senate Majority Leader Lott, House Minority Leader Gephardt, Senate Minority Leader Daschle, Sent February 8, 2000. Accessed from www.ombwatch.org/ia/IIAsign-on.html.

80 Robert H. Frank, *Luxury Fever: Money and Happiness in an Era of Excess*. Princeton: Princeton University Press, 1999, 57.

81 William K. Tabb, Privatization and Urban Issues: A Global Perspective, *Monthly Review*, February 2001.

82 Ibid.

83 Youssel M. Ibrahim, Welfare's Cozy Coat Eases Norwegian Cold, *New York Times*, December 13, 1996.

84 Ibid.

85 Ibid.

86 Physicians' Group Decries 2.4 Million Rise in Number of Americans Lacking Health Insurance, news release, Physicians for a National Health Program, September 30, 2003.

87 Scott Wilson, Venezuelan President Warns of Coup Attempt, *Washington Post*, December 6, 2002.

88 Ibrahim, Welfare's Cozy Coat Eases Norwegian Cold.

89 This research, by century's end, was taken as a given. "Academic achievements of blacks of middle- and upper-middle-income families lag behind those of comparable whites," *US News & World Report* editor-in-chief Mortimer Zuckerman noted in a somber editorial. "On some tests, black children from middle-class and wealthier families have done no better than white kids living in poverty." Mortimer B. Zuckerman, Making the Grade, *US. News & World Report*, May 7, 2001.

90 Pam Belluck, Reason Is Sought for Lag by Blacks in School Effort: Sensitive Issue Debated, *New York Times*, July 4, 1999.

91 One University of California study of SAT scores in California "found that blacks from the highest-income families scored lower than whites or Asians from the poorest families." Students from black families earning $100,000 or more averaged 498 on their math scores, "1 point less than whites from families earning less than $10,000." Annie Nakao, How Race Colors Learning, *San Francisco Examiner*, June 7, 1998.

92 Ibid. The quote is from reporter Annie Nakao's description.

93 Ibid. Another third or so of whites, polls showed, "believe blacks are less intelligent for other reasons."

94 Brent Staples, How the Racial Literacy Gap First Opened, *New York Times*, July 3, 1999.

95 Ibid. Black students often "find themselves confronted by teachers and counselors who cannot conceive of them as academically inclined and discourage them from taking advanced courses."

96 "African-American parents," one black mother told the *New York Times*, "are going to have to step up to the plate and do more." Belluck, Reason Is Sought for Lag by Blacks in School Effort: Sensitive Issue Debated.

97 Black students "who excel are routinely attacked by their friends for 'selling out' and becoming

'white.'" Staples, How the Racial Literacy Gap First Opened.

[98] Nakao, How Race Colors Learning.

[99] Ibid.

[100] "Overall, blacks do worse than whites," Conley noted, "but when the differences in economic endowments that African Americans and whites bring to the educational system are taken into consideration, blacks do better than whites in some measures and the same as whites in others." Dalton Conley, *Being Black, Living in the Red*, University of California Press: Berkeley, 1999, 80.

[101] Alain Jehlen, The Wealth Factor, *NEA Today*, September 2000.

[102] Melvin L. Oliver and Thomas M. Shapiro, *Black Wealth/White Wealth: A New Perspective on Racial Inequality* (New York: Routledge, 1995).

[103] White households owned twelve times more median net worth than black households. Melvin L. Oliver and Thomas M. Shapiro, Race, Wealth and Inequality in America, *Poverty & Race*, November/December 1995.

[104] The quote is from Dalton Conley, who built his work on the foundation laid by Oliver and Shapiro. Conley, *Being Black, Living in the Red*, 5.

[105] Dalton Conley, How to Widen the Black-white Wealth Gap, *Salon*, April 5, 2001.

[106] Ibid. Also see Net Worth of Oldest U.S. Households Rises Sharply, but Younger Americans Don't Fare as Well, and Blacks Still Lag Far Behind, New U-M Study Says, The University of Michigan News Service, February 8, 2000. Accessed from www.umich.edu/~newsinfo/Releases/2000/Feb00/r020800a.html.

[107] Conley, How to Widen the Black-white Wealth Gap.

[108] Loren Schweninger, Black Property Owners in the South, 1790-1915. Urbana and Chicago: University of Illinois Press, 1990, 147.

[109] Ibid., 146.

[110] Ibid., 160.

[111] Ibid., 161. "Including the propertyless, blacks controlled an average of only $76 worth of wealth in 1870, compared to $2,034 for southern whites."

[112] Ibid., 163.

[113] Ibid., 233-235.

[114] Conley, *Being Black, Living in the Red*, 36-37.

[115] Ibid., 36.

[116] "Gates's wealth from securities, stocks and bonds was about $58 billion in 1998. Black wealth from stocks and bonds was calculated at about $11 billion." Courtland Milloy, Sharing the Wealth Is Not

Enough, *Washington Post*, September 19, 1999.

[117] Milloy, Sharing the Wealth Is Not Enough.

[118] Gary Burtless and Timothy Smeeding, America's Tide: Lifting the Yachts, Swamping the Rowboats, *Washington Post*, June 25, 1995.

[119] "To expect civilized behavior from individuals who obtain only hardship from their participation in society," noted historian James Huston near century's end, "appears moronic." James L. Huston, *Securing the Fruits of Labor: The American Concept of Wealth Distribution 1765-1900*. Baton Rouge: Louisiana State University Press, 1998, xxii.

[120] Michael Thomas, Abuse of Wealth Spells Trouble, *New York Observer*, November 13, 2000.

[121] The figures are from Justice Policy Institute analyst Jason Ziedenberg. William Raspberry, 2 Million and Counting, *Washington Post*, December 13, 1999.

[122] Michael Schwartz, Slave Labor Means Big Bucks for U.S. Corporations, *Daily Bruin*, January 31, 2001.

[123] Shifting Focus in L.A. Reflected in Mayoral Race, *Washington Post*, April 9, 2001.

[124] Schoeneman, Putting on the Gated Ritz.

[125] Ibid.

[126] In Arizona, an entire subdivision of neo-fortress homes went up, with the top models priced at $639,000. Roger Lewis, The Neo-Fortress Home: Can the Concept Be Defended? *Washington Post*, September 5, 1998.

[127] Robert Wade, Winners and Losers, *Economist*, April 28, 2001.

[128] David Saltonstall, How Tiny Tax on Stock Sales Could Coin Billions for City, *New York Daily News*, April 20, 2003.

[129] Six of the eight firehouses on the mayor's original shutdown list were set to be closed as of mid-May 2003. Michael Cooper, Mayor Spares 2 Threatened Firehouses After All, *New York Times*, May 20, 2003.

[130] Rene Sanchez, Gold Coast Tarnish: Affordable Housing Is a Parked Camper, *Washington Post*, December 23, 2000.

[131] Quoted in A Review of How Rich Is Too Rich?: Income and Wealth in America, by Economists Herbert Inhaber and Sidney Carroll, *Journal of Post Keynesian Economics*, Fall 1993.

AN IMPERILED NATURAL WORLD

[1] Rachel Carson, *Silent Spring*. Greenwich, Conn.: Fawcett Publications, Inc., 1962, 16.

2 Earth Summit World Leaders See Darkening Future for Planet, Agence France Presse, September 2, 2002.

3 Paul Hawken, *The Ecology of Commerce: A Declaration of Sustainability.* New York: HarperBusiness, 1993, xiii.

4 Ibid., 12. "First, business takes too much from the environment and does so in a harmful way; second, the products it makes require excessive amounts of energy, toxins, and pollutants; and finally, the method of manufacture and the very products themselves produce extraordinary waste."

5 Ibid., 167.

6 Wayne Ellwood, Searching for Sustainability, *New Internationalist,* November 2000.

7 Michael Renne, Overview: The Triple Health Challenge, Vital Signs 2001: The Trends That Are Shaping Our Future, The Worldwatch Institute, May 24, 2001.

8 Earth Summit World Leaders See Darkening Future for Planet, Agence France Presse.

9 Tom Athanasiou, *Divided Planet: The Ecology of Rich and Poor,* Boston: Little, Brown and Company, 1996, 53.

10 These figures are based on per capita Gross Domestic Product. Marc Lee, The Global Divide, Inequality in the World Economy, Canadian Centre for Policy Alternatives, April 18, 2002.

11 Nancy Birdsall, Life Is Unfair: Inequality in the World, *Foreign Policy,* July 1998.

12 Filthy Rich!, *New Internationalist,* September 1994. The world's wealthiest fifth, United Nations researchers would report in 1992, took in 83 percent of the world's income in 1991, the poorest fifth less than 2 percent. Ched Myers, God Speed the Year of Jubilee! The Biblical Vision of Sabbath Economics, *Sojourners Online,* May-June 1998.

13 These nations totaled one-and-a-half billion people. Filthy Rich!, *New Internationalist.*

14 Colum Lynch, U.N. Cites Disparities in Wealth, *Washington Post,* July 13, 1999.

15 Leon Lazaoff, Falling Down, *In These Times,* February 6, 1995.

16 Nancy Birdsall is a senior associate at the Carnegie Endowment for International Peace, Charles Griffin a senior economist at the World Bank. Nancy Birdsall and Charles Griffin, Latin America Must Invest in People to Save Reform, *Houston Chronicle,* January 20, 1999.

17 James K. Boyce, Equity and the Environment: Social Justice Today as a Prerequisite for Sustainability in the Future, *Alternatives,* January-February 1995.

18 Ibid.

19 Athanasiou, *Divided Planet: The Ecology of Rich and Poor,* 54.

20 Ibid., 54.

21 Alan Durning, *How Much Is Enough? The Consumer Society and the Future of the Earth.* New York: W. W. Norton & Company, 1992. 23.

22 Boyce, Equity and the Environment: Social Justice Today as a Prerequisite for Sustainability in the Future.

23 Lance Morrow, The Shoes of Imelda Marcos, *Time,* March 31, 1986.

24 Does Inequality Matter? *Economist,* June 14, 2001.

25 Robert Weissman, Staggering Inequality, *Multinational Monitor,* September 1998.

26 Human Development Report 1996: United States Has Steady Economic Growth, July 17, 1996.

27 Gar Smith, memo to author: quoted from *Our Planet,* bimonthly magazine of the UN Environment Program, 1995.

28 David Holtzman, Ecological Footprints, *Dollars & Sense,* July/August 1999.

29 Holger Jensen, Reports Show Democracy, Prosperity Link Not Firm, *Denver Rocky Mountain News,* December 10, 1998.

30 Josef Hebert, Fuel-efficient Vehicles Outnumbered by Gas Guzzlers, *Star-Tribune* (Minneapolis), October 17, 2000.

31 Bill McKibben, Now or Never, *In These Times,* April 30, 2001.

32 Geneva Overholser, Green Light for Gas-Guzzlers, *Washington Post,* August 7, 2001, quoting data from the April 2001 issue of *Harpers.*

33 Gas prices, adjusted for inflation, actually dropped between 1981 and the end of the century. If they hadn't, motorists would have been paying $2.55 a gallon for gas in 2000. That wouldn't have bothered affluent Americans much at all. Gas prices would have had to have hit $3.66 a gallon in 2000 "to have the same effect" on the pocketbooks of families in the top 20 percent as they had in 1981. For families in the top 5 percent, gas prices would have had to hit $4.47 a gallon. Keith Bradsher, In This Gilded Age, Gilded Model T's, *New York Times,* November 12, 2000.

34 Gas Guzzler Loophole, Friends of the Earth, Friends of the Earth 1025 Vermont Avenue, N.W., Suite 300, Washington, DC 20005. Accessed from www.foe.org/res/pubs/pdf/GG-Report.pdf.

35 An Economist's Case for a 'Maximum Personal

Income,' *Too Much*, June 1997.

36 Sustainable Development, Part 5, *Rachel's Environment & Health Weekly*, December 10, 1998.

37 Ibid.

38 Morgenthau's comments came in 1944 at the Bretton Woods meetings that defined the post-war economic world. David C. Korten, The Limits of the Earth, *Nation*, July 15, 1996. That same spirit of limitless abundance still reigns over conventional economic policy making. A half century after Bretton Woods, U.S. Deputy Treasury Secretary Lawrence Summers reassured Americans that the gospel of more could never backfire. "There are no … limits to carrying capacity of the Earth," Summers noted, "that are likely to bind at any time in the foreseeable future." Quoted in Bill McKibben, A Special Moment in History, *Atlantic Monthly*, May 1998.

39 Sustainable Development: Part 1, Peter Montague, editor, *Rachel's Environment & Health Weekly*, November 12, 1998.

40 Ibid.

41 "This consumption consists of fuels in the form of gas, coal, and oil; quarried materials such as stone, gravel, and sand; industrial minerals such as phosphate, cement, and gypsum; industrial metals such as copper and aluminum forestry products such as sawed timber, pulpwood for paper, and firewood; and agricultural products such as milk, meat, eggs, grain, hay, and produce." Paul Hawken, Waste, *Mother Jones*, March/April 1997.

42 David C. Korten, The Limits of the Earth, *Nation*, July 15, 1996.

43 Bill McKibben, A Special Moment in History, *Atlantic Monthly*, May 1998.

44 Ibid.

45 Sustainable Development: Part 1, *Rachel's Environment & Health Weekly*.

46 John Bellamy Foster, The Heresy of Ecological Economics, *In These Times*, January 20, 1997.

47 Ibid.

48 Herman E. Daly, Sustainable Growth: An Impossibility Theorem, 267, in Herman E. Daly and Kenneth N. Townsend, *Valuing the Earth: Economics, Ecology, Ethics*. Cambridge: MIT Press, 1993.

49 Ibid.

50 Ibid.

51 Sustainable Development, Part 6, *Rachel's Environment & Health Weekly*, December 17, 1998.

52 Jonathan Rowe, The Growth Consensus Unravels, *Dollars & Sense*, July/August 1999.

53 Ibid.

54 Mark Burch, *Stepping Lightly*. Gabriola Island, B.C.: New Society Publishers, 2000, 85.

55 Ibid., 85.

56 Ibid., 120.

57 Romesh Diwan, Relational Wealth and the Quality of Life, *Journal of Socio-Economics*, July 2000.

58 Burch, *Stepping Lightly*, 162.

59 Durning, *How Much Is Enough? The Consumer Society and the Future of the Earth*, 108-109.

60 This notion appears originally in the 1973 book, *Small Is Beautiful*, by the English economist E.F. Schumacher. Burch, *Stepping Lightly*, 27.

61 Diwan, Relational Wealth and the Quality of Life. This discussion of alternate measures relies largely on this paper.

62 To maintain a sustainable world, observes Herman Daly, the basic needs of the future must "always take precedence over the extravagant luxury of the present." Herman E. Daly, *Beyond Growth: The Economics of Sustainable Development*. Boston: Beacon Press, 1996, 36.

63 Rich Hayes, Commencement Address on Consumption, Inequality, and the Environment, University of California at Berkeley Energy and Resources Group, May 21, 1994. Accessed from www.newdream.org/discuss/hayes.html.

64 Athanasiou, *Divided Planet: The Ecology of Rich and Poor*, 105.

65 Akash Kapur, Poor but Prosperous, *Atlantic Monthly*, September 1998.

66 Ibid.

67 Quoted in Ibid.

68 Life expectancy in Kerala: 72 years. Morocco: 62. Infant mortality in Kerala: 16 per 1,000 births. In Colombia: 37 per 1,000 births. W. Alexander, *Exceptional Kerala: Efficient Use of Resources and Life Quality in a Non-Affluent Society*, 1994.

69 In India's Kerala, a Little Equality Works Wonders, *Too Much*, Spring 1996.

70 Richard W. Franke and Barbara H. Chasin, Kerala State: A Social Justice Model, *Multinational Monitor*, July-August 1995.

71 Ibid.

72 The Keralan rate: 93 percent. India overall: 31 percent. Alexander, *Exceptional Kerala: Efficient Use of Resources and Life Quality in a Non-Affluent Society*.

73 Uli Schmetzer, 'The Other India' Harvests Fruits of a Communist Rule, *Chicago Tribune*, January 16, 2000.

74 Akash Kapur, Poor but Prosperous.

75 Bill McKibben, The End of Growth, *Mother Jones*, November/December 1999.

76 Richard W. Franke and Barbara H. Chasin, The Politics of the Kerala Model, *Multinational Monitor*, July-August 1995.

77 Ibid.

78 The quote comes from Will Alexander, an emeritus professor at California Polytechnic State University who spent time studying the wonder of Kerala in the 1990s. In India's Kerala, A Little Equality Works Wonders, *Too Much*, Spring 1996.

79 Kapur, Poor but Prosperous.

80 McKibben, The End of Growth.

81 Schmetzer, 'The Other India' Harvests Fruits of a Communist Rule.

82 Kapur, Poor but Prosperous.

83 Richard W. Franke and Barbara H. Chasin, Kerala State: A Social Justice Model, *Multinational Monitor*, July-August 1995.

84 Ibid.

85 A most useful bibliography about Kerala's development model, compiled by a Keralan, appears at http://216.205.90.100/mallu/keralamodel.htm.

86 Franke and Chasin, Kerala State: A Social Justice Model.

87 Ibid.

88 Adam Hochschild, The Brick Master of Kerala, *Mother Jones*, July/August 2000.

89 Simon Romero, Cashing in on Security Worries, *New York Times*, July 24, 1999.

90 Athanasiou, *Divided Planet: The Ecology of Rich and Poor*, 54.

91 The data are from the Fernand Braudel Institute of World Economics, a research center in Sao Paolo. Romero, Cashing in on Security Worries.

92 Ibid.

93 Brazil grew at a 1.3 percent annual rate in the 1980s, a 2.2 percent rate in the 1990s. In 1991, 52.5 percent of families had no access to sewage treatment. In 1998, 48.5 percent had no access. Adriana Arai, Brazil Rich-Poor Income Gap Hasn't Narrowed in Decade, Dow Jones News Service, April 4, 2001.

94 Richard W. Franke and Barbara H. Chasin, Kerala: A Valid Alternative to the New World Order. *Bulletin for Concerned Asian Scholars*. Accessed from http://csf.colorado.edu/bcas/kerala/ker-rfbc.htm.

95 "The present world political and economic structure," note Richard Franke and Barbara Chasin, "favors models based on private accumulation and

growing inequality over Kerala's emphasis on public services and egalitarian ideals." Richard W. Franke and Barbara H. Chasin, Is the Kerala Model Sustainable? Lessons from the Past. Proposed for presentation at the International Conference on Kerala's Development Experience: National and Global Dimensions. December 9-11, 1996. New Delhi. Accessed from www.chss.montclair.edu/anthro/decconf.html.

96 Franke and Chasin, Kerala State: A Social Justice Model.

97 Franke and Chasin, Is the Kerala Model Sustainable? Lessons from the Past.

98 Sustainable Development: Part 4, *Rachel's Environment & Health Weekly*, December 3. 1998.

99 Ibid.

100 Ibid.

101 Schmetzer, 'The Other India' Harvests Fruits of a Communist Rule.

102 Raymond W. Baker and Jennifer Nordin, A 150-to-1 Ratio Is Far Too Lopsided for Comfort, *International Herald Tribune*, February 5, 1999.

A DYING DEMOCRACY

1 Martha McNeil Hamilton and Frank Swoboda, Labor Seeks Aid for Workers Laid Off in Wake of Attacks, *Washington Post*, September 25, 2001.

2 Ibid.

3 Statement by AFL-CIO President John J. Sweeney on Congressional Decision on Worker Relief Package – Airline Bailout Bill, September 21, 2001.

4 Greg Goldin, Bailout: Another Free Lunch for Fat Cats, *Los Angeles Times*, November 4, 2001.

5 Hamilton and Swoboda, Labor Seeks Aid for Workers Laid Off in Wake of Attacks.

6 That was no oversight, as members of Congress would make clear one year later after reports began circulating about the millions of dollars in "deferred compensation" pouring into airline executive pockets. Lawmakers, acknowledged House Transportation Committee Chairman Don Young, a Republican from Alaska, did not mean to limit airline executive pay when they enacted the bailout. "That was not our intention," he announced. Juliet Eilperin and Greg Schneider, House GOP Refines Air Security Bill, *Washington Post*, November 1, 2001.

7 Insurance Handout, *Ouch! A Regular Bulletin on How Money in Politics Hurts You*. Public Campaign, December 18, 2001.

8 Dean Baker, Restructuring the Tax Code, *Economic Reporting Review*, November 25, 2002.

9 This landmark legislation, the industry promised,

would bring "new choices and lower rates for America's consumers." By the end of 1999, cable TV rates had leaped 21 percent, four times the inflation rate. In the summer of 1998, the Senate killed a proposal that would have simply asked the FCC to study rising cable rates. Micah L. Sifry, How Money in Politics Hurts You, *Dollars & Sense*, July/August 2000.

[10] Banks would remain free to average $1.27 in fees on transactions that cost them about 25 cents to conduct. Ellen S. Miller and Micah L. Sifry, The Coin-Operated Congress, Public Campaign, (Posted June 30, 1999) Accessed from www.publicampaign.org/articles/em6_30_99.html.

[11] Major Challenges Ahead for Injury Prevention After Repeal of Ergonomics Rule, *Occupational Health Management*, May 2001.

[12] Robert S. McIntyre, Director, Citizens for Tax Justice, Testimony before the Committee on the Budget, United States House of Representatives concerning "Waste, Fraud, [and] Abuse in Federal Mandatory Programs," June 18, 2003. Accessed from www.ctj.org/html/corp0603.htm.

[13] The figures come from the federal Office of Management and Budget and the Congressional Joint Committee of Taxation for 1994. Eric Pianin, GOP Barely Draws Blood from Business, *Washington Post*, August 20, 1995.

[14] Ibid.

[15] Ibid.

[16] Of those sampled, 40 percent agreed strongly, 27 percent somewhat. *Business Week*/Harris Poll: America, Land of the Shaken, *Business Week*, March 11, 1996.

[17] Steven Greenhouse, Update on Capitalism: What Do You Mean 'Us,' Boss? *New York Times*, September 1, 2002.

[18] Robert L. Borosage, Budgetmania Misses the Main Event, *Los Angeles Times*, October 10, 1999.

[19] Statement of the American Society of Civil Engineers on the Federal Role in Meeting Infrastructure Needs Before the Subcommittee on Transportation and Infrastructure Committee on Environment and Public Works, U.S. Senate, July 23, 2001.

[20] In 2000, federal "investment in physical capital, education and training, and research and development" stood at 1.6 percent of GDP, down from 2.6 percent in 1980. John Miller, Economy Sets Records for Longevity and Inequality, *Dollars & Sense*, May/June 2000.

[21] "There's a growing sense," one dissenter, Oregon Democrat Peter DeFazio, would note, "that what Congress is doing might make sense for CEOs but that it doesn't make sense for the rest of us." John Nichols, Building a Progressive Caucus, *Nation*, July 5, 1999.

[22] Miller and Sifry, The Coin-Operated Congress.

[23] The sectoral totals: health care industry: $234,724,579, communications, technology: $217,163,009, finance, insurance: $204,257,351, energy, natural resources: $146,813,166, transportation: $137,588,149, retail, services: $98,953,739, manufacturing: $73,464,837, agriculture: $61,257,735, defense: $58,665,973, real estate, construction: $39,659,117. Organized labor, including public employee groups: $ 27,446,586. Paying to Make a Point, *Washington Post*, August 19, 2001.

[24] Americans making $1 million a year or more, after this hike, would pay 4.5 percent more of their incomes in taxes in 1993 than they did in 1992. Author's calculation on data in Therese M. Cruciano, Individual Income Tax Returns, Preliminary Data, 1993, *Statistics of Income Bulletin*, spring 1995, 10.

[25] By 1999, the number of IRS tax staff had been cut by 19 percent over 1990 levels — at the same time the volume of tax returns had increased 13 percent. David Cay Johnston, IRS Is Allowing More Delinquents to Avoid Tax Bills, *New York Times*, October 10, 1999.

[26] The IRS probed 1.36 percent of the tax returns filed by people earning less than $25,000 and just 1.15 percent of returns filed by those earning $100,000 or more. David Cay Johnston, I.R.S. More Likely to Audit the Poor and Not the Rich, *New York Times*, April 16, 2000.

[27] Ibid. This covers a period starting in 1988.

[28] The cut, once fully in effect in 2010, would give Americans earning over $200,000 three hundred times more in after-tax savings than Americans making less than $10,000. The one fifth of taxpayers making up to $10,000 a year will see an increase in after-tax income of 38 cents a week. Taxpayers who make over $200,000 a year will average $127 extra a week after taxes. David Cay Johnston, Tax Analysis Says the Rich Still Win, *New York Times*, July 14, 2002

[29] "In 1997, 9.6 percent of that group's income went to payroll taxes, compared with 5.2 percent going to income taxes." *Effective Federal Tax Rates*, 1979-1997, The Congress of the United States, Congressional Budget Office, September 2001, xvii.

[30] The Gulf Widens, Editorial, *Washington Post*, June 5, 2001.

[31] Under this latest Bush administration tax cut, households earning between $50,000 and $75,000 a year would see their after-tax income jump 1.2

percent. For millionaires, the *Washington Post* reported, the boost in after-tax income would be almost four times that. Jonathan Weisman, Congress Passes $350 Billion Tax Cut Bill, *Washington Post*, May 24, 2003.

[32] Editorial, Has Greed of the Rich Eaten Away Democracy in America? *National Catholic Reporter*, October 21, 1994.

[33] Michael Kazin, One Political Constant, *New York Times*, April 1, 2001.

[34] Mark Green, The Evil of Access, *Nation*, December 30, 2002.

[35] The study was conducted by the Center for Responsive Politics in Washington, D.C. Richard Morin, Playing the Odds, *Washington Post*, November 6, 1994.

[36] David Donnelly, Janice Fine, and Ellen S. Miller, Going Public, *Boston Review*. Accessed from www-polisci.mit.edu /bostonreview /br22.2/donnelly. html.

[37] Jill Abramson, Al Gore's Money Problem, *New York Times Magazine*, May 9, 1999.

[38] Robert L. Borosage and Ruy Teixeira, The Politics of Money, *Nation*, October 21, 1996.

[39] Jamin B. Raskin, Campaign Finance on Trial: Challenging the Wealth Primary, *Nation*, November 21, 1994.

[40] Ruth Marcus, Dollars Dictate Field's Early Exits, *Washington Post*, October 21, 1999.

[41] Ibid.

[42] Ibid.

[43] Ibid.

[44] The Journalist: Everyone Has Been Discredited, *Fast Company*, October 2002.

[45] The exact figures: percentage of U.S. adults giving over $200: 0.28 percent. Percentage giving over $1,000: 0.11 percent. Donor Demographics, opensecrets.org. Center for Responsive Politics, Media Advisory, December 11, 2002.

[46] Bob Herbert, The Donor Class, *New York Times*, July 19, 1998.

[47] Sifry, How Money in Politics Hurts You.

[48] Juliet Eilperin, Capitol Hill Fundraising Cycle Has No End, *Washington Post*, January 28, 2001.

[49] Roper Starch Worldwide surveyed a sample of five hundred people making at least $250,000 in income or holding at least $2.5 million in assets. Richard Todd, Who Me, Rich? *Worth*, September 1997.

[50] Jill Abramson, Gravy Train: Soft Money Goes Through the Roof, *New York Times*, July 8, 2001.

[51] Heineman's fascinating explanation originally appeared in the *Raleigh News & Observer*. Class Unconscious, *Racine Labor*, November 3, 1995. Actually, Heineman is not atypical of people in his comfortable income bracket. Notes *Worth*: "The WorthRoper Starch survey of the top 1 percent found that 57 percent of respondents didn't consider themselves "rich" (and only a quarter thought themselves "upper class"), even though they have a median annual income of $330,000." Richard Todd, Who Me, Rich? *Worth*, September 1997.

[52] Alexander Cockburn, Packwood Pepys, *Nation*, October 2, 1995.

[53] Packwood would actually make a comeback of sorts. He would become, by century's end, a behind-the-scenes lobbyist in the campaign to repeal the estate tax. The Estate Tax: Down but Not Out, *Too Much*, spring 2003.

[54] Borosage and Teixeira, The Politics of Money.

[55] Ibid. "By 53 to 38 percent, the public believes 'we need to make government regulations tougher in order to stop companies from moving jobs overseas, polluting here at home and treating their workers badly' rather than thinking that 'most government regulations go too far now, making it too difficult for companies to grow and create jobs, and costing consumers money.' Big contributors have the reverse view, endorsing the 'government regulations go too far' argument by 58 to 31 percent."

[56] Some 48 percent of large donors opposed lifting the cap, and 42 percent favored it. Celinda Lake and Robert L. Borosage, Money Talks, *Nation*, August 21, 2000.

[57] Kenneth Cooper and Kevin Merida, Many Hill Freshman Are Millionaires, Disclosures Indicate, *Washington Post*, June 15, 1995.

[58] Jonathan Salant, A Richer Congress, Associated Press, December 25, 2002.

[59] Ibid.

[60] Mike Allen, A Senate Hopeful Tests the Power of His Deep Pockets, *Washington Post*, May 6, 2000.

[61] Campaign Finance: Is Mark Warner a Piker? *George*, November 2002.

[62] Dean Murphy, What Costs $75 More Than Manhattan? *New York Times*, April 7, 2002.

[63] Campaign Finance: Is Mark Warner a Piker? *George*.

[64] Dan Balz, High Rolling in California, *Washington Post*, October 6, 1994.

[65] Campaign Spending in '93-94: More Than a Half-Billion Dollars, compiled by Jeannette Beliveau, *Washington Post*, January 23, 1995.

[66] Balz, High Rolling in California.

[67] Ibid.

[68] This discussion of Rossiter's campaign effort is based on his account in Caleb Rossiter, Think Globally, Run Locally, *Nation*, August 23, 1999.

[69] Caleb Rossiter, Think Globally, Run Locally, *Nation*, August 23, 1999.

[70] Robert Dreyfuss, Money 2000: The Election Will Break All Record$. And We'll Lose, *Nation*, October 18, 1999.

[71] Ibid.

[72] Amy Keller, Billion-Dollar Mark Broken Fundraising Hit New Peak in Last Cycle, Roll Call, May 17, 2001. Accessed from www.rollcall.com/pages/news/00/2001/05/news0517a.html.

[73] Mike Allen, A Senate Hopeful Tests the Power of His Deep Pockets, *Washington Post*, May 6, 2000.

[74] Molly Ivins, Tax Plan Would Be Funny if ... Well, No, It Wouldn't, *Sacramento Bee*, March 1, 2001.

[75] Rove made $1.5 million unloading stocks after the media reported he had met with drug industry lobbyists while personally holding $250,000 worth of drug company stock. Bush Aide at Drug Meeting Held Shares, *New York Times*, July 21, 2001.

[76] Charles R. Babcock and Barbara J. Saffir, In Wealth, Clinton Team Doesn't Look Like America, *Washington Post*, July 24, 1997.

[77] High Court Justices Disclose Their Assets, *USA Today*, June 28, 2000.

[78] The State of the Estate Tax, *Washington Post*, June 6, 2002.

[79] Ibid.

[80] William Greider, Unfinished Business: Clinton's Lost Presidency, *Nation*, February 14, 2000.

[81] Ibid.

[82] "A system that relies on private campaign financing tends to produce candidates who reflect the views and values of those who have the money," note political analysts Bob Borosage and Ruy Teixeira. "And in an economy of growing inequality, in which a few make out like bandits while the many struggle to survive, the views of those who pay for the parties are likely to be increasingly divorced from those expected to vote for them." Borosage and Teixeira, The Politics of Money.

[83] Holly Sklar and Chuck Collins, Forbes 400 World Series, *Nation*, October 20, 1997.

[84] Borosage and Teixeira, The Politics of Money.

[85] William Greider, Middle-Class Funk, *Rolling Stone*, November 2, 1995.

[86] Mark Shields, Has Gephardt Got It? *Washington Post*, September 1, 1997.

[87] Kip Sullivan, Greedlock in Congress, *Nation*, February 26, 2001.

[88] Ibid.

[89] Donnelly, Fine, and Miller, Going Public.

[90] Ruth Marcus and Sarah Cohen, The Loophole Lesson in 'Soft Money,' *Washington Post*, March 18, 2001.

[91] John Lewis, Don't Let Money Rule, *Washington Post*, July 10, 2001.

[92] Eben Moglen, Campaign Money Morass, *Nation*, July 3, 2000, and Sifry, How Money in Politics Hurts You. By midway through 2000, the oil and gas, mining, electric utility, and auto industries — the businesses with the most to lose from stiff environmental regulations — had made $48.2 million in political contributions, fifty-nine times more than environmental groups.

[93] Helen Dewar, Campaign Reform Wins Final Approval, *Washington Post*, March 21, 2002.

[94] Ibid.

[95] John Moyers, Reform for Fannie Lou: Measuring Reform, TomPaine.com, March 27, 2001. Accessed from www.tompaine.com/features/2001/03/27/index.html.

[96] An Open Letter to the Reform Community, U.S. PIRG, March 20, 2002.

[97] This argument had been made by the leading Senate opponent of McCain-Feingold, Kentucky's Mitch McConnell. Trying to ban "soft money," McConnell had argued, was "like putting a rock on jello." "You can squeeze it down," he quipped, "but it just goes in different directions." Thomas Edsall and Juliet Eilperin, Debate Heated on Campaign Finance, *Washington Post*, February 12, 2002.

[98] "First authorized in 1975, the 527 committees became popular after a series of IRS and court rulings in the mid-1990s enabled politicians and donors to the committees to escape virtually all regulation." Thomas B. Edsall, Lawmakers Embracing 'Stealth PAC' Advantage, *Washington Post*, April 11, 2002.

[99] Ten to twenty years down the road, McCain added, another group of senators and congressmen will "have to clean it up again." For the Record, *Washington Post*, July 11, 2001, A18.

[100] The Progressive Interviews Sen. Feingold, *The Progressive*, May 2002.

[101] The extra funds are "capped at twice the original amount provided to the candidate." Donnelly, Fine, and Miller, Going Public.

[102] The States Lead the Way, AAHH! An Occasional Bulletin on How *Clean* Money in Politics Can Help You, Public Campaign, July 11, 2001

103 In Missouri and Oregon, citizens tried to enact Clean Money systems via ballot referendums. Special interest cash defeated both efforts. In Massachusetts, advocates did enact a Clean Money system via referendum. But state lawmakers stonewalled the system's implementation. Ellen S. Miller and Nick Penniman, The Road to Nowhere: Thirty Years of Campaign-finance Reform Yield Precious Little, *American Prospect*, August 12, 2002.

104 The 34th Annual *Phi Delta Kappa*/Gallup Poll of the Public's Attitudes Toward the Public Schools, *Phi Delta Kappan*, September 2002.

105 Linda Perlstein, Two Philanthropists to Expand Private School Grants in Cities, *Washington Post*, June 11, 1998.

106 *The Story Behind America's Voucher Movement*, Washington, D.C.: National Education Association, 2000, Appendix G.

107 Vouchers, National Education Association. Accessed from www.nea.org/vouchers.

108 *The Story Behind America's Voucher Movement*, National Education Association, 2.

109 Vouchers, National Education Association.

110 *The Story Behind America's Voucher Movement*, National Education Association, 3.

111 Vouchers, National Education Association.

112 Linda Perlstein, Two Philanthropists to Exapnd Private School Grants in Cities, *Washington Post*, June 11, 1998.

113 Supreme Court Decision on School Vouchers Harmful to Future of Public School Education, National Association for the Advancement of Colored People news release, June 27, 2002. Accessed from www.naacp.org/news/releases/edu-vouchers062702.shtml.

114 George Pillsbury, Laws for Sale, *Dollars & Sense*, July/August 2000.

115 Vouchers, National Education Association.

116 Edward Walsh, Financier's Ads to Urge Public School Alternatives, *Washington Post*, July 11, 2000.

117 The estimate, for the year 2010, comes from Dean Baker, co-director of the Center for Economic and Policy Research in Washington, D.C. Ken Silverstein, Finance, Insurance & Real Estate: With 71 Brokers and Investment Managers on the Mother Jones 400, Privatizing Social Security Looks Like Money in the Bank, *Mother Jones*, March 5, 2001.

118 "Cato and other conservative think tanks have invested millions of dollars in a sophisticated campaign to privatize Social Security." David Callahan, $1 Billion for Conservative Ideas, *Nation*, April 26, 1999.

119 Paul Krugman, Connect the Dots, *New York Times*, April 2, 2002.

120 A point made by Robert Reich. Robert Kuttner, Rampant Bull: Social Security and the Market, *American Prospect*, July-August 1998.

121 Editorial, End Legalized Bribery, *Multinational Monitor*, March 2000.

122 A National Committee for Responsive Philanthropy report estimated that "spending by the top twenty conservative think tanks will likely top $1 billion in the nineties." Callahan, $1 Billion for Conservative Ideas.

123 Goliath Getting Bigger, Moving Ideas, The Policy Action Network, May 6, 2002.

124 Hannah Clark, Read All About It (But Not in the Mainstream Media), *Dollars and Sense*, September-October 2001.

125 Alicia C. Shepard, Moguls' Millions, *American Journalism Review*, July/August 2001.

126 John Stauber of PR Watch estimates that about 40 percent of what Americans "read, see or hear in the mainstream media is a result of government or corporate public relations campaigns." Adds Stauber: "As magazines and newspapers and TV networks and stations downsize journalists, they are not reducing news coverage, they are just using more public relations and passing it off as news." Joel Bleifuss, PR Watch Has Its Eyes Open, *In These Times*, October 17, 2003.

127 Alexander Stille, Emperor of the Air, *Nation*, November 29, 1999.

128 World's Richest People, 2000 list, Forbes.com.

129 Stille, Emperor of the Air.

130 The victory represented a comeback for Berlusconi. A brief earlier stint as prime minister had ended in scandal.

131 David Broder, Proud of Their Fund-Raising Prowess, *Washington Post*, March 12, 1997.

132 During his New Jersey Senate run, Jon Corzine became a "most dependably generous neighbor for an entire state." Noted one reporter: "Covering almost every imaginable base, his campaign has bought dinner tickets from the Dominican Empowerment PAC ($2,000), the United Negro College Fund ($2,550) and the Hispanic American Association for Political Awareness ($1,000), as well as ads from the New Jersey Jewish News ($8,819), the Newark Mayor's Commission on the Status of Women ($2,500), the Montclair St. Patrick's Day Parade ($1,000) and the Newark St. Patrick's Day Parade ($250)." Mike Allen, A Senate Hopeful Tests the Power of His Deep Pockets, *Washington Post*, May 6, 2000.

[133] Harold J. Laski, *A Grammar of Politics*. London: George Allen & Unwin Ltd., 1930, second edition, 157.

[134] Dreyfuss, Money 2000: The Election Will Break All Record$. And We'll Lose.

[135] Lester Thurow, Why Their World Might Crumble, *New York Times*, November 19, 1995.

[136] All references to Vilas in the following discussion come from Carlos M. Vilas, Inequality and the Dismantling of Citizenship in Latin America, *NACLA Report on the Americas*, July-August 1997.

[137] Barbara J Fraser, Rich World, Poor World, *National Catholic Reporter*, January 14, 2000.

[138] Brian Livingston, Should Microsoft's Millionaires Face Social Obligations? *Infoworld*, May 12, 1997.

[139] Ibid.

[140] Christopher Byron, Ted Turner's Million-Dollar Boondoggle, *New York Observer*, October 6, 1997.

[141] Maureen Dowd, Ted's Excellent Idea, *New York Times*, August 22, 1996.

[142] Mark Dowie, *American Foundations: An Investigative History*. Cambridge, Mass.: MIT Press, 2001, 191.

[143] Robert Kuttner, Philanthropy and Movements, *American Prospect*, July 15, 2002.

[144] Ibid.

[145] Randy Cohen, Uncharitable View, *New York Times*, June 20, 1999.

[146] John D. Donahue, *Hazardous Crosscurrents: Confronting Inequality in an Era of Devolution*. New York: The Century Foundation Press, 1999, 18.

[147] Gary Burtless, Growing American Inequality in Income, *Brookings Review*, December 22, 1998.

[148] Scott Martelle, Down-to-Wire Race Fails to Excite Voters, *Los Angeles Times*, October 12, 2000.

[149] Adam Clymer, The Body Politic, *New York Times*, January 2, 2000.

[150] Michale Moore's e-mail News Letter, July 19, 2000.

[151] Dan Balz, Sky Fell Again on Turnout, *Washington Post*, September 2, 2001.

[152] Thomas E. Patterson, Where Have All the Voters Gone? History News Network, November 18, 2002. Accessed from http://hnn.us/articles/1104.html.

[153] Ibid.

[154] Clymer, The Body Politic.

[155] Holly Sklar, States Have Growing Income Gaps and Shrinking Voter Turnout, *San Diego Union-Tribune*, January 20, 2000.

[156] Ibid.

[157] Ibid. Income gaps may also help explain why voting rates in European nations more equal than the United States tower above voting rates in the United States. In Europe, only about a 5 percent difference separates voting rates between people at the bottom of the economic ladder and people at the top. In the United States, affluent people vote at about twice the rate of people at the bottom. The Vanishing Voter: Why Does This Describe Half of the U.S. Electorate? *Democracy*, October 2002. TomPaine.com. Accessed from http://stream.realimpact.net/rihurl.ram?file=realimpact/tompaine/patterson20021017.rm.

[158] Paul Krugman, The Spiral of Inequality, *Mother Jones*, November/December 1996.

[159] Ibid.

[160] James K. Boyce, Equity and the Environment: Social Justice Today as a Prerequisite for Sustainability in the Future, *Alternatives*, January-February 1995.

[161] A. K. Sen, "What Did You Learn in the World Today?" paper presented at the Conference on Visions of Society: Perspectives from the Social Sciences (University of Pennsylvania, October 19, 1990). Quoted in James K. Boyce, Equity and the Environment: Social Justice Today as a Prerequisite for Sustainability in the Future, *Alternatives*, January-February 1995.

A PRICE TOO HIGH

[1] From Jeffrey Garten, *The Mind of the CEO* (Perseus Press, 2001). Quoted in Conventionally: The Mind of the CEO: Cliches, Stock Responses and Vapid Generalisations from Some of the World's Top CEOs, *Economist*, March 17, 2001.

HISTORIC STRUGGLES

[1] Randolph Paul, *Taxation in the United States*. Boston: Little, Brown and Company, 1954, 301.

[2] Frank Kluckhohn, $25,000 Income Limit, Ceilings on Prices, Stable Wages, Taxes, Asked by President, *New York Times*, April 28, 1942.

[3] Paul, *Taxation in the United States*, 301.

[4] Kenneth S. Davis, *FDR, the War President, 1940-1943: A History*. New York: Random House, 2000, 463.

[5] The *New York Times*, after the release of the President's proposal, excerpted editorial opinion at nine different newspapers. Not one of the papers openly blasted the President's $25,000 cap. The *Raleigh News and Observer* captured the general tone: "Nobody — not even the President — will relish some of the things that must be done, but

every American who loves country above ease will enlist." Press Comment on President's Plan, *New York Times*, April 28, 1942.

[6] The tax savings for the top 1 percent came to $218.38 billion, for the bottom 80 percent, $152.32 billion. Citizens for Tax Justice, January 8, 2003. Accessed from www.ctj.org/stim03.pdf.

[7] James L. Huston, *Securing the Fruits of Labor: The American Concept of Wealth Distribution 1765-1900*. Baton Rouge: Louisiana State University Press, 1998, 6. "An important economic corollary of republicanism established primarily by Englishman James Harrington (1611-1677) during the Puritan Commonwealth was widely acknowledged by American revolutionaries: to endure, a republic had to possess an equal or nearly equal distribution of landed wealth among its citizens."

[8] Ibid., 21.

[9] Ibid., 20.

[10] Ibid., 13. As much if not more than "no taxation without representation."

[11] Ibid., 47

[12] Ibid., 204.

[13] Ibid., 73.

[14] Sean Wilentz, America's Lost Egalitarian Tradition, *Daedalus*, Winter 2002.

[15] Ibid. "Inequality, Hamilton declared in 1788, 'would exist as long as liberty existed, and ... would unavoidably result from that very liberty itself.'"

[16] Ibid.

[17] In 1785, critics noted, the Pennsylvania legislature had revoked the charter of the Bank of North America. That institution, its opponents charged, had been dominated by "an upper-class clique" dedicated to "giving loans mostly to well-connected merchants." Kevin Phillips, *Wealth and Democracy: A Political History of the American Rich*. New York: Broadway Books, 2002, 16.

[18] Ibid., 18.

[19] Wilentz, America's Lost Egalitarian Tradition.

[20] Huston, *Securing the Fruits of Labor*, 193-194.

[21] Ibid., 332-333.

[22] Wilentz, America's Lost Egalitarian Tradition.

[23] Ibid. "By expanding the concept of labor to include all gainfully employed persons," notes historian Sean Wilentz, the interests opposing Jackson "at once blurred class distinctions, upheld the labor theory of value, and presented themselves as the true friends of the toiling masses."

[24] Huston, *Securing the Fruits of Labor*, 319.

[25] In 1860, just 7,500 Americans held fortunes larger than $111,000. Sixty percent of these fortunes could be found in the South. Phillips, *Wealth and Democracy*, 22.

[26] Huston, *Securing the Fruits of Labor*, 316.

[27] Ibid., xvi.

[28] Ibid., 185.

[29] Ibid., 189.

[30] Ibid., 57.

[31] Ibid., 200-201.

[32] Ibid., 217.

[33] Ibid., 260.

[34] Ibid., xvii.

[35] Ibid., 260.

[36] The original sources: Edward Pessen, The Egalitarian Myth and the American Social Reality: Wealth, Mobility and Equality in the Era of the Common Man, *American Historical Review*, October 1971, and Robert Gallman, Trends in the Size Distribution of Wealth in the Nineteenth Century, in *Six Papers on the Size Distribution of Wealth and Income*, ed. Lee Soltow. New York: Columbia University Press, 1969. Quoted from Benjamin Schwarz, Reflections on Inequality: "The Promise of American Life," *World Policy Journal*, Winter 1995.

[37] Huston, *Securing the Fruits of Labor*, xv.

[38] Ibid., 111. "From furniture making to coal mining to shoe and boot manufacturing, the nation's economy teemed with small companies with few employees," historian James Huston notes. "English industrialism was born big whereas American industrialization was born little."

[39] Ibid., 283. Explained one reformer, Unitarian minister Theodore Parker, "a man's hands will give him sustenance, not affluence."

[40] Ibid., 134.

[41] Ibid., 140.

[42] Ibid., 79.

[43] Wilentz, America's lost egalitarian tradition.

[44] Ibid.

[45] John F. Witte, *The Politics and Development of the Federal Income Tax*. Madison: The University of Wisconsin Press, 1985, 68.

[46] Sidney Ratner, *American Taxation: Its History as a Social Force in Democracy*. New York: W.W. Norton & Co., Inc., 1942, 67.

[47] Ibid., 73-74.

[48] Paul, *Taxation in the United States*, 10.

[49] Ratner, *American Taxation*, 85.

[50] Ibid., 97-98.

[51] Carolyn Webber and Aaron Wildavsky, *A History of Taxation and Expenditure in the Western World.* New York: Simon and Schuster, 1986, 419.

[52] Ratner, *American Taxation*, 112-13.

[53] Ibid., 124-25.

[54] Paul, *Taxation in the United States*, 27.

[55] Ibid., 143.

[56] Steve Fraser, The Gilded Age Unravels, *Los Angeles Times*, April 1, 2001.

[57] Phillips, *Wealth and Democracy*, 26.

[58] Ibid., 31.

[59] Ibid., 32-36.

[60] Ibid., 39-40.

[61] Ibid., 33-34.

[62] Ibid., 41.

[63] Ibid., 33-34.

[64] Huston, *Securing the Fruits of Labor*, 348-349.

[65] Phillips, *Wealth and Democracy*, 41.

[66] Ben B. Seligman, *The Potentates: Business and Businessmen in American History.* New York, The Dial Press, 1971, 211.

[67] Peter Grier, It's Hip to Be Greedy, *Financial Post*, February 12, 2000.

[68] Michael Lewis, The Rich: How They're Different . . . Than They Used to Be, *New York Times*, November 19, 1995.

[69] *The Prosperity Paradox: The Economic Wisdom of Henry George: Rediscovered*, Compiled by Dr. Mark Hassed, Canterbury, Australia: Chatsworth Village, 2000, 52.

[70] Phillips, *Wealth and Democracy*, 332.

[71] William Graham Sumner, *What Social Classes Owe to Each Other.* Caldwell, Idaho: The Caxton Printers, Ltd., 1961 (original edition 1883), 47.

[72] Ibid., 39.

[73] Phillips, *Wealth and Democracy*, 42.

[74] Sumner, *What Social Classes Owe to Each Other.* 50.

[75] Andrew Carnegie, *The Gospel of Wealth and other Timely Essays*, edited by Edward C. Kirkland. Cambridge: The Belknap Press of Harvard University Press, 1962, xvi.

[76] Ibid.

[77] Phillips, *Wealth and Democracy*, 49.

[78] Huston, *Securing the Fruits of Labor*, 351.

[79] Carnegie, *The Gospel of Wealth and Other Timely Essays*, 21.

[80] Huston, *Securing the Fruits of Labor*, 145.

[81] Ibid., 372.

[82] Ibid., 355.

[83] Paul, *Taxation in the United States*, 30.

[84] Ratner, *American Taxation*, 151.

[85] Ibid., 153.

[86] John D. Hicks, *The Populist Revolt.* University of Nebraska Press, 1961 (original edition 1931), 434.

[87] Ibid., 435.

[88] Norman Pollak, editor, *The Populist Mind.* Indianapolis and New York: The Bobbs-Merrill Company, Inc., 1967, 172.

[89] Pollak, *The Populist Mind*, 174.

[90] Steven R. Weisman, *The Great Tax Wars.* New York: Simon & Schuster, 2002, 124.

[91] Ibid., 138.

[92] Ratner, *American Taxation*, 186.

[93] Witte, *The Politics and Development*, 71.

[94] Paul, *Taxation in the United States*, 35.

[95] Ibid., 37.

[96] Weisman, *The Great Tax Wars*, 158.

[97] Ibid., 148.

[98] Ibid., 160.

[99] Ratner, *American Taxation*, 221.

[100] Michael Kazin, One Political Constant, *New York Times*, April 1, 2001.

[101] Ibid.

[102] Louis W. Koenig, *Bryan: A Political Biography of William Jennings Bryan.* New York: G. P. Putnam's Sons, 1971, 240.

[103] Kazin, One Political Constant.

[104] For the McKinley figure, Louis W. Koenig, *Bryan: A Political Biography of William Jennings Bryan.* New York: G. P. Putnam's Sons, 1971, 231. Bush spent $186 million in 2000. The Center for Responsive Politics, 2000 Presidential Race: Total Raised and Spent. Accessed from www.opensecrets.org/2000elect/index/AllCands.htm.

[105] Phillips, *Wealth and Democracy*, 314. Historian Michael Kazin puts the margin at half that. Kazin, One Political Constant.

[106] Kazin, One Political Constant.

[107] Koenig, *Bryan: A Political Biography of William Jennings Bryan*, 235.

[108] Ibid., 251.

[109] Ibid., 254.

[110] Phillips, *Wealth and Democracy*, 242.

[111] Ratner, *American Taxation*, 237.

[112] Paul, *Taxation in the United States*, 66.

113 Huston, *Securing the Fruits of Labor*, 348-349.

114 Weisman, *The Great Tax Wars*, 192.

115 Ibid., 196.

116 Paul, *Taxation in the United States*, 88-9.

117 Barry W. Johnson and Martha Britton Eller, Federal Taxation of Inheritance and Wealth Transfers, in *Inheritance and Wealth in America*, edited by Robert K. Miller, Jr. and Stephen J. McNamee, New York and London: Plenum Press, 1998, 71.

118 Paul, *Taxation in the United States*, 88-9.

119 Weisman, *The Great Tax Wars*, 206.

120 Phillips, *Wealth and Democracy*, 48.

121 Weisman, *The Great Tax Wars*, 250-251.

122 Ratner, *American Taxation*, 298.

123 Weisman, *The Great Tax Wars*, 240.

124 Ratner, *American Taxation*, 304.

125 The final tally would be forty-two states in favor, six against. Weisman, *The Great Tax Wars*, 264.

126 Phillips, *Wealth and Democracy*, 307-308.

127 Weisman, *The Great Tax Wars*, 279.

128 Witte, *The Politics and Development*, 76-78.

129 Weisman, *The Great Tax Wars*, 284.

130 Ibid., 241.

131 Ibid., 290. The richest 1.6 percent, the study showed, were claiming 19 percent of national income.

132 Ibid., 309. The top forty-four families had an aggregate income of $55 million, the Commission reported.

133 Ibid., 304.

134 Ibid., 305-308.

135 Johnson and Eller, Federal Taxation of Inheritance and Wealth Transfers, in *Inheritance and Wealth in America*, 73.

136 Sprague specifically proposed "that the government take 95 percent of all income earned in excess of the average income of two years before the war." Weisman, *The Great Tax Wars*, 322-323.

137 *Congressional Record*, May 16, 1917, 2403.

138 Jerold L. Waltman, *Political Origins of the U.S. Income Tax* (Jackson: University Press of Mississippi, 1985), 45.

139 *Congressional Record*, May 16, 1917, 2404.

140 Ibid.

141 Weisman, *The Great Tax Wars*, 327-328.

142 Paul, *Taxation in the United States*, 120.

143 Witte, *The Politics and Development*, 85.

144 Austan Goolsbee, Evidence on the High-Income Laffer Curve from Six Decades of Tax Reform, *Brookings Papers on Economic Activity*, Fall 1999.

145 Witte, *The Politics and Development*, 86.

146 By late 1919, the value of the 1913 dollar had dropped from 100 to 45. Robert K. Murray, *Red Scare: A Study in National Hysteria, 1919-1920*. New York: McGraw-Hill, 1964 (originally published 1955), 7.

147 Ibid., 9.

148 Ibid., 8.

149 Ibid., 171.

150 Ibid., 174.

151 Ibid., 91.

152 Ibid., 17.

153 Ibid., 17.

154 Phillips, *Wealth and Democracy*, 57.

155 Ibid., 60.

156 Seligman, *The Potentates: Business and Businessmen in American History*, 301.

157 Paul, *Taxation in the United States*, 165.

158 By the end of Mellon's tenure, in 1932, the top marginal income tax rate would actually drop to 24 percent. Weisman, *The Great Tax Wars*, 315.

159 Ibid., 315.

160 John Kenneth Galbraith, *The Great Crash*. Boston: Houghton Mifflin Company, 1954, 27.

161 Seligman, *The Potentates: Business and Businessmen in American History*, 306.

162 Calvin Coolidge, The Price of Freedom, 389. Accessed from the Calvin Coolidge Memorial Foundation at www.calvin-coolidge.org/index.html.

163 Irving Bernstein, *The Lean Years A History of the American Worker 1920-1933*. Baltimore: Penguin Books. 1966, 53.

164 Ibid., 54.

165 Ibid.

166 Ibid., 64-65.

167 Ibid., 63. "Where 75 persons had paid taxes in 1924 on annual incomes over a million dollars," notes Kevin Phillips, "283 did in 1927, and 519 for 1929." Phillips, *Wealth and Democracy*, 63.

168 Weisman, *The Great Tax Wars*, 2002, 291.

169 Alan Dawley, *Struggles for Justice: Social Responsibility and the Liberal State*. Cambridge, Mass.: The Belknap Press of Harvard University Press, 1991, 338.

170 Bernstein, *The Lean Years A History of the American Worker 1920-1933*, 63.

[171] Ibid., 47.

[172] Phillips, *Wealth and Democracy*, 61.

[173] Galbraith, *The Great Crash*, 57.

[174] Forrest Davis, *Huey Long: A Candid Biography*. New York: Dodge Publishing Company, 1935, 299.

[175] Huey P. Long, *Every Man a King: The Autobiography of Huey P. Long*. New Orleans: National Book Company, Inc., 316.

[176] Witte, *The Politics and Development*, 97.

[177] Carleton Beals, *The Story of Huey P. Long*. Westport: Greenwood Press, 1971 (originally published 1935), 26.

[178] Beals, *The Story of Huey P. Long*, 245.

[179] Long, *Every Man a King: The Autobiography of Huey P. Long*, 295.

[180] Beals, *The Story of Huey P. Long*, 244.

[181] Davis, *Huey Long: A Candid Biography*, 174.

[182] Long, *Every Man a King: The Autobiography of Huey P. Long*, 338-9.

[183] Huey P. Long, *Share Our Wealth: Every Man a King* (Washington, D.C.: 1935), 7.

[184] Beals, *The Story of Huey P. Long*, 292.

[185] David H. Bennett, *Demagogues in the Depression*. New Brunswick: Rutgers University Press, 1969, 127.

[186] Huey Pierce Long, *My First Days in the White House*. Harrisburg: The Telegraph Press, 1935, 143.

[187] Paul, *Taxation in the United States*, 153.

[188] Ronald A. Mulder, *The Insurgent Progressives in the United States Senate and the New Deal, 1933-1939*. New York: Garland Publishing, Inc., 1979, 67.

[189] Howard Zinn, editor, *New Deal Thought*. Indianapolis: Bobbs-Merrill, 1966, 394.

[190] Mulder, *The Insurgent Progressives in the United States Senate and the New Deal, 1933-1939*, 116-17.

[191] Arthur M. Schlesinger, Jr., *The Politics of Upheaval*. Boston: Houghton Mifflin Company, 1960, 325-326.

[192] Ibid., 325-326.

[193] Edwin Amenta, Kathleen Dunleavy, and Mary Bernstein, Huey Long's "Share Our Wealth" and the Second New Deal, *American Sociological Review*, October 1994.

[194] Phillips, *Wealth and Democracy*, 312.

[195] William H. Gates Sr. and Chuck Collins, *Wealth and Our Commonwealth: Why America Should Tax Accumulated Fortunes*. Boston: Beacon Press, 2002, 48.

[196] Roosevelt had largely gone after only the richest of the rich. The top 79 percent rate, in fact, would apply to just one taxpayer, John D. Rockefeller. Bruce Bartlett, The Futility of Raising Tax Rates, Policy Analysis series, Cato Institute, April 8, 1993.

[197] Mulder, *The Insurgent Progressives in the United States Senate and the New Deal, 1933-1939*, 122.

[198] Davis, *Huey Long: A Candid Biography*, 253.

[199] Frances Perkins, *The Roosevelt I Knew*. New York: The Viking Press, 1946, 328-329.

[200] Ratner, *American Taxation*, 495.

[201] Davis, *FDR, the War President, 1940-1943: A History*, 19.

[202] Paul, *Taxation in the United States*, 302.

[203] Kluckhohn, $25,000 Income Limit, Ceilings on Prices, Stable Wages, Taxes, Asked by President.

[204] In a 1936 article published by the American Academy of Political and Social Science, John T. Flynn had proposed new income tax rates that would not permit "the topmost tax-free incomes to exceed $10,000." Ratner, *American Taxation*, 562.

[205] Marriner S. Eccles, *Beckoning Frontiers: Public and Personal Recollections*. Edited by Sidney Hyman. New York: Alfred A. Knopf, 1951, 372.

[206] A point made by historian Lawrence Reed of the Mackinac Center. Amity Shlaes, The Boies Factor, *Jewish World Review*, December 4, 2000.

[207] First Reaction Is Divided on Income Limit, Associated Press, *Washington Post*, April 28, 1942.

[208] Ibid.

[209] Paul, *Taxation in the United States*, 313.

[210] Witte, *The Politics and Development*, 116-18.

[211] Ibid., 117.

[212] Paul, *Taxation in the United States*, 319.

[213] Witte, *The Politics and Development*, 175.

[214] Paul, *Taxation in the United States*, 318.

[215] Witte, *The Politics and Development*, 125.

[216] Ibid., 128.

[217] Wages "went up by 86 percent while the estimated cost of living rose only 29 percent because of price controls." Phillips, *Wealth and Democracy*, 75.

[218] Ibid., 75.

[219] Robert Shogan, For Religious Right, a Dilemma Over Strategy, *Los Angeles Times*, September 19, 1994.

[220] Goolsbee, Evidence on the High-Income Laffer Curve from Six Decades of Tax Reform.

[221] Phillips, *Wealth and Democracy*, 315.

[222] Ibid., 220.

[223] "With the depression still in mind, the tax code seemed to say that there was a social limit to

inequalities of reward." Richard Todd, Who Me, Rich? *Worth*, September 1997.

224 John Balzar, A First-Class CEO's Worth? *Los Angeles Times*, September 18, 2002.

225 Robert Collins, *More: The Politics of Economic Growth in Postwar America*. New York: Oxford University Press, 2000, 42.

226 Ibid.

227 Phillips, *Wealth and Democracy*, 220.

228 Collins, *More: The Politics of Economic Growth in Postwar America*, xi and 240.

229 Bruce Bartlett, The Futility of Raising Tax Rates, Policy Analysis series, Cato Institute, April 8, 1993.

230 The reduction to 65 percent, Kennedy administration officials assured Congress, had become absolutely necessary. The "present rates up to 91 percent not only check consumption but discourage investment." President's 1963 Tax Message. Hearings before the Committee on Ways and Means, Eighty-eighth Congress, First Session, on the Tax Recommendations of the President contained in his message transmitted to the Congress, January 24, 1963. February 6, 7, 8, 1963, 9.

231 Ibid., 544.

232 Ibid., 732. Some Republicans had pushed for a deeper cut, down to 42 percent.

233 Collins, *More: The Politics of Economic Growth in Postwar America*, 60.

234 "Beginning in 1970," economist James Galbraith notes, "the government abandoned the goal of full employment and instead turned its attention to a fight against inflation." That fight was fought with higher interest rates, and those rates sparked a recurring series of recessions that, Galbraith argues, would batter the American middle class. James K. Galbraith, *Created Unequal: The Crisis in American Pay*. A Twentieth Century Fund Book. New York: The Free Press, 1998, 9.

235 Weisman, *The Great Tax Wars*, 357.

236 Ibid., 357.

237 Collins, *More: The Politics of Economic Growth in Postwar America*, 177.

238 Wilentz, America's Lost Egalitarian Tradition.

239 Phillips, *Wealth and Democracy*, 333.

240 "The IRS took such a big chunk of my earnings," he would later recall, "that after a while I began asking myself whether it was worth it to keep on taking work." Collins, *More: The Politics of Economic Growth in Postwar America*, 195.

241 Ibid.

242 William Greider, Stockman Returneth, *Nation*, April 2, 2001.

243 The centerpiece: a 5 percent income tax cut the first year, followed by two years of consecutive 10 percent cuts, for a combined total reduction of about 23 percent. Ibid., 358.

244 *Effective Federal Tax Rates, 1979-1997*, The Congress of the United States, Congressional Budget Office, September 2001, 4.

245 Molly Ivins, Getting Between the Hogs and the Tax Cut Trough, *Sacramento Bee*, February 4, 2001.

246 These amendments also subjected some Social Security benefits, for the first time ever, to the income tax. *Effective Federal Tax Rates, 1979-1997*, 4.

247 David Obey, Who Is Downsizing the American Dream?, Speech to the Center for National Policy, March 11, 1996.

248 *Effective Federal Tax Rates, 1979-1997*, 4.

249 Phillips, *Wealth and Democracy*, 221-222.

250 The maximum tax rate on income from capital gains, 28 percent since 1986, would stick at that level. *Effective Federal Tax Rates*, 4.

251 This includes income taxes and payroll taxes. Phillips, *Wealth and Democracy*, 96.

252 Congressional Budget Office, *The Budget and Economic Outlook: Fiscal Years 2002–2011*, Washington, D.C., January 2001, 139.

253 The law established two new tax brackets, 36 percent for income at $115,000, 39 percent for income over $250,000. Well-to-Do Paid 16% More in Taxes in '93, Study Says, *New York Times*, April 17, 1995.

254 Louis Uchitelle, A Surplus Built on Bricks of Income Inequality, *New York Times*, February 28, 1999.

255 Spencer Rich, Number of Poor Americans Increases to 39.3 Million, *Washington Post*, October 7, 1994.

256 Ibid.

257 James MacGregor Burns and Georgia Sorenson, *Clinton-Gore Leadership and the Perils of Moderation*. Simon & Schuster, 1999, 338.

258 Wilentz, America's Lost Egalitarian Tradition.

259 Clay Chandler, GOP Leaders to Put Spending Cuts Before Tax Relief, *Washington Post*, December 19, 1994.

260 Their signature campaign document, the GOP *Contract with America*, called for a huge tax cut — on capital gains income. About half the $25 billion a year savings from this tax cut, analysts pointed out, would go to taxpayers making more than $200,000

a year. Robert S. McIntyre, Voodoo Economics: The Sequel, *Washington Post*, September 25, 1994, and Iris Lav, Cindy Mason, Pauline Abernathy, The Contract with America Proposal: Assessing the Long-Term Impact, Center for Budget and Policy Priorities, November 9, 1994.

261 Robert McIntyre, A Flat-Rate Consumption Tax? *CTJ Update*, July 1995.

262 Dave Skidmore, Tax Panel Head Vows Open-Mindedness, *Washington Post*, June 15, 1995.

263 Unleashing America's Potential. Report of the National Commission on Economic Growth and Tax Reform, January 1996. Accessed from www.empower.org/kempcommission/kempcommission_toc.htm.

264 According to IRS data. Isaac Shapiro, The Latest IRS Data on After-Tax Income Trends, Center for Budget and Policy Priorities, Revised February 26, 2001.

265 Max Sawicky, Who Wants to Stay a Millionaire? *Los Angeles Times*, July 3, 2000.

266 Gates and Collins, *Wealth and Our Commonwealth*, 2002.

267 Iris J. Lav, Estate Tax Cuts Would Benefit Wealthiest Americans, Center for Budget and Policy Priorities, April 21, 1997, and Max Sawicky, Who Wants to Stay a Millionaire? *Los Angeles Times*, July 3, 2000.

268 Gates and Collins, *Wealth and Our Commonwealth*, 68.

269 Glenn Kessler, Federal Tax Level Falls for Most, *Washington Post*, March 26, 2000.

270 Ibid.

271 Ibid. Bush proposed to cut the top marginal income tax rate from 39.6 to 33 percent.

272 Ibid. The analysis came from the Institute on Taxation and Economic Policy.

273 Andrew Greeley, U.S. Should Try to Reduce Income Disparity, *Chicago Sun-Times*, February 18, 2001.

274 Repealing the estate tax, exclaimed the world's second richest man, Warren Buffet, "would be a terrible mistake," as big a mistake as "choosing the 2020 Olympic team by picking the eldest sons of the gold-medal winners in the 2000 Olympics." David Cay Johnston, Dozens of the Wealthy Join to Fight Estate Tax Repeal, *New York Times*, February 14, 2001.

275 "A single parent with two children," noted reporter Glenn Kessler, "actually doesn't owe federal tax until her income reaches nearly $27,000." Kessler, Federal Tax Level Falls for Most.

276 The votes tallied for the Bush tax cut included twenty-eight House Democrats and twelve Democratic senators. Gar Alperovitz, Tax the Plutocrats! *Nation*, January 27, 2003.

277 David Cay Johnston, The Tax Bill Up Close: Some Facts, Some Tips, *New York Times*, June 3, 2001.

278 Albert B. Crenshaw, Tax Planning May Be Futile, *Washington Post*, June 3, 2001.

279 Albert B. Crenshaw, Alternative Minimum Tax Skews Effect of Cut, Democrats Say, *Washington Post*, June 9, 2001.

280 Glenn Kessler, Poorest Americans to Get No Tax Rebates, Study Shows, *Washington Post*, May 31, 2001.

281 Robert S. McIntyre, Bush's Most-Favored Taxpayers, *American Prospect*, July 2002.

282 Citizens for Tax Justice, Year-by-Year Analysis of the Bush Tax Cuts Shows Growing Tilt to the Very Rich, June 12, 2002. Accessed from www.ctj.org/html/gwb0602.htm..

283 A proposal advanced by Jan Schakowsky, an Illinois Democrat, in the First Things First Act. John Nichols, Political Twist, *Nation*, February 11, 2002.

284 Ibid.

285 Ibid.

286 Citizens for Tax Justice, January 8, 2003. Accessed from www.ctj.org/stim03.pdf.

287 Jonathan Weisman, In 2003, It's Reagan Revolution Redux, *Washington Post*, February 4, 2003.

288 Statement by the Honorable George Miller, Industrial Union Council, AFL-CIO. February 4, 2003. Accessed from http://edworkforce.house.gov/democrats/statement2403.html.

289 These numbers are from an analysis by the Urban Institute-Brookings Institution Tax Policy Center. Robert Greenstein, Richard Kogan, and Joel Friedman, Conference Agreement on Tax Cuts Makes Heavier Use of Gimmicks Than House or Senate Bills, Center for Budget and Policy Priorities, May 23, 2003.

290 Michael Gormley, SUNY to meet soon on tuition increase, *Newsday*, May 19, 2003.

291 Mark Weisbrot, Tax Cut Continues "Class Warfare." Distributed by Knight-Ridder/Tribune Information Services. Published May 26, 2003 by CommonDreams.org.

292 James K. Galbraith, Bush Tax Cuts Will Do a Number on Us, *Newsday*, May 24, 2003.

293 Statement by the Honorable George Miller, Industrial Union Council, AFL-CIO.

294 Huston, *Securing the Fruits of Labor*, 384-385.

CONTEMPORARY OPTIONS

1 Richard Harwood, Opportunity and the New Diversity, *Washington Post*, July 21, 1997.

2 Ibid.

3 Study: New Economy Arrests Worker Mobility, University of Wisconsin, news release, March 8, 2002.

4 Edmund L. Andrews, Fight Looms Over Who Bears the Tax Burden, *New York Times*, January 14, 2003.

5 Alexander Stille, Grounded by an Income Gap, *New York Times*, December 15, 2001.

6 Government Can Fight Inequality, *USA Today*, March 1, 2001.

7 One typical example of this perspective: "In the long run," noted an Urban Institute study co-authored by Edward Gramlich, the dean of University of Michigan School of Public Policy, in 1996, "the most important thing government at all levels can do to address inequality involves education." Edward M. Gramlich and Mark Long, Growing Income Inequality: Roots and Remedies, The Future of the Public Sector series, The Urban Institute, Washington, D.C., June 1996.

8 Robert Kuttner, Is Worker Training Really the Answer? *Business Week*, June 17, 1996.

9 S. M. Miller, Ill Fares the Land: The Wealth of the Nation, *Social Policy*, Spring 1999.

10 Michael Sherraden's book, *Assets and the Poor: A New American Welfare Policy* (M. E. Sharpe, 1992), played a key role in boosting the asset-building campaign. "Why not give the poor," he argues, "at least as much subsidy for saving as everyone else?" Michael Sherraden, Assets and the Poor: Implications for Individual Accounts and Social Security. Invited Testimony to the President's Commission on Social Security, Washington, D.C., October 18, 2001. IDAs, in 1998, would actually be written into law, through a pilot federal demonstration project. An excellent analysis of this effort: Jared Bernstein, Savings Incentives for the Poor, *American Prospect*, May 1, 2003.

11 A family that maxed out on annual "USA" credits and matching payments could end up with $250,000 after forty years, assuming a 5 percent annual return on its savings. Higher-income families, under the proposal, would also receive government credits and matches, only at somewhat less

generous levels. Robert B. Reich, To Lift All Boats, *Washington Post*, May 16, 1999.

12 Ibid.

13 Dalton Conley, How to Widen the Black-white Wealth Gap, *Salon*, April 5, 2001.

14 Reich, To Lift All Boats.

15 Rachel Sylvester, Blair's Big Idea to Improve Society Is the Baby Bond, *Daily Telegraph*, February 15, 2001.

16 Robert Kuttner, Sharing America's Wealth: The Policies and Politics of Building a Larger Middle Class, *American Prospect*, May 1, 2003.

17 Robert Kuttner, Time to Spread the Wealth Around, *Washington Post*, December 27, 1999.

18 For the cost of elementary and secondary education: National Center for Education Statistics. Table 30. Total expenditures of educational institutions, by level and control of institution: 1899-1900 to 2000-01. Accessed from nces.ed.gov//pubs2002/digest2001/tables/dt030.asp.

19 The program, the Abecedarian Project, was conducted by researchers at the University of North Carolina FPG Child Development Institute. Robert E. Slavin, Can Education Reduce Social Inequity? *Educational Leadership*, December 1997/January 1998.

20 Ibid.

21 High-quality Child Care Returns Far More Than Cost — New Report, News release, FPG Child Development Institute (FPG) at the University of North Carolina at Chapel Hill. November 20, 2002.

22 Head Start Reauthorization: Questions and Answers, Children's Defense Fund, February 2003.

23 An "effective education and training program," as the World Policy Institute's Benjamin Schwarz has noted, "would require in essence a substantial redistribution of wealth, in the form of taxation, from those who profit from the economy to those who do not." Benjamin Schwarz, American Inequality: Its History and Scary Future, *New York Times*, December 19, 1996.

24 Jack Beatty, Against Inequality: A Valiant Proposal to Give Every American Twenty-one-year-old the Same Chance to Prosper (or Fail), *Atlantic Monthly*, April 1999.

25 Blaming Workers for Low Wages, *Extra!* May/June 1999.

26 Ibid.

27 *The State of Working America 1996-97*. Washington, D.C.: Economic Policy Institute, 1996. Accessed from http://epn.org/epi/epswa-

in.html.

28 The 1973 hourly wage for employees with a college degree, $19.49. The 2001 rate, $22.58. Change in real hourly wage for all, by education, 1973-2001 (2001 dollars), Data Zone, Economic Policy Institute, Source: EPI authors' analysis from *The State of Working America: 2002-03*, table 2.17.

29 S. M. Miller and Charles Collins, Growing economic fairness, *Social Policy*, Summer 1996.

30 Ibid.

31 Theodore J. Marchese, U.S. Higher Education in the Postwar Era: Expansion and Growth, U.S. Society & Values, U.S.I.A. Electronic Journal, December 1997. Accessed from http://usinfo.state.gov/journals/itsv/1297/ijse/marchese.htm.

32 Barry Bluestone and Bennett Harrison, *Growing Prosperity*. Boston: Houghton Mifflin Company, 2000, 202.

33 Income Inequality: Issues and Policy Options, Remarks by Chairman Alan Greenspan at a symposium sponsored by the Federal Reserve Bank of Kansas City, Jackson Hole, Wyoming, August 28, 1998.

34 The top 5 percent of American income-earners saw their incomes rise 86 percent from 1947 to 1979. The bottom 20 percent saw a 116 percent increase. Chuck Collins and Felice Yeskel, *Economic Apartheid in America: A Primer of Economic Inequality & Insecurity*. New York: The New Press, 2000, 44.

35 Ched Myers, God Speed the Year of Jubilee! the Biblical Vision of Sabbath Economics, *Sojourners Online*, May-June 1998.

36 Ibid.

37 Ibid. Exodus 16:5, 26.

38 Ibid. Exodus 23:10-11.

39 Ibid. Isaiah 5:8.

40 Ibid. Leviticus 25:8, 10.

41 As the Mennonite theologian John Howard Yoder has noted in his classic, *The Politics of Jesus*. Ched Myers, Jesus' New Economy of Grace, *Sojourners Online*, July 1998.

42 Ibid.

43 Ibid. Mark 10:31.

44 Ibid.

45 Ibid.

46 Patricia Ann Lamoureux, Assessing the Value of the Tax Plan, *America*, April 16, 2001.

47 Economic Justice for All, Pastoral Letter on Catholic Social Teaching and the U.S. Economy, U. S. Catholic Bishops, 1986, 202.d. Accessed from www.osjspm.org/cst/eja.htm.

48 Sheldon S. Cohen, Taming the Tax Code, *Washington Post*, August 27, 1995.

49 Molly Ivins, There Are Tax Numbers, and There Is Tax Fairness, *Sacramento Bee*, March 6, 2001.

50 Pechman died in August 1989, four months before he was scheduled to deliver his address. Joseph A. Pechman, The Future of the Income Tax, *American Economic Review*, March 1990.

51 Charles Peters, Besieged and Beleaguered on $200,000 a Year, *Washington Monthly*, June 1990.

52 Bruce Bartlett, The Futility of Raising Tax Rates, Policy Analysis series, Cato Institute, April 8, 1993.

53 Michael Klepper and Robert Gunther, The *American Heritage* 40, *American Heritage*, October 1998.

54 Robert J. Samuelson, Gates Isn't God (or Even Henry Ford), *Washington Post*, August 27, 1997.

55 Robert D. Putnam, *Bowling Alone: The Collapse and Revival of American Community*. New York: Simon & Schuster, 2000, 217.

56 The 1926 Revenue Act gave oil and gas producers the ability to deduct 27 percent of their gross income as depreciation. Lillian Doris, editor, *The American Way in Taxation: Internal Revenue 1862-1963*. Englewood Cliffs, N. J.: Prentice-Hall, Inc., 1963.

57 Kevin Phillips, *Wealth and Democracy: A Political History of the American Rich*. New York: Broadway Books, 2002, 81.

58 Holly Sklar, If Only the Forbes 400 Billionaires Would Listen . . ., *Houston Chronicle*, October 4, 1999.

59 Roy C. Smith, *The Wealth Creators: The Rise of Today's Rich and Super-Rich*. New York: St. Martin's Press, 2001, 3-4.

60 Dan Seligman, Want to Get Rich? Don't Get Born in Afghanistan, *Forbes*, October 13, 1997.

61 David Broder, International Study Shows That Americans — Especially the Rich — Aren't Overtaxed, *Pioneer Press* (St. Paul), March 23, 1995.

62 John Balzar, A First-Class CEO's Worth? *Los Angeles Times*, September 18, 2002.

63 David Rosenbaum, Render Unto Caesar, Pay the Piper or Just Get That Check in the Mail, *New York Times*, April 16, 1995.

64 Sven Steinmo, The End of Redistribution? International Pressures and Domestic Tax Policy Choices, *Challenge*, November-December 1994.

65 Ibid.

66 Ibid.

67 Gar Alperovitz, Tax the Plutocrats! *Nation*, January 27, 2003.

[68] Edward N. Wolff, How the Pie Is Sliced: America's Growing Concentration of Wealth, *American Prospect*, Summer 1995. Wolff, in 2003, would advance a similar wealth tax with 0.8 percent top marginal rate on accumulations over $5 million. The first $250,000 of wealth would be exempt from any wealth tax under this Wolff proposal. The tax would raise an estimated $60 billion a year, with 80 percent of families paying no tax at all. The Wealth Divide: The Growing Gap in the United States Between the Rich and the Rest: An Interview with Edward Wolff, *Multinational Monitor*, May 2003.

[69] AFL-CIO Secretary-Treasurer Tom Donahue, Panel on Wealth at the "Facing the 21st Century" Symposium, National Planning Association, May 5, 1995.

[70] Robert Reich, My Dinner with Bill, *American Prospect*, May-June 1998.

[71] Phillips, *Wealth and Democracy*, 393.

[72] Robert H. Frank, Market Failures, *Boston Review*, Summer 1999.

[73] Ibid. "Phased in gradually," Robert Frank contends, "this tax would slowly reduce the share of national income devoted to consumption and increase the corresponding share devoted to investment."

[74] Robert H. Frank, *Luxury Fever: Money and Happiness in an Era of Excess*. Princeton: Princeton University Press, 1999, 219.

[75] Ibid., 215.

[76] Ibid., 205. The luxury tax Congress imposed on expensive cars in 1990, for instance, did not apply to sport-utility vehicles. The wealthy simply started buying luxuriously outfitted SUVs.

[77] Ibid., 206.

[78] Ibid., 213.

[79] Ibid., 216.

[80] Kenneth S. Davis, *FDR, The War President, 1940-1943: A History*. New York: Random House, 2000, 629.

[81] Frank, Market Failures.

[82] Frank, *Luxury Fever: Money and Happiness in an Era of Excess*, 224.

[83] Ibid., 225.

[84] Robert S. McIntyre, Another Bright Republican Idea. Taxing the Poor, *New Republic*, January 30, 1995.

[85] Unleashing America's Potential. Report of the National Commission on Economic Growth and Tax Reform, January 1996. Accessed from www.empower.org/kempcommission/kempcommission_toc.htm.

[86] Aaron Bernstein, A $50,000 Car and You're Still Not Happy, *Business Week*, February 15, 1999.

[87] The comment came in 1977. John A. Byrne, Executive Pay. Compensation at the Top Is Out of Control. Here's How to Reform It, *Business Week*, March 30, 1992.

A MAXIMUM WAGE?

[1] Remarks by William J. McDonough, September 11 Commemoration, Trinity Church, New York City, September 11, 2002. Accessed from www.ny.frb.org/pihome/news/speeches/2002/mcd020911.html.

[2] David Chanen, Twin Cities Groups Join National Fight Against Poverty, *Star-Tribune* (Minneapolis), April 30, 1996.

[3] Bill McClellan, Maximum Greed, Maximum Wage, *St. Louis Post-Dispatch*, January 13, 1997.

[4] Randolph Paul, *Taxation in the United States*, Boston: Little, Brown and Company, 1954, 30.

[5] Thomas A. Stewart, The Leading Edge: Can Even Heroes Get Paid Too Much? *Fortune*, June 8, 1998.

[6] Ibid.

[7] Ibid.

[8] Henry Phelps Brown, *Egalitarianism and the Generation of Inequality*. Oxford: Clarendon Press, 1988.

[9] Herbert Inhaber and Sidney Carroll, *How Rich Is Too Rich: Income and Wealth in America*. New York: Praeger, 1992.

[10] Ibid., 42.

[11] Brown, *Egalitarianism and the Generation of Inequality*, 465.

[12] Inhaber and Carroll, *How Rich Is Too Rich: Income and Wealth in America*, 43.

[13] Brown, *Egalitarianism and the Generation of Inequality*, 465.

[14] Inhaber and Carroll, *How Rich Is Too Rich: Income and Wealth in America*, 43-44.

[15] Wallace C. Peterson, How Rich Is Too Rich: Income and Wealth in America, by Herbert Inhaber and Sidney Carroll: A Review. *Journal of Post Keynesian Economics*, Fall 1993.

[16] Ibid.

[17] Ibid.

[18] Boris I. Bittker, comments on the Principal Paper by Norman B. Ture in Arleen A. Leibowitz, ed., *Wealth Redistribution and the Income Tax*. Lexington: Lexington Books, 1977, 67.

[19] Brown, *Egalitarianism and the Generation of Inequality*, 19.

[20] Cathy Madison, Don't Buy These Myths: Eleven Misconceptions That Make Us Slaves to Desire, *Utne Reader*, November-December, 1998.

[21] Paul Clolery and Jeff Jones, Intermediate Sanction Rules Finally in Place, *Nonprofit Times*, February 15, 2002.

[22] The IRS employs no exact criteria to determine what may be excessive, judging reasonableness instead by an analysis of the work and its context. Michael R. Yegidis, Court Allows Large Pay to Compensate for Low Salary During Fledgling Years, *Hudson Valley Business Journal*, September 16, 1996.

[23] Carrie Johnson and Christopher Stern, Judge Puts Limits on WorldCom: Freeze on Documents and Executives' Pay, *Washington Post*, June 29, 2002.

[24] Thomas Heath, On Deck, a Labor Showdown, *Washington Post*, July 19, 2001.

[25] This discussion draws from Robert J. Samuelson, Justice, Not Plunder, *Washington Post*, July 27, 2000.

[26] Alan Cottey, Asset and Income Limits for individuals are needed, if the trend to ever greater consumption is to be reversed, April 5, 2001. Accessed from www.uea.ac.uk/~c013/ail/ail.html.

[27] Most notably in his 1991 book, *The Rhetoric of Reform*. This discussion draws from an article along the same theme, Albert Hirschman, The Rhetoric of Reform *American Prospect*, June 23, 1993.

[28] Gene Epstein, What's Behind America's Trend Toward Widened Income Inequality? *Barron's*, October 26, 1998.

[29] The Social Value of Financial Services, An Address by Charles S. Sanford, Jr. Accessed from www.terry.uga.edu/dean/sanford_speech.html.

[30] Andrew Hacker, *Money: Who Has How Much and Why*. New York: Touchstone, 1997, 55-56.

[31] We are using here the preliminary 2003 income estimates used by the Institute on Taxation and Economic Policy Tax Model, as published January 7, 2003. See www.ctj.org/stim03.pdf. The IRS publishes official figures in annual incomes three years after the specific year in question.

[32] These calculations assume married couples as our base. Single taxpayers making the same incomes as married-couple households would, of course, pay a higher Ten Times tax on their incomes, since the 100 percent tax rate would apply to income over ten times the wage of a *single* minimum wage worker. Our figures here, as a result, understate the total revenue a Ten Times Rule would raise.

[33] The figure on 2003 tax rates actually paid come from calculations under the Urban-Brookings Tax Policy Center Microsimulation Model. Preliminary Results Based on Conference Report (H. Rept. 108-126), Table 5.2, Conference Agreement on the Jobs and Growth Tax Relief Reconciliation Act of 2003: Distribution of Income Tax Change by Percentiles, 2003, May 22, 2003. Accessed from www.taxpolicycenter.org/commentary/congress/table5_2.xls.

[34] For this calculation, we have assumed, conservatively, that 135 million tax returns will be filed for 2003. If the richest 1 percent of these average $1,082,000 million, as the Institute on Taxation and Economic Policy Tax Model estimates, 1.35 million households would average $889,184 in tax under the Ten Times Rule.

[35] This is an estimate calculated from OMB numbers released in 2002. OMB estimated that, in 2003, federal individual income tax revenues will make up 49.1 percent of the $2,048,060 in total federal receipts. Receipt Summary: receipts, outlays, and surplus or deficit in dollars and as a percent of GDP from 1940 to 2007, Source: Office of Management and Budget: Fiscal Year 2002 Budget (August 2002). And Percentage Composition Receipts by Source: 1934-2007. Source: Office of Management and Budget: Fiscal Year 2003 Budget (February 4, 2002). Tax Policy Center Tax Facts. Accessed from www.taxpolicycenter.org/TaxFacts/overview/main.cfm. This calculation actually overstates the likely final tally for 2003 income tax collections. It does not take into account 2003 tax law changes.

[36] The federal government, outside of Social Security and Medicare, spent $763.2 billion in 2003. Of that, $364 billion went for defense and another $10.5 billion for military construction, leaving $388.7 billion for all other discretionary federal spending. Fiscal 2003: The Final Cut, *Washington Post*, February 26, 2003.

[37] Gene Epstein, What's Behind America's Trend Toward Widened Income Inequality? *Barron's*, October 26, 1998.

[38] Ibid.

[39] George F. Will, Tax Break for the Yachting Class, *Washington Post*, October 28, 1999.

[40] Robert B. Reich, To Lift All Boats, *Washington Post*, May 16, 1999.

[41] David Campbell and Michael Parisi, Individual Income Tax Returns, 2000, *Statistics of Income Bulletin*, Fall 2002. Table 1. 2000, Individual Income Tax, All Returns: Sources of Income and Adjustments, by Size of Adjusted Gross Income.

[42] David Cay Johnston, Very Richest's Share of Income Grew Even Bigger, Data Show, *New York*

Times, June 26, 2003.

[43] These apologists do not prattle because the claim that higher marginal rates reduce the effort people put into their careers enjoys little research support. "An extensive literature in labor economics," notes Austan Goolsbee, "has shown that there is very little impact of changes in tax rates on labor supply for most people, particularly for prime-age working men." Austan Goolsbee, What Happens When You Tax the Rich? Evidence from Executive Compensation, *Journal of Political Economy*, April 2000.

[44] Ibid.

[45] Ibid.

[46] "But whither will these people fly?" retorted Rep. William Jennings Bryan from the House floor. "If their tastes are English — 'quite English, you know' — and they stop in London, they will find a tax of more than 2 per cent assessed upon incomes." Steven R. Weisman, *The Great Tax Wars*. New York: Simon & Schuster, 2002, 141.

[47] This discussion draws from Alex Callinicos, *Equality*. Cambridge, UK; Polity Press: Malden, Mass.: Blackwell Publishers, 2000, 128-129.

[48] International financiers, one team of Canadian and Russian researchers noted in the late 1990s, are always concocting masterful new schemes that enable "the avoidance of government regulation." The Problem of Capital Flight from Russia: A final report from a joint project on Capital Flight from Russia undertaken by the Institute of Economics, Moscow, and the Center for the Study of International Economic Relations, University of Western Ontario. Accessed from www.warwick.ac.uk/fac/soc/CSGR/current/capfligt.pdf.

[49] At forty hours a week, a full-time minimum wage worker labors 2,080 hours in a year. That means that a minimum wage couple would work 4,160 hours in a year. A $1 minimum wage increase for this couple would translate into a $4,160 annual wage increase. Ten times that would amount to a $41,600 increase in the "maximum wage."

[50] This is based on the American Institute for Economic Research cost-of-living calculator at www.aier.org/cgi-bin/colcalculator.cgi.

[51] If the minimum wage were $8.25, the maximum income would become $343,200. In 2003, a household needed to earn at least $374,000 to enter the lofty realm of the richest 1 percent of income-earners. A household making $374,000, in a Ten Times Rule America with a $8.25 minimum wage, would pay in tax 10 percent of its first $343,200, plus 100 percent of the rest of its income. This household's total tax would be $65,120. That tax, under the Ten Times Rule, would equal 17 percent of the family's total income. In 2003, after the Bush tax cut enacted that year, a family earning $374,000 would have paid about a fifth of its income in federal income tax. Source for 2003 income estimates: Institute on Taxation and Economic Policy Tax Model, January 7, 2003, Preliminary, Citizens for Tax Justice, January 7, 2003. Accessed from www.ctj.org/stim03.pdf. Source for tax rate estimate: Urban-Brookings Tax Policy Center Microsimulation Model. Preliminary Results Based on Conference Report (H. Rept. 108-126), Table 5.1, Conference Agreement on the Jobs and Growth Tax Relief Reconciliation Act of 2003: Distribution of Income Tax Change by Percentiles, 2003, May 22, 2003. Accessed from www.taxpolicycenter.org/commentary/congress/table5_1.xls.

[52] *Popular Culture & Industrialism 1865-1890*, Edited by Henry Nash Smith. Garden City, New York: Anchor Books, Doubleday & Company, Inc., 1967, 309.

LIFE IN A TEN TIMES RULE AMERICA

[1] In the past, high tax rates on high incomes have always had a "restraining effect" on corporate executive compensation. "In 1954," notes *Worth*'s Richard Todd, "a board could plausibly say to its president that compensation in excess of a million dollars was rather pointless, since the government was just going to take 91 percent. It seems reasonable to think that with similar rates in place we would now see fewer $8 million point guards and $12 million CEOs." Richard Todd, Who Me, Rich? *Worth*, September 1997.

[2] Sharon Walsh and Blaine Harden, Wall Street's Season to Be Jolly, *Washington Post*, January 31, 1998.

[3] Ibid. "They all have a number," explains Marlin Potash, a psychologist with a Wall Street practice. "They say to themselves, 'If I have this much money, I am free.' But the number keeps changing."

[4] Income averaging was repealed by the 1986 Tax Reform Act. It has since been reinstituted for farmers.

[5] Without the income averaging, the household would have paid, in its $500,000 income year, a tax of $230,000, a sum that would have equaled 10 percent of the household's first $300,000 of income that year and the difference between the $300,000 maximum and the household's $500,000 income.

[6] "As a rule," notes the best recent book on the

estate tax, "estates that have tax liability give two to three times as much to charity as estates without tax liability." William H. Gates Sr. and Chuck Collins, *Wealth and Our Commonwealth: Why America Should Tax Accumulated Fortunes.* Boston: Beacon Press, 2002, 127-128.

[7] Ibid.

[8] See the discussion in Martin Carnoy and Derek Shearer, *Economic Democracy.* Armonk, N.Y.: M. E. Sharpe Inc., 1980, 316.

[9] This splintering would also open options for ownership innovation: "As fortunes splintered, ownership of companies would fall into more hands, opening up the possibilities of economic democracy at the firm level, through municipal and other public agencies, and through cooperatives." Howie Hawkins, The Guaranteed Minimum Income and the Maximum Income, *Synthesis/Regeneration 9: A Magazine of Green Social Thought,* Winter 1996.

[10] From Introduction, Morton Mintz and Jerry S. Cohen, *America, Inc.: Who Owns and Operates the United States.* New York: Dell, 1971, 16.

[11] The Glass Ceiling: A Women Employed Factsheet. Women Employed Institute, 2002. Accessed from www.womenemployed.org/publications/glass_ceiling.pdf.

[12] The 1,500 include the *Fortune* 1000 Industrial and *Fortune* 500 companies. The Glass Ceiling for African, Hispanic (Latino), and Asian Americans. EthnicMajority.com. Accessed from www.ethnicmajority.com/glass_ceiling.htm.

[13] These figures are for 1998. David Cay Johnson, As Salary Grows, So Does Gender Gap, *New York Times,* May 12, 2002.

[14] Michael Peltz, Investing Outside the Box, *Worth,* April 2002.

[15] John Heilemann, *The Networker,* August 11, 1997, 33.

[16] This story is superbly told by Donna Fenn in her article, The Sweet Smell of Excess, *Inc. Magazine,* February 2003.

[17] Tony Snow, Cry About Fairness Is Taxing, *Baltimore Sun,* February 15, 2001.

[18] Ibid.

[19] And Linux for All, *American Benefactor,* Winter 1998.

[20] Scott Berinato, Linus on Linux: He's Just Having Some Fun, *PC Week,* February 1, 1999.

[21] Science for Science's Sake, Readers Report, *Business Week,* October 7, 1996.

[22] Geoffrey Colvin, What Money Makes You Do, *Fortune,* August 17, 1998.

[23] Ibid.

[24] Daniel Akst, On the Contrary Money Can Motivate. So Can Love of the Job, *New York Times,* April 1, 2001.

[25] Robert H. Frank, *Luxury Fever: Money and Happiness in an Era of Excess.* Princeton: Princeton University Press, 1999, 129.

[26] AARP surveyed 2,366 adult respondents, a much larger sample than the normal national poll. Vivian Marino, Diary: Millionaire? No, Thanks, *New York Times,* May 21, 2000.

[27] Frank, *Luxury Fever: Money and Happiness in an Era of Excess,* 182.

[28] Sustainable Development, Part 5, *Rachel's Environment & Health Weekly,* December 10, 1998.

[29] Herman E. Daly, *Beyond Growth: The Economics of Sustainable Development.* Boston: Beacon Press: Boston, 1996, 203.

[30] Ibid., 36.

[31] Alan Durning, *How Much Is Enough? The Consumer Society and the Future of the Earth.* New York: W. W. Norton & Company, 1992, 150.

A STRATEGY FOR CHANGE

[1] Sven Steinmo, The End of Redistribution? International Pressures and Domestic Tax Policy Choices, *Challenge,* November-December 1994.

[2] Hans Christian Johansen, *The Danish Economy in the Twentieth Century.* New York: St. Martin's Press, 1987, 160.

[3] Todd Gitlin, Unum Versus Pluribus, *Nation,* May 6, 1996.

[4] George H. Gallup, *The Gallup Poll: Public Opinion 1935-1971. Volume One, 1935-1948.* New York: Random House, 1972, 363.

[5] Gitlin, Unum Versus Pluribus.

[6] A decade earlier, only one in four Americans felt that way. Anne B. Fisher, A Brewing Revolt Against the Rich, *Fortune,* December 17, 1990.

[7] This figure had jumped up from 55 percent on the same question in 1987. Susan Mitchell, *American Attitudes.* Ithaca, N.Y.: New Strategist Publications, Inc., 1998, 57.

[8] Survey by Cable News Network, *USA Today.* Conducted by Gallup Organization, January 10-January 12, 2003 and based on telephone interviews with a national adult sample of 1,002. [USGALLUP.200303.Q35] Data provided by the Roper Center for Public Opinion Research, University of Connecticut.

[9] Ibid., Q38. The "too high" group: 25 percent.

"About right": 34 percent.

[10] The numbers: 29 percent strongly agree, 17 percent somewhat agree, 22 percent somewhat disagree, 29 percent strongly disagree. Survey by Henry J. Kaiser Family Foundation, *Washington Post*, Harvard University. Conducted by *Washington Post*, October 12-October 19, 2000. [USWASHP.00ELECN.R42B]. Data provided by the Roper Center for Public Opinion Research, University of Connecticut.

[11] The numbers: 44 percent indicated that having this information would be very important, 30 percent somewhat important, 15 percent not too important, 9 percent not at all important. Survey by Institute for Policy Studies, The *Nation* Magazine. Conducted by Program on International Policy Attitudes, University of Maryland, September 21-September 25, 2000. [USUMARY.00NATIPS.R04] Data provided by the Roper Center for Public Opinion Research, University of Connecticut.

[12] Cynthia Williams, Promoting Corporate Social Transparency, Citizen Works news conference, July 5, 2002.

[13] The AFL-CIO's new Center for Working Capital, in one landmark move, even began publishing a "Key Votes Survey" to help pension funds evaluate how investment managers were voting their shareholder proxies. New AFL-CIO Proxy Voting Guidelines: A Trustee Resource, *Working Capital*, published by AFL-CIO Center for Working Capital, Fall 1998.

[14] Chain Saw Reactions, *America@Work*, January 1997.

[15] Candice Johnson, As Shareholders. CWA Members Challenge Management Missteps, *CWA News*, April 1997.

[16] David Cay Johnston, Teamsters Are Challenging G.E. Chief's Compensation, *New York Times*, March 3, 1997.

[17] AFL-CIO PayWatch Website and New E-Campaign Turns Fed-Up Shareholders into Cyber Activists on Out-of-Control CEO Pay, PR Newswire, April 5, 2001.

[18] Ron Scherer, Soaring Stocks Send CEO Salaries Sky-high, *Christian Science Monitor*, April 8, 1999.

[19] A Nice Return on Our $75 Billion, *Too Much*, Winter 2003.

[20] The meltdowns at Enron and other scandal-ridden corporate giants had cost these funds dearly. The nation's single biggest pension fund, the California Public Employees' Retirement System, and the nation's third-biggest, the California Teachers' Retirement System, together lost $850 million from the WorldCom collapse alone. Mark

Schwanhausser, Pension Funds Urged to Join 'War' for Corporate Reform, *San Jose Mercury News*, March 6, 2003.

[21] Martha McNeil Hamilton, Option Reform Gains Backing, *Washington Post*, March 26, 2002.

[22] James Flanigan, Reforms Could Embolden Employees, *Los Angeles Times*, July 28, 2002.

[23] The research was conducted by Institutional Shareholder Services. Ronna Abramson, Voices in the Corporate Wilderness, TheStreet.com, October 15, 2002. Accessed from http://aol.thestreet.com/ tech/ronnaabramson/10047135.html.

[24] Consulting fees, reformers had noted, gave supposedly independent auditors an incentive to play footsie with executives who cooked their corporate books. Jerry Useem, In Corporate America It's Cleanup Time, *Fortune*, September 16, 2002.

[25] Abramson, Voices in the Corporate Wilderness.

[26] Most small shareholders, for instance, neither attend annual meetings or vote their proxies. That gives managements an immediate leg up, since non-votes count as management votes. Investors Question Executive Pay, Associated Press, May 15, 2001.

[27] Ellen Goodman, Cap Cash Flow to CEOs, *Arizona Republic*, April 16, 1999.

[28] "When we have our contract campaigns, we like to compare the earnings of our members," notes Salvador Bustamante, director of the San Jose office of Service Employees International Union Local 1877, a local involved in SEIU's ongoing justice for janitors campaign, "to the various CEOs for the corporations." Shawn Neidorf, Executive Pay Continues to Outpace Others', *San Jose Mercury News*, June 17, 2001.

[29] Manning Marable, The Maximum Wage: Lower the Top, Raise the Bottom, *Orlando Reporter*, February 1997.

[30] Survey by National Public Radio. Conducted by Greenberg Quinlan Rosner Research & Public Opinion Strategies, June 18-June 24, 2002. [USGREEN.02NPRJL.R17] Data provided by the Roper Center for Public Opinion Research, University of Connecticut.

[31] Reps. Maloney and King introduce Contractor Accountability Act, *Corporate Reform Weekly*, July 21, 2003.

[32] Mark Tapscott, Tomorrow's Car Will Sip Gasoline, Hold Lots of Bags, *Montgomery Journal*, September 30, 1994.

[33] The $20 billion represents inflation-adjusted dollars — and two and half times more than baseball team owners themselves spent on stadium construction. Alan B. Krueger, Take Me Out to the

Ballgame, but Don't Make Taxpayers Build the Ballpark, *New York Times*, January 10, 2002.

[34] Peter Behr, Maryland's 'Must' Deal Comes With Risks, *Washington Post*, March 12, 1999.

[35] Jeffery J. Smith, Geonomics: The Citizens Dividend Liberates Everyone, Geonomy Society. Accessed from www.progress.org/geonomy/geotalk.html.

[36] Price Anderson: Stealth Renewal, *Nation*, December 31, 2001.

[37] Michael Thomas, Sleazy Southern Hypocrite? *New York Observer*, August 21, 2000.

[38] The roots of current-day policy go back over a half-century. During World War II, the federal War Labor Board, by threatening to withhold contracts for war materials, was able to force a number of employers in the overwhelmingly nonunion South to honor the labor rights granted workers by the 1935 Wagner Act. Landon R. Y. Storrs, "Whiteness," Job Segregation, and Working-Class Conservatism in the Southern Textile Industry, *Reviews in American History*, September 2002.

[39] 'Living Wage' Bill Signed into Law by Baltimore Mayor Schmoke, *Solidarity Notes*, January 1995.

[40] Living Wage Successes: A Compilation of Living Wage Policies on the Books, Living Wage Resource Center. Accessed from www.livingwagecampaign.org/victories.php.

[41] History of Women in Sports Timeline, St. Lawrence County Branch of the American Association of University Women. Accessed from www.northnet.org/stlawrenceaauw/timelne4.htm.

[42] Title IX: Gender Equity in College Sports. An AAUP Position Paper, June 2003. Accessed from www.aaup.org/govrel/capthill/2003/titleIX.htm.

[43] Joel Rogers, Revitalizing the U.S. Labor Movement, *Working USA*, November/December 1997.

[44] In Connecticut, a Push to End Tax Subsidies for CEOs, *Too Much*, Spring 1997.

[45] Philip A. Wheeler, Testimony before the Commerce and Labor Committee, State of Connecticut, March 6, 1997.

[46] In Connecticut, a Push to End Tax Subsidies for CEOs, *Too Much*, Spring 1997.

[47] Greg LeRoy, Good Jobs First, Counterpoint: We Are Making Progress! Accountability: The Newsletter of the Business Incentives Clearinghouse, December 1999.

[48] Pushing 'Corporate Responsibility,' *Economic Notes*, April 1996.

[49] David Kameras, Kennedy, Reich Call for Corporate Responsibility, *AFL-CIO News*, February 19, 1996.

[50] John Harris, Clinton Pushes Corporate Citizenship, *Washington Post*, March 24, 1996.

[51] Sarah Anderson and John Cavanagh, Institute for Policy Studies, Chris Hartman and Betsy Leondar-Wright, United for a Fair Economy, *Executive Excess 2001: Eighth Annual CEO Compensation Survey*, September 2001, 16-17.

[52] A Minnesota Congressman Sends CEOs a Message, *Too Much*, Winter 1997.

[53] Craig Cox and Sally Power, Executive Pay: How Much Is Too Much? *Business Ethics*, September-October 1991.

[54] Anderson, Cavanagh, Hartman, and Leondar-Wright, *Executive Excess 2001: Eighth Annual CEO Compensation Survey*, 16-17.

[55] Ibid.

[56] Coralie Carlson, Sabo Renews Call for Legislation to Cut Income Inequality, *Star-Tribune* (Minneapolis), September 15, 1999.

[57] Among those who find Sabo's notion attractive, the *St. Louis Post-Dispatch*. Noted the paper in 1999: "Rep. Martin Olav Sabo, D-Minn., is pushing legislation to limit tax write-offs for executive pay to 25 times what the lowest-paid employee gets. That gives corporate elites an incentive to elevate the standard of living of their entire workforce, not just those in the corporate suites." The Case for a Maximum Wage, editorial, *St. Louis Post-Dispatch*, August 31, 1999.

[58] Anderson, Cavanagh, Hartman, and Leondar-Wright, *Executive Excess 2001: Eighth Annual CEO Compensation Survey*, 16-17.

[59] As defined by Section 501(c)(3) of the IRS Code. Paul Arnsberger, Charities and Other Tax-Exempt Organizations, 1999, *Statistics of Income Bulletin*, Fall 2002.

[60] "In 1996," for instance, "32 million taxpayers claimed just over $86 billion of deductions for charitable contributions, reducing federal revenues by about $22 billion." Budget Options, Congressional Budget Office, March 2000. Accessed from www.cbo.gov/showdoc.cfm?index=1845&sequence=21.

[61] Arnsberger, Charities and Other Tax-Exempt Organizations, 1999.

[62] Elizabeth Schwinn, Falling Through the Cracks, *Chronicle of Philanthropy*, November 14, 2002.

[63] Ibid.

[64] A Gift and a Threat, *American Benefactor*, Spring 1997.

[65] Joe Calderone, HIP Spending the Big Bucks, *New York Daily News Online*, July 4, 1999.

[66] M. William Salganik, House Panel Arriving at Bill on CareFirst Board Changes, *Baltimore Sun*, March 29, 2003.

[67] The *Chronicle of Philanthropy*, in its annual compensation survey, found thirty-four major nonprofits that paid their CEOs more than $500,000 in 2001. Thirty nonprofits, the *Chronicle* reported, also paid other officials, besides their CEOs, over $500,000. Harvy Lipman and Martha Voelz, Big Rise in Pay for CEO's, *Chronicle of Philanthropy*, October 3, 2002.

[68] Schwinn, Falling Through the Cracks.

[69] Ibid. The law also requires nonprofits to blow the whistle on themselves. In the legislation's first six years, only sixteen organizations with budgets over $10 million self-reported themselves to be guilty of excess.

[70] Judith Havemann, Top Foundations Gave Chiefs a Bountiful Raise, *Washington Post*, July 5, 1998.

[71] "There is strong reason to fear that the contracting bonanza will serve only to enrich the Bush administration's corporate cronies rather than the Iraqi people," warned the Corporate Policy Project's Charlie Cray. It's Time to Stop the War Profiteers, October 8, 2003. Accessed from www.corpwatch.org.

[72] Office of Federal Procurement Policy (OFPP); Determination of Executive Compensation Benchmark Amount, Federal Contracts Dispatch, FedGovContracts.com, May 2, 2003. Accessed from http://fedgovcontracts.com/pe03-62.htm.

[73] Ibid.

[74] Sarah Anderson, Executive Compensation and Iraq Reconstruction Contractors, Institute for Policy Studies, September 30, 2003.

[75] Ibid.

[76] Phyllis Bennis, Talking Points: Iraq, the UN, & U.S. Corporations, Institute for Policy Studies, October 2, 2003. Accessed from www.ips-dc.org/comment/Bennis/us-un-corps.htm.

[77] Holly Sklar, Good News, Bad News Economy, KnightRidder/Tribune News Service, October 5, 1999.

[78] Greg Coleridge, Citizens Over Corporations, in *Defying Corporations, Defining Democracy*, edited by Dean Ritz. New York: Apex Press, 2001, 49.

[79] Ibid., 50.

[80] Richard L. Grossman and Frank T. Adams, Taking Care of Business: Citizenship and the Charter of Incorporation, in *Defying Corporations, Defining Democracy*, 65.

[81] Coleridge, Citizens Over Corporations, in *Defying Corporations, Defining Democracy*, 51.

[82] *Defying Corporations, Defining Democracy*, 3.

[83] Richard L. Grossman and Frank T. Adams, Taking Care of Business: Citizenship and the Charter of Incorporation, in *Defying Corporations, Defining Democracy*, 69.

[84] Ward Morehouse, Creating a Model Corporation Code, in *Defying Corporations, Defining Democracy*, 261.

[85] Model State Corporation Code, Revised: June 10, 2001. Program on Corporations, Law, and Democracy. Accessed from www.cipa-apex.org.

[86] Geov Parrish, Impolitics: Killing Corporations, *Seattle Weekly*, July 15, 1999.

[87] Legislative Counsel's Digest, Senate Bill No. 917, Introduced by Senator Alarcon, February 21, 2003. Accessed from www.leginfo.ca.gov/pub/bill/sen/sb_09010950/sb_917_bill_20030221_introduced.pdf.

[88] Marjorie Kelly, Despairing Globally, Hoping Locally: The Promise of State-level Action as an Avenue for Corporate Reform, *Business Ethics*, Spring 2003.

[89] Ibid.

[90] Tax Struggle: Making the Rich Pay Their Fair Share, *UE News*, March 19, 1999.

[91] Larry Rinehart, the Greens/Green Party USA, Thinking Economically, Economic Justice in the New Millennium, *Synthesis/Regeneration 22*, Spring 2000.

[92] *Counterbudget 1995-1996*. A Publication of SENSES. March 1995, 3-4.

LOOKING FORWARD

[1] Michael Bellamy, Looking Backward, 2000-1887: What Happened to Utopian Evolution? *Globe and Mail* (Toronto), January 1, 2000.

[2] Rory Carroll, Wine, Women and the Poor of Pompeii, *Guardian* (UK), June 13, 2000.

[3] Dinesh D' Souza, The Moral Limits of Wealth, *Forbes*, October 9, 2000.

[4] Geneva Overholser, Executive Pay Enters the Stratosphere, *San Jose Mercury News*, September 3, 2001.

ACKNOWLEDGMENTS

IN OUR PERSONAL LIVES, change can often come suddenly. A glance, *Some Enchanted Evening*-style, across a crowded room. The birth of a child. A job offer out of left field. A tragic accident. In the flash of a moment, our lives can career off into entirely different directions.

But sometimes our lives can change more slowly, so slowly we may not even recognize that change is taking place. We go about our daily routines, year after year. Then one day we look up and see a new world all around us — and realize that the lives we lead have been fundamentally transformed.

Over the last quarter century or so, I believe, we Americans have experienced just such a transformation. These pages have attempted to explain the impact of this change — the resurgence of inequality — upon us.

I don't remember exactly when I started thinking about writing this book, or about inequality. I do know that inequality has always struck me as deeply unnatural.

Maybe that's because of where — and when — I was raised. I grew up a half-century ago on Long Island, next door to Levittown, the first super suburb of the postwar United States, the American dream come true. In the 1950s, I lived in what came across to me as an incredibly equal world. I could ride my bike for blocks and blocks, or ride in the backseat of my father's Ford, and never see anything but the same suburban spectacle. Neighborhood after neighborhood of single-family homes. No hovels, no mansions.

Not much pretense either. Some people worked with their hands, some were professionals who never got their hands dirty. That didn't seem to make much of a difference, as far as my eleven-year-old eyes could see. My uncles who drove nails rode in fancier cars than my father who practiced law or my mother who taught school. Nothing strange in that. Some households chose nicer cars. Some spent weekends now and then at some bungalow colony in the Catskills. Some put up vinyl pools in their backyards. People made choices how to spend their money — and everyone seemed to have money to spend.

But not too much. No rich people ever entered into my eleven-year-old line of sight. I knew, of course, that rich people existed, just as I knew that, somewhere, elephants actually existed outside of zoos. But no rich people — or elephants — lived in my neighborhood, or any neighborhood I had ever seen.

My classmates and I did take a school field trip, once, to a rich person's house. The rich person was long dead and gone, the house many times bigger than any house we had ever seen. Nobody lived there anymore. The only visitors seemed to be schoolkids like us. We walked the grounds, climbed the marble steps, tried to tell time by the sundial. The teacher told us somebody named Vanderbilt had lived here a long time ago. Years ago, she told us, a few people did indeed live like this all the time. Wasn't that, she asked, amazing? Certainly was, we nodded.

Our young minds had no trouble processing what our teacher was trying to say. Back then, we understood, people lived backward lives. Nobody had TV or telephones. And some people lived in huge houses. And then we had progress. Now we all have TVs and telephones and nobody lives in huge houses. We were better than people back then. We were smarter. We were more equal.

That sense of the world became — and remains — a part of me. I feel deeply grateful having grown up in that time and place. Without that experience, that foundation, this book could not have been written.

In the years since then, a great many people have helped me build on that foundation. My political mentors in upstate New York. My fellow staffers and activists in the labor movement. My colleagues in good works that range from Progressive Maryland to the Boston-based United for a Fair Economy. My long-time support group of graying local friends, not a Yankee fan among them, still going strong after nearly thirty years.

My deep thanks to all these folks.

And my special thanks to the folks most directly linked to this effort.

Thanks to Ward Morehouse, David Dembo, and Judi Rizzi, the trio at the Council on International and Public Affairs who have given me the time and space, over the past dozen-plus years, to grow my ideas about growing inequality.

Thanks to Jeff Vogel, trade union and environmental advocate extraordinaire and maybe the deepest bass in the New York City Labor Chorus. He dares to envision a truly different and better society — and tirelessly nudges me, and everyone else, in the right direction.

Thanks to Chuck Collins, the co-founder of United for a Fair Economy. His energy and insights never cease to give me inspiration.

Thanks to Nancy Leibold, a most public-spirited South Jersey soul. Her words of encouragement came at just the right time.

And thanks, most of all, to the person who's been bringing home the bacon. Some know her as Tia Toots, some as Dr. Pizzigati. I know her as a life-long partner. Without her, I could never have completed these pages.

Sam Pizzigati
Kensington, Maryland

INDEX

401(k) plans
  costs vs. pension plans, 102, 574n45
  deferred, for CEOs, with insurance/interest paid, 45–46
  government protection of, 381

A

AARP, 524
ABB Ltd., 206, 207
ABC Carpet & Home, xi
Abramson, Jerry, 128
Abramson, Leonard, 33, 285, 602n61
accountants, 278–282, 601n31
Acheson, Sir Donald, 324
Ackerman, Bruce, 460, 462
Adams, John, 416
Adams, Richard, 174
Adelphi University, 291, 603n90
Adler, Felix, 481
Aetna, 33
AFL-CIO, 530–531. *See also* unions
Agassi, Andre, 305
airlines industry, 177, 379, 587n114
Akst, Daniel, 524
Alarcon, Richard, 545
Albeda, Randy, 199, 200, 230, 231
Alcoa, 36
Aldrich, Nelson, 431
Allaire, Paul, 188
Allen, Paul, xii–xiii, 226, 302, 403, 468
Alm, Richard, viii, 113, 248
Alstott, Anne, 460, 462
Amazon.com, 36, 69–71, 183, 570n122, 570n125. *See also* Bezos, Jeff
American Airlines, 298
American Express, 36
American Online (AOL), 13–14, 176, 188, 588n166
AMF, 178
Anderson, Basil, 53
Anschutz, Philip, 227
AOL (America Online), 13–14,

176, 188, 588n166
AOL Time Warner, 176
Apple Computer, 15–16, 559n65
Appleton, Lynn, 242
Applied Magnetics, 562n159
Applied Micro Circuits, 47
Aramony, William, 540
Arbusto Energy Inc., 85
Archer, Bill, 451
Archibald, Nolan, 43
Arizona, election spending in, 395
Armey, Dick, 451
Arno, Peter, 315
Arthur Andersen, 281–282
arts, the
  attendance statistics, 144
  education and, 147–149
  funding, 142–151, 583n76
  future of, 144–145, 148–151
  mid-sized organizations, 144–145
  museum attendance, 141
  performing artists employment, 144–145
  symphony ticket sales, 141
  Ten Times Rule, effect on, 512–513
Artzt, Russell, 25–27, 561n117
Aspen effect, 257
AT&T, 211
Athanasiou, Tom, 362
athletes career length, 304–305. *See also* sports industry
athletes salaries. *See also* sports industry
  average, 2001, 304
  average vs. median, 308
  income gap, fans vs., 296, 307, 605n70
  isolation linked to, 306
  limits to, 299, 487
  performance/compensation link, 307–310
  as tax deduction, 296, 604n48
attorneys, 274–278, 289, 487–488, 601n21
Audet, Christopher, 463
automobile industry, 250–253, 363–365, 598n71, 613n33
average citizens. *See* families (aver-

age); *under* democracy in America

B

Bacon, Sir Francis, xviii
Baechle, Raymond and Carla, 61
Bagdikian, Ben, 399
Bagehot, Walter, 333
Bairoch, Paul, 360
Baker, Dean, 233
Baker, Laurie, 375
Baker, Raymond, 378
Baltimore, Maryland, living wage law, 535–536
Balzar, John, 28, 470
Bank of America, 33, 39
Banks, W. N., 441
Barach, Michael, 594n151
Barbour, James, 417
Barksdale, James and Sally, 127
Barnett Banks, 175
Barnevik, Percy, 206, 207
Barrett, Craig, 63–64, 172–173
Bartlett, Bruce, 468
Barzun, Jacques, xiv, 554n51
Baumol, William, 142
Baxter International, 18, 560n81
Beattie, Dick, 12
Beck, Audrey Jones, 141
Becker, Nancy, 70–71
Bellamy, Edward, xvi, 426, 549
Bellamy, Michael, 549
The Bell Curve (Hernstein and Murray), 352
Belle, Albert, 296
BellSouth, 61
Benabou, Roland, 199
benefactors, the greedy as, 93–94. *See also* greed; wealth inequity
Benioff, Marc, 189
Benjamin, Brent, 150
Bennis, Phyllis, 542
Benson, P. George, 3–5
Beresford, Dennis, 11
Berlusconi, Silvio, 400
Bernhardt, Annette, 105, 106, 458
Bernsen, Thordjorn, 363
Bernstein, Aaron, 214, 477, 593n93
Bernstein, Peter, 221
Bertelsmann, 206, 207

Bertelsmann, Carl, 207
Bertrand, Marianne, 82
Bezos, Jeff, 69–71, 569n118, 570n135. *See also* Amazon.com
Bezruchka, Stephen, 315
Biggs, Morton, 221
Bijan, xi
Bill and Melinda Gates Foundation, 128, 580n6
billionaires, ix, 120, 361, 362
Bingaman, Jeff, 537
Bittker, Boris, 484
Black & Decker, 43
black Americans. *See also* discrimination; slavery
    academic achievement gap, 352–354, 611n89, 611n97, 611n100
    vs. white
        accumulated wealth, 354–356, 612n103
        financial assets, 353–354, 612n103
        income, 1940-1960, 443
Blackwell, Ron, 530
Bloom, Matt, 168, 186, 308
Bloomberg, Michael, 388
Bluestone, Barry, xxi, 213, 214, 215, 464
boards of directors, corporate. *See also* corporate America; shareholders
    compensation consultants used by, 28–29, 75–76, 562n135
    conflicts of interests in, 28, 562n129
    control over management, 29–31
    election procedures, 39–40
    repricing risks taken by, 34–35
    shareholders, accountability to, 39–40, 564n200
    on stock options as compensation, 10–14
    union efforts to unseat, 532
boards of directors, nonprofits, 290–292
Boatmen's Bancshares, 175
Boesky, Ivan, 93
Bok, Derek, 274, 275
Bonilla, Bobby, 296
Bonior, David, viii
Bonsignore, Michael, 174
Booth, Melvin D., 557n126
Borosage, Robert, 384, 392, 618n82
Boswell, Thomas, xiv, 302, 309, 310
Boulding, Kenneth, 367
Bowen, William, 142
Bowles, Erskine, 390
bowling alone syndrome, 332
Boyce, James, 361
Bradsher, Keith, 252

Brandeis, Louis, xix, 170
Brazil, 232–233, 375–376, 403, 595n190, 615n93
Breeden, Richard C., 48
Breslau, Karen, 122
Breyer, Stephen, 289–290
Bristol-Myers Squibb, 188, 531
Britain, 64, 321–324, 326
Broad, Eli, 131
Brobeck, Stephen, 117
Broder, David, 400, 470
Bronfman, Edgar, 89
Brooke, James, 596n210
Brooklyn, New York, housing costs in, 256
Brown, Jeff, 31
Brown, Sir Henry Phelps, 482, 483
Bruhn, J. G., 320
Brundtland, Gro Harlem, 367
Brungs, Heinz, 161
Bryan, Williams Jennings, 426, 428–429
Buffet, Warren
    described, 267
    on estate tax, 626n274
    on his children's inheritance, 266
    philanthropy philosophy of, 128
    on revenue padding, 589n177
    on stock options as compensation, 11
Burch, Marc, 369
Burkhauser, Richard, 96
Burns, James MacGregor, 450
Burns, Scott, 118
Burtless, Gary, 204, 356
Bush (George H. W.) administration, 448–449
Bush (George W.) administration
    campaign finance reform legislation, 393
    Iraq War, 2003, 542, 635n71
    loans to executives, legislation prohibiting, 18
    millionaires in cabinet of, 390, 618n75
    tax cuts for the wealthy
        $1,000,000 income or greater, 382–383, 616n31
        $200,000 income and greater, 616n28
        $50-$75,000 income, 616n31
        Congress, votes approving in, 626n276
        estate tax, 382
        richest 1%, 415, 620n6
        tax-free investment income, 477
        tax plan 2001, 452–455
Bush, George W.

    campaign pledges, 452, 460
    connections role in success of, 84–87
    election spending, 384, 429
    estate tax effect on, 391
    fundraising success, 385
Bussmann, W. Van, 251
Byron, Christopher, 222

C
California. *See also specific cities*
    arts funding, tax cuts affecting, 146
    charitable giving in, 135
    Code for Corporate Responsibility, 545–546
    commuting times in, 257–258
    election spending in, 388
    housing costs, 121–122, 255–256, 579n181–182
    Kerala compared to, 372–373
    public goods and services funding in, 348
    uninsured statistics, 121
    universities vs. prisons built in, 1980-2000, 357
    wealth inequity in, 120–122
California Teachers' Retirement System, 633n20
Callinicos, Alex, 58, 495
CalPERS (California Public Employees' Retirement System), 39, 633n20
Caminer, David, 173
Canada, health care in, 327
Cappellas, Michael, 167
Cappelli, Peter, 54
Caraway, Hattie, 437
CareFirst, 540
Carnegie, Andrew, 129, 266, 424
Carnegie Hall, 140
Carroll, Sidney, 482, 483, 484
Carter, Gary, 296
Carter, Jimmy, 62, 133, 446
Case, Steve, 13–14, 188, 563n184
Casper, Barry, 392
Castle, John K., 58–59, 254
Cawley, Charles, 45
Cello Technologies, 174
Cendant, 34
Central Maine Power, 181–182
CEOs. *See also* boards of directors; corporate America; performance/compensation link, CEOs; *specific individuals*
    of colleges/universities, 291
    consultants used by, 28–29, 31, 75–76, 87, 562n135
    control (sense of) felt by, 57, 323
    foreign vs. U.S., 63–64, 75, 205–208, 235
    post-WWII, characteristics of, xx

Ten Times Rule, effect on, 504–506, 514–515, 631n1
CEOs, income. *See also specific individuals*
1980s-2000, xxiii–xxiv, 217, 563n179
caps proposed for, 37, 48–49, 61, 571n161. *see also* income caps propsals
company size-compensation link, 170–182
competitive benchmarking in determining, 30–31
at corporate health care empires, 285
corporate profits vs., 10, 14–15
deferred (401k) with insurance/interest paid, 45–46
foreign vs. U.S. executives, 63–66, 173, 568n79, 569n88
limits placed on
for airline bailout funds, 380, 615n6
benchmark compensation caps, 542
government compensation limits, 635n71
by IRS, 486, 540–541, 629n22
by public officials, 486
shareholder resolutions for, 531–532
in nonprofit sector, 290–292, 539–541, 634n67
reform efforts, 36–40, 61, 531–534
shareholder profit vs., 15
stock options in lieu of, 15–16
as tax deduction, 37, 539
CEOs, income additional to salary
bonuses, 21, 30, 37, 43, 562n140, 563n179, 603n85
business school education, 570n154
financial planning services, 45
golden parachute, 33, 562n154–155
life insurance premiums, 46
lifetime annuities, 77
loans for stock purchases, 18, 560n88
long-term compensation, 44
perks, 45–46
personal assistants, 45
stock grants, 31–32, 562n147
stock options
1970s, 9–10
1980s, 7–10
1990s, 10–14, 563n179
2000 stock market crash, effect on, 43
Bonus Unit awards,

558n20
Computer Associates example, 25–28, 561n117
critics of, 11–12
gains, 1999, 42–43, 564nn214–215
reforms, 16–18, 560n74
reloadable, 36
stock repricing, 34–35
CEOs, income statistics. *See also specific individuals*
1980s-1990s, 37, 38, 558n2, 559n59
1980s vs.1990s, 36
2000-2004, 41–43, 44, 564n205, 564n226
public disclosure requirement, 564n200
school superintendents vs., 60–61
U.S. Presidents vs., 60–62
CEOs, wealth of. *See also specific individuals*
connections role in, 84–87
corruption tied to, 227–228
downsizing as source of, 180–182
fraudulent accounting practices in, 187–191, 285, 588n166, 589n177
luck as contributor to, 81–83
for media executives, 399
PayWatch Web site monitoring, 530–531
power factor in, 90
public opinion on, 533
support staff role in, 87
talent shortage affecting, 14, 29–31, 51–52, 73–75, 570n148, 570n153, 571n158–159
tax dollars funding, 534–536
CFOs (corporate financial officers), salary, 280
Chambers, John, xxiv, 43
Chambless, Jerry, 53
Chandler, Asa, 590n25
Chang, Chee Jen, 315
charitable giving. *See* philanthropy
Chase Manhattan Bank, 180
Chasin, Barbara, 374
Chemical Bank, 180
Cheney, Dick, 131, 385, 391
Chesterton, G. K., 347
children
arts education for, 147–150
black, academic achievement gap in, 352–354, 611n89, 611n97, 611n100
child care costs, 576n100
education for poor, 213, 335–336, 459–461, 464, 593n93, 609n31, 609n33,

627n7, 627n11
health care for, 350
latchkey, 247, 332
in Norway, 350
poverty rates, 336–337
preschooler education, 461–462
children of the wealthy
Baby Boomers, 572n214
black vs. white, 354–355, 356
economic mobility of, 458
inherited wealth, 88–90, 260, 263, 266, 514, 599n130
parental worries regarding, 265
Ten Times Rule, effect on, 514
in the workplace, 265–266, 290
Chiles, Eddie, 85
China, bowling in, 178
Chirac, Jacques, 359, 360
Christian, Jeff, 52
Chrysler, 9, 63
Churchill, Brent, 181–182
Cisco Systems, 11, 43, 164, 227, 564n214
Citigroup, 45, 64, 227
Clean Money campaign, 395
Clear Channel Communications, 176–177, 587n109
Clendenin, John L., 61
Cleveland, Grover, 427, 428
Cleveland Browns, 302–303
Clikeman, Paul, 280
Clinton (Bill) administration, 37, 382, 537–538, 616n24
Clinton, Bill (William Jefferson), vii, 97, 297, 385, 390
CNET, Inc., 84
Coca-Cola, 565n230
Cochrane, Peter, 211
Coffman, Vance, 542
Cohen, Randy, 405–406
Coleman, 55–56
Collins, Chuck, 451, 464
Collins, Jim, 192
Collins, Robert, 444
Collison, David, 24
Colombia, South America, 372, 614n68
Colton, Charles, xviii
Colvin, Geoffrey, 168
Comcast, 81–82
Comerica Inc., 20
community, alliegence to corporations vs., 403
community as stakeholder, 25, 511–512, 561n104
community involvement, 246–247, 331–333. *See also* relationships; society
Compaq Computer, 13, 167
Computer Associates, 25–27, 532, 561n117
Conley, Dalton, 353

Connecticut, corporate reform efforts, 537
Connif, Richard, 244
Conseco, 18
consumer exploitation. *See also* corporate America
 airlines industry, 177, 587n114
 automobile industry, 251–252
 financial services industry, 175, 380, 615n10
 sports industry, 298–300
 telecommunications industry, 176–177, 300–301, 380, 587n114, 615n9
Continental, 177
Contreras, Miguel, 357
Conwell, Russell, 264
Cook, Philip, 287
Cook, Wade, 222
Cooke, Jack Kent, 261
Coolidge, Calvin, 151, 435
CoreStates, 175
corporate America. *See also* boards of directors, corporate; CEOs; consumer exploitation; employees; shareholders; taxes on corporations
 auditing of, 280–282
 as community, allegiance of wealthy to, 403
 "A Corp" status proposal, 537
 debt offset/reduction schemes, 228–229
 discrimination practices-government contracts link, 633n38
 European corporations vs., 202–204, 206–207
 health care empires of, 285
 history of, 423, 544
 investment capital, sources for, 223–226, 517–520
 market wisdom distortions, 19–23, 560n95, 560nn98–102
 mergers and acquisitions in, 171–178, 180–182, 193, 429–430, 586nn77–78
 operating capital, sources of, 24, 228–229, 595n177
 political influence, 379–380, 382, 393–396, 428–429, 615n6, 616n23, 618n82
 raiders restructuring of, 7–8, 33
 research and development investment, 210–212, 214, 520
 success in, 23–25, 65, 561n104
 telecom phenomenon, 226–228
corporate America, fraudulent accounting practices
 Enron collapse, 281, 531
 HMOs, 285
 revenue padding, 9, 17, 560n74, 588n166, 589n177
 stock repricing, 35
 tax fraud, 187–191
corporate America, Information Age
 bureaucracy as obstacle, 161–163, 586n64
 characteristics of, 170, 179, 191–193, 588n166, 589n177
 deregulation/mergers and acquisitions in, 171–178, 180–182, 193
 gain-sharing plans, 168–170
 requirements for, 586n71
 small firms success in, 170
 workforce downsizing in, 179–182
corporate America, profitability in
 CEO pay gains vs., 14–15
 the ecology of commerce, 359–360, 367–372, 374, 612n4
 low-wage workers in, 113–115, 342–343
 stock options and, 9, 17, 560n74
 stock repricing, 35
corporate America, reforming for pay equity. *See also* income caps propsals
 citizens movement, 544–545
 legislative proposals, 536–538, 540–541, 545–546
 living wage law, 535–536
 pay equity ratio requirements in government contracts, 535
 revoking corporate charters as means of, 544–546
 union efforts, 529–534
Cort, John, 235
Corzine, Jon, 390, 404, 619n132
Costa Rica, 328, 403
Costas, Bob, 301–302
Cottey, Alan, 488
Coulter, David, 33, 562n155
Cox, W. Michael, viii, 100, 113, 248
Cravath, Swaine & Moore, 275, 289
Crawford, Anthony, 355
Crèvecoeur, Michel Guillaume Jean de, 420
crime and wealth inequity, 231–233
Crisman, Craig, 562n159
Crittenden, Ann, 261
Crowe, James, 227
Crystal, Graef, comments Andy Grove's compensation, 64–65

CEOs on boards of directors, 28
 compensation consultants, 29
 greed in CEOs, 36, 90
 income as motivator, 565n1
 income as power dynamic, 90
 income related to company size, 170
 Jack Welch's compensation package, 71, 570n139
 obscene pay levels, 482
 stock grants, 32
 supply-and-demand for CEOs, 571n158–159
Csikszentmihalyi, Michaly, 523
CSX, 46
Cullen, Mark, 318
Curley, John J., 399
Currall, Steven, 166
Curry, Eddy, 306
CVS, 564n217

D

Daimler-Benz, 63
Daisey, Mike, 183
Daly, Herman, 365–367, 368, 377, 525, 614n62
Daly, Martin, 231
Daly, Sharon, 109–110
Daniels, Norman, 329–330
Danone, 206
Daschle, Thomas A., 394
Dauten, Dale, 182
Davis, Edward, 289
Davis, Kenneth, 415
Davis, Marvin, 268
Davis, William, 139
Davos, 205
Deavers, Ken, 96
Debs, Eugene Victor, 430, 432
deca-millionaires, ix
DeFazio, Peter, 616n21
Delevett, Peter, 241
Dell, Michael, 46
Dell Computer, 46
Deloitte & Touche, 282
de Loyola Brandao, Ignacio, 232
Deming, W. Edwards, 168, 585n51, 587n125
democracy and inequality
 basic difficulties of, 400–401
 citizenship undermined by, 402, 620n157
 loss of community as result of, 403
democracy in America. *See also* United States; United States government
 campaign finance reform as, 392–396, 618nn97–99
 civil rights movement as, 443
 corporate influence on, 379–380, 382, 393–396, 428–429, 615n6, 616n23, 618n82

free press vital to, 399–400,
619n126
pay discrepancies endangering
quality of justice, 289–290
Social Security privatization,
398–399
wealth inequity as threat to,
400–402
democracy in America, citizens
(average)
elected representatives responsiveness to, 381–382, 406,
617nn55–56
importance to, 384, 404–405,
618n82
participation in political
process, 384–385, 396–397,
406–407, 430
political perspective of vs.
wealthy, 386–387,
617nn55–56
voting by, 406–407, 429,
620n157
democracy in America, elected representatives
campaign fundraising/spend-
ing, 383–385, 388–389,
392–396, 429, 618n82,
619n132
corporate contributions, 382,
616n23
millionaires among, 387–388,
618n75
responsiveness to voters,
379–383, 406, 617nn55–56
wealth, desire for, 386, 617n53
wealth-gap not addressed by,
392
democracy in America, history
1892 presidential race, 428
1896 presidential race,
428–430
1904 Congressional elections,
430
1910 Congressional elections,
430
Federalists party, 418
Jeffersonian party, 418, 421
Peoples/Populist Party,
426–428
democracy in America, wealth as
threat to
historically, xv, xix, 547
laissez-faire doctrine and, 417,
425
by media control, 399–400
political climate altered,
396–399, 403–406
by political contributions,
384–385, 388–389,
393–396, 428–429,
617nn55–56
positions of importance held
by wealthy, 390–391
Supreme Court ruling of 1895

influenced, 427–428
Denmark, welfare state in,
338–339
Department of Defense (DoD)
schools, 461
Depression years, 436–438
de Vogel, Willem F. P., 26
DeVos, Dick, 397
Diamandopoulos, Peter, 291,
603n90
discrimination. *See also* black
Americans; equal opportunity
civil rights movement and, 443
government contracts and,
535, 633n38
Ten Times Rule, effect on,
516–517
Title IX funding and, 536
wealth inequity and, 351–353
Disney. *See* Walt Disney
Doerr, John, 223
Dole, Bob, xiv
Dole, Elizabeth, 384
Dole, Robert, 385
Domenici, Pete, 476–477
Donahue, John, 405–406
Donahue, Tom, 472
Dost, Valesca, xii
Douglass, Katie Herbert, 482
Dovai, Karl, 502–503
Dowie, Mark, 405
Dow Jones effect, 19–20
Downs, Alan, 181
downsizing of employees. *See also*
layoffs of employees
1980-1993, 104
1990s, 179–180, 584n15
2001-2002, 181
air traffic controllers, 217,
593n113
Deming on inevitability of,
587n125
forced rankings in, 72,
570n144
IRS staff, 616n25
layoffs vs., 179–180
management vs., 584n15
outsourcing as method of, 104
results of, 181–182, 588n139
U.S. vs. Europe, 591n55
Washington Post pressmen,
593n113
Draper, Timothy, 397
Drexler, Millard, 38, 563n184
Dreyfuss, Robert, 390, 401
Drucker, Peter, 162–163, 182,
533, 584n19
D'Souza, Dinesh, 88, 241, 550
duckpin bowlers, 178–179
Duke, Doris, 261
Duke, James Buchanan, xv
Dunea, George, 284
Dunlap, Albert J.
admiration for, 52, 565nn6–7,
566n8

corporate practices, 52–56,
566n11, 566n23
fraudulent practices of, 53,
567n46, 567n49
wealth, importance to,
566n20, 566nn23–24
Dunlop, M. H., 262, 264
Dunphy, T. J. Dermot, 22
Dupont Chemical, 169
Durlauf, Steven N., 593n93
Durning, Alan, 239, 362, 370,
526
Duten, Dale, 597n31

E
Earls, Gregory, 187
Earned Income Tax Credit,
341–342, 610n62
Eastman Kodak, 18
Easton, George, 584n9
Eaton, Robert, 97
eBay, 221
Ebbers, Bernard, 48, 180–181,
225
economic growth. *See also* productivity
1860s-1900 (Industrial Age),
201
as benefit of wealth inequity,
197–201, 444–445, 590n9
defined, 200, 368
demand for goods and services
in, 215–216
environmental unsustainability
and, 367–372, 374
full employment vs. inflation,
1970s, 625n234
increasing, methods of,
592nn74–75
in Japan, 596n216
New Growth economists on,
212
economic growth theory. *See also*
wealth inequity
equality-efficiency conflict in,
198, 590n9, 590n17
Kuznets, 197–198, 590n9
Wall Street model, 208–210,
215, 218, 230
wealth distribution in,
196–199
Economic Policy Institute, xxi, 110
Ecuador, equality and democracy
in, 403
Edelman, Marian Wright, 334,
336
education
academic achievement gap of
black students, 352–354,
611n89, 611n97, 611n100
civic role of public, 459–460,
627n7, 627n11
college graduates, hourly
wages, 463, 627n28
college students, enrollment,

1945-1970
Department of Defense (DoD)
schools, 461
equal opportunity from,
459–463, 627n7
government funding for,
212–213, 303, 381,
461–462, 627n23
income link to achievement,
353–354
for poor children, 213,
335–336, 459–460, 464,
593n93, 609n31, 609n33,
627n7, 627n11
for preschoolers, 461–462,
627n23
school voucher system,
396–398
student loan debt, 277
teachers, inadequate pay for,
287–288, 603nn70–72
Ten Times Rule, effect on, 520
Title IX funding and, 536
universities vs. prisons built,
1980-2000, 357
egalitarianism
Danish welfare reform failure,
338–339
in European business, 66,
202–208
Europeans admiration of in
early U.S., 420
in Japan, 233–235
literature on, xvi
in Norway, 350–351
United States belief in, historically, 416–421, 620n7
Ehrenreich, Barbara, 243
Einstein, Albert, 80
Eisenhower, Dwight D., 442
Eisner, Michael, 13, 67–69, 126,
177, 569n111, 579n209
Eliot, Samuel, 129
Elliott, Robert, 265
Ellison, Larry, 13, 44, 189–190,
269
Elmendorf, Steve, 385
Ely, Leonard, 131
Emanuel, Ezekiel, 329
employee benefits
401(k) plans
costs vs. pension plans,
102, 574n45
deferred, for CEOs, 45–46
government protection of,
381
death benefits, 107
employer expenditures, 1973
vs. 1992, 574n36
health insurance, 100–101,
106–107
retirement
1979 vs. 1998, changes to,
101

corporate revenue state-
ments and, 189
defined-contribution plans,
101–102
Enron losses of, 633n20
government protection of,
381
revenue padding, effect on,
589n177
at Wal-Mart, 107
for temporary/part-time workers, 105
employee empowerment
bureaucracy as obstacle,
586n64
at Hewlett-Packard, 164–165
at Intel, 163, 165
management belief in, 167,
179, 584nn11–13
the mantra of, 159–161
Ten Times Rule, effect on,
505–506, 514–517
employees. *See also* downsizing of
employees; income inequity; layoffs of employees; wages; workplace
anger in, 191
child care costs for, 576n100
commuting times of, 257–258
equality for, U.S. vs. Europe,
202–208
exploitation of
clean room workers, 58
ergonomics legislation, 380
excessive work hours,
181–182, 588n139
immigrant labor, 113–115
job security, 202, 233,
587n124, 596n210
jobs redefined, 1960s vs.
1990s, 104
performance rewards, effectiveness of
Deming on, 585n51
gain-sharing plans for,
168–170
management belief in,
167–168
motivation in, 585n44
negative results, 168,
193–194, 585n48
proof of, 585n45
puzzle players example,
184
public sector, 288–290
retail, 105–108, 214
service sector, 214
temporary/part-time, 105,
114, 575n63
Ten Times Rule, effect on, 524
theft by, 191
turnover, costs of, 185–186
wages and benefits, U.S. world
ranking, 1995, 204

Enrico, Roger, 409
Enron collapse
accounting firms participating
in fraud, 277, 281–282, 531
corporate/political leaders,
effect on, 208
executive compensation affected by, 47
pension funds, losses, 633n20
pension funds safety, effects
on, 381
shareholder voting practices
affected by, 531–532
stock analysts, conflicts of
interests and the, 22, 23
tax evasion and, 190–191
Ensign, John, 390
environmental advocacy, 363
environmental degradation
benefits to participants in,
361–362
damage statistics, globally, 360
by disinvestment in public
services, 348–349
the ecology of commerce,
359–360, 612n4
economic growth/development
choice in, 367–372, 374
economic policy supporting
global, 376–377
industrial production rates,
367
Sao Paolo, Brazil, 375–376
sustainable alternatives
(Kerala), 372–375, 376–377,
615n95
Ten Times Rule, effect on,
525–526
U.S., consumption/waste in,
363–364, 366–367, 614n41
environmental protection legislation, 365, 371
environmental sustainability,
377–378, 525–526, 614n62
Epstein, Gene, 493
Epstein, Helen, 323, 326
Epstein, Lisa, 161
Equality and Efficiency (Okun),
198
equal opportunity. *See also* discrimination
asset building movement,
460–462, 627n11
barriers to, 462–463
education's role in, 459–463,
627n7, 627n11
the poor and, 458–459
sabbath economics, 466–467
Title IX funding for, 536
Ernst & Young, 282
ESPN, 309
Esrey, William, xxiv, 557n124
estate tax
1861, Civil War levy, 422

1898, Spanish-American War-
   time levy, 429
1916 tax act, 433
1917, War Revenue Act, 433
1935, Wealth Tax Act, 439
Buffet on, 626n274
Bush (GW) administration,
   382, 391, 453
Carnegie on, 425
Clinton administration,
   451–452
Gates Sr. on, 80–81, 404
politicians against repeal of,
   404
Rockefeller affected by 1935
   Act, 624n196
Roosevelt (Theodore) proposal
   for, xvii
Ten Times Rule, effect on,
   513–514
eToys, 225, 594n155
Etzioni, Amitai, 246–247
Europe. *See also specific countries*
   CEOs, vs. U.S., 205–207
   employee equality, vs. U.S.,
      202–208
   incarceration rates, 231
   murder rates, 231
   shareholder vs. stakeholder
      position, 24
   voting rates, 620n157
executives. *See* CEOs

F
families (average). *See also* middle
   class; taxes on average families;
   the poor; the wealthy
   in California, 121–122
   happiness of, 239–242,
      246–247
   political perspective of vs.
      wealthy, 386–387,
      617nn55–56
   reference group comparisons,
      241–243
families (average), economics of.
   See also taxes on average families
   consumer debt, 117, 122, 218
   consumption pressures, 218,
      242–245, 248–250,
      509–510
   housing costs, 121–122,
      255–257, 579n181
   New Deal effect on, 438–439
families (average), exploitation as
   consumers
   airlines industry, 177,
      587n114
   financial services industry, 175,
      380, 615n10
   sports industry, 298–300
   telecommunications industry,
      176–177, 300–301, 380,
      587n109, 615n9

families (average), financial assets
   1998 vs. 2001, 578n162
   home ownership, 115–117,
      255–256, 578n146
   retirement savings, 102–103
   stock market investments,
      118–119, 222, 573nn12–13,
      578n153
families (average), income. *See also*
   taxes on average families
   1920s, 435–436
   1939-1945, 441
   1970s-2000, 121
   median
      1980 vs. 2000, 98
      1990s, 450, 579n187
families (average), lifestyle
   1920s, 435–436
   community involvement,
      331–333
   leisure time available, 243,
      247, 332, 509–510, 597n31,
      597n49, 597n53
   workweek hours, 99, 243–244,
      597n28
Fang, Jing, 315
Fannie Lou Hamer standard, 394
Feingold, Russell, 393, 395
Feinstein, Diane, 388
Feldstein, Martin, viii
Fidelity effect, 20–21
Filene, Edward, 471
Filo, David, 20
Financial Accounting Standards
   Board, 11, 35, 560n74
Fiorina, Carly, 166–167
Fireman, Paul, 10–11
firing of employees. *See* downsizing
   of employees
First Union, 175
Fisher, George, 18
Fitzgerald, F. Scott, 261
Fitzhugh, George, 418–419
Flanigan, James, 531
Fleishmann, Ernest, 141
Florida Marlins, 309
flower industry takeover, 519–520
Flynn, John T., 624n204
Forbes, Malcolm, xii
Forbes, Steve, 129–130
Forbes magazine list of 400, ix–x,
   470, 554n23
Ford Motor Co., 21, 25
Forstmann, Theodore, 396–398
Foster, John Bellamy, 367
France
   child poverty rates, 336
   downsizing statistics, 591n55
   incarceration rates, 231
   income caps, public support
      for, 528
   murder rates, 231
   unemployment compensation,
      590n27

union membership in, 203
Frank, Robert, on
   the Aspen effect, 257
   effects of income on career
      choice, 287
   happiness from well-main-
      tained public commons,
      610n66
   income equality, 524, 525
   luxury fever, 241
   material possessions and happi-
      ness, 245
   middle class purchasing, 248
   model feature creep, 254
   opportunities for progress,
      195–196
   progressive consumption tax,
      474–477, 629n73
   self-interest vs. community
      well-being, 486
   wealth and satisfaction, 239
Franke, Richard, 374
Frankfurter, George, 24
Franklin, Benjamin, xviii
Frazier, Owsley Brown, 127
Frick, Henry Clay, 428
friendships. *See* community
   involvement; relationships
Fromstein, Mitchell, 267
Frumkin, Peter, 292
Fuente, David, 57
Fujimori, Alberto, 402
Fuller, Millard, 259
futility thesis of social change,
   489–493

G
Galbraith, James, 336, 338, 341,
   455, 625n234
Galbraith, John Kenneth, 435, 477
Galli, Joseph, 36
Galvin, Christopher, 73
Galvin, Paul V., 570n151
Gandhi, Mahatma, xviii
Gans, Curtis, 406–407
The Gap, 38
Gates, Bill. *See also* Microsoft
   about, 78–79
   art collection of, 139–140
   charitable giving of, 128, 356
   wealth of
      vs. all African Americans
         combined, 356,
         612n116
      growth rate, ix,
         553nn19–20
      progressive tax rates and,
         468
Gates, Bill Sr., 80–81, 404, 451
Geffen, David, 127
General Electric, 46, 71–73, 174,
   570n139
General Mills, 47
Genuine Progress Index, 370. *See*

also quality of life
George, Henry, xvi–xvii, 424, 426, 429
Germany
    CEO income, vs. U.S., 63
    downsizing statistics, 591n55
    employee wages and benefits, 204, 590n27
    mergers and acquisitions in, 586n88
    pay gaps, executive-employee, 66
    productivity vs. U.S., 214
    union membership in, 203
    work year length vs. U.S., 99
Gerstner, Lou, 58, 563n184
Getty, J. Paul, 141, 261–262, 489
Getty, J. Paul III, 261
Gibson Greeting, 12
Gilded Age (1870-98)
    described by Twain, 422
    isolation of the wealthy during, 262
    philanthropy in, 129
    politics influenced by wealth in, xv, xix, 547
    social justice crusades, 481, 502
Gilded Age (1990s), 126, 262, 264, 306
The Gilded Age (Twain), 422
Gillespie, Ed, 384
Gingrich, Newt, 450
Glassman, James, 130, 221
Global Crossing, 188
Goizueta, Roberto, 565n230
Golbart, Stephen, 263
golden parachute, 33, 562n154–155
Goldin, Claudia, xx
Goldman Sachs, 178, 254
Goldstein, Rob, 150
Goodman, Ellen, 24
goods and services. *See also* productivity
    production and distribution of, 365–366
    wages and demand linked, 215–216, 219
goods and services, demand for public
    environmental degradation link to, 348–349
    happiness and, 610n66
    lacking in unequal society, 345–351, 534
    September 11, 2001, attacks, 357–358
    Ten Times Rule, effect on, 512–513
Goodwin, Fred, 64
Google, 83
Goolsbee, Austan, 494
Gordon, David, 162

Gordon, Edmund, 352
Gore, Al, 384, 429, 460
Gorin, Stephen, 327
The Gospel of Wealth (Carnegie), 424
Gould, Jay, xv
Graff, Steffi, 305
Grassi, Anthony, 504–505
greed. *See also* benefactors, the greedy as; wealth inequity
    basic ideas supporting need for, 4–5, 557n1
    benefits from, 93–94
    employee, 191
    as incentive, 5, 564n223
    research as captive of, 211–212
Greed: The Series (television), xiv
Greeley, Andrew, 452
Greenberg, Stan, 264
Greens/Green Party program, 546
Greenspan, Alan, 87–88, 464
Greider, William, xxiv, 391
Grier, Peter, 249
Grieve, Paddy, 222
Griffey, Ken Jr., 296
Grove, Andy, 64–65, 165, 172
Grubman, Jack, 227
Guatemala, equality and democracy in, 403
Guerrand-Hermes, Mathias, xii
Gunther, Robert, 468

H

Hacker, Andrew, 130, 489–490, 493
Haft, Herbert, 259, 599n130
Hall, Peter, 128, 129
Hall, Steven, 73
Hall, Uriel, 427
Hamilton, Alexander, 418, 621n15
Hammer, Armand, 261
Hamptons, housing costs in, 256, 599n109
Hanna, Mark, 383, 384, 428
happiness
    1975 vs. 1999, 246
    components of, 524–525
    desire for wealth and, 241–246
    friendships/community and, 246–247, 260–262, 331, 369
    material possessions and, 244–246, 248–250, 262–263, 369
    public services and, 610n66
    reference group comparisons, 241–242
    satisfaction factor in, 238–239
    wealth as causative, 237–239, 258–259
Harken Energy, 85
Harlan, John, 427
Harrigan, Sean, 39
Harrington, James, 620n7

Harrison, Benjamin, 428
Harrison, Bennett, 213, 214, 215, 464
Harrison James, xi
Hart, Peter, 537
Harvard Business School, 74
Hasan, Malik, 285
Hassett, Janet and Christopher, 346–347
Hastert, J. Dennis, 379
Haughey, John, S.J., 260
Hawken, Paul, 359–360
Hawkes, Albert, 441
Hayes, Rich, 371
health
    psychosocial dimension of, 319–320, 325–328
    tax dollars spent on, 608n107
    in U.S. vs. other industrialized nations, 316–317, 326–327, 606n10, 607n40
    Whitehall study (Britain), 321–322
health, links to good
    income/wealth, 311–318, 606n12, 606n16, 606n23
    social cohesion, 319–320, 325–328
    social status, 321–326, 607n63, 608n77
health care
    for children in Texas, 350
    for-profit corporations, 285
    government funding for, 381
    HMOs, 285
    Medicare/Medicaid, 283, 335–336
    U.S. vs. other industrialized nations, 283, 350
health care industry's government influence, 382
health care reform, 284, 602n58
Heard, Jamie, 46
Hearst, William Randolph, 439
Heckman, James, 458
Heineman, Fred, 385
Heinz, H. J., 47
Hernes, Gudmund, 350
Hernstein, Richard, 352
Herodotus, 237
Hewlett, Bill, 164
Hewlett-Packard, 163–164, 166–167
Hickey, Dave, 150
Hightower, Jim, 90
Hilbert, Stephen, 18, 259
Hilfiger, Tommy, 220
Hill, Michael, 301
Hilton, Rick and Kathy, 357
Hilzenrath, David, 278
HIP, 540
Hiraide, Shoji, 234
Hirschman, Albert, 489
Hirshhorn, Joseph, x, 554n25

Hochschild, Adam, 375
Hockmeyer, Wayne T., 557n126
Hodges, Luther, 444–445
Home Depot, 253
home ownership. *See also* housing
   costs
   black vs. white, 353–354, 356
   by middle class, 97, 115–117,
      255–256
   Ten Times Rule, effect on,
      506–509
homes of the wealthy
   castles, x
   Gilded Age, xv
   landscaping costs, xi
   Neo-Fortress Movement, 357,
      612n126
   prices of, x–xi
   safe rooms, 230
   servants for, xiii, 554n49
   square footage, 255–256
   Ten Times Rule, effect on,
      506–509
Honeywell, 174
Hoover, Herbert, 437
Houghton, Amory, 389
housing costs. *See also* home own-
   ership; homes of the wealthy
   California, 121–122, 255–256,
      579nn181–182
   for middle class, 115–117,
      255–256
   national averages, 255
   in poverty calculations, 109
   Ten Times Rule, effect on,
      506–509
   for the wealthy, x–xi
Houston Astros, 298, 302
Houston Museum of Fine Art, 141
Howard, Cynthia, 286
Howard, Milford, xix
Howard, Richard, 187
Howells, William Dean, xvi
How Rich Is Too Rich? (Carroll and
   Inhaber), 484
Hubbard, Frank McKinney, 237
Huffington, Michael, 388
Huizenga, H. Wayne, 268,
   309–310
Hunt, H. L., 470
Huston, James, comments on
   American belief in egalitarian-
      ism, 419, 455
   American belief in monopoly,
      425
   industrialization in America,
      621n38
   supply-and-demand for CEOs,
      571n158–159
   those who counted in early
      America, 420
   wealth distribution, historical-
      ly, xviii, 197, 416, 417

I
Iacocca, Lee, 9
IBM, 58, 78–79, 189, 211
Idealab, 225, 594n155
immigrants, 113–115, 317, 336,
   607n40, 610n35
incentive
   greed as, 5, 564n223
   income alone as, 558n2,
      565n1
   reasonable and appropriate,
      5–6
   striving for a better life, 3–4,
      557n1
incentives for leaving, CEOs
   accelerated vesting, 32–33
   golden parachute, 33,
      562nn154–155
incentives for performance. *See also*
   CEOs, income additional to
   salary; performance/compensa-
   tion link
   Bonus Unit awards, 558n20
   CEO incentive-setting system,
      28
   stock ownership, 17–18,
      560n79, 560n81
income caps, proposals. *See also*
   corporate America, reforming for
   pay equity; Ten Times Rule
   for athletes, 487
   for attorneys, 487
   benchmark compensation caps,
      542
   disincentives for creating,
      492–493
   for executives, xxvi, 37, 48–49,
      61, 540 541, 546, 571n161
   public support for, 527–528
   social acceptance of, 488–489
income caps, proposals by
   Adler, 481
   Flynn, 624n204
   Keating, 433
   Long, 437–438
   Mazzocchi, 546
   McClellan, 571n161
   Menendez, 541
   Roosevelt (FDR), xxvi, 415,
      440–441, 481, 620n5
income distribution patterns,
   482–485
income equity ratios. *See also*
   income caps proposals; Ten
   Times Rule
   twenty times, 77–78,
      162–163, 546, 584n19
   Income Equity Act legislation,
      538–539, 634n57
   twenty-five times, 634n57
   100 times, soldiers vs. CEOs,
      542
   U.S. vs. other industrialized
      nations, 65–66, 203

income inequity. *See also* wealth
   inequity
   academic achievement link to,
      353–354
   athletes vs. fans, 296, 307,
      605n70
   CEOs vs. soldiers, 542
   entry-level professionals affect-
      ed by, 286–290
   health, correlation to,
      313–318, 320–321, 326,
      327–330
   murder rates relationship to,
      231–232
   school superintendents vs.
      CEO, 60–61
   U.S. vs. other industrialized
      nations, 63–66, 204
   voting rates correlated to, 407,
      620n157
income inequity, executive-
   employee
   1960s, 66
   1980s-2000, xxiii–xxiv, 66,
      569n95
   Drucker on, 162–163, 584n19
   examples of, 125–126
   in gain-sharing plans, 169
   McDonough on increases in,
      479–480
   morality in, 66–67, 480
   nonprofit sector, 291–292
   results of, 163, 165–166,
      183–186, 192–193
   in stock options, 13–14,
      164–165, 183
   U.S. vs. other industrialized
      nations, 65–66, 234
income inequity reform. *See also*
   income caps proposals
   citizens movement, 544–545
   importance of, 549–552
   legislative proposals, 536–538,
      540–541, 545–546
   living wage law, 535–536
   pay equity ratio requirements
      in government contracts,
      535
   revoking corporate charters as
      means of, 544–546
   union efforts, 529–534
income tax
   history, 547
   post-WWII, 442–443, 471,
      624n223
   progressive structure for,
      467–472
   reforms of 1890s, 425–428
   Roosevelt (Theodore) on,
      430–431
income tax legislation
   16th constitutional amend-
      ment, 431–432
   1861, Civil War levy, 422

1864, Civil War levy, 422
as 1894 tariff bill amendment, 427
1916 tax act, 433
1917 War Revenue Act, 433
1926 Revenue Act, 628n56
1932 Revenue Act, 437
1935 income tax, 439–440
1935 Wealth Tax Act, 439
1942 Revenue Act, 441, 442
1981 Economic Recovery Tax Act, 447
1981 Revenue Act, 433
1985 Supreme Court ruling, 427–428
1986 Tax Reform Act, 448
1988 Revenue Act, 433
1997 Taxpayer Relief Act, 451
Kemp-Roth initiative, 446–447
Rockefeller affected by 1935 Act, 624n196
Unlimited Savings Allowance Tax Act bill, 476–477
Victory Tax, 441
independent sector. *See* nonprofit sector
index funds, 19–20
Index of Social Health, 370. *See also* quality of life
Infinity Broadcasting, 587n109
infrastructure
  commons maintenance, 345–351, 357–358, 610n66
  elimination of firehouses, post 9/11, 358, 612n129
  U.S. government investment in, 213–214, 381–382, 520
Inhaber, Herbert, 482, 483, 484
Institute for Policy Studies, 182
insurance, medical, 100–101, 106–107, 121, 574n38. *See also* employee benefits
Intel
  CEO compensation, 64–65
  employee empowerment at, 163, 165
  executive pay, 2000, 42–43
  Late List, 165
  mergers and acquisitions, 172–173
  stock options at, 9
Internet commerce, 73, 225–226, 594n151, 594n155. *See also* Amazon.com
investment capital, sources for, 223–225, 517–520, 594n151, 594n155
Iraq War, 2003, 542, 635n71
Ironite, 161
IRS
  audits of poor vs. rich, 382, 616n26
  capital flight controls,

495–498
  history, 422
  limits to executive compensation, 486, 540–541, 629n22
  staff cuts, 616n25
Isenberg, David, 211
Ishi, Hiromitsu, 234
Italy, media ownership in, 400
Ivins, Molly, vii, 468

J
Jackson, Andrew, 419, 621n23
Jackson, Tim, 165
Jack: Straight from the Gut (Welch), 72
Japan
  CEO income, vs. U.S., 63–66, 569n88
  crime in, 231, 232–233, 595n185
  economic growth, 596n216
  health in, 314, 316–317, 607n40
  incarceration rates, 231
  job security in, 233, 596n210
  mergers and acquisitions in, 586n88
  pay ratios, executive-employee, 65–66
  shareholder vs. stakeholder position, 24
  stock/real estate collapse, 233
  wealth distribution, 233–235, 595n199
  work year length vs. U.S., 99
Jarrell, Sherry, 584n9
Jasinowski, Jerry, 100
Jefferson, Thomas, 417
Jehlen, Alain, 354
Jencks, Christopher, 313
Jenkins, Holman W. Jr., 290
jeopardy thesis of social change, 499–500
Jesus, xviii
Jiacomin, Danielle, 570n153
Jobs, Steve, 15–16, 559n65
job security. *See* unemployment
Joe Millionaire (television), xiv
Johnson, David Cay, 191
Johnson, Lyndon B., 333, 445
Johnson, W. R., 47
Johnson & Johnson, 531
Jones, Charles H., 427
Jones, Jesse H., 141
Jordan, Michael, 304
Jordan, Vernon E. Jr., 84
Josephson, Michael, 482
J. Paul Getty Museum, 141
judges, 289–290

K
Kagann, Stephen, 113
Kalla, Susan, 227–228
Kane, Eugene, 335

Kaplan, George, 313, 327
Kapur, Akash, 372
Kasich, John, 380, 384
Kaus, Mickey, 468
Kavanagh, David, 258
Kawachi, Ichiro, 313–314, 329–330
Kay, Ira, 14, 42
Kay, John, 64, 160
Kay Manufacturing, 170
Kazin, Michael, 428, 429
Keating, Edward, 433
Kellcher, Herb, 173
Kelly, Marcy, 39
Kelly, Marjorie, 24, 545
Kemp, Jack, 446–447, 451, 477
Kennedy, Bruce, 313–314, 329–330
Kennedy, Edward, 453
Kennedy, John F., 444–445
Kennedy, John Pendleton, 420
Kenny, Shirley Strum, 28
Keough, Keith, 335
Kerala, India, 372–377, 614n68, 615n95
Kerrey, Bob, 460
Kersh, Russell, 53
Keynes, John Maynard, 215
Kimberly-Clark, 53, 566nn23–24
Kimel, Martin, 289
Kimsey, James, 14
King, Willford Isbel, 432
Kinsley, Michael, 254
Kirsch, Steve, 127–128
Klein, Ethel, 537
Kleiner Perkins Caufield & Byers, 518
Klepper, Michael, 468
Klinger, Scott, 532
Knight, Christopher, 147
Knight, Phil, 392
Koenig, Louis, 428–429
Kohn, Alfie, 194
Koizumi, Junichiro, 234, 235
Koogle, Timothy, 563n184
Koors, Jan, 32
Korten, David, 366
Kozlowski, L. Dennis, 47, 173
KPMG, 281, 282
Kraft, Alexander, x
Kravis, Henry, 174
Kroc, Joan, 127
Krugman, Paul, xxi, 281, 407
Kucinich, Dennis, 203
Kumar, Sanjay, 25–27, 561n117
Kuttner, Robert, 405–406, 459
Kuznets, Simon, 197, 556n101

L
La Follette, Robert, 437–438
LaGuardia, Fiorello, 438
Lake, Celinda, 386
Lamoureux, Patricia Ann, 467
Lane, Robert, 240, 246, 247, 319

Lang, Eugene, 266
Larcker, David, 90
Lardner, James, 315, 334
Laski, Harold, 185, 401
Lawler, Edward, 160, 161, 168, 170, 584n12, 586n64
lawyers. *See under* professionals
layoffs of employees. *See also* downsizing of employees
　airline employees, 379
　downsizing vs., 179–180
　post-9/11 attack, 379
　U.S. vs. European restrictions, 202, 591n31
layoffs of employees at
　Amazon.com, 70–71
　BellSouth, 61
　Cisco Systems, 227
　Hewlett-Packard, 166–167
　Kimberly-Clark, 54
　Nortel, 227
　Scott Paper, 52–54, 566n29
　Sunbeam, 54, 566n35
　Washington Post, 593n113
Lazar, Edward, 193
Lazard Freres & Co., 84
Lebowitz, Fran, 269
Ledebur, Larry, 199
Ledecky, Jonathan, 140
Lee, William, 584n11
Leggett, William, 419
Leno, Jay, xiv
Lerman, Robert, 113
Lerner, Alfred, 28
Lesar, David, 542
Level 3 Communications, 227
Levin, Carl, 394
Levin, Gerald, 30, 562n140
Levin, Jerry, 55–56, 563n184
Levitt, Arthur Jr., 281
Lewis, John, 393
Lewis, Michael, 67, 174, 264, 346
Licklider, J. C. R., 523
Liebling, A. J., 398–399
life, quality of. *See* happiness; quality of life
life, quantity of, 525
Lillak, Dale, 266
Lily-Tulip, 52
Linfante, Kristen, 145
Linux software, 522–523
Lipman, Samuel, 141
Lippman, Walter, 445
Lloyd, Henry Demarest, 425
Lodge, Henry Cabot, 432
Lofton, Thomas, 291
Long, Huey P., 437–439
Looking Backward (Bellamy), xvi, 426, 549
Lorsch, Jay, 185
Los Angeles Lakers, 604n19
lottery payoff amounts, ix
Lowenstein, Louis, 229
Lucent Technologies, 43, 188

Lucky, Robert, 211
Luxury Fever (Frank), 474
Lynch, John, 327
Lynch, Lorenzo, 299
Lynch, Peter, 133
Lyons, Max, 96

M
Madison, James, 418, 457, 481
Magma Copper, 584n13
Maine, election spending, 395
Malone, John, 226
Mancuso, Frank, 562n161
Marcos, Ferdinand and Imelda, 362
Marcus, George, 128, 129
Marcus, Stanley, 262
Marks, Mitchell, 180
Marmor, Ted, 329
Marmot, Michael, 321–322, 323, 328
Marshall Industries, 169
Martinez, Arthur, 35
Marx, Karl, 196
Maryland, revoking corporate charters, 544–545
Maslow, Abraham, 168, 245
material possessions
　conspicuous consumption of, 474–478, 629n73, 629n76
　creating artificial need, 369
　happiness and, 244–246, 248–250, 262–263, 369
　social pressure felt by families, 218, 242–245, 248–250, 344–345, 509–510
　Ten Times Rule, effect on consumption standard, 509–510
maximum wage history. *See also* income caps proposals; Ten Times Rule
Mays, L. Lowry, 176–177
Mazzocchi, Tony, 546
MBNA, 28, 45
McAuliffe, Terry, 384
McCain, John, 393, 395
McCain-Feingold, 393–395
McClellan, Bill, 76, 481, 571n161
McColl, Hugh, 39
McConnell, Mitch, 618n97
McDonough, William J., 479–480
McGill, William, 523
McGinn, Richard, 43
McGuire, Mark, 304
McGurn, Patrick, 47
MCI, 48–49. *See also* WorldCom
MCI Center, 298, 299
McIntyre, Robert, 453, 476
McKibben, Bill, 364, 367, 374
McKinley, William, 428–429
McNamee, Stephen, 88
McPherson, Michael, 213
Meany, George, 442
media

changes in news reporting, 619n126
　free press and democratic tradition, 399–400
　middle class depicted by the, 242
　wealthy depicted by the, 242
media, influence on
　consumer spending, 242
　desire for wealth, xiv
　sports industry, 300–301, 309
MedImmune Inc., xxiv, 557n126
Mellon, Andrew, 136–137, 435, 623n158
Menendez, Robert, 541
Merrill Lynch, 222
Mesa, Armida, 58
Messier, Jean-Marie, 206, 207
Metropolitan Museum, 139
Mexico, 361, 402
Meyerson, Harold, 121
MFS Communications, 174
MGM (Metro-Goldwyn-Mayer Inc.), 34, 562n161
Michalos, Alex, 270
Microsoft, 11, 57, 78–79, 567n53, 571n174. *See also* Gates, Bill
Middelhoff, Thomas, 206, 207
middle class. *See also* families (average); taxes on the middle class; the poor; the wealthy
　black Americans as, 351–353, 612n103
　consumer debt of, 244
　defined, xxi, 385
　economic mobility of, 458, 460, 464
　emergence/decline of, xx, xxi–xxii, 97, 348, 555nn99–100, 556n101
　in Europe, 203, 338–339
　exploitation as consumers, 241–245, 251–252, 364, 598n71, 613n33
　full employment vs. inflation in 1970s, 625n234
　happiness of, 244–246
　housing costs, 255–257, 358, 506–509, 599n109
　in Japan, 233
　lifestyle, 121–125, 300, 358
　media depiction of, 242
　reference group comparisons, 241–243
　Ten Times Rule, effect on, 506–510
　the wealthy, beliefs regarding, 264–265
middle class, financial assets
　1998-2001, drop in, xxi–xxii. *see also* taxes on the middle class
　black vs. white, 353–354, 612n103

home ownership, 97
net worth, 1992-2001, 119
stock market investments, 97,
117–119, 573nn12–13
middle class, income of the. *See
also* taxes on the middle class
1947(post-WWII) -1973, xx
1947(post-WWII) -1997,
579n203
1960s vs. 1990s, 124
1970s-2000, 121, 556n130
after tax losses, 1970s,
557n130
gains
1947-1973, 125
1979-2000, 113
median, annual, 1980 vs.
2000, 98, 113
physicians vs., 284, 602n63
wage-earners/family, 99,
243–244
Milken, Michael, 12, 57, 567n54
Miller, Ellen, 382
Miller, George, 454, 455
Miller, Heidi, 18
Miller, Matthew, 75
Miller, Mike, 464
Miller, Robert Jr., 88
millionaires
in 1800s, 422, 423
1919 vs. 1929, 436
as cabinet officers, 390
in California, 120
in Congress, 387–388
globally, 2001, 362
growth rate, ix, 120, 253,
553n11
public opinion on, 528
on the Supreme Court, 391
taxation of, 433
Milloy, Courtland, 356
Mills, D. Quinn, 225
minimum wage. *See also* Ten Times
Rule
1950s-1960s, 216–217
1968 vs. 2001, 217, 343
1980s-1990s, 217
2003, 490
cost of living vs., 110–111,
593n111
history of the, xx, 480
incentives for increasing,
484–485, 499
living wage law (Baltimore),
535–536
Ministry of Money, 260
Minor, Halsey, 84
Minow, Nell, 40, 42, 52
Modell, Art, 302, 303, 307
Mogil, Chris, 260
Mohn, Reinhard, 207
Mondale, Walter, 448
Money, Meaning and Choices
Institute, 260

Mongiovi, Gary, 229
Monks, Robert A. G., 38,
563n189
Moore, Gordon, 165
Moore, Stephen, 115
More than Money, 260
Morgan, J. Pierpont, 77–78, 139,
533
Morgan Stanley Dean Witter, 36
Morgenson, Gretchen, 227–228
Morgenthau, Henry, 366, 476
Morocco, 372, 614n68
Morrill, Justin, 422
Morris, Charles, 12
Morrison, Bob, 149
Morrissey, Rick, 306
Motorola, 20, 73, 570n151
Mott, David M., 557n126
Mullainathan, Sendhil, 82
murder rates
income inequity and, 231–232
social status and, 325
for women, Europe, 595n185
Murdoch, Rupert, 304
Murray, Charles, 352
Murray, Robert, 434, 435
Museum of Modern Art, 139
Myers, Ched, 466–467
My First Days in the White House
(Long), 438
Myths of Rich and Poor (Cox and
Alm), 100, 248

N
Nacchio, Joseph, 227
Nader, Ralph, 516
Nakao, Annie, 353
Nasser, Jacques, 21, 25
NationsBank, 33, 175
Naylor, Bart, 530
Neiman Marcus retail, 262–263
Netscape Communications,
220–221
Newbold, Frank, xi
NewTithing Web site, 133
Newton, Sir Isaac, 80
New York (state), election spend-
ing, 389
New York, New York, 256, 258,
315, 349, 536, 607n28
New York Yankees, 296, 307
Nicolosi, Richard, 53
Nitec, 567n49
Nixon, Richard M., 62
nonprofit sector. *See also* philan-
thropy
CEO pay in, 290–292,
537–539, 539–541, 634n67
funding by tax dollars,
142–143, 146, 150,
539–541, 583n76
political influence of, 405–406
Ten Times Rule, effect on,
512–513

Nordin, Jennifer, 378
Norris, George, 437–438
Norway, equality of goods and
services in, 349–351
Novak, Robert, 264
Novell, 82
Noyce, Bob, 163, 165
Nunn, Sam, 476–477

O
Obey, David, 448
Odendahl, Teresa, 135
Office Depot, 57
Okun, Arthur, 198
Oliver, Melvin, 354
Olson, Floyd B., 437–438
O'Neill, Paul, 391
Oracle, 13, 44, 189–190, 221
O'Reilly, Charles, 185
outsourcing of employees, 104
Overholder, Geneva, 552
The Overworked American (Schor),
243
Ovitz, Michael, 67–68, 569n108

P
Packard, Dave, 164
Packwood, Bob, 386, 617n53
Page, Benjamin, 458
Page, Scott, 14
Pagliocchini, Lisa and Steve, 123,
125
Palaima, Thomas, xvii
Palast, Greg, 115
Palter, Peggy, 35
Paraguay, equality and democracy
in, 403
Parenti, Michael, 89
Parsons, Frank, 428
pay. *See* wages
Pearlstein, Steven, 49
Pechman, Joseph, 468, 628n50
Peirce, Neal, 303
Peltzman, Sam, 348
Peltzman's Law, 348
Pelz, Michael, 518
Pen, Jan, 482
Peninsula Hotel, Hong Kong, xii
Pen parade analysis of income dis-
tribution patterns, 482–483
pentamillionaires, 253, 598n79
PepsiCo, 11
performance/compensation link.
See also incentive
for athletes, 305, 307–310
effectiveness for employees
Deming on, 585n51
gain-sharing plans for,
168–170
management belief in,
167–168
motivation in, 585n44
negative results, 168,
193–194, 585n48

proof of, 585n45
puzzle players example,
184
for risk, 57–58
performance/compensation link,
CEOs. *See also* incentive
1980s, 7–10
2000 crash, effect on, 40–44
boards of directors as factor in,
28–31
bonuses not requiring, 21, 30,
562n140
Computer Associates example,
25–28, 561n117
Fidelity effect on, 19–20
post-WWII-1970s, 6–7
reform of WorldCom system,
48
stock analysts effect on, 21–23,
560n95, 560nn98–102
stock options
1970s, 9–10
1980s, 7–10
1990s, 10–14
Bonus Unit awards,
558n20
Computer Associates
example, 25–28,
561n117
reforms, 16–18, 560n74
stock ownership requirement,
17–18, 560n79, 560n81
performance/compensation link,
CEOs lacking performance
Carly Fiorina, HP, 166–167
David Rickey, Applied Micro
Circuits, 47
European CEOs, 206–207
George Shaheen, Webvan,
76–77
Gerald Levin, Time Warner, 30
insuring against, 33
Jack Welch, General Electric,
570n139
James Crowe, Level 3
Communications, 227
Jeff Bezos, Amazon, 70–71,
570n122, 570n125
John Ward, Russell Corp.,
562n145
Joseph Nacchio, Qwest, 227
Larry Ellison, Oracle, 44
L. Dennis Kozlowski, Tyco
International, 173
Michael Bonsignore,
Honeywell, 174
Philip Anschutz, Qwest, 227
Richard Adams, Cello
Technologies, 174
Solomon Trujillo, Qwest, 178
Stephen Sanger, General Mills,
47–48
Steve Jobs, Apple Computer,
559n65

William Smithburg, Quaker
Oats, 174
W.R. Johnson, H.J. Heinz, 47
Perkins, Frances, 440
Perot, H. Ross, 449
Perotti, Roberto, 593n93
Peru, elections in, 402
perversity thesis of social change,
493–499
Petersen, Donald E., 13
Peyrelevade, Jean, 206
Pfeiffer, Eckhard, 13, 136
philanthropy. *See also* nonprofit
sector; *under* the wealthy
by Boston Brahmins, 128–129
NewTithing Web site calculator, 133
poor as recipients of, 135–136,
581n65
purpose of, 129
statistics
1960s, 130
1970 vs. 1999, 581n66
1990s, 130, 134, 136,
580n27, 581n65
2000, 133–134
as percentage of income,
130–131
Ten Times Rule, effect on,
508–509, 512–513, 519,
631n6
the wealthy and
giving by, 130–131,
133–136
untapped capacity of,
132–134
Philip Morris, 35
Phillips, Kevin, 418, 423, 431,
442, 443, 448
Phillips Collection, 140
physicians, 282–286, 602n58,
602n63. *See also* health care
Pierce, Gregory, 66
Pinchot, Amos, 433
Plutarch, xvii
plutocracy. *See also* the wealthy
1870-98 (Gilded Age), xv
1896 presidential race, a win
for the, 428
1950s, xv
1990s-2000, xv, 383, 404–405
concerns regarding, 434, 445
by default of average citizen,
407
demise and resurgence of,
xiv–xv
politicians opposing, xvi–xvii
Populist crusade against, xix,
428
PNC Financial, 564n217
Pollans, Albert, 282
the poor. *See also* taxes on the
poor; working poor
in California, 121

education for children of, 213,
335–336, 459–461, 464,
593n93, 609n31, 609n33,
627n7, 627n11
environmental degradation by,
361–362
immigrants as, 113–115, 336,
610n35
philanthropy as benefit to,
135–136, 581n65
poor, beliefs about held by
economists, 111–113
journalists, 264
lawmakers, 344
politicians, 447, 458
the wealthy, 263–264, 333,
338
poor, incomes of the. *See also* taxes
on the poor
1960s vs. 1990s, 124
1977 vs. 1999, 556n130
1989-1999, California, 121
2001, 119
after taxes, 342
poorest 20%, 112–113,
124–125, 342, 628n34
poorest 25%, 119
poorest 5%, 557n130
poorest 90%, 557n131
post-WWII, xx
poor, socioeconomic elements
anti-hunger campaign,
343–345
budget calculations, minimum
needs, 109–110
equal opportunity lacking,
458–459
food bank usage, 111
Food Stamps for, 336
health care, 283, 335–336
leveling up strategy for social
justice, 457–459
lifestyle, Gilded Age, xvi, 262
material possessions and well-
being of, 245
shelter request increases, 111
social pressures faced by,
344–345, 509–510
Poppendieck, Janet, 343–345
Populist Party, xix
poverty
defined, 108–109, 576n94,
576n96
equality-efficiency conflict for
eradicating, 198
health linked to, 311–312,
324–325
in Japan, 233
leveling down strategy for alle-
viating
futility thesis of, 489–493
jeopardy thesis of,
499–500
perversity thesis of,

493–499
progressive consumption
tax, 474–478, 629n73,
629n76
progressive taxation,
467–472
sabbath economics,
466–467
wealth tax, 472–474,
628n68
murder rates relationship to,
231–232
official guidelines for, 109–110
the war against, 333–334
poverty line, 216–217, 334,
576n110. *See also* working poor
Prada, xi
*The Present Distribution of Wealth
in the United States* (Spahr), 428
Pressler, Margaret Webb, 244
Priceline, 18, 188, 221
PricewaterhouseCoopers, 253,
279, 282
productivity. *See also* economic
growth; goods and services
equality as contributor to, 233
increases, 435, 592n77
increasing, methods of,
200–201, 212–215, 593n93,
593n97
Japanese enterprises, 233
research and development
investment and, 210–212,
214
security spending vs., 230–231
speculative trading vs.,
228–229, 595n177
U.S. vs. European rates of, 214
wages relationship to, 214–215
professionals. *See also specific professions*, e.g. attorneys
characteristics of, 292–293
effect of unequal rewards on
entry-level, 286–290
salary gaps, results of, 289–290
satisfaction of, factors in,
273–274
success defined by, 273–274
trust as vital to, 274, 282–283
Progress and Poverty (George), xvi
Progressive Party, xix–xx
Prothrow-Stith, Deborah,
313–314
psychosocial dimension of health,
326–328
public sector, reform efforts by
unions and, 534
Pulitzer, Joseph, 426
Putnam, Robert, 247, 331–332

Q
Quaker Oats, 174
Qualcomm, 221
quality of life. *See also* happiness

Kerala, India, 372–375,
376–377, 614n68
measurement indexes, 370
Ten Times Rule, effect on,
524–525
Quinn, Michelle, 270, 346
Qwest Communications, 178,
227–228

R
Raber, Roger, 28
racism, 351–353, 611n93,
611n95. *See also* black
Americans; discrimination
raiders restructuring of corporate
America, 7–8, 33
Raines, Franklin, 390
Rainwater, Richard, 85–86
Rakoff, Jed, 48, 486
Ran, Thomas, 564n217
Randolph, Joseph Fitz, 419
Raskin, Jamin, 384
Raskob, John J., 436
Ratner, Sidney, 429
Rawls, John, 339–340
Raytheon, 279
RCN Corporation, 17, 226,
560n74
Reagan (Ronald), presidency of,
217, 447–448, 541, 625n240
Rector, Robert, 112
Reebok, 10–11
Reed, Bruce, 130
Rees, William, 363
Rehnquist, William, 289, 391
Reich, Robert, 217, 450, 473,
493, 537–538
Reingold, Jennifer, 585n45
relationships. *See also* community
involvement
good health linked to,
319–320, 325–326
happiness from, 246–247,
260–262, 331, 369
of the wealthy, 260–262, 267,
306, 346
Rendell, Ed, 111
Rennert, Ira, x
Revlon, 12
Ricardo, David, 196
Rickey, David, 47
Riley, Richard, 148
Ritz-Carlton Downtown, 346
RJR Nabisco, 174
road rage, 258
Roberts, Brian, 82
Roberts, Ralph, 81–82
Robertson, Julian, 222
Robertson, Pat, 442
Robinson, Jackie, 296
Robinson, John, 597n31
Roche, James, 125, 579n209
Rockefeller, David, 139
Rockefeller, John D., ix, 81, 129,

430, 624n196
Rockefeller Foundation, 129
Rodin, Rob, 169
Rodriguez, Alex, 296, 305, 308,
309, 605n77
Rogers, James, 266
Rogers, Joel, 537
Rohr, James, 564n217
Rooney, Mickey, 95
Roosevelt, Franklin D., 61
income cap proposal, xxvi,
415–416, 440–441, 481,
620n5
New Deal, 436–439
tax increases for the wealthy,
440, 624n196
Roosevelt, Theodore, xvii, 430,
432
Rosen, Irwin, 263
Rosenberg, Claude, 132–134
Rosenberg family foundation, 132
Roseto, Pennsylvania, 319–320
Ross, Steve, 10, 12, 558n20
Rossiter, Caleb, 389
Roth, William, 446–447
Rove, Karl, 390, 618n75
Rowe, Jonathan, 369
Royal Bank of Scotland, 64
Rubin, Robert, 390
Rumsfeld, Donald, 391
Ruppik, Erich, 207
Rushin, Steve, 306
Russell Corp., 562n145
Russia, child poverty rates in, 336,
337
Ryscave, Paul, 216

S
sabbath economics, 466–467
Sabo, Martin, 537–538, 634n57
Salk, Jonas, xxiv
Salomon, 227
Salzer, Myra, 263
Samuelson, Robert, 205, 487
Sanders, Bernie, 454
Sanford, Charles S. Jr., 489
San Francisco (Calif.) housing
costs, 255–256
Sanger, Stephen, 47
San Jose (Calif.) commuting time,
257–258
Sapolsky, R. M., 323–324
Saraiva, Ellen, 232
Sarbanes, Paul, 282
Sarbanes-Oxley Act, 47, 565n247
Scanlon, Joseph, 168–169
Schacht, Henry, 217
Schapiro, Morton Owen, 213
Scheiber, Anne, 259–260
Schervish, Paul, 267–268
Schlesinger, Arthur, 439
Schmidt, Eric, 82–84
Schmidt, Ted, 218
Schor, Juliet, 242, 243, 245,

248–249, 597n31
Schrempp, Jurgen, 63
Schumacher, E. F., 370
Schwarz, Benjamin, 627n23
scientific management, 159
Scoones, Eric, 64
Scott, Richard, 285
Scott, Samuel, 73
Scott Paper, 52–54, 566n13, 566n29
Scripps. E. W., 433
Seagate Technology, 32
Sears, 35
Seattle Mariners, 309, 605n77
Sedgwick, Theodore, 419
Selig, Bud, 307
Seligman, Ben, 435
Sen, Amartya, 231, 372, 407
September 11, 2001, attacks
  airlines industry bailout, 379–380, 615n6
  commemoration ceremony, 479–480
  elimination of firehouses following, 358, 612n129
  workforce layoffs after, 379
Seward, William, 419
Shaheen, George, 76–77, 571n164, 571n168
Shanahan, John, 179
Shapiro, Leonard, 305
Shapiro, Thomas, 354
shareholder activists, 38, 531–532, 563n189
shareholders. *See also* corporate America; stock ownership
  CEO income increases vs. profits of, 14–15
  market wisdom of individual investors, 19
  power of management over, 39–40, 531–532, 564n200
  pre-eminence of, 24–25, 561n104
  stakeholders vs. in importance, 24–28, 561n104, 561n117
  takeover industry affecting wealth of, 33, 54–56, 566n35
  voting practices, 633n26
Shaw, Eric, 191
Shaw, George Bernard, 267, 271
Sheen, Charlie, 269
Shellenberger, Lynn, 481
Sherman, John, 420, 427
Sherraden, Michael, 460, 461
Shi, Leiyu, 318
Shields, Mark, 392
Shriver, Sargent, 334
Shugart, Al, 32
Sifry, Micah, 382
Silber, John, 291, 603n85
Silverman, Henry, 34
Simon, Neil, 270–271

Simon, William, 12
Sims, Jane, 107
Singletary, Michelle, xiv
Skadden, Arps, Slate, Meagher & Flom, 275
Skilling, Jeff, 22
Sklar, Holly, 118, 407, 543
Slater, Philip, 261, 262, 270
slavery, 419, 421, 621n25. *See also* racism
Slavin, Robert, 461
Slim, Carlos, 402
Sloan, Allan, 46, 73
Sloan Kettering Cancer Center, 291
Slywotzky, Adrian, 229
Smeeding, Timothy, 204, 356
Smith, Adam, 467–468
Smith, George Davey, 326
Smith, Goldwin, 422
Smith, Logan Pearsall, 270
Smith, Roy C., 8, 82, 287, 558n2
Smith, Tim, 38
Smithburg, William, 174
Snapple, 174
Snow, John, 46
Snow, Tony, 521
Soare, Anastasia, 268
social capital, 247, 331–332. *See also* community involvement; relationships
social cohesion, link to good health, 319–320, 325–326. *See also* community involvement; relationships
social justice. *See also* Ten Times Rule
  economic justice in, 529–534
  leveling down for leveling up strategy
    for education funding, 462, 627n23
    historical belief in, 457–459, 481
    natural range of inequality, 484
  leveling down strategy for wealth distribution
    futility thesis of, 489–493
    jeopardy thesis of, 499–500
    of Native Americans, xvii
    perversity thesis of, 493–499
    progressive consumption tax, 474–478, 629n73, 629n76
    progressive taxation, 467–472
    sabbath economics, 466–467
    wealth tax, 472–474, 628n68
  leveling up strategy for educa-

tion funding, 461–462
Social Security
  black vs. white history, 356
  FICA payroll tax increases, 448
  general public vs. wealthy on, 387, 617n56
  history, xx, 439
  taxation of benefits, 448, 625n246
society. *See also* community involvement
  cohesive, 247, 331–332
  commons maintained in healthy, 345–351, 357–358, 610n66
  Kerala, India, as example of equality in, 372–377
  social/moral obligation in
    civic role of public education, 459–460, 627n7, 627n11
    employee safety nets, 201–202
    food for all in America, 343–345, 610n35
    living wage law, 535–536
    self-interest vs. community well-being, 485–488
    welfare reform, 334–336, 342–343
  social status and
    health, 321–326, 607n63, 608n77
    material possessions, 248–250
    murder rates, 325
Sonnenfeld, Jeffrey, 171
Sooy, Richard, 390
Sorenson, Georgia, 450
Soros, George, 404, 593n123
Sosa, Sammy, 304, 306
South Beach (New York) infant mortality in, 315, 607n28
Southwest Airlines, 173, 587n124
Spahr, Charles B., 428
Spinner, Percell, 299
Spitzer, Eliot, 545
Spock, Mr., 126
sports industry. *See also* athletes; athletes salaries
  1960s vs. 1990s, 297–298
  media effect on, 300–301, 309
  pay gaps, athletes-average fan, 296
sports industry fans. *See also* athletes
  anger in, 302
  attendance statistics, 301, 307, 309–310
  costs increasing for, 298–299, 301–302, 604n19
  declining importance of, 297–301
  Fan Cost Index, 299

income gap, athletes vs., 296
pay gaps, athletes-average fan, 296
sports industry finances
  Fan Cost Index, 299
  franchise revenue/value, 296, 307
  owner profits, 301, 302–303, 307–308
  owner salaries, 296
  revenue, annual, 295–296
  revenue gaps, 307
  stadium costs, 298, 309–310, 403
  tax breaks/deductions, 296
  taxes subsidizing, 302–303, 403
  television broadcast costs, 300–301
  ticket costs, 298–300, 604n19
Sprague, O. M. W., 433, 623n136
Sprint, 11, 35, 36, 180–181
Sreenivasan, Sreenath, 212
The Stakeholder Society (Ackerman and Alstott), 460, 462
Starfield, Barbara, 329
Stauber, John, 619n126
Staw, Barry, 161
Steinbrenner, George, 296, 301
Steinmo, Sven, 471
Stevens, Rick, 257
Stevenson, Howard, 482
Stewart, Jill, 131
Stewart, William, 233
St. Louis Art Museum, 150, 583n76
St. Louis Municipal Opera, 583n78
stock grants, 31–32, 562n147
Stockman, David, 447–448
stock market. *See also* Wall Street
  Dow Jones effect on, 19–20
  Fidelity effect on, 20–21
  manipulation through IPOs, 223–226, 594n151, 594n155
  speculative trading, 228–229, 595n177
  telecommunications industry corruption and the, 226–228
stock market analysts, conflicts of interests, 21–23, 560n95, 560n98–102
Stock Market Primer (Rosenberg), 132
stock options
  Bonus Unit awards, 558n20
  as compensation. *see also*
    CEOs, income additional to salary
    critics of, 16–17
    restrictive nature of, 165
    supporters of, 10–11
  corporate earnings statements

and, 17, 560n74
  in lieu of salary, 15–16
  management-employee gaps, 13–14, 164–165, 183
  taxation of, 9, 558n29
  for telecom executives, 228
stock ownership. *See also* shareholders
  1980s-1995, 573n13
  1983-2000, 573n12
  by middle class, 97, 117–119, 578n153
stock repricing, 34–36
success
  in corporate America, 23–25, 65, 561n104
  defined, 23–25, 65, 273–274
  individual vs. shared achievement in, 65–66, 79–80, 87
  leveling up strategy, 463
  social roots of, 80–81
Sudden Money Institute, 260
Sugar, Ronald, 542
Sullivan, Donald, 30
Sullivan, Ken, 233
Summers, Lawrence, 224, 613n38
Sumner, William Graham, 424
Sunbeam, 54–55, 566n35, 567n37, 567n47
Swartz, Mark, 280, 602n36
Sweden, 231, 314, 336
Sweeney, John, 183
Switzerland, taxation in, 472
Sykes, John, 148–149

T
Tabb, William, 349
Taft, William Howard, 431
Tawney, R. H., 255, 273, 292
tax deductions
  charitable organizations, 508–509, 539, 634n60
  corporations, 37, 303, 539
  insurance premiums for death benefits, 107
  sports industry, 296, 604n8
tax dollars funding
  Bill Gates, early computer research, 79
  CEO wealth, 534–539
  George W. Bush, Arlington Ballpark, 86
  insurance company liability safety net, 380
  nonprofit organizations, 142–143, 146, 150, 539–541, 583n76, 634n60
  Paul Allen, Seahawk Stadium, 302, 403
  public goods and services, 348–349
  sports industry, 302–303
taxes. *See also* estate tax; income tax

avoidance strategies, 343, 443, 468, 494–498, 500–502
  capital flight option, 495–498
  Earned Income Tax Credit, 341–342
  environmental, 359–360
  income averaging for, 507–508, 631nn4–5
  IRS audits, 382, 616n26
  Share-Our-Wealth movement, 437–439
taxes, historical
  1790 excise tax on distilled liquor, 418
  1861 Civil War levy, 422
  1864, Civil War levy, 422
  1873, post-Civil War, 422
  1917 War Revenue Act, 433
  1920- (post-WWI) decreases for the wealthy, 435, 623n158, 623n167
  1932 Revenue Act, 437
  1942 Revenue Act, 441
  1948 Revenue Act, 442
  post-WWI, 435, 623n158, 623n167
  post-WWI decreases for the wealthy, 435, 623n158, 623n167
  post-WWII, 527
  war-time profits, 433, 440, 542, 623n136
taxes on
  401(k) plans, 45–46, 102
  bonds, state/municipal, 500–502
  capital gains, 343, 446, 448, 451, 625n250, 625n260
  net worth, 472–474, 628n68
  oil and gas production, 469–470, 628n56
  property, xvi, 150, 472
  savings, personal, 476–477
  stock market gains, 343
  stock options, 9, 558n29
taxes on average families
  Bush (GW) administration, 382, 452–455
  FICA tax increases, 448
  IRS audits, 382
  Reagan administration, 446–448
  sports industry subsidized by, 302
  Ten Times Rule, effect on, 491, 520–521
  Victory Tax, 441
taxes on corporations
  1981 Economic Recovery Tax Act, 447
  corporate welfare subsidies, 342, 380–381
  "A Corp" status proposal, 537
  deductions, 37, 303, 539

environmental, 359–360
fraudulent accounting for,
187–191, 531, 588n166,
589n177
fraudulent reporting of profits,
190–191
oil depletion allowance loophole, 469–470, 628n56
public opinion on, 381
stock options, 9, 558n29
taxes on the middle class
Bush administration, 382–383
IRS audits, 616n26
Reagan administration, 449
Ten Times Rule, effect on,
484–485, 491
taxes on the poor
1790 excise tax on distilled
liquor, 418
under Bush administration,
453, 616n28
IRS audits, 382
Ten Times Rule, effect on,
484–485, 491
taxes on the wealthy. *See also* estate
tax; Ten Times Rule
Bush (GHW) administration,
449
Bush (GW) administration
$1,000,000 income or
greater, 382–383,
616n31
$200,000 income and
greater, 616n28
$50-$75,000 income,
616n31
congressional votes approv-
ing, 626n276
estate tax, 382
richest 1%, 415, 620n6
tax plan 2001, 452–455
Clinton administration, 382,
449–450, 451–452,
625n253, 625n260
decreases
Bush (GW) administra-
tion, 382–383, 415,
452–455, 616n28,
616n31, 620n6,
626n276
Clinton administration,
451–452, 625n260
Economic Recovery Tax
Act, 1981, 447
Kennedy administration,
444–445, 624n230
Reagan administration,
446–448
Tax Reform Act, 1986,
448
increases
Bush (GHW) administra-
tion increases, 449
Clinton administration,

382, 449–450, 616n24,
625n253
public opinion on, 528
Victory Tax, 441
IRS audits, 616n26
Kennedy administration,
444–445, 624n230
progressive consumption tax,
474–478, 629n73, 629n76
public opinion on, 632n6,
632n8, 632n10
Reagan administration,
446–448
richest 1%, 620n6
Rockefeller affected by 1935
Act, 624n196
tax calculations using the Ten
Times Rule, 484–485,
490–492
U.S. vs. Europe, 591n53
taxes on the working poor,
341–342, 610n62
tax fraud, 187–191, 588n166,
589n177
tax loopholes, 469–470, 628n56
tax rates
calculating using the Ten
Times Rule, 484–485,
490–492
for public goods and services,
350
rich vs. poor, 382–383
on the wealthy, xx, 203, 470,
471–474
tax structure for social justice. *See
also* Ten Times Rule
progressive consumption tax,
474–478, 629n73, 629n76
progressive taxation, 467–472
wealth tax, 472–474, 628n68
Taylor, Frederick Winslow, 159
Taylorism, 159
Teach for America, 287
Teixeira, Ruy, 384, 392, 618n82
Telecommunications Act, 176
telecommunications industry,
176–177, 226–228, 300–301,
380
Ten Times Rule. *See also* income
caps propsals; social justice
concept, xxvi–xxvii
Greens/Green Party proposal,
546
history of, 502–503
income caps and taxation rates
using the, 490–493, 631n49,
631n51
IRS revenue, increases from,
490–492
minimum wage as basis for,
484–485
tax rate calculations using the,
484–485
union negotiating for, possibil-

ity of, 532–534
Ten Times Rule, effect on
charitable giving, 508–509,
512–513, 519, 631n6
education, 520
employee empowerment,
505–506, 514–516
employment, 500–502, 510
environment, 525–526
executives, 504–506, 514–515,
631n1
families
housing, 506–509
latchkey children, 511–512
leisure time, 510–511
tax reductions/income
increases, 520–521
income averaging, 631nn4–5
individuals
happiness of, 524–525
personal fulfillment,
504–514
talented, 505–506
infrastructure, 500–502
innovation/invention/motiva-
tion, 520–524, 525
public goods and services/com-
munity, 512–513
Texas, 135, 350
Texas Rangers, 85–86, 309
The Gap, 38
Thomas, Frank, 305
Thomas, Michael, 356, 535
Thompson, Bob, 269–270
Thompson, Tommy, 335
three-times rule, 109
Thurow, Lester, xxv, 252, 401
TIAA-CREF, 39
Tiger Management, 222
Tilly, Chris, 199, 200, 230, 231
Time Warner, 30, 176, 562n140
Tisch, Larry, 267
Title IX funding, 536
Todd, Richard, xxvii, 264, 333
total quality management,
160–161, 584n9
Tovalds, Linus, 522–523
Townsend, Washington, 422
Trinity Yachts, xii
Trujillo, Solomon, 178
Truman, Harry, 442
Trumka, Richard, 531
Trump, Donald, 473
Trump International Hotel &
Towers, 346–347
Tuck School of Business, 74
Turner, Ted, 174, 176, 404
Turner, Trevor, 265
Twain, Mark, 422
twenty-five times pay ratios,
538–539, 634n57
twenty times pay ratios, 77–78,
162–163, 533, 584n19
Twitchell, James, 250

Tyco International, 173, 279, 280, 602n36
Tyson, Don, 564n229
Tyson, Laura D'Andrea, viii
Tyson Foods, 564n229

U
Ueberroth, Peter, 85–86
Umetani, Kenji, 234
unemployment
   1990s, 97
   1997-2000, 104
   defined, 591n50
   recipiency rates, 590n28
   U.S. vs. other industrialized nations, 205, 233, 234
unemployment compensation, 205, 590n27
Unhealthy Societies (Wilkinson), 313
unions
   1950s-1960s, 216
   1980s-1990s, 217
   contributions to elected representatives, 382, 616n23
   history, xx, 430, 546
   membership statistics, 534
   reforms for pay equity, role in, 529–534
   strikers
      1919 Red Scare, 434–435
      1995 World Series, 297
      permanently replaced, 217, 593n113
   U.S. vs. European restrictions, 202–203
   wages/demand/productivity and, 216, 464
United for a Fair Economy, 89, 182
United States. *See also* democracy in America
   consumption/waste production, 366–367
   crime in, 231, 595n185
   prison population, 230, 231, 357, 373, 595n180
   security spending, 230–231, 595n182
United States government
   control of free press, 619n126
   Department of Defense (DoD) schools, 461
   education, investment in, 212–213, 303, 381, 461–462, 627n23
   infrastructure, investment in, 213–214, 381–382, 520
United States government regulations
   compensation limitations for CEOs, 542, 635n71
   contract requirements imposed for corporate reform,

534–536, 633n38
   health care systems, 284, 602n58
   war-time profits limitation, 542, 635n71
   welfare reform, 334–336, 338, 342–343, 609n27
United States history
   McCarthyism, 443
   national banks, 418–419, 621n17
   New Deal, 438–439
   Red Scare, 434–435, 443–444
United States wars
   Civil War, 421–423
   Cold War, 444–445
   Spanish-American War, 429
   WWI, 432–434
   WWII, 440
United Way, 540
UPS, 190
Uruguay, equality and democracy in, 403
USHealthCare, 33
U.S. Technologies, 187
US West, 177–179
UUNet Technologies, 174

V
Vanderbilt, Cornelius, xv
Vanderbilt, George, xv
Vanderbilt, William, xv, 423
Varone, Antonio, 550
Vasdev, Shawn, 231
Vaughn, Mo, 67, 69
Veneman, Ann, 390
Venezuela, commons supported in, 350
VHI Save The Music Foundation, 148–149
Vilas, Carlos, 402–403, 406
Vinson & Elkins, 276–277
Virginia (Fairfax County), 123, 135, 579n188
Vivendi Universal, 206, 207
Vogel, Ezra, 234
Volker, Paul, 289
von Hoffman, Nicholas, 136, 262
von Mises, Ludwig, 96

W
Wachtell, Lipton, Rosen & Katz, 275
Wackernagel, Mathis, 363
Wade, Robert, 357
wages. *See also* CEOs, income; minimum wage
   demand for goods and services relationship to, 215–216, 219
   gain-sharing plans and, 169–170
   happiness linked with increases in, 525

productivity relationship to, 214–216
   U.S. vs. other industrialized nations, 204, 234
wages, hourly
   1970s-2000s, 99, 463, 574n25, 575n56
   for college graduates, 463, 627n28
   growth of vs. inflation, 556n119
   temps vs. full-time workers, 105
   unions effect on, 216
   at Wal-Mart, 575n80, 576n89
   welfare reform legislation and, 342–343, 609n27
wages, weekly
   1915, 432
   1939-1945, 441, 624n217
   1973 vs. 2001, 99, 574n29, 575n56
Wallis, Jim, xviii
Wall Street. *See also* stock market
   1929 crash, 436
   1980s-2000s (boom), 220–222
   2000-2002 crash, 40–44, 222–223, 564n199
   market wisdom distortions, 19–23
   raiders restructuring of corporate America, 7–8, 33
   share prices
      factors in 1990s boom, 16, 559n66
      investor losses, 2000, 564n199
      profit distributions, 1997, 118
   Social Security privatization, 398–399
   stock analysts, conflicts of interests, 21–23, 560n95, 560nn98–102
Wall Street brokerage houses, income sources, 22
Wall Street investment banks, 223–226, 287
Wall Street model, 208–210, 215, 218, 230
Wal-Mart, 105–108, 575n80, 576n89
Walt Disney, 13, 67–69, 177
Walton, Alice, 259
Walton, John, 397–398
Walton, Sam, 107, 108, 468
Walton family, 107
Wang, Charles, 25–27, 561n117
Ward, John, 562n145
Ward, Ralph, 49
Warner, Mark, 388
Warner Communications, 10, 12, 558n20
War on Poverty, 333–334

Washington Post, 593n113
Watson, Raymond, 67
Watson, Tom, 426
Watt, George, 329
wealth
  burden of, 260, 262–263, 267
  defined, ix
  empowerment of, 267–270
  excessive defined, 482–484
  happiness linked to
    context defining, 238–239
    fallacy of, 258–261
    by material possessions,
      244–246, 248–250,
      262–263, 369
    satisfaction factor in,
      241–242
    Shaw on, 271
  health linked to, 311–318
  hyperagency resulting from,
    268–269
  luck as contributor to, 51,
    78–79, 81–83, 266, 458
wealth, accumulation of. *See also*
  wealth inequity
  black vs. white, 354–356,
    612n103
  Hirschhorn on, x
  post-Civil War, 423
  religion on, xvii–xviii,
    465–467
wealth, believed deserved. *See also*
  Dunlap, Albert J.
  based on a just society, 264
  belief of richest 1%, 263–264
  as divine right of founder,
    77–79
  for hard work, 51, 59–61,
    77–79, 81, 88–90
  for individual achievement,
    80–81, 193
  by information age executives,
    63
  inherited wealth vs., 260, 263
  for intelligence/genius, 51,
    67–68, 77–79
  for risk, 51, 56–58
  for talent, 14, 29–31, 51–52,
    73, 74–75, 505–506,
    570n148, 570n153
  for visionaries, 69–71, 84
wealth, desire for
  CEOs, other industrialized
    countries, 205–207, 235
  elected representatives, 386,
    617n53
  environmental degradation in,
    361–362
  happiness and, 241–246
  historical/religious view of,
    xvii–xviii
  media influence, xiv
  as obsession, xiv
  percentage of Americans, 237

  research communities, effect
    on, 211–212
wealth, distribution of. *See also*
  wealth inequity
  in economic growth theory,
    196–197
  in Japan, 233–235, 595n199
  in Native American society, xvi
wealth, inherited. *See also* children
  of the wealthy
  black vs. white, 354–355, 356
  as guarantee of wealth, 88–90
  guilt resulting from, 260, 263
  predictions for Baby Boomers,
    572n214
wealth inequity. *See also* economic
  growth theory; greed; income
  inequity; wealth, accumulation
  of; wealth, distribution of
  athletes vs. executives, 304
  automobile industry and,
    250–251
  banking industry, conse-
    quences from, 253–254
  in California, 120–122
  crime rates relationship to,
    231–233
  earnings distribution disparity,
    557n129–130
  health and, 320–321, 606n12,
    606n16, 606n23
  literature on, xvi
  morality in, 90, 182, 276
  need for/purpose of, 3–5,
    557n1, 590n9
  progressive tax structure, effect
    on, 467–472
  public opinion on, vii–viii,
    528–529, 632n6, 632n8,
    632n10
  racism and, 351–353, 419,
    621n25
  unions link to, 216
  in Virginia, 123
wealth inequity, benefits perceived
  from
  charitable works, 93
  cultural achievement, 93, 140
  economic growth, 197–201,
    521–522, 590n9
  job creation, 93, 95–96
  to the middle class, 96
  social advance, 424
wealth inequity, chronologically
  1600s, 219
  1700s, 219
  1700s-1800s, xviii–xix, 360,
    416–424, 620n7
  1800s-1900, 129, 262, 264,
    621n25
  1920s, 219
  1945 (post-WWII)-1970s,
    xx–xxii, 216, 442–446,
    464–465, 555nn99–100,

    624n223
  1970s, 216, 445–447,
    557n130
  1980s-1990s, xxii–xxiii, 217,
    219–223
  1998-2001, 557n131
  Industrial Age-present,
    360–361
the wealthy. *See also* children of the
  wealthy
the wealthy. *See also* families (average); plutocracy; taxes on the
  wealthy; the middle class; the
  poor
  beliefs held regarding
    the middle class, 264–265
    the poor, 263–264, 333,
      338
  Boston Brahmins, 128–129
  in California, 120–121
  characteristics of, self-
    described, 51, 81, 129
  defined, ix–x, xxii, 617n51
  environmental degradation by,
    361–362
  financial assets, 1980s-1990s,
    xxii
  relationships of, 260–262, 267,
    306, 346
  Roosevelt (FDR) on, 440
  Roosevelt (Theodore) on, xvii
  social roots of success, 80
  voting rates, 407, 620n157
wealthy, charitable giving of
  arts funding, 139–140, 142,
    143, 148–151
  statistics, 127–137, 580n31
  Ten Times Rule, effect on,
    508–509, 512–513
  untapped capacity of, 132–134
wealthy, governmental influence of
  by contributions, 384–385,
    388–389, 393–396,
    428–429
  Gilded Age, xv, xix, 547
  positions of importance held
    by, 390–391
  Social Security cap, 387
wealthy, income of. *See also specific*
  income groups e.g. millionaires
  1977 vs. 1999, 556n130
  distribution patterns, 483–484
  global statistics, 613n12
  income share, 1947-1973, 125
  sources of, 118, 493–494
wealthy, insulation of
  for athletes, 306
  from greater society, 262, 298,
    346–347, 349, 403
  from intrusion by others, 268
  from poverty, 336
  from reality, 269, 333
wealthy, lifestyles of the
  art collections, 139–140

clubs/memberships, 268–269, 298
Gilded Age, 262, 423–424
home furnishings, xi, 244, 253, 436
homes
  castles, x
  Gilded Age, xv
  landscaping costs, xi, 268
  Neo-Fortress Movement, 357, 612n126
  prices of, x–xi, 256, 599n109
  safe rooms, 230
  servants for, xiii, 554n49
  square footage, 255–256
  Ten Times Rule, effect on, 506–509
personal needs and services
  beauty/grooming, 268
  clothing, designer lines, xi, 253
  Neiman Marcus retail, 262–263
  private security, 230, 357, 595n182
  servants, 268
transportation
  automobiles, 253, 364–365, 629n76
  pay-for-speed lanes, 258
  planes/yachts, xi–xii, 59
  travel, xii–xiii, 59
wealth management services, 253, 598n90
wealthy, speculation by
  in Civil War, 423
  by George Soros, 593n123
  as investment capitalists (angels), 223, 594n151, 594n155
  in Japan, 233–234
  post-Revolutionary war, 418
  stock trading, 219–222, 229
  telecom investments, 226–228
  Ten Times Rule, effect on, 519–520
  as venture capitalists, 223–226, 594n151, 594n155
wealthy, the richest 1%
  40 richest Americans of all time, 468
  accumulated wealth
    1983-1998, xxiii
    1998, xxiii, 556n115
    2003, xxv
  income gains
    1970s-2000, xxiii, 113, 557n130
    1990s vs. other Californians, 120–121
    1993-1997, 120

income share
  1915, 432, 623n132
  1929, 436
  1977-1990s, xxv, 125
  1980s-1990s, 125
  1992-2001, 125, 579n207
  political influence of, 385
  tax cuts benefiting, 415, 451, 453
  wealth believed deserved by, 90, 263–264
  wealth of, credited to, 51
wealthy, the richest 5%
  income share, 125, 579n203, 628n34
  minimum income required, 556n112
  richest 1% compared, xxii–xxiii, 556n115
wealthy, the richest 20%, xxii, 121, 242, 556n109
Wealthy and Wise (Rosenberg), 132
Webber, Carolyn, 348
Webster, Noah, xviii
Webster, William, 187
Webvan, 76–77, 571n168
Weill, Sandy, 45, 64, 140
Weiman, Lori, xxiv
Weinstein, Michael, viii
Weisman, Steven, 431
Welch, Jack
  compensation package, xxiv, 46, 570n139
  connections role in success of, 76
  forced rankings process, 72, 570n144
  genius of, 71–73
  as model for Barnevik, 206
welfare reform
  Denmark, 338–339
  United States, 334–336, 338, 342–343
  wages and, 342–343, 609n27
Wexner, Leslie, 127
Wheeler, Phil, 537, 539
Whitehall study (Britain), 321–322
Whitman, Walt, xix
Who Wants to Be a Millionaire (television), xiv, 69
Who Wants to Marry a Multi-Millionaire (television), xiv
Wigginton, Randy, 121–122
Wilbur, Colburn, 291
Wildavsky, Aaron, 348
Wilentz, Sean, 417, 447, 450, 621n23
Wilkinson, Richard, 313, 322, 323, 325, 326, 328
Will, George, vii, 91, 307, 493
Wilson, Margo, 231

Wilson, Woodrow, 432
Wilzig, Alan, x
Winnick, Gary, 188
Winter, J. Burgess, 162, 584n13
Witte, John, 441
Wolf, Stewart, 320
Wolff, Edward, comments on
  growth rate of super rich, ix, 125
  net worth of average American, xxii
  net worth of wealthiest 1%, xxiii
  on retirement preparedness of Americans, 103
  wealth tax proposal, 472, 628n68
women
  murder rates, 595n185
  Title IX funding for, 536
  in the workplace, 242, 516–517
worker rights, U.S. vs. Europe, 202–208
working poor. *See also* the poor
  1920s, 435–436
  full-time workers as, 105–108, 217
  Santa Clara County, CA, 122
  taxing the, 341–342, 491, 610n62
  Wal-Mart employees as, 105–108
  welfare reform and, 334–336, 342–343, 609n27
workplace. *See also* employees; professionals
  egalitarianism vision of, xvi
  history, 420–421, 621n38
  people of color in the, 516–517
  safety nets, U.S. vs. other industrialized nations, 202, 233, 596n210
  scientific management of the, 159
  wage-earners/family, 99
  women in the, 242, 516–517
workweek, hours in the
  1979 vs. 1997, 243, 597n28
  excessive
    for attorneys, 275, 277
    downsizing driving, 181–182, 588n139
    for immigrants, 114
    poor health related to, 318–319
  Germany vs. U.S., 99
  for the middle class, 243–244
  Ten Times Rule, effect on, 505, 510
  U.S. vs. other industrialized

nations, 99, 204
   at Wal-Mart, 106
WorldCom, 48–49, 174,
   180–181, 189, 486
WorldCom collapse, 633n20
Wozniak, Steve, 164
Wyly, Sam, 532
Wynn, Steve, 149

X
Xerox, 187–188, 211, 281

Y
Yahoo, 20, 221
Yang, Jerry, 20
Yazigi, Monique, 265
Yerger, Ann, 46
Yermack, David, 16

Z
Zandi, Marc, 97